Typical uses: Conversations of many people at home, with friends, on the job • Representations of this speech in stories, plays, movies, comic strips, on radio and television (See pp. 23-25)

Typical uses: Casual conversation • Letters between people who know each other well; diaries, personal writing; writing close to popular speech, as in fiction and some newspaper columns (See pp. 21-23)

Typical uses: Conversation; talks to general audiences • Most business letters and advertising • News and feature stories, newspaper columns • Magazine articles and books on subjects of general interest • Most fiction and other literature for general circulation • Many college papers (See pp. 15-17)

Typical uses: Addresses and lectures to special audiences • Some editorials and business writing • Literature of somewhat limited circulation: essays and criticisms, much poetry, some fiction • Academic writing: reference works, dissertations, most term papers, reference papers, some textbooks • Scientific and technical reports • Books and articles dealing with special subjects for professional groups and experts (See pp. 17, 20-21)

WRITER'S GUIDE AND INDEX TO ENGLISH

Porter G. Perrin

Fourth Edition
revised by

Karl W. Dykema
Youngstown University

Wilma R. Ebbitt
University of Chicago

SCOTT, FORESMAN AND COMPANY

Preface

The fourth edition of *Writer's Guide and Index to English* retains many of the ideas and emphases of the earlier editions but also includes numerous major and minor changes. To the end of his life, Porter Perrin continued to investigate the problems of the freshman course in composition and—because open-mindedness was one of his most characteristic virtues—his investigations influenced his opinions. Some of the most significant changes in this fourth edition are changes decided upon by Porter Perrin. The remainder, we believe, are consistent both with his philosophy and with the present needs of the writing course.

The most obvious change is in the organization of the *Guide*. Although the *Guide* still begins with a chapter on the varieties of English and ends with one on the reference paper, the number of chapters in between has been reduced from eleven to nine, and the order of chapters has been changed. Chapters 2-10 now divide roughly into two parts: composing parts and wholes (2-7) and revising for accuracy and effectiveness (8-10).

The major change in organization, then, is that the *Guide* now launches the student into the writing of papers from the start of the course. In philosophy and arrangement, this change reflects Porter Perrin's thinking. In his essay "Freshman Composition and the Tradition of Rhetoric" in *Perspectives on English* (New York, 1960), he called for "a courageous shift of emphasis" in the composition course, a shift that would subordinate grammar to rhetoric, "taken as the traditional name for the study of the making, the qualities, and the effects of verbal discourse." In this edition, therefore, after Chapter 1 has introduced the student to the varieties of English, Chapter 2 takes up the stages in writing a paper; Chapter 3, a new chapter, deals with methods of developing parts of papers and whole papers; Chapter 4 covers the writing of paragraphs; and Chapters 5-7 discuss and illustrate the types of papers composition students are normally assigned. Chapter 7 incorporates and expands the section on logic formerly included in the *Index*.

Chapters 8-10 give attention to matters particularly important in revising papers—sentences, words and phrases, punctuation, and spelling. Each chapter emphasizes the two stages in revision taken up in separate chapters in the third edition—one, revising to meet the reader's expectations; two, revising to make the expression of ideas effective, not merely acceptable. Grammatical analysis is introduced not as a study in itself but as a means of making the student aware of how his expression can help or hinder him in communicating his ideas. Here, too, the approach follows the advice of Porter Perrin, who wrote in 1960: "Looking at the situation squarely shows that the argument now flourishing over 'traditional grammar' *vs.* 'linguistics' is a secondary issue. The basic question is, How much direct attention to the language should be given in a course in writing? The answer is, As much as is necessary to encourage habits of effective expression."

Most of the exercises in the *Guide* are new. Many more samples of student writing have been included in both the text and the exercises.

Because it has continued to meet with general approval, the format of the *Index* has been retained. Entries have been brought up to date; some new ones have been added; a few old ones that seemed to have outlived their usefulness have been dropped. In general, any shift in the *Index* has been in the direction of helping the student *as writer.*

The publishers wish to express their gratitude to the many teachers of English who contributed to this edition of *Writer's Guide and Index to English* by providing criticism and advice. As a first step in its preparation, comprehensive critical studies were obtained from Paul Roberts, Jayne Harder of the University of Florida, and Wilma R. Ebbitt of the University of Chicago. After Mrs. Ebbitt had joined with Karl W. Dykema of Youngstown University, a participant in the third edition, to undertake the revision, their plan for reorganizing the *Guide* was submitted for criticism to the following teachers: Dudley Bailey, University of Nebraska; George E. Jones, Bloomfield College; Robert Hall, University of South Florida; Edgar W. Lacy and Ednah S. Thomas, University of Wisconsin; T. G. McGuire, Los Angeles Valley College; Louis T. Milic, Columbia University; C. E. Nelson, Washington State University; Robert A. Peters, University of Idaho; Paul Beekman Taylor, Brown University; and Howard A. Wilson, Knox College. The comments of these teachers guided the authors in performing a difficult task. We believe that the task has been performed with success and that the fourth edition of *Writer's Guide and Index to English* effectively carries on the tradition of a great textbook.

The Publishers

Contents *Writer's Guide*

The process of revising

The reference paper: method and form

Contents *Index to English*

The *Index,* pages 465-896, contains articles in alphabetical arrangement that fall roughly into four categories:

a Articles on particular words and constructions such as *continual—continuous; *fiancé, fiancée; *get, got; *like—as; *plenty; *shall—will; *so . . . that; *very

b Articles for correction and revision of papers indicated by longhand abbreviations before the entry word

c Articles on English grammar giving definitions and examples of such matters as *Case, *Conjunction, *Plurals of nouns, *Principal parts of verbs

d Articles on various facts of language such as *American and British usage, *Foreign words in English, *Linguistics

Bibliography

The following works have been most useful in gathering the material for this book. They are frequently referred to (usually by author's name only) in the chapters of the *Guide* and in the alphabetical entries of the *Index*.

American Speech, New York, Columbia University Press. A periodical, founded in 1925, containing much direct observation of current American usage, especially vocabularies of particular regions and vocations.

Baugh, Albert C., *A History of the English Language,* New York, Appleton-Century-Crofts, 1935; revised 1957. A substantial and readable history of the language.

Bloomfield, Leonard, *Language,* New York, Holt, Rinehart and Winston, 1933. A basic work on the general principles of language study.

Bryant, Margaret M., *Current American Usage,* New York, Funk & Wagnalls, 1962. The most recent reliable work on the subject.

Carroll, John B., *The Study of Language,* Cambridge, Harvard University Press, 1953. Chapter 2 is a brief and clear introduction to linguistics.

Curme, George O., *Syntax,* Boston, Heath, 1931; and *Parts of Speech and Accidence,* Boston, Heath, 1935. A very full grammar of modern English, with much historical material. (The second book referred to as Curme, *Parts of Speech*)

Fowler, H. W., *A Dictionary of Modern English Usage,* Oxford University Press, 1926. Although based on British usage and now somewhat dated, still a readable and often illuminating book.

Fries, C. C., *American English Grammar,* New York, Appleton-Century-Crofts (NCTE Monograph No. 10), 1940. A number of points of grammar discussed with special reference to differences between levels of usage. (Referred to as Fries, *AEG*)

Fries, C. C., *The Structure of English,* New York, Harcourt, Brace and World, 1952. Presents a realignment of the parts of speech and a program of sentence analysis based on this realignment. (Referred to as Fries, *Structure*)

Gleason, H. A., *An Introduction to Descriptive Linguistics,* New York, Holt, Rinehart and Winston, 1955; revised 1961. Exactly what its title implies.

Hall, J. Lesslie, *English Usage,* Chicago, Scott, Foresman and Company, 1917. Historical discussion of 141 locutions on which usage has been divided or questioned.

Jespersen, Otto, *Essentials of English Grammar,* New York, Holt, 1933. An abridgment of Jespersen's seven-volume *Modern English Grammar,* the most complete description of English available.

Kenyon, John S., and Thomas A. Knott, *A Pronouncing Dictionary of American English,* Springfield, G. & C. Merriam Co., 1944; addenda 1949. The most systematic guide to American pronunciation of individual words.

Marckwardt, Albert H., and Fred G. Walcott, *Facts About Current English Usage,* New York, Appleton-Century-Crofts (NCTE Monograph No. 7), 1938. Includes the data of the Sterling A. Leonard study (1932) of debatable and divided usage, with additional information.

Mencken, H. L., *The American Language,* 4th Edition, New York, Knopf, 1936; *Supplement I* (1945); *Supplement II* (1948). A mass of material on various varieties of American English, with commentary and references to further sources. References in this book are to the one-volume abridged edition by Raven I. McDavid, Jr. (New York, 1963).

Pooley, Robert C., *Teaching English Usage,* New York, Appleton-Century-Crofts (NCTE Monograph No. 16), 1946. Discussion of a number of debatable locutions, with evidence and recommendations for teaching.

Roberts, Paul, *Understanding Grammar,* New York, Harper and Row, 1954. A good, brief, systematic English grammar.

Robertson, Stuart, *The Development of Modern English,* Englewood Cliffs, Prentice-Hall, 1934; revised 1954 by Frederic G. Cassidy. Gives the background of many points of current syntax.

Skillin, Marjorie, and Robert M. Gay, *Words into Type,* New York, Appleton-Century-Crofts, 1948; revised 1964. A detailed manual of publishers' style.

Summey, George, Jr., *American Punctuation,* New York, Ronald Press Co., 1949. The most thorough and authoritative treatment of punctuation.

United States Government Printing Office Style Manual, Washington, Government Printing Office, revised edition, 1953. Detailed directions for preparing government publications, most of which are generally applicable. (Referred to as *GPO Manual*)

The University of Chicago Press, *A Manual of Style,* 11th edition, Chicago, The University of Chicago Press, 1949. The stylebook of a distinguished conservative publishing house.

More specific works are cited in the various articles to which they are appropriate. A list of current dictionaries will be found on page 363.

WRITER'S GUIDE

Chapter One

THE
VARIETIES
OF
ENGLISH

The circle of the English language has a well-defined centre but no discernible circumference.

Oxford English Dictionary

We began to learn our language by imitating what those around us said, and soon we picked up enough of it to make our wants known and then to talk with others. At first our parents were so delighted to have us talk that they accepted anything that we said, including some of our infantile contributions to the English vocabulary. Milk might be *nuck,* a hammer an *agboo,* an elephant an *umpy-dump.* We used odd forms of words and odd syntax: One youngster, struggling with irregular verbs, said, "Mother did gave me a lot of pants. She shouldn't have gaven me so much pants this summer." For a while the grown-ups thought this sort of language cute, but by the time we were four or five, they began to expect us to talk about as they talked, and because we wanted to conform, so far as we could talk that way, we did.

In school we added to our use of English the ability to read and write it. We also studied "grammar," and were told that "It is I" and other expressions were correct and "It is me" and a lot more were not. If a reason was offered, it was generally something like "The verb *to be* is followed by a predicate nominative." We tried to follow this grammar in the schoolroom, but outside we talked about the same as before. Some of us, though, began to realize that English, which we supposed we just talked naturally, was a pretty complex matter and that opinions about it differed, sometimes violently.

By the time we reach college and find that we are almost ready to take our places in public affairs, we become more concerned about our language. We want to feel confident in our pronunciation and our choice of words. When we write something, we want to have control of the language, to be able to use it readily and presentably. And we want to be able to speak and write effectively in the more demanding situations in which we find ourselves.

Confidence and effectiveness in the use of English come in part from an accurate knowledge of the possibilities of language. We need to know how to choose what is most effective for us, and we need to practice until the sort of English we want to use comes easily and becomes a habit. The habit of using good English comes mainly from reading the work of good writers and listening to good speakers, giving conscious attention to how they gain their effects. But to observe language profitably, we need some knowledge of how it works and some specific guidance; a composition course and a book like this can help.

We all use English with ease and with a good deal of effectiveness in situations where we feel at home. But when we meet new people, perhaps from a different social circle or a different part of the country, or when we have to give a talk or write an important letter, a paper for a college course, or something that will be printed, we may become acutely conscious of *how* we are speaking or writing. Fortunately the greater part of our language raises no questions; it can be used at any time, under any circumstances. The ordinary names of things (*dog, dresses, politics*) and of acts (*walking, swimming, voting*) and thousands of other words are in general use; most of the forms of words are standardized (*theirs, people's, lived*); and the order of words in phrases and sentences is pretty well fixed. But some questions about usage do come up. Sometimes we have to make choices among words and forms and constructions, and because those choices contribute to the impression our talk or piece of writing makes, they are important.

These questions about English usage arise chiefly because there are different varieties of the language that do not fit equally well into every situation. The questions may be simple: Is it all right to say "It's *me*," "Go *slow*," "It's *real* interesting," or "It's *laying* on the table"? Does *phony* fit in this sentence? Is *solon* better than *congressman* here? Or the questions may be more complicated: Should this be one sentence or two? Do these words express what I mean? How can I show the connection between these ideas? What is the best order for these ideas?

The answers to some of these questions are clear-cut and definite, but the answers to others vary with the circumstances. English, like every other widely used language, is not one single set of words and constructions, everywhere and always the same; it is a variety of such sets that have much in common but are still far from uniform. This variety is stressed in this book for two reasons: to show you the immense resources our language offers and to help you form habits of easy and automatic choice in your actual usage—habits that will be appropriate to the varying situations you meet. A mature use of English means speaking and writing the sort of English that is appropriate to the situation in which you find yourself, for *English is not just "good"; it is good under certain conditions.*

Sources of variation in English

The varieties of English that you find around you are all natural growths, and specialists in the study of language are able to describe and in some degree account for them. Understanding the reasons for the differences will give you perspective on the language and will guide you in making some choices.

Variations due to time • Because change has characterized every language whose history has been traced, it appears to be an inevitable trait of every living language. Ordinarily the changes are slow and barely noticeable—slightly different pronunciations, new shadings in the meaning of words, and gradual shifts in grammatical constructions. You know from reading older literature that English has changed greatly in the centuries during which it has been written.[1] A play by Shakespeare needs a good many notes to tell us what some of the words meant to the people who first heard the plays over 350 years ago. If we go back far enough, English looks like a foreign language, though we may recognize in the older forms the ancestors of some of our current words. Language changes as naturally and as steadily as other social habits do.

Words, forms, or constructions no longer in use are called *obsolete.* No one today refers to a *bottle* of hay, or uses *can* in the sense of *know,* or *coy* in the sense of *quiet.* Usages now disappearing from the language are called *archaic.* Fashion

---

[1]For further discussion, see *Index* entries *Change in language and *English language; histories of the English language, especially Baugh (books cited by name of author only will be found in the Bibliography, pp. xiii-xiv) ; Otto Jespersen, *Growth and Structure of the English Language* (various editions) ; Thomas Pyles, *The Origins and Development of the English Language* (New York, 1964) ; *Oxford English Dictionary; Dictionary of American English.*

has just about driven out *betrothed* in favor of *fiancée*. Archaic expressions survive in some situations, such as the *thou* and *saith* of church services. A few archaic or even obsolete words are used in set phrases, such as "much *ado*" and "in good *stead*," and many are preserved in uneducated or dialect speech after they have disappeared from other varieties of English. *Learn* in the sense of *teach, you was* in the singular, *he don't,* and the *double negative[1] were all once in general and reputable use. It is often hard to tell when a word or construction is sufficiently uncommon to be called archaic; a good many words not so labeled in all dictionaries are really used very rarely (like *betimes, deem, doff*).

Because we learn our language chiefly by imitating what we hear and read, obsolete and archaic usage offers few problems, but occasionally in trying to "improve" his language a student will use an archaic expression, and sometimes a strained effort at humor produces words like *quoth* or *wight*.

We cannot know the whole history of our language, nor do we need to, but realizing that it has a history should help us adjust to reading older literature and explain many of the peculiarities of the current language (in spelling and verb forms, for instance) that we need to consider in this book.

Words, constructions, and styles keep changing. Recent years have seen the addition of many words (*cosmonaut, drunkometer, isometrics, thalidomide*), names for scores of new chemical compounds, and so on,[2] the dropping of some from general use, and a tendency toward more concise idioms and constructions.

While new words for new things are natural additions to our vocabulary, it is wise to hesitate before adopting new words for things that have already been named. This is especially true of the abstract words (such as *recreational facilities, urban redevelopment, causal factors*) that higher education and occupational specialization seem to be substituting for the common words for some activities and situations (see Chapter 9, "Big words," pp. 347-348).

New words have sometimes made their way into literary usage rather slowly, but most writers today use a new word whenever it is appropriate. It is important for a writer to make the fullest possible use of the current language. It is the language of his contemporaries, the language they understand best, the language they will expect to read and hear. When

[1]Throughout this book, references to *Index* articles are indicated by an asterisk (*) .
[2]The journal *American Speech* treats many new words as they appear, and the annual supplementary volumes to the principal encyclopedias have lists of such words.

you write naturally, from your observation of the language and your feeling for it, you will normally write current English, and you should aim for no other kind.

Variations due to place • No language is spoken in exactly the same way in all parts of the country or countries in which it is used. We can easily spot an Englishman because some of his pronunciations and some of his words and constructions are different from ours. (See *American and British usage.*) We can also very often tell what part of the United States a person comes from by listening to him talk. Differences in words, pronunciation, stress, phrasing, and grammatical habits that are characteristic of fairly definite regions are called *regional dialects.* Put another way, a regional dialect is speech that does not attract attention to itself in the region where it is used but does outside that area. A pronunciation, a word or meaning of a word, or an idiom that is current in one region and not in others is called a *provincialism* or a *localism.*

Dialects are not peculiar to backward regions, for the "Oxford accent" forms a minor dialect, and the natives of Boston and of New York speak differently from each other. Nor are dialects the result of lack of education or social standing. An educated Westerner will speak somewhat differently from a Southerner or New Englander of a similar degree and quality of education. A dialect may retain traits of the differing British dialects spoken by early settlers or may show the influence of foreign languages spoken by large numbers of people in the region, as in German sections of Pennsylvania or in the Scandinavian sections of the Middle West. It may show the influence of a neighboring language or of the language of an earlier settlement: the dialect of the Southwest contains Spanish elements, the dialect of New Orleans, French.

There are fewer differences among the dialects of the United States than would be expected in a country of such size, many fewer than exist among the dialects in much smaller Great Britain.[1] The relative freedom of movement of the American

---

[1]See Baugh, Ch. 11, especially § 250; Bloomfield, Ch. 19; *Dictionary of American English;* Otto Jespersen, *Mankind, Nation and Individual from a Linguistic Point of View* (Oslo, 1925); G. P. Krapp, *The English Language in America* (New York, 1925), pp. 225-273; Mencken. Many articles in *American Speech* record facts of various American dialects. Linguaphone album L-19 has recordings of twenty-four American dialects. For some results of work on the *Linguistic Atlas,* see Hans Kurath, *Handbook of the Linguistic Geography of New England* (Providence, 1939), *A Word Geography of the Eastern United States* (Ann Arbor, 1949); E. B. Atwood, *Survey of Verb Forms in the Eastern United States* (Ann Arbor, 1953) ; Hans Kurath and Raven I. McDavid, Jr., *The Pronunciation of English in the Atlantic States* (Ann Arbor, 1961) ; and Jean Malmstrom and Annabel Ashley, *Dialects— U.S.A.* (Champaign, 1963) .

people, transportation facilities that have prevented even the Rocky Mountains from marking a linguistic boundary, the educational system, the circulation of books and national magazines, and more recently radio and television—all these factors have helped people who are thousands of miles apart to speak substantially the same language. But words peculiar to a local terrain or to local occupations will probably survive, since they fill a real need and usually have no equivalents in other dialects. The frequent use of localisms on radio and television and in stories may help make one region more tolerant of the language of others, and it may very well introduce into general use words formerly characteristic of a particular locality.

Three major speech areas of the United States have been traditionally recognized: *Eastern* (New England and a strip of eastern New York), *Southern* (south of Pennsylvania and the Ohio River, extending west of the Mississippi into Texas), and *Northern* (extending from New Jersey on the Atlantic, through the Middle West and the whole of our Pacific Coast), also called *General American* or *Western*. Insofar as educated Americans distinguish regional varieties of pronunciation, they do it on this basis. But as a result of the work being done on *The Linguistic Atlas of the United States and Canada,* the boundaries are being more exactly drawn, subdivisions indicated, and lines of influence between areas shown. The major speech divisions are called *Northern, Midland,* and *Southern,* and their boundaries have been projected to include the entire country. Within the three main divisions there are important subdivisions; for example, the Eastern New England type of Northern differs appreciably from the North Central type, which extends from New York State—excluding New York City—west through Iowa to the Dakotas. And other regional varieties exist within each of the three main areas, as in the Ozarks or in New York City, but the differences between the speech of California and Illinois are less noticeable than the differences between either of these and, say, Georgia or Massachusetts. Roughly one twelfth of the population speaks what is generally called Eastern, one sixth Southern, and three fourths Northern or General American.[1]

A professional student of American English observes many differences in speech that the ordinary person might miss, but we are all aware of some of them. Some New Englanders use

---

[1]For a map showing the subdivisions, see Charles K. Thomas, *An Introduction to the Phonetics of American English,* 2nd ed. (New York, 1958).

broad *a*, as in /äsk/, /gräss/, /päst/ where most Americans
have short *a;* they usually slight *r*, as in /bän/ for *barn*.[1] A
Westerner has a distinct, perhaps even a prolonged, *r* after
vowels as well as before. Like most Americans he has /ä/ for
the *o* in *hot, lot, cot.* Like many Americans he rounds the *o* in
hog, frog, log. Beginning in New York State, most speakers in
the Northern region do not distinguish *hoarse* and *horse,*
mourning and *morning,* pronouncing /ōr/ (like the word *ore*)
in all. A Southerner from the lowlands (as distinguished from
the hill country) does not sound *r* after vowels (for example, *suh*
for *sir*, /dōä/ or /dō/ for *door*). The long *i* both in the lowlands and the hills may suggest /ä/, as in the popular spelling
Ah for *I*. Southerners from the hills usually pronounce *r* after
vowels—as all fanciers of hillbilly music know. Each region—
Eastern, Southern, and Northern—also has its characteristic
stress and speech rhythm.

In vocabulary, different words will be found for many common objects. Which of the following is used in your locality,
or is some other word used?

bag—sack—poke
gumshoe—overshoe—rubber
piazza—porch—stoop—veranda
seesaw—teeter-totter—teeterboard
cottage cheese—clabber or crud or curd or dutch or pot or smear or
    sour milk cheese—cruds—curds—smear or smier case
doughnut—fried cake—cruller—fat cake—nut cake—cookie

The accompanying map shows several words that are used
within the relatively close limits of New England for the common earthworm: *angleworm, angledog, easworm* (for *eastworm*), *fish worm.* In other regions it is known by some of
these names and by others as well.

Besides these different names for common objects, creatures,
and things, each region has special words for local features of
the landscape or for occupations that are more or less local:
*coulee, hogback, sierra, mesa; mesquite, piñon; mule skinner,
vara* (a surveyor's measure in the Southwest). And there are
local idioms like the Southern "I'll *carry* [for *take*] you home,"
or like those for telling time—New Englanders generally say
quarter *of* four, Southerners quarter *till* four, and Westerners
quarter *to* four.

---

[1]See Index article on *Pronunciation for key to phonemic transcription.

Dialect Chart for "Earthworm"

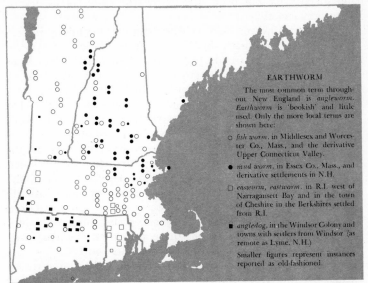

EARTHWORM

The most common term throughout New England is *angleworm*.
Earthworm is 'bookish' and little
used. Only the more local terms are
shown here:

○ *fish worm*, in Middlesex and Worcester Co., Mass., and the derivative
Upper Connecticut Valley.

● *mud worm*, in Essex Co., Mass., and
derivative settlements in N.H.

□ *eastworm, eastworm*, in R.I. west of
Narragansett Bay and in the town
of Cheshire in the Berkshires settled
from R.I.

■ *angledog*, in the Windsor Colony and
towns with settlers from Windsor (as
remote as Lyme, N.H.)

Smaller figures represent instances
reported as old-fashioned.

After Chart 1, *Handbook of the Linguistic Geography of New England*, p.38

People's attitudes toward the use of localisms vary greatly. Some people feel that localisms should be weeded out; others believe that a person should retain as much as possible of the flavor of his native speech. It is a problem everyone has to settle for himself. Educated people tend to shed their more conspicuous local pronunciations, but conscious effort to change to a different pattern often results in an unhappy combination of elements from both. Natural, gradual, unconscious change is best.

Differences between speaking and writing • Language is in origin speech; writing came very late in its development, no more than six thousand years ago, whereas speech, we are assured by anthropologists, archaeologists, and linguists, must go back tens of thousands, perhaps hundreds of thousands of years. And this primacy of speech remains in our own experience of language. We learn to listen and speak long before we learn to read and write, and most of us will continue to talk and listen a great deal more than we write and read. But listening and speaking, reading and writing (not to mention the even greater use of language in "thinking," about which we know so little) are related, overlapping skills. In a language like English, with vast amounts of written and printed material, the relations between speaking and writing are complex and so far have not been sufficiently studied to let us discuss them very exactly.

It is clear, however, that writing cannot be treated as merely a simplified and often inadequate transcription of speech. Spelling, especially in more logically spelled languages than English, does quite satisfactorily indicate the sequence of vowels and consonants in words spoken in isolation: *c-a-t, d-o-g, b-u-l-l-y* provide pretty good instructions as to what sounds are to be uttered to make the three words. But words are never spoken out of context except in nonsense situations like the reading of spelling lists. In context they are always part of a pattern involving pitch, stress, and rhythm, for which marks of punctuation provide only the barest hints; and the sounds in the words themselves undergo alterations, usually subtle, but occasionally radical. Consider the pronunciations given in the Kenyon-Knott *Pronouncing Dictionary of American English* for the word *and;* there are eleven of them, ranging from the full, emphatic form in "John *and* Oscar" to the nonsyllabic *n* in "butter 'n' eggs." A system of transcription which attempted to indicate faithfully such normal spoken variations would be hopelessly cumbersome.

There are several nonlinguistic reasons why writing has developed some characteristics of its own. Readers are often at a distance and may be strangers, with backgrounds different from the writer's. They will probably read silently, no doubt rapidly, and they will expect to find what they read in a form easy to follow. This is one reason for stressing clearness and precision in writing. Another reason is that writing lies on the page and can be examined closely, while speech goes by rapidly. This has led to establishing standards for the written language which, though they have a fairly wide range, are much more uniform than standards for speech. Most of the details of written form have been developed by printers and publishers, who naturally enough wish for consistency in what they publish, and they enforce the details through copy editors and proofreaders, who tidy up copy to meet the standards. This standardization allows for wide circulation of printed matter, one of its greatest assets. Any writer who presents his copy for others to read is expected to approach (though not to meet in every respect) these standards by writing clearly and following the most definitely established conventions of published writing.

The written or printed word serves two rather different purposes, though too few writers are aware of the distinction. It may be intended as the basis of a spoken utterance or it may serve for silent reading only. (Usually, of course, it should lend itself to both purposes.) If it is primarily meant to be spoken, it is merely a set of cues which provide the raw material of what is to be said, cues which rely heavily on our control of the resources of speech to supply all the variations in voice which transform what is visible into natural talk. Many people can't do this and they read aloud as if reciting a list of disconnected words. They don't get their cues. Such writing makes heavy demands on the reader. Most poetry is, essentially, this kind of writing, and many people find reading it pretty hard going because it was written to be spoken.

Writing which is to be read silently should demand much less from the reader. "Invites Public to Tax School" (a newspaper headline) might puzzle us, at least for a moment, because we don't know whether in speech the heavier stress would come on *tax* or *school*. We wonder why the public should be invited to tax a school; but the news item makes clear that the Internal Revenue Service is inviting the public to attend a "school" on tax information.

Many people assume that what they write is a complete transcription of what they would say. Such a transcription is impossible. Linguists have devised symbols which permit a much fuller transcription of speech than does conventional writing, but even it cannot indicate such subtle things as voice quality and fine gradations of intensity. In any case such a transcription is so complex that reading would have to be relearned and even when mastered would be very slow.

A great deal of what we say is redundant. This term does not refer to the obvious repetitiousness that characterizes so much conversation. It refers to what may be called signals, often unnecessary, like *the, is, in,* etc. When we send a telegram we try to eliminate all the words that are not absolutely essential. "The picture is finished" becomes "Picture finished"; "It will arrive in Boston tomorrow" becomes "Arrive Boston tomorrow." And there are many more such signals, especially of pitch, stress, and timing, some of which have no transcription in conventional writing. Though they are often redundant, they are not always so. Occasionally the whole purpose of an utterance depends on one of them. In a detective story, for example, the narrator gives us the remarks of one of the women in the story; the last sentence reads: " 'I understand it's about a tie-up of Nero Wolfe and Dazzle Dan, having Dan start a detective agency?' " Then the narrator adds this comment: "I put the question mark there, though her inflection left it to me whether to call it a question or merely a statement." (Rex Stout, "The Squirt and the Monkey," *Triple Jeopardy*, p. 125.) The resources of conventional writing cannot transcribe all the speech signals, so the writer has to replace them with a verbal explanation, or phrase his writing to avoid the difficulty.

On the other hand, writing has certain advantages over speech, especially over unrehearsed conversation. Most important is the possibility of revision. When we talk we must get our words out at a tremendous rate, often 200 or 300 a minute. We have little chance to plan what we are to say, to choose just the right words to express our ideas. So we are uneconomical, repetitious, unorganized in our expression. This is not necessarily bad. Discursiveness and digression may lead to a wider exploration of a subject, and a repetitive discussion is easier to follow than a concentrated one. Besides, conversations are likely to be leisurely affairs, and an evening of talk will produce hundreds of thousands of words. But the person who is quite willing to sit through two or three hours of talking about a subject in a congenial social situation will probably be quite unwilling to read the same number of words if they carry the subject no further than the talking did.

When we write we set our own pace. Even our first drafts are likely to be better organized, more economically expressed than our talk would be. And we have unlimited opportunity to rearrange, excise, and rephrase. Writing can, therefore, be better organized, more economical, better worded than speech. It can be, but often it is not. After years of practice we are used to talking. Since our practice in writing is negligible in comparison, we find it hard at first to exploit the advantages of writing.

Some minor devices of writing also differentiate it from speech. In this book the special, limited sense in which certain words are defined is shown by capitalizing them. The sentence on page 27 "Most fiction is General or Informal" would make little sense if heard. But after the definitions of "General" and "Informal" on the preceding pages, it is evident that it states that most works of fiction are written in the Informal and General varieties of English. Because these terms have been restricted by definition and their limited sense shown by capitalizing them, the statement can be made in six words instead of fourteen.

The grammar of speech differs somewhat from that of writing, at least of edited, publishable writing. The reference of pronouns is less precise; the pronunciation of prepositions is usually unstressed, so that the *of,* for example, in *a couple of birds* is so reduced that a careless transcription of it might be *a couple birds;* only a few connectives are used, especially *and* and *so;* yet we make ourselves clear. Many of the matters marked on student papers are simply such traits of spoken language transferred to paper. Spoken sentences are usually shorter than written, or if they are long, it is because one statement is added to another rather than because clauses are built together with subordinating conjunctions. Because a reader gets no help from sound as the listener does, he needs more guidance in seeing the relationship between the parts of a sentence.

But written English is not a different language from spoken. Most of the differences are in matters of grammar and style that can be tended to in revising a paper. Others stem from the difference in the situation between speaker-and-hearer and writer-and-reader. The writer often has to fill out constructions which the speaker need not. It is usually best to write nearly the same words that you would speak and then to test what you have written by reading it as a stranger might, making sure that you are telling him what you mean so exactly that he can understand it without hearing you say it, and that you are in general following the conventions of printed English. The best basis for your writing is your more careful speech, reshaped to stand scrutiny on paper. Some languages have entirely different forms for speech and writing, but in English, and especially in present-day English, the relationship is close. We sometimes say someone "talks like a book," meaning that his talk is uncomfortably elaborate or stiff; it is more often a compliment to say "he writes as he talks." Letters and accounts of personal experience are likely to be quite close to speech; most academic work, including term papers for courses, needs to meet the more exacting standards for written communication. A writer must at all times be ready to use as wide a range as possible, drawing on all the resources of spoken and written English that are effective in writing.

Differences due to situation • Many words of similar meaning, though they are in current and general use, cannot be used interchangeably in all situations. Consider these groups:

indigent, impecunious, underprivileged, in want, penniless, poverty-
stricken, *poor,* hard up, broke, flat
spent, fatigued, weary, exhausted, *tired,* worn-out, played out, used
up, dog tired, all in, pooped
stripling, youth, lad, *boy,* youngster, kid, punk

Similarly, many idioms and constructions represent the same
idea but suggest different varieties of speech:

dare not, daren't, *do not dare,* don't dare, dassent
were it not for, if it were not for, *if it was not for,* if it wasn't for,
if it wan't for

Poor, tired, and *boy, do not dare* and *if it was not for* certainly belong to the central part of the language and might
be used by anyone in any circumstance; the same is true of
the words near them in these series. But as we move away
from these central expressions, the words become somewhat
more limited, until those at the ends would be found only in
either quite formal or quite informal situations. Probably
most of us would not use *indigent, spent, stripling*—they suggest old-fashioned or rather bookish usage. We all might use
broke, all in, kid in casual company but not when talking to
someone on whom we want to make a good impression. These
differences are due not to any variation in the central meaning
of the words but to the circumstances in which they have been
generally used and which they suggest. That is, their quality
depends on the social situations in which they have been and
are predominantly used.

There is no well-established system of naming these varieties of English, though they have been often discussed.[1] In
this book we recognize two principal varieties, Standard and
Nonstandard English; and we divide the first into General,
Formal, and Informal English. These varieties are defined in
the table on pages 18-19, and because they are so important
in everyone's judgment of his own language, they are elaborated in the next two sections of this chapter.

Although differences are easily observable between these
varieties, they should not be thought of as mutually exclusive
but as relatively different, shading into each other. A passage
may be considered Formal because it has a few conspicuous
traits characteristic of that variety, and thus a Formal "feel"

---

[1]See, for instance, Bloomfield, pp. 52, 149 ff.; Fries, *AEG,* in which usage is treated according to social varieties; John S. Kenyon, "Cultural Levels and Functional Varieties of
English," *College English,* 1948, 10:31-36; Marckwardt and Walcott; Pooley, Ch. 3.

or "tone," even though the language of most of the passage is in General usage. Although individuals will differ somewhat in deciding where the dividing lines should be drawn, the principal characteristics of the varieties are pretty clear, and the illustrations in the following sections should make it possible to distinguish them.

Standard English

General English—unlimited use • Most speaking and writing situations call for General English, the great central body of words and constructions of our language. In speech we find it in the conversation of educated people and in most talks to general audiences; in writing we see it in letters, in newspapers and magazines, in plays and novels, and in books of all sorts for general circulation—in most of what we read.

General written English lies close to good speech, but it is not speech exactly reproduced, partly because the resources of the written language are somewhat different. The words are likely to be from the central vocabulary, of wide currency in both speech and writing (*roomy* rather than *spacious, rainfall* rather than *precipitation*). They are likely to be concrete, close to experience, referring to things, people, actions, and events more than to abstractions, and familiar to a large number of readers. The constructions reflect those of speech (*look into, give up, take over*), and the sentences are relatively short, made up of one or two clauses without interrupting phrases or involved movement.

General English is especially appropriate to narratives of personal experience and to presentation of people and action, whether in fiction or factual accounts. In the following paragraph, a personal comment by the author of a biography of Columbus, the sentences are short, averaging nineteen words, but not monotonous. With eighteen verbs and six verbals (*shining, to spend*), two bits of conversation, and several phrases that suggest speech (*to check up on, how to get it out*), the passage is clear, fast-moving, and easy to understand.

In 1940, when we were ranging this coast to check up on Columbus, we encountered an old prospector who explained why Veragua had never been properly exploited for gold. Years before, he went up one of the rivers with a partner and an Indian guide. "Where do we find gold?" he asked, after paddling many miles. "Right here!" said the Indian, who pulled out a clasp knife, dug some clay from the river bank and panned out some ten dollars' worth of shining gold grain! The prospector and his partner began at once to plan how to spend their first million dollars. They returned to the nearest town for supplies and lumber and built sluice boxes, the product of which should have made them rich. But in the next freshet all their gear was washed down into the Caribbean. That has happened again and again during the last four and a half centuries. There is still "gold in them thar hills," but only the Indians know how to get it out.—SAMUEL ELIOT MORISON, *Christopher Columbus, Mariner,* p. 136

Ideas, too, though they are by nature abstract and are often presented in Formal English for rather restricted groups of readers, may be expressed in General English. The following definition of the word *sign,* a term important in philosophical discussions of meaning, is presented concretely for general readers by a professor of philosophy. The early specific details lead to the generalization at the end. The constructions are simple, the verbs carry a good bit of the meaning (*the way we will dress*), and the sentences are simple, direct, and short, averaging 22 words. (The longest sentence, the third, is a series of clauses.)

What do all these events have in common that causes us to lump them together as signs? One core similarity: *they all influence the way we tend to react toward something other than themselves.* The alarm tells us the time, the sight of our face in the mirror informs us about our appearance, the newspaper tells us what has happened in the world, the pressure from the oranges or the odor of eggs determines which one we will select, the note to the milkman tells him how we wish him to act. The appearances of the sky or the words of the weather report influence the way we will dress, the way we will behave outdoors. We do not put on our raincoats indoors nor raise an umbrella between us and the newspaper. We eat not the menu but rather what its printed words stand for. Signs denote something other than themselves, other things or other aspects of the thing of which they are a part. The marks on the newspaper stand for happenings in China; the rate of our pulse beat stands for the condition of our heart. Signs influence our beliefs, our preferences, our feelings, our actions with respect to what they signify. They dispose us to react to something other than themselves in one way rather than another.—CHARLES MORRIS, *The Open Self,* pp. 16-17

Though General English is hard to describe by itself, partly because its characteristics are so familiar to us, it will become clearer by comparison with the other varieties that follow. Obviously it has a wide range, shading off into Formal English in one direction and Informal in the other. It is the most useful variety, without the limitations of the others, and since it has such wide currency and in fact can reach practically all readers, it is the most necessary to master, and is the proper goal of instruction.

Formal English—limited use • Formal English is typically found in books and articles intended for circulation in somewhat restricted groups—among teachers, ministers, doctors, lawyers, and other professional people of general or specialized intellectual interests. It is found also in addresses and other formal talks and often colors the conversation of people who do a good deal of reading, but it is more characteristic of writing than of speaking.

Although Formal English will include most of the traits of General English, it will show enough of the Formal vocabulary and constructions to give it a definite tone. The vocabulary has many words seldom used in ordinary speech, specialized words from various scientific and scholarly fields, and words of more general meaning associated with the literary tradition (*desultory, ubiquitous, redoubtable*). It uses a good many abstract nouns, which summarize rather than present experience directly (*luxury, distinction, research*). For people familiar with the words, they often carry a good deal of suggestiveness (*bosky, ominous, paradox, transcend*) and often have some appeal of sound or rhythm (*quintessence, immemorial, memorable*).

In Formal English the constructions are often elaborate and filled out; the short cuts characteristic of General and Informal English are not taken. Contractions are avoided, relative pronouns are not omitted, prepositions and conjunctions are likely to be repeated in parallel constructions, and so on. Sentences tend to be somewhat longer than in General writing, binding more ideas together, with parallel and balanced clauses; the word order may be different from the usual English pattern, and modifiers may come between the main elements of subject, verb, and object. Allusions to literature and to events of the past are common. Deliberate, *studied* choice of sentence patterns as well as words characterizes Formal writing, making its impact quite different from the more casual styles of most General and all Informal English.

NONSTANDARD ENGLISH • *Limited use*
Chiefly spoken • Language not much touched by school instruction; often conspicuously local; not appropriate for public affairs or for use by educated people

STANDARD ENGLISH
Informal English • *Limited use*
More often spoken than written • Speaking and writing of educated people in informal situations; includes shoptalk or slang and some localisms
General English • *Unlimited use*
Both spoken and written • Speaking and writing of educated people in their private or public affairs

Formal English • *Limited use*
More often written than spoken • Speaking and writing for somewhat restricted groups in formal situations

Comments

1. Standard English is here divided into Informal, General, and Formal English because we are mainly concerned with these variations in the English of the cultivated. The same subdivisions could be made in Nonstandard English. (See Kenyon, "Cultural Levels...")
2. The varieties are not to be thought of as sharply defined and mutually exclusive but as shading into each other. A passage might be regarded as Informal, for instance, if it had several conspicuous traits characteristic of that variety even though the greater part of the passage was in General English.
3. Usage is said to be *divided* when choices exist between two usages in General English, both of which are in good standing (for example, the spellings of *catalog* or *catalogue,* or a comma or no comma before the *and* of the last item in a series, or *dived* or *dove* as the past tense of *dive*) .
4. *Slovenly* (impoverished speech, often including obscenity and profanity) and *Stilted* (pretentious and unnecessarily heavy speech or

Typical uses: Conversations of many people at home, with friends, on the job • Representations of this speech in stories, plays, movies, comic strips, on radio and television (See pp. 23-25)

Typical uses: Casual conversation • Letters between people who know each other well; diaries, personal writing; writing close to popular speech, as in fiction and some newspaper columns (See pp. 21-23)

Typical uses: Conversation; talks to general audiences • Most business letters and advertising • News and feature stories, newspaper columns • Magazine articles and books on subjects of general interest • Most fiction and other literature for general circulation • Many college papers (See pp. 15-17)

Typical uses: Addresses and lectures to special audiences • Some editorials and business writing • Literature of somewhat limited circulation: essays and criticisms, much poetry, some fiction • Academic writing: reference works, dissertations, most term papers, reference papers, some textbooks • Scientific and technical reports • Books and articles dealing with special subjects for professional groups and experts (See pp. 17, 20-21)

writing—gobbledygook) may be regarded as the extremes of Nonstandard and Standard English.

5. The varieties are characterized by some differences in word forms, in pronunciation, in vocabulary, and in grammatical constructions and by the avoidance of certain locutions (as Standard English avoids double negatives). The chief differences, and the easiest to discuss, are in vocabulary.

6. Labeling a usage as belonging to any one of the varieties indicates that it is characteristically used as the description of that variety, that its connotation comes from this use, and that it is not characteristic of another variety. Such labeling does not prohibit the use of the word under other conditions but does suggest that it may be inappropriately conspicuous in another variety.

7. Though the writing situations in which Nonstandard and Informal English may appropriately be used are limited, these varieties are used much more often than General and Formal by the total number of *speakers* of the language.

This does not mean that Formal writing need be stiff or dull, though there is danger that it may; but the nature of the language of Formal writing makes its appeal somewhat limited. It often demands considerable concentration and presupposes in the reader an interest in specialized subject matter or in general ideas and some awareness of our cultural tradition. The special audience for which it is written will not only follow the material but, if it is really well expressed, will appreciate the style as well. Formal English appeals to some readers simply because it is different from everyday language.

An example will show some of the traits of Formal English. The words carry a good deal of force and suggestiveness (*high* in a special sense, *guardians of culture, time-honored, outrage*), and some are of rather restricted currency (*occupational disease, disparate, diverse*). Most of the meaning is carried by nouns and adjectives. The sentences are long, averaging 37 words, but their parts are closely and naturally related.

All such perversions of high traditions are intensified by traditionalism, the occupational disease of guardians of culture. The guardians tend to forget that tradition has always been the great enemy of the founders of great traditions: that Socrates was a radical who did corrupt the youth of Athens by impiously urging them to question the time-honored ways; or that the teachings of Christ were an outrage to precisely the most cultivated, respectable, God-fearing people of his time; or that the American Revolution was strictly a revolution, illegal, violent, and bloody. In particular, the traditionalists abuse our Western heritage by singling out some one school of thought as the "essential" or "true" tradition; whereas diversity and nonconformity are the very soul of this heritage. It is the richest tradition that man has ever known simply because it includes so many disparate elements from diverse sources, and has never been at rest.—HERBERT J. MULLER, *The Uses of the Past,* p. 58

Some highly individual styles in literature require detailed study to be understood because of the unusual use of words and the uniquely personal associations of words as well as various departures from the typical patterns of current English —the writing of Carlyle, for example. In the quite different styles characteristic of scholarly and scientific writing at its best, a precise and specialized vocabulary is employed in a compact, impersonal statement. Beyond these are abuses of Formal English: the cumbersome, archaic, and highly repetitious language of most legal documents, and the pretentious, abstract, and equally repetitious style of some bad academic writing and of much of the official writing of government and business, popularly and appropriately known as gobbledygook.

But good Formal English may be the best way (if not the only way) to present certain ideas. The ability to read Formal English is a necessity for educated people and one of the abilities to be perfected in college. Although a good deal of writing is more Formal, or at least more difficult, than it need be, intellectual growth demands its mastery. In some college writing, as in term papers for advanced courses, the writing is appropriately Formal, though it should not be excessively so, never to the extent of seeming affected. A development toward somewhat more Formal expression will naturally come with increased experience in reading college-level material.

Informal English—limited use • Informal English is at the other side of General English and grades off into Nonstandard English. When we write for our own convenience or amusement or when we talk or write to members of our family or to friends, we use the language with more freedom than when addressing strangers or people we do not know well. When Informal English is used publicly, it presupposes a regular relationship of some sort between user and receiver; it may be used in a recurring radio program or newspaper column, or for a distinctly informal situation or subject—amusing little experiences, comment on social foibles, sports, humor.

Informal English has considerable range, sometimes including distinctly Formal traits for contrast or Nonstandard forms for accuracy or novelty. Most conspicuously it uses words and phrases characteristic of familiar conversation, words sometimes marked *Colloquial* in dictionaries (*snooze, in-laws, goner, arty, doohickey*); words of special currency at the moment (*in-group, overkill, escalate*); informal coinages for common things or situations (*TV, hootenanny, go steady*); clipped words (*stereo, hi-fi, psych*). It may include more *localisms than General English ordinarily would, *shoptalk (words from occupations, like *mike, strike* [to dismantle], *hypo, typo*) and *slang, words continually being formed and given a temporary currency in offhand or flashy speech: *flip, flack, flick, funky, fuzz.* Since writer and reader usually have a good deal in common, the writer can take much for granted—in material, in allusion to common experiences, and in the special current connotation of words.

Informal English has its chief use in lively conversation and in writing where the subject and situation warrant a light touch, as in this columnist's comment on the prevalence of candle heating devices for the table:

Gone are the days when a man got his coffee all saucered and blowed and at the right temperature, only to have the latter drop so rapidly that the beverage was stone cold by the time he got his handle-bar mustache parted and ready.... Now a man saucers and blows the stuff and puts it on a little iron cradle over a lighted candle, where the brew starts boiling once more in nothing flat. Then he has to begin all over again. It's going to be hard on commuters until they get the hang of the new gimmick.... The ironmonger is jubilant and the fire insurance companies will be as soon as they get hep to this situation and jack up the rates. It makes for a nice, lively business cycle, with the boys at the firehouse scarce able to get through a checker game before the siren sounds again.—INEZ ROBB, "Candle Is Remarkable Invention," *Seattle Post-Intelligencer*, Feb. 6, 1954

General, Formal, and Informal English are varieties of *Standard English*. Standard English presents, then, a wide range of usage, offering a writer many choices of words and constructions—choices which in any given paper will set its tone and define its possible audience. Some principles to guide these choices will be discussed in the last section of this chapter.

The basis of Standard English is social, the "differences due to situation" described on pages 13-15. Its basis has been well described by C. C. Fries:

On the whole, however, if we ignore the special differences that separate the speech of New England, the South, and the Middle West, we do have in the United States a set of language habits, broadly conceived, in which the major matters of the political, social, economic, educational, religious life of this country are carried on. To these language habits is attached a certain social prestige, for the use of them suggests that one has constant relations with those who are responsible for the important affairs of our communities. It is this set of language habits, derived originally from an older London English, but differentiated from it somewhat by its independent development in this country, which is the "standard" English of the United States. Enough has been said to enforce the point that it is "standard" not because it is any more correct or more beautiful or more capable than other varieties of English; it is "standard" solely because it is the particular type of English which is used in the conduct of the important affairs of our people. It is also the type of English used by the *socially acceptable* of most of our communities and insofar as that is true it has become a social or class dialect in the United States.—C. C. FRIES, *American English Grammar*, p. 13

The attention given to Standard English in schools and colleges is intended to help young people speak and write like educated people so that they will be prepared to take their part in public affairs. Writing in composition courses is practice for later work in college and after college.

Nonstandard English

The everyday speech of many people, relatively untouched by school instruction or by the tradition of printed English, makes up Nonstandard or Vulgate English, the name popularized by H. L. Mencken in *The American Language*.[1] This speech variety is a very real and important part of the English language and is studied by linguists with the same seriousness with which they study other varieties. Its distinguishing traits are not lapses from any brand of reputable or Standard English. It is a different development from the same language stock, representing a selection of sounds, words, forms, and constructions made under different social conditions. It works very well in carrying on the affairs and occupations of millions of people and is consequently worthy of study and respect. It is avoided in business, government, and literature chiefly for social reasons, not because it is inadequate as a means of communication. It is not ordinarily printed, since, for various historical and social reasons, the printed language is a selection of words, forms, and constructions considered appropriate to public affairs and so to Standard English.

Nonstandard English differs most noticeably from the other chief varieties of English in the use of pronoun and verb forms and in the freer use of localisms. Many of its words have a longer history in English than the more genteel words that have replaced them in "society." Some of the forms and constructions have a continuous history back to a time when they

---

[1]See Leonard Bloomfield, "Literate and Illiterate Speech," *American Speech*, 1927, 2:432-439; Fries, *AEG;* Mencken.

were reputable: Chaucer used a double negative occasionally; *an't* or **ain't* and *he don't* were reputable until less than a century ago, **you was* as a singular was standard in eighteenth-century England and America. Many other features of Non-standard English are equally natural developments of the language that by some accident of dialect or other circumstance did not become Standard English.

Nonstandard English is primarily spoken. Forms like *ain't, dassent, scairt, you was* are conspicuous when they appear in print but much less so when spoken rapidly and with appropriate (not exaggerated) emphasis. They occur in many radio and television programs, in plays, and in the conversation of stories. You will find them, often distorted, in many comic strips. Occasionally a Nonstandard form is used in humor or for special effect, as in Josh Billings' epigram: "It isn't so much the ignorance of mankind that makes them ridiculous as knowing so many things that ain't so."

The monolog of the barber in Ring Lardner's story "Haircut" is a fairly accurate representation of Nonstandard. A few traits of pronunciation are shown (though the *of* in "she'd of divorced him" is just a Nonstandard spelling of the normal contraction of *have*—"she'd've divorced him"), adverbs without the *-ly* ending, *seen* for *saw, beat her to it,* and so on.

Jim didn't work very steady after he lost his position with the Carterville people. What he did earn, doin' odd jobs round town, why he spent pretty near all of it on gin, and his family might of starved if the stores hadn't of carried them along. Jim's wife tried her hand at dressmakin', but they ain't nobody goin' to get rich makin' dresses in this town.

As I say, she'd of divorced Jim, only she seen that she couldn't support herself and the kids and she was always hopin' that some day Jim would cut out his habits and give her more than two or three dollars a week.

They was a time when she would go to whoever he was workin' for and ask them to give her his wages, but after she done this once or twice, he beat her to it by borrowin' most of his pay in advance. He told it all round town, how he had outfoxed his Missus. He certainly was a caution.—RING LARDNER, "Haircut," *Roundup*, p. 25

Since the established spellings of English words are those of Standard English, it is not easy to give an adequate representation of Nonstandard English in print. And sometimes the effort to represent it is merely a somewhat more phonetic transcription of pronunciations current in all varieties of

English, like *wuz* for *was, sez* for *says,* and *wimmin* for *women.*

Schools attempt to carry on their work in what they assume to be the language of the upper social classes, Standard English. Students who go into the professions, into many branches of business, and into most white-collar jobs continue to use Standard English more or less consistently. Those who go into manual labor and the less well-paid and less socially elevated jobs often use Nonstandard English. The differences between Standard and Nonstandard are probably decreasing as the result of influences of each on the other.

The objection to Nonstandard is not that its grammar is "bad," but that it is inappropriate to the readers for whom college students and college graduates write and to the subjects they are handling. Nonstandard English may be effective in writing the conversation of some characters in stories, and it may be used occasionally to give a note of realism to portraits of real people who naturally speak it. But ordinarily it is inappropriate in college writing. When an expression in this book is marked "Nonstandard," it should not be used except for good reason. Some Nonstandard practices are discussed in Chapters 8 and 9.

What is good English?

To a student of language, all varieties of English are equally a part of the language, and one variety is to be observed and studied as carefully as another. But to a *user* of English, the varieties are by no means equal. They differ in the impression they make on people and in the ideas they can communicate.

Every educated person normally wants to speak and write what may be called "good English," just as he wants to "make a good personal appearance" and to "be intelligent." But the great range and diversity of the English language raises many questions about usage. The problem of English usage is much like the other social problems which face us. In dress, to take the most convenient parallel, we gradually develop something we call taste or judgment, in part by imitating others, consciously or unconsciously, in part by consulting people who are supposed to know what is good form, in part by following our own preferences. Our usual dress lies between the extremes of work, sport, and formal clothes. It is comfortable; it reflects something of the taste of the wearer; it is appropriate to going about personal affairs, to work in stores and offices, to college classes, to informal social affairs. But a person needs to have and to be able to wear several kinds of clothes, and he needs to know when it is appropriate to wear one kind or another. In the same way, anyone who is going to take his place in public, business, social, or educational affairs needs to know the resources of the various kinds of English and when they can profitably be drawn on. For answers to questions about English usage, you can often consult books, especially dictionaries and handbooks. You can ask people who write well; you can ask teachers who have made the study of the language part of their professional training. And you can always be watching what effective writers do—how the language is handled in the better books and magazines. This observation is especially important, because, as in dress and in manners, more or less conscious imitation of those you approve of or wish to be associated with will bulk large in forming your own habits. Few will ever write with real ease unless they listen and read a good deal and so unconsciously absorb the ways of their language by direct experience.

Basis of good English set by the purpose of communication • Of course, if anyone wants to talk to himself or write for his own amusement, relief, or "self-expression," or if he deliberately sets out to deceive or puzzle, then his usage need not conform to any established practice. And a writer may experiment as much as he wishes, as James Joyce and Gertrude Stein and others have done, creating for themselves a limited audience willing to study out their meaning in spite of handicaps. But the ordinary and principal function of language is immediate and effective communication, making someone understand or feel something, or getting him to do something that we want him to do.

This fundamental purpose in speaking and writing prevents the language, complicated as it is, from falling into chaos, and sets the broad limits of what is permissible. We use words in the meanings they have acquired from their past use and we make our statements in established patterns. From this point of view, Fries defines the basis of good English:

. . . language is a means to an end and that end is specifically to grasp, to possess, to communicate experience. Accordingly, that is good language, good English, which, on the one hand, most fully realizes one's own impressions, and, on the other, is most completely adapted to the purposes of any particular communication.—C. C. FRIES, *What Is Good English?* p. 120

In other words, so far as the writer's language furthers his intended effect, it is good; so far as it fails to further that effect, it is bad, no matter how "correct" it may be.[1]

This definition of good English may differ somewhat from other definitions you have seen. Its emphasis is on the primary purpose of language and it subordinates correctness for its own sake. Isolated details such as spelling, punctuation, capitalization, and Standard usage are important, but always in relation to their appropriateness to the immediate purpose. This appropriateness is threefold: to the subject and situation, to the expected listeners or readers, and to the writer or speaker himself. A consideration of these will yield *principles,* rather than *rules,* to guide actual practice.

Appropriateness to subject and situation • In conversation we automatically adjust our language as well as our topics to the situation. For our talks and papers, whether assigned or voluntary, there should be a similar adjustment. The language of a reminiscence will differ somewhat from that of an explanatory paper for a popular audience or a plea for action or a scholarly discussion of ideas. (See Chapters 5-7 and 11 on types of writing.) The effect on the audience depends partly on the variety of English used.

Choosing the appropriate variety of English is one sign of a practiced, mature writer. Slang may fit in a letter or in a popular newspaper column; it is usually out of place in discussing a serious or elevated subject. Most fiction is General or Informal. Writing on a technical or professional subject is more likely to be Formal. The language of a church service and of religious and philosophical discussion is Formal.

Students—all writers, for that matter, who strive for language appropriate to subject and situation—come at last to the same resolution: *to treat simple subjects simply,* or, in terms of our varieties of English, to treat them in General English. Most subjects are relatively simple, or at least the writer is going to give only a simplified version of them. Amateur writers are often not content to be themselves but assume a dialect that is really foreign to them, too Formal to be appropriate to their subjects.

---

[1]Fries, *AEG,* Ch. 1 (an unusually good statement) ; Fries, *The Teaching of English* (Ann Arbor, 1949) , Ch. 5; Otto Jespersen, *Mankind, Nation and Individual from a Linguistic Point of View* (Oslo, 1925) , Ch. 5; Pooley, Part I.

Students should also avoid writing too Informally in papers which discuss serious subjects. But the better students in a composition course often err in the direction of overly Formal writing, probably because of the emphasis on Formal correctness throughout their school careers.

Though teachers and students will not always agree in their judgments of particular passages, they will agree on a surprising number of them. And once students fully grasp the principle of appropriateness they are not likely to return either to unnecessary pomposity or to unsuitable lightness.

The tone of a passage should be consistent unless the writer has special reason for departing from it. A conspicuous lapse from Formal to Informal or from Informal to Formal should ordinarily be avoided. These examples show obvious and awkward lapses:

Formal to Informal: If our Concert and Lecture program this year is not superior to that of any other college in the country, *I'll eat every freshman lid on the campus.*

Informal to Formal: *I was bowled over* by the speed with which the workmen assembled the parts.

Some writing—in *The New Yorker,* for example, and in many newspaper columns—successfully fuses distinctly Informal words with quite Formal ones. The expressions are unified by the vigor and smoothness with which they are brought together and are not lapses from appropriateness. Superficial consistency is not so important as the fundamental appropriateness to the situation. But for most writers one variety of English should be kept throughout a piece of writing.

Both in a composition course and out of one, keep a Formal style for complex or scholarly subjects and an Informal style for light or humorous ones; write in General English on most matters.

Appropriateness to listener or reader • If you are trying to reach a particular type of reader, you will adjust both your subject matter and your expression to him. To reach him, to really get your points across, you have to be more than merely intelligible: you have to meet him pretty much on his own ground. You already do this almost automatically in your letters, writing in somewhat different ways to different persons. You no doubt adjust your expression to the expectations of different teachers. Certainly in many other situations you pay some attention to the language you believe is expected of you.

Some types of writing are in theory completely adjusted to their readers, notably directions to be followed, newspaper writing, and advertising. Although we realize that they often fail, either from cheapness or from dullness and unintended formality, in a general way they do meet their readers' expectations.

Essays (or themes) are sometimes difficult to write because you lose the sense of having a reader. It is better to try to visualize a particular audience, to direct your paper to some magazine, or, more commonly, to write for the class of which you are a member. Directing your paper to the members of your class will help you select material that will interest and inform them or at least appeal to most of them, and it will help you judge what words and what kinds of sentences are appropriate. Remember that you are not writing for everyone but for a selected audience. Novels are for readers of differing tastes, and even the audiences of best sellers like *The Robe* and *Lolita* are far from identical. In most of your writing a firm General style is probably best, for many people prefer it and anyone can be reached through it.

Clearness.   Since your aim is to convey some fact or conviction, some fancy or feeling to a person or group, appropriateness to a reader means clear expression: exact words and, for the most part, words in the vocabulary of the person you are addressing. If the subject requires words unfamiliar to him, their meaning can usually be made clear from the way they are used. If not, you can throw in a tactful explanation or in some instances resort to formal definition.

Clarity also requires careful sentence construction. Experienced readers can grasp more elaborate sentences than those who read little or hurriedly. But anyone will be pleased with direct, straightforward sentences. Clarity should be one of your main objectives in revising a paper.

Correctness.   Avoiding what a reader might consider errors is a major task for a beginning writer. People tend to judge us by superficial traits, in language as in other matters. Spelling, for example, bulks larger in most people's judgment of writing than it reasonably should. Certainly many people take delight in finding what are (or what they consider to be) errors in language, especially in the writing or speech of those supposed to be educated or of anyone soliciting their favor. Courtesy demands that a writer should do his best in anything he is submitting to another; soiled manuscript, many interlineations, confusion of common forms like *its* and *it's,* misspelling of common words (*similiar* for *similar*) are ordinarily the result of carelessness or thoughtlessness. The chief reason for mastering the "minimum essentials" of English forms (the sort of things discussed in Chapters 8, 9, and 10) is to meet the expectations of educated readers. You need not worry about these matters as you write, but you must reserve some time for revision to bring the paper to the best state you can.

Liveliness.　　There is so much unavoidable dullness in the world that any reader will appreciate some liveliness in writing, in the expression as well as in the material. Striving for novelty is dangerous, and its results are often self-defeating. But students frequently hide behind a flat sort of language, squeezing all the life out of their writing. Your words need not be out of the ordinary; for the most part, they should be those you would use in serious conversation. Your sentences should not be formless or dragged out; they should suggest an alert interest. Refer to things people do and say, use plenty of lively detail to clarify ideas and to keep up interest, and pay special attention to the beginnings and endings of your papers.

Some professional writers have set themselves the rule "Don't write anything you couldn't read yourself." Following this principle means that you will choose your best available material, write it as interestingly as you can, and make it genuinely readable. If you promise yourself that you won't turn in a paper that you couldn't read yourself with interest and perhaps profit, you will not only be accepting responsibility for your work, but you will also be permanently improving your control of expression and laying a sure foundation for continued growth in good English.

In general, satisfy your reader's expectations insofar as you believe they are worthy of respect. But don't aim at your reader's worst, compromising yourself and insulting him. Visualize him in his better moments and write for him as he is then.

Appropriateness to speaker or writer • In the speaker-listener or writer-reader relationship, the speaker or writer dominates. He makes the choices; his judgment or unconscious sense of fitness finally controls. Your language in the long run represents your personality, and you are responsible for the language you use. To take this responsibility, you first need to inform yourself fully of the possibilities of the English language. Observe what is spoken and written, use dictionaries and other reference works, and consult people who have studied English as a language. You can then apply this information in your own work according to your best judgment. There is nothing mysterious about the matter; it is just a natural process of learning and applying what is learned.

The most important step in improving your language habits is to watch your own speech and writing to see what their good qualities are and what shortcomings they may have. Can you confidently pronounce the words you need in conversation or recitation? Does your language tend to be Formal, or is it predominantly Informal, or General? Do you rely too much on slang or on trite words, or do you lapse into Nonstandard expressions? When you talk or write to someone older than yourself or when you write a paper for a college course, do you choose the most appropriate part of your natural language, or do you assume an entirely different sort of English?

And, finally, is the language you use consistent with the rest of your conduct? If you are a rather casual person, informal in dress and manner, we should expect your English to be somewhat Informal; if you are conventional in dress and manner, we should expect your English to be more Formal. It is necessary for you also to realize the direction in which you are moving, for young people, especially in college, are changing, becoming either more flexible or more conventional in their ideas and manners, or making some other change. Their language should be moving similarly. In your first papers in a composition course you should write naturally so that you and your instructor can decide together on the direction your growth should take. Such growth will in part be in the direction of greater appropriateness to yourself.

The three sorts of appropriateness here suggested for arriving at good English (appropriateness to the subject and situation, to the listener or reader, and to the writer or speaker) will not always be in harmony. The subject may seem to demand words that are not appropriate to the reader. The writer can usually solve such a problem either by finding simpler words or by explaining the necessary but unfamiliar ones. The reader's expectation and the writer's natural manner of expression may be different. Such a conflict can be solved by the writer—deciding how essential to his purpose his own turns of expression are, whether he can honorably yield to the reader's expectation or whether his usage is so necessary to his sense of the subject that compromise is impossible. In the long run the writer's sense of fitness, his pride in his work, will resolve most such conflicts.

As a result of this approach to good English you should have confidence in writing. The greatest handicap in writing is fear—fear of pencil and paper, fear of making a mistake, fear of offending the reader's (teacher's) taste. The opposite attitude, cockiness, is a nuisance and is equally at odds with good writing, but fewer students suffer from that than from inhibitions about their language. As yet psychologists can't tell us much about the mental activity involved in thinking or writing, but some of them believe that the fundamental condition for effectiveness is a positive feeling of readiness— which amounts really to a sort of faith that when you prepare to write, language appropriate to the occasion will come. A wide knowledge of the possibilities of current English, backed up by sufficient practice in writing for specific readers and sufficient care in revision, should increase your confidence. With such confidence you can write your best, for good English is not primarily a matter of rules but of judgment.

Exercises

1. Study the language in the passages below and decide what variety of English is used in each (see table, pp. 18-19). Cite specific words and constructions in support of your decisions. Discuss the appropriateness of the style to the subject and to what you judge to be the writer's purpose.

a. One spring day, just after a thunder shower, I walked into the yard of an abandoned farm in upstate New York. The old house had gaping holes in its walls where windows had been, and the swinging doors creaked dismally in the wind. The yard had grown up to tall weeds and grass, which almost covered several flat stones that lay about. I lifted one of them and under it I saw the open burrow of some small animal. Then, in a side chamber off the main tunnel, I found the discarded shells of more than two dozen snails. The empty shells were packed close together in the chamber. What animal had put them there?

Later I returned with two small cage traps, which I set in the tunnel. Within two days I had caught a pair of short-tailed shrews. They were the builders of the tunnel, the tidy housekeepers who were careful not to obstruct their travel way with empty snails' shells. I released the shrews in their tunnel, then set the stone over it just as I had found it.—John Terres, "Just Out from under a Rock," *Sports Illustrated,* May 4, 1964, p. 66

b. *9 Nov 62*   It was bound to happen. The other night I am sitting on my cot minding my own business when an RA (Regular Army) kid across the way looks at me with a pained expression on his face and says, "What did I do? Just tell me what I did wrong?" Later he yells at a group of men talking at the far end of the tent, "I know what you're saying about me!" This kid has always taken the Army too seriously. He has been on the Peanut Patrol and has probably taken all the abuse to heart. On top of that he got a dear john letter. He will be shipped home or shoot someone. The MP that fired the shot has already gone. The men are mumbling that they too are going to crack up just to get out of this hole.—Charles Vanderburgh, "A Draftee's Diary from the Mississippi Front," *Harper's Magazine,* Feb. 1964, p. 44

c. The mentally retarded child makes a normal or increased *amount* of sound in comparison to well children, and vocalizations are qualitatively those that are also heard among healthy children, the only difference being a change in age of appearance. The healthy infant should have done with babbling by twenty-eight months and use exclusively words and phrases and during play make some chanting noises representing some primitive form of singing; he may also imitate sounds of vehicles or animals, but all of his vocalizations seem to fall into distinct patterns. The random aspect of the eight-months-old babbler is conspicuously absent in the healthy child of two and a half. The retardate, however, is heard to make the sounds of the normal eight-months-old at a much later age, the exact occurrence depending on the general rate of development of cognitive function. The sequence of cooing, babbling, words, phrases and sentences is preserved but in severe retardation the final stages may never be attained. As in the normal child, understanding of language is always a bit ahead of production and there must be a close correlation between development of understanding and speaking if the diagnosis is to be maintained. Mutism or highly bizarre sound production such as exclusively meowing like a cat or barking like a dog are definitely not characteristic of mental retardation. Nor should there be any marked discrepancies between the development of the various verbal and language skills. Mental retardation should make it impossible for a child to have the ability to learn long passages of discourse by heart and reproduce them with flawless articulation and grammar in the fashion of an actor. Even in retardates where language is perfectly developed, the semantic content of discourse remains simple, and the sophistications of wit, drama, or propaganda are beyond their comprehension.—Eric H. Lenneberg, "Language Disorders in Childhood," *Harvard Educational Review,* Spring 1964, p. 159

d. The drama of this landscape is in the sky, pouring with light and always moving. The earth is passive. And yet the beauty I am struck by, both as present fact and as revived memory, is a fusion: this sky would not be so spectacular without this earth to change and glow and darken under it. And whatever the sky may do, however the earth is shaken or darkened, the Euclidean perfection abides. The very scale, the hugeness of simple forms, emphasizes stability. It is not hills and mountains which we should call eternal. Nature abhors an elevation as much as it abhors a vacuum; a hill is no sooner elevated than the forces of erosion begin tearing it down. These prairies are quiescent, close to static; looked at for any length of time, they begin to impose their awful perfection on the observer's mind. Eternity is a peneplain.—Wallace Stegner, *Wolf Willow,* p. 7

e. Visitors to our place, instead of being barked at by dogs rushing from under the porch, are squalled at by peacocks whose blue necks and crested heads pop up from behind tufts of grass, peer out of bushes and crane downward from the roof of the house, where the bird has flown, perhaps for the view. One of mine stepped from under the shrubbery one day and came forward to inspect a carful of people who had driven up to buy a calf. An old man and five or six white-haired, barefooted children were piling out of the back of the automobile as the bird approached. Catching sight of him, the children stopped in their tracks and stared, plainly hacked to find this superior figure blocking their path. There was silence as the bird regarded them, his head drawn back at its most majestic angle, his folded train glittering behind him in the sunlight.

"Whut is thet thang?" one of the small boys asked finally in a sullen voice.

The old man had got out of the car and was gazing at the peacock with an astounded look of recognition. "I ain't seen one of them since my granddaddy's day," he said, respectfully removing his hat. "Folks used to have 'em, but they don't no more."

"Whut is it?" the child asked again in the same tone he had used before.

"Churren," the old man said, "that's the king of the birds!"—Flannery O'Connor, "Living With a Peacock," *Holiday,* Sept. 1961, pp. 111-112

f. To a cub reporter breaking into sports in St. Louis 35 years ago, the New York writers were godlike creatures. The kid was, to be sure, almost incredibly naive, but being accepted by the top guys in the dodge was enormously important to him, and with a busher's bat-eyed innocence he regarded anybody who got his stuff published in a New York paper as a top guy per se.—Red Smith, Chicago *Sun-Times,* Sept. 16, 1964

2. Group the following words according to the varieties of English in which they are typically used. Refer to the table on pages 18-19 and consult a dictionary if necessary—it won't distinguish the four varieties but it will give you some hints. For words not typical of General English, give an equivalent General word or phrase.

abrogate	drownded	nonage	sidekick
aperture	edit	often	smog
backlash	escalator	OK (verb)	spunky
blat	gate-crasher	passim	therein
blurt	give up	plethora	this-here
boughten	hiccup	pucker	thrombosis
con (verb)	hungry	redd up	victuals
corpulent	jinx	rend	viewpoint
disparate	juggle	rev (verb)	wacky
domicile	mire	risky	whence

3. Sometimes the sense in which a word is used determines how it should be classified. Decide from the context which variety of English each of these italicized words belongs to—Formal, General, Informal, or Nonstandard:

   a. All night long he heard the *drip* of the water.

   b. My last blind date was certainly a *drip*.

   c. I get bored stiff by all that *jazz* about cybernetics.

   d. What I wanted to do was listen to *jazz* at The Blue Note.

   e. *Irregardless* of his advice, I'm going to major in psychology.

   f. It has been suggested that the word *irregardless* is a blend of "regardless" and "irrespective."

   g. I will *drain* the vegetables.

   h. Two exams a day *drain* a girl.

   i. I *laid* on the bed for an hour.

   j. After we had *laid* the carpet, we moved the furniture back.

   k. John is a great admirer of the poetry of the *Beat* Generation.

   l. After walking all day at the fair, John was *beat*.

   m. He was really *looped*.

   n. They *looped* the curtains back to let in more light.

   o. All we do in class is *yak* about Eliot.

   p. He explained the difference between a *yak* and a buffalo.

   q. We have to *level* the surface before we can paint it.

   r. I want you to *level* with me.

4. Examine the introductory material in your dictionary. What labels does it use to record "Variations due to time" (pp. 4-6), "Variations due to place" (pp. 6-9), "Differences due to situation" (pp. 13-15)? When a word is unlabeled, do you feel free to use it in any writing that you are doing? Why or why not?

5. Keep a speech notebook and write down campus slang, pronunciations, and characteristic expressions. When you have gathered enough material, write a paper on the speech of students at your college. Comment on the differences you have observed in the varieties of speech used by students inside the classrooms and outside.

6. For a period of a few days, examine carefully the language of a newspaper columnist or of the characters in a comic strip. Write a brief report on the variety of English typically used and show that it is or is not appropriate to the subjects discussed.

7. Write a page of dialog in which you discuss with your roommate or a classmate a specific problem you have run into in one of your college courses. Then write a second page of dialog in which you discuss the same problem with the instructor of the course.

8. Examine the following passages from student papers. Decide what variety of English is most appropriate to the subject. Wherever you find the language unsatisfactory or incongruous, rewrite to make the style of the passage more consistent.

a. One day when I was twelve, my mother left the car keys on the hall table. Like any other adventurous he-man, I had always wanted to drive. Twenty minutes later, when the right fender was half ripped off the car, I commenced to speculate on the potential repercussions of my now-apparent ill-advised course of action.

b. My library can not be called large nor even small. It is tiny. One would scarcely notice the unobtrusive metal bookcase set against a wall of my room, for his attention would be captured by the massive desk, the modernistic drapes, and other products of my aberrant fancy, and he would depart without a glance at my collection of literary masterworks. But he would have missed something very important in my life. I love my books. Most of them are shabby and cheap. All of them are my friends.

c. Just then I heard the bell—the last bell signifying that class was to convene. I dashed into the classroom and tried desperately to relax and make myself think that he probably wouldn't call on me anyway. Even if he did, he couldn't flunk me for answering one little question wrong. But it was to no avail; the second question he asked was pointed right at me.

d. It has been affirmed that student government is a democratic organization and all democratic organizations institute effective employment of parliamentary procedure. Parliamentary procedure is necessary to hold down confusion in meetings and discussions.

e. A new word, unfamiliar to the reader, can also cause great difficulty in spelling. This word should be looked up previous to its use. It should, moreover, be written and learned to facilitate its correct spelling henceforth.

Chapter Two

THE
STAGES
IN
WRITING

While we may cheerfully concede that the great writer,
like the poet, is born and not made,
we need not hesitate to say that
the ordinary writer is made and not born.

B. A. Hinsdale

Writing a paper is work, and it should be gone about in a workmanlike manner. There is no mystery about it (unless you find yourself doing much better than you expected) and, like any other job, it should be done in a series of steps. Each step presents its problems, but each makes an important contribution to the finished paper.

For convenience of discussion, writing a paper can be divided into the eight steps, or stages, shown in the table on page 39. Of course, any such analysis is somewhat arbitrary because of the variable conditions involved in a particular paper—the writer's habits and background, his purpose, the complexity of the material, the proposed length of the paper, and the time at the writer's disposal. In writing a letter to a friend, the stages are telescoped and can hardly be distinguished, but in preparing a long, complex paper you must pay careful attention to each stage. In some writing tasks, the stages overlap, especially the early ones; work on the second stage may lead to reconsideration of the first, and so on. Making due allowance, then, for the telescoping of some of the steps, for the overlapping of others, and for the varying weight given to each because of differences between writers and between specific writing projects, we may take them (or all of them except the last) as typical of most writing. This chapter indicates briefly what is involved in each step. In one way or another, the rest of the book develops the general points made here.

Stages in Writing a Paper

1. *Focusing on a subject*—Definition of topic, sensing of problems involved and of possible sources of information
2. *Gathering material*—Notes (in mind or on paper) from memory, observation, interviews, reading, speculation
3. *Deciding on methods of development*—The ways of approaching and exploring the subject
4. *Organizing the paper*—A synopsis or outline of the paper
5. *Writing the first draft*—Tentative copy of the paper
6. *Revising*—Necessary changes in material, corrections and improvements in words, sentences, paragraphs
7. *Preparing the manuscript*—The completed paper, ready for reading or for printing
8. *Seeing the manuscript into print*—The printed copy

As you consider what is involved in each step in the process of writing, you should keep in mind that your background is one of your fundamental resources. Certainly you will put to use your memories, your general attitudes, your ways of thinking, as well as the words and habits of expression that you have accumulated. Out of this background—made up of what you have seen and heard and done, what you have thought and read—comes the entire material for some papers. (See Chapter 5, "Personal experience papers.") From this background should come your point of view, the way you look at a subject, without which a paper is likely to be impersonal and dull. And from it should spring individual words and phrases, illuminating comparisons and illustrations, incidents, information, bits of color and life that can contribute to the main subject in small but important ways.

With each day you live, your background grows. College brings an enormous number of new experiences and ideas to add to those you already have. The new enriches the old, and by considering past and present together, you can bring your total resources to bear on the ideas you are trying to express. If you do this, your papers will sound as though they were written by a living person, not by an automaton; they will sound as though they were written by you, not by somebody else. Both your total experience and your use of language are different from those of any other person. It is these differences that give you your individuality and that can in turn give your writing the stamp of individuality. Although too much insistence on yourself and your point of view will irritate your reader, some indication of the person behind the writing will increase his interest.

Focusing on a subject

The first stage in producing a particular piece of writing is to focus your attention on a definite topic or on some general subject that will yield a definite topic.

In much of the factual writing you will do in college and after graduation, the subject will be assigned or will be dictated by circumstances. As a student, you may be asked to report on a scientific experiment, to compare two characters in a story, or to evaluate the conflicting opinions held by two historians. On examinations you will need to write relevant answers to definite questions. If you are a member of the college newspaper staff, you may be assigned to cover a specific lecture or sports event. Later on, after leaving college, you may need to prepare reports for committees on which you serve, you may be instructed to submit your views on your company's sales campaign, or you may be persuaded to write an account of your travels overseas for your local newspaper or alumni magazine.

Much of your writing, then, is done to order—to meet requirements set for you by others. When the subject has been clearly defined and limited, you need not linger over the first stage of the writing process, except to make sure that you understand exactly what the assignment is. Unfortunately, instead of beginning immediately to investigate the assigned subject and gather material for it, some students waste time at this stage complaining that the topic is dull or unappealing. If you are interested in the subject from the beginning, count yourself lucky; but if you are not, don't feel that life has been hard on you. With a little effort and the exercise of your native curiosity, you can become interested in anything from earthworms to existentialism. In everyday affairs, curiosity is not always a virtue, but in intellectual matters, it is a blessing. Any subject is *potentially* interesting; you can make it *actually* interesting by getting curious about it and by taking steps to satisfy that curiosity.

For some of the papers you write in a composition course, you will probably be encouraged to find your own subjects, or you will be invited to carve out your subject from a very broad area like education or politics. When you are free to make such choices, you obviously have no excuse for complaining that what you have to write about is uninteresting. Without spending too much time waiting for the ideal subject to suggest itself, you should be able to settle on a subject which is not only good but good for *you*. In choosing a subject, you will want to consider the possibilities offered by your own experience, by the college courses you are taking, and by the world around you.

If you have the opportunity, it may prove wise, especially during the first few weeks of a composition course, to select subjects drawn from your own experience. For one thing, you will probably find that you are expected to write longer papers than you did in high school; for another, you will certainly find that you need to meet higher standards in the organization and expression of your ideas. Until you are confident that you can meet these standards, you should not handicap yourself unnecessarily by tackling extremely ambitious and difficult topics. When writing about your own experience, you are thoroughly familiar with the material and can give your main energy to developing, organizing, and expressing it. Sometimes students get bogged down in topics that are hopelessly pretentious or complicated because they have the mistaken notion that their own short lives offer no subjects worth writing about. But remember that your experience, however limited it may seem to you, will have in it many elements that are not shared by others. And as your reading should have made you realize, even the elements that are shared by everyone can be given a fresh and individual treatment. Your family, your friends, your school experiences, your jobs or hobbies or sports, the places you have lived in or visited—all offer subjects that can be developed into excellent papers.

You may also wish to use a "free choice" assignment as an opportunity to find out more about areas or issues that you have not yet had a chance to explore thoroughly. Good subjects can grow out of your desire to extend your experience, to learn more about a topic that has caught your interest in history, literature, economics, or biology. Naturally, you will want to choose a subject in which you will not be merely rehashing ideas gleaned from books or rewriting something you have read. In some of your college courses, it is essential to produce clear and accurate summaries of what you have read; but in a composition course you should aim for a subject which permits you to make your own contribution in the way of application or illustration, attitude or judgment. A survey of the increase in power of the federal government, based on your reading in a course in political science or American history, could be given point and interest if it were shaped into an argument that such an increase in power is or is not beneficial to the nation. Or you might use the historical material as a basis for considering the extension of federal control into a new area, such as the awarding of college scholarships.

Good subjects can regularly be found in new developments in the world around you—either the campus world or the larger one. Dormitory discussions and the daily newspaper will suggest subjects for explanatory and persuasive papers. In October 1962, for example, 90 percent of the students in one composition class chose to write about the Cuban crisis that came to a head during that month. During succeeding months, the same class used as subjects for papers Project Mercury, the Common Market, the desegregation of schools, a local case of censorship, dormitory regulation of women's hours, and a change in the college curriculum—all current, lively issues.

It should be emphasized that most of the examples just cited refer to subjects, not definite topics for papers. Although the first four—the Cuban crisis, Project Mercury, the Common Market, and school desegregation—all relate to specific events or situations, each needed further limitation before it could be handled satisfactorily in a short paper. A superficial and disorganized paper was produced by a student who tried to cover all aspects of the Cuban crisis—military, economic, political, and moral. A much better paper was produced by a student who chose to clarify the various attitudes toward the crisis expressed by the students in his dormitory.

Focusing on a subject means more than finding a general area for investigation and discussion; it means narrowing the area to something definite and manageable. When students are assigned "free choice" papers, the chief danger is that they will not limit their subjects sufficiently. (Occasionally a student selects a subject that is too insignificant for a paper of the length assigned. He finds that he must then build it out by going into trivial detail, by repeating himself, or by dragging in unrelated material.)

Because the purpose of a paper is to enlighten or persuade or entertain the reader, not just to remind him that the general subject exists or to rehash familiar information about it, you should limit your subject to one that can be handled adequately in the length expected. Unless you were writing a very condensed article for a reference work, there would not be much point in writing 1000 words—or even 5000 words—on Benjamin Franklin. But something could be done in a short paper with some phase of Franklin's career—his work as postmaster general, his part in the founding of the University of Pennsylvania, his relations with other statesmen, or his life in Paris. Similarly, "education" or "labor unions" or "J. D. Salinger" are not topics for papers but subject areas within which a great many possible topics lie. Your aim should be to find a topic that can be adequately treated in a paper of the length you are to write.

Perhaps the best way to limit your subject is to work out a sentence statement of your purpose in writing the paper. Try to define your purpose in a sentence or two or in a question that will be answered by the paper. Suppose you are an electronics hobbyist; several different papers could be written in this general area. You could tell about the various kinds of equipment you have built, the kits available, the mechanics of building your own equipment, the abbreviations and special language of electronics, and so on. You might be tempted to say a little something about all of these, and as a result write so generally that you would tell your readers nothing new. But a sentence statement would record your choice among possibilities. It might be: "The development of the printed circuit has cheapened the hobby of electronics." Besides giving you a limited and workable topic, such a statement will prevent you from wandering off the subject in later stages of writing.

Sometimes the subject cannot be definitely limited until after some material has been gathered. This is especially true in writing long papers for which a working bibliography of books and articles must be assembled as part of the preliminary analysis. (See Chapter 11, "Reference papers," p. 428.)

Once you have been assigned a definite topic or have selected and limited one of your own choice, the first stage in writing is over. You should know pretty clearly what the paper is to be about, and you should have some idea of how and where you will get the material for it.

Gathering material

The basic material for your writing comes from memory, from observation and experiment, from interviews and conversations, from reading and studying, from reasoning and reflecting on what you have learned in all these ways.

For letters and short papers about personal experience, you already have the material; but even for writing of this kind you will need to give some time to jogging your memory in order to re-create for yourself the scenes and incidents you want to bring before the reader. Making a conscious effort to recall half-forgotten details and impressions may make the difference between a flat, fuzzy account of an experience and a vivid, effective one. While it is hard to direct and control your memory, thinking about some past experience for a time and then recalling it at intervals can often bring back details which at first were hazy.

Sources of material outside your own mind can be more consciously worked, and skill in handling them can be cultivated. In particular, you can, by attention and practice, greatly improve your command of the direct sources of original material—observation, experiment, interviews. The habit of noticing details can help you in your writing, for a writer's chief distinction often comes from his unique expression based upon his own observation, and the interest and value of many papers rests on the amount of first-hand detail they carry.

Often you will need to make interpretations and judgments of the data assembled, and for critical papers in any field these interpretations and judgments become the central material. (See Chapter 7, "Persuasion papers.") The exercise of common sense and some elementary acquaintance with logic will help you test the soundness of your generalizations and improve the reliability of your evaluations and conclusions. Training yourself to read critically will make you aware of the different kinds of evidence needed to support different kinds of judgment.

For some papers you will need to acquaint yourself with the special techniques of research used by scientists and scholars. (See Chapter 11, "Reference papers.")

Although the material for short papers on simple and familiar subjects can sometimes be carried in your head, you will find that scratch notations help to keep ideas and impressions from slipping away. For more complex subjects you will need fairly extensive notes.

Deciding on methods of development

At the same time that you are assembling material for your paper, you should also be reflecting on possible ways of developing the subject. It is not enough to have a collection of raw data—facts, details, observations, impressions, judgments, generalizations. To produce a rich and interesting paper, you must know how to use the data.

Any subject, even one which has already been defined and limited, can be approached in several ways. If you are in the habit of reading carefully, you are pretty well aware of the methods commonly used in factual prose. You are probably most apt to recognize *description*, in which the writer presents you with a person, place, or object as he has seen or known it, or *narration*, in which he presents an incident or series of incidents or the steps in a process. But you have also read substantial stretches of explanatory or persuasive prose in which an author used *examples* as the chief means of clarifying or supporting his main point. Parts of essays (or even entire essays) may be developed by *definition*, by *comparison*, or by *classification*. Sometimes a subject can be developed most effectively by analyzing the *causes* of a situation or an event; sometimes it is useful to discuss the *effects* which have resulted or might result from a situation or event. Depending on the writer's purpose he might use one of these methods or several of them in treating a specific topic.

Each of these methods is discussed in Chapter 3. You will find it useful, as you are gathering material for a paper, to review the various methods of development and to decide which offer the best possibilities for the paper you are working on. If, for instance, your general subject is the jobs you have held and if you have limited the subject to the extent of formulating the sentence statement "Learning to work in my early years taught me a lot," what are some possible ways of developing that topic?

To a certain extent, producing your sentence statement (in the first stage of writing) has helped you gather material (in the second stage). Presumably you now have a collection of facts and incidents relating to your jobs and some ideas about what your jobs have taught you. But how are you going to bring those threads together? How are you going to approach and develop the subject? One way would be to describe your jobs, one after another, showing what you learned from each. Another would be to write a narrative account of the valuable experiences you have gained through working. Or you might classify your jobs on the basis of the kinds of demands they made (physical and mental) and then indicate which gave you the most pleasure or profit. You might want to open up your subject by comparing yourself with a friend who has never held a job. Again, you might concentrate pretty much on your reasons for going to work in the first place, why you continued working, and what effects your jobs have had on you. You might even (perhaps by contrasting your jobs with your hobbies) write a paper in which the chief aim is to define *work*. (We all use the term all the time, but we don't always mean the same thing by it.)

Considering these possibilities and deciding on one or more of them will lead you to review your statement of purpose and perhaps to revise it to make it more exact. If you have decided to classify your jobs on the basis of the skills they required, you might phrase your sentence statement this way: "The jobs I have held have made me determined to earn my living with my head, not my hands." If you have become interested in defining *work*, you might revise your first statement to "Learning to work in my early years has taught me what *work* means."

Choosing your methods of development will certainly help you in sorting, sifting, and evaluating the material you have gathered; and, if you find you need more material, you can search for it more purposefully. You will be able to estimate the relevance of a fact or generalization; you will know which bits of data are of primary importance and which secondary. Should you discard the descriptive details about your employers, or do you need more of them? Should you jot down more information about the jobs themselves? Do you need more specific evidence about what you have learned from them?

The second and third stages of writing—gathering material and determining the way material is to be used—are the stages most likely to be neglected or skimped by a hurried student. If he has given too little time and thought to assembling raw material and to figuring out how to develop his subject, he should not be surprised if he has trouble writing a paper. Either he doesn't have enough to say, or he doesn't know how to make the most of the material he has.

Organizing the paper

While you are deciding how you will use your material in developing your subject, you will also be thinking about how you will organize your paper. Grouping related material into blocks and then arranging these blocks in a sensible order constitutes the fourth stage in writing. From this stage should emerge a plan for the paper—whether in your mind or in scribbled notes or in a formally prepared outline.

Uses of outlines • How detailed your plan will be and how closely it will guide your writing depends partly on the length of the paper and partly on the conditions under which you find you can do your best work. Short papers on simple subjects obviously require less planning than long papers on difficult ones. Sometimes the organization of a paper grows quite naturally out of the material; in writing description and narration, for instance, you are to a certain extent committed to the order inherent in the scene you are describing or the event you are narrating. In a paper about ideas or policies, your own mind has to determine the topics or divisions of the subject and the order in which they should stand. Because you have more alternatives to choose from, the need for planning becomes more evident. But even in papers of this kind, experienced writers differ widely in their use of outlines.

Some writers like to produce a very detailed outline (really a skeleton of the entire paper) before they begin to write. If they have decided on the shape of the whole, they can give their full attention to one part at a time; they can write with ease and confidence because they do not have to worry whether a particular point goes here or there. Other writers like to use a sketchy outline more as a starting point than as a guide. They find that the actual process of composing suggests new possibilities for expanding the points they have jotted down and new ideas about the order in which they should appear. If they happen to have made a detailed outline before beginning to write, they are not surprised to find that the completed paper differs noticeably from that outline. They are more likely to make a full outline *after* they have produced the first draft and use it as a means of testing the structure and unity of what they have written. (Occasionally, instructors make an outline of a paper they are correcting, to see at a glance the strengths and weaknesses of the organization.)

Which kind of writer are you? If you have trouble establishing a clear direction in your papers, if they are criticized for being scattered and disorganized, you evidently need to make detailed outlines and follow them closely. If, on the other hand, your papers read as if you have just ticked off points one, two, three, then perhaps you are being cramped by your outlines and should train yourself to use them more flexibly. In either case, your teacher, from his knowledge of the typical merits and faults of your papers, can advise you about the kind of outline you should produce and the use you should make of it.

An outline is a schematic statement of the material in a paper, showing the order of topics and the general relationship between them. To make one, you first need to establish the main topics or divisions of the paper. For some papers, the major sections will be pretty much determined by your choice of methods of development. This would be true, for instance, if you had decided to discuss your reasons for going to work, the various jobs you had held, and the beneficial effects of working. Although you would still have to decide on the best order for these sections and the order of points within each section, you would be fairly sure that your paper would have three main parts.

For other papers, especially those which rely on one chief method of development, you need to determine, first, what the large blocks are and, second, in what order these can best be arranged. It may be easier to see your blocks if you list the important points, putting related ones together in columns or on separate slips of paper, or if you draw squares and jot down related matters in different squares. The labels for these groups of material will probably form the main heads of your plan or outline. Usually there will be three to five main heads. A paper with only two, unless it is very short, is likely to break in the middle. On the other hand, a fairly short paper with five or more heads is probably overdivided. In a paper of 1500 words or so, five points would average only 300 words apiece—and 300 words does not say very much. Even magazine articles of 6000 words rarely have more than five or six main divisions. Any outline of more than six main heads should be examined carefully to see whether the material really does require so many main divisions and, if so, whether too much is being attempted.

Next, the small, particular points can be arranged under the main heads to which they belong. Sometimes these points will in turn form several groups, which will stand under subheads in the outline.

After the main blocks are decided on, their order can be determined. What the best order is depends on the nature of the material and your purpose in discussing it. General plans for expository papers are of two chief kinds, each of which can be modified in various ways. One may be called the *order of support*. Its beginning serves as a preview of the whole paper; it states the ideas or main points, sometimes in the form of questions which the paper is to answer. What follows is a series of supporting blocks, each block dealing with a point or question raised in the opening paragraph or paragraphs. Often, when the material is complex or difficult, a paper following this plan ends with a section which restates in a new way the points made at the beginning. The restatement is unnecessary in a short paper but may be valuable in a long one.

Another general plan, which may be called the *order of climax,* begins with a specific fact or situation and then goes on to unfold the subject until at the end it stands complete. In the climax pattern, as the diagram below illustrates, each block of material is built on the preceding one, whereas in the *order of support,* blocks 2-5 are roughly parallel to each other. The *order of climax* is particularly useful when the writer wants to lead the reader to a conclusion that has in it an element of surprise or novelty.

The Order of Support   *The Order of Climax*

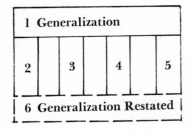

The *support* plan is more common in developing scientific and technical subjects and opinions that are methodically substantiated; the *climax* plan is more common in popular and informal papers. Whichever plan you follow, the last part of your paper should be the most important, meaningful, intense, or interesting—it should emphasize the point or points that you most want to impress upon the reader. The beginning has the double duty of attracting the reader's interest and getting him into the subject. The last point is the one he is to carry with him. (See Chapter 4, "Opening paragraphs," p. 143, and "Concluding paragraphs," p. 147.) In between, the ideas or main points should be arranged according to the most logical and sensible way of advancing the subject.

Types of outlines ∘ *Scratch outline.*   To make it easier for him to write an orderly paper, every writer should work out some method of sorting and organizing his material. Most writing is done from very casual notes, jotted down with due attention to meaning but without regard to form. The points are grouped according to some system of the writer's own devising. Since the scratch outline is an entirely personal document, not to be shown to anyone else, there is no point in making suggestions for its form.

Topic outline.   In this, the most common type of formal outline, the main points are noted in brief phrases or single words, numbered consistently as they are in the following example:

I Have Learned to Work [Title]

Learning to work in my early years has given me money for clothes and for my college education and has established habits that have been useful in many ways. [Sentence statement]

I. Early formation of work habits [Main head]
    A. Parents' warning against the evils of idling [Subhead]
    B. Required chores for all children in my family
    C. A newspaper route for fun and profit
II. Summer vacation work during my high-school years
    A. Necessity of earning money
        1. For various school activities
        2. For my future college expenses
    B. Ways and means
        1. Selling popcorn and candy at baseball games
        2. Selling magazines and subscriptions
        3. Acting as lifeguard at seashore resort

III. Beneficial results of this work
    A. Practical results
        1. Many additional clothes and social activities
        2. A bank account for my college expenses
        3. Skills and contacts valuable for getting jobs during college vacations
    B. More permanent results
        1. Strengthening of character
            a. Avoiding mischief
            b. Developing habit of industry
        2. Realization of value of money
        3. Carry-over of work habits into study habits of academic life
        4. Development of self-reliance

Sentence outline.   A sentence outline differs from a topic outline only in that each head is a complete sentence. It is more formal and requires more effort to draw up. Its chief advantage is that it forces the writer to think through his ideas thoroughly in order to give them complete statement. The following outline is for a paper based on Stephen Crane's *The Red Badge of Courage.*

The Transformation of Henry Fleming

Henry Fleming's romantic ideas of war were destroyed in his first battle, but after running away he returned to his regiment and by overcoming his fear regained his confidence and became a man.

  I. Henry's boyish idea of war underwent a change on the eve of battle.
    A. He had enlisted because he thought of war romantically and pictured himself performing heroic feats.
    B. A few days before his regiment was to have its first engagement, his idea of the glory of war was modified.
        1. He observed his fellow soldiers, listened to their boastful remarks.
        2. He began to doubt his courage, feared he might run from danger.
  II. He failed in the first test.
    A. As the regiment went into the firing line, he wished he had never enlisted.
    B. For a time he remained in the line and did his duty.
        1. He was bewildered.
        2. Feeling himself to be in a "moving box," he did as the others did about him.

    C. Overcome by fear, he finally turned and ran to the rear.

    D. As a skulker, he had a miserable experience.

        1. Discovering that his regiment had unexpectedly held its ground, he felt cheated.

        2. Joining a column of the wounded, he was shamed when asked about his own wound.

III. He regained his self-confidence.

    A. Dealt a blow on the head by a deserter, Henry rejoined his regiment, expecting to be ridiculed.

    B. When his fellow soldiers assumed that he had been wounded in action, Henry saw that his cowardice had passed unnoticed.

    C. In the next day's battle he acted creditably.

        1. Enraged at the enemy, he fought furiously and desperately.

        2. Praised by his lieutenant, he saw himself in a new light.

        3. He became color bearer and urged his fellows on to the charge.

IV. After this engagement, Henry was no longer his old self.

    A. He had had a chance to see himself in a new perspective.

    B. For a time he was tortured by thoughts of his cowardly conduct of the first day.

    C. Then he rejoiced at having become a man and overcome fear.

Paragraph summaries. It is sometimes helpful to prepare for writing a short paper by jotting down in advance the main point of each paragraph. But this method doesn't work well for long papers because it fails to distinguish subheads. This is the only type of outline in which the entries correspond exactly to the paragraphs of the paper.

Most of the conventions of outline form are shown in the examples just given. For more specific comment on them, see *Outline form*[1] in the *Index.*

If the outline is to be part of the final manuscript, it should be revised to represent the actual development of the finished paper. An outline of less than half a page may stand on the first page of a paper with the text beginning below it. A fuller outline should stand on a page by itself, placed before the first page of text.

---

[1]Throughout this book, references to *Index* articles are indicated by an asterisk (*).

Writing the first draft

Of course some writing has been going on in the last three steps, but actual consecutive composition usually takes place as the fifth step in developing a paper. If the preliminary stages have been well done, this writing should be free from worry. The feeling of being ready to write is the prime result of careful work in the early steps and the best guarantee of a good paper.

People's habits of writing differ so much that it is rash to make general statements about what they do (or should do) in the actual process of composition. Experience shows, however, that two faults often hinder students in writing papers: they take too long in getting started, and when they are finally under way, they write too slowly and laboriously, pausing for an undue length of time between one word and the next, one sentence and the next.

Don't worry at the outset about getting an ideal opening— this is really a sort of procrastination. The paper must be started somehow, and it is better to make a tentative start, the best that suggests itself at the moment, and change it later if necessary. After a few pages you will find that your writing is improving, and often you will find that you have a good opening simply by crossing out the first paragraph or two.

Your paper will have more life, your ideas will have better continuity, and your style will be more consistent if you write rapidly. Don't stop to look up spellings or to check mechanics as you write the first draft; these important matters can better be attended to in one operation after you have written the whole paper.

Writing that is repeatedly interrupted by pauses is almost sure to suffer, and so is the writer's work schedule, for the practice is extremely inefficient. If you do pause while writing, try to pause between paragraphs or between the larger stages of your paper. If you are writing from a good outline, it is easy to see the stages in material and so concentrate on one stage at a time. A long paper should be broken up into sections (corresponding to the main heads of an outline), and each section should be written more or less by itself. Writing a paper of 3000 words may appear a dismaying task, but if it is thought of—and written—as a series of three or four discussions of different, though related, aspects of the subject, it will be much more manageable. If the writing of the various sections is done at different times, however, it is well to reread what you have already written before continuing.

Try to make the first draft rather full. You may even include some material that at first may seem trivial or minor, because the inclusion of all the detail will help you later on to see what is relevant and important and what is not. It is always easier to take out unwanted matter than to fill in topics that have been done too sketchily.

Since the first draft shows you for the first time your ideas expressed in writing, you should expect to rework it. To make revision mechanically easy, give the first draft plenty of space on the paper. Leave generous margins and let the lines stand far enough apart so that you can write new words between them. Some writers put only one paragraph on a page or use only the upper half of the sheet in the first draft, so that they have plenty of room for additions and alterations of all sorts. Work out some scheme of physical arrangement on paper so that your revision can be carried on conveniently.

Revising the paper

Few people write so well that their first draft represents their best work. In general, good writing is rewritten writing. With most of the task of actual composition done, you can go over your work and improve it, sometimes in its larger arrangements, almost always in the details. This criticism and reworking should make the paper a more accurate and effective presentation of the subject you are discussing.

In revising, take the point of view of a reader or critic as far as you can. This is hard to do unless you allow some time to elapse between writing and revising. Here is some good advice from a professional writer:

Then you let the writing cool. You leave it alone for long enough so that, when you read it, you will see not what you felt and thought but what is on the paper. You slash and hew. You snatch things from where they are and put them where they fit. This time, or the fifth time, you get from mere black marks on paper all you meant.
—SIDNEY COX, "On Style, Originality, Integrity," *Indirections*, p. 51

In revising, test the paper for material, for organization, for style, and finally for the mechanics of writing.

Material • Make sure that enough material has been put in the paper to achieve its intended purpose. Occasionally, too much will be included, but not often. Usually the writer has become so familiar with the topic that he forgets to put in enough details to inform or interest his readers. The first questions, then, are: Is the material complete enough for my purpose? Do I need more examples or details? Do the facts given need more interpretation?

Check the factual statements for accuracy. Examine the interpretations and generalizations to see that they are as reasonable and convincing as you can make them.

Organization • Check the organization of the paper and test its unity. Is space wasted at the beginning? Will the first few sentences appeal to a reader and make him want to continue? Does the opening make clear what the paper is about? Is the subject advanced by clear-cut stages? Is the relation between one stage and the next shown? A paragraph which sounds like a new start, as if nothing has already been said, needs attention. Perhaps it is in the wrong place in the paper, or perhaps its first sentence needs to be revised to make clear the connection with the preceding paragraph. Does the conclusion leave the reader with the point you want him to carry away? Often irrelevant matters are brought in at the last, or the writing goes flabby or shows signs of haste. The beginning and ending of any paper need special attention in revision.

Style • You should look at the language of your draft, at the qualities of the paragraphs, sentences, and words that together make up its style. (These qualities are discussed in Chapters 4, 8, and 9.) Style is not a question of correctness but of effectiveness. The English language gives you many choices in words and constructions and sentence movement; not all are equally effective. You have read many passages that impressed you as vigorous and direct, accurate and clear, satisfying in their movement and their rhythm. And you have read others that somehow seemed shapeless and clumsy. With this experience to aid you, you can ask such questions as these: Does this word say just what I mean, or do I need to search for a more accurate one? Are there words which should be taken out because they add nothing to the sense? Is this long sentence confusing, or does it carry the reader easily to its end? Does each sentence seem to follow naturally from the preceding one, or do successive sentences appear disconnected? Is the style reasonably consistent? Or have I, without justification, made an abrupt shift from one variety of English to another?

Many questions of this sort can best be answered by reading the paper aloud. The ear catches qualities the eye may not see. You soon learn to recognize a shapeless sentence because it is difficult to read without stumbling.

Mechanics • Finally, in revising, you should check spelling, capitalization, punctuation, and matters of standard usage. At this point, a good dictionary and the *Index* of this book are especially useful, since they answer many particular questions, and Chapters 8, 9, and 10 give background for checking these matters. This is the process of **proofreading* described on page 275. After you have made the final copy of the paper, it, too, should be proofread with great care.

Preparing the manuscript

The final step in writing a paper is preparing the manuscript for another person to read. This may be simply making a fair copy of a first draft, or, as in research papers, it may also involve preparing footnotes and a bibliography. Whether it is a letter, a class paper, or an article or book for publication, the aim is the same—to make a manuscript that reads easily and represents your best work.

In preparing the manuscript, follow the directions given here unless your teacher instructs you otherwise.

Materials • The materials for copy have now been pretty well standardized. Paper 8½ by 11 inches is almost universally used, except in legal documents. For longhand copy, conventional "theme paper" having lines about half an inch apart is best. Odd sizes do not handle or file well, and narrow-lined notebook paper makes hard reading. For typewritten copy use a fair grade of bond paper. Lined paper should not be used if copy is typed, and paper torn out of notebooks with spiral binders is not acceptable. Flimsy paper such as onionskin should not be used because it is difficult to handle and mark. Handwritten manuscripts should be in ink, although some instructors will permit pencil for papers written in class. Pale ink is often illegible, and colored inks are regarded by many as in bad taste; black or blue-black is the best. If you use a ball-point pen, make sure it does not skip. For typewritten manuscripts a good black typewriter ribbon and clean type make a readable page.

The page • Leave comfortable margins at the ends of lines. A good right margin will not only improve the appearance of a page but will reduce the number of words that have to be divided at the end of lines. An inch and a half at the left, an inch at the right, an inch and a half at the top, and an inch at the bottom are typical margins. Very short papers should be centered on the page.

Typewritten copy should be double-spaced. In longhand copy, the ascenders and descenders of letters like *b, l, f, g* should not be allowed to cut across letters on the line above or below, and letters easily confused (*a-o, n-u*) should be made with special care. The letters of a word should be connected so that the reader's eye can grasp the word at a glance.

Paragraphs are indented about an inch in longhand and from five to eight spaces in typescript. In typewritten manuscript it is better to start a new page than to allow the first line of a paragraph to stand alone at the bottom of a page, and it is better to avoid starting a new page with the last line of a paragraph.

Only one side of the sheet should be used.

Pages should be arranged in their proper order (it is surprising how often they are not), and pages after the first should be numbered, preferably in the upper right-hand corner and in Arabic numerals (2, 3, 4).

In longhand manuscript the title should be centered on the top line or about two inches from the top on unlined paper; the text should begin about an inch below. On lined paper leave the line below the title blank. A title should not be underlined or set in quotation marks unless it is an actual quotation. No end punctuation is necessary unless the title is a question or exclamation. Since the title is not a part of the body of the paper but is rather a label put upon it, the first sentence of the text should be complete in itself and not refer back to the title by a pronoun, as in "This subject is of great interest to all musicians."

Common practices that should be avoided are: (*a*) indenting the first line on a page when it is not the beginning of a paragraph; (*b*) leaving blank part of the last line on a page when the paragraph is continued on the following page; (*c*) repeating, as the first word on a new page, the last word on the preceding page; (*d*) putting punctuation marks, other than quotation marks or a dash, at the beginning of a line. A punctuation mark belongs with the word that it follows, not at the beginning of the next construction.

Endorsing the manuscript • Most course papers in college are folded vertically and endorsed near the top to the right of the outside fold, or as the instructor may direct. Teachers usually give a standard form for the endorsement, such as:

> Student's name
> Topic, title, or assignment of paper
> Date submitted

Other facts, such as the number of the paper, the name and section of the course, or the instructor's name, may be included as the instructor requests. Clear and uniform endorsement is a real convenience to the teacher who must handle the papers.

If the papers are to be handed in flat, the endorsement should be on the back of the last sheet or on a special title page, as the teacher directs. Sheets should be held together by paper clips that can be slipped off, not by fasteners that pierce the paper or by pins, hairpins, or string.

Corrections in copy • Some errors may have crept into the final copy, no matter how carefully it has been made. If there are many, or if they are complicated, the page should be done over. If they are relatively minor (for instance, adding a letter to a word or substituting or deleting a single word), they can usually be done neatly without damaging the appearance of the page.

Words that are to be eliminated should be struck out by having a line drawn through them. (Do not use parentheses for this purpose.) Words to be added can be written in the margin or between the lines, and a caret ($\wedge$) inserted at the place where they belong. In correcting mistypings while the paper is still in the machine, erase completely and retype; do not merely strike over the wrong letters.

If you want to indicate the beginning of a paragraph in copy that you have written solid, put the paragraph symbol in the left margin and draw an angle before the first word of the new paragraph, like this:

> In correcting mistypings while the paper is still in the machine, erase completely and retype; do not merely strike over the wrong
> ¶ letters. ⌊If you want to indicate the beginning of a paragraph

in copy that you have written solid, put the paragraph symbol in
the left margin and draw an angle . . . .

If you want to indicate that what you have written as two
paragraphs should be joined as one, write *No* ¶ in the left
margin and draw a line from the end of the preceding to the
beginning of the following paragraph.

The goal is a clean, legible copy that can be read easily by
someone else. Reading this final copy aloud rather slowly will
be a good last check to make sure that mistakes have not
slipped in during the copying.

From manuscript into print

Although the manuscript form is the final state of most college writing, some of the papers in composition courses find
their way into campus periodicals. At any rate, since a college
graduate is almost certain to write something that will see
publication of some sort, he should know something of this
last stage. It may be merely a final check preparatory to
mimeographing, or it may be an elaborate process of editing,
revising at the suggestion of an editor, and proofreading, before the manuscript is finally published. A number of books
dealing minutely with such matters are available. A few of
the more important details are treated in the *Index* articles
*Proofreading and *Submitting manuscripts.

Exercises

1. Choose three of the general subjects below. For each one you
choose, list four specific topics, two suitable for a paper of 400-700
words and two for a paper of 800-1200 words. Be prepared to write
on any of these your instructor assigns.

learning a new language	prestige symbols	jazz
admission to college	college rituals	folk songs
educational television	personality types	sports fans
life in the suburbs	automation	sports cars
values of teenagers	segregation	comic strips
transportation systems	religious training	architecture
slick magazines	national defense	movie idols

2. Rearrange the topics in each of the groups below, placing the most specific at the bottom, the most general at the top. Decide which topics would be best for papers of 500 words, which for papers of 1000-1200 words. Then write an essay on the topic that interests you most.

a. Chesapeake Bay Bridge
   Toll collection on Chesapeake Bay Bridge
   Bridges of the twentieth century
   Modern suspension bridges
   Traffic control on Chesapeake Bay Bridge

b. Humphrey Bogart in *The Maltese Falcon*
   The typical "Bogey flick"
   Campus favorites—foreign films and Bogart revivals
   The Maltese Falcon—a movie classic
   Bogart's tough talk in *The Maltese Falcon*

c. The degree of power a student government should have
   How a student body president should conduct meetings
   Principal duties of a student body president
   Student government
   Electing student officers

d. Choral music of Bach
   Bach's B Minor Mass
   Choral music since Bach
   Choral requirements for Bach's B Minor Mass
   History of religious music

3. Criticize the form and content of the following outline and suggest specific ways of improving it. (See pp. 50-52 and *Outline form.)

American Opera: The First Hundred Years

Though opera in America was limited by circumstances, its gradual but sure development revealed the strong need for this art form among the American people.

 I. The New Setting for Opera
    A. Limited by struggle to live
    B. Opera didn't fit present life
 II. First Performance
    A. *Flora*
       1. February 18, 1735
       2. Charleston, South Carolina
       3. Quality of performance
          a. Singing
       4. Attendance
    B. *The Beggar's Opera*
    C. Audience
       1. Fashions
       2. Divided by classes

III. Types of Early Operas
    A. Ballad operas
        1. Plots concerned with daily life
        2. Used popular tunes for music
    B. Folk Operas
        1. Plots based on folklore
        2. Music derived from traditional tunes
IV. How Presented
    A. Traveling stock companies
        1. Limited wardrobe and settings
        2. Limited number of artists
 V. Expansion of American Opera
    A. French influence
        1. French popularity after Revolution
        2. French operas in New Orleans
    B. Italian influence
        1. Steamboat
        2. Visits by Italian touring companies
        3. Erection of first permanent opera
          house in New York by Lorenzo da Ponte
VI. Conclusion

4. Arrange the following sentences in a three-level outline to support the central statement:

Problems in the social adjustment of a gifted child arise partly from his heredity and partly from his environment.

a. In play, the talented child will prefer older companions, but they may ignore him.

b. Mary K., for example, was capable of becoming an accomplished painter, writer, and even a mathematician.

c. More often the gifted child comes into conflict with his environment.

d. Frequently a person will have remarkable ability in both music and mathematics and cannot decide which should be his vocation, which his avocation.

e. Occasionally problems are created for the gifted child by certain combinations of hereditary traits.

f. Very often the gifted child will be superior in many areas, making vocational guidance difficult.

g. Parents who do not realize a child's superior intelligence may unintentionally retard his development.

h. The gifted child may inherit remarkable musical abilities but may be rather poor in verbal skills.

i. Teachers may have difficulty providing him with enough work and he may become a nuisance.

5. This sentence statement is to serve as the central idea for a paper: "I decided to attend a liberal arts college instead of a vocational school because I think there are other things more important than preparing to earn a living." Of the following points, which ones should probably be discarded as irrelevant? Arrange the rest in five groups, each to be developed as one part of the paper.

a. Today there are great pressures on young people to prepare themselves to earn a living.

b. Computers do the jobs that accountants used to do.

c. For many students, a college degree is just a status symbol.

d. Preparing for one specific vocation is a mistake.

e. Being a responsible citizen means more than paying taxes.

f. I took part in few extracurricular activities in high school.

g. Many jobs have become so specialized that students are told they have to start preparing for them even in high school.

h. The liberal arts are the key to the wisdom of the past.

i. A liberal arts education helps one to be a responsible citizen.

j. In ten years I expect we will have a thirty-hour work week.

k. For the professions that interest me, on-the-job training is best.

l. Standards for admission to college are getting higher every year.

m. While the number of telephones has increased, the number of telephone operators has decreased.

n. Our society emphasizes money and possessions.

o. The study of history helps us cope with today's problems.

p. I do not want to spend my leisure time just watching television.

q. Philosophy has no dollars-and-cents value but it has great value to the individual.

r. Most students should take their high-school work more seriously.

s. Automation is making many jobs obsolete.

t. Making wise use of leisure time is increasingly important.

u. Students do not always realize how much their education costs.

v. I intend to be a journalist or an editor.

w. My grandfather was never so unhappy as in the ten years he lived after retiring from his job as a foreman.

6. Write a paper (700-900 words) on your reasons for attending college, making clear what values you expect your college education to have for you. Submit an outline with the paper.

Chapter Three

METHODS
OF
DEVELOPMENT

*The writer's job is to find the argument,
the approach, the angle,
the wording that will take the reader with him.*

Paul Roberts

For any writer, the ideal situation is to have something to say, to want to say it, and to know how to go about saying it. In approaching a particular writing task, students often lament that they find themselves at either of two unhappy extremes—both far from the ideal situation. One student declares that he is crammed full of facts and feelings and convictions about his subject but is baffled as to how to get them across to the reader. Another protests that *everything* he has to say can be said in one sentence, and so he will have to pad out his paper by repeating the same point a dozen times with minor variations and using fifty words when he knows ten would do.

Probably most of you most of the time find yourselves somewhere between these extremes: you have a few ideas, but you need to struggle hard to flesh them out, to make clear how they relate to each other, and to arrange them in the most effective order. Fleshing out does not mean padding. It means developing the subject with such fullness and direction that the reader feels the discussion was worth his time—and yours.

Whatever estimate you make of your problems in approaching and developing your subject (and no doubt this estimate will vary from paper to paper), you will find it helpful to review the methods of development treated in this chapter—narration, description, comparison, and so on. If you are exuberantly full of ideas but don't know how to present them in a coherent and orderly fashion, this chapter will help you sort your material into manageable parts and so control and organize the content of your paper. If, on the other hand, you are short of ideas, this chapter will give you clues as to how to go about finding something to say—not, of course, by providing you with the actual facts and data for a paper but by suggesting the kinds of thinking and investigating that will lead to the uncovering of useful material. The techniques are not new—you have certainly used all of them to formulate and express your ideas and feelings. But however familiar you are with them, you may not be aware of how generally useful they are in writing different kinds of papers on different subjects. Methods of development are treated here to remind you of some of the resources you can draw on as you think (and write) your way through a paper. Further illustrations and applications of them will be made in Chapters 4-7.

Choosing the methods

A simple example will indicate how these resources can serve a student who feels that all his notions about his subject can be put in a phrase or sentence. (Strangely enough, it is when a student is confronted with a rather easy assignment on familiar material that he is most apt to say that his mind is empty.) Suppose he has been assigned a paper on his home town, and suppose he decides that "everything" he has to say can be summed up in "Fairview is a dull town to live in." Actually, he has the kernel of a paper here, an impression or judgment that could very well serve as its unifying idea. Presumably, too, there is a glimmering of purpose, which he could clarify by deciding what effect he wants the paper to have on his reader. Does he want to re-create the town so as to make the reader feel its dullness? Does he want to explain what makes the town dull and why? Does he want to prove to the skeptical reader that it is indeed dull? Reviewing some typical ways of developing a subject would help him settle on a definite purpose and suggest the kind of material he needs to accomplish it.

Description • If the aim is to create a feeling about the town, the paper needs to be rich in concrete details and specific images to make the reader hear, see, feel, taste, touch, and ultimately absorb the flavor of the town. Details about the streets and buildings, the characteristic activities and interests of the residents would all be selected with a view to creating one unified impression—dullness.

Narration • The entire paper (or a part of it) might recount an incident or a series of incidents that took place while the writer lived in the town. Narration would also be the main method of development if the writer chose to present what he regarded as the unending round of meaningless activities that made up the lives of the residents: a typical day in Fairview.

Example • Though a paper is seldom built on examples alone, concrete illustrations are of first importance in supporting generalizations and judgments—about Fairview or about any other subject.

Comparison and contrast • The student could bring out the dullness of Fairview by contrasting it with a town he considers exciting. Or he might use a variety of comparison (an analogy), introducing it with a sentence such as "Living in Fairview is like being imprisoned on a beautiful summer afternoon in a stuffy lecture hall, with nothing to do but listen to the endless drone of a monotonous voice reciting platitudes about protozoa."

Division • He could enumerate those aspects or features of the town that are relevant to his main idea, and then discuss each one in turn. The topics might be what the town offers— or fails to offer—in the way of satisfying occupations, intellectual stimulation, and entertainment.

Classification • Classifying the people of the town according to their interests and activities or their political and social views could provide the chief substance of the paper.

Causes and effects • After establishing through description, comparison, or other methods the *fact* of Fairview's dullness, the writer might explore the causes of it. Are they to be attributed chiefly to the location of the town, to the industries (or lack of them), to the people it has attracted, or to some other cause? Examining reasons might lead to the conclusion that the town has to be the way it is. Or the student could argue that a little enterprise and imagination—a few alterations in present practices, attitudes, or policies—could make it a very satisfactory place to live in.

Definition • Fairview could be used as a springboard for an explanatory or persuasive paper in which the chief aim is to define the essential characteristics of "small town life." The student might try to persuade his reader that life in a small town is bound to be dull: such is the nature of small towns.

Although the student may very well use several of these methods in developing his paper, one is likely to be dominant, and that one will be determined by his decision as to the purpose of his paper. Sometimes an assignment is so phrased that a specific method of development is clearly called for—"Compare . . . ," "Describe . . . ," "Analyze the reasons for . . ."—but in assignments beginning with "Discuss . . ." or "Write a paper on . . ." you need to establish your own purpose and choose your methods of development. To see how the methods work cooperatively to accomplish the purpose, examine the following two papers—markedly different ones in purpose, material, and development—written in response to this very broad assignment: "Write a paper in which you carve out your own topic from the general subject of American political behavior. You may treat politics on the national, state, or local level; you may discuss the political attitudes or activities of an individual, a group, or the people as a whole."

My Uncle Ralph

On the corner of the intersection of Doris and Meachem Avenues, there is a well-finished two-story house in the morning shadow of a 300-foot water tower. The house is owned by my Uncle Ralph, who works assiduously at renovating his home.

It must have been no more than six years ago—at most seven —when his house appeared decrepit and leprous. One corner of his yard was reserved for scrap metal, which he collected for a foundry in which he worked. His monthly income was 320 dollars. His yard also housed a few rabbits, and, in addition to this, he grew a few vegetables each year. His personal appearance coincided with his environment. The clothes he wore were shabby and unpressed. His hands were grimy from working in the foundry all day, and his face never appeared to be washed. But today he has changed. His hands and face are clean, and his clothes are neat.

What brought about this change in his outlook on life? Well, it began developing about five years ago when he decided to involve himself in politics—county government. The Democratic party would seem to have been the obvious choice for his support, but, no, he wanted to be a Republican. His choice received a great many laughs from those who knew him. A Republican is generally a businessman, usually a person in the middle and upper classes of society. Where did he fit in? He didn't, and his choice was looked upon by others as ludicrous.

After paying a dollar for a booster pin, he became a full-fledged party worker. I often used to wonder who did all the footwork and canvassed the district. I see now that the bulk of the work, such as organizing rallies and putting up thousands of decals which tell you to vote for so and so, is performed by hundreds of uneducated people like my Uncle Ralph. The lower class of people are generally more enthusiastic about politics than are the middle or the upper classes.

My Uncle tells the family of his experiences and how wonderful it is to work for the party. For instance, one time he told us of his shaking Rockefeller's hand at a Republican rally. He said it made him feel like a million dollars.

I once asked him why he enjoyed working for the party. He told me that Dwight D. Eisenhower once said: "Informed citizens are the guardian and spirit of democracy." He then said to me, "What better way is there to be fully informed than being a party worker?" I knew there was much truth to what he had said and questioned him no further.

As time passed I began to fully understand why my Uncle Ralph involved himself in politics. First of all, it made him something he was not. He was looking for prestige and his only opportunity to procure same was if he affiliated himself to a political party. Politics gave him a purpose in society; it made him feel as though he was influencing something. Secondly, politics elevated him from shabby living conditions; it made him conscious of his surroundings and compelled him to take a new outlook on life.

Yes, today my Uncle is undoubtedly a changed man. He is a proud man who appreciates clean living. Politics gave him a new life. You might even say he was reborn.

This paper is intended to demonstrate that involving oneself in politics is a good thing—at least for the Uncle Ralphs of this world. The central method in accomplishing this intention is a *cause-effect* analysis. Note, however, that this analysis occupies comparatively little space; though its importance is signaled by the question which opens paragraph 3, it becomes the chief topic only in the last two paragraphs. Other methods are used in the rest of the paper.

Establishing the *contrast* (paragraphs 1 and 2) is necessary before the causal analysis can be launched. The contrast itself gets its substance from *descriptive details* about Uncle Ralph's house, yard, and personal appearance. (Are all of the details relevant? Should the writer have given more details about the present state of Uncle Ralph and his surroundings? Is the sentence about his wages really useful, or is it a distracting detail?

Questions such as these will be discussed later in connection with paragraph development, Chapter 4, pp. 111-127.)

Paragraphs 3-6 follow a loose chronological sequence. The *narrative* pattern is not overt or obvious, nor need it be. All that is required is to make clear the beginning of the sequence of events that changed Uncle Ralph and to give enough *examples* to demonstrate that the change did occur; the examples, in fact, are more important than the narrative, and the reader could wish for a few more than the generalized ones in paragraph 4 and the specific one in paragraph 5.

The casually phrased *definition* in paragraph 3, though not central to the paper, is quite useful where it appears. Accurate or not as a definition, it represents the general view of Uncle Ralph's friends and so explains why they laugh at his decision.

A number of criticisms could be made of the style of the paper—its words, phrases, and sentences—but for the moment the main thing to notice is that the student has used a variety of methods of development and that these are well adapted to his purpose.

Here is the second paper written in response to the same broad assignment:

Americans in Politics

The attitude of any people toward politics and their activities in this field are good indicators of their character and of the degree of maturity which they have attained. In a political system such as ours, where each person has an opportunity and a responsibility to take an active part in his government, this is especially true. A careful examination of the political attitudes and activities of the American people shows that they are moving toward political maturity. Although their actions are often ridiculous and sometimes dangerous, their strong devotion to the fundamental ideals of democracy and their faith in the ultimate achievement of these goals have maintained American liberty and have made possible gradual improvements and reforms in government. Many things—present-day party politics, poor attendance at the polls, and widespread intolerance—seem to conflict with, and possibly refute, this statement, but the results of American political action show its truth.

One of the traits for which Americans can be criticized is their willingness to let petty partisan squabbles distract attention from the really serious issues of the day. Name-calling on the floor of the Senate, the airing of personal feuds in the press and over radio and television, deliberate opposition to proposed legislation or to executive appointments for purely partisan reasons, widely publicized bickering not only between the parties but also between factions within a party may all be taken as examples of political immaturity and irresponsibility. Yet while Americans often let their sectional interests and private rivalries influence their judgment in unimportant matters, these minor differences are quickly forgotten in time of crisis and actually attract more attention than they deserve in normal times. Again and again, when major matters of foreign policy are at stake, the majorities in both parties have given the administration solid support.

Thus far we have been speaking chiefly of the representatives of the people. What of the people themselves? When only about half of them consider a presidential election important enough to vote in, do they have any real sense of responsibility? Certainly unwillingness to take part in any kind of political activity is a very serious problem in this country, but the very fact that it is generally recognized as such represents a great step forward. The acknowledgment of the situation has resulted in many attempts to change it. Various political and nonpolitical organizations, including the parties themselves, voters' leagues, the Boy Scouts, numerous Chamber of Commerce groups, unions, and private companies have cooperated in providing transportation to and from the polls, baby-sitting services, and adjusted work hours in a concentrated drive for more voters. Gains have already been made, and further improvement is mainly a matter of time.

More important than either of these problems is the spread of political intolerance among the American people. The establishment of the doctrine of guilt by implication, guilt by accusation, and guilt by association has been accompanied by a tendency to identify loyalty with conformity; and the person who does not conform has suffered attacks inspired by fear and hatred, primitive emotions that are associated with the immature mind rather than the adult intellect. Evidence of this intolerance has marred the American political scene at every level, and intolerance in politics is itself clear evidence of immaturity. Yet even while they sometimes fail to live up to their own ideals of liberty and equality, the American people continue to revere and aspire to those ideals, and recent events indicate that the hysteria that led to intolerance is giving way to cooler reasoning, which will lead, inevitably, to justice and fair play.

Thus, while the American in politics squabbles too much, votes too little, and sometimes turns his back on the very principles that make his political system possible, he is moving toward maturity and responsibility. When the chips are down, he joins ranks with his political opponents; when his responsibilities as a voter are made clear to him, he goes to the polls; when he takes the time to reason, he rejects injustice and intolerance. Superficially, his actions are sometimes those of a child, but again and again he has shown the ability to recognize the flaws in his own political system and then, working within the framework of that system, has taken steps to correct them. And this, surely, is the mark of maturity.

To demonstrate that Americans are "moving toward" political maturity, the writer has made a *division* or breakdown of American political behavior into three relevant parts or aspects. As he treats each of these (in paragraphs 2, 3, and 4) he makes use of *comparison*: for each aspect he presents the negative evidence—the signs of political immaturity—and then the positive evidence—the signs of political maturity. Dividing the subject into parts enables the writer to keep his organization firm and clear; comparison enables him to make the point he wants to make. For each topic he chooses to discuss, the writer measures the gap between the way Americans behave in politics and the way they should behave.

An examination of the structure and movement of these two papers shows that a full, detailed statement of purpose (possibly extending to several sentences) will identify the methods to be used in developing the subject and to some extent predict the organization of the paper. If the author of "My Uncle Ralph" had thought through his topic very carefully before he began to write, he might have informally phrased for himself the following detailed statement of purpose: "I want to show that getting involved in politics is a good thing for people. Of course, I can't speak for everybody, but I can speak for Uncle Ralph. Mainly I have to do two things—show what a different man he is now and make the reader see that this change came about as a result of his interest in politics."

Not all writers take the time to clarify their intentions so fully before they begin to write, and perhaps some of them don't need to. Their purpose takes shape as they write—as they work with the material they have collected. An experienced writer no doubt selects his methods of development almost intuitively, choosing this one or that as the best means of saying what he wants to say. But an inexperienced writer runs some risks if he does not know what shape his paper is to take. He may find, on reading his first draft, that he has wandered in several different directions and that a good deal of pruning and rewriting is necessary to produce a unified paper. Sacrificing interesting but irrelevant material *after* it is written is painful; it is much less painful (and less time-consuming) to decide in advance what *is* relevant. Choosing his methods of development will help the inexperienced writer make such decisions.

Using the methods

It is not enough, of course, to make sensible choices among the methods of development; you must know how to handle them effectively. You want to write not just a description, but a *good* description; not just a classification, but a *good* classification. To a certain extent, the same criteria can be applied to all kinds of writing; we can make general statements about the qualities all good writing will possess—whether we are talking about paragraphs (Chapter 4), sentences (Chapter 8), or words (Chapter 9).

But some aspects of good papers can better be discussed in terms of the larger problems of thinking through, organizing, and developing material. This section will suggest some points to keep in mind as you draw on various methods of development in your own papers. The methods are here treated separately, because each raises somewhat different problems; but they rarely occur in isolation, and in writing a paper you will usually find yourself drawing on several methods, not just one. You should remember, too, that they are not imprisoning molds into which you force your material but natural and necessary ways of saying what you want to say.

Description • Two students wrote the following opening paragraphs for papers describing New York City:

New York is the largest city in the world. Its narrow, crowded streets, lined with enormous buildings, make the visitor feel that he is in the bottom of a gigantic canyon. New York's buildings are, in fact, one of the most outstanding things about the city. Its one-hundred-and-three-story Empire State Building is the tallest in the world, and people come from everywhere to see it and the other landmarks of this huge city.

New York is the largest city in the world and, for a great many people, the cruelest city in the world. When hearing about New York, one usually hears about the magnificent buildings, the excellent transportation system, the famous night clubs, the glamorous night spots in Harlem, or the eccentric Greenwich Village. It is true that New York does have these things, and more, but this view of the city ignores the fact that many of the buildings are architecturally ugly, that the subways are dingy and crowded, that many of the night clubs are shoddy clip joints, that most people in Harlem have never been inside the night spots, and that many of the eccentricities of Greenwich Village are by no means attractive.

As one would expect from these opening paragraphs, the first continued with a description of the most impressive "landmarks" of New York City—the United Nations buildings, Rockefeller Center, the Metropolitan Museum of Art, and so on. For the most part, the description was impersonal and objective, limited to informative statistics and details about the physical appearance of the landmarks. The only attitude expressed was the conventional one of awe and admiration.

The second paper described none of these landmarks; instead, the writer limited himself to giving an account of Harlem ("a dirty, run-down district"), of Greenwich Village ("the home of unfortunates"), and of the Bowery and Chinatown. Physical description of these areas was interwoven with an account of the habits and attitudes and activities of the people. All of the details were selected with a view to supporting the writer's opinion that for many people New York is "the cruelest city in the world." The writer made the reader share both his sympathy for the people of the city and his bitterness over the impersonal brutality of life in certain areas of the city.

Description of the first type is often called *objective* or *impersonal;* the second is said to be *subjective* or *personal.* Objective description is primarily intended to convey information about the appearance or characteristics of a place, person, process, or object. The writer aims to render or record what is before him—to present exactly and faithfully what any careful, impartial observer would see. Subjective description does not ignore those characteristics or features that would catch the eye of a careful observer, but its central aim is to present the object as it appears to *one* observer—the writer. Indeed, the details are selected with a view to re-creating in the reader the impression the object made on the writer or the feelings it aroused in him.

It has been said that objective description *shows* us the object and subjective description *gives* us the object. Although the distinction is not always that clear-cut, it is a useful one if it suggests two general kinds of description that, at one time or another, students need to use. If you are a skin-diver, you ought to be able to write a clear, precise account of the sport of skin-diving, the equipment you use, and the skills you employ; you also ought to be able to convey to someone who has never tried the sport a clear, vivid impression of the special feelings and emotions that skin-diving brings you. Although you might do both in one paper, it is important not to shift aimlessly back and forth. You can guard against this fault if you decide in advance what purpose any particular piece of description is to serve. Do you want to convey not only what you have seen but also how you feel about what you have seen? Or do you want to play the role of the impersonal instructor and report the objective facts?

Papers based on personal experience (discussed in Chapter 5) can use both kinds of description but are more likely to rely on subjective description. Explanatory papers (Chapter 6) draw heavily on objective description, both how-to-do-it papers (how to sew, how to swim, how to survive on a desert island) and papers in definition (what a man is, what a mammal is, what a mammoth is). In persuasive papers (Chapter 7), either kind may play a subordinate but essential role: in arguing the need for slum clearance, one writer begins with a graphic, subjective description of life in the slums; another starts from facts and statistics about overcrowding, sanitation, educational facilities.

Perhaps the chief hazard in writing purely objective description is that the paper may end up as a catalog of unrelated details or particulars. It is certainly important to record each "part" or area with precision and accuracy; but it is not less important to relate the parts in such a way that the reader can grasp the object as a whole. The pen is not a camera: a writer cannot simultaneously present all of the parts and at the same time indicate how they fit together. To guide the reader in constructing his mental picture, the writer must find some means of organizing and unifying his description.

One way of doing this is to make clear the physical point of view taken by the observer. If he is standing on the roof of the highest building, he will have one picture of the town; if he is standing on a corner of its busiest intersection, he will have another. The reader needs to be told where the observer is, and he needs to be told when the observer changes his location. A second way of organizing the description (and especially of unifying it) is to establish a generalization which serves as a keynote or unifying theme for the specific details that follow. This device is particularly useful when the material presents a bewildering array of characteristics or features.

Both devices are used in the following passage, where the author undertakes the challenging task of describing a part of the whale's anatomy. Describing a particular whale would obviously offer problems; describing *the* whale offers greater ones simply because there are many different kinds of whales. Sanderson invites the reader to share his vantage point in looking at the whale, and he supplies a key word, *asymmetry*, to generalize about what can be seen.

First, if you stand on top of a whale's skeleton and look down at the head you will find that in many species the left side is quite unlike the right. The single "S"-shaped blow-hole of the Sperm, for instance, is always on the left side of the tip of the snout. This asymmetry can be carried out even to the surface coloring of the skin so that the left-hand side of the jaw may be white, the right black. The Beaked Whales or Ziphoids display the greatest asymmetry. Secondly, the nostrils of whales have, in all but the Sperms, moved back on to the top of the head and the nasal passage goes directly to the lungs without joining the throat. Thirdly, the skin has been reduced to about the thickness, and much the appearance, of a sheet of carbon paper in the larger whales but is backed with a thick layer of fibrous tissue impregnated with oil, a substance called blubber. In the Porpoises, most Dolphins, and the White Whales the skin is thickened to form a very tough leather. The eyes of whales are comparatively small and the ear-openings of the largest will just admit a pencil but they have extremely acute hearing both above and below water. Most whales are completely hairless but some have a few thick bristles on their chins—the Common Porpoise just six—while the curious Grey Whale has lines of hairs all over the upper part of its body.—Ivan T. Sanderson, *Living Mammals of the World*, p. 211

Although a well-chosen generalization can be an excellent device for organizing and unifying a passage of description, it is no substitute for the concrete details that actually do the job of describing. To use it as a substitute is a fault you need to guard against, particularly when you are writing subjective description. It is a mistake to lean too heavily on generalized statements of emotions or impressions. "The appearance of the lake and the warm sun made me feel peaceful and serene" is an assertion, not a description; what you need to do is present the concrete details that make the reader taste, feel, hear, see, touch in such a way as to share your feelings. "It was a bustling, thriving town" is merely an assertion; what you need to do is make the town bustle and thrive before the eyes of the reader. Ordinarily, generalizations such as these—which are hardly organizing devices—should be used sparingly, for in themselves they cannot convey the sense of living reality that is the chief purpose of subjective description. To make sure you are not relying on them too heavily, read through your completed paper, skipping all the generalizations and concentrating on the details. If these alone do not make you feel that you are in the presence of the object you have meant to describe, then you need more images and concrete details.

In thinking through the task of writing a descriptive passage or paper, ask yourself these questions: Is my description to be primarily subjective or primarily objective? If subjective, what is the dominant mood or flavor I want to convey, and what details will convey it? If objective, what physical point of view or other organizing device will enable me to move systematically from part to part and at the same time unify my description? And, after you have written the paper: Are there enough details to make the reader see the object or to know it in the way I want him to know it?

Narration • Narration recounts an incident or series of incidents or the steps in a process. It is the method of essays based on personal experience, of newspaper stories, of biographies and histories. (It is also, of course, the method of all fiction; but our concern in this book is with factual prose.) In papers for college courses, you will use narration in all kinds of "historical" reports—reports which trace the development of a nation, a scientific theory, a philosophical concept, a movement in art or literature, a political party, or a sociological trend. You will use it in writing up laboratory experiments.

Aside from these projects in which the chronological method of development is dictated by the material or your purpose, you will use stretches of narration in parts of papers whose main purpose is quite different. Narration is often the best means of providing the necessary background for an analysis of a current social or political issue. Such is the case with the following passage, part of a discussion of racism in the United States as it affects relations between whites and Negroes:

Racism began in the southern slave states in the early decades of the nineteenth century as a justification for economic exploitation of Negro slaves—a justification needed in a society that proclaimed and believed in democracy and equality. The racist ideology held that Negroes were biologically inferior to whites, that they were not really human beings, and hence that the values of "liberty, equality, and fraternity" were not applicable to them. Racism became stronger after the Civil War (1861-1865) because the legal abolition of slavery left it as the only major argument for the subjugation of Negroes.

After the beginning of the twentieth century, racism began very gradually to lose some of its strength. This was the result of a large number of social changes, including the rising educational level of Negroes; the growth of a protest movement; migration of Negroes to the northern industrialized states; and particularly the diversification of the southern economy, which made it less economically valuable to exploit Negro labor. Racism received its strongest challenge with the Second World War, when increasing industrialization, the growing need for nonagricultural labor, geographic mobility, the exposure of soldiers to foreign influences, and the growing recognition by Americans that their nation had developed responsibilities toward a multiracial world, all tended to weaken an ideology that was developed in an isolated, stable, agricultural economy. It was during the war years that the force of the federal government—particularly of the Supreme Court and the presidency—shifted toward supporting the constitutional principle of the equality of all citizens.

With the economic motive for racism greatly weakened, the major forces maintaining the subordination and segregation of Negroes were those of tradition and the status quo. But the 1954 decision of the Supreme Court, which called for "all deliberate speed" in the desegregation of public schools, provoked concerted resistance by segregationist leaders, especially by southern White Citizens Councils.

Baltimore and a few other cities in border states, as well as Washington, D.C., began to desegregate their schools in 1954, but the Supreme Court decision met determined resistance in most of the South; by the middle of 1956 only about 350 southern school districts out of 6300 were desegregated. By the following year—1957—southern opposition to school desegregation had reached the point of clashes with federal military power. President Eisenhower sent in federal troops to ensure that nine Negro students were allowed to enter Central High School in Little Rock, Arkansas; Governor Orval Faubus had defied federal authority by using state troops to bar the entrance of the Negro students.

Although the use of federal troops stiffened resistance on the part of segregationists, by 1961 Arkansas, Virginia, Louisiana, and Georgia had accepted at least token desegregation. But violence broke out when James Meredith, a Negro, attempted to enroll at the all-white University of Mississippi in October 1962. State officials defied a court order requiring the university to admit Meredith, and federal authorities assigned U.S. marshals to protect Meredith upon his arrival at the university. When segregationists, encouraged by Mississippi Governor Ross Barnett's public statements of defiance, attacked the marshals, the federal government dispatched thousands of federalized Mississippi national guardsmen and regular army troops to the town of Oxford to ensure the execution of the court's orders. Meredith thus became the first Negro student to enter the university. In August 1963 Meredith was graduated from the university with a bachelor's degree.—ARNOLD M. ROSE, "Social Problems of the Contemporary World," in *Contemporary Civilization—Issue Three,* pp. 187-188

This excerpt illustrates two principles that can be helpful to you in planning papers (or parts of papers) that are mainly narrative: selectivity and coherence. You will observe that the treatment of race relations in the United States is very general and highly condensed. The first two paragraphs trace broad trends; no mention is made of specific conflicts or measures such as the Civil Rights Acts of 1866 and 1875 or the famous case of *Plessy* v. *Ferguson* in 1896. In the last two paragraphs the chronological thread becomes more distinct and the treatment somewhat more detailed. It is still, however, highly selective: a comprehensive history of Negro-white relations in this country would fill many volumes. What is presented here is not so much history for its own sake as background material for the writer's analysis of race relations in the 1960's.

The need for selectivity can be just as important in papers where you are working with a much smaller time span. In writing any narrative, you have to decide what has a significant bearing on the action and what is merely coincidental. As it occurs in life, the simplest street-corner incident can be a fairly complex affair: a camera trained on the scene would record a great deal that was unrelated to the central action. As an observer of such an incident, you might intuitively know or very rapidly decide what was central and what was not. When you are writing about such an incident you need to give the reader enough clues so that he can make similar inferences.

Selectivity does not imply merely a bare recital of the action —an accurate reporting of the many tiny incidents that go into an event or episode. Separate links do not make a chain until they are welded together. A piece of narrative will have coherence only if the writer connects the tiny incidents, relating them in such a way that they make up a single, unified action of some significance. Normally a story does not "tell itself," and the reader's interest is likely to fade if the account is limited to "He did this. . . . Next, he did this. . . . Then he did that."

Among the devices for knitting a narrative together are words and phrases to indicate time relationships or to express causal relationships. The reader needs to understand the action as well as to visualize it. Indeed, causal analysis may dominate a narrative as it does at the beginning of the passage quoted on page 76. The chronology in the first two paragraphs is subordinated to an explanation of the origins of racism and of the forces which gradually weakened it.

Since narrative is the staple of personal experience papers, other problems of writing a narrative will be taken up in Chapter 5. The principles of selectivity and coherence are the chief ones you need to keep in mind when thinking through a topic that is to be organized in chronological sequence—whether in papers based on personal experience, explanatory papers, or persuasive papers.

Example • The use of examples is so characteristic of writing of all kinds and so closely allied to the use of details that it requires little discussion here beyond the admonition to *use* examples and develop them fully enough so that they can serve their proper purpose. Even though the writing is correct and the material well organized, a paper may be criticized as "vague," "abstract," "overgeneralized," or "lacking in persuasiveness"—in short, lacking in the telling examples that would clarify the ideas or support the opinions.

Students often limit their examples to a single "for instance." Sometimes this is adequate as in "The Wobblies, like most labor movements, produced some splendid songs. The best-known example is 'Casey Jones.'" But often the example will carry its meaning only when it is developed and explained. "Half a dozen movies—*Tom Jones,* for one—taught me more about life a couple of hundred years ago than all the history books I studied in high school" introduces an example, but it will remain inert and ineffective unless the writer extends and develops it. The following passage shows how an example used to clarify an idea can profitably be extended through several paragraphs:

Different poets concentrate in different ways. In my own mind I make a sharp distinction between two types of concentration: one is immediate and complete, the other is plodding and only completed by stages. Some poets write immediately works which, when they are written, scarcely need revision. Others write their poems by stages, feeling their way from rough draft to rough draft, until finally, after many revisions, they have produced a result which may seem to have very little connection with their early sketches.

These two opposite processes are vividly illustrated in two examples drawn from music: Mozart and Beethoven. Mozart thought out symphonies, quartets, even scenes from operas, entirely in his head—often on a journey or perhaps while dealing with pressing problems—and then he transcribed them, in their completeness, onto paper. Beethoven wrote fragments of themes in note books which he kept beside him, working on and developing them over years. Often his first ideas were of a clumsiness which makes scholars marvel how he could, at the end, have developed from them such miraculous results.

Thus genius works in different ways to achieve its ends. But although the Mozartian type of genius is the more brilliant and dazzling, genius, unlike virtuosity, is judged by greatness of results, not by brilliance of performance. The result must be the fullest development in a created aesthetic form of an original moment of insight, and it does not matter whether genius devotes a lifetime to producing a small result if that result be immortal. The difference between two types of genius is that one type (the Mozartian) is able to plunge the greatest depths of his own experience by the tremendous effort of a moment, the other (the Beethovenian) must dig deeper and deeper into his consciousness, layer by layer. What counts in either case is the vision which sees and pursues and attains the end; the logic of the artistic purpose.

A poet may be divinely gifted with a lucid and intense and purposive intellect; he may be clumsy and slow; that does not matter, what matters is integrity of purpose and the ability to maintain the purpose without losing oneself. Myself, I am scarcely capable of immediate concentration in poetry. My mind is not clear, my will is weak, I suffer from an excess of ideas and a weak sense of form. For every poem that I begin to write, I think of at least ten which I do not write down at all. For every poem which I do write down, there are seven or eight which I never complete.—STEPHEN SPENDER, "The Making of a Poem," *Partisan Review,* Summer 1946, pp. 296-297

Spender's intention in using the pair of examples from music is to clarify the main idea of his opening paragraph. For his purpose, one extended (double-pronged) example is sufficient. But as support for a debatable proposition, a single example is seldom adequate. The method of proof known as *induction* consists of giving clusters of examples or instances designed to support general assertions about *all* or *most* of the members of a class. (See Chapter 7, pp. 242-247.)

Only rarely do examples alone—even large clusters of them—constitute the dominant method of development for an entire paper. More often they are used cooperatively with the other methods of development. Whether they are limited to a single phrase or extend through several paragraphs, examples are indispensable in clarifying generalizations and giving concrete meaning to abstract statements. (See "Details and generalizations," pp. 112-117.)

Comparison and contrast • Comparison and contrast constitute a method of development which sets forth the points of resemblance and the points of difference between two or more entities—objects or places or people or groups or ideas. Strictly speaking, *comparison* implies likeness, and *contrast* implies difference; but ordinarily the term *comparison* is applied to the whole operation of discovering and presenting the similarities and differences between entities.

In our everyday lives, we are, for one purpose or another, constantly comparing one thing with another—two movies, two books, two people, two restaurants, two teams. (For convenience, we shall limit our discussion to two entities, though obviously you can make comparisons among three or even more. You need to do a little more juggling, but essentially the same operation is involved.) A question requiring comparison is a favorite way of testing your knowledge of the content of the course: you will probably be called on to write papers comparing the interpretations made by two historians or the techniques used by two novelists or the fiscal policies recommended by two economists. In such papers, comparison is central; it is used for its own sake as the means of conveying your understanding of the significant likenesses and differences between the two works or authors you are discussing.

Comparison may play a subordinate role in papers whose central purpose is quite different. If, after a year in England, you wanted to explain the British political system to a friend at home, you might decide to develop your subject by comparing the essential aspects of the British system with those of the American. You would be using a "known" as a point of reference to explain or define an "unknown." To establish a generalization about television audiences, you might compare the shows which have proven popular with those which have not. And as you know, comparison is a typical method of conducting an argument. In controversies over which policy should be adopted or which candidate elected, comparison is inevitable.

To make a comparison, you need first to determine on what basis the objects should be compared. This will depend on your interest or purpose. If you are comparing Jefferson and Hamilton as political thinkers you will use different terms (or points of comparison) from those you would use if you were comparing them as prose stylists. What you want is a limited number of terms that will yield significant likeness and difference—significant for your purpose in making the comparison.

It is risky, of course, to generalize about significance before knowing what is to be done with the likeness or difference. In a paper comparing travel by plane and travel by train, the fact that trains have smoking cars appeared as an irrelevant and distracting detail, sandwiched between a discussion of the quality of the meals on plane and train and a comparison of the two means of transportation in terms of safety. In another paper on the subject, the same detail was a relevant bit of support for the contention by the writer (a nonsmoker) that traveling by train is more comfortable than traveling by plane. Clearly, the terms or points of comparison—comfort was one such term for the writer of the second paper—will guide you in selecting from all the "facts" or characteristics or qualities of the two entities those relevant to your particular purpose.

Presenting the material in an orderly way often gives students more trouble than finding points of comparison. Every paper needs a clear, firm structure, but the need is especially urgent in comparison. To concentrate on one entity at the expense of the other produces an ill-proportioned paper. Failure to link the details about one to the details about the other leaves the reader confused about what the similarities and differences are. Some possibilities for building a balanced comparison are illustrated by three passages in which the same material is organized in different ways. Notice that each makes somewhat different demands on the writer in terms of bringing out relationships of likeness and difference.

A) Thomas Jefferson grew up among the landed gentry of Virginia, and he remained a confirmed Virginian throughout his life. He was a thoughtful man, a scholar and a philosopher, always eager to add to his knowledge of the arts and sciences and to meditate on the mysteries of the universe and of the human spirit. Though reluctant to take part in the clamor and conflict of politics, he became a powerful political leader, working for the welfare of his nation. A patriot and statesman, he devoted his life to the development of the Republic he had helped to create. His writings mirror his hopeful view of human nature, his belief that under the right conditions men will improve. That faith is implicit in the great Declaration of Independence, of which he was the author. It is the basis of his dream of a happy land of free men, living together in natural harmony. And that faith is, of course, the root of his objection to any kind of government that would stifle individual liberty and hamper individual growth. Both his faith and his dream became permanent parts of American democracy.

Alexander Hamilton came from a background very unlike Jefferson's. He was born into a poor family on an island in the Lesser Antilles. He became a New Yorker, joining a society of men as competitive and aggressive as himself. A born organizer and administrator, he used his brilliant mind as a weapon with which to fight not only for personal success but also for the practical policies which he supported. His patriotism was as great as Jefferson's, but his view of the future of the young nation to which he devoted his life was dictated by a very different reading of human nature. He believed that men will act upon the same selfish motives whatever the form of government and concluded, therefore, that a government with sufficient authority to impose order and stability is always essential. Only through a strong central government, he thought, could America achieve peace, progress, and prosperity. This idea, powerfully expressed in his *Federalist* papers, had great influence upon the organization of the new republic and upon its subsequent history.

B) Thomas Jefferson and Alexander Hamilton were two of America's most influential statesmen in the early period of the Republic. Jefferson grew up among the landed gentry of Virginia; Hamilton was born into a poor family on an island in the Lesser Antilles. Only with great reluctance did Jefferson accept a political career, with its accompanying clamor and conflict. A thoughtful man, he would have preferred to spend his life in his native state, free to add to his scholarly knowledge of the arts and sciences and to meditate philosophically on the mysteries of the universe and of the human spirit. Hamilton, on the other hand, found his natural *milieu* in New York City, in a society of men who shared his competitive, aggressive spirit, and entered politics with the enthusiasm and efficiency of the born organizer and administrator. His brilliant mind served him admirably in his fight for personal success and for the practical policies which he supported. His *Federalist* papers are among the greatest documents of the period, ranking in historical importance with Jefferson's Declaration of Independence. Both are the works of great patriots.

Jefferson's political philosophy was optimistic; he believed that, given the right conditions, men would improve. By contrast, Hamilton was convinced that, regardless of environment, human nature could not change. Accordingly, while Jefferson dreamed of a happy land of free men, living together in natural harmony, Hamilton worked for order and stability, for system and organization. The Virginian feared the machinery of a strong central government would stifle individual liberty and hamper individual growth; the New Yorker believed that government must have authority in order to ensure peace, progress, and prosperity. Regardless of the differences in their views, both men devoted their lives to the welfare of the new nation, which both had helped to create and which both helped to survive. And their different views had permanent influence upon the history of America.

C) Thomas Jefferson and Alexander Hamilton were fellow patriots and fellow statesmen. Men of true brilliance, the powerful influence that they exerted upon the Republic at the beginning of its history had an effect that has persisted to the present day. To them we owe some of our greatest historical documents—to Jefferson the Declaration of Independence and to Hamilton a number of the famous *Federalist* papers. Both were powerful political leaders, working for the welfare of the new nation, which they had helped to create and which both helped to survive. To it, they devoted their lives.

At the same time, their differences were numerous and profound. They were unlike in background, in temperament, in habit of mind, and in political philosophy. Jefferson grew up among the landed gentry of old Virginia; Hamilton was born into a poor family on an island in the Lesser Antilles. Throughout his life, Jefferson remained a confirmed Virginian, but Hamilton became a New Yorker, flourishing in a society of men as competitive and aggressive as himself. Jefferson shrank from the clamor and conflict of politics; Hamilton had the zeal of a born organizer and administrator. Jefferson was a thoughtful man, a scholar and a philosopher, always eager to add to his knowledge of the arts and sciences and to meditate on the mysteries of the universe and of the human spirit. Hamilton used his mind as a keen weapon with which he fought not only for personal success but also for the practical policies he supported.

They differed profoundly in their views of human nature. An optimist, Jefferson believed that, under the right conditions, men would improve; Hamilton was convinced that, regardless of environment, human nature would never change. Because of their different reading of human nature, they had different views about the role of government. Since he could not believe that a new type of government would result in a new type of citizenry, Hamilton worked for the old objectives—order and stability, system and organization; he sought to build a government with traditional authority, which he considered essential to peace, progress, and prosperity. Just as naturally, considering his philosophy, Jefferson fought against a strong central government, fearing that it would stifle individual liberty and hamper individual growth, seeing it as a threat to his dream of a happy land of free men, living together in natural harmony.

Passage A is sometimes called the whole-by-whole method of comparison; Jefferson is first described in full, then Hamilton. Passage B is the part-to-part method; it treats the two men together in terms of each point relevant to the task of comparison—influence, background, attitude toward politics, intellectual habits, works of comparable importance, political philosophy, conception of the role of government, and contribution to the nation. (These are the same points that made up the substance of A and that, arranged in still another *order,* make up the substance of C.) Passage C is the likeness-difference method. In the example given here, points of likeness come first and then points of difference. For some purposes—if, for example, likenesses rather than differences were to be emphasized—the order might be reversed.

Even when both of the entities are "unknowns," comparisons seldom follow patterns as neat as these, with such a careful balancing of points. Sometimes two of the methods are combined: a complex comparison may use the C pattern in combination with A or B, and other variations are possible. Sometimes a perfect balancing of "part" against "part" would be wasteful. In explaining the British political system to an American, you would give relatively little space to the "known" —the American system—because you could count on the reader's familiarity with it. Nevertheless, these passages are useful models of basic patterns of organization and show the need for selecting *relevant* material. There is no place in the comparison for a treatment of Jefferson's political views unless Hamilton's are treated too. It would be impossible to use the dramatic (but wholly irrelevant) detail of Hamilton's death in a duel with Aaron Burr without seriously distorting the kind of unity now present in the passages.

Your purpose will influence your choice of a pattern of organization, just as it determines what points of comparison—and, therefore, what material—you will use. Questions you should keep in mind are these: Do I need to present a general view of each whole? Should I set side by side certain aspects of each whole to sharpen the comparison of particular points? Do I wish to emphasize the ways in which these entities are alike, or do I wish to stress their differences?

Division and classification • In the kind of thinking and planning they require, division and classification are similar enough to be treated together.

Division (or analysis) is the process of breaking down into its parts a single object or institution or concept; an automobile, a sorority, communism, or democracy can be divided into its basic parts or features. Classification is the process of grouping together related objects or institutions or concepts; automobiles, sororities, theories of government can be sorted into groups on the basis of their similarities and differences. Both are useful methods of explanation, and both procedures may go into the making of arguments.

Sometimes a paper will be assigned in such a way as to require the use of one of these methods; you might be asked to *analyze* jazz as a musical form or to *classify* jazz musicians. At other times, you might choose to use either or both of these methods in conveying your ideas about your topic. Thus, if your general subject is the place of the Republican party in American politics, you might decide to get at the main characteristics of the party's philosophy by analyzing its platform— possibly by dividing it into two broad topics, the position on foreign policy and the position on domestic policy, and discussing each one. Or you might find that it suits your purpose to classify influential Republicans into groups that are representative of different schools of thought within the party. By establishing the groups and indicating significant differences among them, you could represent the range of political opinion included within the Republican party.

Logicians have set up two hard-and-fast rules for making a sound division (or classification). First, in dividing (or classifying), only one principle is to be applied at a time. Second, the dividing must go on until all of the parts of the entity have been identified (or in classifying, until every member or entity has been placed in one of the groups).

Briefly, the first rule warns against inconsistency and overlapping, the second against incompleteness. Taken together, the rules are indispensable in rigorous scientific procedures, and anyone who undertakes even an informal division or classification will find them a guide to clear thinking. You can guard against gross blunders by making sure that the basis of division or classification is followed through consistently, that one part or group does not overlap another, and that no essential part or group is omitted.

Weaknesses in division can be spotted most readily when the subject is a concrete object like an automobile. An elementary division might yield three main parts: chassis, engine and driving parts, and body. Other divisions are possible, and certainly further subdividing would be necessary if you were writing an informative article on how a car works; but as far as it goes, the simple, three-part division is consistent and complete. By contrast, a division into chassis, engine and driving parts, and fenders would strike anyone as faulty, for it is obviously incomplete. And a division into chassis, body, and inexpensive transportation is worse, for it is both incomplete and inconsistent. The third "part" has been arrived at by introducing a new principle of division—expense.

Unlike a car, a concept (or intellectual whole) like patriotism or democracy does not have parts that can be pointed to and separated out in a physical sense. When no mechanical principle of division offers itself, the writer has to find a principle of his own and impose it on the material. That principle will be determined by his interest, his way of looking at the subject, his estimate of what line of division will be most fruitful in accomplishing his purpose. In any informal analysis, the chief task is to single out those aspects of the material that, discussed separately, can increase the reader's understanding of the parts of the subject and, taken together, can permit the writer to come to a significant generalization about the whole. Thus the student who wrote the paper "Americans in Politics" (p. 69) divided the subject of American political behavior into three parts: the behavior and attitudes of representatives; the behavior and attitudes of constituents; the spread of political intolerance among both representatives and constituents. This division is not strictly logical, for the third topic is not precisely coordinate with the other two. Nor is the analysis complete, for other topics could have been treated. Few readers, however, would criticize the paper for being grossly illogical or obviously incomplete, since, when the subject is a large and complex one, division serves its proper function if it enables the writer to proceed in an orderly, economical way as he unfolds his ideas on his subject. In the following paragraph, the author makes a division of the complex activity of listening to music, admits that the division is somewhat arbitrary, and then points out its usefulness for his purpose:

We all listen to music according to our separate capacities. But, for the sake of analysis, the whole listening process may become clearer if we break it up into its component parts, so to speak. In a certain sense we all listen to music on three separate planes. For lack of a better terminology, one might name these: (1) the sensuous plane, (2) the expressive plane, (3) the sheerly musical plane. The only advantage to be gained from mechanically splitting up the listening process into these hypothetical planes is the clearer view to be had of the way in which we listen.—AARON COPLAND, *What to Listen for in Music*, pp. 9-10

Classification, like division, can bring clarity and order into a discussion. But again the basis of the classification should be consistent. Serious blunders can result from ignoring the rule that only one principle is to be applied at a time. The blunder occurs most commonly, perhaps, in classifying people. It is all too easy to shift the basis of classification in midstream, probably because in any rather full classification the writer wants to convey a sense of the reality of each group rather than simply to set up the groups, and in doing so he typically uses several different principles of classification. This is perfectly acceptable so long as one principle has been carried through the whole group before a second one is introduced. But using two or more principles simultaneously will confuse rather than enlighten the reader. Such is the case in a paper written by a student who, describing his own adventures as a Marine, established four groups of Marine transport pilots: the nervous pilot, the old pilot, the ex-jet pilot, and the reliable pilot. This classification is obviously bad, for the groups overlap: an old pilot and an ex-jet pilot might well be nervous, either or both might be reliable, an ex-jet pilot might be old, and an old pilot might be an ex-jet pilot. The student was using several different principles of classification at once. What he needed to do was to apply one at a time—age *or* reliability *or* experience. He could then logically go on to establish subgroups by using either or both of the remaining principles.

Such flagrant violations of the first rule for a sound classification will offend anyone's sense of what is reasonable. The basic trouble, perhaps, is that the student misunderstood the nature and purpose of classification. In thinking through his material he kept his attention focused on individuals, and his "classification" emerged as a series of character sketches. But the classifier has to interest himself in the type, not the individual. He must concentrate not on the idiosyncrasies and complexities which make any two people strikingly different, but on the general characteristics they share in relation to the specific principle of classification he is applying. What the classifier says is that *for the purpose he has in mind* these two people can be put in a compartment with other people, all of whom are different in some respects but alike in terms of a single principle of classification.

It is quite possible that the classifier's interest in the type rather than the individual will require some relaxation of the second rule of the logicians. A too-conscientious effort to observe the rule that a niche should be found for every member of the entire group may result in an extremely cluttered classification in which the large main classes and subclasses lose their clarity by being festooned with "borderline," "miscellaneous," or "other" tiny groups. You will not get into such difficulty if you modify the second rule to something like this: the classification should be as complete as the material allows and the writer's purpose requires. In classifying a large and heterogeneous group, you are not aiming for rigidly distinct categories which will enable you to pigeonhole every single individual. When you say that there are four types of students or statesmen, you are not saying that there are *only* four and that *every* student or statesman fits comfortably in one of the groups; you are saying that four discernible classes can be differentiated in ways that are significant *for the purpose you have in mind.* If the classification is clearly related to that purpose and if each of the classes is substantiated by enough relevant and meaningful details to make it a real one, the reader will be satisfied.

These general observations are illustrated in the following informal classification. The author makes clear his purpose— to explain why foreigners often get the impression that Americans are "brainless and entirely uninterested in the life of the mind." His application of a single principle of classification (the extent to which Americans say what they think) produces two groups—loudmouths and quietmouths. (The grouping is sound enough, even though some individuals may hover between the two classes: they may say what they think in some circumstances but not in others.) The author gives reality to his groups by using those characteristics of each group which are relevant to his principle. Because the classification is made not for its own sake but to serve as a jumping-off point for a discussion of the effect on foreigners of "the quietmouth American," the loudmouth gets less space than the quietmouth.

Foreigners frequently emerge from meetings with Americans convinced—although they probably couldn't say exactly why—that we are brainless and entirely uninterested in the life of the mind. Understandably, they are shaken by this conclusion. But the many small habits which together have created the impression are not really the traits of the stupid American or the anti-intellectual American; they are the natural ways of the quietmouth American.

Let me explain.

Americans can be divided into two groups: the "loudmouths" and the "quietmouths." Loudmouths make a business of expressing their opinions, whether for duty, profit, or pleasure. These are the voices heard by all those who wish to plumb American character, American policy, American public opinion. These are the journalists, ever busy, busy, busy, and forever seeming busier than they are, mainly by the noise they make. These are the politicians or their ghost writers, the captains of industry or *their* ghosts, the clergy moved by a holier Ghost. These are the columnists, writers of books and articles, critics, reviewers, biographers and autobiographers, street-corner loungers and barflies buzzing the news straight from the horse's mouth. These —all these—are the loudmouths. Everybody knows what they think.

All other Americans are the quietmouths. They are the ones who are touching the lives of foreign folk and being touched by them, more and more as time goes on. What do they think? Nobody knows. They don't say.

Not that it is hard to get an American to talk. He is really quite chatty with strangers, ready to say a kind or unkind thing about the weather, baseball, any current event or holiday. Weasels and how they fish will interest him if the barber talks about these as he cuts his hair. He talks to the plumber about plumbing, with the mechanic about cars; if the bus driver, the elevator girl, his secretary, or his children have had a bad day, he commiserates, a good day, he rejoices. But what does he *think*? Nobody knows. Somehow he doesn't say.

Similarly his wife. At the supermarket, the drugstore, the beauty shop, the cocktail party, she converses amiably on what may be amiably conversed about: oddities of husbands, bother of children, vagaries of style, crotchets of neighbors, glories of gardens, monotony of home management, textures of textiles, weight, diet, and taxes. But what does she *think*? She doesn't say.

The American's house reflects his mind. Set back from the street, it offers every passer-by an inviting stretch of green lawn. Like a house in any country, it resembles the houses surrounding it. Usually the green lawns merge with no more to mark boundaries than a hedge which is no barrier to dogs or paper boys. Or eyes. The American's house has a broad porch or a picture window, sometimes both. Entering this house across a welcome mat, you are met by a hearty "Come in," served refreshments with heartwarming informality, and engaged in conversation which, if it veers from the standard safe subjects, veers toward your interests and recent experiences. The evening over, you are pressed to come again, though without definite fixing of a future engagement.—Donald Lloyd, "The Quietmouth American," *Harper's Magazine,* Sept. 1963, pp. 101-102

Whether the reader accepts the grouping of Americans into loudmouths and quietmouths, he is sure to find it original and thought-provoking. It is worth repeating that a classification like this one is not made for its own sake but so that the author can express his ideas about his topic. In the same way, you might classify books on the best-seller list to draw some conclusions about the reading tastes of Americans. Classifications in textbooks often do appear to be made solely for their own sake—that is, as a means of conveying information. But even here the ideas of the author and the nature of his audience will determine some aspects of a classification. Chapter 1 of this book classifies the varieties of English into two major groups: Standard and Nonstandard. Standard is further subdivided into Formal, General, and Informal, and these are differentiated from each other in some detail. Although a corresponding subdivision of Nonstandard could be made, it has not been—simply because it would have no practical value for readers of this book. Their interest is in Standard English.

Causes and effects • Cause-effect connections are made constantly in all kinds of writing. They are conveyed not only by explicit statements (A is the cause of B *or* B is the effect of A) but also by such common transitional words and phrases as *because, therefore, consequently, in order that, as a result,* and, in some of their uses, *for, since, then,* and *thus.* Sometimes the parts of a sentence are linked in such a way as to suggest a causal relation ("The higher the tuition, the better the school"); and sometimes the simple juxtaposition of two statements implies such a relation:

On April 6 Lincoln sent word to the governor of South Carolina that supplies would be shipped to Fort Sumter. On April 12 Confederate guns began to bombard the fort.

The role of causal connections in making a narrative coherent has already been stressed (p. 78). They are equally important in various pieces of informative prose which, though organized chronologically, are not usually thought of as purely narrative—recipes, descriptions of processes, sets of instructions. The following recipe gives as much attention to causal relations (in the form of warnings) as it does to the directions themselves.

If you want your hard-cooked eggs to taste good, don't boil them. If you do, the whites will be leathery. Put the eggs in a saucepan, cover them with water, and add a pinch of salt to keep the shells from cracking. Bring the water rapidly to a simmer, reduce the heat, and continue to simmer for 15 minutes. Immediately after removing the eggs from the heat, drop them into cold water to make them easier to shell and to reduce darkening of the yolks.

Naturally, the causal statements here are spare and undeveloped. The housewife does not learn why egg white becomes tough if cooked at a very high temperature, nor why salt keeps shells from cracking, nor why dousing the cooked eggs in cold water has the double effect of making them easier to shell and reducing discoloration of the yolks. She is told just enough to make her see the need for following the directions.

In a more elaborate set of instructions (how to refinish a piece of furniture, for example, or how to do the butterfly stroke in swimming) statements of cause and effect may be introduced not only to explain each separate direction but also to justify the order in which the directions are given. In an explanation of a process like soil drifting, causal statements show how one stage in the process relates to another. Although they are subsidiary to the writer's main purpose, such statements are extremely useful in helping the reader understand *why* what happens does happen.

In some essays cause-effect analysis becomes the major method of development. The authors of explanatory and persuasive articles frequently probe into the causes of (or reasons for) an event or situation or policy or trace its effects (or results); or they may use both methods in the same discussion—first setting forth the events that led to a particular state of affairs, then revealing or predicting the developments this state of affairs has brought about or can be expected to bring about. Titles like these signal a cause-effect method of development:

The Roots of Juvenile Delinquency
Unemployment—Its Causes and Cures
The Cold War and How It Grew
Why Thoreau Went to Walden Pond
The Decline and Fall of Fraternities

In such essays, the writer's interest is centered not so much on the phenomenon or situation or event as on what led to it or on what it has led to or will lead to. His concern is to present (and perhaps argue for) the relationships and connections he has arrived at by *reasoning about* origins and results.

Reasoning in terms of cause and effect, like any other kind of reasoning, can be done well or badly. A paper that is developed largely in terms of cause and effect will be judged, among other things, on the soundness and plausibility of the causal relations set forth. On the kinds of topics which college students are expected to deal with, it may not be easy to establish convincing cause-effect connections, but neither is it impossible. The students who have most trouble doing it are those who think it is one or the other.

The student who approaches a cause-effect assignment without the proper respect can easily make a fool of himself. Typically, he oversimplifies: Bureaucracy is to blame for high taxes; slavery caused the Civil War; unemployment is the result of automation; the abolition of cigarettes will put an end to lung cancer. He matches one cause to one effect, often without evidence that his one cause is, in fact, a cause at all, and so turns what should be a reasoned discussion into a dogmatic statement of simple-minded opinion.

Another student, overwhelmed by the difficulty of assigning causes or attributing results, goes to the other extreme and refuses to commit himself at all. He becomes so cautious that he loads his paper down with qualifications, presents an endless list of "possible" causes, or traces the "possible" immediate causes back to such large and virtually meaningless causes as "civilization," "heredity," or "environment." Both the student who oversimplifies and the one who overqualifies need to develop a realistic notion of how to go about discovering and presenting causal relations.

Anyone who is accustomed to thinking of cause-effect relations in the context of laboratory experiments in chemistry, physics, or biology readily recognizes that two phenomena are causally related only if the existence of the one *requires* the existence of the other. Thus a causal connection between A and B can be established with certainty only if it can be demonstrated that whenever B occurs, A is present; that B never occurs in the absence of A; that the presence of A always results in the occurrence of B.

The scientist working in the laboratory tries to control one variable after another until eventually he can determine what condition or set of conditions operates as a cause. Laboratory conditions give him the further advantage of being able to run experiments again and again until he has verified his hypothesis, his hunch or his guess that A is the cause of B. The following paragraph sketches the evidence which proves that the causal factor in the flying behavior of bats is an "internal timing device" or biological clock, not, as was formerly supposed, the coming on of evening.

Those who are familiar with the habits of bats will know that each day these animals begin to fly in the early evening just when the insects they feed on are most abundant. The inference that this flying behavior is controlled by some internal timing device is based in part on measurements which have been made on caged bats in controlled conditions. The activity of bats, even when confined to a cage, shows a pattern of active periods followed by rest periods, and this pattern is repeated periodically with a well defined rhythm. Even in complete darkness at a constant temperature this rhythm persists indefinitely. Of course, in such conditions the rhythm no longer has exactly a twenty-four-hour period, but at regular intervals of perhaps 23 or 23½ hours (depending on the individual bat) the cycle of activity repeats itself. Such rhythmic activity patterns occur throughout the animal kingdom, and the rhythms of leaf movement or flower-opening which occur in plants likewise will persist in the absence of a cycle of light and dark. Therefore, although rhythms may be synchronized by an external cycle, they appear to be in no way dependent on it, and the persistence of the rhythms in the absence of external signals is one of their important characteristics. These rhythms are now frequently called *circadian rhythms* because their period is about (circa) a day (diem).—Victor G. Bruce, "Biological Clocks," *Frontiers of Modern Biology,* pp. 64-65

In many of the things that matter most to us, it is impossible to set up controlled laboratory experiments that will nail down cause-effect relations. We cannot call into existence the actual circumstances or conditions in which a crime was committed or an election lost or a battle won. And even if we could rerun episodes and situations of this kind, we would rarely be able to isolate a single cause that inevitably led to the given effect. "In the world of reality," a logician observes, "there is no such thing as *the* cause of anything. There are many causes, or necessary antecedents, for everything that happens." Even a simple event may have to be accounted for in numerous ways. An investigation into a collision of two cars may be concerned with weather conditions, the mechanisms of one or both of the cars, the drivers' observance of traffic regulations, the skill and reactions of the drivers. The investigator may well find that no one "cause" can be isolated, that the accident had many contributing causes. If his job is to assess responsibility, he will try to demonstrate that, given the whole complex set of circumstances, *one* had a more immediate connection with the accident than the others. He may, however, have to content himself with listing three or four, none of which can be said to be crucial in itself.

If a street-corner accident turns out to have several causes, then it is likely that large, complex social problems will have many more. In recent years, statistics have been gathered to show "a marked trend toward early marriage." Various reasons for this trend have been suggested: the dating customs of teenagers, prosperous economic conditions, the impact of the draft, "a search for security in a troubled world." (You may be able to think of others.) If you were writing a paper on the subject, you might, on the basis of observation and reflection, be able to show that each of these is *a* cause, though you might not feel justified in labeling any one as *the* cause. At any rate, the interest and value of your paper would reside not merely in the list of causes but in the demonstration that the relationship between each cause and the effect was indeed a probable one. Why is it likely, for instance, that prosperous economic conditions encourage early marriage? Some of the papers students write are weak simply because the relation between the effect and what is asserted to be the cause is not made to seem convincing. In this connection, you need to recognize that causal analysis usually has an argumentative edge to it. There is no point in writing about cause-effect relations that are obvious to everybody (touching a red-hot burner sears the flesh and causes pain). There *is* some point in exploring and writing about those cause-effect relationships which, even though they cannot be pinned down with absolute certainty, can, when they are shown to be probable, increase the reader's understanding of the subject or guide his actions. And it is demonstration, not mere assertion, that establishes probability.

Demonstration in cause-effect papers, as in all kinds of explanatory and persuasive papers, takes the form of concrete, relevant details. In terms of the organization of the paper, it may also take the form of a movement from less probable causes to more probable causes, from remote ones to immediate ones, or from supposed causes that the writer rejects to the cause that he thinks is the real one. Both kinds of demonstration are illustrated in a paper in which a student analyzes the causes for his failure in a high-school course.

Why I Failed Biology

When a student fails a course, he has to face the disturbing question: "Why?" I failed Biology during my junior year in high school, and it took me some time before I finally recognized the real reason I flunked.

When I first asked myself "Why?" I thought of the usual reasons I had heard classmates give for their failures: "The teacher was no good"..."I didn't get a decent background for the subject"..."I just can't handle that kind of work." But I had to admit that I couldn't use any of those reasons. My Biology teacher had taught me General Science the year before; he was a good teacher, and his General Science course was an excellent introduction to Biology. So it wasn't the teacher's fault, and it wasn't that I had no background. And I couldn't use the alibi of a friend of mine who flunks Math year after year and says that she just doesn't have a mathematical mind. I got the highest grades in the class in General Science, and that proved that I should have been able to handle Biology.

My teacher thought that I failed because I had fallen into poor study habits, and for a while I agreed with him. I found it hard to work at home that year, because my kid brother had reached the noisy age and he and his twelve-year-old pals always had the house in an uproar. Because of that, I got into the habit of putting off my homework until late in the evening, after he'd gone to bed, and then I usually fell asleep over my books. But I never got seriously behind in any of my courses—except Biology. I worked hard at the others, and I did well in them.

I didn't work hard at Biology, and I flunked the course. I remember the day of the final examination: I looked over the questions, and most of the material didn't even sound familiar. I knew some of the answers, but I also knew that I didn't have a chance of passing. In the end, I didn't make much of an effort.

So you might say that I failed Biology because I didn't work at it hard enough. But why didn't I work at it? I finally figured out the answer this last summer, when my parents agreed to let me major in art at college.

My father is a doctor, and he always expected me to study medicine. I planned to, too, until I got interested in painting during my sophomore year in high school. My father thought it was only a passing fancy, and at first he was amused by my attempts; but before long he began to complain. He said I was spending entirely too much of my time on my "oils" and told me I shouldn't let a "hobby" interfere with serious work. He got very impatient, but by that time I knew that I wanted to paint more than anything in the world.

So I failed Biology. I failed it because I didn't work at it, and I didn't work at it because I wanted to become a painter, not a doctor. I knew that I could never argue my father out of his ambition for me, but I knew that he'd give it up if he became convinced that I didn't have the abilities to succeed as a medical student. I was right, too. And now that it's all settled, I'm taking the freshman course in College Biology and doing fine.

In this paper, as in many other causal accounts that are less personal, the causal analysis is combined with a narrative framework, though the analysis, quite properly, dominates the account. The student moves from one generally accepted cause of failure to another, rejecting each in turn and giving evidence why, in his particular case, all these causes are invalid. The real cause, it turns out, was his reaction to his father's attempt to discourage his artistic ambitions. He gives enough evidence about his father's attitude and about his own feelings to make his interpretation of cause fairly convincing.

In a personal causal account like "Why I Failed Biology," it is difficult for the reader to evaluate the accuracy of the analysis. But when the subject is a more general one, the reader can weigh the writer's interpretation against his own. No one outside your immediate family can challenge your account of how you caught measles in kindergarten, but any reader can question your analysis of the causes of the popularity of Jack London's books in the Soviet Union or your reasons for finding one poem better than another. To make your causal analyses acceptable, you must see to it that they are logical; to make them convincing, you must provide evidence to support your point of view.

The preceding examples have dealt with the uncovering and presenting of causes. Sometimes a student's main concern will be to set forth results or effects—the effects of living in a fraternity, the effects of school desegregation, the effects of automation. To a large extent, the problems are similar to those already discussed. The task is to make plausible the relationship between the situation or the phenomenon and the effects attributed to it. Just as extremely remote causes are uninstructive ("The cause of the street-corner accident was the invention of automobiles"), so there is a danger that one may attribute too broad a result to the phenomenon with which he is concerned. We find this tendency in some simplified history texts: the suggestion that the Renaissance period in Europe *resulted* from the Crusades, that the revolution in American morals in the 1920's was the *effect* of the First World War, that the Depression of the 1930's was the *result* of the policies of the Hoover administration. Other historians have demonstrated convincingly that the Renaissance, the change in moral standards, the Depression were the effects of much more complex forces.

It is particularly important to proportion effects to causes when dealing with *future* effects. The politician may feel no qualms about predicting dire consequences for the country if his opponent is elected, but then very few intelligent people take him seriously. If you want an "effects" paper of yours to be taken seriously, you must make sure that, through adequately detailed evidence, you have established reasonable links between the event or situation and the results you say it has brought about or will bring about.

Definition • In many of the papers you write, you will need to compose a clear, concise statement of what a word means in the context of your discussion. This is what is ordinarily thought of as definition—the explanation of the meaning of a word somewhat in the manner of a dictionary definition. Definition of words is worth some attention before we go on to definition as a method of development.

-To know when you need to define a word takes a certain amount of sensitivity to your audience. For example, it is not always safe to assume that your instructor has even heard a term from skiing or skin-diving or sports car racing which you and your friends are all familiar with. (It is not wise either, of course, to assume that he is unfamiliar with every word that has entered the language since World War II.) After estimating whether your reader can be expected to know the word, you must decide how important it is that he know precisely what *you* mean by it. If his understanding of a key term is radically different from yours, you can scarcely hope to communicate your ideas fully, if at all. The decision is easy enough when you are using highly technical terms like *cybernetics* or *synergetics* in a paper addressed to a general audience; these certainly need to be defined. So do everyday words used in the specialized sense they have acquired in a particular subject matter: *set,* for instance, in mathematics; *wealth* in economics; *texture* in literature. A good rule of thumb is this: whenever a word has several accepted meanings and the context does not make readily apparent the meaning you intend, you should specify the sense in which you are using the word. The purpose of a definition of this kind (sometimes called a stipulative definition) is simply to establish common ground between reader and writer. Naturally, the definition must be an accepted one. No reader will pay much attention to you if in a serious discussion you arbitrarily decide, like Humpty Dumpty in *Alice in Wonderland,* that "glory" is to mean "a nice knock-down argument."

The phrasing of a definition requires some tact and sensitivity, too. You have to take into account not only the amount of information your reader already possesses but also the range of his vocabulary. In papers for a general audience, it is obviously unsatisfactory to explain a technical term by other, equally unfamiliar technical terms; the definition will accomplish its purpose only if it is couched in words and phrases that are within the reader's working vocabulary. Using zoological terminology to define *bush baby* is appropriate in a paper for Zoology 101, but such a definition would be pretentious and irritating in a paper describing the attractions of the zoo.

A circular definition like "A linguist is one who specializes in linguistics" is not enlightening and therefore cannot be considered satisfactory even though it appears in good desk dictionaries. You should resist the temptation to quote a definition from your dictionary instead of phrasing it in your own words. Because dictionary-makers are always pressed for space and because they can expect the serious user of their book to move from one entry to another, they do not always supply definitions that are clear and readable. Yours should be. (Another reason to avoid quoting dictionary definitions, particularly in an opening paragraph, is that there are few more certain ways of losing your reader's interest.)

When the writing situation is a formal one, you may want to introduce the definition of a key term with a little pomp and ceremony in order to make sure the reader's attention fixes on it long enough for him to assimilate the meaning. In less formal contexts, the explanation can be slipped in casually and unobtrusively, without delaying the forward movement of the discussion. The first of these calls attention to itself; the others do not.

> By a faction, I understand a number of citizens, whether amounting to a majority or a minority of the whole, who are united and actuated by some common impulse of passion, or of interest, adverse to the rights of other citizens, or to the permanent and aggregate interests of the community.—James Madison, *The Federalist,* No. 10

> The curiously variable wind that sweeps up the Adriatic from Africa, called *sirocco* by the Venetians whether it is cold and wet or hot and dry, turns suddenly chill, and summer is ended.—William Marchant, "Venice Out of Season," *Holiday,* Feb. 1964, p. 52

> In a very general sense, ethics is the name we give to our concern for good behavior.—Albert Schweitzer, "The Evolution of Ethics," The *Atlantic,* Nov. 1958, p. 69

Often an illustrative example or an identifying phrase or synonym will do as much as needs doing toward clarifying the meaning of a word, but sometimes you will find it useful or necessary to construct what is known as a *logical* definition.[1] Many definitions in textbooks fall into this pattern:

term	=	*genus* or *class*	+	*differentia*
A ballad	is	a song		that tells a story
Conchology	is	the study		of shells and mollusks

A logical definition first specifies the *genus* or class to which the term belongs and then differentiates it from other members of the class. Sometimes one differentiating characteristic is sufficient; sometimes several are needed. You will recognize that this process of defining is similar to the procedure followed by the biologist or zoologist in classifying organisms according to genus and species. Although in the examples just cited the process appears cut and dried, a little experimenting will convince you that for many terms a great deal of discriminating thought has to go into the selection of the *genus* and *differentia*. (The traditional rules for testing the soundness of a logical definition are listed in the *Index* entry *Definition.[2]) The ability to frame such definitions is one measure of your understanding of a subject, and that is why you are often expected to produce them on examinations and in term papers. Furthermore, because one extremely valuable device for explaining fully the nature of a thing or concept is to demonstrate its relation to its class and to other members of that class, the logical definition lies at the heart of many full-length essays. Whether or not it appears explicitly, it may provide the basic content and even determine the organization of a paper.

Encyclopedia articles, which are designed to present information not about the meanings of words (as in dictionary entries) but about the things the words stand for, are often built around the core of a logical definition. Scan some encyclopedia articles to see for yourself how logical definitions serve as pegs or anchors for the explanation. Such articles are not, however, models for the essays in definition that you will write. The purpose of encyclopedia articles is to convey information in an objective and impersonal fashion. Although this does not

---

[1] It is sometimes said that a logical definition names the essence of a thing and so is a "real" definition in contrast to the "nominal" definitions (definitions of words) that are found in dictionaries. The distinction is a slippery one because many dictionary definitions do fall into the pattern of the logical definition and because many terms have been given different, apparently equally satisfactory logical definitions even within a single subject matter. What, for example, is the proper *genus* for poetry? Practically speaking, when a student sets out to write a paper in definition, he is concerned with the object or concept itself and, whether or not he frames a logical definition, he will try to produce a "real" one.

[2] Throughout this book, references to *Index* articles are indicated by an asterisk (*) .

mean that they have to be dull, they often are—mainly because they cannot be directed at a particular audience. When
you are writing essays developed by definition, you should
(as in all your papers) aim them at a specific audience. This
does not mean that you will be any less obligated to define
the thing as it really is, but it does mean that in explaining
its nature you will reach into the reader's experience (as well
as your own) for the illustrations, details, comparisons, and
all the other resources which you can draw on in writing an
extended definition.

Sometimes you can start from a typical misconception, one
which the reader is likely to share. Very often the writer of a
popular article or newspaper column does this, for his purpose is not simply to convey information but to sweep away
fuzzy or wrong notions and to replace them with clear or
accurate ones. The following passage, the beginning of a
long article on American deserts, is launched by an engaging
and lively attack on the reader's general attitude toward
deserts, which is shown to be based on a faulty understanding
of what a desert is. The logical definition (at the beginning
of paragraph 7) is stated with formal precision, to be sure, but
it is less formidable and more meaningful because of the
preceding discussion.

Much more desert exists within our country than most of us know,
or will admit. You could drop the whole of England into it and
have trouble finding England again. But the chamber-of-commerce
habit of mind is strong. Deserts do not tolerate large populations and
refuse to yield much in material wealth except in mineral strikes.
Therefore they are usually regarded as unimportant, handicapping,
to be played down, ignored.

That is a downright silly attitude. We should be proud of our
deserts. A country without deserts is incomplete, shut off from much
of the world's wonder and of life's reach. Deserts preserve a balance
in the very nature of things and round out the human experience.

One difficulty, of course, is that most of us cannot even define a
desert. Our minds are fogged with vague remembrances of school-
text pictures of some barren stretch of, say, the Sahara; sand, nothing
but sand, more sand, sand heaped in big dunes, a camel or two plodding across it. That is merely a misleading extreme portrait of one
part of one type of desert. True, all deserts have sand, plenty of it.
Most have extensive dune areas. Most have long stretches of barren-
ness. But all of them have much, much more.

There are two basic requirements: low average rainfall and high
average daytime temperature. Any region where rainfall rarely rises

above ten inches a year and which is within the wide warm belt known as the "horse latitudes"—that is, within about 30 degrees of the equator—is almost certain to be a desert.

And so those two create the dominant characteristic: dryness, aridity, a lack of water at or near the surface of the ground where it can be used by animal and plant life.

The most obvious immediate result is a scarcity of vegetation. None at all in some areas. Elsewhere only isolated plants. Desert plants do not fight for places in the sun; they fight for water rights. In effect, each stakes a claim to its own small empire and holds this against invaders.

A desert is a great arid basin or congeries of basins beyond high mountain ranges lying athwart the course of rain clouds swinging in from the oceans. These mountain ranges shut off desert rainfall. A desert may have mountains of its own, rising abrupt and craggy from the general floor level. It may have a river running through— but this does not belong to it, is independent of it. Invariably such a river rises outside, drains from the barrier-rim mountains. The desert's own "rivers," called so often only by courtesy, are contained within itself, are dry stream beds most of the time. Even those few fed by springs usually meander a short way slowing and dwindling and die into the sands.

A desert may even have marshes, lakes, in season boast many ponds and play host to migrating waterfowl. Since many desert basins have no natural outlets, what rain falls on them is collected in the lowest levels. These "wet" areas are often, for all practical purposes, the most barren.—Jack Schaefer, "Our Challenging Deserts," *Holiday*, July 1958, pp. 56, 90

In the passage just quoted, a prevalent misconception serves as an effective starting point for the essay. A single, explicit negative often accomplishes a great deal in paving the way for a positive definition. Consider, for example, how much is implied in the statement "A composition text is not a book of etiquette." But of course it only paves the way. Defining by negation can be a risky technique for an inexperienced writer: he may end up by telling a great deal about what the subject of his definition isn't, without ever getting around to telling what it is. The method of negation is most useful, perhaps, when the writer is aware that a conflicting definition is firmly held by many members of his audience or when he knows he must persuade his audience that his definition is the right one by contrast with other current interpretations. In such situations he is not likely to evade the task of clear, positive definition. But even though the paper itself gives little or no space to getting rid of misconceptions or false notions, negating is inherent in the thinking process by which you arrive at a positive definition. To define the nature of a thing is to delimit and exclude, to narrow down to the characteristics or properties which set the thing off from other things. It brings you to what will be the center of your paper in definition.

One helpful means of finding that center has already been suggested and illustrated in the logical definition. Many weaknesses in definition papers stem from the failure to give serious thought to the class to which the thing belongs and to the characteristics which differentiate it from other members of the class. The student who built a paper around the statement "A beatnik is a bearded teenager" was off to a bad start. He needed to reconsider the class (many beatniks are not teenagers), and it was hard to take seriously the implication that it was the beard that made the teenager a beatnik. After some further reflection on what traits or characteristics best distinguish beatniks from nonbeatniks, he rewrote the paper, centering his definition on attitudes, ideals, behavior. He included descriptive statements about appearance, dress, and age-groups, but without making them the chief clues to identifying beatniks. The rewrite was a superior paper in definition because it told more clearly what a beatnik is.

Naturally, the chief identifying characteristics will vary with what you are defining. You may find them in the origin of the thing, or in what it is used for, or in what it is made of, or in what it looks like, or in what effects it produces. A physical object like a lathe will be defined in different ways from a concept like patriotism, and a concept will be defined in different ways from a school in literature like Romanticism. Once having decided on the center of the definition, you will find yourself drawing on the other methods of development treated in this chapter. To list all the possibilities would be to review virtually everything that has been said in this chapter, for definition is the most comprehensive of all the methods of development. Instead, it may be more useful to summarize what some students have done in their essays in definition.

The center of a paper defining a stapler was a statement of what it is used for. From there the student went on to show what its parts are, what it looks like, what materials it is made of, and how it operates. The essay was developed mainly by objective description.

A definition of Cubism first placed the movement in time, giving a narrative account of how and why it arose and showing how it differed from other contemporary schools of art. By using examples of famous Cubist artists and describing some of their chief paintings, the student arrived at the characteristics of form, color, and handling of subject that make a painting a representative of Cubism.

A student who defined the "campus intellectual" used division to enumerate the traits and characteristics of the type; exemplified these through action, attitude, and habits; showed how the traits related to each other; and demonstrated that the combination of the traits is what makes the type.

A definition of brainwashing centered on the purpose, contrasted the methods and effects with those used in psychiatric treatment, and drew examples and details from two novels, *Nineteen Eighty-four* and *The Manchurian Candidate*.

These summaries are not intended to represent the only ways of developing definitions, nor the best ones. For each example you should be able to think of other approaches. They are simply intended to show the great variety of resources at hand when you set about the task of defining—description, narration, example, detail, comparison and contrast, classification, division, analysis of causes and effects. But you cannot choose among them at random. You need to select those which will best enable you to make clear the properties or characteristics of what you are writing about—those distinctive aspects which set it off from everything else. Only when you have done this will you have accomplished the purpose of defining.

Exercises

1. Analyze and evaluate the following papers, answering these questions about each one: What is the writer's central idea or main point? What methods does he use to develop this main point? What are the strengths and the weaknesses in the organization and development of the paper? Note that the paragraphs are numbered for convenience in discussion.

Growing Up

(1) After attending college for eight weeks, I find that it is considerably more enjoyable and interesting than high school.

(2) The physical lay-out in the classrooms of high schools and colleges are somewhat different—at least for some of the classes. In two of my college classes, the students sit around large tables. Each person can see the whole class, and as a result there is a better relationship and a greater willingness to take part in a discussion.

In high school, each student sits at a desk. In my college classrooms, the windows open up, but in high school they opened out.

(3) Participation is more important in college because most class work is done by discussion. Written work is done outside of class. In high school most of it is done during class hours. College students are able to express their opinions and to hear the opinions of their fellow classmates. Thus they enjoy their lessons more and learn more from them than they do in high school, where most of the talking is done by the teachers. One of my college classes is done entirely by lecture, though.

(4) Students are able to accomplish more in college than in high school because the classes are longer. Because a student in college has to go from one building to another for different classes, there is ten minutes between classes. In high school there is five.

(5) In college a student is given an assignment, told what day it is due, and then left on his own. In high school, a student is given an assignment, told what day it is due, and then constantly reminded of the deadline date. The college student is treated as an adult: he has to solve his own problems and face his own responsibilities. In high school the student is often treated like a child. Someone is always ready to help him solve his problems.

(6) In college there is a slightly wider range of activities than in high schools, but the activities are pretty much alike. College students have more activities after school hours.

(7) I like college life better than high-school life because in college I feel that I am progressing toward maturity.

Going to College—But Why?

(1) A college degree means a great deal in our country today. Most of us look upon the holder of a bachelor's degree as a person who is more intelligent, better educated, and perhaps a little more ambitious than the average. The facts do not entirely justify this attitude, however. There are many intelligent and ambitious Americans who have never had the opportunity to go to college but who have managed to become well-educated people. And it is unfortunately true that a college graduate is not necessarily intelligent or ambitious or even educated. This is true because education is not necessarily the goal in which the student is interested when he attends college. In my dormitory the students seem to have come to college to achieve various goals. Though it is hard to tell about some of them, I think it is safe to say that the vast majority fall into one of three groups—those who are here to enjoy an active social life; those who want a college degree in order to pursue a career; and those who are actually interested in being educated.

(2) The students in the first group are enthusiastic about college life—outside the classrooms. They attend parties, dances, and other social functions by the dozen. The chief ambition of a student of this kind is to be the most popular boy (or girl) on campus.

Popularity is measured in the number of phone calls made and received, the number of dates acquired, the number of social functions attended, the number of admirers of the opposite sex collected, and the number of friends of the same sex gained. Personal popularity is the only matter that causes the student serious concern.

(3) The second group, made up of those who want a degree because it will enable them to find good jobs, must be subdivided, for the members have quite different attitudes. Some are serious students, determined to learn as much as possible in their chosen field, so that they can advance rapidly in their careers after graduation. Others look upon the degree as a magic key that will unlock the doors of success all by itself; they are determined to get a degree but have no interest in acquiring any knowledge to go with it.

(4) Those in the first of these subdivisions are very ambitious, and most will build up an impressive store of knowledge that will help them in their chosen professions. For them, college has been nothing more than a training school. Those in the second subdivision may be able to obtain degrees, with the help of frantic cram sessions, but they will not really be educated and will not have much of value to offer an employer. For them, college as a place of learning has been a total loss.

(5) Finally, there is that group of students who attend college not for fun, not for future fortune, but for education. They come to learn, to find out more about the world in which they live, to examine old ideas and new theories, to move toward intellectual maturity. For them, and only for them, the college degree marks a forward step in education.

Bits and Pieces

(1) A great deal of American education, from kindergarten to college, is aimed at developing *all* of the student's interests, talents, and whims. Education should be broad, should include many disciplines. A student should be actively interested in all sorts of ideas and activities. So goes the theory.

(2) But the practical result of this emphasis is a scattering of the student's interests. The caption under his high-school yearbook picture says "Football—varsity, tennis—junior varsity, athletic association—treasurer, dramatics club, and school newspaper." Proudly the student displays all his small abilities; the more committees, clubs, and teams he can put next to his name, the better person he feels he must be. He may have had only a small part in the play and only helped fold the school newspaper, but somehow the number of mere experiences is supposed to be educational.

(3) In college, the emphasis on "school activities" is likely to be continued. There the rationalization is likely to be service to the school and "community spirit." The club organizers, those who join every discussion group and cause, are automatically the student leaders. Those few who have a single driving interest, who sit quietly

in a lab, ignoring school politics and service committees, are said to lack community spirit. But who will win the Nobel Prize—the student who spends his time on a pet project or the committeeman?

(4) At all levels the student is encouraged to break up his time and his thought into many small pieces. Through grade school and high school and college, he runs from one study to another, from baseball to a piano lesson, from church committee to newspaper meeting. If, in this tangle of group work, busy work, he ever finds a compelling interest, some problem to work at during his lifetime, he is lucky—and unusual. Most students brought up in this tradition and encouraged to wait a while before looking for a particular interest never do find that interest. They go right on serving on small committees, playing on small teams, cutting up all their time into small, wasted scraps.

2. Review the suggestions for writing a paper on Fairview, pages 65-67. Write three beginnings for a paper on the community where you grew up—the town, the city neighborhood, or the rural area. Each beginning should be at least 150 words long, and each should signal a different method of development. Then, in a paper of about 1000 words, complete the beginning that interests you most.

3. Review the three methods of organizing a comparison and contrast, pages 81-85. Write a paper about 1000 words long based on one of the following topics. Notice that an audience is specified for each.

a. For a sympathetic audience, such as an old friend or a school counselor, compare and contrast your views and attitudes with those of your parents on matters which are especially important to you. (Suggestions: political, religious, or moral views; social activities; dress; education; careers; interior decorating.)

b. For the sports section in a newspaper or magazine, compare and contrast the physical skills required for filling two different positions on a team (such as end and guard in football or center and guard in basketball) or for engaging in two different sports.

c. For a campus newspaper, bring out the similarities and differences between two kinds of music you know well (for example, folk songs and show tunes, jazz and classical music).

4. In a paper of about 750 words, classify some material you know well. Give enough descriptive details so that the reader will be able to grasp the distinguishing features of each group. Here are suggested topics and principles of classification you might apply:

a. People in your neighborhood—their interests and activities

b. Political liberals (or conservatives)—their consistencies and inconsistencies

c. The books you own—what they reveal about you

5. Write an extended definition (500-750 words) of one of the following terms. Notice that an audience is suggested for each; if you wish, choose a different one, but in any case identify it.

a. For a group of high-school seniors, define "success in college."

b. For a group of sixty-year-olds, define a slang term currently popular among teenagers.

c. For a group of liberal arts students, describe and characterize a trend in music, art, literature, or advertising.

6. Examine the following one-sentence definitions to determine which ones satisfy the formula for a logical definition:

term = genus or *class + differentia*

To each that contains a *genus* and *differentia,* apply the rules for testing a logical definition listed in the *Index* *Definition. Which satisfy those rules, and which do not? Finally, review those you have decided are unsatisfactory as logical definitions and explain why you would or would not feel justified in using them in a paper.

a. A lugger pilot is one who pilots a lugger.

b. A bull session goes on all the time in a college dormitory.

c. Loyalty is not conformity.

d. A teetotaler is a person who on principle refuses to drink alcohol.

e. A nursery is a child's bedroom.

f. A nursery is an area where trees, shrubs, or plants are grown for transplanting, for use in budding and grafting, or for sale.

g. History is bunk.

h. History is the memory of things said and done.

i. History is a branch of knowledge that records and explains past events.

j. Sadness is the quality, state, or fact of being sad.

k. Touch football is a type of football in which touching is substituted for tackling.

l. Man is the most glorious maverick in the universe.

m. Man is a talking animal.

n. Slums represent what democracy is not.

o. A plow breaks up and turns over the soil.

p. Poetry is the breath and finer spirit of all knowledge.

q. Ichthyology is the branch of zoology that treats of fishes.

r. Seamanship is the skill of a good seaman.

Chapter Four

WRITING PARAGRAPHS

*B*ut *the first thing to remember is that the division*
     (into paragraphs)
is for the benefit of the reader or hearer.
It is a device for making the whole clear to
     someone else.
This does not in the least make the process less
     valuable to the writer;
it merely forces upon him the right point of view.
A division is good in proportion as it helps a
     hearer or reader to follow.

                                   Charles Sears Baldwin

A paragraph is a group of related statements that a writer presents as a unit in the development of his subject. It appears as a unit to the eye because it is physically set off from what precedes and what follows, either by indention of its first word or by spacing above and below. More fundamentally, a paragraph strikes the mind as a unit because of the relation that exists between the statements it contains. These related statements represent a stage in the flow of the writer's thought.

One function of the paragraph is to join related statements into a unit; the other function is to separate this unit from the other units in the paper. In any single paragraph the continuity of material is the most important feature, but in a series of paragraphs, though each one relates to the subject of the paper, each develops a somewhat different phase of it. The appearance of a new paragraph is a sign to the reader that the thought is going to shift, and he adjusts his attention automatically. Paragraphing therefore offers valuable clues to the movement of ideas within a paper.

Not every paragraph indention in a paper indicates the same degree of separation. Sometimes the writer's shift in thought is very slight. In a series of, say, four paragraphs, a major point set forth in the first is then expanded and developed through the next three. The writer links the paragraphs in such a way that the reader understands they are all related to the major point and together constitute one large block of material which would be represented as a main head in an outline. In a very detailed outline, the subordinate points made by each paragraph in the series could be represented by subheads, which in turn might be further divided.

When the shift is a major one, such as would be indicated by a new main head in an outline, the writer is likely to call attention to it by a *transitional sentence* announcing the phase of the subject to be treated next. If the essay or article is long, he may even devote an entire paragraph to the transition, perhaps summarizing what has already been discussed and mapping out the points to be taken up next.

In a long essay, then, paragraphs may differ widely in their functions. A few may be useful road markers, indicating the structure and plan of the paper. But the bulk of them—and all of them in a short paper—will represent stages in the progressive unfolding of the writer's thought. Taken together, they represent what he has to say on his topic. It is paragraphs of this kind that we shall consider first.

Paragraph development

If a paragraph is to make its proper contribution to the whole paper, it must *do* something. Perhaps it is better to say that it must do *one* thing, for, as we have defined it, a paragraph is a group of related statements dealing with one phase of the material. Looked at in this way, a good paragraph must first of all make a point—convey an idea or impression. It will do this only if each sentence in it contributes to a core of meaning which is the focus of the paragraph and which justifies the inclusion of the paragraph in the paper.

As a student, you have had plenty of experience in extracting the core of meaning or central thought from paragraphs. In your effort to grasp the essential points of a chapter in a textbook and to understand how they relate to each other, you may have made a sentence outline. This would have involved working through the chapter paragraph by paragraph, passing over transitional ones, grouping others together, but making sure that each of the main points was represented by a sentence in your outline. How did you get these sentences? Some were key statements that you copied directly from the text. Others you produced by condensing two or more of the sentences in one paragraph. Still others you composed yourself as the best way of getting at the gist of the paragraph. If you did the job carefully, distinguishing between main and subordinate points, you produced an outline of the chapter that looked like the sentence outline on pages 51-52.

A sentence outline of a chapter or essay is a valuable aid in learning the material. By reviewing the outline several times while the complete reading of the chapter is still fresh in your mind, you can grasp the chief points and see them in relation to each other. But if you put it aside for a few weeks and then return to it, you will be astonished to find how uninformative it is. In the interval you will have forgotten all the concrete particulars—the details, the examples, the evidence—that originally clarified the meaning of those key sentences.

In writing paragraphs, it is well to remind yourself of your experience in reading them. A good paragraph develops a core of meaning that may be explicitly stated in a single sentence (called the *topic sentence*), that may be scattered through several sentences, or that may be the unstated idea which underlies all the particulars making up the paragraph. If the paragraph is to carry a unified impact, the core of meaning needs to be elaborated in all the sentences of the paragraph. In other words, a paragraph needs to be developed.

Details and generalizations • To develop a paragraph is to expand and clarify its core of meaning. The writer aims to have the reader share in the process that led him to *his* view of the matter. The "matter" may be something in the physical world (a scene or incident or process) or it may be something in the world of thought (a conviction being argued for or a concept being clarified). In his discussion of it, the writer will not reproduce the actual course of his thinking, which is rapid, helter-skelter, full of false starts, digressions, and dead ends. Instead, he will prune, arrange, and edit so that the actual flow of thought takes on coherent shape in the mind of the reader. But what he writes will in some degree represent the process of his thinking and not merely the product of it—the core of meaning.

As we formulate and express our thinking in speech or in writing, we make statements which may be roughly divided into two categories, details and generalizations. The details in a paragraph are all those particular statements used to illustrate or make clear or support the writer's point. Some details are statements of images, which call up pictures in the mind of the reader:

The heavy downpour beat the crops into the ground.
We passed a policeman standing knee-deep in swirling flood water.
Dozens of abandoned cars lined the highway.

Other details are particular facts—statements of occurrences that can usually be verified or tested by other observers. Many of the facts are the result of our own observation; some come from the observations of others.

I finished fourth in the race.
The *Daily Record* reported that only two hundred students attended the meet.
A botanist once counted 180,220 minute, glossy black, lens-shaped seeds on a single plant of the common tumbleweed, *Amaranthus albus.*—EDWIN WAY TEALE

The examples above give details about physical objects or events. But a discussion of a novel uses details, too, in its specific statements about the plot, the characters, and the theme. And a discussion of *virtue* would use as appropriate details particular virtues, such as honesty, charity, and so on. Thus, while they do not always refer to concrete experiences or facts, the details in any passage of writing present the particulars of the subject.

By contrast, generalizations reflect our *ideas* about the subject. They are based on particulars but extend beyond them to make more inclusive statements. Sometimes they sum up a large number of observations ("Man still has not succeeded in controlling nature"). Sometimes they interpret the meaning of particular observations or experiences ("I learned what patience was when I had to wait on customers"). Sometimes they express opinions or judgments of particular things or occurrences ("The Administration's policy is unwise").

Many of our generalizations we get from others—from what we have heard and what we have read—but some we make for ourselves. Generalizations can be sound or unsound, depending on how much evidence and thought have gone into their making. One mark of a mature writer is that he appears to have formulated his generalizations by reasoning sensibly from an adequate number of relevant particulars.

The writer's material and his purpose will determine whether he relies more heavily on details or on generalizations. Narrative and descriptive passages are usually long on details, short on generalizations. This is as it should be: "showing" is more effective than "telling" when the purpose is to have the reader share what has been observed or experienced. In the following paragraph, the details are massed, piled up one after another to make a clear and vivid account of New York's blizzard of 1888. The only hint of a generalization is put in a negative way—"this figure gives no conception of the difficulties travelers met." As the reader proceeds through the paragraph, a generalization gradually but unmistakably forms in his mind, something he might phrase as "Travelers met enormous difficulties." This is the core of meaning in the paragraph. So phrased, it is flat and colorless in comparison with the impression made by the accumulation of concrete details. It is also superfluous, for the core of meaning comes through the details and needs no explicit statement.

The actual fall in $53\frac{1}{2}$ hours was 20.9 inches, or more than twice as much snow as had fallen all that winter, but this figure gives no conception of the difficulties travelers met. For the wind continued high, and the soberest observers reported drifts of fifteen and twenty feet. It was almost impossible to walk. A few hacks took to the streets, the drivers charging anything they could get and in some cases forcing whiskey down the throats of their horses in order to keep them alive. Surface cars struggled for a little while, and then stopped; many of them were literally buried. The Third Avenue Elevated Railway, not then electrified, ran a few trains downtown— one car each, with two or even three dinkey engines pushing it—but these too were stalled. In one of them, helpless between stations, were thirty men; but though they could not get down, they were so fortunate as to be in front of a saloon, and hot toddies were hoisted to them by means of a pail and a length of cord, so that the men remained tolerably happy for the fifteen hours of their captivity, and even were heard to sing. Sturdy little boys with ladders went from place to place letting people down out of second-story windows; generally they charged (this being in the days before Boy Scouts) fifty cents for the descent.—DONALD B. CHIDSEY, *The Gentleman from New York: A Life of Roscoe Conkling,* pp. 381-382

In its almost total reliance on details, the paragraph just quoted is unusual. But many paragraphs of description and narration gain their effects in a comparable way: they bring before the reader one detail after another, so arranged that the reader is led to shape for himself a clear impression of what the writer has observed or experienced.

No clear impression will be made unless the writer exercises care in selecting and ordering the details. The details must feed into each other, producing a cumulative, unified impact. No such impact is made by the paragraph below. Instead, it moves in two different directions, the next to last sentence picking up a thread from the second sentence.

From our conversation I learned that he had left home at the age of fourteen. After his home had broken, his father didn't want him and his mother could not support him. He lived alone and financed his way through school in a Wyoming town. On the night of his graduation from high school, where he received the award for outstanding student and athlete award, not one person could he claim as being present for his sake alone. His accomplishments became known to a local politician who aided him in gaining an appointment to the USMA at West Point. He was very successful there. In all that time he had never heard a word from his father. He is now happily married.

A sharp contrast to the detail-packed paragraph by Chidsey on page 114 is the one below, which consists entirely of generalizations:

Religion will not regain its old power until it can face change in the same spirit as does science. Its principles may be eternal, but the expression of those principles requires continual development. This evolution of religion is in the main a disengagement of its own proper ideas from the adventitious notions which have crept into it by reason of the expression of its own ideas in terms of the imaginative picture of the world entertained in previous ages. Such a release of religion from the bonds of imperfect science is all to the good. It stresses its own genuine message. The great point to be kept in mind is that normally an advance in science will show that statements of various religious beliefs require some sort of modification. It may be that they have to be expanded or explained, or indeed entirely restated. If the religion is a sound expression of truth, this modification will only exhibit more adequately the exact point which is of importance. This process is a gain. In so far, therefore, as any religion has any contact with physical facts, it is to be expected that the point of view of those facts must be continually modified as scientific knowledge advances. In this way, the exact relevance of these facts for religious thought will grow more and more clear. The progress of science must result in the unceasing codification of religious thought, to the great advantage of religion.—ALFRED NORTH WHITEHEAD, "Religion and Science," *Science and the Modern World,* pp. 188-189

It is only fair to say that this paragraph is not intended to stand alone; other parts of the chapter in which it appears give support to the large generalizations. Furthermore, in the first paragraph of his chapter the author has warned the reader that his discussion will be couched in generalities— "I wish to speak in the most general way possible, and to keep in the background any comparison of particular creeds, scientific or religious." What is admirable in the paragraph quoted is the great clarity with which the author states and restates his generalizations. The restatement is not simple repetition; each new phrasing makes more emphatic and persuasive the central proposition that it is a distinct advantage to religion to modify its expression of beliefs as scientific knowledge advances.

The paragraph is a good one of its kind, but the kind is hard to do well. The following paragraph, which was part of a 750-word paper on a civil rights demonstration, illustrates the disasters that await the writer who is not really in control of his generalizations.

Segregation is a social phenomenon which has been in existence since the earliest known civilizations. When a group of people join together to live under a certain set of regulations and moral codes, they set themselves apart from others. They put themselves on a certain level of civilization and intelligence in respect to other groups. This is inherent in many people. In the case of the founding of the United States there is a definite exception.

A basic flaw in this very bad paragraph is its failure to explain what segregation is. (That surely is what the writer intended it should do.) The attempt at definition begins with an unmanageable generalization—one that is dubious at best and at any rate needs an immense amount of historical evidence to make it plausible. However momentous the issue, it need not be (and in a 750-word paper should not be) set in the context of the Garden of Eden or the beginning of civilization or even the founding of America. Paragraphs of this sort should be discarded; they are only an encumbrance to the writer and a headache to the reader.

What the topic is, what the writer's purpose is, what the expected audience is—all these have some bearing on the proportioning of details to generalizations. Details make up the chief content of papers in description and in narration, both factual—as in news stories—and fictional. They bulk large in explanations of objects, processes, and situations, and in technical and scientific reports of all kinds. Generalizations are of central importance when the writer's purpose is to interpret, to criticize, to evaluate; they are indispensable in dealing with concepts and ideas. In most of the papers college students write, there is or should be an interplay of details and generalizations, generalizations bringing out the significance of the details and details providing the concrete particulars without which the generalizations might be unclear or unconvincing.

The relation between the details and the generalizations may be of various kinds. Perhaps the simplest pattern offers the details as *examples* to clarify or support an opening generalization. Three examples are used as evidence for the generalization which opens this paragraph:

[Generalization] The few American inventors of that period—from 1790, say, to 1810—could find no one interested enough in new mechanical ideas to back them. (1) John Fitch, the true inventor of the steamboat, died in poverty and despair because neither capitalists nor the government would take any interest in his invention. (2) Oliver Evans, one of the greatest of them all, had to fight against ignorance, superstition and blind prejudice to induce millers to adopt his revolutionary flour-milling machinery. With his steam engines and his "road carriage"—a steam automobile—he had even less success. (3) When Charles Newbold patented an iron plow in 1797, farmers refused to use it because they were convinced that the iron would "poison the soil."—ROGER BURLINGAME, *Machines That Built America,* p. 307

Topic sentences • In the paragraph just quoted, the opening generalization is the *topic sentence;* it summarizes what the paragraph *says* and so comes close to representing the central thought. A topic sentence of this kind stands out as the most comprehensive or general statement in the paragraph. It serves as an anchor for the more particular or more specific statements that move from it or toward it or around it. (As we shall see later, the topic sentence can stand anywhere in the paragraph—at the beginning or at the end or in between.) The following topic sentences all open their paragraphs:

Education is "liberal" in proportion as it assists in the formation of a personal will, develops the faculty of choice, and furnishes that

faculty with a rich reservoir of estimated possibilities.—RALPH BAR-
TON PERRY

Andrew Jackson has long been the symbol of fighting democracy
in American political life.—ARTHUR M. SCHLESINGER, JR.

Plant growth has four basic needs: light, air, water, and a comparatively small amount of such chemical elements as magnesium,
phosphorus, sulphur, silicon, and others.—GEORGE RUSSELL HARRISON

Within only a few decades a curriculum system that had been too
tight and too rigid was made too loose and too sprawling.—RICHARD
HOFSTADTER

In literary composition there is only one fundamental principle:
clarity.—BROOKS ATKINSON

The term *topic sentence* is also often applied to statements
which indicate what the paragraph is to *do* and so signal
the direction the discussion is to take. Such statements are
pointers or guides which prepare the reader for the way the
paragraph is to develop without actually summarizing its main
idea. Examples (again all opening sentences of paragraphs) are:

The reason is very simple.—ALBERT SCHWEITZER

There are several ways of taking notes.—DONALD DEAN PARKER

What, then, can be expected from the future?—ERICH FROMM

There are two prevailing winds in the American theater of the last
few seasons, rather closely related.—FRANK GIBNEY

I can best explain the difference by a reminiscence.—W. T. STACE

Because many paragraphs contain statements of both kinds,
one announcing what the paragraph is to do and another summarizing its central thought, it is sometimes useful to give
them different labels. When necessary, we will indicate the
difference by using *topic sentence* for the kind which summarizes, and *pointer sentence* for the kind which announces
how the paragraph is to develop. The following paragraph
begins with a pointer sentence which leads through details and
interpretations to the topic sentence beginning "The basis of
formal design." This in turn is followed by more details.

Let us analyze the two types of garden treatment and see what
makes a successful example of each. Step first, in imagination, into
a formal garden and look at its design. You immediately become conscious of a strong central axis or imaginary line running down the
middle of the garden. The design on one side of this dividing line
is a duplicate of the other side. This is symmetrical balance. Straight
lines, geometric patterns and forms, and pairs of specimens at all

important points of interest make up the design. The basis of formal design is a completely symmetrical balance of geometrically shaped beds and architectural objects with the boundaries of the area very strongly marked and defined. In such a design the plant material is subordinated to geometrical pattern. Clipped hedges and clipped specimens of trees or shrubs are used to form and accentuate the structure of the design.—JOHN A. AND CAROL L. GRANT, *Garden Design,* p. 8

Not every paragraph has a topic sentence. As we have said, the central thought of a paragraph (especially in description or narration) may be conveyed through the accumulation of details, so arranged that a generalization forms in the mind of the reader. Even in explaining or persuading, the writer may decide (for reasons that have to do with the strategy of the whole paper rather than the strategy of the particular paragraph) not to frame a topic sentence for any one paragraph. But most of the paragraphs that make substantial contributions to an explanatory or persuasive essay do give the reader clues in the form of topic sentences or pointers.

Inexperienced writers can often improve the unity of their paragraphs by getting into the habit of writing topic sentences. With the topic sentence in view, they are less likely to bring in irrelevant or distracting details. Furthermore, the very act of framing a topic sentence can suggest how the paragraph should develop. In reading paragraphs, you naturally look for topic sentences as clues to the writer's main ideas and his method of developing them. In writing paragraphs, it is well to remember that the reader needs and deserves some guidance if he is to grasp your ideas. Of course, when you are intent on formulating and expressing your ideas, you do not consciously decide that *here* or *there* is the place for a topic sentence or that the paragraph is to develop *this way* or *that way.* You follow the flow of your ideas, arranging and shaping the material in the manner that will best convey your thought. But the writing will come more easily if you know in a general way what the paragraph is to *do* and what it is to *say.* Once you are clear on that—once you have your topic sentence in mind—you will find it easier to write a paragraph that is a meaningful unit, not just a collection of statements.

Methods of paragraph development • Some of the passages used to illustrate the methods of development treated in Chapter 3 were single paragraphs, and all of them could have been.

Just as comparison may be the major method of development in a complete essay or a large part of it, so it may be the method of developing a paragraph. This chapter gives further examples of these methods, showing how they are used, singly and in combination, to clarify or support the central point of a paragraph. Within a paragraph many other devices—restatement, qualification, anecdote, and allusion—can serve the same purpose.

In the following paragraph, the first sentence suggests the way the paragraph is to develop. What the author means by his generalization that liberalism "must begin shifting its emphasis" is clarified by *comparison* and *qualification.* Sentences 2 and 3 single out differences between the two kinds of liberalism, sentence 3 restating sentence 2 in more concrete terms. Sentences 4 through 6 qualify those differences by showing how the new liberalism will be similar to the old. The last sentence restates the first one in narrower fashion, preparing the reader for a discussion of differences "in mood and approach."

(1) Liberalism in an age of abundance must begin shifting its emphasis. (2) Instead of the quantitative liberalism of the 1930's, rightly dedicated to the struggle to secure the economic basis of life, we need now a "qualitative liberalism" dedicated to bettering the quality of people's lives and opportunities. (3) Instead of talking as if the necessities of living—a job, a square meal, a suit of clothes, and a roof—were still at stake, we should be able to count that fight won and move on to the more subtle and complicated problem of fighting for individual dignity, identity, and fulfillment in a mass society. (4) The new liberalism implies no repudiation of the old; rather it respects, accepts, and absorbs the triumphs of the New and Fair Deals, regards them as the basis for a new age of social progress, and seeks to move beyond them toward new goals of national development. (5) Nor, should I add, does the distinction between "quantitative" and "qualitative" mean that one form of liberalism requires taxation and spending while the other is cheap and painless. (6) Obviously progress in the "qualitative" area will require government initiative almost as much as the other. (7) Yet a significant difference remains between the two in mood and approach.—ARTHUR SCHLESINGER, JR., "The Future of Liberalism," *The Reporter,* May 3, 1956, p. 9

In the preceding paragraph, the comparison is between two things that are very much alike—two varieties of liberalism. But the comparison may be between things that are strikingly different. In the following, the author clarifies the topic sentence in a memorable way by drawing an *analogy* between the characteristics of a political liberal and the habits of a dog on a walk. On the basis of the analogy, he then makes a literal comparison of the liberal with two other political types.

The liberal holds that he is true to the republic when he is true to himself. (It may not be as cozy an attitude as it sounds.) He greets with enthusiasm the fact of the journey, as a dog greets a man's invitation to take a walk. And he acts in the dog's way, too, swinging wide, racing ahead, doubling back, covering many miles of territory that the man never traverses, all in the spirit of inquiry and the zest for truth. He leaves a crazy trail, but he ranges far beyond the genteel old party he walks with and he is usually in a better position to discover a skunk. The dog often influences the course the man takes, on his long walk; for sometimes a dog runs into something in nature so arresting that not even a man can quite ignore it, and the man deviates—a clear victim of the liberal intent in his dumb companion. When the two of them get home and flop down, it is the liberal—the wide-ranging dog—who is covered with burdocks and with information of a special sort on out-of-the-way places. Often ineffective in direct political action, he is the opposite of the professional revolutionary, for, unlike the latter, he never feels he knows where the truth lies, but is full of rich memories of places he has glimpsed it in. He is, on the whole, more optimistic than the revolutionary, or even than the Republican in a good year.—*The New Yorker,* Jan. 17, 1948. Reprinted by permission. Copr. 1948, The New Yorker Magazine, Inc.

In the next example, the topic sentence gives a commonly accepted notion of what a "practical man" is. The writer then clarifies this *definition* by specifying in more detail the ends that people consider important.

In a more usual sense, perhaps, a practical man is a man occupied with attaining certain ends that people consider important. He must stick pretty close to the business of feeding and preserving life. Nourishment and shelter, money-making, maintaining respectability, and if possible a family—these are the things that give its common meaning to the word "practical." An acute regard for such features of the scenery, and the universe, as contribute or can be made to contribute to these ends, and a systematic neglect of all other features, are the traits of mind which this word popularly suggests. And it is because of the vital importance of these things to almost all people that the word "practical" is a eulogy, and is able to be so scornful of the word "poetic."—Max Eastman, *The Enjoyment of Poetry with Anthology for Enjoyment of Poetry,* p. 4

The topic sentence may forecast an *analysis* or enumeration of parts:

There are certain strange bodily characters which mark man as being more than the product of a dog-eat-dog competition with his fellows. He possesses a peculiar larval nakedness, difficult to explain on survival principles; his periods of helpless infancy and childhood are prolonged; he has aesthetic impulses which, though they vary in intensity from individual to individual, appear in varying manifestations among all peoples. He is totally dependent, in the achievement of human status, upon the careful training he receives in human society.—LOREN EISELEY, *The Immense Journey,* p. 91

A paragraph may develop *reasons* or causes for a situation set forth in the topic sentence. In the following paragraph, sentences 2 through 4 set forth reasons for the difficulty of collecting information; sentence 5 restates in more particular terms the idea expressed in the topic sentence; and the final sentence states that a good effect has followed from that situation.

(1) For a number of reasons it is not easy to collect a body of valid and reliable information on American dialects. (2) The wide spread of education, the virtual extinction of illiteracy, the extreme mobility of the population—both geographically and from one social class to another—and the tremendous development of a number of media of mass communication have all contributed to the recession of local speech forms. (3) Moreover, the cultural insecurity of a large portion of the American people has caused them to feel apologetic about their language. (4) Consequently, they seldom display the same degree of pride or affection that many an English or a European speaker has for his particular patois. (5) Since all dialect research is essentially a sampling process, this means that the investigator must take particular pains to secure representative and comparable samples from the areas which are studied. (6) Happily, the very care which this demands has had the result of developing the methodology of linguistic geography in this country to a very high level.—ALBERT H. MARCKWARDT, *American English,* pp. 133-134

In the way they are developed, all of the preceding paragraphs follow a simple pattern—the expansion of a topic sentence which either states in a general way what the paragraph *says* or forecasts what it is to *do*. In all but one, the phrasing of the topic sentence pretty well determines the kinds of details needed to clarify the generalization. (The one exception is the paragraph developed by analogy, p. 121.) The next paragraph is more complex in development. It begins with a topic sentence that is supported in sentences 2 and 3 by details in the form of reasons and in sentence 4 by a comparison. Sentence 5 is a pointer sentence referring back to the preceding statements in "the magnetism of their instrument" and also forecasting what is to come by classifying jazz pianists into "two groups." Each group is then treated in terms of the distinguishing characteristics of the leaders and their followers. The paragraph ends by narrowing down to the musician who is to be the subject of discussion in the rest of the essay.

In a special way, the piano is the most troublesome instrument in jazz. The pianist in the heat of improvisation not only must keep in mind the niceties of touch, dynamics, tone, and pedalwork but must resist the temptation to use more notes than he needs. For there, in smiling symmetry, are eighty-eight notes, each calling out to be struck at least once in every solo. (Lucky saxophonists and trumpeters and trombonists, who cannot see their notes but can pursue them at will through the maze of their imaginations!) For a long while, the magnetism of their instrument divided jazz pianists into two groups. The first, nurtured principally on ragtime, which dictated five notes where one would have done, were flamboyant and multi-note. Among them were the great "ticklers"—James P. Johnson, Willie the Lion Smith, Luckey Roberts, and Fats Waller. Their descendants were Art Tatum (who checked each note on the keyboard two or three times a number), Duke Ellington, Thelonious Monk, Lennie Tristano, Erroll Garner, and Red Garland. In addition to being show pianists, these men used a lot of notes that were simply to be felt rhythmically. The founder of the second group was probably Earl Hines. A revolutionist, he skirted ragtime and the stride pianists and advanced the proposition of the spare, single-note melodic line. Teddy Wilson, his main admirer, was even more economical. He was followed by Billy Kyle and Nat Cole and Clyde Hart. (Count Basie, at first profligate, became thrifty early in his career, when he discovered that one judiciously placed note easily implied four or five.) Then Bud Powell arrived, to combine the best of these two schools with the teachings of Charlie Parker. He borrowed the brilliant melodic bone hidden in the steam and smoke of Tatum's style and joined it to the dry, logical skeleton of Wilson and Cole and Hart, and he covered this with Parker's freer rhythmic and harmonic approach. He also farmed out the left hand, allowing the drummer and bassist to divide its work between them. His immediate students were Al Haig, George Wallington, Duke Jordan, and George Shearing, who have been succeeded by Hank Jones and Jimmy Rowles and Tommy Flanagan and Bill Evans. Of these, Evans, who is thirty-four, is the most impressive as well as the most elusive.—WHITNEY BALLIETT, "Evans vs. Evans," *The New Yorker,* Sept. 21, 1963, pp. 157-158

Two minor devices for developing paragraphs are the *anecdote* and the *quotation*. They are often useful supporting devices, sometimes extending through a whole paragraph but more often limited to one sentence. The anecdote may be the author's own or it may be one that he has heard or read. The quotation may be direct or indirect. In the following paragraph, the author uses anecdote to introduce a prevailing attitude, then further clarifies it by giving a new application to an indirect quotation from Samuel Butler.

A late nineteenth-century tycoon is said to have remarked in all simplicity that America had no need of artists, since we were in a position to buy from Europe all the treasures of the past that we had any use for. And though there were only a few who had arrived at a conviction so clear and concise, those who thought (or even did not think at all) on the subject, assumed that artistic creation and artistic appreciation were frills—good enough in their way, but best left to elegant, otherwise unemployed women and to those male misfits who were somehow incapable of doing the world's work, while virile and capable men devoted their energies to inventing machines, building factories, and accumulating wealth. If, as the second Samuel Butler said, Englishmen supported the vicars of the Church of England in order to have someone to be virtuous for them vicariously, so even the more enlightened members of the American plutocracy were willing to do no more than give rather contemptuous support to those who would, vicariously, create or admire art for them.—JOSEPH WOOD KRUTCH, "The Creative Dilemma," *Saturday Review,* Feb. 8, 1964, p. 16

Adequate development • A common fault in paragraphs is that the generalizations are not supported with enough particulars to make them clear and convincing. This fault is natural enough, for in the very act of framing general statements the writer has assimilated into his thinking, and so in a sense discarded, the particulars that led him to them. But if the reader is to share in that thinking, he must be taken over some of the same ground. Bare assertions or propositions cannot convey to the reader anything like the fullness of the writer's thought. To make an impression on the reader, it is necessary not just to make a general statement about the subject but to present it, develop it, lead him to understand and accept it.

The following paragraph has a measure of unity but is unimpressive because it lacks telling concrete details:

> When I became a junior, I changed radically. I realized I would be going to college, and school should not be only for having fun. I started working nights and weekends, and my grades were a lot better. My friends and I didn't fool around so much and talked about more intellectual things. Every time we had a meeting with our college counselor we would get into a big argument about which colleges we would apply to. And then we would work harder.

The same weakness appears in lesser degree in the following paragraph, part of the paper reprinted on page 67. The adjectives "decrepit" and "leprous" represent a commendable attempt at vividness, but unfortunately seem pretentious and overdone because they are not supported with relevant details.

> It must have been no more than six years ago—at most seven—when his house appeared decrepit and leprous. One corner of his yard was reserved for scrap metal, which he collected for a foundry in which he worked. His monthly income was 320 dollars. His yard also housed a few rabbits, and, in addition to this, he grew a few vegetables each year. His personal appearance coincided with his environment. The clothes he wore were shabby and unpressed. His hands were grimy from working in the foundry all day, and his face never appeared to be washed. But today he has changed. His hands and face are clean, and his clothes are neat.

Although the paragraph is by no means a bad one, it has two weaknesses besides inadequate development. Because of its position, the third sentence strikes the reader as a distracting detail. It is not hard to see how the student came to put it where he did: mention of the foundry led him to Uncle Ralph's wages. It *could* have been made a relevant detail if it had been presented as an explanation or justification of Uncle Ralph six or seven years ago. But it needs to be shifted elsewhere; in its present position it intrudes between related details about the yard and so damages the unity of the paragraph.

A final criticism has to do with style. If a paragraph is to make a unified impact, the style must be reasonably consistent, or, at any rate, shifts in style must be made to seem appropriate to changes in thought. In this paragraph "His personal appearance coincided with his environment" sticks out like a sore thumb. "Coincided" is the wrong word, and the whole sentence is stilted by contrast with the fairly relaxed style of the rest of the paragraph. When jarring shifts of this kind occur, it is usually at the point where the writer moves from details to generalization, or the reverse.

Adequate development of paragraphs is closely related to their length. Logically, length should be determined by the subject and purpose and by the importance of the idea being expressed. However, length is often largely a matter of convention and fashion, as you can see by examining paragraphs in different kinds of publications.

Short paragraphs can be read more quickly and easily than long ones. Because of the usually simple narratives of news stories and the narrow columns which make long, unbroken stretches of type forbidding, and because they are intended for hasty reading, paragraphs in newspapers run distinctly short; the great majority are under 75 words, 20 to 40 words being typical. Paragraphs in magazines of restricted circulation approach book paragraphs in length, but in popular magazines the paragraphs are rarely 200 words long and typically run from 100 to 150 words. Books show great variety, but as a rule paragraphs of less than 125 words are short and paragraphs of over 250 rather long, except in books intended for a somewhat limited audience. (Fiction shows considerable variety in paragraph length, approximating periodical length.) In any given article, naturally, the paragraphs vary considerably, some points deserving fuller and others briefer treatment.

This does not mean that you should stop to count the words in your paragraphs, but you should be able to visualize their length as they would stand in typical magazine and book form. Look closely at any page of your manuscript that shows more than two paragraph breaks—not because they are necessarily wrong, but because you should be sure they represent actual stages of your material and are appropriate to the subject, to the reader, and to the emphasis you intend. Conspicuously short paragraphs, especially several in sequence, are likely to be symptoms that you are not developing your material sufficiently or that you are dividing your subject into units too small to guide your reader to an understanding of the relationships between points.

Similarly, you should look closely at paragraphs that run over a manuscript page, to see if they are actually unified or if perhaps they should be broken for emphasis or for the reader's convenience. Paragraphs are likely to be longer than average when the thought emphasizes relationships between facts or ideas. In works of criticism, in philosophy and science, the paragraphs are rightly longer than in pictures of the life around us. Length is a symptom of other qualities of paragraphs; it should be considered in the light of subject matter and purpose and should be a sign of adequate and appropriate development.

Paragraph movement

Obviously the thought of a paragraph should move: the reader should be better informed at the end than he was at the beginning. There are numerous kinds of movement, but most of them fall into five general types: movement in time, *narrative;* movement of sense impression, especially of things seen, *descriptive;* and three sorts of movement of facts and ideas, *support, climax,* and *pro-and-con.*

Narrative paragraphs • In terms of the first section of this chapter, narrative paragraphs are made up principally of details. Generalizations are introduced chiefly to furnish background or to point up the significance of an occasional detail or scene. In many narrative paragraphs, the movement is strictly chronological, the details appearing one after another as they happened in time or are imagined to have happened.

In the following paragraph a social historian narrates one of the most shocking episodes in the gangster "wars" in Chicago during the Prohibition Era. The author quickly sets the stage for his "little drama," giving the date, the time of day, and the location. He introduces the victims and the executioners, and then, in four sentences which follow the chronological order of events, he recounts the entire action. Few descriptive details are provided; the report is fast-moving and economical; the terse recital of events needs only the comment made in the first sentence. (This paragraph, unlike many narrative paragraphs, does begin with a topic sentence.)

The war continued, one gangster after another crumpling under a rain of bullets; not until St. Valentine's Day of 1929 did it reach its climax in a massacre which outdid all that preceded it in ingenuity and brutality. At half-past ten on the morning of February 14, 1929, seven of the O'Banions were sitting in the garage which went by the name of the S.M.C. Cartage Company, on North Clark Street, waiting for a promised consignment of hijacked liquor. A Cadillac touring-car slid to the curb, and three men dressed as policemen got out, followed by two others in civilian dress. The three supposed policemen entered the garage alone, disarmed the seven O'Banions, and told them to stand in a row against the wall. The victims readily submitted; they were used to police raids and thought nothing of them; they would get off easily enough, they expected. But thereupon the two men in civilian clothes emerged from the corridor and calmly mowed down all seven O'Banions with sub-machine gun fire as they stood with hands upraised against the wall. The little drama was completed when the three supposed policemen solemnly marched the two plain-clothes killers across the sidewalk to the waiting car, and all five got in and drove off—having given to those in the wintry street a perfect tableau of an arrest satisfactorily made by the forces of the law!—FREDERICK LEWIS ALLEN, *Only Yesterday,* pp. 262-263

Even when the actual events are spread over a long period of time, the writer can keep the chronological movement sharp and clear by specific indications of how the separate details relate to each other in time. In these three paragraphs, a historian gives a clear, orderly account of the main events between the invasion of Normandy and the end of the war in Europe eleven months later. Notice how the last sentence of paragraph 2, introduced by *meanwhile,* brings in necessary information about simultaneous action on the Eastern front. It is brought in at precisely the right point in the narrative; anywhere else it would have been distracting or confusing.

The decision to launch such an invasion had been taken early in 1943. A year of preparation had accumulated almost three million men and well over two million tons of supplies in England. On June 6, 1944, a hundred and seventy-six thousand soldiers, carried by almost five thousand vessels, stormed the Normandy coast. Six days of brutal fighting established a beachhead five miles deep and seventy miles wide. Into this pocket the Allies poured three hundred and twenty-five thousand men, fifty thousand vehicles and one hundred thousand tons of supplies. In the last week of July they broke out of the Normandy peninsula and were on their way to the Rhine. Four columns, one Canadian, one British, and two American, moved swiftly across France. By the end of August they had reached Paris and Brussels.

In the fall of 1944 the Allied drive ground to a halt along a line that ran through Belgium and northern France. It had consumed supplies at a prodigious rate and needed time for regrouping. But the winter was far from leisurely for the troops. They threw back a German counterattack in December and a series of detached battles straightened the line. Meanwhile, the Russians had begun an offensive that carried them through the Ukraine, Poland, Hungary and Czechoslovakia toward Vienna and Berlin.

The final stage of the German war began early in March, 1945, with the seizure of the Remagen Bridge, which permitted a swift crossing of the Rhine. A series of deft encircling movements captured the Ruhr, the cornerstone of Nazi heavy industry, and ended the last serious hopes of German victory. In April, Hitler died by suicide and partisans took Mussolini's life. On May 7, General Eisenhower received the unconditional surrender of the remaining fascist forces.—OSCAR HANDLIN, *The Americans,* p. 376

The two examples above condense a good deal of action into a short space. *Summarized* narrative of this kind can be very vivid and effective, even though the reader is not made to feel part of the action. In *dramatized* narrative, the reader is brought into the action—or feels that he is. In passages of autobiography or biography, various devices are used to create this effect; the action may be given very fully, or conversation may be quoted, or the thoughts of the central figure in the action may be disclosed. All of these devices are used effectively in the following full account of an incident. (The comments to the left bring out some points about the development of the paragraph as well as its movement.)

Setting of incident (descriptive details)	My aunt, Lady Wimborne, had lent us her comfortable estate at Bournemouth for the winter. Forty or fifty acres of pine forest descended by sandy undulations terminating in cliffs to the smooth beach of the English Channel. It was a small, wild place and through the middle there fell to the sea level a deep cleft called a "chine." Across this "chine" a rustic bridge nearly 50 yards long had been thrown. I was just 18 and on my
Beginning of narration	holidays. My younger brother aged 12, and a cousin aged 14, proposed to chase me. After I had been hunted for twenty minutes and was rather short of breath, I decided to cross the bridge. Arrived at its centre I saw to my consternation that the pursuers had divided
Plan (suspense and drama through sharing thoughts of writer)	their forces. One stood at each end of the bridge; capture seemed certain. But in a flash there came across me a great project. The chine which the bridge spanned was full of

young fir trees. Their slender tops reached to the level of the footway. "Would it not," I asked myself, "be possible to leap on to one of them and slip down the pole-like stem, breaking off each tier of branches as one descended, until the fall was broken?" I looked

Time indicator:
meanwhile

at it. I computed it. I meditated. Meanwhile I climbed over the balustrade. My young pursuers stood wonder-struck at either end

Allusion echoes "To be or not to be"
Time indicators:
in a second ...
three days ...
three months
(summary of episode)

of the bridge. To plunge or not to plunge, that was the question! In a second I had plunged, throwing out my arms to embrace the summit of the fir tree. The argument was correct; the data were absolutely wrong. It was three days before I regained consciousness and more than three months before I crawled from my bed. The measured fall was 29 feet on to hard ground. But no doubt the

Return to actual chronology

branches helped. My mother, summoned by the alarming message of the children, "He jumped over the bridge and he won't speak to us," hurried down with energetic aid and inopportune brandy. It was an axiom with my parents that in serious accident or illness the highest medical aid should be invoked, regardless of cost. Eminent specialists stood

The aftermath—details

about my bed. Later on when I could understand again, I was shocked and also flattered to hear of the enormous fees that had been paid. My father travelled over at full express from Dublin where he had been spending his Christmas at one of old Lord Fitzgibbon's once-celebrated parties. He brought the greatest of London's surgeons with him. I had among other injuries a ruptured kidney. It is to the surgeon's art and to my own pronounced will-to-live that the reader is indebted for this story. But for a year I looked at life round a corner. They made a joke about it in those days at the Carlton Club, "I hear Randolph's son met with a serious accident." "Yes? Playing a game of Follow

Anecdote (the writer's father was a politician)

my Leader,"—"Well, Randolph is not likely to come to grief in that way!"—WINSTON CHURCHILL, *A Roving Commission,* pp. 29-30

You will have noticed that the actual chronology is altered midway through the paragraph. Following the sentence "In a second I had plunged, throwing out my arms to embrace the summit of the fir tree," four sentences intervene to summarize the entire incident before the actual chronology is resumed. The interruption is necessary, for the writer has carried the account to the point where he lies on the ground unconscious. To go immediately into "My mother, summoned by the alarming message ..." would have made an unconvincing shift in the point of view—that is, the view from which the action is presented. When the shift does come, the intervening sentences have told us enough so that it is perfectly reasonable for the writer to resume the actual chronology; like any other convalescent, he would have been told over and over every bit of detail relating to the period when he was unconscious.

When the shift in point of view is not made reasonable, it can be irritating and distracting. One device for ensuring consistency in the point of view is to use the same subject or very nearly the same subject (*the four of us, we, we; the man they called Frank, he, Frank*) in each of the sentences that convey the small parts of the continuous action. Another device is to use a connecting word or phrase or clause like *meanwhile, at the same time,* or *while I was doing that.* (For further discussion of narration and of narrative paragraphs in a paper, see pp. 76-79 and 161-181.)

Descriptive paragraphs • Like narrative paragraphs, descriptive paragraphs are made up mainly of details. A generalization may be used to give an overall impression which is then clarified and sharpened by details, but it is often more effective to build the details so that the reader forms the generalization for himself.

When the object described is static, the details are often presented in a spatial order—from outside to inside, from top to bottom, from left to right. A building, for example, might be described in any of these ways. Spatial order is most typical of objective description (see p. 72) where the aim is clear, factual recording of what has been observed. This description of the United Nations General Assembly chamber moves from outside the building to a selection of images of the chamber as seen from the visitors' galleries. (Previously the writer had spoken of the chamber as covered "by a huge inverted tub.")

The chamber is on the second floor of the Assembly Building, that strangely curved northernmost of the U.N. cluster. (The flattish gray dome projecting from its roof is the exterior of the tub's bottom.) From the galleries, the audience looks out over the seated delegates toward the dais—a pyramid of green-carpeted steps leading up to two landings. On the lower landing is the lectern, sheathed in slabs of greenish-black marble, at which the delegates stand when speaking. Above and behind this, on the second landing, is the President's desk, shaped like a judge's bench and finished in oyster-white marble. Still higher, on a shaftlike gilt panel rising behind the President's desk, is fixed a big bronze disc bearing the U.N. emblem—a global map of the world, in white. At the President's desk are places, each with its microphone and glass of water, for three men.—CHRISTOPHER RAND, "A Pageant in Sack Suits," originally published in *The New Yorker,* Jan. 19, 1957, p. 63

In this paragraph the movement is indicated by the phrases *From the galleries.... On the lower landing.... Above and behind this, on the second landing.... Still higher.... At the President's desk.* Other common indications of movement in descriptive paragraphs are *next, beyond that,* and so on. A certain number of these are essential when the writer has begun his paragraph in such a way as to forecast a more or less systematic inventory of the parts of the object or scene he is describing.

In many descriptive paragraphs, clear, factual, objective recording of what can be observed is not the writer's goal. He may want the reader to share his enthusiasm for the external design of a new car; if so, he will focus the reader's attention on the overall appearance as viewed from a distance of, say, ten yards. Or he may want to convince the reader that this same design makes driving hazardous; to do so, he may concentrate on the lack of view from the driver's seat. Even the writer with no special ax to grind will frequently treat in detail just that feature of an object or scene that he considers dominant, filling out the remainder of the picture only as much as he thinks necessary. The spatial relation is still there, but it is subordinated to a dominant impression stemming from the interests, the opinions, or the associations of the writer. In the following paragraph, notice how a few carefully selected details are used not simply to describe the writer's mother but to lend support to the opinion expressed in the first sentence—an opinion so novel that it might, if unsupported, strike the reader as either absurd or meaningless.

The drabness of real life seems to affect taste. If your life is exciting you are likely to decorate in stark Danish and wear simple unadorned black classics. But in my mother's house there is glitter—a dazzling wall clock that bongs every half-hour, an oversized, wood-inlaid painting of Chinese dancers (à la Coney Island), painted figurines of bongo players, and a giant Buddha perched atop the TV. In her clothes my mother prefers bright reds to black. She will choose the flashy fakes over subdued pearls, big beads over smaller ones, and three strands over one. Size, quantity, and glitter always count. Her car is an orange and white Mercury (now in its declining years), and her hair is of rather similar hues—it all seems somehow gayer that way.—Patricia Cayo Sexton, "Speaking for the Working-Class Wife," *Harper's Magazine,* Oct. 1962, p. 131

(For further discussion of description and descriptive paragraphs in a paper, see pp. 72-76, 166-168, and 182-186.)

Basic to narrative and descriptive paragraphs is an order suggested by the material itself. The fundamental movement —through time or through space—will be altered for special effects, but writer and reader can always measure and judge departures from it by reference to something *out there.* In explanatory and persuasive writing, however, no natural order is suggested by the material itself; the writer has to impose his own order on it. That order is determined by several considerations, among them what the writer wants to communicate about his material and how he thinks he can best do it with a particular audience. For any one paragraph, the problem of organization boils down to a question of how to make clear the relation between the details and the main generalization. Paragraphs of support, climax, and pro-and-con represent three ways in which that relation may be set forth. (Paragraphs of support and climax are similar to the two general plans for papers described in Chapter 2, pp. 49-50.)

Support paragraphs • In the support paragraph a generalization comes first and is followed by details or by less general statements that elaborate or support it. This type of movement is often spoken of as "from general to particular." The paragraph by Roger Burlingame on page 117 is the simplest pattern for the support paragraph, and most of those quoted in "Methods of paragraph development," pages 119-124, are support paragraphs.

A support paragraph may begin with a pointer statement announcing the subject to be discussed, as in this example (which for convenience of reading and for emphasis was divided into two closely related paragraphs):

There are several ways of taking notes. One is to copy the exact words of the author. This is the lazy man's way of historical writing, unless you are planning to edit selected documents or excerpts from the materials you use and do not intend to do any interpretative writing of your own at all. Another and better way is to read the paragraph or page at least twice (once for general sense and a second time for detailed analysis), and then to try to put the idea expressed by the author into your own words, copying verbatim only such words, phrases, or sentences as are so expressive or colorful that you want them exactly as the author said them. This second method will insure your understanding what the author is trying to say, for unless you understand his statement you will not be able to paraphrase it in your own words.

A third way is to "boil down" the author's statement to as brief a form as possible, that is, giving a summary. In taking notes it is not advisable to do much summarizing, unless you are certain that the subject summarized is one which you will not need to discuss in great detail later on. It is better to paraphrase at the note-taking stage and then to summarize when you begin to write. Rather have too much than too little when taking notes.—Donald Dean Parker, *Local History*, p. 95

A more complex example of the support paragraph is the following, part of an account of the way of life developed by the Irish immigrants who came to America in the 1830's and 1840's. The topic sentence is a generalization made up of two separate (but related) parts—"community values" and "the old village ideals of mutual help." The characteristics of business life analyzed in the paragraph are all related to one or the other of the two parts of the topic sentence.

Topic sentence	The nature of business life within the Irish community reflected community values and the old village ideals of mutual help. The early Irish businessmen, like most immigrant entrepreneurs, did not have the capital
Fact	resources or the personal connections to make a frontal entry into the main areas of business such as manufacturing, mining, and banking. Rather, they operated in its interstices. They were the blacksmiths, sa-
Result (details)	loonkeepers, grocerystore owners, small contractors, and makers and sellers of soap, leather, meat, and other provisions. Success in these businesses and in the professions of

Condition for success clarifies "community values" (sentence 1)

Example

The first of the unwritten rules clarifies "community values" and is followed by evidence

Reason for later change
Qualification ("Even then")

Second rule clarifies "old village ideals of mutual help"
Example

law and medicine often depended as much on neighborhood goodwill as on financial resources or personal skill. Only if a man and his family before him were well regarded by his fellows would the latter patronize him as a doctor or go to his shop or saloon. There were two unwritten rules the rising tradesmen and professional men usually obeyed. One was to live in the neighborhood. It would be the end of the nineteenth century before any important number of them could safely move away to better neighborhoods. By then, clearly differentiated middle classes had emerged in the Irish community, and a sizable segment of them moved away from original bases. Even then, the better-off families did not detach themselves from the old neighborhood in an isolated or haphazard fashion; they shifted to better sections of the city as part of a general movement of Irish out of old neighborhoods that were being abandoned to newer immigrant groups. The other requirement was a willingness to help the worst off in time of need. If a laborer died without insurance, one of his fellow workers was likely to go from house to house in the neighborhood collecting donations, no matter how small, to make up a purse for the widow and her children. These appeals were frequent. No one who hoped to prosper or be well regarded in the community turned them down.—WILLIAM V. SHANNON, *The American Irish,* pp. 36-37

Because of the focus provided by the topic sentence, a paragraph of support is probably the safest type for a writer who has trouble unifying his material. With the generalization before him, he is more likely to recognize threats to unity in the form of distracting or irrelevant details. One disadvantage is that he may feel that framing the topic sentence is virtually all that is required of him; the paragraph will trail off to a weak ending if he has not seen the need to support the topic sentence with particulars. In a paragraph built on the support plan the details should be interesting in themselves as well as in their relation to the topic sentence. This type of paragraph movement is the most common in factual writing.

Climax paragraphs • A paragraph of climax begins with a detail and continues with others that move toward the point the writer wishes to make. The order is sometimes described as "particular to general." *Climax* may be too strong a name for this natural and common pattern, but the label does emphasize an actual movement frequently found in writing. It allows the writer to pick up the reader's attention quickly and lead him to the end, often a generalization, as in this:

We stopped for half an hour the other afternoon in bright sunshine to watch the digging where the Murray Hill Hotel used to be. There were about forty of us kibitzers, every one a male. A huge Diesel shovel named Lorain was hacking the last few tons of dirt and rubble from the hole and dropping them deftly onto trucks. This was a large-scale operation—big, ten-wheel Mack trucks, plenty of mud and noise and movement. The shovel operator was conscious of his audience and played to it. Bathed in sunlight and virtuosity, he allowed his cigarette to drip lazily from his lips while he plucked his levers as cunningly as a chimemaster. We men in the audience were frozen in admiration, in respect, in wonder. We studied and digested every trick of the intricate operation—the thrust, the hoist, the swing, the release—conscious of the power and the glory. To a man, we felt instructed, elevated, stimulated. To a man, we were at the controls, each one of us, learning the levers, nudging the rocks, checking the swing, clicking the jaws to coax the last dribble. The sun warmed us in our studies. Not a woman, of the many who passed, paused to watch and to absorb. Not one single female. There can be no question but that ninety-five percent of all the miracles in the world (as well as ninety-five percent of all the hell) are directly traceable to the male sex.—*The New Yorker,* Feb. 19, 1949. Reprinted by permission. Cop. 1949, The New Yorker Magazine, Inc.

Often the subject is announced at the beginning but the full idea comes as a climax at the end, as in this series of particular opinions that lead to a final broader generalization:

These observations give a sort of base-line for estimating the effect of pocket-size books on the general cultural level. At their very worst they are immensely better than the comics. Still at their worst, they are a little better than the pulps; often they are written by the same authors, but with somewhat more care and consecutive effort. At their best they are better than any of the mass-circulation magazines—and the statement remains true even if we set aside the pocket-book series that have achieved some literary or scholarly distinction, like Mentor Books, Anchor Books, and Penguins imported from England. Except for a few of the Mentors, these seldom appear at newsstands in shabby neighborhoods, but even there the assortment is likely to include some admirable works that were never before available at low prices. Pocket-size books as a class are making possible a considerable improvement in the reading habits of the American public.—MALCOLM COWLEY, *The Literary Situation,* pp. 105-106

Building up to a conclusion, as the paragraph of climax does, is often an effective way of sustaining the attention and interest of the reader. The element of suspense that comes from withholding the generalization makes the reader feel that he is sharing in the process of discovery. A writer may choose to use it when there is something paradoxical or exciting in the generalization he wishes to convey. Or he may choose to use it because he knows that the generalization is a complex and difficult one; instead of stating it at the beginning of the paragraph, he may wish to lead the reader to it in easy stages. Finally, he may choose the climax pattern when he knows the reader's initial reaction to the generalization would be irritation or dismay. Presenting the evidence first—and making it convincing—is a good way of allaying the reader's hostility and winning his acceptance of the generalization.

The chief hazard of this pattern is that unless the details are well chosen and the relation between them is made clear, the reader may be confused as to what they are supposed to mean. If he has no notion at all about the point the paragraph is to make, his interest may not be strong enough to carry him through the details that lead to that point.

Pro-and-con paragraphs • In its movement, a pro-and-con paragraph is somewhat more complex than a support paragraph or a climax paragraph. The paragraph usually starts with a generalization which is supported by details, as in the support paragraph, but then takes a turn in a different direction (often signaled by *but, however,* or some other contrast). In the paragraph below the writer follows this pattern, first describing a current situation (sentences 1-6) and then attacking the attitude that is responsible for it. The second half of the paragraph, beginning "But I wonder if cause and effect have not become a little confused here," attacks the methods of the experts and argues to the conclusion set forth in the last sentence. (For context of the passage, see pp. 262-265.)

Along with the tremendous increase in popular interest in skiing during the past few years there has been a proliferation of ski litera-ture defining and refining what the skier must do. Experts are every-where. Competition is tougher. Equipment is better. All such changes have created a condition in which the ski expert flourishes. And because the level of competitive performance is improved, the experts' theories seem to be justified. But I wonder if cause and effect have not become a little confused here. There is an absolute necessity for a competitive skier to be in top physical condition—no one could argue otherwise. The question is how he is to be given his physical training. In the case of training at the junior level, it is a question of what is to be done to make him want to receive it. The exhaustion technique is just what its name implies, a matter of forc-ing the skier to push himself beyond his known endurance. Now, if you can instill in the individual the *desire* to do this for himself, without the authoritative voice ordering him to do this or that, he will achieve the same end, but he will have done it for himself. It is the forcing that is wrong and potentially dangerous. Encouraging an individual's desire, instead of compelling him to a predetermined condition, will make him just as good a competitor, and yet will let him retain his own zest for the sport.—Andrea Mead Lawrence, "Let's Not Spoil Their Sport," *Sports Illustrated,* Feb. 3, 1964, p. 20

The pro-and-con movement has other uses besides attacking an opposing position. It may be used simply for the purpose of refining and qualifying the writer's own main point. And when it serves this purpose, the pro-and-con movement may be repeated several times in a single paragraph. In the follow-ing, the regular alternation of negative and positive statements about the average man of Lincoln's generation permits the writer to move judiciously to a generalization at the end that is considerably stronger than the one at the beginning.

The average Western American of Lincoln's generation was funda-mentally a man who subordinated his intelligence to certain domi-nant practical interests and purposes. He was far from being a stupid or slow-witted man. On the contrary, his wits had been sharpened by the traffic of American politics and business, and his mind was shrewd, flexible, and alert. But he was wholly incapable either of disinterested or of concentrated intellectual exertion. His energies were bent in the conquest of certain stubborn external forces, and he used his intelligence almost exclusively to this end. The struggles, the hardships, and the necessary self-denial of pioneer life constituted an admirable training of the will. It developed a body of men with great resolution of purpose and with great ingenuity and fertility in adapting their insufficient means to the realization of their important business affairs. But their almost exclusive preoccupation with practical tasks and their failure to grant their intelligence any room for independent exercise bent them into exceedingly warped and one-sided human beings.—HERBERT CROLY, *The Promise of American Life,* pp. 90-91

Organizing a paragraph on the pro-and-con pattern enables the writer to indicate his awareness of conflicting opinions and of the need to modify and qualify his own generalizations. Handled well, it suggests a certain subtlety and depth of thinking about the material. Handled badly, it can communicate a sense of indecisiveness, as if the writer is merely sitting on the fence, evading the responsibility of making clear what his own ideas on the subject are. A pro-and-con paragraph usually needs to end with a forceful, positive statement that leaves no doubt in the reader's mind as to the writer's final judgment.

Although there is a good deal of variation in the movements described in this section, most paragraphs belong to one of these five kinds—narrative, descriptive, support, climax, or pro-and-con. The writer's purpose, his material, and the audience he is addressing—one or more of these considerations will determine which organization will be most effective in a given paragraph. Ordinarily the paragraphs in a paper should show some variety in movement. To build every paragraph on the same pattern is likely to result in a monotonous, wooden effect. The paragraphs in a good paper differ in the way they are organized just as they differ in the way they are developed and in their length.

Continuity in paragraphs

Whether a paragraph makes its full point depends largely on the way the reader is led from one statement to the next. The relation between the statements should be obvious not only to the writer but also to the reader for whom it is intended. The connection must first exist in the ideas and then be shown in the writing.

The second sentence of the following paragraph does not follow from the first; it seems to make a new start. The whole paragraph needs to be rewritten from a single point of view (either that of the men who for many years have been breeding, raising, and schooling horses in an effort to produce the ideal polo mount or that of the player trying to find one) and the relation between the statements needs to be clarified.

For many years men have been breeding, raising, and schooling different types and breeds of horses in an effort to produce the ideal polo mount. When a player wishes to purchase a high-type pony, he looks for four things—quickness, speed, stamina, and ability to stop easily. A combination of these four essentials is difficult to find in one animal. Several have two or three of the qualifications, but very seldom do you find a pony with all four.

Fortunately there are a number of simple ways to indicate the natural and logical connection between statements. Relationship may be shown by:

1. continuing the same subject from sentence to sentence, using the same words, synonyms, or pronouns
2. using a pronoun referring to a word in the preceding sentence
3. using a conjunction or adverb (*however, but, because, consequently, for example*) to show the thought relationship (contrast, cause or effect, reason, illustration)
4. repeating key words from sentence to sentence
5. making sentences parallel in structure

The following paragraph shows the most common of these signs of continuity (indicated by the italicized words):

(1) Critics have not been lacking, *of course,* who pointed out what a hash democracy was making of its pretensions to government. (2) *These critics* have seen that the important decisions were taken by individuals, and that public opinion was uninformed, irrelevant and meddlesome. (3) *They* have usually concluded that there was a congenital difference between the masterful few and the ignorant many. (4) *They* are the vic-

Suggests continuation from a preceding paragraph	
Subject of 1 repeated	
Pronoun, referring to *critics,* subject of 1 and 2	
Pronoun, as in 3	

tims of a superficial analysis of the evils they see so clearly. (5) The *fundamental difference* which matters is that between insiders and outsiders. (6) *Their* relations to a problem are radically different. (7) Only the *insider* can make decisions, not because he is inherently a better man but because he is so placed that he can understand and can act.

fundamental contrasts with *superficial* of 4; *difference* repeated from 3
Pronoun *Their* refers to *insiders and outsiders*
Insider repeated

(8) The *outsider* is necessarily ignorant, usually irrelevant and often meddlesome, because he is trying to navigate the ship from dry land. (9) *That* is why excellent automobile manufacturers, literary critics and scientists often talk such nonsense about politics. (10) *Their* congenital excellence, if it exists, reveals itself only in their own activity. (11) The *aristocratic theorists* work from the fallacy of supposing that a sufficiently excellent square peg will also fit a round hole. (12) *In short,* like the democratic theorists, *they* miss the essence of the matter, which is, that competence exists only in relation to function; that men are not good, but good for something; that men cannot be educated, but only educated for something.—WALTER LIPPMANN, *The Phantom Public,* pp. 149-150

outsider repeated from 5, contrasting with *insider* in 7

Pronoun *That,* summarizing idea of 8

Pronoun *Their,* referring to the subjects of *talk* in 9
aristocratic theorists echoes *critics* of first sentences; *excellent* echoes *excellent* of 9 and *excellence* of 10
In short, a connective; pronoun *they,* referring to *theorists* of 11; *democratic theorists* contrasting with *aristocratic*

A firm, emphatic final sentence, topic sentence and goal of the preceding statements (climax movement)

It would be impossible to begin reading this paragraph at any sentence without feeling that something had gone before, something needed to get the full meaning of the sentence.

The signs of continuity in a paragraph can be seen more clearly in relation to the development of the paragraph (the relations between details and generalizations as discussed on pp. 112-117). Accompanying the passage that follows, some points are made at the left about development of material and at the right about signs of continuity. The passage is from an advanced textbook in psychology, the opening paragraphs of a chapter on *canalization*. This introduction to the subject is not technical, though much of the treatment that follows is. The interweaving of generalizations and details makes a closely knit passage.

Material		*Continuity*
Topic sentence (generalization)	(1) Needs tend to become more specific in consequence of being satisfied in specific ways. (2) Children all over the world are hungry; their hunger may be satisfied by bread, by ice cream, by peanuts, by raw eggs, by rice, or by whale blubber. (3) Eventually they develop, when hungry, not a demand for food in general, but a demand for what they are used to; in one part of the world peanuts are good food, whale blubber disgusting, and vice versa.	(Starts a new unit)
		Relation obvious
Example (and evidence)		
		Repetition of *satisfied* from 1
Details		
General idea repeated in less general terms		*they* refers to *children* of 2; *hungry* repeated from 2
Repeated in details		
Another example	(4) So, too, over the face of the earth, children enjoy rhythms; the need is satisfied by different kinds of rhythms, different games, different types of music. (5) Soon they find the ones which they are "used to" natural and satisfying; others seem awkward, difficult, unsatisfying.	*So, too,* connective; *children* repeated as subject
Made more specific		
Part of general idea restated		*Soon* suggests continuity, *they* referring to *children*
Idea repeated with two examples	(6) If a person is hungry, oriented toward food in general, he may nevertheless be more hungry for bread than for corn, for beef than for	*hungry* echoes preceding paragraph

	mutton. (7) Attitude toward food is general, the	*Attitude* translates *oriented toward;*
Idea progressively refined and limited	valuation of absent food is general; but specific attitudes are defined within the general, and within the specific there are some still more specific, so that one	*food* and *general* repeated; *specific* repeated from preceding paragraph
Illustration	wants not only currant buns but the one with the	
Compact restatement of general idea	darkest crust. (8) Tastes have become specific.— GARDNER MURPHY, *Personality,* p. 161	*Tastes* echoes *attitudes* and *needs; specific* repeated

The first paragraph follows the support pattern, beginning with the general statement that is developed in more specific terms; the second, the climax pattern, beginning with particulars and ending on a strong general statement. A conspicuous trait is the repetition of the key words of the first sentence: in the two paragraphs *specific* occurs six times (and, contrasting with it, *general* five times), *satisfied* and *satisfying* four times, and *needs* and its equivalents *(demand, attitude, wants, taste)* eight times. Since these words occur in statements which clarify and illustrate the central idea, their repetition is not bothersome but keeps us aware of the main generalization: "Needs tend to become more specific in consequence of being satisfied in specific ways." The last forceful sentence, "Tastes have become specific," is the final source of emphasis.

Paragraphs in a paper

Except in practice writing, paragraphs seldom occur singly. In preparing a paper, you should give special attention to the beginning, to the ending, and to the transitions that show the relationship between paragraphs.

Opening paragraphs • The first few sentences of a paper have a double function: they must get the subject under way, or at least get definitely started toward it, and they should interest the reader enough to make him want to read on. Amateur writers are often tempted to concoct an elaborate "introduction" and so postpone the real matter of the paper, or to begin routinely ("It is the purpose of this paper to show how to select vacation work"), or even to open with an apology ("I realize that nobody of my age could have a sound opinion on this important topic"). The following sentence, so general in its application that it might begin a paper on almost any social topic, actually began one on sharecroppers: "All men are endowed by their Creator with certain inalienable rights, among which are life, liberty and the pursuit of happiness."

Studying the openings of successful essays and articles will suggest possibilities. Of the eight nonfiction articles in an issue of the *Atlantic*,[1] three open with some kind of narrative. The one article which is entirely autobiographical begins quietly with a narrative-descriptive account of the origins of the writer's father.

My father, whose name was Denis Whelan, was a police constable in the Royal Irish Constabulary. He came from a small farm near the hamlet of Stradbally, about fifty miles southeast of Dublin in what was then known as the Queen's County, a region named after Queen Mary I, the wife of Philip of Spain, when it was originally planted and shired by English settlers. It is known today by its old Gaelic name of Laois.—SEAN O'FAOLAIN, "Vive Moi!" p. 81

In another article the narrative opening is impersonal, reporting a recent event which leads the writer into his subject.

In the spring of 1963 the junior senator from Arkansas, the Honorable J. William Fulbright, and the senior senator from Pennsylvania, the Honorable Joseph S. Clark, were quoted at length in a pamphlet issued by the Center for the Study of Democratic Institutions. The occasion was a discussion staged by the center on the subject "The Elite and the Electorate," in which the participants were the two senators, a few guests specially invited to sit in, and two distinguished foreigners: Pierre Mendès-France, former Premier of France, and Quintin McGarel Hogg, Viscount Hailsham, Conservative leader of the House of Lords.

The pamphlet received more than usual attention from the press because it contained two statements which, coming from American politicians, astonished many people.—GERALD W. JOHNSON, "The Art of Being Free," p. 60

---

[1]The *Atlantic*, Jan. 1964.

In a third article the writer makes only brief mention of the historical background because the reader can be expected to be familiar with the main events relating to the Teamsters Union during recent years. The narrative is subordinated to the central point that the union has flourished in spite of bad publicity. (Note the literary allusion—"the sweet uses of adversity.")

The International Brotherhood of Teamsters, the nation's biggest, strongest, and most investigated union, is a monument to the sweet uses of adversity, a testimonial to the proposition that nothing succeeds like bad publicity. For nearly seven years all the awesome powers of the federal government, reinforced by every instrument of mass communication, have been focused on the destruction of the union's iron-fisted president, James R. Hoffa. Yet both Hoffa and the Teamsters have prospered, while the AFL-CIO, which cast them out as a disgrace to organized labor, is sunk in bureaucratic torpor.— A. H. RASKIN, "The Power of James R. Hoffa," p. 39

Three other articles—all of which are intended to persuade the audience to accept the writer's interpretation or judgment —begin with clear, strong statements of the central propositions to be supported.

The American way is not necessarily the best way for all the people of the world. Drastic adaptation is necessary before our methods are transplanted to other cultures. The health center movement provides a good example of how Western practices have been and are continuing to be adapted to provide new organizational patterns for other countries.—CARL E. TAYLOR, "Medical Care for Developing Countries," p. 75

Contemporary Russian writers are not out to reshape Russian political institutions. Divisions in talent, in generations, in intellectual allegiance, have become clear and bitter, but the writers are politicians only in the sense that Russian writers have played political roles these last two hundred years—ever since literature in Russia has had a clear responsibility to its audience to express understanding of the values behind daily political and economic life. Writers today must wish to express a fresh understanding of the role of the Party in the entire life of the nation, including its consciousness; and that is precisely what all the writers and artists have said they wish. Not since Olesha's speech at the 1934 Writers' Congress has anyone publicly announced that artists cannot function within the Party or within the Writers' Union. It is the dogmatists, in their attacks on certain writers, who have made contemporary Russian literature seem to be striving to be anti-Communist.—F. D. REEVE, "Writer versus Bureaucrat in the Soviet Union," p. 69

The thesis of this piece is that the Western writer is in a box with booby traps at both ends. By "Western writer" I do not mean the writer of Westerns; I mean the writer who has spent his formative years in the West. When I say he is in a box, I mean that he has a hard time discovering what is in him wanting to be said, and that when he does discover it he has difficulty getting a hearing. His box is booby-trapped at one end by an inadequate artistic and intellectual tradition, and at the other end by the coercive dominance of attitudes, beliefs, and intellectual fads and manners destructive of his own. The fact that these attitudes control both the publishing media and large portions of the critical establishment is more important than the fact that publishing is concentrated in another region. This is not a complaint against Leviathan. It is only an extension of the observation that, since any writer must write from what he knows and believes, a writer from the West finds himself so unfashionable as to be practically voiceless.—WALLACE STEGNER, "Born a Square— The Westerners' Dilemma," p. 46

Two other articles are on subjects which might be considered to be of less general interest. Notice how in each of them the writer makes a determined effort to catch the reader's attention. The first asks and answers questions in a progressively narrowing sequence. The literary allusion that opens the second gives a light, bright touch to an article which is packed with statistics about the national debt. (Micawber's theory, by the way, is referred to regularly throughout the article to represent the point of view that the author is attacking.)

Do all Pacific salmon die after spawning? Yes. Even the pink salmon, after a life of less than two years? Even the great and powerful king salmon? Even the jacks, the precocious males that come back after only one short year in the sea? Yes, they all die. Not a single one of all the hosts upon hosts that come in from the sea lives to spawn a second time.—RODERICK HAIG-BROWN, "The Death of the Salmon," p. 57

If a man had twenty pounds a year and spent nineteen pounds, nineteen shillings, and sixpence, he would be happy, but if he spent twenty pounds sixpence, he would be miserable.

Thus Mr. Micawber expounded his theory of economics to David Copperfield. In modern terms: Balance the budget and all is well; unbalance it on the minus side and you are on the road to hell.— J. DAVID STERN, "The National Debt and the Peril Point," p. 35

The openings of these articles suggest that it is effective to begin directly with some part of the material that is to be presented. The reader who finds himself in the very first sentence in a definite time and place or faced with an interesting, provocative generalization will want to read on. Considering your prospective audience is important when you begin a paper, and paying attention to the opening sentences will help remove the impression that so many papers give of being written in a void.

Not all writing, of course, needs to make a direct appeal to the interest of the audience. Articles in technical and professional journals seldom begin in such an attractive way. But the readers of such journals turn to them because they are determined to work their way through the articles no matter how forbidding and difficult the material and the style may be. Your task is to make your style and material as attractive as possible without sacrificing accuracy and honesty.

Concluding paragraphs • The last paragraph of a paper, like the first, has a double function: it rounds out the subject and gives the final emphasis. If rightly done, it will leave the reader with exactly the impression the writer intended. It should also sound like a last paragraph; that is, by its subject matter and its style it should satisfy a reader's sense of having reached the end.

A concluding paragraph is usually unemphatic when it is made up of minor details or of references to materials that could be but are not discussed in this particular paper. Instead of concentrating the reader's mind on what has been said, it sends it off in other directions. For example, this ending, at the close of a paper on pitching, suddenly turns to a generalization about the other members of a baseball team:

> Baseball is one of America's favorite sports, and to spend an afternoon at the Yankee Stadium, watching two great pitchers battling for a victory, attracts thousands of fans. What I have said about pitching gives you an idea as to what a pitcher must keep in mind while out there on the mound, or as a substitute on the bench. There are eight other players on the team besides the pitcher and the same can be written about each individual player and his position.

It is true that every subject suggests others and is in some way related to others, and sometimes this relation should be indicated. But bringing it in at the end will only blur the final emphasis.

An apology also weakens the final effect, and attempted cuteness may let a paper die away inconclusively when it should end strongly.

> I guess old Mike was not really an unusual character. Just a plain citizen who had had more than his share of bad luck. Today is the first time I've thought of him. I don't know why he should have been recalled to my memory now. Maybe it's spring, weather, or something else. I really don't know.

Often a writer feels quite properly that his subject needs a better treatment than he can give it; sometimes he needs to explain why the treatment is limited in the way that it is. But the place for such qualifications is early in the paper—though not at the beginning, because that would get the paper off to a weak start.

In a short, informal paper a mechanical summary of content is rarely needed and such bald statements as "In this paper I have shown that" are inappropriate. Summaries are more appropriate in formal academic papers, where they may be necessary if the material is complex or difficult. When a summary is used, it should end with the particular emphasis the writer intends.

The conclusion should leave the reader with the main idea that the writer wants to get across. It is likely to be a generalization, though it may be stated in terms of details. The endings of five of the articles from the *Atlantic* (used to illustrate beginnings on pp. 144-146) show various ways of achieving final emphasis. Three are very short, but the few sentences that make them up all refer back to the situation or problem posed at the beginning of the article and restate vigorously the main point developed in the article.

> Our nation is growing faster than its debt. Those words are the magic formula to lay Micawber's ghost.—J. DAVID STERN, "The National Debt and the Peril Point," p. 38
>
> Senators Fulbright and Clark spoke well in proclaiming education as our hope. But *quis custodiet*—Banker Schmidt was the one to raise the crucial question, who is to educate the educators?—GERALD W. JOHNSON, "The Art of Being Free," p. 64
>
> Just possibly, if our Westerner lived and wrote his convictions, he could show the hopeless where hope comes from, like Aesop's frog which, drowning in a bowl of milk, in the destructive element immersed, swam so desperately that it churned up a little pad of butter on which to sit.

This is not exhortation, neither is it prophecy. It is only, since I am from the West and incorrigible, hope.—WALLACE STEGNER, "Born a Square—The Westerners' Dilemma," p. 50

Two other concluding paragraphs bring out in more leisurely fashion the significance of the topic:

These are the less known titles in the splotchy mosaic that is the Teamsters Union. They are part of a reality that includes almost limitless economic potential in a field unrestricted by any of the usual bonds of union jurisdiction. This is a union that cannot live to itself; it touches too many others too intimately. That is why the character and the aspirations of its leadership, good or evil, have a significance beyond that of any other American labor organization.— A. H. RASKIN, "The Power of James R. Hoffa," p. 45

But until that last strength is gone, the will to live is still in them and finds its expression. At some too close threat of danger they will drive away, upstream or down, in a surge of energy that seems no proper part of their wasted shapes. Bodies white with parasitic fungus, great king salmon somehow hold station over swift-running spawning shallows as though they still could play a part. I see them now on the shallows near my house, often two fish together, slowly forced down by the current, turning fiercely against it as it presses on their broad thin flanks and warns them of their weakness. It is the sort of thing man has glorified in himself as the undying spirit of man. Seeing it here so clearly, long after hope and purpose have gone, I can recognize it for what it is: the undying spirit of animals. I find it no less admirable.—RODERICK HAIG-BROWN, "The Death of the Salmon," p. 59

As these examples show, the concluding paragraph should contribute to the tone of the paper as well as to its content. The style in which the main point of the paper is restated can suggest urgency or humor or meditative calm, or any number of other effects. In writing a concluding paragraph, try to decide what effect as well as what final thought you want to leave with the reader, and make the last sentences express that effect as well as you can.

Transitions between paragraphs • The paragraphs in a paper should show continuity from one to the next, much as the sentences within a paragraph do. The connections between the parts of the subject, the words or phrases or clauses that lead the reader from one thought to another, are called *transitions*.

When paragraphs are short, the signs of continuity may not differ essentially from those used between sentences. The familiar connectives like *and, but, although, moreover, finally, because,* and those that are more exclusively transitional like *for example, on the other hand,* and *on the contrary* can connect paragraphs just as they can connect the sentences within a paragraph. Such connectives are more useful than the flabby *then too* or a mechanical expression like *It is interesting to note,* which are symptoms that the writer has not sensed the actual relationship between the points he is making.

Pointer sentences are often used to make the bridge between one paragraph and the next, sometimes coming at the end of a paragraph and looking forward to the next one but more often standing as the first sentence of the paragraph that is to deal with a related phase of the subject. The following pointer sentences look back to the preceding paragraph (in "another" and "third") and also look forward to the content of the paragraphs they introduce:

Let us look at another aspect of the problem.
There is a third reason for the current emphasis on getting a college degree.

Transitions like these and others which express the relationship between ideas or between phases of the material being discussed can be valuable devices for establishing continuity from one paragraph to another. They are, however, external transitions in which the writer in a sense stands outside his material and points the reader in the right direction. More subtle and often more effective are *organic transitions* in which the language itself makes the relationship clear. These transitions are accomplished by carrying over from the end of the preceding paragraph an essential word or two or an idea expressed in slightly different words. Two examples follow:

... And the statement becomes undignified—if not, indeed, slanderous.
The lack of dignity in such statements is not in the words, nor in the dictionaries that list them, but in the hostility that deliberately seeks this tone of expression.—BERGEN EVANS

... Religion can get on with any sort of astronomy, geology, biology, physics. But it cannot get on with a purposeless and meaningless universe.
If the scheme of things is purposeless and meaningless, then the life of man is purposeless and meaningless too.—W. T. STACE

Transitional paragraphs • Occasionally in a paper of some length a writer may give an entire paragraph to a transition. Some of these transitional paragraphs may be very short indeed, such as Donald Lloyd's "Let me explain" in the passage quoted on page 89. (This is really a pointer sentence which gains emphasis by its separation from the preceding paragraph and from the following one.) Others, somewhat longer, provide the transition by summarizing the previous discussion and preparing the way for the next phase of the topic.

Ordinarily, transitional paragraphs serve as a bridge from one part of a paper to another rather than from one paragraph to another. Unnecessary in short papers, they can be useful structuring devices in long essays, term papers, and reference papers.

Because many paragraphs are "compositions in miniature," much can be gained from studying how good writers develop and organize them. Because many of them carry their full meaning only in the context of the essays of which they are a part, much can be gained from analyzing full paragraph sequences to see how good writers connect one paragraph with another. A study of paragraphs comes close to being a study of composition, and practice in writing paragraphs is excellent preparation for writing complete essays.

Exercises

1. For each of the following paragraphs, *first,* pick out the topic sentence or pointer, or, if the paragraph has neither, compose a sentence that expresses the central idea; *second,* state the method or methods used in developing the paragraph.

a. (1) A baby in America can enjoy an outing in his *baby buggy, baby carriage* or *baby cab,* depending on where he enjoys it. (2) If it's in the North, he may be *wheeled* or *pushed;* if in the South, *rolled, ridden* or *carried.* (3) Back home, he will be *bathed* in most parts of the country, but may be *bath'd* in some parts of Philadelphia and San Francisco. (4) The cows that furnish the milk for his bottle will have been called home by "sook!" in one section, by "boss!" in another and by "co-ee!" in a third. (5) If he's old enough to chew, he may get a *doughnut*—though in Pennsylvania it's likely to be a *cruller* and in some parts of the South a *cookie.* (6) And it may have been fried in a *spider,* a *skillet* or a *frying pan.—*Bergen Evans, "America Talking," *Holiday,* July 1961, p. 92

b. (1) The art of the dramatic monologue demands high gifts in an uncommon combination. (2) The actor-monologuist is one who can project passages and scenes written by others, with perhaps his own adaptations. (3) In presenting that material, he must master a special sort of illusion. (4) In most monologues the presence of others and the words spoken by them must be registered by the single mirroring voice of the monologuist. (5) In others, the monologuist must be able to shift his voice from role to role and yet manage, with a minimum of props, to establish and to build his illusion. (6) When, moreover, he is recording rather than performing to an audience that can see him, the actor-monologuist must forego costumes, scenery, props, and even his own gestures. (7) The voice must carry it all. (8) To carry it off is a test of talent.—John Ciardi, "Cornelia and the Loves of Charles," *Saturday Review,* April 13, 1963, p. 35

c. (1) Nearly half of the world's population is underfed or otherwise malnourished. (2) The lives of the people in the underdeveloped areas are dominated by the scramble for food to stay alive. (3) Such people are perpetually tired, weak and vulnerable to disease—prisoners of a vicious circle that keeps their productivity far below par and so defeats their efforts to feed their families adequately. (4) Because their undernourishment begins soon after birth, it produces permanently depressing and irremediable effects on the population as a whole. (5) Malnutrition and disease kill a high proportion of the children by the age of four; the death rates for these young children are 20 to 60 times higher than in the U.S. and western Europe. (6) Among those who survive, few escape physical or mental retardation or both.—Nevin S. Scrimshaw, "Food," *Scientific American,* Sept. 1963, p. 73

d. (1) Insurrection, a congressman called the Oxford riots. (2) And insurrection they were in the strict legal sense of that term —a revolt against lawful authority. (3) But to those who still love this republic they were far worse than insurrection; they were subversion. (4) And not subversion in the current witch-hunting sense, which sniffs with terror at every dissenting view, but subversion in the honest meaning of that word—subversion of the country itself. (5) For America cannot survive if the American idea is repudiated. (6) Nations are not made by territory, or the greatness of nations by extent of land. (7) Nations are made by commitments of mind and loyalties of heart, and the nobler the commitment of the mind, the higher the loyalty of the heart, the greater the nation. (8) If the American proposition is no longer the proposition to which the American heart and mind were committed at our beginning, then America is finished, and the only question left is when America will fall.—Archibald MacLeish, "Must We Hate?" The *Atlantic,* Feb. 1963, p. 81

e. (1) But Fort Polk had other things. (2) It had several herds of roving cattle, and anything you did to them was a court-martial offense. (3) There were armadillos (also sacred, although I did see two of them running through the woods painted red, white and blue) and razorback hogs. (4) Add to this tarantulas, pigmy rattle-snakes, cottonmouths and coral snakes (none of which gave any warning, not even the pigmy rattler, whose rattle didn't work—and all of which during certain months seek warm places to curl up in at night, like sleeping bags). (5) Finally, there were all kinds of name-less bugs whose main function in life was to provoke revulsion and disgust by crawling out of things: drains, cracks, footlockers, shoes, mess kits and shaving kits.—John Berendt, "Memoirs of a Six-Months Trainee," *Esquire,* June 1964, p. 160

f. (1) Over the years, Americans living and working abroad have often been accused of cutting themselves off from the people around them and making little, if any, effort to find out about the place they were in—a state of affairs that would seem to be an individual reflection of this country's traditional penchant for isolation, the eagerness to avoid "entangling alliances" that began in George Washington's day. (2) Even after the Second World War, when America's responsibilities around the world multiplied and the nation identified itself with the aspirations of colonial people struggling for freedom—many of whom looked to the United States for inspiration and guidance—there was still a conspicuous lack of personal association between Americans living in other countries and the citizens of these countries, and this, as is often pointed out, tended to diminish the effectiveness of our foreign-aid programs. (3) It is true that in many nations the language problem has been a formidable barrier to warm personal relationships—as a rule, Americans are not good linguists—but an even more important factor has been a strange disinclination on the part of most Ameri-cans abroad, whether they represent the United States officially or are engaged in private business, to mix with foreigners other than those on their own immediate levels. (4) And although increasing numbers of Americans have been living abroad for extended periods, far too many still suffer from what has been called a "compound psychology"; that is, they elect to spend almost all their time within their own compounds—their own offices and their own homes, where they generally entertain one another. (5) Naturally, there are ex-ceptions to this way of life—for example, among missionaries, techni-cians, and journalists whose work takes them far afield, and, now-adays, among some members of the diplomatic corps, who in recent years have been quietly advised by the State Department to get to know more people of the countries they are assigned to. (6) By and large, however, Americans have remained insulated, and although more of them than formerly seem aware of their condition, they still seem singularly unwilling to do anything about it.—Robert Shaplen, "Encounters in Barrios," *The New Yorker,* Sept. 28, 1963, p. 50. Reprinted by permission; © 1963, The New Yorker Magazine, Inc.

2. For each paragraph in the preceding exercise (a) identify the type of movement—narrative, descriptive, support, climax, or pro-and-con; and (b) analyze the devices for achieving continuity (see p. 139).

3. Common weaknesses in the development and organization of single paragraphs are: (a) inadequate development—usually because of the failure to supply enough relevant details; (b) lack of focus— no controlling idea in the paragraph; (c) lack of continuity between statements—the absence of connectives indicating the relationships between statements; (d) unwarranted shift in the direction of the thought; (e) weak beginning; (f) weak ending; (g) inconsistency in point of view or style or tone.

And some common weaknesses in a sequence of paragraphs are: (h) overparagraphing—the failure to group together related ideas; (i) underparagraphing—the failure to make logical breaks in the material; (j) poor transition or lack of transition between paragraphs.

Using this check-list as a guide, point out the weaknesses in paragraphing in "Growing Up," Exercise 1, Chapter 3, page 104, and state how each weakness could be remedied.

4. Using as a guide the check-list in the preceding exercise, identify the weaknesses in the passages below and suggest improvements.

a. (1) In the city of Chicago there are many small communities. (2) One of these is called West Pullman. (3) West Pullman has a population of about 15,000 and is at the southwestern city limit. (4) This community was started by the Dutch in 1860, but in the last fifty years the Dutch influence has been disappearing. (5) The community has five large factories which serve the entire nation with its finished products, but you will find that most of the people do not work in these factories. (6) West Pullman has eight churches, one large park, and one railroad station.

b. (1) After I had been working for the company for a couple of weeks, I was introduced to Joyce, the office secretary. (2) I soon discovered that Joyce was quite easy to talk to, and in our conversations she would pour out all her family problems, her health problems, and even some of her personal problems. (3) In one conversation she told me that she saved her money every day so that on Friday she could put on her best dress, go downtown, and eat at an expensive restaurant. (4) Without this wild fling every Friday night she could not face her job Saturday morning. (5) And yet she seemed happy and content with her daily routine. (6) Why?

c. (1) As one learns more about jazz, he sees more clearly the jazzman's attitude toward life. (2) The jazzman strives for beauty and freedom of expression. (3) Jazz is open to everyone. (4) There is no prejudice in the world of jazz. (5) While there is some snobbery of a sort, it is based on personal accomplishment. (6) It has nothing to do with race, religion, or social or financial standing.

d. (1) Another social gathering place in our dorm is the main desk at 11:30. (2) 11:30 is the time of the mail delivery. (3) What a delivery! (4) Can you imagine four floorloads of girls waiting for mail? (5) Well, it's surely a sight!

e. (1) Anyone who goes to college away from home has to develop a certain amount of sophistication. (2) By sophistication I mean the ability to accept and understand people of all kinds. (3) When I left home to go to school, I also left familiar faces. (4) I was exposed to a college and a city devoid of a familiar face. (5) When encountering people, I have had to start learning how to meet them on their own terms because they treat me like an equal. (6) I was short-changed by a taxi driver and by a laundryman when I first arrived, so I now count my change carefully. (7) Since I live in a dorm, I have had to learn to live with all the other fellows in it. (8) Some are noisy, and some are quiet; some are interesting, and some are dull; some are amiable, and some are obnoxious—but they are all my neighbors and I must accept them. (9) I am having to learn about people. (10) I know a man living in my home town who went to our local high school and then went to our local college. (11) His high-school and college schoolmates were the same, and they all now have a large party once a year. (12) He has always lived in our town, except for one summer which he spent in New York. (13) He is a complacent man, he makes a good salary, and he has a nice family. (14) But he has become stagnant; he once told me the world is so dull that he really doesn't feel as if he has anything to live for. (15) This is an unsophisticated man because he doesn't know what man is.

f. (1) "If you can get through registration without losing your mind, you'll have no trouble getting through the year." (2) This well-worn quotation is supposed to serve as a conciliating factor to the confused neophyte who finally emerges from the chamber of horrors where registration is performed. (3) The first step is to fill out the forms. (4) I do not know whether I wrote my name, home address, school address, and degree program ten times or twenty, but I know it was not less than ten. (5) After this Herculean task, one receives not praises but a monstrous list of courses to take. (6) Then one is instructed to stand in line for an appointment with one of the registration clerks. (7) However, while you wait in line, everyone else is filling up the classes at the decent hours. (8) When your turn comes, you find your classes have to be at 8:30 in the morning or after 3:00 in the afternoon or over the lunch hour or on Saturdays. (9) Staggering out of this mess, one finds that his few remaining hours are filled by physical education. (10) Sometime later (who can keep track of the time now?) the class cards are presented to the Bursar in return for a blow to the pocketbook. (11) All my senses numbed, I did not feel the full effect of that blow until later. (12) That is, my parents felt the blow and hit the ceiling.

5. Compose a topic sentence of your own—a generalization about yourself, about college life, about some issue that interests you—or, if you prefer, choose one from the list below. Write three different paragraphs in support of the topic sentence (or pointer). In one, begin with the topic sentence; in another, end with it; in the third, place it in some other position in the paragraph. (As the position of the topic sentence shifts, you may want to alter its phrasing to make it fit more smoothly into your paragraph.) Finally, write a fourth paragraph in which you convey the same idea without putting it in a topic sentence.

    a. Owning a sports car can be a very educational experience.

    b. The child of divorced parents doesn't have any real sense of security.

    c. The choice of a college should be made by the student, not by his parents.

    d. To sell their products, advertisers make appeals which have nothing to do with the quality of the products themselves.

    e. My family has some unusual traditions.

    f. Tolerance and indifference are sometimes confused.

    g. The first week or two of college can be a very difficult time.

    h. Setbacks and disappointments make an important contribution to any young person's growth.

    i. There are fashions in make-up as well as in dress.

    j. Graduating from high school is an astonishing ritual.

    k. Popular songs fall into three main groups.

    l. The books on the best-seller list tell us about our culture.

6. From a current issue of *Harper's Magazine* or the *Atlantic* (or any other periodical your instructor suggests), select a long nonfiction article. Clip it, number the paragraphs, and submit the article with a brief analysis in which you answer these questions: (a) What is the author's main purpose? (b) To what extent do the opening and concluding paragraphs reveal an attempt to catch the reader's interest? In what ways do they relate to the central idea of the article? (c) Which of the paragraphs, if any, are simply structural, in the sense that they do no more than make a transition from one main section of the article to another? (d) Find the longest paragraph in the article. Explain—in terms of the purpose and content of the article—why it is the longest. (e) Find the shortest paragraph in the article. Explain—in terms of the purpose and content of the article—why it is the shortest. (f) Referring to the paragraphs by number, divide the essay into its main blocks or parts. (g) For each of these main blocks of paragraphs, state the chief method of development.

Chapter Five

PERSONAL EXPERIENCE PAPERS

For the energetic and groping mind, writing should be, first of all, a matter of inquiry—of inquiry in the sense both of reminiscence and of exploration.
Harold C. Martin

The four types of papers discussed in separate chapters of this book are likely to be assigned in any composition course. "Personal experience papers" (this chapter) are normally limited to courses in writing, but "Explanation papers" (Chapter 6), "Persuasion papers" (Chapter 7), and "Reference papers" (Chapter 11) are often required in other courses as well. The reference paper has special features and makes special demands, and since it is nearly always assigned at the end of a course, it is discussed in the last chapter of this book. Although the other three types of papers have much in common, they are here treated separately (roughly in order of difficulty) in order to focus on writing problems one by one.

The differences among personal experience papers, explanatory papers, and persuasive papers stem partly but not entirely from the material that goes into them. An account of a childhood trip to the zoo obviously belongs to the category of personal experience, while a discussion of the Common Market does not. Aside from extreme examples like these, however, it is not easy to say that such-and-such material *must* belong to one of these types of papers and not to another. (A paper on the Common Market may be explanatory or it may be persuasive.) As a matter of fact, the material for any of the three types of papers may be based on the writer's own experience, broadly considered. For a personal experience paper, a student who was a skiing enthusiast wrote an account of an afternoon of skiing that ended with his breaking his ankle; for an explanation paper he drew on his own experience and knowledge to describe exactly how to execute a difficult maneuver in skiing; for a persuasion paper he argued that one method used in training competitive skiers is superior to another. Naturally, he selected different material for the three, but for each paper he drew on a reservoir of incidents, facts, and convictions relating to his chief interest.

Material alone, then, need not distinguish the three types. A better basis for distinguishing them is the purpose of the writer. In a personal experience paper, as we are using the term, the writer aims to make the reader *share* what he has seen or done, live the experience as he has lived it. In an explanation paper, he aims to *inform* the reader, to clarify the subject for him, to increase his understanding of it. In a persuasion paper, he aims to *influence* the reader—to make him think or act in a certain way. Of course, either sharing or informing may be a means of influencing, but in a good paper one of these purposes is usually dominant.

The general characteristics of a personal experience paper are easy to state. Essentially the paper is autobiographical. The writer presents what he has seen or done or felt or learned in such a way that the reader believes in the reality of the experience. Incidents and people and places, reactions to and reflections about incidents and people and places—these make up the raw materials for papers intended to present and make real a fragment of the writer's experience.

Beyond this, however, it is hard to go; for even though an assignment may have specified to some degree the kind of experience and the approach to it, the choice of material is in a very real sense the writer's. Some general assignments for personal experience papers are these:

Tell about a single episode (or a series of related incidents) in such a way that the reader will understand the significance it had for you.

Describe a scene of violence you have participated in or have witnessed.

Describe a place that you are familiar with in such a way that the reader will grasp the special flavor and atmosphere it has for you.

Write a chapter of your autobiography representing some important stage in your development.

Give an account of an incident that reflects a sharp disagreement you have had with a friend, a parent, or someone in a position of authority.

Describe a person you know well, using only concrete details of physical appearance, mannerisms, habitual actions to convey something about his personality or character.

For all of these, although some boundaries have been established, you still have great freedom in choosing the material you will write about and the precise effect you will try to produce. And of course you will have even greater latitude if you are asked simply to write about something from your own experience that has struck you as funny or frightening or sad.

Even though the essence of a personal experience paper is that it *is* personal and even though everybody's experience differs from everybody else's, there are a few general guides to the *kind* of material likely to produce a good paper. The chief requirement is that the event or person or place have some meaning *for you*—it should have caught your imagination in some way, made an impression on you, taught you something. In some other types of papers, the writer's lack of interest in his material can to some extent be compensated for by hard work, but in a personal experience paper the damaging effects of lack of interest almost always reveal themselves in writing that is either dull, colorless, and perfunctory, or strained, artificial, and pretentious.

Many writers find that events that happened some time ago supply the best material. Memories of childhood, either pleasant or unpleasant, are often vivid and sharply focused. You may find that a childhood adventure viewed from the perspective of a few years takes on a more coherent shape than an episode you were involved in yesterday afternoon. But whether you are writing about something you experienced yesterday, last week, or ten years ago, choose material that interests you. The event need not be spectacular, the place need not be exotic, the person need not qualify as "the most unforgettable character I ever met"; but the event or place or person must have some meaning for you if you are to make it meaningful for your reader.

Once you have decided on the experience that will be the basic material for your paper, don't waste time fretting about whether it is sufficiently interesting or significant. Give yourself to the telling of it. If you recall the best storytellers you know, you will realize that they are the best not because they always have great stories to tell but because they do a great job of telling them.

"Telling" suggests narration, and because the majority of personal experience papers are cast in a chronological framework, narration will receive most attention in this chapter. Description, to be sure, is likely to be the dominant method of presenting an experience relating to persons or places, but even papers which are primarily descriptive often have a narrative thread running through them. Of the other methods of development discussed in Chapter 3, comparison and contrast and cause-effect analysis occasionally serve as the chief means of developing a paper based on personal experience, but more often they are subordinate to narrating what has happened or to describing what has been seen. Since the general problems of using narration and description in personal experience papers are quite similar, the next sections will deal mainly with the writing of narrative, with comments about writing description introduced as they seem necessary.

Tactical decisions

It is unwise simply to select an experience and begin writing. You need to think through the material and decide how it can be made most interesting to your reader. If the incident you choose is so familiar to you that you take its details for granted, it is helpful to back away mentally and imagine how it would have appeared to an observer. Thinking about some past experience for a time and recalling it at regular intervals helps stir up half-forgotten memories and sense impressions. One image will suggest another—the memory of a certain expression on your father's face on a certain long-ago Sunday afternoon may set up a chain of associations that brings a dozen, two dozen, three dozen details crowding after.

In a preliminary survey of your material you must make some important decisions: the "meaning" that the experience is to convey and how it is to be conveyed, the point of view most suitable to the material, and the style and tone of the paper. All these decisions should be made (at least tentatively) before you begin to write.

The meaning of the experience • Although an account of a personal experience is not expected to develop an abstract idea, it should have some central meaning. It should make a point; it should have a unified impact on the reader. You need, therefore, to decide early in planning your paper what meaning the experience has for you and, correspondingly, what meaning it is to have for your reader. In terms of a narrative, this is the significance of the incident or series of incidents; in terms of a description, it is the dominant impression made by the person or place.

Formulating a one-sentence statement of purpose (see Chapter 2, p. 43) will often help you decide on the precise meaning you want the account of the experience to convey. It is best to keep the statement simple and specific. "The services of the medical profession are of inestimable benefit to mankind" is pretentious in breadth and in style for an account of an appendectomy; much better would be the simple statement "While I was in the hospital for an appendectomy I began to appreciate the work of doctors and nurses." There is no point in using such words as *interesting, impressive, important, exciting* in your statement of purpose—and little point in using them in the paper itself. Adjectives expressing your intention of conveying such-and-such an impression will not persuade your reader you have done your work; on the contrary, they are likely to lead him to suspect that you have settled for the easiest (and least effective) way out.

Once you have decided what meaning the experience is to have for your reader—an attitude or a feeling or a generalization about the significance of the experience—you need to decide how to get it across. Will you tell the reader how you felt, what conclusions you came to as a result of the experience? Or will you let the experience speak for itself?

When the meaning of the experience is stated explicitly—when the writer tells what it meant to him—the statement often comes at the end of the paper, or in the form of a comment or reflection on the episode or event or scene. It may, however, serve as a starting point for the paper, as in the following opening paragraph:

> I cannot imagine how anyone could be so foolish as to assert that childhood is a time of bliss in which one's lack of maturity and knowledge keep him from real suffering. I certainly would not support such a statement, for I can think of not one but many incidents from my own limited experience which caused me to suffer as a child with a pain keener than any I feel now. My twelfth summer was just such a time. I was at camp, not for the first time nor the last.

Following this introduction, the paper narrates an incident at camp which supports the generalization in the opening paragraph. The real meaning of the event is made clear enough, and little further comment is required. The student concludes the paper succinctly and effectively:

> At length I convinced my mother to come for me, though by the time she agreed to do so I had recovered sufficiently to be ashamed

of my ever having been homesick. After all, it was not my first summer away. It was, however, my first contact with the real world, and remembering it now, I feel like crying still.

Comment like this is not obtrusive and is justified if it is made to seem proportionate to the experience. There is a danger, of course, in being too "talky," in sermonizing, or in making the experience assume cosmic importance when it is actually fairly run-of-the-mill. Although a paper on "My First Date" should have sufficient point to be worth writing— and reading—nobody expects it to carry a profound philosophical message. Experienced writers often keep comment to a minimum, believing that it is more effective to have the reader make the comment for himself. Of course, this requires the utmost care in selecting and presenting the details, for they must in a sense speak for themselves. In a narrative entitled "The Day I Killed the Pigeon," a student managed to make them speak most eloquently. The killing was accidental, and the effect on the narrator was profound. But he made no statement about his emotional reaction; there were no tears and no remorse, nor was any sympathy expressed for the dead bird. Instead, the writer made his point through a series of contrasts. Before the incident, everywhere he looked he saw beauty; after it, everywhere he looked he saw ugliness. (No, he didn't use the nouns "beauty" and "ugliness" or the adjectives "beautiful" and "ugly." He used contrasting images —the colors of fallen leaves, the taste of an apple, the glance of a girl; later, the slime and rubbish in the streets, the lurching of a drunken bum, dirty words scrawled on the side of a freight car.)

One way or another, directly or indirectly, a paper on personal experience should "carry" its meaning. What that meaning is, and hence what effect you want to produce in the reader, should be the first thing you settle on when planning the paper and the last thing you check in revising it. The meaning should determine what details you will select and how you will present them; it should also determine to a large extent the tone and style of the paper.

Point of view • Before starting a rough draft, you should decide what point of view is best suited to your material and your purpose. Defined most simply, point of view in narrative means the pronoun by which the writer refers to himself. Novelists experiment with various points of view, and these subtle variations are a complex feature of their technique. In factual narrative, however, point of view is relatively simple; a paper can be written in first, second, or third person.

The *I* (or *we*) paper is by far the most common in narrations of experience. The first person lends itself naturally to autobiographical narrative or to any account in which the writer plays a leading role. You may have been taught that too many *I*'s are offensive, but they are usually less conspicuous than they seem. The "I was there" account has the credibility of personal testimony, the vivid directness of first-hand observation.

The second person is seldom used throughout an entire paper, but it may be effective in a generalized bit of narrative, especially if you are giving directions the reader might follow. Though less intimate than the first person, *you* may have a similar suggestion of participation. It invites the reader to share the experience or the mood. The following paragraph takes the reader directly into the scene:

When you awake in the morning the air is clean and cold in the mouth as water from a hill stream. You listen—and hear the silence. With the odd feeling of having been transported magically into some boyhood memory, you turn your head on the pillow and through the window see the ancient Caledonian pines on the lower slopes and, beyond them, the mountaintops. This is the deer forest and you are here.—NEIL M. GUNN, "Deer Stalking in the Highlands," *Holiday,* Jan. 1957, pp. 60-61

When the context makes it clear that *you* is impersonal, nobody will object to it. But when it is used in such a way that the reader feels pulled into the situation suddenly and without justification, he is likely to retort mentally, "Who, me?" In this paragraph, the *you* of the last sentence invites such a retort.

During the freshman reception I stood in line for an hour to get a cup of punch. No one spoke to me except a gray-haired lady, who asked me if I had seen the dean. "Not since I registered last spring," I answered. She looked at me suspiciously, and I realized my mistake. You often make silly remarks like that in a strange situation where you feel embarrassed and out of place.

Occasionally in student papers the writer refers to himself in the third person, especially when writing about a typical or representative experience of "a new camper" or "the average freshman." This is almost always less effective than the "observer's point of view," in which the writer refers to himself as *I* and to his subject as *he, she,* or *they.*

A final possibility needs mentioning. In an effort to avoid the personal revelation of *I* and the direct address of *you,* students sometimes resort to *one,* which traditionally has substituted for *I, you, we,* "people in general," or anybody. But *one* is less favored now than it was in the past. Current objections to it are that it seems stilted, strained, and unsuitable in most contexts. It still has a place in Formal prose but usually sounds artificial in the more casual style used in most accounts of personal experience. In most of the papers you write, choose *I* or *we.* When the choice is between *you* and *one, you* is preferable. "Looking north, you see the mountains" is satisfactory, unless of course the pronoun changes abruptly to *I* in the next sentence. Occasionally *they* can also be used for the true impersonal. It saves the writer from the over-Formal *one* and from the formidable passive. "Spring, they say, is the season for romance" is simpler, easier, and altogether preferable to "Spring, one says, is the season for romance" or "Spring, it is said, is the season for romance."

For papers based on personal experience, *I* is the best choice for the narrator's "voice." It is simpler, more natural, and actually easier to sustain through a whole paper. Attention has been given to other possibilities because students often mistakenly assume that *you* or *one* or *an average Joe* is self-effacing and therefore more elegant or dignified or otherwise desirable. But a personal experience paper is above all *personal,* and the mask of impersonality often turns out to be a barrier to communication, not a means to it.

Once you have limited yourself to a first-person point of view you should be consistent. The reader may be confused if he is told not only what you are thinking but what everyone else in your story thinks. It is natural to describe what you —the teller—think and feel; but other characters can only be known by their appearance, conversation, and actions. You can say that Uncle Bill *seemed* to be thinking about getting back to the office, but if you say "Uncle Bill was thinking that he should get back to the office," you violate credibility, for in life you never really know what goes on in anyone's mind but your own. Here is an example of shifted point of view:

I pulled over and stopped the car, wondering what the policeman wanted and what I'd tell my father if I got a ticket. [Shift] The policeman thought to himself that kids who can't remember to turn on the headlights shouldn't be given licenses. But he softened up when he saw how scared I was.

[Revised:] I pulled over and stopped the car, wondering what the policeman wanted and what I'd tell my father if I got a ticket. Just as the officer came up to the window I noticed I'd forgotten the headlights. *I suspected* he was thinking that kids who can't remember to turn on the headlights shouldn't be given licenses. But he *seemed* to soften up when he saw how scared I was.

In description, point of view refers not so much to the identity of the writer (the *I* or the *you* or the *he*) as to the actual location of the writer in relation to what he is describing. In a description of a person or a place, the writer may indicate that he is looking at the person or place from a fixed position (across the room or from a hilltop); the reader expects, then, not to see *everything* but only what could logically be seen from that position. In giving a fairly full description of a town, the writer may find it more useful to adopt a moving point of view; he takes the reader on a tour of the town, indicating where one part of the town is in relation to another part, and so on. What can be seen by the writer (and so by the reader who is sharing his point of view) will depend on where he is at any one moment.

The choice of a point of view is very important in description, for it is the chief device in organizing the material. It determines the selection of details—what can be seen from the position of the observer—and the order in which they are presented. Directly or indirectly, the writer should indicate what his point of view is. In the following passage, the point of view is made explicit (the observer is standing on the sidewalk, looking into "the Reader's" office); the only change in the point of view is the natural enlargement of his field of vision as his eyes adjust to the dim light.

I am standing on the sidewalk. It is quiet and dark. The darkness extends into the Reader's office and is only broken by the mellow light of a small desk lamp at the far end of the room. The lamp is old and has a dusty, yellow paper shade. It casts a dim circle of light around the long wooden table. The warm light falls upon the two stacks of books at either end of the table. The light has an ancient color similar to that given off by the oil lamp which Rembrandt used in his portraits. This mellow light gives the room a bygone atmosphere. It also illuminates the Reader. The Reader is hunched over a book and sits in a hard wooden chair on the other side of the table. There isn't much of his gray hair left, and his high forehead has been wrinkled by time. The soft light that darkens these wrinkles also gives him a brown Italian color. A pair of small steel-rimmed glasses pinch in his tired face. He is wearing an old corduroy coat with leather arm patches. It hangs loosely on his thin body. He doesn't move about: he only reads.

My eyes have now adjusted to the dim light and begin to wander around the room. The walls are hidden behind high stacks of dusty books. There are more stacks behind the Reader—they extend upward and then finally merge with the darkened ceiling. An opening in the wall marks a darkened corridor. The corridor simply recedes —it seems to have no end. On the floor in front of the table there are broken shadows suggesting books which have not yet been read. The dim light falls on some books in the casement. Most of them have thick brown leather covers, some are gilt edged but the gold has lost its shine. Right next to the window are two milk cartons with red writing. A few containers have been stacked in with the books. Shadows hide their labels. The Reader moves! Fortunately he is only turning a page and doesn't see me. I have never seen his eyes because of the thick glasses. His old head is again tilted towards the open book. He continues to read—only the magnifying glass is moving. It is late and I return to the dormitory.

In the preceding passage, the point of view is clear and consistent. In the following, it is confusing and inconsistent.

Enter Parkway Gardens from the south on the South Park bus at 66th Street. From this point we see that Parkway is cut off from South Park by a strip of trees. The first courtway, like the other three, is built around a triangle, the center of which is like a miniature park. You will notice that the buildings are either three or eight stories tall. From the eighth floor we get a wonderful view of the neighborhood at night.

In part, the confusion stems from unjustified shifts in the point of view as indicated by the pronouns; the paragraph begins with the imperative "Enter" and then slides into "we," "you," and back to "we." Is the writer directing the reader or accompanying him? Does the second "we" refer to the shared view of writer and reader or to that of the writer and the other residents of Parkway Gardens? Besides this confusion, there is the alarming shift from a bus ride to the view from the eighth floor.

In writing narration or description, choose a point of view that can be made natural and plausible in terms of what you know about your material and what you want the reader to know. When you shift the point of view, give some indication to the reader so that he can go along. (See also Chapter 4, p. 131.)

Style and tone • The style and the tone of a paper are closely related to point of view. The level of language—one important element in both style and tone—should be made appropriate to the point of view. A recollection of a third-grade Christmas party might be written in something close to the language of the child who experienced the party, or it might be written in language that is natural to the adult who is recalling it; but the two should not be awkwardly intermingled.

A falseness sometimes creeps into personal writing, perhaps because the student feels self-conscious in writing about himself, perhaps because he is deeply involved emotionally in his subject and strains for fancy, high-sounding words to express his emotions. Self-consciousness seems to have been the reason for this disastrous first paragraph of a paper:

I invariably meet one evident obstacle when confronted with an autobiographical sketch. This is actuated by the need for explicit exposition of emotional experiences, which in my mind, is of distinct import in this type of writing. Here lies the problem. For the aspects which may appear maudlin to the reader, contrastingly give impetus to the writer. However this writer makes no apology, since the dealing with human emotions makes the use of any large degree of objectivity detrimental to his means.

To make matters worse, the student appears to have misunderstood the very nature of a personal experience paper. Even if he had expressed his point clearly and simply, there was no need for him to make it.

In another opening paragraph, which is by no means as bad, the writer verges on coyness and sentimentality. He gives the reader the impression that he is striking a pose.

A flower delights me. A sunset can hold me spellbound. Churning storm clouds excite and awe me. Nature's every mood, motion and creation affects me. I want to know and understand at once every particular of the cosmos, its relation to the whole, and the meaning of the sum. I often feel frustrated and inadequate because my senses so limit me that I can never realize concurrently the minutest details and the entirety. At the same time I feel joy and gratitude that I have been given so much.

The tone of a paper depends on the distance from which a writer views his subject matter and on his attitude toward it; the tone may be formal or informal, light or serious, subjective or objective. Tone is an intangible quality, easy to sense but hard to analyze. In the following selection the point of view, the language, and the tone are all inconsistent:

> The game that would terminate the Little League play-offs was about to commence. I strolled nonchalantly to the second base bag and gave it a kick, as I had seen professional players do. My dad was sitting in the first row. He was sure that I would bobble the first grounder that came my way. I was confident that nothing so ignominious would occur. My buddy, who was pitching, took his last practice pitch. He desperately hoped that the first batter would not succeed in reaching base. I spotted the catcher heaving the ball down to second and hastened over to take the throw.

Such writing is as distracting as a singer who is off key. The point of view should suit the material, and the language should suit the point of view. With the heavy words (*terminate, commence, nonchalantly, ignominious, hastened*) taken out and the point of view controlled, the passage might read like this:

> The last game of the Little League play-offs was just starting. From the field I spotted my father sitting in the first row. He looked as if he thought I'd bobble the first grounder that came my way, but I was feeling pretty sure of myself. I walked over to the second base bag and gave it a kick the way the pros do. Then I saw my buddy taking his last practice pitch, and when the catcher tossed to second, I ran over to take the throw.

Narrative movement

Kinds of narrative movement • Narratives can be classified in three broad types—dramatized, summarized, and generalized—depending on how much time is covered and how close the reader is brought to the action. All three types have their uses in accounts of personal experience, and choosing among them is relatively easy once the writer has settled on the incident or series of incidents he will present. The nature of the material should suggest the appropriate method or methods.

A *dramatized* narrative presents the action most fully, in direct scenes. As a rule, it includes conversation and details that give a relatively complete picture of what happened. It is the most vivid of the three types because it *shows* the reader an action instead of merely telling him what happened. It is best suited to an account of a single episode—an evening in a coffee house or an interview with the dean or a dispute with a friend.

The following is a passage of dramatized narrative from a student's paper entitled "A College Interview."

I was visibly shaken as I was shown to the creaky door that led into Harvard territory. The room smelled rankly of stale cigars. The odor, added to the way I felt, made me want to get the interview over as quickly as possible. I walked stiffly into the room and came face to cigar, so to speak, with my interviewer. His ruddy face was nearly obscured completely by a tremendous Bering cigar and volumes of dense black smoke.

"How do you do, Neddle?"

"Fine sir, and you?"

"Not too well. My back's been giving me a little trouble and the kids have been sick."

"Oh, that's too bad." I secretly laughed at his misfortune. "Oh sir, by the way, my name is not Neddle, but Neil."

This little interjection did not make the slightest impression on him. He continued to call me by the absurd name of Neddle.

"Neddle, why do you want to go to Harvard?"

"I think it's the best school in the country."

"Oh, I don't know about that, son. The University of Miami is not such a bad school."

"Well sir, yes, but I'd like to live in New England for awhile...."

"No matter, young man."

"Yes sir."

I knew how he was answering the questionnaire, for as he wrote he mumbled the answers. He didn't think I was too enthusiastic about Harvard.

Our conversation was interrupted by a telephone call. During the time my interviewer talked about his latest golf score, I looked around the office. I saw on the far wall a plaque with "the golfer's prayer" engraved on it. On his desk were numerous trophies from college and fraternity meets. I felt that sports were his only interest. I was worried even more by the fact that I was far from the athletic type. I had good reason to worry.

"Neddle, are you active in varsity football?"

"No sir, but I like to swim."

"Neddle, are you a track team star?"

"No sir, but I can swim pretty well."

"Do you play golf, volley ball or frisby?"

"No sir, but I do a lot of swimming."

When I told him that I did not play golf, the cigar had gone out and the fumes had cleared sufficiently for me to see his face. He looked stunned. On the questionnaire he wrote "no athletic activities." I guessed that people did not swim at Harvard.

"How are your grades in high school?"

"Good, sir, I had a straight 'A' average."

"What is your rank in class?"

"I'm first in the senior class, sir."

"Do you participate in any social activities, dancing or anything?"

"Yes sir, I swim and dance."

"Do you belong to any clubs?"

"Yes sir, I am an officer in six school clubs and am a member of other extracurricular activities."

He marked on the form "limited social activities."

At this point the interviewer had a little talk with me about the merits of a small school such as Oglethorpe or Slippery Rock. He thought that I was not the type of person who would like the intellectual atmosphere of Harvard. He felt I emphasized swimming too much over my class studies. I looked a bit dejected at that moment; consequently the interviewer smiled mildly if not mechanically and ushered me swiftly toward the door. By the time I got home I realized that Harvard was not the school for me. I knew that I should go to a school where I could get my degree in the American crawl or back stroke.

In papers like this one, where dialog has more than incidental importance, it can be a useful device for revealing character and motivation and for unfolding relationships, but it needs to be done well if it is to be effective. Many student writers produce conversation that differs from the rest of their writing only by being enclosed in quotation marks. Not only does each character sound like every other character, but all the speeches use the vocabulary, syntax, and style of the narrative framework. Careful observation of how people really talk will show what's wrong with this. To be convincing, dialog must be realistic; it will be realistic only if it uses the words and constructions of spoken English and is suitable to the person represented. Ordinarily that means using contractions and clipped expressions, the grammar natural to everyday speech. The first step in learning to write good conversation is to listen to yourself and others talk. Really *listen*.

Yet a transcript of actual speech will not seem real. We depend so much on facial expression, gesture, and tone of voice that our language transformed into mere written words seems jumbled and unnatural. Credible dialog is a *selection* from actual speech; the writer gives it clarity and consistency.

Speech peculiarities should be suggested, not reproduced literally. Even the most realistic novelists do not give all the profanity and vulgarity of their lustier characters. To represent the grammar of Nonstandard English exactly is not necessary; it can be suggested by avoiding obvious literary and Formal constructions, by inserting an occasional Nonstandard form, and by using the sentence movement of spoken English. Pronunciation also should be suggested, not reproduced. After all, if anyone's talk was spelled phonetically, most of the words would look strange. *Localisms,[1] if appropriate to the speaker and if used sparingly, are more effective in suggesting regional speech than the respelling of every third word. A few dropped *g*'s and a few vowel sounds spelled as the speaker pronounces them (*idee* for *idea,* for example) will do a great deal to suggest the regional or social quality of a person's pronunciation. But only a few are necessary; a whole page speckled with apostrophes and phonetic spellings only distracts the reader.

The speech tags or stage directions (*he said* and *she replied*) should be chosen with care. Used sparingly, specific verbs like "whispered" or "yelled" are more effective than a continuous sequence of *said*'s. On the other hand, it is possible to go too far in searching out unusual variations. Once the give and take of a conversation has been established, tags can be omitted. When they are used, they can be varied in position; the identification of a speaker may introduce, interrupt, or conclude a quotation. (Frank asked, "But what is he doing here?" "But what," Frank asked, "is he doing here?" "But what is he doing here?" Frank asked.) Above all, they should not be made conspicuous, either by monotonously repeating the same ones or by straining too hard for novelty with verbs like *affirmed* or *expostulated.*

To introduce or conclude a quotation, verbs referring to the act of speaking should be used, not verbs referring to facial expressions or gestures. Such sentences are incongruous:

"I wonder where she put the dishes," he *grinned* [... he asked, grinning].

Mac *pointed,* [.] "In the cupboard, I imagine."

---

[1]Throughout this book, references to *Index* articles are indicated by an asterisk (*) .

When conversation is made credible and realistic, it offers an effective means of presenting brief episodes, especially those which reveal significant relationships between individuals. But it is hardly efficient when the central action extends over a period of time. In most papers it is used for only brief stretches of the narrative.

Summarized narrative is the typical method for an account of what happened over an extended period of time. It is more economical than dramatized narrative because it condenses the action. When well written, it gives a sense of rapid movement. It may be less vivid than a dramatization because the reader does not "see" the action taking place, but in some ways it is more flexible. The writer need not try to represent *actual* time as he lived it but can compress long stretches (when that is desirable) or extend those parts of the action that are most significant. Because he usually represents himself at some distance from the action, he can also bring in (more naturally perhaps than in dramatized narrative) his reflections on and interpretations of events. Because summarized narrative permits a wider range in time and place and the full development of an attitude or a situation, it is the usual method of narrating related incidents that together make up a unit of autobiography or biography, such as experiences at a summer camp or an account of a personal relationship that evolved over a period of time.

The following is a personal experience developed through summarized narrative.

My Confirmation

1. Before going into the specific details of my own Confirmation, perhaps it is necessary to relate a few of the laws and customs of the Jewish ceremony of Confirmation, or to use the Hebrew term, Bar Mitzvah. When a Jewish boy reaches the age of thirteen, he has become, for religious purposes, a man. He is responsible then for his own behavior, and his father is no longer held accountable for the boy's misdeeds. This ceremony of being accepted into religious manhood makes up part of an ordinary morning service in the synagogue on a Sabbath about the time the boy is thirteen years old. It is a very joyous occasion and often large parties are held celebrating the event.

2. In synagogues which hold services in the traditional manner, a portion of The Five Books of Moses, or the Pentateuch, is read in Hebrew each Sabbath morning. This reading is divided into seven portions, and for each part a different worshiper is called to chant

the Hebrew blessings for the reading which is to follow. Only a man who has been Bar Mitzvah may chant these blessings, and it is on the morning of his Confirmation that a Jewish boy first performs this religious act.

3. My Bar Mitzvah was scheduled for September 9. Months earlier, in April, my religious school instructor began to teach me the blessings and their intricate melodies. By listening carefully to the teacher and to boys who were further along in their preparations, I gradually mastered the benedictions.

4. Then came the difficult part of my preparation for Confirmation. Immediately after the reading of the portion from the Pentateuch, a section from the Prophets is chanted in Hebrew. The Bar Mitzvah celebrant has the honor of chanting this portion on the Sabbath of his Confirmation. Since these portions can be many pages long, it is impossible to remember the different melodies of each one, and therefore a system of notes has been devised. These notes are small marks which appear above and below the Hebrew letters and show how each word is to be sung. After I had learned the various blessings, I began to study the notes used in the Prophetic readings.

5. By listening to other boys chant the portions that they were preparing for their Bar Mitzvahs, I gradually learned how the notes are used. Then my teacher started to instruct me as to how the notes were used in the portion that I was to chant. At first it seemed like an impossible task, but after a few weeks of constant repetition, I had learned that all-important Prophetic portion.

6. Now it was the end of June, and I had the whole summer vacation in which to practice before my Bar Mitzvah day, the second Saturday in September. A short speech in English is also usually given by the Bar Mitzvah celebrant, but I did not need to begin work on that until the end of the summer.

7. Meanwhile, my family was making plans to celebrate the happy occasion. Mother decided to serve lunch in the community hall of the synagogue after the services. All of the guests at the ceremony and the Rabbi, Cantor, and other officials of the Congregation were invited. She was also planning an "open-house" for Saturday evening especially for those who would not be able to celebrate with us during the day. I was looking forward to these parts of the celebration for two reasons: first, because by that time I would have completed the blessings, Prophetic reading, and speech; and, second, because I would be the center of attention. All of us like to be in the limelight at least once in a while, and I was no exception to this rule.

8. At the end of August my teacher returned from his vacation, and he and I began work on my speech. I wrote a rough outline for it, and he prepared the finished product. The few days remaining before my Confirmation were more than enough in which to learn

the speech and also to rehearse the whole service until I practically knew it by heart.

9. After much anxious waiting, the big day finally arrived. I awoke very early that morning and lay in bed worrying about what would happen if I made a mistake. My father, brother, and I were among the first to arrive for the beginning of the services. My father and brother took seats with the other worshipers, but because I was being confirmed that morning, I sat on the dais with the Rabbi, Cantor, and the President of the Congregation. During the early part of the service I could see many familiar figures—uncles, aunts, cousins, and school chums—taking their seats.

10. I joined in the prayers with the rest of the Congregation, but my thoughts were, of course, on the part I was to play that morning. After about an hour and a half it was time for the part of the service in which I was to participate. The Cantor, in his black robe and elaborate prayer shawl, arose and, in a clear baritone, chanted in Hebrew that I was to come forward. I arose from my seat and proceeded weakly to the reader's lectern. My heart was beating loudly in my chest, and my mind seemed fuzzy; but I remembered the long hours of practice, and I sang the blessings and the Prophetic portion as if I were alone with my teacher.

11. Following the reading from the Prophets came the usual prayers, and then the Rabbi called on me to give my small speech. In it I thanked my parents for seeing to it that I received a good Jewish education and also thanked my teachers for providing that education. I asked the Lord to help me to be a good, observing Jew and to be a loyal American citizen.

12. When my speech was over, I listened while the Rabbi directed his sermon to me. He said what any clergyman would say to a young person at his Confirmation. He told me that I was now a responsible member of the religious community and that I was obligated to continue my study of my religion and the heritage of my people. He stressed also the need for my practicing the religious observances that I had learned.

13. After the services, at the luncheon, all of my friends and relatives who had come to the ceremony congratulated me and said that I had done very well. This, of course, made me very pleased, but, nevertheless, I knew that compliments were paid to every Bar Mitzvah celebrant and that I probably had done no better than the average. I realized that I had accomplished something in preparing for my Bar Mitzvah but that there was an infinite storehouse of knowledge into which I had not yet ventured.

14. Late that night, when all the guests had left and the "open-house" was ended, I began to realize that the words I had spoken that morning were not merely parroted but were a true reflection of

my feelings. I sincerely felt the gratitude I had expressed in my speech for the training I had received, and I was truly resolved to continue my religious education, because I realized how little of the Jewish tradition I really knew and how important it was for me to know of the people from which I come.

The first two paragraphs provide general information about the ceremony (unnecessarily complicated by the ambiguous use of the word "portion") and its significance; the last one sums up the significance of Bar Mitzvah for the narrator himself. Between this introduction and conclusion the student follows a chronological sequence covering the relevant events of the five-month period. In general, this sequence is well handled. The indications of time spans are clear, and there is a sensible telescoping of time spans within which nothing of major significance occurs: "Now it was the end of June"— "At the end of August." Since the summer months are devoted to the study of material already introduced, he takes the opportunity to describe the relevant activities of other members of the family: "Meanwhile, my family had been making plans . . ." Throughout, the events and the order in which they take place are made clear. For an account of this kind, the method of summarized narrative is appropriate.

Some criticisms of the paper should be made, however. For a personal experience paper, it does not give enough insight into the thoughts and feelings of the narrator. Paragraphs 3, 4, and 5 describe the actual tasks the writer has to accomplish in preparation for his confirmation. In general, the description is adequate; we, as readers, see what he was up against. But the writer does nothing to suggest his own feelings during these months of demanding work. We cannot share his sensations of awe or boredom or determination or depression or triumph or achievement, because he never mentions them in his account. The one indication of difficulty—"At first it seemed like an impossible task"—is canceled out in the same sentence with the phrase, "but after a few weeks. . . ." Notice, too, that "it seemed like an impossible task" is used instead of the personal "At first I felt that it was an impossible task."

Paragraph 7 does give an indication of personal emotion: the writer tells us that the celebrations following the ceremony would be, for him, a time of relief and of satisfaction; and in paragraph 9 he mentions worrying on the morning of the "big day." But immediately he passes over this moment of concern, so that, as an element in scale, it seems to be of very minor importance.

When the climactic moment finally arrives, the writer makes some attempt to give his narrative dramatic effect. He speaks of proceeding "weakly" to the lectern, with his heart beating "loudly." But here, too, the moment is over almost before it has begun, and nothing at all suggests the feeling of relief that would naturally follow such an accomplishment.

The modesty of the student upon receiving congratulations leads logically into his excellent conclusion. Despite some trite diction, this final section, revealing as it does the mature outlook of a youngster who has just completed a ceremony symbolizing the attainment of maturity, has the very note of personal intimacy that the earlier paragraphs lacked.

This lack of personality gives "My Confirmation" a kind of flatness, a defect which is best remedied by vivid details. Telescoping time spans is all very well when the period being condensed has no importance to the narrative, but moments of climax deserve precisely the opposite treatment—they should be extended, through specific details, so that their full effect is realized. The reader, after all, wants to share the experience, not just hear about it.

In *generalized* narrative, the least common of the three types, repeated or representative actions are used to describe typical events, to characterize a person in his habitual actions, or to show a way of life by telling of usual or customary actions. The verbs are often formed with *used to* or *would*. Adverbs like *always* or *frequently* also generalize the action, as in this account of a father's automobile driving:

Dad always blamed the clutch for these bucking starts, and in fact carried a face-saving can of Neatsfoot Oil in the tool kit, so that he could anoint the clutch after particularly embarrassing takeoffs which ended in stalls.

To drive with Dad through Nantucket's alley-sized streets was a spine-chilling, as well as a neck-cracking, experience. And it didn't add to our peace-of-mind to know that scores of Nantucketers, including some of the old surrey-driving cap'ns were just learning how to operate cars.

There weren't any stop-streets in those days, but I doubt if Dad would have stopped anyway. He usually chose to ignore warning signs, on the grounds that compliance would only encourage the city fathers to new dictatorial extremes, such as cluttering up the beautiful landscape with even more signs. He also insisted that the Nantucket speed limit, plainly marked at twenty-five miles an hour, was probably meant to apply only to horses.—FRANK B. GILBRETH, Jr., *Of Whales and Women,* p. 224

A student uses generalized narrative effectively in this paragraph from a paper describing dormitory life. (Notice, though, the unnecessary shifts in point of view. *You* would have been a satisfactory choice of pronoun throughout—*If you happen . . . . Even your phone calls . . . .*)

There is no such thing as privacy in the dorm. The most ferocious sign on the door is flagrantly disregarded by a zealous sweater hunter or a frantic procrastinator who wants to know what the assignment is an hour before it is due. If one happens (purely by luck) to be sitting alone and quietly thinking, a friend who wanders in is bound to assume you are in a state of morbid depression. Such a budding young psychologist will not be satisfied until she has uncovered some deep rooted problem as the real cause of your solitary deliberations. Even one's phone calls must take place amidst a group of seemingly nonchalant but actually curious listeners.

The two preceding examples show that generalized narrative can convey a sense of immediacy and drama. But it will do so only if the details are representative and also have some interest in their own right. When badly handled, the method can be vague and aimless, as in the following brief passage:

Summers we spent in our beach cottage. For us children the first week or two was an unhappy time. We really did not know what to do with ourselves. Our parents were kept busy setting up the cottage for summer living. We were in the way. We would miss our friends in the city. After a while, we could adjust to the change. Our activities would fall into a new pattern, and by the end of the summer we were always sorry to have to leave.

The absence of concrete details and specific episodes makes the paragraph a failure. The reader cannot share the experience of adjusting to the pattern of summer life because he is not given the necessary details.

Because it establishes a distance between the writer and the experience, generalized narrative is often appropriate when mood or atmosphere is of chief importance. Even when the details are few—as they often are in generalized narrative— they will, if well selected, convey the essence of a repeated or representative action.

In many personal experience papers, dramatized, summarized, and generalized narrative are used in combination. A paper may begin with a bit of generalized narrative and go on to a series of interlocking summaries and scenes, the less important episodes being presented in summarized narrative and the most important or most revealing in dramatized narrative. The choice of method should depend on the kind of action narrated and the effect to be produced by it. An example of how the three types of movement work together is this incident in the life of a national park ranger and his wife.

[Generalized:] It seems Bill is always on duty. If we are making a social call, driving into the city—inside the park or out—he never passes up anything that looks suspicious, or a person who might be in need of help. [Summarized, the immediate situation:] We were on our way to church one Sunday when he spied a car parked on a deserted stretch of road, and he stopped to look it over. The car was unoccupied, and nothing about it appeared unusual—I would have guessed that it belonged to a fisherman who was down at the river teasing the trout. But before continuing, Bill paused for a quick survey of the surrounding area—and stopped. [Dramatized, direct action:] Barely visible through the dense shrubbery was the deathly white face of a woman staring directly at us.

"You all right?" Bill called.

The woman's lips moved spasmodically, but she made no reply.

"Don't move!" he yelled, seizing his gun from the seat beside me.

He disappeared into the brush, and a moment later I heard a shot. Then he was making his way back to the road with the woman, unconscious in his arms.

"Fainted," he said, laying her on the pine needles while he treated her for shock.

"What happened?"

[Summarized, past events learned from conversation:] It seemed the woman had been attracted by the profusion of wild flowers growing off the road and while preoccupied had stepped on a rattlesnake. Luckily her foot rested so near the snake's head that it couldn't strike, but she knew the second she raised her foot to make her escape it would instantly sink its fangs into her ankle. She had stood there with the snake rattling and curling about her legs for what must have seemed hours before we happened along. When Bill shot off its head, her relief was so intense she fainted in his arms. When Bill asked her afterwards why she didn't jump when she stepped on the snake, she said she had been too frightened to move.—Margaret Merrill, *Bears in My Kitchen*, pp. 145-146

Time sequence • A narrative must have a time order. The simplest pattern is to have one action follow another as it happened in the original experience. The time span of narrative may vary greatly, from a few minutes to several weeks or even years. Generally speaking, the shorter the time span, the fewer problems you will have. If a long period of time is covered by several episodes, clear transitions are needed. If the action is short and continuous, most or all of the narrative can be dramatized. If several events are covered, more of the action must be generalized and summarized.

Occasionally you may want to shift temporarily to an earlier time—the "cutback" or "flashback" used so often in movies, television plays, and fiction. Such an interruption of the time order is often effective in compressing the time span and in avoiding long preliminary explanations. A cutback is usually summarized narrative, but it may be dramatic. The shift in time should be unmistakably clear and should seem a natural part of the paper. It is often signaled by an expression like "I remember" or "that was when." The following selection is from an account of a man's visit aboard a carrier on which he had served twelve years before. The cutback is obviously well suited to such a subject.

The end of the gangway, where I was standing, rested on the hangar deck. The deck looked narrower than I remembered it. There was a bulkhead that hadn't been on the old Randolph. I told this to the petty officer, and he said that there were spaces on the other side of the bulkhead, and that the flight deck above was wider than it used to be, with a greater overhang. I noticed that a couple of whaleboats and motor launches and the captain's gig were stored aft. There were no planes, of course; they were now probably at some naval airfield.

Perhaps it was the absence of planes—anyway, I suddenly remembered the night off Okinawa when I left the after deckhouse and, not realizing how dark it was (the ship, of course, was blacked out), started forward on the hangar deck and soon found myself bumping into parked aircraft. I got down on my hands and knees and tried to crawl between the planes, but, in the intense darkness, I still collided with wheels and propeller blades. Finally, when I was in real desperation, unable to find my way either forward or aft, I spied a tiny dot of light on the starboard bulkhead, and managed to make my way to a ladder and then, feeling very sheepish, to a passageway leading forward.—MONTGOMERY NEWMAN, "Return to the Randolph," originally published in *The New Yorker*, May 11, 1957, p. 130

Occasionally, too, you may want to use the present tense rather than the past tense to describe vivid impressions. In the following passage the use of the "historical present" makes the reader feel that the scene is before his eyes.

A little wait at Dublin station, time enough to write one's name in tin for a penny and weigh oneself for another. The May wind is bitter. Some American women are shivering on a bench, huddled in their plastic cloaks. One of them goes to the refreshment room in search of hot coffee—comes back and says: "Don't go in there, it's just dismal." The train is an omnibus. Four nuns make a quick dash to install themselves by the four front windows, which they open. The wind rushes in; it beats on the plastic garments of the Americans and disturbs their hair nets; they suffer for a while and then one of them goes forward: "Pourdon me, could you close the windows?" But the nuns, in their veiling and men's boots, are feeling the heat; they observe custody of the eyes and pretend not to have heard. If the temperature totters into the forties the Irish, as it were, reach for their solar topees. There are many farmers in the train who have been to an agricultural show; they, too, are feeling the heat, there are sighs and groans and mopping of brows. They scrape manure off their trousers with knives and talk like an Abbey Theatre play. "I've had another anonymous letter from Dooley O'Sullivan." Delicious dinner of bacon and eggs and then we arrive at Limerick Junction. The cold sun is still shining, though it is now half past nine.—NANCY MITFORD, "The Other Island," in *The Water Beetle*, pp. 114-115

Although the preceding paragraph has, as it were, a narrative envelope, it is obviously unnecessary to mark off the passing of time, for the chronology is subordinated to the descriptive details and the revealing bits of conversation. In narratives where it is necessary to keep the time pattern clear, time indicators will be much more prominent. Mainly these are adverbs (*then, later, next, soon, afterwards, instantly*), adverbial phrases (*after dinner, a week later, for the next ten minutes*), and adverbial clauses (*when he had finished, before the bus arrived*). These time indicators ordinarily occur near the beginnings of sentences. It is wise, however, to try to vary their position and to avoid repeating the same ones too often.

Writing the paper

By the time you begin to write, you should have made decisions about the meaning of the experience or the dominant impression to be conveyed, about the point of view to be employed, and about the general style and tone of the paper. If you are writing a narrative, you should have figured out which kind of narrative movement is most appropriate to the material and whether any modification of strict chronological sequence is advisable. In thinking through these matters, you will be refreshing your memory of the actual experience—the best preparation for writing a paper that makes an experience come alive. The three major problems in writing the paper are selecting the details, unifying the paper, beginning and ending the paper.

Selecting details • Papers about personal experience require a high proportion of concrete details. (See Chapter 4, pp. 112-117.) During an actual visit to the dentist or a struggle to land a rainbow trout, sense impressions predominate. Abstractions, if they come at all, come after the experience is over. In narrating the experience, then, you need to convey your sense impressions, not your afterthoughts. Abstractly, *pain* is "a distressing sensation in a part of the body"; concretely, it is the throbbing of an abscessed molar or the whirring of a dentist's drill in a cavity. Which type of presentation is more likely to communicate the effect of an actual experience?

Another advantage of concreteness is that it individualizes an experience. One experience differs from another chiefly in its details. Abstractly, one automobile race is similar to all other automobile races; concretely, each race is unique. The special flavor of an experience can be caught only in images and specific actions.

Concrete details *show* the reader an action instead of merely *telling* him that it happened. The reader can visualize a statement like "Frankie tapped his toe and took quick puffs of his cigarette" and from it deduce that Frankie was nervous or angry. But given a general, abstract statement like "Frankie exhibited signs of nervousness," he cannot convert it into the image that was in the writer's mind. He probably will not visualize anything at all, but if he does, the image is likely to be fuzzy and is sure to be different from what the writer intended. It takes concrete sights, sounds, and smells to recreate an experience.

Students' personal experience papers often suffer from a sparseness of concrete details. Especially in a descriptive paper, the details may be simply too few to permit the reader to form any valid impression of the person or place being described. Or they may be flat, lacking in any individualizing quality. Selecting the right details is as important as having enough of them. When you begin to write a paper, you should have on hand many more details than you can use. From among the thousands of sense impressions that make up any experience, you should select those which convey the essence of it. You should strip away the incidental, everyday details that might be used to describe any person or place and concentrate on those that make the particular person or place distinctive. In the following paragraph, a student has singled out those details of climate that convey an impression of Pasadena as he has seen and known it.

Pasadena is in a partial desert, and if the artificial water supply were removed, Pasadena would revert to its natural condition of aridness. When clouds appear, they look like heavy haze, and usually rain merely splatters on the ground and disappears. The water from the rain does not clean the soot from the buildings but makes a thin layer of mud, which dries the next day. The newer buildings, which are pale in color, soon take on signs of age because of the soot and the absence of rain. When fog comes during the winter, it smells like leather but pleasantly hides the view of the city from the people of Pasadena; but hail cruelly forces the people to seek shelter in the buildings. Not even the sun is a friend, for a clear day reveals a city that reeks with languor and stagnation.

By contrast, this description of sunrise on the seashore is thoroughly unsuccessful; the diction is trite and the images hackneyed.

Already along the horizon a warm tint has appeared. Deep choppy waves and drab sky await in suspense the sun's first appearance. Shortly after the lower clouds have been brightened, the crest of the sun materializes throwing out its beams in mad conquest of Night. These groping rays catch the crests of lively water, adorning them all with sparkling miniature suns. The giant red ball rises with majesty and its warmth falls against sea and rock. Night is defeated and Day's glorious reign continues once again.

Unifying the paper • Many of the matters already discussed in this chapter are devices for achieving unity. Chief among these devices is the choice of the dominant impression or the meaning of the experience that is related. Physical point of view is another such device (What can be seen from your physical location?). Tone or psychological point of view is still another (What is your attitude toward your material?). And the unity of a paper derives in part from the way the details feed into each other to produce the dominant impression.

Students sometimes find it more difficult to unify a narrative than to unify a description. The reason, perhaps, is that the writer takes on two jobs at once: (1) he must supply descriptive details of characterization, motivation, and scene to explain the action and make it appear a coherent whole, while at the same time (2) he must keep the action moving to create the illusion of something happening in chronological sequence. Long passages of static description destroy the unity of a narrative by shifting attention from the action; on the other hand, the absence of descriptive details may impair unity by making the action seem unmotivated. The trick is to find the right tempo or pace for the narrative and to bring in descriptive details without impeding the forward movement of the action.

In the following excerpt from an account of a bullfight, the narrative is kept moving (especially by the well-chosen verbs and verbals), but at the same time enough descriptive details are introduced for the reader to see and understand the action.

As though crazed, the bull loped into the center of the ring, snorting, flinging his body to toss away those splinters of steel that bit ever deeper into his muscles and the red streaks of blood turned to broad, gleaming patches of scarlet that matted the black, bristling hair of his back.

Then, to his right, another man appeared. The bull turned to face his adversary, settling solidly on his four hoofs, then advanced. The man advanced, holding two more red and green and white sticks tipped with steel. Pained, the bull pawed the sand, lowered his horns, sighting his target, and moved forward with quicker momentum, and the two steel tips tore and widened the gash in his neck. On he came and on came the man, and, at the point of meeting, when the horns of the bull seemed about to gore the intestines and you could hear the bull's vast lungs expelling a mighty breath, the man rose into the air, shooting the steel-tipped darts downward and into the gaping, bloody wound. The man was in the air when the sticks left his hands, and, upon landing lightly upon the sand, he leaped aside, veering from the searching horns, escaping to safety.

The bull now stood and lifted his head and bellowed, raging, looking about for the vanished target, heaving his vast black shoulders and feeling the steel slashing his flesh and the streaks of blood now turned to rivulets. The peak of muscle back of his neck gushed blood.—RICHARD WRIGHT, *Pagan Spain*, pp. 101-102

Beginning and ending the paper • The beginning of a personal experience paper should capture the reader's attention. Although a reader may excuse a little dullness in the opening of a paper on a subject he is eager to learn something about, he is not likely to excuse it in a paper which is intended to make him share an experience. From the start, he should be convinced that the experience is worth sharing.

The family's debate about a vacation spot, the task of packing the car, and the values of relaxation would not combine into a good opening for a paper on "Fishing at Rice Lake." Ponderous generalities about the necessity of education in the modern world would alienate the reader of a paper on "A Freshman's First Day." Two unsatisfactory opening paragraphs have been quoted earlier in this chapter (p. 168).

Here are two that do a much better job of setting the tone of the paper and engaging the reader's attention:

"Thrift and swift" was the motto of Sandy's Drive-In, where I used to work. "Thrift" referred to the low prices (hamburgers for 15c) and "swift" to the speedy service. In the noon rush hour as many as 600 hamburgers might be sold. Four men produced the food and drinks—one working at the grill, one cooking french fries, one preparing buns, and one making milk shakes. I was one of the three window men who took and filled orders. We were responsible for the "swift" part of the motto, and the manager made sure that we had something to work for besides our meagre pay. Each window man had his own cash register, which recorded the number of sales. Whoever had waited on the fewest customers by the end of the rush hour had to mop the floor. I was a window man for two years, and I am happy and somewhat proud to say that in my second year I never had to mop the floor.

I was sitting in the cafeteria waiting for Jack and too worried to eat. He had been called to the principal's office an hour ago, and I knew he was in trouble. He had been caught speeding the night before. This wasn't the first time. According to the rules, he would be suspended, and that would ruin his last year of high school. I was still worrying when he rounded the corner and headed for my table. He was coming fast and just when he got close enough to throw his lunch bag at me, he slammed into Mike, who was backing out of his chair.

"Cut it out," snarled Mike.

Suddenly the two of them were on the floor, clawing at each other.

Like the opening of a paper, the ending should be straightforward and to the point. It should not be a series of generalities or a weak apology. Personal narratives seldom need an elaborate summarizing close. The most effective ending may be a brief restatement of the central idea, a descriptive detail, or a bit of dialog—whatever will suggest the overall unity of the experience and strike a note of finality. The conclusions of the two narratives whose beginnings are given on page 185 do strike such a note:

At the end of the line I could sight the regular customers, the clerks, the barbers, and the secretaries who came every day. They were smart enough to wait until the worst of the rush was over, and I was smart enough to give them the best service I could. They never hesitated over an order the way the kids did, never complained about our limited menu the way the tourists did, never wanted to chat the way the old folks did. Some of them never spoke except to say "Same." I used to marvel that they could eat the same thing day after day. But I'm thankful they could. They were the ones who saved me from mopping the floor.

After several long minutes, Jack returned, carrying a broom and dustpan. I expected an outburst of despair, but, as he swept up the broken dishes and scattered food, he only smiled sheepishly and remarked, "Boy, did that make me feel better!"

Exercises

1. Study the paper reprinted below and prepare answers to these questions: (a) What function is served by paragraph 2? By paragraph 3? (b) How successful is paragraph 5 in its handling of the time sequence? In its handling of point of view? (c) Is the paper successful or not in conveying the meaning of the experience?

Spectators

(1) One Friday last fall I was coming home after a trip downtown. After a twenty-minute ride on a horribly crowded train, I was waiting for a bus on the corner of Wentworth and 59th. It was about 5:30, and it was already getting dark. Along with about twenty other people, I waited for the bus that would take me home. Most of them were probably downtown office workers; stenographers, receptionists, and salesgirls. Also, there were several men dressed like laborers, probably a street repair crew. There was no talk. We just stood waiting.

(2) We stood facing the street, directly in front of a small, dingy beer tavern. Across from us also was a tavern. On the diagonal corner was a drug store, and on the fourth corner was another tavern.

(3) I was getting tired from standing, so I walked back to the wall of the tavern and leaned against it. I watched the crowd of people

in front of me and thought about them. Somehow all these silent figures in their cool-weather coats seemed to me to be devoid of sense or feeling. I wondered if they would have reacted at all if someone had stuck pins in them. Anonymous people huddled in a crowd often make that impression on me. They seem to be just blobs of life, not concerned about anything outside of themselves.

(4) I sighed with relief when I saw the bus coming. I thought that it would be good to get home. Out of merely existing, and into my home, where there was food and warmth and rest and life.

(5) The bus was coming to a stop. At this time, I pushed my way into the crowd to get on before some of the others. The doors opened. I felt pushing people behind me and resistance from those in front. Suddenly, I sensed something was wrong, or maybe I heard something. I glanced over my shoulder. I saw an old man (perhaps sixty) with an expression of horror on his face. I was shocked and looked more closely. Behind him was poised a tall, nondescript man. His hands were under the old man's long coat. His right hand found the old man's right hip pocket; his left hand, the left pocket. As if lightning had hit me, I froze. My heart beat furiously. After a moment, I realized what the situation was. Suddenly I felt super-human. I felt as though I could have run a mile in three minutes; I felt as though I could have defended myself against anyone. I realized the old man was only five feet from me. If some man would help me.... But then I was nauseated as I saw the old man struggling futilely. He reached behind him to grasp the robber's hands. He wheezed. His tortured, plump face was deathly pale. His cap fell off, his white hair was mussed. The robber still did not have the wallet. They struggled. I looked at the people flocking on the bus. I felt panic. Still they struggled. I heard the bus driver shout, "Somebody help.... That man is being robbed!" Several women said, "Why doesn't somebody do something?" Still they struggled.

(6) The last person got on the bus, and the driver closed the doors. I watched from the window. Still they struggled. Then the robber spun around, throwing the old man down. He hit him hard, I do not know where but I think near the head. The old man gave up the struggle. The robber turned the old man over, reached into his pocket, and pulled out the wallet. As the bus pulled away, I saw the robber running north, up Wentworth. I also saw the old man, lying face down in the gutter, in the spit, and dirt, and rain water, and cold darkness, alone.

(7) We are scum. We are sheep.

2. Rewrite as summarized narrative the passage from the student paper quoted on pp. 170-171. Then, in a separate paragraph, explain why you judge your rewrite to be more successful or less successful than the original.

3. Relying chiefly on the method of summarized narrative, write a chapter of your autobiography (800-1200 words). Whether you

choose a single incident or a series of related incidents, make clear the significance the incident or incidents had in your personal development.

4. Now rewrite as dramatized narrative one crucial scene from the chapter of your autobiography. Keep descriptive details and comment to a minimum. Aim to recreate the scene entirely through dialogue.

5. Write a brief paper (300-500 words) describing one of your habitual activities as a child or evoking the special qualities of a place that has some emotional associations for you. Generalized narrative would probably be most appropriate.

6. The following passages are from personal experience papers written by students. Decide which are satisfactory and which unsatisfactory, and suggest ways of improving the latter. Here is a check list of points to watch for: Has the student supplied enough concrete details for the reader to share the experience? Are the details brought together in such a way as to make a unified impact? Is the point of view consistent, or, if it shifts, is the shift reasonable and justifiable? Is the time sequence (if there is one) handled satisfactorily? Are the style and tone of the passage appropriate to the material? Is the writing competent in terms of sentence structure, choice of words, and mechanics?

a. The stifling subway ride from Port Authority was finally over. I was sustained only by the mental picture created by the name Forest Hills. As I dragged myself up the last flight of stairs, my nose was the first to detect something was amiss. The "clear forest air" was delicately perfumed by car exhaust and soot. The last step completed my disillusionment. I found myself confronted by a ten-lane monster of screeching, misdirected chromium and steel. Amidst this mangle was a distraught, heavily perspiring young officer. This giant, called Queens Boulevard, plows its way through Queens, and connects with the 59th Street Bridge to Manhattan. Clutching harder all the paraphernalia I had just brought back from camp, I asked a reddish-pink-headed lady where I could get the 108th street bus that would take me to my new home. I waited an hour for the bus (guaranteed to run every fifteen minutes) with my hair sticking to my face, and my grimy camp yearbook forever sliding from under my arm. When the bus finally arrived, I was propelled onto it by about forty other dripping riders. As I boarded it, I couldn't help thinking of the grotesque sense of humor of whoever named Forest Hills.

b. When I was thirteen years old I got an all-summer job cleaning house and baby sitting. I worked from 8:30 to 5:00, six days a week for fifty cents an hour, a rather lowly wage. At 8:30 I walked to my "home," went upstairs and brought the crying five-month-old twins downstairs from their cribs, one by one. Downstairs I left the baby

boy in his bassinet in the dining room, he being the smaller and
the less vociferous of the two, and carried the girl into the den,
placing her on top of a large padded desk. I undressed her and
dropped the acrid-smelling wet diapers into a can. I propped her
between two bath towels to keep her from rolling off the desk and
went into the adjacent closet to get a large plastic basin. This I
brought into the kitchen and filled with warm water. Answering
the cries of a squalling baby left alone, I rushed back into the den,
trying not to slop the water. After a fresh bath she was toweled and
diapered and brought back into the dining room to her bassinet,
while the whole procedure was repeated with her tiny brother, who
was by this time exceedingly red and raging from his extended wait.
    After their formulas were prepared and the bottles heated, break-
fast was served. Later on, this was replaced by baby food, which
was accompanied by angry cries of rejection and frustration. A food-
dabbled bib was wisely left tucked under their fat chins for fifteen
minutes, allowing for burps and upset stomachs to settle things.

    c. I remember the smells most of all in that Indian summer of
1951—the musty smell of a large vacant house; the poignant scents of
the old fruit cellar—plums, peaches, apples, pears; the pleasant odor
of walnuts drying row upon row on the damp cellar floor. Upstairs
I found the funny, small kitchen with, of all things, a smaller room
adjacent to it filled with rows of shelves and cupboards. The dining
room and living room were completely bare, so that the reddish-
brown mahogany woodwork framing the doorways and running
along the lower walls asserted its permanence; then up the wooden
staircase to the second floor. A glance into each of the three large
bedrooms assured me that there would be sufficient lodging for the
family. (Moisture underneath the wallpaper on the ceiling had
produced shapeless patterns of light and dark. I stood there for
several moments forming mental pictures of phantom stallions and
western cowpunchers.) Then I was downstairs again, meeting myself
in the huge wall mirror suspended at the bottom of the stairway; and
pushing the screened-door open, I went outside to inspect the
exterior. (The sprawling front porch held eye-hooks overhead for an
old fashioned seat swing.) Down the steps and turning around for a
full view of the large but modest two-story frame structure. In front,
a flowering pine tree and a drooping willow contrasted east and
west: towering above one side-yard, a top-heavy elm; in the other, a
healthy pear twenty feet high. Running now to the backyard, I
perceived an apple tree, a cherry tree, and behind the simple garage,
two leafless walnut trees. Tripping uneasily over the fallen fruit, I
surveyed the remaining landscape of my new home. That immense
lot east of the house—was that ours too? I felt young pride for the
withering rows of brown corn stalks, piles of decaying matter which
had produced beans, peas, and tomatoes for the family before; and
the very thin stems of drying zinnias and snapdragons. All this was
my new home—and it looked darn big to a boy six years of age.

d. The camp counselors would occasionally take us to a riding stable, where the horses would try to rub us off against fence posts, or to a monster swimming pool, where the sun never shone and the wind always blew. One day I remember as a series of particularly grotesque experiences. It was very hot and we started a forced march down an interminable road, ankle deep in dust. Eventually we arrived at a large deserted quarry, where the rock had been extensively exposed, but not deeply excavated. I wandered off from the group and found myself confronted by two dogs that had apparently died at each other's throats. Their seams had burst and I suppose they would have looked horrible to some, but to me they somehow looked natural in that jumbled rock setting. When I returned to the group I said nothing. Everybody was gathered around a green pond, and a boy named Charlie had just hit a small fish with a large rock. "What a shot!" The fish fluttered down into the reeds, smoking dark brown.

The road back to the shelter was all uphill. Looking back on the day, I see it as a basic lesson in surrealism.

e. I often wandered alone through the old forests that partially surrounded our town. The spirit of the forests entered my body and became part of my being. In these times of loneliness, nature became my friend. My favorite location was hidden from the sight of the townspeople by six-foot hedges on the north and the east, by a forest on the south, and by a haystack on the west. If I waited patiently, I could observe the activity of the hummingbirds in the hedges which had been discontinued by my arrival. Listening to the peeps and squeaks of the young birds, the rustling of the adults, the sound of the wind in the trees and smelling the freshness of the grass, the sweetness of the dandelions and the pansies, the mustiness of old hay, and seeing the flickering of birds in the hedges, the green and brown colors of the hedges, the yellow-brown old haystack with its own content of animal life, the majesty of towering white oaks, the blue sky undisturbed by airplanes. All of the sights, the sounds, the smells of the forest—of nature—all created peace, contentment, and satisfaction.

f. Aunt Sally is an old, wrinkled woman who goes from house to house around the neighborhood asking for old clothes. Her hair is a grizzled gray, what there is of it. She is almost bald now. There are bald spots showing her crusted scalp, and the little bits of gray fuzz left cluster together as though for comfort before they too will be gone. Her sunken mouth is perpetually open in a slack smile disclosing two gold teeth, one on the upper right, the other on the lower left side. On the inside of her lower lip there is a pocket of snuff that frequently dribbles down her chin. The cloudy whites of her eyes are streaked with blue, and the brown pupil gazes up habitually beseechingly as she spies some object she would like to have. Somehow or other, she always manages to get what she wants.

Chapter Six

EXPLANATION PAPERS

*N*o *writer achieves complete clarity. But
the nearer he comes to seeing clearly,
the more his gifts prevail.*

Sidney Cox

The purpose of an explanatory paper is to increase the reader's understanding of the subject. A typical explanatory paper tells what a thing is, how it is made, how it works, how its parts fit together, how it is like or unlike other things. Or, by means of various strategies, it clarifies an attitude, a concept, an idea. Whatever the topic and whatever the methods used to develop the "explanation" or clarification, the writer sets out to share with the reader not so much his *experience* of something (or his reaction to it) as his *knowledge* of it.

Because college courses demand explanatory writing more frequently than any other kind, every student needs to develop competence in presenting information accurately, objectively, and clearly. Some course papers (and examinations) require that and no more. But even when an assignment calls for interpretation, evaluation, and criticism (of a novel, say, or of an economic theory), the paper can proceed successfully only from the basis of an accurate account of what is being interpreted, evaluated, and criticized. Explanatory (or expository) passages are woven into the fabric of most arguments.

Subjects for explanatory papers

The subject for an explanatory paper in history grows out of the course itself, and the material comes from textbooks, lectures, and class discussions. A science paper may be based on all of these and on laboratory work as well. In a composition course, you are likely to be given subjects that you can develop from your own experience and observation as well as from your reading. When you have a choice of topic, select one which you are thoroughly familiar with through experience, observation, and reflection. Practice in analyzing and explaining your own perceptions and ideas is the best preparation for analyzing and explaining the perceptions and ideas of others.

The range of subjects for explanatory papers can only be suggested here. For convenience, sample subjects are grouped into two categories, corresponding to typical ways of phrasing assignments.

Category I • This type of assignment gives guide lines for approaching and developing the paper but leaves the student free to apply the approach and method of development to his specific material. Notice that the first assignment below designates an audience; in the others the student is expected to select an audience and to identify it either in the paper itself or in a note attached to the paper.

For a beginner (someone your own age), give directions for a sports technique such as serving in tennis or putting in golf.

Describe a process, making clear the stages in it and showing how they relate to each other.

Describe a mechanism that consists of at least four distinct parts and explain how the parts work together in the functioning of the mechanism.

Describe the steps in a job—running a paper route, for instance, or selling merchandise, or working in a library.

Prepare a set of do-it-yourself instructions for an activity like repairing a leaky faucet, refinishing furniture, or putting a zipper in a skirt.

Explain how to raise (or train) an animal.

Describe the structure of a college organization or the activities of a club, showing how the structure or activities relate to the purpose of the organization or club.

Give an account of a campus event and indicate how it illustrates characteristic attitudes or interests of college community life.

Write a profile of a person or place you know well.

Compare some aspect of your high school and college experiences or activities (such as methods of instruction, extracurricular activities, social pressures) so as to convey a clear idea of what you consider to be significant similarities and differences.

Compare two sports on the basis of the skills they require.

Compare and contrast the ways in which various racial or religious groups celebrate holidays of religious or national significance.

Compare the styles of two comedians or actors.

On the basis of careful reading of the editorials for the past week or two, make clear the political viewpoint of a local newspaper.

Analyze the sources of humor in your favorite comic strip.

Analyze the format and methods of a television series in relation to its purpose.

Classify the students in your dormitory on the basis of their political views, their attitudes toward religion, their motives in attending college, the ways they spend their leisure time, or some other principle.

Explain why you are attending the college you are attending.

State clearly and give reasons for your political convictions, your religious beliefs, or your moral code.

Choose a term from current slang, illustrate its use, and explain (as best you can) the reasons for its popularity.

Explain the meaning of sin, pain, tolerance, courage, or prejudice —or any other concept that appears to have different meanings for different people.

Define a political *ism* like conservatism or liberalism or radicalism.

Through examples and personal anecdotes, show how a term like *love* or *fear* has come to have a new meaning for you.

Except for the assignment to write a profile of a person or a place, all of these assignments are phrased in terms of one or two of the methods of development discussed in Chapter 3. The profile (see pp. 208-212) offers considerable freedom in approach and may be developed in a variety of ways.

Category II • Another type of assignment focuses on a general subject (often an issue or a problem) but requires the student to make his own approach to the subject, to decide how to develop it, and, of course, to narrow it to something manageable. When specific questions are raised, these are intended only to stimulate the student's thinking, not to limit it or to dictate a particular approach in the paper. In the brief list of possible assignments given below, the second specifies an audience; the others leave the choice of audience up to the writer.

There are many kinds of discrimination in our society—discrimination based on race, color, or creed are perhaps the most obvious, but by no means the only kinds. Write a paper describing one kind of discrimination with which you are familiar through experience, observation, or reading. In thinking through your material, you may wish to ask yourself such questions as: Where does it flourish? How widespread is it? How does it reveal itself? How does it affect the minority group? What influences tend to counteract it? (Your paper should not, however, be merely a series of answers to these questions.)

Write a paper on some group you are familiar with, one which can be identified by its habitual activities; its moral or social standards; its dress, language, or ceremonies. Make clear through concrete details the distinguishing traits of the group, its typical behavior, and the shared attitudes which give the group its unity and explain its actions. Your audience is a class in sociology.

Discuss a campus publication (newspaper, humor magazine, literary review) to show the role it plays in campus life.

Discuss one aspect of your education in politics, art, music, or science. (Education is not limited to the classroom.)

Other "discussion" subjects may be drawn from campus events or issues of current interest; every college community provides dozens of them every year. In using one of them as the basis of an explanatory paper, the student ordinarily has a choice of approaches—describing an event, showing how or why it came about, analyzing its importance or its results, and so on. He should remember, however, that his purpose is to explain, not to defend or to deplore.

Whether an assignment is phrased on the pattern of those in Category I or those in Category II, the student always has the responsibility of focusing more sharply on a specific topic and deciding on the central point that will control and unify his paper. In preparing and writing the paper, he needs to pay careful attention to the stages in writing discussed in Chapter 2 and to the methods of development discussed in Chapter 3. Not all of them can be reviewed here, but the next three sections will make some additional suggestions about those matters which have a special bearing on the chief purpose of an explanatory paper—to present *for a specific audience* accurate information in a clear, orderly, interesting way.

Gathering and selecting material

Since accurate and adequate information is the core of an explanatory paper, the material-gathering stage is particularly important. There is no substitute for getting the facts straight, for knowing what you are talking about; the reader will have confidence in your explanation only if he feels that you have mastered the basic material that goes into it. This is the main reason, of course, why you should always try to choose a topic on which you have first-hand experience and knowledge. While your paper may include information that you have heard or read, its chief interest usually hinges on the amount of relevant material you are able to present from your own experience—what you have done or seen or found out yourself.

From experience and observation • For some topics you can draw entirely on your own past experience, especially if a job or hobby has made you something of an expert on a process or activity. But in reviewing and selecting the material, you need to remember that an explanatory paper takes a different tack and aims for a different effect than a personal experience paper. You might develop "Picking Apples" as a personal experience, describing an afternoon in an orchard and concentrating on those sense impressions (the color and fragrance of fallen apples, the weight of the loaded baskets) that best convey your reactions to the experience. In developing an explanatory paper on the same topic, you would probably divide the activity into its major stages, discussing in turn the methods of picking, sorting, storing, and transporting the fruit. In the first paper, you would be telling of your personal reactions; in the second, even though you might use the framework of a personal narrative, you would be conveying information, using the knowledge gained from your experience as a means of clarifying the procedure. The first would be individualized, a subjective description of your experience for its own sake; the second would be generalized, an objective description of the typical activity of picking apples.

In gathering material for a paper based on your past experience, you may be able to produce enough detail merely by jogging your memory. But more often you will want to check on your memory or add to your store of information by careful observation. Explaining even the most familiar process can present unexpected difficulties. Everyone knows in a general way what a can opener is and how it works, but to perform the very exacting task of saying on paper what it is and how it works, you need to look at it again and again—to really *see* it as a mechanism and not just as the implement of a recognizable shape that you habitually use without effort or thought. The kind of observation—examination or re-examination—that turns up good material for explanatory papers is purposeful, directed, deliberate.

Depending on the nature of the material, you may or may not need to indicate what opportunities you have had for collecting material based on experience and observation. If you are describing something physical and finite like a coffee pot or the engine of an automobile, no such indication is necessary: the reader will assume that you have had the opportunity to examine and re-examine until you are thoroughly familiar with what you are describing. But if you are reporting on the editorial policy of a newspaper or the themes in popular songs or the kinds of television programs available in your area, you will need to indicate how extensive your investigation has been. A student who wrote a paper on "Advertising Appeals in Television Commercials" states that his analysis was based on the commercials shown on NBC between 7:00 and 10:00 P.M. on October 23, 1964, and between 3:00 and 5:00 P.M. the following day. When the potential material for a paper is almost limitless, as it is in this case, it is advisable to let the reader know what sample of material has provided the basis for your generalizations.

From interviews • Often you can get material for your paper by talking with someone: a member of your family, a fellow student, a jet pilot, a jeweler, a kindergarten teacher, a county welfare worker. The technique of interviewing is highly developed by newspaper reporters, who know how to ask pointed questions and how to draw out the answers, and who have trained themselves to remember what is said. You can do the same thing on an amateur scale.

Before beginning an interview you should know something of what you are to discuss and what you want to find out, and you should have some specific questions in mind. Listen carefully, mentally summarizing the less important points, fixing in mind the more important statements, as far as possible in the speaker's words, and perhaps making some notes. If he gives some figures, repeat them to be sure you have them right. If he qualifies a statement with "I think" or "perhaps" or "around," be sure you get the qualification in your notes.

If you are conducting a small-scale Gallup poll (to find out, for instance, the political views of members of your fraternity), make sure that your questions are phrased objectively and that you address the same questions to each member of the group.

In your paper you should name and identify the people who give you facts and specify what qualifies them as authorities. Don't write "Somebody told me..." or even "A local grocer said...," but "Charles Anderson, manager of the Central Food Mart, said. . . ." If his personality is important to your paper, as it would be in a profile (see pp. 208-212), watch for details that may help indicate what he is like and use them in your paper—his gestures, appearance, likes and dislikes, even the room in which the interview took place. In some instances you may also want to quote his exact words. There are two reasons for direct quoting: either a statement summarizes a point in such a valuable way that it deserves exact quotation, or it is put in such an unusual way that it will add interest.

From reading • You may need to do some background reading for your topic to find further details or additional facts. If you were explaining the rules of cribbage, for instance, you would probably write most of the paper from your present knowledge of the game, but you would check up on the points you couldn't remember or weren't sure of. If you know of a magazine article or book with useful information about your subject, it may be a real help.

Material for short papers will come chiefly from your own knowledge, but the content of longer, more comprehensive ones usually needs further support. A useful kind of project combines material from a college course with some first-hand information. A sociology course might provide you with some points about suburban developments that you could illustrate from your experience; a physics or a chemistry course might help you explain some new machine or a new medicine. In your paper you can combine two areas of your knowledge.

When you make use of published material, whether in textbooks or any other books or magazines, you must treat it with respect. In summarizing or paraphrasing, make sure you are accurately reporting the facts or ideas in the source. And be scrupulous in acknowledging your debt. Your instructor will indicate how formal or informal such acknowledgment should be. Informal methods include direct reference within the paper itself ("As Thoreau says in *Civil Disobedience,* . . .") or a note of indebtedness at the end of the paper ("Facts about the pricing of drugs are taken from Richard Harris, 'Annals of Legislation: The Real Voice,' *The New Yorker,* March 14, 1964"). For formal acknowledgment, see Chapter 11, pages 438-445.

Whether the material comes mainly from experience and observation, from interviews, or from reading, you will have the problem of selecting material and adapting it to your audience. For an explanatory paper, as for any other kind, you will have some material so central to the topic that you must include it, and you will have other material so peripheral that you must decide whether or not to use it. The decision depends partly on the length and scope of the paper and partly on the readers you intend to reach. You need to consider your readers' interests and their probable knowledge of the subject. How much knowledge can you assume? There is often a fine line between insulting their intelligence with the obvious and puzzling them with insufficient detail. For a general audience a paper on a scientific or technical subject will need to explain special and unfamiliar terms, make comparisons with common experiences, and perhaps provide some simple drawings to supplement the explanation (though not to substitute for it). For readers with some background in the field much of this would be unnecessary, and details of a more technical nature could be used. There is some danger of writing at too low a level, putting in things that almost everyone will know, but as a rule amateur writers do not explain fully enough or include enough details.

Since the selection of details and the choice of materials will be determined by the audience for which the paper is intended, it is wise to decide arbitrarily what kind of readers your explanatory paper will be addressed to. Having a particular audience in mind will help you focus your paper and maintain consistency in the general approach, the tone, and the style. Depending on the topic, you might address your paper to the readers of a campus publication, a newspaper supplement, or a magazine that appeals to a special group (to photographers, fishermen, teen-agers, travelers). Probably the most challenging task you can set yourself is to inform an alert, interested, educated reader who wants to satisfy his general curiosity about the subject without consulting a specialized journal or reference book. Such a reader will not want to be talked down to. He can assimilate a certain amount of technical or semi-technical information and will make the effort to do so if the material is presented in a graphic and attractive way. Some such reader seems to have been addressed in the article from which this passage on the characteristics and uses of ivory appears. The writer does not hesitate to make certain demands on the reader's intelligence, but he regularly gives the reader all sorts of help in understanding the material. Notice the vivid and illuminating comparisons; notice also the striking bit of detail from the writer's own experience.

● *Explanation papers*

Ivory is highly elastic but as strong as spring steel, and a riding crop made from a lengthwise strip of it is as supple as a willow switch. Cut to the thickness of common typing paper, it is so transparent that standard print can be read through it; at the same time, its structure of concentric rings and small lozenge-shaped whorls, which look like the engine-turning on the back of a watch, becomes visible. Ivory is dentine, from which our own teeth are in large part made. It is "solidified" with phosphate of lime and other minerals including fluoride of calcium (the chief ingredient of tooth enamel), the percentage of which gradually increases in dead ivory to as much as 10 per cent. At the same time the gelatinous component gradually dries out, so that very old ivories tend to crumble (ancient ivory statues are restored by boiling in albumen or gelatin). Hippo and walrus teeth are covered with an immensely hard, flintlike dentine that will strike sparks from iron. It can hardly be cut and blunts files of the hardest tempered steel. . . .

Ivory is cut with very thin circular saws that have to be whetted constantly. For very delicate operations it may even have to be cut under water (oil is seldom used because it is absorbed and stains the finished product.) It is also, of course, sawed by hand and cut and carved with everything from a machete to a dentist's drill. Every scrap of the tusk is used. From the points, which are generally more solid and of finer grain than the rest of the tusk, come billiard balls, chessmen, and other hard-used utilitarian objects. The main shaft is delaminated and the plates used for such items as the handles of cutlery. In fact, this was once ivory's commonest use, and at one time a quarter of it went to Sheffield, England, for that purpose. Another quarter went to the towns of Ivoryton and Deep River in Connecticut and to a few other American cities where the keyboards of pianos were made. The scraps went, and still go, to button manufacturers. The sawdust is used as fertilizer, or is boiled down to make gelatin or a light sizing for straw hats and lace.

It has always been in the arts, however, that ivory has figured most prominently. We have already alluded to the ivories of the ancients, but we have not discussed the utterly amazing art of the Chinese—who still remain, after some four thousand years, the supreme ivory carvers. Their genius has for the most part been displayed in miniature: exquisite statuettes, models of temples and pagodas, animal statuary, and those mysterious series of carved hollow spheres, one within the other, that take years to execute but only a few dollars to purchase. Incidentally, I recall a gift given my mother by the last Manchu emperor, P'u Yi. It was an ivory sculpture of an ordinary clam shell no more than life size, but within its half-opened shell was a complete scene of a Chinese summer pavilion set among trees and shrubs, with a garden sloping down to a pond. On the pond were five ducks wearing collars. A man in a big straw hat stood on the bank holding a string attached to each of the collars. I recall with what amazement I first saw, with the aid of a strong magnifying glass, that each of these strings had been carved in the twisted form of a rope and that all were separately gathered into the minuscule right hand of the man! The ducks were about one millimeter long. How the artist could have done such work, even aided by powerful glasses, is really incomprehensible.—Ivan T. Sanderson, "A Passion for Ivory," *Horizon*, May 1960, p. 94

The impression made by this passage is that the writer has selected, from a vast storehouse of knowledge about his subject, the material that will be most informative and at the same time most interesting to a general audience of educated non-specialists. In presenting his material, he has used such highly effective devices of clarification and illustration that he has produced a model of *readable* explanatory prose.

Organizing the paper

Three main considerations should determine the general plan for the paper—the material itself, the method of development, and, again, the expected audience.

For some explanatory papers, the material and the method of development dictate rather strongly the structure of the paper, or at least the order of parts making up the bulk of it. A description of a process, a set of directions for doing something, an account of an event will all probably follow a chronological movement. Once you are launched into the paper, you will proceed according to the natural order suggested by the material, taking up one state or step or instruction in the time sequence where it actually fits. In the same way, when you are describing an object or mechanism, you will follow a natural order, this time spatial—from left to right, top to bottom, inside to outside, and so on.

Although the natural order (whether chronological or spatial) would seem to present few choices and few difficulties if you are really familiar with your material, you do have some options, and you need to exercise good judgment to make the right choices for a particular audience. The purpose of an explanatory paper, remember, is to increase the reader's *understanding* of the subject. Just as his knowledge and interests should guide you in selecting material, so they should determine the biggest problem in organizing and writing the paper—where and how to start.

Particularly in informal papers, the writer should make a real attempt to put himself in the reader's place, starting where he can best catch the reader's interest and exploit his present state of knowledge. An unsophisticated reader may be greatly helped by first being given an overview of an event that is made up of a rather complicated series of incidents. Or he may profit by being told some practical applications close to his own experience. Notice the device used in the opening of a student's paper on "The Fluorescent Lamp":

> You turn the switch. For an instant, nothing happens. Then light flickers along the tube. And finally there is full, steady illumination. As contrasted with the ordinary bulb, which lights up as soon as its switch is turned, the fluorescent tube always provides a moment of dramatic uncertainty. Why the hesitation?

The rest of the paper provided an answer to the question by describing the operation of the starting circuit. An opening paragraph like this one does forecast, however informally, the chief point to be made by the paper.

Consider now the more austere opening of another paper on the same topic:

> The fluorescent lamp is a device which utilizes a relatively low voltage electric current to provide artificial illumination. Unlike an incandescent light, it employs an electrical discharge through tenuous mercury vapor to convert electrical energy into light energy. The discharge produces invisible ultra-violet light. The long glass tube through which the discharge passes is coated on the inside with a substance that transforms the ultra-violet light into visible radiation. That the visible light comes from this coating rather than directly from the discharge differentiates the fluorescent lamp from other types of discharge lamps.

Beginning as it does with a rather formal definition and classification, this opening paragraph seems to promise a systematic and comprehensive account of the working of the lamp. The paper fulfilled this promise by first describing the parts of the lamp, then moving to the two phases in its operation—the starting phase and the operating phase—and concluding with an explanation of exactly how energy is transformed in the tube to produce ultra-violet light. The starting point for the writer of the first paper ("You turn the switch") had a position about one-third of the way through the second paper but was given no special emphasis.

Each "way in" has its value. The first is appropriate for its intended audience—beginning high school students; the second is appropriate for its audience—college students with some knowledge of physics.

The problem of the "way in" is equally important in those explanatory papers where no natural order is suggested by the material itself and where, consequently, the reader has to impose his own order. Particularly for analytical papers based on reading, you should try to avoid the purely perfunctory beginning which suggests that you are merely fulfilling an assignment ("This paper will deal with the plot, characters, and theme of 'The Snows of Kilimanjaro' by Ernest Hemingway"). Try to start in such a way as to indicate that you yourself are aware of the significance of the material you are dealing with; this in turn will catch your reader's interest and make him feel that he is participating in an analysis or explanation that will yield something of value. The following is a student's successful attempt to indicate the significance of the analysis he is about to undertake.

Religion has always played a major part in the formation and maintenance of both public and private morality. Because morality is, to a large extent, taught primarily as a part of religious instruction and because our moral code is often justified by reference to the Bible, many individuals tend to think of the two as inseparable. In fact, many people think that morality is a set of religious precepts. To them an agnostic ethic is impossible either on the individual or social level. But is it? Can an individual who does not believe in the divine source of morality lead a life as righteous and moral as that of a man who founds his morality upon the revealed word of God? This is the basic question posed by John Stuart Mill in his essay on the "Utility of Religion."

The beginning of an explanatory paper can hardly be considered, of course, apart from the general plan of the whole. Although many variations are possible, most expository papers follow roughly the two plans outlined in Chapter 2, pages 49-50—the *order of support* and the *order of climax*. The support plan, you will recall, opens with a preview of the whole paper, giving the reader a general orientation before taking up, one by one, the main points sketched in the first few sentences. The climax plan leads the reader from particular to particular, building toward some comprehensive generalization or point that will make sense of the particulars. Each of these patterns may be employed in papers which define or classify or divide or analyze causes and effects. A writer may, for instance, start by announcing that his investigation has turned up four main kinds of appeals made in television commercials (identifying each in a sentence or two) and then proceed to discuss each in turn—moving from the least prevalent to the most prevalent, or through degrees of subtlety, or according to some other principle. Or he may start with a description of one commercial, gradually building up the "class" by details and examples, and then moving to a striking example of a different class, and so on. The second plan would highlight individual examples of each class. To choose wisely between these two general plans requires you to size up your material and decide how it can best be explained to your particular audience.

The support plan and the climax plan serve also as general strategies for organizing a paper in comparison and contrast. The terms of the comparison (or the basic similarities and differences) may be made explicit at the start and then each developed in turn, or the reader may be led from one particular point to another and finally to a conclusion, which pulls together and synthesizes the main similarities and differences. Three basic patterns for fashioning the internal structure of the comparison have already been illustrated in Chapter 3, pages 81-85. The whole-by-whole method, the part-to-part method, and the likeness-difference method can all be adapted to the framework of support or climax.

For explanatory papers, as you see, considerable variation in plan is possible; choice of the basic organizational pattern should come from a thoughtful consideration of alternatives. The best plan will do justice to the material, to the writer's purpose in presenting the material, and to the probable state of the reader's knowledge and interests. In any case, the writer owes his reader a clear, firm structure in which there is an orderly progression from part to part or point to point.

Style and tone

Material set down in a disorganized fashion will leave the reader in a state of confusion, the very opposite of that larger understanding which an explanatory paper should produce.

Only slightly less damaging is an unfortunate choice of style and tone that kills the reader's interest. In an effort to avoid chumminess and informality, which are certainly incongruous for explaining some subjects, students often go to the opposite extreme and produce an antiseptic, depersonalized prose that sounds as if it had come into being without benefit of human mind or heart. Aiming to be objective, they detach themselves so completely from their material that their writing is drained of any trace of personality. But this is to mistake the meaning of objectivity.

Objectivity is an attitude toward material rather than a special manner of writing; it implies avoidance, as far as possible, of bias and self-interest. More positively, it means treating the subject honestly and accurately. But in doing so, your writing doesn't have to be as colorless and cold as a tabulation of statistics. In many explanatory papers, the *I* point of view is perfectly appropriate, and in all of them you should aim for details that are clear, vivid, and telling. *My* and *I* are used with unobtrusive ease in the following passage. Without forcing himself into the center of the explanation, the writer does effectively use his experience to bring the reader closer to the technique he is describing.

My principal technique for collecting webs should be easy for anyone to master. I simply spray the web with lacquer and mount it on a sheet of paper. I trudge through the woods for hours carrying my spray can and searching for virtually invisible silken traps. My middle-aged eyes require a bit of aid. At each likely web site I don my bifocals and examine what often turns out to be blank space. Staring into empty air at close range makes one feel ludicrous enough, but spraying that air with paint appears even more so to onlookers who cannot discern the beautiful patterns that occasionally materialize.— C. L. STONG, "The Amateur Scientist: How to collect and preserve the delicate webs of spiders," *Scientific American,* Feb. 1963, p. 160

Although accurate explanation sometimes entails suppression of personal inclinations and attitudes, those convictions and beliefs that give vividness and force to writing of other kinds, some interpretation is woven into most explanatory writing and is indeed an essential part of many explanations. It is hard to conceive of an explanatory essay (outside of a purely technical or scientific report) that fully explains what is known without revealing an attitude toward that knowledge. You can give a fair and impartial account of something, and at the same time make clear your own interpretation of it. Expressing an attitude is by no means incompatible with scrupulous handling of your material. The point is that the interpretation should be based on a fair and impartial survey of the material, not on some preconceived notions that you had long before you really tried to *see* what was before you.

What the reader wants (and deserves) is the assurance that a lively intelligence is at work on the material—making distinctions, clarifying relations, ordering the parts of the discussion in a coherent and comprehensible way. And the reader is gratified when the expression has some liveliness, too. All of the resources of the language can be brought to bear on the basic purpose of clarifying. The words you use, your choice of details, the pattern and rhythm of your sentences, the movement of your paragraphs—all of these can help or hinder that purpose.

Sample explanatory papers

Some of the general points made earlier in this chapter will have more meaning in the context of sample papers. No complete survey of kinds of explanatory papers can be given. The ones represented here are chosen because papers like these are frequently assigned in composition courses. For further illustrations of explanatory papers, both by professional writers and by students, see Chapter 3.

The process paper • With the popularity of do-it-yourself projects, process papers have become familiar to all of us. Magazine articles and even books are often written to describe how something is done or how something works. The term "process" applies not only to a systematic account of series of actions or steps but also to a systematic survey of the parts that enter into the working of a mechanism. While description and narration are the chief means of developing a process paper, the emphasis is more on *how* something works or how it is done than on *what* a thing is or what happens.

A paper that tells the reader how to do something typically follows the support plan. The opening sentences usually identify or describe the process, indicate its usefulness, define any technical terms, and specify the tools, conditions, and materials necessary. Or the process paper may describe how a mechanism or an instrument works. Special attention needs to be paid not only to giving an accurate description of each part but also to showing how each part functions in the working of the mechanism. In terms of composition, this means the writer needs to make the transitions clear and to introduce statements of cause and effect at appropriate points. In the following paper, the student finds a starting-point in the reader's everyday experiences with simple locks, and as he proceeds with his explanation of a more complicated type, he uses various devices to sustain the reader's interest as well as to inform him.

The Release Mechanism of the Combination Lock

Whatever it is attached to, a lock is a device for preventing access by anyone other than its owner. The most common lock, perhaps, is the one used to keep a door from opening or being opened while the owner of a house is away. In this or any other lock there is a basic problem which must be solved: how to enable the lock to recognize its owner. This problem is solved differently in different kinds of locks. The lock on a door is usually of the type that opens with a key. This small piece of metal with a special pattern of bumps and slots along one edge is carried by the owner, who has only to insert it in the lock and turn it to open the door. Thus a lock of this type identifies its owner by his possession of a certain object. This kind of lock has many disadvantages since the key can be lost or stolen, forcing the owner to change the lock and putting him to great inconvenience if not loss of his property. The combination lock, however, identifies its owner by his knowledge of a certain sequence of numbers, called the combination. This means that there is nothing that can be lost, stolen, destroyed, or otherwise made useless to its owner by purely physical means. The only responsibility taken on by the owner is that of remembering the combination.

While combination locks differ widely in the special features of their operation, the simple three-number lock illustrates most of the important principles behind all other combination locks. At the heart of this lock there are three circular discs piled on top of each other like pancakes, only with a small space between the surfaces of adjacent discs. An axle passes through the center of these discs perpendicular to their surfaces, allowing each to turn independently of the others. These discs are very important, for it is their positions which will determine whether or not the lock will open. Usually this is done by three holes, one on the surface of each disc and not far from the edge. When the lock is open, these holes are lined up one above the other so that a shaft running parallel to the axle may pass straight through all three at once. When the shaft has moved thus, the lock mechanism is released. If the discs are not properly aligned, the shaft cannot move all the way, and there is no release.

What is the method of lining up the discs? A combination lock is usually imbedded within the machine it guards, but on the outside portion there is a circular dial with a knob in the middle for turning it. Around the edge of the dial are a series of evenly spaced marks numbered consecutively. There is also a dot on the casing of the machine right next to the dial that shows which number the dial is set on. The lock's inner mechanism is fixed so that the faces of the discs are parallel to that of the dial and the axle passes through the dial's center. The top disc is directly attached to the dial, so that it turns as the dial does. This enables the owner to line up the first disc by simply turning the dial to a certain number, but all of the discs must be properly aligned to work the lock. To give the operator of the lock a means for turning the other two discs, there is a small peg sticking out from the surface of each disc like a candle on a birthday cake. These pegs are put only on the surfaces that face the surface of another disc. They are placed the same distance out from the axle so that if the top disc is turned far enough, the peg on its lower surface will hit the one on the upper surface of the second disc, making it turn.

The operation of this combination lock consists, then, of the following steps: The dial is first turned around twice in one direction to insure that the peg on the first dial has had a chance to hit that of the second dial to move it and that the one on the bottom of the second has also hit that of the third. This means that all three discs turn when the dial turns. Then the dial is set on the number that will line up the hole of the bottom disc. The dial is then turned around once in the opposite direction. This brings the first disc's peg around to hit the peg of the second disc from the other side. The dial is then turned further, pushing the second disc into the proper position. This happens before the peg below the second disc can hit that of the third disc. The two bottom discs are now in place, and the dial is simply turned back in the original direction to the last number, moving the top disc into position. Again this happens before any pegs can collide, so the other discs are not moved. Thus, one by one the discs are lined up so that finally the shaft can pass through them to open the lock.

The profile • Although it will probably contain more interpretation and judgment than the process paper, a "profile" is an explanatory paper. Its aim is to tell readers enough about a person so that they understand him and in a sense know him. It differs from a biography in that it is usually not organized chronologically. It is a "character sketch" written with purpose and direction, arranged somewhat informally by topics chosen for their relevance to the subject.

The subject of a profile should be interesting and distinctive in some way, either in his characteristics or in what he does, has done, or stands for. To write a profile, you need a rather full knowledge (first-hand knowledge is best) of the person, more than you can get from reference books or casual acquaintance. You can collect information about him by talking with him, if he is available, and by talking with people who know him. Sometimes there is material in print, perhaps in newspapers or if he is a student, in the campus paper. But these secondary sources cannot take the place of your first-hand knowledge; consequently, the best profile is written about a person you know—a grandfather, a family friend, a teacher, a teammate, or someone you have worked with.

The first few paragraphs of a profile are likely to give a glimpse of the person and tell why he is distinctive in terms of a character trait (often shown in a direct quotation), or in terms of an occupation or an accomplishment. Something about his appearance may come here. The second block of information usually gives further details of his distinctiveness. Then the profile often goes back to the person's beginnings and gives a brief biography, amplifying incidents that are especially revealing and showing the influences that have made him what he is. This chronological path leads back to the present so that the last part gives some further details of him today and ends either with a brief summary or more often with another glimpse of him in action.

A profile prepared by a professional writer for publication in a magazine often sums up a purposeful investigation extending over several weeks or months, and it may run to many thousands of words. More typical of the kind of profile a student can handle is the following account of the author's grandmother, written as a feature article for a newspaper as a comment on a specific incident. While not explanatory in the narrow sense, this brief profile does a great deal to help the reader understand the seventy-two-year-old woman who chose to go to jail for her principles.

The Mission of Mrs. Peabody

MY GRANDMOTHER . . . THE FLORIDA JAILBIRD

Last Thursday 72-year-old Mrs. Malcolm Peabody, mother of the governor of Massachusetts (Endicott Peabody) and descendant of one of Massachusetts' most distinguished families, posted $450 bond and left her cell in the St. Augustine (Fla.) county jail. She had been held overnight for taking part in a racial demonstration. In the following article, her granddaughter, Frances Fitzgerald, 23, a graduate of Radcliffe and a free-lance writer, tells how the immediate family reacted to Mrs. Peabody's spirited actions.

By Frances Fitzgerald

N.Y. Herald Tribune Special

That Mary Elizabeth Peabody spent last Wednesday night in jail for "trespassing" came as no surprise to her seven grandchildren. We expected such a development. With the clarity of hindsight I think the incident was inevitable.

My grandmother is a passionate woman, dedicated to the Christian ideal of respect for human dignity. Her determination to defend what she believes to be right has led her to undertake a wide variety of humanitarian projects. Such is her sense of justice that merely watching her read the newspapers can be an unnerving experience. Recently I visited "Gaga," as her grandchildren call her, at her house in Cambridge. "It's horrible, absolutely horrible," I heard her exclaim. "A great tragedy!" I thought she had just read of the death of a friend but it was a story of the Kurdish massacres in Iraq that had incensed her. Further down the page she came to an article on the extension of a throughway near Cambridge, which threatened to destroy the life of several suburban towns.

"I don't understand how people can let that sort of thing happen," she complained. A few days later she attended a citizens' meeting to protest the construction and wrote a letter to the governor of Massachusetts, her son.

"Gaga's" compassion and sense of justice were evident from the time she moved with her husband, the Right Rev. Malcolm E. Peabody, to his first parish of Lawrence, Mass. Lawrence was then a mill town, hard hit by widespread unemployment and there, as later in Philadelphia and Syracuse, my grandmother became a leader in the community welfare projects of the Episcopal Church. During World War II she took in refugees from Germany and Austria and afterwards helped them to start their new lives in the United States. At present she works regularly for the American Field Service, the U.S. Committee for the United Nations, and for the many charitable organizations of the church.

Her house in Cambridge, though it stands between the ultra-modern Episcopal Theological Seminary and a towering hotel, has an atmosphere of early, maritime New England with its wooden shingles, its gables and its prints of clipper ships. The house is spare and neat; in spring it is caught up in a bed of daffodils which Mrs.

Peabody plants herself. "Gaga" will have no maid, for she hates to spend money on herself. Her cooking is excellent—although there is a joke in the family that whatever is left over from the main course goes into the salad and from there into the soup.

She is intolerant of vanity and of people who think too much about themselves. From Isabella Stewart Gardner, Boston's grandest grande dame and art collector, she received as a wedding present a Degas painting of a bare-bosomed lady at the opera. Feeling that the picture was inappropriate for a young clergyman's house, she decided that Mrs. Gardner had given it to her out of a desire to impress. The next day she donated the Degas to a rummage sale.

The Peabody house in Cambridge is always full of people—parishioners, relatives and guests. One recent visitor was the smallest grandchild, aged 4 months, who came to stay while his parents went on a trip. He was treated like a helpless, but rather appealing grown-up.

Mrs. Peabody loves to entertain and to go to parties; she was probably one of the few who really enjoyed her son's inaugural ball. Through natural tact she has successfully overcome what might have been her one social impediment—that she will never tell a lie. Once, when visiting a clergyman's house, she was asked what she thought of a particularly ugly chandelier. "It's unusual," she hedged.

Just a few years ago my grandmother challenged me to a tennis match and, to my consternation, won. No wonder. For strategy, she had been teaching herself Russian, and for practice, climbing all the mountains near North East Harbor, Me. Convinced that her own phenomenal energy was the norm, she long worried that her children lacked stamina.

That the oldest of them is a delegate to the United Nations, the second the governor of Massachusetts, the third a clergyman, the fourth a schoolteacher and the fifth the secretary of the Massachusetts Urban Redevelopment Board pleases her but does not impress her in the least. They are simply doing their duty—the duty to be of service to man.

My grandmother is descended from Puritan ancestors who helped to create and to maintain the principles of equal justice and individual liberty that have been America's greatest contribution to the world. Like her abolitionist forebears, Mary Peabody has confirmed values and an unselfconscious determination to speak out for them. When Bishop Peabody was unable, because of other duties, to go to St. Augustine on the request of the Southern Christian Leadership Conference, it was only natural for her to volunteer.

It was only natural as well that her 6-year-old granddaughter Elizabeth should get the news as she did. Elizabeth overheard one of her teachers say to another last Thursday, "Did you know that her grandmother was put in jail?"—Chicago *Sun-Times,* April 5, 1964

Most often, perhaps, we think of the profile as having a person as its subject. But a place may be the subject of a profile, too. Sun City, Arizona—a town created specifically for retired people—was the subject of a lengthy explanatory essay in *The New Yorker*, April 4, 1964, and *Holiday* regularly runs feature articles on places that are in some way interesting or distinctive. You should find it enjoyable to write your own "Notes for a Gazeteer" on a place you know well. While probably including some historical information and some account of the physical layout and the people who live there, such an essay would have its center in your analysis of the distinctive traits or features of the place.

The process paper and the profile are pretty clearly defined *types* of papers that have become familiar to readers of newspapers and magazines. Although much individual variation is possible, the general purpose of such papers is so well established that we are justified in using the labels *process* or *profile* to identify them. Other explanatory papers are more easily typed in terms of the method used to develop them—the essay which explains by defining, for instance, or the essay which explains by comparing. Notice how clearly this opening paragraph signals the student's approach to the general subject of tolerance. Notice, too, the indication that the discussion, like many which undertake to define, will have an argumentative edge to it. The student is not merely going to identify various conceptions of tolerance but will explain why one is genuine tolerance while the others are not.

We Americans are a people who pride ourselves individually on our tolerance in our private lives and collectively on the principle of tolerance on which our country is founded. We have so accustomed ourselves to being spokesmen for international tolerance that we hardly realize that in our dealings with each other we are often misinterpreting, and thereby demeaning, the very cause we wish to further. For there is no doubt but that in America today many attitudes pass for tolerance which are in fact no such thing. Only one of them deserves the respect and admiration we unthinkingly give to all.

Other explanatory papers which rely mainly on one method of development have been illustrated in Chapter 3. To conclude this section, we shall look at a paper which combines several methods in a response to a "discussion" assignment listed earlier in this chapter:

There are many kinds of discrimination in our society—discrimination based on race, color, or creed are perhaps the most obvious, but by no means the only kinds. Write a paper describing one kind of discrimination with which you are familiar through experience, observation, or reading. In thinking through your material, you may wish to ask yourself such questions as: Where does it flourish? How widespread is it? How does it reveal itself? How does it affect the minority group? What influences tend to counteract it? (Your paper should not, however, be merely a series of answers to these questions.)

Learning to Be an Adult

In boring high-school assemblies I often looked around musingly at the 2,000 students spread over the gymnasium bleachers like a brightly-colored quilt, patterned neatly into squares: a block of cashmere sweaters, a block of behind-the-times dresses handed down from older sisters; a block of red football letter-sweaters, a block of wrinkled satin shirts; a block of heads bent over books, a block of chattering mouths; a block of lively, interesting faces, a block of dull eyes and vacant expressions. Even though they are supposed to sit with homeroom groups, Monitor High students contrive to be with their friends in assemblies. Since "friends" in M.H.S. means "kids like me," the small blocks of students are laid out according to the class structure of the school. This class system is prominent in all of school life, and enables students to pick out "their sort of people" almost before they have been introduced.

Perhaps the main reason that the students are so aware of the class structure and so readily accept it is that M.H.S. is the only public high school in the city. Students seem to expect that the class divisions and prejudices of the town itself will show up in the school. And they do—with some differences. Like their parents, the students fit into three layers—the "haves," the "have somethings," and the "have nots," and what first puts a student in his layer is his family's income and place of residence. The cashmere sweaters in the assembly and classrooms are worn by girls whose parents can afford them and who for the most part live in the wealthy West End of town; the unfashionable hand-me-downs are seen on girls from the poorer sections who haven't the money to dress well; in between are the girls with orlon sweaters and old clothes that are still fashionable. Clothes are important in M.H.S.—they indicate prosperity or lack of it—and any new student is first judged on his appearance and soon put in his place.

The system is not so rigid, though, that the upper class is open only to those who have money. Those who have letter-sweaters or other marks of extra-curricular activity—club pins, beanies, choir robes, or committee positions—usually can make their way up. Either a large number of school activities or a few high quality ones will pull a student out of his financial class (and so allow him to look down on those who might normally have been his "friends"). The major school activity, scholarship, has the same effect. Those who have good grades set themselves apart and do not associate with those who are just scraping through. To maintain a position in the upper group or the middle group requires a C average, acquired without sacrificing social life.

With information on money, extra-curricular activities, and scholarship about a student, one can make a good guess as to the group he belongs to. But occasionally someone pops out of his probable place and lands above or below it, usually above. A lively look, good ideas, and a friendly smile can put a girl into one of the exclusively "have" sororities even though she comes from the wrong corner of town and participates in no activity. Less often a surly manner or a maladjusted personality shuts a wealthy, able student out of his proper place. Most of the "have nots" are discriminated against primarily because they haven't the right personality; they are motorcycle fiends in satin shirts, mousy and unattractive "characters" or unsociable people who don't want to be in any class. Unless they have a *lot* of money to spend on others, they're doomed to the bottom class.

The fact that personality is so important is the most important difference between the class structure of the school and that of the town. Though the students reflect the basic class structure of the town (and practice the same kinds of discrimination) the structure is not as rigid, mainly because personality counts for so much. It is probably because students are in closer contact with each other than most adults and get a chance to know each other better. At any rate, they are more aware of personality than their parents and are more influenced by it.

The flexibility of the class system does not preclude great discrimination, however. At M.H.S., as at every large high school, a small group runs things. The "haves" control the Student Council and run it for the benefit of the "haves"; the "have nots" have no committee appointments, no student-sponsored social activities they can afford, and nobody listens to them at open meetings. Each grade is run the same way. The "have-nots" are not elected to office, do not serve on committees, do not feel welcome at class functions such as the Senior picnic, are not chosen for class Talent Shows or plays. Because of their place in the status-structure, they are looked down upon by the upper group as unfit to participate.

Every student is made aware when he *doesn't* belong. And so he gravitates to others who are ignored for the same reason he is. He is restricted to his little block in the bleachers, and he loses a feeling for those outside his block.

Class discrimination on the small scale of a high school carries over outside the school. The students who are part of it (either the "haves" who discriminate or the "have-nots" who are discriminated against) are caught in the cycle of prejudices, snobbery, and warped outlook which passes from one generation to the next. Only the "have something" student (if he's not too busy angling for more) seems to be not permanently affected by the class structure of his high school.

Nor is M.H.S. unique. I have had contact with similar high schools in my state where the same patchwork quilt appears at athletic contests, conventions, and music festivals. I have found the same class-consciousness even in a large high school in one of the largest cities in the country, which is attended by a largely homogeneous group from a particular area rather than by a cross-section of the whole city. If the financial standard does not apply to the same extent, the personality factor simply counts more, and the result is the same. Young people learn their adult roles, their place and position, while still in high school.

Although it could be improved, this paper has decided merits. The student has narrowed the subject to a manageable topic and in treating it has made excellent use of descriptive details. The "way in" is unusually good, and the echo of it in the last paragraph ("the same patchwork quilt") is only one of many devices that unify the paper. The classification could have been handled more smoothly, but it provides a convincing basis for the central point that the student makes. His approach to the material is objective and analytical (note that he does not reveal *his* place in the class structure as he would surely have done in a personal experience paper); at the same time, he does interpret what he has observed, speculating about causes and briefly indicating certain damaging effects. In short, the writer succeeds in large part in doing what he set out to do—increase the reader's understanding of the subject.

Essay examination answers

Answering an examination question in essay form usually means writing a short explanatory paper. The subject or choice of subjects is limited by the question. In studying for the course, you have become familiar with a fairly wide range of information; to answer a specific question you must recall the relevant material, organize it, and present it in essay form.[1]

Reading the questions • Because most examinations have a time limit, students often begin writing feverishly after no more than a glance at the questions. The results of such frantic haste are usually disappointing. It is much better to take a few minutes at the start to read all the questions and directions. If a choice is offered, decide which question to answer and cross out the others. If the questions have different values, divide your time sensibly: a question worth 10 percent should not take up 30 percent of your time. Save a few minutes at the end to check your answers.

Before beginning to write, read the question carefully. Many answers are unsatisfactory simply because the student misinterpreted or forgot the question in his hurry to fill the paper with words. The instructor has planned his questions to test your knowledge in specific areas: he is not asking you to improvise and answer questions of your own making. Examine each question to see what kind of answer it requires. Look for key words. Notice in the following examples how a change in one word affects the whole question:

Explain the
- causes
- effects of the Spanish-American War.

Describe the
- digestion
- reproduction of the frog.
- development

Discuss the
- sources
- structure of *Moby Dick*.
- significance

Since the verb often determines the nature of the answer, take particular care to interpret it properly. Here are some of the verbs instructors commonly use in essay questions.

analyze: give main divisions or elements, emphasizing essential features
classify: arrange into main classes or divisions
compare: point out likenesses and differences

---

[1]This material is adapted from pp. 426-431 of *The Perrin-Smith Handbook of Current English,* 2nd ed., 1962.

contrast: point out differences
criticize: give your opinion as to good and bad features
define: explain the meaning, distinguish from similar terms
describe: name the features in chronological or spatial order
discuss: examine in detail
evaluate: give your opinion of the value or validity
explain: make clear, give reasons for, trace the development of
illustrate: give one or more examples of
interpret: give the meaning or significance
justify: defend, show to be right
review: examine on a broad scale
summarize: briefly go over the essentials

Some of the verbs *(criticize, evaluate, justify)* call for evidence and judgment as well as information. (See Chapter 7, "Persuasion papers.")

Writing the answers • Before beginning to write an answer to a question, remember that the instructor expects you to demonstrate *specific* knowledge about the subject. A succession of vague generalities will not be acceptable. Even if you are discussing a fairly broad general topic, support whatever generalizations you make with specific illustrations. Do not omit essential particulars because you assume that the instructor is familiar with them already. Of course he is; the main purpose of his examination is to find out whether *you* are.

A scratch outline of the main points that you plan to develop in your answer may be useful as a guide in writing. But whether you make an outline or not, make a concentrated effort to set your thoughts down in some logical order: all the sentences should relate to the question asked, and each should lead to the next in an orderly fashion. Many essay answers are unsuccessful because the student, although well-informed, presents information in a haphazard, unrelated fashion, giving the impression that he is thoroughly confused on the subject. Remember that the *length* of the answer is not the criterion of its worth: choosing the right facts and organizing them sensibly impress the reader far more. Since the time you have to write is limited, you should confine yourself strictly to what you know about the question.

Examination answers should be written in acceptable General English. Although the instructor will not expect an essay written in class to be as fully developed and as polished in style as one written at home, he will expect it to be adequate in usage and mechanics of writing. Even if a paper is otherwise accurate, frequent misspellings do much to lower the reader's opinion of it. Take particular care to spell and use correctly any technical terms or names that have been used in the course: *myosis, mercantile, assize, neurosis, imagery, Lamarck, Malthus, Schopenhauer*. An instructor will be understandably disturbed if he thinks you have paid scant attention to terms you have heard in class and read in the text numerous times. Proofreading your answers will help you eliminate careless errors and will give you a chance to fill in gaps in information.

Sample essay answers • Reproduced below are brief essay answers from examinations in biology and history. Read each question carefully, decide what sort of answer is required, and compare the answers given by two students. Then read the criticisms that follow.

Question: Define *dominant* as it is used in genetics.

Answer A

(1) In genetics, dominant is the opposite of recessive. (2) Different characteristics are inherited by the individual by means of genes acquired from the male and female parents. (3) These genes are arranged, or carried, on chromosomes, and are paired, one from each parent. (4) A good deal is still unknown about the behavior of genes, although the science of genetics is making rapid progress. (5) Gregor Mendel, a monk, made discoveries in heredity by doing experiments with sweet peas. (6) He found that certain traits are stronger (dominant) and others are weaker (recessive). (7) Therefore, if two genes carry the same characteristic, one will be dominant over the other. (8) Examples of this are dark eyes, normal color vision, etc.

Answer B

(1) The term *dominant* as used in genetics refers to that situation in which one gene in a pair takes precedence over another in determining a given characteristic in the individual. (2) For example, if a child inherits a gene for blue eyes from one parent and for brown eyes from the other, he will have brown eyes. (3) This is because the brown-eyed gene is *dominant;* the blue is *recessive.* (4) He still carries both genes and may transmit either to his offspring, but one has masked the effect of the other in his physical appearance. (5) Clear dominance does not occur in all pairings, however. (6) Sometimes *mixed dominance* occurs, as in the case of sweet peas, where a cross between a red and a white parent produces pink offspring. (7) Some cases of dominance are *sex-linked;* the

Criticism: Answer A contains irrelevant general information (sentences 2-5) and does not give a clear definition of *dominant*. You cannot explain the meaning of a word simply by naming its opposite (sentence 1). "Stronger" and "weaker" (sentence 6) are poor synonyms because they have such a variety of meanings. The answer also misleads by oversimplification: sentence 7 implies that complete dominance occurs in *all* pairings of genes. It is also not clear to what species of life the two examples in the last sentence refer.

gene for color blindness in humans, for instance, is dominant in the male and recessive in the female.

Criticism: Answer B is satisfactory. The term is clearly defined in the first sentence. Sentences 2-4 give an example of its use, distinguish it from its opposite, and add an important qualification. Sentences 5-7 note two important variants in the meaning of the term. There is no irrelevant material.

Question: Compare and contrast English and Spanish colonial methods in the New World.

Answer A

(1) The Plymouth colony suffered many hardships in the early years of its existence. (2) This was also true of the Roanoke colony, but it eventually failed and did not survive. (3) The climate was more promising there, but it seemed as if the kind of people it included, like gentlemen unused to work, adventurers, and renegades, did not have the patience and religious fervor of the New England settlers. (4) The same was true of the Spanish colonies in Florida and elsewhere —the climate was good, but the men were selfish and had no direction. (5) The Spanish were more cruel toward the Indians than the English, and there was nothing constructive in their aims.

Answer B

(1) The Spanish generally thought of the New World as a reservoir of riches to be tapped. (2) The great Spanish conquerors, like Cortez and Pizarro, were explorer-adventurers whose main aim was to subjugate the native population and wrench from them whatever riches and power they possessed. (3) The Spanish method was usually to impose a military dictatorship upon a restive populace; the domination depended on military force. (4) The English, on the other hand, thought of the New World colonies as a *permanent* extension of English civilization. (5) Their methods were not to immediately extract native riches, but to plant the seeds of English life in the new continent. (6) Unlike the Spaniards, the English generally

Criticism: More than half the answer (sentences 1-3) contrasts *two English colonies* rather than *English and Spanish colonial methods.* Mention of climate in sentences 3 and 4 is also irrelevant to a question dealing with methods. "Selfish" and "had no direction" need further explanation, as do "cruel toward the Indians" and "nothing constructive."

emigrated in family units, placated rather than subdued the native inhabitants, invested labor and capital in the New World soil, and awaited long term fruits. (7) Settlement was their aim rather than exploitation.

Criticism: This answer is much more satisfactory than A. The basic differences in aim and the consequent differences in method are fairly well stated. The first section of the answer (sentences 1-3) describes Spanish methods; the second (sentences 4-7) presents the significant differences in English aim and method.

Exercises

1. The following paper is a student's attempt to explain the basic essentials of rowing to an audience totally unfamiliar with the subject. Evaluate the paper, answering these questions: (a) Are the proportions of the paper satisfactory, or should the student have given more space to some phases of his material and less to others? (b) Are the technical details about the equipment explained in such a way that the layman can visualize the equipment and understand its function? (c) Is the explanation of the actual process of rowing clear and complete? (d) Is the writing competent?

Rowing

Rowing is a thrilling competitive sport. The aim of rowing is simply to win a race. To win a race you need a good shell, called a boat by landlubbers, with eight powerful oarsmen and a smart coxswain working together as a team. The oarsmen who do the physical work of rowing the shell are usually between 150 and 170 pounds of solid muscle. If an oarsman is too heavy he will slow the shell down, and if he is too fat he will tire out too fast during a race. The oarsmen sit in a straight line with their backs to the bow. Each oarsman has a number, which corresponds to his position in the shell. The bow man is number one in position, and the stroke (the one who sets the stroke) is number eight in position. The even numbered men have their oars on the port side (left side), while the odd numbered men have their oars on the starboard side of the shell—the right side. The coxswain is the most important single individual in the shell for he steers it, and he decides how many strokes the crew should do every minute. He also makes sure that each oarsman does his job exactly in time with the others. The coxswain is always much lighter than an oarsman, and the reason of course is that he is not required to do any of the hard physical work of rowing. What he needs is skill.

The shell is a streamlined piece of equipment approximately sixty feet long and two feet wide. An important reason for handling the shell with the greatest of caution is the bottom of it, which is only an eighth of an inch thick. The shell is designed to cut through the water in the most efficient manner possible. The oar that an oarsman uses is a long shaft of wood with a rounded handle at one end and a blade at the other. The handle is usually unshellacked and very rough for the purpose of a better grip. The blade is a thin, smooth, shellacked surface that is slightly curved to offer increased resistance to the water. The middle of the oar rests in an oarlock on an outrigger that is attached to the gunwale of the shell. An oarsman sits on a sliding seat that helps him when he rows. His feet are laced into special shoes that are attached to a small piece of wood a little above the bottom of the shell.

When a team practices, it works on speed and the method of rowing. Special emphasis is placed on the method of rowing because it is with a good individual method that a shell develops the speed it needs to win a race. The movement of a shell is accomplished by a series of "strokes." In a race an eight-man crew uses thirty-eight or forty strokes for a brief dash when it is needed. Technically a stroke includes all the motions of an oarsman from the time he dips his oar to catch the water to the time when it is again in the same position. The oarsmen sit up with their backs straight and their legs in a bent position with their seats forward as far as they will go. When the coxswain yells "Row," they catch the water with the oars and push their feet against the shoes, driving their sliding seats backward until their feet are straight. As they move backward, they pull their oars through the water, creating the power that moves the shell. They then "recover" (part of the stroke, in which the blade is in the air) the blade by "feathering" it by means of a wrist motion, in which the wrist is perpendicular to the arm. They then carry it toward the bow in a nearly horizontal position, until it is squared for the next stroke. If an oarsman fails to clear the water with his blade on the recovery because he has feathered too soon or too much or too little, he "catches a crab." This usually causes the loss of the race.

An oarsman gets satisfaction from rowing at a fast pace and testing his endurance, from eating pure honey on the day of a race to build up his energy, and from the greatest thrill of all, the winning of a race and the opportunity to throw the coxswain in the water for the traditional ceremony.

2. Select an explanatory article from a current magazine, clip it, and then submit it with a brief paper in which you answer these questions: (a) What are the sources of the writer's material? To what extent is it drawn from interviews? From reading? From his own experience, observation, and reflection? (b) Is there any indication in the opening of the article that the writer was making a special attempt to catch the reader's attention or engage his interest in the subject? (c) What techniques or devices of explanation does he use? (d) What audience does he seem to have been addressing?

3. Write an explanatory paper (600-900 words) on any one of the assignments in *Category I*, pages 193-194 (or on the one that your instructor selects). In a separate note at the beginning of the paper, identify the audience you are addressing.

4. Write an explanatory paper (800-1200 words) on any one of the assignments in *Category II*, pages 194-195 (or on the one that your instructor selects). In a separate note at the beginning of the paper, indicate the audience you are addressing; and in a separate paragraph at the end of the paper, summarize the methods you have used in developing your explanation.

5. Find a passage written for a specialized audience—a paragraph or two from a textbook for one of your other courses or from a technical journal. Rewrite it for general readers, people who have some interest in the subject but no special knowledge of it. If necessary, consult a dictionary to find simpler terms for those which are likely to be unfamiliar to your readers, but do not merely copy out dictionary definitions. Aim for a clear, coherent, readable style.

6. The following are excerpts from explanatory papers written by students. Decide which ones do a satisfactory job of explaining and which do not. Rewrite those you find unsatisfactory.

a. Even the common words we use everyday can be very difficult to define. Take the word "courage." No one can pinpoint its exact meaning because the word is subject to the interpretation of each individual. My dictionary states that courage is "the quality of mind that enables one to encounter difficulties and danger with firmness or without fear." But sometimes a person will act so quickly in a dangerous situation that there is doubt as to whether he had courage or was just foolhardy. He may be just acting instinctively. Such a situation often occurs when one person tries to help another. Many double drownings are the result of impulsive acts. One person sees another drowning, and instead of analyzing his own chances as well as those of the other person, he rushes to aid the other person. If the would-be rescuer had carefully, though quickly, studied the situation and then had gone to the drowning person's aid, he would then have courage. In addition, the drowning person would have had a better chance of being saved. The impulsive rescuer often gets himself into trouble, and two people die instead of one. The would-be rescuer had "the quality of mind that enables one to encounter difficulties and danger with firmness or without fear," but he really acted irrationally, not courageously.

By amending the dictionary definition, we can arrive at a more suitable one. The amended definition should be "Courage is that quality of mind which enables one who realizes the circumstances in which he is placed to encounter difficulties and danger with firmness or without fear." This definition is more exact and more in accord with the way the word "courage" should be used.

b. My first introduction to Zen came in conjunction with the exercises we did before our karate lessons. Normally, we spread our legs about twice the shoulder width, and squatted as if we were riding a horse. We usually did this until our calves burned like fire, which only took a few minutes. One day, however, as I endured this torture, I was told to take a deep breath, not into my lungs, but to try to force the air into my stomach. To assist me, the instructor wrapped his long belt from his judo robe tightly around my chest, so the air could only go to my stomach. After a while I was able to accomplish this fairly well, and found it affected me profoundly. My legs did not hurt as much, my head felt clearer, I felt wonderful.

A few weeks later, I received a deeper touch of Zen. I was to try to achieve a state of meditation. The simplest way to accomplish this, I was told, was to do the normal squatting and breathing routine, but then remain squatting, take a very deep breath, force it to my stomach, hold it as long as I could, and then yell. Yell, not as does a frightened female, but more as one grunts from the stomach when picking up a heavy weight. Meanwhile, I was to try to keep my mind blank, and to stare at some point in space between myself and my instructor, who was also doing this. Amazingly, it worked. Suddenly my mind was free. All the world was black and quiet, except for my instructor. The blackness closed in around him until it was about two feet from him, and there it stopped. He was my world. I could only see and hear him. At first my head felt slightly dizzy, but suddenly it soared. It was free of my body, free to communicate completely and thoroughly with my instructor. We did not remain like this for long, yet time was strangely affected, and it seemed forever. After this experience, I began to see that there was far more to the Oriental martial arts than the mere physical.

c. Jazz is usually classified on the basis of "what the music sounds like," or to be more accurate on the musical forms derived by composers, arrangers and soloists from previously existing forms and styles and from their own musical imagination. Thus bop is distinguished from swing because of the use that bop makes of complex chord progressions (often one change per measure) and dissonant intervals, whereas swing employs fairly simple chord progressions and for the most part consonant intervals, intervals that "sound right" to most people. In the light of the current controversy in jazz as to the merit of what is called "the new thing" (abandoning of the melody line, lack of concern with harmony, and the use of extremely disjointed rhythms), it would seem to be valuable to re-classify jazz styles on the basis of the composer's (or soloist's) approach to existing forms. Along these lines jazz styles can be divided into two elements which I shall call the formalist and the expansionist. By a formalist I mean a person whose concern is to embellish upon the previously existing forms; by an expansionist I mean a person who tries to expand the existing forms.

d. Since the people of Barrington are very similar in income, ideology, and social status, it is easy to characterize them. Barringtonians are middle- to upper-class, well educated, Protestant, Republican, and pretty much complacent and apathetic as far as the affairs of the world go. Barrington is a town in which:

One joins the country club and puts a lamp in one's picture window because "everyone else does."

One goes to the Methodist, Presbyterian, or Episcopal church every Sunday and promptly forgets Christianity for a week.

One feels sympathetic toward the cause of civil rights as long as the housing laws still prohibit families of any race other than white.

The main topics of discussion in the hallways of its sprawled-out, modern high school are the recent football game and who is going out with whom next week-end.

Almost every man catches the commuter trains in the morning and evening, complete with his brief case and gray flannel suit.

The League of Women Voters has degenerated into a gossip-over-morning-coffee group.

One of course sends one's children away to boarding school or prep school until they are old enough to enter Smith, Wellesley, Princeton, or Yale—if they can get in.

Practically no one has ever tried to register Democratic at the polls.

Schoolgirls have a strict code of dress and behavior, and generally no one bothers to stray from the norm.

One can look above the plate glass windows in the business district and see store fronts reminiscent of Western movies.

One's future consists of making a sound and acceptable marriage so one can settle down and put one's own lamp in one's own picture window.

Sounds like hell, doesn't it? Of course, it isn't quite so bad. The atmosphere may be intellectually discouraging, but it is not suffocating. Emotionally there is a sort of warm, relaxed naïveté that could be termed charming. Barrington is also a town in which:

One cannot walk down a street and escape the inevitable hellos.

A lost purse is returned promptly with belongings intact.

A student can feel free to visit his teacher at home for additional assistance.

One is never alone when one needs help.

Chapter Seven

PERSUASION PAPERS

*P*eople *listen instinctively to the*
man whose speech betrays inclination.

Richard M. Weaver

In some sense, all good writing is persuasive. A subjective description of a town is persuasive if it makes the reader "see" the town as the writer sees it. An account of an incident is persuasive if it makes the reader feel that "this is the way it really happened." An explanatory paper is persuasive if it makes the reader understand what a thing is or how it works or what it is like. In this broad sense, any piece of writing that accomplishes its author's purpose is persuasive—whatever that purpose may be.

As the term is used in this chapter, however, "persuasion" has a narrower meaning. It identifies the kind of writing in which the author tries to *influence* the convictions or beliefs or actions of his reader. So used, persuasion applies only to matters or issues on which there is a difference of opinion among reasonable men: a persuasive essay is one in which the writer tries to win the reader over from either a neutral or an opposing position. (Political speakers at $100-a-plate dinners for the party regulars ordinarily engage in ritual, not persuasion, for they are exhorting those who are already persuaded.)

This definition draws no distinction between *convincing* and *persuading*. It is sometimes said that a piece of writing aimed at convincing uses logical reasoning whereas a piece of writing aimed at persuading relies on appeals to the emotions and passions. The distinction has some value, but its value is lessened if it is further insisted that appeals to the mind are inherently more honest or more desirable than appeals to the emotions. Most of the world's great arguments make appeals of both kinds; moreover, these appeals are hardly separate and distinct but work cooperatively to reinforce each other. And both may be used for dishonest as well as for honest purposes. It seems better, then, to include under persuasion whatever contributes to the writer's purpose of influencing his audience. Some of the appeals may be labeled "logical" and some "extra-logical" (not illogical but simply outside the province of logic).

The degree and kind of influence will vary. An expression of opinion or preference may have—and may be intended to have—very little persuasive force, but when backed up by reasons, it takes on more. An interpretation of an event or of a poem, however objective the presentation, is usually designed to persuade the reader that it is the right interpretation—or at least a plausible one. Any book review which goes from an account of what is in the book to an evaluation of it attempts to be persuasive, for it argues that the book is good or bad, worth reading or not worth reading. More obviously intended to persuade are speeches and essays which call for action—to elect a candidate to office, to pass a piece of legislation, to change a University ruling.

Many essays and articles fall on the borderline between explanation and persuasion. In the writing that college students do, the chief examples of such borderline cases are reviews and book reports, which we will consider before going on to more sharply argumentative—persuasive—papers.

Reviews and book reports

A review is a description and evaluation of something new. When we think of reviews we think first of books, movies, and plays, but there are reviews published on a large variety of things—television programs, concerts, recitals, recordings and art exhibitions; new medicines and other chemical compounds, from fertilizers to weed killers; new buildings; new machines of all sorts, including each year's crop of new cars. Some of these reviews appear in specialized magazines and go into considerable technical detail, but many are run in periodicals for general circulation, addressed to intelligent readers with an interest in the subject but no first-hand knowledge of it.

Typical content of reviews • Ordinarily a review will identify, classify, describe, and evaluate the subject—though not necessarily in that order.

Identifying the subject.   A review (unless of a single occurrence like a concert) should identify its subject specifically enough for a reader to find it. For a book this means giving title, author, publisher, and usually the number of pages and price; for a movie—title, principals of the cast, and often the producer, director, company and theater where playing; for a concert—principal performers, organization sponsoring it, and time and place; for a product—name (often a trade name), model or type, perhaps catalog number, manufacturer, price.

Classifying the subject.   Usually you will tell what sort of thing your subject is—for instance, whether a movie is a western, a musical, a comedy, a mystery, a serious drama, a documentary, or another kind. This tag will help the reader place the subject in its class and suggest like subjects for comparison. A precise statement about what your subject is and what its purpose is will pave the way for your judgment of how adequately it fulfills its purpose. A drawing-room comedy and a farce are both intended to amuse, but they provoke such different kinds of amusement that they can hardly be judged by the same standards.

Describing the subject.   The bulk of your review will consist of details about the subject, either given in a block of description or scattered as evidence for your evaluation of it.
   Reviewers of books become very skillful in summarizing a story without giving away its outcome and in sketching sample scenes that are either representative or especially successful or unsuccessful. Something of the same sort is appropriate for a review of a movie, together with comment on such technical features as the acting, the setting, lighting, and photography. A review of an automobile gives details of appearance, of the body and accessories, of the motor, and of performance.

Evaluating the subject.   A good eye for detail and for analysis is fundamental to a good review, but you should not limit yourself to description. Even though it may be stated briefly, the important feature of your review is your opinion. It may range from an informal expression of your immediate reaction to a judgment based on considerable study and reflection. As in other persuasive papers, you should give reasons that will make your evaluation plausible. This means, among other things, making clear your criteria for judgment—your beliefs about the proper nature and function of what you are reviewing, its place in society, and so on. Even though your evaluation is not definitive, it will win respect if it flows from standards that are sensible and clearly stated. Resist the temptation to take refuge in vague, subjective reactions or in sweeping verdicts: "I liked it," "It appealed to me," "It is the best," "It is the poorest." One way to avoid this is to supplement your general appraisal with judgments about the success or failure of specific parts or aspects of the subject. Another way is to make discriminating comparisons between your subject and others like it—better ones and worse.

A review often includes other matters (for interest or for what light they throw on the subject), especially background facts, something about the making of the subject or the author's career; but the body of short reviews consists of description and evaluation.

You will find the essential elements in this review. Note that the reviewer begins with some remarks about the trend of presenting history as popular entertainment and then relates the book to that trend.

Contemporary historians have been a good deal criticized for their failure to tell a good story, their neglect of the play of personality and the stir of great events in favor of a more abstract account of trends and forces and factors and developments. But publishing abhors a vacuum, and the need for history as popular entertainment has been filled in various ways. One that has enjoyed very considerable commercial success in the last few years is represented by the kind of book that essentially consists of a group of touching or amusing or exciting anecdotes grouped around an historical event. This slice-of-time or the-day-Lydia-E.-Pinkham-died school of American historiography is utterly innocent of that trafficking with abstractions that has allegedly marooned professional historians on their island of unreadability; it presents the past as pure human interest, and anyone literate enough to deal with a tabloid can read it. Often he won't be able to tell the difference.

In *When the Cheering Stopped* (William Morrow, $5.95), Gene Smith has applied much the same technique to biography. The book is an account of the last years of Woodrow Wilson. After prefatory chapters on the death of the first Mrs. Wilson, the courtship of the second Mrs. Wilson, and the President in Paris at the Peace Conference, the book settles down to its main subject, a portrayal of the years during which the immense hopes for peace based upon Wilson's leadership gradually collapsed—when he decided to take his fight for the League of Nations directly to the people, his breakdown, his tenure of office when he was too sick to work, his last years as a broken and isolated man. All this is presented as a purely personal story, as human interest. No public issue is presented as such; Senator Lodge's reservations to the peace treaty, for instance, must be mentioned at least a score of times, but we are never told what they were, although we are told what kind of furs and what shade of Georgette Mrs. Wilson wore on innumerable occasions.

As a human-interest story, *When the Cheering Stopped* is a decidedly superior performance. It has been carefully researched; Smith has made conscientious use of the extensive archive left behind by Mrs. Wilson, and he is in a position to speak more freely and probably with more authority of that remarkable woman than any historian could have before her death in 1961. He clears away a mass of gossip about her marriage to the President and her role in running the government during his illness. He avoids the various oversimplified or overingenious efforts to explain Wilson's readiness to break with his friends by not explaining it at all, which leaves the impression, perhaps correct, that Wilson was a man with more loyalty to ideas than to men. Details about Wilson's taste in his later years are revealing: he loved the tawdrier forms of theatrical entertainment and liked to look at *Film Fun*. (Scratch a puritan and you'll find a pornographer.)

All this is fascinating. Less fascinating are the endless stories of little boys coming to the door of the house where Wilson lived in retirement and handing in one perfect rose, of old ladies sending the former President sweaters of their own knitting, of people bursting into tears.

The trouble with presenting the past simply as a human-interest story is that in the end it is all reduced to a flat level of triviality. It may be human but it is not very interesting because it denies that the past has any relevance, any significance. Action is replaced by gesture; the little boy proffering the rose is as important as Senator Lodge proffering his reservations, and a great deal nicer.

The later years of Wilson's Presidency raised the most profound questions about leadership in a democracy; the later years of his life raise equally profound questions about human destiny. But *When the Cheering Stopped,* by omitting the issues, offers the reader no evidence on which he can form a judgment of such matters. History as human interest fails on its own terms, because it tells a lesser story than the events; what makes a human being interesting is not in the end the number of sentimental anecdotes that cluster around his name, or the clothes his wife wore, or his taste in movies, but his ability to confront the great issues of life with passion and purpose, and out of their wreckage to achieve some perception of the world, to take upon himself the mystery of things. For all its fascinating detail, some of it genuinely illuminating, *When the*

Cheering Stopped makes a small and manageable and rather sentimental story out of something that was much more like a tragedy. (A Book-of-the-Month Club selection.) —PAUL PICKREL, *Harper's Magazine,* March 1964, p. 117

Course book reports • A report on "outside reading" for a college course in some respects resembles a review. But since the book or article is generally not new and the reader (the instructor) presumably has read it, your report will be more analytical than descriptive. Ordinarily the purpose of the report is to test your ability to apply to your independent reading the techniques of interpretation and criticism used in discussing class assignments.

Subjects for persuasive papers

In a book report, as well as in many term papers for college courses, the material is drawn from reading related to the course itself. The paper is in part explanation, in part interpretation, in part evaluation, and any one of these may receive the chief emphasis. The standards for interpretation and evaluation come largely from the principles and methods of the course. In most persuasive papers that you write for a composition course, you will draw your material from issues of general interest, and make your evaluations and judgments from careful reflection on those issues.

Although a part of any persuasive essay is usually given to explaining what the issue is—describing the situation and outlining the problem (and sometimes indicating various solutions that have been proposed)—the bulk of the paper is taken up with presenting and supporting the writer's judgment and his proposal for settling or solving the problem. The best topic is one which offers you a real problem and at the same time enables you to feel confident that you can offer a reasonable solution to it. A number of timeless questions have been debated for generations—the existence of God, the nature of evil, freedom *versus* determinism, and so on—and, at some time or other, every college student should (and no doubt does) engage in discussion about these matters. But for the papers you write, you are advised to choose narrower, more specific topics derived from your own experience and observation and from your reading in current newspapers and magazines. The following list suggests some areas to consider for possible subjects. Each, of course, would have to be narrowed to a definite, limited topic. (See Chapter 2, pp. 40-44.)

1. *Manners and customs:* reactions to dress and fashion, home or school etiquette, campus morality, dating, engagements
2. *Social affairs:* judgments about family relations, use of leisure time, entertainment, relations between groups of people
3. *Organizations and institutions:* interpretations and evaluations of clubs of all sorts, such as a lodge, a labor union, a church
4. *Education:* your evaluation of educational methods and practices in high school and college; appraisal of specific courses; your opinion on such issues as the criteria for awarding scholarships, religious instruction in public schools, general education *versus* specialized training
5. *Politics:* your conclusions about a campaign or a political party, the conduct of elections, the duties of an office holder, the performance of a person in office, an issue currently debated in Congress or in the United Nations
6. *Economics and business:* a critical examination of pricing, advertising and selling, qualities of products (from a consumer's point of view), buyers (from the point of view of the seller)
7. *Technology and production:* comparison and evaluation of two or more processes, methods, materials, designs; interpretation of some trend in engineering, architecture, or any other special field; the impact of technological advances on our lives
8. *Health and medicine:* an examination of a popular notion or of one with supposedly scientific backing; medicare; the need for or the effect of some new medical development
9. *Science:* estimates of the significance of new developments, methods, applications, hypotheses, and theories
10. *Literature and the arts:* interpretations of and preferences in literature, painting, sculpture, music—of particular works, of the works of one person; evaluation of methods or styles; criticism of the "popular arts" of movies, television, folk music; the issue of censorship of books and movies

A review of the subjects for explanatory papers (see Chapter 6, pp. 192-195) will suggest further possibilities, for often the same basic material can be channeled into either an explanatory paper or a persuasive one. An essay on a college club might be simple explanation, designed to show how the structure or activities relate to the purpose of the club. Or the essay might be shaped into an argument that because the club performs so many valuable functions, it deserves to be subsidized by the college administration (*or* that because of certain activities, it should be censured *or* that because its membership rules are discriminatory, it should be abandoned). In choosing a topic for any persuasive paper, the primary consideration is that you see an *issue* in it—something you regard as desirable or undesirable, beneficial or harmful, wise or unwise. The best topic for a persuasive paper is one about which you have not only adequate information but convictions and beliefs that you want to express.

Supporting the thesis

So far as the content of an essay in persuasion goes, the two essential elements are the thesis and the proof. The thesis (or the central proposition) is the belief or conviction or course of action that the writer tries to persuade his audience to accept. The proof is the evidence advanced in support of it. Thesis and proof represent the *what* and *why* of argument.

A persuasive paper is not just a discussion or exploration of the topic. It affirms something about the topic; it advances a thesis. The thesis may be an opinion or a preference; it may be a judgment or an evaluation or a proposal for action. Whatever its nature, the thesis gives a focus to the paper, a center to the discussion. In a rough way, the thesis corresponds to the sentence statement of any paper and (depending on whether the general plan is one of support or climax) may be set forth at the start of the paper or may be the conclusion toward which the discussion moves. (See Chapter 2, pp. 49-50.)

The development of the thesis makes up the proof, the substance of the paper. Proof in persuasive papers is not the same as scientific demonstration. If we could achieve absolute certainty in all matters, presumably one demonstration would be sufficient for us. But the matters we argue about are those which arouse differences of opinion or judgment, even among sensible men of good will—matters which are not subject to indisputable demonstration. As it applies to persuasion, proof is best defined as what any *reasonable* man would feel obliged to accept as evidence in support of the thesis. It is unfortunately true that few of us are reasonable all of the time. As we are not always temperate, rational, and unprejudiced, so we are not always persuasive nor open to persuasion. But the progress of society depends largely on persuasion; we must learn to use it and to reckon with it.

Two useful approaches to proof may be made. One is through the sources a writer draws on to support his thesis, and the other is through the logical relationships he establishes. The first approach is particularly useful in building up or constructing an argument; the second (treated in the next section of this chapter) is valuable in testing its strength.

In supporting his thesis, the writer gives his reasons for holding a belief or for advocating a policy—reasons of sufficient force, he hopes, to lead his audience to share the belief or agree to the wisdom of the policy.

The reasons may be of many different kinds. Some may be first-hand observations of incidents or situations or characteristics; others may be reflections about relationships; still others stem from the judgments or investigations of other people. The basis for many of the reasons we offer in support of our convictions has already been suggested (see Chapter 3, "Methods of development"). Examples, comparison and contrast, classification, definition, and cause-effect analysis—all can be given an argumentative thrust that shapes them into support for a belief or a proposal.

The following paragraph shows how explanatory material can be given an argumentative edge. The low pay, the nature of prison work, and the kind of employees that prison work attracts—these are presented not as descriptive details but as obstacles to the reforming of the inmates.

Where reformation is concerned, the quality of a prison's employees is of critical importance; yet for reasons which are easy to discern, but difficult to change, it is, generally, abysmally low. Not only is the financial reward for prison employment far below what might attract high-grade employees, but the very nature of prison work is unappealing to most people. Almost nowhere else in modern society can a man wield the direct, personal authority over other men that a prison guard—and, to a lesser degree, a noncustodial prison employee—wields over convicts. This "watchdog" aspect of prison work attracts chiefly men who have sadistic inclinations or who, perhaps to compensate for feelings of inadequacy, find reassurance of personal worth in exercising authority over others.—Hal Hollister, "An Ex-convict's Scheme for More Practical Prisons," *Harper's Magazine,* Aug. 1962, p. 16

The following outline of a student's paper indicates how some of the typical methods of developing a subject can be drawn on for the substance of a persuasive essay. The first section (I) is an explanatory statement about current dormitory regulations, and the last one (VI) is a proposal to abolish all regulations. Sections II-V argue for the proposal, and so constitute the proof.

No Curfews

College students in dormitories should be free to come and go as they choose, unrestricted by hours regulations. [Sentence statement or thesis]

I. Dormitory regulations now in force place many limitations on the student's freedom to choose his own hours.
   A. The rules for men are strict.
   B. The rules for women are even stricter.
II. Because college students as a whole are mature, they should be given the responsibility to make their own decisions.
   A. Maturity is one criterion this college uses in admitting students.
   B. Although many students are under 21 and so not legally mature, they are socially mature and responsible.
      1. They have to assume responsibility for doing independent work in their college courses.·
      2. They have to make sensible decisions about dividing their time between studying, campus activities, and social life.
III. If a student is treated like a child, he will behave like a child.
   A. Some recent examples of students breaking regulations show that they were just rebelling against unfair rules.
   B. My own infraction of the rules was a deliberate protest ·against an unfair regulation.
IV. If a student is treated like an adult, he will behave like an adult.
   A. Fraternity students on this campus have unrestricted hours, yet they behave in a responsible way.
   B. Eubanks College, which has recently abolished all regulations, has fewer disciplinary problems than we do.
   C. When I am at home, I am given complete freedom to choose my own hours, and I do not abuse that freedom.
V. An authority, John T. Rule, offers support for my position.
VI. The administration should immediately abolish all limitations on the hours of dormitory students. [Proposal—the thesis]

As the outline indicates, the writer's first reason (section II) is based on definition; he uses examples to argue that college students belong in the *class* of mature people. His second reason (III) is based on cause-effect relations; he gives instances to prove that dormitory regulations produce bad effects on students. His third reason (IV) is based on three comparisons, each of which is intended to show the wisdom of permitting students to make their own decisions about hours.

The fourth reason (V) is not so clear from the outline. As a method of development, it is more common in persuasive papers than in personal experience or explanatory papers. In using it here, the writer turned from the evidence suggested by his own experience, observation, and reflection to that provided in an essay on a somewhat larger but related problem— the degree to which a college should take responsibility for the moral behavior of its students. He summarized some of the main points made in the article and incorporated this direct quotation into his paper:

To punish all to prevent the transgressions of the few is, on the face of it, unjust. At most the college can, by legislation, limit opportunities for immorality. Such limitation is at heart police action, not educational action. Limiting immorality is not teaching morality. Though it is a much more difficult policy to follow, severity toward those who abuse a privilege is far better than denying everyone the privilege. The college that is willing to accept the headaches such a policy inevitably entails is then in a position to define by its specific disciplinary actions what it considers to be abuse.—John T. Rule, "Must the Colleges Police Sex?" The *Atlantic*, April 1964, p. 58

The use of the testimony or opinions of others is considered to be an *external* source of argument in contrast to the *internal* sources of argument (definition, likenesses and differences, causes and effects), which relate directly to the subject itself. Evidence of this kind is often useful, either for supplying facts or statistics on which only the expert can be reliably informed or (as in the student's paper) for presenting general principles that accord with those advanced by the paper. In most persuasive essays, however, the testimony of an expert or authority, no matter how respected, is—and should be—only a relatively minor part of the total argument.

These comments on the student's outline for his paper "No Curfews" are made not to show that he was right or wrong but to show that he used a variety of reasons in advancing his thesis. The skeleton of the paper consisted of a series of propositions, each of which was given support in the paper and each of which was made to bear on the central proposition or thesis—"Hours regulations should be abolished." Stated most baldly, these propositions and the sources used to support them are:

1. College students are mature (definition, classification, examples)
2. Hours regulations have bad effects (cause-effect relationships, examples)
3. Students behave better when they are not subject to regulations (comparisons, examples)
4. A noted authority supports this opinion (testimony in the form of direct quotation)

Any good persuasive paper is built on a chain of related propositions, all anchored to the main point or thesis that the writer is trying to support. In preparing your paper, you need, first, to establish (in the form of assertions) a chain of propositions that will lead you to your thesis; second, to decide which of those propositions need to be supported; and, third, to decide what kind of proof can be offered for those that need it. Notice the first sentence of the passage just quoted: "To punish all to prevent the transgressions of the few is, on the face of it, unjust." No proof is offered for the proposition; the words *on the face of it* indicate that the author believes no proof is necessary. Any reasonable man, he says in effect, will accept as an axiom, or at least as a tenable assumption, that it is unjust to punish all to prevent the transgressions of the few. Another assumption, also unstated, lurks behind that one: no unjust policy should be pursued. Again, any reasonable man would accept that assumption.

Another example is offered by the first of the reasons sketched in the student's outline. His train of reasoning might be put formally in one of two ways:

1. All mature people are free to choose their own hours; college students are mature people; therefore college students should be free to choose their own hours

or

2. If college students are mature, they should be free to choose their own hours; they are mature; therefore they should be free to choose their own hours.

In thinking through the problem of persuading his audience, the writer had first to decide what would make a compelling train of reasoning, and he fashioned for himself a series of propositions roughly corresponding to those outlined above. He had further to decide what he could take for granted and what needed proof. The first of the propositions, he realized, was self-evident; it would only belabor the obvious to present evidence that his parents, college administrators and teachers, and other people generally held to be mature do indeed have the freedom to choose their own hours. In this example, the vulnerable proposition—the one that needs all the support he can give it—is that college students considered as a group are mature. In advancing his first reason, he gave virtually all his attention to this proposition—and properly so.

To persuade any audience, you need to decide which of your propositions they will take for granted and which will strike them as novel or shaky or even unreliable. Belaboring the obvious will bore your audience; asserting as an incontrovertible truth what is in fact highly debatable will irritate them. In preparing to write a paper intended to persuade or in checking over one you have written, it is a good idea to outline it in the form of a series of propositions and then, for each one, ask yourself: "Is this a basic assumption I can start from, or do I have to give evidence for it? If I need evidence, what will be most convincing? Can I support it through definition and classification, or should I develop causes and effects, or will comparison be the best method of handling this particular point? And what concrete evidence will prove that the definition is reasonable, or the causal analysis sound, or the comparison legitimate? What instances, what examples, and what particulars can I draw from my own experience? What kind of support can I find in the speeches or essays of others?"

To answer these questions intelligently, you need to size up the issue as well as the nature of the audience. Where the issue involves a judgment, making clear the basis of the judgment is quite as necessary as presenting the particulars that lead to the judgment: an evaluation of a poem (as good or bad) should rest on a cogently argued definition of what good poetry is. Where the issue involves a proposal for action, the substance of the paper will demonstrate that the proposed course of action is wise or desirable or necessary. Many action proposals are grounded in definition but are also likely to draw heavily on effects (good consequences will result from adopting this course of action) and on comparisons (this course of action is better than that one).

Once you know the nature of the issue, you can formulate your thesis and then decide what kind of proof can be brought to bear on it. For some of your papers, the phrasing of the assignment will specify the issue. In each of the following assignments, the issue is established for you, and you would be expected to argue for or against a specific course of action: Should comic books be banned? Should *Lady Chatterley's Lover* be sold in drugstores and newsstands? Should movies be censored? Should professional boxing be made illegal? Should a national lottery be instituted to help pay the cost of government? Should gambling be legalized? Should capital punishment be abolished? The argument on any one of these questions may be very subtle and complicated, but the *issue* is given clear statement in the assignment.

In other papers, you may be asked to find your own issue. In many persuasive essays, the writer creates the issue by analyzing a situation or a problem, posing possible alternatives, and then arguing for one of them. A typical pattern is to present evidence that there are only two alternatives, to give reasons why one alternative is unacceptable, and then to urge the adoption of the other. The following excerpts from an essay (its beginning and end) make this pattern clear, as does the title of the essay itself:

The recent changes in the technique of war have produced a situation which is wholly unprecedented. War has existed ever since there were organized states, that is to say for some six thousand years. This ancient institution is now about to end. There are two ways in which the end may come about: the first is the extinction of the human race; the second is an agreement not to fight. I do not know which of these will be chosen....

I have been speaking of dangers and how to avoid them, but there is another thing which is just as important to emphasize, for while fears are at present unavoidable, hopes are equally legitimate. If we take the measures needed to end our fears, we shall thereby create a world capable of such well-being as has never been known and scarcely even imagined. Throughout the long ages since civilization began, the bulk of mankind have lived lives of misery and toil and bondage. All the long burden of misery that has darkened the slow progress of mankind has now become unnecessary. If we can learn to tolerate each other and to live in amity, poverty can be abolished everywhere more completely than it is now abolished in the most fortunate nations. Fear can be so much diminished that a new buoyancy and a new joy will brighten the daily lives of all. The work of science, which while war survives is largely evil, will become wholly beneficent. Nothing stands in the way but the darkness of atavistic evil passions. New technical possibilities of well-being exist, but the wisdom to make use of them has hitherto been lacking. Shall we collectively continue to turn our back upon the things that each one of us individually desires? We can make a world of light, or we can banish life from our planet. One or other we must do, and do soon. A great duty rests upon those who realize these alternatives, for it is they who must persuade mankind to make the better choice.—Bertrand Russell, "Co-existence or No Existence: The Choice is Ours," *The Nation,* June 18, 1955

We shall see later some of the hazards of posing alternatives in such black-and-white, *either-or* terms. For the moment we are concerned with ways of building an argument, and the example above does represent a very common one. Notice that the basis of it lies in an analysis or division of the subject; the procedure is to show that one course of action is unwise or impossible (or, in this case, unthinkable) and that therefore the other *must* be adopted.

A variation on this approach is illustrated by the recommendations for action that conclude a long analysis of the urgent need to increase the food supply of the underdeveloped countries of the world. The author offers several solutions and rejects none; but to him only one is a genuine, long-term solution. (Earlier, he has given evidence to support this conviction.)

What can be done to help the hungry half of the world pull itself up from its undernourished state and speed up the developments that would enable it to feed itself decently?

Even pessimists must note, first of all, that the prospects of the impoverished peoples are brightened by a most remarkable turn in human history. Whereas in the past men have been concerned only with feeding their own families and have fought long and bitter wars for food, we see today a new and remarkable world-wide concern for feeding the hungry wherever they are. Whether this arises out of advanced humanitarianism, the fears of the well-fed or the contest between the West and Communism is less important than the fact that the wealthy countries are taking an interest in the peoples of the poor countries.

During the past nine years the U.S. has sent more than $12 billion worth of its surplus food to these countries. The Food and Agriculture Organization, at the suggestion of Canada and the U.S., has launched an international effort for the same purpose with a $100 million fund as a starter, and it is now conducting a five-year Freedom from Hunger campaign.

This emergency help is not to be underestimated, and one hopes that it will be continued and even enlarged, preferably under international auspices.

A second way in which the developed countries are helping substantially is by example and by technical advice and assistance to the developing areas. The example, again, is important. The U.S. Department of Agriculture has estimated that at the present rate of progress in agricultural productivity the developed countries will be able to produce almost twice as much food as they need by the year 2000. Such an advance cannot fail to infect and stimulate the backward countries.

Yet when all is said and done, these countries must themselves generate the means for their emancipation from hunger. To do so they will have to change long-established habits and attitudes. Neither well-meant exhortations nor government decrees are likely to persuade them—certainly not in a hurry. Concrete steps may, however, speed reforms by quickly convincing the people of their value.

It is easy to list effective projects that the governments of these countries might undertake. Make available to the farmers the seeds and stocks of improved plant varieties and animal breeds. Build chemical-fertilizer plants. Supply agricultural chemicals for pest control and other special purposes. Provide new implements and machinery suitable for the local types of farming. Extend credit to the farmers for their new seeds and equipment. Pay them subsidies to start urgently needed new crops. And above all, establish training programs that will show them how to handle their new materials and equipment and to farm more efficiently.

Education must receive the first priority for the advancement of these countries. The development of each one of the Western countries has been founded on the literacy and knowledge of its population. This applies to their progress in agriculture as well as to their achievements in industrial technology and professional services. To raise itself the underdeveloped country requires a population that understands modern agriculture and nutrition, is equipped with teachers and experts in all the fields of food technology and is led by political and administrative officials who appreciate the possibilities of science and technology.

This will be a long and difficult program for some of the poorly educated and ill-fed nations. But investment in education is a far more practical and effective program for them than investment in big buildings, dams, roads and factories that are put up mainly as visible symbols of progress. Just as the strength of the so-called developed countries lies in their educational systems and their culture, so the great hope and promise of the future for the underdeveloped countries resides in the fact that they too will come to share in the full wealth of mankind's knowledge and contribute to it themselves.—Nevin S. Scrimshaw, "Food," *Scientific American,* Sept. 1963, pp. 79-80

Testing relationships

So far we have sketched some lines of argument that can be profitably explored in supporting a thesis. We turn now to the question of the internal coherence of the paper. To persuade the reader to accept his thesis, the writer must make a good case for it. Among other things, he must convince the reader that in arriving at his conclusion (his interpretation or evaluation or judgment) he has been guided by accurate observation and sound reasoning. He does this by giving sufficient evidence for the key generalizations—those which provide the grounds of his argument—and by making correct inferences from them. His task is first to see relationships, especially between premises and conclusions, and then to communicate those relationships to the reader. Making relationships clear is mainly a matter of continuity of statement, as discussed in Chapter 4, pages 139-143. But the critical reader will insist that relationships be sound as well as clearly stated. Testing them is therefore an essential step in preparing—and especially in revising—a paper.

In testing relationships, the writer can rely to a considerable extent on his own good sense, but he will also find some helpful cues and short cuts in the procedures of logic. Few students in a composition course have had a course in logic, but all of them have a nodding acquaintance with its fundamentals, whether from mathematics or the sciences or from courses requiring close reading. This section will touch on points of logic that are of special importance in testing statements for reliability and validity. Tests for reliability are easy to grasp but hard to apply. Tests for validity are more complicated but, once understood, are easy to apply.

Traditionally, the labels *induction* and *deduction* have been given to two ways of reaching conclusions. In most arguments, inductive reasoning and deductive inference mix freely; but because different methods are used to test the conclusions resulting from them, they will be discussed separately.

Testing induction • An inductive inquiry is grounded in particulars. It moves from the observation of facts, characteristics, attitudes, or circumstances to an inclusive statement or generalization. Strictly speaking, the term does not apply to those investigations in which all the data can be examined. The generalization "All the members of this year's freshman class were in the upper third of their high-school classes" results from an examination of the grade records of *all* the freshmen; it is essentially a nose-counting operation, and if the facts used are accurate, there is no question about its truth. But for an inductive generalization, not all the data have been examined (and, in most cases, not all of them can be).

The distinguishing mark of induction is the *inductive leap,* stemming from the insight or conviction that a characteristic or relationship (because it has been observed again and again) holds true for all data of the same kind. The investigation may have been painstaking and thorough, covering case after case, but at some point the investigator makes a shift from a de-scriptive or statistical statement about *this* member, *that* one, and the *next* one to a confident assertion about the whole class, including those members not available for inspection. Because unexamined data are included in the generalization, the logi-cian says that an inductive generalization (by contrast with nose-counting) is never certain, however high its degree of probability.

Most of us find it hard to accept the logician's cautious atti-tude toward all generalizations based on observation and ex-perience. Some inductive generalizations familiar to all of us do seem to be incontrovertibly true (especially those simple ones that regularly appear in textbooks). "All men are mortal" invites no skepticism whatever. Still, says the logician, it has only a very high degree of probability because men now alive *might* prove exceptions to the generalization. Although this may strike you as hair-splitting, it should serve as a useful reminder that the inductive generalizations that run through your persuasive papers need the best support you can give them.

In using inductive generalizations, students often do them-selves an injustice; they simply assert the generalization, for-getting that what seems like a commonplace to them may very well be both novel and dubious to their readers. It is not enough to convince yourself that your generalization is prob-able; you must convince your reader that it is. And you can do this only by giving him the evidence—citing the instances you have observed and showing that they are representative of the whole class. Unsupported, the generalization "Students on this campus have practically no interest in national politics" does not convince. Backed up by relevant examples, however, it may be overwhelmingly persuasive.

But how many examples do you need to support that gen-eralization, and what kind of examples? One swallow does not make a summer, and probably no reader would be persuaded by one instance—"My roommate never reads the editorials in the newspaper" or "The Socialist Club had to disband last year because of lack of members" or "Only a handful turned out to hear the senator." On the other hand, the reader will resist sheer quantity of evidence if he has reason to believe the instances you cite are not genuinely representative. To decide that students are politically apathetic on the basis of the in- difference shown by your roommate would be premature: the sample is too small. To base the judgment on the indifference manifested by all students majoring in music would be unwise: the sample is not representative.

The word *sample* suggests the kind of inquiry on which television ratings and political predictions are based. Poll-taking often does yield a high degree of probability. Although the sample may be small in terms of the total number of voters, it will, *if representative,* forecast fairly accurately the results of an election in which thousands of times the number of those polled cast their votes. Obviously, when you are gathering evidence for your persuasive papers, you do not have time to conduct comprehensive polls, nor do you have at your com- mand the complicated statistical systems that make polls reli- able. The inductive inquiries you make are necessarily incom- plete and unsystematic. At the same time, in writing as in daily life, you must make generalizations that will serve as a basis for judgment and for action.

One of the surest ways to produce unsound generalizations is to ignore contradictory evidence. An inductive inquiry has its origin in a hunch or hypothesis that such-and-such is so— that your roommate's attitude toward politics is not just a per- sonal idiosyncracy but is a characteristic shared by a great many other college students. On the basis of that hunch you start to investigate. The hypothesis is necessary; without it you could hardly launch an inquiry. But if further investigation proves the hypothesis incorrect, abandon it. Sticking to it in the face of contradictory evidence is foolish. Suppressing the contradictory evidence is dishonest.

Remembering that inductive generalizations yield only prob- ability should keep you aware of the need to back them up with relevant evidence. It should also make you more gen- erous in admitting the existence of negative instances or ex- ceptions. Acknowledging such exceptions will damage your case less than ignoring them. And you can often make your generalizations sturdier by finding reasons for exceptions. To return to our earlier example, you may be able to show that those few students who do have a lively interest in politics come from homes where such an interest is encouraged. They

have maintained their interest in spite of the fact that as college students they have scores of other interests.

Gathering and citing a good many instances will keep you
from "stereotyping," from using loose general labels that ignore more fundamental differences. There are stereotypes for
almost any group—Swedes, schoolteachers, blondes, Baptists,
Rotarians, movie stars, Texans, scientists, and so on. You can
call to mind a dozen more. But if you start thinking about
individuals, you will realize that an individual's membership
in a certain group does not determine his whole make-up and
that his thousand other characteristics make him, in some respects, different from any other person. Intolerant generalizations about racial or national groups all too often result from
the error of *hasty generalization*—jumping to a conclusion on
the basis of one instance or a small number of instances.

So far we have been concerned with the making of inductive
generalizations that describe or classify. (College students are
asserted to be in the *class* of politically apathetic people.) Many
other inductive inquiries are undertaken to establish causal
relations or connections between phenomena, and these need
to be handled with special care, especially when they are given
predictive value as guides to future action. Some causal relations are indisputable: anyone who puts a plastic dishpan
on a very hot burner will not do it a second time. But in other
situations causal connections are much harder to establish. A
college admissions officer is struck by the fact that the last ten
students admitted from Monitor High School have had disastrous college careers. He wonders if any student from M.H.S.
could succeed in college. He forms, however tentatively, a
causal connection between *students-from-M.H.S.* and *failure-
in-college.* Is he right? Probably everyone would agree that the
causal connection is less sure than the one the housewife established. The capacity to withstand heat is not likely to vary
much from one plastic dishpan to the next. But the admissions
officer cannot count on such a principle of uniformity when
he is dealing with the quality of instruction in a high school
from year to year or with the capacity of individual students
to succeed in spite of poor instruction.

Logicians give the label *post hoc, ergo propter hoc* ("after
this, therefore because of this") to the fallacy of assuming that
whatever comes after an event is necessarily a result of it. The
simple fact of temporal succession—one event following another in time—does not necessarily indicate a causal relationship. Did the ten students fail *because* they came from Monitor
High? The evidence at hand might be compelling enough to

suggest this as a hypothesis, but a thoughtful admissions officer would do no more than use it as a starting point for further inductive inquiries about the students who failed, the school they came from, and so on. These inquiries might enable him to confirm the hypothesis; on the other hand, they might force him to alter it or reject it altogether. Determining causes is the most rigorous stage of any inductive inquiry, for only a good deal of analytical skill can distinguish coincidental circumstances from genuine causes.

The British philosopher John Stuart Mill formulated five methods or canons for testing causal hypotheses. They are listed in the *Index* (*Cause). Their value and their limitations are obvious. In every case it is assumed that all of the circumstances can be known and that only a single cause is operating. The methods are peculiarly fitted for controlled experiments which can be repeated; where repetition is not possible, the difficulties of applying them are very great indeed. (The admissions officer cannot put the failing students into another high school and then give them another try at college.) In spite of these limitations, it is useful to acquaint yourself with Mill's methods, for they represent the basic procedures for testing a causal hypothesis, and the very statement of them should remind you of the need to give the evidence that makes the causal relationship plausible or probable. Most of the issues that you will debate—social and political and educational questions—are too complex to be argued on the basis of a single overriding cause. In dealing with such issues, you can recognize the complexity by ranking causes in terms of probability, by classifying different kinds of causes, and by proposing solutions that take into account a variety of causes.

Inductive procedures enter into those generalizations which express comparative judgments—this policy is better than that, this system of teaching a foreign language is better than that. The judgments are arrived at deductively, by referring to other generalizations about values and the ends to be achieved; nevertheless, it is inductive inquiry that yields the points of similarity and difference. And, as in using comparison for explanatory papers, the points of similarity and difference must be made relevant to the issue. (See Chapter 3, pp. 81-85.)

Analogy is a special variety of comparison that works as a partial induction. We reason analogically when we say that because two things are alike in certain respects, it is probable that they are alike in still another respect. We may, for instance, argue that because the period in which we now live is strikingly similar to some period in the past, we should adopt a policy now that proved successful then. Or we may argue that a volunteer corps should be instituted to cope with certain problems in this country because of the success of the Peace Corps in dealing with somewhat analogous problems in foreign countries. Analogy underlies the advertiser's plea to use a product because a man of athletic prowess (or a woman of charm) testifies to its excellence.

These are all examples of literal analogy, in which things of the same class are compared—historical periods, economic or social problems, people. In a figurative analogy, the things being compared belong to different classes. Some kind of imaginative insight uncovers similarities between things that have no obvious resemblance. For example, in the selection on page 121, the characteristics of a political liberal are brought out by the analogy to the behavior of a dog on a walk. Figurative analogies are of value in illuminating a subject, in opening up an avenue of speculation, in giving colorful support to an argument. But generally speaking any conclusions drawn from them are only suggestive and do not constitute proof. They may have great persuasive value in leading the audience to entertain a thesis (about the superiority of liberalism as a political philosophy, say), but in themselves do not prove it.

In sum, many of the generalizations that we use in persuading are arrived at by reasoning inductively about what we have observed and experienced. A generalization may be phrased as a class relationship (or partial definition), as a causal relationship, or as a comparison. In any of these, the two chief features of the inductive procedure are the framing of the hypothesis and the inductive leap. The three chief sources of error are (1) hasty generalizing, (2) mistaken causal relationships, and (3) faulty comparisons and analogies. Knowing the possible sources of error can guide you through the job of testing the reliability of your inductive generalizations.

Testing deduction • In reasoning inductively, we pull particulars into an inclusive generalization; in reasoning deductively, we draw a conclusion from propositions that we accept as true or that we have already proved to be true. We are reasoning deductively when we say "If this is true, that *must* be true." If Jack is a National Merit finalist, he must be smart. Why *must?* Because we take it for granted that all National Merit finalists are smart. The essence of the deductive process is the *must*—drawing an inevitable conclusion from propositions known or assumed to be true.

To test conclusions arrived at deductively, you need to ask two questions: Are the premises true? Is the reasoning valid? Only if you can answer both questions affirmatively is your argument sound.

As we have seen, logic offers some rules-of-thumb for testing the reliability of inductive generalizations. It does not, of course, tell us that a specific generalization is true or untrue, probable or improbable. That can be determined only by an examination of the material—the facts or instances that have gone into the making of the induction. Similarly, logic cannot tell us whether the premises we are working from in deduction are true or false. What it can do is provide rules for testing the validity of the conclusions we draw from our premises.

As a first step, you need to reduce complex propositions to simple ones, to sort out premises from conclusions, to bring into view whatever generalizations are not stated but simply implied in the argument (in the example above, "All National Merit finalists are smart"). In this preliminary analysis, your aim is to reduce your chain of reasoning to a skeletal pattern that will conform to the three-part structure of assertions known as the syllogism. Once your reasoning is laid out in syllogistic form, you can begin testing your premises for reliability and your conclusion for validity.

The three parts of the syllogism are the *major premise,* the *minor premise,* and the *conclusion.* The phrasing of the major premise allows us to distinguish three common patterns: the hypothetical syllogism (If P, then Q), the alternative syllogism (Either P or Q), and the categorical syllogism (All P is Q). An argument can often be reduced to more than one of these patterns, but ordinarily one of them seems more natural and is easier to deal with. (See p. 237 for an example of how the same train of reasoning can be thrown into two different patterns.)

The hypothetical syllogism.   This pattern is familiar to you from mathematics:

Major premise	If P, then Q		If P, then Q
Minor premise	P	*or*	not Q
Conclusion	Therefore Q		Therefore not P

The major premise asserts that if the antecedent P is true, the consequent Q is true. The minor premise asserts that P is true, and the conclusion drawn is that Q must be true. Or the minor premise denies that Q is true, leading to the conclusion that P is not true. These are the two valid forms of inference in a hypothetical syllogism.

Consider the reasoning of the admissions officer who decides to reject a candidate from Monitor High School. He says, "Better not admit this one. He's from Monitor High. Chances are he'll never get through college." Put more formally, his reasoning is:

If an applicant is from Monitor High, he will not succeed in college
This applicant (John Jones) is from Monitor High
Therefore this applicant (John Jones) will not succeed in college

Another chain of reasoning based on the premise that no college should admit students that it knows will fail leads to the decision "Better not admit this one." But first it is necessary to establish the fact (or the probability) that John Jones will fail. We can see that the admissions officer has followed a valid pattern of inference. After asserting the minor premise, he can move to his conclusion. As we have already seen, the major premise ("If an applicant . . .") asserts a causal relation based on induction. *If* it is true, the conclusion is true as well as valid.

Using the same major premise, the admissions officer could, without checking to see which high school Bob Burns came from, infer from his success in college that he was *not* from Monitor High. Here is his reasoning:

If a student is a graduate of Monitor High, he will not succeed
Bob Burns is succeeding in college
Therefore Bob Burns is not a graduate of Monitor High

The minor premise has denied the consequent Q; from this it follows that the antecedent P can be denied.

But look at these two inferences:

Jane Smith is not from Monitor High, so she will succeed in college
Lee Wallek is flunking out of college; he must be from Monitor High

Both inferences are incorrect. The *if . . . then* relationship is not reversible. The major premise has asserted that P implies Q, but it has not ruled out the possibility of other antecedents for Q. Nor has it asserted that Q implies P—that every case of failure in college can be attributed to attendance at Monitor High.

In summary, the two patterns of *valid* inference are:

P, therefore Q (affirming the antecedent entails affirming the consequent)

Not Q, therefore not P (denying the consequent entails denying the antecedent)

and the two *invalid* patterns are:

Not P, therefore not Q (it is fallacious to move from a denial of the antecedent to a denial of the consequent)

Q, therefore P (it is fallacious to move from an affirmation of the consequent to an affirmation of the antecedent)

Let us look again at the conclusions that are labeled invalid: "Jane Smith will succeed in college" and "Lee Wallek must be from Monitor High." It may turn out on further investigation that Jane *does* succeed in college and that Lee *is* from Monitor High—that is, we may discover that both conclusions are true. They are, however, true for reasons *other than* those given in the premises we were working with. You must get used to the unpleasant idea that invalid inference may yield a conclusion that happens to be true, just as valid inference may yield a conclusion that happens to be false. Validity means only that the stated conclusion follows from the premises that have been supplied. For a sound argument, you need valid inference from true premises.

The example we have used for the hypothetical syllogism involves causal relations. The *if . . . then* pattern, although peculiarly appropriate for expressing causal relations, is not restricted to them. The senator who says, "I oppose the Public Accommodations Bill because it is unconstitutional" could put his reasoning into the *if . . . then* framework:

If this bill is unconstitutional, then I oppose it
This bill is unconstitutional
Therefore I oppose it

In his argument, however, he would probably give little attention to establishing the necessary relation between the unconstitutionality of a bill and his opposition to it. His real job is to prove the minor premise, and here he would need to make a very careful analysis of the bill to show that it is unconstitutional. Definition and classification are at the heart of this syllogism, not causal relations.

The alternative syllogism. This pattern offers a natural way of formulating those arguments which move from a consideration of one course of action to another. The basic pattern is:

Major premise	Either A or B
Minor premise	Not A
Conclusion	Therefore B

The list of alternatives may, of course, be extended to three or more; one after another would be eliminated in separate arguments. As the pattern makes clear, the major premise reflects a classification or division of the material under consideration, and the major premise will be true only if it proceeds from a rigorous and accurate analysis of the material. In everyday situations, the alternatives are often provided for us: "John said he would be in the library or in the dormitory; he's not in the library, so he must be in the dorm." If John stuck by his promise, the conclusion is true as well as valid. Other major premises present larger problems. "Either we must co-exist or we will not exist" (see p. 239) asserts that there are only two choices, and moves to the conclusion that we must co-exist because the other choice is unthinkable. If there are other alternatives than the two stated, the conclusion does not necessarily follow.

The first problem, then, in testing an *either-or* syllogism is to determine the truth of the major premise. If other alternatives can be shown to be feasible, the argument is unsound.

The second problem is whether the major premise expresses an *exclusive* or an *inclusive* relationship. In the exclusive relation, one alternative rules out the other. John cannot be in two places at once; we cannot both co-exist and simultaneously destroy ourselves. If common sense or the context makes it clear that A excludes B, then there are two valid forms of inference. The minor premise may deny one alternative (and so affirm the other) or affirm one alternative (and so deny the other). For the exclusive relation, both of these procedures are valid, though in actual argument it is much more common to find the minor premise taking the form *not B:*

Either A or B	Either A or B
Not B	A
Therefore A	Therefore not B

Only the first of these procedures (denying one alternative) results in valid inference when both of the alternatives may be true—that is, when the relation is *inclusive*. Tests indicate, your doctor says, that you have bronchitis or pneumonia. At this stage he cannot rule out the possibility that you have both. If further tests show that you have pneumonia, you may or may not have bronchitis; that remains to be determined. An editorial states, "To curb juvenile delinquency, we must either find jobs for these unemployed young people or we must greatly extend the city's recreational facilities." The implication is that both alternatives are acceptable. But since jobs are simply unavailable, the editorial goes on to argue that the city must commit itself to building a new recreation center. With alternatives such as these, it would have been unrealistic (as well as invalid) to first demonstrate that jobs were available and then go on to say the center should not be built. When the relation is inclusive, there is only one valid form of inference:

Either A or B
Not A
Therefore B

In summary, the conclusion of an alternative syllogism will be unsound:

If the enumeration of alternatives is incomplete;
If, in an inclusive relation, the minor premise is affirmative

A systematic consideration of genuine alternatives offers an excellent way of structuring a persuasive essay. But a shrill insistence on an *either-or* premise that stems from a faulty analysis of the material can be very damaging to your case.

The categorical syllogism.   You will have observed that in the hypothetical and the alternative syllogisms the major premise contains all the terms of the argument. The minor premise brings in nothing new; it simply deals with one part of the major premise. In the *categorical* syllogism, the minor premise does bring in a new term. Both premises are phrased in such a way as to reflect class relationships, and errors in inference are fundamentally errors in handling these relationships.The errors are sometimes harder to detect than flaws in reasoning from *if . . . then* or *either-or* premises because the premises less often receive full statement. "Kangaroos are marsupials, and wallabies are kangaroos; therefore wallabies are marsupials" illustrates the pattern of the categorical syllogism. Essentially it asserts a series of class relationships. The major premise makes a statement about all members of a class, the minor premise relates the subject of discussion to that class, and the conclusion states what necessarily follows. Each statement contains two terms. The major term (P) is the predicate of the conclusion, the minor term (S) is the subject of the conclusion, and the middle term (M) appears in both the premises but (naturally) not in the conclusion.

	(M)		(P)
Major premise	All kangaroos	are	marsupials
	(S)		(M)
Minor premise	All wallabies	are	kangaroos
		(S)	(P)
Conclusion	Therefore all wallabies are marsupials		

The categorical syllogism rarely receives full statement in ordinary prose. One premise may be omitted or the conclusion may be presented first. Here are several ways the chain of reasoning might appear:

(Minor premise) A wallaby is a kangaroo, *(Conclusion)* so it must be a marsupial.

(Minor premise) Since a wallaby is a kind of kangaroo, *(Conclusion)* it is a marsupial.

(Conclusion) Wallabies must be marsupials: *(Minor premise)* they are kangaroos.

(Major premise) Kangaroos are marsupials, *(Conclusion)* and so wallabies must be.

Here are some common patterns, represented by letters, with their counterparts in argument:

1. "Of course this tap water is safe to drink.
   It's city water."

All *city drinking water* is *pure.*	All M is P
This tap water is *city drinking water.*	S is M
This tap water is *pure.*	S is P

2. "We should give this plan serious consideration because it offers a possible solution to
the East-West deadlock."

Any *plan which offers a possible solution to the East-West deadlock* is *a plan which should be given serious consideration.*	Any M is P
This plan is *a plan which offers a possible solution to the East-West deadlock.*	S is M
This plan is *a plan which should be given serious consideration.*	S is P

3. "I know some of my friends are good swim-
mers; they wouldn't be in the water show
if they weren't."

All *participants in the water show* are *good swimmers.*	All M's are P's
Some of my friends are *participants in the water show.*	Some S's are M's
Some of my friends are *good swimmers.*	Some S's are P's

4. "It's unreasonable to suppose that Mr. Laux,
a staunch Republican, voted for a Democratic governor."

No staunch Republican is *a person who votes for a Democratic governor.*	No M is P
Mr. Laux is *a staunch Republican.*	S is M
Mr. Laux is not *a person who votes for a Democratic governor.*	S is not P

The tests for the categorical syllogism are precisely the same
as for the other kinds we have considered: the conclusion
must make a *valid inference* from *true premises*. If you look
back at the premises, you will see that some are statements of
fact, some inductive generalizations; others stem from definitions or causal relations. Though some of the premises would
be easier to prove (or disprove) than others, in each case it is
clear what is being asserted. Often, however, you need to re-
construct the syllogism before you know exactly what is being
asserted as true. In "Jack must be a Democrat because he's in
favor of socialized medicine," the concealed major premise
("Anybody in favor of socialized medicine is a Democrat") is
untrue, and so the conclusion ("Jack is a Democrat") is unsound. In "All fish have gills, and whales are fish, so whales
must have gills," the minor premise is false; and again the
conclusion is unsound.

The propositions that appear in full categorical syllogisms
are of four kinds:

Universal affirmative	All men are mortal
Particular affirmative	Some men are liars
Universal negative	No men are four-legged
Particular negative	Some men are not liars

To put yourself in a position to test the validity of the inferences that you make in your own reasoning, you usually need to make some expansions and translations. *Few* is translated into *some,* and *every* and *any* into *all.* A statement like "Only students who maintain an A or B average are on the Dean's list" is rephrased as a universal affirmative with the term following *Only* appearing as the predicate: "All who are on the Dean's list are students who maintain an A or B average." "The only students on the list are seniors" is rephrased as a universal affirmative with the term following *The only* in the subject position. As a premise in a syllogism, it would read: "All the students on the list are seniors."

For a handy short cut to testing the validity of the syllogism, you need to be acquainted with the concept of *distribution.* A term is said to be distributed when the proposition in which it appears affirms or denies something about the entire class for which the term stands. In the universal affirmative "All men are mortal," the subject term *men* is distributed; mortality is said to be an attribute of the whole of the class. The predicate term *mortal* is undistributed—no assertion is made about the whole of the class. In a particular affirmative ("Some men are liars") both terms are undistributed: *Some* men (not all) are in the class of liars, a class whose limits are not specified. In a universal negative ("No men are four-legged") both terms are distributed: the class of men is excluded from the entire class of four-legged things. In a particular negative ("Some men are not liars") the subject term is undistributed: an assertion is made about some members of the class but not about all of them. The predicate term is distributed, however, for something *is* asserted about the entire class of liars—that some men are not in the class.

Recognizing the type of assertion made and knowing how the terms are distributed provides a quick test for validity, a test which otherwise might entail a rather long and laborious consideration of exactly how the terms are related to each other. We can move now to the seven rules for valid inference in the categorical syllogism.

1. A syllogism contains three terms, and the meaning of these terms is the same every time they appear. Nothing can be inferred if four terms are used, as in

> All banjo players are folk singers
> Pete is always going to hootenannies
> Therefore Pete is a banjo player

Even when only three terms are used, the same kind of error results if the meaning of any of the terms shifts. "Americans have the highest standard of living in the world, and Peruvians are Americans; therefore Peruvians have the highest standard of living in the world." If a term is ambiguous (as *Americans* is here), the syllogism is unsound.

2. The middle term must be distributed at least once in the premises. Failure to observe this rule results in most of the errors in reasoning. It is illustrated in this pattern:

> American flags are red, white, and blue
> This flag is red, white, and blue
> Therefore this flag is an American flag

The middle term *(red, white, and blue)* is undistributed in both the major and the minor premise. No inference can be drawn relevant to *this flag* because neither premise has supplied any information about the *whole class* of red, white, and blue flags.

3. No term can be distributed in the conclusion which was not distributed at least once in the premises.

> All banjo players are folk singers
> No gentlemen are banjo players
> Therefore no gentlemen are folk singers

Folk singers, distributed in the conclusion, is undistributed in the major premise. The inference is invalid because, while gentlemen are excluded from the class of banjo players, they may still be in the class of folk singers.

The remaining four rules will help you tell at a glance whether a syllogistic pattern is invalid:

4. From two particular premises (assertions about some—not all—members of a class), no conclusion is drawn.

5. From two negative premises, no conclusion can be drawn. From "No thieves are honest" and "Some men are not thieves" we cannot infer that some men are honest. (The statement is true, surely, but does not follow from these premises.)

6. If one premise is negative, the conclusion must be negative.

7. If one premise is particular, the conclusion must be particular.

So far we have considered separately the tests for conclusions based on induction and deduction. They can be summed up in two large questions:

1. Are the generalizations (or premises) true? This question relates to both induction and deduction. To answer it may require examining the material for factual accuracy, or it may require a consideration of the definitions, the casual relationships, the comparisons, the classifications, and the divisions which serve as steps in establishing the conclusions.

2. Are the inferences valid? This question applies only to the conclusion of a train of deductive reasoning. We have identified the chief fallacies or errors in reasoning, such as the fallacy of denying the antecedent and the fallacy of the undistributed middle term. *Non sequitur* (does not follow) is a convenient label for all those errors of reasoning in which the stated conclusion does not follow from the premises that have been supplied. But a *non sequitur* may also be simply a lapse in continuity, a failure to make the relationships clear. It can occur whenever you skip a step in the argument and so leave the reader confused about the connection between your statements.

For example, can you make sense of "I read a fascinating book last week, and so I'm saving my money to go to Europe"? Perhaps. But you can see the logical relationships more clearly when the thought is fully developed: "Before last week I had never been much interested in traveling abroad, but after reading Herbert Kubly's *American in Italy,* I changed my mind. I'm saving my money to go to Europe." In this case, the *non sequitur* can be corrected by supplying the missing links in the reasoning. In other cases, where the error lies in the reasoning itself and not in its expression, the relation of the premises must be reexamined.

Two other logical fallacies, not peculiar to induction or to deduction but involving the argument as a whole, are *begging the question* and *ignoring the question.*

Begging the question means assuming the truth of a proposition which actually needs to be proved. "This unfair method of testing must be changed" assumes that the method of testing *is* unfair. The writer hopes to take advantage of a general predisposition in favor of virtue and against vice, but begging the question is an unethical device in arguing. In preparing a paper, examine your propositions (especially the taking-off point of your argument) to be sure that you are not sneaking in unjustified adjectives or adverbs which appear to prove what has not yet been investigated.

One common form of begging the question is arguing in a circle. Reduced to its simplest form, the circular argument asserts that X *is true because* X *is true:* "In our society it is necessary to keep up with the latest styles because it is essential to be fashionably dressed." This evasion is often hard to recognize when it is buried in a long chain of argument, but when it is uncovered, it earns—and deserves—ridicule.

Ignoring the question is a broad term for various kinds of irrelevant argument. It consists in shifting the grounds of the argument from the real issue to one that is not under consideration. In one characteristic form, *argumentum ad hominem*, the attack is not on the issue itself but on those who support the opposing view. At its lowest, it takes the form of invective and abuse.

Finally, in testing an argument, you need to examine the extra-logical appeals that you have used in supporting your thesis. Appeals to emotions and ideals—to pride, to justice, to morality—can be powerful means to persuasion. They are properly used when they are brought to bear on the real issue. To use them to cloud or misrepresent the issue is to pervert the nature of responsible argument.

Corrections and refutations

Testing relationships and scrutinizing the argument for fallacies should be a regular part of revising every persuasive paper you write. It is also the first step in preparing a paper which sets out to correct a misinterpretation or to refute an opinion—but here you are probing logical relationships and searching for fallacies in the speeches or writings of others.

In the background of every piece of persuasion lurks the opposing thesis, and very often it looms in the foreground. In preparing any argument, it is always useful for you to learn what has been said on the other side or to figure out what might be said. Even if you give no explicit recognition to the opposing view in your paper, knowing what arguments its proponents present will help you make sensible decisions about the kind and quantity of evidence that you need to support your thesis. Often, too, it will help you determine which reasons can best support your thesis and the order in which they can best be presented. In some of your papers, you may limit yourself to what is called constructive argument—

the affirmative support of your thesis—but in others you will probably want to meet objections, demolish misconceptions, and in general strengthen your own thesis by showing the weaknesses in the counter-thesis.

Especially when you have reason to believe that your readers hold the opposing view, you may find it useful to open your paper with an analysis of and an attack on that view or on one important element in it. Launching a brief and temperate offensive at the start can clear away obstacles to a sympathetic hearing for your own views. On the other hand, it is ordinarily bad tactics to recognize and deal with other views at the very end of the paper, no matter how briefly; the conclusion should make a strong reaffirmation of your own thesis, accompanied perhaps by a final telling bit of evidence or an indication of the larger significance of the issue. But some consideration of the opposing position will lead your reader to see its weakness and so, in contrast, the strength of your position.

Refutation is an attack on the evidence and the reasoning that make up the argument for the opposition. It occurs when a writer challenges and opposes a fully developed position as set forth in an editorial, a speech, an article, or even a book. In most cases, demolition is not enough; the writer clinches his attack by building an affirmative argument for the opposing issue. The term *refutation,* however, properly belongs only to that part of the argument which proves the opponent to be wrong.

Refutation obviously requires the most careful analysis of the substance of the argument and of the reasoning that leads to the conclusion. Possible lines of refutation are as numerous as the ways of building an argument. Common ones are summarized here:

1. The inductive generalizations may be shown to be based on facts that are inaccurate or a sample of data that is incomplete and unrepresentative. Sometimes this involves challenging the opponent's powers of observation or his opportunities for finding out the real facts of the case. Sometimes it can be shown that he has relied on authorities who are unqualified or biased.

2. An attack may be launched on any of those premises on which the opponent builds his case, not only on the inductive generalizations but also on the definitions, the causal relationships, and the comparisons, including analogies. It may be shown that the opponent has initially made a faulty analysis of the situation and thereby ignored some legitimate alter-

natives to his proposed course of action. And the attack may involve challenging the basic assumptions, which are sometimes explicit but more often lie far below the surface of the argument—assumptions, for example, about the purpose of education or the relation between the citizen and the state or even more fundamental notions about the nature of man.

3. The refutation may uncover errors in reasoning: unwarranted shifts from *some* in the premise to *all* in the conclusion, improper inferences stemming from an undistributed middle term, subtle changes in the meaning of a term.

4. Finally, the refutation may attack those techniques of persuasion which can be shown to be irrelevant to the issue or manifestly unfair (character assassination—*argumentum ad hominem,* devious or overt appeals to prejudice, special interests, and so on).

Full-scale refutation, then, extends far beyond the correction of a small error; to destroy the whole basis for the position, it must go to the roots of the argument. If it is to be convincing, it must attack premises, not merely conclusions; and if it is to win respect, it must scrupulously avoid those tactics which it criticizes in the opponent.

Many newspaper editorials and magazine articles attack specific views held by specific individuals or the proposals they advance. Others, however, attack a general opinion or attitude which is not attributed to any one individual but is common enough to deserve attention. In the following paragraph from the essay quoted in part on page 240, the author describes one "solution" to the problem he is discussing and then shows what is wrong with it.

The simplest way to increase food production, one might suppose, is to bring more land under cultivation and put more people to work on it. The U.S.S.R. and some of the underdeveloped countries have resorted to this straightforward approach, without notable success. It contains several fallacies. For one thing, it usually means moving into marginal land where the soil and climatic conditions give a poor return. Cultivation may quickly deplete this soil, ruining it for pasture or forest growth. It is often possible, of course, to turn such lands into useful farms by agricultural know-how; for instance, a sophisticated knowledge of how to use the available water through an irrigation system may reclaim semiarid grasslands for crop-growing. But the cultivation of marginal lands is in any case unsuccessful unless it is carried out by farmers with a centuries-old tradition of experience or by modern experts with a detailed knowledge of the local conditions and the varieties of crops that are suitable for those conditions. Such knowledge is conspicuously absent in the underdeveloped countries.—Nevin S. Scrimshaw, "Food," *Scientific American*, Sept. 1963, p. 73

In attacking misconceptions, fallacies, or delusions, the writer should not yield to the temptation to misrepresent the opposition through caricaturing or exaggerating the position. Setting up a straw man is one of the easiest and least admirable ways of conducting a refutation. The responsible writer will test his statement of the opposing position by asking himself this question: Have I represented my opponent's case in such a way that he would find it an acceptable statement of his position? If he can answer the question affirmatively, he has the groundwork for a responsible refutation. The student who wrote the following passage as part of a defense of liberal education was far from just in characterizing the position of "the proponents of specialized training":

The proponents of specialized training believe that education consists of knowing everything about virtually nothing. They insist that every course a student takes should lead him directly into his own tiny field of research. They do not care if a student can read or write or think. All they are interested in is having him do a successful experiment on his fruit flies. They do not see a man as a citizen with responsibilities to the entire world; they see him as a mole, burrowing blindly in his own little hole—deeper and deeper until he buries himself.

Scolding, ridiculing, and caricaturing the opponent's views come easy in refutation. Normally a writer undertakes an attack only because he has been stirred into disagreement—and often stirred emotionally as well as intellectually. When you have a chance to write on a subject that arouses you emotionally, by all means do so. Let yourself go; let your rage pour out on paper. But don't submit that draft to your instructor. When you have cooled down (and the act of getting it off your chest will help), go over the paper and dig out its core of solid refutation. Throw away all the insults and sarcasm it did you so much good to write down; then test the core of refutation to make sure it destroys the foe logically and responsibly. When you're sure it does, you can probably afford to restore some of the sharpness of tone. Chances are you've produced an excellent refutation.

In the following passage (three crucial parts of an essay) the writer interweaves her refutation with constructive argument. The essay begins with a statement of the position under attack (paragraphs 1-3), questions it (paragraph 4), and then proceeds to refute it. Notice that the author (winner of two Olympic gold medals in skiing) uses definition to attack the "philosophy" itself and cause-effect relations to show the damaging effects of the philosophy. Notice, too, how effectively her personal experience serves as inductive support for the argument made in the second last paragraph. Like many good arguments, this one not only deals with the specific issue but relates it to a larger context—in this case, the function of sports in relation to living.

Let's Not Spoil Their Sport

If you think of a recreation skier at the start of a marvelous day, the image that comes to mind is likely to be a familiar one—the temperature just right, the sun up for two hours or so, the trees brilliant white under a new snowfall and a whole wide slope of powder stretching out ahead. But if someone stood beside this hypothetical recreation seeker on this perfect slope and told him over and over that he must do this, or do that, or do something else, because otherwise he would not get the most out of his skiing, one main ingredient in the magic of his world would disappear. He would very likely ski better, but regardless of whether he did or did not, a certain amount of the pleasure and satisfaction that would otherwise have been his would now have been taken away.

To a greater extent than is generally recognized, some such hard-sell philosophy of ski training for competitors has become the fashion in this country—and scarcely a voice has been raised against it. For example, it was authoritatively stated recently that the rigorous training that our present Olympic skiers followed "must be copied by each organized racing program everywhere." And what did the training program of the American Olympic team include? Well, on the physical side, there was a daily regimen of tire-course running, high-speed rope jumping, bar workouts, a long mountain hike, wind sprints, full-speed foot races up steep embankments and group exercises with intricate steps—twists, straddles and stomps— performed by the entire troupe with all the precision of ballet dancers. The purpose of this "exhaustion technique," as it is called, is to force the racer to push himself on after he thinks he is exhausted, to show him that he is really able to do more than he thought he could do.

The only questions that interest the present-day theoreticians of the sport are those involved in getting the racer into the starting gate, down the slope and across the finish line as a winner. This is the goal of all the planning and all the training. It is the dominant philosophy in ski competition right now and it could hardly be simpler: win, win, win. The most serious aspect of this is that this hard sell is by no means limited to top-level competition. The same attitude is found in school and club competition—programs that involve thousands and thousands of youngsters from 7 to 17 years old, youngsters who are not ready to face this kind of physical and emotional test.

This new attitude represents a great change in American competitive skiing, and I think it is at least worth wondering for a moment whether or not the change is for the best.

Whatever else American ski racing may have been in the past, it was above all spontaneous. You raced because you loved it, and whatever you achieved came from within yourself. Perhaps because there were so few American skiers—and so little attention was given the meets that were held—a young beginner usually found himself in an atmosphere of casual goodwill with his elders right from the start. Often his elders knew no more about skiing than he did. But now the training of a typical junior team is a matter of barked commands, learning by rote and doing the same thing over and over. And too often you find youngsters coming off the slopes with their eyes glazed with weariness and a sense of inadequacy after the sort of afternoon that, under different training circumstances, could have been among the most exhilarating of their youth.

Winning is one of the pleasures of skiing, as it is of all sports, but there is a subtle difference about winning a ski race that separates it from most of the competitive efforts of mankind. The act of winning itself—even an Olympic medal—is incredibly brief. It takes only a few seconds, the briefest possible fragment of one's lifetime and an appallingly short period to be set as the goal of all one's efforts. But, according to the hard-sell philosophy, all training, mental and physical, must be directed toward it.

• • • •

It is at this point that I strongly disagree. I feel that all the past experiences have their own intrinsic value, that their significance is not contingent on their leading to victory. Those experiences represent moments of elation, hours of exhilaration, days of release and relaxation, the joy of discovery and the thrill of competition. They also involve, for that matter, leaden days of sluggish performance when nothing goes right, periods of hopelessness when one gives up the whole business and the astonishing rediscovery of pleasure when all goes well again. Those past experiences have not only made the skier a winner, they have been woven into the very fabric of his consciousness, making him what he is—and will become—not only as a performer but as a person. Thus what seems to

me to be vitally important is to get the skier into the starting gate
—yes—and through the finish, and then out into the world with all
that has gone before serving as a meaningful part of his daily
existence. This does not happen if all you do is ski to win.

Along with the tremendous increase in popular interest in skiing
during the past few years there has been a proliferation of ski
literature defining and refining what the skier must do. Experts are
everywhere. Competition is tougher. Equipment is better. All such
changes have created a condition in which the ski expert flourishes.
And because the level of competitive performance is improved, the
experts' theories seem to be justified. But I wonder if cause and
effect have not become a little confused here. There is an absolute
necessity for a competitive skier to be in top physical condition—no
one could argue otherwise. The question is how he is to be given
his physical training. In the case of training at the junior level, it
is a question of what is to be done to make him want to receive it.
The exhaustion technique is just what its name implies, a matter
of forcing the skier to push himself beyond his known endurance.
Now, if you can instill in the individual the *desire* to do this for
himself, without the authoritative voice ordering him to do this or
that, he will achieve the same end, but he will have done it for himself. It is the forcing that is wrong and potentially dangerous. Encouraging an individual's desire, instead of compelling him to a
predetermined condition, will make him just as good a competitor,
and yet will let him retain his own zest for the sport.

The danger, obviously, is that we may be depriving the individual of his own urge for accomplishment. I believe, in fact, that
we are cheating today's young skiers of one of the greatest rewards
of competition: the thrill of self-discovery. I remember a race at
Lake Placid in the early '40s. I was 10 or 11, but I was racing in a
senior girls' event. In those days we drove from our home in Vermont to Lake Placid on Friday afternoon, unbundled ourselves and
climbed up the course in preparation for Saturday's race. On the
way up I made my first conscious effort to analyze myself, and I
acquired my first self-knowledge. . . .

• • • •

Finally, setbacks and disappointments have their own contribution to make toward rounding a young skier's personality, and they
do make a contribution if they are not submerged in so much
psychological shock at defeat that they cannot be properly appre-
ciated. One of the most memorable events of my life was the down-
hill race in the 1948 Olympics in St. Moritz. The course was wonderful, fine rolling terrain with wide turns and no trees. I was
doing well as I approached the finish, where you had to make a

turn at the bottom of a little gully, then scurry around and come back up at an angle to a side-hill traverse before pitching down toward the finish line. When I hit the pitch I was going at a speed faster than anyone with any brains would have maintained, and I flew off into the horizon, rolling and rolling into great banks of snow. By the time I picked myself up and got back on the course I was, if not last, the next thing to it. I was not hurt, though I felt a little foolish. And, in fact, despite the record that stands there imperishably in the books—I finished 35th—it was also great fun and I had a fine time doing it. My time before the catastrophe would probably have put me in first place—the winner of a gold medal. But, at 15, I should not have had a gold medal. I was too young, and I did not know enough. I would not have been able to cope with what I had done, or even known why I could not cope. It was, in the last analysis, a good thing that I fell.

In short, that fraction of a second that is decisive in determining whether or not you win an Olympic medal is too brief a period to shape all one's skiing experience. The medal winners are going to be few, no matter what philosophy of competition is followed. What I urge is that we be mindful of the hazards of the hard sell, that we be sure that in placing all the emphasis on winning we do not lose something more important—the endless interest and variety and pleasure of sport. I would beseech the parents of today's thousands of young skiers to understand that the experience of skiing does not end at the finish line. We must not follow a philosophy of sport—or of anything else—that prepares us for winning but leaves us unprepared for all the rest of life.—Andrea Mead Lawrence, "Let's Not Spoil Their Sport," *Sports Illustrated*, Feb. 3, 1964, pp. 19-21

The writer and his audience

The essay just quoted ends with a direct appeal to the parents of young skiers. This is the only mention of a specific audience, but in the approach and method there are several unobtrusive indications that parents—rather than skiing instructors or fifteen-year-old aspirants to championships—make up the intended audience. The opening paragraph, many of the arguments based on consequences, and of course the final paragraph reveal a special awareness of the interests and concerns of parents. So do the smallest details, such as the characterization of the opposing view as "some such hard-sell philosophy of ski training for competitors."

This is not to say that other readers cannot enjoy the article. Readers of all ages and interests (including those who know nothing about skiing and are quite unaware that there are different notions about how a competitive skier should be trained) will not only enjoy the article but will take sides in the debate. For a variety of reasons the essay does have general interest. But its focus and unity stem largely from this fact that it is addressed primarily to *one* group of readers. The kinds of arguments, the order of the arguments, and the choice of evidence—these are all determined to a large extent by the audience. The audience no doubt determines also the tone of the piece (see paragraph 4, for instance). Though the author might well speak with considerably more assurance and dogmatism—in view of her own intimate knowledge of the subject of discussion—it would probably defeat her own case to launch a harshly aggressive attack right at the start. What she chooses to do is adopt a tone of inquiry. Then, as she piles up more and more evidence against the "hard-sell philosophy," she speaks more assertively. In numerous ways, which you will find profitable to analyze, she has adapted (or accommodated) her argument to her audience.

In most of the persuasive essays you read, you will find some such evidence of an awareness of the audience. Some arguments (in philosophy, for instance) do seem to be addressed to mankind through the ages; but the vast majority of them speak to a particular group in a particular place and time. Accommodation to a specific audience is a vital element in most persuasive writing.

Accommodation involves three chief elements and the interrelations among them: the writer, the audience, and the proofs supporting the thesis. In any particular argument, one of these (or one in relation to another) may be paramount. Most important may be the writer's estimate of the probable views his readers hold on the issue. What is the distance between the views they hold and the views he wants them to hold? If it is very great, what is the best means of reducing it so that he can get a fair hearing? Finding common ground, however small, is a necessary first step to persuading.

This does not mean that the writer must start by buttering-up, flattering, or cajoling the audience or by telling a round of jokes just to get his readers in a good mood. A joke may be the way in, particularly when there is something special in the relation of the writer to the audience; but the technique of the after-dinner speaker rarely succeeds in print. Nor does accommodation mean putting yourself and your virtues on public display in an effort to persuade the audience to accept your thesis just because you're you—good fellow that you are. Everyone is familiar with such transparent attempts to curry favor with the audience, to subordinate issues to personalities, to win friends *to* influence people. The devices are used, and often they are effective. But they do not represent accommodation at its best.

Accommodation in a deeper sense means finding ways in which you can bring your audience to feel the force of the reasons which have led you to believe in your thesis. In persuading, you are not selling a piece of merchandise which may be returned tomorrow via the "complaints" department; you are contributing to the responsible discussion of ideas that characterizes educated people. Probably the best guarantee against shoddy devices of accommodation is to remind yourself that whether you "win" the argument or not, you are trying to lead your audience to see the truth as you see it. The best procedure is to find good reasons for supporting the position you hold and then to use all the resources of *responsible* communication to persuade your reader to assent to it.

Exercises

1. Clip a review from a newspaper or magazine and paste it in the center of a sheet of paper. In the space at the right, label each sentence or group of related sentences (identification, classification, description, evaluation); at the left, note the traits of style or indications of tone that are relevant to the reviewer's evaluation.

2. Write a review, making clear the criteria or standards that have led you to your evaluation. Suggested subjects: a sports event, a movie, a play, or a short story in a current magazine; the campus newspaper or literary magazine; a trend that reflects popular tastes— fashions or fads in dress, recreation, slang, popular songs.

3. From the list of general subjects on page 232, select one, narrow it to a definite topic, and write a persuasive paper (800-1200 words). Then, in a paragraph, answer these questions: What is the thesis of your paper? In supporting it, what sources have you relied on most heavily—definition, cause-effect, comparison, or the testimony of others? To what extent have you used inductive evidence, and to what extent have you used deductive inference?

4. From a current issue of a magazine, clip eight or ten typical advertisements. Submit them with a 500-word paper in which you make an inference, *on the basis of the advertisements,* about the kind of audience the magazine addresses itself to.

5. From a campus or city newspaper, clip an editorial (or column) that expresses an opinion or makes a recommendation with which you disagree. Submit the editorial or column with a brief "Letter to the Editor" making clear your reasons for disagreeing.

6. From each of two newspapers or magazines that are known to have basically different political viewpoints (*The National Review* and *The New Republic,* for instance), clip an editorial or column dealing with a topic of social or political importance. (If possible, choose articles on the *same* topic.) Submit them with a 600-word paper in which you compare and contrast the two articles. Give the best explanation you can for the similarities and differences you find in the views stated in the articles, in the assumptions underlying these views, in the kinds of arguments used, and in the style and tone. Be objective; do not express your own opinion on the issue.

7. Select a campus issue that interests you and use it as the basis for two papers, about 750 words each, in which you attempt to persuade two distinctly different audiences to share your judgment or support your recommendation. (An illustration—but only an illustration: Write to the curriculum committee asking that specific changes be made in a course. Write to a friend urging him not to sign up for the course.)

Your two papers will present the same general views about the issue, of course, but they should differ in the space you give to each reason, the order in which you present your reasons, the way you open and close the papers, and the general style and tone. Your task is to accommodate the same argument to two very different audiences and to lead them both to the same conclusion.

8. Study the following passage and write two brief papers based on it. (The sentences are numbered so that you can conveniently refer to them.) (a) Analyze the passage, answering these questions: What is the author's thesis? In supporting it, what is the chief source he draws on—definition, cause-effect, comparison, or the testimony of others? How much inductive evidence (facts, particulars) does he present? What specific words and phrases has he evidently selected for their persuasive value in this context, and what attitudes are these words and phrases likely to induce in three different kinds of readers— those sympathetic to the thesis, those hostile to it, and those neutral to it? (b) Defend or attack the author's thesis. For evidence, draw on your own experience or the experience of other college students you know. In the course of your paper, make clear your view of the proper relationship between "the small college" and its students.

(1) The delusion of which the small college is peculiarly the victim is the delusion that a college is One Big Family. (2) College becomes a home; dormitories, houses; college personnel, housemothers. (3) Students are encouraged to seek out Big Sisters. (4) Big Brother is always watching someone. (5) Students are organized, organized, organized, run twice around the block and given cold gang showers. (7) And in this Louisa May Alcott atmosphere of *Little Men* and *Little Women* they remain, for four years longer, little boys and little girls. (8) The results of the family delusion are the violation of human privacy and the perversion of student government into Grundyism, junior grade. (9) Students are given access to presumably confidential information about other students. (10) They are encouraged to make judgments beyond their competence. (11) And what these student boards and posses lack in experience they make up in numbers. (12) It is possible to find one student out of seven on a typical small college campus engaged in the regular business of judging and jurying his peers. (13) This is not an objection to student government (which is another delusion), or to the governing of students (which is merely an unlikelihood). (14) But the guide for both should be Jeffersonian: the best of either is the least.

(15) Surely the worst effect of the Family delusion is that it diverts energies from the training of the mind to the overseeing of the body. (16) Some of this is unavoidable. (17) But the delusion sets up almost irresistible pressures to turn the college into either a reformatory or a finishing school, thereby driving its better students elsewhere.—SHELDON ZITNER, "Delusions of a University," *The North American Review*, March 1964, p. 67

9. Following are excerpts from students' papers. For each, analyze the reasoning and the kind of argument advanced, and explain why you find it sound or unsound, persuasive or unpersuasive.

  a. One of my acquaintances is the director of an extensive community charity program. This man was the agent for, and the observer of, a hundred acts of charity a day. However, when his son married a young woman of a different religious faith, he disowned the boy. Surely this man knew—with his eyes and with his ears and with his mind—what charity is. But did he ever feel it in his heart? Ask the son.

  b. When I read the works of men like Emerson, who are convinced of the fundamental goodness of man, I find it hard to suppress fits of uncontrollable laughter. Their concept of human nature, which assumes man to be normally motivated by a sort of fraternal benevolence, has, it seems to me, no foundation in fact. Are the bulk of the instances of human relations that we see carried on with consideration for others? I think not. And is there any evidence in nature of a kind of fundamental goodness and charity in the nonhuman world? Nature actually offers a spectacle of death and constant struggle in which the strong continually destroy the weak, where no quarter is asked and none given. I cannot imagine a tiger or lion having pangs of conscience for eating a helpless, harmless, friendly gazelle. This whole process in nature is neatly labeled *natural* selection, a term which implies that this process of dog-eat-dog is a trait inherent in all natural situations. If not from nature, then, from what source comes this most remarkable statement that men are basically good, kind, and full of love for their fellows? The inspiration for it is merely the wishful thinking of Emerson and the rest of the sunny-side-of-the-street gang.

c. The detrimental effects of specialized education are twofold. First, a student who too soon abandons investigation of all the disciplines becomes limited in scope. He cannot understand problems in any frame of reference but his own. In his essay "The American Scholar," Emerson decries fragmentation of the individual, and this is just what specialization does. Instead of "Man Thinking"—Emerson's ideal—there is produced a man thinking in physics, or a man thinking in history, or a man thinking in mathematics. The student who enrolls in a program of specialized education enters as "Man Thinking" and leaves as "man thinking in." Thus he views life through a narrow window, an individual restricted in thought to only one discipline and unable to integrate reality. This happens very frequently, more often, perhaps, than the victim of the other unfortunate result of early specialization. He is the one who discovers too late the other roads he might have taken. When college is completed and graduate work under way, the chance of turning abruptly onto another path is indeed slight. And the disillusioned man is forced to adjust as best he can to the future of working in a field other than the one he prefers.

d. Specialization of labor is an essential part of the progress of humanity. Only to the extent that the functioning elements of a society specialize can the society improve. We see specialization in every branch of industry, in every area of knowledge, in each of the fine arts. It is the specialist who has produced our greatest achievements, whether in mathematics or music. The jack-of-all-trades intellectually speaking—the amateur who dabbles in this field and that—may have some fun and may fool himself into thinking he's a "well-rounded man," but his real accomplishments are small. To achieve anything important in life, you have to concentrate on one thing, rigidly excluding all others. In the world today, it is pretty clear that the great inventions are produced by specialists and the great books written by them. For this reason, every college student should begin specializing in his first year. That's late enough if he is to do anything in the world.

e. I disagree with the proposal that the Pure Food and Drug Administration be given control over the distribution of cigarettes. The Administration performs a necessary function in testing food and drugs for safety before they are put on the market. On many occasions it has protected the public from suffering and disaster; the most recent example was its fourteen-month delay in approving the sale of the drug thalidomide. By the time it became known that its sale in Europe was responsible for the birth of many deformed children, every American citizen was grateful that the Administration has the power it does.

It has been proved that the smoke tars that the drug nicotine combines with form a base for cancerous tissue in the lungs. There is no doubt that cigarette smoking is extremely dangerous to the health of individuals. But I do not believe the Administration should take over the problem of cigarette control and distribution. It has the responsibility to test drugs before they are put on the market. But it performs this function only because the average citizen is not equipped to perform it. In the case of cigarettes, no further testing is necessary. The average citizen now knows the harm cigarettes can do, and the decision as to whether to smoke or not should be left up to him. With thalidomide and other drugs the citizen has no way of knowing whether the drug is safe, but with cigarettes he does know, and what he does next is his problem, not the government's.

f. Liquor is a luxury. The buyer of such a luxury can easily afford a few cents' tax. The tax represents almost no part of the actual initial expense. The liquor buyer will not miss the few cents. But his tax money will go to help the nation. It will be dispensed by the government, a government of the people. It will be used to solve problems that will affect everyone if that money is not spent. Crime and ignorance will be prevented by the building of schools. Diseases will be prevented and cured by hospitals. Slums will be abolished. The national defense will be provided for. We can afford that tax on liquor. We cannot afford not to have it.

g. Though it's great to be hip in a square world, it would be even better if the world were a little more hip than it is. Educated Americans today have a fairly good idea of what goes on in a Shakespearian tragedy when they see one on the stage, but they don't know what is going on in jazz (or in most music that one hears on AM radio, which is influenced by jazz, as are the musical scores for movies, television shows and musical comedies). Intellectuals and pseudo-intellectuals discuss the vast problems of contemporary civilization with ease, yet do not know even the melody line of "Salt Peanuts" or "Bloomdido" or "Work Song"—three songs that are among the most viable music of the past few decades. In their way they tell something about contemporary civilization. Why not study them? No single jazz tune is created in a vacuum—it is a part of an entire culture, and refers to that culture and cannot be fully understood without some understanding of the culture it is created in.

Many schools are now giving instruction in the understanding and appreciation of music, and this is a good thing. But the only music treated is classical music. I believe that "equal time" ought to be given to jazz. It is true that no amount of formal education can make a person dig jazz, but then again no amount of formal instruction can teach a person to appreciate Beethoven. The world needs to be a little more hip. The words "Bird lives" should be spoken in lecture halls as well as scrawled in "L" stations.

h. Everyone would agree that poetry needs rhythm, but some people still cling to the notion that a poem is not a poem unless it has rhyme as well. In connection with this, one is reminded of a woman wearing an extraordinary diamond necklace. The necklace enhances her costume, but whether or not she *needs* it is questionable. The jewelry may be so distracting that perhaps we will not notice the fact that she is not attractive. If she is really beautiful, the necklace will serve only as a charming incidental. Similarly with poetry. If the work is a piece of great writing, rhyme acts only as an incidental. If, however, the work is poor, the rhyme may serve to distract us from that fact.

i. As for decadent movies showing the rottenness of our society, rottenness does exist, and it will always exist until people take a realistic view of the undesirable elements of our society and clean it out. Hiding the rotting stump does not stop the rot. We are forced to live in the world as it is and not as we would have it be. If enough people do not like things as they are, they have the alternative of changing them. To get enough people interested in changing something, they have to know what needs to be changed. If people are forbidden the knowledge of what is, how can they know what needs to be? Movies should portray our society as it is and if people see the undesirable portrayed realistically they can fight decadence, knowing exactly what to fight. Because censors prevent a true picture of our society from being shown, they stand as a barrier to improvement.

j. Movies, as a mass media, can endanger the public as a whole through harmful propaganda spread quickly across the nation or by exceeding the accepted moral standard. Since the general movie-going public consists of diverse mental capacity, no two people will be affected similarly by the same movie. For example, an intellectual may not be disturbed by watching a tragedy. He might derive extreme pleasure from a catharsis of emotion while others may be strongly influenced in the wrong direction. Included in the latter group are children and adults of retarded mental capacity or very low intelligence. Because the majority of persons in this group cannot define where the imaginary ends and the real begins, they could be intrigued, influenced, or induced to commit actions against the public at large. I can remember stories about children who tried to fly like "Superman" or who tied each other up like movie characters being tortured. It is not hard to believe that retarded minds seeing a murder or rape on a movie screen would carry the action to a conclusion in real life. Since movies can endanger the public, the public should look to the government for protection.

Chapter Eight

REVISING SENTENCES

*W*ords and sentences are subjects of revision; paragraphs and whole compositions are subjects of prevision.

Barrett Wendell

Most good writing is rewritten writing. For a few lucky people, ideas seem to emerge whole and clear at once, but the vast majority of us find that our first drafts fall far short of acceptable, effective expression. In revising any paper, you need to consider every aspect of it: content, organization, paragraphing, style, and mechanics—each evaluated in terms of your purpose in writing the paper.

Earlier chapters in this book have given attention to the paragraph and to the whole paper. This chapter and the next two deal with an important stage in writing—revising sentences, word-groups, words, and mechanics. Each chapter outlines the minimum standards your writing must meet to receive favorable attention from anyone who reads it. Parts of this chapter and the next also suggest ways of making your writing not merely acceptable but effective. Because effectiveness is more a matter of style than of simply observing conventions of correctness, final judgments about what is effective or ineffective can seldom be made apart from the context of the paragraph or the whole essay. Still, much can be learned from seeing how good writers produce their effects, and some principles can be given that will help you choose between one acceptable sentence and another, one acceptable word and another.

To improve the smaller units of your writing:

1. Know what is appropriate to General English—the sentence pattern or word form or punctuation used by educated people. Just as you learn what good spoken English is by listening to good conversation, talks, lectures, you learn what good written English is by reading widely and by giving con-

scious attention to sentence patterns and usage. To profit by the criticisms made of your writing, you will need to be familiar with a few of the most useful grammatical terms (*verb, predicative,* and so on) and with the correction symbols used in the margins of your papers—comma fault (*CF*), dangling modifier (*DM*), or whatever. Recognizing the mistakes you have made in a paper is the first step in improvement. The second is rewriting in accordance with the criticisms and recommendations made by your instructor.

2. Train yourself to proofread your papers carefully. We are naturally so familiar with what we have written that we often read it over without noticing spelling or punctuation or phrasing. If you know you are weak on some particular point—pronouns or comma faults, for example—go over your paper once looking for that point alone. Careful proofreading will reduce the number of your mistakes surprisingly, for most college students know, or at least know how to find out, what good usage calls for. Proofread your papers for other courses, too. Read them aloud to see how they sound—it will help them as well as your work in English.

3. Revise unsatisfactory sentences, word groups, words, and mechanics to meet the reader's expectations. Fortunately the greater part of our language raises no questions, but the problems that do arise can cause blunders that are easily spotted by others. Revising to meet your reader's expectations will eventually help you form habits of writing that will produce better first drafts.

4. In revising, remember that often the language offers you various ways of saying the same thing. Choosing the way that is best for your specific purpose will lift your writing from the level of competence to the level of effectiveness. Don't be satisfied with your revision until you are sure that it represents the most effective expression you are capable of.

Analyzing sentences

To write with any degree of competence, we need to have some conscious knowledge of how our language works. To discuss sentences profitably and to revise them intelligently, we need to be able to analyze them and identify their parts. This section reviews the chief grammatical characteristics of written English sentences.

The favorite English sentence • In speech, sentences are marked by various sorts of stress, pitch, and pause that we use and understand automatically. *This is mine,* for example, if said quietly, with a falling intonation, could best be written with a period at the end; if more intensely, with an exclamation point; if with a rising inflection, with a question mark. It can also be said as part of a sentence, which might be written "This is mine, I think." *Yes* can be said so that to a listener it will mean anything from "You are absolutely right" to "I don't really believe what you are saying."

In writing, all these qualities of voice are missing, and the writer has to rely on various patterns of word order and conventions of punctuation to make his sentences "say" what he means.

It is difficult—very difficult—to arrive at a satisfactory definition of a sentence. As a practical matter, about all we can say is that a sentence is a stretch of prose which an experienced writer intentionally punctuates as a sentence (by beginning it with a capital letter and ending it with a period, question mark, or exclamation point) and which, when so punctuated, an educated reader automatically accepts as a sentence. What we mark as a sentence is largely a matter of convention, reflecting our understanding of what readers have accepted and will accept as a sentence. But a sentence could also be many other sentences; its particular, individual construction is only partly inevitable. It represents a choice among various possibilities. The more we know about typical sentence patterns, the easier it is to describe the sentences we have written and to understand, through discussion, why they are acceptable or unacceptable, effective or ineffective.

The pattern most commonly used ("the favorite English sentence," as Jespersen has called it) is centered in a subject and a verb. The vast majority of sentences contain an *independent* subject-verb combination. ("Birds fly" is an independent subject-verb combination; "When birds fly" is not.) But a sentence may have other words in various relations to the subject and verb, and there may be more than one subject-verb combination in a single sentence, so that these simple elements can be used to build sentences of great variety. For convenience in describing the parts of sentences, we can indicate the elements by letters and mark three levels of relation—main, secondary, and third.

Main elements. The typical English sentence is composed of a *subject* S, the starting point of the statement, and a *verb* or a *linking verb* V. This subject-verb construction may be continued by an *object* O or by an object and an *indirect object* ①; the subject-linking verb construction, sometimes called "copula" (*be, become, feel, seem*) is continued by a *predicative* P, which may be either a noun or an adjective. More than 90 percent of the sentences in modern written English are of this type.

These examples show the main elements in ordinary patterns:

    S   V
Alex laughed.
    S   V   O
They bought a sailboat.
     S   V   P
Harold felt tired.
                        S   V   P
The highest ranking student becomes valedictorian.
     S   V   ①   O
Mrs. Jones bought him a dozen eggs.
 S V   O
He said that they ought to know better.

In the last sentence the object, *that they ought to know better,* is a clause with a subject and a verb of its own, but it serves the same grammatical function as a single word. In English, word groups often function as single words do.

Sentences with *anticipatory* or *lesser subjects* s, as in *there is, it is,* have the actual subject after the verb:

 s V P   S
It is hard to know who is right.
   s   V   S   P
There are five in bloom.

In a phrasal verb, the auxiliary element is lower-case v, the main verb is upper-case V:

  S   v   V
They had already parked.

Secondary elements.   In the system of showing sentence parts used here, words, phrases, and clauses that modify main elements in the sentence have their relationship to those elements shown by a number. The primaries are the subject S, object

O, and indirect object ①, and their rank is shown by 1. They
are modified on the one hand by the verb, on the other by
adjectival elements, which are marked 2. These secondaries
may in turn be modified by other elements which are marked
3. In the following example, the subject is *very old men* and
consists of a primary *men,* modified by a secondary *old,* which
in turn is modified by a tertiary *very;* since the verb always
modifies the subject, the number 2 need not be put over it, but
greatly, which modifies *suffer,* is labeled 3. The parts of a main
element are enclosed in parentheses, and the symbol for the
element is placed just before the parentheses:

```
S(3      2     1 )    V        3
Very  old   men   suffer   greatly.
```

Further examples:

```
              2            S    v    V       O          3
    Coming into the open,  he  could see  the tracks  plainly.
     S (       2          1   )  2(S₂   v    V₂                3  )
    The high school   orchestra,  which was directed by Mr. Appley,
    V₁   O(2    1   )            3
    played   two   numbers   between each act.
```

Third elements.   Other words may be related to the pattern
of the sentence by modifying the secondary elements (The
local high school orchestra, *more* plainly). Since their relationship to the secondary elements is similar to that of secondary
elements to the primary, the number 3 makes the function
clear:

```
S(3           2          1   )    V     3( 4        3 )
The local  high school  orchestra  played  unusually  well.
```

There may be further degrees of modification (An almost |
completely | accurate | description), but since the funda-
mental relationship is the same, it is rarely worth carrying the
numbers any further. (Notice 4 for *unusually* above.)

Completing the sentence analysis.   A system for analyzing
sentences completely would be extremely complicated. Fortunately, in discussing our writing we do not often need more
items than those which have been presented. Some less common constructions, such as *appositives or *direct address, are
described in articles in the *Index.* In an analysis they may be

labeled by their full names or by convenient abbreviations —AP, DA. (For comments on individual items, see *Index*.[1])

To discuss the general qualities of sentences it is not necessary to name the individual words of phrases and clauses that function grammatically as single words. The prepositions that introduce phrases and the conjunctions or relative pronouns that introduce clauses are not elements of the whole sentence but belong to the word groups in which they occur.

```
                    3          S     V           3
Phrase: Between the acts,    they  went out   for a smoke.
              3( 3        S₂    V₂    )      s      V     3
Clause: When the party broke up,    there  were  still
S(2    1    )     3
six couples    there.
```

A few other details of analysis will be brought out in later sections of this chapter.

Order of sentence elements.   In English the relation of the elements in a sentence depends mainly on the order in which they stand. This is especially true in writing because the oral devices of pitch, stress, and pause are not available. The more elaborate the sentence is, the more important it is to build it carefully.

The typical order of the main sentence elements is: subject —verb—object or predicative.

```
       S          V              O
Sixty students   got   permission to leave early.
       S          V           P
Ash Wednesday    is   the first day of Lent.
```

No matter how many modifiers may be in the sentence, its basic pattern will usually be S-V-O. This typical order of sentence elements is such a fundamental part of English grammar that we ordinarily identify subjects and objects by their position before or after the verb respectively (Jim beat Frank— S-V-O).

One standard departure from this typical S-V-O order is *inversion,* in which the predicative or an emphatic modifier of the verb stands first, followed by the verb and then the sub-

---

[1]Throughout this book, references to *Index* articles are indicated by an asterisk (*).

ject (P-V-S). Or the object or predicative may precede the subject and verb (O-S-V).

```
    P      S    V    [2]  (appositive, shown by brackets)
Foolish   he   was,  just plain foolish.
    O       S    v    3     V              3
This book   he  was  now  reading  for the third time.
    3        v   S    V           O
Only then   did  he  realize  what he had done.
```

Inversion of subject and verb is the usual order in questions:

```
  V    S   O(2    1   )    3     v    S    V   O
Have  you  a few minutes?  Where did you get  it?
  v    S    V    O(S₂  v₂   V₂ O₂)
Does  he  think      he can fool us?
```

English has only two formal means of connecting modifiers with what they modify: close position and linking verbs. If a linking verb is not used, the secondary elements must be close to what they modify in order to make the relation clear. Often a faulty sentence can be improved simply by changing the order of its parts. The correction symbol *WO* (for *word order*) indicates that such a change is necessary either to make the meaning clear or to make the sentence more emphatic.

Confusing order	*Clearer order*
The jury convicted the defendant of assault and battery *after deliberating two hours.*	*After deliberating two hours,* the jury convicted the defendant of assault and battery.

These basic facts of word order are grammatical, because they are relatively fixed in English. Elements whose position can be varied are discussed later in this chapter.

Kinds of sentences • It is conventional to classify sentences as simple, complex, compound, and compound-complex, according to the number and kind of subject-verb constructions in them. These are grammatical terms. A simple sentence may have a rather complicated structure, and a complex sentence may have a rather simple structure. The first two sentences in this paragraph are simple. The one you are reading is complex.

Simple sentences.   A simple sentence contains one grammatically independent statement—that is, one independent subject-verb combination. About a third of published sentences are simple, but not necessarily short. A simple sentence may be expanded by four kinds of elaboration—prepositional phrase modifiers, phrases with verbals, compound subjects, and compound predicates.

Many English sentences have one or more phrases introduced by prepositions:

> *From my experience in the Navy* I would divide the men into two groups.
> *After a few days of penicillin treatment* she was out of danger.
> A lathe operator must be highly skilled, *with years of experience.*

Phrases made with infinitives (the base form of a verb with *to*), participles (the *-ing* or *-ed* form used as a modifier), and gerunds (the *-ing* form used as a subject or object)—all parts of a verb that do not ordinarily make sentences—are common elements of simple sentences.

Infinitive phrases may be subjects or objects or modifiers:

> As subject: *To review the whole course in three hours* wasn't easy.
> As object: He tried *to avoid work.*
> As modifier [of *efforts*]: His first efforts *to get a job* failed.

Participles may be modifiers of subject or object:

> He watched them *going by in little groups.*   (Modifies *them*)
> *Locked up like that,* he wasn't going to hurt anyone.   (Modifies *he*)

Gerund phrases may be subjects or objects:

> As subject [of *requires*]: *Proofreading your papers* requires close attention to the written marks on the paper.
> As object [of *from*]: He got confidence from *knowing so much* about the subject.

Two or more words may be the subject (compound subject) of a single verb:

$$S_1 \quad S_2 \qquad\qquad S_3$$
Finally the husband, wife, and the two children moved to the city.

Two or more verbs (compound predicate) may have the same subject:

$$v \quad V_1 \qquad\qquad\qquad\qquad\qquad V_2$$

The husband has aged ten years in the last two and looks tired and unhappy most of the time.

Although these sentences contain several constructions, they have only one main clause and so are classified as simple sentences.

Compound sentences. A smaller proportion of sentences in printed material are compound—that is, made up of two or more independent clauses that might often be punctuated as separate sentences. The clauses may be joined by connectives or by punctuation alone.

The majority of clauses in compound sentences are joined by one of three kinds of connectives: coordinating conjunctions—*and, but, for, nor, or, yet*; correlative conjunctions—*both . . . and, either . . . or, neither . . . nor, so . . . as, not only . . . but (but also), whether . . . or;* conjunctive adverbs—*accordingly, also, besides, consequently, hence, however, indeed, namely, nevertheless, so,* and some others.

The first type is by far the most common:

We had expected to get there by noon, *but* the train was late.

Correlative conjunctions are not used much in speaking or General writing, except for *either-or:*

Either the postman hasn't come *or* there isn't any mail for us today.

Conjunctive adverbs have a suggestion of formality, which may be out of place in short sentences—ordinarily *but* is better than *however.* In current writing *indeed, nevertheless, consequently,* and some others are more likely to connect two separate sentences than two parts of the same sentence.

This attitude with respect to the nature of axioms still persists in the minds of many. *Indeed,* in current nonmathematical writings it is not uncommon to see such phrases as "it is axiomatic" and "it is a fundamental postulate of" used to mean that some statement is beyond all logical opposition.—ROBERT R. STOLL, *Sets, Logic, and Axiomatic Theories,* p. 123

For the purposes of writing, it is necessary to note that a conjunctive adverb within a sentence is preceded by a semicolon. This convention sharply differentiates a sentence which contains a conjunctive adverb joining independent clauses from a compound sentence in which the clauses are linked by coordinating conjunctions or correlatives. (See "Revising comma faults," p. 290.)

> We shall not present an axiomatization of set theory here; *instead,* we merely assure the reader that this can be done. . . .—ROBERT R. STOLL

When there is no conjunction between the clauses of a compound sentence, the individual clauses are called *contact clauses*. The conventional punctuation between the clauses is a semicolon:

> For Jung, dreams were often more gripping than wakeful life; he often felt he was living simultaneously in two different ages and being two different persons.—LEWIS MUMFORD

Complex sentences.   According to George Summey, Jr. (see Bibliography), nearly half the sentences used in current writing are complex. We identify them by the connection of dependent (or subordinate) clauses to independent clauses, usually through *relative pronouns* or *subordinating conjunctions*.

Many dependent clauses are connected to the main clause by the relative pronouns *who, whose, whom, which, that, whoever,* and so on. If these clauses modify a noun in the main clause, they are called *adjective clauses*; if they are subjects or objects or complements, they are called *noun clauses*.

> Then there are the people *who are unhappy* and *who never try to hide their feelings.* (Two adjective clauses modifying *people*)
> He had no sense of *what was appropriate.* (Noun clause, object of the preposition *of*)
> The man *whom I met on that trip* became a firm friend. (Clause modifying *man*)

This last type of clause is often made without the relative pronoun (The man *I met on that trip* became a firm friend), but the relation is the same.

Dependent adverbial clauses are usually connected to the main clause by subordinating conjunctions, of which the most common are:

after	because	since	until
*although	before	so that	when
*as	how	that	where
as if	if	though	while
as long as	in order that	unless	why

Some men are sportsmen *because they have a lot of energy.*
When people watch a football game they try to keep their eyes on the man with the ball.

The subordinating conjunction *that* introduces noun clauses, occasionally as subjects but more often as objects:

They didn't know *that the bell had rung.* (Object of *know*)

This type of clause is often made without the *that*: They didn't know *the bell had rung.*

Compound-complex sentences. A rather small number of sentences have two or more main clauses and one or more dependent clauses. This sentence has three dependent clauses (introduced by *if, who,* and *if*) and two main clauses:

If the reckless pilots who break these safety rules can be weeded out, and if the public can be educated to understand the light plane and the private pilot, [First main clause:] the fear of the small plane will disappear, [Second main clause:] and private flying may know the boom now enjoyed by the automobile.

These four types of sentences—simple, compound, complex, and compound-complex—are classified on the basis of the number and interrelations of the clauses in them. Analyzing the clause structure is the first step in revising many unclear or unsatisfactory sentences, for the weakness can often be traced to the order of clauses, the connective that links or introduces them, or the punctuation that separates them.

Minor sentence types ● Most written English sentences belong to the "favorite" type, centered on an independent subject-verb combination. But enough good sentences without this combination occur so that a descriptive grammar must take them into account. These minor sentence types are not to be confused with sentence fragments, discussed in the next section. Nothing is omitted from these sentences, and no words need be "understood" in analyzing them. They are natural forms of expression to be taken just as they are. When they appear in print, they are used deliberately and for a special purpose (for dialog, for emphasis, for brevity, or to avoid colorless and repetitious verbs).

The distinctive feature of a small number of minor sentences is that they have no subject. There are a few of a traditional pattern like *No sooner said than done,* and commands and requests (imperative sentences): *Don't let me ever hear you say that again. Please try.* Other subjectless sentences are confined almost entirely to narrative, in which the subject is easily carried over from the context, or to definitely Informal writing. This type of sentence is most appropriate in representing dialog in stories or in informal sketches of people:

"Guess I can live on the town if I've a mind to. Been paying taxes for thirty years and more."—ERSKINE CALDWELL

They took no interest in civilized ways. Hadn't heard of them, probably.—CLARENCE DAY

Much more common is the minor sentence which has either no verb or no independent subject-verb combination. Several types are habitual in speech and in good, if rather limited, use in writing. The verbs are not "left out"; they are not thought, spoken, or written. The statements are complete and independent without them.

One kind of verbless sentence is the exclamation, from *Ouch!* and other monosyllables to *What a mess!* and on to more intricately and emotionally phrased statements of feeling. Another type is the answer, from *Yes* and *No* and *Not if I know it* to longer and more specific statements:

For instance, how many deans share with their faculty the most recent report of the accrediting agency? Many, but by no means all. —LOUIS JOUGHIN

Often in passages that are chiefly descriptive, especially if the details are given as impressions, the only verb possible would be a colorless *is* or *are* or *has* or *have.* Without a verb there is no loss of meaning and an actual gain in economy and sharpness.

The whole thing was so familiar, the first feeling of oppression and heat and a general air around camp of not wanting to go very

far away. In midafternoon (it was all the same) a curious darkening of the sky, and a lull in everything that made life tick; and then the way the boats suddenly swung the other way at their moorings with the coming of a breeze out of the new quarter, and the premonitory rumble. Then the kettle drum, then the snare, then the bass drum and cymbals, then the crackling light against the dark, and the gods grinning and licking their chops in the hills.—E. B. Wʜɪᴛᴇ, "Once More to the Lake," from *One Man's Meat,* pp. 252-253

Occasionally for emphasis an adjective or other modifier is set beside its noun without a verb:

An understatement, this.—S. E. Mᴏʀɪsᴏɴ
No verb no predication.—P. B. Bᴀʟʟᴀʀᴅ

Minor sentences (sometimes appositional) frequently serve as transitions:

What does the asking price buy? At the worst it will buy, day after tomorrow, the knowledge that we have lived an additional day —and if fear has not paralyzed us, that we got from it what we could, and did what we could. . . .
That, at worst. But it is possible that. . . . —Bᴇʀɴᴀʀᴅ DᴇVᴏᴛᴏ

In rare instances, expressions in the form of phrases or subordinate clauses stand alone as sentences. These are usually light in tone (*Which is another story*), or almost formulas (*Not that it matters*), or *because* or *which* clauses set off for emphasis:

When they are indoors, they sit for a while without doing anything much. Then they suddenly decide to go out again for a while. Then they come in again. *In and out—in and out.*—Rᴏʙᴇʀᴛ Bᴇɴᴄʜ-ʟᴇʏ, "The Children's Hour," *My Ten Years in a Quandary,* p. 165
For twelve years, Max Beerbohm admitted in his valedictory article, Thursdays had been for him the least pleasant day of the week. Why Thursday? *Because that was the day, the latest possible one, he set aside each week to get his writing done.*—Jᴏʜɴ Mᴀsᴏɴ Bʀᴏᴡɴ, "Pleasant Agony," *Still Seeing Things,* p. 310

The minor sentence types discussed in this section are entirely acceptable and appropriate in their contexts. It is important, however, to distinguish them from the sentence fragments discussed in the next section.

Revising to meet the reader's expectations

The preceding section has sketched the chief grammatical characteristics of English sentences as a basis for considering specific problems in revising sentences. This section will deal with some flaws in sentences which are likely to be criticized by any careful reader. It is almost inevitable that some will creep into your first drafts. Correcting them is the first step in winning a sympathetic hearing for the ideas you are trying to communicate.

Revising sentence fragments • A basic convention in the writing of serious factual prose—the bulk of the writing college students do—is that ideas are generally expressed in sentences of the "favorite" type, containing at least one main clause. It is in the consistent use of this type of sentence that published writing differs most markedly from spoken English. Whenever in writing you depart from the convention of building a sentence around an *independent* subject-verb combination, you should be able to justify the departure as an acceptable alternative to the "favorite" type of sentence. It is even better if you can show that in its context your version is rhetorically more effective than the "favorite" type would be.

"Minor sentences" can be so justified. It seems altogether likely that in the case of each illustration in the preceding section of this chapter, the writer would argue that his minor sentence is rhetorically more effective than the corresponding full sentence—"An understatement, this" is more effective (because more emphatic) than "This is an understatement." It is even more likely that in each case the writer used the minor sentence intentionally. Before experimenting with departures from the norm, any writer needs to know what he is doing and why. Among the departures from the norm of the "favorite" sentence type produced by an amateur writer, most are not minor sentences but sentence fragments (usually marked *Frag* in correcting papers). Few of them are intentional, and few can be justified as rhetorically effective.

It is sometimes hard to see any difference between a fragment and a minor sentence. Neither has an independent subject-verb combination; either may take the form of a phrase or dependent clause. But the minor sentence, used sparingly and deliberately for an appropriate purpose, is acceptable, and the sentence fragment is not. In proofreading your papers, analyze each unit that you have punctuated as a sentence to see that it contains an independent subject-verb combination. If it does not, you must decide whether you can let it stand as a minor sentence type or whether you need to revise it. Some examples from student writing will help you make the decision.

In this passage, the series of infinitive phrases is used to give emphasis and a sense of urgency to the writer's own answer to his question:

Why did they sign the treaty? *To stop the war. To put an end to the senseless slaughter of the people. To give the country a chance to bind up its wounds.*

(The writer had to decide whether this version was preferable to an alternative such as:

(They signed the treaty to stop the war, to put an end to the senseless slaughter of the people, to give the country a chance to bind up its wounds.)

Consider two more examples:

And now a word about the honor system.

High school and college differ in many respects. First, in the relationship between teacher and students.

The first might be justified as making a concise and easy transition. Because the second ("First, in the relationship between teacher and students") gives the statement something of the prominence of a main heading in a topic outline, it might be useful in structuring a passage that would continue with other differences, probably identified by *second, third,* and so on. Used sparingly, the device isolates and emphasizes a significant point; overused, it creates an effect of jerkiness or, when the content does not deserve such prominence, of distortion.

Contrast these examples with three more, all of which were unintentional, all of which were marked *Frag,* and none of which could be justified by the students who wrote them:

In an unexpectedly heavy turnout, over ninety percent of the voters went to the polls. *A figure that shows how strongly the citizens felt about the bond issue.*

Military training is taken for granted on most campuses. *While if R.O.T.C. were ever seriously considered here, the students would object violently.*

I should like to give my opinion on an important matter. *This being the change in policy concerning examinations.*

The first two contain subjects and verbs, and the third a verbal (a participle); but in no case does the italicized portion meet the primary condition of the sentence. None of the items contains an *independent* subject-verb combination. All result from a faulty analysis of what has been punctuated as a "sentence." As a general rule, dependent clauses and verbal phrases punctuated as sentences are revised either by joining the fragment to the preceding or following sentence or by rewriting it as an independent clause that can stand as a separate sentence.

Three more items show explanatory phrases punctuated as sentences:

That most people dislike poetry is a reflection of our methods of teaching it. *Not an eternal truth of human nature.*

The jobs the machinist does in this shop vary considerably. *Anything from making a bolt to cutting a gear twenty feet in diameter.*

High school and college differ in many important respects. *Chiefly in the relationship between teacher and students.*

None of these can be defended on grounds of effectiveness. The elements in contrast in the first item would be better juxtaposed, not separated. ("That most people dislike poetry is a reflection of our methods of teaching it, not an eternal truth of human nature.") In the second and third items, parts that belong together are set apart; in both, the fragments create an effect of disconnectedness and they may possibly even confuse the meaning. Compare the third example, "Chiefly in the relationship between teacher and students," with the one previously cited as a minor sentence used to isolate and emphasize a main topic—"First, in the relationship between teacher and students." The difference in effect should be clear.

The remedy for the fragment which is simply an explanatory phrase is usually to join the phrase to the preceding sentence. (In the second example above, *anything* would be deleted.)

Other items, many of them beginning with parenthetical or explanatory remarks, must be classed as borderline cases; they would be criticized by some readers, accepted by others.

They have their own schools, stores, and amusements. *In short, an island of China inside San Francisco.*

He had a fine record as mayor, and everybody respected him. *That is, until World War II broke out.*

If these were to be defended, it would probably be on the grounds that *in short* and *that is* occur regularly enough in contexts like these to be accorded the independent status of the fuller statements for which they substitute. If they were to be criticized, it would be on the grounds that the semantic relationship is so close that the period marks an unduly sharp interruption.

The only protection against the sentence fragment is skill in analyzing and evaluating what you have punctuated as a sentence. When you recognize that what you have produced does not conform to the pattern of the "favorite" type, you need to decide whether it can stand as a minor sentence or whether, as a fragment, it needs to be revised.

Revising comma faults • The term "comma fault" (or "comma blunder" or "comma splice") is fundamentally an error in punctuation. It refers not to all misuses of the comma but to one of a rather special kind. Although it is an error in punctuation, it needs discussion here because (like the sentence fragment) it results from a failure to analyze correctly the clause-structure of the sentence in which it appears. It sometimes occurs when a comma (instead of a semicolon) is used before the conjunctive adverb that joins two independent clauses:

I wanted to see the movie; [not ,] however, I decided I could not spare the time.

More often it appears in a combination of two or more independent clauses not joined by a coordinating conjunction:

The schedule has changed, the main feature begins at 7 P.M. now.

If there is not even a comma between the clauses, the mistake is sometimes called a "fused sentence": "English is not just 'good' it is good under certain conditions." This is not really a different mistake but simply grosser carelessness.

If you can make a sure distinction between an independent clause and a dependent clause, you will find it relatively easy to identify the comma faults in your sentences. Look first to see how many independent subject-verb combinations you have in a group of words punctuated as a single sentence. If there are two independent clauses, look to see if you have a connective between them. If there is no connective but only a comma, you have probably produced a comma fault.

There are four principal ways to revise comma faults: subordinating one or more clauses, rephrasing to make a single independent clause, adding a connective, or repunctuating.

In some sentences, the relation of the clauses is such that the best change is to rewrite one of the independent clauses either as a dependent clause or as a phrase:

Comma fault	*Revised*
The *Ranger's* crew is made up of 26 professional sailors, *most of them* are of Scandinavian ancestry.	The *Ranger's* crew is made up of 26 professional sailors, *most of whom* are of (or: most of them of) Scandinavian ancestry.
While a boy lives at home he is dependent on others, *they* help him out of his difficulties and provide at least for his necessities.	While a boy lives at home, he is dependent on others *who* help him out of his difficulties and provide at least for his necessities.

Many comma faults are due simply to separating ideas that should be written as one statement:

Comma fault	*Revised*
One part receives the stimulus from outside and transmits the impulse to the cell, *this is known as the dendrite.*	One part, *known as the dendrite,* receives the stimulus from outside and transmits the impulse to the cell.
The pressmen were a good-natured bunch who *seldom complained about conditions, instead they usually joked about them.*	The pressmen were a good-natured bunch *who usually joked rather than complained* about conditions.

Another type of comma fault is one in which a second verb is used in a construction that does not require it:

Then came the speeches, some of them *were* very amusing while others *were* very serious.	Then came the speeches, some of them very amusing, others very serious.

In each of the preceding examples there seems to be an idea that can appropriately be put in a single sentence, but the writer did not make his sentence reflect the logical relations of his material. Very often such sentences profit from more drastic revision than is shown in these examples.

Sometimes inserting a coordinating or subordinating conjunction in a comma fault sentence will make the sentence compound or complex in form.

Comma fault	*Revised*
I think it would do a lot of Americans good to read this book, they would get a background on which to form a more exact knowledge of the English people.	I think it would do a lot of Americans good to read this book *because* they would get a background on which to form a more exact knowledge of the English people.
America is said to be a nation of conformists, this is not true.	America is said to be a nation of conformists, *but* this is not true.

Occasionally a comma fault can be corrected by repunctuating with a period or a semicolon. A semicolon can be used when there is a connective indicating a logical relationship or when the clauses are closely related in meaning. In the first sentence below, and possibly in the third, a semicolon would be satisfactory; in the second, a period (or more formally, a colon) would be better.

The vigilantes did not bother with courts, which might cause a wait of six months for satisfaction, [; here] instead they hung their men as close to the scene of the crime as possible and left the body there as an example.

The long days of Front and Market streets were a thing of the past, [new sentence here or :] the store now opened for business at eight in the morning and closed at six-thirty, including Saturdays.

The captain was endowed with great vitality, [; or . depending on emphasis desired] he had what amounted to a genius for survival.

Independent clauses joined without pause or change in pitch are common in speech ("Hurry up, we'll be late"), and recently, with the increasing informality of written style, they have become more common in writing. In books and articles by writers of high standing we occasionally find sentences in which independent clauses (contact clauses) are joined only by a comma:

The need is not really for more brains, the need is now for a gentler, a more tolerant people than those who won for us against the ice, the tiger, and the bear.—LOREN EISELEY. *The Immense Journey,* p. 140

This sentence is effective and would hardly be improved by repunctuating or by making some other revision. Whenever you come upon one like it in good prose, you should analyze it and try to determine why it is effective. Some comments on students' sentences will suggest the lines such an analysis might take.

It is not merely a regulatory board, it is a board of censorship.
Capitalism and socialism are not political systems, they are economic.
Some will gain, others will lose.
Tolerance understands, compassion warms, charity forgives.

The most obvious characteristic of these items is that the clauses joined by commas are short and parallel in form. In addition, the semantic relationship of the clauses is very close, one filling out or amplifying the meaning of the preceding one. In the first two there is a clear pattern of opposition (*not . . . but*), even though the *but* is not explicitly stated. In the last two, the meaning is additive and climactic. (The climactic effect is most obvious in the series of three in the final example.) Another clue—though not a sure one—is to be found in intonation. If you read these sentences aloud in a natural tone, you will probably discover that your voice does not drop at the comma as it normally does when you come to the end of a sentence. Most readers would find the punctuation in these four sentences acceptable.

In deciding whether you can punctuate sentences in this way, you should consider the appropriateness of contact clauses to the kind of writing you are doing and you should remember that there is a widespread prejudice against them—editors seldom let them stand. They are almost always inappropriate in Formal English. They are rare, too, in discussions of ideas, even when the discussions are not very formally written, because the writer needs to show relationships between statements, and that usually means linking them by specific connectives.

Contact clauses are most useful in easy, rapid narrative (factual or imaginative) in which the clauses are relatively short, approaching turns of speech, and in which relationships can be rapidly grasped without connectives. In fact, connectives would often bring an unneeded note of formality into such narrative.

Revising subject-verb agreement • The relation between verb, subject, and object or predicative is most commonly shown by their position, by word order. In the typical sentence the subject precedes the verb and is the starting point of the statement (not necessarily the "doer"; see *Passive verbs). The object ordinarily follows the verb. If both subject and object precede, the first noun is the object (The *book* [object] *he* [subject] had written first). In some constructions the order is inverted:

In questions: *Have you* any kerosene? *Does he expect* us to read all that?

In some conditions [a Formal construction]: *Had he known* then what he knows now, he would have hesitated.

After emphatic adverbs: Never *have I seen* such a mess.

All these basic matters of word order we pick up early and without conscious effort. We also automatically observe the familiar convention that the verb agrees in number with the subject. True, the forms of *be* and a few other verbs which have irregular inflections have to be learned in order to avoid such Nonstandard usages as *we was;* but the vast majority of verbs have regular inflections and, except for -*s* in the third person singular, show no change as the subject changes in number or person (I sing, you sing, he sings, we sing, you sing, they sing).

The few trouble spots that do occur come from slight complications in particular locutions or from the conflicting demands of agreement by form and agreement by meaning. In some instances usage varies: Formal is likely to insist on agreement by form and General to favor agreement by meaning.

Most mistakes in agreement result from the failure to *identify* the subject correctly: the writer makes the verb agree with a word which is not the actual subject (*blind agreement*). The mistake is likely to occur when a long phrase or clause containing plural nouns intervenes between subject and verb:

An analysis of the extent to which audio-visual aids are used in our schools make me conclude that books are no longer the chief means of education [the subject *analysis* requires the singular verb *makes*].

Often the real trouble with sentences such as this is that they are awkwardly phrased; in the following the words in brackets suggest a recasting that would eliminate the problem of agreement:

Here and there a *man such as* [such men as] Columbus, Galileo, and others *has* [have] ventured into the unknown physical and intellectual worlds.

Such mistakes can be avoided if the subject is correctly identified, for in these examples and in countless others agreement by form coincides with agreement by meaning. The formal marker of a few subjects is initially confusing; but the special cases are rare, and consulting a dictionary will resolve doubt. *Analysis,* for example, is singular (plural, *analyses*); in American English, *news* is now always treated as singular, and so are such words as *mathematics* and *politics.* For a very few words, agreement varies according to the sense in which the word is used:

His one *means* of making a living *has* been removed.
The *means are* justified by the end.

In other sentences where a phrase or clause intervenes between subject and verb, there is a conflict between the formal and the rational number. Words like **type, part, series, *kind, *number,* when they are followed by an *of* phrase containing a plural noun, are especially troublesome:

The greater *part* of their inventions *has* no economic importance.
A *series* of articles *was* planned, written, and published.

Formal usage favors the singular; in speech and in some General writing, a plural verb is found because the sense of the closely knit phrase is felt to be plural.

Relative clauses introduced by *who* or *that* or *which* have verbs agreeing with the pronoun's antecedent:

A skunk *that has been captured young* makes a good pet.
Skunks *that have been captured young* make good pets.

In sentences containing the construction **one of those who,* Formal usage has a plural verb for *who* because its antecedent (*those*) is plural; General usage more often has a singular verb because the main idea is singular:

Formal: Dad is one of those men *who see through* people at the first meeting.

General: Dad is one of those men *who sees through* people at the first meeting.

But again rephrasing may be preferable.

Additional patterns of subject-verb combinations are treated in *Subject and verb, §2b. As the examples make clear, choices have to be made when the subject is a collective noun like *athletics* or *jury;* traditionally and Formally, such subjects take singular verbs, but it is common practice to use the plural when the emphasis is on the variety or individuality of the members of the group.

The *jury* [as a group] *has* been out five hours.
The *jury* [the individual members] *have* been arguing for hours.

When the subject is compound, the number of the verb is usually determined by the internal structure of the subject. Compare:

My friend and my Scout leader *have* agreed to speak at the meeting. (two different people)
My friend and Scout leader *has* agreed to speak.... (the same person)

When *either-or* or *neither-nor* links subjects in the singular, and the parts are thought of as clear alternatives or separate units, the verb is singular:

Either blue or grey is suitable.
Neither train nor bus is fast enough.

But sometimes, particularly with *neither-nor,* singular subjects may be construed as plural in meaning. General usage favors the plural verb when there is a strong suggestion of the plural (with a meaning of "Both do not. . . ."):

Neither poll nor straw vote convince me.

Again the pull of meaning accounts for the increasing use of the plural following *none*:

The children are enjoying themselves; none *are* ready to leave. (The Formal *is* would sound strained after *themselves.*)

Minor problems arise in connection with subject-predicative relationships and the subjects of gerunds. When the subject and the predicative are of different numbers, the verb agrees with the subject:

Our chief *trouble was* [not: *were*] the black flies that swarmed around us all during the trip.

The territory comprised what *is* [not: *are*] now Texas and Oklahoma.

The subject of a gerund (an *-ing* verb form used as a noun) is either in the genitive or the objective case. The genitive is more common with pronouns, less common with nouns:

They had never heard of *his asking* for such a privilege.

They had never heard of a person [less common: *a person's*] asking for such a privilege.

Use whichever seems more natural. (See *Gerund for further distinctions.)

You can guard against gross blunders in subject-verb agreement by making a careful analysis of the sentences you have written. Usually the correction is apparent once you have identified the actual subject.

Revising dangling modifiers • The basic S-V-O pattern of the simple sentence may be expanded by verbal phrases—infinitives, gerunds, and participles. (See p. 281.) With a few exceptions that will be noted later, these modifiers do not have independent status in the sentence. Most of them are expansions of the subject or the verb, and the writer needs to make clear their relation to what they are intended to expand. If, instead, he treats them as free-wheeling structures which he can casually insert here or there in the sentence, he is likely to produce the mistake known as the *dangling modifier*.

Questions about modifiers center on their *position* in the sentence and on their *relationship* to other words or word-groups. Often questions about position will lead to questions about relationship; for if the writer fails to place a modifier properly, he will obscure its relationship to the word it is intended to modify. Sometimes the problem is wholly one of relationship: the careless omission of the word which should logically be modified creates an ambiguity or confusion which cannot be cleared up simply by shifting the position of the modifier.

A verbal phrase dangles if, because of its position, it appears to relate to a word which can only make nonsense of the meaning, or if, in a context which demands an explicit relationship, the phrase has no clear relation to any word in the sentence. Blunders in placing and relating modifiers may make sentences unintentionally humorous or preposterous.

Being full of curves, she had trouble keeping the car on the road.
Reaching sixteen, my parents agreed to let me drive.

Every serious writer takes care to be neither unintentionally amusing nor patently absurd. But even if he escapes these embarrassments, he will confuse his reader (momentarily, at least) if he places a verbal phrase before a word—normally, subject—which it cannot logically expand.

Looking far to the south, the spitting iron vats of the steel mills tinge the sky.

The verbal phrase cannot modify *vats*—vats do not look. But the problem is not the simple one of a misplaced modifier. No change in its position would improve the sentence; in fact, any change would be for the worse. The only feasible solution is to rewrite the sentence in such a way that the modifier will be a genuine expansion of a logical subject:

Looking far to the south, I see [*or*: we see, he sees, etc.] the spitting iron vats of the steel mills tinging the sky.

Another, simpler revision would convert the participle into a prepositional phrase:

Far to the south, the spitting iron vats of the steel mills tinge the sky.

(The dangling verbal phrase *Looking far to the south* is related to the larger problem of point of view; blunders like these often result from the writer's unsuccessful attempt to be anonymous.)

Two more sentences illustrate the dangling modifier in other positions in the sentence:

A democracy encourages free discussion of all ideas so that, *when approaching new problems,* old dogmas will not furnish the only solutions.

In the northern half of the area, two cement factories have sprung up, one in each of the last two years, *being the only industry in the town aside from a sawmill that has carried over from the great lumbering era.*

The first sentence demonstrates again the confusion that results when a sentence contains no word which can logically be modified by the participle phrase. Various revisions are possible; at the least, we must introduce a proper subject *(citizens,* perhaps) and rephrase the final clause—"citizens will not depend on old dogmas alone to furnish solutions."

The second example has multiple flaws. The *being* construction (this time consisting of a participle phrase expanded by phrases and a dependent clause) is in a position that makes it appear to be an expansion of the verb *have sprung up.* But again, reordering to correct the obvious error in position would not improve the sentence; it would only emphasize the looseness and inexactness of the expressed relation of the modifier. *Industry* is not an adequate appositive for *cement factories.* The sentence needs to be written afresh, and probably the best course is to make two sentences:

In the northern half of the area, two cement factories have sprung up, one in each of the last two years. Aside from a sawmill that has carried over from the great lumbering era, these represent the only industrial activity in the town.

All of the dangling modifiers considered so far are phrases beginning with participles; they are by far the most common and most troublesome to revise. Simply shifting the position will seldom remedy the weakness; more often drastic surgery is indicated, and this must be preceded by a careful diagnosis of what ails the sentence.

Other modifiers can dangle too, but they are simpler to revise. In these, the italicized part could be rewritten as a dependent clause (in the first, *When I am at home*) or the subject of the independent clause could be changed (When at home, *I* am treated):

When at home, everybody treats me as if I were still a child.
Whether at work or play, self-confidence is the key to a successful life.
To play a musical instrument, nothing is more important than regular practice.

In revising your sentences, check the verbal phrases (especially the participles) to make sure that in each case the word it relates to is *expressed,* not merely understood, and that the position of the modifier leaves no doubt as to which word it modifies.

These precepts, like most so easily stated, need qualification. A few patterns are so well established that they do not demand this kind of explicit relationship. A number of verbals can appear as *absolute phrases,* functioning much like subordinate clauses. A number of verbs for mental activity are so used:

> *Granted the verdict,* what is the penalty?
> *Considering the situation,* more facts are needed.

Revising shifted constructions • The structural pattern of *parallelism* is a characteristic feature of English. Parallelism is the arrangement of words, phrases, clauses, or sentences in a series of two or more grammatically equivalent structures. (In the preceding sentence, *words, phrases, clauses, sentences* are parallel; each noun is the object of the preposition *of.* The grammatical similarity signals to the reader the fact that the words have similar functions in the sentence.) The following pair of sentences demonstrates the value of parallelism in making meaning clear. Although both sentences are grammatically coherent, the patterning of the second makes the meaning easier to grasp.

> One group favors gradual desegregation, while another demands that integration be brought about immediately, and a third group says that it is altogether opposed to integration.
> One group favors gradual integration, another demands immediate integration, and a third opposes integration altogether.

As used here, parallelism introduces clarity and directness into a sentence that is flabby and diffuse. A third version (the way the student wrote it in his first draft) illustrates the chaos which results from the absence of any structural patterning.

> One group favors gradual desegregation, another demanding immediate integration, and from the third group, total opposition to integration.

The reader's expectation that *and* will join the second and third elements of a series of three is thwarted by the grammatical structure of both the second and third elements. The "sentence" is incoherent.

Dozens of other structures which likewise thwart the reader's expectations (though seldom so drastically) are commonly labeled *shifted* (sometimes *mixed*) *constructions*. The term can be used to designate any structural pattern which begins in one way and ends in another and so fails to carry out an implied promise of matching structures.

Since parallelism is a mode of coordination, faulty parallelism may occur in pairs of any kind (where *a* is joined to *b* by a coordinating conjunction) or in a series of three or more.

No complete listing of failures in parallelism can be or need be made. Recognizing such shifts, no matter what forms are involved, is easy enough, once the basic principle of parallelism is understood. Here are a few examples, with comments:

Going home for Christmas, seeing my family, and to find how much they had changed disturbed me.

In the compound subject, the pattern established by the first participle phrase is repeated by the second but broken by the third, with the shift to the infinitive. The simplest revision is to change *to find* to *finding*.

The leaders of our society encourage group activity and at the same time discouraging creative thought.

The simplest revision is to change *discouraging* to *discourage*, making a satisfactory compound predicate.

He was cold, hungry, and envied his brother's superior strength.

Parallelism of adjectives could be established by changing *envied* to *envious of*. But other revisions are possible, such as "He was cold and hungry, and he envied his brother's superior strength."

The reasons students offer for attending college are the social advantages they hope to enjoy, training for a position, because of the uncertainty of their future, or in order to get an education.

The multiple shifts create real confusion. Does the phrase beginning with *because* belong with *training for a position,* or does it signal a third reason for attending college (because they didn't know what else to do with themselves)?

Ideal and practice will only be brought together when the laws are enforced and until observing the laws becomes the accepted thing.

Two patterns collide: *Ideal and practice will only be brought together when* and *Ideal and practice will not be brought together until.* One pattern should be used consistently.

The law serves a double purpose; first, it protects the people, and second, the capture of criminals.

The promise of parallelism of an independent clause following *second* remains unfulfilled.

Faulty parallelism includes incomplete constructions, as illustrated by:

The Great Dane was as big if not bigger than the wolf. (The incomplete comparison invites the reader to fashion the unidiomatic pattern *as big than*.)

Although the problem is stylistic rather than syntactic, shifts in approach to the statement are also blunders in parallelism. Most conspicuous are shifts in point of view (see pp. 163-169) and shifts from active to passive verbs or the reverse:

The other occupants of the bus thought that I was slightly eccentric, for my entire trip was spent talking to myself.

Conspicuous lapses in parallelism, such as those illustrated in this section, are real hindrances in communicating the writer's meaning and should be corrected in revision. The basic question is "What goes with what?" and any writer needs to recognize that in English some combinations are ungrammatical and unacceptable. At the same time, making a fetish of parallelism will have adverse effects on any style. "We need to know who is to censor and by what methods" is clear and acceptable; only an examination of the context would tell whether parallelism would be more effective.

Revising for clear statement • Many problems in revision can be solved by making a faulty sentence conform to standard grammatical patterns and to certain established conventions. But some sentences which violate neither typical structural patterns nor accepted conventions are, nevertheless, bad sentences —bad because they do not convey the meaning they were intended to convey. Very seldom, of course, does a native speaker or writer fail to make himself understood, but he often fails to communicate what he wants to. Especially in writing—because he cannot notice the immediate signs of a lapse in communication, such as the puzzled expression or inappropriate response of a listener—he may confuse the reader, send him off on the wrong track, or, worse, contradict himself.

Many of these problems in written communication are taken up in Chapter 9, but some can better be discussed in the context of the sentence. The discussion is necessarily incomplete and tentative, for often a final decision can be made only after examining the paragraph or essay from which the sentence or sequence of sentences is taken. (For continuity between sentences, see "Continuity in paragraphs," Ch. 4, pp. 139-143.)

Coordination and subordination. Choosing between coordination (two or more independent clauses in a compound sentence) and subordination (dependent clauses combined with independent clauses in complex or compound-complex sentences) is partly a matter of style. Often our meaning can best be communicated by a particular conjunction. "He looked up *when* I spoke" expresses one relationship between events; "He looked up *and* I spoke" expresses a different one. But meaning alone cannot determine every choice. It would be hard to find any significant difference in meaning between each of the following pairs, the first containing a coordinating conjunction, the second a subordinating conjunction:

He studied, *but* I went to the movies.
Although he studied, I went to the movies.

You must pass the test, *or* you will not be admitted to college.
Unless you pass the test, you will not be admitted to college.

He appealed the decision, *for* everyone advised him to.
He appealed the decision *because* everyone advised him to.

When the criterion of meaning yields no basis for choosing between coordination and subordination, a writer may decide to use one rather than the other to achieve a smooth transition, to vary the pattern of preceding sentences, or for some similar reason. Unfortunately, many amateur writers fail to distinguish between situations like these and situations in which *one* pattern is distinctly superior in conveying meaning. Some examples will show how the specialized meaning of some of the subordinating conjunctions make statements clearer and more exact than they would be if *and* (the most popular of the coordinating conjunctions with inexperienced writers) were used:

Inexact connection	*Revised*
Illustrations were given in every case *and* the plan was easily understood, which made it all the more interesting.	Illustrations were given in every case *so that* the plan was easily understood and all the more interesting.
The Stanley Steamer looked like one of those cars of the nineties in every way except its wheels, *and* they were changed so as to use pneumatic tires.	The Stanley Steamer looked in every way like one of those cars of the nineties except for its wheels, *which* were changed so as to use pneumatic tires.
He may have attended both of the preceding classes, *and* by chapel time he begins to feel the desire for a respite from mental work.	*If* he has attended both of the preceding classes, by chapel time he begins to feel the desire for a respite from mental work.

Weaknesses in handling coordination or subordination may stem from the poor choice of a conjunction. One example, however, should make clear why little advice can be given on this point apart from an examination of the context. Most of us, thinking of *and* and *but* in isolation, would immediately say they have different meanings. And very often they do: *and* is additive, while *but* is contrastive. But often a conjunction derives its exact meaning from context; because of the context in which it occurs, the *and* in the first sentence below is different, or conveys a different meaning, from the *and* in the second:

Yesterday I had news of the two Smith boys for the first time since they left home. John is a bank manager in New York, *and* James is a professor at Yale.

Although for years James slavishly imitated his brother John, he finally showed some independence. John is a bank manager in New York, *and* James is a professor at Yale.

In speech, the second *and* would have something of a "what-do-you-know" effect, really closer to the usual meaning conveyed by *but*. In writing, *and* is satisfactory in either sentence, because the context makes the meaning clear.

The choice of a connective (whether in coordination or subordination) depends on what we want to say. We choose the

conjunction that will best clarify the logical relationships of
our statements and so make our meaning clear.

The placing of clauses offers little trouble in coordination
but a good deal in subordination. The reporter who wrote
the following sentence had trouble.

The catcher was the star of the ball game with a double, two
singles, and a walk that drove in four runs.

The clause *that drove in four runs* appears to modify *walk;* if
it was meant to, the statistical foundations of our national
pastime are in dire peril. Dependent clauses take different positions in the sentence, depending on what they modify. But this
does not mean that we can be reckless or casual in placing
them, any more than we can be casual about placing a verbal
phrase. Notice the difference in meaning in this pair:

While he was in Washington, he argued that the bill should be
passed.

He argued that the bill should be passed while he was in
Washington.

It is wise to experiment with the ordering of a dependent
clause until its position makes clear what it modifies.

The position of a dependent clause, even when it does not
mislead the reader, may very well cause momentary lapses in
communication. Consider the following pair, the first as a
student wrote it, the second his revision:

If, as our recent history testifies, extreme individualism is exercised in all phases of human life, anarchy will result.

Our recent history testifies that anarchy will result if extreme
individualism is exercised in all phases of political life.

(Notice that the revision entails something more than simply
shifting the clauses around.)

Interrupting a dependent clause with another clause or a
phrase sometimes leads the writer to repeat unnecessarily the
word which introduced the clause. What is intended to be a
device for clarifying and reminding may make the reader
stumble:

It is only natural *that* with a sudden change in the Administration *that* the people should worry about what new policies might
be instituted.

Incongruous statements.   Other examples show how a writer may carelessly hinder efficient communication. He may put together details that do not belong together, producing a sentence which may raise a question in the reader's mind or even confuse him:

Lady Beaconsfield affectionately called him "Dizzy" and she did everything in her power to make him the success he was. (Combining a nickname and a wife's help in building a statesman's career can only make a reader smile.)

He has a nervous habit of toying with the last two buttons on his vest when thinking and uses his deep voice to the best advantage when excited or angry. (Perhaps these two characteristics could be put together as signs of nervousness, but certainly they are too different to be connected simply by *and*.)

Amateurs write a surprising number of sentences in which one part cancels the other. The sentences below come from an effort to put in a fact that doesn't quite belong, as in the first example, or from a clumsy attempt at qualifying a statement, as in the second:

Her marriage to another writer, who teaches at Harvard, may have some influence upon her style; *however there is no evidence to support this.*

The next day we visited the ancient mosques, where we tried to walk in sandals which fitted—*or rather refused to fit*—over our shoes.

Revising to make sentences effective

In the first section of this chapter, we discussed the chief characteristics of English sentences, commenting on the order in which the parts typically stand. This analysis provided the basis for the discussion in the second section about revising to meet the reader's expectations—making sure that what you write is clear and acceptable. We have seen that one way of achieving clarity—indeed, of making sense—is to observe certain conventions of word order. But much variety is possible in sentences, and a writer should be aware of the opportunities he has for personal choice. Making the right choices leads to effective expression.

English sentences offer various ways of expressing substantially the same basic idea, even a very simple one like this:

That book bored me.   I found that book boring
I was bored by that book.   That is a boring book.
That book is boring.   That book seemed boring to me.
My impression is that that book is boring.

It is easy to imagine different neighboring sentences that would make one of these seem more appropriate than the others. The choice of one or another is not a matter of grammar but of style. The sentences you write may be long or short, direct or involved, emphatic, rhythmical, depending on how successfully you exploit the resources of the language.

Styles of writing can be described but not prescribed. You have to develop a sense of when and where and how a particular style can be used effectively. How others have written is your best guide; it pays to reread and analyze a passage that appeals to you, observing the sentences closely. This section describes several traits of sentences and offers some principles to help you see how other writers produce their effects and how you can develop a more effective style in your own writing.

Variety in sentence length • The most obvious sentence characteristic is relative length. The shorter sentence is characteristic of most newspaper writing, of much business writing and advertising, of familiar writing (as in diaries and letters), of much fiction today, and of many discussions of ideas in both books and magazines—in brief, it is characteristic of Informal and much General English. At worst, short sentences become choppy and jerky, breaking the ideas into units too small to follow conveniently; or they become unemphatic and monotonous, tiring a reader if they occur in long sequences. At best, short sentences permit ideas to come directly, to follow each other naturally as they were thought, or as they might be spoken:

Sadeyes soon wired back to both of us to discontinue our surveys. We were thankful for that. It is not that we were in any immediate danger. But with radiation so intense at such an altitude, that at water level would certainly be lethal. And this wasn't just a point source, it was spread out over an area miles square.—DAVID BRADLEY, *No Place to Hide*, pp. 96-97

Longer sentences, in which several contributing details or generalizations are combined, characterize Formal styles, especially discussions of ideas; they are also fairly common in fiction, especially in descriptive passages, and in newspaper leads, where the most important information of a news item is summarized in a sentence or two. This long sentence specifies several parts of what the writer sees as the relation of style to language and personality:

It is strange how long it has taken the European literatures to learn that style is not an absolute, a something that is to be imposed on the language from Greek or Latin models, but merely the language itself, running in its natural grooves, and with enough of an individual accent to allow the artists' personality to be felt as a presence, not as an acrobat.—EDWARD SAPIR, *Language,* p. 227

There is no special virtue in either long sentences or short ones, but there is a virtue in making the length of any one sentence appropriate to what is being said and in varying the lengths of sentences in a sequence. A short sentence following a series of rather long ones can have a dramatic effect; a long one coming after a series of short ones can pull together details or particulars into an inclusive, satisfying statement.

A "choppy" style results from piling up short sentences, as in this passage:

Probably the hardest job is the handling and treating of grain. The treating consists of running the grain through a machine called a "Fanning Mill." This machine thoroughly cleans the grain and adds a chemical which protects it against winterkill, smut and other common diseases. The most common kind of storage bin for grain is the tank type. It is a round tank with straight sides and peaked roof. These bins have flat bottoms. Grain will not run out by gravity. Someone has invented a simple elevator that can be pushed into the grain to elevate it out.

With some rephrasing, these eight sentences could be made into three—and the three would do a better job of showing the logical relationships of the material.

"Stringy" sentences—sentences drawn out beyond reasonable length—are likely to be aimless or confusing. They often result from an excessive dependence on either subordination or coordination. The following has eight dependent clauses—six of them built one upon another in a sequence known as "tandem subordination." Though the sentence contains no grammatical errors, it leaves even the most patient reader with only a blurred impression of what the writer is up to—except that he means to convey a sense of crisis.

As everyone knows, Chicago has a traffic problem that needs to be solved, because every day that we ignore it brings us closer to the time when the congestion of traffic will be so great that it will paralyze the city, which cannot function at all unless there is an uninterrupted flow of goods and people from one section to another.

There is no handy rule to fix limits to the number of clauses a compound or compound-complex sentence should contain. When the parallelism of clauses is strict enough to establish a predictable pattern or when the clauses build to a climax, step by step, the number may be surprisingly large. But when the parallelism is not marked or when the sentence slides into trivial details, the very long compound or compound-complex sentence will strike the reader as aimless and sprawling. This one dies long before its last words:

The orders were issued at dawn, and the detachment set out, and the men moved down hill, but their progress slowed as the heat increased, and by noon the columns were barely shuffling along, although the officers were doing their best to keep to schedule and nobody was deliberately stalling.

Variety in sentence movement • Groups of sentences of about the same length and general pattern become monotonous. Varying the length helps avoid such monotony, but changing the order of elements in the sentences is equally important. In speech, variety is also achieved by stress and rhythm, the emphasis on individual words, intonation of the various sentence elements, and the pauses between them. Some sense of these qualities carries over even into silent reading, but the chief way to vary written sentences is to change the order of their parts.

Varying the position of modifiers. In a paragraph the arrangement of sentences is governed by the thought patterns of the writer. But in a sentence the writer has to follow established grammatical patterns in the arrangement of words. Since the S-V-O order probably occurs in nine tenths of English sentences, the chief source of variety is in the positions for modifiers.

*   *Revising sentences*

The subject is likely to be conspicuous and emphatic because it comes at the beginning. Therefore a series of sentences beginning with unmodified subjects tends to become monotonous. One way of breaking the monotony is to begin an occasional sentence with a modifier of the subject of the whole sentence. Notice the different movement of these openings:

His first serious attempts were failures.
In spite of their seriousness, his first attempts were failures.
Although he worked with great seriousness, his first attempts were failures.

An occasional sentence beginning with a long phrase or with a subordinate clause takes the stress away from the subject and makes for variety.[1] It also clears away the necessary qualifications so that they will not later interrupt the movement of the sentence or come limping in at the bitter end.

With six similar facts to state in this passage, the author begins half the sentences with the subject and half with modifiers that vary the sentence opening:

[Subject:] *The theoretical type* seeks to grasp the nature of things. [Adverbial modifier of sentence:] *When the reality sought is not local and temporary but cosmic,* we have the religious type. [Adverbial modifier of sentence:] *When not the abstract relations but the persons about one are valued,* we have the social type. [Adverbial phrase:] *In the person for whom individuals are significant not for themselves but as pawns in a game for power,* we have the political type. [Subject:] *The economic type* finds value in the relations of gain and loss. [Subject:] *The esthetic type* values the relations between sensory objects that are directly and immediately satisfying.—GARDNER MURPHY, *Personality,* pp. 283-284

And the sentence may end either with the object or with a modifier of the object, as in the last two sentences in the paragraph above.

Interrupted movement. We seldom put words between the major elements of a sentence unless they are short modifiers

---

[1] George Summey, Jr., found (*American Punctuation,* p. 241) that about half the sentences he studied began with the subject (often with an adjective modifier) and over a quarter began with adverbial modifiers, ranging from connectives like *however* and sentence adverbs like *certainly* to long phrases and *when, if, although* clauses. Francis Christensen has made a study of "sentence openers" in "Notes Toward a New Rhetoric," *College English,* 1963, 25: 7-11.

closely related to one of the main elements (as in "He does *not always* pay his bills promptly"). If the modifiers are long or not very closely related to the main elements, the movement of the sentence is sufficiently interrupted to distract.

My friend's argument bore then—*at the time and afterward*—on my vicious practice, *as he maintained, of postulating for the purpose of my fable* celebrities who *not only* hadn't existed in the conditions I imputed to them, but who *for the most part (and in no case more markedly than in that of Jeffrey Aspern)* couldn't *possibly* have done so.—HENRY JAMES, Preface to the *Aspern Papers,* in *Henry James: Selected Fiction,* LEON EDEL, ed., p. 414

Such interruptions give variety to sentences, but they also make slower and sometimes even difficult reading. They are more characteristic of tightly knit Formal prose; in General writing, such modifiers are likely to precede or to follow the main sentence elements. Usually it is better to allow only very short modifiers to come between the main sentence elements. The following sentences show how awkward interruption may be in ordinary writing.

Interrupted	*Revised*
Ski trails down the sides of the biggest mountains in New England were cleared.	Ski trails were cleared down the sides of the biggest mountains in New England.
Then he impresses on the freshman the fact that he is getting the pictures practically at the price the materials on which they are printed cost.	Then he impresses on the freshman the fact that he is getting pictures practically at the cost of the material they are printed on.

Cumulative and periodic sentences.   Another classification of sentences shows the relation of arrangement to meaningful effect. The sentence you are now reading is so constructed that the completion of its meaning and effect depend on reading it to the very last word. Such a sentence is called *periodic,* as contrasted with the other type, *cumulative*[1] (also called *loose*), of which this is an example—a sentence that might be stopped at several points (in this sentence, after *periodic, type, loose, example,* or *points*).

---

[1]This more accurately descriptive term was first proposed by Francis Christensen, "A Generative Rhetoric of the Sentence," *College Composition and Communication,* 1963, 14: 155-161.

[Periodic] Yet to this day in England, as in Australia and the United States, the tradition survives that boys who are good at killing animals, or propelling balls, or leaping obstacles, or running very rapidly, are healthier-minded, and therefore more attractive, than boys who devote their attention to art or literature. [Periodic] This seems in many ways an admirable tradition. [Cumulative] It renders English intellectuals unassuming, and provides the state and the commercial community with a constant supply of apprentices who lack imagination and are therefore obedient. [Periodic] The disadvantage is that the athlete, after short years of glory, may have to endure an unhappy middle age. [Periodic] Even as the mediaeval knight, who once his hawking days were over found his afternoons lonely and his evenings dull, so also may those who have rejoiced only in the transient marvel of their physical strength discover in later life that their range has become restricted and their interests few. [Periodic] It is thus recommendable that Olympic champions should acquire the reading habit while still young.—HAROLD NICOL- SON, *Good Behavior,* p. 141

Cumulative sentences are characteristic of conversation, in which we typically add grammatically subordinate statements after the main statement. Periodic sentences are somewhat more Formal. The reader's or listener's attention is suspended until the end; he has to hold the complete sentence in mind rather than let later elements modify the earlier parts. The danger of periodic sentences is that they may seem artificial and unnatural; the danger of cumulative sentences is that they may be unemphatic. While there is no reason to strive for either type, especially in a General style, cumulative sentences are so much more common that an occasional periodic sentence contributes not only suspense but variety.

Parallelism and balance.   Earlier in this chapter (p. 300) we learned that putting sentence elements of equal value into parallel constructions was one way of making the sentence easy to understand. More elaborate parallel movement be- comes an element of style. The first two of the following ex- amples of parallelism are natural and simple; the third is rather Formal, but still the parallel locutions are sufficiently varied in length and form so that they are not monotonous:

> To suppose that we can think like men of another time
>   is as much an illusion as
> to suppose that we can think in a wholly different way.—
> LIONEL TRILLING

> The most serious criticism leveled against American civilization is
> not that its work is standardized and its business engulf-
> ing, but that its pleasures are mechanical and its leisure
> slavish.—IRWIN EDMAN

> The materials out of which the latter [Shakespeare] created his works—
> his conception of human dignity,
> his sense of the importance of human passions,
> his vision of the amplitude of human life—
> simply did not and could not exist for Ibsen, as
> they did not and could not exist for his contem-
> poraries.—JOSEPH WOOD KRUTCH

When the parallel constructions, especially clauses, of a compound sentence are noticeably equal in length and similar in movement, the sentence is called *balanced*. Even in a plain style, balanced sentences are fairly common for emphatic statements and especially for comparisons and contrasts:

> They have been educated to achieve success; few of them have
> been educated to exercise power.—WALTER LIPPMANN

Inverted movement.   A less common means of varying pat-terns is inversion, in which the order of the main elements de-parts from the usual S-V-O (see p. 277). Some inversions are purely grammatical, but in sentences like the following they are stylistic:

> Then came the greatest treat of all.
> This job he kept six years.
> A bargain it was, at that price.

Inversion is not common and ordinarily is not used unless the words put first really deserve special emphasis (see p. 323).

Questions.   Since grammatical order in questions is inverted (Can you come tomorrow? How could you say that?), they give variety to the sentences in a paragraph. And they are helpful, if sparingly used, to focus the reader's attention on a change in subject or on an important point, as in this passage:

> ...It is even possible to defend the thesis that the Renaissance
> proper means a regression in the growth of modern science. Is your
> criterion economic, the growth of a money economy, banking, ex-
> tensive trade? Modern research pushes most of these back to the
> Crusades, to the high Middle Ages. Is your criterion the establish-

ment of the territorial state in the place of the feudal congeries of holdings? Surely France and England are both territorial states by the time they begin their Hundred Years' War in the fourteenth century.—CRANE BRINTON, *The Shaping of the Modern Mind*, p. 20

Occasionally a question makes an effective opening for a paper, but it should be a genuine question leading to the subject, and not a general one concocted just to get attention.

Economy in sentences • Economy in writing means efficient communication with an irreducible body of words and constructions. The fewest and simplest words and constructions are not always the most economical, for they may oversimplify the message, or they may limit its readers to those who are practiced in following an over-compact style. But *unnecessary* words and needlessly complicated expressions cannot be economical.

One feature of economy relates to sentences in a sequence. Regardless of its length, each sentence should advance the thought of the essay. Amateur writers sometimes let sentences stand that say little or nothing, as in the examples below:

My first course in math was taken at Riverside High School in Milwaukee. This was first-year or elementary algebra.

The reader feels that he is not getting full value from the individual sentences. The thought might go: I took my first course in math, elementary algebra, . . .

Some useful but commonly overlooked methods of packing more into a single sentence are:

Series.   Two or three details instead of one give more meaning per sentence:

It is not *newspapers, radio scripts, and movies* that spoil our tongue so much as *textbooks, official documents, commencement speeches, and learned works.*—JACQUES BARZUN

Oxford men are *no more brilliant, no better looking, no more cultured and possessed of no greater inherent ability* than countless undergraduates of American universities; but they think they are.—KENNETH ROBERTS

Compound predicates.   Using two or more verbs for a single subject often makes it unnecessary to have several short sentences of little meaning:

A play that *didn't require changes* or *couldn't profit from suggestions* would be a very remarkable one.—LOUIS KRONENBERGER

Modifiers. A common way of making sentences mean more, and one neglected by amateur writers, is a greater use of phrases and clauses:

He was an incarnation, not unengaging, of the eternal malcontent on the campus, the perpetual, surprised discoverer of the way in which the machinery of a university, like the machinery of many other enterprises, defeats its purposes by swallowing them.—IRWIN EDMAN, *Philosopher's Holiday,* p. 52

Recall, however, the difficulty in handling verbal phrases competently. (See "Revising dangling modifiers," pp. 297-300.)

When you revise your papers, combine statements of little meaning into more complete ones or add informative details to statements that seem flat, so that each sentence is effective in its own right.

Amateur writers frequently put into two statements what could more accurately be expressed in one, thereby hampering communication by requiring the reader to rearrange the thought.

Two statements	*One statement*
It was three or four miles to the nearest village and these people used to walk it at least once a day.	These people used to walk the three or four miles to the nearest village at least once a day.
This is only a typical example; the author has more examples.	This is typical of the author's many examples.
When one is in the fresh air most of the time, as a hunter is, it tends to keep a person healthy and to develop his body.	Being in the fresh air most of the time, as a hunter is, tends to keep a person healthy and to develop his body.

In single sentences the chief way to achieve economical expression is to remove wordy expressions in revision. *Deadwood* is a convenient label for a word or phrase that adds nothing to the sense of a sentence. In the following sentences, the bracketed phrases can be omitted with no loss at all in meaning and with positive gain in economy:

Every thinking person these days seems inclined to agree [with the conception] that the world has gone mad.

Anyone acquainted with violin construction knows that the better the wood is seasoned, the better [the result will be as far as] the tone of the instrument [is concerned].

To my surprise the damage was not so bad as I had expected [it to be].

[It was] during this time [that] the greatest number of cases came down.

It was the first time [in my life] I had seen Niagara Falls.

At the end of an hour and a half we arrived at [the spot where] the red flag [was situated].

The following statistics [serve to] give a good idea of the effects of tobacco.

He kept things moving at breakneck speed throughout [the entirety of] the performance.

A common type of dead phrase is the addition of *color* to a word that can mean only color ("green color"), *number* to a number ("nine in number"), *shape* to a definite form ("rectangular in shape"), or locutions like the following:

The architecture [of the houses] and the landscaping [of the grounds] whisper a word of town pride to the passers-by.

A few words are doubly bad in that they not only add useless weight but often take emphasis from more important words:

case: Many of them have been put to death in individual cases. (Revised: Many individuals have been put to death.)

character: These things, though [of a] useful [character], were not what he wanted.

exception: Most young actors experience numerous difficulties in their early appearances. I was no exception. (Revised: Like most young actors I experienced many difficulties in my early appearances.)

fact (the fact that) : He was quite conscious [of the fact] that his visitor had some other reason for coming.

happen: [It happened that] we were exactly the same age.

line: He had always thought he would do something along agricultural lines. (. . . in agriculture.)

nature: He was never popular because he was reticent [by nature].

variety: I bought two kinds of rolls for the dinner—two dozen plain and one dozen [of the] pecan [variety].

Eliminating deadwood is one of the easiest ways to begin the attack on uneconomical writing: simply draw a line through the unnecessary word or phrase. A writer should also avoid circumlocution—the use of too many words in conveying a single notion. In speaking, we inevitably use more words than are necessary; in writing, too many roundabout expressions result in flabbiness, make the style seem immature, and tire the reader.

Wordy	*Revised*
During the time that she was in Los Angeles she had at least six different jobs.	While she was in Los Angeles, she had at least six different jobs.
The way psychologists measure ability is by tests.	Psychologists measure ability by tests.
It has some of the best ski trails in the country and as far as the other cold weather sports are concerned, they have them too, along with one of the most fashionable hotels in the country.	They have a very fashionable hotel, all the cold weather sports, and some of the best ski trails in the country.

Here are some typical examples of circumlocution:

> *destroyed by fire* means *burned*
> *come in contact with* usually means *meet* or *know*
> *the necessary funds* usually means no more than the *money*
> *in this day and age* means *today*

Long and short constructions.   English offers a choice between a longer and a shorter way of expressing certain relationships. Relative clauses may or may not use the relative pronoun: "the professor *I saw*" or "the professor *whom* I saw." The conjunction *that* may or may not be used: "We like to think *that* our scholarship standards are higher than yours" or "we like to think [   ] our scholarship standards are higher than yours." The choice between these forms is a matter of style; Formal English tends to fill out most constructions and General English uses the shorter forms more freely. Short forms obviously make for economy.

Reducing predication.   An "idea"—a small part of our meaning—may be expressed in one of four grammatical units: in a word, a phrase, a subordinate clause, or a full sentence:

Word: The snow *blanketed* the countryside.
Phrase: The snow covered the countryside *like a blanket*.

Clause: The snow, *which lay like a blanket*, covered the country-side.

Sentence: *The snow lay like a blanket*. It covered the countryside.

Obviously the chief difference is between the first two examples (containing one verb) and the last two (containing two predications). Which expression would be more appropriate would depend on the writer's intention and on other traits of his style. Solely from the point of view of economy, the first two are better. One mark of inexperienced writing is the use of a predication for an idea that deserves no more than a phrase or a single word.

Amateur	*More economical*
A few of the fellows *who were less serious* would go to a bar *where they would have a steak dinner and a few glasses of beer.*	A few of the *less serious* fellows would go to a bar *for a steak dinner and a few glasses of beer.*
We taxied back and forth in front of the starting line, waiting impatiently for the sound of the gun *which would mean that the race was started.*	We taxied back and forth in front of the starting line, waiting impatiently for the sound of the *starting* gun.

Writing can be made so compact that it is hard to follow, but most beginning writers need to acquire a more economical style. Length in a paper should not come from piling up *words* but from piling up *material*—ideas and especially details of observation that convey meaning. Proper economy comes from trying to say more in a given number of words.

Emphasis in sentences • The emphasis in a piece of writing comes principally from the use of strong and distinctive words and from a progressive arrangement of statements in paragraphs and of the paragraphs in the whole, but sentences contribute to this general impression. Economy is an important factor, for wordiness buries the meaning, but there are also other means to make sentences emphatic.

Mechanical devices.   Writing and printing have various mechanical means—underlining (italics), capitals, emphatic punctuation—for stressing words and passages. These devices are often used by inexperienced writers in an attempt to make up for deficiencies in style or content or they are used by advertising copywriters as a device to catch the reader's eye.

7-UP YOUR THIRST AWAY!!

No matter who uses them, the effect is still "forcible-feeble." As a writer's skill increases, he depends less on these mechanical devices, more on distinctiveness of expression, position, and other means of giving emphasis to a statement.

Intensives. Meaning may be emphasized by the use of intensives, particularly in speech. A speaker can stress *too* or *very* or *much* so that it will have a good deal of force (and the activity of the stress gives him a certain physical satisfaction). On paper such words are less convincing because the quality of voice is lacking.

A number of adjectives and adverbs are primarily intensives: *much, *very, such, *too, highly, certainly, extremely, tremendously.* They may provide real emphasis in writing, but an overuse of them suggests a lazy style. Most profanity belongs in this category, the words allowing a satisfying stress and bite but not contributing otherwise to meaning.

In writing, intensives often give a flavor of artificiality that weakens rather than strengthens the statement. Deleting the intensives would improve these sentences:

We had [such] a lovely time at your party.
Everybody was [so] tired after the holiday round of parties.
In pushing the product the slogan has [surely] been [unquestionably] of paramount importance.

The colloquial superlative, used to indicate a considerable degree of a quality instead of the greatest, is a typical intensive in conversation, but it is not often appropriate to writing:

She had the nicest manners [for *nice* or some more exact adjective].
He is a most important figure in the book [an important figure].

The pronouns with *-self* are idiomatic intensives both in speaking and writing:

He picked the flowers himself.
I must see Catherine herself.

There are scores of words of rather intense meaning—*thrill, intriguing, devastating, incredible, passion*—all of which have their necessary and legitimate uses and all of which are likely to be abused when applied to some feeling that does not really deserve such a vigorous word.

The use of intensives should be a matter of appropriateness —in writing, appropriateness to the subject; in speech, sometimes also to the person. At their best intensives may represent a vigorous and emphatic personality; at their worst they show insensitiveness to the values of words. In writing, overuse of them is sure to result in weakened statements.

Repetition.   Repetition of words and phrases can be an excellent means of emphasizing or relating ideas, but repetition that serves no function is unpleasant and should be avoided.

Meaningless repetition of words or phrases may be the result of hazy ideas, but most of it is due to plain inattention to writing—certainly to a lack of revision. Both vague ideas and carelessness are back of the five *beautiful*'s (not to mention one *beauty*) in this passage:

The landscape is *beautiful*. There are myriads of *beautiful*, stately trees, which contribute greatly to the *beauty* of the place in every season of the year. There are also many *beautiful* wild flowers and other pretty forms of undergrowth. The climate and the absence of smoke and dust of the city makes it very easy to cultivate a *beautiful* lawn, with flowers and shrubs. The lake is a wonderful part of the landscape. There are many *beautiful* views in different times of the day and season.

More typical of careless repetition are such sentences as these:

This dam was without doubt going to be the largest [dam] in the world.

[The problem of] feeding her ever-increasing population is one of Japan's most acute problems.

Repetition of whole phrases is likely to be more objectionable, because a group of words naturally attracts more attention than a single word:

The next morning we noticed the river had risen considerably and was flowing *at a very fast pace*. We decided to resume our journey immediately, and soon we were once more traveling downstream, but this time *at a much faster pace* [better: *even faster*].

Especially jarring is repetition of the same word in two different senses, an easy pitfall in English because of the number of meanings many words can carry:

My *marks* showed a *marked* improvement.
No President in time of war has dared to fight the powerful financial *interests* of this country who have *interests* in the belligerent countries.

A slightly different form of careless repetition is doubling the meaning of a word unnecessarily. We write *continue on* when *continue* is enough, *repeat again* when we mean merely *repeat*.

The modern college student [of today] . . .
In this modern melting pot, I found people [there] who were unacquainted with the English language.
I believe that colleges should offer scholarships but they should not offer only athletic scholarships [alone].
The [resultant] effect

The remedy for all this loose repetition is the same: careful revision. Reading a paper aloud is perhaps the surest way to spot such expressions, since our ears often catch what our eyes do not.

Unnecessary, careless repetition weakens a style. But some types of repetition are necessary and others are effective. Repetition of the key words of a discussion is unavoidable and because of the context, it does not call attention to itself. If you are writing about the Supreme Court, you will have to mention it frequently, and it is better to repeat *Supreme Court* than to hunt for synonyms (like *the highest tribunal*). Simply see that the sentences are economically constructed to avoid *unnecessary* repetition and that pronouns are used where they can be.

Repetition of words and repetition of the ideas in other words are also useful stylistic devices. Repetition may help hold a passage together, it may emphasize ideas, and it may suggest emotion. A controlled repeating of key words is useful in keeping the reader's attention focused on the subject, and it is especially helpful in binding sentences together. The repetition of *power, imperative,* and *coalition* binds together the thought of this paragraph and emphasizes its meaning:

Intolerant power respects power, not weakness. It is imperative therefore to build and better the balance of power. Conspiracy and incitement prosper in disunion and discontent. It is imperative therefore to build and better the unity and well-being of the free world. We cannot do it alone. It is imperative therefore to build and better the coalition. And here we encounter our greatest danger and our final task. A coalition built on expedient reaction to the common danger will not stand, because the Sino-Soviet alliance has the power to blow hot and cold, like Boreas and Phoebus in the fable; it has the power to relax or increase the tension as it sees fit. But our coalition cannot live by fits and starts; it must rest on an enduring community of interest. And successful communal relations mean give and take, cooperation, consultation, accommodation —a decent respect for the opinion of others. Our coalition is a partnership, not a dictatorship.—ADLAI E. STEVENSON, *Call to Greatness,* pp. 107-108

No writer needs to fear repeating the key words of his subject, and rightly used, their repetition will add emphasis. Various devices will separate elements and so heighten and sharpen the meaning.

Separating elements.   In speaking, one of the most effective means of emphasis is a pause. It allows what has just been said to sink in, or if the voice is suspended, it throws emphasis on what is to follow. It is difficult to transfer this effect to the written page, but something of its value can be had by keeping constructions separate.

The most emphatic separation, of course, is into individual sentences:

Right is right, even if nobody does it. Wrong is wrong, even if everybody is wrong about it.—G. K. CHESTERTON

Internal punctuation (commas and especially semicolons) keeps statements separate and tends to force a pause even in rapid reading:

There are various types of schizophrenia each with special characteristics: quarrelsomeness and delusions of persecution (paranoia); pleasant stupor (hebephrenia); violent tantrums, obstinacy or rigidity (catatonia).—ABRAM SCHEINFELD

In a series of parallel words or constructions, repeating the conjunctions or prepositions may add emphasis to the individual elements. Contrast the movement of the two versions of these sentences:

The collecting buckets *and* tubes *and* jars were very full of specimens—so full that we had constantly to change the water to keep the animals alive.—JOHN STEINBECK and EDWARD F. RICKETTS

The collecting buckets, tubes, and jars were so full of specimens that we had constantly to change the water to keep the animals alive.

In the course of a lifetime of voyaging he went *to* China, *to* India, *to* all parts of Africa, and even *to* the arctic.

In the course of a lifetime of voyaging he went to China, India, all parts of Africa, and even the arctic.

An abrupt break in the direction of the thought—often signalled by a dash—may make for sharp emphasis:

A hardness about this technicolor epic makes it difficult to enjoy all the way through—the eventual hardness of the theater seat.

Position. An important means of emphasis is *position,* ordering the words and parts of the statement so that attention is directed unmistakably to the words you want to stress. The emphatic positions are the end of the sentence and its beginning.

The subject of a sentence is usually important enough to deserve the emphasis of initial position. "Anticipatory subjects" (*there* is, *there* were, *it* is, *it* was) waste this emphasis unless they permit a rearrangement of elements not otherwise possible.

Unnecessary anticipatory subjects
There are many people who read history to raise their self-esteem.

More emphatic
Many people read history to raise their self-esteem.

There is some evidence pointing to the gradual disappearance of hazing in our colleges.

Some evidence points to the gradual disappearance of hazing in our colleges.

Useful anticipatory subject
It is silly to quarrel about words.

Less emphatic
To quarrel about words is silly.

There are in the world a number of interfering, fanatical, greedy, reckless people who, given the chance, will behave in such a way as to make life intolerable and civilization impossible.— CLIVE BELL	A number of interfering, fanatical, greedy, reckless people, who, given the chance, will behave in such a way as to make life intolerable and civilization impossible, are in the world.

Other departures from the normal word order are usually made to emphasize the words put first; but, as these examples suggest, the device is a bit hazardous:

> Charles he had beaten twice, but never his brother.
> Who they should have in jail is that brute over there.

The ends of sentences deserve special attention. In speech we can seldom foresee the ends of our sentences and are likely to add various unemphatic elements which reduce their effectiveness. But in writing we can revise sentences to give them stronger endings:

Unemphatic	*Revised: more emphatic*
In regard to hedging, we had a hard time trying to understand its complexity.	We had a hard time trying to understand the complexities of hedging.
This is nobody's fault but their own with few exceptions.	With few exceptions, this is nobody's fault but their own.

The revision often means putting elements in an order of *climax*—that is, arranging words, phrases, clauses, or sentences in an order of increasing value. The increase may be in mere physical length, for usually in a series of phrases or clauses the longest is put last. The increase may be in forcefulness of meaning or distinction of phrasing. Or the increase may be in complexity of meaning or of emotional or ideal value.

Here is a conventional climax pattern, with the last of the three parallel parts of the object the fullest in expression and the most important for the writer's purpose at the moment:

> We are liquidating in sweat and blood and tears, and at our mortal peril, the fact that we made commitments, asserted rights, and proclaimed ideals while we left our frontiers unguarded, our armaments unprepared, and our alliances unformed and unsustained.—WALTER LIPPMANN, *U.S. Foreign Policy: Shield of the Republic*, p. 5.

Climax is the natural order for arranging the items of a series unless there is some necessary reason for another order. Failing to use a climactic order results in a weak sentence or, if the last member of the series is conspicuously less important than the preceding, in definite anticlimax:

It spoiled the rest of the summer for the boys and disappointed them terrifically.

No degree will be conferred unless the applicant shall have sustained a good moral character, completed the necessary study, and paid all fines to the library.

Intentional use of anticlimax is one of the sources of humor:

"Because Luxembourg is divine," he said, his eyes lighting. "I spent a most wonderful vacation there a year or two ago. It is a cameo, a miniature. It is a little country and everything in it is little: the inns, the mountains, the waiters, the people, the prices."
—IRWIN EDMAN, *Philosopher's Holiday,* p. 65

Sound and rhythm of sentences • Much prose is written without thought of appeal to the ear and is generally read silently, but what it would sound like still has a bearing on its readability. Though we have been taught "silent reading" from our early years, there is still some echo of the sound as our eye goes over the sentences, for we stumble when we come to a word we can't pronounce. In hasty, casual reading, the echo is faint indeed. The average news story, planned for eye reading, becomes a form of punishment when read aloud, as does much other writing. But the echo becomes an important factor in more distinctive prose.

In phrases some combinations of sounds ("A rose-red city half as old as time") seem more pleasant than others ("propelled by the repeated and seemingly needlessly brutal remarks and jabs of the detectives"). What makes them so is a matter of dispute, and people will differ in their judgment of particular combinations, but most will agree that the repetition of unstressed syllables, especially similar ones (seeming*ly* need-less*ly*) is annoying. Your best guide is your ear. But it may be useful to be reminded of two devices of sound that are factors in binding words and phrases together:

Alliteration, the same sound at the beginning of words or of stressed syllables within words, is not uncommon in prose, as in the quotation from Adlai Stevenson on page 322: "It is imperative therefore to *b*uild and *b*etter the *b*alance of power."

Assonance, similar vowel sounds in syllables that have different consonant sounds, is quite common in prose: a perfume escaped on the g*a*le; the re*ti*cence of the pe*ni*tent.

It is apparent that spoken prose has a noticeable if varied rhythm, that stresses differ in intensity and in number and in combination. But the rhythms of prose are more difficult to analyze than those of verse. By reading aloud the contrasting passages in the *Index* entry *Style, you can hear some of the varieties. Read aloud other passages that appeal to you to see what kind of rhythm they have.

Sound and rhythm, like other aspects of sentence-making, can hardly be discussed apart from the context and the writer's purpose. Sometimes writers deliberately choose sound combinations that are harsh and rhythms that jolt. You should remember, therefore, that whatever happy combination of sounds you have chanced upon or contrived, you will not have written effective prose unless the sound serves the meaning. Here, as elsewhere, what you want to say should determine how you say it.

Exercises

1. Make up two sentences for each of the patterns listed below. Add as many secondary elements as you wish, but keep the *main* elements in the order specified.

S-V	S-V-①-O	O-S-V
S-V-O	s-V-S	V-S-O
S-V-P	v-S-V-O	v-S-V-①-O

2. Mark off and identify the *main* elements in the sentences below, using the symbols S V O ① P s v. Example:

$$S \quad v \qquad V \qquad\quad O$$
I have just finished the novel.

a. The author has a fine reputation.

b. His earlier novels won him three coveted awards.

c. That he wrote this one is almost inconceivable.

d. Why he wrote it puzzles me.

e. Why did he imitate Mailer?

f. His own early novels would have given him a better model.

g. Did you see this ecstatic review?

h. My only reaction is that the reviewer couldn't have read the book.

i. Well, he always liked Mailer.

3. The main elements of a sentence and their relation to each other are usually quite obvious, but close analysis may be needed to show how the secondary and third elements are related to the main ones. Consider, for example, these two sentences, which are identical except for the final words but in which the relations of the grammatical elements are appreciably different:

S*   v   V Ⓘ(2   1) P* (2   1)   O (2   1)
She will make some man a good wife.   *or* . . . a good wife.
[But **P** seems more accurate; this is what Otto Jespersen calls a quasi-predicative.]

S   v   V O*(2   1) P* (2   1)
She will make some man a good husband.

Copy the following sentences, leaving space between the lines, and label the main, secondary, and third elements. In analyzing the sentences, you may find it helpful to use the method described in the *Index* article *Immediate constituent. You will need these symbols in addition to the seven listed in exercise 2:

1, 2, 3   show main, secondary, and third elements
( )   show where the parts of an element begin and end; since there may be elements within elements, there may be parentheses within parentheses:

        S   V   P(1 2(S_2 V_2 O(1 (S_3 V_3 O_2))))
        This is the cat that ate the mouse that ate the grain. . . .

S_2, O_3 subscript numbers are used when a second or third subject, object, or verb occurs in the same sentence
c, p, I   show connective (c), preposition (p), and infinitive (I)
* *   show related elements separated in the sentence

a. What we had begun was quite impossible.

b. The men who saw the accident reported that the driver had promised them a very substantial reward.

c. Is it right to keep the money which I found?

d. This year the dean of men appointed me dormitory counselor.

e. Did they find him dead or alive?

f. The legitimate king, who had been so tyrannical to his subjects, was assassinated by the conspirators.

g. That face I was sure I had seen before.

h. Impressive, breathtaking, awe-inspiring it certainly was.

i. They had very nearly reached the top when they started to fall.

4. Copy each item below on a separate card.

First, identify each clause and phrase, using a marking system of your own or one specified by your instructor. For the purpose of this exercise, treat a simple sentence as an independent clause. Label each dependent clause as adjective, adverb, or noun. Distinguish between prepositional phrases and verbal phrases, and for each verbal phrase indicate whether it is made with an infinitive, a participle, or a gerund.

Second, identify the sentence fragments and comma faults. Distinguish between fragments and minor sentence types, and between comma faults and the appropriate use of a comma between contact clauses.

Third, for each item that contains a sentence fragment or comma fault, revise to make it acceptable in college writing.

a. The northern part of the city is residential. On the eastern outskirts are factories. And to the south beaches and parks.

b. Why do we ask this question? Because only by answering it can we begin to understand why he never became President.

c. We have the finest school system in the world, nevertheless we do not have a perfect one. Far from it.

d. We have the best school system in the world, but it is still not perfect. Only the best there is.

e. In New York he appeared on the stage only once, in Boston he played for three months.

f. The good hunter must spend much of his time in silence, for the hearing of his prey is keener than his own, if he is noisy he comes home empty-handed. Empty-handed after a long day's work.

g. The book treats the Revolution under three topics. First, the causes of the war; second, the events; third, the effects.

h. Suddenly the car paused, shuddered, and rose into the air, crashing violently down on its side and rolling over with a final desperate motion it came to rest on its roof.

i. Some people rear their children, others just let them grow up.

j. She asked me to outline my plans. I did. She made no comment. Not a single one. To my surprise, she changed the subject.

k. White, yellow, and grey are the colors most anglers prefer, however, color of the lure is actually of little importance.

l. The building is handsome. Especially when the afternoon sun reflects off the white or gold brick walls.

5. Some, but not all, of the sentences below illustrate failures in parallelism or other unjustified shifts in structural patterns. Describe precisely what the trouble is in each of the faulty sentences, and revise the sentence to make it acceptable.

a. Our ambitions changed as often as our favorite disk jockeys.

b. For all its narrowness, the curriculum did for me what every curriculum should do but does not always succeed: it taught me to think.

c. Their topics of conversation are few—hunting, fishing, the weather.

d. I don't like him because not only is he tactless; he is unconventional in his ideas too.

e. Engineers fit the description as well as medical students.

f. By moving as frequently as it is common these days, people never develop really rewarding friendships.

g. What I disliked most about the school was the small number of students and that most of them were from the same economic class.

h. He has a genius for science, but in poetry he cannot scan a line.

i. It has been said that though both good and evil exist and though we often choose evil instead of good, it has nevertheless been observed that good generates itself, whereas evil destroys itself.

j. Sunlight has a double purpose, one as a source of energy for photosynthesis, and second, it is required for the production of chlorophyll.

k. Driving into Bagby from Mariposa, he found himself more concerned with the steepness of the road than in the scenery.

l. All he wants from life is security in his job, a suburban home, to be respected by his neighbors, and a wife who adores him.

m. Democratic principles are nearer to those of the communist than the fascist.

n. The contractor got all sorts of complaints about the shingles being loose and that the concrete walks were not allowed to ripen properly.

o. He was a statesman whose behavior it was difficult to understand but difficult to disapprove of.

p. Our vacation was dull; there was nothing to do besides swimming or the movies.

q. He never has and never will like living on a farm.

r. Tires should be checked for pressure at least once a week, and you should move them to different wheels once a month.

6. Rewrite each of the items below according to the instructions in parentheses and make whatever other changes are necessary to produce an acceptable sentence or sequence of sentences.

a. Please give us a ring if both your father and mother are coming. (Change *both ... and* to *either ... or*.)

b. Mary's skill is not yet great enough. (Add *to water-ski safely*.)

c. Are any of these engravings to be auctioned today? If so, their future owners are probably planning right now how to rearrange their living rooms to show them off to best advantage. (Add *one* before *of*.)

d. The bicycle is the most popular means of transportation but there are a few cars, but these are usually owned by government personnel. (Rephrase to eliminate the second *but* clause.)

e. Many elections are won by appealing to the public's fear of war. (If the verbal phrase dangles, revise it. Note that here, and in some of the following items, you are asked to rewrite only if you decide that rewriting is necessary.)

f. It began to rain and the golfers took cover, and that ended the day's play. (Make the first clause dependent.)

g. Awakened by a heavy hand tugging at the blankets, his arduous day began long before dawn. (If the verbal phrase dangles, revise it.)

h. A well-known movie star marries for the fifth time, and the story hits page one. If a scientist who is also well known makes a discovery that promises to cure cancer, you find the newspaper puts the story on page ten. (Make the contrast sharper by establishing parallelism.)

i. The main reason I began college in the summer term is that it will take me several years to complete my formal education. The sooner I start, the sooner I will be through. (Make the causal relation clear and logical.)

j. It is important that causal relations be clear and logical. (Eliminate the anticipatory subject.)

k. To succeed in life, luck is as essential as brains. (If the verbal phrase dangles, revise it.)

l. Scientists face many conflicts between their work and moral standards that seem insoluble. (Revise to eliminate the confusion about what *that* modifies.)

m. Because the Chinese mainland was convulsed in civil war, news of the massacre received little world attention. The news was reported by a few foreign journalists on the spot. (Combine into one sentence.)

n. Built in 1900, the age of the school is indicated by its run-down appearance. (Change the subject to clarify the meaning.)

o. College class schedules are fairly confusing, and in some cases a good deal of confusion may arise from them. This particular plague usually strikes the green students, namely, the freshmen. Let me relate to you one such experience which I had. Classes had been in session for a full week, and I thought that after such a comparatively long period I had mastered my class schedule. (Revise for economy.)

p. Most of the major league teams made trades along toward the midnight deadline; at least a few of them did so. (Make up the writer's mind for him.)

q. He looked steadily at the boy, searching for a clue to his behavior. (If the sentence is faulty, revise it.)

r. I am sorry that you cannot offer me the position though I very much hoped you would. (Strengthen the logical relationship.)

s. Seen from across the dimly lit room, she was a pretty woman. Seeing her at close range, her twisted features shocked me. (Examine the sentence openers and, if necessary, revise.)

t. With a bedroom, a kitchen, a living room, and a bathroom up the hall that rented for $75 a month, the apartment was a great bargain. (Make clear what rents for $75 a month.)

u. A student has a problem. Perhaps he has no self-control and wastes all his time playing bridge or dating and he is failing a course. (Make clear what the student's specific problem is.)

v. I feel that the loyalty oath and disclaimer affidavit are an infringement upon our inherent rights as Americans in a free society. They are in direct contradiction to two of our basic freedoms as granted in the Bill of Rights. The freedoms of speech and thought. These are two of the primary rights in our society. Free speech and thought are part of the American way, part of our democratic way of life. Both the loyalty oath and the affidavit curtail free speech and thought. (Reduce the six sentences to one.)

w. Figuring roughly, the tax comes to ten percent of the value of the purchase. (If the verbal phrase dangles, revise it.)

x. Poe's tales and poems are characterized by melancholy; his criticisms by harsh spitefulness. Jealousy of the success of other writers seems to reveal itself in his criticism. The melancholy tone is a sign of his morbid personality. (Clarify the logical relations.)

y. Awakening early, a quick glance outdoors convinced me that it would be a fine day for a visit to Jackson Park. Arriving there before six, a brisk breeze was blowing across the Wooded Island. (Improve the sentence openers.)

z. The sun was coming up over the lake, but the car stalled. (Compose two different sentences to precede this one; one sentence should make the coordination seem reasonable and the second should show the need for subordinating one of the independent clauses.)

7. From any one of the items you have revised in the preceding exercise, select one sentence. Use the idea (though not necessarily the phrasing) as the topic sentence for four paragraphs, each about 150 words long. First, jot down some points in support of the topic sentence. Then present these points in a paragraph (a) using only simple sentences, (b) using only complex sentences, (c) using only compound sentences, and (d) using the variety of sentence patterns most effective for the material. Finally, describe as precisely as you can the *stylistic* effects of the first three of the four paragraphs you have written.

8. Rewrite each of the simple sentences below in at least six different ways, keeping the same basic idea but varying the order of parts, the constructions, and the sentence patterns. Then indicate which versions (if any) would be inappropriate in speech and which (if any) would be inappropriate in Formal or in General writing.

a. This simple exercise gave even the experienced gymnasts aches and pains.

b. For the first and last time in his life he felt humble and grateful.

c. He paced the floor angrily, firing questions but receiving no reply.

d. Her unexpected outburst of temper confused and baffled him.

e. To break established codes requires either courage or foolhardiness.

9. Review the passages listed below (some by professional writers, some by students) from earlier chapters of this book. For the passages in which sentences are handled effectively, list the devices that make for effectiveness (sentence length, variety, and movement; parallelism; repetition; word order; and so on). Rewrite those passages that you consider ineffective to improve sentence clarity, economy, emphasis, rhythm, or other points of style.

Chapter Nine

REVISING
WORDS
AND
PHRASES

*T*he instructed writer is one who understands
      not merely that words are symbols of ideas,
but that they have their connotations and
interrelations, and that unless they are
put together with care they are likely to
get in one another's way, to send the reader
off on false scents, and to produce the
confusion and distress that notes in music
cause us when they are put together without
an understanding of the laws of harmony.
                                    Joseph Warren Beach

The four-point program for revising sentences, outlined at the beginning of Chapter 8, is also helpful in revising words and phrases. In considering the revision of these smaller units to meet the reader's expectations, we can state fairly definitely certain minimum standards and indicate where good usage varies. But our discussion of revising words and phrases for effectiveness is necessarily tentative, for the effectiveness of a word, like that of a sentence, can be judged only in a specific context. A word that is appropriate for one purpose may be thoroughly unsuitable for another. As in our discussion of sentences, however, we can describe some general traits of words that will help you make a choice.

Revising to meet the reader's expectations

The points treated in this section are minor and sometimes trivial details of writing, but competent writers so consistently avoid them that their occurrence in General or Formal English may be called mistakes. They are important from a social point of view because educated readers do not expect to find them in what they read.

As a college student you already have pretty good control of written English, but if you are like most of us, you are often careless in your writing, sometimes from haste, sometimes from not knowing what is expected of you. The correction symbol *X* indicates a mistake so obvious and elementary that your instructor assumes it is the result of carelessness, not ignorance. Typical blunders of this kind—first-draft blunders—are listed in the *Index* entry *Carelessness[1]; if you check such mistakes, you will realize that you can catch them by proofreading the final drafts of your papers. Other mistakes, especially those dealing with the forms of words, are harder to catch, and you may need to review systematically such grammatical matters as the forms of pronouns. Brief comments made here on the smaller structural elements of the sentence should be supplemented by the relevant *Index* articles.

Checking verb forms • A few verb forms cause elementary mistakes that should be caught in proofreading. Since the regular English verb has only four forms (*ask, asks, asking, asked*) those forms raise very few questions, and not many problems occur with verb phrases (*have gone, may go, did see*) that have replaced old special forms. Even the irregular forms for *be and *go are so common that we learn the patterns early and use them automatically.

Most English verbs make their past tense and past participle by adding a /d/ or /t/ sound to the simple (infinitive) form. This sound is ordinarily spelled *–ed* (*asked, hunted, beautified*), but in a few verbs it is *–t* (*kept, slept, wept*); and with some verbs both forms are used (*dreamed–dreamt, kneeled–knelt, spelled–spelt*). In these last examples the *–ed* forms are now the more common.

The "strong verbs" continue to make the past tense and the past participle by another method, changing the vowel sound (*throw, threw, thrown–write, wrote, written*). Some of these have two forms, either because they are changing to the typical past in *–ed* or because two vowel changes are current: infinitive, *dive*; past tense, *dove* or *dived*; past participle, *dived* or *dove*; infinitive, *sing*; past tense, *sang* or *sung*; past participle, *sung*. For other verbs which have alternative forms for the past tense or past participle, see *Principal parts of verbs.

---

[1]Throughout this book, references to *Index* articles are indicated by an asterisk (*).

A few other verbs have forms in Nonstandard English that should be avoided in General English, such as:

Infinitive	Past tense	Past participle
begin	began (NS: begun)	begun
*burst	burst (NS: busted)	burst
drink	drank (NS: drunk)	*drunk
fall	fell	fallen (NS: fell)
see	saw (NS: seen)	seen

Note also *lay—lie, *set, sit, *let—leave, verbs which illustrate particularly well the tendency in written usage to insist on a distinction much sharper than that made in speech—even in the conversation of educated people. In still other verbs, spelling has to be watched and associated with the spoken forms: *choose* /chüz/, *chose* /chōz/, *chosen* /chō′zn/; *lead* /lēd/, *led* /led/. And for a few there are some regional differences. The General English forms for *eat* are *eat* /ēt/, *ate* /āt/, *eaten* /ē′tn/, but in some regions the two past forms are *eat* (pronounced et). The General forms should be used in writing.

For a list of irregular verbs, see *Principal parts of verbs, and for further details on verb forms, see the *Index* entries *Auxiliary verbs, *Linking verbs, *Split infinitives, *Tenses of verbs, *Transitive and intransitive verbs, *Verbs, *Voice.

Checking pronouns • Pronouns are troublesome in writing because their forms are numerous and irregular and because not all of the various functions they serve in casual talk are appropriate in writing. The careful use of pronouns is less a matter of exact meaning—they are seldom ambiguous—than it is of tidiness and conforming to the expectations of educated readers.

Mistakes in the use of the possessive (or genitive) are chiefly spelling mistakes—*it's* or *its'* for *its, who's* for *whose,* and so on. It is helpful to remember that the most usual sign of the possessive of nouns—'s—marks the possessive of *no* pronouns.

Object and subject forms. Confusion between subject and object forms is more typical than any mistake in the possessive. Six of the eight commonly used personal and relative pronouns have distinctive object forms, though nouns and the indefinite pronouns (*anyone, everybody, someone,* and so on) do not. We know the subject-object pairs (*I—me, we—us, he—him, she—her, they—them, who—whom*), but sometimes the formal distinction between them is not observed because in English we rely on word order rather than on word form to tell us the function of words in a construction. Pay special attention to the following uses in Standard English:

1. After prepositions the object form is regularly used: *with him and her,* **between you and me, To whom was this sent?*

2. When a pronoun (usually the first person plural, *we*) is directly joined with a noun, the appropriate case form is used (*Subject: We children* used to make a wide circle around the cemeteries. *Object:* They used to terrify *us children*).

3. After forms of the verb *be,* Formal English usually has the subject form, General English frequently the object form (*Formal:* I was hoping it would be *she. General:* I was hoping it would be *her*). Much fuss has been made over the *It's I—It's me* construction. All responsible grammars now present *It's me* as the usual form. Since it can scarcely occur except in a conversational setting, the writer seldom has to make the decision. (See **It's me.*) When the construction is followed by a dependent clause, the pronoun is in the subject form. (It is *he* who planned the strategy and won the election.)

4. Usage is divided on *who* or *whom* as the object form when it precedes a verb or preposition. *Whom* has practically disappeared from the spoken language, so that we naturally and regularly say, "*Who* were you with last night?" In writing, most editors and teachers try to keep the object form, "*Whom* were you with last night?" In Informal writing the subject form is proper in this kind of construction; in Formal and General writing the object form is preferred, though it will strike some readers as artificial; perhaps it is wiser to avoid the construction or to substitute "Who was it you were with last night?" (See **who, whom.*)

Agreement in number.   The student who wrote this sentence forgot whether he was using a singular or plural notion:

The value that *a person* can receive from understanding *these* give-and-take methods will stand *them* in good stead for the rest of *their* lives.

This sentence could be improved by making the reference consistently singular: will stand *him* in good stead for the rest of *his life.* But the notion seems actually plural—a statement of general application—so that a slightly better revision might be to change *a person* to *people.* It is not always the pronoun that needs to be changed.

When errors in agreement between pronoun and antecedent occur, it is sometimes because there is a lengthy separation between the pronoun and its antecedent. The best protection against such blunders is analyzing the sentence to *identify* the antecedent. In other sentences, uncertainty arises because there is a conflict between agreement by form and agreement by meaning. When we have a collective noun as subject in conversation, we frequently make its verb singular and make a later pronoun referring to it plural. This shift in number is frequently found in writing too, especially when the meaning is clearly plural. But it is better avoided:

The club is sponsoring a dance, and *they* [better: *it*] will give the proceeds to charity.

Sometimes there is a lot to do and the *crew is* [better: *crew are*] not allowed to run things to please *themselves*.

A shift in number is especially likely to occur in references to the collective pronouns: *anyone, *each, everybody, everyone*. In speech these are almost universally referred to by plural pronouns; in writing, the singular is ordinarily used or the subject is changed to a plural:

Anyone who has spent part of *their* [better: *his*] time abroad can see *their* own [better: *his own*] country in a different light. (Or, the *anyone* could be changed to *people: People* who *have* spent part of *their....*)

It is a rule that before entering an operating room everyone must scrub *their* hands thoroughly. (Change *their* to *his* or change *every-one* to something like *all doctors and nurses*.)

(See *Collective nouns and *every and its compounds.)

Misleading or vague reference. Sometimes an amateur writer's pronouns seem to just happen, as in this:

We pulled out our spare, which was under the seat, and put *it* on. *It* sort of dampened our spirits but we decided to try *it* again.

The first *it* refers to the spare tire, the second to the operation of changing tires, and the third to the road or trip. A sentence like this needs to be rewritten. Usually the situation is simpler:

Students and teachers are working at the same job but sometimes *they* don't seem to realize it and seem to be competing with *them*.

The *they* seems to refer to both students and teachers but by the end of the sentence we see it should refer to students only. The sentence could be revised:

Students are working at the same job as the teachers, but sometimes *they* don't seem to realize this and seem rather to be competing with *the teachers*.

But readers should not be perverse and pretend there is misunderstanding when there is none. In this sentence the context keeps the meaning of *he* and *him* straight, even though two people are intended:

He hoped *his* grandfather wasn't in because *he* always scolded *him*.

Sometimes a statement including pronouns referring to different nouns can be made clear by making one of the nouns (and its pronoun) plural:

One way to approach criticism is to compare *an inferior work* with *good ones* to see what *it* [the inferior one] lacks that *the others* [the good ones] have.

A common reference fault is using a pronoun to refer to a noun that is only implied in the statement:

The actual sport of sailing has changed very little from the time when only the wealthiest had the pleasure of owning *one*. (Better: of owning a sailboat.)

The other fellow enlisted about two years ago and had spent a year of *it* in Persia. (Better: The other fellow, who had enlisted about two years ago, had spent a year of his service in Persia.)

Frequently, of course, *this, *that, and *which refer to the whole idea of a preceding statement, not to any single word in it or to any word implied in it:

The mud was eight inches deep, *which* made the road to Edward's Bay impassable.

The addition of *condition* after *which,* insisted on by some purists, adds nothing to the clarity of the sentence, and makes it heavier; but care should be taken in such a construction not to use a pronoun that may seem to refer to a particular noun:

I proceeded to go to the phone, *which* decided my fate for the rest of the summer. (Better: Answering that phone decided my fate for the rest of the summer.)

(For other examples, see *Reference of pronouns.)

English lacks a comfortable indefinite pronoun to refer to people in general. Since *one is stiff and formal, we use *they* or *we* or *you.* The indefinite use of these pronouns should not be confused with their definite use. In speech the distinction is clear because there is less stress on the pronoun used indefinitely. (Compare *They say* meaning "People in general say" with the same words meaning "The people over there say.") The chief problem in the use of indefinite pronouns is consistency. Use whichever pronoun seems most natural in a passage, but avoid shifting from one to another unless there is a genuine shift in point of view. (See "Point of view," Ch. 5, p. 163, and *he-or-she.)

Revising modifiers • Next to the subject-verb-object relation, the most important is of *modifier* to a principal word or construction, called the *headword.* We distinguish between modifiers of nouns and pronouns (*adjectives*), and of verbs, adverbs, and other modifiers, and complete statements (*adverbs*).

Adverb forms.   There are few problems of form in adjectives and adverbs, though some adverbs without the usual *–ly* ending are worth noting. The typical English adverb is made by adding the suffix *–ly* to an adjective: *dim, dimly; hurried, hurriedly.* Some common adverbs, however, have the same form as the adjective, and have had for centuries. We can say either "Go slow" or "Go slowly"; "Don't talk so loud" or "Don't talk so loudly." In General English the shorter form is usually preferable, though the *–ly* form is often used when the adverb comes in the middle of a construction: They drove *slowly* back and forth in front of the school.

In Nonstandard and Informal English the adverbs without suffixes tend to be more numerous, and such words as *easy* and *real* are used where written English has *easily* and *really. Special* and *considerable* are found for *specially* and *considerably.* In writing, use the *–ly* form of these and other adverbs that do not have accepted short forms. A list of the more common ones will be found in *Adverbs, types and forms, §1. (See also *bad, badly.)

Position of adjectives and adverbs. The relation of adjectives to what they modify is shown by position; single modifiers usually precede the headword (the *tallest* buildings) and longer modifiers usually follow it (the buildings *of the new plant,* the buildings *that are tallest*). The position of some adverbial modifiers is less fixed. Those modifying specific words are usually near those words (He *drove* fast; an *almost* imperceptible breeze), and those modifying the whole statement tend to stand first or last in the sentence (*Certainly* you know who did it; *Since the trolleys had given way to buses,* most of the tracks had been torn up; It was impossible to keep up with them *because the traffic was so heavy*).

Often there is a choice of position for an adverb, allowing for variety and a little different emphasis. (He turned the dial *slowly.* He *slowly* turned the dial. *Slowly* he turned the dial.) A good deal of useless effort has been spent on the placement of *only*. Formal usage tends to put it directly before the element it modifies (There have been *only* four presidents whom most people admire). General usage tends to place it next to the verb (There have *only* been four presidents most people admire). But adverbs should not be carelessly placed so that they are misleading or seem to belong to words they are not intended to modify: Using several pen names, the two editors had *almost* written every article in the magazine. Revised, this would read: Using several pen names, the two editors had written *almost* every article in the magazine.

Comparison of adjectives and adverbs. Adjectives and adverbs alike may be compared in two ways: by adding *–er* and *–est* to the basic form or by preceding it with *more* or *most*. (For examples, see *Comparison of adjectives and adverbs.)

Predicate adjectives. *Be* and a number of other verbs (*become, feel, grow, taste*) are used as linking verbs (or copulas). Since a modifier following one of these relates to the subject, it is an adjective rather than an adverb (He became *silent.* The tree grew *straight.* This tastes *flat.* She looked *sad*). Such predicate adjectives should be distinguished from the adverbs that modify these same verbs or other verbs (He felt the edge *carefully.* She looked *sadly* out of the window). (See *Linking verbs.)

Revising unidiomatic expressions • Every language has a number of expressions that cannot be easily analyzed according to its general grammatical patterns and yet are in good use. You can use thousands of words as subjects or verbs of sentences, but you cannot substitute any other adjective in the phrase *in good stead,* and the number of sentences you can make on the pattern of *you had better* is distinctly limited. These single or very limited patterns are called *idioms.* Some idioms are survivals of early patterns of expression: *many is the time, come fall, good-by, a dollar a pound.* Others are made for convenience or to fill some need: *let's don't, to make good, easy does it.*

Proponents of Formal English have sometimes discouraged such idioms, even some in widespread use, like *"I don't think so and so is"* instead of *"I think that* so and so *is not."* And they have been highly critical of *try and* do something, *go and* get something, instead of the more conventionally formed *try to, go to.* Other readers find idiomatic writing easy and natural, and they point out that straining to avoid idioms results in a stilted style. Idioms should, of course, be used in their standard form: *on the whole* (not *on a whole*); *if the worst comes to the worst* or *if worst comes to worst* (not *if the worse comes to the worst*). (See *Idiom and idioms.)

Idiomatic prepositions. A number of words are convention-ally related to other words by a specific preposition:

belief *in* technocracy
conform *to* public opinion (but: in conformity *with* public opinion)
conscious *of* his position

Since the prepositions in these expressions are not used in their earlier specific meanings, they have to be learned in phrases, with the words to which they belong. We acquire these idioms by hearing them, and in learning new words we should see them in use, see how they fit into sentences, not learn them as isolated "vocabulary." Dictionaries generally show the con-ventional preposition used with particular words.

A word may occur in idioms with different prepositions, like *agree on* a plan, *agree with* a person, *agree in* principle; for some of these idioms, usage is divided.

When two words which conventionally call for different prepositions are used with a single object, both prepositions should be given:

We know for a fact that most of our players lost a great deal of respect *for* and confidence *in* the coach.

Though the use of a single preposition in an idiom is the usual practice in Standard English, there are exceptions, like *sick to* or *at* or *in the stomach.*

Infinitive or gerund. Some words are followed conventionally by an infinitive and some by a gerund, as illustrated by the following examples:

Infinitives	Gerunds
able *to work*	capable *of working*
take pains *to write*	the idea *of writing*
the way *to cut*	this method *of cutting*
neglect *to say*	ignore *saying*

With a number of words either is used:

no reason *to express* them—no reason *for expressing* them
a chance *to learn*—a chance *for learning*

Gerunds may be used to emphasize their noun aspect (The *trusting* of women is a mark of a gentleman) or their verb aspect (*Trusting* women is the mark of a gentleman). The latter construction is more direct and is increasingly used in General writing. (See *Gerund.)

Idioms for comparisons. The idioms for simple comparisons are not troublesome: He is *younger than* I thought; It was the *hardest* fight of his career. But when other elements are involved, there are some questions of idiom.

Most people say "The summer was *as* dry if not *drier than the last.*" Formal and usually General English would complete both constructions: "The summer was *as* dry *as* if not *drier than* the last" or "The summer was *as* dry *as* the last, if not *drier.*" (See *as . . . as.)

Other is used in a comparison between things of the same sort but not between things of different sorts:

This picture is a better likeness than the other portraits.
This portrait is a better likeness than the bust.
There is not a more enjoyable light novel by any writer. (Not: by any other writer.)

The two things compared should be actually comparable. This means using a possessive if the name of the first thing is not repeated:

His muscles were firm, like an athlete's. (Not: like an athlete.)
The president's recommendations were more practical than the committee's. (Not: than the committee.)

Revising "wrong words" • The correction symbol *WW* (wrong word) does not mean that the word is in itself "wrong"; it means that the word does not convey a meaning that makes sense *in the context*. For example:

An educated man seems to have an expression signifying shrewdness, *comprehensibility* [The writer seems to have meant *comprehension*], and originality.

Usually such errors occur when a writer is attempting to use a vocabulary in which he is not at home (note the *signifying*) or when he confuses two words of similar sound (*temerity—timidity, mystification—mysticism, moral—morale, inequity—iniquity*). Confusion is especially likely to occur between words of opposite meaning (*concave—convex*). Confusion in the use of words that are pronounced alike (homonyms) is a matter of spelling rather than of meaning (*meat—meet*). Even if the context makes the meaning clear, such inaccuracies are a mark of carelessness. But most "wrong words" result from uncertainty about the meaning of the word. For this there are two remedies—consulting a dictionary and familiarizing yourself with the meanings of words *in context* by paying attention to what you read. (See *Boners.)

Revising for effectiveness

The principles of appropriateness given as the basis of good English (pp. 25-32) apply to all phases of our use of language but are easiest to demonstrate in discussing particular words in particular contexts. Obviously the choice of many words is determined by the subject. But others are not specifically demanded by the subject—one writer might use them, another might not. In making a choice, some balance must be struck between the reader's expectation, his knowledge and taste, and the writer's specific purpose. No rules can tell you what words to choose, but some account of the traits of words will suggest guidelines.

Choosing appropriate words • Amateur writing is often less effective than it might be because of an excessive reliance on vague words, trite words, euphemisms, or "big" words. And often it could be made more effective by giving careful attention to synonyms.

Vague words. Some words used regularly in conversation are too general to make exact reference. Words like *fine, bad, good* should usually be replaced in writing by more definite adjectives, and even words like *interesting* or *important* frequently stand for some particular sort of interest or importance that could better be named, so that the reader's thought is brought nearer to the writer's intention. (See *Counter words.) Many phrases could be replaced by single exact words with a gain in economy and sometimes in definiteness:

The men with axes would then trim off the branches, while the men with crosscut saws cut the *large part of the tree* [*trunk*] into ten-foot lengths.

Last year in a nearby city an *occupant* [*prisoner*] in the county jail escaped.

The other thing that I have in mind [*My other intention—hope— plan?*] is to go to France.

Such words are usually marked *D* (*Diction) on papers.

Trite words. A *trite expression* (or a *cliché* or a *hackneyed term*) is a phrase that has been overused. Obviously, the repetition of certain necessary function words—*a, the,* the prepositions, the conjunctions—is inescapable; the actual names of things and acts and qualities do not wear out; and formulas like *How do you do* and *Yours truly* may be used over and over without attracting attention at all. Expressions that are direct and exact do not deserve to be called trite. We can call for *bread* as often as we need to—but *staff of life* is quite a different matter, stylistically. It is a figure of speech, once bright and perhaps startling, now threadbare.

We should not be too severe about triteness in ordinary conversation, where the common expressions have their place and prevent awkward hesitation. But the use of many trite expressions in writing is a symptom that the writer isn't trying to find the words that will express what *he* means.

Most trite expressions will be found to be outworn figures of speech, frayed quotations, or phrases that are repeated intact more often than is pleasing.

- *Revising words and phrases*

1. Worn-out figures of speech:

Father Time	tide of battle	flowing with milk
history tells us	irony of fate	and honey
darkness overtook us	commune with nature	trees like sentinels
better half [wife]	crack of dawn	run like a flash
Mother Nature	bolt from the blue	a watery grave

(See also "Figurative use of words," p. 350.)

2. Frayed quotations: Shakespeare has so many magnificently quotable lines that a writer who confines himself to the most used (All the world's a stage—Uneasy lies the head—To be or not to be—Not wisely but too well) makes his readers suspect that he has never actually read Shakespeare or he could make fresher choices. The Bible is similarly sinned against, though so many of its phrases have passed into the General language that it is not always fair to label them trite. If you want to illustrate a point by quotation, however, it is safer to take one from your own reading than to rely on these overused expressions.

3. Stock phrases: The commonest sort of triteness comes from set phrases—adjectives that are too often found with the same nouns, adverbs that come with the same verbs. Here is a brief sample:

We dedicated ourselves to the task and searched far and wide for the missing child. Finally, to our amazement and consternation, he emerged, cool as a cucumber, beneath our very noses.

You can make a similar collection from any "field of endeavor."

Your instructor, as a professional reader with a longer exposure to clichés, may find more trite expressions in your writing than you realize are there. Of course you should not slow up your first writing by stopping to find original phrases, but you should become sensitive enough to triteness to remove it from your copy in revision. The remedy is nearly always the same: look squarely at what you are writing about and present it as simply and concretely as possible. (See *Trite.)

Euphemisms. A *euphemism* is a pale or comfortable word or phrase used instead of the more explicit or abrupt name for some discomfort or suffering, or for something presumed to be offensive to delicate ears. The substitute is often more vague, less harsh in sound or connotation, than the more exact and literal term it displaces; and it is often an abstract word or one derived from Latin rather than a native English word.

The largest group of euphemisms has a somewhat prudish origin, for it consists of substitutes for the vigorous monosyllabic names of certain physical functions and unpleasant social situations: *perspire* for *sweat; expectorate* for *spit; intoxicated* for *drunk; odor* for *stink* and *smell; abdomen* for *belly;* and so on. The *aged* or *old people* are *senior citizens. Dull* children become *retarded* or even *exceptional.* Those *out of work* or *jobless* are the *unemployed,* perhaps the victims of *technological unemployment* (an accurate but distant noun); and the *poor* are the *underprivileged.* Some of these terms have so nearly displaced the older ones that a writer can hardly avoid using them, but he should keep clearly in mind the specific unhappiness and suffering they name.

Euphemisms show one side of the relation between language and social attitudes. They sometimes indicate timidity, but more often they are a conscious seeking for "respectability." At a more serious level, newspaper euphemisms like *companionate marriage, love child, social diseases* once allowed prudish people to talk about matters they would never have mentioned by their more common names.

Except for some journalistic and commercial terms and some taboos of radio and television networks, movies, and newspapers, the prevailing temper is now against euphemisms in writing; and unless circumstances actually demand a substitute for the ordinary names of things and situations, a writer should call a spade a spade—simply and without unnecessary emphasis. Fowler's comment is true: "Euphemism is more demoralizing than coarseness." But the college writer should not be misled by the explicitness of some modern fiction to assume that he may abandon good taste. Appropriateness is the guide, and whatever might seem offensive to your audience is not appropriate. (See *Euphemism, *Obscenity, *Profanity.)

Big words.   The term *big words* covers several common faults of writing that come from an unhappy choice of words. The words may not be long or uncommon (*deem, doff, dwell*), but they are big in that they are *too heavy for their place.*

There is little objection to long words when they are called for by the subject, come naturally to the writer, and are appropriate to the reader. Long words are the only and necessary names for many ideas and for many things, and they must be used in much technical, scientific, and professional writing —though they may be overused even in the writing of specialists. *Sphygmograph, schizophrenia, Pleistocene* all have their place, though it is a restricted one. (If one of these words is needed in ordinary speech, a shorter form or a substitute usually arises, like *DDT* for *dichloro-diphenyl-trichloroethane*.) Some longer words may be needed, especially in Formal writing, for their rhythm or connotation: *multifarious, provocative, infinitesimal, anticipation*.

Big words are words that do not fit, that are too heavy or too pretentious for the subject. The writer may use them because he is writing carelessly or trying to show off, but he may also use them in a serious attempt to "improve" his expression. As a matter of fact, he will improve his writing not by translating his thought into pretentious words but by expressing it in more exact and suggestive words. It is perhaps natural for a person to feel that his own speech is not good enough to use in public appearances and in writing. It may not be—but the remedy lies in improving and extending its best features, not in striving for an unnatural language.

Big words are a special curse today in much government writing or gobbledygook, in the more pretentious journalism, and in some academic writing, especially, it seems, in the social studies. Try putting into your own words the following (quite true) statement:

> Out of the interstimulation of conversation there emerges an interweaving of understanding and purpose leading to co-individual behavior. Of course the conversation may be divisive, as well as integrating. But even these divisions may be regarded as mere differentiations within the general synthesis of human behavior. Thus in conversation is found that mutual understanding and common purpose essential to effective and continuous cooperation.

The continued use of big words not only alienates readers, but it may make you write without feeling or even without really knowing what you are saying. Try reading aloud what you have written. If you find it conspicuously different from how you would *tell* the same thing to a friend, examine the words carefully and see if you can't find simple ones that are natural to you.

Synonyms.   When you make the effort to improve your choice of words, consider synonyms. A *synonym* is a word of nearly the same meaning as another. Often the real difference is in their *connotations*. There are very few pairs of genuinely interchangeable words. Even names of specific things differ, like *rhu-*

barb—pieplant, bucket—pail, flicker—yellow-hammer; although they refer to the same objects, and so have the same *denotation,* their connotations are not the same because one of the pair is used mainly in one part of the country, or by a specific group of people, or under certain circumstances, and so it cannot be regularly substituted for the other. English is especially rich in words of slightly different shades of meaning: *joke—jest; obedient—dutiful—yielding—compliant—obsequious; multitude —throng—crowd—mob.* Because of these differences in connotation, merely trying to escape repetition of a word is not a sufficient motive for using a synonym. (For further discussion of connotation and denotation, see "The suggestion of words," p. 373.)

When a writer looks for a synonym, what he usually wants is a word that can give his meaning in the particular sentence more exactly than the word he has on hand. The important point, then, in looking at two or more words of similar meaning is to know how they *differ.*

As a rule, testing the appropriateness of words is a matter of revision. Only when they stand in a context can they be tested for exactness of reference and appropriateness to the subject and reader. Sometimes a single word can take the place of a long phrase; sometimes a more specific word can replace a general or ambiguous one: *funny* might be *amusing, laughable, odd, queer, different, peculiar;* or *walk* might be replaced by a more descriptive word—*stroll, trip, saunter, stride, pace, tiptoe, amble, march.* Sometimes the change is to bring a word in line with the variety of usage of the rest of the paper; choosing one either more or less Formal: *want—wish—desire; roomy—spacious; fast—rapidly.*

There are various tools at hand. Dictionaries group words of similar meaning and indicate the general distinctions between them. The most popular of the various books of synonyms is Roget's *International Thesaurus* (Third edition, New York, 1962), which lists words by topics, giving words of opposite meaning in parallel columns, and offers a wide range from slang to Formal and even obsolete words. Since it does not give definitions, its chief use is to remind a person of those words he recognizes but does not use readily. In this way it helps the writer to bridge the gap between his recognition and active vocabulary and is often useful in revising a paper.

But lists of synonyms are somewhat hazardous to use. To pluck a word from a list of synonyms and use it solely on the basis of a dictionary definition may produce something inexact and even ludicrous. The prime source of synonyms, as of other words, is conversation and reading. Paying attention to the use and meaning of new words you meet is the best background for using the "right" words in your own writing.

Figurative use of words • Although we may not be aware of it, we use figurative language in our conversation all the time. Practically all writing, even reference works and scientific or scholarly papers, makes some use of it. When carefully used to make our expression more exact, more interesting, or more effective, figures of speech are a valuable resource in writing.

Many words which originally had narrowly restricted senses have come to be used figuratively and have extended their reference. *Head* still has its old literal denotation as a part of the body but is also applied to the highest or foremost or principal part of a wide variety of things—of a screw, nail, pin, army, the force of a stream of water, bay, news story, stalk of grain, hammer, bed, golf club, beer, boil, barrel—not to mention parts of a number of machines and the leaders of all sorts of institutions and governments and movements. Ordinary speech is full of these figures: we *play ball* when we work with others; we may *chime in* by adding our voice to others.

Such figurative uses have become new "senses" of words, as *head* of a pin or nail has—there is no other word for it and it is listed as one of the regular definitions of *head* in dictionaries. These figures are no longer alive but are what may be called petrified figures of speech. We are here concerned with more or less fresh extensions of words to new referents that will add interest to our writing.

The following sections describe some of the commonest and most useful figures, grouped according to the contribution they make to meaning. Though the names given to them, often derived from Greek, are rather forbidding, the examples will show that the figures themselves are quite familiar.

Comparison: metaphor, simile, analogy. Metaphors and similes and analogies all make comparisons, but in different ways. A *metaphor* is the shortest, most compact. Two ideas are involved: the one we are concerned with and the one we are comparing it to, and we substitute the latter for the former. For "Mary is a malicious, spiteful, vindictive girl" we substitute "Mary's a cat." Another example:

> . . . for *the waves* cast by a *pebble of thought* spread until they reach even the nitwits on *the shores* of action.—IRWIN EDMAN, *Four Ways of Philosophy*, p. 100

Where the metaphor implies the likeness, a *simile* asserts that one is like the other, using the words *like* or *as*. A literal statement of similarity is not a simile—"the Congress is like a state legislature" is plain statement of fact. A simile is a comparison between two essentially unlike things which may be strikingly alike in some one way that illuminates the writer's immediate purpose:

> The shepherds of Sardinia are elemental men. Short, square, silent, they look like the rocks of their rocky land, like faintly sentient boulders.—*Time,* April 24, 1964, p. 103

An *analogy,* unlike the metaphor and simile, ordinarily notes several points of similarity instead of just one. Suggestive analogies often bring home or emphasize an idea, as in this sentence:

> The channels of genuine political and religious speculation were choked, until the Great Rebellion loosed the pent flood of books and pamphlets which covered the land for twenty years, cutting far and wide new river-beds in which the thought and practice of our own day now run, and leaving when it subsided not a little of pure gold on the sands of the spent deluge.—G. M. TREVELYAN, *England Under the Stuarts,* p. 162

Relationship: metonymy, synecdoche.   Metonymy and synecdoche are two figures of speech which substitute for the exact name of something the name of something closely associated with it. Strictly, *synecdoche* gives the name of a part when the whole is meant (so many *mouths* to feed, a *sail* in the offing, plant employing sixty *hands*), or of a whole for a part (the *army* adopts a policy). *Metonymy* is the use of one word for another that it suggests: (a) the material for the object made of it: *rubber* for footgear made of rubber; (b) the maker or source for the thing made: *Shakespeare* for Shakespeare's plays; *Java* for Javanese coffee; (c) any word or phrase closely associated with the object: *grandstand* for the audience.

Metonymy, a common figure of speech (common in both Formal and General usage), illustrates one way in which the meanings of words change. Long use of *crown* for *king, heart* for *courage* or *sympathy* and similar use of hundreds of other words have given these words definite secondary meanings.

Degree of statement: overstatement, understatement, irony. Overstatement (or exaggeration or *hyperbole*) is a figure of speech when it is used not to deceive but to emphasize a statement or situation, to intensify its impression. Overstatement may involve simply choosing a word of broader or more intense meaning than literal accuracy would call for (like *perfect* for *excellent, starved* for *hungry, rout* for *retreat*), or it may involve developing a more complex statement, as in the following passages:

But the feelings that Beethoven put into his music were the feelings of a god. There was something olympian in his snarls and rages, and there was a touch of hell-fire in his mirth.—H. L. MENCKEN, "Beethoven," *Prejudices: Fifth Series,* p. 89

A too free use of superlatives or of intense adjectives is weakening and should be avoided:

Within the limits of Colorado, New Mexico, Arizona, and Southern California there are four centers of sublime and unparalleled scenic sublimity which stand alone and unrivaled in the world.

Overstatement is a frequent source of humor, both literary and popular. Many American anecdotes and tall tales hinge on it; the Paul Bunyan stories make a cycle of popular exaggeration. Overstatement is just as much a part of more sophisticated humor and satire:

Englishwomen's shoes look as if they had been made by someone who had often heard shoes described, but had never seen any, and the problem of buying shoes in London is almost insoluble—unless you pay a staggering tariff on American ones. What provokes this outburst is that I have just bought a pair of English bedroom slippers and I not only cannot tell the left foot from the right, but it is only after profound deliberation that I am able to distinguish between the front and the back.—MARGARET HALSEY, *With Malice Toward Some,* pp. 99-100

Understatement, the opposite of overstatement, may mean stating an idea in negative terms (*litotes*) or in less strong words than would be expected: "Joe Louis was not a bad fighter." It is often used in unfavorable criticism:

Having hinted that "Captain Newman, M.D." is something less than a landmark, I feel obliged to note that, under the circumstances, Mr. Peck does a remarkable job....—BRENDAN GILL, "The Current Cinema," *The New Yorker,* Feb. 29, 1964, p. 123

Irony implies something markedly different, occasionally even the opposite, from what is actually said. Light irony is a form of humor, severe irony usually a form of sarcasm or satire —though exact definition in such matters is difficult and rarely fruitful. The following example illustrates both understatement and irony:

A revolution is always distinguished by impoliteness, probably because the ruling classes did not take the trouble in good season to teach the people fine manners.—LEON TROTSKY quoted by H. J. Muller in *The Uses of the Past,* p. 295

Word play.   Occasionally we try experiments in words, either by making old words do new tricks or by inventing new ones. The results are often disastrous—in fact usually so—but now and then the effect comes off. Clipped words of recent creation seem slangy or familiar (*natch, psych, ex-pug*), though older ones are thoroughly respectable—[*taxi*] *cab,* [*omni*] *bus, exam* [*ination*]. The same is true for *blends. The commonest experiment with words is the pun: More trouble is made by in-laws than by outlaws; Don't learn traffic laws by accident. Even in academic writing a pun may occasionally fit:

In other words, we must in fact regretfully admit that earthquakes, in view of our limited knowledge of their incidence and frequency in ancient times, are a shaky basis on which to build a precise chronology.—SIR MORTIMER WHEELER, *Archaeology from the Earth,* p. 43

Word play is risky because the failures are conspicuous, but a full use of language calls for some risks. If you try word play, review carefully what you have done to make sure it comes off.

Allusion.   Sometimes a writer makes reference to matter which is not directly pertinent but which adds interest or explains more clearly or emphasizes what he is saying. This may be an allusion, a brief reference to literature, to history, to things, to people and what they do. Since it is a voluntary addition of the writer, its effect is stylistic—a way of saying something that could have been put differently—and may properly be included in a study of the choice of words.

Many writers have read widely and have found some of what they read so memorable that allusion to it naturally appears in their explanation of other matters. (They may use quotations, too, but we are talking of less specific reference to their reading.) Speeches from two Shakespearean plays are referred to in the following passage:

There is nothing new in heaven or earth not dreamt of [Hamlet] in our laboratories; and we should be amazed indeed if tomorrow and tomorrow and tomorrow [Macbeth] failed to offer us something new to challenge our capacity for readjustment.—CARL L. BECKER, *The Heavenly City of the Eighteenth Century Philosophers,* p. 23

Allusion to written literature is more characteristic of Formal than of General English, which is apt to borrow from proverbs, current phrases, advertising, and the great stock of colloquial phrases (more fun than a barrel of monkeys). Homely, everyday phrases can be used to advantage in any Informal discussion:

The thing for the faculty of the University to do is to take it easy. Don't get excited. Walk, don't run to the nearest exit and enjoy life in the open. In a few months the sun will shine, water will run down hill, and smoke will go up the chimneys just the same.— WILLIAM ALLEN WHITE, *The Emporia Gazette*

Writers often allude to outstanding events in the past—to Waterloo, Gettysburg, D-Day, and to the lives and characters of important persons:

The voice of duty speaks differently to Savonarola, to Cromwell, to Calvin, to Kant and to the contemporary communist or fascist.— IRWIN EDMAN, *Four Ways of Philosophy,* p. 292

Detailed historical reference is rather characteristic of Formal writing; brief reference to better known events characterizes General writing.

More typical of current writing is allusion to current events, persons in the public eye, immediate affairs. But one difficulty with such casual allusions is that in time they become hard to identify—a reason why Shakespeare's plays and other older literature need explanatory notes. This was written in 1921:

Suppose a young man, just out of college and returned to his moderate-sized home town in Ohio (why not Marion?), honestly tries to make those contacts with the national culture which Mr. Sherman so vigorously urges him to make.—HAROLD STEARNS, *The Bookman,* March 1921

"Why not Marion?" is meaningless to young people today, and many of their elders will have forgotten that it was President Harding's home town, often referred to in 1921. But missing the allusion does not interfere with the basic point of the passage. As with other such references, if a reader does recognize the allusion, he has an added pleasure. Such topical allusions are best for immediate consumption, and since most of us are not writing for the ages, they help make our writing seem more alive, as though the writer knew what was going on around him.

One of the most fertile kinds of allusion, and one that is open to everybody, is to the things that people do, the things around us, our work, our sports, our hobbies. It was natural for Carlo Levi, an M.D., to write "The sky was a mixture of rose, green, and violet, the enchanting colors of malaria country" (*Christ Stopped at Eboli*, p. 63). The directness of modern style encourages such allusions to the life around us. An allusion that has its roots in the writer's experience gives his style life and vigor and the stamp of individuality.

Use of figures of speech. Since figures of speech are likely to be a little conspicuous, they need to be used with care. It is wiser to do the best possible with literal words unless a happy and accurate figure comes to mind.

Effective figures are natural, consistent, and appropriate. Figures should come from the way the writer sees his subject and should be the sort that he might use in his conversation. They should not be tacked on or used just "to make an impression"—they should bring the reader closer to the writer's actual sense of his subject. In speech there are many figures, especially comparisons (*tired as a dog, lap of luxury*), which are pretty threadbare but which still work when we're not too fussy about the effect we are making on our listener. In writing we should be more careful. "Trees that stand like sentinels" is an example of the lazy, trite, and really useless figure. Trees of course do stand as sentinels did—but we don't see sentinels in our experience, so it would not occur to us to say so if we hadn't heard the phrase before. Struggling for freshness usually brings on either these trite figures or strained ones. The figures to use need not be unusual, just the ones that come easily to your mind when you are trying to give an exact account of the subject. They should fit in their context and—most important—add something to the sense.

If a figure is continued through more than one phrase, sometimes it becomes "mixed"—inconsistent in some way (called the *mixed metaphor*). The sophomore who wrote "My father is a limb in a chain of the business cycle" couldn't have been thinking either about his father or about his writing. Sometimes, however, mixed figures are used intentionally as a sort of easy but occasionally effective humor—like those attributed to Samuel Goldwyn ("They're always biting the hand that lays the golden egg").

Since figures are used to make a passage in some way more effective, they should be accurate enough to contribute to the meaning and they should be in the same tone as the subject and style. This is out of key:

> In learning more about him I found that he was just about the kindest man I have ever met. He had the heart of an elephant and the mind of a genius.

And these figures seem much too violent to suggest even voracious reading:

> He sank his teeth into the throat of the book, shook it fiercely until it was subdued, then lapped up its blood, devoured its flesh and crunched its bones.

Range and liveliness • The qualities of words that we have been discussing contribute not only to communicating information and ideas but also to the life and force of writing, to its readability. Colorless and impersonal writing may at times be adequate and even appropriate, as in some reports and scholarly papers, but it does not make an impression, and it limits the readers to those already having a concern for the subject.

The following paragraph is quite accurate but quite colorless—that is, it is deadly dull.

> Our way of life is menaced today and we are concerned about its defense. The first step in the defense of democracy (as we realize more readily in times of crisis, though it was just as true in easier days of security) is to ensure an understanding and appreciation of its essential values and of the obligations it entails. So many young people have grown up thinking of the advantages of democracy in terms of their personal liberty to do what they like, and so devoid of any sense of the claims of democracy upon their service, that we are now able to see clearly how seriously our educational institutions have been failing to transmit our ideals and to play their part in developing the attitudes and loyalties on which our free society depends for its very survival.

One of the chief traits of contemporary writing is the range and vigor and suggestiveness of the words used. We do not need to go to works that make primarily a literary appeal to find these qualities. This paragraph from a factual discussion of recent American painting has a lively, vigorous style. The writer's attention is firmly centered on his immediate subject, but he has not switched off the rest of his mind. He takes words and instances as he finds them, puts them to work, and conveys not only his ideas but a sense of life. An outstanding trait is the *range* of the vocabulary, from Informal to rather technical words. Note the vivid (and vicious) characterization of "the European portraitist" as a "third-rate member of the pretty-pretty school of eyelash affixers," a characterization which gives point to the "grievance" of the American artist.

Another irritant contributing to the drift of the American artist into his present state of forthright nationalism was his old grievance against the European portraitist, usually a third-rate member of the pretty-pretty school of eyelash affixers, who crosses the Atlantic to batten on portrait commissions from the culturally illiterate. These "artists" are merely commercial limners, skillful in surface flashiness and clever masters of the technique of publicity and social flattery. Americans who try to click heels with them usually end up on an elbow. The news and society reporters (not the art critics) give them yards of publicity with photographs dramatizing their records among European royalty. A visit to Washington would produce sittings from Congressmen, a member of the Cabinet or even the President—every American ruler since 1912, except F. D. R., patiently sat to some foreign painter, for "reasons of state." After a year among our dollar aristocrats, the "artist" would carry back across the Atlantic with him as much as $50,000—his departure attended by the futile curses of better but less suave American portraitists. It is a condition that obtains even today. American taste in the upper brackets being what it is, our lords and ladies of breeding and position like to feel that the same brush that painted Duchess Thisque or Countess Thatque can be hired by Mrs. Smith to outshine Mrs. Jones.—Peyton Boswell, Jr., *Modern American Painting,* p. 73

You can aim to express your ideas with similar life. Through observant listening and reading, plenty of good talk, and practice in using the full range of your vocabulary, you will come to write with increasing effectiveness. The real problem in choosing words is deciding whether *in the context* they do what you want them to do. You will have a greater range of choice if you acquaint yourself by wide reading with the resources of the English vocabulary. This is the best way to become sensitive to what words can and cannot do for you as you use them to express your thoughts and feelings. The next section gives some background to sharpen your awareness of the resources of the language.

Learning about words

Anyone who is at all concerned with his speaking and writing gets interested in words. He gets curious about their meaning and how they are used; he becomes conscious that there are words he lacks but really needs, and that there are others he only partially knows. This section discusses a selection of points about the meaning of words[1] and their use, about what words can and cannot do for us in attempting to tell others something or in understanding what they are trying to tell us.

Learning new words • The exact number of English words cannot be known. The "unabridged" dictionaries have about half a million word entries; many of these are compounds (*lamplight, combat fatigue*) or derivatives (*rare—rarely, rarefy, rarity*), and a good many are obsolete words to help us read older literature. But a good many of the "words" have several definitions, and sometimes one "word" will have two or more senses at least as different as those for two separate entries. One definition of *dog*, for example, is "andiron"; this is less like the commonest sense (a domesticated animal) than "canine" is. Yet *canine* gets an entry of its own, while the definition of *dog* as "andiron" does not. Equating the number of words in a language with the number of entries in an unabridged dictionary is misleading at best. And dictionaries do not attempt to cover completely many large groups of words: slang, localisms, the terms of various occupations and professions; words used only occasionally by scientists and specialists in many fields; foreign words borrowed for use in English; or many of the thousands of new words or new senses of words that come into use every year and that often disappear leaving scarcely a trace.

---

[1]Students of language are not agreed on what they will regard as "a word," preferring to analyze language into smaller elements (*Phoneme, *Morpheme), but as amateurs we can use the rule of thumb that what an educated person would separate in writing or print is a word. In this text we are more interested in the use of words—how they are combined to "say something"—than in theories about them.

It would be conservative to say that there are over a million English words which any of us might meet in our listening and reading and which we may use in speaking and writing.

The individual's vocabulary. Since we cannot decide just what we will count as a word, how many words an individual uses cannot be exactly measured either, but there are numerous estimates. Professor Seashore concluded that first-graders enter school with at least 24,000 words and add 5000 each year, so that they leave high school with at least 80,000. The average for college students he puts at twice this number.[1] These figures are for *recognition* vocabulary, the words we understand when we read or hear them. Our *active* vocabulary, the words we use in speaking and writing, is considerably smaller.

In the following paragraph of academic prose some of the words illustrate possible distinctions between a recognition and an active vocabulary. They are italicized for later discussion.

Language exists in a *potential* state: it is a system of signs stored away in our memories, ready to be *actualized, translated* into physical sound, in the process of speech. Language, then, does not consist of sounds in the physical sense, but of *sound-impressions* left behind by the actual sounds we have ourselves pronounced or heard from others. These sound-impressions are made up of *acoustic* and *motor* elements: we remember the quality of the sound and the *articulatory* movements we performed when pronouncing it, and with these impressions is combined a *disposition* to repeat the same movements. The difficulty some people *experience* in pronouncing a foreign sound shows that the process of *innervation* has not been completely successful. Other elements of the *linguistic* system—words, grammatical forms, syntactical constructions, etc.—are likewise deposited in our memories as impressions, patterns and dispositions. The *precise* psychological nature of these impressions is not directly *relevant* here, though the *behavioristically* minded could regard them as "engrams": "*residual* traces of an *adaptation* made by the *organism* to a *stimulus.*" Be that as it may, the essential point is that language is potential whereas speech is actualized.—STEPHEN ULLMANN, *Semantics: An Introduction to the Science of Meaning*, pp. 19-20

Probably most college students would recognize and understand after a fashion all the words in this passage except *inner-*

---

[1] Robert H. Seashore, "The Importance of Vocabulary in Learning Language Skills," *Elementary English*, 1948, 24: 137-152; "How Large Are Children's Vocabularies?" *Elementary English*, 1949, 26: 181-194.

vation and *engrams.* Most of them would not use *actualize, acoustic, articulatory, linguistic, precise, relevant, behavioristically, residual, adaptation,* and *organism* in speech, though a few of these words might crop up in their writing. *Translate, motor, disposition, experience, stimulus* would occur in any student's speech, but not in the senses they have here: *translate* has approximately the sense of *transformed, motor* is used as an adjective rather than in its more common noun function and refers to muscular coordination as well as willingness, *experience* is a verb rather than a noun, and *stimulus* is used in a biological sense. *Sound-impression* is self-explanatory but rather special in application, as is *potential.*

It is quite proper that many of these words should be nothing more than a part of the recognition vocabularies of most educated people. The paragraph is a specialized one, and most educated people are not going to become specialists in semantics or even in linguistics, of which semantics is a branch. The extent to which such words will become a part of the individual's active vocabulary depends on how precisely he masters the concepts for which they are the signs. When he controls the concepts, the signs will be actualized, translated into words which he will speak—and write.

You cannot always produce a word just when you want it, as you probably know from the exasperating experience of fishing for the name of a casual acquaintance. But striving to express yourself in the most exact words will help get them into your active vocabulary.

Increasing vocabulary by learning new subjects. "But my vocabulary is so small!" is a common complaint of students in composition courses. Or they say, "I know what I mean but I can't put it into words." They seem to think that some sort of injection of new words will magically transform them into good writers, as though having an inadequate vocabulary was an affliction like myopia or hay fever, to be remedied by contact lenses or by an antihistamine.

If your vocabulary is small, that is only the symptom and not the disease, for words cannot be considered apart from their senses and uses. If you have a good grasp of what you want to express, you won't have much trouble finding the words to do it. There are sense impressions, moods, and feelings—a variety of subjective sensations—for which you may have no specific words, but in most of your writing you are not discussing these. Not being able to "find the words" usually means not being able to think out your ideas very clearly.

The words you already have are in the areas of your knowledge and your interest. Consequently, the most natural way to increase your stock of words is by learning something more, something new, perhaps from observation or conversation or from reading a magazine or a college textbook. You can't take facts and ideas away with you unless they are in verbal form. The easiest way to extend your vocabulary is through new experiences. New words come from every experience—every job, every sport, every art, every book; from every field of thought and study—electronics, surfing, music, astronomy.

But new words are not a usable part of your vocabulary until you know what they stand for. Explain to someone what you have just learned, talk it over with somebody who knows nothing about it, or write about it.

In college your stock of facts and ideas increases enormously, with a corresponding increase in vocabulary. As you come to understand what *registrar, curriculum, honors course, schedule, conflict* stand for, you will find yourself using them easily and naturally, as well as the colloquial and slang vocabulary of the campus (*dorm, poly sci, home ec*); you may take up a new sport or some other activity and acquire more words; and a course in a new field will probably add three or four hundred new words to your vocabulary, some of them technical and of restricted use, many of them of more general application. Acquiring the vocabulary of biology or sociology or history is essential to learning biology or sociology or history.

You should try to learn these words accurately *the first time you meet them:* look at their spelling, pronounce them as you hear them in class or as a dictionary specifies, and study their exact meaning. Probably a good deal of students' trouble in courses comes from only partly understanding the specialized words when they are first met. Once these words are understood, they should be used. Many of them will be called for in class discussions or examinations or term papers, but using them in talking over the course work or using them casually in conversation will help impress on your mind what they stand for, and make the words themselves come more easily.

Basic to increasing your vocabulary is a desire to learn—to learn both subject matter and words; you need an inquiring and receptive attitude, almost recapturing the youngster's open curiosity and continual "What's that?" by which we all acquired our first few thousand words. The essential point is that you are not merely "increasing your vocabulary." You are acquiring more meaningful and useful ideas, increasing your powers of understanding, and extending your range of interests, as well as adding to your command of the enormous supply of English words needed to think, speak, and write in the manner of educated people.

The use of dictionaries ● The most useful single tool for a writer, in or out of a composition course, is a good dictionary. Nowhere else can you find so much information about words and their use. You will use your dictionary most in revision and should get the habit of turning to it frequently while revising a paper and preparing the final copy.

There is no such thing as *the* dictionary, one which can be quoted to settle any question about words. Dictionaries obviously vary in three fundamental respects (as well as in minor matters like typography and arrangement of entries): in date, in size, and in responsibility of editing.

A dictionary should be up to date because words are continually being added to the general stock of the English language, other words are used in new senses, some drop out of use, and spellings and pronunciations change. Although some alterations are made between printings, the date of compilation—not of printing—is the important one. Bookstores handle only recent editions, but if you are buying a second-hand dictionary, look at the copyright statement on the back of the title page.

For specialized reading and detailed work with words it is necessary to go to an "unabridged" dictionary. For everyday work, the smaller "college" size, costing usually from five dollars up, according to binding, is more convenient and is generally adequate.

The date and size of a dictionary are easily determined, but it is more difficult to judge the editing. Responsible editing is what makes the dictionary really useful and gives it whatever "authority" it may have. It should be a compilation from a vast accumulation of actual recorded uses of words, not a patchwork from existing word books. This raw material should be worked over by specialists in various subjects and by trained editors, who digest the evidence and compose the dictionary's brief entries. Since it is difficult to determine how well dictionaries have been edited, most people have to rely on reviews or on the advice of someone who has studied them.[1]

---

[1]See Allen Walker Read, "Desk Dictionaries," pp. 547-550, and James Sledd, " 'Standard' is a Trademark," pp. 551-552, in *Consumer Reports*, Nov. 1963. See also dictionaries listed, with critical notes, in Constance M. Winchell, *Guide to Reference Books* (7th ed.; Chicago, 1951, and supplements) , pp. 217-220; dictionaries of special subjects, pp. 220-226.

The following dictionaries, listed alphabetically, are currently available; instructors usually recommend certain ones for students to buy:

American College Dictionary (Random House, 1965; 1421 pp. plus supplements to 1444 pp.). Simplified pronunciation key and pronunciations based on current usage; comprehensive treatment of technical words; good synonym studies; all words (general words, proper names, abbreviations) in one alphabetical list; common meanings of each word come first in entry; frequently revised.

Funk & Wagnalls Standard College Dictionary (Funk & Wagnalls, 1966; 1565 pp. plus supplements to 1606 pp.). All entries in a single alphabetical arrangement; definitions arranged on the basis of frequency of current use; synonym and antonym lists for certain words, with cross references; labels for usage levels, dialect distribution; grammar; useful introductory sections and appendices.

Thorndike-Barnhart Comprehensive Desk Dictionary (Scott, Foresman and Company, 1951; 896 pp. plus supplements to 925 pp.). Contains 80,000 entries as contrasted with the 100,000 to 150,000 in the "college" dictionaries listed here; synonym studies; simplified etymologies; simplified pronunciation key and especially accurate record of current American pronunciation; usage notes; common meanings first in entry; one alphabetical list of all words; frequently revised.

Webster's New World Dictionary of the American Language, College Edition (World, 1964; 1702 pp. plus supplements to 1724 pp.). Uses simplified definitions even for technical terms; many Informal words and phrases; related meanings grouped and entered in historical order, with technical senses usually last, etymologies unusually full; all words in one alphabetical list; new words added annually.

Webster's Seventh New Collegiate Dictionary (G. & C. Merriam, 1965; 1041 pp. plus supplements to 1220 pp.). Based on *Webster's Third New International Dictionary of the English Language, Unabridged* (1961); careful treatment of usage problems and general vocabulary; four alphabetical lists of words: (1) common and technical words and foreign words and phrases, (2) abbreviations, (3) biographical names, (4) geographical names; synonym studies; earliest meaning of a word stands first in each entry; appendixes; special attention to scientific and technical words.

Uses of a general dictionary.   To use a dictionary efficiently, you must first read the introductory sections carefully. Lexicographers—dictionary makers—probably have to reject more available material in preparing their final copy than do the editors of any other kind of book. Naturally they will resort to space-saving devices wherever possible. These devices and the purposes and policies of the editors will be explained in the introductory sections. Study these sections.

After you have studied the introductory sections and acquainted yourself with the arrangement of material in the book, read a page or two consecutively; look up a few words that you know and a few that are new to you to see how they are handled. Try pronouncing some words, familiar and unfamiliar ones, to see how the pronunciation key works. The next sections describe in some detail the main features of a typical dictionary and their uses.

1. Spelling: A word is entered in a dictionary under its usual spelling. As a rule you can come close enough to this to find a word you are in doubt about, but sometimes you have to keep in mind other common spellings of a sound—so that if you fail to find *gibe* you will look under *jibe*. When more than one spelling is given, both are in good use: *esthetic, aesthetic; although, altho.* Ordinarily take the first of two forms unless the second for some reason is more appropriate to other traits of your writing. The entries in a dictionary show where a word should be hyphenated at the end of a line, as in *mor ti fi ca tion, dis par ag ing ly.* They also show whether the editors have found compound words most often as two words, as one word, or with a hyphen. (Most dictionaries suggest the use of more hyphens than are necessary for General writing.)

2. Pronunciation: Dictionaries respell words in specially marked letters to show their pronunciation, as you will notice in these examples. The exact sounds represented by the symbols are usually shown at the bottom of the page and are further explained in a discussion of pronunciation in the preface.

ac·cli·mate (əklī′mĭt, ăk′ləmāt′). *v.t., v.i.,* **-mated, -mating.** *Chiefly U.S.* to habituate or become habituated to a new climate or environment. [t. F: m.s. *acclimater,* der. *à* to + *climat* climate]   **—ac·cli·mat·a·ble** (ə-klī′mĭtəbəl), *adj.* **—ac·cli·ma·tion** (ăk′ləmā′shən), *n.*

cer·ti·o·ra·ri (sûr′shĭərâr′ī), *n.   Law.* a writ issuing from a superior court calling up the record of a proceeding in an inferior court for review. [t. L: to be informed (lit., made more certain)]

ac·cli·mate \ə-'klī-mət, 'ak-lə-,māt\ *vt* [F acclimater, fr. a- (fr. L ad-) + climat climate] : ACCLIMATIZE — **ac·cli·ma·tion** \,ak-,lī-'mā-shən, ,ak-lə-\ *n*

cer·tio·ra·ri \,sər-sh(ē-)ə-'re(ə)r-ē, -'rär-ē\ *n* [ME, fr. L, to be informed; fr. the use of the word in the writ] : a writ of a superior court to call up the records of an inferior court or a body acting in a quasi-judicial capacity

Dictionaries are somewhat imperfect guides to pronunciation.[1] Their chief source of material, published books and articles, naturally contains very little evidence about pronunciation. Pronunciation must be studied from actual speech, and an adequate record of the actual speech of a large country like ours is hard to make. Sometimes a dictionary gives full or "platform" pronunciation, which if followed exactly would slow up a person's speech and make it sound quite stilted. Ordinary speech uses less distinct vowels than the usual dictionary symbols suggest, and stress may vary with the position of a word in a phrase. Furthermore, our dictionaries do not recognize sufficiently the regional variations in American pronunciation. But people can usually rely on dictionaries for the pronunciation of unusual words, and they are likely to learn the sound of common words from hearing them.

Dictionaries show divided usage in the pronunciation of many words, as in the examples of *acclimate* shown above. If more than one pronunciation is given without qualification, each is acceptable. A speaker should use the pronunciation most common among the educated people of his community.

3. Definition: The definitions of words take up the bulk of space in a dictionary. Definitions of unusual words help you get the full sense of a passage that treats new material. But often you will need more information than a dictionary has room for, and will need to go to an encyclopedia or other work or wait until you have heard or seen the word used several times.

It is not so much the definitions of uncommon words, like *hackbut, pyrognostics,* or *zymurgy,* that you need, as of those that are almost but not quite in your active vocabulary. Nearly any series of dictionary entries will illustrate these words, and also the scope and method of dictionary definition:

---

[1]Systematic guides to American pronunciation are the Introduction to John S. Kenyon and Thomas A. Knott, *A Pronouncing Dictionary of American English* and "A Guide to Pronunciation" by Edward Artin in *Webster's Third New International Dictionary.*

luminous intensity *Physics* The luminous flux emitted from a point source of light per steradian.

lum·mox (lum′əks) *n. U.S. Informal* A stupid, clumsy person. [Origin unknown]

lump[1] (lump) *n.* **1.** A shapeless mass, especially a small mass: a *lump* of dough. **2.** A protuberance or swelling. **3.** A mass of things thrown together; aggregate. **4.** A heavy, ungainly, and usually stupid person. **— a lump in one's throat** A feeling of tightness in the throat, as from emotion. **— in a** (or **the**) **lump** All together; with no distinction. **—** *adj.* Formed in a lump or lumps: *lump* sugar. **—** *v.t.* **1.** To put together in one mass, group, etc. **2.** To consider or treat as one mass, group, etc.: to *lump* all the facts together. **3.** To make lumps in or on. **—** *v.i.* **4.** To become lumpy. [< ME, prob. < Scand.]

lump[2] (lump) *v.t. Informal* To put up with; endure: You can like it or *lump* it. [Origin uncertain]

lum·pen (lum′pən) *Informal adj.* Having little genuine claim or substance; defective; shabby; phony: used in combination: *lumpen-intellectual.* **—** *n.* One who is lumpen. [< G, rag, tatter < *lump* contemptible person]

lump·fish (lump′fish′) *n. pl.* **·fish** or **·fish·es** A bulky, clumsy fish (*Cyclopterus lumpus*) of the North Atlantic, with rows of bony tubercles on the skin and a sucker enabling it to cling to rocks. Also **lump′suck′er** (-suk′ər).

lump·ish (lum′pish) *adj.* **1.** Like a lump. **2.** Stupid; clumsy. **— lump′ish·ly** *adv.* **— lump′ish·ness** *n.*

lump sum A full or single sum of money paid at one time.

lump·y (lum′pē) *adj.* **lump·i·er, lump·i·est** **1.** Full of lumps. **2.** Covered with or having lumps. **3.** Lumpish. **4.** Running in rough, choppy waves: a *lumpy* sea. **— lump′· i·ly** *adv.* **— lump′i·ness** *n.*

There are three points to remember in using dictionary definitions. *(a)* A dictionary does not *require* or *forbid* a particular sense of a word but *records* the uses that have been found for it. Now and then a word is in the process of acquiring a new sense or somewhat altering its usual one. *(b)* The dictionary definition is for the most part a record of the denotation of a word and often cannot give its connotation. For this reason it is safest not to use a word unless you have heard or read it and so know it in part from experience, at least what suggestion it carries if it is not a simple factual word. *(c)* Finally and most important, the words of the definition are not the *meaning* of the word; they, along with the examples or illustrations, are to help you understand what, in the world of objects or ideas, the word refers to.

4. Labels of usage: Words that are unlabeled in a dictionary are supposed to belong to the general vocabulary; other words are labeled *dialectal, obsolete, archaic, foreign, colloquial, slang, British, United States,* or are referred to some field of activity—*medicine, law, astronomy, baseball, printing, electricity, philosophy.* These labels are rough guides to usage, but a writer should bring his own observation and judgment to bear on individual words. Many that carry no label are

rarely used (*impavid, ustulate*) and would mar most writing. Usually the dictionary editors' point of view is rather cautious, and many words marked *Dial.* or *Colloq.* would fit perfectly well into Informal or even General writing. It must be clearly understood that these labels are descriptive terms and are not intended to prohibit or even to discourage the use of the words so labeled. *Colloq.* in a dictionary, for example, usually means that the word is characteristic of the ordinary conversation of educated people and of General rather than Formal writing. (Some dictionaries have abandoned *Colloq.* because readers persist in thinking the label derogatory.)

5. Synonyms: Most dictionaries gather words of similar senses into a group and show in what ways they are alike and in what ways different, as in the following entries which appear after the word *discuss* in *Webster's New World Dictionary*:

> **SYN.—discuss** implies a talking about something in a deliberative fashion, with varying opinions offered constructively and, usually, amicably, so as to settle an issue, decide on a course of action, etc.; **argue** implies the citing of reasons or evidence to support or refute an assertion, belief, proposition, etc.; **debate** implies a formal argument, usually on public questions, in contests between opposing groups; **dispute** implies argument in which there is a clash of opposing opinions, often presented in an angry or heated manner.

From *Webster's New World Dictionary, College Edition,* copyright 1964 by The World Publishing Company, Cleveland, Ohio.

The discrimination of synonyms is often a helpful addition to the definition in selecting the right word to use. (See p. 348.)

6. Linguistic information: A dictionary entry indicates the part or parts of speech in which a word is generally used, the transitive or intransitive use of verbs, the principal parts of irregular verbs, plurals of irregular nouns, and any other distinctive form a word may assume. (It is useful to remember, however, that this information, based on edited printed material, cannot always accurately reflect general cultivated practice.) The history of the word—its etymology—is usually given. Sometimes this is merely a statement of the language from which the word came into English; sometimes it is a more complicated chain of source and change of form, as in this statement:

> **sil·ly** \'sil-ē\ *adj* [ME *sely, silly* happy, innocent, pitiable, feeble, fr. (assumed) OE *sǣlig*, fr. OE *sǣl* happiness; akin to OHG *sālig* happy, L *solari* to console, Gk *hilaros* cheerful] **1** *archaic* : HELPLESS, WEAK **2 a** : RUSTIC, PLAIN **b** *obs* : lowly in station : HUMBLE **3 a** : weak in intellect : FOOLISH **b** : contrary to reason : ABSURD **c** : TRIFLING, FRIVOLOUS **syn** see SIMPLE — **silly** *n or adv*

By permission. From *Webster's Seventh New Collegiate Dictionary,* copyright 1965 by G. & C. Merriam Co., publishers of the Merriam-Webster Dictionaries.

Though etymologies are often interesting, they may have little bearing on the present meaning of a word.

7. Miscellaneous information: Most dictionaries contain some reference material, such as lists of places and prominent historical figures, abbreviations, foreign words and phrases. Sometimes these are placed in the back of the volume, sometimes in the main alphabetical listing.

Larger dictionaries. Dictionary making (lexicography) is a highly specialized art, or applied science. The general dictionaries are supplemented by some larger ones and by several specialized ones.[1]

1. Unabridged dictionaries: The most complete dictionaries of present-day English are called unabridged, meaning that they are not selections from larger works as—in effect—the college size are. Two important, but dated, unabridged dictionaries available in most libraries are the *Century Dictionary and Cyclopedia* (Century Company, 1911; 12 vols.) and *Funk & Wagnalls New Standard Dictionary of the English Language* (Funk & Wagnalls Company, 1913, 1947; 2895 pp.). The most up-to-date unabridged dictionary is of course *Webster's Third New International Dictionary of the English Language* (2718 pp.), which was published in 1961. As with most departures—however slight—from what has become accepted, the *Third* met with disfavor in some popular reviews. Most scholarly reviews of it, however, were favorable.[2]

2. Historical dictionaries: The *Oxford English Dictionary,* published in ten large volumes, is the great storehouse of information about English words. It traces the various forms of each word and its various senses, with dates of their first recorded appearance and quotations from writers illustrating each. There is a *Supplement* giving material on new words and evidence on earlier words not found in the original work. An abridgment, the *Shorter Oxford English Dictionary,* in two volumes, is also very useful for interpreting past literature.

The *Dictionary of American English* (4 volumes, 1938-1944), on the same plan as the *Oxford,* gives the histories of words as they have been used in the United States. An entry begins with the first use of the word by an American writer and continues, with quotations, to 1900. In this way it is especially

---

[1] *A Survey of English Dictionaries* (New York, 1933) by Mitford M. Mathews is a history of English dictionaries. *Dictionaries British and American* (New York, 1955) by James R. Hulburt and *Dr. Johnson's Dictionary* (Chicago, 1955) by James H. Sledd and Gwin J. Kolb are more recent surveys.
[2] See James Sledd and Wilma R. Ebbitt, *Dictionaries and THAT Dictionary,* (Chicago, 1962).

useful in reading American writers. The more recent *Dictionary of Americanisms* (1951) selects from, interprets, and supplements this work.

Besides these there are dictionaries for Old English and for Middle English, and other period dictionaries are being compiled, like the *Dictionary of Early Modern English* (1500-1700).

3. Dialect dictionaries: Besides Joseph Wright's *English Dialect Dictionary* (6 volumes), giving words in the various dialects of England, there are a number of special word lists from different regions, which appear in books and in periodicals like *Dialect Notes* and *American Speech*. (See Ch. 1, pp. 6-9.) Eric Partridge's *Dictionary of Slang and Unconventional English* is a historical dictionary of English slang.

4. Dictionaries in special subjects: Because the general dictionaries cannot give the complete vocabulary of specialized fields, they are supplemented by a growing group of dictionaries in special subjects, like the following:

Alsager, C. M., *Dictionary of Business Terms*
Ballentine, J. A., *Law Dictionary*
Dorland, W. A. N., *Illustrated Medical Dictionary*
English, H. B., and English, A. C., *A Comprehensive Dictionary of Psychological and Psychoanalytical Terms*
Good, C. V., *Dictionary of Education*
Hackh, I.W.D., *Chemical Dictionary*
Henderson, I. F., and Henderson, W. D., *Dictionary of Scientific Terms* (biological sciences)
Rice, C. M., *Dictionary of Geological Terms*
The International Dictionary of Applied Mathematics

The meaning of words • One of our commonest and most important questions in listening or reading is "What does he mean by that?" And in our own speaking or writing we often wonder "Will they see what I mean by this?" In speech we may repeat a remark in different words if we are not understood; in revising a paper we can change words or phrases to make our intention more nearly unmistakable. In speech the way we manipulate our voice does much of the work of indicating what we intend, but in writing, our words may need to be chosen differently, because there is nothing else to reinforce our intention.

The nature of meaning.   The meaning of words is studied in the division of linguistics called *semantics*. A complete study of meaning involves other fields too, especially psychology and philosophy. In spite of a great deal of study by specialists in recent years, the explanations of meaning are less satisfactory than of other aspects of language, but there are a number of particular ideas on which there is considerable agreement.[1]

Strictly speaking, words have "meaning" only as they are used in particular statements. They can be studied individually, but as they are recorded in a dictionary, for instance, they have only typical or potential meaning. One way to show that meaning is *not in the isolated word* is to consider some words which are homophones—words which sound the same but have different senses: *right, wright, rite, write,* which though spelled differently sound the same; or the word *sound* itself, which though spelled in only one way has at least three derivations and several different senses. Which sense is intended is made clear by the sentence in which it is used—that is, by the *context*. Though it is the context which actualizes the potential senses of words, without these potential senses no sentence could have any meaning other than a grammatical one.

All full words—words whose function is not merely grammatical, like *the, and,* etc.—can be considered on the basis of three terms: *name, sense, thing.* The *name* is the word itself, its sound in speech, its spelling when seen; *atom,* for example. The *sense* is the ideas the name conjures up in speaker and hearer; they are not necessarily the same in speaker and hearer, as the example *atom* can show, since the nuclear physicist and the man in the street will have quite different ideas of an atom—the first, precise and complex; the second, vague and highly elementary. Finally there is the *thing* itself, which, paradoxical as it may seem, is not really important from the point of view of meaning. The two different ideas of *atom* just mentioned demonstrate this. The man-in-the-street's notion is much further from the reality than the physicist's, but even the latter would admit that he is still somewhat in the dark as to exactly what an atom is. And sometimes the sense is all that exists: for *ghost* we have a name and a sense but no reality. The *meaning* of a word is "the reciprocal and reversible relationship between name and sense: if one hears the word one will think

---

[1] Three elementary books lead to the more difficult original works: S. I. Hayakawa, *Language in Thought and Action* (New York, 1949) to the "general semantics" of Alfred Korzybski (Books cited by name of author only will be found in the Bibliography, pp. xiii-xiv); Hugh Walpole, *Semantics* (New York, 1941) to I. A. Richards' contribution; and Stephen Ullmann, *Semantics: An Introduction to the Science of Meaning* (New York, 1962) to his own more elaborate work. Bloomfield, Chs. 9 and 24, and Eugene A. Nida, *Morphology, The Descriptive Analysis of Words* (Ann Arbor, 1946) are more specifically linguistic. Max Black, *Language and Philosophy* (Ithaca, 1949) evaluates the principal writers on semantics up to 1949.

of the thing [not always accurately], and if one thinks of the thing one will say [or write] the word."[1]

This definition of meaning suggests how perilous communication can be. We assume that there is a neat three-aspect path: The (1) word or symbol *atom* stands for an (2) idea which accurately represents the (3) referent or thing. Unfortunately there is no assurance that the thing is accurately represented by the idea. Consider such a sentence as this:

We cannot speak English unless we know its grammar.

The word *grammar* will be "understood" by everybody; that is, the word has a *sense* for every speaker or listener. The sentence is therefore meaningful because "if one hears the word one will think of the thing [grammar], and if one thinks of the thing [grammar], one will say the word." But the thing thought of will not necessarily be the same for all speakers and listeners. Read the entry *Grammar in the *Index*. Four *things* or referents for the *name* "grammar" are listed. By putting any of these definitions in place of the word *grammar* in the sentence above, a different communication would result.

Meaning, then, is the relationship, "reciprocal and reversible," between a name and a sense. It may be objected that this exclusion of the thing symbolized, of the referent, sanctions "wrong meanings." But this is to approach the explanation of meaning prescriptively and to evade the crucial problem of accurate communication. Whether we like it or not, people assume that they know what a word means when they feel a relationship between name and sense. To communicate accurately, we must make certain that for our audience the relationship between the name and the sense is that which we intend. For the careful and responsible writer, this is the problem of meaning.

The dictionary definition of a word is not, then, its meaning but an attempt to provide a basis for meaning which will approximate the meaning which the word has for educated people. If the basis is something tangible—like *hoe,* for example —the dictionary may reinforce the verbal definition with a picture of the object so that we may visualize the referent. Words for such concrete objects are fairly easy to define. But when the referent is intangible (like *light*) or abstract (like *beauty*), not only does the definition become more difficult but the

[1]Stephen Ullmann, *Semantics: An Introduction to the Science of Meaning*, p. 57.

variability of meaning among all speakers and listeners, writers and readers increases. The following three classes of words show varying degrees of definiteness.

Concrete words.   Concrete words have meanings established by more or less regular reference to actual objects. *Hoe,* for example, has a definite core of meaning because it is used to apply to a kind of tool. Even though people might disagree over a particular untypical *hoe*—there are garden hoes, mortar hoes, weeding hoes, etc.—almost always the meaning of *hoe* would be definite enough for one's purposes. The specific image that a word raises in the minds of different people will vary somewhat: at a given moment *robin* may be pictured by one person as *robin-pulling-at-a-worm;* by another, as *robin-on-a-nest;* by another, as *robin-crying-rain;* but in each there is a core of meaning for *robin.* A word with which a person has had no experience (perhaps *spandrel, tenon, farthingale, rickrack,* or *tachistoscope*) will have no meaning for him.

A speaker or writer would not as a rule use these concrete words without a fairly definite knowledge of their core of meaning; a reader or listener will either know this meaning, be able to approach it through a dictionary definition or through other reading, ask someone who knows, or learn it by observation. It is lucky for all of us that such a large part of our vocabulary consists of these fairly exact words and that we can be pretty sure that other speakers of English understand them as we do.

Relative words.   The referents of words for qualities are less definite. What they refer to in a given instance depends a good deal on the experience and intention of the user. *Red,* for instance, runs from orange to violet and for a reasonably definite meaning needs to be qualified by another word, *light, dark, orange.* To a person in "the upper brackets," a family with $4000 a year might be *poor,* but to someone out of work, that family might be *well-off.* Similarly, *warm, heavy, thick, rough, pretty, honest, tall* are relative in reference. Although attempts have been made to provide an exact or standard referent for some of these words, as in the scale for exact naming of colors in art, or in the standardized weights and measures of physics, or in definitions by law of words like *drunk* and *speeding,* these arbitrary definitions are useful only in certain situations.

In using these descriptive words, especially those that record our attitudes and judgments, it is important to distinguish various degrees, to provide as exact shading as possible. The general method for attaining approximate accuracy in relative or evaluative statements, when accuracy is desirable, is to consider a series (known as a *graded series*) of possible terms between the extremes, from *good* to *bad, light* to *dark,* and to remember that the terms and the statements in which they occur can be made more exact by qualifiers: *more, less, rather, extremely,* and so on.

Abstract words. Like relative words, abstract words do not have specific observable referents. The most definite of them refer to acts or relationships or directions: *trading, murder, cost, citizenship, nation, height.* Other abstract words are collective; they stand for a number of individual items—*college, jazz, the administration* (of a college or of the United States) and summarize one or more common traits belonging to a number of particular people or things or situations. Although they have a pretty definite core of meaning, they may be used with very different values. Unfortunately, in using such words we often lose sight of the particular individuals or things for which they stand. *Personnel,* for instance, may conceal the notion of living people and lead us to make statements that we never would make if we visualized clearly even a dozen of them. *Capital* usually means employers and investors collectively, and *labor* stands for workmen. But as the words are often used, they are more likely to suggest vast, impersonal forces than actual people.

Many other words do not have referents even as commonly agreed on as these. The meaning of such words as *beauty, art, the good life, culture, evil, education, Americanism* is a complex of reasoning and feeling that varies from person to person. Defining the term is a prerequisite to discussing the concept.

We cannot expect that more or less haphazard people, as we all are, will always use these words carefully, but we should strive to be as exact as possible. One way to do this is to translate our meaning into other terms and by giving two or three versions reach something approaching exactness. Another way is to give wherever possible specific, concrete examples of what we intend. One reason for the concreteness of much modern style is the attempt to attain fairly exact communication. (Compare pp. 112-117 on details and generalizations.)

The suggestion of words • The denotation of a word, its factual and informative reference discussed in the preceding section, is what we ordinarily think of as its meaning. But this may be considerably modified by the circumstances in which the word has been generally used and by the particular context in which it occurs. This suggested quality is called its *connotation*. It is an essential part of the meaning of many words, separated from their denotation only in more or less arbitrary analysis.

The connotations of words. The words in each of the following groups have substantially the same denotation, but their connotations vary, so that their total meanings are often quite different:

average (factual) ; *mediocre* (derogatory)

childlike (approving) ; *childish* (derogatory)

saliva (factual, slightly Formal, with scientific suggestion) ; *spit* (the usual word but to many people "an ugly word")

antique (generally approving) ; *old-fashioned* (factual, though often suggesting disapproval) ; *antiquated* (derogatory) ; *passé* (slightly derogatory)

drunk (in General use) ; *intoxicated* (more polite); *under the influence* (euphemistic—minimizing) ; *pie-eyed, soused, loaded* (Informal speech)

reporter (factual) ; *journalist* (slightly pretentious) ; *newshawk* (usually with slight derogatory or humorous note) ; *legman* (shoptalk)

slender (factual, tending to approval) ; *thin* (factual, tending to disapproval) ; *skinny* (disapproving) ; *scrawny* (derogatory) ; *sylphlike* (Formal) ; *svelte* (fashionable)

The connotations of these words suggest an attitude or a feeling of the person using them and would usually arouse a similar attitude or feeling in most readers or listeners. The context in which the word has been generally used, the variety of usage it comes from, and the general social attitude toward its referent and toward the people who generally use it (politicians, advertising men, teachers, children, seamen)—all contribute to the connotation. The force of slang and of much profanity comes mainly from the connotation of the words. The connotation may change as the words or their referents move up or down in social esteem. *Methodist* and *Quaker* started as words of dispraise but are now simply factual or often words of esteem. Until fairly recently *propaganda* meant a means of spreading a truth or a faith, but it now often implies a deliberate attempt to misinform or deceive.

Besides connotations that are more or less permanent characteristics of words and may therefore be given some attention in a dictionary definition, there are more immediate connotations that come from context or from the way words are used at a specific time. In speaking we can alter or even invert the usual meaning of a word by our tone of voice or facial expression or gesture. We can call a person a liar in such a way that he will know he is being flattered. In writing, the tone is set by the general style and by the tenor of ideas expressed. *Democracy, communism, monarchy* are denotative words for types of social organization, but they may also carry suggestions of loyalty or suspicion or hate. The full implication of many words cannot be indicated by a dictionary; consider what would be omitted in a standard definition of such words as *fascism, income tax, ball game, quintessence, the founding fathers, scab, the forgotten man, horse and buggy era.*

The use of connotative words. Connotative words give writing a quality that is called *suggestion.* They are often referred to as emotive, evaluational, intentional, loaded, or slanted words. As most of these names themselves suggest, connotative words are often regarded with suspicion. It is true that their use is often an abuse of statement. It is easy to find slanting—in newspaper headlines, columns by news "analysts," advertisements, political and social discussions—that may range from inconsequential to deceptive and malicious. Reducing such material to neutral statements is a good exercise, necessary for clear thinking. But outside of strictly scholarly and scientific writing, nonconnotative statement is rare. In everyday life and in literature, suggestion—the connotative force of words— is essential. As human beings we have feelings, attitudes, opinions, desires which we need to express, and we should express them.

But we live among people and have a responsibility to them. If we wish to deceive, language offers us the means; by intentional misuse of words or by an irresponsible manipulation of the emotional suggestion in words, a "propagandist" (or anyone else) can distort truth and make error prevail, at least for a time. The difficulty is less in the words than in the intentions of the person using them. An honest attempt at communication can succeed. Although we sometimes fail because we make a careless or unhappy choice of words, or because we don't make full use of the facilities of our language, a determined effort to convey material we really know can be successful.

Absolute exactness is not always desirable. A person who in conversation is overexact or overcareful is likely to become a bore, sacrificing immediate appeal to unnecessary precision. Often in a poem so much depends on the connotation of the words that several "meanings" are possible, and properly enough, so long as a reader does not insist that his interpretation is necessarily the one the writer intended. In attempts to persuade and in any sort of emotional speech, the connotation counts for much. Our aim should be to fit our use of words to a reasonable view of the particular situation and to a reasonable purpose.

For self-protection in our reading, a useful device is to think of other ways the statement might be made. We probably won't be able to judge its accuracy but we can judge the way the words are used. Without being captious we can translate the idea, especially if it represents an opinion or attitude, into other words which are neutral or have a different connotation. Various people, for example, might state what they think (and feel) is the central reason for rising prices:

Slanted phrasing	*Neutral*
Continued wage grabs by big labor	Higher wages secured principally by labor unions
Inflated corporation profits given away as dividends	High corporation profits paid out in dividends to investors
Outrageous bonuses paid to company big shots	Large bonuses to top executives

This device of translating will not necessarily produce "the truth," but it may keep us from being too easily taken in by irresponsibly slanted statements—even when they fit our own views.

For the protection of our readers, the first step is to examine our own views to see that they are based on the best evidence available to us and represent our whole and better selves. It may be helpful to state directly, or at least imply clearly, what our general approach or bias is.

The second step is to be aware of other people's attitudes and feelings, especially of those differing from our own. On most important questions, opinions may legitimately differ—otherwise they would be facts rather than opinions. The serious opinions of others should be met squarely and in their best expression, not their shoddiest. A decent regard for the feelings of others will also reduce the thoughtless, loose, insensitive, or even hostile use of words. Such a concern will reduce the offensive epithets for races, nationalities, occupations, social groups of all sorts and the oversimplification of complex situations—perhaps even some of the unanalyzed terms of virtue we wish to apply to ourselves—*rights, liberty, free enterprise, peace, the Free World.* Within the limits of reasonable attitudes and of understanding, we still have the right to express ourselves strongly.

To communicate his ideas so that others can understand them, a writer needs to have a sure grasp of the denotative meanings of the words he uses. To make the choices that lead to responsible, effective expression, he needs also to be sensitive to the connotations of words.

Exercises

1. Examine the items below, paying particular attention to the forms of verbs and pronouns, to the reference of pronouns, and to the use of adjectives and adverbs. Revise any unsatisfactory item to make it acceptable in General writing.

a. After they had lit a roaring fire, they drunk a toast to the queen, and jollily forgot all their troubles.

b. Us boys wanted to help but didn't know whom to ask.

c. There is a slight resemblance between her and I.

d. My hound's eyes are the soulfulest I have ever seen.

e. He asked me whom I thought would win the election.

f. As soon as the dough rises, sit it in a warm place and leave it stay there for an hour.

g. It is natural for a human being to strike back when struck, because they have an instinct for self-preservation.

h. When the Dean came to call on my father and I, we were flattered.

i. He failed the spot quiz because he can only handle those kind of questions leisurely.

j. He took refuge in the Fifth Amendment, which is his privilege.

k. Under the leaves we found a caterpillar rolled up tight.

l. He receives letters from many people of whom he's never heard or seen.

m. Everybody in the first four cars are Congressmen or the wives of Congressmen.

n. To get a cup of coffee, all you had to do was put a dime in the slot, which I did.

o. Millions of people who never visit Grand Canyon enjoyed its beauty. This has been made possible by motion pictures.

p. The only correct standard of English is that which is appropriate to the occasion and accepted by the people with whom you are.

q. The main fault of black powder were the dense clouds of smoke it generated.

r. Probably the reason for this unfortunate situation are that salaries are low and that the profession is not in higher esteem.

s. If, while an important international story was breaking, a movie star decides to jump out of a hotel window, the *American* would give the headline to the suicide.

t. This newspaper puts its own interpretation on political matters and often withholds information that conflicts with their viewpoint.

u. He passed the examination, which surprised nobody more than he.

v. He fell into a puddle, which broke his leg, and now he is laid up.

w. The tomb had laid buried in the desert for centuries.

x. Many people take pills without a doctor's prescription. This is unwise. They begin by taking habit-forming sedatives only when they cannot sleep or when they are tense. But it is not long before they can't do without them, and they increase the dose until all it does is make them worse.

y. Suddenly the Doctor heard screams. Rushing toward them, he found that a locomotive had ploughed into a train loaded with coal miners. He springs into action, operating on the miners with whatever instruments he can lay hands on. He works alone for an hour. Finally, help arrived in the form of a well-equipped ambulance.

z. That day the Doctor saved the lives of ten miners and alleviated the pain of many others. As I look back on the incident, I see him in the role of a great humanitarian. He is the hero in my home town and always will be.

2. Some, but not all, of the items below are confusing or ineffective because of wordy, unidiomatic, inept, or inexact expression. State precisely what the trouble is with each faulty item, and revise to make it satisfactory in General writing.

a. This book is written on the order of a biography.

b. Since his son died, he seldom ever appears in public.

c. Football commands a predominating interest in this country.

d. It is ironic that we are diffident to jazz, which we created.

e. The door was a mystery as to its function.

f. We plan on driving home Tuesday.

g. In this day when the words "balance of power" are bantered about, a ban on nuclear weapons is paramountly important.

h. The history of human thought takes vehement issue with the idea that the scientist can live in an ivory tower.

i. From the desk you have a perspective into my back yard. View-wise it isn't much—a few scraggly pines, some spindly bushes, and a lawn fractured by the feet of kids who won't stick to the path.

j. With no other alternation before me, I hitchhiked home.

k. Every teacher has a different method to teach poetry.

l. The snow covers the dead foliage and dormant ground, and transposes the world into a sparkling fairyland.

m. His parents were too dominant and showed him no affection.

n. The exercises are found on the page opposite of the rules.

o. He is as competent if not more so than the previous mayor.

p. Students should not be regulated to a fixed position because of their parents' social status or wealth.

q. Many of her actions are synonymous of a thirteen-year-old.

r. Camping tests your ability of roughing it in the open.

s. Because I have been to Niagara Falls a number of times I have learned a numerous amount of facts about this phenomena.

t. This chain reaction of discoveries influenced society greatly.

u. The people all looked as if they were either coming or going back to a soft office job.

v. As a critic he is seldom if ever fair.

w. In my opinion, I think his harsh criticism stems from jealousy.

3. Study the choice of words and phrases in each of the items below, paying particular attention to imagery, to figures of speech, and to words used for their connotative values. For each item, explain why you consider the choice of words effective or ineffective.

a. Ireland is an old sow that eats her farrow.—JAMES JOYCE

b. Using a language may be compared to riding a horse; much of one's success depends upon an understanding of what it *can* and *will* do.—RICHARD M. WEAVER

c. In the argument between Snow's "two cultures," the humanities certainly have the advantage of their spokesmen's much greater mastery of the weapons of controversy. In the hands of Barzun, the word becomes a sharp rapier, used with the skill of a fencing champion.—EUGENE RABINOWITCH

d. White is one of those people who write the word intellectual in quotation marks, as though holding it at a distance in the tweezers of disdain. "The 'intellectuals' within the old Administration . . ."—*Newsweek,* June 8, 1964

e. Miss Tyler, eye-catching in a white wool suit with large black buttons, flashed a restrained smile as she entered the marble-columned caucus room. Once seated, her face froze into a mask of smoldering irritability as photographers swarmed around the witness stand snapping pictures.—Chicago *Sun-Times,* Feb. 27, 1964

f. Like a giant caldron the screen boils with life, and Kurosawa's telescopic lenses, spooning deep, lift the depths to the surface and hurl the whole mess in the spectator's face.—*Time,* Sept. 21, 1962

g. Adjustment is the word. So it would seem that the overall purpose of most primary education in modern America is to turn out friendly people free of neuroses and the critical sense which makes its possessor gnash his teeth at the calculated insults to the human intelligence perpetrated by politicians and advertisers in a television-consumer society. Nice work if you can get it; even nicer work if you can get away with it indefinitely.—HUGH MAC-LENNAN

h. So it's swish, thump, bumpbumpbumpabumpitybump and we are aground in Lima, Peru, storied Lima, sparkling jewel midst a fairyland of sparkling palm trees, sparkling Spanish eyes and sparkling soda pop.—RICHARD BISSELL

i. The quarrel between stay-at-home and expatriate is a blistering and unattractive one. Young writers, actors and directors who find Canada too bland and parochial for their taste, have left because they are bored and because there is no more than farm-club opportunity for them at home. But the stay-at-home has it that only those who prefer being big fish in a small pond have stayed behind. Well, yes, possibly, but not quite. Naturally there are many who appear to be whales because they limit their splashing to the shallow standards of the Canadian pond, but as a Canadian living in London I must admit that while many expatriates are well-known, nobody has made himself artistically indispensable here.—MORDECAI RICHLER

j. Books for children should be imaginative, not realistic. A child's fancy is fragile and will wither soon enough. Why, then, subject it sooner than necessary to the cold frost of adult reason?

k. Our new house is going to be splendiferous and right up to the minute.

l. So at last, to make a long story short, he is caught between the devil and the deep blue sea.

m. From the beach at the edge of the fishing village, the ocean and sky seemed like the flat backdrop of a stage on which ruddy sails and sun had been painted.

n. Impassioned, impersonal Gargantuan stage upon which thousands of unheard of, ne'er mentioned dramas are enacted daily by thousands of unheard of, ne'er mentioned actors. Graveyard of frustrated desires and shattered hopes. Concrete juggernaut whose massive wheels, propelled by the expediency of the moment, ceaselessly crush, grind, and remold the lives of countless millions of men and women. Yet through this chaos a certain order and efficiency is maintained in the mundane matters of workaday world; there is birth and there is death; there is love and there is hate; there is happiness and there is sorrow. This is New York.

o. The lurid, greenish glow of the streetlight showed a woman covered with blood. Thick, ropy blood oozed slowly from angry abrasions on the side of her head, and a stream of bright gore spouted like a geyser from a cut on the bridge of her nose.

p. Of course, girls should have a college education. A man wants more than a brood sow for a wife.

q. A grey mist overhung Nature like a pall. The somber shroud wrapped in oblivion lifeless forms which had been so beautiful in their summer splendor. The branches of the trees, shorn of their green raiment, appeared like spectral fingers reaching up to the somber, low-hanging clouds. Stunted shrubs, less bold, groveled to the ground. Closer still to the earth huddled withered blades of grass, corpses of the gallant, green-clad knights of early May. The staunch little soldiers of spring and summer were no more; they had succumbed in the battle with wind and storm. Faded autumn leaves stirred restlessly with every puff of wind, but seemed unwilling to leave the protection of Mother Earth's embrace.

r. The oak trees on our street were honest and forthright. The bark was not just a grey skin but was solidly rigid and dark. In the winter they stood heavy and black against the sky, while other trees threw up mere bundles of twigs. In the spring, they did not creep out in pale green mistiness, like the other trees; they waited until they were sure, and then they came out in great confident clots. When summer winds blew, the oaks never trembled. They surged mightily, sighing fiercely. And in the fall, their leaves fell like stiff wrapping paper, and their seeds, which were not of membrane and cotton but of wood, bounced smartly when they fell on the sidewalks, and popped loudly in the fires.

4. Review the passages listed below, some by professional writers, some by students. For each passage in which you consider the writer's

choice of words to be unusually good, single out the words and phrases that contribute most to the effectiveness of the passage, and explain the effect they create. Rewrite any passage you find to be ineffective, improving it in any way you can.

Terres, p. 32
Student, "Bits and
  Pieces," pp. 106-107
Balliett, pp. 123-124
Stegner, p. 146
Berendt, pp. 152-153

Student, pp. 166-167
Wright, p. 184
Student, exercise 6a, p. 188
Student, exercise 6e, p. 190
Sanderson, pp. 200-201
Zitner, p. 269

5. Examine your dictionary and write out answers to these questions: What is the title, the date of original copyright (on the back of the title page), the date of the latest copyright, and who is the publisher? What supplementary sections are included at the beginning and end? Approximately how many entries are there? Is there a supplement of new words? Where are biographical and geographical names listed? Where is the key that explains the symbols used in giving pronunciations? When several definitions of a word are given, in what order do they appear—in historical order, in order of frequency, or in some other order? What usage labels (or restrictive labels) does your dictionary use, and what does each label mean?

6. Look up the words below in your dictionary to see what usage labels, if any, are applied to them. If different dictionaries are used by your classmates, compare labels. How do you account for differences?

bobby	dead set	honeymoon	pester
bogus	dead pan	honky-tonk	snide
clepe	enthuse	hush puppy	tizzy
clime	fain	nobby	whiz

7. From newspapers, conversations, and television and radio programs, make a list of new words—words too recent to be included in your dictionary. For each word, explain how you know or can guess at the meaning intended by the speaker or writer.

8. Class exercise: Take four or five minutes to write down all the connotations and associations which a given word (suggested by your instructor) has for you. Then on the blackboard put the core of meaning (denotation), the connotations common to the members of the class in order of frequency, and the personal connotations peculiar to individual members of the class.

9. Select a current issue that has stirred up a good deal of controversy. From your reading in newspapers and magazines, find two discussions of the issue, one in which words are used in an irresponsible or slanted fashion and one in which words are used responsibly. Write a page or two comparing and contrasting the two passages.

Chapter Ten

REVISING PUNCTUATION, MECHANICS, AND SPELLING

*Good punctuation is possible only in good writing.
If sentence structure is lame or stiff, punctuation
is only patchwork,
helping after a fashion but also showing how bad the
word pattern is.*

George Summey, Jr.

For most writers, the final stage in revising a paper is checking its punctuation, mechanics, and spelling. Carelessness in
such matters is seldom excused—even by readers who are
chiefly interested in the content—and this stage should never
be hurried. Punctuation is not always absolutely necessary to
make printed or written material intelligible, as is evident
from school exercises which require the student to supply the
proper marks in an unpunctuated group of words; if the student couldn't understand how they were related, he couldn't
punctuate them. Spelling mistakes, too, however eccentric,
seldom leave a reader totally bewildered as to what word was
meant. Nevertheless, there are two compelling reasons for the
proper use of punctuation and other mechanics such as capital
letters and italics: first, to make the material easier to read
and, second, along with correct spelling and Standard English,
to make it acceptable to cultivated readers.

Punctuation and mechanics

Punctuation is closely related to sentence structure. Punctuation marks are signs that indicate the relationship of words
within a sentence (and of sentences within a paragraph). They
join words and word groups, they separate words and word-

groups, and they perform other important functions. Therefore, a thorough knowledge of the structure of the sentence is
essential to an intelligent application of the conventions of
punctuation. Though accurate punctuation cannot redeem a
confused sentence—one that needs rewriting—it may save a
weak sentence from hopeless ambiguity, and it can make a
complicated sentence clear and meaningful.

For the writer, punctuation[1] is an indispensable aid to clear,
efficient communication. Properly used, punctuation reflects
and supplements the spoken signs of meaning. Misused, it
distorts those signs and confuses the reader. The placing of a
comma after one word rather than another can significantly
alter the meaning conveyed.

Some of the punctuation marks in written English are a
substitute for, or a reminder of, elements in our speech for
which we have no written equivalents; thus, in some of their
uses, the comma, the semicolon, and the period are visual
indications of patterns of pitch and pause in our speech. This
correspondence between punctuation and certain features of
speech is so imprecise, however, that no writer can afford to
rely on it to any great extent. Moreover, a mark like the
apostrophe (sometimes discussed as an aspect of spelling) corresponds to nothing in our speech, and its uses in writing must
be learned as an arbitrary set of conventions.

The placing of the apostrophe and the conventions governing the use of capital letters and some other matters of
mechanics are so well established that every careful writer observes them. But though some rules seem to be fixed and invariable, others need to be stated with qualifications and
exceptions. When a writer has a choice among alternative
methods of punctuating, he may be guided by such matters as
emphasis, tone, and movement in the sentence or perhaps by
the intention of an entire paragraph. He needs to consider also
the choices offered him in terms of "open" and "close" punctuation.

One group of marks can illustrate the choices often possible.
The comma, semicolon, and period may be used to separate
elements or statements, depending on the degree of separation
to be indicated. A comma makes a slight separation, a semi-

---

[1]See Summey for the most thorough study of current punctuation practices (books cited
by name of author only will be found in the Bibliography, pp. xiii-xiv) ; see also Harold
Whitehall, *Structural Essentials of English* (New York, 1956), Ch. 10. The stylebooks of
publishing houses treat punctuation and have had an important influence in establishing
current practices because the editors change the manuscripts they print to conform to
these rules. Though the practices vary somewhat among publications, they agree on
most points.

colon a somewhat greater separation, and a period a complete separation. Look at these versions of the same statement:

1. The person, the time, the place, the purpose, the preliminary assumptions—these enter into all discussions of human affairs; it seems impossible to conceive of any discussion without these features.

2. The person; the time; the place; the purpose; the preliminary assumptions: these enter into all discussions of human affairs. It seems impossible to conceive of any discussion without these features.

3. The person. The time. The place. The purpose. The preliminary assumptions. These enter into all discussions of human affairs. It seems impossible to conceive of any discussion without these features.

The first version is the most rapid, holding the elements most closely together; the second is more emphatic and slower; the third gives still more emphasis to each element but moves much more rapidly than the second. Charles A. Beard actually wrote it the third way (*The Discussion of Human Affairs,* p. 14), giving the statements still more emphasis by having them stand as a complete paragraph. The second version seems unnecessarily Formal and not likely to be used. The first would be appropriate to a more General style.

Another group of marks that have much the same meaning but different tone consists of two commas, two dashes, or parentheses used to "set off" part of a statement. Consider the emphasis on *but actually turns out to be a help* in these four versions of the same sentence:

1. One thing which at first seems to be an obstacle for an athlete but actually turns out to be a help is the fact that he usually has less spare time than a nonathlete.

2. One thing which at first seems to be an obstacle for an athlete, but actually turns out to be a help, is the fact that he usually has less spare time than a nonathlete.

3. One thing which at first seems to be an obstacle for an athlete— but actually turns out to be a help—is the fact that he usually has less spare time than a nonathlete.

4. One thing which at first seems to be an obstacle for an athlete (but actually turns out to be a help) is the fact that he usually has less spare time than a nonathlete.

The first version might be found in a General style using as few marks as possible. The second, with commas, throws more emphasis on *but actually turns out to be a help,* the idea that

The Principal Punctuation Marks

1. *Sentence marks,* used principally to mark the end of sentences:

   .   *Period,* at the end of statements (and after abbreviations, in decimals, dollars and cents, and so on)

   ?   *Question mark* (interrogation point), at the end of questions: He said, "Do you want to come?" Not used after indirect questions: He asked if we wanted to come.

   !   *Exclamation mark* (exclamation point), at the end of an exclamation or vigorously stressed sentence

   ...   *Ellipsis,* after a statement that is left uncompleted, or a speech that is allowed to die away

2. *Internal marks,* used to separate or to indicate the relation between elements within a sentence:

   ,   *Comma,* the most common mark, basically a mark of slight separation between words, phrases, or clauses. It has a number of routine uses, as in *dates.

   ;   *Semicolon,* indicating a degree of separation greater than that marked by a comma and slightly less than that marked by a period

   :   *Colon,* a mark of anticipation, pointing to what follows. It is used after the salutation of a business letter and to introduce formal quotations, explanatory statements, or series too long or too heavy to be prefaced by a comma or a dash.

   —   *Dash,* a mark of separation more intense than a comma. It is used when the construction of a sentence is abruptly broken or when a note of surprise or feeling is indicated. Two dashes may set off a parenthetical expression.

   ( )   *Parentheses,* used to enclose an explanatory statement not built into the construction of a sentence

   [ ]   *Brackets,* used to enclose matter that has been inserted in quotations and as parentheses within parentheses

3. *Quotation marks* (" "), used to enclose speeches in real or imagined conversation and any short quoted words or statements

4. *Apostrophe* ('), used to indicate the possessive (genitive) case of nouns; also the omission of letters in contractions

is to be developed in the rest of the paper; the dashes emphasize it still more, while the parentheses subordinate it, make it
less essential than the writer intended it to be.

More complicated (not necessarily longer) sentences need
more and heavier marks (semicolons rather than commas,
perhaps) to guide the readers; shorter and more direct sentences need fewer. The preference in General English today is
for rather open punctuation, using the marks conventionally
expected and only as many more as may be required for clarity.
Writers who use more marks often do so because they need
them in their rather elaborate sentences but often also because
they follow a tradition of close punctuation. The following
passage, given with close punctuation and then with open,
illustrates some of the differences between the two styles:

Close punctuation

Now, the chief literary and dramatic vice of the scientists and philosophers is that they seldom begin at the point of the reader's or hearer's interest. Here, for example, is a book on botany. It begins with a long ac-count of the history of botany, and continues with an even longer account of the general principles of the science. But what do you, or what do I, want to know about the feeble begin-nings of botany? We want to know—provided, of course, that we want to be something more than the ladylike botanists who know only the names of flowers— we want to know what the prob-lems of botany are; in what direction botanical research is tending; what differences all this botanical research makes anyway; why it is worth studying.

Open punctuation

Now the chief literary and dramatic vice of the scientists and philosophers is that they seldom begin at the point of the reader's or hearer's interest. Here for example is a book on botany. It begins with a long account of the history of botany and con-tinues with an even longer ac-count of the general principles of the science. But what do you or what do I want to know about the feeble beginnings of botany? We want to know, provided of course that we want to be some-thing more than the ladylike bot-anists who know only the names of flowers, we want to know what the problems of botany are, in what direction botanical research is tending, what differences all this botanical research makes anyway, why it is worth study-ing.

Because students typically write in rather short and direct
sentences, they usually are encouraged to follow the open
custom. The movement of this forty-four-word sentence, from

an article in the *Saturday Review* on "Theatre in Cleveland," shows how directness removes the need for internal marks.

Is the pattern of community theatre changing from what it was not so many years ago when its function was to present a menu of light comedies and glamorous dramas that had received the stamp of approval from Broadway critics a few seasons earlier?

In the following review of the principal punctuation situations, special attention is given to those in which usage is divided or a choice of marks is possible. (Articles on the individual marks will be found in the *Index*.)

At ends of sentences • In the great majority of sentences no question arises about end punctuation. Most sentences (and minor sentences) are statements and are marked by a period.

A question mark is used after a clear-cut question: *How did the rebels plan the attack?* It stands immediately after a question that is included within a sentence: *What do all these facts prove? you may ask.* (A comma might be used here, giving a good deal less emphasis to the question: *What do all these facts prove, you may ask.*) A question mark is not generally used after a request phrased as a question (*Will you please give this your immediate attention.*), though it might be used in rather Formal style. A question mark is not used after an indirect question: *He asked his mother why he could not leave the house on Saturday.* (The direct question would be: *He asked his mother, "Why can't I leave the house on Saturday?"*)

The exclamation mark is used mainly in transcribing speech and is therefore seldom appropriate except in writing conversation. It indicates strong emotion, usually feelings of surprise, incredulity, or determination. The single-word exclamations range from strong ones like *Ouch!* that would almost always carry an exclamation mark to mild ones like *Oh* that might warrant one or might deserve only a comma. But aside from dialog, exclamation marks are little used except in advertising and in some excited personal writing.

Between subjects, verbs, objects • Commas should *not* be used between the main elements of a clause or sentence, between its subject and verb or between its verb and object or complement, or between a preposition and its object. The temptation to punctuate these elements is strongest when they are long or are themselves clauses. There should be no mark where the brackets stand in the following sentences. (Do not be misled by the fact that in speech there would often be a pause where the brackets are.)

Subject and verb: My friend estimated that the average news program that is fit to be put on the air [ ] takes one man approximately five hours to prepare.

Verb and object: We all know [ ] that the person who is hard-working and willing has a good deal put over on him.

The manager frequently said [ ] if he had his way the project would be abandoned. (The clause is a direct object, not a quotation formally introduced by a construction like *He said*. See p. 398.)

Preposition and object: He would not have done it except [ ] that everyone was daring him to.

Formal, old-fashioned writing occasionally uses a comma between a long subject and its verb; for example, it might add a comma after *air* to the sentence above beginning "My friend estimated . . ." but this practice is not current and not advisable in student writing.

The verbs in a compound predicate (two verbs having the same subject) should not be separated by a comma unless one is needed to prevent misreading or to point up a contrast.

Compound predicate: Thus in fifteen years rabbit raising has ceased to be a hobby [ ] and has taken a definite place among the industries of the world.

Pop could talk himself out of trouble [ ] and also talk himself into a lot of trouble. (A comma might be used in this sentence to emphasize the contrast.)

Sometimes several subjects of the same verb (compound subject) are summarized by a word like *all*. This summarizing word is usually preceded by a dash.

The characters, the plot, the theme, the scene—all are trite in this play.

Between coordinate clauses • A comma between the clauses of a compound sentence connected by *and, nor, or, yet* emphasizes their distinctness and gives the writing a slightly slower pace. Formal writing ordinarily has a comma; General writing is less likely to have one unless the clauses are long or have different subjects. The use of a comma is advisable if its absence allows the possibility of misreading.

They read novels by the dozen and they write a report on every one. (Closely related clauses; comma unnecessary.)

Most textbooks have tended to encourage close punctuation, and students sometimes try to see how many commas they can put in. (Clauses have different subjects; comma optional but convenient.)

These increased orders meant a demand for labor, and workers began to stream in from all parts of the state. (Clauses have different subjects; comma necessary so that the reader will not be misled into reading *a demand for labor and workers.*)

Commas are ordinarily used between clauses connected by *but* or *for*:

There are recognizable dialects in the United States, but they show fewer differences than would be expected in a country of such size.

Yet this is not a characteristic test, for the same reaction is given by several other aromatic compounds.

When there is no connective between the clauses, or when they are connected by a conjunctive adverb (*however, therefore* . . .), a semicolon is used:

No connective: In rather formal papers for college courses and in theses, Formal usage should be followed; in other college papers, either General or Formal may be used, as the instructor prefers.

Conjunctive adverb: Medical schools keep requesting the colleges not to teach "medical subjects"; however [,] they still give the advantage in admissions to students with a good deal of chemistry and zoology.

(See also "Revising comma faults," Ch. 8, pp. 290-294.)
When the second clause of a compound sentence repeats the idea or makes specific the meaning of the first, a colon is used:

There is one thing that I am sure of now: at this stage of his experience he should have followed my advice.

When the writer shifts his construction abruptly or wishes to emphasize the separateness of the clauses, a dash may be used:

How many times she must have said this before—I shuddered at the simple thought.

Clauses of the type *the more . . . the more* or *the more . . . the greater* ordinarily have no mark:

Just when she had scrubbed the last corner, a wall receded and the room grew larger, and the more she scrubbed the greater the room became—until finally she was scrubbing a multitude of limitless rooms with cold marble floors.—Edna O'Brien, "Lovely to Look At, Delightful to Hold," *The New Yorker,* Mar. 28, 1964, p. 42

After preceding subordinate elements • A comma is used after a subordinate clause or long phrase that precedes the main clause, especially in Formal style. A comma is not used in General writing if the preceding element is short and closely related to what follows, especially if the two clauses have the same subject.

Comma not necessary: As soon as they register they must pay their fees.

Comma optional: When we lost the fourth of the six games, [or no mark] we just about gave up.

Comma needed: Because so much of the land has been taken for farms, regions where birds and wild animals can live have been greatly reduced. (Clauses have different subjects.)

Comma with long phrase: In a society without hereditary social standing, a person's job is the chief sign of his status.

Short preceding modifiers should not be punctuated unless a comma is necessary to give special emphasis or to prevent misreading:

Soon [ ] we were at the gym and in less time than usual were in our uniforms.

In my opinion [ ] these youthful marriages are absolutely justifiable.

Several times in recent years [ ] one of the heavy tractors has sunk out of sight in the thick winter mud.

When you do think it wise to separate a subordinate element from the rest of the sentence, be sure to use a comma, not a semicolon:

Because learning to live together is so much harder than learning to fight each other, [not ;] the nations of the world make little progress toward peace.

Before subordinate elements • The punctuation of words, phrases, and clauses coming after the words they modify depends on the closeness of the semantic relationship between the modifier and its headword.

Close or restrictive modifiers—no commas. A modifier that closely limits or restricts the meaning of its headword is not set off by commas. The principal type is the restrictive adjective clause:

Boys *who are supposedly wild* should not be sent to a strict preparatory school. (Not all boys are supposedly wild.)

The man *who had the aisle seat* had to get up four times.

The house *that burned* was pretty well gone to pieces anyway. (Most adjective clauses beginning with *that* are restrictive.)

The first three cars *we saw* were going the wrong way. (See "Long and short constructions," p. 317.)

Other close modifiers are epithets and occupations that are treated as part of a name (Charles the Good, Lang the baker) or that obviously limit a noun (His friends Jock and Harry were the first to arrive) and adverbial clauses that would be spoken without a pause:

He must have left *because he had another appointment.*

A freshman has a chance to see all that is going on at a fraternity *when he is a guest at dinner.*

Loose or nonrestrictive modifiers—commas. A modifier that does not limit the headword (in the sense of altering the meaning) but simply adds descriptive details is marked by a comma, or by two commas if it does not come at the end of the sentence.

Another time Frank spent an unforgettable week with his father, *who had broken a leg and was unable to go to the office.*

A. T. Fowler, *assistant professor of zoology,* teaches the course.

His best friend, *Jock,* was the first to come.

Old Nat, *who had been a great fisherman in his day,* wouldn't believe our story.

He must have left, *because his coat and hat are gone.*

One helpful test is to read such sentences aloud. Contrast the sound of these sentences:

The man *who was standing at the head of the line* had been there since five o'clock. (No pause or tone change—restrictive, no comma)

Bill, *who was standing at the head of the line,* had been there since five o'clock. (Slight pause and drop in tone on *Bill*—non-restrictive, commas)

He must have left *because he had another appointment.* (No pause or tone change—close modifier, no comma)

He must have left, *because his coat and hat are gone.* (Slight pause and tone change—loose modifier, comma)

Frequently a writer has a choice of using or not using commas with a following modifier, using them if he wants to emphasize a slight relation, not using them if he wishes the sentence elements to seem more closely related. In sentences like the following, commas might or might not be used around the italicized expressions, depending on the emphasis desired:

The man *who had previously glanced at us* now really stared.

We must *of course* face the facts.

The atmosphere is completed when you are greeted by the doorman *dressed up like a vaudeville admiral.*

The best test is reading the passage aloud, using commas if you change your voice and pause slightly before the modifier, not using them if you read without change.

A phrase modifying the whole clause is set off by a comma:

The time per sample varies, *depending on the nature of the sample being run.*

"How'd you like to go to the game tomorrow?" he asked, *much to my surprise.*

"Why, I would like to very much," I answered, *hoping he was serious.*

Do not use a semicolon to set off the sort of modifiers just described:

It takes quite a bit of courage to start *War and Peace,* [not ;] because it is not only long but has a lot of characters with curious Russian names.

Around interrupting elements • A phrase or clause that interrupts the direct movement of the sentence should be set off by *two* commas, not just one:

This last semester, *if it has done nothing else,* has given me confidence in myself.

Over in the corner, *beside the dark and broken window where a newspaper was stuffed to keep out the rain,* sat Verona.

Did intelligent people, *he asked himself,* do things like that?

Usage is divided over setting off short parenthetical words and phrases like *incidentally* and *of course.* Sometimes their use or omission makes a difference in emphasis:

These early attempts, of course, brought no results.

These early attempts of course brought no results.

The famous artist, oddly enough, preferred the company of common laborers to that of his own kind.

The famous artist oddly enough preferred the company of common laborers to that of his own kind.

Adverbs that modify the verb or the statement closely should not be set off by commas when they are in their natural position:

Perhaps [ ] they had never intended to come.

They had never intended to come, perhaps.

When a *conjunctive adverb[1] stands after the first phrase .in its clause, as it often does, it is set off by commas, and often it is set off when it stands first in the clause:

The next morning, however, they all set out as though nothing had happened.

The second plan, therefore, was the one determined upon for the holiday.

However, [or no comma] they all set out the next morning as though nothing had happened.

But and other coordinating conjunctions are a part of the clauses in which they appear and should not be followed by commas:

I was positive that if someone would just give me some guidance I could do much better, but [ ] the semester continued the same as before.

---

[1]Throughout this book, references to *Index* articles are indicated by an asterisk (*).

Dashes are occasionally used to emphasize a parenthetical expression:

They think that they are the last radicals—and the greatest—and that their ideas and their works will live forever.

Parentheses are used to enclose added details or illustrations not built into the construction of a sentence or to subordinate a side remark by the writer.

The few verb endings that English now retains (*–s, –ed, –ing*) are being still further reduced in ordinary speech.
The largest additions to the territory of the United States (the Louisiana Purchase and Alaska) were gained by purchase.

A punctuation mark belonging to a part of a sentence that includes parentheses comes *after* the second parenthesis:

There are several words of foreign origin that keep their original plural forms (like *alumnae, alumni, analyses*), and many that have two forms (like appendix, cactus, formula) .

Square brackets [ ] are used chiefly as parentheses within parentheses or to mark words supplied in a direct quotation which are not those of the person quoted:

Each pronunciation of *process* (/pros′ es/ and [much less commonly] /prō′ ses/) has a history.
According to Dr. Roberts, "It [the institution of private property] is in our time under attack in many parts of the world."

(See *Parentheses and *Brackets.)

In lists and series ● Commas separate the items of a series of three or more short elements:

When to get up, when to eat, when to work, when to have fun, when to go to bed were all laid down in the regulations.

Commas are not used when the items are joined by connectives:

Fire insurance and life insurance and accident insurance and car insurance and all other forms of insurance are bets placed on odds more or less scientifically determined.

Usage is divided as to a comma before the last member of a series when it has a connective (literature, painting, sculpture, music, and drama, / literature, painting, sculpture, music and drama) unless some misinterpretation would result, as when the last item itself contains a connective (tired, dirty, and black and blue). A writer should be consistent in this use or nonuse of the final comma, but he has the option of choosing whichever practice is more appropriate to the other traits of his style. If he is writing for a particular publication, he should follow its style (see *Series):

The typical freshman's program includes English, social studies, a language[,] and some sort of science.

Two items connected by *and* are not punctuated:

In high school the student is paid ten dollars a month for helping the teachers in their work [ ] and for doing odd jobs about the school building.

A construction formally introducing a series is followed by a colon (a mark that looks ahead, as the salutation of a letter [*Gentlemen:*] looks ahead to the text of the letter):

The town has four landmarks: the Town Hall, the Baptist Church, the Memorial Library, and Lincoln Park.

The colon is not used if the sentence continues past the series:

The town's four landmarks—the Town Hall, the Baptist Church, the Memorial Library, and Lincoln Park—have been carefully preserved by the citizens.

When several adjectives modify a single noun, commas are used between them:

When the long, cold, lonesome evenings came, we would gather about the old wood stove and eat the chestnuts.

In this sentence there are commas between *long—cold—lonesome* because each stands in the same relation to the noun *evenings*. But there is no comma between *old* and *wood* because *old* modifies *wood stove* rather than just *stove*. A comma following *old* would throw more emphasis upon *wood* and might sometimes be wanted. Compare these two versions:

The room presents a colonial effect with its old-fashioned, cross-beamed ceiling and gray, brick fireplace.

The room presents a colonial effect with its old-fashioned cross-beamed ceiling and gray brick fireplace.

Either version is acceptable but in the first *cross-beamed* and *brick* stand out as separate modifiers of their nouns.

For clarity and emphasis • A comma tends to keep distinct the constructions it separates and to emphasize slightly the construction that follows the mark:

Temporarily the wine industry was all but ruined, and farmers turned to dairying, and to cooperation to give them a market.

This is especially true when a connective is omitted:

And afterwards I told her how I felt, how I kept feeling about her.

Often a comma can guide a reader in interpreting a sentence and make it unnecessary for him to go back over it for meaning because he has mistaken the grouping of the words. *For* or *but* may be either a conjunction or a preposition, and confusion may be avoided by using a comma before either when it is used as a conjunction:

He talked about Germany but he never went, for money was too scarce to spend on voyages. (To avoid reading "went for money")

The surgeon's face showed no emotion, but anxiety and a little nervousness must be seething behind that impassive mask. (To avoid reading "no emotion but anxiety")

It is not necessary to have a session like this very often, but when you do, get everything off your mind that is disturbing you. (Not: but when you do get everything off your mind. . . .)

After all, the students had gone quietly. (Not: After all the students. . . .)

When the same word occurs consecutively a comma may be used, though usage is divided:

What the trouble really is, is of no interest to him.

Around quotations • Quotation marks are used to enclose real or imagined speeches, conversation, and short excerpts from printed matter. Either double quotations marks (" ") or single quotation marks (' ') may be used for a quotation, though the double marks are much more common. If there is a quotation within a quotation, the marks are alternated:

"The first eight I called on answered, 'Not prepared,'" Miss Stoddard complained.

Or: 'The first eight I called on answered, "Not prepared,"' Miss Stoddard complained.

When a speech is introduced by a formula like *he said,* the quotation is preceded by a comma. If the speech is built into the construction of the sentence, there is no preceding comma:

We are taught that "thou shalt not kill," but in war we ignore it.

The following passage shows the typical uses of quotation marks and paragraphing for conversation:

A man and a woman stood on the observation platform of a large eastern airport. In the distance a light plane roared down the runway and took off toward the far horizon.

The man said, "That's the way to travel. No waiting around. When you feel like going, you go."

"Well!" The woman seemed shocked. "You'd never get me into one of those things!"

"What? But you've flown before."

"In an airliner, yes," the woman said, "but that's different. Why, I'd no more trust my life in one of those—those kites than...."

Most American publishers put a comma or a period inside the closing quotation mark, regardless of whether it belongs to the quotation or to the sentence as a whole. A colon or a semicolon, on the other hand, is conventionally placed outside the closing quotation mark.

Exclamation points and question marks stand inside the quotation marks if the quotation is an exclamation or question:

Then suddenly he shouted, "Get out of here, all of you!"
You don't mean that he actually said "You're another"!
She asked, "Won't you please try to do it for me?"
Did she say, "Please try to do it"?

In expository matter quotations of more than one sentence are often indented and printed in smaller type without quotation marks—as is frequently done in this book. In longhand manuscript simply indent such quotations about half an inch; in typed copy, indent and single space. (For further details see *Quotation marks.)

In conventional positions • Besides indicating parts of sentences, periods and commas have several conventional uses; some of the more common ones are listed here. Uses of the period:

1. *Abbreviations:* Dec. N.C. e.g. vol. When the letters of the abbreviation are frequently spoken instead of the words they stand for, the period often is not used: CIO, TVA, USSR (see *Abbreviations § 3).

2. *Dollars and cents:* $12.48 $0.87 (but not in 87 cents, 87¢). See *Money.

3. *Decimals:* .4 .04 14.33 (but 4%, 4 percent).

Some conventional uses of the comma are:

1. *In dates,* between the day of the month and the year: May 20, 1965. When only the month and year are given, a comma is not necessary (May 1965), though it is frequently found (May, 1965). See *Dates.

2. *In addresses,* between town and state or city and country when they stand on the same line: Waco, Texas; Seattle, King County, Washington; Casablanca, Morocco.

3. *After the salutation of personal letters:* Dear Fred,

4. *In figures,* grouping digits by threes: 6,471,063

5. *After names followed by titles or degrees:* A. H. Hazen, Ph.D.; Arthur Garfield Hays, Esq.; J. F. Forsythe, Jr.; Annie T. Bowditch, Secretary.

6. *After exclamations* like *well, oh, why* when they are not emphatic.

Using apostrophes • The apostrophe has three chief uses:

1. It is the graphic sign of the possessive (genitive) of nouns. In a singular noun the apostrophe ordinarily comes before the *−s: the secretary's report, today's lesson, my driver's license, the company's retirement plan.* In a plural noun the apostrophe ordinarily comes after the *−s: the doctors' offices, the secretaries' records, the companies' retirement plan.* (See *Genitive case for exceptions.)

2. It also marks the possessive of the indefinite pronouns— *anybody's, anyone's, everybody's, somebody's, somebody else's.*

3. An apostrophe is used in contractions, indicating that a sound is omitted in speaking an unstressed syllable, especially when *not* is reduced to *n't: aren't, can't, doesn't, isn't, I'll, it's*

(as the contraction of *it is:* It's late). Only one apostrophe is used in *shan't, won't.* An apostrophe is also used in such phrases as *the class of '66.*

An apostrophe should not be used in the possessive of personal pronouns. No apostrophe is used in *his, hers, its (its* end, *its* cause), *ours, yours, theirs, whose.* Nor is it used in conventionally clipped (shortened) words: *ad, phone, varsity.*

Using capital letters • The principal uses of capital letters in English are well standardized and give very little trouble. These are: first words of sentences, names of people and places, proper adjectives derived from these names, days of the week, months, the important words in *titles, ordinarily the first word of a line of verse, the pronoun *I*, the exclamation *O*, nouns and pronouns referring to divine beings, and names of companies and organizations.

Some items formerly capitalized are no longer: the seasons, points of the compass (except when they refer to a region, *the Southwest*), common nouns derived from proper names when they have lost the suggestion of the name (*paris green, jersey, macadam, volt, fedora, shrapnel*).

Many class nouns are capitalized when they refer to an individual thing or person: *I dislike all professors* [but] *I dislike Professor Weems. He was taking geography* [but] *He was taking Geography 106.*

Names of members of a family are not capitalized when used as common nouns (*my father, his brother*), but when used specifically, like a proper name, they usually are: *We told Mother what we had done.* Similarly, either *He was in the army* or *He was in the Army* might be used, the first indicating that he was in *an* army, the latter that he was in the United States (or Canadian or French or British) Army. Titles of officials are capitalized when those titles designate specific persons but not otherwise: *the Duke of Normandy* [but] *the dukes and counts joined forces.* The one exception is familiar: the title of the chief executive of the United States is capitalized whether or not the reference is to an individual (President Johnson; the President has the power of the veto).

In the title of a book, article, play, or movie, the first and last words and all other words except articles and the short prepositions and conjunctions are capitalized: *The Brothers Karamazov; A Short History of the United States;* "The Garden Party" (a short story).

Most magazines and books use capitals on words like *street, river, church, hotel, park* when they are parts of proper names, although newspapers do not. Most General writing follows book conventions: *Bond Street, Potomac River, Drake Hotel.*

Capitals may occasionally be used for stylistic reasons, as for emphasis (Her precious Intuition, I suppose), but the practice is now rare and is not recommended. Students tend to use more capital letters than necessary and should limit them to the conventional situations. (See *Capital letters.)

Underlining for italics • Words or statements that would be printed in italics are underlined once in manuscript. Formal, especially academic, writing follows the conventions of book publishing, using italics in a number of standardized places; General writing is more likely to follow newspaper usage, which often replaces italics with quotation marks. The principal uses of italics are:

1. To indicate the titles of books, plays, motion pictures, and other complete works. (Titles of articles, short stories, and short poems are put in quotation marks.)

2. To indicate the titles of periodicals and newspapers: *Harper's Magazine, The New York Times* (or The New York Times). See *Titles of articles, books, etc.

3. To mark words and expressions considered as words rather than for their meaning: There is a shade of difference between *because* and *for* used as conjunctions.

4. To mark words from foreign languages that are not yet regarded as English: *persona non grata, coup d'état, Götterdämmerung;* but not such naturalized borrowings as "chassis," "coup," "blitzkrieg." (For a list see *Foreign words in English.)

5. To emphasize words or statements, especially in factual writing. Spoken emphasis may be represented, though this device is best used sparingly: It was *his* night, all right.

The following *Index* articles deal more fully with problems of punctuation, mechanics, and related matters:

Spelling

No one is a complete master of English spelling, but with the help of a dictionary everyone can manage to spell well enough to meet the expectations of educated readers. First a student needs to understand something of the social pressure for uniform spelling and accept the responsibility for meeting it, and then he needs to discover the sources of his own difficulties, many of which are due to the inconsistencies in English. The rest is work.

The social demand for uniform spelling • Spelling exists only in writing and is therefore not a part of oral language. But it is the very essence of alphabetic writing, and a reasonably consistent spelling is a genuine convenience to a reader because he has become accustomed to the conventional visual form of whole words or phrases. Unusual spellings distract him, make him look twice or even force him to guess at the word, and so interfere with easy communication. Standard spelling makes it easier to list and to find items given in alphabetical order. And it is imperative in some occupations: for secretaries (since many employers need to buy their spelling); for editors, proofreaders, and compositors, who prepare material for printing; and, in general, for people whose writing goes to others without passing through the hands of someone professionally trained in bringing it up to established and accepted standards.

Our present standard spelling was established largely by printers and editors, who naturally wished for consistency in what they printed and now usually revise manuscripts according to the dictionaries or according to their own stylebook lists, which are based on the spellings of the dictionaries.

Mistakes in spelling are easily noticed, even by people who would have difficulty with some of the more complex departures from Standard usage. Consequently, spelling has become a convenient test of literacy and even of respectability. The main reason for "learning to spell" is that educated readers expect to see words in the standard forms and are likely to undervalue a person who does not use them. Employers of college graduates frequently complain that "they can't spell," implying that they do not meet a minimum requirement of education and intelligence. Correct spelling is an important—if superficial—trait of good English.

Reasons for difficulties in spelling • The spelling of English is admittedly bad, compared for instance with that of Italian. We represent the 40-odd sounds of our speech with an alphabet of 26 letters, 3 of which—*c* (or *k*), *q,* and *x*—merely duplicate the work of other letters. The 23 active letters singly and in combinations like *th, ea, sh* have to represent more than 40 distinctive sounds. The difficulty is greatest in the vowels: *a,* for instance, spells the vowel sounds of *lay, lap, far, fare, was,* not to mention untypical words like *many* and the sound of the second *a* in *comparative.*

But the limitations of the alphabet could be largely overcome, as they have been in the spellings of most languages— Italian again, for example—if we could somehow keep pace with our gradually but steadily changing pronunciation. English spelling tradition was established by the thirteenth century and was stabilized chiefly by the printers of the sixteenth and seventeenth centuries. Meanwhile the pronunciation of many words changed, but the spelling did not. This fact accounts for many curious English spellings: *meat* and *meet* once were pronounced differently; *colonel* was a word of three syllables, spelled with an *r* between the *o*'s and pronounced ko-ro-nel; the *gh* in *night, through,* and other words was sounded, as it still often is in Scotland.

The English habit of borrowing words generously from other languages is responsible for such groups as *cite, sight, site,* and for hundreds of words that do not follow conventions of English spelling—*bureau, croquet, hors d'oeuvre, khaki, onomato- poeia.*

An even greater problem comes from our perpetuating spellings that were significant in another language, like the pairs of Latin endings *-ance, -ence* and *-able, -ible.* Each pair is now pronounced the same and has the same meaning so that it is very difficult to remember which one is expected in a particular word.

These facts suggest that though English spelling cannot be defended, both its general confusion and the form of a particular word can be explained by reference to the history of the language.[1]

---

[1]Henry Bradley, *Spoken and Written Language* (Oxford, 1919) ; W. A. Craigie, *English Spelling* (New York, 1927) ; Thomas R. Lounsbury, *English Spelling and Spelling Reform* (New York, 1909); Robertson-Cassidy, Ch. 11, pp. 330-335, 353-373); (books cited by name of author only will be found in the Bibliography, pp. xiii-xiv) K. W. Dykema, "Spelling" in *Encyclopedia Americana,* 1950 and later printings; Donald W. Emery, *Variant Spelling in Modern English Dictionaries* (Champaign, 1958) . The section "Orthography" at the front of the Webster dictionaries, especially the International size, contains a great deal of information about English spelling.

However, when all has been said about the failure of spelling to keep pace with pronunciation, it must also be said that the discrepancy between correct pronunciation and spelling is not such a common cause of misspelling as might be expected. We usually remember the spellings of words that seem furthest from their sound, like the *-ough* words and those with silent letters (de*b*tor, *p*sychology, sa*l*mon), but often misspell words like *arctic* (or *Arctic*), because we fail to pronounce the middle *k* sound, and *sophomore,* in which the second *o* is almost never spoken, and words like *accidentally* and *occasionally,* in which the *-al* is not spoken or is very much cut down in speech. And some words are misspelled because in speech we do not clearly distinguish certain consonants like *t* and *d,* as in *latter* and *ladder;* or the words have variant pronunciations, as in *absurd* and *absorb,* where the *s* may be sounded either as /s/ or /z/.

Occasionally, too, a Nonstandard pronunciation is reflected in spelling (*athelete* for *athlete*), or an unstressed syllable leads to a substitution (*undoubtably* for *undoubtedly*) or to the omission of a letter: *ever* or *evry* for *every, tenative* for *tentative, quanity* for *quantity, continous* for *continuous.*

Suggestions for improving spelling • In spite of its admitted difficulty, fairly correct spelling is possible for anyone, though if you have reached college age without having acquired the knack, it will mean a great deal of work. The goal for a poor speller is to know when and how to check possible errors. The fatal mistake is to give up, to enjoy poor spelling as a hypochondriac enjoys poor health.

The first step, if you are really a poor speller, is to recognize that the demand for standard spelling is an inescapable social fact; in insisting on it your instructors are merely representing the community. The next step is to take the responsibility for your own improvement, to want to improve, and to do something about it. Since difficulties in spelling are highly individual matters, the suggestions that follow will not be equally helpful to everybody. But they are worth trying.

Keep a list of difficult words.   The old suggestion of keeping a spelling notebook is sound. Working on the words that you have misspelled is more valuable than using lists made up by others. Copying short passages that contain words you need to use helps fix them in mind, and writing them from dictation is even better. This lets you write the word in its context and so helps you get accustomed to putting it in a natural setting.

Visualize words in reading.   In reading you do not look at each individual letter of a word but at the word as a unit, and then usually as part of a phrase. In recent years great efforts have been made in the schools to increase the speed of silent reading. As a result, students probably have less clear images of individual words. Since in rapid reading the vowels especially are not seen, the majority of spelling mistakes are in vowels. People vary greatly in the accuracy with which they remember visual images. If your visual memory is weak, you may have to make a special effort to look at some words as you read—particularly common words like *physicist, quiet, quite, pamphlet, separate, similar.*

Use a dictionary.   A college-size dictionary will have all the words you need, and more, and is the best help in checking spelling. If you are quite unsure of a word, you may have to look in more than one place: it may begin with a *g* or a *j* or a *k,* or the first vowel may be an *e* or an *i.* Don't rely on a roommate or someone else who happens to be around—his guess may be no better than yours. Get the dictionary habit, and keep searching.

Learn new words accurately.   With new words, learn both the spoken and written forms at the same time. Making a word your own is chiefly a matter of attention to its sound, its appearance, and its meaning.

Work on confusing forms.   Two closely related words sometimes show differences in spelling that are hard to keep separate: f*ou*r—f*o*rty, compar*a*tive—compar*i*son, consci*ence*—consci*ous,* curi*ous*—curi*o*sity, pron*ou*nce—pron*u*nciation. A vowel may be dropped or changed when an ending is added to a word: ent*er*—ent[ ]rance, disast*er*—disast[ ]rous, maint*ai*n—maint*e*nance. Or the vowel may be retained: temp*er*—temp*era*ment, mount*ai*n—mount*ai*nous. Because such words usually don't show any difference in sound, their spelling has to be learned.

One of the greatest nuisances in our language is a group of prefixes and suffixes with two different forms: **en-, in-; *in-, un-; *-able, -ible; *-ance, -ence; *-er, -or.* The following samples show how common and necessary these groups of words are:

en- (or em-) : embark, enable, enclose (or inclose), encourage, enforce

in-: infuse, inquire, insure (or ensure), instruct

in- (not) : inactive, incompatible, infrequent, impractical
un-: unacceptable, uncontrollable, unrecognizable
-able: advisable, changeable, desirable, laughable, usable
-ible: audible, credible, eligible, flexible, irresistible, legible
-ance: (noun) , -ant (adj.) : attendance—attendant, intolerance—intolerant, resistance—resistant
-ence (noun) , -ent (adj.) : confidence—confident, independence—independent, persistence—persistent
-er: advertiser, consumer, manufacturer, subscriber
-or: administrator, conqueror, editor, proprietor, ventilator

Similar as a spelling problem is this group: *precede, proceed* (but *procedure*), *recede, supersede.*

English is rich in *homonyms, pairs of words pronounced alike but often spelled differently: *pair—pare, piece—peace, plain—plane, coarse—course, stationary—stationery, lead* (noun) *—led.* The context keeps their meaning clear. Since most of them are in common use, confusing them in writing is usually the result of carelessness. If you have trouble with any of them, try writing them in phrases or sentences that will show their meaning.

The *capital* of California is Sacramento.
The *capitol* has a gilded dome.
the city *council—counsel* for the defense—good *counsel*
the *principal* of the high school—4% on the *principal*—a man of *principle*

Affect—effect, weather—whether, which are homonyms in most people's speech, also belong in this group.

Proofread carefully. Students usually know how to spell most of the common words they miss on papers. In conference they will frequently spell a word right that they have misspelled on a paper. To close the gap between knowledge and performance, careful proofreading of the final copy is necessary.

Spelling has to be checked in revision. Don't stop when you are writing to look up a word or even to worry about it. You will almost certainly lose something more important if you do—the trend of your thought, the movement of your sentence, at least. If you are suspicious of a word, you may mark it in some way (with a ? or $\sqrt{}$), and then check up on all dubious spellings when working over what you have written. Always scrutinize the final copy for careless spellings. Close reading of a paper for spelling alone is the best advice for anyone who is likely to make mistakes. To make your eye slow down, if you need to, read with a pencil point just below the line so that you will see every syllable. Some students have found that reading a paper backward forces them to look at each word afresh, and so brings spelling errors to their attention.

For continued improvement, see your spelling words in three groups. First be sure of the common everyday words (*companies, definite, professor,* and so on). Then learn the words for subjects that interest you and especially those needed in your college courses. Beyond these you can go as far as you wish in the vast wordstore of English.

Choice in spelling • To complicate matters still more, a writer now has a choice of simpler spellings in some hundreds of words. Which he will use depends upon his feeling of appropriateness. Formal writers are conservative; General writers use the shorter forms more readily. Scientific and business English are most open to changes in spelling. In the Informal writing of personal correspondence many people are more adventurous than in writing intended for strangers.

The basis of choice is the extent to which the shorter form is used. *Altho, tho,* and *thru* are in fairly general use in advertising and in familiar correspondence and are found in enough periodicals so that they are included in recent dictionaries as alternate forms. Many instructors prefer—and some insist on—the longer form. For many words (*catalog—catalogue, program —programme, esthetic—aesthetic*) usage is divided, and the shorter forms are becoming the more usual.

In general, when good usage is divided in spelling a given word, choose the simpler form. Most people writing today, and certainly anyone who has difficulty with spelling, will ordinarily prefer:

1. The more modern of two equally reputable spellings of common words: *plow, mold, theater* rather than *plough, mould, theatre.*

2. The simpler form of a less common word if it has attained currency among people who use it most: *anesthetic, medieval, sulfur* rather than *anaesthetic, mediaeval, sulphur.*

3. American rather than British spellings (though both spellings are usually current to some extent on both sides of the Atlantic): *center, color, labor, pajama, story* (of a building), *traveler* rather than *centre, colour, labour, pyjama,*

storey, traveller. Of course, in spelling British proper names or in direct quotation, British spelling should be kept, as in "the Labour Party."

Much sheer memory work is necessary to become a good speller, but there are a few rules and word groups that may simplify the task. Because you've heard them since the early school grades, they are not repeated here, but for your convenience they are given in detail in the *Index,* often with word lists.

In addition to the entries already mentioned in this chapter, see especially the following:

*-al ly   **-er, -re*

*-ce, -ge   **-ize, -ise*

*Doubling final consonants   **-le words*

*E § 5   **-or, -our*

*-ed   *Silent letters

*-ei-, -ie-   *Spelling

Exercises

1. Copy the items below, supplying appropriate punctuation and mechanics. If a mark of punctuation is optional, bracket it. If you have chosen between acceptable alternatives, give reasons for your choice.

a. here is a letter that gives a clue to his mysterious behavior and perhaps explains his mona lisa smile

b. isnt this the letter the clue to the mystery

c. when the war ended the trials of the traitors began

d. when the war ended the general returned to the pentagon

e. the constitution guarantees us our civil rights but does not set up the machinery to investigate violations of these rights

f. the constitution guarantees us our civil rights unfortunately it does not set up machinery to investigate violations of them

g. we walked in the park at night as though we were in our own garden

h. he told us we could feel perfectly safe walking in the park at night as though we needed reassurance

i. we walked in the park at night as though we were in our own garden because the grounds were always well patrolled

j. the election of jackson brought one era of our history to a close it represented the triumph of the masses over the classes

k. an era ended with jacksons election the masses had triumphed over the classes

l. adamss administration ended one era jacksons election began another

m. it is the student who works diligently and steadfastly who succeeds

n. the office girls who have worked hard all year deserve a day off

o. its the worlds oldest profession he says

p. these were lincolns words four score and seven years ago in 1776 our fathers brought forth on this continent a new nation

q. hers is a happy life she trusts her parents she likes her work she has many friends and a grey cat

r. all of us have some beliefs we cannot prove by induction or deduction basic assumptions standards of value articles of faith

s. not all superstitious people are ignorant however superstition usually stems from ignorance

t. its not only ignorant people though who are superstitious

u. the difference between man and mans is a matter of case

v. the difference between man and boy is hard to state

w. as we drove along we found that chile was just like the travel posters towering mountains winding roads wayside chapels and glimpses of the blue blue pacific

x. the storm was violent but freakish straws were driven into concrete posts feathers were blown off chickens trees were stripped of branches yet frail flowers remained undamaged

y. packed in his suitcase were a few clothes including a turtle neck sweater two pairs of socks and a handkerchief the bible a hymnal and a pocket dictionary and a loaded revolver

z. at laredo tex the flooding rio grande forced 2500 persons from their homes and about the same number fled from homes on the mexico side of the river in the worst inundation in ten years maybe even in twenty

2. Supply appropriate punctuation for the following passages, from which all marks have been removed. First, glance through a passage to get a general idea of the content and to decide whether Formal or General punctuation is appropriate. Then copy the passage, inserting punctuation, mechanics, and paragraph symbols, but making no other change.

a. had a good preparation for sampling religion in harlem a hot night of tropical rain bouncing white kindled by flares of lightning the sort of rain that seems naked and gives voices to the buildings in the morning the sky is heavily gray the planes sound low coming into la guardia sunday is steaming the streets are almost empty— V. S. PRITCHETT, "A Stranger in New York, Part II," *Holiday*

b. the progress of a nation depends first and foremost on the progress of its people unless it develops their spirit and human potentialities it cannot develop much else materially economically politically or culturally the basic problem of most of the under-developed countries is not a poverty of natural resources but the underdevelopment of their human resources hence their first task must be to build up their human capital to put it in more human terms that means improving the education skills and hopefulness and thus the mental and physical health of their men women and children the way to start seems obvious and quite uncomplicated build schools and launch a massive program of primary and secondary education and technical training but the problem is not really that simple these countries are not in a position to adopt any such crash program their limited funds for investment in education must be placed where they will do the most good moreover the shotgun approach may create more difficulties than it solves in some countries the training of more engineers for example may produce nothing but trouble in any country developed or underdeveloped education can become socially malignant if its people do not have a chance and incentives to use it—FREDERICK HARBISON, "Education for Development," *Scientific American*

c. the tundra is also a densely populated nesting ground for birds that we generally see only on migration driving through the park during the late afternoon we had found practically every roadside pond occupied here a red throated loon looking in the low light like a plate by louis agassiz fuertes there a pintail with half grown young farther on a family of horned grebes the adults in their rich nuptial plumage with several of the tiny young riding on the mother birds back now a soft whistle caught our ear on the top of the next rise was a golden plover that had made the long overseas flight from its winter home in the hawaiian islands what a strange sensation to meet in the mountains hundreds of miles from salt water birds that one always associates with sand beaches or the sea shorebirds dont belong in trees but a lesser yellowlegs screamed at me from the tip of a scraggly spruce and an arctic tern had buzzed me so close that i heard the whoosh of his wings as i explored the delta area where both were nesting short billed gulls were everywhere along the road and the gravel bars and above the rolling tundra hovering and plunging like a sparrow hawk was a long tailed jaeger startlingly beautiful in form and motion with his black cap and white throat and needlelike tail a sea hawk that winters at sea in the southern hemisphere.—PAUL BROOKS, "Alaska: Last Frontier," The *Atlantic*

d. the brilliant young renaissance prince had grown old and wrathful the pain from his leg made henry ill tempered he suffered fools and those who crossed him with equal lack of patience suspicion dominated his mind and ruthlessness marked his actions at the time of his marriage with catherine parr he was engaged in preparing the last of his wars the roots of the conflict lay in scotland hostility between the two peoples still smouldered ever and again flickering into flame along the wild border reviving the obsolete claim to suzerainty henry denounced the scots as rebels and pressed them to relinquish their alliance with france the scots successfully defeated an english raid at halidon rig then in the autumn of 1542 an expedition under norfolk had to turn back at kelso principally through the failure of the commissariat which besides its other shortcomings left the english army without its beer and the scots proceeded to carry the war into the enemys country their decision proved disastrous badly led and imperfectly organized they lost more than half their army of ten thousand men in solway moss and were utterly routed the news of this second flodden killed james v who died leaving the kingdom to an infant of one week mary the famous queen of scots—WINSTON CHURCHILL, *The New World*

e. on the night of july 22 1933 oklahoma oil millionaire charles f urschel and his friend walter r jarrett together with their wives were playing bridge on urschels screened porch in oklahoma city two masked intruders armed with a machine gun and a pistol entered okay whos urschel one man asked when neither urschel or jarrett answered the gunmen took them both warning the women not to call for help as soon as the man left mrs urschel phoned the fbi—MARTIN OLIVER, "Rogues' Gallery," Leavenworth *New Era*

3. In the following student paper, correct the errors in spelling and punctuation. Then write a brief evaluation of the content, organization, and style.

My History as a Speller, or Non-Spellar

1 My problem is an old one. I have never been able to spell. Over
2 the past twelve years I have spent a lot of time, energy, and
3 money trying to learn how to spell.
4 Probably I was introduced to spelling in the first grade although
5 I don't really remember. To me first grade seems like a dream,
6 I sat in the last seat of the last row and spent most of the time
7 pertending my pencil was a rocketship. When I reached second
8 grade I could neither read nor spell. I remember my first real
9 attempt to lick my spelling problem. In preparation for the
10 weakly spelling test I would copy the words on my desk the day
11 before, and then for the test I would mearly copy the words onto
12 my paper. This must have worked well until I was discovered. I
13 had to stay after school, and clean off the desk, and thus ended

14 my first and last attempt at cheating.

15 Soon after that I stopped taking spelling tests, instead I was
16 given extra reading instruction. My parents have told me that the
17 teacher was more worried about my inability to read than my
18 inability to spell, they have also told me that I appeared to be a
19 bright child and excelled in science and mathematics so everybody
20 was confused by my inability to read or spell. At one time I was
21 taken for psychological testing. I remember a man showed me
22 pictures and asked me to make up a story about them; I even
23 remember working at a peg board putting square pegs in square
24 holes and round ones in round holes. I don't think anything was
25 done as a result of the tests.

26 In fourth grade I began to do better on spelling tests. By
27 working very hard with my mother, I could memorize enough
28 words to pass, but there were some words that no matter how hard
29 I tryed I could not memorize; an example is the word "does."
30 Until last year I could not have spelled this word to save my life,
31 and I can now only by associating it with "doe." In fifth grade I
32 learned to read. I read *Mrs. Pickeral Goes to Mars* and ever since
33 I have been an avid reader.

34 By the end of grammar school my spelling was a real problem.
35 Although I could usually get a decent mark on a test, I always
36 forgot the words right after and made mistakes when I wrote. My
37 teachers kept pounding away at the fact that my work would be
38 unacceptable in high school.

39 It was the same way in high school! I could pass spelling tests
40 but could not spell when I wrote. In the summer after my 11th
41 year I was tutored by a Mr. Case who was a remedial speling
42 instructor. He was puzzled as all my teachers had been by my
43 inconsistancy in spelling. I would spell "accept" correctly and
44 then five minutes later I would write "aceptable." He tried to
45 teach me all the rules of spelling, phonetic and otherwise. After
46 several weeks I was making progress; I was able to figure out, on
47 the basis of rules how to spell some words I had not memorized.
48 However, when I returned to school I found to my dismay I still
49 could not spell when I wrote and still could not recognize my
50 own mistakes.

51 Last year I worked with the reading teacher in our school. Her
52 theroy was that the more senses you used when learning a word
53 the longer you would remember it, and she was right. I did not
54 have an opportunity to spend much time with her, but long
55 enough to see it helped to say the word, see the word, and write
56 the word with my finger in the sand that she kept in a box on her
57 desk. She solved my problem with "does." I could learn words
58 for a test faster and easier. But even her help had little affect on
59 my writing; when I conquored one problem I would create a
60 new one to take its place.

61 In college I am still trying to learn to spell. I spend more time
62 going over my papers for spelling than for anything else. The one

63 new trick Ive learned is to read by papers backward, word for
64 word. My first paper this year had thirty spelling mistakes. I
65 wonder how many this one has.

4. To the following words add the suffixes indicated and give alternate forms if they exist. Study *Doubling final consonants, *E § 5, and *-ce, -ge, before you work out this exercise.

drop + ed	quarrel + er	ridicule + ous
kidnap + er	dine + ing	profit + able
courage + ous	acknowledge + ment	mile + age
control + ed	travel + ed	prove + able
service + able	desire + ous	singe + ing
like + able	repay + ed	worship + er
bias + ed	refer + al	equip + age
endure + ing	deter + ent	parallel + ed
confer + ed	tie + ing	infer + ence
grieve + ous	clot + ed	shoe + ing

5. You can often learn to distinguish between words of similar spelling by using them accurately in sentences. For each pair or trio of these frequently confused words, make up a sentence showing their correct use. Example: After *awhile* they rested *a while*.

accept—except	its—it's
affect—effect	lead—led
already—all ready	loose—lose
breath—breathe	moral—morale
capital—capitol	principal—principle
choose—chose	quiet—quite
complement—compliment	site—cite—sight
conscience—conscious—	stationery—stationary
conscientious	there—their—they're
council—counsel—consul	weather—whether
formerly—formally	whose—who's

6. In your spelling notebook keep a list of words that you will have to use in various courses. Also list words you have misspelled and new words you want to use in your writing. To fix the spelling more definitely in your mind, divide the words into syllables as you enter them; consult your dictionary for this purpose. Use the names of your subjects for headings, for example:

History	*Psychology*	*Zoology*	*General*
me di e val	ap per cep tion	car ti lag i nous	dor mi to ry
Med i ter ra ne an	cor re la tion	ap o neu ro sis	soph o more
Ren ais sance	ho me o sta sis	Eu sta chi an	sched ule

7. Review the *Index* entry *Spelling. If possible, have a friend read off the words to you. Enter in your spelling notebook any words you have misspelled. Review them at regular intervals.

Chapter Eleven

REFERENCE
PAPERS

There are three distinguishing marks of a University;
a group of students, a corps of instructors, and a
collection of books; and of these three the most
important is the collection of books.
                    Chauncey Brewster Tinker

Preparing a reference paper gives excellent training in developing critical judgment—one of the major objectives of college education. It also provides a student with his best opportunity to exploit the resources of the library. Self-reliant use of the library is necessary not only in getting an education but in continuing the activities of an educated person in later life. A college graduate isn't expected to know everything, but he should know how to find out about almost anything. This chapter deals with one phase of library work—using material drawn from close reading to write a long, documented paper, here called a reference paper. Other names for it, sometimes with rather special senses attached, are library paper, term paper, research paper, source paper, or investigative paper.

Preparing a reference paper in your composition course will give you practice in finding material, taking notes on it, evaluating it, and presenting it. The emphasis put on the method and form of the reference paper will give you the techniques you will need to prepare such papers in later courses. Advanced work, especially in literature, history, and the social sciences, depends on this sort of study, and in sciences a laboratory experiment is often supplemented by research in records of previous experiments. These same methods, more elaborately developed, are the basis of graduate work in the various professional schools, where theses, dissertations, and monographs are required; they are also the basis of many sorts of reports and industrial studies. A glance at the "learned journals" in a college library shows that in every field of knowledge there are periodicals containing research articles written by specialists for other specialists. A freshman reference paper is an important first stage in the scholarship that extends through the advanced courses in college to the work of professional people who are steadily adding to our knowledge of the past and the present. It is also practice for research that you may do later as part of a business project, as an investigation of questions raised in your day-to-day experience, or as a service for some special group.

Besides offering training in research methods, a reference paper challenges your best efforts at every stage (see chart, p. 39). Because of the length of the paper and the complexity of the material, each stage becomes particularly important. Choosing an appropriate subject is crucial, because a poor selection will make all later work a tiresome chore; gathering the material is by far the largest part of the task; selecting and organizing the material are essential to make the paper a coherent whole; and preparing the manuscript requires special attention because of the footnotes and bibliography. Each stage takes time, patience, and judgment.

Your own contribution to a reference paper may seem slight. The material comes from sources outside your experience, the style is impersonal, the language is rather Formal, and the primary intention is to inform and to interpret rather than to express your own feelings and ideas. But serious work on a paper will show how large a part you actually play. You not only uncover the material (a process often calling for ingenuity), but you use your judgment in selecting material that fits your topic and purpose. And though the methods of gathering material have been worked out by thousands of research workers before you and the forms of the manuscript standardized, the actual content and organization of your paper represent your own thought and judgment.

Furthermore, a reference paper is not just a listing of facts. Facts must be *interpreted,* for only the most common knowledge can stand without some comment on its meaning. Questions of causes, of results, of significance are not settled merely by presenting data; a mind must work on the facts and ideas to establish their relationships and to see their meaning in perspective. This is what is meant by critical judgment.

For the writer, much of the interest as well as the profit in preparing a reference paper comes from the material itself, from acquiring new knowledge and becoming something of a specialist in a small field. The choice of topic is therefore of special importance. If you are given a wide choice of subject, don't choose "just any subject" at random. If you do, you will regret it. Preparing a reference paper is a long job; it will become a bore or at least a waste of time unless you pick a subject that interests you and that will add something to your stock of knowledge. It is a good idea to make your selection only after weighing the merits of several possibilities. Although any topic is possible, some are better avoided, especially those that are too commonly chosen or that do not represent a genuine personal choice.

Chapter 2, pages 40-44, offers suggestions for focusing on a subject and narrowing it to a manageable topic. What is said there is relevant to the subject for the reference paper, for, even though the reference paper typically runs much longer than the average course paper, the thorough analysis of material that is required makes it imperative that you have a fairly limited subject for your paper. Choose one that you can explore in depth, one that you can develop in enough detail to really inform the reader, not just enumerate the commonplace facts. Thoughtful and early attention to limiting your subject will make all later stages of the work easier and more profitable.

One caution before we turn to the actual preparation of the reference paper—during the time you spend on it, you will need to strike a balance between your interest in the subject for its own sake and your interest in the procedures of research. Exclusive absorption in either is costly and unwise. At first you may feel a certain impatience about following a rigid pattern in preparing your paper, particularly if you begin by simply wanting to know more about your subject. Meticulousness in recording bibliographical data and taking neat notes may seem to be a waste of good hours. But in the long run the process of preparing the paper may be more valuable to you than the paper itself.

This is not to say that the *writing* of the paper is unimportant. Organizing your material into a whole that has a unity and integrity of its own presents as many challenges as hunting for sources. It is as unwise to concentrate solely on method as it is to slight it. The student who becomes absorbed in the minutiae of preparing extensive bibliographies and taking full notes may exhaust his interest and enthusiasm as well as his time before he faces the major task of writing the paper. Note-taking is not an end in itself, and it is only by knowing what you are taking notes *for* that you can make an intelligent selection of material.

Sources of references

Almost everyone starts work on a reference paper with one or two sources in mind—a discussion in a textbook, a magazine article, the name of a writer, the title of a book. Very often, preliminary reading furnishes references to other works, and these make a natural starting point for the working bibliography. But efficient assembling of possible useful sources depends on informed use of the resources of the library. There are several aids planned specifically to direct you to books and periodicals that you can use. No matter what your choice of topic, you will invariably want to consult your library's card catalog, its periodical indexes and its special bibliographies, and its other general and special reference works.

The card catalog • The library card catalog lists all the books in the library by *author,* by *title,* and by *subject* (sometimes under more than one subject heading). If you know of an author who has written on your subject, find his name in the card catalog. If you know a book title dealing with your topic, find it in the catalog. And look up the subject you are writing about, watching for cross references made by *see* and *see also* cards. If you are looking for material on athletics, you may find a card headed ATHLETICS, SEE SPORTS; this indicates that in your library the cards relating to athletics are filed under the subject SPORTS. When you look up SPORTS, you may find, in addition to a number of cards with that heading, a card labeled SPORTS, SEE ALSO GAMES, indicating that additional related material will be found under the subject heading GAMES. *Analytic* cards refer you to a part of a book (a chapter, for example, on a specific subject, or a story in a volume of short stories); they are also used to identify authors and titles of self-contained volumes in a series like *The New American Nation Series.*

The library subject card at the top of the next page (PUBLIC WELFARE) illustrates the information given about a book. Items 2, 3, 4, and 5 would be transferred to a bibliography card. The entry on the bibliography card should resemble that in the final bibliography as closely as possible (p. 444) so that making the final bibliography will be simply a matter of arranging the cards alphabetically and copying the entries, inserting conventional punctuation.

1. Card catalog
   subject heading
2. Library call
   number
3. Author
4. Title
5. Facts of
   publication
6. Relevant
   facts about
   the book
7. Subject index
8. Information
   for librarians

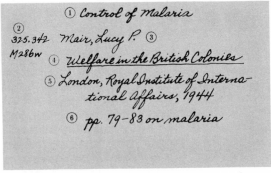

(2) (1) PUBLIC WELFARE – Great Britain – Colonies

325.342
M286w **Mair, Lucy Philip, 1901–** (3)
(4) Welfare in the British colonies [by] L. P. Mair. (5) London,
The Royal institute of international affairs [1944]

(6) 115 p. 21½ᶜᵐ.

"First published 1944."
Bibliography at end of each chapter except the first.

(7) 1. Gt. Brit.—Colonies—Soc. condit.   I. Royal institute of international affairs.   II. Title.

44–9322

(8) Library of Congress   HN398.A5M3

[4]   325.342

Library Subject Card

1. Topic of paper
2. Call number
3. Author
4. Title
5. Facts of
   publication
6. Pages on the
   specific subject
   (added from
   the book)

(1) *Control of Malaria*
(2) *325.342* *Mair, Lucy P.* (3)
M286w (4) *Welfare in the British Colonies*
(5) *London, Royal Institute of Interna-*
tional Affairs, 1944
(6) *pp. 79–83 on malaria*

Bibliography Card

Periodical indexes • Next to the card catalog the most useful
sources of references are *Readers' Guide* and other periodical
indexes. *Readers' Guide* indexes magazines published since
1900 and gives, under author and subject entries (see illustration below), references to articles in some 200 current magazines of general interest. It appears twice a month (except July
and August, when it is published only once a month); later
cumulative volumes cover one or more years. It is one of the
most valuable sources for topics of current interest. The following is an excerpt from the *Guide* for February 10, 1964:

LABORATORY technicians
  Danger in our medical labs. M. Pines. Harper
  227:84-7+ O '63: Discussion. 227:4+ D '63
LACEBARK pine. See Pine
LACERDA, Carlos
  Hammer & the anvil. il por Time 82:53-4
  N 15 '63
  Milk, motherhood and the American flag.
  New Repub 150:10-11 Ja 4 '64

LACHAISE, Gaston
    Radiating sex & soul; exhibition at Los
    Angeles' County museum of art. il por Time
    83:66 Ja 17 '64
LACY, Joe M.
    Shopper's park. Am City 78:73-5 D '63
LADA-MOCARSKI, Polly
    Modern French book art. Craft Horiz 24:36-
    41 Ja '64
LAFARGE, John
    Voices out of a wilderness of hate. Sat R 46:
    42-3 D 14 '63

Readers' Guide uses abbreviations, explained on a page at
the beginning of each issue, for the titles of magazines indexed, for the months, and for various facts about the articles.
Be sure to write out all important words on your bibliography
card when using the *Guide,* to avoid later questions and to
have the data in correct form for future use. In the references
the number before the colon refers to the volume and the
numbers after the colon refer to the pages of the articles
(227:84-7+ means volume 227, pages 84 to 87 and continued).
Putting quotation marks around the title and capitalizing the
important words will give the entry the proper bibliographical
form. A bibliography card for the first entry follows:

1. Topic of paper
2. Author
3. Title
4. Facts of
   publication
5. Description
   of content

① The Need for Medical Technologists
② Pines, Maya
③ "Danger in Our Medical Labs"
④ Harper's, Oct. 1963, 227:84-87, 92-93
⑤ (Shortage of trained personnel
a threat to reliable tests)

Bibliography Card from a *Readers' Guide* Entry

A number of other magazine indexes list articles from specialized periodicals not covered by *Readers' Guide.* Most of
them appear annually. The ones marked with a † in this list
are the most generally useful.

Agricultural Index, 1916-   . Subject index to a selected list of
periodicals, books, bulletins, documents
    Art Index, 1929-   . Author and subject index to fine arts
periodicals and museum bulletins

Bibliographic Index, 1937-   . Subject index to bibliographies in books and periodicals

†*Biography Index,* 1946-   . Subject index to biographical material in books and periodicals

†*Book Review Digest,* 1905-   . Author, subject, and title index to published book reviews. Gives extracts and exact references to sources

Catholic Periodical Index, 1930-   . Subject index to a selected list of Catholic periodicals

Dramatic Index, 1909-   . Index to articles and illustrations concerning the American and English theater

†*Education Index,* 1929-   . Author and subject index to educational periodicals, books, and pamphlets

Engineering Index, 1884-1905; 1906-   . Subject index to technical periodicals; transactions and journals of engineering and other technical societies; reports of government bureaus, engineering colleges, research laboratories

Index to Legal Periodicals, 1926-   . Author, subject, and book review index to legal periodicals

†*Industrial Arts Index,* 1913-1957. In 1958, it became two separate indexes: *Applied Science and Technology Index* and *Business Periodicals Index.* Subject index to a selected list of engineering, trade, and business periodicals

†*International Index to Periodicals,* 1907-   . Author and subject index to periodicals from various countries; devoted chiefly to the humanities and the social sciences

†*Nineteenth Century Readers' Guide,* 1944-   . An index to periodicals, 1890-1899 and to some omitted from *Readers' Guide,* 1900-1922

Poole's Index to Periodical Literature, 1802-1906. Subject index to American and English periodicals, many of which are no longer published but are still important; precedes coverage of *Readers' Guide*

†*Public Affairs Information Service,* 1915-   . Subject index to books, periodicals, pamphlets, and other materials in economics, government, and other public affairs

Quarterly Cumulative Index Medicus, 1927-   . Author and subject index to medical literature in many languages

United States Government Publications; Monthly Catalog, 1895-   . A bibliography of publications issued by all branches of the government

Ulrich's Periodical Directory (8th ed., 1956) lists periodicals under subjects they treat, answering the question: What periodicals are there in this field? It also tells where each is indexed so that it becomes an indirect guide to the contents of all magazines.

The New York Times Index now appears semimonthly and runs back to 1913. Although it indexes only *The New York Times,* it can be used as a rough general index to material in other newspapers, since the dates indicate when the news stories were breaking throughout the press. Through this index you can find many speeches and important documents as well as news stories of significant events.

Special bibliographies • Besides these periodical indexes there are many annual bibliographies in the learned journals in special fields and bibliographies in one or more volumes that survey a complete field. Most of these are more elaborate than you will need for your reference paper, but when you begin to work in detail in a particular field in your college major, you should know the special bibliographies that serve it.

The key to these special lists is Besterman's *World Bibliography of Bibliographies* (3rd ed., 3 vols., 1955-1956), a standard and comprehensive work, or the shorter Ireland's *An Index to Indexes* (1942). The following are standard bibliographies in history and literature:

Articles on American Literature, *1900-1950* (Leary), 1954

Bibliographical Guide to English Studies (Cross), 10th ed., 1951

A Concise Bibliography for Students of English (Kennedy), 4th ed., 1960

Bibliography of Writings on the English Language . . . to the end of 1922 (Kennedy), 1927 and supplement

Cambridge Bibliography of English Literature, 1941, 4 vols., *Supplement,* Vol. V, 1957

Literary History of the United States (Spiller and others), 1948; 3rd ed., 1963

Contemporary British Literature (Manly and Rickert), 1935

Contemporary American Authors (Millett), 1940

Literature of American History (Larned), 1902 and supplement

Bibliographies in American History (Beers), 1942

Guide to Historical Literature (Dutcher and others), 1931; repr. 1949

These miscellaneous indexes are useful for many research projects:

Vertical File Service Catalog, 1932- . An annotated subject catalog of pamphlets, booklets, brochures, leaflets, circulars, folders, maps, posters, charts, mimeographed bulletins, etc.

United States Catalog: Books in Print (1899-1934). Four editions and their supplements, constituting a comprehensive record of American book publication from 1898 to 1934

Cumulative Book Index, 1898-   . Supplement to the *United States Catalog;* since 1930 an author, subject, and title index to books printed in English

Catalog of the Public Documents of Congress and of All Departments of the Government of the United States for the Period 1893-1940 (1895-1945, 25 vols.)

Biography Index, 1946-   . A quarterly index to biographical material, with annual cumulations

Essay and General Literature Index, 1900-   . Author and subject index to essays and articles in collections and miscellaneous works

Granger's Index to Poetry and Recitations (1904-1944). Author, title, and first line index to poetry in collections; 5th ed. completely revised and enlarged, 1962

Play Index, 1949-1952. Augments but does not supersede the *Index to Plays*

Short Story Index, 1953-   . Index—by author, title, and in many cases by subject—to some 60,000 stories published in 1949 or earlier; supplements, 1953, 1956, 1960

Song Index (1926-1934). Author and title index to more than 19,000 songs in collections

Index to Plays (1927-1935). Author and title and subject index to plays in collections or separately published from 1800 to 1935; 4th ed., 1963

Index to Reproductions of American Paintings, 1948

Portrait Index (1906). Subject index to portraits of persons in books and periodicals; *Readers' Guide* and other periodical indexes now indicate portraits in periodicals

Reference works ● The reference department of a library has a large number of general and special works which furnish varied and plentiful information. Since the articles in reference works almost always refer you to authoritative specialized works, they are a good starting point for compiling a bibliography—but only a starting point.

A comprehensive list of reference works of all kinds is given in *Guide to Reference Books,* by Constance M. Winchell, 7th edition, 1951, based on 6th edition by Isadore G. Mudge, with four supplements from 1952 to 1962. *How and Where to Look It Up: A Guide to Standard Sources of Information,* by Robert

W. Murphey, 1958, provides a variety of reference sources, and the organization of the book makes it easy to locate the many items of fact it contains.

There are numerous general encyclopedias, these varying in size from the single-volume *Columbia* to the several-volume-with-supplements *Britannica*. Though by no means infallible and always in need of revision (the larger ones revise some articles for each new printing), they are convenient store-houses of information on a vast number of subjects. Here are the names of a few; near them on the reference shelves you will find others:

Chambers's Encyclopaedia
Columbia Encyclopedia
Encyclopedia Americana
Encyclopaedia Britannica
Encyclopedia International
New International Encyclopaedia

Even more important for college work are special reference works—the encyclopedias and general reference works in specific fields. Their articles usually go into greater detail than those in the general encyclopedias, and their approach is more specialized. They also give brief, carefully selected bibliographies. Some of the best known are:

Agriculture: *Cyclopedia of American Agriculture* (Bailey), 1907-1909, 4 vols.

Architecture: *A History of Architecture* (Fletcher), 17th ed., 1961

Art: *Harper's Encyclopedia of Art*, 1937, 2 vols. *Bryan's Dictionary of Painters and Engravers*, 1903-1905, 5 vols.

Biography (American): *Dictionary of American Biography*, 1928-1937, 20 vols. and index; supplements 1944, 1948. *Who's Who in America*, biennially since 1899. *Who Was Who in America*, Vol. I, 1897-1942, Vol. II, 1943-1950, Vol. III, 1951-1960 (*Who's Who* subjects who died during those years); *Who Was Who in America*, Historical Volume, 1607-1896, 1964.

Biography (British): *Dictionary of National Biography*, 1885-1940, 22 vols. and supplements. *Who's Who*, annually since 1848.

Biography (General): *Current Biography*, monthly since 1940, with annual cumulation. *International Who's Who*, 1935-   . *World Biography*, 5th ed., 1954

Business: *Encyclopedia of Banking and Finance* (Munn), 6th ed., 1962

Chemistry: *Thorpe's Dictionary of Applied Chemistry,* 4th ed., 1937-1949, 9 vols; Vols. 10-12, 1950-1956; 12 vols.

Education: *Cyclopedia of Education* (Monroe), 1911-1913, 5 vols. *Encyclopedia of Educational Research* (Monroe), 3rd ed., 1960

Government: *Cyclopedia of American Government* (McLaughlin and Hart), 1914, 3 vols.

History (General): *An Encyclopedia of World History* (Langer), 3rd. ed., 1952. *Cambridge Ancient History* (Bury and others), 2nd ed., 1923-1939, 12 vols. of text and 5 vols. of plates. *Cambridge Medieval History* (Bury and others), 1911-1936, 8 vols., 1 vol. of maps. *Cambridge Modern History* (Ward and others), 2nd ed., 1926, 13 vols. and atlas

History (American): *Dictionary of American History* (Adams), 2nd ed., 1942, 5 vols. and index; *Supplement I* (1940-1960), 1961

Literature (General): *Dictionary of World Literature* (Shipley), new ed., 1960. *Columbia Dictionary of Modern European Literature* (Smith), 1947

Literature (Classical): *Oxford Companion to Classical Literature* (Harvey), 2nd ed., 1937. *Oxford Classical Dictionary* (Cary and others), 1949

Literature (English): *Cambridge History of English Literature* (Ward and Waller), 1907-1927, 15 vols. *Oxford Companion to English Literature* (Harvey), 3rd ed., 1946

Literature (American): *Cambridge History of American Literature* (Trent and others), 1917-1921, 4 vols. *Oxford Companion to American Literature* (Hart), 3rd ed., 1956. *Literary History of the United States* (Spiller and others), 1948; 3rd ed., 1963. *Twentieth Century Authors* (Kunitz and Haycraft, eds.), 1942; first supplement, 1955

Music: *Grove's Dictionary of Music and Musicians,* 5th ed., 1954, 9 vols.; supplement (Vol. 10), 1961. *International Cyclopedia of Music and Musicians* (Thompson), 8th ed., 1964

Philosophy and Psychology: *Dictionary of Philosophy and Psychology* (Baldwin), 1910, 3 vols. *Encyclopedia of Psychology* (Harriman), 1946. *The New Dictionary of Psychology* (Harriman), 1947

Quotations: *Bartlett's Familiar Quotations,* 13th ed., 1955. *The Home Book of Bible Quotations* (Stevenson), 1949. *The Home Book of Shakespeare Quotations* (Stevenson), 1937. *The Home Book of Quotations, Classical and Modern* (Stevenson), 8th ed., 1956

Religion: *Catholic Encyclopedia,* 1907-1922, 17 vols. *Universal Jewish Encyclopedia,* 1939-1944, 10 vols. *Encyclopedia of Religion and Ethics* (Hastings), 1908-1927, 13 vols. *New Schaff-Herzog Encyclopedia of Religious Knowledge* (Jackson), 1908-1914, 12 vols. and index. *Dictionary of the Bible* (Hastings), 1898-1904, 5 vols.; new ed., 1963

Science: *Dictionary of Scientific Terms* (Henderson), 7th ed., 1960. *Harper Encyclopedia of Science,* 1963. *Hutchinson's Technical and Scientific Encyclopedia* (Tweney and Shirshov), 1935-1936, 4 vols. *Space Encyclopedia,* 1957; 2nd ed., 1960. *Van Nostrand's Scientific Encyclopedia,* 3rd ed., 1958

Social Sciences: *Encyclopedia of the Social Sciences* (Seligman and Johnson), 1930-1935, 15 vols.

General and special dictionaries are described on pages 362-369.

Yearbooks, etc. For facts and figures, various publications are valuable for the information they contain or can direct you to.

World Almanac and Book of Facts, 1868- . This and the following one are the general reference works that anyone with a serious interest in affairs should have on his own bookshelf.

Information Please Almanac, 1947-

The American Yearbook, 1910-1919, 1925-1950. Annual record of events in the United States

The Americana Annual, 1923- . Annual supplement to the *Encyclopedia Americana*

The Britannica Book of the Year, 1938- . Annual supplement to the *Encyclopaedia Britannica*

The New International Yearbook, 1907- . Annual supplement to the *New International Encyclopaedia*

Statistical Abstract of the United States, 1878- . Summary statistics on the industrial, social, political, and economic organization of the United States

Social Work Yearbook, biennially since 1929. Social work and related fields

Statesman's Yearbook, 1864- . Descriptive and statistical information about world governments

Reference Shelf, 1922- . Reprints of articles, bibliographies, and debates on topics of current interest

University Debaters' Annual, 1915- . Constructive and rebuttal speeches from college and university debates

Yearbook of the United Nations, 1956-

Besides specific sources like these, you will always find some references indirectly. Almost every article or book will refer to some other source or give some clue that you can follow up. Talking with experts in the field will produce suggestions. The sources of material spread out like a fan—one source leads to another, and if you work long enough in a field, friends and sometimes even strangers may give you clues without being asked. Systematic work and ingenuity in following up hunches will almost always enable you to turn up plenty of material.

Since one reason for the assignment of reference papers is to train students in research methods, you should do as much as possible without help. The library has reference librarians, but you should not bother them until you have exhausted your own resources.

The working bibliography

Before you concentrate on gathering material for your topic, you should compile a *working bibliography* of sources you expect to consult. Check reference works of the kind described in the preceding section, and consult the appropriate subject headings in the card catalog and the periodical indexes. To make sure that enough material on your subject is available in the library, compile the working bibliography before actually starting to take notes. This preliminary survey of materials saves time and worry in the actual reading and makes possible intelligent selection of books and articles.

Everyone should have a consistent method of keeping track of references and of taking and keeping the notes from which he works. For casual study, notebooks and odd sheets may do, but for large and important jobs and for training in research methods, the most flexible and efficient materials are standard filing cards or slips, either 3x5 or 4x6 inches, the latter probably more convenient, since they hold more and allow for more generous spacing and labeling of material. *There should be a separate bibliography card for each reference.* Later, note cards on the content of the reference will be added to your file of material for the paper.

Form of bibliographical entries • The bibliography card records all the facts about a book or an article needed to identify it, to find it in the library when you want it, and to make the formal bibliography that will appear at the end of the paper. Each card should carry these facts:
For the formal bibliography:
   1. *The author's or editor's name,* last name first; *ed.* after editor's name. If no author or editor is given, omit this item and start with 2 below.

2. *The title* of the article (in quotation marks) or of the book (underlined to represent italics); put *a, an, the* after the title.

3. *The facts of publication:*

a. Of a book, the city and date, and the name of the publisher if you need to use it.

b. Of a magazine, the name of the magazine (underlined), the volume, the date, the pages on which the article appears.

c. Of a newspaper story, the name of the paper (underlined), the date, the page, and, if you wish, the column number.

For your own use:

1. *The library call number* or location—preferably in the upper left corner, as it is in the card catalog; if you are working in two or more libraries, be sure to put some identifying symbol before the call number.

2. *Any other facts* that relate to the use of the reference, such as the pages that treat your subject or the value of the source —preferably at the bottom of the card.

3. *A subject heading,* a phrase for the particular part of your topic that the reference pertains to, at the top center of the card. This label is familiarly known as a *slug.*

4. *A code reference* in the upper right corner. This reference may be a number, a letter, or the author's last name. Using it instead of a full citation on each note card taken from this source will save a great deal of needless copying.

The form and arrangement of bibliography cards are illustrated on page 430.

Bibliography cards • Your bibliography cards should be kept in alphabetical order according to author, or first important word of the title if no author is given. If you have only a few, they can be held together with a paper clip or kept in an envelope or an expanding pocket file. For large accumulations, use a filing box.

The number of references depends on the nature of the topic. Graduate research papers should show that all the pertinent material has been examined; undergraduate papers should represent adequate coverage of the subject. Glance at all available sources and select those which are neither too technical nor too general for your purpose. No paper should be written from only one or two sources, but of course for a short paper done in a limited time, a student can easily be weighed down by too much material. Papers of 2000-5000 words typically have from 6 to 15 or 20 sources, depending on the nature of the subject and the length of the work.

1. Subject (slug)
2. Call number
3. Author
4. Title
5. Facts of publication
6. Specific part of book
7. Your code reference

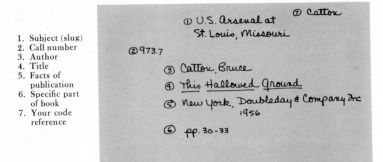

Bibliography Card for a Book

1. Subject (slug)
2. Author
3. Title
4. Facts of publication
5. Your code reference

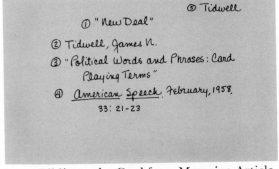

Bibliography Card for a Magazine Article

1. Facts of publication
2. Headline
3. Description of content
4. Your code reference

① The New York Times, Aug. 14, 1958,
    p.1, col.5; p.8, col. 8

② "President Hints at Gains in Sea
    Water Conversion"

③ (Reduction in cost of de-salting
    sea water and purifying
    brackish inland water)

④ N.Y. Times

Bibliography Card for a Newspaper

Taking notes on reading

Good notes are crucial in the preparation of a reference paper. Illegible handwriting, meaningless phrases (clear when the note was taken but not when it's "cold"), and inadequate labeling of the source may send you back to the library when you should be settling down to write your paper. As you become experienced in note-taking, you will learn to evaluate the importance of a source and to vary the kind, length, and number of notes you take accordingly. From some sources you may need only a few particular facts or statistics; from others you want direct quotations in addition to careful summaries of whole paragraphs, sections, or even chapters; from a few you may simply jot down a sentence or two describing the content and giving a brief evaluation of it. The note-taking methods described in the following sections are widely used by many research workers.

Form of notes • Notes are usually made on 3x5 or 4x6 slips or cards because they are easy to sort, discard, rearrange, can be accumulated indefinitely and kept in good order by the use of guide cards with tabs on which subjects can be written. Even for a relatively small job, such as a course reference paper, they are the most convenient form for notes. The three essential parts of a note card are: (1) the *material,* the facts and opinions to be recorded; (2) the exact *source,* title and page number, from which they are taken; (3) a *subject label* or slug for the card, showing what it treats.

Since footnotes must refer to the exact page from which material comes, you should keep track of the source and the page, preferably recording them first because it is easy to forget to write them down after the note is taken. The sample card on page 432 shows a convenient form. In the upper right-hand corner put the author's name, a number, or a letter —just enough to make reference to the full bibliography card easy and sure. Before writing the note, set down the exact page on which the material was found. Inclusive pages (such as 87-92) should not be used unless the note actually describes or summarizes what those pages say. The slug is best placed in the upper left corner and should identify the subject matter of that particular card, making it possible for you to sort the cards when you get ready to outline and write.

Label

Note
with
page
reference

*First Harvard Commencement   Morison, Founding
                                    of Harvard Coll.*

257 1ˢᵗ Harvard Commencement Sept. 23, 1642
*Gov. Winthrop, his guard, the magistrates of
the Colony come from Boston by ferry or barge*

Sample Note Card

Don't put too much on a single card; it should contain
only one point or a few facts that bear on one point. If unrelated bits of information are included on one card, you will
find, when you are sorting the cards, that one bit belongs here
and another there. One hundred items of information on one
hundred cards can be organized and reorganized speedily and
efficiently; fifty items on ten cards will result in confusion, ex-
asperation, and error.

Use only one side of the card. Cards written on both sides
are difficult to handle, and you will certainly forget to turn
some over if you use both sides. If only a few words remain
at the end of a statement, they can be written on the back, but
over should be put on the front as a reminder.

Not all notes need be taken in full sentences—words, phrases,
and topics are enough, if you are sure the note will be meaningful after you have laid it aside for a while. Take notes in
ink as you do the reading, but don't bother to recopy them
except for some very good reason. They are means to an end
(a good paper), not works of art themselves.

Suggestions for note-taking • Exact rules for taking notes cannot be given; your judgment will improve as you gain experience, and you will formulate your own rules. But it is wise to
begin by first glancing through the article or chapter to see
roughly what it contains for your purpose. Then go over it
again, this time making the necessary notes. From your first
few sources you will probably take a good many notes, but

after you have accumulated material, a new reference may give only a few additional facts. In taking notes:

1. Distinguish between the author's facts and his opinions. Label the opinions "So-and-so thinks. . . ." In general pay most attention to the *facts* presented (unless of course your paper is something like "What reviewers said of Hemingway's short stories"). You will need the facts as the basis of your own interpretations and as evidence to support them in the paper.

2. Distinguish carefully between direct quotation and summary. What is copied literally should be carefully enclosed in quotation marks and should be taken down exactly as it appears. After an obvious error in the source, write **sic*[1] (thus) in brackets to indicate that the error was in the original. (Actually [*sic*] is seldom necessary in student papers, but you should know what it means when you find it in your reading.)

In the early stages of note-taking, before you have a clear idea of the proportions and focus of your paper, you may want to quote rather fully. Although direct quotations may not be numerous or extensive in the final draft, having a quotation before you as you write will help you work the summary into your discussion more gracefully and more effectively. In the later stages of note-taking, quotations should be taken only for good reason: unusually important material, crucial for your paper; a striking statement that you want to quote for its vividness or its conciseness; controversial or difficult material that you need to think about before deciding exactly what it means for your subject. Other material may be digested in your own words and so reduced to the scale of your paper.

3. Distinguish between what you take from a source and any comments of your own. Put the latter in brackets or encircle them and write your initials alongside.

The summarizing note • The summary is the note most difficult to do well. Material to be summarized must be read more than once, the number of readings depending upon the difficulty of the material and the use to be made of it. First watch for the main ideas and note how each is developed. If the book or magazine is your own, underline the main ideas; otherwise, make notes. You can use a decimal system for recording a location on a page: If a key passage occurs about one third of the way down page 344, mark it 344.3 in your notes. In reading an article to summarize it, work from the general to the spe-

---

[1]Throughout this book, references to *Index* articles are indicated by an asterisk (*).

cific; that is, try first to determine the overall meaning, then the main points, and then the subdivisions supporting each main point. The author's transitional expressions are useful clues to the pattern of his ideas. As in any other note-taking, you must be sure you understand and write down the author's ideas, not your own, even though you disagree violently with the author's point of view. Your summary should not be interrupted or distorted by your personal opinions.

Your success in producing a good summary will depend partly on the care with which you read the original and partly on your skill in cutting unnecessary passages and in condensing the author's language. A good summary reproduces as faithfully as possible the ideas, the structure, and the spirit of the original. Condensation is accomplished by eliminating nonessentials—anecdotes, descriptive details, digressions, illustrations, and all kinds of repetition—and by using appositives, series, and verbals to make the phrasing more compact.

Original	*Summary*
Louisiana leads the nation in fur production and in conservation of fur resources. The state realizes about 5 million dollars annually from its raw fur crop and collects more than $200,000 a year in fees and dues of various kinds for use in maintaining the fur business.—Ruben L. Parson, *Conserving American Resources,* p. 279	Louisiana leads the nation in production of raw furs, and annually realizes about 5 million dollars from them and over $200,000 from fees charged the fur industry.
Government is the "benevolent despot" of conservation, and no one else can play that important role. None but the national government could adequately preserve our aesthetic resources. Only government can prescribe and finance conservation of such scope as flood prevention, forest fire protection, and range restoration. Only government can establish and enforce regulations for cleansing our streams and purifying the air we breathe.—*Ibid.,* pp. 8-9	Only the national government can preserve our aesthetic resources, conduct large-scale conservation, and control water and air pollution.

Many words from the original necessarily reappear in your summary. But if you deliberately use a phrase exactly as it appears in the original, enclose it in quotation marks and cite the page number in parentheses or in a footnote.

Evaluating material

Because preparing a reference paper is largely an exercise of judgment, it is important to evaluate the sources being used. "I found a book in the library that said. . ." is a confession of uncritical work. Your aim should be to find the best books and articles, the most recent and most reliable material on the subject. When you find contradictions or differing estimates in two sources, you should investigate to determine which is more accurate or more probable. Since most of us cannot evaluate references until we have done a good deal of work in a field, we must at first rely on the judgments of others. In your reading you are likely to find remarks about other investigators—that one is the recognized authority, that another misinterprets facts, and so on. Judgments like these should be noted and, if possible, substantiated or disproved by further investigation.

For recent books it is often possible to find reviews that will give some indication of their value. The best sources of reviews of serious works are the learned journals—the *American Historical Review* for historical works, for instance. The *Book Review Digest* will lead you to reviews of less specialized works.

After you have worked on a subject for a while, you can evaluate a good deal of the material yourself, and your considered judgment should influence your further choice of materials. (It is often helpful to enter a brief critical note—your own or one you have found—on a bibliographical card.)

Sources are often classed as *primary* (or *original*) and *secondary*. A primary source is a first record of facts or the closest that a person writing now can come to the subject he is discussing; a secondary source is something written by someone else using original sources. In a paper on a literary subject, for instance, the primary sources are the works written by the man you are discussing—letters, diaries, and so on written by him or by others who knew him; secondary sources are what a critic or historian has written about him and his work. In a science, primary sources are records of observation or experiments;

secondary sources are discussions of such records. In history, primary sources are records of all sorts or reliable reproductions of them—letters, diaries, documents—and remains such as coins, tools, or buildings; secondary sources are historians' accounts based on this evidence. Most textbooks and reference works are secondary sources.

Graduate research relies chiefly on primary sources. Undergraduate papers are drawn principally from secondary sources, but a student who is trying to do a thorough job should use some original ones where possible. He certainly should come as close as he can to the first record of the facts he is to use, and in choosing his material he should try to determine and find the most reliable facts available.

You will find that it is helpful to make a tentative outline— a *tentative* one—fairly early in the note-taking stage. In the first few days of looking for material, you will no doubt have in mind a few points you want to develop; but if these rigidly guide your note-taking, you will overlook many interesting approaches to your topic. On the other hand, if you have only a hazy notion of your subject, you can hardly take notes intelligently and economically; and, because your full notes represent a sizable investment of time and energy, you may later find yourself working desperately to incorporate them into a paper which cannot logically accommodate them. Some notes are bound to be wasted; every researcher duplicates information and jots down irrelevancies. But you can reduce the duplications and irrelevancies if you keep a tentative outline beside you as you take notes and if you revise it regularly. After every three hours or so of reading, while your notes are still fresh in your mind, spend some time studying, modifying, and developing your tentative outline.

Reviewing and sifting your material in this fashion will prepare you to make an exact formulation of the topic and purpose of your paper. Such a statement, usually called a *thesis sentence,* enables you to see the emphasis of your ideas more clearly and makes your research more purposeful. It is often a difficult sentence to write, requiring considerable juggling and cutting. But once it has been worked out, it will guide you in selecting pertinent material. In a careless, hastily prepared paper, the selection is random, including practically everything turned up in the course of the investigation. In a good paper, the selection is deliberate, guided by a controlling idea or thesis.

As you survey your notes and make your final outline, you will be sorting your facts into those that must be used, those that will probably be used, those of incidental importance or interest that may be used, and those that clearly do not belong. It is a good idea to indicate in the margins of your note cards the most important points. You may want to sort your note cards into four groups: *Must, Probably, Maybe,* and *No.* The final selection of material takes place during the actual writing, of course, but the clearer the plan you have in mind before you begin writing, the more easily the paper will move and the more satisfactory it is likely to be.

Planning and writing

After the material has been gathered, the work of planning and writing a reference paper resembles that of any other explanatory or persuasive paper. (See Ch. 2, pp. 47-59 and Chs. 6-7.)

Because of the quantity of material and the length of the paper, you should have your outline clearly in mind—and on paper—before you begin to write. Try to group the material in from five to eight stages—not more unless the paper is unusually long. The main divisions grow out of your material, your approach, and your purpose. To check the plan and to enable your instructor to examine it and make suggestions, cast it in one of the standard outline forms—see Chapter 2, pages 50-52 and *Outline form.

By the time you have come this far, you should be thoroughly familiar with your material. But it may be wise to read your notes through once or twice more to get them fully in mind. This review will also help you put the material into your own words, get it away from the form in which you found it, and work it into the proportion suitable to your paper. Digesting the material into your own words is important; otherwise you will follow your sources too closely. A research paper is not a string of quotations stitched together. It is the intention of the assignment that you take information from various sources and work it into a form of your own. Direct quotation should be kept to a minimum and should always be indicated by quotation marks (see p. 399) or, if it is more than three lines long, by indention as a "display quotation." Often a part of a sentence will be all that needs quoting; the rest of the material you will summarize in your own words.

Because the finished paper gives credit in footnotes to the sources used, you will want to indicate those sources in the first draft. You can put an abbreviated reference to the source used in parentheses after a statement (see the draft reproduced on p. 460), or write the reference in the margin of the paper. **Either method** enables you to transfer the data to a footnote when you make your final copy.

The traditional style of reference papers is Formal and impersonal. It is not usually necessary for the writer to refer to himself at all, and, if he does, the reference should be brief. But impersonal writing does not have to be dull. Aim for compact, direct, readable prose.

The audience for term papers in advanced college courses is ordinarily a specialist in the field—the instructor. But in a composition course, where all sorts of subjects may be treated, the approach may vary from that of a specialist, if you are very much at home in the field of your subject, to that of a writer for a general magazine. Your instructor will explain the approach most appropriate for the course and for the subject. Usually, the best approach is to direct your paper to an intelligent reader who knows little about your subject but has a desire to learn more.

Footnotes and final bibliography

Any paper based on the writings of others should acknowledge the sources used. Not only is it common courtesy and honesty to give credit where credit is due, but it is a sign of scrupulousness to tell the source of a statement, so that a reader can judge for himself the evidence it is based on. It also allows the reader to turn to the sources for further information. College students are expected to draw their materials from various sources, but they are also expected to make a frank acknowledgment of these sources. (See *Plagiarism.)

In formal academic papers—reference papers, term papers, theses, dissertations—it is conventional to give exact references in footnotes. The forms differ slightly, but the aim of all is the same—*to record in some brief and consistent form the author, title, facts of publication, and exact page from which each quotation and each fact or opinion is taken.* Giving these facts about sources of material is called *documentation*. The style of footnotes and bibliography suggested in this chapter is suitable for documentation in a college reference paper. This style follows the recommendations of the *MLA Style*

Sheet, revised edition, which has been adopted by most journals in literature and history and by many university presses. In scientific papers other styles of reference are often used; these are given in the *Index* article *References in scientific papers. *Be sure to learn from your instructor what style of documentation he wants you to follow.*

Footnotes are needed *for all direct quotations* (except well-known bits from the Bible or other literature that are used for style rather than content; for these the source is given in parentheses directly after the quotation) *and for all important statements of facts or interpretations that are summarized from written sources.* Obviously statistics, dates, descriptions of situations, scientific data, opinions, and the like that are not common knowledge and that are presented to advance the thesis of the paper need a stated source.

Although the number of sources referred to in a paper must vary with the type of subject and the kind of sources used, a typical student reference paper might average from two to five footnotes for a page of typewritten manuscript. Material from conversation, from lectures, or from any other source that a reader cannot turn to is best acknowledged in the text of the paper or in a prefatory note. The source of a diagram, map, table, or other illustration is not given in a footnote but under the illustration (see p. 9).

The reference figure is placed slightly above the line after the statement or quotation whose source is being given, usually but not always following a mark of punctuation. The notes are numbered from 1 up throughout the paper. In books they are usually numbered from 1 up on each page, but this practice is rare in college papers.

The footnotes are placed at the bottom of the page on which they belong or all together at the end on a separate sheet headed *Footnotes.* If you put them at the bottom of each page, look ahead in the rough draft to see how many footnotes will be needed on a page; put a light pencil mark where you should begin the footnote series; separate the footnote from the bottom line of the text by a triple space. The first line of each footnote is indented like a paragraph; following lines, if any, begin flush with the left margin and are single-spaced.

The footnote reference number should be slightly raised above the line as in the text; additional footnotes are separated by a double space. (For footnotes on separate sheets you may be instructed to double-space within footnotes and triple-space between them.)

Form of footnotes • The purpose of a citation footnote is to tell the reader the exact source of a statement. Uniformity is a convenience for the reader and is obligatory in scholarly papers and articles intended for publication. This section gives a pattern for use in undergraduate papers.

Books. The *first* reference to a book gives the author's full name (first name first), the full title copied from the title page and underlined, the place and date of publication in parentheses, the page or pages, and a period at the end of the footnote:

> [1]Everett Dick, Vanguards of the Frontier (New York, 1941), p. 450.

Variations on this basic form are introduced for the following reasons, illustrated in order below: (1) more than one author, (2) an edited work, (3) a translated work, (4) a compilation by an editor, (5) an item in a collection, (6) a work in more than one volume, (7) an indication of an edition, (8) a work whose author is not known, (9) material quoted at second hand.

(1) [1]James Bradstreet Greenough and George Lyman Kittredge, Words and Their Ways in English Speech (New York, 1901), p. 185.

(2) [2]H[enry] L[ouis] Mencken, The American Language..., The Fourth Edition and the Two Supplements, abridged, with annotations and new material, by Raven I. McDavid, Jr., with the assistance of David W. Maurer (New York, 1963), p. 521, n.1.

The periods after the title show that it has not been quoted completely; the rest of it is *An Inquiry into the Development of English in the United States.* The brackets after *H* and *L* show that the full first names were not given on the title page but only the initials followed by periods. The material from "The Fourth" to "Maurer" might have been reduced to "ed. Raven I. McDavid, Jr., and David W. Maurer." After the page number "n. 1" means "[foot]note 1."

(3) [3][Thomas] Urquhart and [Peter Antony] Motteux, trans. The Works of Rabelais (London, n.d.), p. 331.

Since this is a well-known translation, the names of the translators are given first; but the note might have read: "[3][François] Rabelais, *The Works,* trans. Urquhart and Motteux (London, n.d.), p. 331."

(4) [4]Letters of Noah Webster, ed. Harry R. Warfel (New York, 1953), p. 49.

(5) [5]Wilfrid Mellers, "Music," The New Outline of Modern Knowledge, ed. Alan Pryce–Jones (London, 1956), pp. 342–365.

(6) [6]William James, The Principles of Psychology, American Science Series—Advanced Course (New York, 1890), II, 403.

Though this work is part of a series, the indication of that fact is not vital here; in other instances it may be.

(7) ⁷Albert C. Baugh, <u>A</u> History <u>of</u> <u>the</u> English Language, 2nd ed. (New York, 1957), p. vii.

(8) ⁸<u>Britain</u>, <u>an</u> Official Handbook, prepared by the Central Office of Information (London, 1962), p. 147.

(9) ⁹Ludwig Wittgenstein, <u>Philosophical</u> <u>Investigations</u> (1953), pp. 65–67, quoted in Barbara M. H. Strang, <u>Modern</u> <u>English</u> <u>Structure</u> (New York, 1962), pp. 2–3.

Pamphlets and government bulletins are referred to in the same form as books. The items always appear in the same order (author, title, place, date, page).

For *later* references to the same book, use a short form, enough to identify the work in the bibliography; the author's last name is sufficient if only one work by the same man is used:

³Dick, <u>Vanguards</u>, p. 128.

Magazine and newspaper articles.   In the *first* reference to a magazine article, give the author's name in normal order, the title of the article in quotation marks, the name of the magazine underlined, the volume in capitalized Roman numerals, the year in parentheses, and the page or pages (number only):

⁴David B. Davis, "Ten–Gallon Hero," <u>American</u> <u>Quarterly</u>, VI (1954), 114.

For magazines that number pages separately in each issue (instead of consecutively through a volume) and for newspapers, give the complete date of issue and page; the volume number may be omitted:

⁵Bernard DeVoto, "Birth of an Art," <u>Harper's</u> <u>Magazine</u>, CCVII (December 1953), 8.

A magazine article with no author given would be referred to as above, but the note would begin with the title of the article.

Reference to a newspaper story or untitled item in a magazine includes the name of the periodical underlined, the date, and the page. The column number may be given. If there are sections paged separately, the section should also be given. Headlines are not ordinarily given because they are often changed from edition to edition.

⁶The New York <u>Times</u>, July 17, 1964, Sec. II, p. 1, col. 6.

A *later* reference to a magazine article or newspaper item may be shortened to the author's last name, the name of the magazine, and the page; or the periodical's name and the page:

⁷DeVoto, <u>Harper's</u>, p. 12.

Unsigned encyclopedia articles may be given by the title of the article or simply by the name of the encyclopedia:

> [12] "Rhetoric," <u>Encyclopaedia</u> <u>Britannica</u> (Chicago, 1964), XIX, 247.
>
> [12] <u>Encyclopaedia</u> <u>Britannica</u> (Chicago, 1964), XIX, 247.

Unsigned publications of organizations are listed by title:

> [13] <u>American</u> <u>Education</u> <u>and</u> <u>International</u> <u>Tension</u> (Washington, National Education Association, 1949), p. 32.

In a footnote *ibid.* means "in the same place"—that is, in the same book or article as the preceding footnote. It is used to refer to the work cited in the immediately preceding footnote. Though useful, it should not appear very often in a good paper; a long succession of *ibid.*'s shows excessive reliance on one source.

> [8] Edward Everett Dale, <u>Cow</u> <u>Country</u> (Norman, Oklahoma, 1945), p. 53.
>
> [9] <u>Ibid.</u>, p. 96.

Ditto marks are not used in footnotes or in the bibliography.

Split note.   If part of a reference is given in the text of the paper, it need not be repeated in the footnote: if the author's name is in the text, the footnote begins with the title; if author and title are in the text, only the facts of publication and the page are in the footnote. This system can be used for material at second hand: if you give the original source in the text, cite in the footnote the secondary source in which you found it.

Informational footnote.   In some scholarly books, you may find an additional fact, a statement of a different opinion, a quotation, or a reference to other sources given in a footnote, but in college writing it is well to use footnotes only for citations of sources; everything else belongs in the text.

Law cases.   The following form is used to cite law cases: the plaintiff's last name, *v.* (*versus*, meaning "against"), the defendant's last name, the volume number of the reports where the case is given, an abbreviation for the report series, the page on which the case begins, and the year in which the decision was rendered:

> [16] Lochner <u>v</u>. New York, 198 U.S. 539 (1905).

Bible.   Books of the Bible are not underlined. The reference form is name of the book, chapter, verse:

> [17] Genesis 4:16 (or 4, 16).

Common abbreviations. The following abbreviations are commonly used in footnotes. Although you are not likely to use them all, you should know what they mean. Those from Latin should be underlined to represent italics.

art.—article

c.—copyright

ca. or *c.* *(circa)* —around a given date *(ca.* 1480)

ch. or chap.—chapter; chs. or chaps.—chapters

col.—column; cols.—columns

ed.—edited by; edition (2nd ed.)

f.—following (one following page: 386 f.); ff. (more than one following page: 286 ff.) Exact references are preferable: pp. 286-287; pp. 286-291

ibid. *(ibidem)* —in the same place

l.—line; ll.—lines

MS.—manuscript; MSS.—manuscripts

n.—note (to refer to a footnote in a source: p. 135n.) ; nn.—notes

n.d.—no date of publication

n.p.—no place of publication

N.S.—new series of a periodical

O.S.—old series of a periodical

p.—page; pp.—pages

tr. or trans.—translated by

vol.—volume; vols.—volumes (vol. and p. are not used when figures for both are given: vol. III *or* p. 176; but III, 176 or 3:176)

The following abbreviations were formerly in general use but are less common now:

cf. *(confer)* —compare (used to cite other related passages)

et al. *(et alii)* —and others (used for multiple authorship; English words are now more common: Maurice Frink and others)

infra—below (referring to something discussed later in the paper)

loc. cit. *(loco citato)* —in the place cited (referring to a passage cited in a recent footnote; not followed by a page number)

op. cit. *(opere citato)* —the work cited: Dick, *op. cit.,* p. 128; now a shortened form of the title is more common: Dick, *Vanguards,* p. 128

passim—here and there (indicating that a matter is discussed in several places in a book or an article)

q.v. *(quod vide)* —which see (used for cross reference; now generally replaced by "see")

seq. *(sequentes)* —following (replaced by *f.* and *ff.*)

supra—above (referring to something discussed earlier in the paper)

s.v. (*sub verbo*)—under the word (used to refer to an item in an alphabetical listing)

vide or *v.*—see (now replaced by the English word)

Any description of the form of footnotes makes their use seem harder than it really is. If you have good notes with the sources carefully recorded, it is relatively simple to keep track of the necessary citations in the first draft and then to place them in the final manuscript in proper form.

The final bibliography • The bibliography of the sources actually used in the preparation of a reference paper comes at its end. It contains not all of the sources consulted but only those which have actually furnished material. Its purpose is to enable a reader to identify the works cited in the footnotes. Though the form of bibliographies has been pretty well standardized, some variations are illustrated in *References in scientific papers; check any of them that your instructor prefers you to use. The forms recommended for a book and for a magazine are as follows:

```
Dick, Everett.  Vanguards of the Frontier.  New York, 1941.
Davis, David B.  "Ten-Gallon Hero," American Quarterly, VI
     (1954), 111-125.
```

Note that authors' names are inverted and hanging indention is used. Your instructor may ask you to double-space between entries.

In short bibliographies all the items are run in one list, alphabetically arranged. When no author is given, the first important word of the title (omitting *a, an,* or *the*) is used as the key word for alphabetizing. Very long bibliographies are sometimes grouped by type of material: Primary Sources, Secondary Sources; Works by an Author, Works about Him; and so on. They should not be grouped according to type of publication, such as books and periodicals, except in a list of the works of a single writer.

Typically the completed paper comprises these units (those in brackets are optional):

Title page: Give the title of the paper, the writer's name, the date submitted, and any other information required, such as course and section number.

[*Preface*: In a preface the writer talks about his work. You will not need a preface unless you wish to thank someone for special help, call attention to some unusual material, or note some point that you wanted to develop or should develop but were unable to. The preface stands on a page by itself.]

Outline and table of contents: Make the type of outline assigned. Be sure that it conforms to the order of material in the finished paper. Check its form by referring to Chapter 2, pages 47-54, and *Outline form. The outline can serve as a table of contents if you give at the right of each main topic the page on which it begins.

Text of the paper: This is the final copy of the paper, complete with footnotes and diagrams or any other illustrative material used. Put the title at the top of the first page and follow the manuscript form required by your instructor. Before making this final copy, go through pages 440-444 of this chapter and the sample paper on pages 451-461 to make sure that your footnotes follow the form suggested.

Bibliography: On a separate page, list in the form suggested on page 444 the books and articles actually used in writing your paper.

[*Appendix:* Occasionally a paper needs a table of statistics too long to work into the body of the paper, or it may require a long quotation, such as part of a treaty or other document that much of the paper is based on. Such material can be placed in an appendix, but it is rather rare in student reference papers.]

Because it is chiefly in its form and method that a reference paper differs from the other papers you write in a composition course, these are the matters that have been stressed in this chapter. Finding sources, preparing a working bibliography, and taking notes on reading—these steps, none of which have any place in, say, a personal narrative, are central activities in preparing a reference paper. And these steps make the two types of papers differ even in physical appearance: the reference paper looks different because of its documentation, the demonstration through an elaborate apparatus of footnotes and bibliography that the statements made have a scholarly basis.

But it is a mistake to regard the reference paper as totally unlike all other kinds of writing you have done. Following the conventions of proper footnote form is an indispensable obligation in writing a reference paper, but discharging that obligation does not guarantee that the paper itself will be worth reading. To produce a really effective paper, you need, first of all, to find in your subject a problem you want to solve, one that stimulates your intellectual curiosity. The feeling that a problem exists and that you want to solve it can turn what might be a dreary canvassing of sources into a coherent, purposeful investigation—an investigation that is interesting to you and, ultimately, interesting to your reader. Whether the paper itself is to be historical or analytical in approach, it is not likely to be satisfactory unless it gives the impression that in writing it you have found out something you consider worth knowing. It will do this if—first of all—solving the problem interests you.

A second requisite of a good reference paper is that in the actual process of composition, your intelligence and your intellectual curiosity dominate your research. Fatigued by his hours in the library and confronted by an enormous stack of note cards, a writer sometimes loses both his confidence and his enthusiasm and proceeds to mechanically fit together the bits of information he has assembled, much as he might piece together a jigsaw puzzle. A paper composed in this fashion is bound to be unsatisfactory, either because its proportions are bad, or because its many segments don't join smoothly, or because no single thesis emerges. Your reader's main interest is in the conclusion you come to, your solution of the problem you have set out to solve. Only if that solution, or an approach toward it, is clearly set forth can your reader judge the pertinence and value of the evidence given to support it. A good reference paper—like any other kind of effective writing—gives the impression that a mind has been at work analyzing the material, interpreting it, and organizing it. To be of real value either to yourself or to your reader, your paper must show that you have weighed and evaluated the material, not just collected it.

In preparing your reference paper, you are, perhaps for the first time, systematically imitating some of the characteristic activities of the scholar. Among the immediate satisfactions are those of making your way deeply into a subject, of thinking critically about a problem that interests you, and of achieving a degree of mastery over the small area of knowledge you have set yourself to explore. You will have proved to yourself that you can bring order out of diversity and that you can organize your thoughts into prose that will interest and inform others. The long-range values are quite as important: the research techniques you learn will be useful to you again and again as you move into more advanced courses and as you cultivate new intellectual interests.

Exercises and sample reference paper

Sample reference paper

On the following right-hand pages a sample reference paper is presented in the style of documentation described on pages 440-444. On the left-hand pages are comments on the paper, possible variant styles in documentation, and further exercises. If your instructor asks you to use any of the variants in your paper, star them in the book and later copy them into your notebook for reference.

Exercises

1. The subjects in the following list are too broad or too general for successful treatment in a reference paper of moderate length. Select two that interest you and make up for each at least four topics that could be treated adequately in papers of the length assigned for your course.

American magazines	Medicare
Atomic Energy Commission	Metalworking
Beaux-arts	Metropolitan Opera Company
Bridges	Modern productions of *Hamlet*
Blood bank	Music in industry
Censorship	Nonobjective painting
Civil rights	Pan-African movement
Detective stories	Parent Teachers Association
Diamonds	Peace Corps
Eskimos	Plastics
Euthanasia	Primitive peoples
Existentialism	Prison conditions
Foreign policy	Public libraries
Frozen foods	Radar
Game laws	Satellites
Grand Canyon	Simplified spelling
Grease paint	Space exploration
Hemingway's novels	Stereophonic sound
Hydroelectric plants	Teaching of poetry
Israeli	Television
Lewis and Clark	Testing procedure
Libel laws	United Nations Peace Force
Linguistics	Utopias
Logical positivism	Volcanoes
Marine Corps	Witchcraft

2. Choose a subject on which you would like to write a reference paper, and prepare brief answers on the following points:

   a. Your reason for choosing this subject

   b. Your present knowledge about the subject and the gaps you would have to fill in

   c. The audience you have in mind and the information you assume this audience already has about the topic

   d. The bibliographies, indexes, and other reference works that would be most useful for the topic you have selected

   e. The main points you will make and the methods you will use to develop them

Comment

The outline below is a preliminary version of the outline of the paper, as given on the opposite page. Study it and prepare to answer the questions in Exercise 3 on the opposite page.

```
              The Cowboy Legend (rough outline)
      The cowboy is a popular hero, and his popularity is largely due
   to characteristics that are not authentic.
   I. The cowboy and his horse
      A. Horses in the movies
      B. Actual cowboys were hard on horses.
      C. Tom Mix and Tony
  II. The Virginian
      A. Published in 1902
      B. Set a pattern that is still popular
      C. High Noon
 III. W. S. Hart
      A. Continued the Virginian type of hero
  IV. The life of the cowboy in the 1870's is the basis of most
      movie cowboys.
      A. By 1890 this life had changed.
      B. An employee of a corporation
      C. In the 1870's he was carefree and adventurous.
      D. Reasons for the change in his way of life
      E. The blizzard of 1887
   V. Cowboy costumes
      A. Movie costumes
      B. Expensive buckskin vests
      C. Actual cowboys
  VI. Singing cowboys
      A. Gene Autry
      B. Songs of actual cowboys
      C. Sentimental songs
```

VII. Gunplay

    A. Marksmanship exaggerated

VIII. Cowboys and homesteaders

    A. Early drives

    B. Movie plots

    C. Johnson County War

  IX. Conclusion

Exercises

3. Compare the preceding outline and the one below and analyze the changes that were made.

a. Why is the revised thesis sentence more satisfactory? Why has the order of topics been changed? Which sections of the original outline overlap? Why is "Conclusion" unnecessary in the outline?

b. Convert the following sentence outline to a topic outline, making each item a noun phrase.

The Cowboy Legend

Although some of the characteristics that have popularized the cowboy as a legendary hero are based on reality, others are imaginary.

  I. The cowboy hero is an anachronism.

    A. The cowboy's free and easy life flourished in the 1870's.

    B. By 1888 his life had changed.

    C. In the legend his life has been made more pleasant.

 II. The _Virginian_ set the basic pattern.

    A. Owen Wister thought that he was describing a vanishing American.

    B. W. S. Hart continued the Virginian tradition.

    C. The Virginian type is still popular.

III. Tom Mix popularized two aspects of the cowboy hero.

    A. The devoted horse is not wholly authentic.

    B. The elaborate costume is also exaggerated.

    C. Actual cowboy dress was more functional than decorative.

 IV. The singing cowboy like Gene Autry has become familiar.

    A. Actual cowboys sang on night guard or around the campfire.

    B. Their singing was very different from movie versions.

  V. Miscellaneous aspects of the legend are also a mixture of fantasy and reality.

    A. The cowboy's proficiency with a gun is exaggerated.

    B. His difficulties with homesteaders have some basis in fact.

    C. His recreations have been revised considerably.

Comment

In a manuscript prepared for a printer, footnotes should be placed on a separate page, following the bibliography, and this form may be used for course papers. Sometimes footnotes are included in the text and set off by two horizontal lines. For example, footnote 4 on the opposite page would come immediately after the line in which its reference number appears and would be set up as follows:

much in New York if a way could be found to get it there.[4]

---
[4]Everett Dick, Vanguards of the Frontier (New York, 1941), p. 450.

The railroad provided the way. Young Americans, many of

Most students and instructors feel that drawing or typing so many lines across the page is a waste of time. The natural place for footnotes is at the bottom of the page, where the eye can pick them up easily and relate them to the material in the text.

The first line of a footnote is usually indented, but it may be written flush with the left margin, in which case the reference number is even with the line:

4. Everett Dick, Vanguards of the Frontier (New York, 1941), p. 450.

A line across or partially across the page may be used to separate the footnotes from the text. An extra space, however, is usually considered adequate (see opposite page).

Variant forms for a footnote to a book differ mainly in content. Sometimes the publisher is included; sometimes the place and year are omitted:

[4]Everett Dick, Vanguards of the Frontier (New York: D. Appleton–Century, 1941), p. 450.
[4]Everett Dick, Vanguards of the Frontier, p. 450.

In some styles the year precedes the volume number of a magazine, and the volume number may be in ordinary (Arabic) numerals:

[2]David B. Davis, "Ten–Gallon Hero," American Quarterly, 1954, 6:114.

Exercises

4. If you are using a style of documentation in your paper which differs from the one followed in this sample paper, rewrite the footnotes on pages 1 and 2 of "The Cowboy Legend" in the form specified.

The Cowboy Legend

The cowboy is the most popular legendary hero America has produced. Evidence of his popularity surrounds us all day long; a grim-faced cowboy stares from a box of morning cereal, and his twin brother gallops through the late movie. His appeal is sometimes explained as a modern longing for the days when life was simple.[1] David B. Davis believes that the cowboy is a symbol of our national adolescence, "the last image of a carefree life."[2] A Swedish critic calls Westerns the American mythology and explains their similarity by saying that any myth requires repetition and "a ritualistic passivity" in the audience.[3] Whatever the reasons, the cowboy's popularity is indisputable and must be mainly due to the cowboy hero himself. His characteristics are partly inventions and partly distortions or exaggerations of actual traits.

The cowboy of movies and television is an anachronism. He represents life on the cattle range in the 1870's and early 1880's. After the Civil War the industrial North offered a market for Texas cattle, which outnumbered people six to one and were of little value. A steer worth three to five dollars in Texas would bring ten times as much in New York if a way could be found to get it there.[4] The railroad provided the way. Young Americans, many of them former soldiers, assumed duties once performed by Mexican herders. The northern drives to the railroad and to grazing lands in Montana and Wyoming are the cowboy's heroic age. Round-ups, river crossings, stampedes, the chuck wagon, and the wandering cowboy date from this period. As early as 1888 Theodore Roosevelt wrote that "In its present form stock-raising on the plains is doomed, and can hardly outlast the century. The great free ranches...

[1] "Just Wild About Westerns," Newsweek, L (July 22, 1957), 51.

[2] "Ten-Gallon Hero," American Quarterly, VI (1954), 114.

[3] Harry Schein, "The Olympian Cowboy," trans. Ida M. Alcock, The American Scholar, XXIV (1955), 311.

[4] Everett Dick, Vanguards of the Frontier (New York, 1941), p. 450.

Comment

Quotations can often be blended more smoothly into the text and reduced in bulk by the use of the *ellipsis (...). In citation 5 the quotation itself seemed necessary because of the authority carried by Roosevelt's actual words. The following was omitted: ... *with their barbarous, picturesque, and curiously fascinating surroundings, mark a primitive stage of existence as surely as do the great tracts of primeval forests, and like the latter.*... Since the words add nothing to the student's paper, he is free to cut them as long as he does not distort the meaning of the original. Short quoted phrases like those in the first paragraph of the sample paper do not require an ellipsis.

Note 5: In the citation of a book or an article by two authors, both names are given.

Note 6: A book by more than two authors may also be cited as follows:

⁶Maurice Frink, W. Turrentine Jackson, Agnes Wright
Spring, When Grass Was King (Boulder, Colorado, 1956), p. 58.
⁶Maurice Frink et al., When Grass Was King (Boulder,
Colorado, 1956), p. 58.

Note 7: The first reference to a book or an article should be complete enough to enable the reader to find it. Later references should be condensed. Note 7 could also be handled as follows:

⁷Brown, op. cit., p. 130.
⁷Brown, Trail Driving Days, p. 130.

If lengthy, the title may be shortened but not abbreviated; *Days* would be acceptable. The use of *op. cit.* (work previously cited) is decreasing. If one book is used, the author's last name (see example) is adequate. If two books by the same author are used, a shortened title is necessary to indicate which one is being cited.

⁷Brown, Days, p. 130.

Exercises

5. Bring to class a quotation of about three sentences from a source that you are using in your paper.

a. Summarize it in your own words.

b. Reduce it by leaving out words and inserting an ellipsis.

c. Pick out a brief usable phrase and blend it into a sentence of your own.

must pass away before the onward march of our people."[5]

The end of an era is difficult to pinpoint. Perhaps the cowboy's way of life began to change with the invention of barbed wire in 1874. Its use spread widely; 80,500,000 pounds had been sold by 1880.[6] It brought the small farmer, closed off the northern trails, and forced cattlemen to grow hay for winter feed. The open range was doomed. The passing of the early cowboy might also be dated from the blizzard of 1886–1887. Millions of cattle starved or froze to death. The next spring many unemployed cowboys became homesteaders; others went to work for the large corporations that survived the debacle. The carefree cowboy became a cowhand, who spent much of his time stretching fence, haying, digging wells, and dehorning cattle. In the late 1880's on the huge new XIT (ten counties in Texas) ranch, drinking, gambling, and carrying firearms were forbidden.[7]

Creators of the movie cowboy have eliminated most unpleasantness from his existence. The loneliness and boredom of a life in which memorizing labels on tin cans was a major recreation[8] are seldom shown. The swirling dust in the face of a cowboy at the rear of a cow column, the prairie dog holes into which his horse might stumble, the swift current that imperiled a man riding downstream of a swimming herd--such hazards have been cut in favor of melodramatic encounters with rustlers and bandit-leaders masquerading as respectable bankers. The legendary cowboy has been raised to an enviable status which inspires respect but requires no work. Cowboy movies in which cattle are not even seen are common.

In 1902, when the cowboy seemed a vanishing American,

[5]Quoted in Dee Brown and Martin F. Schmitt, Trail Driving Days (New York, 1952), p. 231.

[6]Maurice Frink and others, When Grass Was King (Boulder, Colorado, 1956), p. 58.

[7]Brown, p. 130.

[8]Philip Ashton Rollins, The Cowboy (New York, 1922), p. 185.

Comment

Note 9: A lengthy title may be shortened in the first citation if the full title is given in the bibliography.

Note 10: The author's name and title of the book are given in the text. Only what is not given in the text is presented in the footnote. If the book had been cited previously, only the page number would be needed, and it might be given in the text in parentheses. The small Roman numeral indicates a page in the preface.

Note 11: When two sources supply information for the same sentence, they are cited in one footnote and separated by a semicolon. The necessity for this type of note seldom arises. The author of the magazine article was given by initials only, "S.P."

Note 12: The author's name is not repeated because it appears in the text.

Exercises

6. Draw the floor plan of the reference library, or that part of the library where you will be gathering material, and show the location of the following reference works, and any others assigned, using the letters as listed below. If you are unable to locate some of the references, consult the card catalog to see whether your library has them.
   a. *Readers' Guide*
   b. *International Index*
   c. *Encyclopaedia Britannica*
   d. *Encyclopedia Americana*
   e. *New York Times Index*
   f. *Oxford English Dictionary*
   g. *Current Biography*
   h. *Dictionary of National Biography*
   i. *Britannica Book of the Year*
   j. *Dictionary of American Biography*

7. Read at least two articles in general encyclopedias on your topic and one in a special encyclopedia. (See the list on pages 425-427.) Contrast these articles as to (a) date of publication; (b) completeness of treatment; (c) emphasis, or possible bias; (d) approach, whether popular or technical; (e) interest and general value of the articles for your purpose.

Owen Wister wrote a novel that standardized the legendary
cowboy's personality. The Virginian has sold more than
1,600,000 copies[9] and has been popular as a play and as a
movie. In his preface to the novel, Wister announced that
the cowboy had disappeared and "rides in his historic yesterday."[10] The real-life cowboy, perhaps; but the soft-
spoken Virginian galloped straight into the plot of High
Noon and a thousand other movies.

Although Broncho Billy, the first movie cowboy, began
making short films in 1908, William S. Hart was the first
to number his fans in the millions.[11] A former stage actor,
he continued the Virginian tradition of a taciturn
hero, honest and upright and true.

The Virginian is as reluctant to fight as Achilles. He
endures insults and indignities but sets a limit which
must not be passed: "When you call me that, smile." He
postpones his wedding while he walks out to meet the
villain who killed his pal. Of course, he lets the villain
fire first. His phlegmatic chivalry and devotion to a
friend set a pattern for his successors. Bernard DeVoto
called the Virginian "a sun god in leather pants" but complained that because of "caste snobbery" Wister put his
hero on the side of the cattle barons.[12] Whatever his
allegiance may be, the Virginian, erect on his beloved
"hawss," is the original legendary cowboy.

Although the cowboy's horse was essential in life, it
is indispensable in legend. Tom Mix, who rose to fame
about the same time as W. S. Hart, popularized the devoted,
intelligent horse that can pick a lock, untie knots, and

[9]Seth M. Agnew, "Destry Goes On Riding...," Publishers'
Weekly, CLXIX (August 22, 1952), 746.

[10](New York, 1902), p. x.

[11]S.P., "50 Years Going That-a-Way," New York Times
Magazine (April 5, 1953), pp. 20-21; Daniel Blum, A Pictorial
History of the Silent Screen (New York, 1953), p. 10.

[12]"Birth of an Art," Harper's Magazine, CCVII (December
1953), 8.

Comment

As is shown in the sample note cards below, the page number is written first to prevent memory lapses. On the first card, a part of a sentence is taken as a quotation in case the author's words are wanted in the paper. In quoting, use an author's exact words and enclose them in quotation marks; in summarizing, do not use his words.

In the second sample card, several facts have been taken on the same card because they will obviously be used at the same point in the paper. Note that they were not used in the same order in which they were found and that the second point was not used at all. Single quotes around the last point indicate a quotation in the original.

Slug   Source

Page
Notes

Rollins

Horses

275 – One pony good at cutting out, another at driving stock, another at roping, etc.

There, "to an efficient cowboy on a large ranch were assigned several ponies, one animal for one class of work, another for another."

Slug   Source

Page
Notes

Rollins

Clothes

105 – hat used for eye-shade, water bucket, fan for campfire, pillow, etc.

106-7 – bandana pulled over nose and face in dust or cold

109 – vest always worn (ordinary civilian type), pockets for matches and tobacco, left arms free

114 – two-inch heels kept heels from slipping through stirrups

117 – 'cattle country, thoroughly masculine; "hung its clothes on the floor, so they couldn't fall down and get lost." Only saddles, bridles, lariots, and firearms received considerate care.'

Use of *ibid.*: Because footnotes 14, 15, and 16 refer to Rollins, *ibid.* (in the same place) is sufficient.

Exercises

8. Bring to class three note cards and be prepared to discuss how the information may be used in your paper.

anticipate every thought of his cowboy costar. To some
extent, the mutual affection of cowboy and horse is a substitute for a love-plot, which most patrons of cowboy
movies would find objectionable. Beautiful palominos and
Arabians, the movie horses are far different from actual
cow ponies. In fact, a cowboy had a string of horses, each
valued for a particular skill such as cutting out or night
herding.[13] At round-up and on a long drive he was hard
on horses and used them up fast. If he felt a special
fondness for one horse, it was often a memory of a horse
he had once owned.

Tom Mix is also chiefly responsible for the elaborate
cowboy regalia. His white sombrero, white gloves, and
jewelled spurs have been imitated by most of his successors. Although an actual cowboy might take pride in his
appearance when he left the ranch, he ordinarily was careful only of his saddle, bridle, lariat, and gun. In the
cattle country clothes were hung on the floor "so they
couldn't fall down and get lost."[14]

The dress of an actual cowboy was functional. Every item
of his apparel had its purpose--from the two-inch heels,
which enabled him to brace against the stirrups when
roping a calf, to the sombrero, which he could use to fan
a campfire or to carry water to his horse.[15] His cloth
"civilian" vest, which left his arms free and provided
pockets for matches and tobacco,[16] contrasts sharply with
the embroidered, pearl-encrusted garment for which a movie
cowboy may pay several hundred dollars.

To the legend established by the Virginian and glamor-
ized by Tom Mix, Gene Autry added a new element--singing.
Actual cowboys sang on night guard because of a superstition that cattle were soothed by the sound of a human.

[13]Rollins, p. 275.

[14]Ibid., p. 117.

[15]Ibid., p. 114; p. 105.

[16]Ibid., p. 109.

• *Exercises*

Comment

A quotation of three or more lines may be indented and single-spaced; it should not be enclosed in quotation marks unless the quotation marks appear in the original source, as they did in the two notes on the opposite page.

Long blocks of quoted matter often indicate too much reliance on sources. The inclusion of three quotations on a single page (see the page opposite) is rather unusual, but the quotations are appropriate to the material. There is no set way of introducing a display quotation. Compare the three ways used in the sample paper.

Note 18: The citation of an unusual source like a phonograph record (Note 18) or a mimeographed pamphlet that does not fit any of the conventional forms should resemble as closely as possible the style used for other footnotes. It should ordinarily describe the unusual source briefly in parentheses.

Exercises

9. Write out in full these entries from the *Readers' Guide,* using the form recommended by your instructor. Consult a recent volume of the index for the meaning of any unfamiliar abbreviations. What information in these entries would you omit in your footnotes and bibliography? What additional information might you need?

COLLEGES and universities

Attendance

Sheepskin explosion; bumper crop of incoming freshmen. il Bsns W p23-4 Je 20 '64

GOLDMAN, Eric F.

Summer Sunday; excerpt from Incident in Coatesville. Am Heritage 15:50-3+ Je '64

SACCHARIDES

Intestinal disaccharidases; absence in two species of sea lions. P. Sunshine and N. Kretchmer. biblio il Science 14:850-1 My 15 '64

SHAKESPEARE, William

Comedy of errors

Shakespeare with a few tears; Royal Shakespeare company's version. R. Brustein. New Repub 150:30-2 Je 13 '64
Theatre; Royal Shakespeare company's production in New York. H. Clurman. Nation 198:592 Je 8 '64

voice.[17] They sang also to let off steam on their rare
trips to town and to pass the time around the campfire.

> "Well, after they'd tied up their night horses, and the
> day's work was done, why, they'd always build up a camp-
> fire and sit around till they was ready to go to bed.
> Then they'd always see which was the finest singer and
> knew the most songs."[18]

Their songs and their manner of singing were far different from the movie hero with a guitar slung from his
saddle who bursts into song at the drop of a rustler. The
songs were of all kinds, but some of the favorites were
surprisingly sentimental like the following:

> Close the brown eyes gently,
> Beautiful Mable Clare,
> For no more shall I gather wild flowers
> To braid in your shining hair.[19]

No one seems to describe the singing as melodious.

> "...the average puncher's voice and the songs he sings
> ain't soothing. Mostly he has a voice like a burro with
> a bad cold, and the noise he calls singin'd drive all
> the coyotes out of the country."[20]

The cowboy's proficiency as a gun-slinger is probably
as exaggerated as his ability as a ballad-singer. He
usually wore one forty-five and carried a rifle to protect
the herd from wolves, but he was "only a fair marksman
with a pistol."[21] The movie cowboy firing from the hip
with both hands has often been repudiated, and the legend
of "fanning" a hammer is even less credible.

[17]Edward Everett Dale, Cow Country (Norman, Oklahoma,
1945), p. 53.

[18]Harry Stephens of Denison, Texas, in a recorded interview with John A. Lomax, "Cowboy Songs, Ballads, and Cattle
Calls from Texas," ed. Duncan Emrich (Record L28, issued
by Music Division, Library of Congress).

[19]Dale, p. 128.

[20]Ramon F. Adams, Western Words (Norman, Oklahoma,
1944), p. 144.

[21]Dale, pp. 122-123.

- *Exercises*

Comment

A rough draft should be triple-spaced or written with wide margins to leave room for revisions. Notice in the sample rough draft below that a brief citation in parentheses records temporarily the source of material used. If footnotes are put at the bottom of the page in a rough draft, one or two may be overlooked because the draft and the final copy will not correspond page for page.

In the sample below, the writer was carried away by his interest in a phase of his subject irrelevant to his purpose and gave it more space than it deserves. Notice the condensation and the single footnote to cover a summary of four pages in the sample paper.

The ~~dislike of~~ *animosity between* cowboys and homesteaders is ~~factual~~ *based on fact*. *Kansas and Missouri* ~~Farmers to the North~~ did not like the first *N*orthern *D*rive *in 1866* because of their belief that cattle carried "Spanish fever." (Brown, 6) Many cowboys ~~also~~ *also,* came from the South, and their ways probably shocked the ~~northerners~~ *transplanted Yankees* in the farm states. In 1892 ~~cattlemen in Johnson County, Wyoming~~ *warfare broke between stockmen and homesteaders broke out in Johnson County, Wyoming.* ~~formed a society known as Regulators to attack the homesteaders. (Brown, 228) They arrived in Casper Wyoming, on April 7 and moved into Johnson County. (Brown, 229) They attacked the ranch of Nate Champion, a leader of the homesteaders. The homesteaders organized an army and moved against them, and fighting was stopped only by the arrival of the U. S. cavalry. (Brown, 231)~~ *(Brown, 228-31)*

Exercises

10. Bring your rough draft and your outline to class or to an individual conference with your instructor. Be prepared to explain your methods of revision and to bring up points on which you need to ask your instructor's advice.

The animosity between cowboy and homesteader is based
on fact. Kansas and Missouri farmers opposed the first
northern drive in 1866 because of their belief that Texas
cattle carried "Spanish fever."[22] Also, many cowboys were
Southerners, and their ways probably shocked the transplanted Yankees in the farm states. In 1892 warfare between stockmen and homesteaders broke out in Johnson
County, Wyoming.[23] It is doubtful, however, that every
homesteader had a daughter to fall in love with a cattle-
man, as in most movie treatments, and thus resolve the
feud.

The cowboy's recreations have been revised drastically.
His drinking habits have been toned down. When he was
paid off and came to town, a real cowboy's drinking was
uninhibited and rapid.[24] The hero calling for sarsaparilla
or milk must have been far less common than in Western
movies. The movie cowboy is hedged in by a long list
of taboos: he cannot spit, swear, chew tobacco, drink
whisky, or kiss the heroine. He has, however, been
granted wider latitude in gambling. Although gambling was
widespread in the cattle country and there are stories of
ranches being lost on the turn of a card, poker games for
high stakes must have been rare among ordinary cowboys.
The fact seems indisputable when one learns that a cowboy's
monthly wage was from thirty to thirty-five dollars.[25]

While the cowboy on America's movie and television
screens may ride the old range and fight the old fights,
he is as different from his historic counterpart as exaggeration, distortion, and invention can make him. But to
his millions of fans this fact will hardly make a difference—he represents what cowboys should have been like,
whether they were or not.

[22]Brown, p. 6.
[23]Ibid., pp. 228-231.
[24]Rollins, pp. 187-188.
[25]Frink and others, p. 10.

Comment

The sample cards are for entries 6 and 8 in the bibliography on the facing page. Note that publishers are not given. If they were, the first entry might read:

```
Adams, Ramon F. Western Words. Norman, University of
Oklahoma Press, 1944.
```

The two entries *without* authors are given by title, alphabetically.

	Call Number	Slug	Code

F 596   singing   Dale
D25

Author   Dale, Edward Everett

Title   Cow Country

Publication data   Norman, Oklahoma, 1945

Comment   singing and night-herding, pp. 52-54

Book

	Location	Slug	Code

west stacks   Virginian   DeVoto

Author   DeVoto, Bernard

Title   "Birth of an Art"

Publication data   Harper's Magazine

CCVII (December 1953), 8-9

Comment   pretty anti-Wister; Virginian set pattern for western movies

Magazine

Exercises

11. Evaluate the sample paper as a piece of writing. Pay particular attention to the organization, to the development of the thesis, and to the quality of the writing.

Bibliography

Adams, Ramon F. <u>Western</u> <u>Words</u>. Norman, Oklahoma, 1944.

Agnew, Seth M. "Destry Goes On Riding—or—Working the
    Six-Gun Lode," <u>Publishers'</u> <u>Weekly</u>, CLXIX (August 22,
    1952), 746-751.

Blum, Daniel. <u>A</u> <u>Pictorial</u> <u>History</u> <u>of</u> <u>the</u> <u>Silent</u> <u>Screen</u>.
    New York, 1953.

Brown, Dee and Martin F. Schmitt. <u>Trail</u> <u>Driving</u> <u>Days</u>.
    New York, 1952.

"Cowboy Songs, Ballads, and Cattle Calls from Texas," ed.
    Duncan Emrich (Record L28, issued by Music Division,
    Library of Congress).

Dale, Edward Everett. <u>Cow</u> <u>Country</u>. Norman, Oklahoma,
    1945.

Davis, David B. "Ten-Gallon Hero," <u>American</u> <u>Quarterly</u>,
    VI (1954), 111-125.

DeVoto, Bernard. "Birth of an Art," <u>Harper's</u> <u>Magazine</u>,
    CCVII (December 1953), 8-9.

Dick, Everett. <u>Vanguards</u> <u>of</u> <u>the</u> <u>Frontier</u>. New York, 1941.

Frink, Maurice and others. <u>When</u> <u>Grass</u> <u>Was</u> <u>King</u>. Boulder,
    Colorado, 1956.

"Just Wild About Westerns," <u>Newsweek</u>, L (July 22, 1957),
    51-54.

Rollins, Philip Ashton. <u>The</u> <u>Cowboy</u>. New York, 1922.

S.P. "50 Years Going That-a-Way," <u>New</u> <u>York</u> <u>Times</u> <u>Magazine</u>,
    April 5, 1953, pp. 20-21.

Schein, Harry. "The Olympian Cowboy," trans. Ida M. Alcock,
    The <u>American</u> <u>Scholar</u>, XXIV (1955), 309-320.

Wister, Owen. <u>The</u> <u>Virginian</u>. New York, 1902.

12. Put the following references to source material in consistent footnote form as they would appear in a reference paper. Keep them in the present alphabetical order.

    a. To page 225 of this book.

    b. To an editorial in the Boston Traveler on December 2, 1940, entitled The Responsibility of the Press.

    c. To pages 139 and 140 in the second volume of a book by George Philip Krapp called The English Language in America. The book was published by the Century Company of New York and the date on the title page reads MCMXXV.

    d. To pages 228 to 231 inclusive of the book mentioned in a.

    e. To an unsigned article called Carping about a Candidate in volume 83 of Time for June 19, 1964, page 36.

    f. To page xvii in the Introduction of a book called Burke's Politics. The book has a subtitle Selected writings and speeches of Edmund Burke on Reform, revolution and war. It was edited by Ross J. S. Hoffman and Paul Levack, and was published in 1949 by Alfred A. Knopf in New York.

    g. To an article entitled Letters to the Editor as a Means of Measuring the Effectiveness of Propaganda, written by two men, H. Schuyler Foster, Jr., and Carl J. Friedrich and printed in The American Political Science Review for February 1937, pages 71 to 79. This issue was part of volume 31.

    h. To the same pages of the article mentioned in g.

    i. To a quotation by Dr. Raymond B. Nixon in the June 1945 issue of Journalism Quarterly, quoted on pages 78 to 79 of The First Freedom, a book by Morris L. Ernst published in 1946 in New York by The Macmillan Company.

    j. To an unsigned article called Isle of Man in the 1941 edition of the Encyclopedia Americana, a thirty-volume work published in New York and Chicago by the Americana Corporation. This article appeared on page 414 of volume XV.

13. Put the items above in proper form and order for a bibliography.

14. Write a brief report in class on one of the following topics:

    a. A summary or précis of your paper, giving the essential ideas and emphasis of the original

    b. Different methods by which you could have developed your paper, and why you chose the one you did

    c. The sources you found most useful and why

    d. Some problems you encountered in organizing your paper and how you solved them

    e. Some by-products of your research—what you have learned about finding material, about the subject itself, or about further areas for investigation

INDEX TO ENGLISH

To make the maximum use of this Index, *first read* Ch. 1 *of the* Guide *so that you will understand the general principles involved, and then read a few consecutive pages of the* Index *articles (or a selection of them) to see those principles applied. With this preparation the articles should prove of immediate use in your writing.*

The sources most used in gathering the material for this book are usually referred to by the author's name only. The exact titles of these sources will be found in the Bibliography on pp. xiii-xiv.

A full discussion of the symbols by which pronunciation is represented appears in the article *Pronunciation § 1, p. 761.

An asterisk preceding a word or phrase indicates a reference to another article within the Index.

This *Index* contains articles in alphabetical arrangement that fall roughly into four categories:

Articles on particular words and constructions • such as *continual–continuous; *fiancé, fiancée; *get, got; *like–as; *plenty; *shall–will; *so ... that; *very. Information about their standing in current usage is given. Since in these discussions classifying labels like Nonstandard, Standard, General, and Formal are used, you should read Ch. 1 of the *Guide* in order to make certain of the meaning of these terms as they are employed in this *Index.* The entry words are not capitalized.

Articles for correction and revision of papers • indicated by longhand abbreviations before the entry word. A list of these articles is given on the end papers at the back of this book. These subjects are so important that they are likely to be studied in class and so are usually treated in the chapters of the *Guide;* but for convenience in revising papers the basic points are given in the *Index* article, with a page reference to the treatment in the *Guide.* These entries are capitalized.

Articles on English grammar • giving definitions and examples of such matters as *Case, *Plurals of nouns, *Principal parts of verbs, which are necessary for a description and understanding of the language. Entries are capitalized.

Articles on various facts of language • such as *American and British usage, *Foreign words in English, *Linguistics, that are designed more for general information than for immediate application. Entries are capitalized.

A • In standard spelling the letter *a* represents several different sounds, which are also spelled by other letters. They are
listed here by their traditional names because these are well-
known though not phonetically accurate:

1. *"Short a,"* the /a/ of *hat* and *stack,* differently spelled in
plaid.

2. *"Long a,"* the /ā/ of *game* and *famous*; other spellings
occur in *aid, gauge, say, break, vein, weigh, they,* and *Gaelic.*

3. *"Broad a,"* the /ä/ of *hard, father,* and *calm,* differently
spelled in *heart* and *sergeant.* Speakers of Standard British
English and some speakers in the United States and Canada
use this vowel in a fairly large group of words like *ask, bath,
craft, demand, half,* and *laugh.* In eastern New England these
words are often pronounced with a vowel between /a/ and /ä/,
known as "intermediate *a.*" But the great majority of Americans and Canadians pronounce the *"ask*-group" with the /a/
of *hat.*

Some speakers try to substitute the broad *a* or intermediate *a*
for their natural short *a* in these words. But this attempt to
imitate a type of pronunciation not naturally acquired usually
calls attention to itself, especially since the imitated vowel may
be introduced into the wrong words: British *glass* /gläs/, for
example, may lead to /läs/ for *lass,* which British speakers
pronounce /las/. The best practice is to pronounce this group
of words in the way that is natural to you.

4. The /ā/ of *care* and *parent,* differently spelled in *fair, pear,
prayer, their,* and *where.* In these words the vowel varies re-
gionally between the /ā/ of *gate* and the /a/ of *hat.*

5. The /o/ of the first syllable of *swallow* (/swol'ō/, rhyming
with *follow*), more commonly spelled with *o,* as in *rock* and
novel. Many speakers have /ä/ in these words.

6. *"Open o,"* the /ô/ of *tall* and *warm,* differently spelled in
broad, maul, draw, soft, taught, and *thought.* Here, too, pronunciation varies in different regions; many use this vowel
only before *r,* pronouncing the other words so that *stalk* and
stock, caller and *collar* are identical.

7. The *"schwa"* /ə/ of *soda* and *about.* This *neutral vowel
sound occurs only in unstressed syllables and is also spelled
with the other vowel letters, as in *society, pencil, lemon, circus.*

(Reference: *Webster's Third New International Dictionary,*
"A Guide to Pronunciation," p. 34a.)

a • The prefix *a-* (from Greek meaning *not*) forms many
words in the Formal and scientific vocabularies (*amoral, asex-
ual, asymmetrical, atypical, achromatic*). It is usually pronounced /ā/.

An Old English prepositional prefix *a-* is found in many words (*abed, aloud, asleep, alert, afraid*), and survives in such regional and Nonstandard phrases as *going a-fishing, a-hunting.*

a—an •
1. The choice between *a* and *an* depends on the initial sound, not on the initial letter, of the word that follows:

A is used before all words beginning with *a consonant sound* —that is, before all words spelled with initial consonant letters except silent *h*, as in *hour*—and before words spelled with initial vowel letters that represent combined consonant and vowel sounds, as in *eulogy* /ū′lə jē/, *unit* /ū′nit/: *a business, a European trip, a D, a usage.*

An is used before all words beginning with *a vowel sound,* including words spelled with initial silent *h* (see *H): *an apple, an F, an hour apart, an honor.*

In words beginning with *h* but not accented on the first syllable, as in *histo′rian, hyste′rical, h* was formerly not pronounced, so that *an* was used. Although the *h* is now often pronounced, some people continue to say and write *an histor′ical* event (but *a his′tory*). In contemporary usage *a* is the more common in such locutions, but an individual may use whichever comes more easily.

2. Repeating *a* or *an* before each noun of a series tends to keep the various words distinct and make the expression emphatic: *a pen, a sheet of paper, and an envelope* (*a pen, sheet of paper, and envelope* would be less emphatic).

3. *Awhile, a while.* The adverb **awhile* is written as one word (He came *awhile* ago) but not the noun (He came for *a while*). The *a* is also separate in *a lot, a bit, a little.* (See *half for *a half hour, half an hour,* etc. See also *kind of a, sort of a.*)

Abbreviations •
    Revision: Write in full the abbreviation marked.
Ab

1. *Appropriateness.* Abbreviations are appropriate in manuals, reference books, business and legal documents, scholarly footnotes, and other works in which saving space is important. They also fit in Informal writing—notes for one's own use, letters to friends. In college papers and most Formal writing, abbreviations are held to a minimum.

*Shoptalk, familiar conversation, and *slang use many abbreviations for the names of things frequently mentioned: *d.t.'s—delirium tremens, VIP—very important person.*

2. *Standard abbreviations.* Dr., *Mr.,* *Mrs.,* *Messrs.* are always abbreviated when used with names. A number of abbreviations, such as *St.* (see *Saint), **a.m.* and *p.m.,* and abbreviations for government agencies such as *TVA* and *SEC,* are commonly used. In Formal writing, titles like *Reverend, *Professor, President,* and *Senator* would not be abbreviated at all, but in most other writing they are found abbreviated *when initials or given names are used:* not *Prof. Hylander,* but *Professor Hylander* or *Prof. G. W. Hylander.*

English still has many abbreviations of Latin words:

A.D.	*Anno Domini*—in the year of our Lord (see *Centuries)
cf.	*confer*—compare (for which *see* may be used)
e.g.	*exempli gratia*—for example
*etc.	*et cetera*—and so forth
ibid.	*ibidem*—the same (used in footnotes)
i.e.	*id est*—that is

Such abbreviations are not italicized, unless there is a special reason for italics (as when *ibid.* represents the title of a book), since they are regarded as English words. Less commonly used abbreviations from Latin are usually italicized: *c.* or *ca.* (*circa,* "about," used with uncertain dates), *seq.* (*sequentes* or *sequentia,* "following").

Dictionaries give frequently used abbreviations in the main alphabetical list of words or in a special list. (See Ch. 11, p. 443 for abbreviations used in footnotes of reference papers.)

3. *Period with abbreviations.* Most abbreviations are still normally followed by a period; where standard practice requires the period, its omission is a careless slip. Only one period is used after an abbreviation at the end of a sentence.

The omission of the period after an abbreviation that ends with the last letter of the word abbreviated is chiefly British: *Dr, Mr, Mrs, vs, Wm.*

Periods are increasingly omitted with the abbreviations of names of government agencies (*SEC, TVA, FBI*) and of other terms if the abbreviation is generally used instead of the name (*AFL-CIO, UNESCO, NATO, CBS*), and of phrases like *mph, hp, kwh, rpm* in scientific contexts or when used with figures (*780 rpm*).

Abbreviations that are pronounced as words (*Wac, Nazi, UNESCO*) are called *acronyms.* The number of these has been increasing; over 12,000 of them are listed in *Acronyms Dictionary: A Guide to Alphabetical Designations, Contractions and Initialisms* [of nonprofit organizations] (Detroit, Gale Research Co., 1960).

(For information on abbreviation of dates, see *Months; of names, see *Given names; of references in scientific papers, see *References in scientific papers § 1c. Compare *Contractions, *Origin of words § 3c.)

ability to • The idiom with *ability* is *to* and an infinitive (ability *to do,* not *of doing*): *He has the ability to design beautiful buildings.* The idea is often better expressed by an adjective or verb: *He is able to [He can] design beautiful buildings. He designs [is designing] beautiful buildings.*

able to • *Able to* is rarely followed by a passive infinitive (like *to be done* or *to be ended*) because the construction sounds awkward.

Awkward: This was not able to be done because of lack of time.
Improved: This could not be done because of lack of time. [Or] They were not able to do this because of lack of time.

Though *able to* may sometimes be replaced by *can* or *could,* it is mandatory to express some time relationships: *will be able, might be able.* (See *Tenses of verbs § 1.)

-able, -ible • These two suffixes, alike in meaning, cause trouble in spelling because we pronounce them alike. In earlier English they were pronounced differently, as they are in Latin and French, but the English tendency to obscure the vowels in unstressed syllables has obliterated the distinction. Since pronunciation is of no help, we must learn the spelling of each word. The suffix *-able* is by far the more common form and should be used in coining occasional words like *jumpable* or *come-at-able.*

1. *-able.* This list contains a few of the many words ending in *-able*:

advisable	imaginable	movable	teachable
applicable	incurable	noticeable	tolerable
changeable	indispensable	perishable	unbearable
comfortable	inseparable	presentable	unbelievable
desirable	intolerable	receivable	unmistakable
detestable	justifiable	serviceable	unpronounceable
eatable	laughable	sizable	unspeakable
excusable	lovable	suitable	usable

2. *-ible.* The following rather common words have *-ible*:

accessible	convertible	edible	impossible
audible	corruptible	eligible	incredible
combustible	credible	feasible	indefensible
compatible	digestible	flexible	indelible
comprehensible	discernible	gullible	inexhaustible
contemptible	divisible	horrible	intelligible

invisible	permissible	responsible	susceptible
irresistible	plausible	reversible	tangible
legible	possible	sensible	terrible
negligible	reducible	suggestible	visible

3. *-able* or *-ible*. Several words are found with either *-able* or *-ible*. The more common form is put first: *collapsible—collapsable, collectable—collectible, preventable—preventible*.

about • Like most English preposition-adverbs, *about* has a variety of uses, a few of which have raised questions.
1. *about—around*. In describing physical position these are nearly interchangeable, though *around* is the more common (about the barn—around the barn). In the sense of *nearly* or *approximately, about* is more common (about 70°) but both are Standard usage.
2. *about—almost*. In the sense of *almost* (about finished), *about* is Standard but slightly Informal.
3. *at about*. Strictly speaking, something would be either *at* or *about,* but the two words are frequently used together (At about four o'clock we crossed the line), with the *about* then best regarded as an adverb, emphasizing the indefiniteness. (See *at about, at around.)
4. *About* followed by an infinitive is a convenient idiom for *on the point of* with the added advantage of allowing a future or anticipated act to be put into past time: *He was about to make a third try.*

above • *Above* is primarily used as a preposition (above the clouds) or adverb (dark above and light below). Its adverbial use in such phrases as "the evidence cited above" is common in contemporary prose; but many writers prefer "the evidence already cited" or some such expression. The use of *above* as an adjective (the above prices, the prices above) or as a noun (the above is confirmed) is often found in commercial and journalistic writing, the adjective use the more frequent, but it is usually avoided elsewhere. (Reference: Bryant, pp. 3-4.)

Abridged clauses • See *Clauses § 3b.

Absolute constructions • Absolute constructions like *The narrows passed* in "The narrows passed, we went along at a fairly good speed," modify the sentence as a whole. They are "absolute" not because they are independent but because they lack connectives defining their relationship to other sentence elements, being joined to the rest of the sentence only by their position, by contact. When absolute phrases follow the main clause, they are a convenient way of adding details:

She walked slowly, big flakes falling on her lamb coat and cling-ing to hair over her ears, the lazily falling snow giving her, in her thick warm coat, a fine feeling of self-indulgence.—MORLEY CAL-LAGHAN, *A Native Argosy,* p. 135

Here everything except the main clause, *She walked slowly,* is in what are usually known as absolute phrases.

(See *Participles § 3, *Infinitives § 5. References: Francis Christensen, *College English,* 1950, 11:401-403; Jespersen, *Modern English Grammar,* V:6; Bryant, pp. 145-146.)

Absolutes, comparison of • See *Comparison of adjectives and adverbs § 4.

Abstract and concrete words •
Abst *Revision: Replace the abstract word or words with a concrete word or words.*

Nouns that name qualities, conditions, actions, or sum-maries of particular facts are abstract: *love, civilization, dan-ger, age, flying.* They contrast with concrete nouns, which name persons and things that can be seen and touched: *bus, schoolhouse, tree.* Abstract nouns are necessary in discussing ideas but in many kinds of writing they are less exact and forceful than concrete words. (See Ch. 9, "Concrete words," p. 372, and "Abstract words," p. 373; and compare Ch. 4, "Details and generalizations," p. 112.)

Academic writing • One conspicuous trait of academic writ-ing—that is, the publications of teachers and scholars and others engaged in research and in originating ideas—is its documentation, the devices of bibliography and footnote ref-erence that give the sources of material used in preparing the paper. Scrupulousness in giving exact references to those materials sets scholarly writing off from popular books and arti-cles. (See Ch. 11, "Footnotes and final bibliography," p. 438.)

Another trait of academic writing is its Formal style. When scholarly articles and monographs deal with the results of experiments, of historical research, or of special investigation in any field, they naturally show the specialized vocabulary, compactness, and impersonality of *scientific and technical writing.

Partly because many works by scholars and research workers are written more impersonally than they need be, "academic" is often used to describe writing that is unpleasantly abstract, distant, and dry, and to describe the style of many books sup-posedly for general reading that do not show sufficient adaptation to the desired readers. But such partial failures in communication should not hide the importance of academic writing. Very often the men engaged in discovering new facts, in originating interpretations of facts, are not particularly interested in popularizing them and leave that task to others. This passage, itself in the Formal style of academic writing, discusses the language of specialists:

> The truth is that the language of science and scholarship and that of ordinary literature are different engines of communication, though they have something in common. It is essential for academics to write as far as possible in normal language, and desirable for them to write well. It is essential for them to explain what they are doing to nonspecialists and this task, if it is to be carried out adequately, requires them to write well. But they will not themselves judge the value of academic writing by literary standards. When a mathematician or nuclear physicist speaks of beauty and elegance—and he speaks of both as often as the composer or chessplayer, and may strive for both as hard as the poet—he has not in mind the proper ordering of words, but of ideas. And for him, as for Spinoza, their beauty may be so great that it altogether dwarfs the lesser beauties of the word. But those of us who do not share his aesthetics, and perhaps cannot understand them, are ill at ease.—"The Language of Scholarship," *The Times Literary Supplement*, Aug. 17, 1956, p. viii

Accent • In this *Guide-Index* the term *stress* rather than *accent* is used for the prominence given certain syllables in speech; in English it results from greater force of exhalation. (See *Pronunciation § 2a, and b.)

Accent marks • French words in English sometimes keep the accent marks of their original spelling:

Acute: café   outré   attaché   fiancée
Circumflex: crêpe   tête
Grave: frère   suède

Though the accent marks are regularly used in Formal writing and Formal publications, in General writing they are usually dropped, though both forms of some words are found —for instance, *fete* and *fête*, *role* and *rôle*. Newspapers rarely use accent marks. (See *Foreign words in English, and for particular words consult a recent dictionary.)

An accent mark is sometimes used in English to show that a syllable is pronounced, especially in verse. The grave (') is best used for this, though sometimes an acute is found (belovéd).

accept, except • See *except, accept.

Accusative case • In English six distinctive pronoun forms have survived which are often called accusative (or objective) forms and usually occur in the object function (but see *It's me): *me, her, his, us, them, whom. You* and *it* do not have such distinctive forms. English nouns have no distinctive form to show the object function; noun objects of verbs and prepositions are in the common case form. (See *Case; *Objects; *Infinitives § 5; *Gerund § 2; *who, whom.)

Acronyms • See *Abbreviations § 3.

Active voice • See *Voice.

actually • *Actually* has been a convenient word of spoken emphasis (Did you actually see him?) usually better omitted in writing. Its usefulness even in speech has been damaged for the present, however, by repetition as a filler in television interview responses: *"Well, uh, actually, Jack . . . ."*

ad • *Ad,* the clipped form of *advertisement,* is spelled with one *d* and no period. Like other clipped words it belongs to General and Informal speech and writing.

adapt, adopt, adept • The first two are verbs; the third is an adjective: They *adopted* a boy who proved *adept* at *adapting* himself to his new home. *Adept* is used with both *at* and *in,* the latter probably more common except with *-ing* words: *adept in architecture, adept at designing.* Either is Standard idiom.

addresses • When the various parts of a person's address are written on the same line, they are separated by commas:

Miss Louise Finney, 48 Adirondack View, Middlebury, Vermont, is a native of Carroll County, Virginia, and a graduate of Smith College.

(See *Letters § 1b, c, and 2 for addresses in and on letters.)

Adjective clauses • See *Clauses § 2b, *Relative clauses, *Restrictive and nonrestrictive.

Adjectives, definitions • See *Parts of speech.

Adjectives in use • Adjectives should add something to the exactness of a writer's statement or to the definiteness of his picture. As Herbert Read puts it, "appropriate epithets may be either exact or happy." Final judgment about the effectiveness of a particular adjective can only be made by considering the context in which it appears, but some general criteria for appropriateness can be suggested. In *briny* ocean, the *briny* does not add, because all oceans are briny; *stark* does not add much to the meaning of *tragedy,* or of *madness* either. Very general adjectives like *good* or *bad* or *nice* or *beautiful* or *wonderful* do not as a rule add; the reader wants more specific detail, a particular sort of *good* (*generous, affable, efficient*). Many adjectives that are exact enough have been used too often with certain nouns (*fond* farewell, *beady black* eyes) and are merely trite. Because most people do not use exact adjectives in conversation, they often fall back on these flat and stale modifiers in writing—and professional writers sometimes fall back on them too. (See Ch. 9, "Trite words," p. 345.)

A writer may try too hard to make a picture exact. Most of the adjectives in the following paragraph from a student theme are exact—that is, they add to the meaning. But there are too many of them; the writer has been too conscientious. The passage would be more readable if those in brackets, and probably others, were taken out.

In a hotel dining room there is not the [*clamorous, raucous*] bedlam of its *immediate* surroundings, but a *refined, subdued* atmosphere, pervaded by *distinct,* faintly *audible* sounds. The orchestra, with a barely *perceptible* diminuendo, concludes the [*melodic,*] *slow-tempo* arrangement, climaxed by the [*beautiful*] strains of the "Merry Widow" waltz—*rising, falling, fading* with *plaintive* supplication. Then later, while a *modern, rhythmic* melody is being played, the *hushed* clash of cymbals, the [*musical*] tinkle of the chimes, and the *muted* blare of brass blend harmoniously with the [*pulsing,*] *vibrant* voice of the *featured* soloist, only to be anticlimaxed by the *perfunctory* applause of the diners. The [*constant,*] *relentless* shuffle, shuffle, shuffle of *dancing* feet becomes *monotonous* with its [*endless*] repetition and *imperceptible* variation, while *trite* conversation is often interrupted by the *affected* voice of the *solicitous* waiter. The whispers and [*gay*] laughter, the *discordant* clatter of dishes upon trays, and the [*careless*] scraping of chairs blend into the room's *distinctive* personality.

But a sensible and sensitive use of adjectives is necessary. In most factual writing the first requirement of adjectives is exactness; they must answer the needs of the material, like the italicized words in the next paragraph:

Many counselors on *public* relations had *one* foot in commerce and the other in politics—even *international* politics. The most *eminent* figure in *this* class was the *late* Ivy Lee. It seems a pity that he died silently, leaving behind, so far as anyone knows, no *real* record of *his* activities. The *candid* reminiscences of Ivy Lee would be as *useful* to a *future* historian as Pepys' Diary—and perhaps as *interest-*

ing to the student of *human* souls. He began *his larger* career as counselor for *certain* Rockefeller interests. He was *careful*, nevertheless, not to identify himself with the Rockefellers or *any other* group, so leaving himself *free* to serve *all* clients. He had a hand in an agitation for recognition of Russia as a means of increasing our *export* market. Indeed, he may have directed *this* campaign. So, too, when an element among the bankers decided that cancellation of *European war* debts would benefit *American* finance, they used Lee's talent for sweetening *unpopular* causes. And in the *last* year of his life he was advising the *new German* government on ways and means for making *Nazi* principles and methods less *hateful* to the *average American* citizen.—WILL IRWIN, *Propaganda and the News*, pp. 267-268

In writing that makes a definite attempt to capture the feelings and sensations of the reader, the adjectives must be exact (as they are in the following paragraph) but they must also deserve the epithet "happy"; that is, they must seem to fit and at the same time lead the reader to the writer's feeling, perhaps by making an imaginative appeal. In describing an actual experience Ernest Hemingway presents a picture rather than merely a series of facts:

In the *five* days I saw a *dozen* or *more kudu* cows and *one young* bull with a string of cows. The cows were *big, gray, striped-flanked* antelope with ridiculously *small* heads, *big* ears, and a *soft, fast-rushing* gait that moved them in *big-bellied* panic through the trees. The *young* bull had the start of a spiral on *his* horns but they were *short* and *dumpy* and as he ran past us at the end of a glade in the dusk, *third* in a string of *six* cows, he was no more like a *real* bull than a *spike* elk is like a *big, old, thick-necked, dark-maned, wonder-horned, tawny-hided, beer-horse-built* bugler of a bull-elk.—*Green Hills of Africa*, p. 138

Notice that the relatively insignificant *glade, dusk,* and *trees* are not modified but that the *gait* is *soft, fast-rushing*. The gait needed to be described; the dusk and the trees are merely part of the background.

Adjectives sometimes tend to make a slow movement in writing partly because many of them have a falling rhythm—that is, the stressed syllable is followed by one or more unstressed syllables. They may contribute to a leisurely, relaxed effect:

The sheltering trees only emphasized the ashen deadness of the wrinkled clapboards.

Too many of them result in an excessively slow movement.

Carl Sandburg has been credited with advising a writer, "Think twice before you use an adjective." This is probably sound advice for anyone who is writing a good deal and who automatically attaches an adjective to every noun. And according to E. B. White, "The adjective hasn't been built that can pull a weak or inaccurate noun out of a tight place." But it is also important for a writer to fix his eye on his subject and write about it as he really sees it. Without stuffing in adjectives he should fill in the qualities that are needed for the reader to re-create the picture or idea for himself. The adjectives then should be at least exact, and some of them may be happy.

(Compare *Adverbs in use.)

Adjectives, types and forms •

1. *Forms.* Many adjectives can be identified by the fact that they are compared by adding *-er* or *-est* to the positive (or base) form or by preceding the positive form with *more* or *most*:

Positive	*Comparative*	*Superlative*
warm	warmer, more warm	warmest, most warm
talkative	more talkative	most talkative

(See *Comparison of adjectives and adverbs for further examples and discussion of use; see also *unique.)

Many adjectives have come down from an early period of the language (*high, handsome, civil*) without a distinctive adjective form, but many have been made and are still being made by adding a derivational ending or *suffix to a noun or verb. Some suffixes that are still active are:

-able (*-ible*)—translatable, edible
-al—critical, hypothetical
-ed—sugared, four-footed
-ful—playful, soulful

-ish—darkish, womanish
-less—harmless, fearless
-ous—callous, ferrous
-y—cranky, dreamy, corny

2. *Position of adjectives.* We recognize adjectives in sentences chiefly by their position in relation to the nouns that they modify, especially by the fact that they can stand between an article (*a/an, the*) or words like *our, this, some* and a noun: an *old* parka, our *youngest* son, this *characteristic* gesture, some more *favorable* opportunity.

According to its position in a sentence, an adjective is either *attributive* or *predicate*:

a—Attributive adjectives are placed next to their nouns, usually preceding, as in *tiny* brook, *horseless* carriages. Sometimes there is good reason for placing an adjective after its noun:

a woman *sweet, simple, home-loving* (Two or more adjectives sometimes follow the noun.)

the outfit *complete* (For emphasis)

court *martial,* attorney *general* (Following French patterns)

a good plan *gone* wrong (Participle modified by adverb)

a plan so *complicated* no one could follow it (The adjective modified by other words)

a *white* cap, *small* and beautifully *made* (Avoiding an awkward piling up of adjectives before the noun)

b—Predicate adjectives (see Ch. 9, p. 341), also called *predicatives,* come after some form of the verb *be* or some other linking verb, stated or implied (*taste, feel, turn*), except in inverted sentence order (*Silent* was the night).

The day is *warm.*	That pie smells *good.*
The train was *crowded.*	For a while I felt *bad.*
The dog was *old.*	They found the man *dead.*

(See *Linking verbs, *Predicate adjective.)

3. *Types of adjectives.* Adjectives are conventionally regarded as of three types according to their meaning or the character of their modification:

a—Descriptive adjectives, the most common type, are said to modify the noun by naming a quality or condition of the object named: a *gray* shutter, *vivid* colors, *difficult* words. They are ordinarily compared and may themselves be modified by intensive and qualifying adverbs, words like *almost, very, quite.* Participles (*laughing, wrecked*) function like them but usually are not compared or modified by qualifying or intensive adverbs. Because this class of words has no definable limits and new members are constantly being added, it is called an *open class.*

b—Proper adjectives, derived from proper nouns, originally are limiting: *French* possessions, the *Puritan* colonies—but often become descriptive: *French* culture, *Puritan* manners. Sometimes they mingle both functions, as *Elizabethan* in the *Elizabethan drama* both limits drama to a period and brings to mind qualities of a group of plays.

Often a proper adjective is used so frequently in a merely descriptive sense that it loses its relation to the proper noun from which it came and becomes a simple descriptive adjective, written without a capital: *bacchanalian, pasteurized, diesel, india* ink, *paris* green. They are, like descriptive adjectives, an *open class,* and may even be compared: *He is Frencher than the French.*

c—Limiting adjectives, a loose and not very numerous group of words, placed in a separate category by some recent grammarians, point out in some way the object named (*this, that, his, other, former*) or indicate quantity or number (*two, second, both*). Several of the first group are pronouns regularly used in the function of adjectives. The articles *a, an,* and *the* are often included in this group. Limiting adjectives cannot ordinarily be compared or modified by other words. They also differ from *a* and *b* in being a *closed class*; new ones are not added. (See *Possessive adjectives.)

4. *Adjective function.* The function of an adjective is to modify a subject, object, or indirect object, that is, to restrict or limit it. Since phrases, clauses, and words which are usually other parts of speech also perform this function, we can speak of adjectival functions performed by them.

   a–Phrases and clauses used in adjectival function:

   The man *with his hat on* is Harry.
   I like the one *on the end* best.
   a bird *with a long bill* (=a *long-billed* bird, a descriptive adjective)
   Everyone *who approves of this* will please raise his right hand.
   That was the summer *we went to Yellowstone.*
   He asked the first man *he met.*

   (See *Clauses § 2, *Restrictive and nonrestrictive for further examples and discussion.)

   b–*Other parts of speech in adjectival function.* One of the outstanding traits of English is the use of nouns in the adjective function: a *glass* jar, the *Churchill* government, a *hurry* call, *store* bread, *ski* pants, *adjective* modifier, the *high school* course, a *stretcher* case, the *horse and buggy* days. (See *Parts of speech.)

   Participles are *verbals which function like adjectives: a *coming* man, a *deserved* tribute.

5. *Adjectives as subjects and objects.* Preceded by an article, words that are ordinarily adjectives occur in the functions of nouns: the *just,* the *rich,* the *unemployed,* a *high* (of weather), an all-time *high,* a new *low.* As a rule such words do not have genitive or plural forms.

Adverbial clauses • See *Clauses § 2c, *Purpose, *Result.

Adverbs, definitions • See *Parts of speech.

Adverbs in use • What has been said about the use of adjectives (*Adjectives in use) can be said again about the use of adverbs: adverbs, too, should be either exact or happy or both. When an amateur writer wants to portray rapid or violent action, he is quite likely to make too free a use of adverbs and kill the whole effect. In this paragraph we would be relieved— and could picture the scene more clearly—if the student writer had deleted his adverbs:

Shrill horns scream *threateningly*. Automobiles career *wildly*. Giant buses lumber *dominantly* along. Policemen shout *warningly* and then *desperately*. Pedestrians scurry across the broad avenue.

Some writers tend to qualify too much, to make a statement and then draw part of it back with such words as *probably*, *apparently*. It is better to choose the most accurate word available and use that.

I shall [probably] try to read your paper tonight.

Many of the longer adverbs are unemphatic because they are unstressed toward the end, and when two or more of them come close together they make a clumsy or unpleasant sounding phrase. The repetition of the *-ly* calls attention to itself.

She sang *resonantly*, if *slightly nasally*, between the towering walls of the adjacent buildings.

They respond to recurrent temperamental differences, and to analogous though *chronologically distantly* separated social conditions.

Many of the adverbs we regularly use in conversation are superfluous and are better omitted in writing:

The college student meets [up with] a different type of instructor in English than he had in high school.

Sometimes writers use an adverb plus an adjective or a verb when an accurate adjective or exact verb would be neater and just as expressive.

Scholarships should be kept for those who are *studiously inclined*. [That is, for those who are studious.]

When no one was looking I took the goggles and *swiftly made my way* out of the store. [The simpler *hurried* would say as much.]

(See *Prepositions § 3b; *very)

Adverbs, types and forms •
  Revision: Revise the form of the adverb marked (§ 1).

Adv

Traditionally the parts of speech category of adverbs has been a sort of rag bag, including a variety of words that modify verbs, adjectives, other adverbs, and whole clauses and sentences. (Some words in the category, like *almost, very, quite, yes, no*, obviously differ in certain respects from typical adverbs—they cannot be compared—and could be set off as different parts of speech; but because some of their functions resemble those of adverbs, they have also been regarded as a group of adverbs.) Grammarians are formulating other categories for some of these words, but since there is as yet no widely accepted grouping, this article follows the traditional grouping. (See *Parts of speech, *Particles.)

1. *Forms of adverbs.* Most adverbs are adjectives or participles plus the ending *-ly: badly, deservedly, laughingly, surely.* Some adverbs have developed from Old English forms without a special adverbial sign: *now, quite, since, then, there, where.*

There are a number of adverbs with the same forms as adjectives, most of them in use for hundreds of years. For example:

bad	doubtless	hard	much	slow
better	early	high	near	smooth
bright	even	late	new	straight
cheap	fair	loose	right	tight
close	fast	loud	rough	well
deep	first	low	sharp	wrong

Most of these also have forms in *-ly,* so that we can write "He sang *loud*" or "He sang *loudly.*" The *-ly* forms are likely to be preferred in Formal English and the shorter forms in speech and Informal writing. The choice between the two is chiefly a matter of style. The shorter forms are often more vigorous than the longer:

Go *slow.* Don't talk so *loud.* It was so windy that I had to hold on *tight* to the iron stand to keep from being blown away.

In speech and Informal writing some other short forms of adverbs are used: Take it *easy.* It came *easy.* He talked *big.*

In Nonstandard usage the adverb sometimes occurs without the *-ly* which characterizes it in Standard, such as *real, special, considerable* for *really, specially, considerably.* This practice should be avoided in writing. When in doubt consult a good dictionary.

Most adverbs are compared, either by adding *-er* and *-est* or by preceding them with *more* and *most.* (See *Comparison of adjectives and adverbs.)

2. *Functions of adverbs.* Adverbs are used typically in four functions:

a–Modifying a single word or sentence element:

He will come *today.* (Modifying verb *come*)
She was *rather* shy. (Modifying adjective *shy*)
Almost immediately we saw them. (Modifying adverb *immediately*)

b–Modifying whole sentences:

Perhaps he will come today. *Unfortunately* there were no more left. *Later* I was sorry. *That evening* I was sorry. *As soon as I said it,* I was sorry.

c–Connecting clauses and also modifying their meaning (see *Conjunctive adverbs):

We agreed to call the matter closed; *however,* they were by no means convinced.

The museum, we discovered, was closed on Fridays; *consequently,* we drove on to the next city.

d–Introducing questions:

When did you begin to feel this way?
Where was the car when you first saw it?

3. *Adverbs grouped by meaning.* Adverbs have been traditionally identified by considering their meaning, according to what question they answer (a classification which tells little about their grammatical function):

a–How? (Adverbs of manner)

alike so worse keenly openly painstakingly

b–When? In what order? (Adverbs of time and succession)

afterwards when finally late lately never soon

c–Where? (Adverbs of place and direction)

below far north there upstairs

d–How much? To what extent? (Adverbs of degree and measure)

all almost less little much quite completely equally

e–Why? (Adverbs of cause and purpose)

consequently therefore

f–Yes or no. (Adverbs of assertion, condition, and concession)

yes no certainly doubtless not perhaps possibly surely
Informal: O.K. nix absolutely

4. *Other constructions in adverbial function.* Nouns may be used in the function of adverbs (see *Genitive § 2):

He came *mornings.* He plans to stay a *month.*

Phrases may have the functions of adverbs (see *Phrases):

He came *in the morning. After the examinations* he quit.

Clauses may have the functions of adverbs:

When it came time to go, he didn't know what to do. He stayed on and on *because he didn't know how to leave.*

5. *Position of adverbial modifiers.* Unlike the position of adjectival modifiers, the position of adverbial modifiers in a sentence is variable and cannot be used as a way of identifying them with certainty. They should be placed in a position that is natural for a native user of the language and that will represent his desired emphasis.

Single word adverbs modifying single words tend to be placed next to the word modified: the *almost* perfect state, the *most disagreeably* certain result, they *certainly* tried, they all worked *hard.* Adverbial phrases and clauses precede or follow the main construction. These versions of the same sentence show some typical variations in the position of adverbials:

1. *When the tide turned,* all the boats *hurriedly* headed *for the channel.*

2. All the boats *hurriedly* headed *for the channel when the tide turned.*

3. All the boats headed *for the channel hurriedly when the tide turned.*

4. *Hurriedly* all the boats headed *for the channel when the tide turned.*

5. All the boats, *when the tide turned, hurriedly* headed *for the channel.*

6. All the boats headed *for the channel when the tide turned hurriedly.*

All of the first five would be possible, though four and five only if special emphasis was wanted on *hurriedly* or *when the tide turned.* In the sixth the position of *hurriedly* relates it to *turned,* and thus conveys a different meaning.

(Reference: Curme, *Parts of Speech,* pp. 73-86; all grammars give some information.)

advice—advise • The first is the noun—*to give advice*—the second, the verb. The General idiom with the verb is an infinitive: *He advised me to forget it.* Possible, but more Formal, is: *I advised his forgetting it.* The business use of *advise* meaning *inform*—erected into a monumental cliché in *beg to advise*—continues an older use of the word and is often, in addition, *deadwood: "We beg to advise that your chair is done" means no more than "Your chair is done." But it remains in good General use for information rather formally given: *The President was also advised that . . . .*

-ae-, -oe- • Words of Greek and Latin origin that contain the digraphs *-ae-* and *-oe-* have been for a long time variously spelled in English. (Most printers do not now use the ligatures *—æ, œ*—except in works dealing with the ancient languages.) Both *-ae-* and *-oe-* are pronounced as though written *e* (either long or short). Many spellings have simplified in the past: *economics, pedagogy, penal* were formerly *oeconomics, paedagogy, poenal.* Medicine has adopted many of the simpler forms like *anesthetic* (for *anaesthetic*). The long series of words beginning with *haem-* (meaning "blood") now preferably begin with *hem-* (*hematic, hemoglobin, hemorrhage,* and

so on). The American Historical Association long ago adopted
*medieval. Dictionaries now give such words as *ameba, cesura,
dieresis, esthetic, subpena* as alternate spellings. For a particular word consult a good recent dictionary. Formal style
tends to keep the older two-letter forms, General to use the
simple *e.*

Latin plurals in *ae* still keep the two letters: *alumnae, an-
tennae, formulae* (see *Plurals of nouns § 4); and in Greek and
Latin proper names the two letters are kept: *Boeotia, Caesar,
Oedipus.*

affect—effect • Since a distinction is seldom made in pronouncing these words /ə fekt′/, it is easy to confuse their spellings.

Affect is usually a verb, meaning "influence" or "put on"
(compare *Affectation) or "pretend": *This will affect thousands. He affected a stern manner. He affects boredom.*

The noun *affect* is a technical term in psychology.

Effect is usually a noun, meaning "result": *The effects of
this will be felt by thousands. What is the effect of doubling
the amount?*

Effect is also a verb in Formal English, meaning "bring
about": *The change was effected peaceably.*

Affectation • We learn our language as children by imitating
the speech of people around us, and we expand our language
later in life by imitating what we hear others say or what we
find in reading. So long as these changes furnish us with more
varied and more exact ways of expressing ourselves, they are
proper and necessary and represent a healthy growth. But
sometimes we are led to adopt different pronunciations or
different words or different constructions not so much to make
our speech more effective as to make it seem more elegant, or
even for the effect of the language itself rather than for what
it is conveying. Such changes are affectations and are unpleasant because they are not part of our variety of English. Writing is usually more precise than speech, but writing in a style
quite different from one's speech is affectation.

Affectation is most easily spotted in pronunciations. In some
parts of the United States /bēn/ for *been,* /rä′ᴛHer/ for *rather,*
and /ī ᴛHer/ for *either* are common pronunciations, but consciously adopting them is affectation in regions where /bin/,
/ra ᴛHer/, or /ē ᴛHer/ are usual. For many people *one should*
or *shouldn't one* is an affectation, and so are Briticisms like
early on and *that which* for *what.* Using slang except for
humorous effect is an affectation in someone who knows little
slang and seldom uses it in natural speech.

The line between natural and affected speech is hard to draw, since it depends chiefly on motive. In general, picking up expressions not commonly heard from the educated people of a community is risky. Increasing the expressiveness of one's speech is praiseworthy but just trying to be "different" will usually result in bad English. The way to avoid affectation is to consider the appropriateness and expressiveness of language and to shun big words when such language is unnecessary to convey your meaning. (See Ch. 1, "The varieties of English," *Pronunciation § 3.)

after • *After* is an element in numerous verb-adverb combinations: *look after the children, takes after his father, go after the largest one, came after a cup of sugar.* Its basic prepositional meanings of "behind" (in space) and "later" (in time) have allowed a number of extensions, especially in common idioms: *after all, after dark.* In crediting illustrations it means "redrawn from another's work": *after Rubens.*

aggravate • In Informal usage *aggravate* means to "annoy" or "irritate": *I was never so aggravated in my life.* In Formal and usually in General English *aggravate* means "to intensify or increase something unpleasant," as to *aggravate suffering* or *a wound* or *a crime.* The same distinction is made with the noun *aggravation.*

Agreement •
Revision: Make the pronoun or verb marked agree in form with the word to which it is related: its antecedent if it is a pronoun, its subject if it is a verb.

Agr

Certain parts of speech which vary in form for gender, person, or number agree in Standard English when they stand in relationship to each other:
1. *Subject* and *verb* agree in number (The *man is* old; The *men are* old) and person (*I go* tomorrow; *He goes* tomorrow). (See Ch. 8, "Revising subject-verb agreement," p. 294; *Subject and verb, *Collective nouns.)
2. When a *pronoun* has an antecedent, it agrees with the antecedent in number (The *boy* had lost *his* way; The *hikers* had lost *their* way), in gender (The *girl* found *her* keys; Every *question* has *its* answer), and when conveniently possible in person. (See *Reference of pronouns, *each, *every and its compounds.)
3. A *demonstrative adjective* usually agrees in number with the noun it modifies (*That coat* is expensive; *These shoes* cost

more than my old black suede pair did). (See *Demonstrative adjectives, *this, *kind, sort.)

The chief cause of lack of agreement is that since formal agreement in English is not vital for intelligibility, we tend to ignore the form of what we started with. This is especially true if the subject is a collective noun or pronoun or if several words, some of them plural, come between a singular subject and its verb, so that we are tempted to use a plural verb. Another cause is that there may be a conflict between agreement by form and agreement by meaning. (See Ch. 9, pp. 337-338.)

In Formal English, agreement by form is quite strictly followed, but there are many locutions in which variations have become acceptable in General and Informal English. (See, for example, *either, *one of those who, *who, whom.)

agree to, agree with • One agrees *to* a plan and agrees *with* a person. One thing agrees *with* another. Other idioms are: I agree *in* principle; we agreed *on* a plan of attack.

ain't • *Ain't* is one of the commonest and most easily identifiable Nonstandard words, and prejudice against it among educated people has been almost unanimous for the last half century or so, though it is directly descended from formerly accepted contractions. In conversation it could be an economical single form for *am not, is not, are not, has not, have not,* but the schools' condemnation of it over the past century has been very effective because it is learned as one word and like an oath can be easily identified.

Used in the first person, especially in question form (*ain't I*) where there is no easy natural contraction—*amn't* is hard to pronounce—*ain't* is occasionally heard among educated speakers and was marked "disputable" and "almost established" in the Leonard study of 1932. *Aren't* is often used in this construction, especially in England: *I'm making real progress, aren't I?* Though in the first person, both *ain't* and *aren't* may perhaps be regarded as Informal, other uses of *ain't* are Nonstandard. Except in dialog, *ain't* is Nonstandard in General and Formal writing.

(See *Divided usage. References: Curme, *Parts of Speech,* p. 248; Marckwardt and Walcott, pp. 48, 95-96; the entry *ain't* in *Webster's Third New International Dictionary.*)

a la • *A la* is regarded as an English preposition, meaning "in the manner of": *a la Whistler, a la The New Yorker.* In Formal writing and modish advertising (as of cosmetics and fashionable clothes), the accent mark is usually kept (*à la*); elsewhere it is written *a la*. The other French forms, *à l'* and *au*, occur only in borrowed phrases: *au gratin*. *Alamode* (whether meaning "in the fashion" or referring to ice cream on pie) is usually written as one word without the accent mark. The French form *à la mode* is now rare.

albeit • *Albeit* is archaic as a conjunction and heavy as a preposition: *It has a kind of structure, albeit a kind of structure that almost defies description. Even though* (or *although*) is more appropriate to General English.

all and its compounds • Watch the following words and phrases:

all ready (adjective phrase) : At last they were all ready to begin.
already (adverb of time) : They had already begun.
*all right (adjective phrase) : The seats seemed all right to me.
*all the farther (adverb, equivalent to *as far as*) is a localism: That's all the farther I'll go.
all together (adjective phrase) : We found them all together in an old trunk. There were six all together.
altogether (adverb, equivalent to *wholly*): That's another matter altogether.

all of • In General and Informal usage *all* is followed by *of* in many constructions where the *of* is less likely in Formal writing:

All of the milk was spilled.
They passed all of the candidates.
You can't fool all of the people all of the time.

All of is required with a pronoun in Standard English.

All of them went home.
They wanted all of it but got only half.
He gave all of us some candy.

all right—alright • *All right* is the usual Standard spelling of both the adjective phrase (He is all right) and the sentence adverb, meaning "yes, certainly" (All right, I'll come).

Alright is a natural analogy with *altogether* and *already* but at present is found mainly in advertising, comic strips, in unedited writing, and, rarely, in fiction. Though it is gaining respectability, the prejudice against it is still strong.

all-round • *All-round* is usually hyphened: *an all-round athlete, an all-round education*. Many readers still object to *all-around*. In either version, the word has been so overused that it has become trite.

all the farther • Although *all the farther* is often heard in Informal and General speech, it is Nonstandard in writing. (Reference: Bryant, pp. 19-20.)

Alliteration • *Alliteration* is the repetition of the same sound usually at the beginnings of several words in a series or at the beginnings of stressed syllables within several words close together. Besides contributing to the pleasure that a reader may find in the similar sounds, alliteration serves to bind the phrase, or sometimes a whole series of phrases, into a unit:

... the *c*rowded, *c*loistered *c*olleges of Oxford.—PAUL ELMER MORE

... ran over the *s*tarry *s*moothness of the lagoon, and the water between the piles lapped the *s*limy timber once with a *s*udden *s*plash.
—JOSEPH CONRAD

Alliteration is one of the figures of sound that contribute to the musical effect of poetry, though not one of the most important:

Here I a*m*, an old *m*an in a dry *m*onth,
Being *r*ead to by a boy, waiting for *r*ain.
T. S. ELIOT

The *s*ilken, *s*ad, un*c*ertain, ru*s*tling...
EDGAR ALLAN POE

In ordinary expository prose conspicuous alliteration is usually out of place because it tends to attract attention to the expression at the expense of the idea. Its use in Formal prose, especially in prose with an oratorical or poetic background, is more appropriate.

Alliteration is one of the chief weapons of advertising sloganeers and makers of flashy titles, who simply push to a conspicuous point the natural binding power of the figure:

*F*ilter, *f*lavor, *f*lip-top box   *M*ealtime *M*agic with *M*ilk

Alliteration is also characteristic of humorous verse and prose of any mannered writing on the light side:

Tell me, what is a man to do
When the *l*ady his *l*ife is based upon
Likes to be *w*ooed but *w*on't be *w*on?
OGDEN NASH, *Hard Lines*, p. 58

Allusion • See *Echo phrases.

-al ly • English has a number of adjectives with the (Latin) endings *-al* and *-ical*: *fatal, final, medical, historical, political*. Usually an adverb is made by adding *-ly* to this. This ending should be remembered in spelling these words, especially since the unstressed final sounds give the impression that there are fewer syllables than must be spelled.

accidental	accidentally	mental	mentally
fundamental	fundamentally	political	politically
incidental	incidentally	practical	practically

Several adjectives ending in -*ical* show a tendency to drop the -*al*: *alphabetic, biographic, geographic, philosophic* following the course of *academic, frantic, emphatic, poetic,* and others that have already shed the final syllable. But the two forms may vary somewhat in meaning: Compare *historical fact* (a fact of history) and *historic fact* (a memorable fact in history). Although *public* and a few others have adverbs without the -*al*- (*publicly*), most reinstate that ending before -*ly*:

academically	dramatically	prolifically
athletically	heroically	specifically
automatically	idiotically	terrifically

alma mater • An anglicized Latin term ("fostering mother") meaning one's school or college; rather pretentious in General writing. Pronounced /al′mə mā′tər/, /äl′mə mä′tər/, /al mə ma′ter/.

almost • See *most, almost.

already • See *all and its compounds.

alright • This is not yet an accepted spelling. (See *all right.)

also • *Also* is weak as a connective; ordinarily *and* works better:

He came with tents, cooking things, *and* [better than *also*] about fifty pounds of photographic equipment.

(See *Conjunctive adverbs.)

alternative • *Alternative* comes from the Latin *alter,* "the second of two." Some Formal writers, in deference to the word's origin, confine its meaning to "one of two possibilities," but it is regularly used to mean one of several possibilities, and is so defined in dictionaries.

although, though • *Although* and *though* connect with the main clause an adverbial clause of concession—that is, a statement that qualifies the main statement but does not contradict it. *Although* is more likely to introduce a clause that precedes the main clause, *though* one that follows:

Although [Though] the rain kept up for almost three weeks, we managed to have a pretty good time.

We managed to have a pretty good time, though [although] the rain kept up for almost three weeks.

Here there is no distinction in meaning; the choice between the two may be based on sentence rhythm. *Although* is a heavier and slightly more Formal word and hence occurs less frequently. (Reference: Bryant, pp. 216-218.) As a conjunctive adverb only *though* is used: *He did it, though.*

Often one of two clauses connected by *but* can be thrown into an *although* clause to vary the sentence pattern:

We had rehearsed that act time and time again, but we all missed our cues the first night.

Although we had rehearsed that act time and time again, we all missed our cues that first night.

The spelling *altho* has made more headway than *tho* and *thru* and is appropriate in Informal writing and in some General writing (if editorial or course policy approves), but would not be used in Formal writing. (See *but. Reference: Curme, Syntax,* pp. 332-340.)

alumnus • Four Latin forms of this word exist in English:

One male graduate is an	alumnus /ə lum′nəs/
Two or more male graduates are	alumni /ə lum′nī/
One female graduate is an	alumna /ə lum′nə/
Two or more female graduates are	alumnae /ə lum′nē/

By common practice *alumnus* and *alumni* are used for graduates of coeducational institutions. Because of this clumsy complication of forms, *graduate* and *graduates* are increasingly used. *Alum /ə lum′/* is used in some institutions.

a.m. and p.m., also A.M. and P.M. • These abbreviations (for *ante meridiem,* "before noon," and *post meridiem,* "after noon") are most useful in tables and lists of times. In General writing they are used only with figures for specific hours: *from 2 to 4 p.m.* (Not: *I'll see you this p.m.*)

Though *M.* is the abbreviation for noon (*12 m.*), *12 noon* is more common; midnight is *12 p.m.*

Ambiguity •
Revision: Make the meaning you intend unmistakable.

Amb

Although inexact writing is common enough, actually ambiguous writing, in which there is possibility of confusing two meanings, is relatively rare. The context usually shows which of two possible meanings must be taken. The most common sources of actual ambiguity are:

1. *Inexact reference of pronoun,* especially in *indirect discourse:

> He told his father he had been talking too much.

Such a sentence usually needs re-forming, perhaps as:

> He admitted to his father that he had been talking too much.
> He criticized his father for talking too much.

(See *Reference of pronouns.)

2. *Modifiers*

a—Squinting modifiers that may refer to either of two words or constructions:

> The governor penalized those office holders who had opposed him *for good reason.* (The governor had good reason for penalizing those who had opposed him. *Or:* The governor penalized those who had had good reason to oppose him.)

> Some people *I know* would go there anyway. (Some people whom I know. . . . *Or:* Some people would go there anyway, I know.)

b—Modifiers temporarily misleading, as in headlines:

> Police repair man killed by car
> Horse bites off ear of owner—Man says he will keep biting mare

Such sentences are usually clear in spoken English, and even in writing the intended meaning can be wrung out by rereading. But the writer should not require his reader to be a detective. (See *Hyphen § 2c.)

3. *Incomplete idioms,* especially in comparison:

> "I like Alice as well as Will" might mean "I like Alice as well as Will does," "I like Alice as well as I do Will," or "I like both Alice and Will."

4. *"Yes" or "no" after negatives. Yes* or *no,* in response to a negative question or in commenting on a negative statement, often needs a clause to make the meaning clear.

> You haven't any more red ink, have you? (*Answer:* "Yes, I have" or "No, I haven't.")

> Let's not use such a long quotation. (No, let's not.)

5. *Changing meanings.* Many words in English are undergoing changes in meaning. Sometimes the transition can be completed without risk of ambiguous communication because the context makes the intention clear. As *car* came to apply primarily to an automobile rather than a railroad or street car, such restricting words as *motor, railroad,* or *street* prevented misunderstanding. But when such safeguards are not present, serious ambiguity may occur. Examples: *disinterested—unin-

terested, *imply—infer, *transpire, *grammar, inflammable—
flammable, *incredible—incredulous, *censor—censure.

6. *Intentional ambiguity*. Incomplete or ambiguous statements are sometimes intentional, like the sign in an airport
limousine, "Tipping for this service not required," which drew
tips from most passengers.

(See *Comma § 7 for information on using a comma to
avoid ambiguity.)

American • Since there is no word to describe the United
States (as *Italian*, for example, describes Italy), *American* is
ordinarily used. It is obviously inexact, since Canadians and
Mexicans are also American. But it is no more inexact than
many other words and is generally used in this sense. Perhaps
we can take an Englishman's judgment:

> The use of *America* for *the United States* & *American* for *(citi-
> zen) of the U.S.* is open to as much & as little objection as that of
> *England* & *English(man)* for *Great Britain (& Ireland)*, *British* &
> *Briton*. It will continue to be protested against by purists & patriots,
> & will doubtless survive the protests.—H. W. FOWLER, *A Dictionary
> of Modern English Usage*, p. 18

It is more exact to use *the United States* as the name of our
country, but the use of *America* is common. Use *American* as
the adjective and the name of an inhabitant. (Reference:
H. L. Mencken, "Names for Americans," *American Speech*,
1947, 22:241-256.)

American and British usage • For several reasons the spoken
and written English of the United States differs from that of
England. Since the seventeenth and eighteenth centuries, when
the English language was brought to North America, the language used on both sides of the Atlantic has changed in somewhat different ways.

The people in the United States and England live under
different governments; they are educated in different school
systems. Social stratification, affecting the ideals and habits of
large classes of people, is considerably different. In spite of the
mutual circulation of publications, visits of lecturers, professors, and government officials, and interchange by way of
movies, radio, and television, many of the factors that tend to
keep the speech within the British Commonwealth more like
that of England cannot operate as effectively between England
and the United States. Finally, dialectal varieties which were
brought from England in the seventeenth and eighteenth centuries have sometimes remained influential in this country
while losing ground in England.

The differences in language have led to interesting emotional attitudes on both sides. In the past Britishers have scorned "vulgar Americanisms." The maker of the glossary to the London edition of Sinclair Lewis' *Babbitt* went beyond simple definition when he wrote for *ice cream soda,* "Ice cream in soda water. A ghastly American summer time drink." Fowler says that the realization that Americans had dropped the *u* from words ending in *-our* stopped the British from making the same change. Some Americans used to look upon British accent and vocabulary as ludicrous or at best snobbish, but these attitudes are becoming less prevalent.

In the written language some spelling differences stand out. The British tend still to prefer *-re* to *-er* in words like *center* and **theater,* though they use both forms; they still keep *-our* in a number of words (see **-or, -our*), though they are gradually simplifying; they use *x* in a few words like *inflexion*; they tend to double more consonants, as in *traveller, waggon*; and there are various individual words that differ, such as *tyre* (automobile *tire*). But these distinctions affect only a small number of words, and actually for most of them usage is divided in both countries. They are just pervasive enough to show that a book is of British or American origin, but they do not interfere with reading. Such differences can be used to make a good argument for allowing more individual freedom in spelling, but they continue to offer a problem to a publisher who wishes to circulate a book in both countries.

For a number of years scholars in the United States have been at work discovering and describing our speech. The magazine *American Speech,* which was founded in 1925, has published specific observations of usage and more general articles. George Philip Krapp's *The English Language in America* (New York, 1925) and John S. Kenyon's *American Pronunciation* (Ann Arbor, 1950) are scholarly works. The four editions of H. L. Mencken's *The American Language* (New York, 1919-1936) have given a good defense of American as against British usage. Mencken is not quite fair in that he usually pits American Nonstandard against formal British, but his main point, the existence of a distinctive popular speech in the United States, is well proved (though not his implication that there is a distinct American language); Raven I. McDavid's large abridgment of Mencken's work (1963, with the assistance of David W. Maurer) includes many additions and presents a more balanced approach. *The Dictionary of American English* and *The Dictionary of Americanisms* present the record of many words as they have been used in the United States.

There are of course several varieties of English in use on both sides of the Atlantic; and Great Britain presents a greater variety than the United States, in part because of sturdy remains of older dialects in the various counties, in Scotland, and in Wales. Among Englishmen and Americans of average education and social position, differences in pronunciation are likely to be particularly striking. There are different intonations, different values for the vowels, differences in particular words like the British /trā/ *trait,* /prō cess/, /con tents'/, /lef ten' ənt/ *lieutenant,* /ral' i/ for the American /rô' lē/ *Raleigh,* and in general a more rapid speech and a tendency to drop the secondary stress (such as an *-ar* in *dictionary*). The slower, fuller pronunciation of most Americans seems wasteful and provincial to some Britishers.

Everyone knows some of the differences in vocabulary in certain common words: In England an *elevator* is a *lift, radio* is *wireless, crackers* are *biscuits* (*cakes* and *muffins* are also different from those in America), a *sit-down* strike is a *stay-in* strike, a *run* in a stocking is a *ladder, daylight saving time* is *summer time, installment buying* is the *hire-purchase system, white-collar* workers are *black-coat* workers. From the group word *tin can* the British have taken *tin,* Americans *can.* A *truck* is a *lorry,* an *automobile* is a *motor car* (though both are compromising on *car*), *gasoline* is *petrol,* sold in a *gallon* much larger than the American measure. A *billion* is a thousand million in America (and France) and a million million in England (and Germany). But recent innovations are more likely to get the same names in both countries.

There is a Nonstandard speech in both England and America, an array of slang that baffles readers on the opposite side of the Atlantic, and many colloquialisms unique to each. In a book or play *no end* and /rä ᴛʜėr'/ are supposed to identify an Englishman as clearly as *guess* or *reckon* is supposed to identify an American. But it is not easy for a writer to catch the distinctive differences, as a reading of a modern detective story by a British writer will show; if Americans are introduced, their speech doesn't ring true. One reason for careful study of the differences between the spoken language in England and in this country has been the vogue of realistic fiction, which necessarily made use of more colloquial English and more colloquial American. In fact, the increased informality of modern prose in both England and the United States has tended to emphasize the distinctions between the two.

The grammar of the popular levels of English and of American differs somewhat—contrast the speech of ordinary people in novels of the two countries. But in the General writing of the two there is less difference in grammar than in vocabulary.

Collective nouns are more likely to be plural in British usage (*the government intend*); British writers differ in small matters like the position of **only,* the proper preposition with **different,* the use of **shall,* and various idioms. (See Stuart Robertson, "British-American Differentiations in Syntax and Idiom," *American Speech,* 1939, 14:243-254.)

A fairly long catalog of such minor differences between these two branches of English could be drawn up, but their importance should not be exaggerated or allowed to obscure the fundamental fact that the resemblances far outnumber the differences and that the speech of the two countries represents two different strands of the English language.

For an American there is no virtue in consciously cultivating British pronunciations or adopting British words and idioms (Briticisms). If he uses generally accepted American English, he will reach his proper public, and if what he writes is interesting or important enough, he can reach British readers too. (Many particular entries in this *Index* note differences between British and American usage.)

among—between • See **between—among.

amount—number • The distinction between these words is that *amount* is used of things viewed in bulk, weight, or sums; *number* is used of things that can be counted in individual units:

> a large *amount* of milk (but a large *number* of cans of milk)
> a small *amount* of time, an *amount* of money
> a large *number* of seats, a *number* of people, a *number* of mistakes

No native speaker substitutes *number* where *amount* is conventionally used, but *amount* sometimes replaces *number*: *the amount of people, an amount of books.* This usage is better avoided.

Ampersand • *Ampersand* is the name for the & sign (originally a linking of the letters of *et*), called also *short and.* Its primary use, obviously, is to save space; therefore it belongs only where abbreviations are appropriate. In addressing firms, use the form they habitually use (...*and Company* or ...& *Company*), and in quoting, follow your original carefully. Use *and* in college papers.

Analogy in language • *Analogy* is the name for the natural tendency in users of a language to make their speech more regular by forming new words like some existing ones, bringing old words closer together in form, or bringing constructions in line with familiar patterns. It results from the fact that, in general, language is a complex of consistent patterns (noun plurals end in *-s*, past tenses in *-ed*, etc.). It is easiest to watch analogy in the attempts of children to master their language. Before they learn the irregular conventional forms used by grownups, they regularize on the basis of the patterns they are familiar with: Most children for a time say *mans* before they learn to say *men, singed* for *sang* or *sung, digged* for *dug*, or they may say *dag* instead of *dug*.

Analogy is the force that has disposed of many irregularities in the main body of language. Out of various plural forms used in Old English, *-s* has won in all but a few words, and analogy is still bringing more words to that form, like **formula, formulas*. Words occasionally are changed in spelling by analogy, as the *-b* was rather recently added to *crumb* and *thumb* from analogy with *dumb*; and *humble* suggested *crumble*; and so on. *Cole slaw* is often replaced by *cold slaw* by folk etymology, *cole* (from Dutch *kool*, cabbage) being unfamiliar. *Adviser* is now changing to *advisor* from analogy with *advisory* and words like *inspector, distributor*. *Alright* is slowly making its way from analogy with *already* (see *all right). New words are formed on analogy with old ones, like *avigation, aerobatics*.

The extension of *was* to the plural—a common form in Nonstandard English, based on the analogy of most English verbs in the past tense (*I did—we did, he went—they went*)—illustrates not only the force of analogy but the fact that the result, however logical and consistent, is not necessarily acceptable. The *was-were* distinction is the sole survival from a considerable group of verbs in Old English which had different forms for the preterit singular and plural—*sing, drive, choose*, for example. To be accepted the analogical form must be frequently used by educated writers and speakers—and *we was* is not. (See *Change in language, *due to, the words starred in this article, and various other examples of analogy treated in particular *Index* articles. Reference: E. H. Sturtevant, *Linguistic Change*, Chicago, 1917, p. 38 ff., Ch. 6. See also the indexes of most works on language for their treatment of analogy.)

-ance, -ence (-ant, -ent) • Two of the most troublesome groups of words in English spelling are those ending in *-ance* (*-ant*) and *-ence* (*-ent*). Most of them are nouns and adjectives descended from verbs of different Latin conjugations whose stem vowels are generally represented in these endings. Our pronunciation of the endings is the same—both get the neutral vowel ə: /di fen′dənt/, /di pen′dənt/. There is a slight tendency for printers to adopt the ending with *e,* but for the present all we can do is learn the individual forms by memory or consult a dictionary.

Here are some of the commoner words of these types:

-ANCE, -ANT

appearance	reluctance, reluctant
attendance, attendant	repentance, repentant
balance	resemblance
defendant	resistance, resistant
descendant (or descendent)	significance, significant
extravagance, extravagant	tolerance, tolerant
intolerance, intolerant	vigilance, vigilant

-ENCE, -ENT

competence, competent	
confidence, confident	innocence, innocent
consistency, consistent	insistence, insistent
dependence, dependent	obedience, obedient
existence, existent	persistence, persistent
independence, independent	reverence, reverent
	turbulence, turbulent

A group of similar nouns end in *-ense:*

defense   dispense   expense   offense   pretense   suspense

and •

1. *Appropriate uses of "and." And* is the most used connective, joining two or more elements in a series, usually of equal grammatical rank:

Adjectives: a *pink* and *white* apron; a *blue, green,* and *white* flag
Adverbs: He drove *very fast* and *rather carelessly.*
Nouns: trees and *shrubs; trees, shrubs,* and *plants*
Verbs: I *found* the book and *opened* it at the exact place.
Phrases: in one ear and *out the other*
Dependent clauses: While the boys were swimming and *[while] the older folks were resting,* I was reading.
Independent clauses: The first generation makes the money and *the second spends it.*

2. *Inappropriate uses of "and."* In careless writing, elements of unequal grammatical value are sometimes connected by an unnecessary *and:*

Main verbs and participles: Three or four men *sat* on the edge of the lake with their backs to the road, [and] apparently *watching* the ducks.

Independent and dependent clauses: *A contract has been let to install new copper work on the Post Office [and] which will require 4500 pounds of lead-coated copper.* (See **which* § 4.)

And is often used in amateur writing where no connective is needed or where some other connective would show more clearly the logical relation:

The freshmen have a number of required courses and [but] the upperclassmen almost none.

3. *At beginning of sentences.* In current writing of all varieties, *and* sometimes stands at the beginning of sentences. If this usage becomes conspicuous, some of the *and*'s should be dropped or two sentences put together as a compound sentence.
4. *Omission of "and."* In some compact writing *and* is omitted between series of items. Judiciously used, this omission makes for economy, but overused contributes to a *"telegraphic" style, which is usually inappropriate for General writing.

(These *Index* articles involve *and*: *between you and me, *Compound predicate, *Compound sentence, *Compound subject, *Conjunctive adverbs, *Coordinating conjunctions, *Series, *which.)

and etc. • See *etc., et cetera.

and/or • Though *and/or* was originally a legal and business locution, it is useful when three alternatives exist (*both* circumstances mentioned or *either one* of the two): *fruit and/or vegetables* means "fruit" or "vegetables" or "fruit and vegetables." *And/or* is increasingly found in General writing, but many readers object to it because of its business connotation and odd appearance. Before you use it, consider its probable effect on your reader.

angle • *Angle* is often *deadwood and suggests a colloquial or business phrase that is rather out of place in General writing:

In a preparatory school the masters go at the matter from a different angle [that is, *differently*] and make the same kind of literature more enjoyable.

Anglo-Saxon • See *English language § 2.

Antecedent • *Antecedent* is the grammatical term for the word or statement to which a pronoun or *pronominal adjective refers. It may stand before or after the pronoun:

We did not hear their call again and when we found the Thompsons they were almost exhausted. (*The Thompsons* is the antecedent of the pronominal adjective *their* and the pronoun *they*.)

(For relations between antecedents and their pronouns see *Agreement, *Reference of pronouns.)

anti-, anti • The prefix *anti-,* meaning "against" in its various senses, is hyphened only before root words beginning with *i* and before proper nouns:

antibiotic	antifreeze	anti-intellectual	anti-Semitic
anti-British	anti-imperialistic	antimonarchic	antisocial

Anti- is pronounced /an'ti/, an'tə/, or often /an'tī/. *Anti* is an Informal noun, meaning "a person opposed to something"; plural *antis: The pros spoke amid boos from the antis* (/an'tīz/ or /an'tēz/).

Anticipatory subject • See *it, *there is, there are.

Anticlimax • An *anticlimax* is an arrangement of a series in order of descending importance of the elements. It may be intentional, as a form of humor (as in Pope's "Men, monkeys, lap-dogs, parrots, perish all"), or unintentional because of a lapse of judgment on the writer's part ("She had a warm and sympathetic personality, a quick and perceptive intelligence, beautiful features and a lovely figure, and she could play Scrabble"). Such lapses should be corrected.

Antonym • An *antonym* is a word that means approximately the opposite of another word: *hot, stingy, boring* are antonyms of *cold, generous, entertaining.* Most books of synonyms also give antonyms, as do the synonym entries in dictionaries.

any, and compounds with any •
1. *Any,* deriving from the same source as *one, a, an,* is used primarily as an adjective (any member of the family, Any dog is a good dog) but also as a pronoun (Any will do).

In comparisons of things of the same class, *idiom calls for *any other: This book is better than any other on the subject.* But: *I like a movie better than any book* (different class of things).
2. *Compounds with "any." Anybody, anyhow, anything,* and *anywhere* are always written as single words. *Any rate* is always two words: *at any rate. Anyone* is written as one word when the stress is on the *any* (Anyone /en' ē wun/ would know that), and as two when the stress is on the *one* (I'd like any one /en ē wun'/ of them.)

Anyway is one word when the *any* is stressed (I can't do it anyway /en' ē wā/), and two when the stress is about equal (Any way /en' ē wā'/ I try, it comes out wrong). If the word

whatever can be substituted for the *any* (Whatever way I try, it comes out wrong), *any way* should be written as two words.
3. *Pronouns referring to "anybody," "anyone."* *Anybody* and *anyone* are singular in form and take singular verbs (Anybody [Anyone] feels bad at times). They are referred to by *he, his, him* (*Anybody* knows what *he* deserves), or, since they are often felt to be collective, Informally by a plural pronoun:

> . . . and a top that goes up and down without *anybody* losing *their* temper.—THORNTON WILDER (letter), *Theatre Arts,* Nov. 1940

(See *Divided usage. Compare *every and its compounds; Fries, *AEG,* p. 50.)
4. *Informal forms* (not appropriate in college writing). *Any place* is Informal for *anywhere* (He wasn't any place I looked). *Anyways* is regional for the generally used *anyway,* and *anywheres* is Nonstandard for *anywhere. Any more = now* is a Standard idiom in a negative context (You don't see that any more). Its regional use in an affirmative context (Any more I do that) is Nonstandard outside quotation marks.

Aphorisms • See *Epigrams.

Apostrophe (') •

Apos   *Revision: Insert an apostrophe where it belongs in the word marked; or take out a wrongly used apostrophe.*

The apostrophe is one of the most useless anachronisms in our traditional system of spelling, as Bernard Shaw demonstrated in his printed works; but you must know the conventions governing its use and follow them.
1. *In genitives.* The most common use of the apostrophe is in spelling the *genitive (possessive) case of nouns and of the indefinite pronouns (*anyone, nobody, someone*—See *Pronouns § 8): *Dorothy's* first picture, The *companies'* original charters, *Everybody's* business is *nobody's* business, The *boys'* dogs.

It should be kept in singular genitives of time even though they carry no idea of possession: a *day's* hike, this *month's* quota.

It is often omitted from plurals that can be regarded as nouns used in the function of an adjective especially when used as proper names: *teachers* college, a *girls* school. (See *Genitive for discussion of special examples of possessive form.)
2. *In contractions.* The apostrophe is used to show the omission of one or more letters in contractions: *can't, I'm, I'll, it's* [*it is*]. (See *Contractions.)

3. *In plurals.* An apostrophe is ordinarily used in plurals of figures, letters of the alphabet, and words being discussed as words: *three e's, the 1920's, the first of the two that's.* There is some tendency to omit this apostrophe:

The legendary Miss Millay, the feminine Byron of the *1920s.* . . . —Louis UNTERMEYER

4. *In representing speech.* An apostrophe may be used to show that certain sounds represented in the usual spelling were not spoken:

"An' one o' them is the new schoolmaster," he said.

This is a legitimate use, but too many apostrophes make a spotted page and confuse the reader. It is better to suggest occasional pronunciations of this sort than to try to represent them conscientiously. In the example the indicated pronunciations are in fact Standard.

5. *Personal pronouns.* Apostrophes are not used in the genitive of the personal pronouns: *his, hers, its, ours, theirs, yours.*

6. *Simplified spellings.* No apology is needed for simplified spellings that are entered in the dictionary: (*altho,* not *altho'*; *thru,* not *thro'.) Till* is a word, equivalent to *until,* not *'til.* In some college classrooms, simplified spellings are acceptable; in some they are not.

appearing • *Appearing* is an inflated (or unnecessarily Formal) substitute for *looking: a comfortable looking* [better than *appearing*] *street, a fine looking* [better than *appearing*] *moraine locust.*

appendix • The English plural *appendixes* is now commoner than the Latin *appendices* and is the better form except in quite Formal usage; it is the only plural form used in referring to the appendix of appendicitis.

Apposition, appositives • *Apposition* is the placing of a construction next to another so that the second either complements or supplements the first. The complementary relationship is called close or restrictive apposition because the second element completes the first; it is not set off by commas. The supplementary relationship is loose or nonrestrictive; it is usually set off by commas.

Close (restrictive, complementary)	*Loose (nonrestrictive, supplementary)*
Coach Bradley	Our coach, Bradley,
William the Conqueror	William I, conqueror of England,

My aunts Mary and Agnes (He had more aunts.)	My aunts, Mary and Agnes, (He had only two.)
Fletcher the grocer	Fletcher, our grocer,
The fact *that he had been over the road before* gave him an advantage.	This fact, *that he had been over the road before,* gave him an advantage.

An appositive pronoun agrees with its headword in number and case:

He called the two of us, *John and me* [object].
The two of us, *John and I* [subject], were going together.

(References: Curme, *Syntax,* pp. 88-92; Jespersen, pp. 93-95; articles in *American Speech,* 1952-1956.)

apt—likely—liable • See *likely—apt—liable.

Arabic numerals • See *Numbers § 3.

arise, rise, get up • See *rise.

around—round • See *round—around.

Articles • Traditionally *a* and *an* are known as *indefinite articles* and *the* as the *definite article.* They belong principally with nouns and as a part of speech are regarded as a class of adjectives, being modifiers of a sort, or in other systems as *function words. They are usually omitted in *telegraphic style. (For some details of usage see *a, an, *the.) Many languages do not have corresponding words and even those that have them use them differently from English.

as • *As* is one of the most common and versatile words in English. Some of its more important uses can be conveniently listed under traditional part-of-speech categories:
1. *Conjunction. As* occurs most commonly as a conjunction, introducing several kinds of clauses.

Degree or manner: . . . *as* far *as* I could.
Time (=while) : *As* I was coming in he was going out.
Cause: *As* it was getting dark, we made for home.

Such a handy word is of course much used in speech, which often prefers *counter words to more exact ones. But the very variety of possible uses makes *as* a problem in written English. It is necessary in comparisons (We went *as* far *as* he did) and for attendant circumstances (*As* we walked along he told us stories) though *while* is preferable if the emphasis is on the time or the action (*While* we were walking along he told us stories).

As may be used as a weaker *because.* But usually *since* or *because* fits better in writing and certainly better in Formal English:

Informal: As it was almost time to go, we were getting more and more exasperated.

More exact and emphatic: Since it was almost time to go, we were getting more and more exasperated. Or: *Because* it was almost time to go, we were getting more and more exasperated.

(Reference: Bryant, pp. 27-28.)

2. *Preposition. As* occurs as a preposition with the meaning "in the position of" (She had a job *as* stenographer); "in the role of" (He was in the cast *as* Mercutio). In the Informal construction "I don't like him *as well as her*" (meaning "I don't like him *as well as I like her*"), *as her* may be construed as a prepositional phrase: Who would want to go with such a poor skater *as me*? (Formal usage would often have ". . . with such a poor skater *as I* [*am*].")

There is a growing tendency to use *as* as a preposition where *like* or *such as* would be preferred by many: *Some writers, as Faulkner, take their material from a particular region.* This probably results from uncertainty about the distinction between *like* and *as* and a conviction that *as* is the lesser risk.

3. *Adverb. As* occurs as an adverb of degree: *I came as soon as I could.* It also introduces appositives: *There were several kinds of shellfish,* as *scallops, oysters, crabs, lobsters.*

4. *Pronoun.* In Formal English *as* occurs as a pronoun usually with *same* or *such* as antecedent: *It was such a day* as *one rarely sees.*

As a common Nonstandard relative pronoun, it takes the place of *who* and *that: Everyone* as *has his ticket can go in.*

(Compare *like—as. References: Curme, *Syntax,* pp. 269-271; *Parts of Speech,* pp. 78-82, and index references in both books.)

as . . . as •

1. *In double comparisons* we sometimes do not complete the first construction with a second *as:* He is fully *as* tall if not taller than his older brother. The pattern is completed if we add the second *as:* He is fully *as* tall *as,* if not taller than, his older brother. But since the interrupted sentence movement is somewhat artificial in General English, it may be better to complete the first comparison and then add the second: He is fully *as* tall *as* his older brother, if not taller.

2. *In negative comparisons* Formal English slightly prefers *not so . . . as:* The winters are *not so* long *nor so* cold *as* they used to be. The winters are *neither so* cold *nor so* long *as* they

used to be. General English does not as a rule make this distinction: The winters are *not as* long *or as* cold *as* they used to be. Which idiom is to be used depends on the formality of the context and the taste of the writer.

as if, as though • In Formal English the *subjunctive is used after *as if* or *as though*: He acted *as if* [*as though*] *he were* losing his temper. In General English the subjunctive is often replaced by the indicative: He acted *as if* [*as though*] *he was* losing his temper. Often in Informal English and sometimes in General, *like* is used instead of *as if*: He acted *like he was* losing his temper. The subjunctive is never used with *like*. Many readers are irritated by these General constructions. (See *like—as.)

as it were • This set expression now seems old-fashioned and is better avoided.

as—like • See *like—as.

as though • See *as if.

as to • *As to* is often a clumsy substitute for a single preposition, usually *of* or *about*:

> Practice is the best teacher as to [in, for, of] the use of organ stops.
> If the question contains words as to the exact meaning of which [of whose exact meaning] you are uncertain, by all means get out your dictionary.

But it is fairly common in all varieties of written English.

> *As to* as a sentence opener emphasizes a word by pulling it out of normal position: *As to my father, everyone likes him.*

as, when, if • See *when, as, and if.

Asides, apologetic • See *Parentheses.

asset • Something of value, currently overused for *advantage, aid, benefit, property,* and so on.

Assonance • *Assonance* refers to the like sound of vowels in syllables having different consonants (*brave—vain, lone—show*). It is a common and effective sound element in verse and is also common in prose, especially in an emotional or heightened style:

> that id*ea*l country, of gr*ee*n, d*ee*p lanes and high gr*ee*n banks.
> —OSBERT SITWELL

Asterisk (*) • Except in reference works, the asterisk or star is not used so much now as formerly, because it is a conspicuous mark and attracts more attention than is necessary.

1. In works which have very few footnotes, an asterisk may be used as a reference mark, placed after the statement calling for the note and again at the beginning of the footnote; but numbers are more common; for example [31]. (See Ch. 11, "Footnotes and final bibliography," p. 438.)

2. Asterisks sometimes indicate a rather long omission in a quotation, a stanza or more from a poem, or a paragraph or more from prose, though spaced periods are now more common. (See *Ellipsis.)

3. In fiction a group of asterisks has been used to suggest that action is omitted or to indicate passage of time between movements of a story, but here again a line of spaced periods or extra space between the movements is more common. (See *Ellipsis.)

at about, at around • It can be argued that since an arrival is either "at seven" or "about seven," "at about seven" is redundant. But in informal speech and writing the construction is common. Since *at* or *about* alone seems more precise, the single word is preferred in General and Formal writing. (Reference: Bryant, pp. 31-32. Also see *about § 3.)

athlete, athletic, athletics • Watch your spelling and pronunciation of these: /ath′lēt/, /ath let′ik/, /ath let′iks/.

When *athletics* refers to sports and games it usually takes a plural verb and pronoun: Our athletics *include* football, basketball, and baseball. When *athletics* refers to skill or activity it usually takes a singular verb and pronoun: Athletics *is* recommended for every student.

at last, at long last • See *last, at long last.

Attributive • An adjective that stands next to its noun is attributive (a *blue* shirt; a shirt, *blue* and *clean*), as contrasted with a predicate adjective that is related to its noun by a *linking verb (The shirt is *blue*). A noun modifying another noun (*horse* race, *football* field) is used *attributively*. (See *Adjectives, types and forms § 2a.)

atom—atomic • We have the choice of *atomic* (adjective) *bomb* or *atom* (attributive noun) *bomb* and usage favors the latter. More debatable is *atomic age* or *atom age*. The former is more widely used, but the latter occurs.

-augh • See *-ough, -augh.

Auxiliary verb • A verb used with another verb to form a phrasal tense or voice is called an *auxiliary verb* or *helping verb*:

I *am* going.　He *will* go.　They *were* lost.　He *should* watch out.

Be, do, have are the commonest auxiliaries; *can, may, shall, will, must, ought, should, would, might* are primarily used as auxiliaries; *get, let, need,* and *used* sometimes. (See *Index* articles for these verbs, the general article *Verbs, *Modal auxiliaries. Compare *Function words.)

awake • See *wake.

awful • In Formal English *awful* means "inspiring with awe." In Informal English it is a convenient utility word of disapproval—"ugly, shocking, ludicrous" (*awful* manners). As a result of this contamination the word is seldom used in General writing. *Awfully* is common in speech as an intensive, but in writing it is an example of *schoolgirl style.

awhile, a while • *Awhile* is an adverb (They talked awhile). Strictly, a prepositional phrase in which *while* is a noun should be in three words (for a while, in a while), but *awhile* is sometimes found. (See *a, an § 3, *while.)

Awkward •

Revision: Rewrite the passage marked to make the phrasing smoother and more effective.

Awk (K)

A rather general word of disapproval sometimes used in correcting themes. It may refer to clumsy phrases, unnatural word order, unnecessary repetition of a word or phrase, or other phrasing that attracts unpleasant attention or handicaps a reader. The remedy is to recast the sentence or passage.

aye • Used for *yes* in voting: pronounced /ī/.

B • The letter *b* occurs frequently in English spelling as a *silent letter and therefore is a possible snare in spelling and sometimes in pronunciation. Many silent *b*'s, especially after *m,* represent *b*'s that were pronounced in Old English but perhaps have not been generally sounded for hundreds of years: *climb* /klīm/, *comb* /kōm/, *dumb* /dum/, though the *b* is pronounced in the Formal or archaic *clamber,* in *limber,* and in a few other words. A *b* not in Old English has been added in *crumb* and *thumb.* Other silent *b*'s represent sounds that had been in the Latin ancestor words but that were dropped as the sound disappeared in Old French, from which the words came into English: *debt* (from *debitum*), *doubt* (from *dubitare*), *subtle* (from *subtilis*). Some of these *b*'s were inserted by Renaissance scholars because they wished to tie English closer to Latin: Chaucer wrote *det* but we do not.

When *b* comes next to *p* the two sounds sometimes are assimilated to one: *cupboard* /kub′ ərd/, *subpoena* /sə pē′ nə/.

Back formations • See *Origin of words § 3e.

bad—badly • *Bad* is an adjective of varied application: *a bad man, a bad cold, a bad night, a bad accident, bad weather, bad news, a bad light, a bad taste.*

In "I feel bad about it," "She looks bad," *bad* functions as a predicate adjective. In "I feel badly," *badly* is in the position normally filled by a predicate adjective. Perhaps the form in -*ly* was introduced under the misapprehension that the modifier had an adverbial function. Whatever the reason, the -*ly* form is now about as common as the other in Standard speech and not uncommon in Formal writing. The analogous "He looks badly" is objected to by many authorities. (See *Linking verbs.)

Both *badly* and *bad* are also used as adverbs, the latter only in very Informal usage.

He draws *badly*. The starter has always worked *badly* [Informal: *bad*].

(References: Lillian M. Feinsilver, "How Bad(ly) Do You Feel?" *American Speech,* 1949, 24:161-170; Bryant, pp. 35-36.)
Badly, meaning "very much" (He wanted it *badly*), is in Standard use.

Worse, worst, the comparative and superlative of *bad,* of course come from a quite different root. They were earlier used in comparing *evil* and *ill,* and when *bad* acquired the meaning of those words, *worse* and *worst* were used for it too.

Bad grammar • *Bad grammar* is used as a term of reproach and is applied to all sorts of locutions from "I ain't got none" to imaginary confusions in the use of *shall* and *will.* It is too vague and emotional a term to be useful. (See Ch. 1, p. 25, *Grammar.)

Basic English • *Basic English* is a simplified form of English devised by C. K. Ogden and intended to facilitate international communication. It has a vocabulary of only 850 words. (Reference: C. K. Ogden, *The System of Basic English,* New York, 1934.)

be • Some grammarians prefer not to call *be* a verb, restricting that term to words that conform more consistently to one established pattern. Here we shall classify its principal uses according to traditional categories.

1. *Forms.* Be has forms from three originally separate verbs (as in *are, was, been*). Though the forms are irregular, we use them so much that they give little trouble:

Present: I am, you are, he is; we, you, they are
Present subjunctive: I, you, he, we, you, they be
Past: I was, you were, he was; we, you, they were
Past subjunctive: I, you, he, we, you, they were
Infinitive: be
Present participle: being
Past participle: been

Some old forms survive in stock phrases ("the powers that be") and in the Nonstandard "You ain't (sometimes be'n't) going, be you?" Nonstandard also uses *was* in the plural ("Was the Adamses there?"), leveling the past tense to one form (*was*), like the past of other English verbs.

2. *As a linking verb. Be* is the most common *linking verb, joining, without adding specifically a meaning of its own, a subject and a predicative:

Predicate nominative: Jerome was the secretary.
Predicate adjective: She is sick.

With the *finite parts of *be* the predicate noun or pronoun is usually in the nominative form in written English; such constructions are rare in writing, and their variation from the spoken ones makes them uncomfortably artificial:

It was *he.* (Informal: It was *him.*)

"It's I" is Formal for the General "It's me." (See *It's me.)

When the infinitive has a subject and complement, both are in the accusative form: I wanted *him* to be *me.*

When the infinitive has no subject, Formal usage has a nominative as the complement (I wanted to be *he*), but General usage would more often have an accusative (I wanted to be *him*).

3. *As auxiliary verb.* Forms of *be* are used with the present participles of other verbs to form the progressive tense form:

I *am* asking   he *was* asking   you *will be* asking

Forms of *be* with past participles form the passive voice:

I *am* asked   you *will* be asked   he *was* asked

4. *As verb of complete predication. Be* is a verb of complete predication when indicating states or positions:

He *was* at home anywhere.   The fire *was* just across the street.

In the sense of "exist," "live" (Hamlet's "To be, or not to be," "Can such things be?"), *be* is now rather rare. (See *Subjunctives, *Subject and verb, *ain't.)

because • *Because* introduces a subordinate clause giving the reason for the independent statement in the independent clause:

Because we were getting hungry, we began to look for a convenient restaurant.

Since and *as* can be used in such clauses, but they are less definite, more casual, and more characteristic of easy speech than of writing:

In a small rural school these young children have to stay for the rest of the day's session, *because* [more definite than *as* or *since*] there is no one to take them home.

For, which also introduces reasons, is a slightly more Formal word, rather rare in conversation and General writing. It also often has the sense of giving evidence for the statement, for the writer's knowledge of the fact stated:

General: I know he is reliable, *because* I have traded with him for years.

More Formal: I know he is reliable, *for* I have traded with him for years. ("He is reliable *because* [or *for*] I have traded with him for years" would not be exact.)

(See *reason is because, *for, *as. For *because of,* see *due to.)

Beginning paragraphs •
Revision: Revise the opening paragraph to make it lead more directly into your subject and to arouse your reader's interest.   *Beg*

(For discussion of qualities of beginning paragraphs and examples, see Ch. 4, "Opening paragraphs," p. 143; Ch. 5, "Beginning and ending the paper," pp. 184-185; Ch. 6, pp. 202-203.)

beside—besides • *Beside* is a preposition referring to place, "by the side of," as in "beside the road," "beside her," and is used figuratively in a few rather Formal idioms like "beside the point," "beside himself with rage." (*Beside* is less commonly used as an adverb, with the meaning of *besides*.)

Besides as adverb or preposition means "in addition to" or "except":

We tried two other ways *besides*. (adverb)

Besides our own members, . . . (preposition)

It is also used as a conjunctive adverb: *He didn't think that he ought to get into the quarrel; besides, he had come to enjoy himself.* (Notice the punctuation.)

between—among • *Among* implies more than two objects: *They distributed the provisions among the survivors.*

Between is most strictly used of only two: *They divided the prize between Kincaid and Thomas.* But the attempt to limit *between* to use with only two items has failed. As the *Oxford English Dictionary* shows, it has from the first been used of several: *Between sobs and groans and tears. He showed the relationship between peoples, races, and cultures.* When a group is treated as a collective unit, only *among* is used: *Divide the books among the poor.* (Reference: Pooley, pp. 135-137; Bryant, pp. 38-40.)

between you and me • Since the accusative form of the personal pronoun ordinarily follows a preposition, the expected form is *between you and me, for you and me, to you and me* (or when the pronouns are objects of a verb, "He will take *you and me*").

But *between you and I* is frequently heard, perhaps because the speakers remember the prejudice against *It's me* and carry over the taboo to a different construction; or because *you and I, he and I,* etc., are felt as unalterable units; or because *I* is felt to be more genteel than *me*. The locution *between you and I* should be avoided.

Bible, bible • When referring to the Christian Scriptures, the word is capitalized but not italicized: "You will find all that in the Bible, and more too." In the sense of an authoritative book or a book much consulted or quoted, the word is not capitalized: "Gray's *Manual,* the botanist's bible, . . ."

The usual form of particular references to parts of the Bible is:

the Old Testament and the New Testament [capitalized but not italicized]

The Ten Commandments are in Exodus xx [or: in Exodus 20].

The Ten Commandments are in Exodus 20:3-17.

I Corinthians 4:6

The adjective *biblical* ordinarily is not capitalized.

Bibliography • See Ch. 11, p. 438, and *References in scientific papers.

Big words •
Revision: Use a simpler, more natural word instead of the Formal or heavy one marked.   Big W

Good writers avoid pretentious or "big" words; they prefer *home* rather than *domicile, think* or *believe* rather than *deem, happen* rather than *transpire,* and so on. (For discussion of big words and suggestions for avoiding them, see Ch. 9, "Big words," p. 347.)

biography • Pronounced /bī og′ rə fē/ or /bi-/. A biography is the life of a person written by someone else; an autobiography is the life of a person written by himself. (Compare Ch. 5, which deals mainly with autobiographical papers, and Ch. 6, "The profile," p. 208.)

Blend • A *blend* is a word made by fusing two words, often with a syllable in common: *paratroops, cinemactress, imagineering, smog, motel, beautility, snoopervise.* (See *Origin of words § 3c.)
Until a blend has established itself in the language, as *electrocute* (from *electric* and *execute*) has, it is usually more appropriate to Informal than to General or Formal writing. (See *New words.)

blond, blonde • Following the French gender distinction, *blond* would be used of a man, *blonde* of a woman:

He is a *blond.*   She is a *blonde.*   a peroxide *blonde* (or *blond*)

But in both the noun and adjective use, the *-e* is gradually disappearing. Some write *blonde* when it refers specifically to a woman (a *blonde* Helen) and *blond* elsewhere, including *blond* hair.
Brunet, brunette are in the same situation: masculine *brunet,* feminine *brunette.*

Boners • Confusion of two similar words, mistaken constructions, combinations of ideas that don't belong together have always been a source of fun for everyone except the persons who made them. Volumes of these boners have been gathered and several periodicals run specimens that they find in other publications. Here are a few that have cropped up in themes:

My papers have a decided tendency toward longevity.

He is descended from one of the most virulent [really *poisonous?* or merely *virile?*] families in the U.S.A.

Jean is no plastic saint.

For the lowly freshmen are moved by sediment rather than by intellect in their voting.

The arduous loves of movie stars are not always convincing.

Many times I started for the library to do some research on Gestalt's psychology.

Keep your eye out for boners in manuscript and in print and get what fun you can from them—but most of all scan your own writing to catch them before they come to anybody else's attention.

born—borne •

1. A useless distinction in the spelling of the past participle of *bear* was introduced in the eighteenth century; in most of its senses it is now spelled *borne*:

They had *borne* this poverty without complaining.

The ship, *borne* along by the breeze, was soon out of sight.

Bear in most of these senses is somewhat Formal; *carry* or *endure* would be more common. But in "It was more than I could *bear*," *bear* is less Formal than *endure* would be.

In the sense of "give birth to," the past participle of *bear* is spelled *borne* except in the (very common) passive when not followed by *by*:

Of the four children *borne* by his wife.... (but... *born* to his first wife)

He was *born* in 1891.   A *born* liar.

The children, *born* in Chicago....

Passion *born* of hatred....

2. In autobiographical papers students often become self-conscious or humorous in giving the facts of their birth: "I saw the light of day first on June 28, 1948," "No planets blazed on the night of June 28, 1948, when a squally infant appeared in the home of Mr. and Mrs...." Neither of these is as satisfactory as the simple and natural statement "I was born June 28, 1948."

Borrowed words • See *Foreign words in English, *Origin of words § 2b, *English language.

both • *Both* is a favorite way of emphasizing two-ness:

The twins were both there. They are both alike. Both Harry and his brother went.

Though none of these *both*'s is necessary, each gives a legitimate emphasis.

"The both women got along well enough together" is a localism for "The two women got along well enough together." But "The both of them" is a fairly common spoken idiom.

both . . . and • See *Correlative conjunctions.

Brace { or } • A brace is the mark used to group two or more lines of writing. Its use is chiefly in technical writing, especially in tables and formulas. Examples will be found in the article *English language.

Brackets [ ] • Brackets are rarely used in General writing and are not in the standard typewriter keyboard, but in much academic and professional writing they have specific and convenient uses. If they are needed in typing, you can make them by using a diagonal and two underscores (/ /), or you can put them in by hand.

Brackets are primarily editorial marks, in this example used to show where some explanation or comment has been added to the text, especially to quoted matter:

The preposition *due to* is not more incorrect than the preposition *owing to,* which is approved by the same dictionary [the *Concise Oxford Dictionary*], but it is not yet so thoroughly established in the language.—G. O. CURME, *Syntax,* p. 561

In quoting material, *sic in brackets is sometimes used to indicate that an error in the original is being reproduced exactly: "New Haven, Conneticut [sic] . . ."; or a correction may be inserted in brackets: "When he was thirty-eight [Actually he was forty-three] he published his first novel."

Brackets function as parentheses within parentheses, particularly in legal documents or in footnotes to theses, etc.

In this *Index,* brackets are used in examples of faulty writing to enclose words that might better be left out or to suggest an improved expression:

Throughout [the course of] the year I read such books as *Oliver Twist* and *Boots and Saddles.*

The continuously moving belt makes a noise *similar to* [*like*] a concrete mixer.

bring up • *Bring up* is the General idiom (that's the way I was *brought up*) for the more Formal *rear* or *nurture;* it also means "to introduce" (a subject). (See *raise—rear.)

British usage • See *American and British usage.

Broad reference • A pronoun referring to a preceding idea rather than to a particular antecedent is said to have a broad reference. (See *Reference of pronouns § 1.)

brunet, brunette • See *blond, blonde.

bunch • In Formal English *bunch* is limited to objects that grow together or can be fastened together (a bunch of carrots, roses, keys). The Informal "bunch of kids" is the Formal or General "group of children."

burst, bust • The principal parts of *burst* are *burst, burst, burst*:

One *bursts* almost every day. Two tanks *burst* yesterday. One tank had *burst*.

Bust, in origin a variant pronunciation of *burst,* has the principal parts *bust, busted, busted*. It is used in Nonstandard English in the sense of *burst*. But it also occurs in Informal English in the sense of "being broke" or "being demoted," and in General English in the sense of "busting a broncho" or "busting a trust."

bus • The plural is spelled *buses* or *busses,* the first much more common American usage.

Business English • The writing of business English has attained a very high standard of mechanical form. The layout, spacing, and mechanics of most business letters and reports are excellent, reflecting the skill of professional typists; and the skill of layout men and printers is available for printed matter.

But the usage and style of business communications vary considerably. Most firms at present pay a good deal of attention to the style of their written and printed matter. The old clichés—*in re, the above, Yrs. of 23d inst. rec'd and contents noted, and oblige*—have practically disappeared. Naturally all degrees of Formality and Informality are found. The prime virtues of good business writing are *directness* and *adaptation to reader*. Adapting the style to the reader is especially difficult in writing advertising and business letters, since usually the writer is not acquainted with his reader and in spite of elaborate market analyses may not size him up correctly. If the letter is sent to many people, there is the difficulty of making it *seem* personal when it really cannot be. For most purposes "business English" is merely good English applied to the specific needs of industry and trade.

Business people have adopted a General style and have handled English with the freedom a living language deserves.

They have pioneered in the much needed simplifying of our spelling. Business writers have used all the native resources of the language in making new names and in brightening style— outright coinages like *kodak, vaseline, fabrikoid,* blends like *servicenter, unisteel, sunoco,* compounds and respellings like *cutex, denticuring* (preventive dentistry), *tudor* (cars), *lubritory.* Though many such words are ludicrous or overcute or in poor taste, some are expressive and are normal language developments. They are much better than attempts at false dignity (*client* for *customer, favor* for *letter,* *business world* for *business, cheque* for *check*).

The question of fitness arises when certain words with obvious business connotation are used in other contexts. Some are frequently borrowed and are useful: *deal,* *asset, feature, bank on,* and *take stock in* are in General usage. But many people, for various reasons, are offended by *beg to advise,* *angle,* *and/or,* *contact,* *realtor.* Such words are out of place in Formal writing and in discussions of ideal rather than practical affairs, but in General writing, business locutions are often useful. H. S. Canby used ordinary business terms to point up a comment on current literature:

> No; public taste, ease of publication, variety of interest, even editorial capability, have all arisen with the intellectual development of the country; only the professional writers, as a class, have not progressed. They have become astonishingly clever, as clever as the mechanism of a Ford; but as a class they have not moved ten feet towards literature. *They have standardized their product without improving the model.—Saturday Papers,* p. 56

(See *Letters, *man, woman, *Reports; *Shoptalk; Ch. 9, "Euphemisms," p. 346.)

business world • *Business world* is a pretentious term for *business* or *businessmen*: *I expect to enter the business world* (I expect to go into business).

but • *But* is the natural *coordinating conjunction to connect two contrasted statements of equal grammatical rank. It is more natural than the Formal *however* or *yet,* and more emphatic than *although.*

1. *Connects equals.* The locutions connected by *but* should be of equal grammatical rank:

Adjectives: not blue *but* green.

Adverbs: He worked fast *but* accurately.

Phrases: He didn't come in the forenoon *but* in the early evening.

Clauses: The first day we rested, *but* the second we got down to work.

Sentences: Enigma of the semitropics, the Rio Grande defied the best engineering minds of two countries for a century. *But* $10,000,000 in flood control work has harnessed the treacherous stream.

(See *which § 4 for comments on *but which.*)

2. *Connects statements in opposition.* The statements connected by *but* should be actually in opposition. Contrast the first example with the second and third:

He knows vaguely that the nation is not much good any more; he has read that the crust of the earth is shrinking alarmingly and that the universe is growing steadily colder; *but* he does not believe that any of the three is in half as bad shape as he is.—JAMES THURBER, *My Life and Hard Times,* Preface

He supported a wife and three children on this pittance *and* [not *but*] he seemed very proud that he wasn't on relief.

Our view was limited to about twenty yards down Tuckerman Ravine; [not *but*] beyond that everything was in clouds.

3. *"But" with "however."* *But* should be used efficiently, carrying its real meaning. It should not be doubled by a *however,* which can add nothing (see *however):

The students wanted to extend the Christmas vacation a day beyond New Year's, *but* [*however* not needed] the Administration couldn't see their point of view.

4. *At beginning of sentences.* *But,* like *and,* often stands at the beginning of sentences, especially if the sentences are short; neither *and* nor *but* should be overused as a sentence opener.

5. *Punctuation.* Two clauses connected by *but* should ordinarily be separated by a comma. The contrast in idea suggests the use of punctuation even when the clauses are relatively short.

I couldn't get the whole license number, *but* it began with A30.

But is part of the clause in which it stands and should not be separated from it by a comma. A parenthetical phrase following the *but* may be set off by commas, especially in Formal English.

His speech was supposed to be extemporaneous, *but* he had really been practicing it for a week.

His speech was supposed to be extemporaneous, *but,* to be quite truthful, we must add that he had practiced it for a week.

6. *Minor uses of "but."*

a—As subordinating conjunction, after *no doubt,* in questions with *know,* and in a few other constructions:

There is no doubt *but* [or *but that,* or more Formally, *that*] he had.

Who knows *but* everything will come out right?

Nothing would do *but* I must spend the night with them.

b–As a preposition, equivalent to *except* (no comma preceding):

We didn't get anything *but* a couple of shad.
No one could have done it *but* me.

c–As a rather Formal adverb, equivalent to *only*:

If he *but* stops to think, he can interpret his own reactions.

d–With "not." *But* is sometimes used after *not* in Standard usage, especially in speech: *There aren't but three eggs left.* This construction develops from "There are *but* three eggs left"; evidently *but* was felt as not strong enough and *not* was added.

(See also *Correlative conjunctions. References: Fowler, article "but"; Curme, *Parts of Speech*, index; Bryant, p. 147.)

but that—but what • *But that* is the more usual conjunction in written English; *but what* is Informal and General:

He didn't know *but that* [Informal: *but what*] the other car could still turn out.

Informal and General: I don't doubt *but that* he will come. [Or: I don't doubt *but what* he'll come.]

Formal: I do not doubt *that* he will come.

(Reference: Bryant, pp. 46-47.)

but which • See *which § 4.

C • In Old English *c* represented two related /k/ sounds: One remained /k/—*cruma*, "crumb," *celan*, "to cool," *cyning*, "king"; but before *e* or *i* the other soon became /ch/ (*ceosan, ciepan, cild*) and is spelled *ch* in Modern English: *choose, cheap, child.* The Norman Conquest complicated *c* spellings, for it brought in many French words in which *c* spelled the /s/ sound. Today *c* is an unnecessary letter, doing work that could more clearly be done by *k* and *s*. Many words spelled with *c* must be respelled with *k* or *s* to show pronunciation: /sit'ē/ (*city*), /sel/ (*cell*), /fôrs/ (*force*), /kōld/ (*cold*), /kum/ (*come*), /ärk/ (*arc*).

Before *e, i,* or *y, c* regularly represents /s/: *cent, civil, cynic;* before *a, o, u,* and any consonant but *h, c* is regularly /k/: *can't, coffee, cute, fact.* Marked with a *cedilla, as in *façade, c* has the /s/ sound before *a, o,* or *u.*

C may represent /sh/: *ocean* /o'shən/, *conscience* /kon'shəns/, *special* /spesh'əl/; and /ch/: *cello* /chel'ō/.

C is silent in *czar, indict, muscle,* and a few other words.

Before *e* or *i*, *cc* spells /ks/: *accident, occident, success, vaccine*; otherwise it is /k/: *acclaim, accommodate.* The pronunciation of *cc* as /s/ in some words like *accessory* and *flaccid*, though widespread, is objected to by many speakers. (See *ch.)

c., ca. • See *Abbreviations § 2.

calculate, guess, reckon • *Calculate* (cut in Nonstandard to /kalk′lāt/ or even to /kal′āt/) and *reckon* for localisms for the *think, suppose, expect* of General English. They should be avoided in writing unless the audience addressed uses them habitually in writing as well as in speaking. *Guess* has moved into General English in the United States.

can—may (could—might) •
1. In General English *may* occurs rather rarely except in the sense of possibility:

It may be all right for her, but not for me.

Can is generally used for both permission and ability:

Can I go now? You can if you want to.
I can do 80 miles an hour with mine.

This is in such widespread usage that it should be regarded as Standard English in speaking and in writing and is so described in modern dictionaries.

Can't almost always takes the place of *mayn't* in the United States:

Can't I go now? We can't have lights after twelve o'clock.

2. In Formal English a distinction is sometimes made between the auxiliary *can,* with the meaning of ability, "being able to," and *may,* with the meaning of permission:

You may go now. He can walk with crutches. You may if you can.

May also indicates possibility: *He may have the right one.*
3. *Might* and *could. Might,* originally the past of *may,* and *could,* the past of *can,* are now used chiefly to convey a shade of doubt, or a smaller degree of possibility. And in General English *could* often replaces *might.*

It might be all right for her, but it isn't for me.
It might have been all right for her, but not for me.

Adverbs are likely to be used instead of *may* or *might* in such constructions, especially for the past tense:

Perhaps it was all right for her, but not for me.

Can and *could, may* and *might* are often interchangeable, except that *could* and *might* are perhaps more deferential or tentative; compare:

May I help you?   Can you help me?
Might I help you?   Could you help me?

Could also suggests doubt or qualified possibility:

Perhaps I could write a poem, but I doubt it.

Be able to tends to replace *can* and *could* when the idea of ability needs emphasis:

I am able to live on my income.

(See *Divided usage. Reference: Gladys D. Haase, *College English,* 1950, 11:215-216.)

cannot, can not • Usage is divided; *cannot* is more common.

can't help but, can't seem to • There are three possible idioms:

Formal: I cannot but feel sorry for him.
General: I can't help feeling sorry for him.
General: I can't help but feel sorry for him.

The last is an established idiom, though avoided by many writers. *Can't seem to* appears to be restricted to Informal speech and writing. At the same time, a locution like "I *can't seem to* get started" makes excellent sense—"I'm not sure just why, but I can't get started"—and is more natural than "I seem to be unable to . . . ." (See *seem.)

Capital letters •
Revision: Capitalize the word marked, for one of the reasons shown in this article; or, if the word marked is written with a capital, make it a small letter.

Cap

*Proofreading marks can be used for correcting themes. Three lines under a small letter means: make this a capital. A slanting line drawn through a capital means: make this a small letter (see *Lower case).

march 15   He came from West of Buffalo.

Certain uses of capitals, as at the beginning of sentences or for proper names, are conventions followed by everyone; certain others show divided usage or are matters of taste. Formal English tends to use more capitals than General English, and newspaper usage tends to cut them to a minimum.

This article summarizes the principal uses of capitals in current writing. Further discussion and examples will be found in the articles marked by asterisks.

1. *Sentence capitals.* The first word of a sentence is capitalized. In quotations, the first word of a quoted sentence or part

of sentence is capitalized, but when the quotation is broken, the second part is not capitalized unless it is a complete sentence:

He said, "The first time I came this way almost none of the roads were hard surfaced."

He said, "Perhaps," and went on.

"The first time I came this way," he said, "almost none of the roads were hard surfaced."

"That was your last chance," she said. "Don't ever ask again."

Complete sentences that stand in *parentheses are capitalized always if they stand between other sentences, but if they stand within sentences they usually are not.

A complete sentence standing after a *colon is not capitalized if it is short and closely connected to the preceding words, but may be if it is long or if for some reason the writer wants to emphasize it or keep it distinct:

Charles Sumner wanted to know his opinion on European law journals: what should he say?—H. S. COMMAGER, *Theodore Parker*

He promised this: The company will make good all the losses.— *New York Times Style Book* (1962) , p. 30

2. *Proper names.* Proper names and abbreviations of proper names are capitalized: names of people, places, races (Indian, *Negro, Caucasian), languages (French, Latin), days of the week, months, companies, *ships, institutions, fraternities, religious bodies, historical events (the Revolutionary War), documents (the Constitution), *courses.

The names of the *seasons (summer, fall, midwinter) are not capitalized except for stylistic reasons.

The points of the compass (north, southwest) are not capitalized when they indicate direction, but are usually capitalized when they denote a region (though this practice is now declining):

He started west in 1849.

He was much more popular in the West than in the East.

Army, Navy, and so on, are not capitalized unless they refer to the organized forces of a particular nation: United States *Army,* the British *Navy,* and even *the Army* when referring to that of a particular nation. Also:

He went to college.

He went to Beloit College.

He went to the College (if a particular college is clearly understood in the context) .

Proper nouns that have become common nouns (*tweed, sandwich, burnsides, plaster of paris, silhouette, guillotine*) are not capitalized nor are proper adjectives in senses that no longer suggest their origin: *Paris fashions* (fashions originating in Paris), but *paris green*.

3. *Lines of verse.* The first letter of a line of verse is capitalized unless originally published without a capital, as in the second example below:

> Burly, dozing humble-bee,
> Where thou art is clime for me.
>
> RALPH WALDO EMERSON, "The Humble-Bee"

> the Cambridge ladies who live in furnished souls
> are unbeautiful and have comfortable minds
>
> E. E. CUMMINGS, "the Cambridge ladies"

4. **Titles of articles, books, etc.* The usual convention is to capitalize the first word, all nouns, pronouns, verbs, adjectives, and adverbs as well as prepositions that stand last or contain more than four (sometimes more than five) letters:

With Malice Toward Some   *The Book of a Naturalist*
You Can't Take It with You   *Pity Is Not Enough*

5. *"I," "O."* The pronoun *I is always capitalized. The exclamation *O is capitalized, but *oh* is not unless it begins a sentence or is especially emphatic.

6. *Names of relatives, individuals.* In personal and Informal writing, as a matter of courtesy, and in General writing, when they are used as proper nouns, names for members of one's family are often capitalized:

> She talked it over with Father, however, just to see what he'd say.
> —CLARENCE DAY, *Life with Mother*, p. 117

They are not usually capitalized when used as common nouns: *My sister and two brothers are older than I.*

President referring to the President of the United States is always capitalized, and ordinarily titles of people in high office when referring to an individual (the Senator). Other titles may be capitalized when referring to individuals (The Colonel was there). (See **Titles of persons*.)

7. *References to Deity.* *God, Jesus,* nouns such as *Savior,* and pronouns referring directly to them are capitalized—though practice is divided on the pronouns:

> Webster for the first time in an English Bible rendered Jesus's saying as He said it.—HARRY R. WARFEL, *Noah Webster*, p. 411

> As we think of him [God], do we think of what he has done or what he can do for us? Do we love him so much that we would keep him for ourselves?—S. K. YEAPLE, *Your Money and Your Life*, p. 30

Pronouns referring to pagan deities (Zeus, Jove, Venus) are not capitalized.

8. *Street, river, park,* etc. Usage is divided over capitalizing such words as **street, river, park, hotel, church* when they follow a proper name. Typically, books and conservative magazines would use capitals; General writing, as in many magazines and most newspapers, would not:

Formal:	the Mississippi River	Thirty-second Street
General:	the Mississippi river	Thirty-second street

An organization is likely to capitalize more words pertaining to its functions than an outsider would, as the Government Printing Office capitalizes many words having to do with government.

9. *Abstract nouns.* Abstract nouns are likely to be capitalized, more often in Formal writing than in General, when the concept they refer to is personified or when they refer to ideals or institutions: *The State has nothing to do with the Church, nor the Church with the State.*

10. *Stylistic capitals.* Some writers, usually in a rather Formal style, use capitals as a form of *emphasis, to lead the reader to stress certain words a little or give them more attention:

And a woman is only a woman, but a good Cigar is a Smoke.— RUDYARD KIPLING, "The Betrothed"

Such unconventional use of capitals is now rare and is usually better avoided. Sometimes, however, the device works:

They will learn, like the boy who cried wolf, that people who mock the Last Laugh are incinerated by it when it finally sounds.— *The New Yorker,* "Talk of the Town," Sept. 21, 1963, p. 33

(For additional information on capitals, see *Foreign words in English § 3, *Proper adjectives, *References in scientific papers. Also consult the stylebooks of periodicals and publishers, such as the GPO *Style Manual.*)

Cardinal numbers • See *Numbers § 5.

Carelessness •
> *Revision: Correct the obvious and apparently careless mistake marked.*

X

Conferences with students on their themes show that well over half the mistakes and slips that an instructor has to mark result from carelessness, not ignorance. Everyone is liable to careless lapses in hasty work. But a course paper is not supposed to be hasty work. Slips like *it's* for *its* (or the other way around), *detract* for *distract,* most *comma faults and *fragmentary sentences, and scores of others are due to lack of attention in the final stages of preparing a paper. An instructor can sympathize with lack of knowledge but not with lack of care; in fact, he has every right to refuse to read an obviously careless paper.

Sometimes carelessness will show itself in your writing because you do not know what is expected by your readers or because you have not paid enough attention to your reading or to previous English teaching, and sometimes simply because of inattention at the time of writing; sometimes it will show itself in the use of Nonstandard forms or constructions, either because of social background or laziness. If you make elementary, careless mistakes, take steps to eliminate them. In some cases you may need to review systematically such grammatical matters as the forms of verbs or pronouns. Brief comments on the smaller structural elements of the sentence treated in Ch. 9 should be supplemented by reading the relevant *Index* articles.

Because the most obvious and elementary mistakes are usually the result of carelessness, not ignorance, they can easily be eliminated by attentive proofreading.

In hasty writing it is easy to leave out an occasional letter—the *n* in *an,* a final *-y* or *-ed.* Watch especially *used to,* because even though "use to" seems a more accurate spelling of what we *say,* we must write "used to": He had a hard time getting *used to* college; We *used to* do it the other way. (See *-ed.)

Be sure to put in end punctuation marks, especially the question mark (not a period) at the end of a question and the closing quotation mark after something quoted.

Do not run small words together. Watch especially for those that frequently seem to form units: *a / lot*; *in / turn*; *any / more*; *on the other / hand*; *in a / while.*

Sometimes small words, usually connectives, are carelessly repeated:

On this one point I have already commented *on.* [Either *on* could be kept; probably the first is preferable in writing.]

Some words are commonly confused, and it may take a moment's thought to see which one fits. See *a—an, *to, *too, and *then—than. In addition to these three common confusions, the following word pairs often cause trouble: affect—effect, whether—weather (or wether), quite—quiet, principal—principle. You can probably add to the list. Some of these are discussed in the *Index;* see also Ch. 9, "Revising 'wrong words,' " p. 344; Ch. 10, p. 406; and *Homonyms.

A careful reading of your final manuscript is a most useful educational discipline. It will make the paper more presentable (and worth a better grade), as well as give you the satisfaction that comes from seeing a job through to the best of your ability. (See Chs. 8, 9, and 10, especially the suggestions for proofreading, p. 407.)

Caret (∧) • This inverted v-shaped mark put in or under a line of manuscript shows that something between the lines or in the margin should be inserted at that point:

```
          Yes, they were smart, but there wasn't any reason
                                  because
          why they shouldn't be, ∧ all they did was study.
```

This is an acceptable way to revise papers (it was used in the original copy of our Constitution) and should be used to improve a paper to be handed in or to make a correction suggested by an instructor. Too frequent use shows lack of care in the preliminary writing and revision.

A caret may be used by an instructor as a correction mark to show where something should be inserted.

Case • One of the relationships between a noun or pronoun and another element in a sentence is called *case*. In languages like Latin and German, whose nouns, pronouns, adjectives, or articles are elaborately declined, the case endings of the nominative, genitive, dative, and accusative (and ablative in Latin) are important clues to the relations of the words in the sentence. In English, the few forms which survive are much less useful as clues. Our adjectives have no case endings; regular nouns have only two forms, the common form (*soldier*) and the form ending in *s* for genitive and plural, distinguished only in writing (*soldier's—soldiers*); and the personal pronouns are reduced to three, a nominative, genitive, and, except for *it* and *you,* accusative (*I—my—me*), or two (*you—your—you*).

We signal the relation of nouns and pronouns to other sentence elements through *word order* (an object following its verb or preposition, for example) and by means of *prepositions* (*to Fred* instead of a dative ending). The few problems that we have come chiefly from the surviving dative-accusative form of pronouns (*It's me; *who, whom).

This *Index* has articles on four cases to call attention to the few functions in which the case forms are significant, to note problems in usage that are due to case forms, and to make possible some comparison between English and the languages which rely more definitely on case forms to signal relationship between words:

*Nominative (or subjective)—the subject of a verb, complement of a linking verb

*Genitive (or possessive)—indicating not only possession but various adjectival and adverbial relations

*Dative—principally notions of interest or location or "indirect objects"

*Accusative (or objective)—the object of a verb or preposition

Fuller accounts of the grammatical points involved will be found in the articles on the various functions indicated: *Subject and verb, *Objects, *Infinitives § 5, *Linking verbs, *Gerund § 2, *Nouns, *Pronouns, types and forms; *Word order. For more complex treatments of problems of English cases, see Jespersen, Ch. 14 (the two-case system); Curme, *Parts of Speech,* pp. 127-136 (the four-case system).

case • Some of the commonest bits of *deadwood in writing are various locutions with the word *case.* *Case* has a number of specific meanings known to everybody. As a general filler for prose, it is unnecessary and annoying. "In some cases," "in the case of," and "in that case" are pat phrases which do no harm if used sparingly; often they can be replaced with a more meaningful word or phrase.

The delegates drank very moderately except in a few scattered cases. [Most of the delegates drank very moderately.]

catalog, catalogue • Spelling usage is divided, with the shorter form gaining. More than half the colleges in the United States now use *catalog* as the name of their annual bulletin of announcements.

Cause • The use of cause-effect analysis in developing a paper is discussed in Ch. 3, p. 91, with later references in Chs. 6 and 7; Ch. 7, p. 246, treats the problem of testing a causal hypothesis. Following (with very simple examples) are the five methods or canons formulated by John Stuart Mill for testing causal relationships:

1. *The method of agreement.* If two or more instances of the phenomenon under investigation have only one circumstance in common, the circumstance in which alone all the instances agree is the cause (or effect) of the given phenomenon. (If several people have an attack of food poisoning after eating lunch in the same cafeteria, and if it is learned that the one item their meals had in common is smoked fish, it is probable—but not certain—that the smoked fish caused the food poisoning.)

2. *The method of difference.* If an instance in which the phenomenon under investigation occurs, and an instance in which it does not occur, have every circumstance in common save one, that one occurring only in the former; the circumstance in which alone the two instances differ, is the effect, or the cause, or an indispensable part of the cause, of the phenomenon. (If two people had exactly the same menu except

that one added smoked fish and if he became sick while his companion did not, the fish probably—but not certainly—was the cause of his illness.)

3. *The joint method of agreement and difference.* If two or more instances in which the phenomenon occurs have only one circumstance in common, while two or more instances in which it does not occur have nothing in common save the absence of that circumstance, the circumstance in which alone the two sets of instances differ is the effect, or the cause, or an indispensable part of the cause of the phenomenon. (This method combines the first two; it suggests the process of testing over an extended period of time used by doctors to isolate, through elimination of various possibilities, the cause of an allergy.)

4. *The method of residues.* Subduct from any phenomenon such part as is known by previous inductions to be the effect of certain antecedents, and the residue of the phenomenon is the effect of the remaining antecedents. (If only four people could have committed a crime and three can be proved not to have done it, then the fourth is presumed guilty.)

5. *The method of concomitant variation.* Whatever phenomenon varies in any manner, whenever another phenomenon varies in some particular manner, is either a cause or an effect of that phenomenon, or is connected with it through some fact of causation. (If a field which is heavily fertilized yields a better crop than one which has received half as much fertilizer and a much better crop than one which has received none at all, the farmer concludes that there is probably a connection between the amount of fertilizer he uses and the yield of the crop.)

For discussion and criticism of Mill's canons, see textbooks in logic. Detailed treatments are in Irving M. Copi, *Introduction to Logic,* 2nd ed., 1961, pp. 363-407, and Philip Wheelwright, *Valid Thinking,* 1962, pp. 228-238.

-ce, -ge • A few special spelling problems arise from the use of *c* for the sound of *s,* and of *g* for the sound of *j.*

A word ending in *-ce* (pronounced /s/) or *-ge* (pronounced /j/) normally keeps the final *e* before suffixes beginning with *a, o* or *u* to indicate the pronunciation: *courageous, noticeable, peaceable, vengeance* (but *mortgage, mortgagor* or *mortgager*). Before a suffix beginning with *e* or *i,* the final *e* is dropped: *diced, noticing, encouraging.*

Usually a word ending in *-c* (pronounced /k/) adds a *k* before an ending beginning with *e* or *i* or *y* so that it will still be pronounced /k/: *colic, colicky; mimic, mimicking; picnic, picnicked, picnicking.* (See also **-ei-, -ie-.*)

Cedilla • The cedilla is a mark under the letter *c* (ç) to show that before *a* or *o* it is pronounced /s/. In English spelling the cedilla persists in words originally French: *façade, Français, Provençal, garçon, aperçu, soupçon.* It is also used as a phonetic alphabet symbol.

censor—censure • When we *censure,* we condemn or blame or disapprove. When we *censor,* we delete or suppress. But the adjective *censorious* refers to *censuring.*

center around • *Center around* (The story *centers around* the theft of a necklace) is the General idiom. The Formal idiom is *center on* or *upon.*

Centuries • Remember that the fifth century A.D. ran from the beginning of the year 401 to the end of the year 500, the nineteenth century from January 1, 1801, through December 31, 1900. Thus to name the century correctly, add one to the number of its hundred. It will help to remember that you live in the *twentieth* century.

Popularly the distinction is not closely kept, since people feel that the century changes when the figure for the hundreds changes: there were celebrations for the beginning of the twentieth century on January 1 of both 1900 and 1901, and there was debate over whether the second half of our century began with 1950 or 1951.

Because of errors made in this scheme of indicating centuries, the practice of naming the hundred can be used, even in Formal writing (the seventeen hundreds).

The abbreviation A.D. once regularly stood before a date. It was not used with centuries, since it stands for *anno Domini,* "in the year of our Lord." But like B.C. (before Christ) it commonly follows the year (431 B.C., 1681 A.D.), and even historians use it to designate centuries (the fifth century A.D.).

cf. • See *Abbreviations § 2.

ch • *Ch* usually spells the sounds *tsh* (pronunciation symbol /ch/), as in *arch, bachelor, chatter, check, cheese, child, church.* When the sound is not at the beginning of a word, it is often spelled *tch* (*batch, watch*) and *ti* in such words as *question, Sebastian.* Compare also *righteous* /rī′chəs/ and *literature.* It is spelled *c* in *cello, cemballo.*

In some words from French, *ch* has the French sound /sh/: *champagne, chagrin, mustache, machine.*

In a number of words from Greek, *ch* is sounded /k/: *chemist, chimera, chorus, echo.*

chairman, chairwoman • Although *chairwoman* is entered in some dictionaries, it is no more necessary to indicate the sex of a presiding officer than of a beginning college student (*freshman*). *Chairlady* is not in good use.

Change in constructions • See *Shifted constructions.

Change in language (oral and written) • The inevitability of change in language is attested by the records of all languages whose histories have been traced. Sometimes changes appear to be relatively sudden and far-reaching, as after an invasion, but ordinarily they are slow—the accumulation of slightly different pronunciations and gradual shifts in grammatical forms and constructions. Vocabulary varies much more rapidly and less consistently than the basic structure of a language.

English shows many changes during the centuries in which it has been recorded. (See *English language.) When we think of the millions of people using our language and of the wide territory over which it is spread, the wonder is that change is not more rapid. Although schools, radio and television, books, periodicals, and newspapers may tend to stabilize the language somewhat, English continues to change. One of the fundamental principles of linguistics is that this change in language is natural and inevitable.

Attempts to direct the course of English have not been very successful. Beginning in the eighteenth century the speech and writing (or at least the writing) of a small and influential group were modified by the application of a formal grammar, but the language of most users of English was unaffected.

Even the transcription of the language—which, it must be remembered, is not the language itself, though most people think of it as such—has been little affected by so sensible and needed a movement as that for simplified spelling. At present, advertising is the chief source of spelling change, though some teachers and nearly all linguists believe that our spelling should be modified.

Conservative influences like schools and publishing houses have taken a pretty firm stand against change, some of them even now presenting usage of the middle nineteenth century. It is to be hoped that this will not always be true.

A person interested in writing needs to be aware of the naturalness and necessity of change in his language and should cultivate the habit of watching the small signs of change that he hears and sees in speech and writing. He needs also to decide whether he is going to oppose change, to welcome it in all its forms, or to try to discriminate, adopting in his own work those new words and forms and constructions that seem to be more convenient and more expressive than older ones. Following cautiously the direction in which English has already been moving (as the increase in nouns making their *plural with -s) is a good general principle to follow.

Several discussions in this *Guide-Index* treat points of change in current English. Reading them will suggest what to watch: *Analogy in language, "The meaning of words" (Ch. 9, p. 369), *Origin of words, "Spelling" (Ch. 10, p. 403), and specific articles like *all right—alright, *-al ly, *due to, *like—as, *shall—will.

The study of the changes that have taken place in English is fascinating, and ample materials exist for carrying it on. The *Oxford English Dictionary* gives the history of individual words from their first appearance in the language, recording their changes in form and in meaning. Histories of the language, like those by Albert C. Baugh and Stuart Robertson, tell the story in detail. The general and orderly process of change is described in Otto Jespersen, *Language,* Part IV, and in E. H. Sturtevant, *Linguistic Change* (Chicago, 1917). See also Bloomfield, Ch. 20 ff.

Chapters • Chapters are numbered in Roman (I, II, III) or Arabic (1, 2, 3) numerals, the latter increasingly used. In bibliographies lower case Roman numerals (i, ii, x) are now more common than capitals (I, II, X), and Arabic are also common.

In Formal book style, references to titles of chapters are usually in quotation marks. In General writing they may simply be capitalized.

Formal: Kennedy, Chapter XIV, "Improvement of the English Language."

General: Kennedy, Chapter 14, Improvement of the English Language.

Charts • See *Diagrams, graphs, etc.

check, cheque • *Cheque* is the regular British spelling, but its use in the United States is pretentious.

Chinese • Preferable to *Chinaman, Chinamen,* because of an offensive connotation sometimes carried by those words. Use *a Chinese, the Chinese.* In Formal compounds *Sino-* /sī′nō/ or /sin′ō/ is used: the *Sino-Japanese War.*

Christian names • See *Given names.

Circumlocution • See *Wordiness § 1.

Cities • The name of the country or state need not be given with the name of a well-known city: Athens, Berlin, Chicago, Hollywood, London, New York, Rome, San Francisco. But many American cities and towns bearing the same names need identification if there is a possibility of confusion: Athens, Georgia; Berlin, New Hampshire; Roanoke, Illinois. (See *Proper names, *Comma § 9b.)

Clarity • See *Ambiguity, *Clearness, *Comma § 7.

Clauses •
1. *Definition.* A clause is an element of a compound or complex sentence that ordinarily has a subject and a finite verb. (But see § 3 and § 4.) By means of a conjunction or of an implied connection the clause construction is related to the rest of the sentence. A simple statement, like "The bird flew higher and higher in slow, easy circles," is usually called a sentence, not a clause.

Compound sentences have two or more independent clauses of grammatically equal value (coordinate), connected usually by *and, but, or, for,* or another *coordinating conjunction. (See *Coordination.) Complex sentences have at least one independent (also called *principal* and *main,* though this does not mean they are of chief importance in meaning) clause, grammatically capable of standing alone, and one or more dependent (because not grammatically independent—also called *subordinate* or *relative*) clauses, joined to the independent clause or clauses by *as, because, since, when,* or some other *subordinating conjunction, or by a *relative pronoun, such as *that, who, which*:

[Compound sentence, first independent clause:] A government as totalitarian as the Chinese has to maintain a vast army of officials, [second independent clause, coordinate with the preceding one:] and it is far in excess of the number of educated men available. [Complex sentence, dependent clause:] Although all have nominally some knowledge of the basic principles of Communism, [independent clause:] their acquaintance with them is often hazy or perverted.— GUY WINT, *Spotlight on Asia,* p. 87

2. *Functions of dependent clauses.* These clauses are classified according to the grammatical function they serve in the sentence:

a–*Noun clauses are subjects and objects of verbs or objects of prepositions:

[Subject, usually Formal:] *That herons fed at night* was not news to him.

No one knew [Object:] *which way they had gone.*

b–Adjective clauses modify nouns:

The man *whom they met* [or: The man *they met*] did not return.
The cement road turned into a macadam road, *which in time turned into a clayey unsurfaced road.*

c–Adverbial clauses are used for notions of time, place, cause, effect, concession, etc.:

When they finally got that straightened out, it was too late.
They were discouraged *because they had tried very hard.*

Here is a passage of nineteen sentences in which four (6, 7, 9, 18) are simple, two are compound-complex (11, 16), and the others complex. The dependent clauses are in italics, and at the end of the passage are the conventional grammatical interpretations of them.

(1) Without question a young man *who is not a radical about something* is a pretty poor risk for education. (2) The relevant question to ask is, *What does this young man's radicalism express?* (3) In general, *if it is doctrinaire,/if he has learned all the answers to the world's problems out of a book or from a wise guy outside,* the worth of his beliefs is slight, both to him and to society. (4) The cut-and-dried patter must first be got out of him *before his mind will give a clear tone.* (5) It is true *that the reasons for the early adoption of ready-made beliefs often deserve sympathy.* (6) Poverty, injustice, a sense of wrong connected with a physical or other defect, are predisposing causes. (7) In other instances it may be great intellectual curiosity coupled with a yearning for absolute truth. (8) This is *why students—though the Trustees do not trust it—can go easily from the doctrine of Karl Marx to the doctrine of Saint Thomas.* (9) By means of these systems, converts can act out their dissent from the regular way and secure the comforts of a vast intellectual edifice.

(10) But dissent of a different type remains the really fruitful element in undergraduate thought; *though here again quality is important.* (11) Dissent from teacher *because he is an authority* is meaningless, but the defiant conviction *that it is no atrocious crime to be a young man, born later, with a different world impressed on the mind, with the consciousness of untried powers and unlimited courage*—that form of dissent is without doubt the one quality to nurture when found and to shield *if need be* against all literal conformity. (12) For *what it fulfills* is the solitary truth rattling through the empty periods of the Commencement orator *when he says:* "Young man, the future is in your hands."

(13) Imagine a generation of young men *who did not think/ they could govern better than their fathers,/ who did not want to revolutionize the world with new inventions or make T. S. Eliot's laurels fade.* (14) *If they do not believe/ they can do this,* who will

tell them? (15) Certainly not the institutions *that rightfully nurse a Tradition.* (16) But a tradition lives by being added to, and it is the young men *who must make the effort of creation.* (17) It is irrelevant to suggest *that this ambition moves thousands of hearts every year and ends in workaday routine and indolence.* (18) That is to look only at the husks. (19) *As long as we cannot prophesy/ who will turn out a winner,* we have no right to question initiative and self-dedication—JACQUES BARZUN, *Teacher In America,* pp. 238-239

1. Adjective clause modifying *young man*
2. Noun clause, predicative after *is*
3. Two adverbial clauses (condition), modifying the independent clause
4. Adverbial clause (time), modifying the independent clause
5. Noun clause, postponed subject of *is*. (Obviously here the "main" idea is in the "subordinate" clause.)
8. Noun clause (*why . . .*), predicative after *is*; adverbial clause (*though . . .*), modifying the *why* clause
10. Adverbial clause modifying the independent clause (though it has the value of a coordinate clause, as is borne out by the punctuation)
11. Adverbial clause of reason (*because . . .*) on the face of it (but what does it "modify"?); noun clause (*that . . .*), in apposition with *conviction*; adverbial clause of condition (*if . . .*), modifying *to shield*. *When found* could be regarded as a subjectless clause of time.
12. Noun clause (*what . . .*), subject of *is*; adverbial clause of time (*when . . .*), modifying the independent clause, or it could be regarded as modifying the quotation. A quotation is conventionally regarded as a noun clause, object of the verb of saying.
13. Two adjective clauses modifying *young men*; noun clause (*they could . . .*), object of *think*
14. Adverbial clause (condition), modifying the independent clause; noun clause, object of *do believe*
15. Adjective clause, modifying *institutions*
16. Adjective clause, modifying *young men*
17. Noun clause, object of *to suggest*
19. Adverbial clause of time, modifying independent clause; noun clause, object of *prophesy*

3. *Verbless clauses.* The typical clause has a subject and verb, but some items without finite verbs can be analyzed as clauses:

a—Elliptical clauses, in which a verb can be supplied from another part of the sentence or can be added with some certainty because of the frame of the sentence:

I don't believe it any more than you [Supply: *do,* or *believe it*].
When [Supply: *he was*] sixteen, he had gone to work.

b–"Abridged clauses" in which no verb element stands. These should not be construed as elliptical clauses, since no verb ever enters the speaker's or listener's mind. They are better interpreted as idiomatic formulas. Two familiar sayings illustrate the abridged clause:

The more[,] the merrier.
The better the day, the better the deed.

4. *Clause and phrase.* Dictionaries define *clause* approximately as in § 1 above and *phrase* as in the *Index* article for that term. But since phrases centered on verbal elements function much like clauses, it has been argued that they should be classified as a kind of clause. (See *Phrases and *Verbals.)

(See Ch. 8, "The favorite English sentence," p. 276, *Adjectives, types and forms § 4, *Adverbs, types and forms § 5, *Purpose, *Result, *Conditions, *Coordination, *Contact clauses, *Noun clauses, *Relative clauses, *Restrictive and nonrestrictive, *Subordination, *that, *when, *where. References: Curme, *Syntax,* Ch. 10; Roberts, pp. 343-345.)

Clearness • Clearness, or clarity, is one of the fundamental virtues of writing, perhaps *the* fundamental virtue, but it is hard to discuss helpfully. No accumulation of small virtues or banning of particular faults will guarantee clarity. Pronouns should match their antecedents, verbs and subjects should agree, constructions should not be wantonly shifted. These traits, somewhat ignored in speech, and usually with little or no consequent loss of communication, require closer attention in writing.

Determination to convey to the reader your ideas and feelings will increase the clarity of your writing. But though clearness is a major virtue of prose—it enables the author to carry out his fundamental purpose, communication—writing has other purposes too: influencing people, entertaining them. And expressiveness also has other virtues. Preoccupation with clarity for its own sake may produce clear writing that is also cold and dry. If a paper is not clear, it will certainly be bad, but clearness alone may not make it good. Certain situations demand suggestion; the sensibilities of readers must be considered, as well as the writer's own feeling for the material. All of these elements may reduce in some small way the immediate clearness yet add to a complete understanding of the whole and so be essential to good writing. If the writer has thought his subject and its implications through, has decided on the relation of the parts to the whole, and thought of his reader as "looking over his shoulder," his writing is likely to be clear. (See *Comma § 7.)

Cliché • See *Trite.

Clipped words • See *Origin of words § 3d.

Close modifiers • See *Restrictive and nonrestrictive.

Cognate • *Cognate* means "related, of the same family." It is applied to languages that are from the same stock, as Spanish and French are both descended from Latin. *Cognate* is often used of words in different languages which are modern forms of some one word in an older ancestral language: German *Wasser,* English *water*; also for borrowed words: English *literature* from French *littérature.*

Coherence •

Coh

> *Revision: Make the relation between the parts of this sentence or between these sentences or paragraphs exact and clear to a reader.*

Coherence—the traditional name for *relationship, connection, consecutiveness*—is a difficult but essential virtue in writing. It is essential because the reader's mind differs from the writer's; the reader does not see the relationships, and must be led through the writer's thought, guided from one stage, from one sentence, to another. It is difficult because in a coherent presentation the writer has triumphed over his natural human casualness and has arranged his thought so that it can be grasped by others.

Coherence is a quality of finished writing to be checked in the final revision. A writer cannot be always worrying about the connection between his statements while he is at work. There is, of course, always some relation between his consecutive "thoughts," but the relation may be apparent only to him. Careful consideration of material before starting to write should help the coherence of a paper, especially if some sort of plan is drawn up, arranging the different stages in a natural and sensible order. But coherence must be tested after writing. The writer should try to go over his copy impersonally to see if what he has written hangs together not only for him but for those who will read it. He should ask, "Is the relation between these statements clear? Can a reader pass from this sentence or from this paragraph to the next without feeling a break?"

A natural arrangement of material is not enough for this; there must often be signs of the relationship between sentences and paragraphs. These signs, various suggestions pointing toward coherence, and examples of successful and unsuccessful attempts at coherence are discussed in this *Guide-Index,* especially in *Conjunctions, *Prepositions, *Reference of pronouns, *Transition, Ch. 2, "Organizing the paper," p. 47, Ch. 4 (Writing paragraphs), and Ch. 8 (Revising sentences).

Coinage of words • See *Origin of words § 2a.

Collective nouns •
Revision: Change, according to the conventions outlined in this article, the verb and/or the pronoun to agree with the collective noun marked.

Coll

1. A collective noun is one whose singular form names a group of objects or persons or acts. Some common collective nouns are:

army	company	gang	*number
*athletics	contents	group	offspring
audience	*couple	herd	politics
band	crowd	jury	*public
class	dozen	*majority	remainder
*committee	flock	mankind	team

When the group as a whole is intended, the collective noun takes a singular verb and singular pronoun; when the individuals of the group are intended, the noun takes a plural verb and plural pronoun:

The *crowd* that *has* been noisily engaged in finding *its* seats *settles* down and the incessant murmur of voices slowly quiets.

The *crowd* that *have* been noisily engaged in finding *their* seats *settle* down and the incessant murmur of voices slowly quiets.

The first *couple* on the floor *was* Tom and Janet.

One day when we were near where the old *couple were* living, we dropped in to see *them*.

The rule is simple enough; its application is more complicated because (1) some collectives have regular plural forms (*army, armies*), others do not (*athletics, offspring*); (2) even in the same sentence the sense may shift from singular to plural (see § 2 and § 3 below); (3) words which are not ordinarily collectives may be so used (the baseball *nine* were . . .); (4) some collectives more commonly take singular verbs (*herd, mankind*); others, plural verbs (*people*).

British and American practices differ somewhat; for example, *government* and *party* referring to political groups are plural in England, singular here.

2. In writing, especially Formal writing, a collective should not be treated as both singular and plural in the same context:

The *company was* organized and immediately sent out *its* [not *their*] representatives.

Mess is over and the guard *have* [not *has*] a busy morning ahead of *them* [not *it*].

In using a collective noun there is often a temptation to try to keep it singular when the meaning really calls for a plural construction. Often the writer slips unconsciously from singular to plural in such a passage:

Into the church *troops* the entire *town, seats itself* on the uncomfortable wooden benches and there *remains* for a good two hours, while an aged curé preaches to *them* [consistency demands *it*] of *their* [*its*] wicked lives and awful sins. [This might better have started "All the people of the town troop into the church, seat themselves. . . ."]

In making constructions consistent you will often find, as in the sentence above, that it is the first member, the collective subject, that needs to be changed, rather than its pronouns.
3. In speech (and consequently in some Informal and in much unedited writing) our tendency not to continue constructions across intervening words usually operates: The verb, which comes close to the noun, is singular, but a pronoun at some distance tends to refer to the individuals, in the plural.

Spoken: The team *was* called together for last minute instructions and sent out to *their* positions.

Written: The team *were* called together for last minute instructions and sent out to *their* positions.

Spoken: The election committee *has* from the beginning misused *their* rights in issuing false instructions for absentee ballots.

Written: The election committee *has* from the beginning misused *its* rights in issuing false instructions for absentee ballots.

4. The plural of a collective noun signifies different groups:

The audiences of New York and Chicago differed in their receptions of the play.

5. In measurements and amounts a plural noun is often followed by a singular verb:

About 80 pounds of carbon disulfide *is* [or *are*] added.

(See *Subject and verb § 2; *Reference of pronouns § 2, *every and its compounds § 1. References: Curme, *Syntax,* pp. 539-540, 50-51; Fries, *AEG,* pp. 48-50, 54, 57-59; Jespersen, pp. 210-212; Pooley, pp. 85-88.)

Colloquial English • Usage that is characteristic of speech is *colloquial.* In modern writing there is not so sharp a division as formerly between what is spoken and what is written, but some spoken usages may be inappropriate in writing, just as some features of written English are inappropriate in speech.

(For discussion of the traits of colloquial English see
*Spoken and written English § 2, *Vernacular, and Ch. 1,
"Informal English," p. 21.)

Colon (:) •
Revision: Use a colon here.

Colon

The colon is a mark of anticipation, indicating that what
follows the mark will supplement what preceded it. Its function differs from that of the semicolon, which is a stop, almost
a period. Most students could profitably use more colons than
they do; often they mistakenly use a semicolon instead:

Yesterday I received a clipping from home, the essence of which
is as follows: [not ;] . . . .

The principal uses of the colon are:
1. *Anticipatory use.* A colon is used after an introductory
expression, as in the second line above, and after the salutation of formal letters:

Dear Sir: [*Contrast the comma in informal letters:* Dear Fritz,]

It is generally used to anticipate quotations in factual writing (not in fiction), especially if the quotation is a complete
grammatical unit and runs to more than one sentence. Whether
or not a colon is appropriate with shorter quotations depends
in part upon the formula with which they are introduced. If
the quotation is closely built into the sentence, a comma is
usual (*says,* in the quotation below); if the introduction is more
formal, a colon is usual (below, *was added:*).

A card made out at 10:45 P.M. on Nov. 4, 1928, says, "Arnold
Rothstein, Male, 46 years, 912 Fifth Avenue, gunshot wound in
abdomen, found in employee's entrance, Park Central Hotel, 200
West Fifty-sixth Street. Attended by Dr. McGovern, of City Hospital.
Removed to Polyclinic Hospital. Reported by Patrolman William
M. Davis, Shield 2943, Ninth Precinct." Two days later the word
"fatal," in parentheses, was written in after the word "abdomen,"
and a second report, with more detail, was added: "Rothstein apparently had been engaged in card game with others in Room 349
on third floor of Park Central Hotel when an unknown man shot
him and threw revolver out of window to street. Body found by
Lawrence Fallon of 3164 Thirty-fourth Street, Astoria, employed as
house detective for the hotel."—MEYER BERGER, *The New Yorker,*
Nov. 26, 1938

2. *Between clauses.* A colon is used between clauses when the
following one is either an illustration, a restatement in different terms, or an amplification of the first:

If a gunnery officer can't explain what he wants done, one of two things is going to happen: either the gun won't be fired or he'll have to do it himself.

Lazy minds give up in despair: "I can't write anyhow," say students to me year after year; they mean they won't think.—BARRETT WENDELL, *English Composition*, p. 136

The supposition that words are used principally to convey thoughts is one of the most elementary of possible errors: they are used mainly to proclaim emotional effects on the hearers or attitudes that will lead to practical results.—H. R. HUSE, *The Illiteracy of the Literate*, p. 21

3. *Conventional uses.* There are a few conventional uses of the colon, though they vary among publishers:

a—Between hours and minutes expressed in figures:

11:42 a.m.   3:28 p.m.
(or, especially British: 11.42 a.m., 3.28 p.m.)

b—In formal bibliographies and formal citations of books:

Between volume and page—The Mt. Adams Review, 160:129-40
Between chapter and verse in citing the Bible—Genesis 9:3-5
Between author and title—Stuart Chase: *Men and Machines*
Between place of publication and publisher—New York: Holt, 1958

In the last two of these a comma would often be found.

c—In proportions when the numbers are written as numerals:

Concrete mixed 5:3:1.

4. *Stylistic use.* Some writers prefer colons where most would use commas or semicolons:

It [a castle] is a shut place that commands by its shutness the open place about it. A castle is builded of the stone of its world: it rises from the stone of its world: it *is* the stone of its world. A castle is austere toward the world which it defends. It is invariable, forbidding: its strength is that of a perpetual shutting-out of all which lies outside it. Sun beats on the castle wall: inside it is dark. Moon melts its bastion and bathes its county blue: it is harsh and rigid. Water and wind make song of the green hills: the castle is silent. It is the lord of its county because it is apart from it. A castle is hot in a cold land: a castle is cold in a hot land: a castle is high in a low land: a castle is full in a land of dearth: a castle is dry in a land of verdure.—WALDO FRANK, *Virgin Spain*, p. 108

This is a matter of taste rather than of correctness and is usually (as here) Formal. The mark ordinarily attracts some slight attention to itself when used this way.

5. *Capitals following.* After a colon either a capital or a small letter may be used. The capital is more usual when the matter following the colon is in the form of a complete sentence, a small letter when it is a subordinate element. (See *Capital letters § 1.) That the deciding factor is largely the closeness of thought relation between the two parts of the sentence is suggested by the following quotations from a single article:

Thus the task of democracy has always been a twofold one: to prevent political privilege from reëstablishing itself, and to make peaceful settlement of disputes possible in a society without privilege.

Those who believe that fascism is simply a tool which Big Business created as soon as it found democracy dangerous overlook one important fact: the opposition of Big Business to democracy is much older than fascism.

The ways in which the kings settled social disputes were very different, in spirit as well as in technic: The kings of France, after having subdued the rebellious nobles, protected the social privileges of the nobility to the point of subjecting both citizens and peasants to cruel oppression; the kings of Prussia, who occasionally liked to be called "kings of beggars," without fully living up to the implications of that title, tried to restrict exploitation of the masses; so, much earlier, did Elizabeth of England.—CARL LANDAUER, in *The American Way,* ed. D. C. Coyle et al.

(For other uses of the colon see the *GPO Manual* and other style books.)

Comma (,) •

Revision: Insert or remove a comma at the place marked, in accordance with one of the sections in this article.   *Comma*

1. *Between coordinate clauses.* C_1

a–A comma is used before the conjunction when the independent clauses are rather long and when it is desirable to emphasize their distinctness, especially if the clauses have different subjects:

The frozen steel edges shrieked as they bit into the ice-covered turns, and the driving sleet slashed against their goggles and jackets with such force that it was impossible to keep clear vision.

A comma is not used when the coordinate clauses are short and closely related in meaning, especially in easy narrative:

There was a knock at the front door [   ] and Mary ran to open it.

b–A comma is generally used between two coordinate locutions joined by *but* or *not* to emphasize the contrast:

I can remember Mother telling me that a book was one's best friend, but I couldn't understand how anyone could feel that way.

Those who hold these ideas are to be pitied, not blamed.

Uses of the Comma

The following list of uses of the comma outlines the treatment in this article. The numbers and letters refer to sections and subsections. Brackets mean that a comma should be avoided.

1. *Between coordinate clauses*
   a–Between rather long coordinate clauses
   b–Between clauses connected by *but, not*
   c–Between clauses connected by the conjunction *for*
2. *With dependent clauses*
   a–After a dependent clause or long phrase preceding the independent clause
   b–Before a dependent clause following the independent clause and not closely related to it
3. *With nonrestrictive modifiers*
4. *With interrupting and parenthetical elements*
   a–Around interrupting constructions
   b–Around conjunctive adverbs not standing first in their constructions
5. *In lists and series*
   a–Between units of a list or series
   b–Between coordinate adjectives in the same relation to their noun
   c–[Not between two words or phrases joined by *and*]
6. *For emphasis and contrast*
7. *For clearness*
   a–Before words of two possible functions (*for, but*)
   b–To prevent a noun being mistaken for an object
   c–To prevent wrong interpretation
   d–To separate consecutive uses of the same word
8. *With main sentence elements (S-V-O)*
   a–[Not between a short subject and its verb]
   b–Sometimes after a long or heavily modified subject
   c–[Not between a verb and its object]
   d–[Very rarely between compound predicates]
9. *In conventional uses*
   a–In dates   *b*–In addresses
   c–After salutations of informal letters
   d–After names in direct address   *e*–In figures
   f–With degrees and titles   *g*–With weak exclamations
   h–[Not to show omission of a word]
10. *With other marks of punctuation*
    a–[Not with a dash] (*Dash § 6)
    b–With parentheses (*Parentheses § 4)
    c–With quotation marks (*Quotation marks § 4, b and c)

c–A comma is generally used between clauses connected by the conjunction *for,* to avoid confusion with the preposition *for*:

Conjunction: They are obviously mistaken, *for* all intercollegiate sports are competitive.

Preposition: Our English instructor had assigned us *Lord of the Flies for* a book report.

(For commas between complete clauses that could stand as separate sentences, see Ch. 8, "Contact clauses," p. 292, and *Comma fault.)

2. *With dependent clauses.* C_2

a–A comma is used after a dependent clause (or a long phrase) that precedes the independent clause or is not closely connected to it:

If that lake wasn't frowning at something or other that night, I'll drink it down to the last drop.

Although willing to use his athletic ability, he wouldn't study hard enough to become eligible.

When the preceding clause or phrase is short and closely related in thought to the main clause (especially when the subjects of the two clauses are the same), there is usually no comma following it:

Without a doubt [ ] Jack is the best linesman our school has.

When we had all gathered near the fence [ ] we could see that they were bums. (Subjects the same)

When appropriations are before the House [ ] he continually checks the Democrats' expenditures. (A close relationship)

b–A comma usually stands before a dependent clause (or long phrase) that follows the main clause if the relationship in thought is not close:

Kemal Ataturk's death had come as a blow to a nation of 14,000,000 people, though he reformed their social customs, their religion, and their economics with dictatorial zeal and speed.

They had tried four times to start it, the starter every time giving just a short whine.

3. *With nonrestrictive modifiers.* Modifiers which do not limit C_3
the meaning of a noun or verb but add a descriptive detail are nonrestrictive and are set off by a comma or commas. The expressions in italics are nonrestrictive:

From where I was standing, *almost directly above the treasure,* I could see many articles that had been lost. [The clause *that had been lost* is restrictive and so is not set off by a comma.]

Pigeons breed in the spring and the hen lays two eggs, *one of which usually hatches into a cock and one into a hen.*

A restrictive modifier, one that is essential to a correct understanding of the word it modifies, is not set off by punctuation.
The expressions in italics are restrictive:

Wouldn't it be as just to remove from his suffering a person *who
has committed no crime* as to make suffer one *who has committed a
crime?*

Great tracts were left, eaten bare of the grass *which had kept the
soil in place.*

The best clue is that in reading aloud a nonrestrictive clause
there is a slight pause and drop in voice; before a restrictive
clause there is no such change of voice.

Many modifiers may be considered either restrictive or nonrestrictive, and their punctuation should follow the writer's
sense of the closeness with which they limit the word they
modify; this can be shown by the way he reads the sentence
aloud. The expressions in italics might or might not be set off
by commas, depending on the writer's intention:

A winding road *that seemed to lead nowhere in particular* passed
through the village.

It was quite a satisfaction *after working a difficult logarithm problem* to know that something had been accomplished.

(Further examples of restrictive and nonrestrictive expressions will be found in *Restrictive and nonrestrictive and in
Ch. 10, "Before subordinate elements," p. 393.)

C4 **4. *With interrupting and parenthetical elements.***

a–A phrase or clause that interrupts the direct movement of
the sentence should be set off by commas—*two* commas:

Next summer, no matter what comes up, we will go to Europe.
The prank, I dare say, seemed amusing to you then.
Mr. Devant, as was customary with him, stopped at the tavern on
his way home.

Usage is divided over setting off short parenthetical words
and phrases like *incidentally, of course.* Setting them off with
commas is more characteristic of Formal than of General writing, though there is often a difference in emphasis according
to whether or not commas are used:

Mr. and Mrs. Crayton, of course, were late.
Mr. and Mrs. Crayton of course were late.
The speaker, naturally enough, was irritated by the interruption.
The speaker naturally enough was irritated by the interruption.

Adverbs that modify the verb or the statement closely should
not be set off when they are in their natural position:

Undoubtedly [ ] this package was intended for Smith.
This package was intended for Smith, undoubtedly.

b–When a *conjunctive adverb stands after the first phrase of its clause, it is usually set off by commas, and often it is set off when it stands first in the clause:

His ridiculous proposal, nevertheless, was the one adopted.

Furthermore, all leaves are canceled until February 15.

But and other lighter conjunctions are a part of the clauses in which they appear and should not be set off:

Hart had received permission to finish his experiment after class. But [ ] he filed out with the others when the bell sounded.

5. *In lists and series.* C_5

a–The comma is the natural mark to use between the units of enumerations, lists, series (unless the units are long or contain commas within them, when semicolons would be used— see *Semicolon § 1).

There are, among others, an actor out of a job, a murderer, a Mexican dipsomaniac, a man obsessed with a philosophical concept of time, an Indian oil millionaire who prefers waffles to any other food, and assorted females, mostly tough.—*The New Yorker,* Nov. 26, 1938

Commas ordinarily are not used when conjunctions stand between the units of the series.

A bit of tarnish on the brass work [ ] or untidy life preservers [ ] or matches on the decks seem to be of little concern to him.

Sometimes a comma is needed to make the meaning clear; otherwise usage is divided on the comma before the last item in a series: *celery, onions, and olives,* or *celery, onions and olives.* (See *Series.)

b–Adjectives in series. In the sentence

Although it was a hot, sticky, miserable day, Mrs. Marston looked cool in her fresh gingham dress.

there are commas between *hot—sticky—miserable* because each stands in the same relation to the noun *day.* There is no comma between *fresh* and *gingham* because *fresh* modifies *gingham dress* rather than just *dress.* A comma following *fresh* would throw more emphasis upon gingham and might sometimes be wanted. Compare these two versions:

The bright, red draperies showed to advantage against the dark, gray walls.

The bright red draperies showed to advantage against the dark gray walls.

Either version is satisfactory, but in the first, *red* and *gray* stand out as separate modifiers of their nouns.

c–Two items connected by *and* are not usually punctuated:

Old Mrs. Clayton was always ready to watch over the young children in her neighborhood [ ] and to help their mothers with light housework.

C₆ 6. *For emphasis and contrast.* The pause indicated by a comma tends to keep distinct the constructions it separates and to emphasize slightly the construction that follows the mark:

The office manager was delighted with the prestige of his new position, and with the increase in pay.

This is especially true when a connective is omitted:

He repeated the story many times, repeated it when it no longer had any meaning.

In idioms like *the more ... the greater,* Formal usage tends to have a comma, General does not:

... And the more meaning the Grammarian finds crowded into the verb [,] the happier he is.—P. B. BALLARD, *Thought and Language,* p. 87

C₇ 7. *For clearness.* Often a comma can guide a reader in interpreting a sentence and make it unnecessary for him to go back over it for meaning. Two such constructions are especially helped by commas:

a–When a word has two possible functions. *For* or *but* may be either a conjunction or a preposition, and confusion may be avoided by using a comma before either when it is used as a conjunction:

The crowd hurried, for the river was rising swiftly. [*Not:* The crowd hurried for the river....]

b–When a noun might be mistaken for the object of a verb:

When the boll weevil struck, the credit system collapsed and ruined a great part of the landowners and tenants. [*Not:* When the boll weevil struck the credit system....]

Soon after the inspector left, the room was crowded with curious onlookers. [*Not:* Soon after the inspector left the room....]

c–Sometimes a faulty interpretation of word grouping can be prevented:

A great crowd of early shoppers milled around inside, and outside hundreds more were storming the doors.

d–Ordinarily when the same word occurs twice consecutively a comma should be used:

What Janice does, does not concern me.

C₈ 8. *With main sentence elements.*

a–Short subjects. Care should be taken not to separate short subjects from their verbs:

The first family to come [ ] sends word back to those left in the Old Country.

The six boys [ ] all came on the run.

b–Long subjects. When the subject of a sentence is a long phrase or a noun followed by modifiers—that is, when it is a locution of five or six words or more—Formal usage often puts a comma between it and the verb, but General usage does not:

Whether a program is appealing or not [*Formal* (,)] is quickly reflected in the sale of the sponsor's product.

c–Verb and object. There is some temptation to put a comma after a verb, separating it from its object or complement. This is especially true after verbs which in speech would be followed by a slight pause. Punctuation does not exactly represent speech, and such commas should be taken out in revision:

Since they know nothing whatsoever about their future occupation, they must start what might be termed [ ] a second schooling.

She always thought [ ] that I would never be a success.

d–Compound predicates. Except very rarely (and then only if the verbs are separated by several words), no comma is used between the verbs of a compound predicate:

We watched television until seven [ ] and then hurried over to the auditorium for the first of the lecture series.

After the supervisor's lecture, the girls returned sullenly to their tasks [ ] and whispered furtively the rest of the morning.

9. *In conventional uses.*

C_9

a–In dates, to separate the day of the month from the year: *May 26, 1965.* When the day of the month is not given, a comma may or may not be used: *In September, 1965* or *In September 1965.* The neater use is without the comma. In *26 May 1965* no comma is used.

b–In addresses, to separate town from state or country when they are written on the same line:

Washington, D.C., is too hot and humid to be a nation's capital.
Chicago, Illinois   Berne, Switzerland
Hamilton, Madison County, New York

c–After salutations in informal letters: *Dear Dot, Dear Len,*
d–After names in direct address: *Jim, try that one again.*
e–In figures, to separate thousands, millions, etc: *4,672,342.*
f–To separate degrees and titles from names:

Elihu Root, Esq.   Charles Evans Hughes, Jr.
Wallace W. Emmett, A.B.   Wallace W. Emmett, A.B. '36

But not in *J. W. Smith III* or *King George III.*
g–After a weak exclamation like *well, why, oh.*

h–A comma is not now commonly used to show the omission of a word that is required to fill out a grammatical construction:

He must have taken the right-hand turn and I [,] the left.

C₁₀ **10.** *With other marks of punctuation.*

a–A comma is now rarely used with a dash. (See *Dash § 6.)

b–When a parenthesis comes within a construction that would be followed by a comma, the comma stands after the parenthesis. (See *Parentheses § 4.)

c–For use with quotation marks see *Quotation marks § 4, b and c. (Reference: Summey, index entries under *Comma*.)

Comma fault •

CF

Revision: Revise the sentence marked by changing the comma to a semicolon or a period, or by inserting an appropriate conjunction, or by rephrasing to make it a more effective sentence.

You should do more than merely remove the comma fault; you should make certain that you have written an effective sentence.

A comma fault (comma blunder, comma splice, *fused sentence) is two or more statements (independent clauses) that are punctuated as a single sentence—that is, with a comma between them (or even run together with no mark at all). Occasionally sentences of this sort may be effective (see Ch. 8, "Contact clauses," p. 292), but here we are considering only those that are unjustified either because of their form or the thought relation between the clauses or both.

There are various remedies for a comma fault:

1) The most obvious remedy is to put a semicolon or a period in place of the comma, but often a period inserted makes two weak sentences instead of one.

2) If the constructions really belong together in one sentence, they may be joined by a conjunction that shows the relationship, and ordinarily the comma is retained.

3) Often the sentence needs to be rephrased—perhaps a relative pronoun used instead of a *this* or *these*—or to be completely rewritten. Remember that the aim is to make an effective sentence.

The following examples show some common types:

Comma fault	*Suggested revision*
He took a couple of steps, stopped, reached out and turned a valve, as he did that he told us	He took a couple of steps, stopped, reached out and turned a valve. As he did that he told us

that all the valves were right-hand valves.	that all the valves were right-hand valves.
Charley then crossed the room and threw a switch which started a motor, returning he wiped the perspiration from his forehead with the back of his hand.	Charley then crossed the room and threw a switch which started a motor. Returning he wiped the perspiration....
They still produce aluminum tips for broken skis, these are very successful as a device for temporary repair.	They still produce aluminum tips for broken skis, which are very successful as a device for temporary repair.

Carelessly run-together sentences are serious blunders in amateur writing. Notice that your reading of the items in the left column was interrupted by the comma faults. If you haven't yet learned to avoid them, you will need to take extra pains to eliminate them.

(For a more complete discussion and more examples of comma faults and of successful run-on sentences, see Ch. 8, "Revising comma faults," p. 290. See also *Contact clauses, *Conjunctions.)

Commands and requests • Direct commands (also called *imperatives*) are expressed by the simple (infinitive) form of the verb:

Hurry up!   *Shut* the door, please.
Fill out the coupon and *mail* it today.

In speech the force of the command or request is shown by the stress and tone of voice, which are hard to represent on paper. Emphatic commands are punctuated with an exclamation mark, less emphatic with a period. The form with *do* is often emphatic (*Do* come!). Negative commands are expressed with *not* and the *do* form of the verb: *Don't go yet.*

Softened or more polite commands and requests depend on phrasing and usually involve auxiliaries or adverbs of courtesy. Often they are in the pattern of a question, written either with a period or a question mark, depending on the intonation intended.

Try to get them in on time.
You will write at least six pages.
Please think no more of it.
Would you be willing to take part in this program?
Would [or *Will*] you please close the window.
Let's go around and see what we can do with him.
Suppose we say nothing more about it.

In indirect discourse a command becomes an infinitive with *to* or a clause with *should*:

He told us to write a 5000-word paper. [*Or*] He said that we should write a 5000-word paper. [*Direct form:* Write a 5000-word paper.]

He wired me to come at once. [*Direct:* "Come at once."]

(For further discussion of forms of commands see Curme, *Syntax*, pp. 419, 430-436; Ralph H. Long, *The Sentence and Its Parts*, pp. 76-79.)

Commercial English • See *Business English.

committee • *Committee* is a *collective noun, usually construed as singular but sometimes as plural when the writer is thinking of the several individuals who compose it. In the latter situation we are more likely to write *the members of the committee*. The singular would usually be the desired form:

The committee meets today at four.

The committee [*or:* the members of the committee] get together once a month.

Common case form • See *Accusative case, *Case.

comparative, comparatively, comparison, comparable • These words are so spelled in our inconsistent practice. *Comparable* is pronounced /kom'pə rə bļ/.

compare—contrast. • *Compare* is used: (1) to point out likenesses (used with *to*); (2) to find likenesses or differences (used with *with*). *Contrast* always points out *differences*.

He compared my stories *to* Maupassant's [*said they were like his*].

He compared my stories *with* Maupassant's [*pointed out like and unlike traits*].

When the things compared are of different classes, *to* is used:

He compared my stories *to* a sack of beans.

In the common construction with the past participle, either *to* or *with* is used:

Compared *with* [or *to*] Maupassant's, mine are pretty feeble.

In comparison *with* [not *to*] Maupassant's, mine are pretty feeble.

Idioms with *contrast:*

He contrasted my work *with* [sometimes *to*] Maupassant's.

In contrast *to* [rarely *with*] Maupassant's, my stories are feeble.

Note the difference in stress between *contrast* /kon'trast/ the noun and *contrast* /kən trast', kən tras'təd, kən trast'ing/ the verb.

Comparison and contrast • For comparison and contrast as a method of developing paragraphs, parts of essays, or entire essays, see Ch. 3, pp. 81-85, Ch. 4, pp. 120-121.

Comparison of adjectives and adverbs •
Revision: Change the form or construction of the adjective or adverb marked, in accordance with the section below that applies.

Comp

Adjectives and adverbs change their forms (see § 5) to show a greater degree of what is named in the simple word (*long, longer, longest*). The forms are simple enough but a number of questions arise in using them.

1. *Uses of the comparative.* The comparative degree expresses a greater degree (It is *warmer* now) or makes specific comparison between two units (He was *kinder* [*more kind*] than his wife).

The two terms of a comparison should be actually comparable:

Comparable: His salary was lower than a shoe clerk's [Or: *than that of a shoe clerk.* Not: *His salary was lower than a shoe clerk.*]

Comparable: His face was round and healthy looking, like a recent college graduate's. [Not: *His face was round and healthy looking, like a recent college graduate.*]

With a comparative, idiom calls for *other* when the comparison is with something in the same class of things but not when the comparison is with things of a different class:

She is a better dancer than the other girls.

She is a better dancer than the boys [*than any of the boys*].

The comparative is frequently used absolutely, with no actual comparison involved (*higher education, the lower depths, older people*), or the reader is left to supply a comparison (*Look younger—Live longer*). (Reference: Esther K. Sheldon, "The Rise of the Incomplete Comparative," *American Speech,* 1945, 20:161-167.)

2. *Uses of the superlative.*

a–The superlative is used to indicate the greatest degree of a quality among three or more people or things (He was the *jolliest* of the whole group; This is the *brightest* tie in the showcase). The form with *most* is also used as an intensive to indicate an extreme degree (You are *most kind;* She is *most clever*) in which no specific comparison is intended.

Superlatives are not completed by *other*:

The Egyptians had obtained the highest degree of cultivation in medicine that had up to that time been obtained by any [not *other*] nation.

b–In many instances the same idea may be expressed by the comparative and the superlative: *He was taller than the other boys. He was the tallest of the boys.*

c–In Informal English a superlative is often a form of emphasis: *We saw the loveliest flowers when we visited her garden. Hasn't she the sweetest voice?*

d–It is also used in comparing two items: *His new novel is the best of the two.* Fries says (p. 101): "The use of the superlative rather than the comparative for two, thus ignoring a dual as distinct from a plural, is a fact of Standard English usage and not a characteristic limited to Vulgar English." (Reference: Russell Thomas, "The Use of the Superlative for the Comparative," *English Journal* (College Edition), 1935, 24:821-829; Bryant, pp. 201-202.)

3. *Idioms with comparatives.*

a—*as much as if not more than.* In "The styles vary as much, if not more than, the colors," two constructions have been telescoped into one: "The styles vary as much as the colors; perhaps the styles vary even more than the colors." The telescoped form is more economical and therefore occurs in Standard speech and even in Standard writing. Prescriptive textbooks have condemned it since the eighteenth century, but the more legitimate objection is to its stylistic awkwardness. Possible solutions are:

The styles vary as much *as* if not more *than* the colors.

The lobby is as strong *as* if not stronger *than* it was in 1955. [Or: *The lobby is as strong as it was in 1955, if not stronger.*]

(Reference: Bryant, pp. 57-58.)

b–*as . . . as.* In the sentence below the use of *than* instead of the second *as* is not Standard:

I paid ten times as much for it *as* [not *than*] for the bigger bus ticket.

(See *as . . . as.)

4. *Comparison of absolutes.* Purists raise objections to the comparison of *black, dead, excellent, fatal, final, impossible, perfect, *unique,* since their meaning is thought to be absolute so that there are no degrees of *deadness* or *blackness* or *impossibility.* But in common use these words are frequently compared: "This was even *more impossible*"; and the Constitution has ". . . to form a more perfect union. . . ." Many are used figuratively with less absolute meanings (This is the *deadest* town I was ever in), which naturally admit comparison. (See *Divided usage. Reference: Bryant, pp. 58-59.)

5. *Choice of forms.* English adjectives and adverbs are compared in two ways:

a–By adding *-er, -est.*

	Positive	Comparative	Superlative
Adjective:	early	earlier	earliest
	hoarse	hoarser	hoarsest
	unhappy	unhappier	unhappiest
Adverb:	fast	faster	fastest
	soon	sooner	soonest

b–By using *more, most.* The change in degree may be shown by prefixing *more* and *most* to the positive form. This form is generally used for adjectives and adverbs of three syllables or more, and for many of two syllables. But no absolute rule can be formulated. It may also be used with those of one syllable, so that for many comparatives and superlatives there are two forms.

	Positive	Comparative	Superlative
Adjective:	exquisite	more exquisite	most exquisite
	empty	emptier, more empty	emptiest, most empty
	able	abler, more able	ablest, most able
Adverb:	comfortably	more comfortably	most comfortably
	often	oftener, more often	oftenest, most often
	hotly	more hotly	most hotly

Words with a short vowel followed by a single consonant double the consonant to indicate the short sound (*thin, thinner, thinnest*). Words ending in *y* change the *y* to *i* before the endings: *dry, drier, driest; shy, shier, shiest* (sometimes *shyer, shyest*).

The meanings of the two forms (*-er* or *more*; *-est* or *most*) are essentially the same, so that whichever seems better can be used. But the *-er* or *-est* form necessarily places the stress on the root part of the word and so tends to emphasize the quality (kind'er), whereas the *more* or *most* form allows the stress to fall on the sign of the degree (more' kind; you are most' kind) so that there could be some difference in the suggestion value of the two. This stress pattern is, however, exceptional.

(References: Curme, *Parts of Speech*, Chs. 11, 13; *Syntax*, Ch. 25; Fries, *AEG*, pp. 96-101.)

Complement • *Complement* (also *predicative*) often refers to the noun or adjective completing the meaning of a linking verb and modifying the subject:

He was *busy*. He became *the real head* of the concern.

In some grammars *complement* is used to include direct and indirect objects. (See *Linking verbs, *Predicate adjective.)

complement—compliment • *Compliment* has to do with praise.

His progress deserved a *compliment*.

Complement means a number or amount that makes a whole, or an allotment (related to *complete*):

The regiment was brought up to its full *complement*.

Complex sentences • See *Clauses.

Compound-complex sentences • See *Compound sentence.

Compound predicate • Two or more verbs having the same subject, together with their modifiers, form a compound predicate: Ruth *wrote* and *mailed* three letters.

Compound predicates are one of the chief devices of economy in writing. Note how far removed these sentences are from the one-small-idea-to-a-sentence type so often used by immature writers:

They (1) accepted the quinine and, in their gratitude, often (2) kissed the hygienists' hands. Heeding their advice, they (1) graveled the village roads, (2) began to drain their lands, (3) enlarged the windows of their dwellings, (4) built sidewalks, sanitary backhouses, and concrete platforms for manure, and so on.—LOUIS ADAMIC, *The Native's Return,* p. 318

(For further discussion see *Subject and verb.)

Compound sentence • *Compound sentence* is the term usually applied to two or more potentially independent syntactical units each with a subject and complete verb but linked to form a single grammatical unit. In speech the voice inflection at the end of the clause links the units. (See Ch. 8, "Compound sentences," p. 282, *Clauses.)

1. *With coordinating conjunction.* Usually the clauses of a compound sentence are connected by one of the coordinating conjunctions, most commonly by *and, but, for, or,* and the combinations *either . . . or, neither . . . nor*:

What a fool he was to be thus startled *but* always he had hated cats from childhood.—WALTER DURANTY, *Babies Without Tails,* p. 11

Either you learned these simple things in high school *or* you will have to learn them in college.

2. *Without connective.* A compound sentence may stand without a connective (see *Contact clauses). Such sentences are usually punctuated with a semicolon:

They are generous-minded; they hate shams and enjoy being indignant about them; they are valuable social reformers; they have no notion of confining books to a library shelf.—E. M. FORSTER, *Aspects of the Novel*, p. 33

Since each of these clauses could be written as a separate sentence, it is apparent that the traditional definition of sentence is somewhat arbitrary.

3. *With conjunctive adverb.* The clauses of a compound sentence may be connected by a conjunctive adverb *(however, moreover, whereas, consequently, therefore...)*:

The F.B.I. had proved themselves expert in publicizing their solution of crimes; consequently some local police gave them only grudging support.

4. *Compound-complex.* Since one or more of the coordinate clauses of a sentence can be modified by dependent clauses, we have the category of *compound-complex sentences*:

He was an old man with a long beard, whose clothes were rags; but Mr. Kiddle had all the way wished to tell some one how proud he was of Ada, who did all the running, so he was glad to have even a tinker to talk to.—T. F. POWYS, *Mr. Weston's Good Wine*, p. 66

This sentence has three independent clauses (making it compound): *He was an old man ... but Mr. Kiddle had all the way wished ... so he was glad to have ...;* and three dependent clauses (making it compound-complex): *whose clothes were rags, how proud he was of Ada, who did all the running.*

Compound subject • Two or more elements standing as the subject of one verb are called a *compound subject*:

Capitalists, militarists, and ecclesiastics co-operate in education, because all depend for their power upon the prevalence of emotionalism and the rarity of critical judgment.—BERTRAND RUSSELL, *What I Believe*, p. 53

The verb following a compound subject is usually plural:

Christianity and humanity *have* gone hand in hand throughout history.

(Some special cases are described under *Subject and verb § 2. See also Ch. 8, p. 281.)

Compound words • Compound words in written English are combinations of two or more words which are written as one word or hyphened: *doorknob, notwithstanding, quarter-hour, father-in-law, drugstore.* But the conventions of writing ignore a large number of compounds which though written as separate words express more than the sum of the parts: the *White House, high school, post office.* In speech these are usually distinguished by the stronger stress on the first words: compare *a white house* and *the White House.*

(Questions about the use of the hyphen in compound words are discussed in *Hyphen, and questions about their plurals in *Plurals of nouns § 5. See also *Group words and check your dictionary.)

Compounding or combining elements of words • See *Origin of words § 3.

Concluding paragraphs •

Concl

Revision: Revise the end of your paper to round out the discussion of your subject or to make the paper end more strongly.

(For discussion of concluding paragraphs and examples, see Ch. 4, "Concluding paragraphs," pp. 147-149; Ch. 5, "Beginning and ending the paper," pp. 184-186.)

Concrete words • See *Abstract and concrete words.

Conditions • A conditional clause states a condition or action necessary for the truth or occurrence of the statement made in the independent clause that the conditional clause modifies. *If* is by far the most common conjunction for conditional clauses, with its negatives *if not* and *unless* (=*if not*), and *whether* (=*if . . . if, if . . . or if*). Somewhat more Formal words and phrases introducing conditions are *in case, provided, provided that, on condition that, in the event that.*

1. *Simple conditions.* Simple (or practical) conditions are statements of actual or reasonable conditions under which the main statement will hold. The indicative (ordinary) verb forms are used:

If the red light is on, you know a train is in that block of track.
He will be there *unless something happens to his car.*
Whether he comes or not, I shall go just the same.

An older type of condition survives in some proverbs:

Spare the rod and spoil the child. [*If you spare the rod,* you will spoil the child.]

In speech, we often express condition by a compound sentence:

You just try that and you'll be sorry.

2. *Less vivid conditions.* Less vivid (theoretical or hypothetical but still possible) conditions are usually made with *should. . . would* or with the past tense:

If he should raise his offer another $100, I would take it. [Or: *If he raised his offer,* I would take it.]

If you revised your papers carefully, your writing would improve and would receive a higher grade.

3. *Contrary to fact conditions.* Conditions that cannot be met, or that are untrue, contrary to fact, are indicated by the past tense of the verb used in a present or future sense (If he *was* here [now], we would have seen him). In some Formal English, especially in writing, the plural form of the past tense is not unusual in the third person singular, usually called a subjunctive (If he were here . . .); and *If I were you* is a firmly established petrified construction. Formal English also sometimes uses a rather archaic inversion (*Were* he here. . .). The whole situation in cultivated practice has become almost hopelessly confused as the result of prescriptive teaching.

General: If I was going to be there, I'd be glad to help.

Formal: If I were President, I would change that.

General: If I had known what I do [or *know*] now, I would [*I'd*] never have let him go.

Formal: Had I known what I now know, I should never have let him go. [Inversion with no conjunction]

General: If he was only here, he. . . .

Formal: If he were only here, he. . . .

(See also *if, *Subjunctives. References: Curme, *Syntax,* pp. 317-332, 421-429; Fries, *AEG,* pp. 104-107; Jespersen, p. 254 ff.)

Conjugation • *Conjugation* of a verb is the set of inflected and phrasal forms in which it may occur to show person, number, voice, and tense. (See *Verbs, *Tenses of verbs, *Principal parts of verbs.)

Conjunction • *Conjunction* is the traditional term for a limited group of words without distinctive formal traits which introduce and tie clauses together and join series of words and phrases. In this *Guide-Index* conjunctions are discussed according to their conventional classification:

*Coordinating (*and, but, for,* etc.)
*Correlative (*either . . . or, not only . . . but,* etc.)
*Conjunctive adverbs (*however, therefore, consequently,* etc.)
*Subordinating (*as, because, since, so that, when,* etc.)

There are also articles on many of the particular conjunctions: *although, *and, *as, *because, *but, and so on. The article *Contact clauses discusses joining clauses without connectives; pp. 290-294 discuss in detail contact clauses and comma faults.

Since many words which function as conjunctions also have other functions, especially adverbial ones, identifying them as a part of speech is not always possible, nor is the distinction between coordinating and subordinating conjunctions always apparent.

(See *Particles. References: Fries, *AEG*, pp. 206-240; Roberts, pp. 231-242; Harold Whitehall, *Structural Essentials of English*, New York, 1956, pp. 65-77; all grammars have discussions.)

Conjunctions, use •

Conj
    Revision: Make the conjunction marked more accurate (§ 1) or more appropriate to the style of the passage (§ 2).

1. *Accurate conjunctions.* An exact use of conjunctions in fitting together clauses is a sign of mature, practiced writing. In everyday speech we get along with a relatively small number—*and, as, but, so, when,* and a few others—because we can emphasize shades of meaning and exact relationships by pauses, tones of voice, gestures. In writing, careful choice of connectives goes a long way toward making up for the absence of these oral means of holding ideas together.

Accurate use of conjunctions needs to be stressed. There are some easy temptations, like using *but* when there is no contrast between the statements (see *but § 2). Some conjunctions vary in definiteness of meaning: *As* means *because,* but means it very weakly (*as § 1); *while* may mean *although* or *whereas,* but the core of its meaning relates to *time. For examples of such refinements in the use of these words see the discussions in the articles on the particular conjunctions.

2. *Weight.* Conjunctions should be appropriate to other traits of style. Their weight should fit with the weight of other words and with the formality or informality of constructions.

A common fault is the use of the *conjunctive adverbs (*however, therefore, consequently* ...) in General writing. These words fit best in rather Formal style. Although *but* and *however,* for example, both connect statements in opposition, one cannot always be substituted for the other. Whereas *but* fits in all varieties, *however* is often too heavy for General writing:

The entrance and registration desk didn't strike me as beautiful. From here, *however,* I went upstairs and then I could see what they meant. (*But* from here. ...)

The English language has a number of long connecting phrases that will weaken a written style when used in place of shorter, more compact conjunctions:

At that time going to the movies was the usual evening pastime *in the same manner in which* [better: *as*] watching television is today.

(See *Conjunctive adverbs and *Function words.)

3. *Repetition of conjunctions.* Repeating a conjunction at the beginning of each element of a series gives distinctness to each element, avoids possible confusion, and achieves the advantage of clear-cut parallelism. This is more characteristic of Formal writing and often gives a definite rhythm:

... designs of spears *and* shields *and* bastions *and* all the pomp of heraldry.—NORMAN DOUGLAS, *Siren Land,* p. 152

For these five days *and* nights the Australians lived *and* ate *and* slept in that gallery of the mine of death, ... —JOHN MASEFIELD, *Gallipoli,* p. 165

On the other hand, omitting *and* before the last member of a short series results in a crisp emphasis:

Last week multimillion-dollar expansion programs were announced by Lockheed in Georgia, International Paper in Alabama, Reynolds Metals in Florida, Allied Chemical in South Carolina. —*Time,* June 19, 1964, p. 84

(See *Series, *Telegraphic style.)

4. *Coordination versus subordination.* For discussion of this phase of the use of conjunctions see *Coordination, *Subordination and Ch. 8, "Coordination and Subordination," p. 303.

(References: Curme, *Parts of Speech,* Ch. 7, and *Syntax,* §§ 19 and 21, and index references.)

Conjunctive adverbs •

1. A number of words primarily adverbs are used also as connectives. They are called *conjunctive adverbs* (or *transitional adverbs* or *adverbial conjunctions* or *sentence connectors* or *sentence adverbials*). They are essential to the construction in which they occur as adverbs, but they do not occur unless there is a preceding utterance to which they are related; hence their conjunctive or transitional traits (as *hence* in this sentence). Ordinarily, they join the independent clauses of compound sentences. The most common are:

accordingly	furthermore	*namely
*also (See *too)	hence	nevertheless
anyhow	*however	*so (See § 4)
anyway (colloquial)	indeed	still
*besides	likewise	*then
consequently	moreover	*therefore

Adverb: No campaign, *however* violent, could make him vote.

Conjunction: The results were poor; *however* we were not surprised.

2. *Weight and use.* Because most of the conjunctive adverbs are relatively heavy connectives, they are most appropriate in

Formal writing and in sentences of some length and complexity; they are less appropriate in General writing. They are now more likely to occur in constructions written as separate sentences than as elements within the same sentence.

Note these appropriate and inappropriate uses:

It is, *therefore,* unfortunate that at a time like the present, which plainly calls for a Socrates, we should instead have got a Mencken. [Appropriate, as is suggested by the Formal sentence structure; connects with thought of preceding sentence]—Irving Babbitt, *On Being Creative,* p. 205

When morning came, *however,* I was still sick; *nevertheless,* when the bugle blew, I got up. *Consequently,* I looked very white at breakfast. [*However* could be omitted; *consequently* replaced by *but.*]

3. *Position.* Conjunctive adverbs are often placed within their clauses instead of at the beginning. This helps take the initial stress from them and gives it to more important words. When they are so placed, they are usually set off by commas as in the sentences in § 2 above.

4. *Punctuation.* A clause introduced by a conjunctive adverb is preceded by a semicolon; however, with *so* a comma is sufficient:

The whole forenoon had been a complete bore, *so* we wanted to make sure that we had a good time after lunch.

The advice sometimes given to strengthen *so* and *then* by adding *and* ("*and so* we wanted to make sure...") is usually wrong, since *and* adds nothing to the meaning of the connective. A better way to improve the illustrative sentence above would be to rephrase it:

The whole forenoon had been such a complete bore that we wanted to make sure we had a good time after lunch.

connected with, in connection with • These are wordy locutions, usually for *in* or *with*:

The social life *in connection with* a fraternity [in a fraternity] will be something you have never experienced before.

Connectives • See *Conjunctions, *Conjunctive adverbs, *Function words, *Relative pronouns.

Consistency in constructions • See *Parallel constructions, *Shifted constructions.

Construction • A construction is a group of words which stand in some grammatical relationship to each other, as that of modifier and head-word (*black cat*), preposition and object (*to* the *roof*), or subject and predicate (*They walked slowly*).

A grammatical pattern may be spoken of as a construction, as in the phrases *sentence constructions, *parallel constructions.* (For some of the commonest deviations from Standard practice, see Chs. 8 and 9.)

contact • The objections to certain recent uses of *contact* ("Will you contact Mr. Hubble?") rest on the fact that the uses came out of salesmanship—and many people have unpleasant associations with being "contacted" or with brokers' "contact men." Others object to using business terms in nonbusiness contexts. But the usage seems to serve a purpose in many fields besides business and, with the qualifications just mentioned, must now be considered established in Standard English. (See *Divided usage. Reference: *College English,* 1955, 16:247.)

Contact clauses • Two or more clauses of a sentence written together without a connective between them are known as *contact clauses.* Many compound sentences are in the form of contact clauses, as in the famous, "I came, I saw, I conquered" or in "But in him the pretence is justified: he has enjoyed thinking out his subject, he will delight in his work when it is done" (MAX BEERBOHM, *Yet Again,* p. 77). Clauses which in meaning seem subordinate are occasionally set beside the main clause without a connective:

Give your decision, it will probably be right. But do not give your reasons, they will most certainly be wrong.—BERNARD HART, *The Psychology of Insanity*

This very old type of sentence punctuation has largely disappeared in print, though never quite abandoned by writers. In recent years it has re-emerged as a more convincing transcription of a natural and common form of speech.

On land, the Florida scenery is mostly man-made, concocted; it is not a terrain, it is just real estate.—STEPHEN BIRMINGHAM, "The Florida Dream," *Holiday,* Dec., 1963, p. 65

Contact clauses have a definite bearing upon one of the perennial problems of writing, the "comma fault," since many sentences containing clauses put together without expressed connectives are really effective as they stand and need no expressed connective. They are especially common and appropriate in rapid narrative where specific labeling of causes and results would slow up the movement. They are less common in straight exposition but occasionally occur. Many, of course, are the result of carelessness, but, as these examples suggest, they may produce the effect of a rapid and natural style. Deciding on the justification for contact clause punctuation is one of the more difficult problems of students and teachers.

A more common type of contact clause, which is always restrictive and therefore never set off by punctuation, is the relative clause not introduced by a pronoun. Usually it is one in which the absent pronoun would be the object of the clause; but other constructions also occur: *He has found the key you lost yesterday. This is the boy we spoke of. There is a man below wants to speak to you. I am not the man I was.* The construction is an old one in English and firmly established in all varieties of the language. (References: Jespersen, *Modern English Grammar*, III: 7; Bryant, pp. 174-176.)

(Successful and unsuccessful contact clauses are discussed fully in Ch. 8, "Contact clauses," p. 292, "Revising comma faults," p. 290. See also *Comma fault. References: Curme, *Syntax,* pp. 170-173; Jespersen, pp. 360-361.)

content, contents • *Adjectives*: The stress is on the second syllable both for the rather Formal *content* (He would be content with less) and the more common *contented* (He would be contented with less): /kən tent′/, /kən ten′təd/.

Nouns: In American English the stress is on the first syllable; *content* is used more as an abstract term (the content of the course) and in amounts (the moisture content); *contents* is rather more concrete (the contents of the box, the contents of the book): /kon′tent/, /kon′tents/.

Context • In writing, the *context* is the discourse that surrounds and limits a word or passage that is being separately discussed: "By itself the word might seem insulting, but in its *context* it could not possibly give offense."
1. The context is tremendously important in revealing the particular meanings of words. What, for instance, does the word *check* mean? By itself no one can tell which of the forty dictionary senses of the word is meant. Yet in actual use, in definite contexts, it gives no trouble:

They were able to *check* the fire at the highway.
The treasurer's books *check* with the vouchers.
He drew a *check* for the entire amount.
The tablecloth had a red and white *check*.
He moved his bishop and shouted *"Check!"*
With difficulty he held his temper in *check*.
He had the *check* list on the desk in front of him.

And so on. *Check* has more senses than most English words, but a very large proportion of our words have more than one sense so that their particular meaning must be gathered from the context—and ordinarily it can be. Context is important not only in indicating the particular denotative sense of a word, as illustrated with *check,* but also in indicating the connotative value of the word, as suggested in the quotation in the first paragraph of this article.

2. Statements of ideas depend for full understanding upon the context in which they stand, and in quoting or alluding to a writer's thought we should be careful to take the context into account. Cardinal Newman's definition of a gentleman as a man who never inflicts pain is often referred to as though it represented Newman's ideal, but in its context (*The Idea of a University,* Discourse viii) he was showing that this gentleman is all very well but without religious conviction he falls far short of being an ideal type. Taking care that allusions and quotations are true to the context in which they occur, that they really represent the ideas of their authors, is a basic requirement of an honest writer. In speech there is also the *situational context,* the whole set of conditions in which words are uttered. (See Ch. 9, "The use of connotative words," p. 375.)

continual—continuous • Dictionaries define *continual* as "frequently or closely repeated," with little or no time between:

> Dancing requires continual practice.
> He continually interrupted the lecture with foolish questions.

Continuous they define as "without interruption, unbroken":

> A continuous procession of cars passed during the hour.
> He has been continuously in debt for ten years.
> *But:* He is continually running into debt.

Sometimes the context rather blurs the distinction: *The roar of the planes overhead continually disturbed us* (or: *was continuously disturbing*).

Contractions • This term is applied to the written forms of words in which an effort is made to indicate the colloquial pronunciation, usually by substituting an apostrophe for one or more letters of the standard spelling. They are appropriate in Informal English and usually in General English but are ordinarily out of place in treatments of dignified subjects and in a Formal style, whether in routine exposition (as in academic papers) or in more literary compositions. You could probably read through a chemistry textbook without finding a single contraction, but you would find a story with the dialog printed without any contractions excessively stilted.

A more Formal style is not achieved merely by writing out the contractions of Informal speech. "I have not time" is not good Formal English for the Informal "I haven't time." For Formal writing another idiom is often needed: "I have no time."

In General English the fitness of a contraction is usually determined in part by the naturalness with which it falls into place, in part by the rhythm:

It wasn't that way to start with, when the Air Force first contracted for the plane in 1957.—*Newsweek*, May 18, 1964, p. 90

Contractions are necessary in reporting most conversation and in writing dialog for plays and stories:

"That's right. She's had a chance to think it over and realize how foolishly she was behaving. I'd even go so far as to make a guess that she's laughing over it by now. They're very changeable, you know."

"They're just like chameleons.... Why you wouldn't believe it."
—EVAN S. CONNELL, JR., "The Suicide," *Saturday Evening Post*, May 2, 1964, p. 49

An apostrophe ordinarily stands in the place of the omitted letter or letters (*doesn't, can't, shouldn't, he's*), though only one apostrophe is used in *shan't, won't*, and *ain't*.

(See *have, *shall—will.)

Contrary to fact conditions • See *Conditions § 3.

contrast—compare • See *compare—contrast.

Conversion • A word most commonly used in one part-of-speech function when used in another part-of-speech function is said to have undergone *conversion* or *functional shift*: a *must* book; a *commercial* (adjective used in the function of a noun, meaning the advertising part of a television program); in the *know*; and (less well established) I wouldn't *fault* him. Sometimes a writer will use the noun form in preference to the adjective form:

... affected by the *monster* growth of London....—SIR CHARLES GRANT ROBERTSON, *England Under the Hanoverians*, p. 337

The principle of functional shift is well established, but a writer should be cautious in experimenting with new conversions. The student who wrote the following sentence was experimenting—unsuccessfully:

She stooped as if *to negative* her height.

Although conversion is not peculiar to the English language, it is facilitated by the absence of those distinctive forms for the parts of speech so characteristic of Latin, for example. *Round* is identified in dictionaries as *adj., n., v., adv.*, and *prep.*, but there is nothing in the form of the word itself to identify it as any of those. (For further discussion see *Parts of speech.)

Coordinate clauses • See *Clauses, *Compound sentence.

Coordinating conjunctions •
1. The principal coordinating conjunctions are: *and, *but, *for, nor (=and not), *or, *yet. Only (I'd come, only I have a class) and *while (He's an expert, while I know nothing about the game) and other connectives are also occasionally used informally as coordinating conjunctions. The *conjunctive adverbs (therefore, however, and so on) are coordinating connectives, as are the *correlative conjunctions (either . . . or, not only . . .but, and so on).
2. Coordinating conjunctions are used between words, phrases, clauses, or sentences to connect elements of equal grammatical rank and substantially equivalent in thought:

   Words: books and papers; books, pamphlets, or magazines
   Phrases: in one ear and out the other
   Clauses: I would venture to say *that his description is perfect,* but *that there are some who would not agree with that verdict.*—
Bonamy Dobrée, *Modern Prose Style,* p. 69

   Independent clauses: What they talk of was in the books, but there was the stimulus of personality.—Arthur E. Hertzler, *The Horse and Buggy Doctor,* p. 181

3. For different effects of repeating or omitting conjunctions in a series see *Conjunctions § 3 and *Series.
4. For coordination versus subordination see Ch. 8, pp. 303-306, *Coordination and *Subordination. For various uses of coordinating conjunctions see *Conjunctions, *Clauses § 1, and articles on individual conjunctions.

Coordination •
Revision: Correct the faulty coordination.

                                                      Coord

   Two or more grammatically equivalent words, phrases, or clauses joined by a coordinating conjunction are said to be coordinate. (See *Coordinating conjunctions § 2.) Many *shifted constructions result from the writer's failure to put grammatically equivalent elements into matching structures. As used here, the term "faulty coordination" refers not to all such weaknesses but only to those relating to independent clauses. Faulty coordination is not a lapse in grammar or usage but a failure to make clear the logical relationships of the material. Often, therefore, it can be discussed satisfactorily only in the context in which it appears. A combination of independent clauses that is perfectly appropriate in one context might be puzzling or ineffective in another. Faulty coordination means that in the particular context the material calls for a relationship or emphasis different from the one reflected in the writer's use or arrangement of independent clauses.

1. Sometimes faulty coordination can be corrected by turning one of the independent clauses into a dependent clause. "He went to France for the summer, and his novel was published" suggests that there is an obvious causal relationship between his going to France and the publication of his novel. In some contexts, this might make sense. But if the only relationship that can be established is a temporal one—two events happening at about the same time but not otherwise related—the sentence needs to be revised: "When he was spending the summer in France, his novel was published" or "At the time his novel was published, he was spending the summer in France," or in some other way.

2. In the example above, coordination might be confusing or misleading. Sometimes it is simply ineffective: "When I reached the intersection, I found a group of people gathered around the body of a man. The left front tire had had a blowout, and the car had gone out of control and rolled over, and the driver was obviously dead." The independent clause "the driver was obviously dead" needs to be taken out of the coordinate relationship it is in; to gain its proper effect, it should be made a separate sentence.

For further discussion, see Ch. 8, "Coordination and subordination," p. 303, and *Subordination. Reference: James Sledd, "Coordination (Faulty) and Subordination (Upside-Down)," *College Composition and Communication,* 1956, 7: 181-187.

Copula • See *Linking verbs.

Copy • Manuscript before printing is *copy.* (For points of form see *Typewritten copy and Ch. 2, "Preparing the manuscript," p. 56.)

Corrections in copy • See *Proofreading.

Correlative conjunctions •
1. Some coordinating conjunctions are used in pairs:

both . . . and   either . . . or   neither . . . nor
not so . . . as   not only . . . but [but also]   whether . . . or

2. Except *either . . . or* and *both . . . and,* these correlative conjunctions are slightly Formal, showing a more conscious planning than is common in Informal or General English:

Not only was the water muddy, *but* it had tadpoles swimming in it.

3. Since these correlatives are coordinating conjunctions, they provide the skeleton for two parallel constructions. In practice, especially in speech, the parallelism is not always complete (I wondered whether *I should go* or *to beg off*). It is sometimes said that in writing, the more complete the parallelism, the more satisfying the result is likely to be. This means not only that the elements connected by the conjunctions should be of equal value but also that the constructions linked by the conjunctions should have the same word order, as in the first part of this sentence. But too strict adherence to this principle may make for artificiality, and variations, such as the shift from active to passive in the last example below, are common:

Nouns: He said that both *the novel* and *the play* were badly written.

Adjectives: He must have been either *drunk* or *crazy*.

Phrases: They can be had not only *in the usual sizes* but also *in the outsizes*.

Clauses: Whether *the sale was for cash* or *a mortgage was given*, it seemed too much to pay.

(See also *Parallel constructions. Reference: Lillian Mermin, "On the Placement of Correlatives in Modern English," *American Speech*, 1943, 18:171-191, and 19:66-68. For number of verb in constructions with *either . . . or*, see *Subject and verb § 2b, and as references, Dorothy J. Hughes, *College English*, 1941, 2:697-699; Bryant, pp. 62-64.)

could—might • See *can—may.

Counter words • Words which also have more restricted precise senses but are used frequently as general terms of approval or disapproval have been called *counter words*. Their popularity is a matter of fashion and is related to slang, except that they are ordinary English words and lack the element of surprise that good slang has. In Elizabethan times *fair* was such a word; recently *fabulous, definitely, mixed-up* have had such currency. In ordinary speech *colossal, cute, fine, fix, grand, lousy, lovely, nice, gorgeous, poor* are samples, and in more educated circles words like *adjusted, creative, dynamic, structure, vital, challenge, charismatic,* and often epithets like *red, radical, conservative, reactionary* are used as vague expressions of like or dislike without regard to more exact meaning.

In advertising and other more or less forced writing, *super-, -conscious* (we are *air-conscious, flower-conscious, defense-conscious* by turn), *-conditioned, -type, -wise* all enter into counter words. They are appropriate in Informal English (in which *certainly* has the sense of *yes*) but seem out of place in serious writing because their vagueness makes them inexact.

couple •
1. The primary meaning of *couple* is two persons or things associated in some way, typically as in "a married couple." In speech it is equivalent to the numeral *two*: *a couple of pencils*; or equivalent to *a few*: *a couple of minutes*.
2. Since in speech *of* is usually reduced to /ə/ before a consonant and assimilated to the preceding unstressed syllable, we may interpret what we hear as the omission of *of* and write:

He'd had a couple drinks.   I'll be gone only a couple days.

This transcription occasionally finds its way into print in General writing:

Mr. Freeman's statement left unanswered a couple [ ] pertinent questions: ... —*The New Republic,* June 16, 1952, p. 15

Course names • In general discussions, only the names of college subjects that are proper adjectives (the languages) are capitalized. In writing a list of courses including one or more of these proper adjectives, it is possible to capitalize them all for consistency (and courtesy), though the distinction would usually be kept, as in the first example:

My program is biology, chemistry, European history, English composition, and French.
My program is Biology, Chemistry, European History, English Composition, and French.

In referring to the various departments of an institution, all names would be capitalized, as they would also when preceding the number of a course:

the Department of History   History 347

In newspaper style *department* and *school* would probably not be capitalized when they follow the proper name.

criterion, criteria • *Criterion* and *criteria* are respectively the singular and plural forms; dictionaries also list *criterions* as a plural.

cupfuls, cupsful • See *spoonful, spoonfuls.

curriculum • *Curriculum* has the Latin plural *curricula,* and the English *curriculums.* The adjective is *curricular,* and the compound adjective with *extra* is ordinarily written as one word: *extracurricular. Curriculum* is also used as a modifier:

... the guidance of college students, curriculum and instructional problems at the college level....—*Current Issues in Higher Education,* 1955, p. 220

D • In our spelling this letter usually represents the first sound in *die, do,* the second in *addict, addle,* and the last in *pod; d* represents the /t/ sound when it follows the sound of /f, k, p, s, ch, sh, or th/ in the same syllable: *walked* /wôkt/, *blessed* /blest/ (but /bles′id/), *kicked* /kikt/, *raced* /rāst/, *telegraphed* /tel′ə graft/, *fished* /fisht/, *matched* /macht/, *toothed* /tütht/. The /t/ sound is produced exactly like the /d/ sound except that in its production the vocal chords are not vibrated; it is voiceless, /d/ is voiced. With the loss in Early Modern English of the vowel of the suffix spelled *-ed,* the /d/ was next to a voiceless sound and lost its voiced quality.

In Standard English in the seventeenth and eighteenth centuries /d/ before an unstressed /y/ sound usually became /j/: *grandeur* /gran′jər/, *soldier* /sōl′jər/. Spelling pronunciation has now restored the /iə/ pronunciation in some of these words and the older /j/ sound is heard only in the speech of some older or Nonstandard speakers: *Indian* /in′jən/. British and American practice also differ: British English often has /i mē′jit/ for *immediate* but /kôrdiəl/ for *cordial.* There are local extensions of the sound to stressed *u* syllables: /jü′ti/, *duty.*

Dangling modifiers •

Revision: Revise the sentence so that the expression marked is clearly related to the word it is intended to modify.   DM

A construction which from its position in a sentence seems to modify a word which it cannot sensibly modify is said to "dangle" (or to be "misrelated"). Careful writers take particular pains to avoid such constructions. See Ch. 8, "Revising dangling modifiers," p. 297.

A participle which is used in the function of an adjective should modify accurately either a noun or pronoun:

Looking further to the left, we saw the spire of a church. [*Looking* clearly modifies *we.*]

Defined in psychological terms, a fanatic is a man who consciously overcompensates a secret doubt. [*Defined* clearly modifies *fanatic.*] —ALDOUS HUXLEY, *Proper Studies,* p. 220

A verbal that precedes the main clause and does not relate to the subject of that clause is dangling.

Upon telling my story to the advisor, he stopped and thought. [For: *When I told....*]

Motoring down Route 17 toward New York City, numerous signs read "Visit Our Snake Farm." [For: *Motoring down Route 17 toward New York City, we saw numerous signs that read....*]

What if, forced to climb over this solid cloud bank, ice should form on the wings and force them down into the wild country? [The ice isn't forced to climb.]

Born in England in 1853, John MacDowell's seafaring activities began after he had emigrated to this country. [His seafaring activities were not born in England.]

Dangling participles are to be avoided simply because educated readers do not expect to find them. As a rule there is no real question of the intended meaning of the sentence, though sometimes the faulty reference of a participle is ludicrous, as it is in Arthur G. Kennedy's gem: *Having swelled because of the rains, the workman was unable to remove the timber.* In Informal use, some constructions of this sort are common: *If possible, I'll call before five.* (Reference: Robert M. Browne, *College English*, 1959, 21:100-101.)

Such dangling constructions should not be confused with *absolute phrases, in which the participial phrase is equivalent to a subordinate clause and is effectively used, especially for adding details: *He had worked for four hours, copy piling up quite satisfactorily.* (See *Participles for further examples of these constructions. References: Curme, *Syntax,* pp. 158-160; Reuben Steinbach, "The Misrelated Constructions," *American Speech,* 1930, 5:181-197; Bryant, pp. 64-65.)

Infinitive phrases may be dangling:

Imprecise: To get the most out of a sport, the equipment must be in perfect condition. [The equipment does not profit from the sport.]

Improved: To get the most out of a sport, you must have your equipment in perfect condition.

This construction should not be confused with an absolute infinitive phrase which is well established in Standard English:

To judge from his looks, he can't be more than forty-five.

(See *Infinitives § 5.)

Prepositional phrases sometimes dangle:

At eleven, our family moved to Kansas City. [Clearer: *When I was eleven, our family moved to Kansas City.*]

Dash • Three dashes of varying lengths are used in printing: – (en dash), — (em dash, the usual mark), and —— (2-em or long or double dash). On the typewriter use a hyphen for the first, two hyphens not spaced away from the neighboring words for the usual dash, and four hyphens for the long dash.

The em dash, the one we have in mind when we say just *dash,* has aroused more discussion and more violent feeling than a mark of punctuation seems to deserve. Some textbooks and some publishers forbid its use generally, while others specify minute shades of meaning which they believe it indicates. Some writers rarely use it. Others, especially in matter not intended for publication, use it at the expense of other marks.

Most dashes are roughly equivalent to commas—that is, they separate units within a sentence—but the separation is sharper and the dashes suggest a definite tone, usually a note of surprise, an emotional emphasis. Some other mark could always be substituted for the dash, but there would be a difference in movement and suggestiveness in the sentence. At its best it is an abrupt, emphatic, and effective mark of punctuation.

1. *To mark a sharp turn in thought.* Most typical is its use to indicate a sharp turn in thought or syntax:

The old nations still live in the hearts of men, and love of the European nation is not yet born—assuming that it ever will be.— RAYMOND ARON, "Old Nations, New Europe," *Daedalus,* Winter 1964, p. 66

2. *Before a final summarizing statement.* It is often used before an inserted or added phrase, usually one that summarizes what has just been said or that gives contrasting or emphasizing details of what has been said, or often a striking apposition. This dash has the force of a vigorous comma:

The waiting, the watching, the hundreds of small necessary acts about the sickroom—all this was past.

The elements of every story are these five: character, incident, nature, fate, and milieu—the social, historical, vital background.—D. H. PARKER, *Principles of Aesthetics,* p. 236

He [the Englishman of the 1870's and 80's] was strongly in favor of peace—that is to say, he liked his wars to be fought at a distance and, if possible, in the name of God.—GEORGE DANGERFIELD, *The Death of Liberal England,* p. 7

3. *Between independent clauses.* A dash is sometimes used between two independent clauses for abrupt separation:

The "womanly" woman became as obsolete as the buggy. The nurse must tend the children, the cook must order the meals—life must be spectacular, not frittered away in little household dullnesses.—IRENE AND ALLEN CLEATON, *Books and Battles,* p. 92

4. *To enclose parenthetical statements.* Dashes may be used for parenthetical statements that are more closely related than parentheses would indicate, separating the expression from the context more than commas but less definitely than parentheses would:

The general effect upon readers—most of them quite uneducated —is quite different from what the serious messiah intends.—T. S. Eliot, *After Strange Gods,* p. 36

5. *Overuse.* The overuse of dashes detracts from their special quality and proves that they are, as Bonamy Dobrée says, "a sandy joint." (See also *Schoolgirl style.)

She [Marlene Dietrich] was turned into a static image of lorelei charm, frozen in a lovely pose—and to bring that image to life, there seems to be no proposal except to point again to its overpublicized legs, and its—by this time—rubber-stamp "allure."

6. *With other marks.* Formerly a dash was often combined with other marks, especially with a comma or a colon, but this use has declined. The dash adds nothing in the salutation of a letter (*Dear Sir:—* means no more than *Dear Sir:*). Within sentences the old comma-dash combination has very generally disappeared also, so that now we find either a comma or, if a desire for emphasis makes it useful, a dash alone.

7. *Other uses.*

a—In place of a colon when the statement ends with a question mark: *How do you explain this?—"English 23, F."*

b—To precede a credit line, as at the end of the quoted passages in this book. (See §§ 1-4 above for examples.)

c—After introductory words which are to be repeated before each of the lines that follow:

We recommend—
That a constitution be drawn up.
That it be presented to the student council.

d—To separate run-in questions and answers in testimony:

Q. Did you see him?—A. No.

8. *Double dash.* Besides some arbitrary uses prescribed by particular publishing houses and in incomplete names (Mr. S——), the 2-em dash is chiefly an *end-stop in dialog when a speech is interrupted:

"...I can't say, of course, whether or not my layman's logic adds lustre to the gladsome light of jurisprudence——"

"Your reasoning is consistent as far as it goes," cut in Markham tartly.—S. S. Van Dine, *The Greene Murder Case,* p. 220

9. *En dash.* A writer does not need to worry about the en dash, slightly longer than a hyphen, but printers use it between inclusive figures (*1837–1901*) and instead of a hyphen when one or both elements of an expression ordinarily requiring a hyphen are made up of two words: *the New York—Bar Harbor express*. (Reference: Summey, pp. 101-104.)

data • Pronounced /dā′tə/ or sometimes /dat′ə/ or (affecting Latin) /dä′tə/. (See *Latin and English.)

Data is the plural form of the Latin noun whose singular, *datum*, is little used in English; *data* is the usual English form for both singular and plural. Its meaning is actually collective and may sometimes stress a group of facts as a unit and so be used with a singular verb. When it refers to the individual facts, *data* is used with a plural:

Singular idea: The actual data of history *consists* of contemporary facts in the form of remains and documents.—MORRIS R. COHEN, *Reason and Nature,* p. 381

Singular idea: Data concerning measurement of social attitudes *has* been included in the next chapter. . . .—LUELLA COLE, *Psychology of Adolescence,* p. 102

Plural idea: When the data *have* been secured the task is to analyze, to sift, to select and to arrange those data which *bear* upon each particular phase of the object or event examined until at the end the scientist has what one might call a logical construct.—G. D. HIGGINSON, *Fields of Psychology,* p. 10

Either possible: These data *are* [This data *is*] unpublished.

The singular verb can be safely used in any but the most Formal writing. (See *Plurals of nouns § 4. Reference: A. Bartlett in "Current English Forum," *College English,* 1954, 15:417.)

date • *Date* is Informal for "appointment, engagement" (I had a date for the evening) and for "a person with whom one has an engagement" (After all, she was his date); as a verb, "to have or make an appointment with.": *Blind date* is a useful and economical Informal expression, saying in two syllables something that would take several words in Formal English. (Reference: Bryant, pp. 67-68.)

Dates • The commoner form for writing dates is: *August 19, 1965*. The form *19 August 1965* is increasingly popular (partly as a result of its use by the armed services) and has a small advantage in that it makes a comma unnecessary.

Never write the year out in words except in formal social announcements, invitations, etc. Expressions like "January in the year 1885" are wasteful. *January 1885* is enough. If saving space is important, or in business or reference writing, months having more than four letters should be abbreviated:

Jan. Feb. Mar. Apr. Aug. Sept. Oct. Nov. Dec.

In Informal writing, figures are convenient: 8/19/65, 11/27/65. (In England and other European countries the day usually comes first: 27-11-65, sometimes with a Roman numeral for the month: 27 XI 65.)

Better style now usually omits the *st, nd, rd, th* from the day of the month: May 1 rather than May 1st.

In Formal style the day of the month may be written in words when the year is not given (September seventeen or September seventeenth).

Roman numerals are rarely used for the year except for decoration, as on the title page of a book.

(See *Months, *Numbers § 1a, *Letters, *Social correspondence.)

Dative case • English has no distinctive form for the dative function, which in some inflected languages indicates the indirect object of a verb, and can hardly be said to have a dative case in any sense. A noun in a construction that in another language might have a dative is in the common case form and a pronoun is in the accusative case form. Usually we have a phrase made with *to, for,* or *on.* (See *Case, *Objects § 2.)

Deadwood •

Dead *Revision: Remove the unnecessary word or words, revising the sentence if necessary.*

Deadwood is a convenient label for a type of *wordiness in which a word or phrase adds nothing at all to the meaning of the statement.

[In] many [cases] students have profited by this.

He was a handsome [looking] man.

The book is divided into various sections, all dealing with [the matter of] unemployment.

Many phrases of this sort make writing flabby and are a mark of amateur or careless writing. (For further examples and discussions see Ch. 8, "Economy in sentences," p. 314, *case, *Wordiness.)

Declension • *Declension* is the change of form of nouns and pronouns (and in many languages the form of adjectives and participles also) to show number (singular or plural), gender (masculine, feminine, neuter), and case (nominative, genitive, accusative, etc.). The English noun has only two regular forms (the genitive form and the common form, which is used for all other relationships), and the variations in pronoun forms are not regular; English has no declension in the sense that Latin has. (See *Case, the articles on the various cases, *Plurals, and the articles referred to there.)

definitely; He was definitely worse than usual; She definitely disapproves of those methods; But definitely!) instead of in its more limited sense of "clear-cut, in a definite manner."

At present *definitely* is overused as a *counter word to give emphasis or in the sense of "certainly, quite" (I will not do it, *definitely*; He was *definitely* worse than usual; She *definitely* disapproves of those methods; But *definitely*!) instead of in its more limited sense of "clear-cut, in a definite manner."

Definition • Various sections of the *Guide* give attention to those problems in definition that have special relevance to writing. The "meaning of words" is discussed briefly in Ch. 9, p. 369, and dictionary definitions in Ch. 9, p. 371. The definition of key terms and definition as a method of development are treated in Ch. 3, p. 98, with further applications in Chs. 6 and 7.

Definitions are of different kinds to suit different purposes. The *logical* (or formal) definition falls into the strict pattern of

$$term \ = \ genus \ or \ class \ + \ differentia(e)$$

as illustrated in "Man (term) is a rational (differentia) animal (genus)." The uses and limitations of the logical definition are discussed in Ch. 3, p. 100. The following are traditional rules for testing the soundness of a logical definition:

1. The definition must be neither too broad nor too narrow. In "A bachelor is a person who is unmarried," the genus *person* is too broad; it should be limited to *man*. In "A shoe is a leather covering for the human foot," the definition is too narrow; the differentia *leather* excludes shoes made of other materials.

2. Unless privation or negation is the distinguishing characteristic (as in bachelor, *not* married; orphan, *without* parents) the definition should be positive, not negative. "Liberty is the state of not being restrained" violates this rule for a logical definition.

3. The definition should not be circular, as in "Hostility is the state of being hostile."

4. The definition should not be expressed in figurative language. This rule excludes the famous definition of Karl Marx, "Religion is the opiate of the people."

Constructing logical definitions and testing them by these rules gives training in precise, literal statement. It should be remembered, however, that many excellent definitions are not —and are not intended to be—logical definitions.

Degree • See *Comparison of adjectives and adverbs.

Degrees • Ordinarily a person's academic degrees are not given with his name except in college publications, reference works, and articles and letters where the degrees indicate competence in a particular field, as in a doctor's comment on a medical matter. When used, they are separated from the name by a comma and in alumni publications are often followed by the year in which they were granted:

Harvey J. Preble, A.B.   Harvey J. Preble, A.B. '08
James T. Thomson, M.A.   James T. Thomson, A.B. '21, M.A. '24
Robert Bernath, M.D., gave the principal address.
Royce Walton, B. Arch., discussed Wright's mile-high building.

As a rule, except in reference lists, only a person's highest degree in an academic professional field need be mentioned.

If the institution granting the degree is named, the following forms are usual:

George H. Cook, A.B. (Grinnell), A.M. (Indiana), Ph.D. (Chicago)
D. C. Browning, B.A. (Oxon. [= Oxford])
J. H. Plumb, Ph.D. (Cantab. [= Cambridge])

Two kinds of degrees are granted by American colleges and universities. *Earned* ("in course") degrees are given at the completion of a required course of study. Some of the ones commonly granted are:

A.B. (*or* B.A.)—Bachelor of Arts
B.S.—Bachelor of Science
B.E.—Bachelor of Engineering
B.D.—Bachelor of Divinity
B. Mus.—Bachelor of Music
B. Arch.—Bachelor of Architecture
Ph.B.—Bachelor of Philosophy
LL.B.—Bachelor of Laws
A.M. (*or* M.A.)—Master of Arts
M.S.—Master of Science
M.E.—Master of Engineering
M.Ed. (*or* Ed.M.)—Master of Education

M.B.A.—Master of Business Administration
M.F.A.—Master of Fine Arts
M.Ped.—Master of Pedagogy (*or* M.Ed., Ed.M.—Master of Education)
Ed.D.—Doctor of Education
Ph.D.—Doctor of Philosophy
S.T.D.—Doctor of Sacred Theology
M.D.—Doctor of Medicine
D.D.S.—Doctor of Dental Surgery

Honorary ("honoris causa") degrees are granted by institutions as a token of respect. Of the following, the first four are the most common:

LL.D.—Doctor of Laws
D.D.—Doctor of Divinity
Lit(t).D.—Doctor of Literature
   or Letters

Sc.D.—Doctor of Science
D.C.L.—Doctor of Civil Law
L.H.D.—Doctor of Humanities
Eng.D.—Doctor of Engineering

British and other European degrees are similar but less numerous.

Delete • *Delete* means "take out, erase, remove." It is a direction to printers made by putting a Greek small *d* (δ-delta) in the margin and drawing a line through the matter to be removed. (See *Proofreading.)

To delete material in your manuscripts, simply draw a line through it (don't use parentheses or black it out completely).

Demonstrative adjectives and pronouns • *This, that, these, those* are called demonstrative adjectives or demonstrative pronouns, according to their use in a sentence:

Adjectives:
This car we bought in May.
Those fellows never think of anyone else.

Pronouns:
This cost a good bit more than *those*.
That's a good idea.

(See *Agreement, *that, *this, *kind, sort.)

Dependent clauses • See *Relative clauses, *Clauses.

Derivation of words • See *Origin of words.

descendant • *Descendant* spells both adjective and noun, as does *descendent*. The adjective has an added sense. Consult a good dictionary.

Description • See *Adjectives in use, *Adverbs in use.

detail • Pronunciation is divided: /di tāl′/, /dē′tāl/, the first older, the second especially common in situations where the word is used a great deal (army life, architecture, composition, etc.).

Details •
Revision: Develop this topic more fully by giving pertinent details.

                                               Det

Adequate development of a topic in writing usually comes from the use of details—images, facts, evidence, bits of observation, and so on. They not only help the reader understand what you are discussing but they are chiefly responsible for making a paper interesting and convincing. (For the various uses of details see Ch. 4, p. 112. See also "Example," Ch. 3, p. 79, and Ch. 9.)

develop • *Develop* is the usual Standard spelling for the verb and *development* for the noun; *develope* and *developement* are now extremely rare.

Development • See *Outline form. For method of developing a paper, see Ch. 3.

devil • *Devil* (and *hell*) seldom receive the courtesy of a capital except for stylistic emphasis.

Diacritic marks • See *Pronunciation § 1.

Diagramming sentences • Diagramming sentences by placing sentence elements in an arbitrary graphic organization in an effort to show their function in the sentence is of questionable value for any purpose other than learning the rules of a game. This exercise, however, seems to have appealed to a good many teachers and even some students. The futility of diagramming has been demonstrated repeatedly; two studies are: Harry A. Greene, "Direct versus Formal Methods in Elementary English," *Elementary English,* 1947, 24:273-285; Anthony L. Tovatt, "Diagramming, A Sterile Skill," *English Journal,* 1952, 41:91-93. (For a simple, useful method, see Ch. 8, pp. 275-282.)

Diagrams, graphs, etc. • The function of diagrams, charts, graphs, and illustrations is to make a writer's meaning more clear and more concrete than his words alone could. They cannot be a substitute for a discussion in words, but they can make it easier for readers to grasp figures, to understand relationships, and especially to make comparisons between facts that can be graphically portrayed. The making of graphs, charts, maps, and so on is discussed in technical and specialized manuals. (References: Herbert Arkin and Raymond R. Colter, *Graphs—How to Make and Use Them,* New York, 1940; Frederick E. Croxton and Dudley J. Cowden, *Applied General Statistics,* 2nd ed., New York, 1955, Chs. 4 and 6; and W. O. Sypherd, Alvin M. Fountain, and V. E. Gibbens, *Manual of Technical Writing,* Chicago, 1957, Ch. 7; chapters on graphic methods in other introductions to statistics.)

Dialects • A dialect is the speech (words, sounds, stress, phrasing, grammatical habits) characteristic of a fairly definite region or group, or, more accurately, it is speech that does not attract attention to itself among the residents of a region (*re-*

gional dialect) or among members of a group (*group* or *class dialect*) but that would be recognizably different to, an outsider. In linguistics a dialect is any development from a parent language: French and Italian are dialects of Vulgar Latin.

Localism is used in this book for a regional dialectal usage. Conspicuous dialectal words are usually out of place in General and Formal writing except to give a local flavor. They are more effective in speech, in fiction, and in Informal writing. (For description of dialects in the United States, see Ch. 1, "Variations due to place," p. 6, and for the use of conversation in writing, see Ch. 5, p. 170 ff.)

Diction •
Revision: Replace the word marked with one that is more exact, more appropriate, or more effective.

Diction here means primarily the choice of words in speaking or writing. Good diction means that the words seem to the reader or listener well chosen to convey the meanings or attitudes of the writer or speaker; faulty diction, that the words either fail to convey the meaning fully or accurately or do not satisfy the reader's expectation in some other way. Ch. 9 discusses many problems of diction. Many specific words have articles of their own (*contact, *drunk, *hope, *however, *notorious, *ye = the). Often the solution to a question of diction can be found in a dictionary. (See also *Usage, *Words.)

Dictionaries • Not every dictionary is reliable and no dictionary can be depended on entirely. A good dictionary is one with a recent copyright date and a clear indication that a scholarly staff was responsible for the editing of the book. Even an unabridged dictionary is not complete, and all smaller ones are necessarily even less complete. The information in the entries varies in reliability according to the difficulties involved in getting and presenting it: spellings are most reliable, pronunciations least. Definitions are abbreviated and often overcompressed because of lack of space. (See also p. 362 ff.)

Dieresis • Two dots placed over the second of two consecutive vowels to show they are to be pronounced separately are referred to as a *dieresis* /dī er′ə sis/: *reëxamine, coöperation*. A hyphen is often used to indicate that the vowels are to be kept separate, especially in words with *re-* (*re-enlist*). There is a tendency not to use either dieresis or hyphen in the more commonly used words, so that *cooperation* and *zoology*, for example, are now the more usual forms. Do not confuse this mark with *umlaut in German words, which when placed over *a, u,* or *e* makes separate alphabetical entities.

different • In American writing the commonest preposition after *different* is *from:*

His second book was entirely different from his first.

Sharon was so different from what we expected that we were all surprised.

But General usage is divided, with *than* sometimes and *to* rarely replacing *from* (*different to* is a common British idiom). *Different than* is common when the object is a clause:

The house was a good deal different than he remembered it. [This idiom is neater than "different from what he remembered."]

Since many people still object to *different than,* students should avoid it in their Formal writing. (References: D. L. Bolinger, *English Journal,* 1939, 28:480; Gladys D. Haase, *College English,* 1949, 10:345-347; Bryant, pp. 69-70; Bergen and Cornelia Evans, *A Dictionary of Contemporary American Usage,* New York, 1957, pp. 135-136.)

Digraph • Two letters used together to spell a single sound are known as a *digraph.* English spelling has many digraphs:

ea as in *head* or *heat*	*ee* as in *seed*
ei as in *either* or *neighbor*	*oa* as in *coat*
oo as in *book* or *food*	*ph* as in *physics*
sh as in *shall*	*th* as in *then* or *thin*

dining • *Dine, dined, dining, dining room* all have to do with eating—as does *dinner* with two *n*'s and a short *i*; *dinning* (short *i*) has to do with *din,* "noise."

Dine and *dining* are Formal words. *Dinner* is used in all varieties.

Diphthong • A *diphthong* is a vowel-like sound made by moving the tongue, jaw, and lips from the position for one vowel to that of another while vibrating the vocal cords. (The term has also been used as equivalent to *digraph.*) The standard method of transcribing these glide sounds is to use two vowel symbols, which are to be interpreted as indicating where the diphthong begins and where it ends. The common distinctive diphthongs of American English are: /ī/, /ä to i/; /oi/, /ô to i/; /ou/, /ä to ü/; and /ū/, /i [y] to ü/.

Most English vowels have some diphthongal quality. (For further details about American diphthongs, see J. S. Kenyon, *American Pronunciation,* § 327 ff, and the discussions of pronunciation in good modern dictionaries.)

Direct address • *Direct address* is the term used to describe the construction in which persons (or objects) are addressed in speaking, reading, or writing:

My friends, I wish you would forget this night.
What do you think, *Doctor,* about his going home now?
Rain, rain, go away.

Words in direct address are separated from the rest of the sentence by a comma or, if in the middle of the sentence, by two.

Direct objects • See *Objects § 1.

disinterested—uninterested • From its first recorded uses in the seventeenth century, *disinterested* has had two senses: (1) impartial, not influenced by personal interest; (2) indifferent, inattentive, uninterested. (See *Oxford English Dictionary* and the 1933 *Supplement.*) The context usually indicates the sense:

The rules [for criticism] may be given in one word: by being disinterested. And how is it to be disinterested? By keeping aloof from practice; by resolutely following the law of its own nature, which is to be a free play of the mind on all subjects which it touches; . . .— MATTHEW ARNOLD, "The Function of Criticism at the Present Time"

Next was the question: Are modern students actually disinterested in reading?—RUTH DAVIES, "We Join the March of the Moderns," *English Journal* (College Edition) , 1939, 28:203

Recently there have been a number of attacks on the use of *disinterested* in the sense of *uninterested.* Usage records the word in both senses, but stylistically (in part because of the honorific connotation of *disinterested,* which *impartial* and *objective* have not acquired) sensitive readers prefer the first sense. A writer should take their preference into account.

The noun *disinterest* means "lack of interest" (and is probably one reason for the increased use of the adjective to mean "uninterested"):

He instances religious corruption, political corruption, and disinterest of the well-to-do.

(Reference: Robert J. Geist, "Usage and Meaning," *College Composition and Communication,* 1955, 6:88-91.)

disremember • See *remember.

Ditto marks (") • Ditto marks are used with lists and tabulations in reference works instead of repeating words that fall directly below. In typewritten manuscript, use quotation marks for ditto marks:

```
m, as in man, men, mine, hum, hammer
n, "  "  no, man, manner
```

Ditto marks are not used in consecutive writings nor in footnotes or bibliographies. In general they are much less used than formerly.

Divided usage • Usage is said to be *divided* when two or more forms exist in the language, both in reputable use in the same dialect or variety. *Divided usage* is not applied, for example, to *localisms, like *poke* for *sack* or *bag,* or to differences like *ain't* and *isn't* which belong to separate varieties of the language. It applies to spellings, pronunciations, or constructions on which those of similar education might differ.

There are many more of these divided usages within Standard English than most people are aware of. For instance, most dictionaries record these and hundreds of other instances of divided usage:

In pronunciation:

/ab'də mən/—/ab dō'mən/
/ad'vər tīz'mənt/—/ad vėr'tis mənt/—/ad vėr'tiz mənt/
/lev'ər/—/lē'vər/
/ī'sə lāt/—/is'ə lāt/

In spelling:

buses—busses	millionaire—millionnaire
catalog—catalogue	although—altho

In verb forms:

Past tense—*sing: sang* or *sung*; *ring: rang* or *rung*
Past participle—*show: shown* or *showed*; *prove: proved* or *proven*

It is hard for some careful users of the language to realize that others may speak or write somewhat differently from themselves and still be following Standard practice. Before calling a person to account, either seriously or playfully, for a usage, we should make sure that his is not a variant that is as reputable as the one we may prefer; that is, we should avoid emotional attitudes and useless disputes whenever possible. This is not always easy. Words (usage) can acquire powerful associations. For instance: The past tense of *eat* pronounced /et/ is for many Americans associated with lack of education, though it is used by many educated Southerners. In England both /et/ and /āt/ are in widespread Standard usage, yet Fowler (in the entry for *eat*) is quite dogmatic: "The past is spelt *ate* (rarely *eat*) and pronounced /ĕt/ (wrongly /āt/)." British dictionaries show that "wrongly" is not accurate; but Fowler evidently felt strongly about it. If he, a distinguished and competent lexicographer, could object so violently to a

Standard pronunciation, other people, lacking his linguistic background, will have similar prejudices even less well-founded.

The point about divided usages is that both are acceptable. A person who has learned to say /rash'ən/ for *ration* need not change to /rāsh'ən/ nor the other way around. When you may choose between variants of equal standing, choose the one that you use naturally, that is appropriate to your style, or, if you are taking pains to be tactful, the one that is customary among the audience you are to reach.

The entries in this *Index* include a number of divided usages. When one or the other of two acceptable usages is likely to disturb many readers or listeners and arouse emotional attitudes, evidence is usually presented: there is security in knowing what is dangerous ground. For examples, see:

Words: *can—may, *drought—drouth, *enthuse, *farther—further
Forms: *-ed, *It's me, *slow, slowly, *Principal parts of verbs
Pronunciations: *either
Constructions: *different from, *due to, *like—as, *reason is because

Division of words •
Revision: Break the word at the end of this line between syllables.

Div

Whenever it is necessary in manuscript or in print, a word is divided at the end of a line by a hyphen ("division hyphen"). But in preparing manuscript you will not be forced to divide many words if you will leave a reasonable right hand margin. A good habit is to divide words only when the lines will be conspicuously uneven if the last word is completely written or completely carried over to the next line. In manuscript for publication most publishers prefer an uneven right margin to divided words.

When you are not sure how to divide a word, consult a dictionary. Both the divided parts should be pronounceable, though this does not necessarily mean that the established printing practice records the actual spoken division of syllables; words of one syllable, like *matched, said, thought,* should not be divided at all. English syllables are difficult to determine, but in general they follow pronunciation groups: *autocratic* would be divided into syllables *au to crat ic,* but *autocracy* is *au toc ra cy.*

The following words are divided to show typical syllables:

mar gin   ca ter   hy phen   chil dren   long ing
hi lar i ous   cat ty   ac com plished   ad min is trate

Double consonants are usually separable:

ef fi cient   com mit tee   daz zling   bat ted

A single letter is never allowed to stand by itself: do not divide at the end of lines words like *enough* (which would leave a lone *e* at the end of a line) or *many* (which would put a lone *y* at the beginning of a line).

Words spelled with a hyphen (*half-brother, well-disposed*) should be divided only at the point of the hyphen to avoid the awkwardness of two hyphens in the same word.

Division of words is primarily a printing and editing problem and fuller directions will be found in the stylebooks of publishing houses (like the *Manual of Style* of the University of Chicago Press).

do • *Do* is one of the most important auxiliary verbs in English. Its conjugation follows the regular strong verb pattern (the past tense and past participle are formed by a change in vowel) except for the pronunciation of the third person singular *does* /duz/ and of the contracted *don't* /dōnt/.

1. *"Do" in verb phrases.*

a–Do is used to form what are called emphatic verb phrases with all verbs except the modal auxiliaries (*can, may, shall* . . .) and usually *be*:

Present	*Past*
I, you do wish	I, you he, she did wish
he, she does wish	we, you, they did wish
we, you, they do wish	

*b–*With *not* (in speech contracted to *don't, doesn't, didn't). This is the Standard way of negating all English verbs except the modal auxiliaries and usually *be*:

He did not feel well enough to go out. I don't expect to go.

*c–*In questions:

Do you think I was right?

Did you like the show as well as you expected to?

2. *"Do" as a pro-verb.* *Do* is used to avoid repetition of a simple verb that has just been used:

I like him better than you do [than you like him].

3. *"Do" in idioms.* *Do* has many idiomatic meanings and is part of many idiomatic phrases: A girl *does* her hair; a steak is well *done*; we *do away* with things; *do for* (which may mean "be enough"—That will *do* for you—or "put the finishing touches on"—That *did* for him—or, in some localities, "work for, serve"—She *does* for Mrs. Lawrence); *done for*; *do in*; *do over* ("redecorate"); *do up* ("wrap up, launder").

(References: Fries, *AEG,* pp. 146-149; Fries, *Structure,* pp. 96-97, 149-151.)

don't • *Don't* is the contraction of *do not,* universally used in conversation and often in writing when *do not* would seem too emphatic or when the rhythm seems more comfortable with the shorter form.

Until about 1900 *don't* was the usual third person singular in Informal speech, and the usage still often finds its way into familiar speech and even into casual writing: "He don't look as well as he used to." Educated people now avoid it, though Atwood found that *Linguistic Atlas* evidence for the Eastern states showed nearly half of the cultured informants using the construction. In another study of *Atlas* material, Malmstrom found *he don't* unevenly distributed in the speech of the cultivated: Middle Atlantic, 75 percent; South Atlantic, 50 percent. But in the New England, North Central, and Upper Midwest areas *he doesn't* predominated. (References: Karl W. Dykema, "An Example of Prescriptive Linguistic Change: 'Don't' to 'Doesn't,' " *English Journal,* 1947, 36:370-376; E. B. Atwood, *A Survey of Verb Forms in the Eastern United States,* Ann Arbor, 1953, p. 28; Jean Malmstrom, "Linguistic Atlas Findings versus Textbook Pronouncements on Current English Usage," *English Journal,* 1959, 48:191-198; Bryant, pp. 73-74.)

Dots • See **Ellipsis,* **Leaders.*

Double comparison • See **as . . . as.*

Double genitive • See **Genitive* § 1c.

Double negative •
1. *In Standard English.* Two negative words in the same statement are not used in Standard English to express a single negation (Not: "He could*n't* find it *no*where," but "He could*n't* find it *any*where" or "He *could* find it *no*where").

There are, however, occasional constructions in which one negative statement modifies another negative statement to give a qualified meaning or a meaning with some special emphasis. In Informal and General English, mostly in speech: "He is not sure he won't slip in at the last minute" does not mean "He will slip in at the last minute" but "He may possibly slip in. . . ." "And don't you think he isn't clever" stands for something more complex than "He is clever"—for "I've found out he's clever" or "You'd better believe he's clever (though I know you don't yet)." Other examples are: "I couldn't not invite her, could I?" "I couldn't just say nothing." In Formal

English: "A not unattractive young woman." "Not for nothing did he sacrifice himself."

2. *In Nonstandard English.* Although double negatives are probably not so common in Nonstandard English as comic writers suggest in their cartoons and stories, two or more negatives are very often used to make an emphatic negative in this variety. "I do*n't* have *no*thing to lose" makes negative two parts of the idea and emphasizes the negative; if the *nothing* isn't stressed, it is a simple negative in two parts, as French uses *ne . . . pas.* Such a double negative is not a backsliding from the idiom of more Formal English but the survival of a desire for emphasis. In earlier English two negatives were used in all varieties of the language. Chaucer wrote:

> In al this world *ne* was ther *noon* him lyk
> A bettre preest, I trowe that *nowher noon* is.

The objection to a double negative is not that "two negatives make an affirmative," for they do not. The objection is simply that the construction is not now in fashion among educated people.

3. *Hardly, scarcely.* Students sometimes fall into a concealed double negative when using *hardly* or *scarcely. Hardly* means "not probably" and *scarcely* means the same a little more emphatically. Consequently in Standard English a sentence like "For the most part our college paper contains *hardly nothing*" should read "For the most part our college paper contains *hardly anything,*" and "For a while we *couldn't scarcely* see a thing" should read "For a while we *could scarcely* see a thing." (Reference: Bryant, pp. 75-76, 106-107.)

Double prepositions • See *Prepositions § 3b.

Doubling final consonants •

1. Words of one syllable ending in a single consonant following a single vowel (*brag, fat, win*) double the consonant before adding a syllable beginning with a vowel (*-able, -ed, -er, -ing, -y*):

brag: bragged, bragging
win: winner, winning
scrap: scrapper, scrapping, scrappy

fat: fatted, fatter, fatty
Exception—gas: gassed, gassing; *but* gaseous, gasify

The consonant is not doubled in words with two vowel letters before the final consonant (*daub, daubed; seed, seeded*) or in words ending with two consonants (*help, helped; hold, holding*).

2. In words of more than one syllable ending in one vowel

plus one consonant, the final consonant is traditionally doubled if the word is accented on the last syllable. A few words so accented are very common:

con trol': controlled, controller, controlling
re fer': referred, referring
Also: confer' equip' excel' infer' occur' prefer'

If the accent of the lengthened word shifts to an earlier syllable, the consonant is not doubled:

infer'—in'ference   prefer'—pref'erence   refer'—ref'erence

If the word is not accented on the last syllable, the consonant need not be doubled, and in American usage preferably is not doubled, though usage is divided on many words:

com'bat [or com bat']: combated or combatted, combating or combatting, *but always* com'ba tant

A few are never doubled:

ben'e fit: benefited, benefiting
o'pen: opened, opening
par'allel: paralleled, paralleling

Usage on *bias, diagram, kidnap, quarrel, travel, worship* is divided, but usually one consonant is preferred.

3. The part of the rule for doubling final consonants that applies to words of one syllable is useful, because it keeps distinct a number of pairs of words similar in appearance:

bat: batted, batting—bate: bated, bating
din: dinned, dinning—dine: dined, dining (*but* dinner)
grip: gripped, gripping—gripe: griped, griping
plan: planned, planning—plane: planed, planing
scrap: scrapped, scrapping—scrape: scraped, scraping

The boy who wrote "The scene in which she almost kills her husband is griping" did not convey the meaning that he intended.

4. Words already ending in a doubled consonant keep both consonants before suffixes beginning with a vowel but may lose one consonant before suffixes beginning with another consonant:

enroll: enrolled, enrolling; *but* enrolment or enrollment
install: installed, installing, installation; *but* instalment or installment
fulfill: fulfilled, fulfilling; *but* fulfillment or fulfilment
skill: skilled; *but* skillful or skilful

These rules are of some help, but they also suggest that the safest way to be sure of the established spelling of any word is to check it in a good dictionary.

doubt • Idioms with *doubt*:

1. *Negative* (when there is no real doubt), *doubt that*:

Formal: I do not doubt that he meant well.

General: I don't doubt but that [sometimes: but what] he will come.

2. *Positive* (when doubt exists), *that, whether, if*:

Formal: I doubt whether he meant it that way.

I doubt that he meant it that way. [indicating unbelief really more than doubt]

General: I doubt if he meant it that way.

draft, draught • The second spelling is now chiefly British.

drought—drouth • Both forms are in good use, *drought* probably more common in Formal English, *drouth* in General. Two pronunciations also occur, /drout/ and /drouth/, which do not always correspond to the spellings.

It is true the longest drouth will end in rain.—ROBERT FROST

drunk • It seems to take courage to use this General word. We either go Formal—*intoxicated*; or grasp at respectability through euphemisms—*under the influence of liquor* or *indulged to excess*; or make a weak attempt at humor with one of the dozens of Informal phrases like *looped, bombed, stoned*. But *drunk* is the word.

due to • The preposition *due to* is especially interesting as an illustration of the difficulties a new locution has in getting textbook recognition.

Due was originally an adjective and is still most strictly used as one: "The epidemic was *due* to the brown rat," in which *due* modifies *epidemic*. But *due to* as it is used in "The Mediterranean has its share of minority problems and they have become more prominent *due to* Italo-British tension in that area" (*Kaltenborn Edits the News,* p. 99) has long been popular, in magazine writing as well as in literature by writers of undisputed respectability. Advocates of strict usage have set themselves sternly against it, forgetting perhaps that *owing to,* which they have suggested should be substituted for it, has come from a participle to a preposition in exactly the same way.

An excellent example of a linguist's approach to a matter of divided and debatable usage is John S. Kenyon's treatment of *due to* in *American Speech,* 1930, 6:61-70. He presents an imposing number of quotations from current writers, discusses the history of the phrase, and concludes:

Strong as is my own prejudice against the prepositional use of *due to,* I greatly fear it has staked its claim and squatted in our midst alongside of and in exact imitation of *owing to,* its aristocratic neighbor and respected fellow citizen.

A study reported by Bryant shows that in some thousands of pages of books, periodicals, and newspapers, *due to* as a preposition occurred in 56 percent of the instances, *because of* in 25 percent and *owing to* in 19 percent ("Current English Forum," *College English,* 1954, 15:478). And in her *Current American Usage* (1962), Margaret Bryant presents further evidence to confirm the established status of the practice (p. 81). A person may not care to use *due to* as a preposition, but in view of actual usage today he hardly has the right to deny it to others.

E •

1. The "long *e*" sound /ē/ is found variously spelled in stressed syllables: b*e*, s*ee*d, rec*ei*ve, sh*ie*ld, m*ea*t, p*eo*ple, k*ey*, qu*ay*, *ae*gis, Ph*oe*be, mach*i*ne.

An unstressed or lightly stressed *e* may vary in pronunciation from long /ē/ in platform delivery of a word such as *descend* /dē send′/ to a short /i/ or /ə/ in ordinary speech /di send′/; *hero* and *zero* may be /hir′ō/ or /hē′rō/, /zir′ō/ or /zē′rō/.

2. The "short *e*" sound /e/ is also variously spelled, as in f*e*d, l*ea*ther, b*u*ry, m*a*ny, s*ai*d, l*eo*pard, fr*ie*nd, s*ay*s.

Before final *r* or *r* plus a consonant, short *e* represents the sound in *learn, fern, err* marked /ėr/—/lėrn/, /fėrn/, /ėr/.

3. "unstressed *e*" (as in *kindness, difference*) represents a slight and rather obscure sound in speech. It may represent short /i/ /kīnd′nis/, or the neutral vowel sound represented in this book by /ə/ /kīnd′nəs/.

Before *l, m, n,* and *r* unstressed *e* is often a part of the consonant ("syllabic" *l, m, n, r*). In this book such syllables are represented by ə or by ļ m̞ n̞ r̞: *settle* /set′əl/ or /set′ļ/, *wooden* /wood′ən/ or /wood′n̞/.

4. Miscellaneous sounds represented by *e*: *e* may represent /ã/ before *r,* as in *there* /ᴛнãr/; /ä/ as in *sergeant* /sär′jənt/ and many words in British usage which in the United States have /ėr/ as in *derby* /dėr′bē/ and *clerk* /klėrk/.

5. Silent or mute *e*: In general, words spelled with a final silent *e* drop the *-e* before additions beginning with a vowel and keep it before additions beginning with a consonant:

change: changed, changing; changeless (*but* changeable)
grease: greased, greaser; greasewood
like: likable, liking; likeness

pursue: pursuant, pursued, pursuing
use: usable, used, using; useful, useless
Exceptions: argument, awful, duly, ninth; judgment (*sometimes* judgement)

A few other exceptions keep *-e* to indicate pronunciation, chiefly after *c* and *g* before suffixes beginning with *a* or *o*:

change: changeable   courage: courageous   notice: noticeable

(See *-ce, -ge.)

In a few words the *-e* is retained to avoid confusion with other words or to keep the connection with the root word obvious:

lineage /lin'e ij/ vs. linage /līn'ij/
singeing /sin'jing/, dyeing /dī'ing/

each •
1. *Each,* though singular in form, never occurs without an expressed or implied reference to more than one. Since the idea of plurality is always present when *each* is used, it inevitably attracts plural forms. In speech and increasingly in writing, *each* is regarded as a collective when the plural idea is uppermost (compare *every):

Each of these people undoubtedly modified Latin in accordance with *their* own speech habits.—ALBERT C. BAUGH, *A History of the English Language,* p. 32

2. In Formal usage *each* is singular:

Each of the three *has* a different instructor.
Each ran as fast as *his* legs could carry *him.*

3. As an adjective, *each* does not affect the number of the verb; when the subject modified by *each* is plural, the verb is also plural:

Each *applicant has* to fill out the blank in full.
Three *students,* also from this county, each *receive* a scholarship.
They each *feel* keenly about it.

(Reference: Russell Thomas, "Concord Based on *Meaning* versus Concord Based on *Form,*" *College English,* 1939, 1:38-45.)

each and every • *Each and every* may have its place, but the phrase has been greatly overused.

each other • *Each other,* basically used of two, is also in good use for more than two, though Formal usage more often has *one another.*

General: The men were shouting to each other.

Formal: The men from farms on both sides of the river were shouting to one another.

(See *Reciprocal pronouns. References: Russell Thomas, " 'Each Other' or 'One Another'?" *College English,* 1957, 18: 422-424; Bryant, pp. 82-83.)

Early Modern English • See *English language § 4.

Echo phrases • Sometimes it is convenient to form a phrase on the pattern of one well known or to echo one less known but apt. This is a type of allusion. The echo phrase may be either serious or light:

I have seen American textbooks in which lesson after lesson is devoted to the lofty purpose of eliminating *got.* As though the fear of *got* were the beginning of wisdom. ["The fear of God is the beginning of wisdom."]—P. B. BALLARD, *Thought and Language,* p. 205

... but democracy means simply the bludgeoning of the people by the people for the people.—OSCAR WILDE, *The Soul of Man Under Socialism*

Ask not what broadcasting can do for you. Ask what you can do for broadcasting.—NEWTON N. MINOW, an address to the National Association of Broadcasters, May 9, 1961

In General writing, echoes of common phrases usually fit, and in more Formal writing there is certainly no harm in a writer showing that he has done some reading, but a parade of echo phrases may seem pretentious.

-ed • A conspicuous spelling problem is the omission of *-ed* in past verb forms (§ 1) and in modifiers made from verbs (§ 2) and from nouns (§ 3). Students often raise questions about these forms, and teachers are much concerned about them. They must also be a problem for editors, who have to insert many *-ed*'s in copy. The *-ed* is rarely omitted in published works, but it is frequently missing in unedited copy—in menus, in signs, and in letters.

To understand the situation it will help to consider the processes that have already led to many accepted forms without *-ed.* In the development of Modern English a final /d/ sound has become a /t/ sound before voiceless consonants /f, p, s, t .../: *watched* /wocht/ *pot* /pot/. Often the words in *-ed* come before *to* or other words beginning with *t* so that the two sounds are assimilated to one: *relieved to hear* /ri lēv tə hir/, *released time* /ri lēs tīm/.

1. *In verb forms.* This trait of pronunciation has led to the complete loss of the /d/ sound in the past tense and past participle of a few verbs, or to an optional form without the end-

ing: *bet, burst, cast, knit, quit, wed.* (Compare the verbs in § 4 that are regularly spelled with a final *t.*)

But carrying this practice into the spelling of past forms of regular verbs irritates educated readers. In these verbs it is well to remember that in spite of omission or assimilation of the *-ed* in speech, *the written form of the past tense and of the past participle should have -ed.* In proofreading go by your eye rather than your ear.

> He was *unprejudiced* toward all.
>
> I am forced to admit I *liked* the show.

(See *used to—the most common offender in this group.)

2. *In modifiers from verbs.* The past participle is commonly used as a modifier: *abandoned farms, dressed chickens.* The same features of pronunciation are at work here, and many fixed phrases without *-ed* are Standard usage: *butter pecan, frame house, grade school, ice cream, oil cloth, salt pork, skim milk.* (Many of these were opposed when they first appeared.) Others of the same type are sometimes found in print but are debatable: *advance headquarters, bottle beer, whip cream.* In all of these except *whip cream* the resulting form could be regarded as a noun used in the function of an adjective so that these expressions seem natural to English speakers.

A routine solution would be to go by a dictionary, but dictionaries will be found to vary, and many of the terms have not attracted the attention of dictionary makers. Two principles may help: (1) For a word group that is well established in speech, the oral form is likely to be appropriate in a written context reflecting its common use; (2) for others, appropriateness to other traits of style will be a useful guide. In Formal writing only those that have been generally accepted, as in the first group of the preceding paragraph, should be used. In Informal writing, especially if it suggests speech, more could stand. In General writing the more conventional form of *-ed* is advisable.

3. *In modifiers from nouns.* Frequently *-ed* is added to nouns to form adjectival modifiers: *barbed wire* (wire with barbs), *long-haired, moneyed, one-armed.* No verb is involved in the derivation of these terms. Consequently when the *-ed* is dropped the result is a noun used in the function of an adjective, a construction that is increasing in current English. In many group words the form without the *-ed* is well established: *one-arm bandit* and *barbwire* occur, and there are *blue-back speller, high-heel shoes, seven-room house, king-size cigaret, hard-surface road, wing chair.* (See *size.)

Forms like these are appropriate in writing and similar forms are also, if they can be taken as nouns used as modifiers.

When a noun is not suggested or if the modifier is not conventionally bound to the headword, the *-ed* should be kept: *advanced courses, middle-aged, old-fashioned, one-sided.* (References: Curme, *Parts of Speech,* pp. 260-296; W. Nelson Francis, "More of the Lost *-ed,*" *Word Study,* Oct. 1954, pp. 6-7; Ralph H. Lane, "Passing Participles," *Word Study,* Feb. 1955, pp. 1-3.)

4. *-ed or -t.* In the past tense and past participles of verbs in which the *-ed* is (or may be) pronounced as /t/, simpler spelling has *-t.* A few words have been rather generally adopted with sound and spelling and with alteration of the root vowel: *crept, dreamt* /dremt/, *leapt* /lept/, *slept;* also *spelt.*

5. *-ed or 'd.* When *-ed* is added to words that are formed unusually, *'d* is sometimes used instead, as in *shanghai'd, ok'd.*

Editorial we • See *we § 2.

-ee • This is an ending derived from French denoting the one who receives or is directly affected by an act or grant of power, the opposite of nouns ending in *-er* (*payer,* one who pays; *payee,* one who is paid): *employee, draftee, grantee.*

It takes two people to say a thing—a sayee as well as a sayer. The one is as essential to any true saying as the other.—SAMUEL BUTLER, "Thought and Language"

In French one *e* would indicate masculine, two feminine, which distinction sometimes leads to the spelling *employe* in English.

effect—affect • See *affect—effect.

e.g. • See *Abbreviations, *namely and other introductory words.

-ei-, -ie- • Words with *-ie-* are much more common than words *-ei-* and on the whole give less spelling trouble. The most common sound represented by *-ie-* is /ē/.

Some words with *-ie-* are:

achieve	field	hygiene	priest
belief	fiend	mischief	shriek
believe	financier	niece	siege
cashier	friend	piece	sieve
chief	grieve	pier	view

Plural of nouns ending in *-y*: *academies   companies   lotteries*

Third person singular present of verbs in *-y*: *cries   fortifies   fries*

After *c*, *-ie-* is seldom used, but it does occur: *ancient, species.*

There are fewer words with *-ei-*, but their spelling needs careful watching. The most common sound spelled *-ei-* is /ā/:

deign	freight	neighbor	skein
eight	heinous	reign	sleigh
feign	inveigle [or /ē/]	rein	veil
feint	neigh	seine	weigh

A number of words spell the sound /ē/ with *-ei-*, especially after *c*:

ceiling	leisure	receive
conceive	neither	seize
either	perceive	weird

And a few words spell other sounds with *-ei-*

counterfeit   forfeit   height   heir   their

Again pronunciation is not a reliable guide.

In some words *i* and *e* stand together but are parts of different syllables:

fi ery   headi er   si esta

(Reference: Donald W. Lee, *College English,* 1944, 6:156-159.)

either •

1. *Either* means primarily "one or the other of two," as an adjective (either way you look at it) or as a pronoun (bring me either). For emphasis the pronoun is usually supported by *one* (bring me either one). Used of three or more objects (either of the corners), it is loose and rare; "any of the corners" is the more usual idiom.

Either is usually construed as singular, though its use as a plural is increasing (Fries, *AEG*, p. 56):

Either Grace or Phyllis is [*or:* are] expected.

2. *Either* with the meaning "each" is rare in present English and definitely Formal: *broil the fish on either side, with one turning—on either side of the river. Each* or *both* (*both sides*) would be more common in such expressions.

3. The pronunciation /ī'ᴛʜər/ or /ī'ᴛʜə/ has not made so much progress in the United States as in England, and outside some communities in New England and a few families or circles that radiate from New England it is usually an affectation. Say /ē'ᴛʜər/, unless your family or social group generally says /ī'ᴛʜə(r)/. Similarly, *neither* is usually /nē'ᴛʜər/, occasionally /nī'ᴛʜə(r)/.

4. *Either* is also used as an adverb of emphasis: He didn't *come either.* (For its use with *or* see *Correlative conjunctions.)

elder, eldest • These archaic forms of *old,* which survive in Formal English, are used only for members of the same family —"the elder brother," "our eldest daughter"—and in some phrases like "the elder statesmen."

Ellipsis (...) •

1. A punctuation mark of three or sometimes four spaced periods to indicate that something is omitted is called an *ellipsis* (plural *ellipses*). Formerly asterisks (***) were used, but they have been generally discontinued because they are too conspicuous. When an ellipsis comes at the end of a statement marked with a period, that period is added, as in the first and third instances in this passage:

As Beret drank in these words the tenseness all left her; the weapon she had seized dropped from her hand; her body straightened up; she looked about in wide-eyed wonder.... Were those church bells she heard? ... But the voices were beginning again on the other side of the wall.... Hush! Hush!—O. E. Rölvaag, *Giants in the Earth*

2. *a*–The ellipsis is an editorial mark showing where a word or more, which is not needed for the purpose of the writer using the quotation, has been left out. The preceding sentence might be quoted with the *which* clause omitted: "The ellipsis is an editorial mark showing where a word or more ... has been left out." Every such omission in quoted matter should be indicated by an ellipsis. If the omission is a line or more in a verse quotation, the periods should be extended to the full length of the line.

b–An ellipsis is also used to show a series or enumeration continued beyond the units named; it is equivalent to *et cetera*:

the coordinating conjunctions (and, but, for ...)

3. In narrative an ellipsis is used to mark hesitation in the action, suggesting passage of time, as in the quotation above from *Giants in the Earth,* and in the quotation below from Conrad Aiken:

"Well—I can see this much. You *are* in love with her. Or you couldn't possibly be such a fool. But it's precisely when you're in love that you need to keep your wits about you. Or the wits of your friends.... You *mustn't* marry her, Harry."

"Well—I don't know."

"No! ... It would be ruinous."—Conrad Aiken, "Spider! Spider!"

It is also used as an *end-stop to mark a statement that is unfinished or is let die away:

I go away to a town, a big strange town, and try to hammer out a good book. The days come, the days go, and big ships sail into the harbor.... —Albert Halper, "Young Writer Remembering Chicago"

4. An ellipsis is sometimes used in advertising copy or in instructions to separate statements for emphasis:

RINSE BY HAND . . . Rinse thoroughly to remove all soap . . . DO NOT WRING . . . as wringing will tend to add wrinkles.

5. For the use of the word as a grammatical term, see the next entry.

Elliptical constructions • *Ellipsis* and *elliptical* refer to a construction in which an element that can be supplied from a neighboring construction is not expressed:

I work a good deal harder than you [*Supply*: work].

The notion of ellipsis has often been misused to apply to the shorter way of expressing a notion. A person may write either:

We went through the same experience that you did. [*or*]
We went through the same experience you did.
"Are you going?" "No, I can't (go)."

It can of course be argued with considerable cogency that in the first two constructions above there is an ellipsis following *did*. But for ordinary purposes of grammatical analysis it is safer to deal only with the words actually expressed. The second construction is not necessarily elliptical but an alternative one; a *that* is not "omitted," it just isn't thought or spoken or written. The choice between the longer and shorter constructions is a matter of style rather than grammar. Formal English uses the longer ones, tends to fill out all constructions. General and Informal English use the shorter constructions freely. (See Ch. 8, "Long and short constructions," p. 317, and compare *Clauses § 3a. References: Curme, *Syntax*, p. 2 and index references; Jespersen, *The Philosophy of Grammar*, p. 306 and index references.)

else •
1. Because *else* follows the word it modifies (usually a pronoun), as the last word in a noun phrase, it takes the sign of the possessive:

I hated wearing somebody else's clothes.
At first he thought the book was his, but he finally decided it was somebody else's.

2. *Else* is sometimes used in speech as an *intensive, but in writing it is likely to be *deadwood and should be removed:

Finally I started talking, just to hear something [else] besides the roar of the motor.

3. *Nothing else but* is sometimes used for emphasis in speech, but the *else* would not ordinarily be used in writing:

Written: There was nothing but wheat as far as you could see.

Spoken: There was nothing else but wheat as far as you could see.

emigrate—immigrate • *Emigrate* means to move out of a country or region, *immigrate* to move into a country. An *emigrant* from Norway would be an *immigrant* to the United States.

Emphasis •
Revision: *Strengthen the emphasis of this passage by one or more of the methods suggested below.*   *Emph*

The purpose of emphasis is to get your reader to accept your ideas with the same degree of importance as you do—the most important as most important, the less important as less important, the incidental as incidental.

Ways in which emphasis can be conveyed are discussed more fully in other sections of the *Guide-Index*, referred to in this summary.

1. *Position.* In most types of writing, except news stories and reference works, the most emphatic position is the end and the second most emphatic position is the beginning. Emphasis by position applies to sentences (see *Word order and Ch. 8, p. 323), to paragraphs (pp. 133-139), and to whole papers (pp. 143-149, 184-186).

2. *Mass or proportion.* Position is supported by the amount of space given to a particular point. Roughly speaking, the more important an idea the more space it deserves. Watch the last topics in a paper, which are likely to be so hurried over and hence underdeveloped that they do not seem as important as their writer intends.

3. *Distinction of expression.* In general, *big words and long *function words and phrases weaken a statement, as do abstract and indefinite words. Fresh, concrete words in direct and economical constructions make for a clear-cut emphasis. (See Ch. 9, p. 372.)

4. *Separation, distinctness.* Careful paragraphing clarifies and emphasizes the relationship between main blocks of material. A short simple sentence following a sequence of fairly long or elaborately constructed sentences can be an excellent means of emphasizing an idea.

5. *Repetition.* Repetition of significant words drives them home, and repetition of statements either in similar or different words, perhaps figurative expressions, is a useful form of emphasis if it is not overdone. (See p. 320.) Repeating a structural pattern (especially in a series that builds to a climax) is a device for emphasizing as well as clarifying. (See pp. 321-323.)

6. *Intensives.* Words added to intensify meaning are generally used in speaking but they are less useful in writing. (See *very and p. 319.)

Labeling a statement "It is interesting to note," "This is an important phase of the subject" is seldom effective. Such phrases can be eliminated in revision by making the fact or opinion stand out in other ways.

7. *Mechanical devices.* Writing and printing have various mechanical means—*underlining (italics), *capitals, emphatic punctuation—for stressing words and passages. These devices are often used by amateur writers in an attempt to make up for deficiencies in style or content. (See p. 318.)

(Compare *Exclamations, *Negatives § 1.)

employee • This spelling is much more common than *employe.* (See *-ee.)

en-, in- • *In-* is either a native English prefix or a prefix of Latin origin; *en-* is the same Latin prefix modified in French. (*Em-* and *im-* are variant forms.) For several common words usage is divided, though usually one form is more prevalent. Fowler and other British sources are not safe guides to American usage on this matter because Americans tend to use *in-* more than the English do. The safest way is to consult a recent American dictionary, but even American dictionaries do not always agree, so that the choice is often a matter of style.

Here are a few samples with the dictionaries' preference first where there seems to be one:

encase—incase
enclose—inclose
encumber—incumber
endorse—indorse
engulf, rarely ingulf
entrust—intrust

encrust—incrust
infold or enfold
inquire—enquire
insure—ensure (Always *insure* in the financial sense, *insurance,* etc.)

-ence, -ance (-ent, -ant) • See *-ance, -ence.

End-stop • *End-stop* is a mark of punctuation—usually a period, exclamation mark, or question mark—used at the end of a sentence. In writing conversation, the double or two-em dash (——*Dash § 8) is used as an end-stop when a speech is interrupted. The *ellipsis (. . .) is often written as an end-stop for a sentence that is intentionally left unfinished or that is let die away.

When two end-stops would fall together at the end of a sentence, as when a question stands within a sentence, only one mark, the more emphatic or more necessary for meaning, is used:

> When we say, for example, that Miss A. *plays* well, only an irredeemable outsider would reply, "Plays what?" So, too, ...—C. ALPHONSO SMITH, *Studies in English Syntax,* p. 8

(For further comment on end-stops see the articles on the individual marks. See also *Verse form.)

English language •

1. *Indo-European.* English is one of a group of languages deriving from what is called Indo-European, a parent tongue for which no written records exist. The family includes most of the languages of Europe, a number of languages of India, the languages of Persia and of certain adjoining regions. It is usually classified into nine branches, English belonging to the group known as Germanic. (On p. 598 is a diagram showing the relations in greatly simplified form.)

A brief selection of facts about the different periods of our language will show some of the roots of the richness—and complexity—of Modern English.

2. *Old English, 450-1050.* The Angles, Saxons, and Jutes brought to England from their old homes in northwestern Europe somewhat differing Lowland West Germanic dialects. They pushed back the native Celts from the part of the island they conquered, so that Celtic speech contributed almost nothing to English but survived as Welsh, Cornish, and Highland Scotch. The conquerors' languages developed into several main dialects—Northumbrian, Mercian, Kentish, West Saxon—which together are known as Old English (or Anglo-Saxon). These dialectal variations still leave their marks in the regional speech of various parts of England. Most of these dialects made some contribution to the Standard language, but it was principally from the East Midland dialect, a descendant of Mercian, that Modern English developed.

Perhaps a quarter—no precise figures are possible—of the total present English vocabulary goes back to the words of Old English. The modern descendants of Old English words are often changed in meaning and almost always in pronunciation, according to regular processes: Old English *stan* /stän/ becomes Modern English *stone, ban* /bän/ becomes *bone,* etc. Our common verbs (*go, sit, eat, fight, whistle*), many of our most common nouns (*meat, house, breakfast, land, water*) and adjectives (*fast, slow, high*) go back to Old English words, so that though less than a fourth of the words in an unabridged dic-

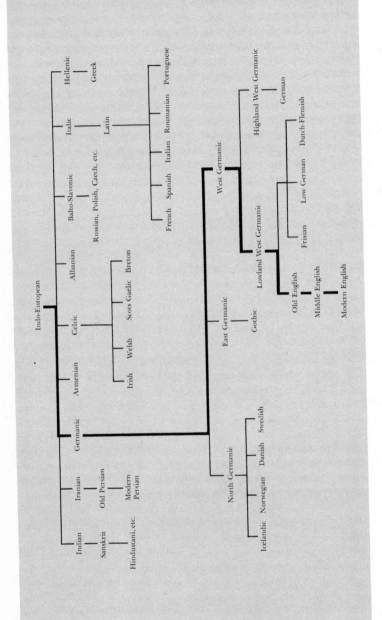

tionary are of this "native" origin, they play a part in our speech out of all proportion to their number.

Furthermore, most of the machinery of our language is from Old English: the articles *a, an, the*; most of the pronouns (*I, we, us, . . .*); the inflectional endings of nouns: house—house*s*, boy—boy*s*, boy'*s*; of adjectives and adverbs: merry—merri*er*—merri*est* or *more* merry—*most* merry; harsh*ly*, kind*ly*; the forms of verbs: pass, pass*es*, pass*ed*, pass*ing*. These endings are applied to words taken from other languages (*indict-ed, politi-cal-ly*), so that although three quarters of the vocabulary may come from Romance or other languages, the borrowed words are built into an English pattern. And when we consider word order, we see that the texture of English is Germanic too. For all these reasons, English must be regarded as a Germanic language. Furthermore, our habits of pronunciation have remained Germanic. Unlike most other Indo-European languages, we show heavy accent by greater loudness and lack of accent by absence of loudness, and we like the accent to stay put, usually on the first syllable of a word.

Within the Old English period the practice of absorbing words from other languages was already strong. A number of Latin words, some of them originally Greek, were taken in, most of them pertaining to the church (*abbot, priest, school*), though there was still a tendency to translate the elements of the Latin words into Old English elements, so that we have *gospel* from the Old English *god spell,* meaning "good news," which is a translation of the Greek-Latin *evangelium.*

In the ninth century the east and north of England was conquered by the Danes, whose language left a large number of words and forms, both because it was closely related to the language then spoken in England, and because of the contact between the two peoples. The *sk* words are likely to date from this mixture—*sky, skin, scream, skirt* (a cousin of the Old English *shirt,* both related to *short*), place names ending in *-by* and *-thorp,* and a number of common words like *odd, anger, egg.*

A number of the most conspicuous irregularities of Modern English existed in Old English: **be, is, are, was, were, been* as forms of the verb "to be"; *may, might, shall, should, ought,* and the other auxiliaries; pronouns—*I, my, me, we, our, us, he, it. . . .* These words are in such common use that they retain patterns of inflection which have otherwise disappeared. Here and there we have remnants of Old English forms that lost out in the development of the language, like the plurals *children, oxen, men, geese,* instead of the regular plural in *-s.*

A considerable body of writing from the Old English period survives. It includes poems, sermons, riddles, history, translations from Latin, and most conspicuously the *Anglo-Saxon Chronicles, Beowulf,* and the large group of writings and translations in West Saxon made by or at the court of Alfred the Great, King of the West Saxons, 871-901. Some 30,000 different words are found in this literature.

3. *Middle English, 1050-1450.* The conquest of England by the Norman French in 1066 coincided with the beginning of Early Middle English. The speakers of Old English in the main became serfs, servants, everything but leaders in affairs. Their language was seldom used in official proceedings and rarely written. One result was the loss of the more elevated and abstract Old English words that had been used in poetry.

As a result of the Old English habit of pronouncing unaccented words and syllables lightly, the endings of most words were obscured and could no longer be distinguished. A far-reaching development of this period was therefore the further decline and in some instances complete loss of the inflectional endings of Old English. The definite article no longer had distinctive forms (our *the* is the sole descendant of ten grammatically significant forms in Old English); *-n* disappeared from the infinitive of most verbs; and other unstressed endings also dropped away. This process went far to make English one of the least inflected of Indo-European languages and far more dependent on word order to show the relations of words in sentences than Old English had been.

On the other hand the vocabulary of the invaders made headway. The words for the acts of the ruling class—*war, government, law, social activity*—were Norman French and they have generally come down to Modern English: *siege, soldier, judge, jury, suit, dinner, servant, obey.* The majority of the Norman French words were ultimately from Latin, though considerably changed in form. For many notions Modern English has two roughly synonymous words, one Latin or French, one Old English: *dress—clothes, aid—help, cottage—hut, solitary—lonely.* Some French spellings made their way into English, like *gu* for hard *g—guest, guess*; *qu* for *cw—queen* for Old English *cwen.*

In 1362 English was restored as the language of the law courts, an official recognition that it had established itself once more in higher circles. The speech of the region around London was now the basis for future development not only of the spoken language but of the literary language. How far English had incorporated French resources can be seen from a few lines by Chaucer, written in the 1380's, French in italics:

> "What folk ben ye, that at myn hoomcominge
> *Perturben* so my *feste* with *cryinge?*"

> Quod Theseus, "have ye so greet *envye*
> Of myn *honour*, that thus *compleyne* and *crye*?
> Or who hath yow misboden, or *offended*?
> And telleth me if it may been *amended*;
> And why that ye ben clothed thus in blak?"
> —GEOFFREY CHAUCER, "The Knightes Tale"

Except for the Old English *misboden* ("insulted"), all of these words, both native and French, are in use today, though *quod* (quoth) is archaic, and *feste* is *fête*; in spite of some differences in spelling, the passage can be read by anyone. Many of the words show inflectional endings that have since been dropped or changed: *ben* (for *are* or *be*), perturb*en*, tell*eth*, and the final *e* of nouns.

4. *Early Modern English, 1450-1700.* In this period we have the beginnings of conscious concern for the language and actual or attempted "improvement" by manipulation of words and constructions—"schoolmastering the speech." The early printers, from 1476 on, felt the need for uniformity, especially in spelling and choice of word forms, and began the domination in these matters that has been exercised by publishers ever since. Translators and writers sometimes considered the language rough, unpolished, incapable of doing what Latin and Greek had done and what Italian could do. They set about enlarging the vocabulary, chiefly by transliterating words from Greek and Latin. A substantial portion of Modern English words are pretty directly from classical languages, and very often we have two words that go back to the same Latin original, one brought in by the Norman French and one taken in directly later: *paint—picture, certainty—certitude.* Latin was the language of the Church at the beginning of this period, though after the Reformation the Book of Common Prayer, and after 1611 the King James translation of the Bible, became tremendous forces for elevated English. Most books of the learned world were in Latin, and college classes were conducted in Latin, even in America, until two centuries ago.

The spoken language was vigorous and was written down in some popular literature, but most literature that has survived was from the hands of educated men and conscious stylists. Shakespeare shows the complete range, from formal, Latinized lines to rough-and-tumble lines, often combining the elevated and the simple in a single speech:

> No, this my hand will rather
> The multitudinous seas incarnadine
> Making the green one red.

Prose style lagged behind poetic, especially in sentence sense, producing "sentence heaps" running to hundreds of words. In the sixteen hundreds the wealth of experiment of the preceding century was analyzed and many words and phrases were disposed of. The less useful and more ponderous of the Latin importations were dropped, and interest in native words increased the proportion of native words in use. Prose style especially developed in directness and sureness until in Dryden Modern English prose is usually said to be established. In spite of small differences in idiom and word order, the following two paragraphs do not seem 300 years old:

To begin, then, with Shakespeare. He was the man who of all modern, and perhaps ancient poets, had the largest and most comprehensive soul. All the images of Nature were still present to him, and he drew them, not laboriously, but luckily; when he describes anything, you more than see it, you feel it too. Those who accuse him to have wanted learning, give him the greater commendation: he was naturally learned; he needed not the spectacles of books to read Nature; he looked inwards, and found her there. I cannot say he is everywhere alike; were he so, I should do him injury to compare him with the greatest of mankind. He is many times flat, insipid; his comic wit degenerating into clenches, his serious swelling into bombast. But he is always great, when some great occasion is presented to him; no man can say he ever had a fit subject for his wit, and did not then raise himself as high above the rest of the poets,

Quantum lenta solent inter viburna cupressi.
[As the cypresses tower among the humbler trees.]

The consideration of this made Mr. Hales of Eaton say, that there was no subject of which any poet ever writ, but he would produce it much better done in Shakespeare; and however others are now generally preferred before him, yet the age wherein he lived, which had contemporaries with him Fletcher and Jonson, never equalled them to him in their esteem: and in the last king's court, when Ben's reputation was at highest, Sir John Suckling, and with him the greater part of the courtiers, set our Shakespeare far above him.—JOHN DRYDEN, *An Essay of Dramatic Poesy* (1668)

5. *Modern English, 1700-* . This *Index* gives a partial picture of current English, especially as it appears in print, and suggests in some of its specific articles changes that have taken place in the last few generations. Such articles may be taken as continuations of this brief historical sketch, for by 1700 English had become substantially the language we now know and use. The vocabulary has been enlarged in the last two centuries chiefly from two sources: borrowings from India and America and from peoples touched by British and American traders; and through scientific coinages, chiefly from Greek and Latin roots. There has been, especially in recent years, a tendency toward shorter and more direct sentences. The paragraph has become a more distinct unit in written expression. One important development has been the study of the different varieties of usage, and different traditions of style, especially Formal, General, and Informal styles.

Today English as the native language of England, the British Commonwealth, and the United States is spoken by about 300,000,000 people—certainly the largest group of people who can easily understand each other in their native language. In addition English is probably the most important second language in the world today.

The result of this varied history is a language full of anomalies, but of unusual range and flexibility, capable of great subtlety and force of expression.

(See also *American and British usage. *Analogy in language, *Basic English, *Business English, *Change in language, oral and written, *Experiment in written English, *Foreign words in English, *Latin and English, *Linguistics, *Newspaper English, *Origin of words, *Parts of speech, *Pronunciation, *Reading and writing, *Shoptalk, *Spoken and written English, *Style, *Usage. References: Baugh; Robertson; Otto Jespersen, *Growth and Structure of the English Language* (various editions), which describes the accumulation of the English vocabulary, and his *Language*, New York, 1923, Part iv, which discusses language change especially apropos of English; Morton W. Bloomfield and Leonard Newmark, *A Linguistic Introduction to the History of English*, New York, 1963; Thomas Pyles, *The Origins and Development of the English Language*, New York, 1964.)

enormity—enormousness • Because *enormity* looks like a more compact way of expressing the idea of *enormousness,* it is sometimes used in that sense. But it usually means "enormously evil," "great wickedness"—as in "the enormity of the crime."

en route • Pronounced /on/ *or* /en/ *or* /in rüt′/; or imitating French, /än rüt′/. "On the way" or "going to" often fits a sentence more naturally:

They were en route [on the way] to Philadelphia.

enthuse • *Enthuse* is a back formation (see *Origin of words § 3d) from *enthusiasm*. Many people object to it, and some dictionaries label it "colloquial" or "informal." But *enthuse* seems to be an improvement over the only locution we have for the idea, the clumsy *be enthusiastic over* or *about.*

Epigrams • An *epigram* is a short, pithy statement, in verse or prose, usually with a touch of wit. In prose this means really a detached or detachable and "quotable" sentence. In consecutive prose, epigrams sometimes become too prominent, attract too much attention to themselves, or suggest straining for effect. But they can focus attention or put a fact or opinion so that a reader can remember (and perhaps repeat) it:

Conscience is the inner voice which warns us that someone may be looking.—H. L. MENCKEN, *The Vintage Mencken*, p. 231

It's no disgrace to be poor, but it might as well be.

Bees are not as busy as we think they are. They jest can't buzz any slower.—KIN HUBBARD, *The Sayings of Abe Martin*

Closely related to epigrams are *aphorisms*—pithy statements but more likely to be abstract and not necessarily witty. The essays of Francis Bacon are packed with aphorisms, and some modern essayists use them too:

To spend too much time in studies is sloth; to use them too much for ornament, is affectation; to make judgment wholly by their rules, is the humour of a scholar.... Read not to contradict and confute; nor to believe and take for granted; nor to find talk and discourse; but to weigh and consider.... Reading maketh a full man; conference a ready man; and writing an exact man.—FRANCIS BACON, "Of Studies"

Proverbs are often-quoted, concrete expressions of popular wisdom. They are likely to make observations on character or conduct. As a rule their authors are unknown:

It never rains but it pours.

Still waters run deep.

It's hard for an empty sack to stand upright.

A special type of epigram is the *paradox,* which makes a statement that as it stands contradicts fact or common sense or itself and yet suggests a truth or at least a half truth:

All generalizations are false, including this one.

Dr. Richards is no mystic; he is a behaviourist, a behaviourist being a psychologist who does not believe in psychology.—P. B. BALLARD, *Thought and Language*, p. 265

(Reference: *Oxford Dictionary of Proverbs*, Oxford, 1936, compiled by William G. Smith.)

-er, -or • Names of persons or things performing an act (nouns of agent) and some other nouns are formed in English by adding *-er* to a verb (*doer, killer, painter, thinker*), but many end in *-or*, chiefly nouns taken from Latin or French (*assessor, prevaricator*).

Since the two endings are pronounced the same /ər/, it is hard to tell whether *-er* or *-or* should be written. Here are a few as samples; a dictionary will have to settle most questions.

With -er:

advertiser	consumer	peddler (or pedlar)
better (or bettor)	debater	promoter
condenser	manufacturer	propeller

With -or:

accelerator	conductor	motor
administrator	distributor	objector
author	editor	proprietor
bachelor	governor	spectator
carburetor	inventor	sponsor
chiropractor	(or inventer)	supervisor
competitor	legislator	ventilator

There are a few nouns of agent ending in *-ar*: *beggar, burglar, liar.*

-er, -re • Many words formerly ending in *-re* are now spelled *-er* in American usage. This group includes the following:

caliber	luster	*meter	somber
center	maneuver	scepter	specter
fiber	meager	sepulcher	*theater

British usage tends to *-re* in most of these words, though Fowler says they are being changed to *-er* one by one, because "we prefer in England to break with our illogicalities slowly."

An American writer who wishes a slightly Formal flavor will tend to use the *-re* forms; most will naturally use the *-er* forms.

Theater is divided in spelling, partly because it is found in a good many proper names of buildings and companies which were set up when *theatre* was the more common spelling, partly because of prestige associations of *theatre.* Keep the form actually used in proper names and whichever you prefer elsewhere.

Acre, lucre, massacre, mediocre keep the *-re* to represent a *c* pronounced /k/, and *ogre* is the current form, though some words with *g*, like *meager,* have changed. We also keep *-re* in *macabre, cadre.*

err ∘ Standard pronunciation of *err* was /ėr/; but as it occurred infrequently in speech, the tendency to pronounce it /ãr/, by *analogy with error /ãr′ər/, has established /ãr/ as an alternative pronunciation.

Esq., Esquire • Written following a man's name in the inside and outside address of a letter, *Esq.* or *Esquire* is Formal, with archaic or British suggestion, and in the United States is not often used except occasionally to professional men, chiefly to lawyers. If used, no other title (*Mr., Dr., Hon.*) should precede the name: *Harry A. Kinne, Esq.*

etc., et cetera • *Etc.,* spoken as *et cetera* or *and so forth,* has been appropriated so extensively for communication in business that it is not conventionally used in serious writing. When it is used, *etc.* is preferred to *et cetera.*

The case is suitable for prints, maps, etc.

In consecutive writing most people prefer the English "and so forth" (or "and so on," "and the like"). But it is better to avoid these end tags (which really take away from emphasis by putting a catchall at the end of a clause or sentence) by rephrasing the list, preceding it by *such as* or some other warning that the list you are giving is not exhaustive:

The case is suitable for large sheets *such as* prints and maps.

Using *and etc.* shows the writer doesn't realize that the *et* of *etc.* means *and*; in effect, he is writing *and and so forth.*

(See also *Abbreviations § 2, *Ellipsis § 2b.)

Etymology • See *Origin of words.

Euphemisms • A euphemism is a softened word used in place of one that names more vigorously something unpleasant, or something regarded as not quite nice: *natural son* for *illegitimate son* or *bastard, separate from the college* for *expel* or *flunk out.*

Occasionally euphemisms are warranted to avoid embarrassment or hurting someone's feelings. But in general it is safer—and better style—to call things by their right names, even if they are somewhat unpleasant. (For further discussion and examples see Ch. 9, "Euphemisms," p. 346, *Obscenity, and *Profanity.)

Euphony • See *Alliteration, *Assonance, *Style § 2b, *Repetition § 3.

every and its compounds •

1. *Every, everybody, everyone* in the early development of the language were treated as singulars and are often so used today:

Every man on the team did his best.
Everybody likes the new minister.
Everyone took his purchases home with him.

But these words are very often treated as collectives in all varieties of English. A verb immediately following *everyone* or *everybody* is usually singular, but a pronoun referring back to it from a little distance is likely to be plural:

Everybody in the room is taking off their hats.

This construction, especially common in British printed practice, is reasonable, since the reference is to a number of people. To make these expressions conform to Formal American written usage, it is often better to change the *everybody* to a more accurate plural or collective than to change the later pronoun:

They all did their best.
The crowd are taking off their hats.

(Reference: Fries, *AEG*, p. 50.)

2. *Everybody* is always written as one word; *everyone* is usually written as one word, but when the *one* is stressed, as two:

Everybody knew what the end would be.
Everyone knew what the end would be.
Every one of the family knew what the end would be.

3. *Every so often, every bit as* are useful General idioms:

Every so often someone in the crowd would give a terrific shout.
They are every bit as happy as they expected to be.

4. *Every place* is an adverbial phrase, more widely used than *any place* (See *any § 4):

Every place I looked the people said the same thing.

Examples • See *Details.

except, accept • *Except,* verb, means to "leave out, exclude": *He excepted those who had done the assignment from the extra reading.* It is decidedly Formal, and *excused* would be more natural.

Accept means to "receive" or to "answer affirmatively" and is slightly Formal: *I accept with pleasure. He accepted the position.*

Exclamation mark (!) • An *exclamation mark* (or *point*) is used after an emphatic interjection, after a phrase, clause, or sentence that is genuinely exclamatory, and after forceful commands. Clear-cut exclamations offer no problem:

Oh! Ouch! No, no, no!
"But," he protested, "it's the chance of a lifetime!"

But many interjections are weak and deserve no more than a comma:

Well, well, so you're in college now.

Often sentences cast in exclamatory pattern are really statements put that way for variety (See *Exclamations) and the exclamation mark is optional. Its use would depend chiefly on appropriateness.

Exclamation marks are more characteristic of imaginative writing, especially of fiction, than of factual writing. In factual writing it is well to remember that in some newspaper offices the exclamation mark is known as a screamer—and that its overuse is a mark of nervousness or of *schoolgirl style.

In typing, the mark can be made with a period below an apostrophe.

Exclamations • *Exclamations* are expressions of strong feeling or emphatic statements of fact or opinion. They range from the simple and often involuntary *Oh!* or *Ouch!* to fully developed sentences.

One word exclamations may be punctuated as full sentences if they deserve that much emphasis: *Oh! You nearly upset my plate.* They may be punctuated as parts of sentences if they seem to belong with other sentence elements: *Oh! you're here at last!* or *Oh, you're here at last!*

Many exclamations begin with *what* or *how*: *What a view! How could you! How lucky you are!*

An exclamation expressing an emphatic opinion gives not only emphasis but variety in a passage:

> But the methods chosen for the transition must always bear those human values in mind, for a whole new social order must inevitably result from a new kind of economic system, and in the process of slow nurture and growth initial trends may be all-important. Compulsion is a bad way to make men free!—ALFRED M. BINGHAM, *Insurgent America,* p. 6

Used just for variety or to give emphasis to what are really commonplaces, exclamations are ordinarily ineffective and give the effect of a strained or *schoolgirl style:

> Think how often you have judged a person by the way in which he speaks! Think of a salesman who is a poor talker! It sounds like the height of unreality, but what a situation in this highly competitive world! Think of a college professor who could not intelligently lecture to his classes because he had not learned the art of elocution!

(For a summary of characteristics of exclamations, or interjections, see *Parts of speech.)

excuse—pardon • Small slips are *excused*; more considerable faults (and crimes) are *pardoned*. "Pardon me" is sometimes considered more elegant than "Excuse me" in upper-class social situations. Either is appropriate for the numerous perfunctory apologies we make in everyday life. *Excuse* also has the special meaning of "giving permission to leave."

expect • *Expect* means "to look forward to" and also "to look for with confidence." In Formal English it is usually kept close to some meaning involving anticipation, but in Informal usage its meaning is extended and weakened to "suppose"—"I expect you'd better be going."

Experiment in written English • Language and literary style tend to become stereotyped; as the same kinds of words are used over and over in the same kinds of constructions, their effectiveness in conveying individual impressions decreases. The more skillful writers escape monotony by the force of their message or the individuality of their expression, and most of them more or less consciously either ignore some conventions of language or experiment with words or constructions.

We might call any departure from the commonly written and printed English an experiment—if it is not just the result of carelessness or ignorance. Almost anyone with an interest in writing will experiment in his own private and Informal writing, trying unusual words or combinations of words, unorthodox sentence patterns, even variations in spelling. Some writers also experiment in their published work. Strikingly "experimental" writing is more characteristic of fiction than of non-fiction. Most of us have quite enough to do learning to exploit the tremendous resources of the language within accepted, conventional patterns.

Expository writing, exposition • Most of the writing required in college courses is explanatory—writing that is intended primarily to inform and enlighten the reader (See Ch. 6). *Exposition* (or *expository writing*) is a term commonly used for writing of this kind. Some textbooks extend the term *exposition* to include what this book calls "persuasive papers." (For the distinctions among the kinds of papers treated in this book see Ch. 5, p. 158.)

extracurricular • *Extracurricular* means "outside the course of study" (extracurricular activities); it is sometimes hyphened but usually not.

F • The sound /f/ occurs spelled *f*, *ff*, *ph*, and *gh* (see *-ough*, -*augh*). The words with *ph* go back to Greek words with *phi* (Φ): *philosophy, telephone*; a few have been simplified to *f*: *fantasy, sulfur*.

Nouns ending in -*f* often have the corresponding voiced sound /v/ in the plural: *leaf—leaves, loaf—loaves, wife—wives*; *beef* has either *beeves* or *beefs*. But not *golf, gulf, oaf, safe, tiff, whiff.*

Factual and imaginative writing • The fundamental distinction between factual and imaginative writing is that in the first the writer's primary responsibility is to present, analyze, and reason about material that can be made available for others to observe, study, and discuss; in the second he has the liberty of shaping any action or picture or idea that may serve his purpose.

The principal types of factual writing are news stories, interviews, characterizations of people, biography, history, explanatory articles of all kinds, reviews, editorials, critical articles on all sorts of subjects, personal essays, and discussions of more general ideas such as demonstration of hypotheses, theories, ideals, philosophical concepts. Whatever other qualities these articles may have, whatever their virtues or faults, they are fundamentally good or bad according as they approach the truth and correspond to some strand of human observation or experience. (This book discusses some of the types of factual writing in Chs. 5-7 and 11.)

The imaginative types, in which the writer's conception is the controlling factor, are poems, plays, short stories, novels.

famed • When *famed* is used for *famous* or *well-known*, it usually suggests a journalese style, or a *staccato one:

famed eating place   famed Nobel prize winner
At seven-thirty we anchored off the famed yachting center.

It is often a sign of amateur writing to label as *famed* (or as *famous,* for that matter) merely well-known people.

farther—further • In Informal English little distinction is made between *farther* and *further* in their adverbial and adjectival functions. As a verb, however, *further* is now the only one in use.

In Formal English a distinction is often made between *farther* and *further,* confining the first to expressions of physical distance and the second to abstract relationships of degree or quantity:

We went on twenty miles *farther.* He went *farther* than I, but neither of us reached the town.

He carries that sort of thing *further* than I would.

He went *further* into his family history. He got *further* and *further* into debt.

In General English, *farther* is usually used of distance, *further* for both distance and degree. In the superlative *farthest* is commoner than *furthest*. (Reference: Bryant, pp. 209-210.)

faze • *Faze* has worked its way from dialect (*feeze*, to disturb) into General usage. It means "to daunt or disconcert" and is almost always used negatively (The bawling out didn't faze him). Do not confuse this word with *phase,* meaning "state" or "stage of development."

fellow • *Fellow* is General and Informal when used to mean "person" but Formal in the sense of "associate." It is most commonly used in writing in the function of an adjective: *his fellow sufferers, a fellow feeling* ("a similar feeling," or "sympathy"). Especially among young people it means a young man as contrasted with a young woman (girl).

female • Usage now restricts *female* to designations of sex, usually in scientific contexts. This leaves English without a single comfortable word for female-human-being-regardless-of-age; somewhat the same comment applies to *male.*

fewer—less • See *less—fewer.

fiancé, fiancée • A century ago the English *betrothed* was replaced by the French word (probably by "society" journalists), and now we are cursed not only with accent marks but with separate forms for the man (*fiancé*) and the woman (*fiancée*). Pronunciation for both is /fē′ən sā′/, with a tendency to /fē-än′sā/. The plurals are *fiancés, fiancées.* In newspapers and much General writing the accent is dropped, and it will probably soon disappear.

Figures • See *Numbers.

Figures of speech •
Revision: This figure of speech is inappropriate, inconsistent, or threadbare. Revise the passage.

Fig

Words can be used in their usual meaning, or they can be borrowed to apply to other things. We can talk of music in terms of color, or moral problems in terms of a game, and so on. Fresh and appropriate figures can help a reader see and understand what you are talking about, but careless or tasteless figures detract. They may be threadbare, used as often as "a ribbon of concrete" or "old man Winter." This sentence has one trite and one fresh figure:

The strident shriek of a siren [Trite:] shattered the silence and [Fresh:] two searching fingers of light swung around the corner as if feeling for the scene of the disturbance.

They may be strained and unnatural, as in this description of dawn:

Over yonder hill Apollo thrust the blade of his golden sword, severing the filmy mist that blanketed the paths of old Onondaga.

Or they may be inconsistent ("mixed"), as in this mélange:

But then the molehill of annoyance grew into a mountain of hate and chased love out of the home.

Such figures stamp a writer as immature or careless.

The effective use of figures of speech is discussed in *Style § 2h and in Ch. 9, "Figurative use of words," p. 350. The most common figures (metaphors, similes, metonymy, irony, over-statement, and understatement) are described in Ch. 9. Other figures are discussed in *Index* articles: *Alliteration, *Epigrams, *Imitative words and phrases, *Negatives, *Personification, *Puns.

fine • *Fine* is widely used as a *counter word of general ap-proval, slightly more vigorous than *nice,* but is of little value in writing and better omitted:

Spring football practice has one aim, to weld eleven men into a [fine,] coordinated team.

It may, of course, be used in any of its more restricted senses. (Reference: Bryant, pp. 87-88.)

Fine writing • *Fine writing* is generally a term of dispraise, applied to writing that is too pretentious for the material or the purpose. Fine writing betrays itself chiefly in the use of big words and in strained, artificial figures of speech. (See Ch. 9, "Choosing appropriate words," p. 345, "Figurative use of words," p. 350, and *Figures of speech.)

Finite verbs • *Finite verb* is a grammatical term indicating that the verb form is limited (Latin *finis,* "end, limit") in *per-son* (by one of the pronouns or by a subject), in *time* (by a tense form: *goes, went*), or in *number* (singular or plural). By contrast, the "nonfinite" parts—the infinitives (*go, to go, to have gone*), participles (*going, gone*), and verbal nouns (*going*) —are not limited in person or number. These are combined with auxiliaries to form verb phrases which function like sim-ple finite forms (he *is* going, he *will* go, he *has* gone).

Finite verbs can be main verbs in clauses and sentences (I *had gone* before he *came*); nonfinite parts are ordinarily in subordinate constructions: Before *coming*; *Gone* with the wind. (But see *Infinitives § 5 and *Participles § 4.)

first—former, last—latter • See *former—first, latter—last.

fish • The plural is also *fish* (We got only six fish after fishing all day), except in speaking of various species of fish, as in "Most of the income of the island is from these fishes: cod, halibut, and sword." This distinction is not always made in speech.

fix • In Formal usage *fix* means to "fasten in place"; in General usage it means to "repair" or to "put in shape." *Fix* as a noun meaning "predicament" (to be in a fix) is Informal, as is its sense of "a bribed arrangement."

flaunt—flout • *Flaunt* /flônt/, to "wave, display boastfully," and *flout* /flout/, to "insult, treat with contempt," are sometimes confused.

folk—folks • Formal English and some local speech use *folk* as the plural; General usage has *folks,* especially in the sense of "members of a family." (Reference: Bryant, pp. 91-92.)
   Folklore and *folkway* are written as one word, *folk dance, folk music, folk tale* usually as two; *folk song* and *folksong* are both used.

Footnotes • See *Asterisk § 1, *References in scientific papers, Ch. 11, "Footnotes and final bibliography," p. 438.

for • For distinction between *because* and *for,* see *because.
   A comma is usually needed between two coordinate clauses joined by *for*; without it the *for* might be read as a preposition:

He was glad to go, for Mrs. Crane had been especially good to him. [*Not*: He was glad to go for Mrs. Crane....]

   Since *for* almost always comes between the clauses it joins, it is usually classified as a coordinating conjunction, but the clause it introduces is often actually subordinate: *He was exhausted, for he had gone two nights without sleep.* (Reference: Henry L. Wilson, "The Classification of the Conjunction 'For,'" *American Speech,* 1952, 27:257-260.)

Foreign words in English •
1. *Anglicizing foreign words.* English has always borrowed words and roots freely from other languages and is still borrowing, especially from Greek and French. Most borrowed words that have been used for a long time cannot be told from

native English words, but those taken in recently often raise questions. They usually cross the threshold of English with their foreign spelling, perhaps with un-English plurals or other forms, and no established English pronunciation. The process of anglicizing brings them more or less in line with English usage, but they may keep some of their foreign quality, like the *i* of *machine*, the silent *s* in *debris*, the *t* where English is tempted to put a *d* in *kindergarten*.

Many loan words are in a transition stage, showing two or more spellings (*naif, naïf, naive, naïve; naïveté, naiveté, naivety, naïvety; role, rôle*); with others we are experimenting with pronunciations, the winner not yet clearly seen (*melee*: /mā lā′/, /mā′lā/, /mel′ā/, and /mē lē/; *zwieback*: /tsvē′bäk/, /tswē′bäk/, /swī′bak/, /zwī′bak/; *menu*: /men′ yoo/, /män′yoo/). Some words that have been in English a considerable time are still changing, especially in stress (*debris*: /də brē′/—/deb′rē/) and in consonant sounds (*massage*: /mə säzh′/—/mə säj′/). These words show how a rough compromise is worked out between English practice and the original form.

The speed and degree of anglicizing depends on how frequently the word is used, the circumstances in which it is used, and the people who use it. The attitude of linguists is that if a word proves useful it will assume a natural English form. *Hors d'oeuvre* is a useful word, but it looks conspicuously un-English. If menu makers would spell it *orderve*, we could all be happy with it. The solution with *maître d'hôtel* has been to clip it to *maitre d'* /mātər dē/.

Formal writers and conservative editors tend to keep the foreign spellings longer than General writers and editors. If the words come in through the spoken language, like those of the automobile vocabulary, they usually become English or near-English sooner than if they come in by way of literature: we have *chassis* (/shas′ē/ or /shas′is/, sometimes /chas′is/), *chauffeur* (/shō′fər/—the spelling lagging), *garage* (/gə räzh′/ or /gə räj′/—in England /gar′ij/), *detour* (/dē′tür/. Words that come in through and remain in literary, scholarly, or "polite" circles change more slowly, in both spelling and pronunciation: *tête-à-tête, faux pas, nouveau riche, laissez faire.*

2. *Use of borrowed words.* The best reason for using an unnaturalized or partly naturalized word is that it supplies a real lack in English—perhaps says in one word what English would have to use a phrase or sentence to express. *Entrepreneur,* "one who undertakes business, especially assumes commercial risk," is useful since the English *undertaker* has a special meaning of its own. *Beige,* "the color of unbleached wool or cotton," *suede, tableau, protégé* are useful. We have also taken in a

number of words and phrases of doubtful usefulness: *entre nous,* when we have *between ourselves,* or *in confidence; affaire du coeur* for *love affair, raison d'être* for *reason for being,* and so on.

Sometimes the gain is in force or tone or suggestion, as *ersatz* is stronger than *substitute,* and *liaison* brings either a connotation of social unconventionality or of military activity, depending on the context. *Nouveau riche* brings its suggestion of dispraise, replacing an earlier borrowing, *parvenu,* which in turn displaced the more blunt *upstart.* French words are often used for tone, especially in discussing (and more especially in advertising) women's fashions: *chic, svelte, lapin* (*rabbit* in other places)—and even *sacque,* which doesn't exist in French. A couple of generations ago French was used a good deal for polite social euphemisms, to avoid plain English: *demi-monde, fille de joie, femme de chambre, enceinte, accouchement.* Now these have generally gone out of use, their place once more taken by straight English, except with the falsely modest. Parading foreign words, a temptation to some who are learning a language or have just returned from abroad, is usually in bad taste, and their use even by people wholly at home with the languages is likely to be inappropriate. Fitness to material, to readers, and to the writer himself will usually determine whether a foreign word should be used.

3. *Handling borrowed words in copy.*

a–Italics. Words which have not been completely anglicized are printed in italics in magazines and books and should be underlined in copy. Newspapers do not use italics for such purposes, and their practice of course has tended to lessen the use of italics by others. There are always many words on the borderline which will be found sometimes in italics, sometimes not. Formal writers tend to use more italics; General, fewer. Consult a recent dictionary for doubtful words—remembering that it can never quite represent present usage.

b–Accent and other marks. Words recently taken in from French are usually written with accent marks if they were so written in French. Newspapers do not use accent marks except sometimes in departments like the editorial, art, music, and fashion pages. After they have been used for a time in English, the accents are usually dropped unless they are necessary to indicate pronunciation. *Matinee, melee, role* do not need marks; *blasé* does. Similarly *cañon* is now usually spelled *canyon,* but: *piñon.* A *cedilla shows that a *c* before *a* or *o* is pronounced /s/: *façade, soupçon.*

In German all nouns are capitalized, and recent or infrequent borrowings from German are capitalized in English, particularly if they are still printed in italics (*Anschluss, Real-*

politik, Weltanschauung, but hinterland, kindergarten, blitzkrieg). The *umlaut can be replaced by an *e* after the vowel: *Mädchen* or *Maedchen.*

c—Plurals. English usually brings borrowed words into its own system of conjugation and declension, though some words change slowly, especially words used mainly in Formal writing (**formulae*). *Beaus* is now as common as *beaux,* and *tableaus* is gaining on *tableaux.* (See *Plurals of nouns § 4.)

A few French adjectives may keep both masculine and feminine forms: **blond, blonde; naïf, naïve.*

4. Pronunciation. For pronunciation of borrowed words, see the examples given in § 5 or consult a dictionary. Because the speech sounds of one language differ somewhat from those of another, it is almost impossible to say a foreign word the way it is spoken in its original language unless you are thoroughly familiar with that language. If there is an established English pronunciation, you should use it, especially since you are more likely to be understood.

5. *List of borrowed words.* This list contains a small selection of loan words in fairly common use. Those in italics would ordinarily be italicized in print. When two forms are separated by a dash, they are both common. A form in brackets is less common than the other. Pronunciations are indicated for words which might offer difficulty. For words not given here consult a recent dictionary. (See *Pronunciation § 1 for key to symbols.)

aide-de-camp—aid-de-camp /ād' də kamp'/
*a la
à la carte
a la mode
bourgeois /bùr'zhwä—bùr zhwä'/
brassiere /brə zir'/
buffet /bu fā'—bù fā'/
bushido /bü'shē dō'/
café—cafe /ka fā'—kə fā'/
chic /shēk—shik/
cliché /klē shā'/
coiffure /kwä fyoor'/
communiqué /kə mū'nə kā'—kə mū'nə kā/
corps; plu. corps /kôr; plu. kōrz/
coup; plu. coups /kü; plu. küz/
coup d'état /kü dā tä'—kü də tä'/
coupé—coupe /kü pā'—küp/

crèche—creche /kresh—krāsh/
crepe—crêpe—crape /krāp/
crescendo /krə shen'dō—krə sen'dō/
debut /di bū'—dā'bū—dā bū'/
debutante /deb'yù tänt—deb'yə tant/
dirndl/dėrn'dl/
Don Juan /don jü'ən—don hwän'/
Don Quixote /don kwik'sət—don kē hō'tē/
dramatis personae /dram'ə tis pər sō'nē/
éclair—eclair /ā klār'—i klār'/
entrée—entree /än'trā/
fete—fête /fāt/
hara-kiri—hari-kari /har'ə kir'ē—hä'rə kir'ē/
lingerie /lan'zhə rē'—län'zhə rā'/
matériel—materiel

matinee /mat ə nā'—mat'ə nā—
mat'nā'/

mayonnaise

menu /men'ū—mā'nū; French
pronunciation not current/

milieu /mē lyœ'—mēl yü'/

monsieur /mə syœ'/; plu. messieurs—messrs. /mā syœ'/

muzhik—moujik /mü zhik'—
mü'zhik/

negligee—négligé /neg'lə zhā'—
neg'lə zhā'/

obbligato—obligato
/ob'lə gä'tō/

papier-mâché /pā'pər mə shā'/

passé /pa sā'—pas'ā/

précis /prā'sē—prā sē'/

premiere—première /pri mir'—
prə myer'/

protégé (masc.), protégée (fem.)
/prō'tə zhā/

quasi /kwā'sī—kwā'zī [kwä'sē]/

questionnaire [questionary]
/kwes'chən är'/

rendezvous /rän'də vü/;
plu. rendezvous /rän'də vüz/

repertoire /rep'ər twär
[rep'ər twôr]/—repertory

résumé /rez'ū mā'/

ricochet /rik ə shā'—rik ə shet'/

salon /sə lon'—sä lôn'/

slalom /slä'lōm [slä'ləm]/

status quo /stā'təs kwō—stat'əs
kwō/

stein /stīn/

suede—suède /swād/

vs.—vs /vėr'səs/

Weltschmerz /velt'shmerts'/

(See *English language, *Latin and English, *Origin of words. References: Kenyon and Knott, § 122; Brander Matthews, "The Englishing of French Words," *Society for Pure English Tracts*, Tract V, 1921, 3-20; T. R. Palfrey, "The Contribution of Foreign Language Study to Mastery of the Vernacular," *Modern Language Journal*, 1941, 25:550-557.)

Form classes • See *Parts of speech.

Formal correspondence • See *Social correspondence.

Formal English •
Revision: The word or passage marked is too Formal for the subject or for the style of the rest of the paper. Revise, making it more General.

Form

Formal English is the usage characteristic of people who work a good deal with books, particularly members of the various professions. It is the appropriate variety for discussions of ideas, for scientific and scholarly writing, for addresses to audiences of considerable education, for literary works that are intended for a somewhat restricted reading public. Formal English is not so appropriate for day to day speaking and writing, for accounts of personal experience, casual comment, and other sorts of writing intended for the general reading public. (For discussion and examples, see Ch. 1, "Formal English," p. 17. See also *Academic writing, *Gobbledygook,

*Legal language. Other *Index* articles dealing with Formal usage include *Abbreviations, *Agreement, *Alliteration, *Collective nouns, *Contractions, *Dates, *Gender.)

former—first, latter—last • *Former* and *latter* refer only to two units:

> The mountain and the squirrel
> Had a quarrel,
> And the former called the latter, "little prig";
> —RALPH WALDO EMERSON, *Fable*

First and *last* refer to items in a series, usually of more than two:

> The first president had set up a very informal organization.
> His last act was to advise his family on their future.

Latest refers to a series that is still continuing (the latest fashions). *Last* refers either to the final item of a completed series (their last attempt was successful) or to the most recent item of a continuing series (the last election). *Latest* for *last* is archaic: His *latest* breath. Note the spelling of *latter,* sometimes confused with *later.* (See *last—latest.)

Forms of discourse • For the last hundred years or so it has been conventional to divide writing into "four forms of discourse"—narration, description, exposition, and argument. The chief value of this classification is that it emphasizes purpose as the controlling element in a piece of writing. Studying the forms one by one allows concentration on certain traits of material, organization, and style peculiar to each type. The categories are not, however, sharply distinct—description contributes to all, notably to narration; many essays which are primarily argumentative include long stretches of exposition, and so on.

formula • The plural is *formulas* or *formulae,* the former the more common.

Formulas • Every language has some constructions that have become fixed by long usage in certain situations and whose total meaning is largely independent of the words in it: *Once upon a time, Ladies and gentlemen, Good morning, How are you? How do you do? Best wishes, Dear Sir, Yours truly.* Occasionally fresh substitutes can be found for these, but more often the attempt merely calls attention to itself. Such phrases, though stereotyped, are too useful to be called *trite, and they are not, as most trite expressions are, substitutes for some simpler locution. They should be used without apology and without embarrassment whenever they are needed. (See *Idiom and idioms, *Subjunctives § 2a.)

Fractions • Fractions are written in figures when they are attached to other figures (72¾), or are in a series that is being written in figures (½, ⅔, 1, 2, 4), or are in tables or reference matter. In consecutive writing they are usually written in words (In the local newspaper three fourths of the space was given to advertising, one eighth to news, and one eighth to miscellaneous matters). Hyphens may be used between the numerator and denominator if neither part itself contains a hyphen, but they are less used than formerly and are not used at all when the numerator has the value of an adjective (as in "He sold one half and kept the other").

seven tenths [seven-tenths]   eight twenty-sevenths
twenty-nine fortieths—twenty nine fortieths

Decimals are increasingly used in place of fractions in factual writing, since they are more flexible and may be more accurate. They are always written in figures: .7   .42   3.14159 (See *Numbers.)

Fragmentary sentence •
Revision: The construction marked is not a satisfactory sentence. Revise by completing its form, by joining to a neighboring sentence, or by rewriting the passage.

Frag

A fragmentary sentence (sentence fragment) is a part of a sentence—usually a phrase or dependent clause—carelessly or ineffectively punctuated as a whole sentence. By its form, it suggests dependence on another construction, and editors usually make sure it does not stand as a sentence. Ordinarily one should be joined to the preceding or following sentence or made into an independent sentence. In college writing, fragmentary sentences are usually the result of carelessness; they are one of the most obvious blunders and should be eliminated in revision.

Three common types with suggested revision follow:

Fragmentary sentence	*Revised*
Since 1939 we had been walking slowly in the direction of war. [Phrase:] Step by step until finally there was no other alternative but to declare war.	Since 1939 we had been walking slowly in the direction of war, step by step, until finally there was no other alternative but to declare war.
He talked for fifty minutes without taking his eyes off his	He talked for fifty minutes without taking his eyes off his

notes. [Participial phrase:] Apparently not noticing that half the class was asleep.

notes. Apparently he did not notice that half the class was asleep.

The first six books I looked for couldn't be taken out of the library. [Dependent clause:] Because they were on reserve for an advanced history course.

The first six books I looked for couldn't be taken out of the library because they were on reserve for an advanced history course.

(For further discussion and other examples see Ch. 8, "Revising sentence fragments," p. 287. See also *Clauses, *Phrases.)

freshman, freshmen • Since these words are pronounced alike /fresh′mən/, their spelling is sometimes confused, not so often when they are used as nouns (a freshman, forty freshmen) as when *freshman* is used as a modifier (freshman class, freshman spirit). *Freshmen* should never stand before a noun in this construction.

It is not necessary to capitalize *freshman* (or *sophomore, junior, senior*), but courtesy or emphasis sometimes makes a capital appropriate, and often one is used when speaking of an entire class—the Freshman Class, the Junior Class.

-ful, full • When the adjective *full* is used as a suffix to nouns of measure (*basketful, spoonful*) or of feeling or quality (*peaceful, sorrowful, soulful*) it has only one *l*.

The plural of nouns ending in *-ful* is usually made with *-s*: *spoonfuls, basketfuls* (also *basketsful*). (See *spoonful, spoonfuls.)

Function words •
1. Some words carry relatively little independent meaning in themselves, serving rather to indicate relationships, to point out grammatical functions. They are also called *form-words, structure-words, empty-words*. Since they are limited in number—new ones are rarely added to a class—they belong to *closed classes*. Some such words are:

Prepositions, which join nouns to other words in a construction; the *of* in the phrase form of the genitive (of the man) is conspicuously a function word.

Conjunctions, which show the relation between sentence elements.

Auxiliary verbs when they indicate time, person, number, of a verb (*is* asking, *has* asked, *did* he ask) without otherwise modifying meaning. (See *have § 1, 2.)

*Some of what are traditionally called *adverbs and *adjectives,* for example, *more* and *most* in comparisons of adjectives and adverbs (more handsome, most handsome), or *the, a, an.*

2. *Stylistic qualities of function words.* Different varieties of usage have some characteristic habits in the use of function words. In the more elaborate sentences of Formal English, heavier connectives, such as *conjunctive adverbs (however, accordingly ...)*, are more appropriate; General style tends to rely more on coordinating conjunctions (*but, for, and ...*) and subordinating conjunctions (*although, because, since ...*).

Informal English shows a good many compound or group prepositions, for many of which Formal English would use a single preposition: *in back of (behind); in regard to (about).* Too many of these long connectives tend to give a sentence a rather weak movement and a rhythm without many strong stresses. In rapid speech they are passed over easily, but they sometimes become conspicuous in writing.

(See *Parts of speech, *Conjunctions, *Prepositions. See also *Wordiness, *Newspaper English § 3, *Telegraphic style. Linguists vary in their definitions of function words. A full treatment is in Fries, *Structure,* Ch. 6.)

Fundamentals • The selection of what can be regarded as fundamentals in estimating a piece of writing depends on judgment, and judgments vary. Suggestions follow for one approach to fundamentals:

1. *The content* of the paper (always considered in relation to the writer's purpose) deserves most weight in evaluating a piece of writing. Nothing can take the place of important and interesting material.

2. *The treatment* of the material by the writer is of next importance. He may use too few details or too many; he may select them according to an intelligent or an unwise or biased principle; he may have an exaggerated idea of the importance of his subject, or approach it with too much or too little sentiment, reverence, humor, or realism; he may or may not direct his statements to readers.

3. *The plan* of an essay is important, since in part through it the writer guides the reader to see his sense of the matter. Too slow a beginning and too trivial an end are serious faults, as is failure to show relation between parts.

4. Finally, a piece of writing is affected by the *mechanics and style* of the writer, which may either hinder the reader or increase his satisfaction. Poor material presentably written has no future, but worthwhile material even if poorly written can with sufficient work be made presentable.

We consciously or unconsciously make some such balancing of qualities in deciding what we think of what we read. Realizing the relative worth of these qualities makes it easier for student and teacher to understand each other's judgments.

funny • In Formal English *funny* means only "comical," "laughable," but in Informal English it also means "odd": *"That's funny. I thought he did."* See that the meaning intended is appropriate to the variety of English being used.

further—farther • See *farther—further.

Fused sentence • A *fused sentence* is the name sometimes given to two grammatically complete sentences written with no mark of punctuation between them (The dress shop was sponsoring a style show they asked Jeanine to model since she was a steady customer). It usually results simply from exceptional carelessness in writing, one step worse than the typical comma faults. (See Ch. 8, "Revising comma faults," p. 290, and *Comma faults.)

Future tense • See *Tenses of verbs, *shall—will.

G • *G*, like *c*, spells a "hard" and a "soft" sound. The hard sound is more common than the soft.
1. *"Hard g"* /g/. *G* is hard before *a, o,* and *u* (except in *margarine* and the British *gaol* [*jail*]): *garrulous, gong, gutter;* when doubled: *doggerel, noggin, toboggan;* at the ends of words: *beg, dig, fig;* before another consonant in the same syllable: *togs, glen;* frequently before *h, l,* and *r*: *gherkin, glow, great;* and sometimes before *i* and *e*: *begin, gig, girl, eager, gear, get.*
    Gu, taken from French, spells hard *g*: *guard, guess, guide, guernsey.*
2. *"Soft g"* /j/ is found typically before *e, i,* and *y*: *gem, gentle, genus, giblet, gin, gym, gyrate.* It is often spelled *ge* or *dge*: *age* /āj/, *edge* /ej/, *fudge* /fuj/; other spellings of the sound are *joy, exaggerate, verdure, grandeur, soldier.*
3. *G* is sometimes pronounced /zh/, chiefly in partly anglicized words from French: *garage, massage, mirage.* These words tend to have a soft *g* after they have been in English a long time (*carriage, marriage*): *garage* is often /gə räj′/ (in England, /gar′ij/); *massage* is tending toward /mə säj′/.
4. *"Silent g."* Initial *g* is silent in such words as *gnaw, gnat, gnome, gnu,* and within a word *g* is often silent before *m* or *n*: *diaphragm, sign.* It is sounded in some derivatives of this latter type of word: *signal.*
5. *"Dropping g's."* In Formal and much General speech the present participle ends in the single nasal consonant sound

spelled *ng*; in Informal speech this /ng/ sound is often replaced by the /n/ sound, written *n'*: *singin', laughin'*. Because of the spelling, this is usually referred to as "dropping *g's*," though none of the sounds spelled by *g* alone are involved. Of the participle forms ending in these two different nasal consonants —/ng/ and /n/—the form ending in *-n* is the older. Originally the present participle ended in *-and* and later in *-en* or *-in*, and this has always been the form for the majority of speakers of English. In the speech of London and vicinity, which became the basis of written English, the present participle was confused with the verbal noun, ending in *-ung*. Now everyone *writes* the participle with *-ing*, but many continue the old pronunciation with *-in*. (See Milton Ellis, *English Journal*, 1937, 26:753. Compare *ng*. Reference: Kenyon and Knott, *-ing*; *Webster's Third New International Dictionary, -ing*.)

-ge, -ce • See *-ce, -ge.

Gender • *Gender* as applied to English is the indication of sex or sexlessness, literally or figuratively. In the many languages which have special endings for masculine, feminine, and neuter nouns and for articles and adjectives modifying them, gender is primarily a grammatical concept, but English had lost this system six centuries ago. Now, except in the pronouns *he, she, it* and a few nouns with endings such as (feminine) *-e, -ess, -a, -ix, -euse,* and (masculine) *-or, -us, -er, -eur* (blonde, blond; actress, actor; alumna, alumnus; aviatrix, aviator; masseuse, masseur), gender can be determined only from the meaning of a word: *man—woman, nephew—niece, rooster—hen.* And even in the pronouns and suffixes, gender is rather a matter of meaning than of grammar. Compounds, partly to show gender, partly for emphasis, are common and expressive: *she-witch, he-bear, boy friend, girl friend.* Nouns referring to inanimate objects are neuter. For most English words gender is identifiable only by the choice of the meaningfully appropriate pronoun (*he, she, it*) and is consequently hardly a grammatical category:

> The speaker hesitated, choosing *his* next words deliberately.
> The novelist has presented *her* chief character effectively.

In Formal, literary English there is a weak sort of personification (or animation) in which the sun or moon or a ship or almost any object may be referred to as *he* (The sun sent forth his cheering beams) or more often *she* (The moon has cast her gentle light). In Informal English *she* frequently replaces *it*, especially if intimacy or affection is involved. A car or a college or a country or any object may be a *she*.

We lack a singular pronoun to represent either-he-or-she; in the plural English is noncommittal: *they* refers indifferently to male, female, inanimate in any combination. Referring to a baby or an animal of unknown sex, *it* is the usual solution; otherwise *he*. (See *he-or-she, *blond, blonde, *naive-naïve.)

General English • *General English* is a variety of Standard English—the central body of words and constructions of our language. (For discussion and examples, see Ch. 1, "Standard English," p. 15. *Index* articles dealing with General usage include *Abbreviations, *Business English, *Contractions.)

Genitive •
1. The genitive (or possessive) function in English is shown in four ways:
a–The *s*-genitive. *'s* is the spelling of the genitive of all singular and a few plural nouns and noun phrases in which the word is pronounced with an added /s/ or /z/ sound and of the indefinite pronouns (*anyone, everybody* . . .):

boy's	horse's	one's	King of England's
men's	brother-in-law's	somebody's	anyone's

An apostrophe alone may be added to words that already end in an /s/, /sh/, or /z/ sound, as in regularly made plurals in -*s*; the last three could also add an *s* after the apostrophe:

horses'	coaches'	*Jones' (singular)
Joneses' (plural)	Moses'	conscience' (for conscience' sake)

Words of one syllable ending in these sounds have either the apostrophe alone or *'s,* pronounced as an added syllable:

Charles' /chärlz/—Charles's /chärl'zəz/   coach's /kōch'əz/
fish's /fish'əz/   Zeus' /züs/—Zeus's /züs'əz/

The apostrophe is a visual mark which signals the genitive only in writing; in speech the genitive is distinguished from the plural by its position before a noun (the doctor's first case) or as a predicate where the context would make a plural impossible (The criticism is Gamble's). In writing, the genitive plural is distinguished from the singular by the position of the apostrophe, but in speech the number is not always clear: *I saw the boy's (boys') books.* (See *Jones—plural and possessive forms.)

When two coordinate nouns are in the genitive, the apostrophe is often added only to the last one:

Fred and Bert's first attempt. [*Formal:* Fred's and Bert's].
He had never thought of his wife and children's future.
[*But:*] Mary's and Tom's bicycles. (Separate objects possessed)

***b*—The *of*-genitive.** The term *genitive* derives from the Greco-Roman grammarians, who used it only to describe inflections; since in English the function of the genitive can often be performed by an *of*-phrase, the term *of*-genitive is used to describe the construction: *He had never known the love of a child* (= *a child's love*); *the plays of Shakespeare.*

The *of*-genitive always stands after the noun it limits: *the leaves of the tree* (= *the tree's leaves*).

The *of*-genitive is rather more common with names of inanimate objects than the *s*-genitive is, but both are used; the *s*-genitive is the more common form with names of people, though both are used:

the car's rattles	the rattles of the car
the field's flowers	the flowers of the field
a day's work	the work of a day
Doctor Clark's house	the house of Doctor Clark

(References: "Current English Forum," *College English,* 1953, 14:236-239; 1954, 16:55-56; Bryant, pp. 93-94.)

In most instances sound—euphony and rhythm—decides whether the *s*- or *of*-genitive is used. Since the *of*-form is longer, it often fits into sonorous and emotional phrases (at the home of Doctor Clark) and allows a more characteristic English rhythm than the compact *s*-genitive.

There is also a possible difference of meaning between the two forms. "Jane's picture" would usually mean a picture belonging to Jane, though it might mean a picture of Jane. "A picture of Jane" can only mean that Jane is represented in the picture.

***c*—Double genitive.** Using both the *s*- and *of*-genitives together is an English idiom of long and respectable standing. It is especially common in locutions beginning with *that* or *this* and usually has an informal flavor:

that boy of Henry's   friends of my father's   hobbies of Jack's

It is useful in avoiding the ambiguity mentioned at the end of § b above: "Jane's picture" is resolved either as "the picture of Jane" or "the picture of Jane's."

***d*—Genitive of the personal pronouns.** The personal and relative pronouns have genitive forms without an apostrophe:

my   your   his   her   its   our   their   whose

It is as important *not* to put apostrophes in these pronouns (and in the forms used without nouns: *ours, yours, theirs, hers*) as it is to put one in a noun in the genitive. (See *Possessive adjectives, *Pronouns § 1, *its, *which, *who, whom.)

2. *Uses of the genitive.* The most common function of the genitive is to indicate possession:

the professor's house   my son   Bert's wife

The genitive also indicates a number of other relationships:

Description: a man's job   children's toys   suit of wool

Doer of an act ("Subjective genitive") : the wind's force   the force of the wind   Sinclair Lewis' second novel   with the dean's permission   with the permission of the dean (The subjective genitive usual with gerunds) : the doctor's coming relieved the strain. (See *Gerund.)

Recipient of an act ("Objective genitive") : the policeman's murderer   the murderer of the policeman   the bill's defeat

Adverb: He drops in of an evening.

(See Ch. 10, "Using apostrophes," p. 400. More details of these and other genitive relations will be found in the large grammars. References: Curme, *Parts of Speech,* pp. 133-136, *Syntax,* pp. 70-88; Fries, *AEG,* pp. 72-88; Bryant, pp. 74-75.)

Gerund •

1. *Form and use.* A *gerund*—also called a verbal noun—is the form of the verb ending in *-ing* used in the function of a noun. It has the same form as the present participle but differs in use:

Gerund: Running a hotel appealed to him. (*Running* is the subject.)

Participle: He was busy *running* a hotel. (*Running* modifies *he.*)

A gerund may take an object (as in *running a hotel*) or a complement (*being a hero*), and it may serve in any noun function:

Subject: Looking for an apartment always fascinated her.

Object: He taught *dancing.*

Predicate noun: Seeing is *believing.*

Used as modifier: a *fishing* boat (a boat for fishing, not a boat that fishes) , *boiling* point, a *living* wage.

When not in one of these constructions, a gerund is related to the rest of the sentence by a preposition (§ 3).

Gerunds may show tense:

	Active	*Passive*
Present:	Just *seeing* the fire was enough.	*Being seen* was bad enough.
Perfect:	Just *having seen* the fire was enough.	*Having been seen* was bad enough.

Gerunds may be modified by adjectives when the noun function is uppermost or by adverbs when the verb function is emphasized:

Modified by adjective: Good boxing is first-rate entertainment.

Modified by adverb: Playing well was his great pride.

2. *Subject of a gerund.* The subject of a gerund sometimes has the genitive and sometimes the accusative (or common) case. In Formal writing the genitive is more usual; in General writing, both occur. Use whichever seems more natural.

a–When the subject is a personal pronoun or a word standing for a person, it is usually in the genitive:

His coming was all that she looked forward to.
She looked forward to *Bob's coming.*

b–If the subject is a plural noun, it is likely to be in the common form. Note that in speech it is impossible to decide whether *students* is genitive, but in writing, a decision must be made:

I don't approve of *men drinking.*
I don't approve of *students coming and going* as they like.
With a pronoun: I don't approve of *them drinking.* [*Or:*] I don't approve of *their drinking.*

c–If the subject is abstract or the name of an inanimate object, it is usually in the common form:

It was a case of *imagination getting* out of control.
The *roof* [or *roof's*] *falling in* was only the first disaster.

d–When the subject is modified by other words, it is in the common form:

In spite of the *plan* of the committee *being voted down* no one could offer a better one.
The principal's *contract running out* gave an excuse for letting him go.

e–When the subject is stressed, it is usually in the accusative, even if it is a pronoun:

Who would have thought of *him* [stressed] *getting* the prize?
Have you heard about *Gertrude* [stressed] *getting* a job?

f–If the subject has no genitive form (*this, many,* etc.) the common form is inescapable:

We disapproved of so *many being taken.*
He could not conceive of *this being done.*

3. *Phrases with gerunds.* Gerunds are often used in phrases that have the value and function of dependent clauses (see *Verbals):

In coming to an agreement, they had compromised on all points.
It's the best thing *for coughing at night.*

The relation of the gerund phrase to the word it modifies should be immediately apparent. In the first two examples below, though there is no real ambiguity since only one interpretation is possible, there is likely to be some interruption of the flow of communication as the reader pauses to make sure just what it is that the writer intended:

Dangling: In coming to an agreement, a compromise had to be voted. [The compromise did not come to the agreement; *they* or some other word meaning the voters should be made the subject.]

Dangling: After reading sixteen books, the subject is still a blank to me.

Immediately clear: After reading sixteen books, I am still blank about the subject.

(See Ch. 8, "Revising dangling modifiers," p. 297.)

4. *Without "the."* In current style there is a tendency to use gerunds without *the* and with a direct object rather than an *of* phrase. This exploits the verbal force of the word and makes for economy and emphasis:

His chief amusement is *telling jokes* on the President. [Rather than: His chief amusement is *the telling of jokes* on the President.]

In *revising the first draft,* a writer can check all the spellings. (Rather than: In *the revising of the first draft....*)

5. *Idioms with gerunds.* Some words are characteristically followed by gerunds, others by infinitives. For example:

Gerunds	*Infinitives*
cannot help *doing*	compelled *to do*
capable *of painting*	able *to paint*
the habit *of giving*	the tendency *to give*
an idea *of selling*	a wish *to sell*
his object *in doing*	obligation *to pay*

With many words, especially common ones, either idiom is used: the way *of doing* something, the way *to do* something.

(See Ch. 9, "Infinitive or gerund," p. 343. Compare *Participles, *Infinitives. Reference: Curme, *Syntax,* Ch. 24.)

get, got •

1. *Forms.* Principal parts: *get, got, got* and *gotten*:

I am getting a new racket.   I got six inside an hour.

I had already got [gotten] mine.

Rebel though I was, I had got the religion of scholarship and science.—LINCOLN STEFFENS, *Autobiography,* p. 127

Gotten was brought to America by the colonists of the seventeenth century, when it was the usual English form, and has remained in general American usage ever since, while in England (less so in Scotland) the form has largely given way to *got* except in compounds (*beget, forget*). Today both forms are used by Americans as the past participle (except in "have got," as in § 2 below), the choice between them depending largely on the emphasis and rhythm of the particular sentence and on the user's speech habits. *Gotten* is probably the more common.

He could have [*gotten* or *got*] here by now.

In the past I have [*gotten* or *got*] a good meal here.

2. *Have got.* *Got* (not *gotten*) is used as an informal way of intensifying *have* in the sense of possess or of being obligated (Have you got a pencil?—I've got to study now). The *have* alone could carry the meaning, but it is unemphatic, especially when contracted, because it is so frequently used as a mere auxiliary of tense that we are not accustomed to feeling it as a verb of full meaning. Consequently *got* has a considerable advantage in speech. Some Formal writers avoid it, but the idiom is in General use and is appropriate in any but the most Formal situation. (References: Albert H. Marckwardt, " 'Have Got' in Expressions of Possession and Obligation," *College English,* 1955, 16:309-310; Thomas L. Crowell, *"Have Got,* a Pattern Preserver," *American Speech,* 1959, 34:280-286.)

3. *"Get" in idioms.* *Get* is one of the most popular verbs in idiomatic phrases, in most of which it doesn't have its original meaning shown in the sentences under § 1 but is a relatively colorless linking verb. Most of these idioms are Informal:

get cold	get sick	get tired	get scared
get going	get to go	get in touch with	get supper
get left	get on my nerves	get away with	get along with
get me?	get it across	get together	get with it

"But I got to," she cried. "I just have to talk to somebody. I didn't go home. I got worried, awful scared."—ARTHUR SOMERS ROCHE, *Shadow of Doubt,* p. 63

The first *got* in this passage would be preceded by *I've* in Standard Informal writing. Transcribing the locution as *I got* makes it look worse than it often sounds; in speech *I've* is often spoken with such reduced stress and so rapidly that the /v/ sound is virtually inaudible.

4. *"Get" as a passive auxiliary.* *Get* is increasingly used as an Informal emphatic passive auxiliary:

He got thrown out inside of an hour. Our house is getting painted.

(See Adelaide C. Bartlett, *College English,* 1949, 10:280-282; Curme, *Parts of Speech,* p. 218; Pooley, pp. 148-151.)

get up, arise, rise • See *rise.

Given names • Ordinarily either spell out or use the initial of *given names* (also called Christian names) rather than such abbreviations as *Chas., Thos., Wm.*:

C. T. Graves	or	Charles T. Graves
T. W. Lane	or	Thomas W. Lane

glamor—glamour • The first would be the normal American spelling (see *-or, -our), but in the fashion and entertainment "worlds" *glamour* is more common (glamour girl). The adjective is generally *glamorous*.

go •

1. *Go* is a useful little word, especially as a *linking verb in a number of idioms, most of which are Informal:

go blind	go mad	go dry
go steady	go hard	go wrong

2. *Go and* is a spoken form of emphasis: *Go and try it yourself* [no actual movement meant]. *She went and shot the bear herself.* These are primarily oral expressions, but they are appropriate in some Informal and General writing.

Gobbledygook • A suggestive label for an abuse of Formal English, characteristic of some government and business communications, marked by overheavy (abstract) words and confusing, pseudo-legal or pseudo-scientific sentences. What relatively simple statement is being made in this sample?

By encouraging and maintaining a reciprocal interest between the prime contractor and his subcontractors in the business matter of fulfilling the obligations of the prime contract, contractual requirements, particularly inspection, can be greatly assisted in furnishing the consignee with the required information that material has received inspection in accordance with the contract.

(See Ch. 9, "Big words," p. 347.)

good—well • *Good* is usually an adjective in Standard English; *well* is either an adjective or an adverb: "I feel *good*" and "I feel *well*" (adjectives) are both usual but have different meanings (*good* implying actual bodily sensation, *well* referring merely to a state, "not ill").

In Nonstandard usage *well* is rarely used, *good* taking its place ("He rowed good" for "He rowed well"). In Informal speech *good* is occasionally heard when the subject is an inanimate object: *The motor runs pretty good.* Perhaps this is because *good* is felt as modifying *motor*. But this usage is not yet appropriate in writing. (Reference: Bryant, pp. 100-101.)

good and • *Good and* is a common spoken equivalent of *very* (I'm good and mad) but is seldom appropriate in writing. (Reference: Bryant, pp. 99-100.)

good-by—good-bye • Both are in use, often without the hyphen.

got, gotten, get • See *get, got.

grade school—graded school • *Graded school* is the older word but *grade school* is much more common, and always appropriate.

graduate • The idiom *to be graduated* from an institution has generally gone out of use except in Formal and somewhat archaic writing and has been replaced by *graduated from*: *He graduated from Yale in 1902.* Omitting the *from* is Nonstandard: *He graduated high school in 1957,* perhaps a confusion with the acceptable *finished.* (Reference: Bryant, pp. 102-103.)

Grammar • *Grammar* derives from the Greek *gramma,* meaning a written symbol; the first grammarians were teachers of writing and reading. In the Middle Ages, to know grammar meant not only to know how to read and write Latin but to possess the powers of a literate man in a largely illiterate society. In modern English, *grammar* is used in several senses:

1. *The basic structure of a language.* Every language is a complex of patterns developed over a long period of time by the people using it. In the English sentence *You see it,* we know *you* is the subject (here the actor) and *it* is the object (the thing seen), because *you* precedes the verb and *it* follows it. In French, however, the sentence would be written, *Tu le vois,* with the subject first, object second and verb last. The order of the elements, as well as their form, depends on the conventions of the particular language. Every native speaker learns these and a host of other patterns in his language as a child and can understand and use them automatically. These patterns may be called the complete or total grammar of the language; in this sense English grammar is "the English way of saying things."

2. *Descriptive grammar.* This is an attempt to describe as systematically and objectively as possible the total system of a language. In his method, the descriptive grammarian attempts to be scientific: he observes the language as it is in an effort to discover its underlying system but without trying to guide the language habits of speakers and writers. Since a language is extensive, complex, varied, and elusive, a particular grammar will never be complete but will depend on the limitations the grammarian has set himself and those imposed on him; he will usually limit himself to one variety of the language (ordinarily that used by the educated because the material is most readily available), and he will be limited by his training (the

linguistic philosophy he embraces), the information available to him, and, of course, his individual competence.

When the description of a language covers a considerable period of time, describing the evolution of words and forms and constructions, perhaps explaining present usage in the light of the past, it is called *historical* (or *diachronic*) *grammar*. When several related languages are compared, as English might be with Latin or German, it is called *comparative grammar*. When one stage of a language is described, it is called *synchronic grammar*.

For one variety of the language there will be one basic structure, one underlying system, one grammar in the sense of § 1 above. Every attempt to describe this grammar will be a grammar; in this second sense there may therefore be several grammars. A brief account of the three principal types of these follows:

a—Classical. This is a rather arbitrary and somewhat misleading name, chosen because *descriptive* has already been applied to all three types. It has the justification, however, that the grammarians who developed it attempted to work within the Greco-Roman grammatical tradition, and that they are the earliest modern grammarians—Jacob Grimm, for example, first published his *German Grammar* in 1819—to attempt a systematic description of a language on the basis of a careful examination of it. Though fully aware of the primacy of speech as language, they were able to break away only gradually from the habit of depending on written records for their evidence, especially as they were much concerned—Grimm again, for example—with the history of the language. Nevertheless their achievements have been enormous, and they established the firm foundations of modern linguistics.

Among the more important grammars in this tradition are Henry Sweet, *A New English Grammar,* 2 vols., 1892, 1898; H. Poutsma, *A Grammar of Late Modern English,* 4 vols., 1904-1926; Otto Jespersen, *A Modern English Grammar,* 7 vols., 1909-1949 (a convenient brief example is Jespersen's *Essentials of English Grammar,* 1934); and in this country, George O. Curme, *Syntax,* 1931, and *Parts of Speech and Accidence,* 1935.

b—Structural. This approach, to which Americans have been major contributors, carries through much more rigorously two principles of the classical descriptive grammars: the primacy of speech and the importance of the structural patterns of the language in conveying grammatical meaning (see *Lexical meaning). Structural descriptive grammars therefore begin with the *phoneme, go on to the *morpheme, and attempt to identify the syntactical devices by which grammatical relations are signalled.

Among the more important grammars in this tradition are Charles C. Fries, *The Structure of English*, 1952; W. Nelson Francis, *The Structure of American English*, 1958; James Sledd, *A Short Introduction to English Grammar*, 1959; H. A. Gleason, *An Introduction to Descriptive Linguistics*, 1961.

c—Transformational and generative. This most recent approach—again American—assumes that the very large total of sentence patterns which can be described for a language is based on a relatively small number of kernel sentences. As we learn our language we unconsciously acquire the rules by which these kernel sentences can be transformed into others. We gradually master the capacity to generate an increasing proportion of the total possible sentences. The task of this kind of grammarian is to discover the basic sentence patterns and the rules by which these can be transformed.

An account of the various transformational grammars will be found in Emmon W. Bach, *An Introduction to Transformational Grammars*, New York, 1964. An elementary presentation is given in Paul Roberts, *English Sentences*, 1962, Ch. 10.

3. *Prescriptive grammar.* Besides these uses of the term *grammar* we also speak of *prescriptive* or *normative grammar*. A prescriptive grammar is a body of rules presented as guides to expression, statements of how, in the belief of the writer, people should speak and write. Many English grammars of this type, represented principally by textbooks prepared for the use of students, are now in disrepute because they are out of touch with descriptive grammar and with actual usage. Too many school grammars represent either older usage or traditional rules that are not consistently followed and some that have never been followed by users of English. To the extent that they are describing a variety of English actually used, they present Formal English as the only (or best) English and discourage General and Informal usage.

One unfortunate result of prescriptive grammar is that the teaching of Formal English has seemed so unreal to students that, unable to separate the useful from the useless advice, they have paid almost no attention at all to it. If they talked as their textbooks said they should, they would be laughed at; consequently they have usually continued their old habits.

Although the usage recommended in schools will probably always be a little more Formal than that being practiced by actual writers, school grammar is now gradually getting away from traditional prescriptive grammar and is coming closer to the actual usage of the educated as presented in the descriptive grammars.

4. *Grammar as remedy.* Many people are occasionally oppressed by a feeling of inadequacy in their use of English.

They believe that all their deficiencies, real or imagined, in vocabulary, effective expression, spelling, usage, and punctuation would be removed if they studied "grammar" conscientiously. This is back of the demand for "More grammar!" in the schools. This demand is really based on a desire for more varied and more acceptable *usage*, "good English" as discussed in Ch. 1, pp. 25-32. The best remedy is wide listening and reading and practice in using language effectively. Grammatical terms play a useful but subordinate part in summarizing and describing the facts of the current language, but they are not themselves the remedy.

When you use *grammar* in speaking or writing, you should be aware of its various meanings and varied uses, and if necessary indicate the sense in which you are using it. In this book the term is restricted to the first two senses described in this article, the exact meaning being shown by the context.

The terms used in grammar deserve a comment also. The analysis of language is a discipline more than two thousand years old, going back in Western culture to the philosophers and rhetoricians of ancient Greece. The terminology devised by the Greeks was used with little modification until modern linguistics made its inadequacy for the description of other languages apparent. Some of the old terms have been kept and given more restricted or more precise definition and new terms have been introduced. Some grammatical and linguistic terms are still not standardized, but by making their reference clear we can and must use them in discussing language.

Many people steadfastly refuse to learn the technical terms of grammar. Students who gaily toss about *schizophrenic, marginal utility, Hanseatic League, dicotyledonous,* or *trinitrotoluene* will not learn the pronunciation and meaning of *predicative, metonymy,* or even *apostrophe* or *agreement,* and some teachers of the subject try to work without naming exactly what they are talking about. Many of the words are a bit difficult—Greek or Latin names that have been taken into the language—but they are not nearly so difficult as the vocabulary of psychology or chemistry. This book uses a good many of these terms, without apology, though when there is a choice of name the simpler and more suggestive has usually been taken. It is only good sense to gain control of the words that name common facts of usage and style, words which are an essential part of the English vocabulary of educated people.

(See *Linguistics, *Latin and English § 3. References: The works in the bibliography at the beginning of this *Guide-Index,* specifically Fries and Pooley, discuss many of the particular rules of prescriptive grammar besides offering their own observation of usage; see especially Fries, *AEG*, Chs. 1, 2, 11, and Robert C. Pooley, *Teaching English Grammar*, New York, 1957; also the descriptive grammars mentioned in § 2 above.)

grammatical, ungrammatical • These adjectives will have senses derived from definitions § 1 and § 3 of the article *Grammar: for § 1, *grammatical* means fitting into the system of the language, *ungrammatical* means not fitting in (*It's me* would be grammatical; the Frenchman's literal translation *She [the table] is large* would be ungrammatical); for § 3, *grammatical* means fitting into arbitrarily prescribed rules, *ungrammatical* means not fitting those rules (*It's I* would be grammatical, *It's me* ungrammatical). *Bad grammar* is approximately synonomous with the § 3 sense of *ungrammatical*. Obviously these terms should be used with great caution.

Group words • In English many groups of two or more words (that is, phrases) function like single words. Often the division of the elements into separate words in print is quite arbitrary. *High school* is not the noun *school* modified by the adjective *high* so much as a noun in its own right just as *highway* is. But established practice is to spell the first as two words, the second as one. Many of our verbs are made up of a verb plus an adverb: *close up, hold off, look into* (see *Verb-adverb combinations); many prepositions are phrases: *according to, in opposition to*.

Other typical group words are:

Nouns: hay fever   back door   holding company   home run
safety razor   baby blue   school year   sacrifice hit
Verbs: dig in   back water   back step (military)   flare up
follow through   follow up   show up   blow up
Prepositions: in spite of   in consequence of   previous to
due to

"In such cases," George P. Krapp wrote, "it is contrary to the idiom of the language to try to analyze the groups into their constituent parts so as to give every word, standing alone, a clearly defined structural value." Consequently in this book we ignore the superficial difference between a part of speech written as a single word and one that is written as a group of words. "Noun" or "verb" or "preposition" refers both to single words and to *group words* functioning as noun or verb or preposition. (References: Curme, *Syntax*, Ch. 30; George P. Krapp, *The Knowledge of English*, New York, 1927, pp. 313-316, where such phrases are called "function groups.")

guess, calculate, reckon • See *calculate, guess, reckon.

H •

1. As a distinctive sound, *h* /h/ always occurs at the beginning of syllables: *harsh, heel, high, horrible, ahead.*

2. *H* is likely to be silent at the beginning of unstressed syllables: *forehead* /fôr′id/, *behind* (when spoken rapidly in unstressed part of phrase), /bi īnd′/, *he, his, her,* etc., when lightly spoken (Give it to *him′* versus *Give′* it to [h]im).

H is silent in *rh* words—*rhetoric, rhyme, rhythm.*

In many words from French the *h* was formerly not pronounced: *habit, history, hotel* ... but now is except in *heir, honest, honor, hour,* and sometimes in *herb, hostler, huge, humble, humor.* So long as the *h* was not pronounced, *an* was used before these words, and it is still by some people in the forms in which the stress is not on the first syllable: *an historical work, an habitual error,* though *a* is now more common. (See *a—an, *wh.)

Habitual action • *Habitual action* is expressed in English in a variety of ways, of which the following are samples:

He would always go by the longer way.

I get up every morning at six.

He came here every week.

He used to go by the longer way.

He usually went by the longer way.

Hackneyed • See *Trite.

had better, had rather • *Had better* is the usual idiom for giving advice or making an indirect command:

You had better take care of that cold.

You'd better go.

The assimilation of the *d* of *you'd* by the *b* of *better* has given rise to the Informal construction without *had*:

If he asks you to do it, you better do it.

Had rather and *would rather* are both used to express preference, the latter the more Formal:

He would rather ski than eat.

He had [He'd] rather ski than eat.

Since the *had* or *would* is unstressed in speech (and the contraction *he'd* is frequently used), it is impossible to tell which is being said.

half • The more Formal idiom is *a half*; the General, *half a*:

Formal: He ran a half mile; a half hour.

General: He ran half a mile; half an hour.

A half a (a half an hour) is a redundancy sometimes found in Informal and Nonstandard speech but not in Standard written English.

hanged—hung • In Formal English the principal parts of *hang* when referring to the death penalty are *hang, hanged, hanged,* the archaic forms kept alive by legal phrases such as "hanged by the neck until dead"; in other senses they are *hang, hung, hung*: Murderers are *hanged,* pictures are *hung*.

General and Informal usage does not keep this distinction, often using *hang, hung, hung* in all senses:

> They hung the Turk that invented work
> In the Big Rock Candy Mountain.

Hanging indention • See *Indention.

hardly • See *Double negative.

have •

1. *Auxiliary.* Have occurs most frequently in the perfect tenses, for which it is now the sole auxiliary in English (in earlier English *be* was also used). *Have* plus a past participle makes the perfect tense (They have come); *shall have* or *will have* plus a past participle makes the future perfect tense (They will have gone by then); *had* plus a past participle makes the past perfect (They had gone to the beach before we arrived). In this use it is a *function word—a signal of tense. (See *Tenses of verbs.)

2. *Independent meaning.* As a verb of independent meaning *have* means to "own, possess" in a literal (have a car) or transferred sense (have the measles). There are many idioms with *have* such as:

> to have a look   the book (or gossip) has it that
> have it your own way   to have it out
> *Informal:* He had his arm broken.
> *General:* He had a broken arm.
> *Formal:* He suffered a broken arm.

Because *have* occurs so frequently as an "empty" auxiliary word, its meaning as an independent word is often reinforced by *got*. (See *get, got § 2.)

3. *Contractions.* In speech, *he, she, it* and unstressed *has* are contracted to *he's, she's, it's* (He's not tried to in years; It's rained for over a week). This contraction is indistinguishable from that of *is; He's gone* may be *He has gone* or *He is gone. I, you, we, they have* are contracted to *I've, you've, we've, they've*.

Would have, wouldn't have are sometimes written *would of, wouldn't of,* an unacceptable transcription of what is spoken as *would've, wouldn't've.*

4. *Had ought* and *hadn't ought* are idioms with *have* that occur frequently in speech. *Hadn't ought* (He hadn't ought to lie like that) is regional and Informal. *Had ought,* on the other hand, is a common Nonstandard idiom, although it, too, is sometimes heard in Informal speech.

Nonstandard: He had ought to take better care of himself.

Standard: He ought to take better care of himself.

5. *Have to* and *must* are nearly synonymous in the affirmative (*I have to* or *must go now*), but in the negative there is a difference (*I don't have to go, I mustn't go*). *Have to* has the advantage that it can be conjugated in all tenses. In present tense forms the last consonant is unvoiced: /haf′tə, has′tə/.

6. *Other idioms.* For *have got* see *get, got § 2. See also *had better, had rather.

he-or-she • Since English has no third person singular pronoun to refer to individuals of either or both sexes, English speakers are faced with a problem unique in Indo-European languages; in all the others the third person singular pronouns have grammatical reference, not sexual (see *Gender). As we must often refer to nouns that name either or both male and female, the language has developed three ways of making up for the lack of an accurate pronoun:

1. The prescribed way is to use *he* or *his* alone even when some of the persons are female:

There is considerable discussion whether a man or a woman will be appointed to the vacant cabinet post. Whoever receives the appointment will find *his* task a difficult one.

Mr. Brown and Miss Trevor led the discussion, each giving *his* opinion of the poem.

Sometimes when the typical individuals or the majority of the group referred to are women, *her* is used in the same way:

Each of the teachers in this school is required to submit *her* report to the principal in person.

2. A common way in General usage is to resort to a plural pronoun because it evades the question of sex:

Neither [a man and a woman] tasted what *they* ate.—KATHERINE ANNE PORTER, *Flowering Judas,* p. 26

3. Sometimes both *he* and *she* are used:

A teacher gives *his* or *her* own opinions on matters of politics and religion and often influences a pupil to think as *he* or *she* does.

(Either of the two pronouns would be better in this sentence than both of them).

Every student wishes to participate in some activity authorized by *his* or *her* college. (*His* or *her* sounds pedantic here; *his* alone would be better.)

The two pronouns are almost always clumsy and really no more accurate, since the meaning is determined by the antecedent. (Reference: Bergen and Cornelia Evans, *A Dictionary of Contemporary American Usage*, New York, 1957, entries for *his* and *they*.)

Headword—head • A *headword* or *head* is a word modified by another word, especially by one or more adjectives (his first long *sleep*) or a verb modified by one or more adverbs (*run* slowly around the rim). The term is used variously by different linguists, but always to mean a word that is regarded as primary in a word group. (See Harold Whitehall, *Structural Essentials of English*, New York, 1956, Ch. 2; Paul Roberts, *Patterns of English*, New York, 1956, pp. 77-105; Ralph B. Long, *The Sentence and Its Parts*, Chicago, 1961, p. 490.)

healthful, healthy • *Healthful* meant "giving health"; places and food were healthful. *Healthy* meant "having good health"; persons and animals were healthy. This distinction is still attempted by some writers and speakers, but many simply use *healthy* in both senses.

Heightened style • See *Style.

hell • See *devil.

help but • See *can't help but, can't seem to.

hence • See *Conjunctive adverbs.

high school • Capitalize only when referring to a particular school (some newspaper styles do not use capitals even then):

I graduated from high school at seventeen.
I graduated from Bismarck High School in 1964.

highbrow • After a period of slang overuse, *highbrow* (and *lowbrow* too) has settled down as a useful General word.

There is a widespread belief that chamber-music makers are long-haired musical intellectuals, bloodless esoterics, highbrows with a G string.—JOSEPH WECHSBERG, "The Music of Friends," *Horizon*, Nov. 1962, p. 45

Middlebrow, a more recent coinage, has also established itself.

himself, herself • *Himself* and *herself* are used in two ways:
1. As reflexive pronouns, referring to the subject of the sentence:

George has always taken himself pretty seriously.
She looked at herself in the window and gave her hat a little pull.

2. As *intensives for emphasis:

He told me so himself.
I looked up and there was Mrs. Goodenow herself.

(Compare *myself, *self.)

home, homely •
1. *Home* is used in the function of a noun, verb, adjective, or adverb—an example of the English habit of making one form serve several functions (see *Parts of speech):

Noun: His home was now in Cleveland.
Verb: They homed the missiles in by radar.
Adverbial modifier: He came home unexpectedly. His remark went home.
Adjectival modifier: He reports to the home office.

In "They are home," *home* is a General expression for *at home. To home* is Nonstandard and regional.
2. *Home—house.* For a realtor a *home* is any house; in sentimental (and some Formal) use a *home* is only the "place of one's domestic affections." But in General use *home* is a lived-in house (or any extension needed for animal, plant, or object).
3. *Homely.* In some contexts, particularly in British usage, *homely* has the sense of "informal, unassuming, characteristic of home life." In the United States, however, *homely* usually means "ugly in appearance." In this country it is therefore safer to use the word only in the second sense.

Homonyms, homophones • Two words of different meanings that are pronounced alike (*bear, bare; plain, plane*) are called *homonyms* or *homophones.*

English has a great many such pairs of words, most of them in common use. They have developed for various reasons. Some Old English words once different in sound have come to be pronounced alike because of changes in form through the centuries: *bear* (the animal) from *bera, bear* (the verb) from *beran; plain* and *plane* both go back to Latin *planus,* but the spelling of the first was altered in coming through Old

French. Many words are from different languages, having fallen into similar forms by accident: *rest* meaning "peace" is from Old English, *rest* meaning "remainder" is from French; *bark* of a tree is from Scandinavian, *bark* of a dog from Old English, and *bark*, the vessel, a more recent borrowing from French-Italian.

There is little chance of misunderstanding such words because their context will tell which is which—though their similarity is often exploited in *puns. Where real conflict exists, the resolution has usually been by one or both words going out of use. The verb *halve* hardly exists in speech anymore because of almost certain confusion with *have*: "We'll halve (have) the pie." But homophones like *plain—plane* make a good deal of trouble in spelling. Much of this confusion is really carelessness, for the words are common. Try to visualize the troublesome ones in phrases that show their meaning, something like these:

priest at the *altar*—who can *alter* human nature?
Father gave his *assent* to the marriage—the *ascent* of Mount Everest
bearing pain—*baring* his arm
a lower *berth*—his tenth *birth*day
born in June 1947—*borne* by the wind
the *bridal* party, *bridal* suite—a horse's *bridle,* the *bridle* path
the *capital* of Illinois is Springfield—the *capitol* has a gilded dome
every woman likes *compliments*—the *complement* of the angle
there are five members of the *council—counsel* is advice—*counsel* for the defense
a *dual* personality—a pistol *duel*
a *mantle* covered her—the trophy cups on the *mantel*
a *piece* of paper—*peace* or war
air*plane*, *plane* geometry—the Great *Plains*, a *plain* statement
pore over a book—*pour* coffee
he *rode* horseback—the *road* was macadam—he *rowed* a dory
a box of *stationery*—a *stationary* engine—*stationary* desks
tea to drink—*tee* on a golf course

(See *Spoken and written English. Reference: Arthur G. Kennedy, *Current English,* Boston, 1935, § 82.)

Honorable • As a title of respect, for persons in political office of some prestige, this word is capitalized and is usually preceded by *the*; it may be abbreviated in addresses when initials or first names are used:

the Honorable Ernest Gruening   The Hon. Ernest Gruening
the Honorable Member from Alaska

hope • Both *in hope of* and *in hopes of* are in General usage, with the former perhaps preferred because of sound:

After leaving Montreal we drove on *in hope of* [or: *in hopes of*] reaching Quebec as soon as possible. [Or: *in the hope of* reaching]

The participle *hoping* is probably more usual:

After leaving Montreal we drove on, *hoping* to reach Quebec as soon as possible.

Hours • In consecutive writing, especially if it is Formal, hours are written in words: *at four o'clock.*

In newspapers and in much General writing, figures are used, especially if several times are mentioned:

at 4 p.m.   just after 9 a.m.   from 10 to 12

(See *a.m. and p.m., *Numbers § 1b. See also *Period § 2d.)

house—home • See *home, homely.

however • As a connective, *however* is more appropriate to the fully developed sentences of Formal style and is especially useful as a connective between sentences:

Occasionally the beat man writes his own story in the press room of the public building in which he is stationed, and sends it to the office by messenger. This, however, is unusual as it involves loss of time.—C. D. MacDougall, *Reporting for Beginners,* p. 65

Amateur writers are likely to overuse *however; but* is usually more appropriate, especially in simple, direct writing:

During the eight weeks I was in the hospital, Al visited me twice, assuring me that as soon as I was able, I could have my old job. But [better than *however*] after four weeks of convalescing at home, it was time for me to go to college.

Clauses in one sentence connected by *however* are conventionally separated by a semicolon. (See *Conjunctive adverbs, *but.)

When two contrasts must be stated in sequence, *however* is useful to avoid repetition: *I got there on time, but he came late; however, he had a good excuse.*

Humor • See *Epigrams, *Malapropism, *Puns, *Spoonerism.

hung—hanged • See *hanged—hung.

Hyphen (-) • The hyphen is a mark of punctuation, rather than of spelling, that is used sometimes to join and sometimes to keep distinct two or more printed units. Its commonest use is to mark the division of a word at the end of a line of manuscript or type (see *Division of words). Other uses of the hyphen are somewhat variable: dictionaries and publishers' stylebooks do not always agree on specific practices. Consequently they are in part a matter of style, with Formal writers tending to use more hyphens than General writers. The following uses are fairly well standardized and may be taken as a guide for General writing.

1. *In compound words.* Many compound words will be found written in three ways: as two words, or hyphened, or as one word (*prize fighter, prize-fighter, prizefighter*); as a rule the form does not affect meaning. In the past, words that were becoming fused into compounds passed through a probationary period with hyphens before being written as single words. *Baseball,* for instance, was hyphened for a time, and so were *football* and *basketball.* There is less tendency now, except in quite Formal writing, to use such hyphens, and compounds are made immediately without hyphens if the words are needed.

Two words of one syllable are most often written solid (*bedroom, kickback, lineman, skylight*), especially when the first element is more heavily stressed in speech; but a hyphen is likely if the first is not a simple modifier of the second: *by-pass, close-up, cure-all, hair-do.* A hyphen is more likely to be used when one of the elements, especially the first, has two or more syllables, though two words is always an option:

... and we have even seen their guilty simulacra in tenement-house and shopfronts.—LEWIS MUMFORD, *Sticks and Stones,* p. 180

Schoolbook is usually written solid; *reference book* is two words.

A hyphen is conventional in three groups of words:

a–In the compound numerals from twenty-one to ninety-nine, and in fractions, though this use is not universal:

forty-seven   ninety-ninth   one hundred sixty-two
three-sixteenths   one thirty-second

b–In names of family relationships:

Hyphened: father-in-law, daughter-in-law
One word: stepson, stepdaughter, stepmother
Two words: half brother, half sister (sometimes hyphened)

c–In compounds with *self-,* which are usually hyphened in dictionaries but are often found in print as two words:

self-contained   self-government—self government
self-help—self help   self-importance   self-pity—self pity

Selfhood and *selfless* are written as one word. (Compare *-wise.)

A hyphen or a separation is used if the first member of the compound ends in the same vowel that the second begins with (*fire-eater, fire-escape* or *fire escape*) or if a misleading or awkward combination of consonants would result from joining the words (*mess hall* or *mess-hall, bell-like*).

If a compound word raises a question, consult a reliable recent dictionary both under the entry for the word and in the discussion of hyphens and compounds. If no information is forthcoming, use a hyphen or not as your taste dictates.

2. *In modifiers.*

a–A number of adjectives composed of two words are conventionally hyphened when they precede a noun:

clear-cut	easy-going	up-to-date
clear-eyed	first-class	would-be
clear-headed	narrow-minded	

The more commonly used ones are given in dictionaries. Most of them are an adverb plus a verbal; and other phrases formed on this pattern are hyphened when the adverb does not end in *-ly*:

a late-flowering iris	slow-moving goods
a well-marked trail	[but] a plainly marked trail

Usually such modifiers are not hyphened in predicate position:

a clear-eyed boy   [but]   The boy was clear eyed.

Such phrases should not be hyphened in a verb construction:

a well-matched pair   They were well matched.
They were well suited to each other.

Short, frequently used combinations are generally hyphened:

a two-year term   a small-town sheriff   a no-hit, no-run game

Longer phrase modifiers are usually hyphened:

on a pay-as-you-go basis
a 5-cent-an-hour wage increase
a detailed question-and-answer sheet
two-hundred-pound, six-foot-two halfbacks

b–Usage is divided on hyphening noun phrases when used as modifiers, as in *seventeenth century philosophy*. Formal writers would usually write *seventeenth-century*; General, *seventeenth century*. This distinction applies to such expressions as the following:

a Seventh Avenue shop   summer vacation freedom

c–Occasionally some pairs of modifiers might be ambiguous without a hyphen: *a light yellow scarf* might be either a light scarf that was yellow or a scarf that was light yellow, so that *light-yellow* is safest for the latter meaning, and *light, yellow scarf* for the first. There is a possible distinction between a *great-grandfather* (indicating relationship only) and a *great grandfather* (indicating quality of a grandfather), and between a new car-owner and a new-car owner. In speech the distinction might be achieved through intonation, but in both speech and writing a re-ordering of the sentence elements would prevent possible ambiguity.

d–A numeral as part of a modifier (5-cent, 27 9-inch boards) and a letter linked to a noun (H-bomb, T-square, X-ray) are hyphened.

e–A hyphen may be used to carry the force of a modifier over to a later noun ("suspension hyphen"):

The third-, fourth-, and fifth-grade rooms have been redecorated.

In both thirteenth- and fourteenth-century texts

3. *With prefixes.* In certain types of compounds of a prefix and a root word a hyphen may be used to avoid confusion, or for emphasis or for appearance:

a–Between a prefix ending with a vowel and a root word beginning with the same vowel (though a *dieresis is used by some publishers) :

re-elected   re-enter   pre-eminent   pre-existent

(See *pre-, *re-.)

Usage is divided on words made with *co-,* the more common ones now generally being written solid:

cooperate or co-operate   coordinate or co-ordinate

b–To avoid confusion with another word:

re-collect—recollect   re-cover—recover

c–Between a prefix and a proper name:

pre-Sputnik   ex-President Truman   pro-Eisenhower

d–When the prefix is stressed:

ex-husband   ex-wife   anti-vivisection (or antivivisection)

4. *Miscellaneous uses.*

a–Between the letters showing how a word is spelled:

The loser spelled *receive* r-e-c-i-e-v-e.

b–Often to show syllabication:

hy-pos-ta-ti-za-tion

Hyphening is more an editor's worry than a writer's. A publisher may wish for uniformity in principle and may struggle to get it in printing particular words, though absolute consistency is impossible. The manual of the Government Printing Office devotes over fifty pages to rules for hyphening, and stylebooks of newspaper and other publications have numerous rules, many of them arbitrary choices of form made simply to insure consistency. In a person's ordinary writing, he does not need to be so particular. For words in common use he can consult a dictionary or do as he finds reputable publications doing.

The conclusion one comes to after a serious consideration of current habits in the use of hyphens is well put by John Benbow in *Manuscript & Proof,* the stylebook of the Oxford University Press of New York: "If you take hyphens seriously you will surely go mad."

(References: *GPO Manual,* pp. 63-120; Summey, Ch. 10; and discussions in recent dictionaries.)

I •

1. *"Long i"* /ī/. The sound of long *i* is a diphthong, gliding from /a/ or /ä/ to short /i/ or short /e/: *ice, wild, find, guide, night, tiny.* It is also spelled as in *aisle, ay, aye, height, eye, by, buy, bye, lie, choir.*

In unstressed syllables /ī/ has a similar sound but is somewhat shorter: /dī am′ə tər/.

2. *"Short i"* /i/ as in *bit, city.* This sound is spelled in a number of other ways: s*ie*ve, dut*y,* forf*ei*t, all*ey,* mess*a*ge, Sund*ay,* marri*a*ge, foreh*ea*d, mount*ai*n, min*u*te, bisc*ui*t.

3. *"Continental i"* /ē/. In a few words the Continental (European) value of *i* is preserved: *machine* /mə shēn′/, *police* /pə-lēs′/, *visa* /vē′zə/, and in recent unanglicized borrowings.

4. *As a consonant* /y/. *I* may represent a /y/ sound before a vowel, especially in rapid pronunciation: *opinion* /ə pin′yən/. (For the plural *-ies* see *Plurals § 1b and *Y. See also *-ile and *J.)

5. *Before* r. *I* may spell the sound represented by /ė/: *bird* /bėrd/, *third* /thėrd/.

I •

1. *Capital.* The pronoun *I* is written as a capital simply because in the old manuscripts a small *i* might be lost or get attached to a neighboring word, and the capital helped keep it distinct. No conceit is implied.

2. *As first word.* The notion that *I* should not be the first word in a letter (sometimes even that it should not be the first word of a sentence) is not justified by prevailing cultivated practice. *I* should be used wherever it is needed, though if it opens several consecutive sentences the repetition becomes irksome. People with only average concern for themselves need not worry; the conceited will give themselves away anyway.

Circumlocutions to get around the natural use of *I* are usually awkward and likely to attract attention to themselves:

There is a feeling in me [I feel] that relief projects are unsound.

The best way to avoid conspicuous use of *I* (or of any other word) is to keep it out of emphatic sentence positions, especially from the stressed beginning of a sentence. A dependent clause or longish phrase put first will throw the stress off the *I*:

After a long struggle I decided to go. [*Instead of*: I decided to go, after a long struggle.]

3. *Omission of I.* In clipped personal writing—diaries, casual and Informal letters—*I* is often appropriately omitted if the style is also clipped in other respects:

Talked to John. Very informative. He doesn't think it can be done.

(See **It's me, *myself, *we* § 2.)

ibid. • See **Abbreviations* § 2.

-ible, -able • See **-able, -ible.*

idea • The word *idea* is frequently used as a substitute for *intention, impression,* and similar words in constructions that are usually wordy:

I got the idea [I thought] that every policeman was my enemy.
Wordy: We started out with the idea in mind of going to a dance.
Improved: We started out intending to go to a dance.

Idiolect • An *idiolect* is the set of speech habits of an individual. A dialect or a language is the speech patterns of people with similar idiolects, the similarities being closer in the former.

Idiom and idioms •
Revision: The expression marked is not idiomatic.
Revise it, referring to an article in this Index *or to a*   *Id*
dictionary if you are not sure what it should be.

The word *idiom* is used in two different, almost opposed, senses:

1. It may mean *the usual forms of expression of a particular language,* as we may compare German idiom with English idiom, meaning the ways in which words are characteristically put together in the two languages. German, for example, has suspended constructions (*Ich habe den alten Mann schon gesehen*—I have the old man already seen), separable prefixes,

and participial constructions, whereas English tends to complete its constructions immediately. In French, adjectives usually come after the nouns they modify (*une maison blanche*), in English they usually come before (*a white house*). "Idiomatic English" connotes natural English. It ordinarily is contrasted with stilted usage and suggests a mastery of the basic constructions of General English.

2. The word *idiom* may also mean *an accepted phrase that differs from the usual construction of the language,* either in not submitting to the typical grammatical analysis (like *somebody else's,* in which the sign of the possessive is added to the adjective rather than to the noun) or in having a total meaning not obviously suggested by the meanings of the parts (like *to center around,* or *in respect to,* which are ridiculous when analyzed). These idioms are usually particular phrases which we learn as separate items—easily in our own language, with difficulty in another—differing from the idioms discussed in the preceding section, which are patterns for large numbers of locutions.

Collecting English idioms is good sport and so is trying to analyze them. Considering them grammatically and literally, what can you make of these?

to come in handy	be your age
how do you do	strike a bargain
to catch fire	to be taken in (deceived)
catch his eye	takes after her mother
a hot cup of coffee	look up an old friend

These expressions are thoroughly respectable members of the language. No one need apologize for using them, for they are part of the stock in trade of the language and most of them are appropriate in all varieties. If they defy conventional analysis, it is because of the inadequacy of the analytical procedure.

The dictionaries give a great many idioms, usually listed under the most important word in the phrase. The *Oxford English Dictionary* is especially rich in idioms.

(See *Comparison of adjectives and adverbs § 3, *Gerund § 5, *Phrases, *Prepositions; see also *Ambiguity § 3, Ch. 9, "Revising unidiomatic words," p. 341; for idioms with verbs see *do § 3, *doubt, *get, got § 3, *go § 1, *have § 4, 5. References: *Oxford English Dictionary*; Logan Pearsall Smith, *English Idioms,* Oxford, 1927; V. H. Collins, *A Book of English Idioms, A Second Book of English Idioms, A Third Book of English Idioms,* London, 1956, 1958, 1960.)

-ie-, -ei- • See *-ei-, -ie-.

i.e. • See *Abbreviations § 2, *namely and other introductory words.

if •

1. *Subordinating conjunction.* If is a subordinating conjunction introducing a condition:

If the weather holds good, we shall stay another week.

If they had known the beacon was out, they would have come in before sunset.

(See *Conditions. Reference: Fries, *AEG,* pp. 224-225.)

2. *"If" and "whether."* In Formal and General usage, *if* is used for conditions, and *whether,* usually with *or,* is used, though not consistently, in indirect questions and in expressions of doubt:

Simple condition: If the weather holds, we will come.

Indirect question: He asked whether the mail had come in. He asked whether they were all going or only some of them.

Doubt: They had all been wondering whether the doctor would get there in time.

From the first returns they could not be sure whether the state was Republican or Democratic.

In Formal English *if* is not used with *or:*

No matter whether [not *if*] the boy goes to preparatory school or high school, his father has to pay local school taxes.

In Informal English *whether* is rarely used:

He asked if they were all going or only some of them.

He asked if the mail had come in.

He was so old, and so shrunken, that it was difficult to tell, at first, if he was a man or woman.—WILLIAM MARCH, *The Little Wife*

3. *For "although" or "but."* In some idioms *if* or *even if* is used for *although* or *but:*

She was a good dog, if she did bark at strangers.

4. The use of *would have* after *if* rather than *had,* though increasing, is not established in Standard written English:

If he had [not *would have*] been there...

(See *as if, *like—as, *when, as, and if.)

-ile • Usage is divided on the pronunciation of words ending in *-ile*. Some of the more common are:

agile /aj′əl [aj′īl]/

fertile /fėr′tl̟ [fėr′tīl]/

futile /fū′tl̟ [fū′tīl]/

gentile /jen′tīl/

hostile /hos′tl̟ [hos′tīl]/

infantile /in′fən tīl/, /in′fən tl̟/

juvenile /jü′və nl̟/, /jü′və nīl/

reptile /rep′tl̟/, /rep′tīl/

senile /sē′nīl/, /sē′nil/

textile /teks′tl̟/, /teks′tīl/

British pronunciation more commonly has -īl: /fėr′tīl/, /hos′tīl/, /rep′tīl/.

ill, sick • See *sick, ill.

illiterate • Both *illiterate* and *literate* are used in a narrower and a wider sense: "(in)capable of reading and writing"; "(un)acquainted with what is written, hence (un)educated." Usage that is often loosely referred to as *illiterate* is called Nonstandard in this book. (See Ch. 1, "Nonstandard English," p. 23.)

illusion • *Illusion*—"a deceptive appearance," as *an optical illusion, an illusion of wealth*—is, because of similarity in pronunciation, sometimes confused with *allusion,* "a reference to something": *He opened his talk with an allusion to recent events.* A *delusion* is a self-deception.

They all saw the oasis, but it turned out to be a mirage, an optical *illusion.*

In *Paradise Lost* Milton makes many *allusions* to the Bible.

He suffered from *delusions* of grandeur.

Illustration (Pictorial) • *Pictorial illustration* may greatly help the interest and understandability of an article—though it cannot (in spite of the picture magazines) take the place of text. Illustrations for articles and books are often arranged for by the publisher, but the writer can suggest possibilities or he can submit drawings or photographs. Many feature articles are accepted by newspapers and magazines largely because of their illustrations.

A student can often add considerably to the value of a paper by drawings or by snapshots. These can be inserted by tucking the corners into slits cut in the manuscript pages, so that they can be taken off after they have served their purpose; or gummed corners available in stationery shops may be used. Travel papers, narratives of experience, and explanations of processes profit especially from illustration. (Compare *Diagrams, graphs, etc.)

Imagery • An image is a word or group of words that may make an appeal to one of the "senses": sight (*bright, yellow, thick brown hair*), hearing (*rumble, faraway shouts, three loud booms*), taste (*sweet, sour, a pickled pear*), smell (*jasmine, a blown-out candle*), touch (*smooth, glassy, a tweed coat*), and the muscular tension known as the kinesthetic sense (*squirm, jogging heavily along*). Obviously a word may appeal to more than one sense (*tweed, glassy, jasmine*), though in a specific context one would usually be dominant. Whether a reader's senses are actually "aroused" depends chiefly on his suggestibility. Some people are easily stimulated by words; some are more sensitive to one sense than to another. For the use of imagery in writing, it is enough that words *capable* of suggesting sensory images are present; we cannot be sure of the response of anyone but ourselves. But images—actually sensed or potential—are the foundation of much writing, of all in fact that does not deal principally with ideas.

Imagery is especially characteristic of poetry, in which ideas, states of mind, and feelings are often represented by images:

> Jack Ellyat felt that turning of the year
> Stir in his blood like drowsy fiddle-music
> And knew he was glad to be Connecticut-born
> And young enough to find Connecticut winter
> Was a black pond to cut with silver skates
> And not a scalping-knife against the throat.
> —STEPHEN VINCENT BENÉT, *John Brown's Body,* p. 22

Fiction, too, since it must present pictures of people and places and actions, has much imagery:

> The sun came in warm in long streaks across the floor, and the giant geranium plants made a pattern across its gold. When we touched our glasses, white circles of light would move on the walls and ceiling, and the cut-glass dish with the peaches in it made a rainbow-bar on the cloth.—JOSEPHINE JOHNSON, *Now in November,* p. 83

In explanatory prose, images are the basis of discussions of people, of experience and situations, of things and processes. Even in expressions of opinion and discussions of ideas, most writers keep in close touch with the visible and touchable world. Current writing is conspicuously concrete and imagistic.

Studying the images in a writer's work will usually show what has impressed him in his experience, what appeals to him—colors, lines, odors, what not—and your writing also should show images drawn from your experience. Images that come from your own experience and that definitely appeal to you will carry over clearly to a reader and are infinitely better than the trite roses and violets of literary tradition. Don't take out of your writing an image that really appeals to you, unless you realize that in the context it is misleading. (See Ch. 9, "Figurative use of words," p. 350, *Style § 2g.)

Imaginative and factual writing • See *Factual and imaginative writing.

Imitative words and phrases • A number of words seem to imitate, or at least suggest in their pronunciation, particular sounds: *bang, buzz, clank, swish, splash, whirr, pop, clatter, cuckoo, ping pong.* These words are established in the English vocabulary and will be found in dictionaries. It is possible to make new ones to fit specific sounds, and they are often necessary, especially in fiction. Sometimes it is better to use the conventional forms even when they are not very exact (*humph, uh huh*) rather than make new ones, which may do nothing except puzzle a reader.

When such words are used for special effect in writing they form a trait of style known as *onomatopoeia* /on′ə mat′ə pē′ə/. Imitative words or sounds in a series that suggest the action or idea or tone of the subject matter are a useful form of intensification of meaning, as in these justly famous lines from Pope's *An Essay on Criticism*:

> 'Tis not enough no harshness gives offense,
> The sound must seem an Echo to the sense:
> Soft is the strain when Zephyr gently blows,
> And the smooth stream in smoother numbers flows;
> But when loud surges lash the sounding shore,
> The hoarse, rough verse should like the torrent roar:
> When Ajax strives some rock's vast weight to throw,
> The line too labours, and the words move slow;

> ALEXANDER POPE, *An Essay on Criticism*, lines 364-371

Often a picture or a narrative can be sharpened by using an imitative word instead of a general or colorless word like *said* or *walked*: *barked, droned, snarled, whined*; *clattered, stamped, strutted.* Conspicuous striving for such words will make a passage seem melodramatic, but accurate words that come naturally will add to its effectiveness.

In *The Red Badge of Courage* Stephen Crane frequently uses imitative words to good effect:

> The regiment snorted and blew.... The song of the bullets was in the air and shells snarled among the tree-tops.... Near where they stood shells were flip-flapping and hooting.... Occasional bullets buzzed in the air and spanged into tree trunks....

Immediate constituent • Some linguists use *immediate constituent,* usually abbreviated to *IC,* to indicate one of the elements into which a specific expression can be analyzed. The *IC*'s of a typical English sentence are the complete subject and the complete predicate, each of which may be made up of *IC*'s, which in turn may be analyzable into smaller elements. The analysis can be carried down to the elements of words (morphemes) and to the sounds (phonemes) of which they are composed. (For a phonemic analysis the sentence would have to be phonemically transcribed.)

The	o l d	e s t	b o y	s
Article (determiner)	Base form	Superlative suffix	Base form	Plural suffix
Article (determiner)	Adjective	Adjective	Noun	Noun
Article (determiner)	Noun phrase	Noun phrase	Noun phrase	Noun phrase
Complete subject	Complete subject	Complete subject	Complete subject	Complete subject

Shown at left and below is a diagram analysis of the immediate constituents and smaller elements of the sentence: *The oldest boys walked the greatest distances.*

w a l k	e d	t h e	g r e a t	e s t	d i s t a n c e	s
Base form	Past tense suffix	Article (determiner)	Base form	Superlative suffix	Base form	Plural suffix
		Article (determiner)	Adjective	Adjective	Noun	Noun
		Noun phrase	Noun phrase	Noun phrase	Noun phrase	Noun phrase
Verb	Verb	Object	Object	Object	Object	Object
Complete predicate	Complete predicate	Complete predicate	Complete predicate	Complete predicate	Complete predicate	Complete predicate

Like other diagrams, this is a device for analysis and exposition, useful to a specialist, a student of the language. Analyzing a sentence of average complexity requires a considerable amount of linguistic knowledge, especially if the suprasegmental *phonemes of pitch and juncture are included. The concept of immediate constituents, however, is basic to any analysis of language, especially for syntax, which examines the relations between elements in utterances. This approach makes visually clear the patterns of sentence structure and helps us to see how sentences are built. (References: Fries, *Structure*, pp. 256-273, and most recent books on linguistics.)

immigrate—emigrate • See *emigrate—immigrate.

Imperative • A verbal construction used in commands and requests is called an *imperative*; in such constructions usually no word occurs as a separate subject. (See *Commands and requests.)

imply—infer • A distinction is made by most careful educated users of English, and in college papers it is wise to keep the distinction. A writer or speaker *implies* something in his words or manner; a reader or listener *infers* something from what he reads or hears.

The dean implied, by the way he tilted his head and half closed his eyes, that he doubted my story.

One might infer from his opening words that the speaker was hostile to all social change.

But *infer* has been used so much in the sense of suggesting, expressing indirectly, that it is also given as a definition of *imply* in dictionaries.

in •
1. *Uses.*

Preposition: in the box   in town   in the rain
in a circle   in training   in words   in bronze
Adverb: mix in   They are not in.   Put in the butter.
[Local: She wants in.]
Adjective: the in box
Noun: the ins and the outs
Verb: [local] to in the beets, to in the car

2. *In combinations.* In speech *in* is often used in combination with another preposition: *in back of, in behind, in between.*

In most writing these would be simply: *back of, behind, between.* (See *Prepositions § 3b.)

in-, en- • See *en-, in-.

in—into—in to • *In* generally shows location (literal or figurative); *into* generally shows direction:

He was in the house.   He came into the house.
He was in a stupor.   He fell into a deep sleep.

Informally *in* is often used for *into*:

He fell in the brook.

In to is the adverb *in* followed by the preposition *to*:

They went into the dining room. They went in to dinner.

in-, un- • *In-* or *un-* (variants *im-, il-*) prefixed to many words gives them a negative meaning: *inconsiderate, incapable, uneven, unlovable, unlovely, unloved.* If you are not sure whether a word takes *in-* or *un-*, you will have to consult a dictionary—an American dictionary, since British usage differs in many words. *Un-* is likely to be used with words from Old English and *in-* with words from Latin, but this is not a safe guide (witness *indigestible, undigested, inequality, unequal, inadvisable, unadvised*). A sample list follows:

inadequate	†indistinguishable	immoral	uncontrollable
inadvisable	inept	impractical	uncontrolled
inartistic	†inescapable	unacceptable	undistinguished
inaudible	inexperienced	unadvised	unessential
incommunicable	infallible	unalterable	unnamed
incompatible	†infrequent	unbelievable	unnatural
incomplete	†insubstantial	uncertain	unnecessary
incomprehensible	†insupportable	uncollected	unrecognizable
inconclusive	illiberal	uncommu-	unresponsive
inconsequential	illiterate	nicative	unsustained
†indecipherable	immoderate	uncompleted	unversed

Those marked † are also found with *un-*.

Not all words beginning with *in-* are negatives (*innate, insure, intoxicate*), and *invaluable* means having a value so great it cannot be determined; *inflammable* has apparently come to be considered so ambiguous as a warning that *flammable* has displaced it on tank trucks (see *Ambiguity § 5); *un-* is also tricky (see *unbend, unbending* in a dictionary).

in connection with, connected with • See *connected with, in connection with.

in hope of, in hopes of • See *hope.

Incoherence • Writing is incoherent when it lacks connection within itself or when the relationship between parts (of a sentence, of a paragraph, of a whole paper) is not evident. (Various examples of incoherence are discussed in *Dangling modifiers, *Participles, Ch. 8, and Ch. 4, "Continuity in paragraphs," pp. 139-143. See also *Coherence.)

Incomplete sentence • See *Fragmentary sentence.

incredible—incredulous • A story or situation is *incredible* ("unbelievable"); a person is *incredulous* ("unbelieving"). (See *Ambiguity § 5.)

Indefinite article • See *a—an.

Indefinite pronouns • See *Reference of pronouns, *you.

Indention or indentation ○ *Indenting* in manuscript or printed copy is beginning the first line of a paragraph in from the left-hand margin. In longhand copy, paragraphs are indented about an inch, in typewritten copy about five spaces.

Hanging indention is setting in all lines below the first line, as in many newspaper headlines, outlines (see Ch. 2, pp. 50-53), headings, and addresses of *letters. If a line of verse is too long to stand on one line, the part brought over to the second line should be indented (see *Poetry):

> A line in long array where they wind betwixt green islands,
> They take a serpentine course, their arms flash in the sun—
>> hark to the musical clank,
>>>> —WALT WHITMAN, "Cavalry Crossing a Ford"

Aside from these uses, indention is mainly a publisher's problem, treated in detail by the stylebooks (For information about indenting quotations, see *Quotation marks § 1d.)

Independent clause • See *Clauses.

Indicative mood • *Indicative mood* is a term from Latin grammar for the set of verb forms which express fact; in English it is applied to the usual form of the verb in sentences and clauses:

> They *sat* on the porch even though it *was* late October.
> *Will* you *come* if you *are invited*?

(See *Verbs; compare *Subjunctives, *Mood.)

Indirect discourse (Indirect quotation) • Quotations that are paraphrased or summarized in the writer's words instead of being quoted exactly as originally spoken or written are in indirect discourse:

> *Indirect:* He said he wouldn't take it if they gave it to him.
> *Direct:* He said, "I won't take it if they give it to me."

Notice that the tense of the verb changes in indirect discourse. (See *Quotation marks § 2b, *Tenses of verbs § 4, *Mood; see also *Commands and requests.)

Indirect object • See *Objects § 2.

Indirect question • An *indirect question* is a question restated at second hand:

> *Indirect:* He asked if everyone was all right.
> *Direct:* He asked, "Is everyone all right?"

(See *Questions § 2, *Tenses of verbs § 4, *whether.)

Indo-European languages • See *English language.

infer—imply • See *imply—infer.

Infinitives • *Infinitive* is a Latin grammatical term for a verb form expressing the general sense of the verb without restriction as to person or number. In English, there is no longer a distinctive infinitive form; instead, the bare form of the verb is used in the infinitive function. Usually *to* precedes the bare form, but after certain auxiliaries *to* does not occur. So-called infinitive constructions cause great difficulty to foreign learners of English, but native speakers generally need be concerned only with the divided usage discussed in the last part of § 5 and in *Split infinitive.

1. *Tenses.* What are traditionally called the infinitive forms are:

	Active		Passive
	simple	*progressive*	
Present:	(to) ask	(to) be asking	(to) be asked
Perfect:	(to) have asked	(to) have been asking	(to) have been asked

The present infinitive indicates a time the same as or future to that of the main verb: He is here now *to ask* you. . . . They had come *to ask* you. . . . He is coming (future) *to ask* you. . . .

The perfect infinitive primarily indicates action previous to the time of the main verb: I am glad *to have been* one of his boys. (See *Tenses of verbs § 3c, 4.)

2. *The "to" infinitive.* To is the "sign of the infinitive" used in most infinitive constructions—that is, it connects the infinitive to the *finite verb—but it is not part of the infinitive.

They all tried *to get* in first.　　　He set out *to get* it.

3. *The "bare" infinitive.* After a few verbs (*can, may, must, shall, will, do, dare, need,* etc.) *to* is never or seldom used:

I can *see*.　　　He must *carry* it.　　　We might *be seeing* him
He does *care*.　　　It does me good *to see* him.

With some other verbs usage is divided:

I helped him *to learn* to drive.　　　I helped him *learn* driving.
You had better not *go*.　　　You had *to go*.
He *dared* to go.　　　He *dared* go.

In short, clear, unemphatic series of infinitives in parallel constructions, the *to* is not repeated; in more Formal series, when the actions are not part of one general process, or when the separate verbs deserve emphasis, the *to* is repeated (see examples under § 4 [Subject] below).

4. *Other uses of infinitives.*
Subject:

To sit and *smoke* and *think* and *dream* was his idea of pleasure.

To walk around among these exhibits, *to see* the horse races where runners, trotters, and pacers with Kentucky and Tennessee pedigrees compete on a mile track, and then *to listen* to the political speakers discussing "purr-ins-a-pulls" and "the Const-ti-too-shun"—this made a holiday for the farmers and city people who came.—CARL SANDBURG, *Abraham Lincoln: The Prairie Years,* 2:6

Object:

He wanted *to go* fishing.   He tries *to do* it every day.

Adjectival modifier:

wool *to spin,* money *to burn.*   They have plenty of fish *to eat.*

Adverbial modifier (to show purpose, result, etc.):

He bought *to sell* again.
Reporters are constantly on the move *to cover* important events.
Television tends *to become* a nuisance.

With auxiliaries:

He will *pass* this time. He didn't *dare* go along.

5. *Subject of infinitive.* Infinitives are increasingly used in subordinate constructions as alternatives to finite verbs:

It would be better *for you and me to discuss the matter* before calling in the others.

as the alternative to:

It would be better *if you and I discussed the matter* before calling in the others.

If the subject of the infinitive is a pronoun, it is in the accusative:

Supposing *them to be new men,* we all shouted, "Get off the grass."

Often these constructions are *absolute constructions:

To judge by the appearances, the party must have been pretty rough.
To make a long story short, they didn't go.

For the pronoun after the infinitive of a linking verb that has no expressed subject, General English usually has the accusative pronoun; Formal would probably have a nominative, but the locution makes the pronoun prominent and might better be phrased differently.

General: I always wanted to be *him.*
Formal: I always wanted to be *he.* [*Or:* He was the one I always wanted to be.]

(Compare *Participles § 3, 4; *Gerund; see Jespersen, *Modern English Grammar,* VII:6.)
6. *Split infinitive.* See *Split infinitive, *Latin and English § 3.

(References: Curme, *Syntax,* Ch. 23; Jespersen, *Essentials of English Grammar,* Ch. 32; Roberts, pp. 359-367.)

Inflection • In grammar *inflection* refers to the change of form by which some words indicate certain grammatical relationships, as the plural of nouns or the past tense of verbs. It includes *Declension, *Conjugation, and *Comparison. (For English inflections see *Case and the articles referred to there, *Plurals of nouns, *Pronouns, types and forms, *Verbs, *Comparison of adjectives and adverbs. Reference: Curme, *Parts of Speech*.)

Informal English •
Revision: The word or passage marked is too Informal for the subject or for the style of the rest of the paper. Revise, making it more appropriate.

Inf

Informal English, as described on pp. 21-22, is appropriate in writing for some personal narratives and light topics, but its words and constructions in General or Formal papers, except for an occasional intended effect, violate the tone. A conspicuously Informal expression marked on a paper should be changed to one more characteristic of General English. (*Index* articles dealing with Informal usage include *Collective nouns, *Dates, *Function words.)

institutions of higher learning • This is a clumsy phrase, and more abstract than *colleges and universities*. It would be convenient if we had one word for the notion, or a group word as economical even as *secondary schools* for "high and preparatory schools." Either *colleges* or *universities* is often used to apply to both.

Intensive (reflexive) pronouns • See *myself, *Pronouns, types and forms § 4.

Intensives • Adverbs like *very, too, much,* and some constructions, like the superlative of adjectives and adverbs, are used to emphasize meaning. (See Ch. 8, "Intensives," p. 319, *very, *Comparison of adjectives and adverbs § 5, *himself, *myself, *self. References: Fries, *AEG*, pp. 200-206; Curme, *Parts of Speech*, pp. 48-50.)

Interjections • See *Exclamations, *Parts of speech.

Interrogation point • See *Question mark.

Interrogative pronouns • See *Pronouns, types and forms § 3.

Interrogative sentences • See *Questions.

Interrupted sentence movement • See *Commas § 4.

into—in to—in • See *in—into—in to.

Intonation • *Intonation* is a general term for the "melody" of a language, used by linguists to include somewhat varying groups of sound qualities but primarily patterns of pitch variation. Since these variations in pitch are closely bound up with stress and other related features of speech, the total phenomenon is difficult to analyze; some account of it is given under *Phonemes § 2. We acquire the intonation of our own language by unconscious imitation and rarely make a mistake in it, but it is usually the last quality attained in learning a second language—witness the odd melody of someone who has learned English as a second language in his later years. And you may assume that your intonation of the modern foreign language you have studied sounds just as odd to a native speaker of that language. Intonation is one of the most conspicuous differences between British and American English, especially obvious in questions.

intramural • *Intramural* has no hyphen. It means etymologically "within the walls," specifically college activities carried on by groups of the same college.

Intransitive verbs • See *Transitive and intransitive verbs.

Introductions • See *Beginning paragraphs.

Introductory words • See *namely and other introductory words.

Inversion • *Inversion* means placing the verb before its subject—a rather uncommon order in English except in questions. It also occurs, however, in a few established constructions: *What a fool is he! Long may it wave. Out gushed the water. Among the callers was Mrs. Brown.*

   In questions inversion is the regular syntactical pattern, with the auxiliary before the subject and the infinitive or participle after it: *Is he coming? Will she go? Did he like it?* (See Ch. 8, pp. 279-280, 313.)

invite • The word *invite* is ordinarily a verb. Its use as a noun /in′vīt/ is hardly even Informal except facetiously in speech: *Did you get an invite?* (Reference: Bryant, p. 116.)

Irony • *Irony* is implying something markedly different, sometimes even the opposite, from what is actually said. (See Ch. 9, "Degree of statement," p. 351.)

irregardless • *Irregardless* is not used in reputable writing and better avoided in speech. The second negative, the prefix *ir-*, is perhaps an effort to reinforce the *-less* suffix, perhaps the result of analogy with *irregular, irresistible, irresponsible.*

Irregular verbs • See *Principal parts of verbs.

-ise, -ize • See *-ize, -ise.

it • *It* is the neuter third person singular pronoun, used to refer to an object, a situation, or an idea. *It* is also used to refer to a baby or an animal whose sex is unknown or unimportant for the statement (The dog wagged *its* tail) and in certain impersonal statements about the weather and events in general (impersonal *it*):

It rained all night.   It's the way things go.

It is also used to refer to the idea of a preceding statement:

We changed two tires in record time. It is not easy to do on a dark and rainy night.

Sentences beginning "It is . . ." or "It was . . ." (anticipatory subject) are often wordy and weakening, since they have put a colorless locution in the emphatic beginning of the sentence:

[It was] then [that] his wife had taken to going with other men.

But this *preparatory it* may be useful when what it represents could not conveniently be placed in the usual position:

It is no use trying to evade the question asked you.

It may also stand in the object position:

He always made it a rule to check every one of his quotations.

It is also used in a number of idiomatic constructions:

There would have been no party if it hadn't been for your help.
You'll catch it if you don't hurry home.
We'll make a night of it.

(See *there is, there are, *its, *It's me. References: Emerson Beauchamp, Jr., "A Study of 'It': Handbook Treatment and Magazine Use," *American Speech*, 1951, 26:173-180; for history see Jespersen, *Modern English Grammar*, VII:6.)

its—it's • The possessive pronoun does not have an apostrophe:

The dog wagged its tail.   A car is judged by its performance.

Associate *its* with *his* and *hers*.
It's is the contraction of *it is* or *it has*:

It's going to rain.   It's rained for over a week now.

It's me • The argument over "It's me" is a case of narrow theory versus established practice. The theory is that after the verb *be* the subject form should always be used, but this theory is consistently contradicted by the actual usage of good speakers (see *be § 2).

We tend to use the nominative form of a pronoun when it is the subject and stands close to the verb—usually before it—and to use the accusative in most other positions, especially when it comes after the verb—in "object territory," as Fries calls it. (Compare *who, whom.)

All the large grammars of English regard *it's me* as acceptable colloquial usage—and since the expression is not likely to occur except in speech, that gives it full standing. Fowler approves it, and one of the "judges" in Marckwardt and Walcott's *Facts about Current English Usage* (p. 108) wrote:

> *I* sounds quite mad in certain cases; e.g., pointing to a photo: "Which is I?"!!! "Oh, I see, that's I"!!! Absolutely non-English, hang all the grammarians on earth.

Us and *him* after *be* are less common, but usage is divided. *Current English Usage* found "If it had been *us,* we would admit it" uncertainly established and "I'll swear that was *him*" and "I suppose that's *him*" disputable. Very often speakers who try to be correct resort to some circumlocution, saying instead of "It was *she* (or *her*)" "That's who it was."

The upshot of the discussion is that in their natural settings "It's me," "It was him all right," "Something was wrong—was it him or the crowd?" are appropriate. (See *Case. References: Marckwardt and Walcott, pp. 77-78; Wallace Rice, "Who's there? Me," *American Speech,* 1933, 8: 58-63; Robertson, pp. 492-503; Fries, *AEG,* p. 91; Bryant, pp. 120-121.)

Italics • In manuscript, both longhand and typewritten, italics are shown by underlining. (Specific uses of italics are listed in *Underlining. See also Ch. 10, "Underlining for italics," p. 402, *Foreign words in English § 3, *Ships' names, *Titles of articles, books, etc.)

-ize, -ise • English has many verbs ending in the sound of /īz/, some of which are spelled *-ise* and some *-ize;* in many, usage is divided. American usage, differing somewhat from British, prefers *-ize,* as in the following common verbs of this class:

anesthetize	dramatize	revolutionize	sympathize
apologize	memorize	sensitize	visualize
characterize	realize	standardize	

In the following, *-ise* is the usual spelling:

advise	despise	exercise	surmise
arise	devise	revise	surprise
chastise	disguise	supervise	

Both *-ize* and *-ise* are commonly found in:

advertise—advertize   analyze—analyse   criticize—criticise

In general, follow American usage. When in doubt, consult a good dictionary.

Some readers object to recent extension of the verbs in *-ize,* such as *concertize, finalize, picturize,* but aside from the fact that any new word is a bit disconcerting, there seems little reason for the objection unless the new verb duplicates in meaning one already in common use. Sometimes the form expresses something the already existing word cannot do: *Moisturize* the air in the house (*moisten* would hardly do).

J • *J* is a common spelling for the "soft *g*" sound at the beginning of syllables: *jam, jet, jibe, journey, jury.* At the end of a syllable the sound is variously spelled, often by *-dge*: *edge* /ej/, *judge* /juj/. (For other spellings of the sound see *G § 2.)

An approximation of some foreign sounds of *j* is attempted in particular words: Latin /y/, *Hallelujah*; French /zh/, *bijou* /bē′zhü/, *jabot* /zha-bō′/; Spanish /h/ *marijuana* /mä′ri-hwä′nə/, German /y/, *jaeger* /yā′gər/.

In the alphabet of the Romans, *i* and *j* were merely different forms of the same letter; though the letter had both a vowel and a consonant function in Latin, no attempt was made to distinguish those functions in writing. Only in recent times have the two forms gained a separate place in Western alphabets and come to represent different sounds.

Jabberwocky • Linguists have found the *Jabberwocky* opening stanza from Lewis Carroll's *Alice Through the Looking Glass* ('Twas brillig, and the slithy toves/ Did gyre and gimble in the wabe. . . .) a convenient device to show that it is possible to recognize the forms and grammatical functions of English words without reference to meaning. Similarly you have no difficulty in identifying four parts of speech and four inflectional forms in: *The harbiger ligs' sollips drave brustrily in the stroks.*

Jargon •
1. *Applied to style.* Sir Arthur Quiller-Couch popularized *jargon* as the name for verbal fuzziness of various sorts—wordi-

ness, abstract for concrete words, big words, and the use of words that add nothing to the meaning of a statement. (See Ch. 8, pp. 315-317; Ch. 9, "Choosing appropriate words," p. 345; "Concrete words," p. 372; "Abstract words," p. 373; *Legal language. Reference: Sir Arthur Quiller-Couch, *On the Art of Writing,* New York, 1916, pp. 100-126.)

2. *Linguistic sense. Jargon* (also *pidgin* and *creole*) is a word used among linguists to mean a dialect composed of the mixture of two or more languages. Jargons involving English are used by non-English-speaking peoples in doing business with the English. The best known of these are the Chinook jargon of the Pacific Northwest, beach-la-Mar (or *bêche-de-mer*) of the Pacific islands, and the Chinese-English jargon, pidgin English. (References: Otto Jespersen, *Language,* New York, 1922, pp. 216-236, and the sources referred to there; R. B. LePage (ed.), *Proceedings of the Conference on Creole Language Studies,* London and New York, 1961.)

job, position • *Job* is General for the Formal *position*: *He got a job at an oil refinery.* The word *position* has more dignity and what it refers to is usually thought of as better paid. *Job* is Informal for *something made,* such as an automobile or refrigerator ("a nice little job there").

Jones—plural and possessive forms • The plural of *Jones* and of most nouns ending in an /s/ or /z/ sound is formed by adding *-es*, pronounced as a separate syllable: *Joneses* /jōn′zəz/, *consciences* /kon′shən səz/, *Jameses.* When two syllables ending in an /s/ or /z/ sound are in the root word, usage is divided: *the Moses* or *the Moseses.*

In the possessive, usage is divided. We may write (and, less frequently, say) *Dr. Jones'* /jōnz/ *office*; or write and say *Dr. Jones's* /jōn′zəz/ *office.* Probably the first form is the more common in writing. Also: For *goodness'* sake, *Charles'* collection, though *Charles's* /chärl′zəz/ is equally reputable.

The possessive plural is pronounced the same as the plural and is written by adding (') to the plural form: *Joneses', Moses'* or *Moseses'.*

Journalese • See *Newspaper English.

judgment—judgement • *Judgment* is the more common American spelling.

Juncture • See *Phonemes § 2c.

just • Most readers find *just* redundant in expressions like *just exactly* and *just perfect*.

K • The /k/ sound, as in *keep*, is spelled *c* (*call, actual, cute*), *cc* (*accord*), *ck* (*back, track*), and also with other letters (*queen, chord, ox, strength, cheque*). *K* before *n* is now silent in a number of words (*knave, kneel, knife*) from Anglo-Saxon, where it was pronounced.

Business sometimes changes *c* to *k* and *qu* to *kw* (*Kwick Kleaners*), either to make the alliteration more obvious or to make a trademark. (See Louise Pound, "The Kraze for 'K,'" *American Speech*, 1925, 1:43-44.) Such substitution is not acceptable in ordinary writing.

kid • As a noun *kid* is Informal for "child," "youngster"; *kids* is the plural (*kidders* is a local plural). As a verb it is Informal for "joke," "tease"; from this verb comes the Informal noun *kidder*.

kind, sort • *Kind* and *sort* are both singular nouns in form:

This kind of person is a menace at any party.
This sort of thing shouldn't be allowed.

As singular nouns, they are expected to take singular demonstrative adjectives in General and Formal writing:

That kind of story doesn't interest me.
Problems of this sort bother him.

But *kind* and *sort* are so closely associated with the noun they stand before that they seem like modifiers and in speech and Informal writing the demonstrative adjectives used with them agree with the principal noun of the construction:

Those sort of ideas in his head and that sort of life with his wife. . . .—A. S. M. HUTCHINSON, *If Winter Comes*, p. 324

You next reach the conclusion that, as these kind of marks have not been left by any other animal than man. . . .—T. H. HUXLEY, "The Method of Scientific Investigation"

The *Oxford English Dictionary* has examples of *these kind of* and *these sort of* from the fourteenth century to the present, many of them from the "best authors." Fries found the plural regularly used with *kind* and *sort* by his Group I (Standard English) writers (*AEG*, p. 58). Only the unnodding vigilance of editorial copy readers keeps the construction from being as common in writing as in speech. Jespersen, p. 202, even suggests that *kind* and *sort* be regarded as unchanged plurals and therefore correct. But the construction is still felt by many to be Nonstandard. (References: Curme, *Syntax,* pp. 544-546; Bryant, pp. 215-216.)

kind of, sort of • *Kind of* and *sort of* are used as Informal adverbs, equivalent to *rather* or *somewhat* in more Formal usage:

I feel kind of logy today.   It was sort of dull, but he said a lot.

Especially in writing, these would be:

I was rather [somewhat, a little, very, pretty] tired.
It was pretty [very, rather] dull, but he said a good deal.

In educated speech, *sort of* and especially *kind of* are preferred to *rather* or *somewhat*. But in writing one of the last two would be usual. (Reference: Jean Malmstrom, "Kind of and Its Congeners," *English Journal,* 1960, 49:498-499.)

kind of a, sort of a • Though there is objection to *kind of a* and *sort of a,* they are very common in General English and fairly common among respected writers:

I want to find someone on the earth so intelligent that he welcomes opinions which he condemns—I want to be this kind of a man and I want to have known this kind of a man.—JOHN JAY CHAPMAN, *Letters,* p. 124

Now, suppose the battle of Salamis had been fought, not in the full light of Greek history, but in the misty dawn of the Epos, what sort of a story should we have had?—GILBERT MURRAY, *The Rise of the Greek Epic,* p. 200

These two sentences from the same short story show the two idioms in differing degrees of Formality, in different tempos:

... he had never once brought her a comical, stuffed animal or any sort of an object with a picture of a Scottie on it.

Bob McEwen wasn't the sort of man to do a sentimental thing like that unless he meant it.—SALLY BENSON, *People Are Fascinating,* pp. 30-31

In Formal writing *kind of a* and *sort of a* should be avoided, but they are accepted General idioms.

L • *L* is a "liquid" consonant that varies considerably in quality in the speech of individuals and groups and with its position in a word: *land, leaf, almost, silly, fill*; it is the only letter to represent this group of related sounds (*phoneme) in English.

L is silent in a few common words: *almond* (usually), *folk, half, salmon, talk, walk, would, yolk.* It is often not sounded in other words as in *golf course* /gôf′kôrs′/. Despite its frequency in spelling, the doubled *l* sounds just like the single one; compare *collar—color, llama—lamb, fell—fail.*

In many syllables no specific vowel is sounded before an *l,* and the pronunciation can be indicated by "syllabic *l*" /l̩/: *marble* /mär′bl̩/, *tickle* /tik′l̩/.

lady • See *man, woman; compare *female.

laissez faire, laisser faire • The spelling is still French, and the pronunciation /les′ā fãr′/ still an attempt at French, but the word is not italicized except in conspicuously Formal writing.

Language • See *English language.

Language study • See *Linguistics, *Usage.

last, at long last • A recently revived archaic idiom, *at long last* is slightly more emphatic than *at last,* at least when it is spoken, but the phrase may have a British or Formal connotation, as in this:

An economic power born of the travail of men at long last asserts its title to political dominance.—Harold J. Laski, *The Rise of Liberalism*

last—latest • In Formal usage *last* refers to the final item of a series; *latest,* the most recent in time of a series which may or may not be continued:

His latest (we hope it won't be his last) biography is of Peter Cooper.

This distinction is not strictly kept, so that both words are used as superlatives of *late.*

last—latter, former—first • See *former—first, latter—last.

later—latter • See *latter—later.

Latin and English •
1. *Latin words.* Many Latin words came into English in early periods of the language, either directly or through French, and are no longer felt to be foreign words: *patience, candle, receive, wine* (see *English language). Most borrowings from Latin are subject to the same process of anglicizing as other *foreign words in English, and in general they are pronounced

as English words—*agenda* /ə jen′də/, *erratum* /i rā′təm/ or /i rä′təm/—instead of according to the system of pronunciation now taught in Latin classes.

Since Latin is dead as a first language and rare as a second language, new borrowings come in through written rather than spoken use and belong to the Formal dialects, used chiefly in science, law, religion, medicine, and academic work. Since practically all college work was carried on in Latin until about 1750, and a good deal of it later than that, considerable Latin is preserved in college use. Many diplomas are in Latin, and at some institutions the commencement formulas are in Latin. At a more routine level, several Latin words and abbreviations are used in the footnotes of academic research (*ibid., passim, supra, infra, loc. cit.*), though there is a tendency to use English words for many of these. Prefixes of Latin origin (*ante-, ex-, in-, pre-, re-, sub-*) and other compounding elements, such as *uni-* (*unilateral*), *bi-* (*biweekly*), are active in forming new English words. At present scientific words are being formed more from Greek than from Latin elements.

2. *Latin forms.* English continues to use the Latin forms for some words that are used principally in the Formal dialects (**alumnus—alumna, bacillus—bacilli*), but those commonly used have either English plurals or both (*formula, formulas* or *formulae; focus, focuses* or *foci; stadium, stadiums* or *stadia*). (See *Plurals of nouns § 4, *data.)

3. *Latin and English grammar.* The first and most later English grammars were composed by men thoroughly familiar with Latin, many of whom believed that English should be a language like Latin. As a result, English, which was a Germanic language in structure, was described in terms of Latin grammar, and rules were devised for making the language fit the picture.

The fact that English was first described in terms of Latin grammar may be one reason for the old taboo of the *split infinitive (which would be impossible in Latin because the infinitive is one word, as in *laborare,* where English has *to work*) and of putting a preposition at the end of a sentence (*Prepositions § 3d), which almost never occurs in Latin but is a characteristic English idiom.

Only recently has English grammar begun to be based squarely on a careful examination of the English language itself and freed from some of the categories and rules of Latin grammar. (See *Linguistics. Reference: K. W. Dykema, "Where Our Grammar Came From," *College English,* 1961, 22:455-461.)

latter—last, former—first • See *former—first, latter—last.

latter—later • *Latter* /lat'ər/ and *later* /lā'tər/ are often carelessly confused in spelling. The habit of reading your copy aloud to yourself should catch this type of error. (See *former —first, latter—last.)

lay—lie • In much spoken English the work of these two verbs is done by one (*lay*; *lay* or *laid*; *laid*). In writing they are regularly distinguished:

lie ("to recline," intransitive), lay, lain
lay ("to place," transitive) , laid, laid

In Standard English the distinctions are these: You *lie* down for a rest or *lie* down on the job; a farm *lies* in a valley. You *lay* a floor, *lay* a book on the table, *lay* a bet, *lay* out clothes. Yesterday you *lay* down to rest (in speech often indistinguishable from *laid*); you *laid* a book on the table. Egg laying is *lay, laid, laid.*

-le words • A large and interesting group of English verbs ends in *-le—fiddle, giggle, meddle, tickle, waddle, whistle, whittle*—in which the ending usually suggests an action continued or habitually repeated. In spelling, lab*el*, mant*el* (the shelf), mod*el*, and nick*el* give some trouble because they are exceptions to the usual English spelling of this final syllable.

lead—led • *Lead* and *led* show the confusion we suffer because English spelling represents one sound by different symbols. *Lead* /lēd/, the present tense of the verb, gives no trouble; but *led*, the past tense, is often incorrectly spelled with *ea* by analogy with *read* /rēd/, *read* /red/, and the noun *lead*.

Please *lead* the horse away.
Lead poisoning *led* to his death.

Leaders • *Leaders*, or *period leaders*, are a line of spaced periods used to guide the reader's eye across a page. They are often used in statistical tables and the table of contents of a book:

		Page
1. Laying the groundwork	. . . . . .	1
a. Defining the problem	. . . . .	2
b. Constructing the preliminary outline	. . .	3

In typed copy, hyphens are often used instead of periods.

Leading question • See *Questions § 3.

learn—teach • Nonstandard English often uses *learn* in the sense of *teach*: *He learned me how to tie six kinds of knots.*

Standard usage makes the distinction: *He taught me how to tie six kinds of knots. I learned how to tie knots from him.*

leave—let • See *let—leave.

led—lead • See *lead—led.

-ledge, -lege • Two common words are spelled with the ending *-ledge*: *acknowledge* (*acknowledging, acknowledgment*), *knowledge*. Do not confuse them with words spelled with *-lege*: *allege* (*alleged, alleging*), *college*, *sacrilege* (*sacrilegious*); also *ledge* but *legend*.

Legal language • Most legal matters are carried on in a style bristling with long series of synonyms ("do hereby give, grant, bargain, sell and convey"), archaic or foreign (French, Latin) words for everyday things and situations, abbreviations and stereotyped phrases that puzzle laymen and sometimes lawyers themselves. The need for certain technical words is great, but the reason for much of the jargon is unconsidered tradition. Perhaps it must be tolerated in legal business, but lawyers and others who have much to do with law should realize that it is a trade dialect (*shoptalk).

Many lawyers and judges write with distinction, using only the technical terms demanded by the subject. Although they use an appropriately Formal style and must allude to cases that give precedents, they still find room for allusion to general experience, without any loss of exactness.

A brief dissenting opinion of Mr. Justice Holmes illustrates a compact but readable judicial style. A majority of the Supreme Court had decided that the State of Ohio could tax a membership in the New York Stock Exchange owned by a resident of Ohio, on the ground that it was personal property, not like real estate, which would be taxed by the state in which it lay.

The question whether a seat in the New York Stock Exchange is taxable in Ohio consistently with the principles established by this Court seems to me more difficult than it does to my brethren. All rights are intangible personal relations between the subject and the object of them created by law. But it is established that it is not enough that the subject, the owner of the right, is within the power of the taxing State. He cannot be taxed for land situated elsewhere, and the same is true of personal property permanently out of the jurisdiction. It does not matter, I take it, whether the interest is legal or equitable, or what the machinery by which it is reached, but the question is whether the object of the right is so local in its foundation and prime meaning that it should stand like an interest in land.

If left to myself I should have thought that the foundation and substance of the plaintiff's right was the right of himself and his associates personally to enter the New York Stock Exchange building and to do business there. I should have thought that all the rest was incidental to that and that that on its face was localized in New York. If so, it does not matter whether it is real or personal property or that it adds to the owner's credit and facilities in Ohio. The same would be true of a great estate in New York land.—*Representative Opinions of Mr. Justice Holmes,* edited by Alfred Lief, pp. 265-266

(References: Benjamin N. Cardozo, *Law and Literature,* New York, 1931, pp. 3-40; F. A. Philbrick, *Language and the Law,* New York, 1949.)

lend • See *loan as a verb.

less—fewer • *Fewer* refers only to number and things that are counted:

Fewer cars were on the road.   Fewer than sixty came.

In Formal usage *less* refers only to amount or quantity and things measured:

There was a good deal less tardiness in the second term [amount].
There was even less hay than the summer before.

Fewer seems to be declining in use and *less* often takes its place:

Less hands were required for this work. . . .—KENNETH BURKE, *Attitudes Toward History,* p. 175

. . . but polled only a sliver of additional votes and won three less seats.—*Foreign Policy Bulletin,* Mar. 3, 1950, p. 2

Many readers find this usage stylistically objectionable.

less, lesser • Both are used as comparatives (of *little*)—*less* more usually referring to size or quantity (less time, less food); *lesser,* a Formal word, referring to value or importance (the lesser of two evils, a lesser writer).

let—leave • A common Nonstandard idiom is the use of *leave* where Standard English has *let*. Both uses are shown in this sentence by a student obviously making a transition between the two varieties:

In high school I was cured of the practice of leaving [Nonstandard] notebooks go, but I fell into the habit of letting [Standard] homework slide.

Let: let it go, let it lie where it is.
Leave: And so we leave him going happily away. Leave it where it is.

The meanings of *leave* and *let* are so close—dictionary definitions use one in defining the other—in all varieties of English that it is hardly surprising to find the semantic function of *let* in one variety being performed by *leave* in another and the other way around. The history of the two words also shows this fluctuation, even in Standard English. But recent dictionaries in their description of Standard practice indicate substitution only in *Leave* (or *let*) *me* (*him, her*) *alone*. (Reference: Bryant, pp. 127-129.)

let's • *Let's,* the *imperative contraction of *let us,* needs an apostrophe. Though *let's us go, let's you and me go* are common in speech, they have no place in writing.

Letters •
1. *General observations on correspondence.*

a—Materials. A good quality of stationery is worth its cost in the good impression it helps make on the reader. The stationery stores are full of novelties, which may appeal to one's taste, but the standard sizes and styles of paper are never outmoded and are usually cheaper and of better quality:

Note paper—A four-page sheet to be folded once across the middle for the envelope.

Club paper—A sheet about 7¼ by 11 inches, with two folds fitting an envelope 3¾ by 7½.

Business letter paper—8½ by 11 inches, to be folded twice across for a long envelope or folded across the middle and then twice more for the ordinary envelope about six inches long.

b—Styles. The pages should appeal to the reader's eye: good margins, centering the body of the letter on the page so that the whole presents a neatly proportioned appearance, spacing the parts of the letter so that they are distinct but still form a unit, and so on. The paragraphs are usually short, three or four sentences or less, and spaced distinctly.

Ingenuity can usually find a way of subduing even long addresses that must sometimes be used in headings. Find an arrangement of the lines that looks well in your typing or longhand.

Style in indenting at the end of display lines is divided. In typed letters a straight lining at the left of the heading and inside address is more usual now than *indention:

Straight form—more common	*Indented form—less common*
Graham, Sutton and Company	Graham, Sutton and Company
1007 E. Newgate Street	1007 E. Newgate Street
Chicago, Illinois 60603	Chicago, Illinois 60603

In longhand letters the indented form is perhaps more common.

The form of the address on the envelope should be consistent with that used for the heading and the address on the first page of the letter; either the straight or the indented form should be used throughout. Commas are not now used at the ends of the lines of address or heading:

Indented form

Graham, Sutton and Company
1007 E. Newgate Street
Chicago, Illinois 60603

Straight form

Graham, Sutton and Company
1007 E. Newgate Street
Chicago, Illinois 60603

c–Envelopes. The first requirements of the address on the envelope are completeness and clearness, for the sake of the post office. Address your mail to street and number. Always include the ZIP codes of both the mailing address and the return address.

2. *Business letters.* Since business letters usually pass between people who are not acquainted or at least for whom the immediate occasion for writing is not friendship, certain matters of form are important in handling routine information.

The writer's complete address is necessary, either in a printed letterhead or in a written heading, to serve as an address for the reply. An inside address is conventional (and useful when the letter is dictated or when several are being written at the same time or when a carbon is to be filed). In addressing a firm, *Messrs.* is not often used in the United States. The salutations are:

Dear Sir: Gentlemen: Dear Sirs:
Dear Madam: Ladies: [Formal or showy, *Mesdames:*]

When a letter is intended for a particular member of a firm, this form is sometimes used:

> Graham, Sutton and Company
> 1007 E. Newgate Street
> Chicago, Illinois 60603
>
> Attention Mr. Stephen Lange
>
> Gentlemen:

A less Formal and more direct form of address is more common.

> Mr. Stephen Lange
> Graham, Sutton and Company
> 1007 E. Newgate Street
> Chicago, Illinois 60603
>
> Dear Mr. Lange:

The body of a business letter should be clear, direct, and as brief as is consistent with clearness. A separate paragraph is used for each item or for each subdivision of the message. The tone may be curt in routine matters—amateurs are apt to indulge in unnecessary explanation—or it may be full and persuasive. All relevant information should be given, especially in letters asking questions or outlining plans.

The desire for brevity should not lead to a telegraphic style or shortcuts in expression. The old tags like "Yours received and contents noted," "In reply to your favor of the 12th inst.," and "Would say" have disappeared entirely from the correspondence of careful business houses.

The best way to become informed on business letters is to study the practice of reputable companies. If you are specially interested in business correspondence, start a collection of the best examples that come your way. The close of a business letter is:

Yours truly,   Sincerely yours,   Very truly yours,

or some such formula. Only the first word is capitalized and the phrase is followed by a comma.

Although in Formal correspondence a woman does not use *Mrs.* or *Miss* with her name in her signature, in Informal and business correspondence it is frequently used and is a courtesy to the receiver of the letter, who may otherwise not know whether to reply to *Mrs.* or *Miss.* The title should be restricted to the typed signature, which should always be included as well as the written one.

(Mrs.) Dorothy Olson   (Miss) Dorothy Olson
Dorothy Olson   (Mrs. Henry Olson)

(See *Business English. Recent manuals of business writing will give further details of form and suggestions for content.)
3. *Personal letters.*

a–Form. The form of personal letters varies with the intimacy between the writer and recipient. No heading except the date is needed between regular correspondents, but the writer's address in the heading is often a convenience and a necessity in letters to occasional correspondents.

The salutation varies:

Dear Bob,   Dear Miss Breckenridge,
Dear Miss Breckenridge: (The colon is more Formal.)
Formal: My dear Miss Breckenridge:

Formal personal letters, especially between professional men who are not intimate, may have the salutation "Dear Sir:" and the recipient's name and address at the bottom, flush with the left margin.

The complimentary close ranges from "Yours" or any other expression of sentiment to "Yours sincerely," "Cordially yours,"

"Yours very truly," between people little acquainted.

b–Tone and style. Letters to relatives and friends are like conversation, and the style will ordinarily be Informal or whatever you would use when face to face with the recipient. But, as in so much conversation, we often sink to our laziest in letters to the people we write the oftenest. It is worth while occasionally to read over a letter to see if *we* would enjoy receiving it, to see if we have told enough to make the incidents interesting, to see if we have written with reasonable care and are paying our readers the courtesy they deserve in neatness and appropriate expression.

(For Formal invitations and so on, see *Social correspondence.)

Levels of usage • In earlier editions of this book the varieties of usage in English were called *levels*. But since *levels* suggests a value judgment, *varieties* (a more accurate term) is now used. (See Ch. 1.)

Lexical meaning • In linguistics a distinction is often made between grammatical or structural meaning and lexical meaning. In *Birds were killed,* the information which *bird* and *kill* give us is of the sort regularly provided by a dictionary or lexicon—hence lexical meaning; the information given by the *s* of *birds* (plural), *were* (past tense, passive voice), and the *ed* of *killed* (past participle in this position) is of the sort provided by our awareness of the structure or grammar of the language—hence grammatical or structural meaning. When we fully understand the sentence we have grasped its total meaning.

Lexicography • See *Dictionaries.

liable—likely—apt • See *likely—apt—liable.

lie • See *lay—lie.

lighted—lit • Both forms are in good use as the past tense and past participle of *light. Lighted* is more common as the adjective and past participle:

a lighted lamp   He had lighted a fire.

Lit is perhaps more common as the past tense.

He lit a cigaret. [Or: He lighted a cigaret.]

lightning, lightening • The flash before the thunder is *lightning; lightening* comes from the verb *lighten, to make lighter,* meaning to reduce either weight or darkness.

like—as •

1. *As prepositions.* In all varieties of English *like* is used as a preposition introducing a comparison:

The description fits him like a glove.

Habit grips a person like an octopus.

She took to selling like a duck to water.

As seems to be increasing in use in this position:

He was built as a sword fish. . . . —ERNEST HEMINGWAY, *The Old Man and the Sea*

2. *As conjunctions.*

a—In all varieties of English *as, as if,* and *as though* are used as conjunctions introducing clauses of comparison:

People try to get to college as they used to try to get to heaven.

Habit grips a person as an octopus does.

It looked as if he would land flat, but he entered the water perfectly.

He walked as though he was hurt.

b—*Like* appears in both educated and uneducated usage as a conjunction introducing clauses of comparison. Probably the most widely known recent example is:

Winston tastes good like a cigarette should.—*Advertising slogan*

c—In the last few years the use of *like* as a conjunction has greatly increased, and it is certainly now within the range of Standard English:

She looked now like she had looked the last times he had seen her. —MORLEY CALLAGHAN, *Now That April's Here,* p. 22

"Suddenly everybody wanted to look like he came from Harvard, or like he thought everyone looked at Harvard," says Grossman. —*Time,* Feb. 28, 1964, p. 83

Historically both forms have a respectable ancestry, since both are parts of the older *like as* ("Like as a father pitieth his children . . ."). The speakers of some regions have taken *as,* of others *like.* A case might be made for *like* as preferable from the standpoint of meaning, because *as* has more meanings and so is relatively less exact in a comparison. But many people are prejudiced against the use of *like* as a conjunction, perhaps because they associate it with advertising and radio comedy programs, and consequently writers should avoid it except in distinctly Informal papers. It is a good instance of change in usage, and of resistance to it. *Like for* rather than *like* alone is common in speech, especially in the South, but is rarely found in print. (References: Curme, *Syntax,* pp. 281-282; Pooley, pp. 153-155; "Current English Forum," *College English,* 1952, 13:463-464; Bryant, pp. 133-135.)

3. *Like* also functions as a noun, verb, adjective, and adverb; *as* also functions as an adverb and pronoun.

like, similar to • See *similar to.

likely—apt—liable • The principal meanings of these words are:

likely: expected, probably

apt: tending toward, naturally fit

liable: possible (of an unpleasant event); responsible (as for damages)

Likely is the most commonly needed of the three. *Apt* is widely used in the sense of *likely,* as well as in its own narrower meaning, and is so recorded in dictionaries. The use of *liable* in the sense of *likely* is common, but because of the prejudice against the usage it should be confined to Informal speech:

It's *likely* [or, *apt*; or, Informally, *liable*] to rain when the wind is southwest.

Limiting adjectives • See *Adjectives, types and forms § 3c.

line • *Line* is business English (What's your line?—a line of goods) or Informal (He handed her a line). As a *counter word it is usually *deadwood and could better be left out:

My own experience along business lines [that is, *in business*] has been slight.

Another book along the same lines as *Microbe Hunters* [similar to *Microbe Hunters*], but with a fine story, is *Arrowsmith*.

Linguistics • Linguistics has been defined as the scientific study of language. A more modest definition would be the systematic study of human languages. Scientific study is today commonly associated with such natural sciences as physics, chemistry, and biology, whose conclusions lend themselves to objective verification more readily than those arrived at by investigators of human behavior. Since speech is a uniquely human phenomenon, the systematic study of it remains, despite the assistance received from other disciplines, a humanistic study, a study whose ultimate objectives are based on humane values. Linguistics is scientific, nevertheless, both in the rigor and objectivity of its methods and in the technical help it has received from the natural and social sciences.

Any language—in this book our examples are drawn mainly from English—is an extraordinarily complex phenomenon. The more thoroughly languages are analyzed, the more astonishing their complexity becomes. This complexity suggests a structure, and even the earliest ancient Greek investigators of language recognized the existence of a structure.

Since language is sequences of sound, and sound is invisible, we cannot see its structure as we can, for example, see the bony structure of a body—its skeleton. As we recognize the basic elements of the linguistic structure we invent names for them and attempt to describe the total structure part by part. It is one of the great beauties of plane geometry that its structures can be seen in their entirety. Though the native speaker seems to have a full grasp of the total grammatical structure of his language, we have no way of describing that structure so that it can all be seen at once. Instead we must break it up into what seem to be its most significant or at least its most conveniently describable parts and present them one after another. This is a most exasperating approach. All the parts are interrelated and necessary to the functioning of the whole, and a native speaker controls them all, utilizes them simultaneously, and never gives a conscious thought as to how he is using the structure to communicate his ideas. We know our English but we seldom know how it works. So we find it irritatingly hard to learn a lot of names for what we do so easily and unconsciously. It is the function of linguistics to discover the structure, to find names for its parts, and to use those names to explain how the system operates. Some of the basic areas of linguistic investigation are briefly defined below:

1. *Phonology* studies and attempts to describe the primary sound units of speech. Two related approaches are made in phonetics and phonemics. (See *Phonemes.)

2. *Morphology* studies and attempts to describe the primary meaningful units of speech; these are called *morphemes.

3. *Syntax* studies and attempts to describe the arrangement of morphemes in meaningful utterances, usually called *sentences.

4. *Grammar* is a term with a number of senses. Linguistics is concerned with the first two which are defined in the article *grammar.

5. *Semantics* studies and attempts to describe meaning. In this definition "meaning" is not used in the same sense as in § 2 above. Morphological meaning is restricted to the linguistic unit itself; the *s* on *cats* means "plural" and is recognized as such even though we don't know what a cat is. For example, if the sentence "I saw a *dat*" is changed to "I saw some *dats*," we know that *dats* is plural though we have no notion of what a *dat* is. Semantics studies the relationship between the word and what it stands for; the relationship between *cat* and the concept of a feline which it represents for us is its meaning.

Semantics gets us into what is called metalinguistics—studies that go beyond linguistics—matters that involve more than the language itself. Most of the concern of this book is metalinguistic because it deals with such matters as *spelling, *dictionaries, *rhetoric, *dialects, *jargon, as well as the *lexical meanings of words. The structures of meaning, in so far as they exist, are certainly far less apparent than the structures examined in phonology, morphology, and syntax. The modern linguist has therefore given most of his attention to these more obvious aspects of language. There is an irony in this because the layman is far more interested in what an utterance means than in how it is structured. And his attitude is right to this extent: Language does have as its primary purpose the communication of meaning. But the educated layman tries to have some understanding of all the more significant aspects of his environment. Language is the most important of these and he should therefore have some understanding of it. This linguistics tries to provide.

A language is a human phenomenon, which will differ somewhat even from person to person; it will differ far more from one place to another and from one time to another. These variations in persons, times, and places give rise to such studies as *dialectology, linguistic geography, historical* and *comparative linguistics*; and, collaborating even more with other disciplines, *lexicography,* the making of dictionaries, *orthography,* the study of spelling, and *paleography,* the study of ancient texts.

1. *The analysis of languages.* In the last few decades linguists have developed a rigorous technique for the analysis of languages, in part in reaction against previous methods of study, particularly philology, which was concerned chiefly with the Indo-European languages and based largely on the study of literature, especially of written literature. A basic principle of linguistics is that language is primarily speech; the methods of analyzing speech (such as establishing categories by comparing "minimal pairs," two locutions alike in all but one linguistic feature—*cat, rat*) have become relatively standardized and have been applied to other aspects of language. Perhaps the most difficult aspect of linguistics has been the separating (for the purposes of analysis) of linguistic activities from the current of life in which they appear. The words *structure* and *structural,* often applied to linguistic study (sometimes almost with a mystical or magical overtone), emphasize this separation. Structural linguistics isolates the linguistic activity and stresses that despite the variety in a language there is a system or a series of patterns which can be

discovered and described by linguistic methods and which alone are the proper subject of linguistics.

Because of the tremendous importance of language in life, there have been numerous pressures for practical applications of the methods and findings of the new science. To date, the notable successes have been in recording and analyzing languages not previously written, recording many that were on the point of extinction, and in teaching the spoken form of a second language through more detailed and accurate analysis.

2. *The reanalysis of English.* Considerable progress has been made in describing English in newer and more precise terms. Features like word order and intonation patterns have been more systematically explored. Real advances have been made in abandoning or at least minimizing some categories inherited from Latin grammar but not significant for English, such as forms for case in nouns and mood in verbs; in defining various categories more objectively, such as the parts of speech (or form classes)—defining them by reference to form and function rather than to meaning; in giving more definite recognition to the phrase patterns basic to syntax; and in providing a syntax grounded in observation of speech.

3. *Linguistics in a composition course.* The purpose of a composition or communication course is to further the communicative skills of the students. Its organization and general direction should aim toward this end, based on the principles of composition—rhetoric. The current language is the medium, and consequently the rhetoric must be presented on the basis of this language. (In the last few generations "grammar" has often triumphed over "rhetoric," partly because of the uncertain control of Standard English by many students and partly because the elementary facts of language have seemed more definite and consequently easier to present and test.)

The description of English should be as accurate as possible, and gradually linguistics is furnishing a more complete and consistent description. Even now there are gains in using some of the terms and categories of linguistics: a few topics such as sentence boundaries and restrictive punctuation can be more accurately presented than formerly, even though the precise definitions of the terminals (see *Phoneme § 2d) involved are uncertain.

But a composition course is not an introduction to linguistics and can hardly spare time for a very secure grounding in such a technical field—though some teachers with specialized training in the field report considerable success in using linguistics as the basic material of the course.

The language part of a composition course, beyond a few pretty elementary topics, is certainly in the area of metalinguistics, involving social habits and attitudes. Most of the questions are of the order of "Shall I say or write this in this situation?" Linguistic generalizations, whether in traditional or more scientific form, can help in presenting general patterns, in summarizing general practices, but they do not go far in guiding choices between similar expressions when both are in the range of Standard English. To make these decisions students need not only the paradigms but a wide knowledge of the varieties of current usage, what educated people say and write. Since this knowledge by itself will not answer the questions, principles are also needed, especially principles of appropriateness. These involve value judgments, the cultivation of taste and some sensitivity to styles.

(See *Style, *Usage, Ch. 1. References: The linguistic works in the bibliography: Bloomfield, Carroll, Fries — *Structure,* Gleason, and those listed under *Grammar; also Archibald A. Hill, *Introduction to Linguistic Structures,* New York, 1958; Charles F. Hockett, *A Course in Modern Linguistics,* New York, 1958; Barbara M. H. Strang, *Modern English Structure,* London and New York, 1962; W. Nelson Francis, *The English Language: An Introduction,* New York, 1965.)

Linking verbs • When a verb is used so that it has little *lexical meaning but functions chiefly in connecting a subject with a modifier, it is called a *linking verb* or *copula.*

The most commonly used linking verb is *be,* followed by modifiers which function as adjectives or nouns (single words, phrases, or clauses), traditionally known as *predicate adjectives* and *predicate nominatives,* respectively. (In this book *predicative* designates both.)

This bottle *was* full.   The man *is* a carpenter.

Many other verbs are used as linking verbs—Curme counts about sixty in current English. Instead of having a verb of full meaning like *colden,* English uses the nearly meaningless verb *turn* or *get* and the adjective *cold* (which carries the chief part of the meaning) in such a sentence as "The weather turned cold." Many verbs are used both with full meaning of their own (as *fell* in "The tree fell into the water") and as linking verbs (*fell* in "She fell silent" or "He fell ill"). Some typical linking verbs are:

He *became* a doctor. The butter *tastes* rancid. She *felt* sad. He *acts* old. The ground *sounds* hollow. He *grew* moody. He *appeared* to be gaining ground. This *looks* first rate. His story *seemed* credible.

The construction "He felt badly" is puzzling. The tendency in English is for the adjective form to supplant the adverb form, as is apparent in Nonstandard "He worked bad," where the limiting word *bad* obviously restricts *worked,* not *he.* But in "He felt badly," the connection of *badly* is with *he,* a relationship which might be expected to reinforce the use of *bad* from earlier stages of the language when *bad* was the regular form. The plausible explanation is that the proscription of *bad* after such verbs as *played, worked, ran,* etc., and the prescription of *badly* in this position has led speakers to distrust *bad* in any postverbal position and to play safe by using *badly* in all positions. The same thing has happened with *sad, sadly.* When the adjective and adverb have the same form, such ambiguities as "The cat looked longer than the dog" can occur. (See *look.)

(See *be § 2, *Predicate adjective and noun. References: Curme, *Parts of Speech,* pp. 66-69, *Syntax,* pp. 26-28.)

Lists and series • See *Series.

literary • *Literary,* as applied to style, usually means possessing traits that are characteristic of an older tradition of English literature. Its connotation may be "distinguished" or it may be "bookish." (See Ch. 1, "Formal English," p. 17.)

literate • See *illiterate.

Litotes • See *Negatives § 1.

little • *Little* can be overused to the point of sentimentality ("little dear" and so on); but such English diminutive suffixes as those in "lamb*kin,* ring*let,* duck*ling*" don't have as much vitality as those in some other languages (French *-ette,* German *-chen* and *-lein*), and *little* in part supplies the need.

loan as a verb • In spite of attempts to restrict *loan* to a noun function and to make *lend* the corresponding verb, *loan* is regularly a verb, at least in American usage:

Verb: I loaned [or *lent*] him two dollars.
Noun: He got a loan of two dollars.

Loan words • See *Foreign words in English, *Origin of words § 2b.

Localisms •

Local   *Revision: The expression marked is in local use only. Replace it by a word or construction in General American use.*

A *localism,* or *provincialism,* is a word or other expression in regular use by many speakers in a limited region but not in the entire area. Localisms are appropriate to conversation and to Informal writing but are usually out of place in General and Formal writing. (See Ch. 1, "Variations due to place," p. 6, *Dialects.)

locate • *Locate* is used for *settle* (The family located near the present town of Nashua) and for *find* (I can't locate the letter now) where *settle* and *find* would be preferable. It is *dead-wood in defining the location of specific places or people:

He is now [located] with the Ford Motor Company in Detroit.

Locution • *Locution* is a handy term for referring to a word or a unified group of words; that is, it may be applied to a single word or to a phrase or clause considered as a meaning group. *Phrase, a meaning group, that is* are three locutions.

Logic •
Revision: Reexamine and revise the logical relationship that is expressed or implied.

Logic

Logic is a complex and difficult subject covering a broad range of topics, from vagueness and ambiguity in statements to the methods of scientific investigation. But "logic" is also a necessary part of our daily lives, whether we are making a judgment, deciding on what action to take, or simply trying to understand what goes on around us. It is equally important in our attempts—spoken or written—to communicate with each other. Everyone (whether he's ever heard the term *logic* or not) has at some time or other protested, "That doesn't make sense" or "That doesn't follow from what you just said." Everyone, that is, has some notion of the difference between logical and illogical reasoning.

Logic has a place in a composition course, if only because what is written should "make sense"—should reflect clear and responsible thinking about the material. Clear thinking in itself by no means guarantees good writing, but no paper is good unless the thinking that has gone into it is clear. A mechanically perfect paper that presents a nonsensical argument is unacceptable by college standards. Unclear thinking may reflect itself in all aspects of a paper—irrelevant material, faulty organization, sentences that don't "hang together," and imprecise choice of words. More narrowly, it shows up in errors in reasoning, in faulty relationships between one idea and another, one statement and another.

Logic will not help you learn the "truth" about your subject; it does not give you information or ideas or insights. But it does furnish techniques for testing the relationships that you have set forth in a paper. Being aware of the possible fallacies or errors in reasoning doesn't guarantee that you won't fall into them, but it should make you more alert to detecting and correcting them once you have set them down on paper.

For a discussion of the kinds of reasoning by which we reach conclusions and for illustrations of the possible sources of error, see Ch. 7, "Testing relationships," pp. 242-258. They are summarized in the following check list.

The chief fallacies in *inductive* reasoning are: hasty generalizing, *post hoc propter hoc* (faulty causal reasoning—see also *Cause), faulty comparisons and analogies.

In *deductive* inference, fallacies are of various kinds, depending on the type of syllogism.

In the hypothetical syllogism (If P, then Q; P; therefore Q), the conclusion is invalid if the minor premise denies the antecedent or affirms the consequent.

In the alternative syllogism (Either A or B; not A; therefore B), the conclusion is invalid if the enumeration of alternatives is incomplete or if, in an inclusive relationship, the minor premise is affirmative.

In the categorical syllogism (M is P; S is M; therefore S is P), the conclusion is invalid if the meaning of one of the three terms shifts, if the middle term is undistributed in both premises, if a term that is distributed in the conclusion was not distributed in the premises, if both premises are particular, or if both premises are negative.

Other common fallacies, which have to do with the material rather than the inferences drawn, are *begging the question, ignoring the question,* and *argumentum ad hominem.*

(References: Three of the many excellent textbooks on logic are Morris R. Cohen and Ernest Nagel, *An Introduction to Logic and Scientific Method,* New York, 1934; Irving M. Copi, *Introduction to Logic,* 2nd ed., New York, 1961; Philip Wheelwright, *Valid Thinking,* New York, 1962.)

Logic and language • Sometimes items of usage are objected to as being "illogical," as *he don't, the *reason is because.* The former is a matter of history and of language variety, *he doesn't* being Standard English and *he don't* now generally Nonstandard. When the objection to the second is elaborated, it is usually "that an adverbial clause (because . . .) is equated with a noun (reason)"; these terms are from grammar rather than from logic. Logic proper is not involved in either objection.

A great many *idioms are not the cumulation of the meaning of their separate words: *get sick, hard to come by, a little water, many is the time, out of order.* These show, more clearly than the equally arbitrary general habits of the language, that language is a human development, the result of millions of speech situations, not a preplanned system; it is not illogical but simply nonlogical. The wonder is that it is as systematic as it is.

Probably arguments from logic had an influence in establishing the *double negative as Nonstandard English, since in language ordinarily the more negatives there are, the more definitely negative the statement is. But arguments from logic have had few such successes, and the term *logical* cannot be applied to language in its technical sense but only in its most general popular sense of "more or less systematic."

Long function word • See *Wordiness § 2.

Long variants • Some amateur writers are tempted to add an extra prefix or suffix to a word that already carries the meaning they intend. They write *irregardless, though *regardless* already means "without regard to," or *doubtlessly* for *doubtless*. Some like to use sonorous suffixes that add nothing to the meaning, like the *-ation* in *origination*. Some other long variants usually to be avoided are:

> *analyzation* for *analysis*
> *certificated* for *certified*
> *confliction* for *conflict*
> *emotionality* when only *emotion* is meant
> *commercialistic* for *commercial*
> *ruination* for *ruin* [*ruination* is an older emphatic form of *ruin*]
> *hotness* for *heat*
> *intermingle* for *mingle*
> *orientate* for *orient*
> *repay* when simple *pay* is meant, as in paying dividends
> Unnecessary *-al* endings, as *transportation*[*al*] system, *government*[*al*] policy
> *utilize* when only *use* is meant

Some of these words are not in good use at all (*analyzation*) and show lack of observation of language by anyone who uses them. Others are respectable but should be used sparingly. They can occasionally produce an effect, but the more compact form is usually preferable. (Occasionally the longer form acquires a special sense: A *certificated* teacher is one who has a certificate from the state licensing him to teach.) If a number of long variants are used they will weigh down a piece of writing and make it flabby. (See *Origin of words § 3; compare Ch. 9, "Big words," p. 347. Reference: Fowler, "Long variants.")

look • When used as a verb of complete meaning (to use the eyes, gaze), *look* is modified by an adverb: *look searchingly, look longingly.* As a linking verb, equivalent to *appear, look* is followed by an adjective which modifies the subject: He looks *well,* or *healthy,* or *tired.* . . . (See *Linking verbs.)

lose, loose • Associate the spelling of these words with the pronunciation and meaning:

    lose /lüz/—lose a bet, lose sleep, lose money
    loose /lüs/—loose a knot, a loose screw
    loosed /lüst/—He loosed the boat from its moorings
    lost /lôst/—a lost road, a lost soul, lost his way, have lost

lot, lots of • Both *a lot of* and *lots of* are in General use. But they tend to be avoided in Formal writing, particularly *lots: We tried a lot of different kinds. He has lots of friends . . . a lot of money.* (Formal: *He has many friends . . . a good deal of money.*) Do not spell the article and the noun as one word: *a lot,* not *alot.*

lousy • Except when meaning "infested with lice" (a sense in which it is rarely needed any more), *lousy* is a strong Informal word of abuse, now weakened to a *counter word of disapproval, expressive if not used too often, but offensive to most ears.

lovely • *Lovely* is a *counter word of approval, popular perhaps because its pronunciation can (by some people) be drawn out indefinitely and practically sung: *We had a love-ly time.*

Lower case •
    *Revision: Use a lower case (small) letter instead of a
    capital in this word.*

    lc

(See *Capital letters, Ch. 10, "Using capital letters," p. 401.)

-ly forms • See *-al ly, *Adverbs, types and forms § 1.

M • The sound represented by the letter *m* is a nasal consonant made with the lips closed: *music, diamond, drummer,* *sum, lamp*; *m* is the only regular spelling for this sound, but it often occurs with other letters which are not sounded: *so*me, *sole*mn, *co*mb.

M may represent a syllable by itself ("syllabic *m*"): *stop 'em* /stop'm̩/. Some people tend to make a syllable with *m* in words like *elm, film* (/el'əm/, /fil'əm/) instead of using the more standard pronunciations: /elm/, /film/.

m. • See *a.m. and p.m., also A.M. and P.M.

madam • As a formula of address *Madam* or *Dear Madam* is used for both married and unmarried women. The French spelling *madame,* better pronounced /mad'əm/, is sometimes used as the title for a foreign married woman, often for a woman musician, and sometimes in social and commercial contexts. In speech *madam* is usually *ma'am*: *Yes, Ma'am,* /mam/ or /mäm/. As a word of address or in social use (journalistic or Formal) the plural of *madam* is *mesdames* /mā däm'/. (See *Titles of persons.)

Magazine references • See *References in scientific papers.

Main clauses • See *Clauses. See also *Absolute constructions; *Adverbs, types and forms § 5; *Comma § 2; *Subordination § 3.

maintain, service, repair • See *service.

majority—plurality • Strictly *majority* means "more than half of" a certain number; *plurality* means "more than the next highest." *Plurality* is not much used now in the United States, the meaning *majority* being extended to "an excess of votes over all others cast"—and even often used in the exact sense of *plurality,* simply the excess of votes over the next highest. In an election with three candidates and 12,000 votes cast, one received 7000, one 3000, and one 2000; the winner would have a *plurality* of 4000 (in common usage, a majority of 4000); strictly speaking, he would have a *majority* of 1000.

Informally *majority* is often used of amounts or quantities as well as of numbers:

Informal: We spent the majority of the day there.
General: We spent most [or: the greater part] of the day there.
Wordy: The majority of students are interested in football.
Better: Most students are interested in football.

Malapropism • A *malapropism* is a confusion of two words somewhat similar in sound but different in meaning, with a consequent ludicrous kind of sense, as *arduous* love for *ardent* love. Malapropisms are the cause of many *boners but are often intentionally used for humorous effect, as they were by Richard Brinsley Sheridan in creating the part of Mrs. Malaprop in *The Rivals*. It is, of course, the speeches of Mrs. Malaprop that have given the name to these confusions in language:

> "I would by no means wish a daughter of mine to be a progeny of learning. . . . Then, sir, she should have a supercilious knowledge in accounts;—and as she grew up, I would have her instructed in geometry, that she might know something of the contagious countries. . . ."
> —RICHARD BRINSLEY SHERIDAN, *The Rivals*, Act I, Scene ii

man, woman • These are preferred to the more pretentious *gentleman* or *lady,* except when *man* or *woman* would sound conspicuously blunt.

Ladies and gentlemen is a *formula in addressing an audience.

The singular forms alone are used as modifiers:

manpower   manholes   woman hater   woman suffrage

(Compare *freshman, freshmen.)

Manuscript form •

MS   *Revision: Your manuscript does not have the proper form. Revise or rewrite as directed.*

(See Ch. 2, "Preparing the manuscript," pp. 56-59, for details of good manuscript practice. See also *Typewritten copy, *Division of words, *Proofreading, *Submitting manuscript.)

Material for papers • See relevant sections of the *Guide* for discussions of selecting, checking, evaluating, and outlining material for papers; also *Fundamentals, *Originality.

may—can • See *can—may.

may be, maybe • *Maybe* is an adverb meaning "perhaps," a reduction of *it may be. May be* is a verb form:

Maybe you'll have better luck next time.   He may be the next mayor.

In speech *maybe* often becomes /me′bi/, with the /ā/ sound becoming /e/ as it has in the *break* of *breakfast*.

me • See *Pronouns, types and forms § 1, *between you and me, *It's me.

Meaning •
Revision: *The word, phrase, or sentence does not make
sense in this context. Replace it with one that conveys
the meaning you intend.*

Mng

When the reader questions the meaning of what you have
written, it indicates a rather drastic failure in communication.
Ordinarily the problem is not simply the use of one word for
another that is reasonably close to it in sound or meaning—
comprehension for *comprehensibility,* for instance. This would
be marked *WW* ("wrong word"); the reader knows the word
is "wrong" because he knows what the "right" one is. But
Mng suggests that the reader cannot make an intelligent guess
at what you were trying to say. Rethinking and rewriting are
in order. (See *Ambiguity.)

For discussion of the meaning of words, see Ch. 9, p. 369.

media—medium(s) • The plural of *medium* is usually *medi-
ums*—always in the spiritualistic sense, practically always in the
general sense. *Media* is most used in scientific contexts and in
the phrase *mass media* (of communication) and usually now as
applied to the different advertising *media* (newspapers, magazines, television, billboards, etc.)

medieval • Some years ago the American Historical Association decided to change their spelling of this word from *mediaeval* to *medieval,* now the commoner form. Pronunciation is
/mē′di ē′vl̞/ or /med′i ē′vl̞/, rarely /mid ē′vl̞/. (See *-ae-, -oe-.)

messrs. • *Messrs.* is the abbreviation of French *messieurs,*
which in English is pronounced /mes′ərz/. It is used as the
plural of *Mr.* (*Messrs. Ives and Johnson*) and sometimes,
though rarely now in American usage, used in addressing firms
(*Messrs. Brown, Hubbell and Company*). The occasions for its
use are Formal. (See *Abbreviations § 2.)

meter • *Meter* is now a more common spelling than *metre.*
The second *e* drops out in derivatives: *metrical, metrics, metric
system.* (For a description of English meters see *Verse form,
also see *-er, -re.)

Middle English • See *English language § 3.

might—could • See *can—may.

Misrelated modifiers • See *Dangling modifiers.

mix, mixer • *Mix* is Informal for "associate with," *mixer* for "sociable person" or for "the person who develops new acquaintances readily." Though slang in their origin, they seem excusable because of the colorlessness of the more reputable words. *Mixer* is also used as a noun to mean "social gathering."

Mixed usage • Experienced writers sometimes deliberately shift from one variety of English to another to achieve special effects, but many weaknesses in expression spring from the *unintentional* mixture of different varieties of usage. Conspicuously Informal words or *idioms may stray into Formal writing; Nonstandard locutions or words usually confined to law or business may appear in General writing. Distinctly Formal words and idioms are equally inappropriate in General writing. (They often appear because the writer is trying to avoid some natural expression.) The principal way to develop in language is to cultivate feeling for different styles and their fitness for a given job. (See Ch. 1.)

Modal auxiliaries • *Can, could, may, might, must, ought, *shall, should, will, would* are called *modal auxiliaries* (though they have nothing to do with grammatical "mood"). They differ from other verbs in having no *s* in the third person singular, no participles, and therefore no compound forms, and they always occur as part of verb phrases, complete or elliptical. *Dare* and **need* are also sometimes used as modal auxiliaries. (See *Elliptical constructions.)

Modern English • See *English language § 5.

Modifiers • *Modifiers* are words or word groups that stand in a sentence in a secondary relationship to other words or word groups (*Headwords). Typically they limit and make more exact the meaning of the headword. In these examples the words in italics modify the words in small capitals:

a *cold, windy* DAY   He FAILED *miserably.*   a *truly* GREAT—a *truly great* MAN   *Coming around the corner,* WE met him head on. *As we came around the corner,* WE SAW HIM BOARDING A TROLLEY.

(See Ch. 8, "Revising dangling modifiers," p. 297, Ch. 9, "Revising modifiers," p. 340, *Absolute constructions, *Adjectives in use, *Adverbs in use, *Ambiguity § 2, *Apposition, appositives, *Clauses § 2b, c, *Dangling modifiers, *Gerund § 1, *Hyphen § 2, *Infinitives § 4, *Nouns § 2, *Participles § 2, *Phrases, *Restrictive and nonrestrictive, *Verbals.)

Money •
1. Exact sums of money are usually written in figures:

72¢ $4.98 $5 $168.75 $42,810

Round sums are more likely to be written in words: *two hundred dollars, a million and a half dollars.*

In factual books or articles involving frequent references to sums of money, however, figures are often used throughout.

2. In consecutive writing, amounts are usually written out when they are used as modifiers: *a million dollar* project. Informally, figures are often used: *an 85¢ seat.*

3. Commas and periods, $ and ¢ signs are used as in the examples in § 1 above. (For an example of writing sums of money in text, see the paragraphs of illustration in *Numbers § 2.)

Monosyllables • A *monosyllable* is a word of one syllable:

asked   bright   feel   fill   longed   word

Monosyllables should not be divided at the end of lines, not even words like *asked, longed.* (See *Division of words.)

A *polysyllable* strictly has three or more syllables, but since we use *dissyllable* (having two syllables) rather rarely, *polysyllable* usually means a word having two or more syllables.

Months • In reference matter and Informal writing, the names of months with more than four letters are often abbreviated in dates:

Jan. 21, 1965   16 Aug. 1966   Dec. 25, 1966
[But:] May 1, 1967   June 30, 1967   4 July 1968

When only the month or month and year are given, abbreviation would be rare:

Every January he tries again   January 1959

In Formal writing, the names of the months would not be abbreviated at all. (See *Numbers § 1a, *Dates.)

Mood • By the forms of *mood* (occasionally, *mode*), verbs in many languages may distinguish the way in which a statement is regarded by the writer. Modern English verbs hardly have moods in the Latin grammar sense, but the terms are still conventionally used:

Indicative:	[as a fact, a statement]	I am
Subjunctive:	[as a wish, possibility, doubt]	If I were
Imperative:	[as a command]	Stop!

(See *Indicative mood, *Subjunctives, *Commands and requests, *Verbs.)

moral, morale • Although the *e* is not in the French noun we borrowed as /mə ral´/ ("a confident mental state"), it is a convenient and natural English way of showing there is something peculiar in the pronunciation. It also distinguishes this *morale* from *moral* ("concerning right conduct").

more, most • See *Comparison of adjectives and adverbs § 5b.

Morpheme • *Morpheme* is a term in linguistics for what is most briefly described as the smallest grammatically meaningful unit in a language. It may be a word—"free form"—(*boy, tall, Massachusetts*) or a part of a word that can combine with other elements—"bound form"—(*-s, -ing, anti-, -ness*). (For a sentence analyzed into morphemes see *Immediate constituent. See also *Linguistics, *Parts of speech, *Origin of words. Reference: Gleason, especially Chs. 5-8.)

Morphology • See *Linguistics, *Morpheme.

most, almost • In speech *almost* is often reduced to *most*: *A drop in prices will appeal to most anybody. Most,* used thus, is Informal and ordinarily out of place in written English. If you can substitute *almost* for *most* in a sentence (*almost* always, *almost* anywhere), *almost* is the word you need.

Mr. • Usually abbreviated, this title is written out only when it represents spoken usage and when it is used without a name:

They're only two for five, mister. [But:] Mr. Schlesser

(See *Abbreviations § 2, *Titles of persons.)

Mrs. • This title is usually written out only to represent Nonstandard usage and is then spelled *missis* or *missus*:

Standard: Mrs. Dorothy M. Adams   Mrs. Adams
Nonstandard: Where's the missis?

Mrs. is not combined with a husband's title except in small town journalese. Write *Mrs. Dodd,* not *Mrs. Prof. Dodd.* (See *Abbreviations § 2, *Titles of persons. For suggestions on the use of this title with a signature see *Letters § 2.)

MS. • *MS.,* usually in caps, is the conventional abbreviation for *manuscript*; plural *MSS.* The shoptalk word for manuscript intended for publication is *copy.*

must • *Must* has recently become an adjective modifier in General use:

the President's must legislation
This is a must article for every intelligent American.

It has long been a noun in newspaper shoptalk, a *B.O.M.* being a *Business Office Must,* a story that has to be run because of some advertising tieup. (See *Auxiliary verb.)

myself • *Myself* is a reflexive or intensive pronoun, referring back to *I* when used as an object or as an intensive:

Object: I shave myself.
Intensive: I saw the whole thing myself.

Myself and the other -*self* pronouns are used as the second part of compound subjects or objects commonly in speech but rarely in writing. They are seldom appropriate in good written style:

Informal: Another fellow and myself saw the whole thing.
General: Another fellow and I saw the whole thing.
Informal: Sam invited John and myself to dinner.
General: Sam invited John and me to dinner.

(See *Pronouns, types and forms § 4; *self; *himself, herself. References: Josephine M. Burnham, "The -Self Forms as Personal Pronouns," *American Speech,* 1950, 25:264-267; Bryant, pp. 141-143.)

N • /n/, as in *now, gnaw, inning, been. N* may be a syllable by itself ("syllabic *n*"), as in *cotton, hidden, couldn't* (/kot'n̩/, /hid'n̩/, /kud'n̩t/), where the intrusion of a vowel sound between the consonants is often considered Nonstandard (see Kenyon and Knott, ¶ 114); *n* is the only regular spelling for this sound, but it often occurs with other letters which are not sounded: *kn*ife, *p*neumonia, *gn*aw.

N is generally silent in *kiln* and in a number of words after *m*: *autumn, damn, hymn, solemn.* The sounding of *n* in derivatives of such words varies with each word. It is not sounded in *hymned* /himd/ and in *damned* only in archaic or ultra poetic contexts /dam'ned/. It is sounded in *autumnal, damnation, hymnal, solemnity,* and in general before a suffix when the suffix begins with a vowel.

An *ñ* (the wavy line is called a *tilde*) is found in some words from Spanish (*señor*). If the word is commonly used, the spelling is usually changed to *ny* (*canyon* instead of *cañon*). (See *ng.)

naive—naïve • The form without the dieresis (*naive*) is gaining over *naïve.* It is unnecessary to keep the French masculine

form *naïf* in English because we do not have the grammatical
*gender which requires it. *Naive* can do all the work. Pronounced /nä ēv′/.

namely and other introductory words •
1. The beginning of wisdom with "introductory words" like
namely, that is, for example, such as is to use them as seldom
as possible. *Namely, viz., i.e., e.g.,* and some others are often
found in Formal scholarly prose, but *for example, for instance,
such as* are more appropriate to most writing. Very often such
words can be omitted altogether in compact, General writing:

> He instructed us in the mysteries of punctuation: [such as] semi-
> colons between clauses of a compound sentence, position of quota-
> tion marks with other marks, commas with nonrestrictive clauses.

2. In Formal style or in a long, rather complicated sentence,
an introductory word is usually preceded by a semicolon:

> The interview is of value, then, because it aids in discovering cer-
> tain traits; e.g., emotional and temperamental attitudes—which do
> not submit so readily to other modes of attack.—G. D. Higginson,
> *Fields of Psychology,* p. 395

When one of these words introduces a series of short items,
it is often followed by a comma rather than by a colon:

> The boys in training are thoroughly grounded in the fundamental
> processes of the work, for example, planning, building, and launch-
> ing.

No comma should follow *such as*:

> Large animals, such as bears, moose, and elk, are often found here.

Names • In factual writing all names used should be complete
and accurate. In current writing, made-up names and other
dodges are not used much except in humor. In the following
they stamp the paper as amateur:

> Across the table sat Cornelius Van Stuck-up between two feminine
> admirers whose names I will not mention but will call Miss X and
> Miss Y. Miss X said to Miss Y....

Use the real names of people and places unless there are cogent
reasons for avoiding them; if there are, invent convincing
names or use pronouns or *a man* or a less conspicuous device. The use of actual names makes a style seem concrete,
immediate, and current.

> (*Index* articles providing information on points of usage
> include: *Capital letters, *Esq., Esquire, *Given names,
> *Nicknames, *Professor, *Proper names, *Reverend, *Ships'
> names.)

necessary • *Necessary* is spelled with one *c* and two *s*'s. Very often a verb is more direct and emphatic but less polite than a construction with *necessary*:

You *must* [or *have to,* rather than *It is necessary that you*] pay.

necessity • The idiom is *necessity of* or *for* doing something (not *to do* something):

I don't see *the necessity of* [or: *for*] *reading* so many pages to get so few facts. [Or, more concise: I don't see *the need for reading* so many pages....]

need—needs • Both are third person singular of the verb *need,* but used in different idioms. *Needs* is the form in affirmative statements, *need not* or *does not need* in negative statements, *need* or *does . . . need* in questions:

He needs a haircut.
He needs to have a haircut. [Infinitive with *to*]
Does he need a haircut?
Formal: He need not come. [Infinitive without *to*]
General: He doesn't need to come. [Also:] He needn't come.
Formal: Need she come?
General: Does she need to come?

Need followed by the past participle rather than the present infinitive is a localism:

General: It needs to be covered.
Local: It needs be covered.

Negatives • The meaning of a negative in language is not always equivalent to its meaning in mathematics, where —3 is as much less than 0 as +3 is more than 0 and — (—3) = +3 because the only mathematical alternative of — is +. In language a contrary is likely to be stated by another positive (*good—evil, white—black*); the negative usually means "less than" or "different from"; *not good* is *less than good* but not necessarily *evil,* and *not white* is *different from white* but not necessarily *black.* This quality of negation provides the weakened positive which results from a negated negative: in *not uncommon,* we get a reduced reduction; *uncommon* is *less than common, not uncommon* is *less than less than common* or *not quite common.*

On the other hand, when two (or more) negatives in a sentence affect different words (In *He can't never do no work, n't* affects *can* and *never,* and *no* affects *do* and *work*), they actually reinforce the negation. But this cumulative effect is no longer used in Standard English. (See *Double negative.)

Sometimes the negative form shows unexpected variation from the affirmative: *must go* and *have to go* are nearly synonymous; *mustn't go* and *don't have to go* are not. (Reference: Otto Jespersen, *Philosophy of Grammar,* New York, 1924, Ch. 24.)

1. *Emphasis.* A statement may sometimes be made more emphatic or striking by being put negatively (in a figure of speech known as *litotes* or *understatement*):

He carried not only his own burden but hers too.

He made not just one great discovery but several.

The assimilating power of the English language is not less remarkable than the complexity of its sources.—J. B. Greenough and G. L. Kittredge, *Words and Their Ways in English Speech,* p. 147

2. *Separation from positive.* Within a single sentence words of positive and negative import usually need to be separated because the constructions in which they occur will not be parallel:

I have learned through this practice to overcome stage fright, and I have gained in vividness of speech. [Not: *I have learned . . . to overcome stage fright and vividness of speech.*]

3. *Double negative.* See *Double negative.

(For a discussion of negative comparisons see *as . . . as.)

Negro • Capitalize, like *Caucasian, Indian.* Plural, *Negroes.*

neither • *See* *either, *Correlative conjunctions.

Neutral vowel • A good many words give spelling trouble because they contain various spellings for the vowel sound represented in this book by /ə/ (*schwa): /ə kad'ə mē/ (*academy*). This is Standard pronunciation, so that no drill in sounding the syllable can help. A number of these words are related to others in which this syllable has a stress, making the vowel stand out. Such pairs as the following may help you spell accurately the vowel italicized in the first word:

academy—academic	despair—desperation, desperado
affirmative—affirmation	extravagance, extravagant—
angel—angelic	extravaganza
comparable—compare	hypocrisy—hypocritical
competition—compete	medicine—medicinal
definitely—definition	preparation—prepare
degradation—degrade	repetition—repeat
democracy—democratic	ridicule—ridiculous

But for the great majority of words with the neutral vowel either a good memory or a good dictionary is essential.

New words • New words are coming into English more rapidly than ever. They originate in various ways (see *Origin of words § 2, *Conversion). Many of them stand for new concepts and provide the means of communicating those concepts. Others are novelties and irritate the many readers and listeners who dislike mere innovation. When you use a new word, always consider the effect it may have on your audience. This does not mean that you necessarily avoid all new words which might disturb. Shock effect may be an appropriate device. But be aware of what you are doing.

Newspaper English • Joseph Pulitzer's famous motto for workers on the old *New York World* still stands as the ideal for the material and style of newswriting—*Accuracy, Terseness, Accuracy.* Complete accuracy is not easy for a reporter who has perhaps only a few minutes to get the facts of a complicated event, and terseness is not easy either for a man who writes habitually, often of very similar happenings, with little personal interest in his material. The result is that newspapers contain some of the worst writing that gets into print and some of the best.

There is no special dialect for newswriting, though the organization of a newspaper story is, of course, likely to be different from a historical account of the same event. Papers have some conventions for giving ages, names, places of residence, and other routine matters, but good newspaper English is simply General English applied to the daily recording of affairs. It is a style written to be read rapidly and grasped by the eye; except in headlines, tricks of sound—*alliteration, rhyme, *assonance—are out of place. The sentences are typically short and direct; the words are concrete and from the General vocabulary.

1. *Journalese.* The two most common sins of newswriting are inflation (*big words) and triteness, which we can lump as symptoms of *journalese.* Granting that *our fair city, ample outlet for her histrionic ability,* and scores of such trite phrases belonging to paleo-journalism are not found now outside small town papers, there is still a vast amount of wordy and lazy writing in newspapers. Every *stylebook contains a list of journalese expressions to be avoided. Triteness (see *Trite) is the next worst offense in journalese.

2. *Headlines and headlinese.* While writers of news stories have to write with an eye on inches of space, headline writers have to watch every letter. A given style of head has a "count" of so many letters, and, as the compositor says, "there ain't no rubber type." This necessity for compression and a desire to

"sell the papers" give rise to the punch of headlines. As the Waterbury, Conn., *Republican* style sheet puts it:

> PUT PUNCH IN HEADS
> SAYS OLD SLOT MAN
> Wants Accurate, Terse, Positive
> and Pungent Guides to
> News
> BEGS FOR ACTIVE VERBS
> Bald-Domed Editor Wants Blue
> Pencil Novices to Lay Off
> Fuzzy Words

This leads to the omission of *function words (*a, an, the,* connectives) and to the use of short words and clipped forms:

Fly ocean; tell fight with gale 3 miles in air—12 Navy planes battered

To save space, short words are used, nouns are used as verbs, verbs as nouns, and any words or even long phrases as adjectives:

Superintendent and Supervisor Refute
Charge of Spying on *Traction Company*
Bus Drivers' Union Enrollment Meeting
Senate Set for Votes on Trade Bill Curbs

Worrying that headline style will ruin our language is silly; nobody ever talks headlinese—it's too concentrated. The feeble circumlocution of the stories that often stand below the heads is a greater menace to our language than the clipped heads.

(References: There are many textbooks on newspaper writing. Two of the most useful are: Curtis D. MacDougall, *Interpretative Reporting*, New York, 1948, and George C. Bastian and Leland D. Case, *Editing the Day's News*, New York, 1943. The stylebooks of newspapers are important. Some, like those of *The Detroit News* and *The New York Times*, 1962, are for sale. The magazine *Editor & Publisher* is the best source on current American journalism.)

Newspaper titles • See *Titles of articles, books, etc.

ng • /ng/ is the pronunciation symbol for the sound produced with the back of the tongue against the soft palate and the air coming through the nose with the vocal cords vibrating, most frequently spelled *ng* (*long, bringing*) but also spelled *n*: *anchor* /ang'kər/, *angry* /ang'grē/, *sink* /singk/, *uncle* /ung'kl̩/.

Pronunciation is divided when a syllable ending in *n* is followed by one beginning with *g* or *k*: *congress* /kong'gris/ but *congressional* /kən gresh'ən l̥/ or /kən gresh'nəl/.

nice • *Nice* is a *counter word indicating mild approval, useful in speech but so general in meaning that it is of little use in writing. One of the word's former meanings, "exact, precise," is seen in a *nice distinction.* (Reference: C. C. Fries, "The Meanings of Words," *English Journal,* 1927, 16:602-606.)

Nicknames • *Nicknames* are rarely appropriate in Formal writing. In other writing they are often appropriate and should be used naturally, without apology. Some writers will put a nickname in quotes the first time it is used but not when it is repeated.

no • See *yes.

No. • The abbreviation *No.* for *number* (from the Latin *numero,* "by number") is written with a capital. It is appropriate chiefly in business and technical English. In the United States *No.* is not written with street numbers.

nobody, nothing, nowhere • All are written as single words. *Nobody* and *nothing* are singular in form and are usually treated grammatically as such, though *nobody* is Informally treated as a collective (see *every and its compounds):

Formal: Nobody thinks that his own dog is a nuisance.
Informal: Nobody thinks their own dog is a nuisance. Nothing is further from the truth. The dog could be found nowhere.

nohow • Nonstandard: *We couldn't get there nohow;* Standard: *... no matter how we tried* [or] *... any way we tried.*

Nominative case • A noun or pronoun that is the subject of a finite verb is sometimes said to be in the *nominative* (or *subjective) case.* The form of the nominative singular is the common form of the noun, the form to which, typically, the endings for the genitive and for the plural are added. *I, you, he, she, it, we, you, they* are the nominative forms of the personal pronouns; *who, which,* and *that* are the nominative forms of the relative pronouns. These forms are the usual ones for the nominative function; but see *It's me and *Pronouns. (See also *Case, *Subject and verb.)

Nonce words • Strictly, a *nonce word* is a word used but once as far as existing writing shows; a word coined for the occasion and not attaining a general use, as *thrillier* in a theater sign: "Thrillier than *Diabolique.*"

none, no one • *None* is a single word, but *no one* is often used instead of *none,* for emphasis. *None* may be either singular or plural but is now more common with the plural:

As only ten jurors have been chosen so far, none of the witnesses were called [or: *was called*].

She tried on ten hats, but none of them were attractive.

I read three books on the subject, no one of which was helpful.

(Reference: Fries, *AEG,* pp. 50, 56.)

Nonrestrictive and restrictive • See *Restrictive and nonrestrictive.

Nonstandard English •
> *Revision*: *Change the Nonstandard word, form, or idiom to one appropriate to Standard usage.*

NS

(See Ch. 1, p. 23.)

nor • See *Correlative conjunctions.

not hardly, not scarcely • See *Double negative § 3.

not to exceed • *Not to exceed* is a business and legal locution; in other contexts *not more than* is usual:

The undersigned will be liable for property damages, not to exceed $500 for one accident.

The enrollment in the course was to be not more than fifty.

Not more than two people could live on that pay.

Notes • See *Letters, *Social correspondence.

nothing • See *nobody, nothing, nowhere.

notorious • *Notorious* means "well known for unsavory reasons": *a notorious cheat. Notable* is "worthy of note, remarkable." *Famous* is "well known for accomplishment or excellence": *a famous writer, aviator. Infamous* means "odious, detestable": *an infamous deed. Noted* is journalistic for "famous, well known."

Noun and verb stress • Though identical in spelling, some nouns and verbs, mostly from French, are differentiated in speaking by stressing the first syllable in the noun and the last in the verb. When this shift occurs, the verb often has an altered vowel sound. Some of these are listed below:

Noun	Verb
com'press	com press'
con'duct	con duct'
con'flict	con flict' [often *con'flict*]
con'trast	con trast' [often *con'trast*]
con'vict	con vict'
de'crease [and *de crease'*]	de crease'
di'gest	di gest'
es'cort	es cort'
ex'tract	ex tract'
in'cline	in cline'
in'crease	in crease' [often *in'crease*]
in'sult	in sult'
ob'ject	ob ject'
prod'uce, pro'duce	pro duce'
rec'ord	re cord'

Several of these verbs in common use show the natural English tendency to put the stress on the first syllable. The following words are both nouns and verbs with the same stress:

ac'cent   cos'tume   dis'count   im'port

Noun clauses • A *noun clause* is a construction having a subject and *finite verb and functioning typically in a sentence as a subject or object. Many noun clauses are introduced by *that*, some by *what, who, whoever, whatever, why, when,* and other connectives.

Subject: *That anyone could raise his grades by studying* had never occurred to him. *Whether or not he should go* had bothered him.

Object: He knew *that it would never happen again.* [Or:] He knew *it would never happen again.*

Predicate noun: His favorites were *whoever flattered him.*

Object of preposition: Sam is always sure of *what he does.*

Appositive: The doctrine *that we must avoid entangling alliances* was first stated by Washington.

That and *whether* clauses as subjects are, as the examples above show, distinctly Formal constructions. (See *Clauses § 2a, *reason is because.)

Nouns •

1. *Forms.* In English an important way in which we identify nouns is by their forms.

Most nouns have two: a plural form in an /s/, /əz/, or /z/ sound, spelled s or es: *hats, kindnesses, lecturers* (minor types are described in *Plurals of nouns); and a genitive form with the same sound but written with an apostrophe: *boy's, boys', cat's, church's.* (See *Genitive.)

There are a few distinctive endings found in groups of nouns, such as *-er* or *-or, -ness, -th, -tion.*

A very few nouns in English have different forms for masculine and feminine: *actor—actress, confidant—confidante, executor—executrix.* (See *Gender.)

Nouns may be single words or compound words written solid, as two words, or hyphened: *bathroom, bookcase, hub cap, go-getter, stick-up.* (See *Group words, *Hyphen.)

2. *Position and functions.* Nouns are also identified by their typical positions in sentences: standing before a verb as subject or after it as object, being preceded by an article (*a, an, the*) or demonstrative (*this, that,* and so on), or being the *headword in a prepositional phrase.

The principal functions of nouns in sentences are listed below:

Subject of a sentence: The *wind* blew for three days. (See *Subject and verb.)

Object of a verb: The wind blew the *silo* over. (See *Objects.)

Object of a preposition: in the *night,* behind the *house,* after *breakfast,* of the *president* (See *Prepositions.)

Predicative: He had become *president* of the firm. (See *Predicate adjective.)

Possession: the *woman's* first dress for two years (See *Genitive § 2.)

Apposition: The first settler, *Thomas Sanborn,* came in 1780. (See *Apposition, appositives.)

Modifiers of other nouns: a *baby* hippopotamus; the best *high school basketball* team in years (See *Genitive, *Parts of speech, *Adjectives, types and forms § 4.)

Modifiers of verbs or statements: He came two *months* ago. *Mornings* he would work a little. (See *Adverbs, types and forms § 4.)

3. *Classes of nouns.* Nouns are conventionally classified by their meaning, as follows:

a–Proper nouns, names of particular people and places, written with capitals and usually without *the* or *a: Anne, George W. Loomis, London, Georgia, France, the Bay of Naples.* (See *Proper names.)

In contrast with these proper nouns, all the other groups are *common nouns.*

b–Concrete nouns, names of objects: *leaf, leaves, road, panda, manufacturer.* (See Ch. 9, "Concrete words," p. 372.)

c–Mass nouns, names of materials in general rather than materials in particular forms: *water, coffee, cement, steel, corn.*

d–Collective nouns, names of a group of things regarded as a unit: *fleet, army, company, committee, trio, bevy.* (See *Collective nouns.)

e–Abstract nouns, names of qualities, actions, ideas: *kindness, hate, manufacture, idealism, fantasy, concept.* Many of these are *gerunds: *fishing, drinking, manufacturing.* (See Ch. 9, "Abstract words," p. 373.)

(For additional information see *Capital letters, *Case, *Infinitives § 4. References: Curme, *Parts of Speech,* Chs. 1, 9, *Syntax,* Chs. 2, 4, 26, and other references; Fries, *Structure,* pp. 65-79.)

nowhere • See *nobody, nothing, nowhere.

nowhere near • Though occurring in print, the usage has an Informal tone: *It was a good score but nowhere near as large as we'd hoped for.* (Preferable in writing: *not nearly so large as.*)

(Reference: Bryant, pp. 148-149.)

nowheres • *Nowheres* is Nonstandard for *nowhere.*

Number • *Number* in English grammar is the singular and plural aspect of nouns and pronouns and verbs. The indication of number is of great importance in nouns and pronouns (though *you* is ambiguous), of little importance in verbs, which in most forms cannot show number. (See *Plurals of nouns, *Subject and verb, *Reference of pronouns.)

number • *Number* is a collective noun, taking a singular or plural verb according as the total or the individual units are meant; *a number* takes plural:

A number of tickets have already been sold.

A number of pages were torn.

The number takes singular:

The number of tickets sold is astonishing.

The number of pages assigned for translation was gradually increased.

(See also *amount–number.)

Numbers •
Revision: Revise the figure or figures in this passage according to conventional usage.   Num

1. *Uses.* Figures are used for:

a–Dates. Only in Formal *social correspondence are dates written out in words; *1st, 2nd (2d)*, and so on may be used when a date is given without the year, but not ordinarily with the year:

Oct. 4, 1960   October 4, 1960   October 4   October 4th

Years are always written in figures.

b–Hours when *a.m. or p.m. is used:

5 p.m. [But:] five o'clock

c–Street numbers (with no comma between thousands):

2841 Washington Avenue   Apartment 3C, 781 Grand Street

d–Pages and other references:

page 642   pp. 431-482   Chapter 14 [Or:] Chapter XIV
Act III, scene iv, line 28

e–Sums of money, except sums in round numbers or, in Formal style, sums that can be written in two or three words:

$4.98   75¢   a million dollars [Or:] $1,000,000

f–Statistics and series of more than one or two numbers within a sentence:

In the political science class mock election the Republicans gained 50 seats in the House, 6 seats in the Senate, and 13 new governorships.

2. *Figures or words.* Usage varies in writing numbers that are parts of consecutive sentences. In general, newspapers and Informal writing have figures for numbers over ten, words for smaller numbers; magazine and book styles (most General writing) have figures for numbers over 100 except when the numbers can be written in two words:

Informal (newspaper) : four, ten, 15, 92, 114
General (book) : four, ten, fifteen, ninety-two, 114. [But practice is not uniform.]

This passage illustrates a typical book style in use of figures and sums of money:

With a well-integrated, rapidly growing organization, Swedish coöperators were ready to go forward to new triumphs—over galoshes this time. It sounds funny but it is not at all; the victory over the galosh cartel—really the rubber cartel—was a very tangible achievement. Galoshes are a necessity in the Swedish winter, to say nothing of the Swedish spring and the Swedish fall. And four manufacturing firms, formed into an air-tight trust, exploited this necessity for years. Annual profits of 60 per cent, 62 per cent and even, in one exceptional year, 77 per cent were recorded. On a capital of less than a million dollars the four factories realized in fourteen years more than twelve and a half million dollars and voted many stock dividends besides. As in the case of the milling cartel, the public yelled long and loud but with no visible results.

... Within a few weeks, merely on the basis of this announcement, the cartel reduced the price of a pair of men's galoshes more than fifty cents, with corresponding reductions all down the line.... The result, within a year, was another seventy cents sliced off the price of a pair of galoshes. Having achieved this, K. F. began the manufacture of automobile tires at the Gislaved plant and by 1932 was producing 50,000 tires a year.—Marquis W. Childs, *Sweden—The Middle Way,* pp. 12-13

When most writing was longhand it was conventional to express numbers in words and then repeat them in figures in parentheses. In clear copy, especially in typewritten copy, this is not done except in legal or important business documents.

Except in dates and street numbers, a comma is used to separate thousands, millions, etc., though it may be omitted in four-digit numbers:

1952 [the year]   1,952 [Or:] 1952 bushels $4,682,921

Numbers in two words between 21 and 99 are usually hyphened, though the practice is declining: *forty-two* or *forty two.*

In consecutive writing a number at the very beginning of a sentence is written in words rather than in figures:

Two to 3% of loading and up to 10% is common and 20 to 30% in specially surfaced papers.... —"Paper Manufacture," *Encyclopaedia Britannica,* p. 234

3. *Arabic and Roman numerals.* Arabic numerals (*1, 2, 146* ...) are used in almost all places where numbers are not expressed in words. Roman numerals, either lower case or capitals (i, ii, cxlvi ...; I, II, CXLVI ...), are occasionally used to number units in rather short series, as in outlines, chapters of a book, acts of a play, though now less often than formerly. The preliminary pages of books are almost always numbered with Roman numerals, because a new pagination is begun with the body of the book. Sometimes they are used on title pages for the date and on formal inscriptions.

In Roman numerals a small number preceding a larger is to be subtracted from the larger (ix = 9, xc = 90). The following table shows the common Roman numerals (lower case):

1	i	7	vii	13	xiii	25	xxv
2	ii	8	viii	14	xiv	27	xxvii
3	iii	9	ix	15	xv	29	xxix
4	iv	10	x	19	xix	30	xxx
5	v	11	xi	20	xx	40	xl
6	vi	12	xii	21	xxi	41	xli

49	xlix	80	lxxx	110	cx	600	dc
50	l	90	xc	199	cxcix	900	cm
51	li	99	xcix	200	cc	1000	m
60	lx	100	c	400	cd	1500	md
70	lxx	101	ci	500	d	1968	mcmlxviii

4. *Plurals of figures.* The plural of a figure is written either with *'s* or *s*:

> *Six fives*: six 5's, six 5s   *By tens*: by 10's, by 10s

5. *Cardinal and ordinal numbers.* The numbers in simple counting, indicating number only, are *cardinal numbers*: *1, 2, 3, 68, 129....* The numbers indicating order, *first, second, third* ... are *ordinal numbers.* Except in numbering items in a rather routine enumeration, ordinals should be spelled out rather than abbreviated to *1st, 2nd, 3rd....*

Since the simple forms *first, second,* and so on can be either adjective or adverb, the forms in *-ly* (*firstly*) are unnecessary and now are rarely used.

(See also *Fractions, *Money, *No., *Comma § 9e, *Hyphen § 1a, 2d, *References in scientific papers § 1c, 2.)

O • Speakers of English vary in their pronunciation of the *o* spellings as they do of the *a* spellings. Because of this widespread variation, pronunciation of particular words, especially with short *o*, can be indicated only roughly.

1. *"Long o"* /ō/, the sound in *go, hoe, oh, oats, note, shoulder, soldier, sew, slow, beau.*

Before spelled *r* the sound of long *o* is somewhat modified, as in *door* /dōr/, and may approach "open *o*" /ô/, as in some pronunciations of *horse, born,* and so on. (See *R.)

In unstressed and rapidly spoken words the sound of long *o* is shorter and may differ in quality: *obey* /ō bā′/ or /ə bā′/, *hotel* /hō tel′/.

2. *"Short o"* /o/. A rounded short *o* is not very frequent and is more characteristic of New England than of other parts of the country, where it is best illustrated in the first vowel of *gonna* (going to). The more common American sound is the unrounded or "open *o*" /ô/ or, especially in Northern English, broad *a* /ä/: *soft* /sôft/, /säft/, /soft/; *pond* /pônd/, /pänd/, /pond/. Since there is no single pronunciation of these words throughout the United States, the symbol /o/ is used for them without indicating the regional variants.

3. *"Open o"* /ô/, most clearly identified in its spelling *aw* (*law, lawn, spawn*) but also the vowel sound in *lord, all, fault, fought, taught, cloth, broad, talk* /lôrd/, /ôl/, /fôlt/, /fôt/,

/tôt/, /klôth/, /brôd/, /tôk/. In some areas this sound is distinguished from the /ä/ sound only before *r*: *for* and *far* are different, but *taught* and *tot* are the same.

In unstressed syllables *o* may spell the *neutral vowel (*schwa) /ə/: *actor* /ak′tər/, *nation* /nā′shən/, or it may entirely disappear as in most people's pronunciation of *chocolate* /chôk′lit/ or sophomore /sof′mōr/.

O represents several other vowel sounds—/ü/ as in *move*, /ů/ as in *wolf*, /u/ as in *son, money*, /ė/ as in *work*. (See also *ou.)

O, oh • *O* is always capitalized, and usually it is so closely related to some other word, often a name in direct address, that it is not followed by a mark of punctuation:

O dear, I suppose so. O yes. O God, unseen, but ever near.

Oh is an exclamation, followed by a comma if the force is weak, by an exclamation mark if the stress is strong. It is capitalized at the beginning of a sentence but not in the middle of a sentence:

Oh! Don't do that! Oh, I wish he would.

In Informal writing the distinction between *O* and *oh* is not always kept, and *O* is often found where traditional usage would have *oh*.

Objects •

1. *Direct objects*

a–An *object of a verb* is the noun element (noun, pronoun, noun clause) *following* a verb and intimately related to it, though less so than is the *subject (see also *Adjectives, types and forms § 5, *Infinitives § 4). In meaning it ordinarily names what is affected or effected by the action of the verb. In those pronouns with an accusative case form (*me, him, her, us, them, whom*), that form is used as object after verbs and prepositions:

They made the *boat* themselves.
Terry chased the *cat* up a tree.
He took *her* to the three formals of the year.
I don't believe *that he told the truth.*

Occasionally, for emphasis, the object precedes both the subject and the verb:

This boat [object] the boys [subject] built themselves.

b–It has been conventional to call the object in certain passive constructions a "retained object" and even to forbid the construction on the ground that a passive verb by definition is incapable of taking an object. But since the position and the relation to the verb are no different from the typical object's, it is simpler to say that a passive verb may take an object:

He was given a *subscription* to a book club.

2. *Indirect objects.* With verbs of asking, telling, giving, and so on there is often a second or "indirect" object that names the receiver of the message, gift, etc.:

He gave the *church* a memorial window.
In desperation she showed *him* the snapshot album.

In American usage the indirect object usually comes before the direct object, as in the sentences just given. A prepositional phrase is common for the indirect object when it follows the direct object:

He gave a memorial window *to the church.*
In desperation she showed the snapshot album *to him.*

3. *Objects of prepositions.* The object of a preposition is the noun element whose relation to some other part of the sentence is shown by the preposition, as *some other part of the sentence* is the object of *to* and *the preposition* is the object of *by* in this sentence. The *what* clause in *Your grade will depend chiefly on what you do on the examination* is the object of *on.* (See *Prepositions.)

4. *Objects of adjectives.* A few adjectives take objects:

It was worth *a fortune.*
Are you sure *that she will come?*
He is like *his father.*

Obscenity • Certain words have acquired connotations offensive to prevailing notions of morality and decency and, especially when written or printed, are considered disgusting or repulsive. To the extent that such words are entered in dictionaries at all, they will be labeled *vulgar* or *obscene.* They obviously can have a powerful shock value, and they are more precise than the *euphemisms and circumlocutions which ordinarily replace them in most cultivated speech and writing. They appear in print, but they very rarely have any place in the writing of college students. (See *Profanity.)

occasion, occasional, occasionally • All three of these words are spelled with two *c*'s and one *s.*

-oe-, -ae- • See *-ae-, -oe-.

of, off • Besides its use as a preposition of numerous meanings, *of* is used to make the phrasal genitive: *of a man = man's,* and so on. (See *Genitive case.)

Of is frequently used in speech in the doubling of prepositions—*inside of, off of, outside of. Inside of* and *outside of* are sometimes used in Informal writing, *off of* less so and should usually be reduced to *off*: *He stepped off* [of] *the sidewalk.*

Of is occasionally used by fiction writers to give a Nonstandard tone to dialog by spelling the contraction of *have* as it usually sounds, but this spelling should not be used in General writing:

He *should have* [possible but awkward: *should've*; not *should of*] known better.

(Reference: Bryant, pp. 115-116, 150-151.)

often • The usual Standard pronunciation is /of'ən/. The *t* is sometimes sounded, but the pronunciation /of'tən/ is regarded as an affectation by most people.

OK, O.K. • *OK* or *O.K.* is Business and Informal English for "correct, all right, approved": *The foreman put his OK on the shipment.* Occasionally it is spelled *okay.* As a verb the forms are *OK; OK'ed* or *OK'd; OK'ing; Oke* and *okeydoke* are slang.

(Reference: For the most extensive treatment of the history of *OK,* see the series of studies by Allen Walker Read in *American Speech,* 1963-1964.)

Old English • See *English language § 2.

Omissions • See *Apostrophe § 2, *Ellipsis, *Elliptical constructions.

on the part of • See *part, on the part of.

one •

1. The use of the impersonal pronoun *one* is characteristically Formal, especially if it must be repeated:

Formal: One can't be too careful, can one?

General: You can't be too careful, can you? [Where *you* is really impersonal.]

Repetition of *one,* to avoid *I* or when *you* would be more natural, is deadly.

American usage normally follows older English practice in referring back to *one* by pronouns of the third person—*he, his, him* (or *she, her*):

One is warned to be cautious if he would avoid offending his friends and bringing their displeasure down upon his head.

(See Ch. 5, "Point of view," p. 163, *they, *you.)

2. *One* may be used to avoid repeating a noun in the second of two compound elements:

Fred took the new copy and I took the old one.

The plural *ones* is often used; the apparent lack of logic need not concern us because *one* is not only a number but an indefinite pronoun.

She has two velvet dresses and three silk ones.

3. *One* is very often *deadwood, reducing the emphasis on the adjective which carries the real meaning:

The plan was certainly [an] original [one].

(Reference: Fries, *AEG,* pp. 245-246.)

-one • *One* is written solid with *any-, every-, some-* in making an indefinite pronoun; but when the *one* is stressed it is written as a separate word:

Anyone can do that. Any one of the four will be all right.
Everyone may study late. Every one of us was surprised.
Someone ought to tell her. Some one of the plans will work.

(See *any § 2, *every and its compounds, *some.)

one another • See *Pronouns, types and forms § 5.

one of those who • In written English the clause following *one of those who* and similar locutions is usually plural:

He is one of those people who believe in the perfectibility of man. [*Who* refers to *people.*]
That's one of the books that make you change your ideas. [*That* refers to *books.*]

In Informal speech and writing and sometimes in General writing the second verb is attracted to the singular by the emphatic main subject:

He is one of those people who believes in the perfectibility of man.

(See also *Subject and verb § 2d. References: John S. Kenyon, " 'One of Those Who Is,' " *American Speech,* 1951, 26:161-165; Bryant, pp. 11-13.)

only •
1. The importance of the position of *only* has been greatly exaggerated. "Logically," perhaps, it should stand immediately before the element modified:

I need only six more to have a full hundred.

But usage in this construction is conspicuously in favor of placing the *only* before the verb of the statement. There is no possible misunderstanding in the meaning of:

I only need six more to have a full hundred.

There are instances in which the placing of *only* can produce a rather ludicrous statement ("with only a face that a mother could love"). But placing *only* with the verb is a characteristic and reputable English idiom:

In reality we only have succession and coexistence, and the "force" is something that we imagine.—HAVELOCK ELLIS, *The Dance of Life,* p. 91

They only opened one bag and took the passports in and looked at them.—ERNEST HEMINGWAY, *The Sun Also Rises,* p. 94

(References: Gladys Haase, "Current English Forum," *College English,* 1950, 12:400-402; J. S. Kenyon, "Current English Forum," *College English,* 1951, 13:116-117; Bryant, pp. 155-156.)
2. In this respect *even, ever, nearly, just, exactly,* and other such limiting adverbs are similar to *only.* But since they are used much less than *only,* and some of them only in Formal English, the idiom is not so common. Like *only* they can be placed so that they spoil the emphasis:

The way I can stand in front of a store window and persuade myself that I need some novel article even surprises me [surprises even me].

Onomatopoeia • See *Imitative words and phrases.

onto, on to • When *on* is an adverb and *to* a preposition in a separate locution, they should be written as two words:

The rest of us drove on to the city.

Used as a preposition, they are written solid:

The team trotted onto the floor. They looked out onto the park.

Onto is frequently used as a double preposition in speech where *on* or *to* by itself would be more common in writing:

They finally got on [Spoken: *onto*] the bus.
The crowd got to [Spoken: *onto*] James Street.

(Reference: Bryant, p. 152.)

or • *Or* is a coordinating conjunction and, like *and, but,* and *for,* should connect words, phrases, or clauses of equal value. (See *Coordinating conjunctions, *Compound sentence, *Series.)

Words: He must be drunk or crazy.
Phrases: We could go by car or by train.
Clauses: We could go by car or we could go by train.

Two subjects joined by *or* take a singular verb if each is singular, a plural verb if both are plural or if the one nearer the verb is plural:

Cod liver oil or halibut oil is often prescribed.

Cod liver oil or cod liver oil capsules have the same effect.

Cod liver oil capsules or cod liver oil has the same effect.

The second construction is more usual than the third. (See also *Subject and verb § 2b.)

Or correlates with *either* and sometimes with *neither*:

General: Either /ē′ᵻ̄н ər/ or /ī′ᵻ̄н ər/ is correct.

Less common: Neither /ā′ᵻ̄н ər/ or /ī′ᵻ̄н ər/ is widely used in America.

General: Neither /ā′ᵻ̄н ər/ nor /ī′ᵻ̄н ər/ is widely used in America.

(See *Correlative conjunctions.)

-or, -er • See *-er, -or.

-or, -our • American spelling prefers *-or* in such words as *color, governor, honor.* When referring to Jesus Christ, *Saviour* is frequently spelled with the *u* but in other senses without it. *Glamour* is used in advertising and social contexts to elevate the tone.

British usage is divided on this point, though of course to an American reader the words in *-our* are conspicuous. Fowler said that the American change to *-or* has actually hindered the simplification that was going on in England:

Those who are willing to put national prejudice aside & examine the facts quickly realize, first, that the British *-our* words are much fewer in proportion to the *-or* words than they supposed, &, secondly, that there seems to be no discoverable line between the two sets so based on principle as to serve any useful purpose. By the side of *favour* there is *horror,* beside *ardour pallor,* beside *odour tremor,* & so forth. Of agent-nouns *saviour* (with its echo *paviour*) is perhaps the only one that now retains *-our, governor* being the latest to shed its *-u-.*—H. W. FOWLER, *A Dictionary of Modern English Usage,* p. 415

In quoting directly from British writings and in referring to British institutions, like the Labour Party, their spelling should be exactly followed; otherwise use *-or.* (References: Fowler, "-our & -or"; *Oxford English Dictionary,* "-or"; John Benbow, *Manuscript & Proof,* New York, 1937, pp. 75-77, discusses spelling in American books that are to be circulated in England.)

oral, verbal • Etymologically, *oral* means "spoken," and *verbal* means "in words"; but *verbal* has been so long used in the sense of *oral* that the sense is recognized in dictionaries:

He delivered an oral message.   He had only a verbal agreement.

Organization •
Revision: Improve the organization of your paper and/or correct the form of your outline.

Org

General methods of organizing papers are discussed in Ch. 2, pp. 47-52. Guides to organizing particular types of papers will be found in Chs. 5-7, 11. Methods of organizing paragraphs are discussed in Ch. 4, pp. 127-139.

Outlines are discussed in Ch. 2, pp. 47-51, and in *Outline form.

Origin of words •

1. *The study of word origins.* Every word has a history. Some, like *chauffeur, mores, television, parapsychology,* are relatively new in English; some have been in the language for centuries, like *home, candle, go, kitchen*; others have recently acquired new meanings, like *satellite* (from a Latin word for "attendant," a term in astronomy which probably now means for most people a man-made object which orbits the earth, moon, or other celestial body). *Etymology,* the study of word origins, traces the changes of forms and combinations of word elements (as in *dis/service, wild/ness, bath/room, room/mate*) and pursues the word or its component parts to Old English and beyond or to the foreign language from which it came into English, and so on back to the earliest discoverable forms. Of some words, especially Informal words like *dude, stooge, rumpus,* earlier forms are unknown; of others, like *OK* or *blizzard,* the sources are debated. But the efforts of generations of scholars have discovered pretty full histories for most words. These are given briefly in most dictionaries and more fully in the *Oxford English Dictionary* and in special works.

Most people working with words have some curiosity about where they came from and about how new ones can be made. They find that many of our everyday words come down directly from Old English (*brother, go, house, tell*) or, if they are of foreign origin, that they were borrowed many centuries ago (*candle, debt, pay, travel*). The vocabulary of high society has many French words, of both early and recent borrowings (*debutante, gallant, fiancée*). The vocabulary of philosophy and abstract thought has a large Latin element (*concept, fallacy, rational, idealism*), and the vocabulary of science has many Greek elements (*atom, hemoglobin, seismograph*).

The sources of words will often reveal something about our history, as the many Norman French and Latin words in law (*fine, tort, certiorari, subpoena*) remind us of the time, following 1066, when the government of England was in the hands of the Norman French. But it is more interesting to discover what meanings the words have had in their earlier career in English and in the foreign languages from which they have come. *Supercilium* in Latin meant "eyebrow"; *rehearse* is from a French word meaning to "harrow again"; *sarcophagus* is, according to its Greek originals, "a flesh eater," referring to the limestone coffins that hastened the disintegration of bodies; *profane* (Latin) meant "outside the temple" and gathered the meaning of "against religion, the opposite of sacred"; *alcohol* goes back to an Arabic word for a finely ground powder, used for painting eyelids, and from its fineness the word became applied, in Spanish, to specially distilled spirits, and so to our alcohol.

Following up the biographies of words makes a good hobby —and it may sharpen a writer's sense for the exact meaning and for the suggestion carried by a given word, even though he must use it in its present sense. This article chiefly presents the various ways in which words have arrived and are still arriving in English. There are two general processes—making new words, either created or borrowed, and compounding or clipping words and parts of words that are already in the language. Then this stock of words is increased in usefulness by changes in the meanings of the forms which are established.
2. *New words.*

***a*–**Creation of words. Outright creation, "coinage," of words is rare. Even *gas,* first used by Van Helmont (1578-1644), a Belgian scientist, probably had the Greek *chaos* as well as a Dutch or Flemish word behind it. *Kodak* is probably an actual creation, as are a good many other trade names, some of which are quite familiar so long as the advertising of them is kept up. Informal words like *dud, burble* were also creations, good sounding words someone made up. F. Gelett Burgess (1866-1951) invented *blurb,* defining it as "self-praise; to make a noise like a publisher." *Imitative words like *buzz, honk, swish, whiz* are attempts to translate the sounds of nature into the sounds of language. Various exclamations of surprise, pain, scorn, may have started as unconsciously emotional noises— *ow, ouch, fie, phooey*—and then became regular words, used by anyone. Of course in the first stages of a language the words were created somehow, but just how is guesswork.

A word that is coined for a special occasion is a *nonce word (used but once). One might write that a certain person "was the acme of hasbeenivity" and *hasbeenivity* would be a nonce word, and would probably remain one. As a rule arbitrary coinages do not stick. Outright creation is a very minor source of new words.

***b*–**Borrowed words. English has always borrowed words freely, from Latin, German, French and from other languages with which English-speaking people have come in contact. It has assimilated words of quite un-English form: *khaki* (Hindustani), *seersucker* (Persian, Hindustani), *tycoon* (Japanese), *ski* (Norwegian), *hors d'oeuvres* (French), *intelligentsia* (Russian). The various words for *porch,* itself Norman French but the oldest and the most English-seeming of the group, come from various languages: *piazza* (Italian), *portico* (Italian), *stoop* (Dutch), *veranda* (Anglo-Indian).

Borrowing is still going on, though perhaps more slowly than at some periods. Some words come into Formal English and remain Formal words: *intelligentsia, bourgeois, chef-d'oeuvre, objet d'art, Zeitgeist, Anschluss,* and many others of political, philosophical, scientific, or literary bearing. *Sphygmograph* and many other scientific words are recent compoundings of Latin and especially of Greek words which are not otherwise in English usage, so that they may be regarded as borrowings as well as compounds. Others come in as General words, especially when large numbers of people go abroad, as during a war (*blitzkrieg, camouflage, ersatz*) or when a foreign invention becomes suddenly popular, as in *chauffeur, garage, chassis* of the automobile vocabulary. Some words brought by immigrants have stuck: *sauerkraut, kohlrabi, pronto, pizza, kosher, goulash.*

Many are dropped before they gain any general currency. The useful words are more or less adapted to English spelling and pronunciation and become true English words. (See *English language, and for suggestions about the use of recently borrowed words, *Foreign words in English.)

3. *Changes in form of words.*

a–Word composition. Most new words are made by putting together two or more elements to make a new word of different meaning or function, as *un-* added to *interesting* gives a word of the opposite meaning, *uninteresting,* or *-ize* added to the noun *canal* gives a verb, *canalize.* The fact that dictionaries separate words formed with prefixes into two groups, those to be defined and those which are self-explanatory, shows how deceptive affixes can be. The elements may be a prefix placed before the root word (*mis-related*), or a suffix added (*foolishness*), or a combining element like *mono-* (*mono-syllable, mono-rail*), or two independent words built together (*book-case, basket-ball, gentle-man*). *Group words like *high school, out of town,* though not written as single words, could be included as a type of word composition.

A list of prefixes and suffixes that are still active in English would take several pages. Here are a few of the more common:

*a- (not) : asymmetrical, amoral, atypical
ante- (before) : anteprohibition era

anti- (against) : antiprohibition
bi- (two) : bivalve, biplane, bicycle
dis- (not) : disinterested, dispraise
in- (in): income, impart, instill
in- (not) : inelegant, impractical
mis- (wrong): mistake, misnomer
*pre- (before): preview, prenatal, preempt
*re- (again) : revise, redecorate
up- (up) : upend (verb) , upswirl (noun)

A few suffixes are:

-en (to form a verb) : heighten, lighten, weaken
-ful (full) : playful, spoonful
-fy (to make) : electrify, horrify
-ish (to form an adjective) : dryish, foolish, smallish
-ize (to form a verb) : circularize

(See also *-er, *-ous, -us.)

Combining elements include a number of words or roots, many of them Greek:

-graph- (writing) : biography, photograph
micro- (small) : microcosm, micrometer, microphone, microbiology
mono- (one) : monotone, monorail
-phil- (loving) : philanthropy, philately, Anglophile
-side-: sidewall, sideswipe, ringside
-smith: locksmith, silversmith, gunsmith
tele- (distant) : television, telemeter
-trop- (turning) : geotropic, heliotropic

At first a compound has no more than the meaning to be expected by putting its elements together: *unable = not able.* But often a compound will develop an independent sense which can hardly be guessed at from the meanings of its elements: *cupboard, loudspeaker.*

Several pairs of prefixes and suffixes have the same meaning, so that often two words of the same meaning but somewhat different in form exist side by side, especially words with *in-* (not) and *un-* and nouns with *-ness, -ity,* or *-tion*:

aridness, aridity	indistinguishable,
completeness, completion	undistinguishable
corruption, corruptness	torridness, torridity
ferociousness, ferocity	unobliging, disobliging

When such a pair exists, take the one that is more familiar to you or that fits best in the rhythm of the sentence. But don't make your style conspicuous by coining a form when there is already a similar word in good use. The only sure way to know whether there is one available or not is to consult a good dictionary.

b–Phonetic alterations. For a variety of reasons, one word may have two or more developments in its pronunciation, each form emphasizing a different shade of the older word's meaning. Here are four Anglo-Saxon words which have had such double developments: from *ān* we get *one* and *a, an*; from *of* come *off* and *of*; from *thurh, through* and *thorough*; and from *ūtera, utter* and *outer*. There are, of course, many more, especially if we go further back. Many such doublets are not so obvious because the spellings do not differ, though the pronunciations, functions, and meanings do: *con'duct,* noun; *con duct',* verb, etc.

c–Blends. Informal English has a number of words that show the liberties that the users of language have always taken with their words and always will take. Some of their experiments have proved useful and have become a part of the main English vocabulary.

One common type is *blends,* or portmanteau words, made by telescoping two words into one, often making a letter or syllable do double duty. *Squish* is probably a blend of *squirt* and *swish, electrocute,* of *electro-* and *execute; smog,* of *smoke* and *fog.* They are common in business: *servicenter, corrasable* (a paper—*correct* plus *erasable*), the names of many firms and products. In humor they abound: *posilutely, absotively, solemncholy, absogoshdarnlutely,* and also in more serious conversation, often presenting two ideas at once: *snoopervize* (*snoop—supervise*), *politricks, happenstance, anecdotage, slanguage.* They may be useful in a humorous context or to suggest derogation.

d–Clipped words. One of the commonest types of word change is clipping, dropping one or more syllables to make a briefer form: *ad* from *advertisement, bus* from *omnibus, taxi* from *taxicab* (earlier from *taximeter cab*), *quote* from *quotation, mob* (an eighteenth-century clip from *mobile vulgus*), *auto, movie, plane, phone,* and so on. *Shoptalk has many clips—*mike* for *microphone* or *micrometer.* The speech of any closely related group is full of clips; campus vocabulary shows a full line: *econ, home ec, phys ed, grad, prom, dorm, ad building, varsity, lab, exam, gym, prof, pre-med,* and scores more. Clipped words are written (when they are appropriate to the context) without apostrophe or period.

e–Back formations. A back formation differs from clips like *exam* and *auto* chiefly in that it is formed on *analogy with other words and is usually needed to serve as a different part of speech. *Beg* was formed from *beggar,* corresponding to *hunt, hunter.* A number of back formations have made their way, like *diagnose* from *diagnosis, edit* from *editor;* some, like *enthuse,* are slowly making their way; but most are formed in

fun, like *burgle,* and are used either in humor or in a derogatory sense, like *orate. Donate* seemed unnecessary, since we had
give, though it has acquired the specialized sense of a publicized giving to charity; *enthuse* is more justifiable, since it
takes the place of the clumsy *be enthusiastic over.*

f–Common nouns from proper names. A number of words
have come into general use because of some association with a
person or place: *boycott,* from the name of an Irish land agent,
Captain Boycott, who was so treated; *macadam,* from the inventor of the road surface, John L. MacAdam; *sandwich* from an
Earl of Sandwich; *jersey,* from the island of Jersey; *pasteurize,*
from Louis Pasteur, who developed the process.

g–Playful formations. Blends and back formations are likely
to have a playful note and so do some other word shifts that
can't be classified. Some, like *hire education,* are convenient
puns. Some become quite generally used: *dingus, doodad,
beanery. Jalopy* seems a perfect word for its meaning.

Watching these recent and familiar formations may lead to
a study of the earlier and less obvious origins of words in the
General English vocabulary.

(References: The great authority on the origin of English
words is the *Oxford English Dictionary,* and now the *Diction-
ary of American English* and the *Dictionary of Americanisms*
are supplementing it for words peculiar to the United States.
Besides general books on English, the following pay special
attention to origin of words: Otto Jespersen, *Growth and
Structure of the English Language,* various editions; George
H. McKnight, *English Words and Their Backgrounds,* New
York, 1923; J. B. Greenough and G. L. Kittredge, *Words and
Their Ways in English Speech,* New York, 1901.)

Originality • *Originality* is applied to writing in two somewhat different senses:

1. The first sense refers to material. Material is "original"
when it is gathered by the writer from his experience, from his
observation of people, events, or places, or from documents
like letters and newspapers. Secondary or second-hand material
has been worked over by someone else, as in textbooks, encyclopedias, most magazine articles and books. This material has
been organized and given form in words. Original material has
to be sorted, selected, and laid out by the writer. Obviously
one can learn more and find more profitable practice in handling significant original material than in handling most secondary material.

Most student papers should contain some original material.
The content may come entirely from the writer's experience.

At least the central idea, the purpose can come from his present desires, some of the examples, details, or applications can come from his observation, and the opinions and the point of view can represent the way he thinks. Merely rewriting a magazine article is not a very profitable exercise in composition. Putting together material from several such secondary sources is more useful, since it requires selection and comparison of material. But the most useful work for growth in writing is composing papers in which a good deal of the material is original. The writing is a little harder, but it is more fun, and the gain is much greater than in simply working over what others have done. (Compare *Plagiarism.)

2. Originality in expression, in style, is a different matter. The English language has been used a long time, and absolutely new words and phrases are rare. The most threadbare figures and phrases can be avoided, and an honest attempt to tell exactly what the writer sees and believes will ordinarily result in straightforward, readable writing, which is more valuable than mere novelty. The one sure fact is that striving too hard for originality is almost certain to result in strained writing, uncomfortable to writer and reader alike. When a style deserving the label *original* appears, it is usually the by-product of an active and independent mind, not the result of trying to be different.

Orthography • See *Spelling.

other • See *any, and compounds with any § 1.

ou • In the *Pronunciation key (§ 1) /ou/ represents the sound in *bout, out, house*; the sound is also spelled *ow* in *cow* /kou/, *ough* in *bough* /bou/.

Words spelled with *ou* are variously pronounced: *trouble* /trub'l/, *soul* /sōl/, *soup* /süp/, *trousseau* /trü'sō/.

-ough, -augh • A handful of words containing *-ough* and *-augh* are one of the many scandals of English spelling. They are common words, so that we learn to spell most of them well enough—but it is hard to believe we should be asked to do so.

The objection to these forms is not so much that they are cumbersome, as that they "spell" such different sounds—*although, bough, cough, thorough, through, bought, taught, laugh*. This can be explained by the history of the pronunciation of the individual words, chiefly by the fact that the pronunciations now generally current have come from different localities of early English speech—but that does not justify them.

For a while *altho* and *tho* and to a less extent *thru* and *thoro* were used somewhat in personal writing and in business writing, especially in advertising, and even in a few periodicals and in some books—though most publishers went by traditional stylebooks. They are still given as permissible spellings in the recent dictionaries, but their use seems to be declining. They are out of place in Formal writing, and their use in General writing should depend chiefly on their appropriateness to other traits of style and to the expectations of readers. (The *Chicago Tribune,* which once championed their use, has abandoned them.)

ought • See *should—would § 2, *want.

-our, -or • See *-or, -our.

-ous, -us • *-ous* is an adjective ending: *fictitious, ominous*; *-us* is a noun ending: *cactus, campus, impetus.*

out • Though *out* has adjective, adverb, noun, preposition, and verb functions, it gives little trouble except in the Nonstandard locution *want out* for "want to go" or "come out."

out of date • *Out of date, out of doors, out of town* are usually hyphened when they stand before a noun but not otherwise:

He has an out-of-date model.   His model is out of date.

Outline form •
1. *The title.* The title of the paper should stand over the outline, but it is not a part of the outline and should not be numbered. The heads should carry their full meaning and not refer back to the title by pronouns. (See *Titles of papers.)
2. *Sentence statement.* It is a good idea to put a sentence stating the subject and scope of the whole paper between the title and the first main head. If this is done it should be a full, meaningful sentence, not a mere announcement of the topic.
3. *Numbering systems.* The most widely used numbering system alternates letters and figures, as shown in the examples in Ch. 2, pp. 50-52. Avoid intricate or confusing schemes of numbering.
4. *Indention.* Write the main heads flush with the left margin and indent subheads two or three spaces from the left—enough to place them clearly in a different column. Heads that run over a single line should be further indented, as in the sentence outline on p. 51.
5. *Punctuation and capitalizing.* No punctuation is needed at the end of lines in a topic outline. In a sentence outline the

punctuation should follow regular sentence practice. Only the first word of a head and proper names are capitalized; an outline head is not a title.

6. *Heads*

a–Meaningful heads. Each head should be understandable by itself. It is especially important that heads convey clear, full meaning if the outline is to be shown to someone for criticism. The following would do as a scratch outline but would not be satisfactory for other purposes:

My Vocation
   I. The work I am interested in
  II. Why I prefer this type of work
 III. What my responsibilities would be
  IV. The chances for success

Subheads, too, should carry full meaning. In this section from an outline for a paper on "The House of Morgan," the subheads are far too general to indicate what the actual content of the subdivisions will be:

A. Started by Junius Spencer Morgan
      1. What he did
B. Succeeded by J. P. Morgan I
      1. What he did
C. Succeeded by J. P. Morgan II
      1. What he did

b–Heads of equal importance. The main heads of an outline, those usually marked by Roman numerals, should show the several main divisions of the material. Similarly, the immediate subdivisions of these heads, those usually marked by capital letters, should designate logical divisions of one phase of the subject. The same principle applies to further divisions under any subhead.

Unequal headings:	*Equal headings:*
Books I Have Enjoyed	Books I Have Enjoyed
I. Adventure stories	I. Adventure Stories
II. Historical novels	II. Historical novels
III. *The Old Man and the Sea*	III. Character studies
IV. Autobiographies	IV. Autobiographies
V. What I like most	V. Books on ethics and religion

c–Headings in parallel form. Parallel heads or subheads are expressed in parallel grammatical form. A sentence outline should use complete sentences throughout; a topic outline should use phrase heads only. Such heads or subheads should use parallel phrasing for all heads of the same rank; that is, the heads in one series should be all nouns or all adjectives or all phrases, or whatever is the most appropriate form.

Heads not parallel:	*Parallel heads:*
The Art of Putting	The Art of Putting
I. The stance is fundamental	I. The stance
II. The grip	II. The grip
III. Importance of the back-swing	III. The backswing
IV. Stroking the ball	IV. The contact with the ball
V. Follow through with care	V. The follow-through

7. *Division of main points.* Since a topic is not "divided" unless there are at least two parts, an outline should have at least two subheads under any main head—or none at all. For every heading marked *I* there should be as least a *II,* for every *A* there should be a *B,* and so on.

Illogical single heads	*Proper subdivision*
The Tripartite System of Government	The Tripartite System of Government
I. The executive branch	I. The executive branch
A. President and Cabinet	A. President
	B. Cabinet
II. The Legislative branch	II. The Legislative branch
A. The House	A. The House of Representatives
B. The Senate	B. The Senate
1. Functions	1. Special functions
	2. Special privileges
III. The judicial branch	III. The judicial branch
A. The Supreme Court	A. The Supreme Court
	B. Lower courts

If there is a single detail, it may be included in the heading. For example, for an organization in which the whole executive power lay in the president the head might be:

  I. The executive branch (The President)

Sometimes an exception is made for an outstanding illustrative example, which may be put in an outline as a single subhead:

  B. Injustice of grades in figures
    1. Example: My almost-Phi Beta roommate

8. *Introductions and conclusions.* Ordinarily a paper does have a beginning, a middle, and an ending (or an introduction, a body, and a conclusion), but you should not use labels such as these in the outline. For one thing, they are too general to reflect the specific content of your paper. For another, the beginning and ending can rarely be represented by heads that are coordinate with the others. The first and last topics in the outline are from the main body of material, chosen with a special view to their fitness for meeting and for taking leave of a reader.

over- • Compounds with *over-* are not usually hyphened:

overanxious   overalls   overdraft   overseas

P • *P* spells the sound as in *purr, tip, puppy*. It is silent in a few common words (*corps, cupboard, raspberry, receipt*) and in a number of words from Greek (*pneumonia, psalm, pseudo-, psychology*).

After *m, p* is often silent in such words as *empty* /em′tē/, and a /p/ is generally sounded after /m/ in words such as *dreamt* /drempt/ and *warmth* /wôrmpth/. In *pumpkin* two pronunciations are recognized, /pump′kin/ and /pung′kin/, and the variant spelling *punkin*.

paid—payed • *Paid* is the spelling of the past tense and past participle of *pay* (He paid his bills) in all senses except *payed out a line, rope,* etc., and occasionally in that sense also.

pair • In General usage the plural of *pair* is ordinarily *pair* when it comes after a number: *six pair of socks.* In other positions *pairs* is the usual plural.

pants, trousers • The Formal word is always *trousers*; the General and Informal, *pants* (clipped from *pantaloons*) or *trousers* —but always *ski pants*.

Paradox • See *Epigrams.

Paragraph indention, No paragraph indention •
Revision: Indent here for new paragraph; or join this paragraph to the preceding one.   ¶, No ¶

(For a discussion of paragraph division, see Ch. 4, "Adequate development," p. 124.)

Paragraphs •
Revision: This paragraph is unsatisfactory. Revise or rewrite it.   Par

The most common faults in paragraphs are:
1. *Underdevelopment*—lack of details to establish the picture or idea intended.

2. *Lack of connection*—either because it contains unrelated statements or the relation between statments is not made clear to a reader.

(Ch. 4, "Paragraphs," p. 111, gives a full discussion. See also checklist of faults in paragraphs, Exercise 3, p. 154.)

Parallel constructions •
> *Revision: Make the two or more elements in this series parallel in form.*

Paral

Typical shifted (unparallel) constructions are these:

Shifted:	*Made parallel:*
To me orientation week seems both [noun:] a necessity and [adjective:] worth while.	To me orientation week seems both [two adjectives:] necessary and worth while.
Jack has received offers from Hollywood not only [phrase:] for his fishing experiences but [clause:] because he resembles the late Will Rogers.	Jack has received offers from Hollywood not only [two phrases:] for his fishing experiences but for his resemblance to the late Will Rogers.

(For other examples and suggested remedies see *Shifted constructions; Ch. 8, "Revising shifted constructions," p. 300, and "Parallelism and balance," p. 312.)

Paraphrase • A *paraphrase* is a restatement of a writer's ideas in different words. It is now usually applied to digesting the contents of a passage in one's own words, as in note-taking. (See Ch. 11, "The summarizing note," p. 433.)

pardon—excuse • See *excuse—pardon.

Parentheses ( ) •
1. *For additions.* Parentheses (also called *curves* and by printers called *parens*) are sometimes used in writing, chiefly to enclose words, phrases, or whole sentences that add to the clearness of a statement without altering its meaning and that are allowed to stand outside the construction of the sentence. These additions are likely to be (1) illustrations, (2) definitions, or (3) added information thrown in for good measure, as in the first sentence of this paragraph.

He has a scholarship at Cornell (Iowa) .

This bill, commonly called the Lockport plan, has been the basis of all later city-manager charters (there are now 438) .

Can we historians of this present day and age, let alone those yet to come (who will have been nurtured and educated exclusively in artificial surroundings), succeed in recovering imaginatively what

that old milieu of thousands of years ago was like?—CARL BRIDEN-
BAUGH, "The Great Mutation," *American Historical Review,* Jan.
1963, p. 317

His concerts were well received in most cities (in Chicago the
reviews were so enthusiastic that he was given a return engagement),
but he was still dissatisfied with his performance.

These uses are slightly stiff, belonging most appropriately to
rather Formal exposition, and should be used sparingly.

2. *For apologetic asides.* Sometimes parentheses are used to
mark an apologetic aside, as much as to say "You know this,
but let me remind you"—though this use is less common today
than formerly:

Madison (the fourth president) enunciated the doctrine in 1823.

3. *To enclose numbers in an enumeration.* Parentheses are
often used to enclose the letters or figures used to mark items
in an enumeration, as in § 1 of this article, though this tends
to make the numbers or letters more conspicuous than they
deserve to be.

4. *With other marks.* When the parenthetical unit is a complete sentence, the period comes *inside* the curves, but it is
usually omitted if the expression falls within a sentence. Punctuation marks belonging to the sentence including the parenthesis come *after* the second curve.

Some words have various meanings with different prepositions, as
agree *with* (a person), agree *to* (a suggestion), agree *in* (principle).

(See *Capital letters § 1 for a discussion of capitalizing sentences in parentheses. Do not confuse parentheses and brackets;
see *Brackets.)

part, on the part of • *Part* or *on the part of* is often a rather
clumsy way of saying *by, among, for,* and the like:

It resulted in less wild driving on the part of [*by*] young people.
In the past ten years there has been a definite move on the part
of [*by* or *among*] our religious leaders to unite all Protestants in one
church.

Participles •
1. Forms of participles.

	Active	Passive
Present:	asking; singing	being asked; being sung
Past:	having asked; having sung	asked, having been asked; sung, having been sung

The simple participle forms (*asking, asked*) are used in
various verb phrases:

I am asking   I am being asked   I have asked   I have been asked

Because the participles do not indicate definite time themselves but time in relation to the context in which they are used, the terms *first participle* and *second participle* have been suggested, as well as others. But *present* and *past* are firmly established as names for them and work well enough if we remember that they are grammatical terms, not descriptions of meaning. (See *Tenses of verbs.)

2. *As modifiers.* When not a part of a phrasal verb form, the participles are most commonly used like adjectives. They have qualities of adjectives in that they modify nouns and pronouns (the pen *used* in signing the treaty; a *coming* era; the leaves *falling* in the street). They have qualities of verbs in that they may take an object (*Following these clues,* he soon found her) and be modified by adverbs (The car, *rolling crazily* ...). (See *Adjectives, types and forms § 3a, 5.)

Sometimes in analyzing a sentence it is difficult to tell a participle used like an adjective from a participle which is a part of a passive verb form. Since grammatically the constructions are indistinguishable, the decision rests on whether the meaning requires the participle to modify the subject as a predicate adjective with a linking verb, or whether it describes an action.

Passive voice: The candidate of the Republican party *was defeated.*

Predicate adjective: The candidate was *defeated* but happy.

When used as a modifier, a participle should refer clearly to some particular noun or pronoun:

Opening his shirt at the neck, he went back to his chopping. [*Opening* modifies *he.*]

A college education, looked at from this point of view, may be a liability. [*Looked* modifies *college education.*]

There should be no reasonable doubt of what is modified. A modifying participle "dangles" or is "misrelated" when it seems to refer to a word the writer does not mean it to refer to:

Dangling: Walking on the campus, several of my class pass by.

Clearer: Walking on the campus, I usually meet. ...

Dangling: Combined with his scientific understanding, Dr. Hertzler is a man who would have made his name for wisdom in any profession.

Clearer: Dr. Hertzler's scientific understanding would have made him a name in any profession.

(See *Dangling modifiers and Ch. 8, "Revising dangling modifiers," p. 297.)

3. *In absolute constructions.* The participle-as-adjective should not be confused with the participle in a phrase which relates to the whole sentence (to the situation) rather than to a particular word. Some such phrases are very common, even *formulas:

> Judging from her looks, she isn't under fifty.
> Beginning with the class of 1965, the tuition was raised $50.

(See *Verbals.)

4. *Stylistically objectionable participles.* Amateur writers often use participles in constructions in which a subordinate clause would sound better:

> Uncle Joe was prompt, *necessitating our hurrying* [so that we had to hurry].
> The sea was running heavily, *being boosted* by a strong southeast wind. [Omit the *being.*]

Especially conspicuous are clumsy "nominative absolutes," made like Latin ablative absolutes:

> Then, *the feature being ended,* everyone began to file out of the theater. (Then, after the feature was over...; *or, perhaps:* The feature over, everyone....)

(For *very* with participles see *very § 2. Compare *Gerund. References: Curme, *Syntax,* pp. 158-160; C. A. Smith, *Interpretative Syntax,* Boston, 1906, pp. 55-59; Reuben Steinbach, "The Misrelated Constructions," *American Speech,* 1930, 5:181-197; H. C. Wyld, *A Short History of English,* pp. 237-258.)

Particles • Of the eight traditional parts of speech, four have no inflected forms in English—*adverbs, *prepositions, *conjunctions, interjections—and appear never to have been inflected in the Indo-European languages. They are sometimes lumped together under the term *particles.* To the grammarian they cause some discomfort. In the classical languages, nouns, adjectives, and pronouns have elaborate declensions, and verbs have elaborate conjugations, so a grammarian can always start with a detailed description of all those forms. And even in English there are at least remnants of inflection for all these words. But for the particles, descriptive comment—aside from listing them—must be entirely about their syntax, their use in utterances. And since syntax is the most elusive part of descriptive grammar, discussion of the use of particles is especially difficult. (See *Idiom and idioms.)

Parts of speech • Certain sentence functions are regularly filled by certain kinds of words which are not ordinarily used

Parts of Speech in English: Summary of Characteristics

Formal characteristics (as spelled)	Some derivational endings	Central syntactical functions	Common secondary functions
Nouns: Plural -s, -es or equivalents; Genitive 's, s'	-ance, -ee, -er (-or), -ism, -ment, -th	Subject or object of verb; object of preposition	Modifier of another noun; apposition; adverbial modifier
Pronouns: See *Pronouns, types and forms	(A closed class— no alterations possible)	Subject or object of verb; object of preposition	In altered (possessive) form, modifier of noun; apposition
Verbs: -s, -ing, -ed, or equivalents; in phrases after auxiliaries	-ate, -ize, -en, -fy	Predicate	As a gerund or infinitive, a subject or object; as an infinitive or participle, a modifier of noun
Adjectives: Comparison with -er, -est or more, most	-able, -al, -ant, -ary, -ic, -ish, -ous	Modifier of noun	Subject or object when preceded by a/an, the
Adverbs: Comparison with -er, -est or more, most (Except almost, very, etc.)	-ly, -wise	Modifier of verb, adverb, adjective, clause, or sentence	Connective; occasional modifier of noun; rarely subject or object
Prepositions: (Invariable)	(A closed class— no alterations possible)	Forming phrase with noun or noun equivalent as headword	Joining phrase to a word or sentence
Conjunctions: (Invariable)	(A closed class— no alterations possible)	Coordinating: joining words, phrases, clauses Subordinating: introducing, forming a clause and joining it to another clause or to some other sentence element	

Interjections, or exclamations, may be regarded as a subtype of Adverbs

Typical position in sentences	Principal subtypes	Word groups with same function	Traditional definition
Before and after verb; after *a/an, the, our, this, some,* etc.; followed by *of*-phrase	Common, proper; abstract, concrete; mass, collective, etc.	Clauses with *that, whoever,* etc. Gerund and infinitive phrases	The name of a person, place, thing, relationship, etc.
Before and after verb; after preposition	See *Pronouns, types and forms	Often a noun or noun equivalent	A word used in place of a noun
Following subject in statements; often first in commands and questions	Open class: most verbs Closed class: linking verbs; auxiliaries (See *Verbs § 1.)	Verb-adverb combination	A word indicating action, state, or being
Between *a/an, the,* etc., and noun; after linking verb	Descriptive, limiting, proper	Clauses with *who, that,* etc.; wide variety of phrases	A word qualifying, making more exact, the meaning of a noun
Variable; after verb plus object	See *Adverbs, types and forms	Clauses with *when, since, although,* etc.; wide variety of prepositional phrases	A word modifying a verb, adjective, or another adverb
Before a noun or noun and its modifiers; often at end of construction	(None)	(None)	A word relating a noun to another word
At beginning of clause or sentence	Coordinating, subordinating, correlative, conjunctive adverbs	(None)	A word joining two words, phrases, clauses, or sentences

in other functions. In *The teacher who realized it has died,* the words cannot be rearranged to replace each other. *The realizes who teacher it has died* is as impossible as *It teacher realizes the who has died* or any other rearrangement. Some words in English play more than one part (*round* the corner, *round* shape, *round* of ammunition, etc.) but the functions of most words are so sharply restricted that it is apparent that speakers of the language have them classified into categories. Hence the traditional name, *parts of speech.* In some highly inflected languages like Latin, *form* (declensions, conjugations, derivational endings) is a reliable basis for assigning words to the parts of speech, though there is always a residue of *particles with only one form. In English, change of form works moderately well in identifying nouns, verbs, adjectives, and adverbs, which are consequently often referred to as *form classes.* Even in these classes, however, there are exceptions and minor variations, like our nouns with plural in *-en* instead of the usual *-s,* or with a foreign language plural, or with only a singular or a plural form; and there are adverbs that are not compared (such as *almost, quite, very*) and verbs with only one form (such as *must* and *ought*). Many languages have derivational endings that indicate the part of speech; English has a few, like *-ize* to make a verb from a noun (*dramatize*) and *-ed* to make an adjective from a noun (*fair-minded*), but such endings indicate the part of speech of a very small number of words.

Since form is not always a reliable way of classifying words in English, their *typical function in sentences* is used as supporting data or as the main data. Typically, English uses the same word form in the function of more than one part of speech.

Sometimes a word develops the forms characteristic of more than one part, as *radio* has the forms of verbs (*radios, radioing, radioed*) and of a noun (*radios* as the plural and the same form spelled *radio's* or *radios'* as a genitive), or *yellow* has the forms of an adjective (*yellower, yellowest*), of a noun (*yellows, yellow's*), and of a verb (*yellows, yellowing, yellowed*). In a dictionary or other general discussion of words, such words have to be given as "belonging to" (that is, having the basic characteristics of) more than one part of speech. In a specific sentence, the syntactical function, the way the word is used, is the final clue, as *walk* is a noun in *Let's go for a walk* and a verb in *They would rather walk than ride.*

Often, however, a word is used in the function of another part of speech without acquiring the characteristic changes of form; *bomb* has the forms and functions of a noun as well as those of a verb but is used as a modifier (as in *bomb shelter*) without acquiring the comparative forms of an adjective. In the past there has been much loose description of this trait.

Stone in *stone cabin,* for instance, has been called "an adjective" or, somewhat more accurately, has been said to be "used *as* an adjective." Actually it is used *like* an adjective, in the function of an adjective—that is, as the modifier of a noun. Some linguists use separate terms for the parts of speech and for these functional shifts or for phrases and clauses used in the function of a part of speech. Most commonly they add the suffix *-al* to the name of the corresponding part of speech. An adjective used in the function of a noun (The *poor* are always with us) or a clause used in a typical function of a noun (*What she said* didn't matter to him) is called *nominal* or *nounal*; nouns used like adjectives (the *house* mother) are sometimes called *adjectivals*; nouns used like adverbs (Then we went *home*) are sometimes called *adverbials*; and so on. In this book, words used in such functional shifts are labeled by their function in a sentence, as subject or verb or modifier: *the light headed* might be a subject or object; in *Whoever was in that car saw it,* the clause is the subject. Referring to clauses as noun, adjective, or adverb clauses or to phrases as adjective or adverb phrases is a convenient way of saying that they are used *like* the part of speech indicated.

Linguists have not yet agreed upon a system for describing the parts of speech in English, though they are quite sure that such categories exist unconsciously in the minds of native speakers of a language and that those speakers have devices for using the words only in their appropriate functions. This book therefore uses basically the traditional categories with somewhat more precise criteria in their definitions. The table on pp. 728-729 lists the principal points regarding the parts of speech; some further details will be found in the *Index* article for each.

(References: Sumner Ives, "Defining Parts of Speech in English," *College English,* 1957, 18:341-348, is a good introduction to the problem. All books intended for use in the study of English treat the parts of speech.)

party • See **person.*

passed, past • The past tense and the past participle of *pass* are *passed* (He passed the first post; He had passed), though *past* is fairly common as the participle. *Past* is the adjective (past favors), preposition (past the crisis), and adverb (past due; They went past). Pronunciation: /past/ or (Eastern) /päst/. (See **A § 3.)

passer-by • Usually hyphened: plural *passers-by.*

Passive verbs •
>   *Revision: Change the passive verb or verbs to active.*

Pass

Amateur writers tend to use passive statements when active verbs would sound more natural ("The music *was enjoyed* by us" instead of "We *enjoyed* the music"). Awkward passives are sometimes used to avoid *I*:

> *Passive*: The situation was taken in by me with great amusement.
> *Active*: I took in the situation with great amusement.

This passage shows both effective and ineffective passives:

> The year 1965 is here. With it comes a host of '65 model automobiles. Most of these cars *were heralded in* during the closing months of 1964. They *were awaited* in anxious curiosity by the buying public. In many instances, they *were looked forward to* with too much anticipation.

Although an awkward phrase, *were heralded in* is a legitimate passive, because the "heralders" need not be named; the passive *were awaited* places *the buying public* at the end of the sentence for emphasis and would not be noticeable if it was not followed by *were looked forward to,* which clearly shows that the writer was not paying attention to his work. Those two sentences might better stand:

> The buyers awaited them in anxious curiosity, often with too much anticipation.

The use of passive verbs is often objectionable because it involves a thoughtless shift from the active voice and adds to the wordiness of what is usually already wordy and fuzzy writing. (For the formation of the passive voice and its profitable use see *Voice.)

Past tense • See *Tenses of verbs.

peeve • Informal for *annoy* and *annoyance, peeve* is a back formation from *peevish* (see *Origin of words § 3e). It is used most commonly as a modifier: *peeved.*

per • *Per* (Latin, "through, by, by the, among," etc.) is most appropriate when used in phrases that are still close to their Latin originals—*per capita, per cent,* or in a definitely commercial setting—*$18 per week, $2.60 per yard, forty-four hours per week,* or in certain standardized technical phrases—*revolutions per minute.*

Because of its commercial and technical connotation, *per* is less appropriate in General writing, where the English equivalent usually fits more naturally: *$18 a week, 20¢ a quart, four times a year.*

per-, pre- • Do not spell the *per-* words with *pre-*: write *per*form, *per*spire, *per*fect, and so on. Remember that *pre-* means "before" (*pre*war, *pre*school, *pre*eminent).

percent • *Percent* is not followed by a period, and is sometimes written as two words. In Informal and General writing it is often used instead of *percentage* or even of *proportion*: *Only a small percent of the class was* [or *were*—collective agreement] *there.*

With figures the percent sign (%) is ordinarily used: 97.6%.

Perfect tense • See *Tenses of verbs.

Period (.) •
1. *At the end of statements.* The principal function of the period is to mark the end of a statement—that is, the end of every completed sentence not definitely a question or exclamation.

Sometimes sentences in the form of exclamations or questions are really to be regarded as statements. After such a sentence a writer may use the exclamation mark or question mark, but he will usually have a period if the tone is lacking in emphasis or if he wishes to minimize the emphasis of the sentence form he has chosen. (See *Rhetorical questions.)
2. *Miscellaneous conventional uses.*

    a–After *abbreviations: Oct.   n.b.   Mr. Wm. Fraser

    b–In sums of money, between dollars and cents: $5.66. The period is not used unless the dollar sign is used: 66 cents or 66¢; $0.66.

    c–Before decimals, or between the whole number and the decimal: .6, 3.14159, 44.6%.

    d–A period is sometimes used between hours and minutes represented in figures (2.36 p.m.), though a colon is usual in the United States (2:36 p.m.).

    e–Three spaced periods (. . .) are used as *ellipses, to mark the omission of words; several are often used to guide a reader's eye across the page. (See *Leaders.)

    f–After a letter or number denoting a series. The dash after *f* at the beginning of the preceding line, for example, could be a period.
3. *Period with quotation marks.* Most American publishers place a period coming at the end of a quotation inside the quotation marks: "The longer you put it off," he said, "the harder it's going to be." (See *Quotation marks § 4b.)

The period is also called a *full stop,* especially in British usage. For other uses see a stylebook.

Periphrastic verbs • See *Phrasal verb.

Person • Pronouns are classified according to *person* (first, second, and third) and *number* (singular and plural):

First person, the one speaking: [Singular] *I, my, me;* [Plural] *we, our, us*

Second person, the one spoken to: [Singular and plural] *you, your* [Archaic: *thou, thy, thee*]

Third person, the one spoken of: [This singular also shows masculine, feminine, and neuter; more accurately, male, female, and inanimate] *he, him, his; she, her; it, its;* [Plural] *they, them, their*

Nouns go with the third person form of the verb.

Except in the verb *be* (I am, you are, he is . . .), English verbs have only one form to distinguish person and number—the third singular of the present tense: *I have, you have, he has; we, you, they have;* and the *auxiliary verbs don't have even that.

person • *Person* is the ordinary word for referring to a human being. *Individual* has the same meaning (though it is applied also to single objects and animals as well) but emphasizes the person's singleness, aloneness, and is slightly heavy or pretentious unless that emphasis is needed. *Party* is legal or light. In British usage *person* sometimes has an unfavorable connotation. Often *people* is used rather than *persons*:

There was one person waiting.

There were several people [not *persons*] waiting.

Personally is sometimes used as a conversational *intensive ("I personally think") but is usually inappropriate in writing.

Personal letters • See *Letters.

Personal pronouns • See *Person, *Pronouns, types and forms § 1, *Possessive adjectives. See also *Apostrophe § 5.

Personification • *Personification* is a *figure of speech in which an object or animal or quality or ideal is given some attributes of a human being:

> Deal gently, *Love,* with him and her
> who live together now!
> REX WARNER, *Poems,* p. 71

It is less common today than formerly, and less common in prose than in verse. Flat and unnecessary personification is likely to have an amateur sound: *No steam engine can brag of such efficiency.*

ph • *Ph* is a *digraph for the /f/ sound in words of Greek origin: *phlox, photography, photograph.*... In *Stephen* (and formerly in *nephew*), *ph* represents /v/.

Most words with *ph* belong to the Formal vocabulary, so that the simplification to *f* is very slow. In a few, like *fantasy* and *sulfur* the *f* form is now the commoner.

In *diphtheria* and *naphtha* the *ph* is pronounced /f/ and also /p/.

phenomenon, phenomena • *Phenomenon* is the singular and *phenomena* the plural (phenomena of the mind).

Originally *phenomenon* meant "any observable event," but now it also means "something remarkable," and *phenomenal* is almost always used in this sense. Often a shorter or more exact word is preferable.

phone • *Phone* is a clip for *telephone,* in General use as noun, verb, and modifier (on the phone; phone me later; the phone book). It is written without an apostrophe.

Phonemes • In linguistics *phoneme* is the term for the smallest distinctive unit, hence the smallest contrastive unit in speech. It may more easily be understood as what speakers of a variety of a language hear as "the same speech sound." "The same sound" actually is a range of sounds similarly produced. We make the /p/ at the beginning of *pit* by closing our lips, building up a pressure of air in the mouth, then opening the lips suddenly with a consequent audible explosion. The /p/ at the end of *stop,* on the other hand, can be clearly recognized merely from the abrupt cutting off of the vowel sound resulting from closing our lips; we don't have to open them again. In these words beginning and ending with /p/, the initial and final sounds are evidently different. Yet we call them "the same sound" because we interpret what we hear as the same thing. Each one of these phonetically different but similar sounds is called an *allophone*; they are actual noises; our interpreting them as "the same sound" results from our experience of learning our native language. Our capacity to do this permits us to classify the thousands of slightly different sounds of speech into a manageable number of categories (between 40 and 50), which exist, of course, only in our minds and are called phonemes.

Phonemes are of two kinds: those called *segmental* are more or less accurately represented by the letters of the conventional alphabet; those called *suprasegmental* may for the moment be described negatively as those devices of speech which are not represented by letters.

1. *Segmental phonemes.* The distinctive and contrastive function of the phoneme is most easily shown through the segmentals. The word *cat* is a sequence of three speech units, *c-a-t*, and forms a segment of speech; *rat* is another. The two are distinguished solely by the differing initial units. *I saw the cat* and *I saw the rat* are different statements because *c* contrasts with *r*. There are other differences in the sounds of *cat* and *rat*; getting from *c* to *a* involves movements in the mouth which differ from those in getting from *r* to *a*. But in learning English we have unconsciously trained ourselves to disregard these (subphonemic) differences. Therefore the smallest significant contrastive units are the *c* and the *r*.

In English the correspondence between the letters of the alphabet and the segmental phonemes is at best approximate (for the consonants), at worst quite bad (for the vowels and diphthongs). Accurate indication of the phonemes requires a phonemic transcription; the one most widely used is based on the International Phonetic Alphabet (IPA), which can be found in any book on linguistics and in some dictionaries. The phonemes of one language or even of one variety of a language may differ from those of another.

2. *Suprasegmental phonemes.* An alphabet is itself a recognition of segmental phonemes; therefore the inventors of an alphabet must have analyzed their language to determine the segmental phonemes, though of course they didn't use that term. The history of our system of writing shows no comparable analysis of stress, pitch, juncture, terminals, and rhythm. One is tempted, therefore, to assert that though they are a characteristic part of the language, they are not an essential part. But such an assertion assumes that conventional writing tries to represent all aspects of speech; it obviously does not. Since the systematic analysis of the suprasegmental features is much more recent than the analysis of the segmental ones, it is hardly surprising that there is disagreement about what they are, how many there are, and even whether they should be called phonemes. The following discussion is therefore tentative and, since this is primarily a book for writers, necessarily brief and incomplete.

In English speech we can observe that some syllables seem more prominent than others, the pitch of the speaker's voice varies, there are variations in the time and manner of getting from one word to the next, the speaker's voice in some way marks the ends of clauses and phrases, and there is a perceptible rhythmical pattern in the succession of syllables.

These features are more difficult to isolate than the segmental phonemes, partly because they are interdependent, partly because as their name suprasegmentals—above, beyond, in addition to the segmentals—suggests, they complement the vowels and consonants. What follows is only the sketchiest account of the suprasegmentals.

a–Stress. This is the most obvious. The greater prominence of the first syllable of *daily* and of the last syllable of *today* is evident to anyone. This light and heavy stress distinguishes words with the same segmental phonemes from each other: *impórt* (verb), *ímport* (noun). Often a third degree of stress is apparent, as in *óratòry,* where the prominence of the third syllable is greater than that of the second and fourth but not so great as that of the first. Occasionally a fourth degree becomes significant. (Symbols: ´ primary, ˆ secondary, ` tertiary, ˇ least—usually not shown). The stress patterns of *irritàting* and *óratòry* are the same; but to emphasize one or the other of the words in a phrase, we make the first syllable of one word a bit more prominent than the first syllable of the other: *irritàting óratòry* or *írritàting óratòry.*

b–Pitch. It is also obvious that speakers of English vary the pitch of their voices as they speak. But the significance of that variation is much harder to discover than for stress. Linguists usually identify four distinctions in relative pitch, marked by superior figures from 1 to 4, 1 now usually indicating low pitch and 4 high, with 2 representing the common pitch of utterance. Frequently, especially in terminal syllables, the pitch glides within the syllable, as *here* in *Look here* might start on 3 and end on 1. In *He's never late, oh no* if the emphasis is on *he,* the pitches might go: ³*He's* ²*never late, oh* ³*no*¹. Pitch is closely associated with stress, and it takes a good deal of training to be able to distinguish it with accuracy.

c–Juncture or transition. In English, syllables and words usually follow each other without any breaks. *This is a board* or *This is aboard* would be indistinguishable in sound. The name given to this usual kind of transition is *close,* and in a transcription it is not ordinarily shown. But sometimes we get from one syllable to the next in such a way as to mark clearly the end of the first and the beginning of the second. In the old rhyme *I scream, you scream, we all scream for ice cream,* we can distinguish *I scream* from *ice cream* by putting the open transition (symbol +) in different places: *I+scream* and *ice+cream.* Context usually makes the distinction provided by this juncture superfluous, and the history of some English words suggests that speakers have not been much concerned about it (*a newt* for Anglo-Saxon *an ewt; an apron* from Middle English *a napron*). But it is a resource which is available, and occasionally speakers may use it to make significant contrasts.

d–Terminals. These are the combination of pitch changes and pauses that occur at the ends of phrases. They are far more significant than junctures, and three are usually recognized: sustained, symbolized by $\rightarrow$ or | ; rising, symbolized by $\uparrow$ or || ; and falling, symbolized by $\downarrow$ or #. For example: *John here? No, he's not.*

$$\uparrow \quad \rightarrow \quad \downarrow$$

e–Rhythm. Rhythmical patterns occur in English speech because there are two major contrasts in stress—primary and least—plus two lesser ones—secondary and tertiary—and the weak and strong stresses tend to alternate. The gradations in intensity are actually far greater than the two or four significant ones just mentioned. It is these finer gradations—repetition with variation—which provide the pleasure we find in both verse and prose rhythm. And since the inherent rhythm of English comes through to some extent even in silent reading, the latent rhythmical patterns are important to the writer.

This account of the suprasegmentals does not give an adequate indication of how integral a part they are of English speech. They obviously convey a good deal of the meaning of speech. A native speaker learns them unconsciously and rarely "makes a mistake" in them, except perhaps from nervousness or inattention, as when a radio announcer reads a commercial mechanically, without sensing what he is reading. Neglect or misuse of them reveals the speaker as a foreigner or as one who is speaking artificially. The proper formation of the segmentals is essential to intelligibility, and of the suprasegmentals for effective oral communication. But the suprasegmentals are rarely essential to mere intelligibility, as is evident from their virtual elimination in song and their general omission in writing.

An understanding of the suprasegmentals is helpful in learning a second language (see *Intonation) and in describing scientifically the sounds of English, especially in finding the boundaries of constructions. In resolving occasional ambiguities in printed sentences, we supply the suprasegmentals; a man and a woman speaking the sentence *"I can be just as stubborn as any man"* would use different suprasegmental patterns with *any man*. Understanding of these features—with or without a knowledge of the term—is also helpful in revising one's writing where they have some bearing on punctuation; but since the written language has had a somewhat independent development they cannot be accepted as infallible guides.

(References: Gleason, Chs. 4 and 16.)

Phonology • See *Linguistics.

Phrasal verb • A verb formed by an auxiliary and an infinitive or past participle is called a *phrasal verb*: *will go, must go, has gone, had gone, should have gone.* Even in the tenses which have simple forms (goes, went), we get different shades of meaning by using phrasal forms (went, did go, was going, etc.). Phrasal verbs are also called *periphrastic* verbs. (See *Verbs.)

Phrases • A *phrase* is a group of two or more grammatically related words without a subject and finite verb that functions as a unit in a clause or sentence. Phrases are conventionally classified in terms of their elements:

Prepositional: in the room   before the war   because of that
Participial: coming into the room   pasted on the wall
Gerund: learning French
Infinitive: to live peacefully   to have seen him

Though the elements in a phrase usually stand together, they need not do so. In *He puts it off,* we have a verb phrase, *puts off,* interrupted by its object, *it.*

Other word groups that function as syntactical units are also referred to as phrases (have gone, a large house) in this article. Phrases function like single sentence elements:

Nouns: [Subject] *The first four games* were lost. [Object] He lost *the first four games.* [Genitive] the work *of the masters*
Adjectives: a heart *of gold*   *Crossing the street,* he nearly was hit by a car.
Adverbs: beyond the town   *in the morning*   He did it *in the Dutch manner.*
Prepositions: Because of John we were late.

(See *Absolute constructions, *Adjectives, types and forms § 4, *Adverbs, types and forms § 4, 5, *Dangling modifiers, *Gerund § 3, *Idiom and idioms, *Immediate constituent, *Participles, *Prepositional phrase, *Prepositions. See also Ch. 8, "Revising dangling modifiers," p. 297.)

picnic • Before endings beginning with a vowel, *k* is added to the second *c* to make sure the /k/ sound is retained:

picnicker, picnicked, picnicking
trafficked, panicked

Pitch • See *Phonemes § 2b.

Plagiarism ◦ *Plagiarize* is defined in *Webster's Seventh New Collegiate Dictionary* as "to steal and pass off as one's own (the ideas or words of another)." *Steal* is an ugly word, but plagiarism is an ugly thing. If anything can be said in extenuation of it, that something is to be found in the explanations of why students do it.

First in importance, perhaps, is the fuzziness of their awareness of what plagiarism is. And for this there are justifications. Most of our ideas and some of our phrasings come from others. We can hardly talk or write without to some extent parroting the ideas of others, occasionally even in their exact words, though quite unconsciously and unintentionally.

The second explanation is to be found in the student's earlier educational experience. He may have been called upon to provide reports or criticisms, the material for which he could not possibly have obtained except from printed sources. Often he has simply copied the material without bothering to indicate his source. Since his teacher knew he had done this and he knew his teacher knew it, no deception was intended or achieved. But a careless habit was established.

As a third explanation there is the possibility of panic. Sometimes in college a combination of assignments put off and of tasks utterly overwhelming puts a student into such a state of terror that his sense of values is confused and he stoops to devices which in a normal state he would shrink from.

Finally, of course, there is the dishonest person. For him, no doubt, there is also an explanation but no justification.

A large part of the problem can be solved by careful self-examination of one's ideas and by an awareness of the procedures to be followed in writing so as to give credit where credit is due.

If a student copies from dishonest motives, he must take the consequences, which are likely to be severe. If he copies from fear or ignorance of proper practices, he deserves consideration and help. Whatever the motive, the penalty—failing the paper or perhaps, if it is an important one, failing the course—does not represent the vengeance of the instructor but the failure of the student, failure in the fundamental purpose of a composition course, which is to increase students' skill in communicating their information and ideas to others. Copying from the work of another is the most complete failure possible.

The student who is scared or puzzled should go at once to his instructor and discuss his situation frankly, the reasons for his difficulties, the present faults in his work, and ways to overcome them. Serious effort intelligently directed should bring improvement. A student who feels he is moving in the right direction, even if he is moving slowly, is doing something valuable, and in the long run work is more satisfying and less wearing than worry.

The student who has not learned how to handle material obtained from reading and study needs guidance in the fundamentals of study and scholarship. A writer expects that what he has published will be read and will be used; but he has a right to expect that his exact words will not be used without his receiving credit and that his facts and ideas will not be used in print without his permission. His rights in these matters are legal, covered by copyright, and violation of them through plagiarism exposes the plagiarist to prosecution.

Anyone using published material, then, has a twofold responsibility: first, of absorbing the ideas into his own thought and, second, of giving credit to important sources. A student—or anyone else—is not *composing* when he is merely copying. He should read and digest the material, get it into his own words (except for brief, important quotations that are shown to be quotations). He should be able to *talk* about the subject before he *writes* about it. Then he should refer to any sources he has used. This is not only courtesy but a sign of good workmanship, part of the morality of writing. In an informal paper the credit can be given informally, perhaps a note on the cover saying "This paper is based on..."; or it may be in the body of the paper: "Professor Keane said in a lecture...," "Walter Lippmann wrote recently...," or "So-and-so said...." Or credit may be given more formally in footnotes at the bottom of the page (as described in Ch. 11). Footnotes must be used in a research paper and are in order in any paper for which a student has found material in print. The greatest temptation to plagiarize is in a research paper, in which the material is ordinarily based on reading various sources. But a research paper also offers the best opportunity for learning how to gather, digest, and give credit for material from published sources. At any rate it is necessary for college students to learn how to use such material—by getting much of it into their own words and then giving appropriate credit to sources used. (See *Originality.)

play • See *show.

plenty • As an adverb (I was plenty worried; The car is plenty large) *plenty* is marked colloquial by some dictionaries and is in Informal use; it is not found in Formal writing and is usually inappropriate in college writing.

The omission of *of* after *plenty* in speech (*plenty* [ ] *time*) results in an adjectival use. The idiom is rarely found in print.

Pleonasm • *Pleonasm* is using two words for the same grammatical function (My *Uncle Fred, he* said he would give me twenty-five cents for every bird I could find and name). It is quite common in speech and for emphasis occasionally appears in writing; but it should not be used in writing except for very good reason.

plurality—majority • See *majority—plurality.

Plurals of nouns • The plural of the great majority of English nouns is made by adding an /s/ or /z/ sound, spelled -s, to the singular form of the noun. This -s is pronounced as part of the syllable to which it is added:

buckets   rats   days   rooms   trees
There are ten *Romes* in the United States.

Since this is the usual way of forming the plural, dictionaries list only the exceptional plurals under the entry for each irregular noun. But several groups of words form their plurals in other ways. The discussion which follows deals only with the spelling of plurals. Pronunciations of plurals are sometimes exceptional: The plural of *edge* has two syllables, though only an *s* is added in the spelling; the *s* of *house* becomes a /z/ in *houses*; etc.

1. *Special groups in "-s" or "-es":*
   a–Nouns ending in *-ch, -s, -sh, -x,* or *-z* add the spelling *-es*:

   birches   churches   bridges   ledges   *buses [or *busses*]
   kisses   bushes   *Joneses   axes   fixes   buzzes   quizzes

   b–Common nouns ending in *-y* preceded by a consonant change *y* to *i* and add *-es*:

   beauties   bodies   caddies   cherries   cities   cries   enemies

Exceptions to this rule are proper nouns (*Henrys*) and a few common nouns: *stand-bys, emptys* (bottles).
   Words ending in *-y* preceded by a vowel (except *-quy*) add *-s*:

   bays   boys   moneys [sometimes *monies*]   monkeys   toys

   These plural forms should not be confused in writing with the genitive singular in *'s: beauty's, body's, caddy's,* and so on.
   Nouns ending in *-quy* replace *y* with *ies: soliloquies.*
   c–Words ending in *-o* preceded by a vowel make regular plural with *-s: cameos, folios, radios, studios.*
   Words ending in *-o* preceded by a consonant vary and have to be remembered or looked up in a dictionary. Some of the commoner of these are:

   With *-s* only: banjos   cantos   dynamos   Eskimos   Filipinos
   pianos   silos   solos   sopranos
   With *-es*: echoes   heroes   Negroes   noes   potatoes   tomatoes
   torpedoes   vetoes

Several words ending in -*o* are used with either -*s* or -*es*. The -*es* form is usually the more common, but the increasing number of -*os* forms suggests that English is gradually reducing these irregular words to the regular plural form:

cargoes, cargos   desperadoes, desperados
zeros, zeroes   hoboes, hobos

d–Nouns ending in -*i* usually add -*s*:

skis [but] taxis, taxies

e–Nouns ending in -*oo* add -*s*:

cuckoos

f–Some common nouns ending in -*f* or -*fe* use -*ves*:

calf, calves   half, halves   knife, knives   leaf, leaves   loaf, loaves
self, selves   shelf, shelves   thief, thieves   wife, wives   wolf, wolves

But proper nouns do not: *Wolf, Wolfs*
Many words ending in /f/ sounds are regular:

beliefs   chiefs   dwarfs   fifes   gulfs   proofs   roofs

Some have two forms:

elf, elfs—elves   hoof, hoofs—hooves   scarf, scarfs—scarves
staff, staffs—staves   wharf, wharfs—wharves

2. *Same form for both singular and plural*:

Names of some animals, especially as game: fowl, sheep, fish [*fishes* for varieties of fish]
All words in -*ics*: athletics, civics, mathematics, politics
Common measurements: foot, pair, ton
A number of words rarely, if ever, used in the singular:

bellows	headquarters	odds [in betting]	smallpox
billiards	means	pants	species
gallows	measles	pincers	tactics
goods	morals	scissors	trousers

3. *Survivals of older English plural forms*:

In -*en*: child, children   ox, oxen   brother, brethren [Church use]
Change of vowel: foot, feet   goose, geese   louse, lice   man, men
mouse, mice   tooth, teeth   woman, women

4. *Foreign language plurals.* English keeps the foreign form of many words that have been borrowed from other languages. As they become more commonly used, the plural is usually formed regularly in -*s*; words used chiefly in scientific or Formal writing tend to keep the foreign form longer. *Antenna*, for instance, makes *antennae* in biology but *antennas* in electronics. When the word is in transition, both forms will be found.

A few borrowed words that now regularly have plurals in -*s* or -*es* will suggest the extent of the change to English forms:

area	campus	encyclopedia	museum
arena	circus	era	panacea
asylum	dilemma	ignoramus	panorama
bonus	diploma	metropolis	plateau
bureau	dogma	minus	quota

Some common words that still have the foreign form or sometimes are found with the foreign plural (as in Formal, academic, or scientific writing) are:

addendum -da	diagnosis -ses	nebula -las, -lae
alumna -nae	erratum -ta	neurosis -ses
*alumnus -ni	focus -ci (scientific),	nucleus -clei, -cleuses
ameba -bae, -bas	-cuses (General)	oasis oases
analysis -ses	*formula -las, -lae	opus opera
apparatus -tus,	fungus -gi, -guses	ovum ova
-tuses	gladiolus -luses, -li	parenthesis -ses
appendix -dixes,	hiatus -tuses, hiatus	psychosis -ses
-dices	hypothesis -ses	radius radii, radiuses
automaton -ta,	index indexes,	rostrum -trums, -tra
-tons	indices	species species
axis axes	larva -vae	stadium -diums, -dia
bacillus -li	libretto -tos, -ti	stimulus -li
basis bases	locus loci	stratum -ta, -tums
beau beaus, beaux	madame mesdames	syllabus -bi, buses
cactus -ti, -tuses	matrix -trixes,	synopsis -ses
chateau -teaus,	-trices	synthesis -ses
-teaux	*medium -dia,	tableau -bleaus,
cherub cherubs,	-diums	-bleaux
cherubim	memorandum -da,	terminus -nuses, -ni
(scriptural)	-dums	thesis -ses
crisis crises	momentum -tums,	trousseau -seaus,
criterion -teria	-ta	-seaux
curriculum	monsieur messieurs	vertebra -brae, -bras
-lums, -la	moratorium -iums,	vortex -tices, -texes
datum *data	-ia	

Because the languages English has borrowed from form plurals in so many different ways, speakers of English are sometimes confused by the variety and produce some odd forms. *Data* is a Latin plural, but because it is sometimes used with a singular verb we get the Nonstandard *datas*. *Bus* is a shortened form of the Latin *omnibus,* already a plural, from which those with a smattering of Latin formed *omnibii,* which has not survived. (See *Foreign words in English § 3c.)

5. *Compound and group words.* Most compound words and group words add *-s* to the end of the group, whether written as one word or several:

bookcases	high schools	cross-examinations

In a few the plural sign is added to the first element:

daughters-in-law   courts-martial   mothers-in-law   *passers-by
attorneys general   postmasters general   poets laureate [also *poet laureates*]   sons-in-law

6. *Plurals of figures, words, letters.* Usually the plural of a letter of the alphabet, of a word discussed as a word, or of a figure is written with *-'s*:

> There are two *c*'s and two *m*'s in *accommodate*.
> Three 2's   six 8's
> Don't use several *that*'s in a row.

(See *Numbers § 4.)

7. *Plural substitutes.* A plural notion is expressed often by a phrase that remains grammatically singular:

> College after college has gone in for intramural sports.
> The coach, with the captain and manager, makes up the schedule.
> The coach, together with the captain and manager, makes [often *make*] up the schedule.

(Other *Index* articles dealing with the formation of plurals include *Apostrophe § 1, *Genitive § 1, *-ful, full. Singular and plural constructions are treated in *Subject and verb, *Reference of pronouns. References: Curme, *Parts of Speech*, pp. 112-127, *Syntax*, pp. 539-548; Fries, *AEG*, p. 40 ff.)

p.m., a.m. • See *a.m. and p.m., also A.M. and P.M.

Poetry • When verse is quoted, it should be lined off as written. If possible, the quoted lines should be approximately centered on the page, indented according to the scheme of the original. When so spaced, quotation marks are not needed around lines of verse quoted and inserted in a prose passage. The first word of each line should be capitalized if it was capitalized in the original. (See *Verse form, *Capital letters § 3.)

politics • *Politics* is construed as either a singular or plural word but should not be both in the same passage:

> In almost any group, politics is a controversial subject.
> Republican politics were offensive to the Federalists.

Polysyllables • See *Monosyllables.

position, job • See *job, position.

Positive degree • The *positive degree* of adjectives and adverbs is the simple adjective form (*poor, high, golden*) or adverb form (*slow, slowly, bitterly*). (See *Comparison of adjectives and adverbs.)

Possessive adjectives • *My, your, his, her, its, our, your, their* (the genitive case forms of the personal pronouns) are often called *possessive adjectives* when they modify a noun:

my car   his first lecture   their experiences

Possessive case • See *Genitive.

practical • *Practical* and its derivatives give some trouble in spelling:

practical, adjective: a practical scheme, He has a practical mind.

practically, adverb: They were practically inclined [Informal in phrases like *practically all there*]

practicable, adjective: a practicable method

practicability, noun: They questioned the practicability of the idea.

pre- • The prefix *pre-* means *before* in time (*preexist, pre-Victorian*), or in place (*precerebral*), or rank (*preeminent*). For the spelling of words beginning with *pre*—written solid or hyphened—consult your dictionary.

pre-, per- • See *per-, pre-.

Precious, preciosity • Applied to style, *precious* and *preciosity* (or *preciousness*) mean "excessive fastidiousness in the use of language." The terms were borrowed from French and, though sometimes useful, have limited currency.

Précis • A *précis* /prā′sē/ is a concise summary of facts or, more often, of an article or other written document, giving in a brief space the essential content, the attitudes, and the emphasis of the original. Writing a précis can be an excellent device for testing your comprehension of a chapter, an article, or even a book.

Predicate • The *predicate* of a clause or sentence is the verb with its modifiers—object, complement, etc.—and predication is the function of a full verb in a clause or sentence. The subject and predicate are the two main elements of a sentence. The predicate may be a simple verb of complete meaning (The big bell *tolled*), a verb and adverbial modifier (The sun *went behind the cloud*), a transitive verb and its object (He *finally landed the big fish*), a *linking verb and complement (The oldest member of a family *is usually the first to go*).

Two verbs depending upon one subject are known as a *compound predicate:

The three of them *washed* and *wiped* the whole lot in fifteen minutes.

(See *Subject and verb, *Compound sentence, *Objects, *Verbs, Ch. 8, "Complex Sentences," p. 283, "Reducing predication," p. 317.)

Predicate adjective and noun •
Revision: Use an adjective here, since the verb is a linking verb.

P Adj

Adjectives and nouns that follow linking verbs are called *predicate adjectives* and *predicate nouns* (or *nominatives*), or *predicatives*.

Predicate adjective: The horse is *fast*. I feel *bad*. It is going to turn *warm*. It got *colder*. That one is *best*.

Predicate noun: Gibbon was a *historian*. Jackson became a *doctor*.

(See *Adjectives, types and forms § 2b, *Nouns § 2, *Linking verbs, Ch. 9, "Predicate adjectives," p. 341.)

Predicative •
Predicative is an inclusive term for *predicate adjective* and *predicate noun*.

predominant •
Predominant is the adjective: *a predominant sentiment, a sentiment predominant in the village. Predominate* is the verb: *This sentiment predominated in the village.* The present participle *predominating* is often used adjectivally.

prefer •
To is ordinarily used with *prefer*:

I prefer *Babbitt* to *Main Street*.

He preferred going by train to going in their car.

Would (or **had*) *rather. . .than* is less Formal and more used:

He would [or *had* or *He'd*] rather go by train than in their car.

Prefix •
A *prefix* is an element that can be placed before a word or root to make another word with a different meaning or function: *anti-* (*antiprohibition*), *bi-* (*biweekly*), *mis-* (*misfit*). (See *Origin of words § 3a. See also *Latin and English, *Hyphen §3, *Long variants.)

Prepositional phrase •
A *prepositional phrase* is a phrase made up of a preposition and its object: *without hope, in a hurry, toward a more abundant life.*

Prepositional phrases are modifiers, used in the functions of adverbs or adjectives:

Adverbial modifier: They came *at just the right time.*
Adverbial modifier: He lives *in the white house.*
Adjective modifier: The woman *in the black dress* has left.

To suggest the importance of prepositional phrases in English, here is a sentence of 42 words in which 27 stand in prepositional phrases (in italics), 15 in other constructions:

The settings *of the novels* ranged *from the fiords of Norway to the coasts of Tasmania,* and every page betrayed that intimate knowledge *of a foreign country* which can only be acquired *by a thorough study of the chattier sort of guide-books.*—STEPHEN VINCENT BENÉT, *Thirteen O'Clock,* p. 71

Prepositions •

Prep

Revision: Change the preposition, making it more exact or idiomatic (§ 3a) or less conspicuous (§ 3b), or making the construction less Informal (§ 3d).

1. *Definitions.* Prepositions are *particles with no distinctive form which belong to a closed class; therefore they are identified by us partly by our having learned them all, partly by the way they are used. Many words function as prepositions, adverbs, or conjunctions; recognition of them as belonging to the preposition class is therefore not enough. Their prepositional function becomes clear to us through a combination of our awareness that they can function as prepositions plus our recognition of their standing in a characteristic prepositional position in relation to other words:

Preposition: The wettest summer *since* the Flood.
Conjunction: *Since* the price was so low, we took three.
Adverb: He hasn't been around *since.*

The principal function of a preposition is to signal the unity of the phrase it introduces: *in turn, after the first try, for a long time.* The phrase then takes its place in a sentence as a unit, and the preposition, partly through its meaning, helps relate it to some other sentence element: to a verb (He showed her *to* her room), to a noun (the click *of* flying wheels), or to an adjective (old *in* experience). A noun following a preposition is called its object (*room, wheels, experience* in the examples just given). Prepositions may be word groups as well as single words: *in regard to, according to.*

There has lately been a tendency to minimize the *lexical meaning of prepositions. In concrete senses they carry as much meaning as other words: being *under* a bed is quite different from being *on* a bed. Even in more abstract contexts, prepositions have meaning, though it may seem more arbitrary: *beneath* contempt, *for* love, *in* or *with* haste, agree *to* a proposal or *with* a person. These meanings, like those of abstract nouns, are learned in a context of language rather than of physical experience, but none the less learned.

2. *List of prepositions.* The following list shows characteristic uses of the commoner prepositions. Many of them show both a concrete and an abstract meaning (*at* home, *at* odds). Fries estimates that nine of them (*at, by, for, from, in, of, on, to, with*) account for over 92% of prepositions used.

   aboard   aboard the airliner [Formal: *on board*]
   *about   about the town, about her, about his work
   *above   above the clouds, above the average, above suspicion
   according to   according to the reports, according to Hoyle
   across   across the bow, across the street
   *after   after supper, we all ran after him [Technical: for a drawing based on another's drawing—*after Newcourt*]
   against   against the door, against the grain
   ahead of   ahead of his generation, ahead of time
   along   along the shore, along the route
   alongside   alongside the dock [Informal: *alongside of*]
   amid (amidst)   [Formal] amid the smoke, amidst the ruins
   among   among the lucky ones [used of three or more]
   apart from   apart from the others, apart from his own earnings [rather Formal]
   apropos   [Formal] apropos our discussion; *or,* apropos of our discussion
   around   around the edge, around the town
   as   as judge, as chairman
   as far as   as far as the door, as far as New Orleans
   *as to   as to the objection, as to your interest
   at   at home, at Johnstown, at his suggestion, at midnight
   back of   back of the screen, back of the house, back of the proposal. *Back of, in back of* are less likely to occur in Formal writing than *behind.*
   because of   because of the war, because of his need
   before   before the flood, before an audience, before replying
   behind   behind the door, behind the pretense
   below   below the surface, below our level
   beneath   beneath the surface, beneath contempt [more Formal than *below*]
   *beside   beside the sea, beside the point, beside oneself
   besides   besides those named, no other besides this
   *between   between New York and Philadelphia, between life and death
   beyond   beyond the river, beyond reach

by   by the house, by an inch, by force, by himself, by night

concerning   concerning my friend, concerning our interest

considering   considering the difficulty

contrary to   contrary to orders, contrary to our expectation

despite   [Formal] despite hostile criticism

down   down the chute, down the slope, down the list

*due to   due to an error, due to carelessness

during   during the last ten years, during the services

except   except the children

following   following the rule

for   for you, for profit, for the community

from   from the attic, from the Far East, from fear

in   in the country, in the house, in the Bible, in trouble

in back of   (see *back of, behind*)

in place of   in place of the old regulations

inside   inside the house, inside ten minutes [Often, somewhat Informally, *inside of*]   inside of ten minutes

in spite of   in spite of the law, in spite of his prejudices

in view of   in view of these concessions

into   into the mountains, into the subject (see **in—into—in to*)

like   like a horse, like a tornado

near   near the window, near the top, near exhaustion

*of   of Wisconsin, of the same color, of my opinion, of the king

off   off the path, off the platform [Redundant, *off of*] off of the path

on   on the road

on account of   on account of the weather, on account of his belief

onto   onto the train, onto the beach

opposite   opposite the house

out   out the window

out of   out of the auditorium, out of sight

over   over the fence, over the plains, over her head

owing to   owing to the emergency, owing to our inability

past   past the stores, past the mark, past the hour

*per   per day, per pound

round   round the Maypole, round the town

since   since his election, since Victorian days

through   through the first barrier, through accident

throughout   throughout the day, throughout his speech

*till   till morning, till the intermission

to   to Los Angeles, to the ocean, to Governor Smith, to the point

*toward   toward Fort Worth, toward dinner time, toward the truth

under   under the awning, under cover, under the arch

until   until dusk, until two o'clock (see **till, until, 'til*)

unto   [Archaic] unto death, unto the last drop

up   up the slope, up the scale

upon   upon a sure foundation, upon further investigation
up to   up to this point
via   via United Air Lines
with   with his fellows, with caution, with the affirmative
within   within bounds, within the city, within a year
without   without money

3. *Use of prepositions.*

a–Exact or idiomatic prepositions. A number of words are accompanied by certain prepositions, as contented *with* conditions, *in* my estimation. Some words have various meanings with different prepositions: agree *with* (a person), agree *to* (a suggestion), agree *in* (principle).

You can add indefinitely to the following list:

deprive *of* pleasure	hindrance *to* advancement
eligible *for* membership	means *of* winning
fascinated *by* this glamor	pride *in* his college
fear *of* fire, fear *for* his safety	unconscious *of* their stares

The customary preposition does not give much trouble with words that we use commonly, because we learn the words by hearing or seeing them in their usual constructions. Obviously it is safer to learn words as they are actually used, to learn *acquiesce in* (acquiesce in a decision) rather than just *acquiesce*. If a person uses an unidiomatic preposition, it is probably because he is not at home with the word or is confused because usage is divided on that particular locution (as *different *from* or *than* or *to*). Dictionaries give the appropriate preposition used with particular words. This book treats a few idioms that are likely to raise questions: *ability (to); *agree to, agree with; *all of; *compare—contrast; *different. (See also *Idiom and idioms.)

A special reminder is needed that when two words are used which are completed by different prepositions *both* prepositions should be used, though in Informal speech the omission of the second preposition often passes unnoticed:

The first lesson learned by the sturdy Italian boy just over from the "old country" was *obedience to* and *respect for* others besides his parents. (Not: obedience and respect *for* others)

Some people cannot reconcile their *interest in* and their *fear of* snakes.

The committee acknowledged its *interest in,* but denied its *responsibility for,* housing conditions.

When both words call for the same preposition, it need not be repeated:

The box office refused to make any *allowance* or *refund for* tickets purchased from an agent.

There are, of course, instances of *divided usage: abound *in* or *with,* hanker *after* or *for,* the necessity *of* or *for.* (See *between, among; *different; *sick.)

b–Prepositions bulking too large. English has a number of group prepositions (according to, in regard to, by means of) that sometimes become conspicuous. They can hardly be called wrong, but used in any noticeable numbers they tend to weigh down the style. Often a shorter preposition will do better.

In these examples, sometimes one or more of the italicized words (in brackets) can be omitted or a simple preposition (in brackets) can be substituted:

We made supper [*out*] *of* beans, fried potatoes, and steak.

Consumers Union attempts to furnish reliable information *in regard to* [*about*] all sorts of goods and services.

For politeness' sake the pronoun of the first person stands last when used [*in connection*] *with* other pronouns: "He, you, and I had better do it."

It has been said that in six months after graduation from college a man can pick up as much practical knowledge *connected with* [*of*] business administration as a nongraduate can in ten years.

... recent demonstrations *on the part of* [*by*] certain students....

Prepositions sometimes bulk too large in writing because we carry over to paper our tendency in speech to use double prepositions: *in back of* for *back of, outside of* for *outside, off of* for *off.* ... These are not appropriate in Formal English, which at its best makes one word do maximum duty, but in Informal English they may help give an easy tone if they do not become too noticeable. The writer should decide whether these idioms are appropriate to other traits of his style. (For further examples and discussion see the articles *as to, *of, off, *onto, and so on.)

c–Omission of prepositions. Spoken English shows not only a frequent piling up of prepositions but the opposite tendency too—dropping a preposition that would ordinarily be used in writing. Prepositions, especially *of,* receive so little stress that they naturally drop out entirely in rapid speech, and this same trait is now increasingly found in writers whose style is conspicuously Informal. A few examples (with the preposition usual in General English in brackets) will suggest the tendency:

The color [of] cloth she preferred was out of stock.

The most notable piece of equipment was an apparatus which made it possible to run the presses [at] almost twice their former speed.

A *couple [of] days later....

d–Prepositions at end of sentence. It was once fashionable for textbooks to put a stigma upon prepositions standing at the end of their constructions (What did you do it *for?*). But postponing the preposition is a characteristic English idiom, even though it runs contrary to our usual tendency to keep words of a construction close together. In fact it is so generally the normal word order that the real danger is in clumsiness from trying to avoid a preposition at the end of a clause or sentence:

Tell me what it is to which you object. [Natural: *what you object to*].

Extreme cases are possible (like the boy's: "What did you bring that book for me to be read to out of for?"), but there is no reason for hesitating to let a preposition fall at the end if natural idiom and rhythm place it there.

Placing the preposition at the end is such a firmly fixed habit that sometimes we use one at the beginning and end:

... in the lives of individuals *with* whom he had come in contact *with*.

Obviously such a sentence shows lack of revision.

(In addition to *Index* articles already referred to in this discussion, see *Parts of speech, *Function words, *Objects § 3. References: Curme, *Syntax,* pp. 566-569; Fowler, pp. 457-459 and other index entries; Fries, *AEG,* Ch. 7; Hall, pp. 213-217; M. Bertens Charnley, "The Syntax of Deferred Prepositions," *American Speech,* 1949, 24:268-277.)

Present tense • See *Tenses of verbs.

Pre-writing • The term *pre-writing* is currently used to refer to the thinking that a writer must do before he can produce even the rough draft of an essay or paper. It applies to that part of rhetoric traditionally called *invention* or *discovery,* the part that deals with the problem of finding something to say. The nature of the problem is often misconstrued by the student writer, who either strains to say something new and original or resolutely suppresses his own thoughts and feelings in order to play safe. What he needs to realize is that the problem of pre-writing is that of finding something to write about that is real and convincing to *him*. Without this personal grasp of his subject, a writer can at best parrot the thoughts of others in prose that is likely to be empty and stereotyped. With it, even the most trivial subject can be made to come alive. It is the minimal requirement of good writing.

Instead of seeking out words and arranging them in sentences and paragraphs, a writer during the pre-writing stage is concerned with arranging the material of his thoughts, feelings, memory, and imagination. The virtues, then, that make a composition formally good (for example, appropriate usage, adequate and orderly development), as well as the habits of mind that produce them, are not the same as those that make the pre-writing stage effective. Nor is the pre-writer much concerned with the thoughts, feelings, and expectations of his eventual audience. According to Gordon Rohman and Albert Wlecke, the central requirement of pre-writing is an "absolute willingness to think one's own thoughts, feel one's own feelings." Further, the pre-writer must be ready to explore the sensory details, the particulars, of his subject, for concrete details are more likely to elicit a purely personal response, more likely to appeal to his own sense of the real, more likely to be convincing to himself than abstractions and generalities.

The aim of pre-writing is not to make all writing personal but rather to make sure that all writing is motivated by a personal concern. From faithfulness to one's own experience can come a controlling attitude, a point of view from which the writer can order his impressions. After the writer has a personal commitment to the truth of his own vision and emotion, he can begin to plan the paper or essay: take notes, search for additional material, draw up outlines, decide on methods of development, write thesis sentences, and so forth. Good pre-writing does not guarantee good writing, but without good pre-writing, good writing can only be a lucky accident.

(References: D. Gordon Rohman and Albert O. Wlecke, *Pre-Writing: The Construction and Application of Models for Concept Formation in Writing,* U.S. Office of Education Cooperative Research Project Number 2174, East Lansing, Michigan, 1964. A briefer discussion can be found in D. Gordon Rohman, "Pre-Writing: The Stage of Discovery in the Writing Process," *College Composition and Communication,* 1965, 16:106-112.)

principal—principle • Associate *principal* as an adjective (the *principal* reason—the *principal* man of the town—the *principal* force involved) with other adjectives ending in *-al*: historic*al*, politic*al*, music*al*.

Principal as a noun is probably an abbreviation of a phrase in which it was originally an adjective: the *principal* that draws interest was once *the principal sum*; the *principal* of a school, *the principal teacher*; the *principal* in a legal action, *the principal party*; the *principals* in the cast of a play or movie, *the principal actors*. These are the only common uses of *principal* as a noun.

The noun meaning "a general and fundamental truth" (the

principles of science, the *principles* of government) or "a rule of conduct" (a man of high *principles*, a matter of moral *principle*) is *principle*.

Principal parts of verbs •

Revision: Change the verb form to the one in good use, as given in the list below or in a dictionary.   Prin

The principal parts of a verb are the bare form or infinitive (*ask*), the past tense form (*asked*), and the past participle (*asked*). Most English verbs are "regular"—that is, their past tense and past participle are formed by adding *-ed* to the bare form. A number, most of them descended from Old English strong verbs—verbs which formed their past tense and past participle forms by altering their root vowels—retain the older pattern (*ride, rode, ridden*). Some of these are becoming regular (*shined, weaved*), and many are made regular in speech and Nonstandard usage (*blowed, growed*).

The following list includes a number of verbs with these irregular parts or with some other question of form. A form in parentheses is decidedly less common in writing, and those labeled *NS* (Nonstandard) would not ordinarily occur in current writing. A recent dictionary should be consulted for other verbs. But usage is by no means uniform, even among speakers and writers of Standard English, and dictionaries do not record all variations.

Infinitive	Past tense	Past participle
arise	arose	arisen
bear	bore	borne
		*born (given birth to)
begin	began (NS: *begun*)	begun (NS: *began*)
bid (to offer)	bid	bid
bid (order)	bade	bidden, bid
bite	bit	bitten, bit
blow	blew (NS: *blowed*)	blown (NS: *blowed*)
break	broke	broken
		(Inf. or NS: *broke*)
bring	brought (NS: *brung*)	brought (NS: *brung*)
*burst	burst	burst
catch	caught	caught
choose /chüz/	chose /chōz/	chosen
come	came (NS: *come*)	come
dig	dug (Archaic: *digged*)	dug
dive	dove, dived	dived, dove
*do	did (NS: *done*)	done
draw	drew (NS: *drawed*)	drawn (NS: *drawed*)
dream	dreamed, dreamt	dreamed, dreamt

Infinitive	*Past tense*	*Past participle*
drink	drank (Archaic and NS: *drunk*)	*drunk (*drank—drunken*; the latter, adjective only)
drive	drove	driven
eat	ate (Local and British: *eat* /et/; see *Divided usage)	eaten (*eat*)
fall	fell	fallen
find	found	found
fit	fit, fitted	fit, fitted
flee	fled	fled
fly	flew	flown
forget	forgot	forgotten, forgot
freeze	froze	frozen (NS: *froze*)
*get	got	got, gotten
give	gave (NS: *give*)	given
go	went	gone (NS: *went*)
grow	grew (NS: *growed*)	grown
hang	hung	hung
hang (to execute)	hung, *hanged	hung, hanged
hear	heard	heard
kneel	knelt, kneeled	knelt, kneeled
knit	knitted, knit	knitted, knit
know	knew (NS: *knowed*)	known
*lay	laid	laid
lead	led	led
lend (*loan*)	lent	lent
let	let	let
lie (see *lay)	*lay	lain
light	*lighted, lit	lighted, lit
lose	lost	lost
pay	*paid (of ropes: *payed*)	paid (*payed*)
plead	pleaded, plead, pled	pleaded, plead /pled/, pled /pled/
prove	proved	*proved, proven
ride	rode	ridden (NS: *rode*)
ring	rang, rung	rung
rise	rose	risen
run	ran (NS: *run*)	run
say	said	said
see	saw (NS: *seen*)	seen
set	set	set
shine	shone, shined	shone, shined
show	showed	shown, showed
shrink	shrunk, shrank	shrunk

Infinitive	Past tense	Past participle
sing	sang, sung	sung
sink	sank, sunk	sunk
sit	sat (NS: *set)	sat (NS: set)
slide	slid	slid (slidden)
sow	sowed	sown, sowed
speak	spoke	spoken
speed	sped, speeded	sped, speeded
spit	spit, spat	spit, spat
spring	sprang, sprung	sprung
stand	stood	stood
steal	stole	stolen
stink	stank, stunk	stunk
strive	strove (also strived)	striven, strived
sweat	sweated, sweat	sweated, sweat
swim	swam (NS: swum)	swum
take	took	taken
tear	tore	torn
throw	threw (NS: throwed)	thrown
tread	trod	trodden, trod
wake	waked, woke	waked, woke (woken)
wear	wore	worn
weave	wove (weaved)	woven, wove
win	won	won
wind /wīnd/	wound (Nautical: winded)	wound /wound/
wring	wrung	wrung
write	wrote (Archaic: writ)	written (NS: wrote; Archaic: writ)

The evidence of the *Linguistic Atlas of the United States* is already providing for revision of some of these descriptions. The past participle *drank* is much more prevalent in Standard English, especially in New England, than dictionaries suggest; *shrunk* seems to be more common in the Upper Midwest as a past tense than *shrank* (see H. B. Allen, "Current English Forum," *College English*, 1957, 18:283-285); both popular and Standard usage favor *knit, laid, pled, fit,* and *sweat* as the past tense forms of *knit, lie, plead, fit,* and *sweat* (see E. Bagby Atwood, *A Survey of Verb Forms in the Eastern United States,* Ann Arbor, 1953. References: Fries, *AEG,* pp. 59-71; Mencken, pp. 527-528; Bryant, pp. 55, 78, 125-126, 194, and 203.)

principle—principal • See *principal—principle.

prior to • *Prior to* is heavy for *before*: *Prior to (Before) coming here he had been at Stanford. Prior to* suggests legal language. *Before* is usually more appropriate in General writing.

process, procedure, proceed • *Process* and *procedure,* the nouns, are spelled with one *e* after the *c*; *proceed,* the verb, has two *e*'s. (The spelling situation is further confused by the verb *precede*.) The pronunciation /prō′ses/ is British rather than American, but not uncommon here. /Pros′ə sēz/ is rather affected for the plural; say /pros′es əz/.

Proceed means "to go," strictly in a rather formal fashion, and is best kept for movement: *We proceeded at a decent rate of speed. We proceeded to unpack* usually means no more than *We unpacked* or *Then we unpacked.*

Profanity • Styles change in the handling of "cuss words" and profanity. At present most writers, most editors, and most publishers are much more liberal than formerly. In college writing such words should be used only in dialog where they are spoken by a character, and you should be quite sure they are fitting and called for. Both cussing and cursing are primarily oral, matters of muscular release more than of meaning, and in print they often attract more attention to themselves than they deserve. You can't put on paper all the vulgarity proper to a vulgar person's speech; the effect will be suggested by an occasional sample. In the writing of biography, criticism, and miscellaneous informational articles there is less freedom, and double dashes and euphemistic blankety-blanks are sometimes found. Such devices ordinarily give the impression of a writer who is playing at being tough but hasn't the courage to use language he believes is really appropriate. Use the expressions the subject seriously calls for, compromising as little or as much as your temperament and circumstances demand. In material submitted to magazines, editors will make whatever alterations their policies demand. (See *Obscenity.)

Professor • Write:

Professor Tewksbury [or] Prof. E. W. Tewksbury [or] E. W. Tewksbury, a professor of electrical engineering

[or, as a Formal title] E. W. Tewksbury, Professor of Electrical Engineering

The colloquial *prof* is a clipped word, not an abbreviation, and if it is written should not have a period:

He said all profs were a little crazy anyway.

Strictly speaking, *professor* should be confined to names of assistant professors, associate professors, and (full) professors. When the title comes before the name (without the *of* phrase), *Professor* is used for all three ranks; when it follows the name and has the *of* phrase, the exact rank is usually indicated: *Professor A. B. Plant; A. B. Plant, Assistant Professor of Eng-*

lish. Applying it to instructors is sometimes a well-meant courtesy but more often carelessness. In official and business usage an *instructor* who has a Ph.D. is often addressed as *Doctor.* It would be better to address all teachers as *Mr.* or *Miss* or *Mrs.*—as many professors would prefer; but students should follow the conventions of their own campus. (See *Abbreviations § 2, *Titles of persons. For an account of the title's history in this country, see Robert L. Coard, "In Pursuit of the Word 'Professor,' " *Journal of Higher Education,* 1959, 30:237-245.)

Progressive verb forms • The grammatical term *progressive verb forms* is applied to verb phrases made with *to be* and the present participle: I *am asking,* he *was asking,* they *have been asking.* (See *Tenses of verbs, *Verbs.)

Pronominal adjectives • Several types of pronouns, used also like adjectives, are called *pronominal adjectives*:

Interrogative:	*Which* way did he go?		
Demonstrative:	*that* way	*this* book	*those* boys
Possessive:	*my* hat	*his* idea	*your* dog	*their* seats
Indefinite:	*some* people	*each* person	*all* men

Pronouns, types and forms •
Revision: Change the form of the pronoun marked to the one expected in the grammatical construction in which it stands.

Pron

Pronouns in the English language are hard to define because traditionally this part of speech includes several groups of quite different words. They all are used in the principal syntactical functions of nouns, serving as subjects and objects, and a number have genitives. Perhaps it is enough to say that a pronoun is a word that can be replaced by a noun in a specific context. Many, like nouns, have an –s genitive and also a plural.

The uses of pronouns are described in *Reference of pronouns. This article lists the various types of pronouns and their forms.

1. *The personal pronouns.* Some of the most common grammatical problems come from the fact that separate nominative and accusative case forms survive for personal and relative pronouns though not for nouns (see *Person, *between you and me, *It's me, *who, whom § 2, 3).

		Nomina- tive forms	Genitive forms	Accusa- tive forms
1st person	*Singular:*	*I	my, mine	me
	Plural:	we	our, ours	us

2nd person	*Singular:*	you	your, yours	you
	Plural:	you	your, yours	you
3d person	*Singular:*			
	masculine:	*he	his, his	him
	feminine:	she	her, hers	her
	neuter:	*it	its (of it)	it
	either gender:	*one	one's	one
	Plural:	they	their, theirs	them, 'em

Archaic forms of the second person singular, *thou, thy* or *thine, thee,* are used only in religious services, by the Society of Friends (*thee* only), and occasionally in poetry.

Mine, formerly used before words beginning with a vowel (*mine eyes*), is no longer so used: *my eyes.* Under *Genitive forms,* the one before the comma is used before nouns, the one after the comma in predicative position; *its* and *one's* do not occur as predicatives in Standard English:

> The money is *mine* [*ours, yours, hers, theirs*].
> *Yours* came a whole week before *mine.*
> Rarely: Baby *mine.*

2. *Relative pronouns.*

Nominative forms	Genitive forms	Accusative forms
*who	whose	whom
*that	of that	that
*which	of which, whose	which, whom

Whoever, whichever, whatever (and archaic: *whosoever, whichsoever, whatsoever*) are less definite than the simple relatives and may have an accent of surprise, emphasis, or playfulness.

3. *Interrogative pronouns.* *who, *which, what; occasionally whoever, whatever

4. *Reflexive and intensive pronouns.* These pronouns are the personal pronouns plus the suffix *-self* or *-selves.* The Standard forms do not follow a consistent pattern; the suffix is added to *my, our, your* (genitive); *him, them* (accusative); *her, it* [*s*]. They are called *reflexive* because the action of the verb is directed toward the subject of the construction: He shaves *himself*; She bought *herself* two hats. (See *himself, herself, *myself.*)

When used as intensives, these words are usually construed as pronouns in *apposition:

> The mayor himself delivered the address.
> I can finish the job myself.

5. *Reciprocal pronouns.* *Each other and *one another,* reciprocal pronouns, are used only as objects of verbs or prepositions. In Formal usage some writers keep *each other* to refer to two,

one another for more than two. General usage has *each other* in all senses:

> They had hated each other for years.
>
> *Formal:* For the first time all the members really saw one another.
>
> *General:* For the first time all the members really saw each other.

6. *Numeral pronouns.* The cardinal numbers (one, two, three ...) and the ordinals (first, second, third...) are used as pronouns: *Three* were there; The *eighth* won.

7. *Demonstrative pronouns.* (See *Demonstrative adjectives and pronouns.)

> *this, these   *that, those   (Compare *kind, sort)
> the *former, the latter, the first, the second ...
> *such, *so (I told you so)   *same

8. *Indefinite pronouns.* A large number of words, of greater or less indefiniteness, often function as pronouns:

all	everybody (see *every § 2)	nothing
another	everyone	*one, oneself
*any	everything	other
anybody	few	several
anyone	many	*some
anything	much	somebody
*both	neither	someone
*each	*nobody	something
each one	*none	*such
either	no one	

9. *Impersonal pronouns.* See *it.

(For a discussion of questions on the uses of pronouns see *Reference of pronouns. See also *Agreement § 2, *Ambiguity § 1, *Apostrophe § 5, *Case, *Gerund § 2, *Parts of speech. References: Curme, *Parts of Speech,* Ch. 10, and *Syntax,* index references; Fries, *AEG,* index references.)

Pronunciation •

1. *Pronunciation key.* The pronunciation of words is indicated in this *Guide and Index* by respelling them with the letters and diacritical marks (with some few exceptions) used in the Thorndike-Barnhart Dictionaries, as follows:

a	apple /ap'l/, fact /fakt/
ā	age /āj/, say /sā/, inflate /in flāt'/
ã	care /kãr/, air /ãr/
ä	far /fär/, father /fä'ᴛʜər/
b	back /bak/, robber /rob'ər/
ch	child /chīld/, literature /lit'ər ə chur/, question /kwes'chən
d	do /dü/, did /did/
e	bet /bet/, effect /ə fekt'/

ėr	urge /ėrj/, bird /bėrd/, term /tėrm/
ē	equal /ē'kwəl/, see /sē/, police /pə lēs'/
f	fat /fat/, stuff /stuf/, cough /kôf/, photo /fō'tō/
g	go /gō/, baggage /bag'ij/
h	hotel /hō tel'/, boyhood /boi'hůd/
hw	wheel /hwēl/, whether /hweᴛн'ər/
i	if /if/, pithy /pith'ē/
ī	ice /īs/, buy /bī/
j	jam /jam/, edge /ej/, age /āj/
k	king /king/, back /bak/, cocoa /kō'kō/
l	life /līf/, silly /sil'ē/, fill /fil/
m	am /am/, meet /mēt/, sample /sam'p ̣l/
n	note /nōt/, inner /in'ər/
ng	sing /sing/, song /sông/, rank /rangk/
o	rock /rok/, stop /stop/
ō	open /ō'pən/, hope /hōp/, go /gō/
ô	bought /bôt/, ball /bôl/, caught /kôt/, four /fôr/
oi	voice /vois/, boil /boil/
ou	house /hous/, out /out/, cow /kou/
p	paper /pā'pər/, cap /kap/
r	reach /rēch/, try /trī/
s	say /sā/, listen /lis'ṇ/, yes /yes/
sh	she /shē/, rush /rush/, cushion /kůsh'ən/, nation /nā'shən/
t	tie /tī/, sit /sit/, kitten /kit'ṇ/
th	thin /thin/, both /bōth/, bath /bath/
ᴛн	that /ᴛнat/, bother /boᴛн'ər/, bathe /bāᴛн/, thee /ᴛнē/
u	cup /kup/, butter /but'ər/
ů	book /bůk/, put /půt/
ü	tool /tül/, rule /rül/, move /müv/
ū	useful /ūs'fəl/, music /mū'zik/
v	very /ver'ē/, salve /sav/ or /säv/, save /sāv/
w	will /wil/, with /wiᴛн/ or /with/, won't /wōnt/
y	young /yung/, yellow /yel'ō/
z	zero /zir'ō/, breeze /brēz/
zh	measure /mezh'ər/, rouge /rüzh/
ə	Called schwa /shwä/, represents the indefinite vowel sound of many unstressed syllables. It is variously spelled: *a* in *sofa* /sō'fə/, *e* in *secretary* /sek'rə ter'ē/, and by the other vowels and combinations of vowels.

/ḷ, ṃ, ṇ, ṛ/ Syllabic consonants, used in unstressed syllables when no vowel sound can be distinguished: little /lit'ḷ/, wooden /wood'ṇ/. When spoken slowly these syllables have /ə/, and are sometimes so respelled.

The stress of syllables is represented by a ′ for a main stress and a ′ for a lighter stress, placed after the stressed syllable: /ag'rə kul'chər/.

A vowel sound in a stressed syllable will be more fully sounded than one without stress. Contrast the *o* of *below* /bi lō′/ and of *obey*—which ranges from /ō bā′/ to /ə bā′/. In unstressed syllables they tend to become the "neutral vowel" /ə/, as in the italicized vowels in *again, academy, dormitory, cursory, circus.* (For suggestions on spelling such words see *Neutral vowel.)

An *r* following a vowel alters the vowel's sound, as in *care, sere, core, sure,* but a separate symbol is not used to represent the change (except for /ėr/ as in *term* /tėrm/): /kãr/, /sēr/, /kôr/, /shùr/. (Further details of the sounds represented by each letter of the alphabet, with examples, will be found in the articles on the separate letters, *A, *B, *C, and so on, in this *Index.* See also *Voiced, voiceless sounds.)

2. *Special points in pronunciation.*

a–Stress. In general, English is a rather strongly stressed (accented) language. The force of the stress varies a good deal among individual speakers. The stress of particular words (*detail, address) varies with their meaning and with their position in sentences. (See also *Noun and verb stress.)

b–Secondary stress. A word of three or especially of four syllables is likely to have a main and a secondary stress: *secondary* /sek′ən der′ē/, *incidental* /in′sə den′tl̥/. One of the differences between British and American pronunciation is that we tend to keep secondary stresses in many words in which the British have but one:

necessary: American /nes′ə sar′ē/; British /nes′əs rē/

dictionary: American/dik′shən er′ē/; British /dik′shn̥ rē/

(See *American and British usage.)

c–*Pronunciation and spelling.* Words really live in their oral forms, and any guide to pronunciation must start with the spoken words, not the written. But our spelling represents, often very approximately, the sounds of words, or at least the sounds they once had.

When words are acquired from reading rather than from hearing, they are very often overpronounced, in what are known as "spelling pronunciations." *Sophomore* on most campuses is two syllables, /sof′môr/, but people who see it more than they hear it are likely to sound the middle *o* slightly /sof′ə môr/; *yearling* is /yėr′ling/ where it is regularly used, /yir′ling/ as a spelling pronunciation. Spelling pronunciation may introduce sounds that are not in the Standard pronunciation of the word (*soften* as /sôf′tən/). Sometimes these pronunciations become acceptable, usually as a minor pronunciation (*often* as /of′tən/), occasionally even forcing out the older established pronunciation (*Indian,* formerly /in′jən/). Genuine familiarity with words is shown by using the established oral rather than a spelling pronunciation.

3. *Standards of pronunciation.* Standard written English is virtually the same in all parts of the United States. But standard speech varies somewhat in different parts of our country and is basically that of the educated people of the region. It shows some regional qualities, though less than the speech of uneducated people. (See Ch. 1, "Variations due to place," p. 6. See also *Affectation, *Divided usage.)

A person's pronunciation should be appropriate as far as possible to the situation in which he is speaking. The elaborateness of "stage" pronunciation is out of place in conversation, even in "cultivated" conversation. Too conscious attention to pronunciation will handicap the speaker and irritate the listener. Pronunciation in speaking to groups must necessarily be somewhat slower, more distinct, but fundamentally it is a refinement of the speaker's better conversational style.

The problem of a person going to live in a different part of the country is more complex. Should he drop his native speech and do as the Romans do? If he makes a specific and hasty effort to pick up the new speech, he will be almost sure to make mistakes—that is, he will confuse the two. If he can stand off the first attacks on his speechways, he will soon find that he will attract less attention. Then he will naturally acquire, bit by bit and without forcing, many of the new ways. He need not be ashamed if traces of his native speech remain.

The words to worry about are not those in everyday use so much as the new ones acquired in taking up new work or a new social status or new ideas or, in college, new subjects of study. Care should be taken to get a conventional pronunciation of these new words (*acclimate, desultory, schizophrenic* ...) as they are learned, to be at home with them from the beginning.

As Fowler puts it (p. 466), "The broad principles are: Pronounce as your neighbors do, not better." For the majority of words, your neighbors are the general public. For words in more restricted use, your neighbors are the group that uses them. Consequently there will be more local flavor in General and Informal speech, less in speaking to limited and special audiences. It is more important to avoid Nonstandard pronunciations than the regional pronunciations of educated people.

4. *Pronunciation list.* The following list is in part to raise questions of pronunciation. The pronunciations suggested should be tested by comparing them with those you hear. For most words that raise questions of pronunciation, consult a good recent dictionary.

Pronunciations of other words will be found in the articles on each letter of the alphabet, *Foreign words in English, *Spelling, *Proper names, and in various articles on particular words.

When two forms are given, no choice is implied; a distinctly less common form stands in brackets. A large number of words are spoken in two or more ways in good usage.

An asterisk before a word means that the *Index* has a separate article on that word.

abdomen /ab'də mən/,
  /ab dō'mən/
absorb /ab sôrb'/, /ab zôrb'/
absurd /ab sėrd'/, /ab zėrd'/
acclimate /ə klī'mit/,
  /ak'lə māt/
adult /ə dult'/, /ad'ult/
advertisement
  /ad vėr'tiz ment/,
  /ad vėr'tis ment/,
  /ad'vər tīz'mənt/
ally (noun) /al'ī/, /ə lī'/;
  (plural more often) /ə līz'/;
  (verb) /ə lī'/
*alma mater /al'mə mä'tər/,
  /äl'mə mä'tər/, /al'mə mā'tər/
alternate (verb) /ôl'tər nāt/,
  /al'tər nāt/; (adjective and
  noun) /ôl'tər nit/, /al'tər nit/
amateur /am'ə chər/, /am'ə tər/
apparatus /ap'ə rā'təs/,
  /ap'ə rat'əs/
applicable /ap'lə kə bl̩/,
  /ə plik'ə bl̩/
Aryan /ar'ē ən/, /är'yən/
atypical /ā tip'ə kl̩/ (see *-a)
aviation /ā'vē ā'shən/,
  /av'ē ā'shən/
aye (yes) /ī/
bade /bad/, /bād/
*biography /bī og'rə fē/,
  /bi og'rə fē/
bureaucracy /byu̇ rok'rə sē/
business /biz'nis/
chauffeur /shō'fər/, /shō fėr'/
chic /shēk/, /shik/
combatant /kəm bat'ənt/,
  /kom'bə tənt/

*contents /kon'tents/
coup /kü/
coupon /kü'pon/, /kū'pon/
coyote /kī ō'tē/, /kī'ōt/
*data /dā'tə/, /dat'ə/, /dä'tə/
debut /dā'bū/, /dā bū'/
decade /dek'ād/
desperado /des'pər ā'do/,
  /des'pər ä'dō/
diphtheria /dif thir'ē ə/,
  /dip thir'ē ə/
diphthong /dif'thông/,
  /dip'thông/, /dif'thong/,
  /dip'thong/
disputable /dis pūt'ə bl̩/,
  /dis'pyə tə bl̩/
drama /drä'mə/, dram'ə/
economics /ē'kə nom'iks/,
  /ek'ə nom'iks/
*either /ē'ᴛHər/, [Brit.]
  /ī'ᴛHər/
electricity /i lek'tris'ə tē/,
  /ē'lek tris'ə tē/
Elizabethan /i liz'ə bē'thən/,
  /i liz'ə beth'ən/
err /ėr/, /ār/
exquisite /eks'kwi zit/,
  /eks kwiz'it/
finance /fə nans'/, /fī nans'/,
  /fī'nans/
formidable /fôr'mə də bl̩/
fortnight /fôrt'nīt/,
  /fôrt'nit/
gibbous /gib'əs/
gladiolus /glad'ē ō'ləs/,
  /glə dī'ə ləs/
gunwale /gun'l̩/
harass /har'əs/, /hə ras'/

heinous /hā'nəs/

human /hū'mən/

idea /ī dē'ə/

impious /im'pē əs/

indict /in dīt'/

isolate /ī'sə lāt/, /is'ə lāt/

juvenile /jü'və nḷ/, /jü'və nīl/

kimono /kə mō'nə/

laugh /laf/, /läf/

launch /lônch/, /länch/

leisure /lē'zhər/, /lezh'ər/

lever /lev'ər/, /lē'vər/

lilacs /lī'ləks/, lī'laks/

matrix /mā'triks/, /mat'riks/

menu /men'ū/, /mā'nū/

mischievous /mis'chə vəs/

news /nüz/, /nūz/

oasis /ō ā'sis/

orgy /ôr'jē/

parliament /pär'lə mənt/

patriot /pā'trē ət/,
   [Brit.] /pat'rē ət/

penalize /pē'nḷ īz/, /pen'ḷ īz/

percolator /pėr'kə lā'tər/

pianist /pē an'ist/, /pē'ə nist/

pleasure /plezh'ər/, /plā'zhər/

premier /pri mir'/, /prē'mē ər/

presentation /prez'ṇ tā'shən/,
   /prē'zən tā'shən/

process /pros'əs/, [Brit.]
   /prō'səs/

pronunciation
   /prə nun'sē ā'shən/

quay /kē/

ratio /rā'shē ō/, /rā'shō/

real /rēl/, /rē'əl/

reel /rēl/

research /ri sėrch'/,
   /rē'sėrch/

rodeo /rō'dē ō/, /rō dā'ō/

rotogravure /rō'tə grə vyùr'/,
   /rō'tə grā'vyər/

route /rüt/, /rout/

sociology /sō'sē ol'ə jē/,
   /sō'shē ol'ə jē/

strictly /strikt'li/ also /strik'li/

sumac /sü'mak/, /shü'mak/

the /ᴛнə/, /ᴛнi/; [stressed] /ᴛнē/

tomato /tə mā'tō/, /tə mä'tō/

usage /ūs'ij/, /ūz'ij/

vaudeville /vô'də vil/,
   /vōd'vil/

white /hwīt/

worsted (yarn) /wùs'tid/

(References: Kenyon and Knott; J. S. Kenyon, *American Pronunciation,* Ann Arbor, 1950; C. K. Thomas, *Phonetics of American English,* New York, 1958; *Webster's Third New International Dictionary,* especially the "Guide to Pronunciation.")

Proofreading • A check of copy is the last act before giving a manuscript to anyone for serious consideration. Proofreading the final copy of a paper for mechanical mistakes that may have slipped into the last draft is an important part of the work in a composition course—and one that pays dividends far beyond the mental effort required.

After copy has been set in type it must be checked for typographical and other mistakes before it is ready to be printed. A tentative print is made on long sheets known as *galley proof.* After the type has been corrected and made up into the pages which are to be finally printed, *page proofs* are taken and read for a last check.

Corrections are indicated in proof by abbreviations and symbols placed at one side of the line to be changed, with a *caret (∧) inserted at the exact point in the line where the change is to be made. Proofreader's marks are illustrated below. See publishers' stylebooks for further details.

Proofreader's Marks

ℒ	Delete	em/	Insert em dash
ℒ	Delete and close up	en/	Insert en dash
ℓ	Reverse	⊙	Insert semicolon
⌒	Close up	⊙	Insert colon and en quad
#	Insert space	⊙	Insert period and en quad
⌒/#	Close up and insert space	?/	Insert interrogation point
¶	Paragraph	⊙	Query to author
□	Indent 1 em	⌒	Use ligature
⊏	Move to left	ⓢ	Spell out
⊐	Move to right	tr	Transpose
⊔	Lower	wf	Wrong font
⊓	Raise	bf	Set in **bold face** type
∧	Insert marginal addition	rom	Set in roman type
⋁	Space evenly	ital	Set in *italic* type
✗	Broken letter— used in margin	caps	Set in CAPITALS
↓	Push down space	sc	Set in SMALL CAPITALS
=	Straighten line	lc	Set in lower case
‖	Align type	✗	Lower-case letter
⋀	Insert comma	stet	Let it stand; restore words crossed out
⋁	Insert apostrophe		
⋁	Insert quotation mark	no¶	Run in same paragraph
=/	Insert hyphen	ld in	Insert lead between lines
		hr#	Hair space between letters

From *A Manual of Style*, The University of Chicago Press.

Proper adjectives • Proper nouns used like adjectives and adjectives directly derived from proper names and still referring to the place or person are capitalized. After proper adjectives lose the reference to their origins, they become simple adjectives and are no longer capitalized:

the French language American interests
the Indian service [but *india ink*]
a Paris (or Parisian) café [but *paris green*]
the Roman Forum [but *roman type*]

Practices of capitalizing differ radically for other languages so that students studying foreign languages should be careful to keep the English and foreign practices separated.

Proper names • Considerable care needs to be taken to spell and pronounce the names of people, places, companies, institutions as the people most concerned with them wish to have them spelled and pronounced. Many are rare or in some way unusual—*Thames* /temz/, *Worcester* /wŭs′ter/, *San Joaquin* /san′wô kēn′/. Analogy cannot be relied on: it is *Waco* /wā′kō/, Texas, but *Saco* /sô′kō/, Maine; *Cairo* /kī′rō/ for the Egyptian city, /kā′rō/ or /ke′rō/ for the one in Illinois.

In place names the recommendation to use the pronunciation current in the place is complicated because the inhabitants often do not agree. *Chicago* is /shə kô′gō/, /shə kä′gō/, and /shə ka′gō/, with other minor variants. English has tended to anglicize many foreign place names and even to prefer an alternative name for some: *Paris* /par′is/ instead of /pä rē′/; *Munich* for *München* and *Finland* for *Suomi*.

Many fairly common names occur in various forms: *Burns—Byrnes, Harvey—Hervey, Cohen—Cohn—Kohen, Mac—Mc—M′*, and so on. Special care is needed with names having silent letters or some peculiarity of spelling or phrasing: Pittsburg*h* (but Gettysburg), the John*s* Hopkins University; Pennsylvania State University and the University of Pennsylvania are different institutions.

Dictionaries and encyclopedias give the pronunciation and spelling of the names of the best-known people and places. For foreign names in current news, we can try to follow the national newscasters. They will show some variation, but they usually make an effort to find a reasonable pronunciation. Getting proper names in the right form is courtesy as well as accuracy. It is especially important to do so in all published work.

(For a discussion of capitalizing proper names, see *Capital letters § 2. See also *Course names. References: Allen W. Read, "The Basis of Correctness in the Pronunciation of Place-Names," *American Speech,* 1933, 8:42-46; *Webster's Biographical Dictionary; Webster's Geographical Dictionary;* W. Cabell Greet, *World Words,* New York, 1948; Thomas Lee Crowell, *NBC Handbook of Pronunciation,* 3rd ed., New York, 1964; Kenyon and Knott; recent dictionaries.)

proposition • The use of *proposition* as a business word for *offer, plan, proposal* has made it inappropriate in General usage, though it is common in Informal English. "*I have a proposition for you*" = "*I have a plan....*"

proved—proven • As the past participle of *prove, proved* is much more common than *proven* and is always acceptable (*He had proved . . .*). But *proven* is often used (*It had proven quite satisfactory*), especially where the rhythm is more comfortable with two syllables or in an adjective function (*a proven friend*). (Reference: Bryant, pp. 165-166.)

provided—providing • Both are used as conjunctions: *He should be home soon provided* [or: *providing*] *the buses haven't been held up.* There is some prejudice against *providing* in this use. (See *Divided usage. Reference: Bryant, p. 166.)

Provincialisms • See *Localisms.

psychology, psychiatry • Watch the spelling of these words: *psychiatry* /sɪ kɪ'ə tre/, *psychiatrist* /sɪ kɪ'ə trɪst/, and *psychiatric* /sī'kē at'rik/, *psychology, psychologist, psychoanalyze,* and *psychoanalysis.*

The pronunciation of *psychiatry, psychiatrist* with short *i* in the first syllable is about as frequent as the one given above.

public • *Public* is a *collective noun and takes either a singular or plural construction depending on whether the writer wishes to stress the whole group or the individuals:

The *public is* invited. The *public are* invited.

Consult the libraries and you will find that the ordinary public do not read poetry.—P. B. BALLARD, *Thought and Language,* p. 250

Punctuation, No punctuation •
Revision: Correct the error in punctuation by either inserting appropriate punctuation or deleting confusing or unnecessary punctuation. If the change to be made is not clear to you, consult the Index *article on the particular mark.*

Pn,

No Pn

A discussion of the function and general uses of the punctuation marks, and of differing styles of punctuation ("open" and "close") will be found in Ch. 10.

Details of the uses of the individual marks will be found in the *Index* articles on each:

'	*Apostrophe		,	*Comma
*	*Asterisk		—	*Dash (including the
{ }	*Brace			long dash ——)
[ ]	*Brackets		. . .	*Ellipsis
∧	*Caret		!	*Exclamation mark
:	*Colon		-	*Hyphen

....	*Leaders	" "	*Quotation marks
( )	*Parentheses	;	*Semicolon
.	*Period	——	*Underlining (for
?	*Question mark		italic type)

(See also *Division of words, *Letters, *Restrictive and non-restrictive, *Series, *Whitespace.)

Puns • A *pun* is a *figure of speech in which a word is used in two senses at once (*the nut that holds the wheel* = *automobile driver*) or in which a word is substituted for another of similar sound but different meaning (*hire education*). Reasonable punning, funny or serious, is a healthy use of language. Objection is often made to puns because of their overuse or because they involve sound and not meaning. Good puns are appropriate to Informal usage, usually giving an accent of ironic humor (as in Dorothy Parker's "a girl's best friend is her mutter") or of mild satire:

Ironically, the mansion of American education has many rooms, but the storehouse of many of its basic concepts and categories is the Attic.—WILLIAM RILEY PARKER, *PMLA,* 1964, 79 (No. 4, Pt. 2):7

But the problem of the reign in Spain is anything but plain.— *Time,* May 15, 1964, p. 47

(Compare *Homonyms.)

purist • A *purist* is one who believes in and tries to practice nicety of choice in the use of materials of expression. In language he is likely to fall into a rigid adherence to traditional and often inaccurate "rules." The term is therefore often used disparagingly for a person who wishes everyone to follow the rules of prescriptive grammar (*Grammar § 3) and who tries to hold words to narrower and older meanings. Dictionaries and scientific grammars are descriptive and consequently reflect the actual situation more accurately.

Purpose • Adverbial clauses of purpose are most commonly introduced by *so that*:

He is packing tonight *so that* he can start early in the morning.

That used alone is more Formal, almost archaic; and *in order that* is wordy. Informally *so* is used alone:

He is packing tonight *so* he can start early in the morning.

put in, put over, put across • *Put in* is good Informal usage for *spend* as "put in time." *Put over* as "a plan, a sale," *put across* as "a scheme, an idea" are also Informal.

Q • This letter is unnecessary in the English alphabet. It was brought into English spelling in words borrowed from French, originally derived from Latin (*question, quarter, quit*), and later borrowings directly from Latin added to the number (*quorum, quota*). Some Old English words with the /kw/ sound (spelled *cw*) were respelled with *qu*: *quick* (from *cwic*), *queen* (from *cwen*), *quench* (from *cwencan*).

Q is always followed by *u* in English except in a few foreign place names (*Gulf of Aqaba*). *Qu* is ordinarily pronounced /kw/ (*quite, quill, quadrilateral*), though in a few words the French value /k/ is kept: *coquette* /kō ket′/. Final *-que* is /k/: *antique* /an tēk′/, *unique* /ū nēk′/. The French pronunciation should not be attempted in words that have been anglicized: *Quebec* /kwi bek′/, *questionnaire*.

Question mark (?) •
Revision: Punctuate this sentence as a question.   *Ques*

1. The principal use of the question mark is as the end stop of a direct question:

What was the real reason?

2. A question mark may or may not be used after a request that is phrased as a question, depending on the Formality of the style:

Formal: Will you please return this at your earliest convenience?
General: Will you please return this at your earliest convenience.

(See also *Commands and requests.)

3. A question mark is not used after an indirect question:

He wanted to know what the real reason was.

(See also *Questions § 2.)

4. A question mark is used to show that a statement is approximate or questionable, as with uncertain dates:

Geoffrey Chaucer 1340?-1400 [or] Geoffrey Chaucer 1340 (?) -1400

5. A question mark in parentheses as a mildly sarcastic comment or as a label for would-be witticisms is now out of fashion and is better omitted:

In those days no fashionable (?) woman would think of going to a football game unless she looked like a giant squirrel.

6. When a question mark and quotation mark fall together, the question mark is outside if the quoting sentence is the question, inside if the quotation is the question:

He asked, "Did you really say that?"
Did you really say "I thought you were older than that"?

After a double question only one question mark is used.

Did she ask, "How many are coming?"

(See also *Quotation marks § 4a.)

Questions •

1. In speech, questions are identified by word order, interrogative words, and intonation. The intonation patterns for questions are complex; some questions end with the voice rising, some with it falling. Since in writing, these patterns must all be summed up by the question mark—which does not appear until the end of the sentence—a written question is most easily identified by interrogative words and word order. It may be introduced by an interrogative word:

Pronoun: Who was that? *What* would you do in his place?

Adjective: Which way did he go? *What* book shall I read next?

Adverb: Where shall we eat? *When* will you be coming back? *How much* is that one? *Why* didn't you say so in the first place?

A question may be indicated by inverted word order, the verb coming before its subject. In older English any verb could stand first (*Came* he yesterday?), but now this order is found only with *be, have, shall, will, can, may, must, need,* and *ought* (*Was* he there?) and in Informal, usually spoken, subjectless sentences (*Want* this one?). Ordinarily a phrasal verb is used, with the auxiliary coming before the subject to provide the inversion (*Do you think* he would go if he was asked?). A statement may be turned into a question by an inverted clause at the end (He didn't try, *did he?*).

A direct question that is parenthetically part of another sentence sometimes begins with a capital and sometimes not:

He felt a strong urge—as indeed who doesn't?—to write a really good modern novel.—NOEL COWARD, *To Step Aside,* p. 9

2. An indirect question is a question that is not quoted directly but is made a subordinate member of another sentence. An indirect question is not marked either with a question mark or with quotation marks; the tense of the verb is changed, if necessary, to fit the sentence and often a subordinating conjunction is introduced (*if, *whether):

Direct: "What are our plans for tomorrow?"

Indirect: He asked what our plans for tomorrow were.

Direct: He asked, "Do you really understand what you have read?"

Indirect: He asked us if we really understood what we had read. He always asks us whether we understand what we have read.

3. A "leading question" is one phrased to suggest the answer desired, as *You wouldn't do that, would you?* (contrasted with *Would you do that?*).

4. For the stylistic use of questions, see Ch. 8, "Questions," p. 313, and *Rhetorical questions.

Quotation marks (" ") •
Revision: Make the quotation marks conform to conventional usage.

Quot

1. *Methods of indicating quotations.*

a–Double quotes (" ") are the usual marks. The mark before the quoted matter is the *open-quote*; the one after is the *close-quote.*

b–The use of single quotes (' ') is common in England and is increasing in the United States. The single quotes are as accurate as the double and are much less spotty on the page.

c–For quotations within quotations, double and single quotes are alternated. If you begin with the double marks: " ' . . . ' "; if you begin with the single: ' " . . . " '. If there are quotations within two such quotations, continue to alternate the double and single quotes.

d–Indenting is used to indicate quotations, especially in factual writing involving numerous quotations of some length, as in this book. No quotation marks are used, and in print the size of type is usually reduced. Publishing houses have rules about how long a quotation must be to be reduced and indented—that it should run to at least five lines, for example, or consist of more than one complete sentence. In double spaced typewritten copy, such quotations are usually indented and single spaced; in longhand copy they are indented.

e–When a long quotation which is not indented includes more than one paragraph, the marks are placed at the beginning of each paragraph of the quotation but at the end of only the last paragraph.

2. *Principal uses of quotation marks.*

a–Quotation marks are used to indicate all passages taken from another writer, whether a phrase or a page or more (except when the quotation is indented). The quoted matter may stand by itself or may be worked into the constructions of the writer's own sentence:

The most that could be said for Haig was said by Churchill: he "was unequal to the prodigious scale of events, but no one else was discerned as his equal or better." (Lloyd George, more succinctly, said he was "brilliant to the top of his army boots.")—GEOFFREY BARRACLOUGH, *The New York Review of Books,* May 14, 1964, p. 3

When speeches or a short conversation are not given for their own sake but to illustrate a point, they are usually put in the body of the paragraph:

Do these instances of the beginnings of new words give us any hints in the search for those new words for which every passing month shows the urgent need? I think they do. First, simplicity and euphony—though not simplicity at all costs. Many years ago, I was chaffing an old friend about the deficiency of his native Welsh. "It's very lacking in the most ordinary scientific terms," I remarked. "For example?" "Well, what's the Welsh for *galvanometer?*" I asked. "And if it comes to that, what's the English for it?" A very proper rejoinder which, correctly interpreted, means that *gas* is preferable to *aeriform fluid,* and *drop-counter* to *stalagmometer.* All within reason, of course: does it follow, for example, that *foreword* is better than *preface?*—ALLAN FERGUSON, "The Scientist's Need for New Words," *The Listener,* Apr. 21, 1937

b—There are no half quotes. A sentence is either an exact quotation in quotation marks, or else it isn't and so is not quoted. A speech summarized or quoted indirectly is not marked:

Direct quotation: The manager told me, "I work harder in one day keeping the girls busy than they work all week."

Indirect quotation: The manager told me that he worked harder in one day keeping the girls busy than they worked all week. [Not: *The manager told me "That he worked harder in one day keeping the girls busy than they worked all week."*]

c—Some writers of fiction do not use quotation marks in the dialog of their stories, but the practice is not common, and omitting the marks is somewhat confusing. (See Ch. 5, p. 170 for their use in dialog.)

3. *Miscellaneous uses of quotation marks.*

a—Many magazines use quotes around titles of books and periodicals, for which Formal writing uses italics:

We come upon passages that contain, all unknowing, whole futures in Nabakovian art. On one page we discover an episode that is destined to expand into a component of "Speak, Memory," on another we greet an infant revolver that will commit major execution in "Lolita," and on another we discern a suggestion of the scheme for "Pale Fire."—DONALD MALCOLM, *The New Yorker,* Apr. 25, 1964, p. 198

In academic style, which uses italics for titles of books and the names of periodicals, quotes are used for titles of written works shorter than volume length, for single poems, short stories, magazine articles, and ordinarily for chapter titles. (See Ch. 11, "Form of bibliographical entries," p. 428; *Titles of articles, books, etc. See also *Ships' names § 3.)

b—In Formal writing words that are used as words—as often in this book—rather than for their meaning are put in italics (underlined in manuscript); in General writing they would often be put in quotes:

"Capitalism" is thus a shape, a form, which speaks, commands, fights, runs away. Asked to define it, the debater on the left introduces more abstractions: "Absentee ownership," "surplus value," "class struggle," "private ownership of the means of production," "exploitation of the masses," "imperialism," "vested interests," "proletariat," "bourgeoisie," the "profit system," and many more. The great words roll.—STUART CHASE, *The Tyranny of Words*, p. 275

c–In Formal writing a word from a conspicuously different variety of speech may be put in quotation marks, but this practice is less common than formerly. In General writing there is less need for these apologetic quotes, because there is greater latitude in choice of words. If the word is appropriate, use it without apology, and if it isn't appropriate, don't use it.

Everybody told Bib what a sucker [not "sucker"] he was, but he still had confidence in the designer of the plane.

After the Yale man had said his piece, the Dartmouth frosh started to blow his horn again. [The question here is whether *said his piece, frosh,* and *blow his horn* are appropriate in the context of the paper; if they are not, quotes will not make them so or rescue the sentence.]

Common figures of speech do not need to be quoted:

After just one chorus, the trio settled to its work and was soon in orbit. [Not "in orbit"]

d–A word may be put in quotation marks to show that the writer refuses to accept its conventional sense in the context in which he has used it:

In numerous cases it is impossible to maintain on any solid grounds that one pronunciation given is "better" than another, as, for example, that one pronunciation of *swamp* is better than the others given; . . .—JOHN S. KENYON and THOMAS A. KNOTT, *A Pronouncing Dictionary of American English*, p. xxvii

e–Practice differs in writing single words that are spoken or thought:

Stephen said "Yes," so we went to work at once.
Stephen said *yes,* so we went to work at once.
Stephen said Yes, so we went to work at once.

Probably the first form is the most common.
4. *Quotation marks and other marks.*

a–When a question mark or an exclamation mark ends a quotation, it is placed inside the quotes:

"Don't go near that wire!" he shouted.
Then in a calm voice she asked, "Why didn't you say so before?"

When a question mark or exclamation mark belongs to a sentence that includes a quotation, it is placed after the quotes:

What kind of work can a man put into "the cheapest building that will last fifteen years"?—Lewis Mumford, *Sticks and Stones,* p. 172

b–Most American publishers put commas and periods inside the close-quotes, whether they belong with the quotation or not, because the quotes help fill the small spot of white that would be left if the comma or period came outside. Some writers follow the conventions that apply to the exclamation and question marks, putting comma or period inside the quotes if it belongs with the quotation, outside if it belongs with the quoting sentence, but this usage is much less common.

Semicolons usually stand after the quotation mark.

c–Introductory words and stage directions are set off by a comma, or by two commas if they interrupt the quotation:

Robert said, "I should think that by now you would have learned that."

"History," it has been said, "does not repeat itself. The historians repeat one another."—Max Beerbohm, *Works,* p. 43

(Note that *does* is not capitalized after the interruption because it does not begin a sentence.)

When quoted phrases are closely built into the construction of a sentence, they are not set off by commas:

I hurried past the zero case with its cream molds, just barely saying "Hi!" to Danny and the girls behind it.

"I give him the book" has two equally correct passives: "He is given the book" and "The book is given to him."—E. H. Sturtevant, *Linguistic Change,* p. 138

A Formal introduction to a quotation is usually followed by a colon, as in the statements introducing the examples in this article.

5. *Indicating quotations in foreign languages.* The methods of indicating quotations are different for other languages. If you have occasion to quote a passage in another language which includes a quotation, you should consult a stylebook.

R • /r/ as in *ready, arch, arrears, car.*

The pronunciation of spelled *r* varies more from region to region than does that for any other consonant symbol—from a tongue trill in Scotland to replacement by *schwa (door* as

/dōə/) or even omission in much British as well as Eastern and Southern American speech.

The pronunciation of *r* also varies according to its position in a word. It is strongest, in all regions, before a vowel: *real, rob, cheering, fairy.* Before a consonant sound it varies, as from /bäk/ to /bärk/ for *bark.* Final *r* is most apparent in Western pronunciation, less conspicuous in the pronunciations of New England, the South, and metropolitan New York.

In Eastern and Southern speech *r* after a vowel often becomes /ə/ or disappears entirely (*farther,* /fä′тнə/), except when the *r* is final and comes before a word starting with a vowel (*far away,* /fär′ ə wä′/). In areas where *r* is treated in this way, many speakers intrude an /r/ between a word ending with a vowel and one beginning with a vowel (The idea-*r* is good). In the rest of the country *r* after a vowel is altered to a special vowel which is, however, interpreted by the hearer as /r/.

In this *Guide and Index* the /r/ symbol as an indication of pronunciation is to be interpreted to mean the sort of /r/ sound the speaker is used to making. (For further details on the varieties of *r* in American pronunciation see Kenyon and Knott §§ 26, 82-85.)

racket • The spelling *racquet* is British. Write *tennis racket.*

Racket in the sense of an illegitimate way of making money, usually involving threats of violence, has made its way from slang into the General language. When used to mean a business or a particular way of making money (the baseball racket, the lumber racket), it is Informal unless used to imply illegitimate means.

raise—rear • *Rear* is now a Formal verb in the sense of *rearing* a child or of being *reared.* *Bring up in this sense is current in all varieties of usage. *Raised* is General usage: *I was born and raised in Kentucky.* (Reference: Bryant, pp. 168-169.)

rarely • *Rarely* means "seldom" (or in archaic and Formal English, "with rare skill," as "a rarely carved panel").

Rarely ever (I rarely ever go), probably a telescoping of *rarely if ever,* is an established spoken idiom. (Reference: Bryant, p. 169.)

re- • The prefix *re-,* meaning "again," is hyphened when the form with hyphen can have a different meaning from the form without:

   reform, to change, improve—*re-form,* to shape again
   recover, to regain—*re-cover,* to cover again

and (rarely) for emphasis, as in *now re-seated in fair comfort,* or in Informal or humorous compounds: *re-re-married.* In other cases, there is no hyphen: *rearrange, reexamine, refine, remit.*

-re, -er • See *-er, -re.

reaction • *Reaction* has escaped from chemistry and the biological sciences to become a General word for any response of feeling or idea:

> Let me have your reaction to [Often: *on*] this.
> She reacted violently when he appeared.

Because it is used so loosely, it has tended to crowd out more appropriate or more exact words; careful users of the language therefore often avoid it.

Reading and writing • We read for entertainment and for instruction; inclination leads us to the first, and either inclination or necessity to the second. Besides these fundamental motives for reading, anyone interested in writing has another—reading to set a goal for his own writing. This does not mean conscious imitation of *Time* or *The New Yorker* or Walter Lippmann, Ernest Hemingway, or E. B. White. Rather it means reading with attention and occasional analysis the writers who genuinely appeal to us and allowing their work to influence ours casually and naturally.

This sort of reading influence is especially necessary in college because a student must read so much in textbooks and reference books and in the literature of earlier periods. Textbooks provide information, and the earlier literature is a necessary and valuable part of education; but the former, unfortunately, are seldom appealing, and the latter may cause the reader to lose touch with the idiom of his own time. If you are interested in writing well, you should supplement this college reading by reading as widely as you can in the better current magazines and books, fiction and nonfiction. The material you read is likely to be better than what you write, and a good background for judging your own work can come from a sensitive and critical reading of the somewhat similar work of the more important writers of your own time. The biographies of writers show that most of them probably formed their styles to a considerable extent on what they read. Though extensive reading cannot in itself make a good writer, it is the most valuable single formative influence.

In college you also have a chance to hear a great variety of spoken English, some of it well worth listening to. Although it would be a mistake to assume that good written styles are mere transcriptions of good speech, a written English which has an echo of the spoken in it is likely to be lively and interesting. Among your classmates there will be a few who talk especially well. And among your teachers there will be some who use language with remarkable skill. You will soon learn who the good talkers are; make a practice of listening to them as receptively as you can. Attentive listening is necessary in the college classroom, and if the teacher is a good talker, you will unconsciously absorb a good deal that will improve your written English. (See *Spoken and written English.)

real—really • *Real* is used as an adjective in Formal and General English: *a real experience, a real chore. Really* is the adverb: *a really successful party; It really went off well.*

In Nonstandard English and Informal conversation, *real* is often used adverbially: *Write real soon. It's real pretty. It went off real well.* This use is inappropriate in writing except to report conversation. (References: Pooley, pp. 161-163; Bryant, pp. 169-170.)

realtor • This business coinage has an advantage not possessed by most of its class, since it is much more economical than *real estate agent.* The National Association of Real Estate Boards contends that only a member of that group may call himself a *realtor.* Pronounced /rē'əl tər/.

rear—raise • See *raise—rear, *bring up.

reason is because • In Formal English the construction beginning "The reason is" is usually completed by a noun or a noun clause to balance the noun *reason*:

The reason for my poor work in French was [noun:] my intense dislike of the subject.

The reason for my poor work in French was [noun clause:] that I disliked the subject intensely.

Since in speech not many noun clauses are introduced by *that,* and *because* is the connective that most obviously stresses the notion of cause, in spoken English we usually find:

The reason for my poor work in French was because I didn't like the subject.

The reason is because is also frequently found in writing:

In general it may be said that the reason why scholasticism was held to be an obstacle to truth was because it seemed to discourage further enquiry along experimental lines.—BASIL WILLEY, *The Seventeenth Century Background*, p. 7

Bryant writes: "*Reason ... is because* occurs in standard usage. In formal English *reason is that* occurs somewhat more frequently, but *reason ... is because* is a variant, which occurs more often in speech than in writing." (p. 170)

Because of widespread prejudice against the construction, students should usually follow Formal usage. (References: Pooley, pp. 134-135, and *College English,* 1956, 18:110-111; F. N. Cherry, "Some Evidence in the Case of 'is because,'" *American Speech,* 1933, 8:55-60.)

recipe—receipt • /res'ə pē—ri sēt'/ Both words have meant "a formula, directions for making something." *Recipe* is now the more common in General English, though occasionally one or the other may be preferred by cooks, and then they are interchangeable in meaning. *Receipt* also means "a written acknowledgment for something received."

Reciprocal pronouns • See *each other, *Pronouns, types and forms § 5.

reckon, guess, calculate. See *calculate, guess, reckon.

Redundancy • See *Deadwood, *Repetition, *Wordiness.

Reference of pronouns •

Ref
> *Revision: Change the pronoun marked (or revise the sentence) so that its reference will be exact and obvious and the pronoun itself will be in the conventional form.*

The syntax of a personal, relative, or demonstrative pronoun, as well as its complete meaning, often depends in part on its relation (or reference) to a previous noun in a passage, called its *antecedent*. This fact makes the accurate use of pronouns more complicated than the use of other words. Five of the personal pronouns and one of the relative pronouns—*who* —are further complicated by having a separate accusative form, as English nouns no longer do. There are some differences between speech and writing in the forms and references of pronouns, differences which become apparent when spoken practice is carried over into writing because when we read we can reexamine the phrasing at our leisure, something we cannot do when we listen. Therefore the conventions of pronoun usage as found in print should be followed in writing. A writer needs to check his pronouns in revising a paper to make sure that they are appropriate in form and in reference. Since a college student almost always knows the form that is appropriate in a given sentence, the choice of pronouns is simply a matter of care. This article runs over the main points in the use of pronouns in Standard written English.

1. *Exact and clear reference.*

a–If the meaning of a pronoun is completed by reference to a particular noun, the reference to this antecedent should be exact and obvious, as in the following examples:

The first hundred miles, *which* we covered before lunch, were rough, but *they* seemed to go faster than the sixty we did in the afternoon. [The noun *miles* is the antecedent of *which* and of *they*.]

All purchases for the University pass through a central purchasing office. *These* include books, trucks, building materials, food, and hundreds of other items. [*These* refers to *purchases*.]

Swimming may be more fun than calisthenics, but *it* can't give such a general development. [*It* refers to *swimming*.]

On July 3 Mr. Havermeyer asked Mr. Page to come to *his* house. [*His* refers to *Mr. Havermeyer*. Although another name has been mentioned, only a perverse reader would fail to understand the statement. *The former's* instead of *his* would be pedantic here.]

Professor Frank thought that McKinly was grateful to *him* for allowing *him* to graduate. [Actually no ambiguity is possible here and the sentence would be all right in speech and General writing.]

Confusion may arise when the pronoun seems to refer to a nearby noun to which it cannot sensibly refer or when there is no noun nearby; when it refers to a noun used subordinately in the preceding construction, perhaps to one used as a possessive or as an adjective; and when two or more pronouns are crossed so that the exact reference isn't readily clear. Usually to improve such a reference, the sentence must be revised, as in the following examples:

He isn't married and doesn't plan on *it*. [... and doesn't *plan to marry*.]

The next year he had an attack of acute appendicitis. *It* broke before the doctors had a chance to operate. [*It* cannot refer to *appendicitis* in the statement made. The second sentence should begin *His appendix broke*. Slips in reference are common when the pronoun refers back to a noun in the preceding sentence.]

A legislator should be a man who knows a little about law and government and he should know how to apply *them* to the best interests of his people. [For *them* put *his knowledge*.]

Bill provided more excitement one afternoon when he was skipping rocks across the swimming hole and cut open *a young girl's head who* was swimming under water. [... and cut open *the head of a young girl who* was swimming under water.]

To many of us the word *geology* means little in our everyday lives. Yet *it* deals with materials in use for making our homes and factories, metals of which our cars are made, and the fuel which enables us to drive them. [*It* should refer to *geology*—the science—not to *the word*. To revise, drop *the word* and remove the italics from *geology*.]

Businessmen without regard for anyone else have exploited the mass of workers at every point, not caring whether *they* were earning a decent living wage, but only whether *they* were getting a lot of money. [The first *they* refers to *workers,* the second to *businessmen.* The sentence needs complete rewriting, but the second part could be improved somewhat by saying: . . . *not caring whether they paid a decent living wage, but only whether they were getting a lot of money.*]

Remember that clear reference is a matter of *meaning,* not just of the presence or position of certain words.

b—General English uses *which, that, this,* and sometimes *it* to refer to the idea of a previous clause. Formal usage tends to avoid this type of reference or to limit it to *this.*

General: Her friend was jealous of her clothes and money and had taken this way of showing it. [*It* refers to the idea in *was jealous.*]

Formal: Her friend was jealous of her clothes and money and had taken this way of showing her feeling.

General: He never seemed to realize when academic tempests were brewing, which was probably a good thing.—J. R. PARKER, *Academic Procession,* p. 86 [*Which* refers to the idea of the first clause.]

Formal: He never seemed to realize when academic tempests were brewing. This was probably a good thing.

General: From his firm grip, piercing eyes, and stern mouth I could see that he was not to be trifled with, which was well proved later. [*Which* refers to the *that*-clause.]

Formal: From his firm grip, piercing eyes, and stern mouth I could see that he was not to be trifled with. This was well proved later.

c—In conversation the reference of pronouns is freer than in writing. The following examples, which would probably pass unnoticed in a conversation, show one reason why, in written work, we sometimes find pronouns that seem inexact. Your written work should be read with a cold eye to find and correct inexact pronoun reference.

Spoken	*Written*
Gordon's mother asked me to take him fishing because he was so interested in *it* but had never caught *one.*	Gordon's mother asked me to take him fishing because he was so interested in *it* but had never caught a *fish.*
Everyone likes to dance and knew they would get plenty of *it* during the party weekend.	Everyone likes to dance and knew he would get plenty of *dancing* during the party weekend.
In aquaplaning the ropes	The ropes should never be

should never be wound around the wrists, because if thrown *he* would be dragged along and injured.

wound around *the planer's* wrists, because if thrown *he* would be dragged along and injured.

2. *Agreement of pronoun with antecedent.* Pronouns referring to specific antecedents generally agree with the antecedents in number, gender, and person.

a–Agreement in number. A pronoun agrees with its antecedent in number: singular antecedent, singular pronoun; plural antecedent, plural pronoun.

Singular: *Jimmy* tried to go quietly, but *he* couldn't keep from whistling.

Plural: The boys had tried to go quietly, but *they* couldn't keep from whistling.

In Formal American English, *each, every, everyone* are generally referred to by singular pronouns (see *every and its compounds § 1):

Almost *everyone* has some little superstitions which *he* would not violate for love or money.

In spoken English these words are treated as collectives and are found usually with a plural pronoun:

Almost *everyone* has some little superstitions which *they* would not violate for love or money.

Maugham takes *anyone* from a gigolo to a lord and develops *them* [Formal: *him*] with equal ease and finesse.

This colloquial agreement is sometimes found in print, but editors usually bring it in line with Formal usage before publication. (Reference: Russell Thomas, "Concord Based on *Meaning* versus Concord Based on *Form*: The Indefinites," *College English,* 1939, 1:38-45.)

A *collective noun is referred to by either a singular or a plural pronoun, depending upon its meaning in the sentence:

Singular: When a *gang* of rabbit hunters spreads out over a field, *it* doesn't lose any time.

Plural: When a *gang* of rabbit hunters spread out over a field, *they* don't lose any time.

Often when a pronoun does not agree with its antecedent, the antecedent should be changed rather than the pronoun:

Putting himself in the shoes of the *slave owner,* Lincoln realized that *they* had a right to feel as they did toward emancipation. [This could be made consistent by making *slave owner* plural better than by changing *they* to *he*.]

Labor's third and major contention is that *they* do not receive an adequate return for the services they render. [Here changing *Labor's* to *The workers'* would be more accurate than changing the pronouns to the singular.]

b–Agreement in person. Except in indefinite pronouns (§ 3 of this article), there is little difficulty with agreement:

First person: *I* wish Mr. Patterson had told *me* before.
Second person: *You* should have thought of that *yourself*.
Third person: *The woman* had said *she* was over twenty-one.

A relative pronoun agrees with its antecedent:

I, *who* am your nearest relative, would help you. [Because of the unusualness of the *who am*, it would not ordinarily be said or written: *I, your nearest relative*....]

He is one of those *people who* do just what *they* want to. [*They* refers to *who*, which refers to *people*.]

c–Form of pronouns. The form of a pronoun depends upon the construction in which it stands, not upon its antecedent. The form of a pronoun does not necessarily show its function; see the discussion of *Case and the articles there referred to (*between you and me; *It's me; *who, whom).

3. *Indefinite reference.* Often pronouns are used to refer to the readers or to people in general instead of to specifically mentioned people. English has no well-established pronoun like the German *man* or the French *on* to refer to a person in general. Our *one* has a definitely Formal and stiffish connotation. *We* and *you* seem to be slightly more personal, more expressive, and are very generally used, as in many pages in this book. This is a question of style rather than of grammar, and whether *you* or *they* (They say ...) or *we* or *one* or *people* or some other noun is used depends on its fitness in the passage.

Care should be taken to keep indefinite pronouns consistent, not shifting from *one* to *you*, for example:

When *you* have worked a day here *you* have really earned your money.

[*Or*:] When *one* has worked a day here *he* has really earned ....

[*Not*:] When *one* has worked a day here *you* have really ....

An indefinite pronoun should not be substituted for a definite personal pronoun:

For *me* there is no fun in reading unless *I* can put myself in the position of the characters and feel that *I* am really in the scene. [Not: For *me* there is no fun in reading unless *you* can put yourself in the position of the characters and feel that *you* are really in the scene.]

The indefinite pronouns (*all, any, each, everybody, few, nobody,* and so on—*Pronouns, types and forms § 8) have no expressed antecedent, so that their use involves consistency but not agreement with an antecedent.

Since English has no single pronoun to mean he-or-she, the masculine *he* is conventionally used (see *he-or-she):

The time comes to every senior when *he* [Not: *he or she*] anxiously looks forward to that eventful day.

The best way out of the difficulty is to use the plural:

The time comes to all seniors when they. . . .

4. *Avoiding pronouns.* Pronouns are necessary and convenient, but since they sometimes lead to inconsistent uses (that are marked by teachers and editors), some writers tend to avoid them, using a noun instead. The result is usually unidiomatic or clumsy English:

That's the reason I hesitate to picture the owner of *a grip* from the appearance of *the bag*. [Better: That's the reason I hesitate to picture the owner of *the bag* from *its* appearance.]

Arrest of *the woman* yesterday followed several days of observation of *the woman's* [Better: *her*] activities by agents of the Stores Mutual Protective Association.

Pronouns are especially useful to bind together clauses and sentences. In the following paragraph each sentence seems to be a new beginning, but with pronouns instead of *Mr. Frothingham,* the paragraph would read more smoothly:

Roland W. Frothingham died at his home on Commonwealth Avenue on Tuesday. Mr. Frothingham [He] was born in Boston in 1868 and had lived here ever since. Mr. Frothingham's [His] ancestors came from Ipswich. Mr. Frothingham [He] was educated at Harvard College.

5. *Omission of pronouns.* In Informal writing and in conversation, pronouns, especially *I,* are often omitted (see *I § 3; Ch. 8, "Minor sentence types," p. 284), and in all varieties of English the relative pronoun is often not used in relative clauses (see *Contact clauses): *The first man (that) I met had never heard of such a street.*

(For the classes and forms of pronouns, see *Pronouns, types and forms; for further instances of their use, see the articles on particular pronouns, *I, *we, *who, whom, *himself, herself, *myself. See also Ch. 9, "Checking pronouns," p. 336. References: All grammars treat the use of pronouns. Curme and Jespersen discuss many special uses.)

References in scientific papers • Research papers in the sciences use a system of reference to sources quite different from the system of the humanities and social sciences described in Ch. 11. The references have the same purpose—giving the author, title, and facts of publication of articles and books used, to acknowledge the source of material and to make it possible for a reader to go directly to a source if he wishes further information. The details of form vary considerably among the different scientific and technical fields and often among the books and journals within a field. If you are writing a paper on a scientific or technical subject, you will have to select among the systems given in this article (or follow your instructor's specification of which to use) or study the form of a particular journal and follow its practice. Many of these journals publish stylesheets: the *Manual for Authors* of the American Mathematical Society, for example.

1. *General points.*

a–A few scientific journals give references to sources in footnotes at the bottom of a page, but most of them, and most scientific books, use footnotes only for explanatory comments or for additional facts, as in this one from *Annual Review of Physical Chemistry* (Palo Alto, 1963), p. 145:

[3a]The lowest temperature at which super-conducting transition has been found, $0.016°K$, was reported for a $Nb_{.30}Mo_{.70}$ alloy at the St. Louis meeting of the American Physical Society (1963) by R. Blaugher, R. A. Hein, and J. W. Gibson at a post deadline paper.

Such footnotes are kept few and brief.

b–The reference to a source is usually given in parentheses in the text, immediately following the writer's name or following the relevant statement, as illustrated in § 2 and 3.

c–The references and the bibliographical entries are made as economical as possible:

Arabic numerals rather than Roman are used for volumes: 24:62-63. Sometimes the volume number is printed in boldface type (**24**:62-63), indicated in manuscript by a wavy line under the figures, or in italic type (*24*:62-63), indicated by one line under the figures; but most often they are in ordinary type.

Sometimes authors' names in a bibliography are printed in capitals and small capitals: BROWNE, C. A. (Small capitals are indicated by two lines under the letters in manuscript.) But most often they are in ordinary type.

In titles usually only the first word and proper names are capitalized, and the titles of articles are not put in quotation marks. Usually the titles of periodicals or other series (bulletins, monographs) are in italics (underlined in manuscript).

Prepositions are often omitted in the titles of periodicals: *J. Nutrition, Jour. Forestry* (for *Journal of Nutrition, Journal of Forestry*).

The names of journals and other series of publications are usually abbreviated. Some common abbreviations are:

Bull.	Bulletin	Mon.	Monograph (s)
J. (Jour.)	Journal	Proc.	Proceedings

Pub.	Publication (s)	Sci.	Science
Rev.	Review	ser.	series

Abbreviations are given for commonly used words, like Am. (American), Assoc. (Association), Soc. (Society), and the names of fields (Biol., Geol.), and of well-known organizations, like IRE (Institute of Radio Engineers). The Latin abbreviation *et al.* (*et alii,* "and others") is used when a work has more than two authors, and *op. cit.* (*opere citato,* "in the work cited") occasionally for later references to a work.

d–In some systems the title of a periodical article is not given:

Mermin, N. D., *Ann. Phys.* (N.Y.) , **81,** 421 (1962).

e–When the reference is to the general method described in a relatively short article or to the general conclusion of a work, specific pages are not given.

f–Little direct quotation is used, but when it is, the source is given between the closing quotation marks and the period ending the sentence:

. . . although it might be added that "the oldest unit of the Detroit River group, the Sylvania sandstone, is succeeded respectively by the Amherstburg dolomite, the Lucas dolomite, and the Anderson Limestone" (Ehlers, 1950, p. 1455) .

g–Since dates are especially important in scientific work—a scientist presumably is familiar with previous work on his subject and builds upon it—they are usually given prominence by being given first or last in the facts of publication of the bibliography and are used as a key item in the reference system described in § 3.

h–Acknowledgment of special assistance of individuals is made either in a footnote early in the article or under a heading *Acknowledgments* just before the bibliography.

i–The bibliography at the end of an article may be headed *References* or *Literature cited,* but most often *Bibliography.*

j–In general, then, the source material used in a scientific paper is indicated by the combined reference in parentheses in the text and an entry in the bibliography. The two most common systems are given in § 2 and 3. Use one of these unless you have reason to use some of the variations indicated.

2. *References by bibliography numbers.* In this system the items of the bibliography are arranged alphabetically by author (the rare unsigned item usually under *Anonymous*) and then numbered from 1 up. The parenthetical references in the text are to these numbers in the bibliography.

Here are some sentences from an article (Robert A. Gardner and John L. Retzer, "Interpretive Soil Classification: Timber,

Range, and Watersheds," *Soil Science,* 1949, 67:151-157), with the reference numbers in parentheses. The sentences occurred in the order in which they stand, though not consecutively.

Kittredge (9) pointed out the advantages that natural forest areas offer to the study of soils, long undisturbed, in relation to forest type —advantages that cultivated soil areas cannot offer.

Veatch (15) has made extensive use of soil-forest relations in approximating areas and kinds of original forest cover in Michigan, and Roe (12) has grouped soil types of the originally forested part of the lake states. . . .

The more important relatively permanent criteria of use in the natural classification of forest soils listed by Lutz and Chandler (10) are also of importance in crop production.

The nutritive value of pasture forage as related to soils has received considerable study (1, 11) , but in the main the nutritive value of range forage as related to soils is an almost untouched field (3) .

The bibliography entries referred to in these sentences are given at the end of the article as follows:

(1) Browne, C. A. 1938 Some relationships of soil to plant and animal nutrition—the major elements. *U.S. Dept. Agr. Yearbook* 1938: 777-806.

(3) Cardon, P. V., *et al.* 1939 Pasture and range in livestock feeding. *U.S. Dept. Agr. Yearbook* 1939: 925-955.

(9) Kittredge, J., Jr. 1928 The use of soil surveys in forestry. *First Internatl. Cong. Soil Sci. Proc. and Papers* (1927) 4 (Comn. V) : 562-565.

(10) Lutz, H. J., and Chandler, R. F., Jr. 1946 *Forest Soils.* John Wiley and Sons, Inc., New York.

(11) McMurtrey, J. E., Jr., and Robinson, W. O. 1938 Neglected soil constituents that affect plant and animal development. *U.S. Dept. Agr. Yearbook* 1938: 807-829.

(12) Roe, E. I. 1935 Forest soils—the basis of forest management. Lake States Forest Exp. Sta., Processed Rpt.

(15) Veatch, J. O. 1932 Soil maps as a basis for mapping original forest cover. *Papers Mich. Acad. Sci., Arts and Letters* (1931) 15: 267-273.

This bibliography does not use capitals or quotation marks in article titles. The year is given before the title. Only inclusive pages (for the whole item referred to) are given. This would handicap a reader who wanted to refer to the source, especially for entry 10, which is a whole book. Usually in references of this type the pages directly involved in the statement are given in the parenthetical references:

. . . in the natural classification of forest soils listed by Lutz and Chandler (10, pp. 262-266) . . . .

A variation of the numbered bibliography system is listing the sources in the bibliography in the order in which they are referred to in the text—1 for the first mentioned source, 2 for the second, and so on. This works well for quite short bibliographies but becomes a nuisance if there are many items. In this system the pages referred to are usually made part of the bibliography entry rather than being put in parentheses.

3. *Reference by author and date.* Perhaps the most widely used system gives the author and date of publication. The items of the bibliography are arranged alphabetically by author. The reference is in parentheses in the text and includes author, date of the publication, and pages when the source to be indicated is only a part of the item.

These examples are from Floyd H. Allport, *Theories of Perception and the Concept of Structure,* New York, John Wiley & Sons, 1955.

In this first example, the full data (in parentheses) stands at the end of a paragraph:

The term meaning has been further extended to apply to the experience of *insight* into one's behavior; for behavior with insight is an evidence of the existence of some manifest ego-field organization. (Koffka, 1935, pp. 175-176, 382.)

If the author's name is given in the sentence, as it frequently is, only the date and page (or chapter of a book) are given in the parentheses. If the reference is to the whole work, only the date is needed:

Hebb has presented his own account of insight and the "meaning of meaning" (1949, pp. 126-134).

The case for perceptual and cognitive learning has also been well stated by Hilgard (1948, Chapter 12).

We recall the experiment performed by Stratton (1897) and Ewert (1930).

If there is more than one item by the same writer, they are identified by the years of publication, and if there is more than one by the same writer in the same year, each is given a letter in addition to the date:

The first type, the associationistic, or S-R, theories are best represented by Hull's objective theory of behavior (1943b, 1951, 1952).

If the item specifically referred to is included in another work, the reference is to the latter (in the bibliography McCleary and Lazarus is not listed):

This proposition, the most challenging of all the directive-state hypotheses, was tested in its various parts by McGinnies (1949) and by McCleary and Lazarus (see Bruner and Krech, eds., 1950, pp. 171-179).

The bibliography of Allport's book is very extensive. The works referred to in the quotations just given are entered as:

Bruner, J. S., and D. Krech. 1950. *Perception and personality: a symposium.* Durham: Duke Univ. Press.

Ewert, P. H. 1930. A study of the effect of inverted retinal stimulation upon spatially coordinated behavior. *Genet. Psychol. Monogr., 7,* Nos. 3 and 4.

Hebb, D. O. 1949. *The organization of behavior.* New York: Wiley.

Hilgard, E. R. 1948. *Theories of learning.* New York: Appleton-Century-Crofts.

Hull, C. L. 1943*a*. The problem of intervening variables in molar behavior theory. *Psychol. Rev., 50,* 273-291.

Hull, C. L. 1943*b*. *Principles of behavior: an introduction to behavior theory.* New York: Appleton-Century-Crofts.

Hull, C. L. 1951. *Essentials of behavior.* New Haven: Yale Univ. Press.

Hull, C. L. 1952. *A behavior system: an introduction to behavior theory concerning the individual organism.* New Haven: Yale Univ. Press.

Koffka, W. 1935. *Principles of gestalt psychology.* New York: Harcourt.

McGinnies, E. 1949. Emotionality and perceptual defense. *Psychol. Rev., 56,* 244-251.

Stratton, G. M. 1897. Vision without inversion of the retinal image. *Psychol. Rev., 4,* 341-360; 463-481.

This bibliography shows one of the standard systems of capitalizing and of punctuating entries, with the period the usual mark between elements except that commas are used within the parts of a periodical reference.

Familiarity with the practices of their scientific field is useful for majors in the scientific and technical departments, both for reading material in the field and for writing papers in advanced courses.

Referent • The term, pronounced /ref′ər ənt/, is used in semantics for what a word refers to. The referent of *book* is either a particular book being discussed or a generalized notion based on our observation of various books. (For discussion see Ch. 9, "The nature of meaning," p. 369.)

Reflexive pronouns • See *myself, *Pronouns, types and forms § 4.

regard, regards • Standard English uses the prepositional phrase *in regard to*; Nonstandard often uses *in regards to*. (Reference: Bryant, p. 115.)

regardless • *-less* is a negative ending and makes the word mean "without regard to"; prefixing an *ir-* (**irregardless*) doubles the negative and makes a word which is as yet unacceptable in writing, though common in speech. (See **Long variants.*)

Relative adverbs • The group of connecting words which may be called *relative adverbs*—though they also have other functions—includes *as, after, before, that, since, until, when, whenever, where, wherever.* (For some examples of their use see **Relative clauses.*)

Relative clauses • Because these clauses are usually introduced by a **relative pronoun* (*that, which, who,* etc.) or a **relative adverb* (*where, when, why,* etc.) without a connective (see the last adjective example below and **Contact clauses*), they usually function like adjectives and are often called adjective clauses; but they may also function as nouns and adverbs in a sentence:

Adjective function:

The rain *that began in the morning* kept on all night.

The coach was now abused by the alumni *who two years before had worshiped him.*

The road to the left, *which looked almost impassable,* was ours.

The first place *where they camped* turned out to be impossible.

The man *I met that afternoon* has been my friend ever since. [Formal: The man *whom* I met. . . .]

The ideas *we held in common* were few indeed. [Formal: The ideas *that* we held . . . .]

Noun function:

Whoever says so is a liar.

He will take *what you offer him.*

He laughed at *what I said.*

Adverb function:

I sing *when I can.*

I go *wherever I like.*

An adjective clause stands after the noun it modifies. In the first sentence above, the clause modifies *rain*; in the second, *alumni*; in the third, *road*; the fourth, *place*; the fifth, *man*; and the sixth, *ideas*. (See **that, *who, whom, *which, *Restrictive and nonrestrictive.*)

Several relative clauses in succession make for an awkward, or at least conspicuous, house-that-Jack-built sentence that should be avoided:

People *who* buy houses *that* have been built in times *which* had conspicuous traits of architecture *which* have been since abandoned often have to remodel their purchases completely.

Relative pronouns • One group of connecting words which introduce *relative clauses is called *relative pronouns* and includes *who (whose, whom), which (of which, whose), that, what, whatever, whoever (whomever)*, and occasionally *as*; of these, *what* and *whatever* introduce only noun *clauses.

> Somebody, *who* [or: *whom*] I don't know, shouted, "Put 'em out."
> The Senator, *whose* term expires next year, is already worrying.
> I haven't read the same book *that* [*as*] you have.

That refers to persons or things, *who* to persons. *Which* in Standard English now refers to animals or objects or situations, and also to collective nouns even if they refer to persons:

> The army which mobilizes first has the advantage.
> The Board of Directors, which met on Saturday . . . .
> The Board of Directors, who are all bankers, . . .

In older English—and still in Nonstandard—*which* applies also to persons:

> "Our Father which art in heaven. . . ."—*The Bible* (King James), Matt. 6:9.

(Particular points in the use of these relatives will be found in separate entries on each, especially those on *that, *which, *who, whom. See also *Subordinating conjunctions, *Restrictive and nonrestrictive.)

remember • In Nonstandard English the idiom is often *remember of*: *I don't remember of doing that.* In writing, the *of* is not used: *I don't remember doing it; I don't remember that at all.* Informally *disremember* means *forget.*

Renaissance—Renascence • *Renaissance* is the more common spelling. It is pronounced /ren'ə säns'/ or /ren'ə zäns'/, or, less commonly /ri nā'sns/; *Renascence* is usually pronounced /ri nas'sns/. The word is capitalized when it refers to the period of history, but not when it refers to a revival, as "the prewar renaissance (renascence) in poetry."

repair, maintain, service • See *service.

Repetition •

Rep   *Revision: Revise so as to remove the ineffective repetition of word, meaning, or sound.*

Repetition of word, meaning, or sound may be an effective trait of style, contributing especially to emphasis. Unsuccessful and successful repetition is discussed in Ch. 8, "Repetition," pp. 320-322. This article reviews only some kinds of repetition that ordinarily require revision:

1. *Of words and phrases.* The subject of a paper or of one of its important parts must be mentioned frequently, though pronouns and economical sentences can reduce the repetition. An attentive reading of the following sentences should have led the writers to revise them, removing the obvious repetitions and other *deadwood too:

The Indian's culture was so different from the white man's [culture] that he has done very well to change as much as he has in such a short [period of] time.

From here on there was no trail, and if there had been it would have been snowed under [by the snow of] the night before.

Especially conspicuous is repetition of a word used in a different sense:

Our club is as much a fraternity as any house along the row. Our unity and fraternity [Substitute: *brotherhood*] have brought us real satisfaction and much success.

2. *Of meaning.* Meaning of single words or of longer groups is often repeated in near synonyms:

... where he did very successful work [there].

In *many* books the setting [very often] is in some foreign country.

At eight-thirty [in the morning] you punch the time clock for the start of the day.

New leg kicks are shown him, new arm stretches are demonstrated, and different ways of breathing illustrated. [Rewritten: *He is shown new leg kicks, new arm stretches, and different ways of breathing.*]

3. *Of sound.* Jingles and rhyming words are out of place in prose and so are repetitions of unstressed syllables, especially the *-ly* of adverbs and the endings of some abstract nouns, like *-tion,* which are unpleasant when noticeable.

Reports • A *report* is essentially an orderly presentation of data arranged for a specific purpose. In business or technical reports the purpose may be to present the results of laboratory or field research; to give a routine account of some activity, process, or advance; or to recommend some action or decision after going over the evidence upon which the recommendation is based.

Reports vary in form, including memorandums, form reports, letter reports, and the "full" technical report. Since in some fields the exact form of the report is rigidly specified, it is wise in preparing such reports to follow the procedures outlined in one of the texts listed below.

A report needs to be clear and compact, quickly understandable to the readers for whom it is intended. Since its sole aim is presentation of data gathered for a specific purpose, it does not lend itself to amateur practice, but a student would do well to familiarize himself with the type of report likely to be used in the field he expects to work in, and if possible make a collection of reports for future guidance.

(Detailed discussions of report writing will be found in books devoted to the subject, such as the following: John Ball and Cecil B. Williams, *Report Writing,* New York, 1955; Robley Winfrey, *Technical and Business Report Preparation,* 3rd ed., Ames, Iowa, 1962; N. B. Sigband, *Effective Report Writing,* New York, 1960; J. N. Ulman and J. R. Gould, *Technical Reporting,* rev. ed., New York, 1959; B. H. Weil, ed., *The Technical Report, Its Preparation, Processing, and Use in Industry and Government,* New York, 1954.)

Requests and commands • See *Commands and requests.

Research papers • See Ch. 11, "Reference papers," p. 416.

researcher • *Researcher* has been added to the English vocabulary as a needed shortening for *research worker.*

Resolutions • An organization usually passes a resolution as a formal recommendation of action, expression of sympathy, or record of sentiment. The style is Formal and the expression arranged in a standardized formula:

WHEREAS, The experiences of the past few weeks have shown . . . ; and

WHEREAS, Our expectations of a more favorable attitude on the part of . . . ; therefore be it

RESOLVED, That this body feels it its duty to inform . . . ; and be it further

RESOLVED, That a copy of these resolutions be sent. . . .

John W. Appel, Secretary

rest • There are two *rest's* in English, both in good standing. *Rest,* "repose," is from Old English *rest*; *rest,* "remainder," is from French *reste.*

Restrictive and nonrestrictive •

Rest

Revision: If the modifier marked is restrictive, it should not be separated from the word it modifies by a comma; if it is nonrestrictive, it should be set off by a comma or by two commas.

1. *Restrictive, or close, modifiers.* A restrictive modifier defines, limits, identifies the word it refers to; that is, it provides information essential to the meaning of the sentence. In speaking or reading aloud, there is little pause before the restrictive modifier and the voice is usually sustained, kept level. Actually the modifier becomes closely attached to, practically a part of, the element modified. If the modifier is omitted, the statement either becomes meaningless, as in the first sentence below, or else it takes on a new meaning, as in the second:

It was a quite different looking person *who walked out into the cold, frosty air a few minutes later.*

The right of the dictatorships *to decide how long this wholesale killing goes on* is unquestioned.

The italicized elements in the following sentences are restrictive and should stand as they are here, without commas:

His opponent appeared at one of the really important rallies *with a drink too much in him.*

Reform should be an application *to wider fields* of methods *with which people are already familiar* and *of which they approve.*

In many states parole boards still persist in turning loose prisoners *who should remain behind bars.*

Mr. Colman proves his versatility as an actor *when he philosophizes one minute and punches his brother on the nose the next.* He portrays a man of action *if the occasion requires* and at the same time a mild-mannered, soft-spoken individual *who gives the impression of being able to think.* He has to make important decisions *when his brother and Margo tell him that this Utopia is a lot of hooey.* Mr. Colman is the only actor I have ever seen *who can show that he is thinking.*

2. *Nonrestrictive, or loose, modifiers.* Modifiers which do not limit the meaning of a noun but add a descriptive detail are nonrestrictive and are set off by a comma or commas. In speaking or reading aloud, there is usually a slight pause and change in level of voice, a drop in tone, before and after a loose modifier. As a rule a nonrestrictive modifier can be omitted without altering the fundamental meaning of the statement.

The new road, *for which appropriations have been made,* will pass just north of here.

The building program includes a new building for the English department, *which now has classes all over the campus.*

Sophomores, *who were freshmen just last year,* have an exaggerated sense of their maturity.

A modifier that follows a proper noun is usually nonrestrictive, since the name itself identifies exactly the person or place mentioned:

Josie, *aged 16,* told Ma and Pa Pansky a thing or two.

Just below Poughkeepsie, *which we reached in a little over two hours,* we had another breakfast in a roadside lunch wagon.

3. *Optional punctuation.* Not all modifiers are clearly restrictive or nonrestrictive: there are degrees of closeness. Use of commas emphasizes a slight relationship, lack of commas suggests a closer relation. Some modifiers can be spoken or read with pause and drop in tone, or not, with some slight change in emphasis. The difference in such sentences is more of tone or movement than of meaning. The italicized modifiers in these sentences might or might not be set off by commas:

These physicians *who so vigorously oppose state medicine* have definite bases for their opinions.

They had *of course* more experience by then.

The sound of swing music reached my ears from a room down the hall *even before I heard the tramping feet that seemed to go with it.*

In open punctuation fewer commas are used, tending to bind the parts of a sentence closer together. As a rule the safest test is reading the sentence aloud, using commas if you pause and change your tone of voice before the modifier.

(See Ch. 10, "Before subordinate elements," p. 393. Reference: W. Paul Jones, "Punctuating Nonrestrictives," *College English,* 1948, 10:158-162.)

Result • Adverbial clauses of result are introduced typically by *so that, so, so . . . that, such . . . that,* and *that. So* is rather Informal, *such . . . that* and *that* likely to be Formal. The most common is *so that.*

He had been taught always to expect the worst, so that [so] he wasn't surprised.

He was so used to suffering that one more disaster made little difference.

The house was such an expense that they were giving it up.

Reverend • It is better form to use *Reverend* as a title only when the full name or the initials and the last name of the person to whom it refers follow; the abbreviation is used in newspaper and more or less Informal writing:

Reverend James Shaw	Rev. James Shaw
Reverend J. T. Shaw	Rev. J. T. Shaw

But *Reverend* before the surname alone, corresponding to *Doctor* or *Professor,* is increasingly found: *Reverend Shaw, Rev. Shaw.*

The Reverend before a name is rather more Formal: *the Reverend James T. Shaw, the Reverend Mr. Shaw.*

The reverend used instead of a clergyman's name (The reverend wasn't there) is distinctly Informal.

In the salutation of a letter, after an inside address, write *Dear Sir* or *Dear Mr. Shaw.*

Revision • See *Proofreading.

Rhetoric • *Rhetoric* is the study of the theory and practice of composition, both oral and written.

Rhetorical questions • *Rhetorical questions* are really statements in the form of questions, since no direct answer is expected and the writer does not intend to give one. In conversation they often carry some special accent, of accusation, for example: *Could you have done any better?*

... Why out of the first forty-six names in the Hall of Fame, have twenty-six of them from one to three relatives of national renown? Does it not argue that they probably belong to great breeds, truly noble strains of blood?—ALBERT EDWARD WIGGAM, *The New Decalogue of Science,* p. 46

right • *Right along, right away, right off* are Informal idioms.

In the sense of "very," *right* is a localism, in good standing in the South: *We'll be right glad to see you.*

rise • In referring to standing up or getting out of bed, *arise* is Formal and poetic; *rise* is Formal; *get up* is General.

role • In Formal usage *role* (a role in a play) is still sometimes printed with the circumflex (*rôle*) but more often without.

Roman numerals • See *Numbers § 3.

round—around • In General usage *round* and *around* are used interchangeably.

In Formal English there is some tendency to keep *around* to mean "here and there" or "in every direction" and *round* for "in a circular motion" or "in a reverse motion":

I have looked all around.   There aren't any around here.
He is going round the world.   Everyone turned round.

Around is Informal in the sense of "about, near":

He had around $200 in bills. Is anybody around [that is: *around here*]?

All-round and *all-around* are overused General adjectives (an all-round flour, an all-around athlete).

Round has no apostrophe.

run • *Run* is in good General use in the sense of "manage, operate": *He runs a hotel in Florida.*

S • *S* represents principally two sounds, /s/ and /z/: /s/ as in *so, sorry, biscuit, crops*; /z/ as in *easy, was, Jones*. In a few words *s* spells /sh/: *tension, sure, sugar*; and in some /zh/: *leisure, pleasure, measure.*

S is silent in several words, most of them from French: *aisle, debris, rendezvous, island, Arkansas, Louisville,* often in *St. Louis,* and usually in *Illinois.* (See *sh; for plurals in -*s,* *Plurals of nouns § 1, *Jones; for the genitive of words ending in -*s,* *Genitive § 1a.)

said • As a modifier *said* (the said person, the said idea) is legal usage; it is not used in ordinary writing.

saint • The abbreviation *St.* is commonly used in names of places (St. Albans, St. Louis); *Saint* is more often written out with the name of a canonized saint (Saint John, Saint Anthony of Padua). The plural of the abbreviation is SS. (SS. Peter and Paul). Occasionally the French feminine form, *Sainte,* is used (Sault Sainte Marie). The abbreviation of the feminine form is *Ste.*

same • *Same* is used as an adjective (the same color) and as a pronoun in such expressions as *The same happened to me once* and popularly in *I'll take the same, more of the same. . . .*

Same as a pronoun is also characteristic of legal and outmoded business use—*and enclose check for same*—where better style would have *it* or *them* instead.

Sarcasm • Sarcasm is a quality of bitterness or reproach in a statement—ironical (that is, to be interpreted differently from the actual statement) or direct. (See Ch. 9, p. 353.)

say • *Say* is the usual word for "speaking." *Talk* implies a continued "saying." *State* implies a formal "saying" and is better kept for this meaning [Not: *Mr. Owen stated that he was ready if we were*].

Say in the sense of "suppose," "perhaps," "for instance" is Informal: *Say they went sixteen miles.*

scarcely • See *Double negative § 3.

Schoolgirl style • A *schoolgirl style* is characterized by sentimental *counter words (*lovely, cute*), by exaggeration, and by reliance on all sorts of mechanical forms of emphasis—exclamation marks, dashes, capitals, and one, two, and even three underlinings. These serve as satisfying release to the writer and may add a sort of glow to a letter, but they should not be transferred to the printed page, and any suggestion of the style should be avoided, except to help portray a character.

schwa (ə) • *Schwa* /shwä/ is the name for the neutral vowel sound frequently occurring in unstressed syllables: *a*head, ang*e*l, def*i*nite, *o*ccur, s*u*ggest; the symbol for it is /ə/. (See *Neutral vowel.)

Scientific and technical writing • The ideal of scientific writing was expressed very early in the modern scientific movement in Thomas Sprat's *History of the Royal Society* (1667). The members of the Society, he said, tried:

... to return back to the primitive purity, and shortness, when men delivered so many things, almost in an equal number of words. They have exacted from all their members a close, naked, natural way of speaking; positive expressions; clear senses; a native easiness: bringing all things as near the mathematical plainness as they can; and preferring the language of artizans, countrymen, and merchants, before that of wits or scholars.

Exactness rather than grace or variety, or even emphasis, is the goal of most scientific and scholarly writing done by members of a profession to be read by other members. Occasionally it attains the ideal of "delivering so many things, almost in an equal number of words":

A stable, stainless, organic mercury compound solution of high germicidal value, particularly in serum and other protein media.

But today Thomas Sprat would find that much scientific writing has departed far from "the language of artizans, countrymen, and merchants."

The chief reason for the *big words that seem to a layman the most conspicuous trait of scientific writing is that scientists have discovered and named qualities and things of which the average person is quite unaware. Their descriptions are more detailed than people in general need. Here is a description of the *h* sound—/h/—from a book on phonetics:

The fricative /h/ occurs as the breath stream passes through the glottis. The vocal bands obstruct the stream sufficiently to produce a slight degree of friction. This whispered sound in therefore known as the glottal fricative sound.—ARTHUR J. BRONSTEIN, *The Pronunciation of American English,* p. 94

Though ordinary people speak of *biliousness* and *eyestrain*, the words have no definite meaning for doctors or oculists. In contrast to the rather imprecise senses of words in General usage, scientific writers try to use words in a single specific meaning. Some scientific words are taken from the General vocabulary and given special meanings, like *magnitude* in astronomy, *force* in physics, *complex* in psychoanalysis, *dip* and *incline* in geology. But the tendency now is to build new words from Latin or more often from Greek roots and give them exact definitions: *photomicrography, bioluminescence, telesthesia*.

The sentence structure and other traits of style in scientific writing are Formal, appropriately so because its audience is specialized. The style is impersonal—completely impersonal in monographs, textbooks, and articles in the scientific journals, less so in popular treatments of scientific subjects. Three levels of scientific writing are illustrated in the following quotations. The first paragraph is a simple statement of fact:

> The nature of the force exerted by a wave upon any obstacle, such as a cliff or beach, depends in part upon the type of wave and its condition at the moment of collision with the obstacle. If an un-broken oscillatory wave strikes a vertical wall or cliff the base of which reaches down to deep water, the wave is reflected back. At the instant of contact the crest of the wave rises to twice its normal height and the cliff is subjected to the hydrostatic pressure of this unusually high water column. The absence of any forward thrust of the water mass under these conditions is shown by the behavior of boats which have been observed to rise and fall with successive waves without touching the vertical wall only a few feet distant. Hagen concludes that under such circumstances débris must accumulate at the base of the wall and that therefore the prejudice against vertical sea walls and harbor walls, based on the fear of undermining by wave action, is ill-founded.—Douglas W. Johnson, *Shore Processes and Shoreline Development,* p. 57

This is part of an informative treatment of wave action, accurate and compact. It would be read, however, only by someone who was consciously looking for knowledge of the subject. The following passage is intended for a more general audience, though one limited to people with a strong interest in more than the superficial appearance of their world. The facts are presented with a minimum of technical language and made more vivid by the use of familiar comparisons ("rather like relays of messengers . . .").

> These molecules move with very high speeds; in the ordinary air of an ordinary room, the average molecular speed is about 500 yards a second. This is roughly the speed of a rifle-bullet, and is rather

more than the ordinary speed of sound. As we are familiar with this latter speed from everyday experience, it is easy to form some conception of molecular speeds in a gas. It is not a mere accident that molecular speeds are comparable with the speed of sound. Sound is a disturbance which one molecule passes on to another when it collides with it, rather like relays of messengers passing a message on to one another, or Greek torch-bearers handing on their lights. Between collisions the message is carried forward at exactly the speed at which the molecules travel. If these all traveled with precisely the same speed and in precisely the same direction, the sound would of course travel with just the speed of molecules. But many of them travel on oblique courses, so that although the average speed of individual molecules in ordinary air is about 500 yards a second, the net forward velocity of the sound is only about 370 yards a second.—Sir James Jeans, *The Universe Around Us,* p. 101

For a still more popular audience the subject matter must be further simplified and the facts made dramatic, if possible, by being presented in action. Some technical words are used, but they seem to be incidental, even decorative, rather than fundamental as in Formal scientific writing:

We now turn to consider the frequency of sound waves. Differences of frequency are detected by the ear as differences of *pitch,* that is, of the shrillness or depth of the musical note, for every musical note corresponds to a particular frequency. The higher the note, the greater the frequency; the lower the note, the smaller the frequency.

Perhaps the easiest way to show this is to take a fine hair comb or nail file and run a stiff card along it: the more quickly the card is made to wave—that is, the more frequently the card is pulled aside and allowed to return—by the passage over the teeth, the higher the note. A better way to show it is to make use of a small wheel with teeth all around the edge: when this is kept turning at a steady measured rate, and a stiff card or thin sheet of metal held so as to touch the teeth, the frequency of the disturbance, corresponding to the pitch of the note produced, can easily be measured. The number of times a second that the wings of a humming fly or bee go up or down can be measured by matching the note of the humming with the note produced by the wheel made to turn at the right speed.— E. N. da C. Andrade, *Physics for the Modern World,* p. 60

Beyond such popularizations are the sensational treatments of scientific subjects which we associate with the magazine sections of some Sunday papers. Because of the cheapness and the inaccuracy of many of these articles, scientists and scholars have tended to scorn all popularizing of their materials. But in recent years there has been an increase of reliable and interesting scientific writing for general readers as more specialists have found a challenge in seeing how much of their subject matter they can find a way of conveying to them. They are now leaving less of the work of popularizing to writers not sufficiently trained to do it accurately.

Until a person can write with authority about a specialized subject, he will most likely be doing popular or semipopular papers. Students in college can try their hand at preparing material for a somewhat limited but nonprofessional group of readers. The style of such papers would be rather Formal, and it has one real danger. The necessity for using genuine scientific words often leads to using *unnecessary* *big words. Writers in the social sciences especially have substituted unfamiliar words or *long variants for words of the General English vocabulary, as in "It is necessary to structure into a complex culture like ours a congruent hospitality to change in all institutional areas." If such writers visualized their readers, they would make more use of the General English vocabulary. P. B. Ballard puts the general principle admirably from the reader's point of view: ". . . when the common language fails in clearness, in dignity, or in freedom from ambiguity, it should be eked out by the language of the laboratory and of the study. Technical jargon is an evil, but a necessary evil. And necessary evils should be kept to a minimum." It is worth trying to see how much of your specialized information you can make available to an intelligent general reader.

An increasing number of jobs now depend on some competence in writing scientific or technical letters, reports, or articles. The director of research in a large corporation has this to say on the subject:

If you can't tell in written or oral English what your results are, it is impossible to get along in any industry. For instance, the laboratory worker must submit a condensed report of his experiments to his laboratory head. This man must in turn condense the reports of many workers and send a new report on to his superior. And so on, all the way up the line. If you can't put your thoughts and figures on paper in concise readable language, you're sunk.

(See *Reports, *References in scientific papers. References: Meta Emberger and Marion Hall, *Scientific Writing*, New York, 1955; W. O. Sypherd, Alvin M. Fountain, and V. E. Gibbens, *Manual of Technical Writing*, Chicago, 1957—with useful bibliography, pp. 545-553; Sam F. Trelease, *The Scientific Paper*, 2nd ed., Baltimore, 1952.)

Seasons • *Winter, spring, summer, fall, autumn, midsummer,* and so on are not capitalized except for stylistic emphasis, as sometimes in poetry or nature essays.

seem • *Seem* is often used as a counter verb (*deadwood), making a statement needlessly qualified or distant:

The letters of Flaubert [seem to] bring us as near to the writing of *Madame Bovary* as we can come.

Can't seem may be "illogical," but it is a useful idiom for *be unable*: *I can't seem to learn physics.*

self • *Self* as a suffix forms the reflexive and intensive pronouns: *myself, yourself, himself, herself, itself, oneself, ourselves, yourselves, themselves.* These are used chiefly for emphasis (I can do that myself) or as a reflexive object (I couldn't help myself). (See *himself, herself, *myself.)

As a prefix, *self* is joined to the root word by a hyphen: *self-control, self-explanatory, self-made, self-respect.*

When *self* is the root word there is no hyphen: *selfhood, selfish, selfless, selfsame.*

(See also *Hyphen § 1c.)

semi- • *Semi-* is a prefix meaning "half or approximately half" (*semicylindrical*), "twice within a certain period" (*semiweekly, semiannual*), or "partially, imperfectly" (*semicivilized, semiprofessional*). It is not usually hyphened except before proper names (*semi-Christian*) or words beginning with *i* (*semi-invalid*). Pronounced /sem′i/ and often /sem′ī/.

Semicolon (;) •
Revision: Use a semicolon as the mark of separation between these sentence elements.   *Semi*

A *semicolon* is used to mark a degree of separation between sentence elements considerably greater than that marked by a comma, nearly as great as that marked by a period. (The suggestion made by Bonner that we call it *semiperiod* has much to recommend it.) Although its use rather than that of another mark is largely a matter of style (§ 4), there are a few situations in which a semicolon is mandatory.

1. *To separate units that contain smaller elements separated by commas.* These may be items in a *series, enumerations, figures, scores, or clauses with commas within them:

Other periodicals not entirely dissimilar were John Harris's *The English Lucian*, 1698; Ward's *Weekly Comedy*, 1699; "Sylvester Partridge's" *The Infallible Astrologer*, 1700; and the *Merry Mercury*, 1700.—GEORGE CARVER, *Periodical Essays of the Eighteenth Century*, p. xviii

Three things which a social system can provide or withhold are helpful to mental creation: first, technical training; second, liberty to follow the creative impulse; third, at least the possibility of ulti-mate appreciation by some public, whether large or small.—BERTRAND RUSSELL, *Proposed Roads to Freedom*, p. 169

2. *To separate coordinate clauses not closely related.*

a–Between contact clauses. A semicolon is used, especially in somewhat Formal writing, between two *contact clauses (clauses with no expressed connective) if the separation in thought and structure is conspicuous. Usually the two state-ments could stand as separate sentences, but the writer wishes to have them considered part of one idea. Contrasting state-ments are often punctuated with semicolons, as here:

Words and sentences are subjects of revision; paragraphs and whole compositions are subjects of prevision.—BARRETT WENDELL, *English Composition*, p. 117

Your religion does not promise you a perfect life on earth, nor freedom from suffering; it does guarantee you the strength to bear suffering. Your religion does not expect you to be free from sin or mistakes in judgment; it does promise you forgiveness for your mis-takes. Your religion expects you to continue making the best efforts you can on behalf of others; it does not guarantee that you or anyone can arrange the lives of people as he pleases.—HENRY C. LINK, *The Return to Religion*, pp. 68-69

(See Ch. 8, "Revising comma faults," p. 290.)

b–With heavy connectives. A semicolon is used between clauses connected by the weightier conjunctive adverbs (*how-ever, moreover, nevertheless, consequently* . . .). These usually link longer clauses in a rather Formal style:

This program implies better orientation of individuals to the mani-fold problems of adjustment; therefore, certain character traits, as well as specific abilities, should show positive change.—*English Journal*, June 1937, p. 456

A comma is now usually more common between clauses con-nected by the lighter conjunctive adverbs (*so, then* . . .). (See *Conjunctive adverbs.)

c–With coordinating conjunctions. A semicolon is used be-tween clauses connected by coordinating conjunctions (*and, but, for, or* . . .) if the clauses are long or if the connection is not close, if they contain commas, or if for some reason (often for contrast) the writer wishes to show an emphatic separation between them:

History as actuality includes all that has been said, felt, done, and thought by human beings on this planet since humanity began its long career; and, if Darwin is right, since the evolution of the human organism began in the primeval dawn.—C. A. BEARD, *The Discussion of Human Affairs*, p. 69

She already had some furniture of her own, including what she could take from Truda; and Louis could let her have some of his— yes?—G. B. STERN, *The Matriarch*, p. 199

Therefore those teachers who cannot admit that they may be wrong should not teach English composition; nor should those who never suspect that their pupils may be abler than they.—L. R. BRIGGS, *To College Teachers of English Composition*, p. 19

The semicolon is used to separate parts of the sentence which are of more importance, or which show a division more distinct, than those separated by commas; or to separate sections already separated by commas.—JOHN BENBOW, *Manuscript & Proof*, p. 89

3. *Semicolon and colon.* Do not use a semicolon, which is a mark of *separation* as the examples in this article show, in place of a colon (:), which is a mark of *anticipation*:

There are two principal considerations in the use of semicolons: the degree of separation to be indicated between statements and the formality of the style of the passage.

(See *Colon § 4.)

4. *Semicolons and other traits of style.* Except for the specific situations described in § 1, the use of semicolons is in part a stylistic matter. They are more appropriate, more necessary, in rather Formal styles and in long, aggregating sentences. They tend to slow up the reading and are consequently fewer in narrative than in exposition. In General styles commas would be used in preference, or if the distinction between the clauses is considerable, two sentences would be written. In the following passage Malcolm Cowley has chosen to rely on semicolons. Commas and periods that might have been used in a more Informal writing of the same passage are put in brackets.

College students inhabit an easy world of their own; [.] except for very rich people and certain types of childless wives they form the only American class that takes leisure for granted. Many, of course, earn their board and tuition tending furnaces, waiting on table or running back kick-offs for a touchdown; what I am about to say does not apply to them. The others—almost always the ruling clique of a big university, the students who set the tone for the rest—are supported practically without efforts of their own. They write a few begging letters;[,] perhaps they study a little harder in order to win a scholarship; [,] but usually they don't stop to think where the money comes from. Above them, the president knows the source of the hard cash that runs this great educational factory; [.] he knows that the stream of donations can be stopped by a crash in the stock market or reduced in volume by newspaper reports of a professor gone bolshevik; [.]he knows what he has to tell his trustees or the state legislators when he goes to them begging for funds. The scrubwomen in the library, the chambermaids and janitors, know how they earn their food; but the students themselves, and many of their professors, are blind to economic forces; [.] society, as the source of food and football fields and professors' salaries, is a remote abstraction.—MALCOLM COWLEY, *Exile's Return,* pp. 36-37

Students tend to use more semicolons than would be used by professional writers today in General writing. They should consider the weight of the mark in view of the general movement of their writing and make sure that the movement of the particular sentence needs the degree of separation marked by the semicolon. (Compare *Comma, *Colon. Reference: Summey, pp. 97-101.)

Sentences •
> *Revision: Eliminate the fault in the sentence marked.*

S

The grammatical characteristics and the chief problems in writing sentences are discussed in Ch. 8 and in the following *Index* articles:

*Agreement
*Clauses
*Comma fault
*Commands and
   requests
*Conjunctions, use
*Contact clauses

*Dangling modifiers
*Emphasis
*Fragmentary
   sentence
*Fused sentence
*Idiom and idioms
*Immediate constituent

*Parallel constructions
*Reference of
   pronouns
*Shifted constructions
*Subject and verb
*Wordiness
*Word order

seq. • See *Abbreviations § 2.

Sequence of tense • See *Tenses of verbs § 3.

Series • Commas are used between the items of a series of three or more short items:

> The supposed contents of the physical world are *prima facie* very different from these: [four short clauses:] *molecules have no colour, atoms make no noise, electrons have no taste, and corpuscles do not even smell.*—BERTRAND RUSSELL, *Mysticism and Logic,* p. 145

> There are two or three large chests, a bedstead, the inevitable cradle occupied by the latest addition to the family. The small windows are seldom curtained. There are shelves for pots and pans, spoons and forks (often wooden), jars of gherkins, bottles of this and that, loaves of bread, sacks of flour, baskets of dried fruit.—LOUIS ADAMIC, *The Native's Return,* p. 271

Usage is divided over the insertion of a comma before the last item of such a series. A comma helps to prevent ambiguity, especially if one member is compound. But many writers, especially in General and Informal styles, do not use one, particularly when the series is short:

Ministers, teachers [,] and journalists all united against the proposal.

If the members of the series are long, or not closely connected, or if the members have commas within them, they are separated by semicolons:

Quite a few people get credit lines in this big, handsome and heavy book: Dr. Albert Sirmay, who did the arrangements; Frederick E. Banbery, who painted the pictures; Newman Levy, who wrote an introduction to each show.—HERBERT KUPPERBERG, review of *The Rogers and Hammerstein Song Book, New York Herald Tribune Book Review*, Dec. 7, 1958

(For further examples and details see Ch. 10, "In lists and series," p. 396; *Comma § 5, *Semicolon § 1. Reference: R. J. McCutcheon, "The Serial Comma Before 'and' and 'or,'" *American Speech*, 1940, 15:250-254.)

service • The verb *service* (to service a car, a refrigerator) is needed and is appropriate in all varieties of English. It means more than *repair* and has a different connotation from *maintain* or *keep up*.

set—sit • In writing Standard English, people and things *sit* (past: *sat*) or they are *set* (past: *set*)—that is, are "placed":

I like to sit in a hotel lobby.
I have sat in this same seat for three semesters.
She set the soup down with a flourish.
The post was set three feet in the ground.

A hen, however, *sets* (on her eggs) and the sun *sets*. Though *set* replaces *sit* in the speech of many people, it is felt by most cultivated speakers to be Nonstandard.

settle • See *locate.

sh • *Sh* is a digraph for a sound which is not a combination of the sounds usually represented by *s* or *h*: *shall, shove, ash*. The *sh* sound—/sh/—is represented by various other spellings: *machine* /mə shēn'/, *tissue* /tish'ü/, *conscientious* /kon'shē en'shəs/, *ocean* /ō'shən/. Compare *zh.

shall—will • Future time is expressed by a number of locutions in English:

I am going to ask for a raise.
I am asking for a raise tomorrow.

There is to be a dance Friday.
He may go next week.

He comes next week.
Come again.
It's time he left.
He is sure to come tomorrow.

If he had the money tomorrow,
he would pay it.
I'll try to be on time.
I shall try to be on time.
I will try to be on time.

Expressions like the first nine are probably more common than the last three, so that it is hardly accurate to say that the future is expressed only with *shall* and *will*. But since distinctions between these auxiliaries have been regarded as an important item of reputable usage, it is necessary to discuss them in more detail than they deserve. Their use has never been uniform in English, though some grammarians have attempted to insist on uniformity. The general practices in the common situations needing these words are as follows:

1. *General usage.*

a–Simple future. In speech and writing the prevailing use in the United States, and in many other parts of the English-speaking world, is *will* in all persons (I will ask, you will ask, he will ask . . .).

b–Emphatic future. In expressing determination in the future or for some special emphasis, General usage is divided. In speech the determination is expressed by stress, which may be used on either word: *I shall' go, I will' go.* There is some tendency to use *shall* in all persons as the emphatic form, because *shall* is so rare that it makes a more emphatic word than *will*: *I, you, he, she, we, you, they shall ask.* Other constructions (I have to go . . .) are also used.

c–Contractions. In speaking and Informal writing in which contractions are used, the future becomes *I'll, you'll, he'll,* and so on, which do not discriminate between *shall* and *will*. *Won't* is used for *will not* (formed from an obsolete *woll* and *not*) and *shan't* for *shall not,* the latter even more rare than the uncontracted form.

d–In questions. In asking questions *shall* is likely to be used in the first and third persons and *will* in the second, but practice is not consistent. Even here *shall* is likely to be avoided, replaced where possible by *'ll*:

Shall I go?
What shall [What'll] we do now?
What shall [What'll] he do?
Will you go?
What will [What'll] you do now?
What will [What'll] he do with it?

The significant difference between *Shall I go?* and *Will I go?* is weakened or nonexistent for most cultivated speakers of American English in *I shall go* and *I will go.*

In the negative, *won't* is much the more common:

Won't I look funny in that?
What won't he think of next?

e–Shall is usual in laws, resolutions, etc.:

A permanent organization shall be set up within a year.
No singer shall receive more than $700 a performance.

The Biblical *thou shalt not* would now be expressed by *you must not*.

2. *Formal usage.* Some writers use *shall* in the first person and *will* in the second and third persons in making the future tense, following handbook "rules" rather than usage.

First person:	I shall ask	we shall ask
Second person:	you will ask	you will ask
Third person:	he, she will ask	they will ask

In the emphatic future, expressing determination of the speaker, Formal English theoretically reverses this use of *shall* and *will*:

First person:	I will ask	we will ask
Second person:	you shall ask	you shall ask
Third person:	he, she shall ask	they shall ask

In asking questions a few people even use the form of *shall* or *will* in a question that the answerer would use in his reply. This usage is distinctly Formal and usually sounds unnatural:

Shall you go? [Answer: *I shall (shall not) go.*]

The efforts of purists to establish this Formal usage as General is now declining, and few editors today change copy to conform to it.

3. *Overuse of "shall."* The stress that schools have put on *shall* sometimes leads to an unidiomatic use:

Whether or not Congress *will* [not: *shall*] favor or pass laws against lynching is not for me to guess.

(See *should–would. References: Much has been written about the use of these words. As a beginning: Curme, *Syntax,* pp. 362-371; Fries, *AEG,* pp. 150-168, a good short summary of actual usage; C. C. Fries, "The Expression of the Future," *Language,* 3:87-95; Jespersen, Chs. 25, 26 for British practice, though also illuminating for American usage; Amos L. Herold, *English Journal,* 1936, 25:670-676; Robertson, pp. 516-520; Bryant, pp. 182-183.)

shan't • There is only one apostrophe in the contraction of *shall not*.

shape • *Shape* is Informal in the sense of "manner, condition": *They were in good shape for the trip.*

she-or-he • See *he-or-she.

Shifted constructions •

Shift   *Revision: Make the constructions marked consistent (parallel) in form.*

Two or more sentence elements that have the same relationship to another element in the sentence should be expressed by words in the same grammatical construction; that is, the constructions should be parallel. A specific verb form should be continued in a similar construction; a verb should be kept consistently active or passive in a sentence or passage; adjectives should be paralleled by adjectives, nouns by nouns, and so on. (The *should be* constructions in the preceding sentence are parallel.)

Shifting from one form to another may confuse or disturb a reader because it is a failure to follow established patterns of writing. Shifts should be removed in revision.

Some commonly shifted constructions are:

Shifted	*Consistent*
1. Shift in subject	
The *car* starts easily, runs smoothly, and *you won't have* any trouble with it.	The *car* starts easily, runs smoothly, and *won't give you* any trouble.
2. Adjective—Noun	
This book seems *interesting* and *an informative piece of work.*	This book seems *interesting* and *informative.*
3. Personal—Impersonal	
In fact going to summer school is worse than no vacation at all, for when *you* have no vacation *you* do not think about all the things *a person* could do if *he* had one.	. . . for when *you* have no vacation *you* do not think about all the things *you* could do if *you* had one.
4. Adverb—Adjective	
Along these walks are the cottages, many of which have stood *since the founding* [adverbial phrase], and others *more recent* [adjective].	. . . many of which have stood *since the founding,* and others of which have been built *more recently.*

5. Noun—Adverb

Associating [noun] with these fellows and *how to adapt myself to live with them* [adverbial phrase] will be helpful to me when I am through college.

Associating with these fellows and *adapting* myself to live with them will be helpful to me when I am through college.

6. Noun—Adjective

Anyone who has *persistence* [noun] or is *desperate* [adjective] enough can get a job on a ship.

Anyone who is *persistent* or who is *desperate* enough . . .

7. Noun—Clause

The most important factors are *time* and *temperature,* careful *control* at every point, and *the mechanical equipment must be in perfect operating condition at any time of the day or night.*

. . . and *mechanical equipment in perfect operating condition at any time of the day or night.*

8. Participle—Clause

How many times have you seen a fisherman *trying* to get to his favorite fishing spot without scaring all the fish away but instead *he sends out* messages with his rhythmical squeak-splash, squeak-splash.

. . . but instead *sending out* messages . . .

9. Phrase—Clause

I have heard complaints *about the plot being weak* and *that the setting was played up too much.*

. . . and *the setting being played up too much.*

(See also *Parallel constructions. For other examples see Ch. 8, "Revising shifted constructions," p. 300.)

Ships' names • The names of ships are indicated in three ways:

1. In most books and generally in Formal writing they are italicized (underlined in the manuscript):

The *Caryatid,* in ballast, was steaming down the river at half-speed. . . .—WILLIAM McFEE, *Casuals of the Sea,* p. 317

2. In newspapers and personal writing there is a growing tendency to regard the names of ships simply as proper names, capitalizing them but not otherwise setting them off:

The Magellan weighed anchor at 9:20 A.M. and moved slowly to her berth at Pier H, Weehawken, N.J.—*The New York Times,* Feb. 3, 1950

3. Occasionally ships' names are found in quotation marks:

The summer of 1926 David spent as a junior member of the American Museum Greenland Expedition. . . . on the stout little schooner "Morrissey." [Jacket of *David Goes to Greenland*. In the book *Morrissey* is italicized.]

The pronoun used in referring to a ship is usually *she*.

Shoptalk • *Shoptalk* is the offhand talk of people about their occupations, from medicine and law to ditchdigging and pan-handling. It varies with the social class and personal taste of its users, from the talk of a garage hand to that of an automotive engineer or professor of physics. Its distinguishing feature is vocabulary. Many of the words are the necessary names for materials and processes and tools and for the people—for everything that is commonly referred to in a line of work—like *em, en, pica, pi, spreaders, platen, rule, chase,* from a printing shop. Such words are usually given in dictionaries with the name of the occupation to which they belong. Shoptalk may also include technical and scientific words, as in the conversation of interns and nurses, but it is set off from Formal technical and professional writing by the conversational tone and by the presence of the jargon of the field, sometimes called *cant,* which would not be found at the Formal level.

Shoptalk has a vigorous and often figurative vocabulary, in which words are formed with great freedom. Especially convenient are short substitutes for long technical words. (See *Abbreviations.) A *mike* may be a microphone in a radio studio, a microscope in a laboratory, a micrometer in a shop; *hypo* is a fixing bath to a photographer and a hypodermic injection in a medical context; *soup* is the name of a pourable mixture in scores of manufacturing processes. Racing has *place, show, on the nose, tipster, bookie;* unlisted securities are *cats and dogs;* football players have *skull practice;* a student pilot must *dual* for many hours before he is allowed to *solo;* a *gagman* makes up the comedian's lines; and so on.

Some of these words, like *fade-out* from the movies, are useful in discussing other subjects, and they may become a part of the General vocabulary, like *third degree.* Shoptalk is appropriate and necessary in speaking or writing about the particular occupation in which it is used, usually with some explanations required for readers who are not acquainted with it. It is often appropriate in Informal writing, but it is usually out of place in General writing, almost always in Formal writing.

(References: *American Speech* and the *Publications of the American Dialect Society* have many articles dealing with the vocabularies of particular occupations and groups.)

should—would •

1. *Should* and *would* are used in statements that carry some doubt or uncertainty about the statement that is being made. They are also used in polite or unemphatic requests:

They should be there by Monday. [Contrast: *They will be there by Monday.*]

Would you please shut the door on your way out? [Contrast: *Will you please....*]

In the first person both *should* and *would* are used:

I would be much obliged if you could do this.
I should be much obliged if you could do this.

Usage is so much divided on the choice between these forms that one's feeling is probably the safest guide. But it is desirable to follow one or the other usage consistently in a piece of writing.

2. *Should* as an auxiliary used with all persons expresses a mild sense of obligation, weaker than *ought*:

I should pay this bill. [Contrast: *I ought to pay this bill.*]

In indirect discourse *should* and *would* represent the future tense of direct speech, following the "sequence of tenses." (See *Tenses of verbs § 4.)

Direct: "I will be ready at three," Mildred said.
Indirect: Mildred said she would be ready at three.

Would has some currency in the Informal or half-humorous idiom *That would be her picture,* meaning "That is her picture, isn't it?"

show • *Show* is Informal or theatrical *shoptalk in the sense of "a play"; is usually humorous or Nonstandard for a dignified public performance, as of a concert; General when applied to the movies (short for *picture show*). It is Informal for "chance" (They didn't have a show of winning).

show up • *Show up* is Informal for "appear" (He didn't show up for two hours) and for "expose" (I showed him up, all right).

sic • *Sic* (Latin for *thus, so*; pronounced /sik/) in *brackets is sometimes used to mark an error in quoted matter. It shows the reader that the deviation from Standard practice was in the quoted material, and was not made by the quoter:

The letter was headed "Toledo, Ohia [sic], Jan. 2."

sick, ill • *Ill* is the more Formal, less common word. In America they mean the same. In British usage *sick* is usually restricted to mean "nauseated." In the United States *sick* in that sense is made clear by adding a phrase: *It made me sick to my stomach.* This idiom has two Standard variants: *sick at* and *sick to.* The spoken idioms *take sick* and *get sick* also occur. In the Informal *I feel sick about that,* the speaker is not referring to his health.

Silent letters • English spells a great many words with silent letters—that is, letters which do not represent any speech sound. A few of them are the result of mistaken analogies, like the *s* of *island,* which is there from confusion with the French *isle,* though it comes from Old English *igland* and has never had the *s* sounded. Renaissance scholars inserted a number of letters that corresponded to those in the Greek and Latin words from which the English ones derived but that had never been sounded in English: Chaucer could write *det,* but we must write *debt* because the scholars recognized the word's descent from *debitum*; and the addition of the *h* to Middle English *trone* has established a spelling pronunciation for *throne.* (See *Pronunciation § 3c.)

But most of our silent letters act, as Thomas R. Lounsbury put it, "as a sort of tombstone to mark the place where lie the unsightly remains of a dead and forgotten pronunciation"; the pronunciation has changed but the spelling hasn't, or hasn't changed enough. There they stand, those final *b*'s in *bomb, comb, climb,* the initial *g*'s and *k*'s in *gnarl, gnash, knack, knave,* the *p*'s in Greekish words like *pneumonia* and *psychology,* the *gh*'s in *through* and *night* and *caught.*

Silent letters are sometimes defended because they tend to remind us of a word's ancestry, but that fact is of use only to scholars, and there are not enough scholars of that kind to justify spelling the language for them. Besides, it's not always true: *delight* is from French *delite,* the *gh* being by analogy with *light.* Some people think these spellings have an esthetic value, that *night* has a beauty not in *nite* or that the superfluous *h* gives *ghost* a special weirdness. But this reason doesn't seem very substantial, since we learn these words from hearing them, and whatever quality *ghost* has as a word comes more likely from the tone in which we have heard it spoken.

Though some of these silent letters have been dropped in the past hundred years—*apophthegm* has lost its *ph*—most of the silent letters hold firm, making spelling more difficult.

Sometimes people who are not familiar with the sound of a word are led to pronounce a silent letter, giving a "spelling pronunciation," as pronouncing *indict* /in dikt′/ instead of /in dīt′/. (See Ch. 10, "Reasons for difficulties in spelling," p. 404, *Pronunciation § 1c. For groupings of silent letter words see W. A. Craigie, *English Spelling,* pp. 36-39, 67-73.)

similar • The last syllable is *-lar*. Contrast *familiar*. Note the pronunciations: /sim′ə lər/, /fə mil′yər/.

similar to • *Similar to* is often a wordy way of saying *like*:

It was my first wreck and I hope I may never have another similar to that one [like it].

since • See *because, *so.

Sino- • See *Chinese.

sit—set • See *set—sit.

situated • *Situated* is often *deadwood:

I was staying with friends in a little town in Canada called Picton, [situated] in the province of Ontario.

size • As a modifier, *size* (a small size hat, king size) is in General spoken usage. In writing, it is often better omitted (a small hat). (See *-ed § 3.)

ski • The plural is *skis,* sometimes *ski*. The verb is *ski, skied, skiing*. The pronunciation is /skē/ (or British, following the Scandinavian, /shē/).

Slang • It is hard to draw a line between slang and other sorts of Informal English. Many people use the term too broadly—for almost any word not in the General vocabulary—and dictionaries have been too generous with the label, marking as "slang" many words that perhaps suggest spoken rather than written style. (Actually dictionaries include very few genuine slang expressions, because by the time they appear in their collection of quotations they have almost necessarily achieved considerable currency in print.)

The central characteristic of slang comes from the motive for its use: a desire for novelty, for vivid emphasis, for being in the know, up with the times, or a little ahead. These are essentially qualities of style, and the tone and connotation are as important as the central meaning of the words. Other varieties of language have ways of expressing the ideas of slang words, but they are often roundabout and their tone is quieter, more conventional. Young people like novelty, as do fashionable and sporty grown-ups, and comedians need it in their trade. Slang is especially common in talking about sports and amusements and all sorts of everyday activities for which the ordinary terms seem to have worn thin.

Slang words are made by natural linguistic processes. Their slang quality may lie in the intonation of a phrase (*or what have you, you and who else*). Slang abounds in clipped words (*razz, natch, hood*), and in compounds and derivatives of ordinary words (*screwball, sourpuss, cockeyed*). Many are borrowed from the *shoptalk of sports and the popular arts, especially jazz (*square, cool, real gone*). And a great many are figurative extensions of General words (*fierce* as a term of approval, *hack around, rock* for a hard guy, and the words for human stupidity, like *numb, feeble*). To *park* a car is General English; to *park* a hat or a piece of gum is probably still slang. In the desire for novelty and emphasis one word leads to another, as *square* went to *cube*. Sound is often an important factor, as in *goof off, booboo, barf*.

Since many slang words have short lives, any discussion of slang in print is bound to be somewhat out-of-date. *Skidoo, twenty-three, vamoose, beat it, scram, hit the trail, take a powder, drag out, shag out, cut out, split* have succeeded each other almost within a generation. Words for being drunk (*soused, plastered, bombed*), for girls (*baby, doll, chick*), and words of approval (*tops, tough, a wow, neat, the most, cool*) and disapproval (*all wet, screwy, a fink*) change almost from year to year. Many slang words prove more permanently useful and become a part at least of the Informal vocabulary (*blind date, boy friend, go steady*). Others have in time become General English (*ballyhoo, *highbrow, lowbrow*).

Slang belongs primarily to familiar and rather flashy speech and comedy, to which it can give a note of freshness. This freshness wears off after some hundreds of repetitions so that the prime virtue of the words is lost. In writing, slang is less often appropriate, partly because of triteness and partly because many of the words name general impressions instead of specific ones, so that they rank with *nice* and *good*. Though occasionally used by practiced writers for special effects, slang is ordinarily out of place in Formal writing. It should not be used in General writing unless it adds a quality that is appropriate. In Informal writing it is more appropriate, especially in recounting personal experiences and for discussions of sports and campus affairs, though even with such subjects the taste of expected readers should be considered. If slang expressions are appropriate, they should be used without apology (that is, without quotation marks); if not appropriate, they should not be used. The chief objections to slang, aside from its possible conspicuousness, are to its overuse and to its use in place of more exact expressions.

Notice that many of the illustrative words in this discussion look like items in the General vocabulary. Their slangy quality results from the context in which they occur. That is why few words can be labeled slang solely on the basis of their form. (See also *Abbreviations, *Shoptalk.)

slow, slowly • Both *slow* and *slowly* are adverbs in Standard English, each going back to an Old English adverb form (*slawe* and *slawlice,* respectively). Use whichever sounds better in the sentence. *Slow* is rather more vigorous: *Go slow.* There is, however, a rather strong prejudice against adverbial *slow*. (See *Adverbs, types and forms § 1; *Divided usage; compare *bad–badly.)

Slurred vowels • See *Neutral vowel.

so • Informally, especially in speech, *so* is used as a subordinating conjunction to introduce clauses of purpose (see *Purpose):

Informal: He started early so he could get good seats.

General: He started early so that he could get good seats; . . . in order to get good seats; . . . to get good seats.

So is similarly used in clauses of result (see *Result), in which General English would usually have *so that* or change to a *since* construction:

Informal: I wondered what they would do with the logs, so I followed them through the woods.

General: Since [Because] I wondered what they would do with the logs, I followed them through the woods.

Informal: He is a fast reader, so he got through before I did.

General: Since he is a fast reader, he got through before I did.

Formal English would also use *so that* or the more exact *because* or *since* in these two constructions.

As an *intensive *so* is common in speech and is often stressed (He's *so* handsome! I was *so* excited.) and has been called the "feminine *so.*" But it is sometimes also used as an intensive in General writing: *This confinement was hard for him—he had been so active all his life.* (References: Fries, *AEG,* pp. 226-227; Russell Thomas, "The Use of *So* as an Intensifier," *College English,* 1951, 12:453-454; Bryant, pp. 190-193.)

so . . . as • See *as . . . as.

so . . . that • Even when several words come between *so* and *that* no comma should precede *that*:

All strands of the story are so artfully and inextricably interwoven [ ] that anything but the author's desired effect is impossible.

(See *so, *Result.)

so-called • If you have to use *so-called,* don't duplicate the idea by putting the name of the so-called object in quotes: not *the so-called "champion,"* but *the so-called champion.* The word is rather stiff and in General writing quotation marks would often be used instead (the "champion").

So-called is usually hyphened when it precedes its principal word but not when it follows:

Their so-called liberal views were merely an echo of the conservative attitude. [Their "liberal" views were . . . .]
Their justice, so called, smacked of partiality.

Social correspondence •
1. *Informal notes.* The form and tone of Informal social notes —invitations, answers to invitations, thank you letters—are those of personal letters. (See *Letters § 1, 2.) Giving all the necessary information of time, place, and so on, being prompt in answering notes, and maintaining a tone of courtesy are more important than mechanical form. If the correspondents are not intimately acquainted, a more Formal style and more details of address may be needed than if they are intimates.
2. *Formal notes.* Formal social correspondence—announcements, invitations, answers to invitations—is impersonal and standardized. It is used for social events indicating, usually, formal dress or a gathering with distinguished guests.

For further details consult a book of etiquette.

Solecism • A *solecism* /sol′ə siz əm/ is a deviation from accepted practice; in language it implies an error in the use of words or constructions. The term is now distinctly Formal.

some, and compounds with some •
1. In written English, *some* is usually an indefinite pronoun (Some travel and some don't) or an adjective (some people, some ideas).
2. As an adverb, *some* is Informally used with comparatives (He felt some better), instead of the more Formal *somewhat.* It is also Informal when used with verbs (We talked some that afternoon).
3. The compounds *somebody, someway, somewhat, somewhere* are written as one word. *Someone* is usually one word (Someone is coming) but may be two if the *one* is stressed (Some one of them). *Someday* is written as one word or as two.
4. *Some place* is Informal for *somewhere* (I lost it some place). *Someway* and *someways* are also Informal, and *somewheres* is Nonstandard. (Compare *any, and compounds with any.)

sooner . . . than • After *no sooner* the preferable connective is now *than* rather than *when* or *but*:

The fly had *no sooner* hit the water *than* [not *when* or *but*] a huge trout snapped at it.

sophomore • Often pronounced as two syllables, /sof′môr/, the word is both noun and adjective. The adjective *sophomoric* /sof′[ə] môr′ik/ refers to supposed undesirable traits of sophomores (conceit and immaturity), as in *a sophomoric style* or *sophomoric conduct.*

sort, kind • See **kind, sort.

sort of, kind of • See **kind of, sort of.

sort of [a], kind of [a] • See **kind of a, sort of a.

Sound • See **Alliteration, *Assonance, *Homonyms, *Repetition § 3, *Style § 2b.

species • *Species* has the same spelling in both singular and plural; in pronunciation: /spē′shēz/, /spē′shiz/, /spē′sēz/.

Specie /spē′shi/, meaning money in coin, is a separate word, a collective noun without plural form.

Spelling •
Revision: Correct the spelling of the word marked, referring to a dictionary if necessary.   *Sp*

Chapter 10, p. 405, makes some specific suggestions for improving spelling habits. It is useful also to study groups of words that have some trait in common. The following *Index* articles treat such groups. Those articles marked † give the most useful rules or suggestions for mastering large groups of words.

-able, -ible (desirable, legible)
-ae-, -oe- (esthetic, ameba)
† -al ly (fatal, politically)
-ance, -ence (-ant, -ent) (attendance, existence)
Apostrophe (Bob's picture, the companies' charter)
Capital letters
† -ce, -ge (peaceable, courageous)
Contractions (didn't, he'll)
† Doubling final consonants (refer—referred)
† E § 5, silent or mute *e* (changeable, likeness)
-ed (exceptions to rule)

† -ei-, -ie- (feign, receive, achieve)
  en-, in- (encourage, inquire)
  -er, -or (debater, objector)
  -er, -re (luster, scepter)
  Foreign words in English (chauffeur, ersatz; accent marks)
† Homonymns, homophones (words pronounced alike but usually
  spelled differently: plain, plane; altar, alter)
  Hyphen (un-American, father-in-law)
  in-, un- (incapable, unedited)
  -ize, -ise (apologize, advertise)
  -le words (meddle, nickel)
† Neutral vowel (comparable, repetition)
  -or, -our (honor, Saviour)
  -ough, -augh (although, laugh)
  Plurals of nouns (beauties, birches, heroes, knives)
  Principal parts of verbs
  Pronunciation § 4
  re- (reform, re-form)
  Silent letters (debt, night)

The following list contains many words that give difficulty in spelling. It is not exhaustive and is by no means a substitute for a dictionary, but it can be used as the basis for improving your spelling. Perhaps it can be most useful if you check the particular words in it that you are not sure of and occasionally study those to fix them better in mind. A profitable exercise might be to have a classmate read the words for you to write out. In the margins add others that have troubled you—in every way possible make it *your* list.

A word preceded by * (for example, *advice*) has an *Index* article discussing it.

A dash separating two words (*adviser—advisor*) means that the two forms are about equally common.

A second form in brackets (*encyclopedia* [*encyclopaedia*]) means that the form in brackets is now less common than the other.

A few words are identified by pronunciation in slashes or definition in parentheses.

The division of words into syllables indicates how they would be hyphened in writing and may assist in visualizing them more accurately.

ab sence
ac a dem ic
ac cept, -ance, -able
ac cess, ac ces si ble
ac ci den tal ly
ac com mo date
ac com pa ny ing,
  ac com pa nied,
  ac com pa ni ment
ac cus tom
ache
a chieve

ac quaint, -ed, -ance
ac quired
a cross
ac tu al, -ly
ad ap ta tion
ad dress
ad o les cence
*ad vice (noun)
ad vise (verb)
ad vis er—ad vis or
*af fect (to influence)
a gainst
ag gra vate
ag gres sion, ag gres sor
air plane [aeroplane]
aisle (of a theater)

al co hol
al lege
all read y
*all right
al lu sion
*al ma ma ter
al read y
al tar (of a church)
al ter (to change)
*al though—al tho
al to geth er
*a lum nus, a lum ni,
    a lum na, a lum nae
am a teur
a nal o gous, a nal o gy
a nal y sis
an a lyze [analyse]
an es thet ic [anaesthetic]
an gel /ān'jəl/
an gle /ang'gl̩/
an nounc er
an nu al
an swer
anx i e ty
a pol o gy
ap pa ra tus
ap par ent
ap pear, -ance, ap pear anc es
ap pre ci ate
ap prox i mate
arc tic

ar gue, ar gu ing, ar gu ment
a roused
as cent (going up)
as sas sin
as sent (agreement)
as so ci a tion
*ath lete, ath let ics
at tacked
at tend, -ance, -ant
at ti tude
at tor ney
at trac tive
au di ence
au to bi og ra phy
aux il ia ry

bach e lor
bal ance
ba sis, bas i cal ly
bat tal ion
be gin ning
be lieve
ben e fit ed, ben e fi cial
berth (a bed)
bib li og ra phy
birth (being born)
breath /breth/
breathe /brēŦH/
brid al (of a bride)
bri dle (of a horse)
bril liant
Brit ain (Great Britain)
bu reau
bu reauc ra cy
*bus, bus es—bus ses
busi ness

ca fe te ri a
cal en dar (of days)
cal i ber [calibre]
can di date
can't
can vas (sailcloth)
can vass (to go about)
cap i tal (city) , -ism
cap i tol (building)
cap tain

car bu re tor
care, -ful, -less
car goes
cas u al ties
cat e go ries
ceil ing
cen ter [centre]
cer tain ly
chal leng er
cham pagne
change a ble
chap er on [chaperone]
char ac ter is tic, char ac ter ized
chauf feur
chief, -tain
choose, choos ing (present)
chose, cho sen (past)
cig a ret—cig a rette
col lar
col le gi ate
colo nel
col or
co los sal
col umn
com e dy
com ing
com mit
com mit tee
com par a tive
com par i son
com pel, com pelled
com pet i tor
com plaint
com ple ment (to fill out)
com pli ment (to praise)
con cede
con ceive
con cer to /kən cher′tō/
con demn
con nois seur /kon′ə sėr′/
con quer or
con science
con sci en tious
con scious, -ness
con sen sus
con sist ent
con tempt i ble

con tin u ous
con trol, con trolled, con trol ling
con tro ver sy, con tro ver sial
con ven ient, con ven ience
con vert i ble
co op er a tive—co-op er a tive
    [coöperative]
corps /kôr/
corpse /kôrps/
coun cil (a group)
coun ci lor—coun cil lor
coun sel (advice)
coun sel or—coun sel lor
cour te ous, cour te sy
crept
crit i cism, crit i cize
cu ri ous, cu ri os i ty
cur ric u lar (adjective)
*cur ric u lum (noun)
cur tain
cus tom
cy lin dri cal

dair y /dãr′i/
damned
dealt
de bat er
de ceased /di sēst′/
de ceive
de cent /dē′sṇt/
de fend ants
def i nite, def i ni tion
de pend ent (adj. or noun)
de scend ant
de scent /di sent′/
de scribe, de scrip tion
de sert /di zėrt′/, (leave)
des ert /dez′ərt/, (waste)
de sire, de sir a bil i ty
de spair, des per ate
des sert /di zėrt′/, (of a meal)
de vel op [develope]
dex ter ous—dex trous
di a gram ma tic
di a phragm
di a ry /dī′ə rē/
die, dies, dy ing

die sel
di e ti tian [dietician]
dif fer ent
di lap i dat ed
din ing room
din ning (noise)
diph ther i a
dis ap pear ance
dis ap point ment
dis as trous
dis cre tion
dis eased /də zēzd'/
dis gust ed
dis patch [despatch]
dis si pate
dis trib u tor
dis turb ance
di vide
di vine
dom i nant
don't
dor mi to ry
dry, dri er, dri est
du al (two)
du el (fight)
dye, dyed, dye ing

ech o, ech oes
ec sta sies
ef fect
ef fi cient, ef fi cien cy
el i gi ble, el i gi bil i ty
em bar rass
em pha size, em phat ic,
    em phat ic al ly
em ploy ee, em ploy ees
    [employe, employé]
en cy clo pe di a [encyclopaedia]
en er get ic
en force
en vi ron ment
e quip ment, e quipped
es pe cial ly
es thet ic—aes thet ic
ex ag ger ate
ex am ine, ex am in ing,
    ex am i na tion

ex ceed, ex ces sive
ex cel, -lence, -lent
*ex cept (to omit)
ex cit a ble
ex er cise
ex haust ed
ex hil a rat ing
ex ist, -ence
ex pe di tion ar y
ex pense
ex pe ri ence
ex per i ment
*ex tra cur ric u lar
ex trav a gant
ex treme ly
ex u ber ance

fac ile, fa cil i ty
fair way (golf)
fal la cy
fa mil iar
fan ta sy, fan ta sies
fas ci na tion
fa vor ite
Feb ru ar y
fi an cé, fi an cée
fic ti tious
fier y
fi nal ly
fi nan cial ly
fin an cier
fli er—fly er
fore head /fôr'id/
for eign
for feit
for mal ly
for mer ly
for ty-four—for ty four
fourth
frame house
fran ti cal ly [franticly]
fra ter ni ties
*fresh man
friend, -li ness
ful fill—ful fil
fun da men tal, -ly
fur ni ture

fur ther

gauge—gage
gel a tine—gel a tin
ghost
gov ern ment
gov er nor
*grade school [graded school]
gram mar, gram mat i cal, -ly
gray [grey]
grief
grue some [grewsome]
guar an tee, guar an teed
guard i an
guer ril la—gue ril la (fighting)
guid ance

hand i cap, hand i capped
hand ker chief
hand some
hang ar
hap pi ness
hear
here
height
he ro, he roes, her o ine
hid e ous
hin drance
hoard
hoarse (in throat)
horde
hor i zon tal
hors d'oeu vre /ôr dėrv'/
huge
hu man /hū'mən/
hu mane /hū mān'/
hu mor ous
hun gri ly
hur ried ly
hy giene
hyp no sis, hyp not ic, hyp no tize
   [hypnotise]
hy poc ri sy, hyp o crite
hys ter i cal

ig no rance, ig no rant
il log i cal

im ag ine, im ag i na tion,
   im ag i nar y
im me di ate ly
im ple ment
im promp tu, im promp tus
in ad e quate
in ces sant ly
in ci den tal ly
*in cred i ble
in de pend ence
in dict ment /in dīt'mənt/
in dis pen sa ble
in flu ence, in flu en tial
in gen ious
in gen u ous
in i ti a tion
in nu en do, in nu en does
in oc u late
in struc tor
in tel lec tu al
in tel li gent
in ter est
in tern [interne]
in ter pre tive [interpretative]
in ter rupt
in tol er ance
in ven tor—in ven ter
ir rel e vant
ir re li gious
ir re sist i ble
ir rev er ent
*its, it's
it self

ja lop y
john ny cake
jol li ty
*judg ment [judgement]

kha ki
kid nap, kid naped [kidnapped]
ki mo no, ki mo nos
kin der gar ten
kitch en ette
knowl edge

la bor, -er, -ious ly ·

lab o ra to ry
lat er /lā′tər/
*lat ter /lat′ər/
lau rel
lax a tive
*lead, led
leg a cy
le git i mate
lei sure ly
length, -en ing
li a ble
li ar
li brar i an
li cense
light en ing (making lighter)
*light ning (a flash)
lik a ble [likeable]
like, -ness, -ly, -li hood
li queur
liq uor
liv a ble [liveable]
live li hood
lone, -ly, -li ness
loose /lüs/
*lose /lüz/, los ing
lux u ry

mack er el
mag a zine
mag nif i cent, mag nif i cence
main tain, main te nance
man tel (the shelf)
man tle (the cloak)
man u al
man u fac tur er
mar riage
math e mat ics
mean, meant
med i cine
*me di e val [mediaeval]
me di o cre
Me di ter ra ne an
met al
met tle
mil lion aire
min i a ture
min ute

mis chief, mis chie vous
mis spelled
mold [mould]
mo not o nous
*mor al /môr′əl/, -ly
mo rale /mə ral′/
mort gage
moun tain ous
mur mur
mus cle
mus tache
mys te ri ous

*na ive—na ïve
nat u ral ly
nec es sar y, nec es sar i ly
*Ne gro, Ne groes
nei ther
nick el
niece
nine ty-ninth—nine ty ninth
no tice a ble, no tic ing
no to ri e ty
nui sance

o bey, o be di ence
o bliged
ob sta cle
*oc ca sion, -al ly
oc cur, -ring, -rence, oc curred
of fi cial
oil y
o mit, -ted, o mis sion
one self
op er ate
op po nent
op por tu ni ty
op ti mism
or gan i za tion [organisation]
or gan ize [organise]
or i gin, o rig i nal
out ra geous

*paid
pa ja ma [pyjama]
pam phlet
pan to mime

par al lel, par al leled
par lia ment
pa roled
par tic i pate
par tic u lar ly
*passed, past
pas time
ped es tal
per ceive
per form
per ma nent
per mit, per mis si ble
per se ver ance
per sist ent
per son al
per son nel
per spi ra tion
per suade, per sua sion
phase
Phil ip pines
phi los o phy
phys i cal
phy si cian
pi an o, pi an os
pick le
*pic nic, pic nicked
piece
pique /pēk/
pi qué /pi kā′/
plain
plane
planned
play wright
pleas ant
pneu mat ic
pneu mo nia
*pol i tics, pol i ti cian
pos si bil i ty
po ta to, po ta toes
prac ti ca bil i ty
*prac ti cal
prac tice [practise]
pre cede, pre ced ing
pref er ence, pre ferred
prej u dice
prep a ra tion
pres ence

prev a lent
prim i tive
*prin ci pal
prin ci ple
priv i lege
prob a ble, prob a bly
pro ce dure
pro ceed
pro fes sion
pro fes sor
pro gram [programme]
prom i nent
pro nounce, pro nun ci a tion
prop a gan da
pro pel ler
pro te in
psy cho a nal y sis,
    psy cho an a lyze
*psy chol o gy
psy cho path ic
psy cho so mat ic
pub lic ly
pump kin, punkin
pur sue, pur suit

quan ti ty
quan tum
quar an tine
quay [quai] /kē/
qui et
quite
quix ot ic
quiz, quiz zes

re al ly
re ceive
*rec i pe, re ceipt
re cip i ent
rec la ma tion
rec og ni tion
rec om mend
re-en ter
re en ter
re fer, ref er ence, re ferred
re for est a tion
rel a tive
rel e gate

rel e vant

re lieve

re li gion, re li gious

re mem ber

rem i nisce

*Ren ais sance [Re nas cence]

ren dez vous

re pel lent

rep e ti tion, rep e ti tious

re sem blance

res er voir

re sist ance

re spect ful ly

re spec tive ly

res tau rant

rev er ent

rhet o ric

rhyme [rime]

rhythm, rhyth mi cal

ri dic u lous

room mate

sac ri fice

sac ri le gious

safe ty

sal a ry

sand wich

sax o phone

scan dal ous

scar /skär/

scare /skãr/

sce nar i o

scene, sce nic

sched ule

sec re tar i al

seize

se mes ter

sen a tor

sense, sen si ble

sen tence

sep a rate, sep a ra tion

ser geant /sär′jənt/

sev er al

se vere ly, se ver i ty

shear (verb)

sheer (adj.)

shin ing

sieve

sig nif i cance

*sim i lar

sin cere ly, sin cer i ty

site (of a city)

skep ti cal [sceptical]

*ski, skis, skied, ski ing

slim y

slug gish

soc cer

sol u ble

so phis ti ca tion

*soph o more

source

speak, speech

spe cif i cal ly

spec i men, spec i mens

spec ter [spectre]

spic y, spic i ness

spon sor

stac ca to

sta tion ar y (fixed)

sta tion er y (paper)

stat ue

stat ure

stat ute

stom ach ache

sto ry [storey] (of a building)

straight

strength

stretched

stud y ing

sub stan tial

sub tle [subtile]

suc ceed, suc cess

suc cess ful, suc ces sion

suit /süt/

suite /swēt/

sul fa

sul fur—sul phur

sum ma ry, summed

su per in tend ent

su per sede

sup pose

sup press

sur prise

sus cep ti ble

sus pense
syl la ble
sym bol
sym me try, sym met ri cal
syn or y mous
syph i lis
syr up—sir up

use, -ful, -less, us ing
u su al ly
u ten sil

vac u um
var ies
var i ous
veg e ta bles
*ta boo [tabu]
tar iff
tech nique [technic]
tem per a ment,
   tem per a men tal
tend en cy
than
*the a ter [theatre]
their
the o ry, the o ries
then
there
there fore
they're
thor ough [thoro]
though—tho
thought
thou sandths
through—thru
to, too, two
to day [to-day]
to geth er
traf fic, traf fick ing
trag e dy, trag ic
tries, tried
tru ly
Tues day
typ i cal
tyr an ny

venge ance
ven ti late, ven ti la tion
ver ti cal
vice (evil)
view
vig i lance
vig i lan tes
vil i fy
vil lain
vise [vice] (the tool)
vis i bil i ty
vi ta min [vitamine]
vol ume

war rant
war ring
weath er
weight, -y
weird
wheth er
whis key [whisky]
whole
whol ly
whoop
who's (who is)
whose
wool en [woollen]
wool ly—wool y
write, writ ing, writ er, writ ten

un doubt ed ly
un nec es sar y
un prec e dent ed
un til (*till)
un u su al

yacht
yield
you're (you are)

zo ol o gy [zoölogy], zo o log i cal

For a discussion of English spelling see p. 403. *Index* articles that discuss spelling include: *American and British usage, *Analogy in language, *Apostrophe § 6, *Change in language, *Divided usage, *Pronunciation § 2c.

Split infinitive • The word order in which an adverb comes between the *to* and the verb (The receptionist asked them *to kindly sit down*) is called a *split infinitive*.

Since the adverb modifies the verb, its natural position is next to the actual verb form, and writers of General English have never taken very seriously the puristic efforts to prohibit the construction. Changing the position of *silently* gives each of these sentences a different meaning:

He prepared silently to go along.
He prepared to go along silently.
He prepared to silently go along.

There is no point in rearranging a sentence just to avoid splitting an infinitive unless it is an awkward one. But awkward split infinitives are to be avoided:

Awkward: After a while I was able to, although not very accurately, distinguish the good customers from the sulky ones.

Improved: After a while I was able to distinguish—though not very accurately—the good customers from the sulky ones.

(See also *Latin and English § 3. References: Curme, *Syntax,* pp. 458-465; Fowler, "Split Infinitive," for overprecise distinctions; Fries, *AEG,* pp. 132, 144; W. H. Smith, "The Split Infinitive," *Anglia,* 1959, 77:257-278.)

Spoken and written English •

1. *Speech and writing.* Language originated as speech; the writing of it came very late in its history, some 6000 years ago. The number of significant differentiations in sound which a speaker uses is considerably larger than the number of symbols available in most established systems of writing. In English we have about forty speech sounds, four levels of pitch, four degrees of stress, and varying durations of sound and silence. (See *Intonation, *Phonemes, *Pronunciation.) To represent these elements of our speech, we have twenty-six letters, nine marks of punctuation, and a few devices like capitals and italics. As an exact representation of speech, our system of writing is obviously unsatisfactory.

The inventors of systems of writing were no doubt less concerned with transcribing every significant detail of the spoken language than with providing a reliable system of verbal communication which had permanence and could be understood visually. The fact that the heavy accent falls on the first syllable of *daily* but on the second of *today* need not be shown because the five symbols arranged in their familiar order tell the reader what word is intended; as soon as he recognizes the word, he knows where to accent it. Even with *desert,* the context will tell him whether the noun or the verb is intended and therefore whether the accent falls on the first or second syllable. Sometimes, in fact, the written forms provide more information than we really need, as a stenographer can testify from the fact that *bread* and *bred, two* and *too,* and all other homophones will look the same in shorthand and yet most will be intelligible. Although writing is never a complete transcription of speech—is no more than a good hint at exactly what might be spoken—it is a satisfactory system of communication.

Even with its limitations, writing can be a very powerful and effective medium. It is therefore legitimate to speak of the written language (or at least of the *written styles* of a language) as an entity in itself. Although *writing,* to some, suggests a weak reflection of speech, the enormous and vital prose literature of the last two or three centuries proves that such a connotation is incorrect. Most prose literature was written to be communicated through the eye, not the ear; and though oral reading often increases its effectiveness, its survival depends mainly on its capacity for communicating without the direct use of sound. What the printed material would sound like if read aloud is still important to its effect, but the actual hearing is not crucial. Many native speakers of English whose pronunciation of French is atrocious can read French prose with delight—Voltaire, for example—though they may find that even the greatest French verse—Racine or Victor Hugo—is unrewarding.

There are some instances in which the written language does better than the spoken; sometimes it makes clear what is almost impossible to communicate in speech, such as detailed instructions, which must be read repeatedly; extensive use of brief quotations, especially quotations within quotations, which can be efficiently indicated by the punctuation; some homophones which would be ambiguous in speech: *We'll halve it,* which could be mistaken for *we'll have it.*

The written language must retain a relationship to the spoken, but it should be an immediately understandable one that does not require the reader to puzzle out from inadequate transcription what would be obvious in speech. Sometimes this means the spoken language must be rephrased for writing. For instance, in *more competent men, more* might modify either *competent* or *competent men.* In speech the distinction would be shown by greater stress on *more* if it modified *competent men.* In writing, the distinction might be shown by *more men who are competent,* or if *more* modified *competent* only, by adding a modifier as in *more really competent men.*
2. *"Colloquial" English.* Dictionaries formerly marked words *Colloq.* to suggest that in the editors' judgment they were more common in speech than in writing. Many people took this

label to mean that the dictionary frowned upon the use of these words, but even the 1934 Webster definition of *colloquial* shows that this was not true:

acceptable and appropriate in ordinary conversational context, as in intimate speech among cultivated people, in familiar letters, in informal speeches or writings but not in formal written discourse (*flabbergast; go slow; harum-scarum*). Colloquial speech may be as correct as formal speech.—By permission. From *Webster's New International Dictionary,* Second Edition, copyright 1934, 1939, 1945, 1950, by G. & C. Merriam Co.

The three expressions given as examples show that *colloquial* was not being used as a word of dispraise or even of suspicion, for though *flabbergast, go slow,* and *harum-scarum* may be more appropriate in speech than in Formal writing, they are accurate, expressive words that could be used in most General as well as Informal writing. But since a good many people continue to interpret *colloquial* as condemnatory, the label is not used in the most recent dictionaries and is used in this book only infrequently and cautiously. If a usage is more common in speech than in writing, that fact is stated; if the word or expression is in good use but would rarely be found in General or Formal writing, it is labeled Informal.

Of course there are different varieties of spoken English, from Nonstandard and even slovenly to distinctly Formal. Many educated people, especially in the professions, get most of their information from periodicals and books, so that their speech reflects the written language. Sometimes the written language may determine the spoken. Topics important in certain limited areas—especially the upper levels of scientific, scholarly, and professional fields, and in some literature—may be much more frequently written than spoken about and may almost never be discussed in ordinary speech. Here the written forms may become the norms, imitated in speech. But for the greater part of the written language, speech, somewhat condensed and made more precise, is the basis.

The closeness of the written literary English to the spoken English of the time has varied from period to period. In the nineteenth century the two were rather far apart—consider Hawthorne and, even more, the rank and file of lesser writers. Since 1880 or so in England and since 1910 in the United States, there has been a closer approach of written to spoken style. Today, how closely one's written style should approximate his spoken style depends upon appropriateness; he should feel free to use words and constructions characteristic of speech when they fit naturally with other traits of his style (see *Style).

(See Ch. 1, "Differences between speaking and writing," p. 9, Ch. 5, p. 171.)

Spoonerism • A *spoonerism* is an exchange of the initial sounds of two words, as in *a half-warmed fish* for *a half-formed wish*—either unintentional or for humorous effect.

spoonful, spoonfuls • The Standard plurals of *spoonful, tablespoonful, teaspoonful* are *spoonfuls, tablespoonfuls, teaspoonfuls* (similarly, *basketfuls, carfuls, cupfuls, shovelfuls, tubfuls*).
   Cupsful, carsful, shovelsful, and so on are often heard, though they appear less frequently in written English.

Squinting modifier • See *Ambiguity § 2.

St. • See *street.

St., Ste. • See *saint.

Staccato style • A staccato style has—as its principal characteristic—short, emphatic sentences, often exclamations or questions, usually without expressed connectives between the statements. The words, especially verbs, are likely to be vigorous. It is effective in short passages that deserve sharp stressing but is likely to be tiresome and to lose its emphasis if it is long continued:

   Hindenburg was shortening his lines. He was quitting northern France and Belgium. But he was holding the Argonne. Day by day the representatives of our G. H. Q. had shown us the map with every enemy division and reserve force marked. Hindenburg had thirty-two reserve divisions at the beginning of our Argonne drive. When November began two or three remained. What had become of an army of German reserves?—GEORGE SELDES, *You Can't Print That!* p. 35

   (Compare *Telegraphic style.)

Standard English • See Ch. 1, "Standard English," p. 15.

state • See *say.

still • *Still* is an adverb in the sentence *It's still raining* and a conjunction (*Conjunctive adverbs) in *I can see your point of view; still I don't agree with you.*

strata • *Strata* is the plural of the singular *stratum*. It is pronounced /strā′tə/ or /strat′ə/.

street • In many newspapers and in some Informal writing, *street* is not capitalized as part of an address. In Formal and most General writing it is capitalized (41 High Street).

The abbreviation *St.* or *st.* is not much used except to save space in newspapers, lists, or reference works.

Stress • See *Noun and verb stress, *Phonemes § 2a, *Pronunciation.

Strong verbs • See *Principal parts of verbs.

Style • Style has been the subject of a number of well-known aphorisms: "Proper words in proper places make the true definition of a style" (Jonathan Swift); "Style is the dress of thoughts" (Lord Chesterfield); "Style is this: to add to a given thought all the circumstances fitted to produce the whole effect that the thought ought to produce" (Stendhal); "Style is the ultimate morality of mind" (A. N. Whitehead); and, most often quoted of all, "The style is the man" (Comte de Buffon).

These are all provocative statements, and properly idealistic, but they tend to defeat profitable discussion; a student of literature or a writer needs something more explicit. Although *style* may be defined variously, it is basically the characteristics, the qualities of the language in a particular piece of discourse. (There are oral styles as well as written, but in this brief treatment only the written will be discussed.) A writer has a wide range to choose from for words, constructions, sentence patterns, and arrangement and emphasis of his material. The style is the choices he makes, consciously or unconsciously, among the options offered by the language. The formation of most noun plurals and the past tense of most verbs, the agreement of subjects and verbs, the standard word order of English are part of the structure of the language and not distinctive traits of style. But the relative length and complexity of sentences, the variations in the order of sentence elements, the use of long or short constructions, the choice and especially the connotation of words may be. The study of style is an effort to discover what qualities of the language used in a particular story, essay, or article give rise to certain of the reader's impressions of it, especially to his response to the tones that are aside from its denotation, the part of the meaning that would be largely lost in a summary or paraphrase of the passage.

1. *The study of style.* The study of style is, then, one emphasis in the study of language. It is closely related to linguistics (some books in linguistics have a term for it, usually "stylistics") and will increasingly use the methods and data of that discipline. But the study of style is interpretive as well as descriptive; it is concerned primarily with the study of specific items of discourse rather than with the general system of the language, and it takes account of meaning and effect, matters at least currently not much explored in linguistics. The aim of the study of style is increased awareness of the qualities of language in use, viewed especially as the source of a reader's impressions.

The first step in studying a style is a natural, attentive reading, usually more than one reading. It is a good idea to make notes of the traits of language that you believe will repay further investigation and of your early impressions, perhaps describing the style as compact or diffuse, literal or allusive or figurative, flat or emphatic, direct or involved, and so on—however it strikes you as a whole.

The next step is a detailed, analytic reading of the passage. Some counting (of kinds of words, types of phrases, length and type of sentences...) is in order, not to accumulate statistics but to gather evidence for the rightness of your first impressions (this reading may of course prove to you that your first impressions were mistaken) and to enable you to demonstrate the validity of your judgment of the style to others. (It is surprising what previously unnoticed traits will force themselves on your attention while you are concentrating almost mechanically on, perhaps, adjectives or metaphors.)

Finally, read the piece again for its own sake and to see the individual traits as a part of the whole. This reading should be more perceptive and more rewarding than the first. Such occasional careful studies of particular pieces should increase the fullness of your first response to others.

2. *Elements of style.* There are no standard categories for the study of style, but some are needed to guide observation. The headings given in this section will serve to organize most of the elements of language usually considered as traits of style. Many of the topics are discussed in chapters of the *Guide* from the point of view of a writer, but the same points can be used to begin the observation and discussion of something already written. The three short passages on p. 836 will be referred to for illustrating some of the points.

a–Thought movement. It is hard to substantiate objectively impressions such as *thin, diffuse, pithy, meaty, dense,* but they can be pretty well demonstrated by looking at the contribution made by individual sentences. The rapidity or slowness of movement, the kind of statement (simple, complex, or compound; periodic or loose...), the marks of continuity, the interrelations of details and generalizations vary widely among writers and contribute to the stylistic impression. The Orwell passage is closely packed with visual detail; the Thurber is more relaxed, a series of individual impressions bearing on the generalization of the first two sentences; the Conrad passage, though organized as narrative, is chiefly visual detail elaborating the narrative movement.

(Ch. 4 discusses thought movement in some detail.)

b–Qualities of sound. There is a question how big a part sound plays in a literature that is written primarily for silent reading. It is obviously important in verse, but it has some importance in prose literature as well. Inattention to sound is responsible for some of the shortcomings of much journalistic and "bureaucratic" prose—it is obviously not "heard" by the writer. We have to be especially cautious in discussing the *intonation: for example, an American would read aloud a passage by a British writer rather differently from the way its author would read it, and a Northerner's reading of a story by a Southern writer would be different from the writer's in some respects.

Even in reading silently we are somewhat conscious of the possible sounds, and in reading slowly we may almost form them—certainly part of our impression of a passage comes from its "sound." The important sounds are those in stressed syllables. There may be a conspicuous series of the same sound, or more often of sounds similar in some phonetic respect: voiced consonants (b, g, v, z, and so on) or unvoiced (p, k, f, s) or "stop" consonants (b, d, g, k, p, t); back vowels /ō/, /ü/, /ô/, or front vowels /ā/, /ē/, /a/; nasals or sibilants. Or there may be a marked variety (as the vowels in the last Orwell phrase are all different: /ō/, /ā/, /ī/, /u/, /a/, /ou/, /ô/, or marked contrasts in individual sounds or groups of sounds, as in the last part of the last Conrad sentence (". . . a land from which the very memory of motion had forever departed").

Three sequences of sounds are named: *alliteration, the same initial sounds (*m*emory of *m*otion), helps bind phrases together; *assonance, syllables with the same vowel but different consonant sounds (m*i*xture of c*i*nders), and consonance, syllables with the same consonants combined with different vowel and consonant sounds (Rou*nd* ma*ny* weste*rn* isla*nds* have I bee*n*).

There has been a good deal of study of prose rhythm. The older method was to scan the units of prose as verse is scanned, by dividing them into feet (iambic, dactylic, etc.). But the units of prose, actually sense units, are usually longer than a metric foot, so that dividing into feet means even less in prose than it does in verse. The sound movement in prose is essentially the intonation patterns, and the methods of linguistics—

Passages Illustrating Points of Style

The canal path was a mixture of cinders and frozen mud, criss-crossed by the imprints of innumerable clogs, and all round, as far as the slag-heaps in the distance, stretched the "flashes"—pools of stagnant water that had seeped into the hollows caused by the subsidence of the ancient pits. It was horribly cold. The "flashes" were covered with ice the colour of raw umber, the bargemen were muffled to the eyes in sacks, the lock gates wore beards of ice. It seemed a world from which vegetation had been banished; nothing existed except smoke, shale, ice, mud, ashes and foul water.—GEORGE ORWELL, "North and South," *The Road to Wigan Pier*, p. 138

The notion that such persons ["writers of light pieces running from a thousand to two thousand words"] are gay of heart and carefree is curiously untrue. They lead, as a matter of fact, an existence of jumpiness and apprehension. They sit on the edge of the chair of Literature. In the house of Life they have the feeling that they have never taken off their overcoats. Afraid of losing themselves in the larger flight of the two-volume novel, or even of the one-volume novel, they stick to short accounts of their misadventures because they never get so deep into them but that they feel they can get out. This type of writing is not a joyous form of self-expression but the manifestation of a twitchiness at once cosmic and mundane. Authors of such pieces have, nobody knows why, a genius for getting into minor difficulties: they walk into the wrong apartments, they drink furniture polish for stomach bitters, they drive their cars into the prize tulip beds of haughty neighbors, they playfully slap gangsters, mistaking them for old school friends. To call such persons humorous, a loose-fitting and ugly word, is to miss the nature of their dilemma and the dilemma of their nature. The little wheels of their invention are set in motion by the damp hand of melancholy.—JAMES THURBER, *My Life and Hard Times*, Preface

In the stillness of the air every tree, every leaf, every bough, every tendril of creeper and every petal of minute blossoms seemed to have been bewitched into an immobility perfect and final. Nothing moved on the river but the eight paddles that rose flashing regularly, dipped together with a single splash; while the steersman swept right and left with a periodic and sudden flourish of his blade describing a glinting semi-circle above his head. The churned-up water frothed alongside with a confused murmur. And the white man's canoe, advancing upstream in the short-lived disturbance of its own making, seemed to enter the portals of a land from which the very memory of motion had forever departed.—JOSEPH CONRAD, "The Lagoon," *Tales of Unrest*, p. 187

the stresses (´ ^ ˋ ˘) and junctures (the pauses and rising and falling terminals)—can probably be developed into a workable scheme for describing it. (See *Phonemes § 2.)

Any discussion of the rhythm of prose would have to be very detailed to be accurate or helpful. Reading aloud the passages on p. 836 will give some idea of the variety in length of rhythmical units, in intensity of stresses, in position of stresses (especially at the ends of sentences and of important constructions within them), and of the general contribution of sound to the impression of styles.

c–Visual traits. Although the appearance to the eye is not so important for prose as for verse, there is some slight contribution to the effect of prose from such matters as length of paragraphs, use of italic type, stylistic use of capitals (*Capital letters § 10), and even from punctuation marks—close punctuation usually suggesting a slower movement than open (see Ch. 10). There is just enough effect from these matters to warrant including them in a discussion of style.

d–Minor points of syntax. In contemporary style the smaller elements of syntax are perhaps more important than the frame of sentences. There are some options in word forms: adverbs ending with -*ly* or without (*Adverbs, types and forms); choice between two plurals of nouns from other languages (*Plurals of nouns § 4); *comparison of adjectives and adverbs with -*er*, -*est* or with *more, most*; choice between two past forms of a few verbs (*Principal parts of verbs); the use or nonuse of active or *passive verbs and of *subjunctive forms. There is some variation possible in the position of adjectives (an immobility *perfect* and *final*) and more in the position of adverbial modifiers (frothed *alongside with a confused murmur*).

There are distinctly different impressions from constructions with nouns as *headwords (by the *subsidence* of the ancient *pits,* the *stillness* of the *air*) and those centered on verbs (as in Thurber's series of mishaps—*they walk . . . drink . . . drive . . . slap . . .*) and the constructions with *verbals that often have the syntax of nouns or adjectives with some of the action qualities of verbs (*mistaking* them for old school friends, *describing* a *glinting* semi-circle). A good deal has been written about the stylistic impact of the various parts of speech. People probably differ in their sensitiveness to this trait, but there are differences between styles with nouns especially prominent and those with verbs, and also differences that depend on the number and quality of modifiers (*Adjectives in use, *Adverbs in use). The Orwell passage has very few adjectives, the Conrad several emphatic ones. Pronouns and other personal words are associated with narrative, but they give ease and rapidity to exposition, as in the Thurber passage.

There are numerous devices that make for compactness: two or more verbs with one subject; noun modifiers rather than prepositional phrases ("the *stone* house" instead of "the house *of stone*"); adjective clauses without the introductory pronoun or still further reduced ("ice the colour of raw umber" instead of "ice which was the colour of raw umber"). (These qualities are discussed in Ch. 8, "Economy in sentences," p. 314.)

Taken together these syntactical traits contribute to impressions of diffuseness or compactness and emphasis; to pace, a sense of slowness or rapidity; and often to the degree of Formality or Informality.

e–Sentences. A writer has wide latitude in how much he will put in a single sentence, of which the physical length is the external symptom. Our three passages are too short for any generalizations, but they show some range. The Orwell sentences run from 4 to 50 words, averaging 25.5; Thurber's 9 to 50, averaging 23.2; and Conrad's 9 to 42, averaging 29. Often there is contrast in arrangement, as Orwell's 4-word sentence follows one of 50, and Conrad's 9-word sentence comes between one of 42 and one of 33 words.

(Sentence length and some of the other more important variations in sentence patterns are discussed in Ch. 8.)

f–Words. English offers a wide range in the choice of words. They differ in the variety of English they come from, in their familiarity, in their degree of concreteness or abstractness, in their precision of meaning, and in their connotations—their tone, the associations from experience or from literature they bring to mind. The three passages show considerable range in words, from the precise words from experience of Orwell to the literary ones of Conrad.

Words are the most familiar element of style. Chapters 1 and 9 will furnish the basic points to consider.

g–Imagery. *Imagery (picture-forming) is a quality of words, but its importance is sufficient to warrant a separate heading. Imagery can be interpreted as roughly equivalent to concreteness. A concrete word calls up a sense impression; an abstract word ordinarily does not. But readers vary: what is an image-bearing word for one person will evoke no image at all or a very different one for another person. Much depends on the experience of the reader and on his habits of thinking.

Verbal images differ in the senses they represent (sight, sound, taste, smell, touch); sight so predominates in imagery that the use of the other senses often has unusual force. The verbal images may be simple, as in the Orwell passage, or complex, involving movement, as in the Conrad. They may be the substance of the piece, as in the Orwell and Conrad passages, or secondary, supporting an idea, as in Thurber. They differ greatly in precision, sometimes forcing an exact picture on a reader, more often allowing him considerable leeway in what image he will produce from his memory. They may be sampled, highly selective, or massed—as in a detailed description. Their connotations are usually more from the objects named than from the words, so that they may seem to be actually symbols, and often the feeling or mood associated with the objects is aroused in the reader.

h–Figures of speech. Figures of speech, which contribute a great deal to imagery, have always been a part of the treatment of style. The term is rather vague and certainly flexible (some of the old lists of figures of speech ran to over 280), but basically figures of speech include words and phrases that come from a context, an area of meaning, other than the subject being presented; expressions that are intensified or altered in some way; and also turns of phrase that are in some way out of the ordinary. The idea of figures of speech was originally based on the supposition that people used language basically in a literal, referential sense and that other uses were a substitution for this ordinary language—for ornament or impressiveness. We now know that all people use figures of speech freely in their everyday talk and writing—children use many figures—and that the point about metaphor and the figures is not so much their departure from literal meaning as what they contribute to the meaning. This contribution is often to the tone and the connotation, bringing into one context some quality or attitude associated with another—with a resulting freshness and emphasis.

Figures may be relatively pale—the metaphor in Orwell's "beards of ice" seems a familiar and almost literal expression, and the personification implied in the verb *wore* is so slight that it seems chiefly grammatical, allowing a more active verb than a flat *had*. Conrad's "bewitched into an immobility" and "a land from which the very memory of motion had forever departed" are more literary and allusive. The naturalness of figures is shown by Thurber's metaphors, exaggerations, allusions, and the extended metaphor or analogy of the last sentence, and even the relatively rare *chiasmus,* two constructions in which the order of keywords is reversed (the nature of their dilemma and the dilemma of their nature).

It is not necessary to be able to name all of the departures from a precise, literal use of words (most of the figures have Greek names that seem strange to us), though we should be able to identify more than metaphors and similes. The important thing is to see what they add, what associations, connotations, attitudes (many are used just for fun), and emphases the figures bring to bear on the subject being presented.

(Several groups of figures are discussed in Ch. 9, "Figurative use of words," p. 350, and others in *Index* articles such as *Epigrams, *Imitative words and phrases, *Negatives, *Personification, *Puns.)

3. *Generalizations about style.* The impetus to the study of style is to understand and appreciate particular items of discourse, but naturally such studies lead to generalizations, if for no other reason than to help in summarizing observations.

There are many terms for general impressions of a style (some have been mentioned earlier in this article): flexible, varied—rigid or monotonous or mannered; conventional, traditional—individual, original, fresh; tense—relaxed; simple—complex; and so on; as well as terms that emphasize separate qualities: literal—figurative; direct—involved; abstract—concrete, imagistic.

Since the earliest rhetoricians there have been efforts to classify styles in general, and in spite of various experiments in terms they come back to the polarities of the *plain,* the more literal and direct, and *heightened,* the more elaborate, using more of the devices of language, especially with emotional suggestion. In between these is a gradation, often called simply *middle* or *mixed* styles, with a conversational base but showing some of the devices of more elaborate styles. The three passages on p. 836 illustrate this range: Orwell, the plain; Conrad, the heightened; and Thurber, the middle.

Since it is difficult to talk in detail about style by itself, it is natural to go to its relationships, Style and ——. There are obvious relationships between the individuality of the writer and his style, though asserting specific relationships is risky. There are some traits of style characteristic of various types of writing (fiction, science, advertising, polemic), of various subject matters (politics, religion, law), and of the literary perspectives of humor, satire, tragedy, and so on.

And finally there is the theoretical question of style and meaning, which is easier to sense than to state. Traits of language certainly affect the precision, intensity, emphasis, tone, and suggestiveness of the central message. Neglecting the style in discussing meaning may lead to misinterpretation, as neglecting the intonation of a *yes* or a *no* in a conversation may. A full and accurate understanding of the meaning of a passage depends in part on a sensitive response to the style.

4. *Style and an individual's writing.* For a practiced writer, style is not a conscious concern but a by-product of his effort to make language carry out his purpose. Most writers start under the influence of some other writer and may even intentionally imitate him for a time. But better is a good deal of varied reading that will show the possibilities of the language. You will unconsciously pick up traits that suit your material, your purposes, and your temperament. Occasional rereading and reading aloud from a writer whose work you would like yours to resemble in some way may help. But nothing can take the place of your own experiments and your own purposeful writing. Your style will develop as you improve in effective completion of your own writing projects.

(*Index* articles treating aspects of style, in addition to those starred in context, include: *Colon § 4, *Conjunction § 2, 3, *Fundamentals § 4, *Jargon § 1, *literary, *Originality § 2, *Scientific and technical writing, *Semicolon § 4, *Subjunctives, *Telegraphic style, *Usage. The following references will provide a guide to a fairly full study of style: Paul F. Baum, *The Other Harmony of Prose,* Durham, 1952—the best starting point for a consideration of prose rhythm; Bonamy Dobrée, *Modern Prose Style,* Oxford, 1934—discussion of passages of prose grouped by subject matter; Edith Rickert, *New Methods for the Study of Literature,* Chicago, 1927—a program of detailed analysis; George Saintsbury, *A History of English Prose Rhythm,* London, 1922—comments on various aspects of the style of past periods; R. A. Sayce, *Style in French Prose,* Oxford, 1953—a topical discussion with various suggested devices; Norton R. Tempest, *The Rhythm of English Prose,* Cambridge, 1930—the analysis of rhythm by metrical feet; Stephen Ullmann, *Style in the French Novel,* Cambridge, 1957—an application of linguistics to style; Richard M. Weaver, *The Ethics of Rhetoric,* Chicago, 1953—stylistic qualities of the parts of speech; W. K. Wimsatt, Jr., *The Prose Style of Samuel Johnson,* New Haven, 1941—one of the more detailed studies of the style of an individual writer.)

Stylebooks • For editors and printers *style* means the method of handling various mechanical matters such as capital letters, punctuation, forms of plurals, division of words, details of typography. Since usage is divided on many of these points, a publisher chooses what form will be used in his publications. Most newspapers, magazines, and publishing houses have stylebooks—documents ranging from a single page to an elaborate volume containing the particular rules to be followed in preparing copy for specific publications. They often show arbitrary choices, to attain a consistency that most publishers feel is desirable. One factor in recent changes in practices in writing and printing has been the decision of some of the book publishers to let authors' copy stand nearly as written, so long as it is consistent.

Most newspaper stylebooks are not generally available, though that of *The New York Times,* revised 1962, is for sale.

The University of Chicago Press *Manual of Style,* eleventh edition (Chicago, 1949), is the most influential stylebook among book publishers. The *United States Government Printing Office Style Manual* (Washington, D.C., 1953) is one of the best stylebooks.

Subject and verb •

1. *As sentence elements.* The backbone of the typical English sentence is a subject and a verb. The subject names the starting point of the statement, and the verb advances the statement. The subject is the noun or substantive in most intimate relation to the verb. Except in inverted sentence order the subject stands before the verb, and its position there is the main grammatical device we have to identify it as the subject, just as the position of the object after the verb identifies it. In the sentence *The submarine sank the cruiser* we know that the submarine and not the cruiser did the sinking because *submarine* is in the subject position in the sentence.

2. *Agreement of subject and verb.* When the verb form permits it, a verb shows agreement with its subject in number and person. This usually means with the grammatical number of the subject. But since, except for the verb *be,* our verbs have only one form for both numbers and for all persons except an *-s* in the third singular present (and the *modal auxiliaries lack this -s*), relatively few problems in agreement can arise. Users of English can rely very little on formal indications of relation between subject and verb; therefore lack of agreement in form seldom causes ambiguity, though it may be felt by the hearer or reader to be a serious mistake: *I is,* for example, is entirely intelligible but it is also certainly Nonstandard.

Singular: *I am* more tired than usual. *A chair was placed* in the corner. *This job takes* four weeks. *The job took* four weeks.

Plural: *We are* more tired than usual. *Three chairs were placed* along the wall. *These jobs take* four weeks. *The jobs took* four weeks.

The problems that arise in the agreement of subject and verb come either from a construction in which the grammatical number of the subject is uncertain or is blurred by other words, or from the meaning of the subject rather than its grammatical form as the basis for agreement.

a–Collective nouns. Agreement according to meaning is seen most clearly in collective nouns, which take either a singular or plural verb, depending upon whether the speaker or writer is emphasizing the group as a whole or the individuals of which it is composed. In writing, the verbs and pronouns of a given sentence should be all plural or all singular in referring back to a collective subject.

Emphasizing the unit: The class *is* the largest in six years.

Emphasizing the individuals: The class *are* by no means all intellectual giants, but *they* have done very well. [More likely: *The students in this class ....*]

(For further examples and discussion see *Collective nouns.)

b–Compound subjects. Ordinarily a compound subject has a plural verb:

Alice and Francis *were* the first to arrive.

The text of the poem and the commentary *make* good reading.

When the two elements of a compound subject refer to the same person or thing, the verb is singular:

The best teacher and the best scholar here *is* Professor Babcock.

The spirit and accomplishment of these men *speaks* for itself.

The verb is often singular when a compound subject follows:

There *is* both health and wealth in this way of life.

For the winner there *was* a large cash prize and weeks of glory.

When a second part of the subject is connected with the first by *with, together with, as well as,* the agreement varies. In Formal English such a construction is kept singular. In General English a plural is often found if the expression is equivalent to a compound subject:

The rudder is the only essential control in taxiing, and this together with a regulative speed *keeps* the plane going in a relatively straight line.

The winner with the four runners-up *were* given a reception. [To make this more Formal, the *with* should be changed to *and,* rather than the *were* to *was.*]

He is not a good speaker, since his hesitating manner with long "uh's" interspersed in the address *make* [Formal: *makes*] him hard to listen to.

Subjects connected by *or* or *either ... or* take a singular verb if both are singular, a plural verb if both are plural or if the one nearer the verb is plural, and often a plural verb if the idea is felt to be plural (especially in questions, where the verb precedes); similarly with *neither ... nor,* with the plural more common:

A novel or a biography *is* to be read outside of class.

Novels or biographies *were* the same to him.

A novel or five short stories *were* to be read.

Either a dentist or a doctor *is* to treat such cases.

Do Tim or any of the others want to come?

Since neither chemistry nor physics *were* [more Formal: *was*] required, most students had no basic physical science.

When the two elements of the subject are pronouns in different persons, the verb is usually plural:

You and I *are* sure to go, anyway.

Either you or he *are* likely to go. [*Is* is possible here to emphasize the singleness of choice.]

Neither you nor I *are* fit for that job.

In questions the plural is common:

Are [or: *Is*] Fred or Harry in?

c–Plural modifier of singular subject. When a rather long plural modifier of a singular subject comes between it and the verb, Formal and General English usually have a singular verb, but Informal often has a plural verb:

This *group* of essays *is* [not: *are*] concerned with problems in sociology and philosophy as they are related to biology.

The *form* of your bibliography and footnotes *is* not standard.

To a beginner on the organ the *array* of stops and pistons, couplers, and pedals *seems* [Informal: *seem*] at first quite bewildering.

Two thousand dollars' *worth* of pictures *were* [Formal: *was*] destroyed.

d–Relative pronouns. A relative pronoun referring to a singular noun has a singular verb (The person *who takes* enough pains can do it) and one referring to a plural noun has a plural verb (The people *who take* pains win in the long run). In idioms like *This is one of the most discouraging things that has come out of the situation,* Formal usage requires *that have come,* since the antecedent of *that* is *things*; Informal often and General occasionally have *that has come,* because the central idea (of *one*) is singular.

Formal: Jeffrey is one of those moderns *who are* making *their* money talk.

Informal and, less often, General: Jeffrey is one of those moderns *who is* making *his* money talk.

(See *one of those who.)

e–Subject and complement of different number. The verb agrees with the subject:

A day's work is four trips.   Four trips make a day's work.

f–Plural subject with singular meaning. When the idea conveyed by a plural subject is singular in intent, the verb is usually singular: *Five years is a long time.*

(References: Curme, *Syntax,* Ch. 4; Fries, *AEG,* pp. 188-190, 249-250, and index references; Pooley, pp. 78-88.)

3. *Punctuation between subject and verb*. Since the subject and verb are part of one construction, they should not normally be separated by a comma:

Another example of what can happen [ ] is furnished by the experience of two young women who were staying at the hotel.

(See *Comma § 8. Discussion and other examples of subject and verb relations will be found in Ch. 8. "The favorite English sentence," "Minor sentence types," and "Revising subject-verb agreement," pp. 276, 284, 294, Ch. 10, "Between subjects, verbs, objects," p. 389.)

Subject of a gerund • See *Gerund § 2.

Subject of an infinitive • See *Infinitives § 5.

Subject of a sentence • See *Adjectives, types and forms § 6; *Agreement § 1; *Compound subject; *Gerund § 1; *Infinitives § 4; *Shifted constructions; *Subject and verb.

Subjective case • See *Nominative case.

Subjunctives • It is not necessary to use the Latin grammar subjunctive mood in describing English verbs. It is probably inaccurate to do so for two reasons: very few forms can be surely identified as "subjunctives," hardly enough to furnish a paradigm; and the use of the few identifiable forms is so irregular that no definite syntactical criteria can be stated to define it.

This article presents some facts about the nontypical subject-verb agreement traditionally called the subjunctive.

1. *Form of subjunctives.*

a–Simple subjunctive. In current English the form called subjunctive is identifiable only in certain forms of *be* (I, you, he ... *be*; I, he ... *were*); in forms made with *be* (he *were asking*); and in the third person singular of most verbs (*he ask* instead of *he asks*; *he have* instead of *he has*).

b–Subjunctive with auxiliaries. Some grammarians include as subjunctives all the locutions that can be used in expressing ideas that may also be, or have at some time been, expressed by the subjunctive, or the forms that could be used in translating subjunctives found in other languages. Under this system several auxiliaries—*may, might, should, would, let, have to,* and others—become subjunctives. This broad interpretation makes consideration of the subjunctive more complicated than is necessary, since the meaning and connotation of such constructions come from the meaning of the auxiliary or from adverbs.

For that reason, in the following discussion only the simple subjunctive—that is, a verb form differing from the one ordinarily expected—is considered.

2. *Uses of the subjunctive.* Because of the paucity of forms, English makes much less use of the mood than most of the modern European languages do. There are a number of idioms in which the subjunctive may be used in English, especially in Formal English, though it is almost always possible to use other verb forms. It is fairly common in wishes, conditions, qualified or doubtful statements, and in *that*-clauses and after expressions like *It is necessary*. The following examples illustrate typical uses of the subjunctive and give alternative idioms that would be more common.

a–Formulas. The subjunctive is found in numerous formulas, locutions surviving from a time when the subjunctive was used freely. Most of these are no longer common idioms; that is, we do not make other sentences on the pattern of *Far be it from me. . . .*

Suffice it to say	Heaven forbid	Heaven help us	Be it said
If I were you	God bless you	Be that as it may	As it were

Many mild oaths have this form: *Confound it; Psychology be hanged.*

Some of these formulas are used in all levels of the language; some, like *Come what may*, are rather Formal, and the oaths are chiefly Informal.

b–In *that*-clauses. The subjunctive is mandatory in idioms for recommendations, resolutions, demands, and so on. These idioms are usually in a Formal context. Note the following examples:

Formal: We recommend that the Commissioner *designate* for this use the land formerly belonging to Mr. Brewster.

Formal: I ask that the interested citizen *watch* closely the movements of these troops.

General: I ask the interested citizen to watch the movement of these troops closely.

Formal: . . . the order that he *be* dropped

General: . . . the order to drop him

Formal: It is necessary that every member *inform* himself of these rules.

General: It is necessary for every member to inform himself of these rules. It is necessary that every member should inform himself of these rules. Every member must [should] inform himself of these rules.

c–In conditions. The subjunctive may be used in *if*-clauses when there is doubt of fulfillment of the condition, or when the condition is "contrary-to-fact"—impossible or not believed by the writer:

If one good *were* really as good as another, no good would be any good.—IRWIN EDMAN, *Four Ways of Philosophy*, p. 80

The meaning here does not require the less common *were*, since the contrary-to-factness is conveyed by the use of a past form (either *was* or *were*) with a present or future meaning. Edman's idea would certainly be as clear if he had written "If one good was as good as another, no good would be any good," but the tone would be a little different.

In fact, few writers make such a distinction and a large proportion of the "subjunctives" found are in "simple" conditions:

Formal: If the subject of a verb *be* [More usual *is*] impersonal, the verb itself may be called impersonal.—ARTHUR G. KENNEDY, *Current English*, p. 296

The fellow who worked next to him in the plant had been turned off, and Jim could not help wondering if that *were* [More usual: *was*] a sign that some of the rest of them would be discharged, too.— ERSKINE CALDWELL, *Kneel to the Rising Sun*, p. 129

(See *as if, as though, and *Conditions.)

In all of these constructions a speaker or writer has a choice between the "subjunctive" and a regular form of the verb (which may be an "auxiliary") or an infinitive. Charles C. Fries found that in both Standard and Nonstandard English the subjunctive was used rather seldom, in considerably less than one fifth of the locutions in which it might be. Actually "subjunctives" are a trait of style rather than of grammar and are used by writers, consciously or unconsciously, to set their language a little apart from everyday usage rather than for basic meaning. The school insistence on the *were* form has even led to its use in statements of fact. (Reference: William M. Ryan, "Pseudo-Subjunctive 'Were,'" *American Speech*, 1961, 36:48-53, and 1962, 37:114-122.)

Students in foreign language courses should remember that very few French, Latin, and German subjunctives can be satisfactorily translated by an English subjunctive. They should try to find the natural idiomatic way of expressing the idea that is idiomatically expressed by the subjunctive in the language they are translating.

(References: The point of view presented in this article will be found in general in Fowler, article "Subjunctives"; Fries, *AEG*, pp. 103-107; Hall, pp. 311-314; Jespersen, Ch. 27; Marckwardt and Walcott, pp. 30, 37, 88, 89; Pooley, pp. 55-59; Thyra J. Bevier, "American Use of the Subjunctive," *American Speech*, 1931, 6:207-215. A different point of view will be found in Curme, *Syntax*, Ch. 20; C. A. Lloyd, "Is the Subjunctive Dying?" *English Journal*, 1937, 26:369-373; Charles D. Cannon, "The Subjunctive Mood in English," *American Speech*, 1959, 34:11-19.)

Submitting manuscript • The conventions for submitting a manuscript for publication depend a good deal on its destination. Increasingly, publishers specify in style sheets how the material should be submitted.

In general the manuscript should be carefully typed, double spaced, on good paper (see *Typewritten copy). Generous margins should be left for editorial operations. Plenty of space, half a page or so, should be left around the title. A carbon copy should be kept for reference.

The writer's name and address may be put in the upper left-hand corner of the first page. The approximate length in words may be put in the upper right-hand corner. Additional facts, such as an account of sources of material or suggestions for illustrations, may be given in an accompanying letter.

Mail in a roomy envelope. Photographs or drawings should be clearly labeled and carefully packed between stiff cardboard.

Enclose an envelope large enough to hold the manuscript as it is folded, addressed to yourself, and carrying sufficient postage for its return.

Subordinate clauses • See *Clauses, *Comma § 2.

Subordinating conjunctions • The most common subordinating conjunctions—words that connect subordinate clauses with the main clauses of sentences—are:

after	*because	since	unless
*although	before	*so	*when
*as	how	*so that	*where
*as if	*if	though	*while
as long as	in order that	*till	why

The relative pronouns (*who, which, that, what*) function also as subordinating conjunctions. (See also *for.)

Subordination •

Revision: Correct the faulty subordination.

Sub

Subordinate sentence elements may be single words, phrases, or clauses that expand other elements in the sentence; but the term "faulty subordination" applies specifically to the handling of dependent clauses. Dependent clauses are introduced by the connectives listed in *subordinating conjunctions or by relative pronouns. The clauses are used in the grammatical functions of nouns, adjectives, and adverbs. Three types of faulty subordination are commonly distinguished:

1. "Tandem" or excessive subordination is the piling up of one dependent clause after another, each modifying an element in the preceding clause. The weakness is in style, not grammar:

Tandem: For his teachers, he had carefully selected those who taught classes that had a slant that was specifically directed toward students who intended to go into business.

Revised: For his teachers, he had carefully selected those who slanted their courses toward students intending to go into business [or: *toward future businessmen*].

2. "Thwarted" subordination occurs when *and* or *but* is added to a dependent clause that is already connected with the independent clause by its subordinating conjunction or relative pronoun. It is a grammatical lapse most commonly found in the form of *and which* and *but which* (see *which § 4):

Thwarted: In the first semester of the course we used three textbooks, and which were continued for the second semester.

Revised: In the first semester of the course we used three textbooks, which were continued for the second semester.

(Compare the appropriate use of a coordinating conjunction to join two dependent clauses that are parallel: "Tolerance is a virtue [which] all of us praise but [which] few of us practice.")

3. "Upside-down" or inverted subordination is not a blunder in style or in grammar but a failure to use subordination in such a way as to make the relationship between statements sensible and logical. It is therefore harder to discuss in isolated sentences, for often it is only the context that determines when subordination is "upside-down." In one writing situation, "Pearl Harbor was attacked when Roosevelt was President" would be satisfactory; in another, "When Pearl Harbor was attacked, Roosevelt was President" might be much better. Without a context, we cannot make a choice as to which statement should be put in the independent clause and which in the dependent clause. But the nature of the statements may make the choice apparent. It is hard to think of a context in which this sentence would not sound odd or absurd: "When I was in class, President Kennedy was assassinated." The relationship of dependent to independent clause needs to be changed; the revision might be "I was in class when the news of President Kennedy's assassination reached the campus." Ordinarily, upside-down subordination is corrected by simply turning the dependent clause into an independent clause and vice versa. Sometimes rewriting is advisable.

See also Ch. 8, "Coordination and subordination," page 303, and *Coordination.

Substantive • *Substantive* is a term that includes nouns and pronouns and other words or groups of words used in the functions of a noun.

such • As an *intensive, *such* is somewhat Informal (It was such a hot day; such energetic people). In Formal and most General writing the construction would usually be completed by a *that* or an *as* clause (It was *such* a hot day *that* the tar melted; I have never seen *such* energetic people *as* they are). (Reference: Russell Thomas, "*Such* as an Intensive," *College English,* 1954, 15:236-238; Bryant, pp. 199-201.)

Idiomatic constructions with *such* are:

There was such a crowd *that* [not: *so that*] we couldn't even get to the door.

The invitation is extended to such nonmembers *as* are interested. [*As* here is a relative pronoun. The General construction would be: *The invitation is extended to all nonmembers who are interested.*]

A good lecturer? There's no such thing. [*No such a thing* is questionable.]

The following constructions with *such* are possible but not very common and seem somewhat stiff:

His condition was such that he could not be moved. [More usual: *His condition would not allow him to be moved.*]

Psychologists could probably find various reasons why it is regarded as such. [. . . why it is so regarded.]

such as • As a coordinating conjunction, introducing examples, *such as* has a comma before but not after:

He was interested in all sorts of outlandish subjects, such as palmistry, numerology, and phrenology.

(See *such, *namely and other introductory words.)

such . . . that • See *such, *Result.

Suffix • An element that can be placed after a word or root to make a new word of different meaning or function is called a *suffix*: *-ize* (*criticize*), *-ish* (*foolish*), *-ful* (*playful*), *-th* (*warmth*). (See *Adjectives, types and forms § 1; *-ce, -ge; *Origin of words § 3a.)

Suggestion • Making use of the associations, the connotations of words, is called *suggestion*. The words *liberty, immemorial, mystical, butcher, homey,* and thousands of others have acquired associations from their past use that may call to a listener's or reader's mind some feeling or attitude that goes beyond their original core of meaning. Relying on suggestion may be misleading or at least may be a substitute for exactness, but a responsible use of suggestion adds color and often pleasure and keeps writing from flatness. (For discussion see Ch. 9, "The suggestion of words," p. 373.)

Sunday school • Capitalize only the *Sunday* except in names of particular Sunday schools:

Sunday school   the Methodist Sunday School

Superlative degree • See *Comparison of adjectives and adverbs § 2.

sure • *Sure* in Standard written English is primarily an adjective (sure footing; as sure as fate; Are you sure?). As an adverb, *sure* instead of *surely*—equivalent to *certainly* or *yes*—is Informal (Sure, I'm coming; That's sure fine of you) and would not ordinarily be written.

swim • The principal parts are *swim, swam* or rarely *swum, swum. He swam half a mile* is the written form rather than *He swum half a mile.*

Syllabication • See *Division of words, *Monosyllables.

Syllogism • See *Logic.

Syntax • *Syntax* means the relationship between the words or word groups in a sentence. (Many articles in this *Index* discuss points of syntax, as, for example, *Adjectives in use, *Style § 2d, *Subject and verb, *Verbs § 3, *Word order.)

T • /t/ as in *type, quote, attach, Thomas.*
   -ed is pronounced /t/ after the sound /f/, /k/, /p/, or /s/ in the same syllable: *laughed, fixed, confessed, tipped, picked; t* is silent in *Christmas, listen, thistle, mortgage, mustn't,* and many other words, and in ordinary speech it is absorbed by the *d* in word groups like sit down /si doun'/; *ti* is pronounced /ch/ in such words as *question,* and /sh/ in such words as *nation, notion.*
   The *t* sound /t/ is produced exactly like the *d* sound /d/ except that the vocal cords do not sound; /t/ is called a voiceless consonant. (Compare *D.) Double *t* usually is pronounced like single *t: latter, later.* In much of the United States *t* (and *tt*) between vowels is voiced and not clearly distinguishable from *d*: compare the pronunciations of *writer* and *rider*

in your community. (Reference: Donald J. Sharf, "Distinctiveness of 'Voiced T' Words," *American Speech,* 1960, 35:105-109.)

taboo—tabu • *Taboo* /tə bü'/ is more generally used than *tabu,* except in anthropology. The plural is *taboos;* the past tense of the verb, *tabooed.*

Taboo in language • A number of words not used in certain circles—many of them not even appearing in dictionaries—are said to be *tabooed.* Communication in the subjects to which they belong is often carried on by accepted substitutes. (Compare Ch. 9, "Euphemisms," p. 346. References: Jespersen, *Language,* p. 239; Edwin R. Hunter and E. Gaines, "Verbal Taboo in a College Community," *American Speech,* 1938, 13:97-107.)

Tabulations • Series of facts can often be more clearly presented in a table systematically arranged in convenient and meaningful columns. (See examples of tabulations in *Tenses of verbs § 2.)

Occasionally in the body of a paper it is convenient to arrange a series of parallel statements in a numbered tabulated form. The device should not be overworked, but it is a good way of securing emphasis by display:

The English textbook of the future, to sum up, must recognize the social nature of language, and English in particular, by

1. acknowledging that language is the tool of the social group,

2. granting that utility is the only valid basis for the creation or perpetuity of a language form,

3. pointing out the part each individual speaker plays in the retardation or acceleration of change,

4. regarding the written language in its proper light as the secondary and partial representation of the real language.—ROBERT C. POOLEY, *Grammar and Usage in Textbooks on English,* p. 151

(Reference: University of Chicago Press, *Manual of Style,* pp. 158-172.)

talk • See *say.

Tandem subordination • See *Subordination § 1.

teach—learn • See *learn—teach.

technic • *Technic* /tek'nik/ is a variant form of *technique.* It is also used, especially in the plural (*technics*), for *technology.*

Technical writing • See *Scientific and technical writing.

Telegraphic style • Telegraphic style refers to writing in which many *function words (especially articles and connectives) are omitted. It suggests also compact constructions and vigorous words. It is not appropriate in ordinary writing but is used in some reference works to save space and in newspaper headlines for vigor: *Gang Flees Cops; Find Loot—Ditch Guns, Stolen Cash Near River.* (Compare *Staccato style.)

Tenses of verbs •
Revision: Make the tense of this verb conventional in form (§ 2) or consistent with others in the passage (§ 4 and 5).

~~Tense~~ *Tense*

1. *Tense and time.* In grammar a tense is a distinctive form or phrase of a verb (*ask, asked, have asked*). The traditional names of the tenses are mainly words indicating time (*past, present, future*); it is therefore assumed that the function of tense is to show time and that the time shown is that suggested by the name of the tense. Both assumptions are only partly true. In *He was here, He is here,* and *He will be here,* the tenses of *be* are respectively past, present, future; the times indicated are also past, present, and future; and the function of the verb is primarily to show time. But in *When did you say you were going home?* only one tense, the past, is used; but two times, past and future, are indicated. And in *Art is long but life is fleeting,* though the tense is present, the time is of little consequence. (In the Latin form of the aphorism no verb is used—*Ars longa, vita brevis.*)

In English most sentences require a *finite verb, and the verb necessarily occurs in a tense form. But the indication of time in the sentence may be supplied by an adverb, or the adverb may modify the time suggested by the verb. In *He plays well,* the verb, despite its present tense form, does not declare that his playing is good only at the present moment; we infer, rather, that it is good at all times. But in *He plays tomorrow* the adverb restricts the time to the future, though the tense is still present. In *I've got two letters from him already, I've got time now,* and *I've got two exams tomorrow,* the tense is the same—perfect—but the times are respectively past, present, and future.

The tense names in English should be considered, then, as convenient but rather arbitrary terms used to identify verb forms and phrases, the actual function of the verb in each sentence being finally determined by other elements in the construction.

2. *Tense forms.* It is customary to distinguish six tenses in English, corresponding in name to the six in Latin. Of these only the present and the past can be single words (*ask, asked*). Like the other four tenses, they also occur as phrases (*is asking, was asking,* progressive; *does ask, did ask,* emphatic). The following table presents forms most commonly associated with time distinctions along with their traditional names:

		ACTIVE	PASSIVE
PRESENT TENSE		he asks he is asking he does ask	he is asked he is being asked
PAST TENSES	*Past perfect* (Past of some time in the past)	he had asked he had been asking	he had been asked
	Past (A time in the past not extending to the present)	he asked he was asking he did ask	he was asked he was being asked
	Perfect (Past, extending to the present)	he has asked he has been asking	he has been asked
FUTURE TENSES	*Future* (Future, extending from the present)	he will ask he will be asking he is going to ask	he will be asked
	Future perfect (Past from some future time)	he will have asked he will have been asking	he will have been asked

"Strong verbs" show a change of vowel in the past tense instead of the -*ed* ending (*he begins, he began; he rides, he rode*) and also in the past participle, often with the ending -*en* (*he has begun; he has ridden*). (See *Principal parts of verbs. References: Curme, *Parts of Speech,* pp. 241-333; Fries, *AEG,* pp. 59-71, 128-198; Mencken, pp. 235-247, 525-542; Jespersen, Chs. 23-26; Leah Dennis, "The Progressive Tense: Frequency of Its Use in English," *PMLA,* 1940, 55:855-865.)

3. *Special tense functions.*

a*–*The "progressive phrases" (*is asking, was asking, has been asking . . .*) tend to emphasize the actual activity and are increasingly being used in English.

b–The present tense is used to make a statement that is generally true, without reference to time:

Oil *floats* on water.

The Captain reminded the ladies that the equator *is* an imaginary line.

c–Participles and infinitives express time in relation to that of the main verb. The present infinitive expresses the same time as the main verb or, often with an adverb, a time in the future:

Our team is playing *to win.*   I hope *to go abroad* next summer.

A perfect infinitive expresses action prior to that of the main verb:

I am sorry *to have disappointed* you.

A present participle generally refers to the time of the main verb:

Rounding a turn in the road, he came suddenly in full view of the lake.

d–The present tense with an adverb may show future time: *He leaves tomorrow.*

4. *Sequence of tenses.* When the verb of a main clause is in the past or past perfect tense, the verb in a dependent clause is also past:

Frank knew that the Statlers were visiting us.

Frank knew that the Statlers would visit us the following week.

The old man wondered whether the train had arrived.

I have never seen Slim when he *hadn't* [or: *didn't have*; not *hasn't*] a wad of tobacco in his mouth.

A present infinitive is, however, usual after a past verb:

I thought you would have liked *to ride* [not: *to have ridden*] in their car.

They intended *to stop* [not: *to have stopped*] only an hour in the village.

The perfect infinitive is used chiefly to indicate action previous to the time of the main verb: *She is sorry to have started the gossip.*

5. *Consistent use of tenses.* It confuses a reader to find tenses shifted without definite reason, as in this paragraph:

I *sit* down at my desk early with intentions of spending the next four hours studying. Before many minutes *passed,* I *hear* a great deal of noise down on the floor below me; a water fight *is* in progress. Study *was forgotten* for half an hour, for it *was* quite impossible to concentrate on Spanish in the midst of all this commotion. After things *quiet* down I *begin* studying again, but I *have* hardly *started* when a magazine salesman *comes* into the room, hoping to snare a large sale. After arguing with him for several minutes I finally *got* rid of him.

Shifts of this sort should be carefully avoided.

In single sentences the inconsistency usually comes from carelessness, especially from forgetting the form of the first of two parallel verbs:

Last fall in the Brown game I saw Bill Geyer hit so hard that he was knocked five feet in the air and then *land* [for *landed*] on his head. [The writer forgot the tense of *was knocked*.]

(Reference: Curme, *Syntax*, Ch. 18.)

textbook • Now usually written as one word, it is often shortened simply to *text*.

th • *Th* spells a single voiceless sound /th/ as in *path* /path/, *think* /thingk/, and a single voiced sound /ᴛʜ/ as in *paths* /paᴛʜz/, *the* /ᴛʜə, ᴛʜi, ᴛʜē/, *bathe* /bāᴛʜ/. *Th* is silent in *isthmus* and pronounced /t/ in *Thomas, Thames,* and *thyme.* (See *ye=the.) In some proper names the older *t* sound /t/ has been partly or completely replaced by /th/ on the basis of the spelling: *Theodore* and *Arthur*—always /th/ (but *Ted* and *Art*); *Anthony*—/th/ and /t/ (but *Tony*).

than •
1. *Conjunction. Than* as a conjunction introduces the second member of a comparison in which one thing or situation is greater than the other:

Their house was bigger than ours.
Nobody was more aware of the need for action than he was.

Than is the idiom after *no sooner*:

He had no sooner opened the door than the flames flared up.

(For other idioms, see *Comparison of adjectives and adverbs.)
2. *Preposition. Than* is often a preposition. Since the clause with *than* is usually verbless (*than he, than I*), *than* here seems to be a preposition rather than a conjunction and frequently in Informal usage, especially in speech, is followed by an accusative:

Formal and General: You are certainly faster than I.
Informal: You are certainly faster than him.

In the Formal *than whom, than* functions as a preposition:

We admire the power of Jack Kramer, than whom there is no greater tennis player.

(References: Jespersen, p. 133; Pooley, pp. 166-170.)

3. *Confusion with "then."* *Then* is often carelessly written for *than.* (See *then—than.)

(See *different. Reference: Dwight L. Bolinger, "Analogical Correlatives of 'Than,' " *American Speech,* 1946, 21:199-202.)

that •

1. *Conjunction.*

a—That should usually be repeated with each of a series of parallel dependent clauses:

Rejecting scientific fatalism, he is convinced that society is not a machine or a biological organism, that the person exists apart from his actuarial status, that he has opportunities to make decisions, that artists and intellectuals influence even mass culture, that behaviorists have not accurately denoted the terms of our lives.—WYLIE SYPHER, "The Uses of Yes and No," *Book Week,* Feb. 6, 1966, p. 15

b—That should not be repeated within a single clause:

Many people seem to think that if an article is advertised by a joker they like or an athlete they admire [not: *that*] it is a good product to buy.

That is usually needed for clarity in the second of two parallel clauses:

I had hoped that the book would be finished by June and that it would be published by January [*that it* could be omitted, changing the clause-pattern of the sentence, but if *it* is kept, *that* should be kept too—not *and it would be*].

2. *Relative pronoun. That* refers to persons or things, *who* usually to persons, *which* usually to things:

The number of men *that* [or: *who*] fell within the age limits of the draft was 3,500,000.

He solved in five minutes a problem *that* [or: *which*] I had struggled with for five hours.

Which usually introduces clauses that are nonrestrictive; *that* more often introduces clauses that are restrictive but may also introduce nonrestrictive clauses:

The book *that she selected for her report* [restrictive] was the longest on the list.

The privilege of free speech, *which we hold so dear* [nonrestrictive], is now endangered. [*That* is also possible here.]

3. *Clauses without "that."* Clauses are often made without the introductory *that.* These constructions are not elliptical (for *that* is not "omitted" or to be "understood") but are a commonly used shorter idiom. They are Standard usage in both speech and writing:

He said he would go. [Or: He said that he would go.]

I remembered my mother's birthday fell on March 10. [Or: I remembered that my mother's birthday fell on March 10.]

The first man he met turned out to be Alexander. [Or: The first man that he met turned out to be Alexander.]

The *that* is necessary when the clause comes first (That one could be punished for such a thing had not occurred to him); in appositive clauses after such nouns as *wish, belief, desire* (My hope that he would finish today was not fulfilled); and with anticipatory *it* (It is not true that I promised to pay the whole sum at once), though in short constructions, especially in speech, it is not needed (It isn't true he likes me better than he does you). (See *Contact clauses. References: Curme, *Syntax,* index references; Jespersen, pp. 350-351.)

4. *That which. That which* is Formal and rather archaic for *what*:

He had no clear idea of *what* [not: *that which*] he was trying to say.

5. *Referring to an idea. That* (or *this*) is used to refer to the whole idea of a preceding statement when the reference is clear:

While I was studying, he sometimes turned on the radio. That was annoying, but I didn't object.

If the *that* refers to an idea suggested but not contained in a particular word, the sentence should be revised to make the reference clear:

Vague reference: My uncle is a doctor, and that is the profession I intend to enter.

Exact: My uncle's profession is medicine and that is going to be mine too.

(Reference: Bryant, pp. 172-174.)

6. *"That" as an adverb.* Adverbial *that* is General English in such constructions as *I didn't go that far.* It is sometimes used in constructions like *I'm that hungry I could eat shoe leather,* but *so* would be more common.

7. *Demonstrative pronoun and adjective*:

I like that.   I like that book.

In this function *that* has a plural, *those.* The use of *them* as the adjective plural is Nonstandard (them books).

8. *That there chair* is Nonstandard, though *that chair over there* is Standard in speech, about the only way it could occur. (Reference: Bryant, pp. 213-214.)

that, so . . . that, such . . . that • See *Result.

that is • *That is* introduces a statement the equivalent of, or the explanation of, what precedes. It is a Formal connective and is best kept to introduce series or complete statements. In such a use it is usually preceded by a semicolon and followed by a comma:

The men worked continuously for three whole weeks to complete the dam on time; that is, they worked twenty-four hours a day in three shifts, seven days a week.

In briefer constructions a comma would be more usual, and the *that is* would not be used:

Formal: They used the safest explosive for the purpose, that is, dynamite.

General: They used the safest explosive for the purpose, dynamite.

(Compare *namely and other introductory words.)

the •

1. Repetition of the article before the various nouns of a series emphasizes their distinctness:

The color, *the* fragrance, and *the* beautiful patterns of these flowers make them universal favorites.

The color, fragrance, and pattern of these flowers are distinctive.

2. In the idiom *the . . . the,* the second *the* is a survival of the Old English instrumental case form of *the* and functions adverbially.

Usage is divided over the punctuation. In Formal writing a comma is frequently used between the phrases, in General usage not:

General: The greater one's economic insecurity the greater the tendency to sacrifice spiritual independence.—STUART CHASE, "The Luxury of Integrity," *The Nemesis of American Business*

Formal: The greater one's economic insecurity, the greater the tendency to sacrifice spiritual independence.

3. Sometimes a possessive pronoun is used where *the* would be more idiomatic:

We stopped to see *the* [rather than *our*] first unusual sight.

4. Keep *the* with the name of our country: *the United States.*

5. *The* is given minimum stress in speech, with the pronunciation /ᴛʜə/ before consonants, /ᴛʜi/ before vowels. In rare instances where *the* has demonstrative force and is emphasized, it is pronounced /ᴛʜē/:

He is *the* man for the job.

theater, theatre • Both spellings are used, the second especially in names established some time ago. (See *-er, -re.)

their • *Their* is the genitive of *they. Theirs* is the emphatic or absolute form: *This table is exactly like theirs.*

Informally *their* is often used to refer to the collective indefinite pronouns (*anybody, anyone, everybody, everyone*), though these are singular in form:

Informal and sometimes General: Everybody found their coats.
General and Formal: Everybody found his coat.

(See *every and its compounds.)

them • *Them* as a demonstrative is Nonstandard: *These, those books* (not *them books*). (Reference: Bryant, p. 215.)

themselves • See *himself, herself; *myself.

then • *Then* is an adverb of time, frequently used as a connective (conjunctive adverb). Often the connection between clauses is made closer by using *and* with the *then*:

The next three hours we spent in sightseeing; *then* we settled down to the business of being delegates to a convention.

He ate a good meal, *and then* he took a nap before starting home.

then—than • *Then* is an adverb of time, *than* a conjunction in clauses of comparison:

Then the whole crowd went to Louie's.
The Big Sky was better *than* any other novel I read last year.

Although etymologically *then* and *than* come from the same source, they must now be carefully distinguished in writing.

then too • *Then too* is overused as a connective in amateur writing:

A reader enjoys a fast moving story; then too he may enjoy something that will set him thinking.

[Better:] A reader enjoys a fast moving story, but he may also enjoy something that will set him thinking.

Then too is an especially mechanical connective when used between paragraphs.

there is, there are •
1. *There* is a lesser, preparatory, or anticipatory subject, used with the real subject following the verb. *There is* is usually followed by a singular subject (though often, especially in speech, by a plural), *there are* by a plural:

There is a size for every need.
There are several ways in which this can be done.

A singular verb (there *is*, there *was*) followed by a plural sub-ject is common, and the choice between a singular or plural verb is pretty much a matter of taste when the first element of the compound subject is singular:

> There is too much starch and fat in the food we eat.
> There was both affection and pride in her message.

(References: Fries, *AEG*, p. 56; David S. Berkeley, "Agree-ment of Subject and Verb in Anticipatory Clauses," *American Speech*, 1953, 28:92-96; Robert J. Geist, "Current English Forum," *College English*, 1952, 14:115-116; 1954, 16:188-189.)
2. Frequent use of these impersonal constructions results in a loss of emphasis:

> There was a vague feeling of discontent evident in everyone's manner.
> *Direct*: A vague feeling of discontent was evident in everyone's manner.
> There are a good many college students who are easily discouraged.
> *Direct*: A good many college students are easily discouraged.

(See *it.)

therefore • The conjunctive adverb *therefore* is a rather heavy connective. It should be—but is often not—used sparingly in ordinary writing:

> *Formal*: My experiences in preparatory school had been very un-pleasant; therefore I was surprised to find college students and college teachers so agreeable.
> *General*: My experiences in preparatory school had been so un-pleasant that I was surprised to find college students and college teachers so agreeable.

therein • *Therein* is archaic or Formal for *in it, in that respect*.

they • *They* is often used as a pronoun of indefinite reference (They say . . .); though it occurs in all varieties of English, a more compact construction is usually preferable in writing:

> They have had no serious accidents at the crossing for over two years. [More compact: *There have been no serious accidents . . . .*]

(Reference: Bryant, pp. 211-212.)

thing • *Thing* is often *deadwood in writing:

> The other thing that I have in mind is going to France.
> *Improved*: I am also thinking of going to France.
> The first thing you do is to get a few small twigs burning.
> *Improved*: First you get a few small twigs burning.

An even more superfluous expression is: *The thing of it is that* . . . .

this •
1. *This,* like *that,* is regularly used to refer to the idea of a preceding clause or sentence:

He had always had his own way at home, and this made him a poor roommate.

The company trains its salesmen in its own school. *This* [More Formally: *This practice*] assures it a group of men with the same sales methods.

(Reference: Paul Roberts, "Pronominal 'This': A Quantitative Analysis," *American Speech,* 1952, 27:171-178; Bryant, pp. 172-174.)
2. *This* is used Informally as a sort of intensified definite article: *This old man went into this restaurant.* Such a use is ordinarily out of place in writing.
3. *This here chair* is Nonstandard, though *this chair over here* is Standard in speech, about the only way it could occur. (Reference: Bryant, p. 213.)

thou • *Thou, thy, thine, thee* are archaic pronouns for the second person, now used in Standard English only in the Formal language of church services. Amateur poets should avoid them except in archaic contexts. Although they correspond grammatically to the second person pronouns of various European languages, and as late as the seventeenth century had much the same force that the pronoun now has in those languages, they preserve none of that connotative force and should not ordinarily be used in making translations.

though • Colloquially *though* is used as a word of qualification or hesitation: "I didn't think he would do it, though." This use is less common in writing. If used, *though* would normally be set off by a comma or commas.

(For use as a conjunction see *although, though.)

Thwarted subordination • See *Subordination § 2.

Tilde • The *tilde* is a mark (~) placed over a letter, as in the Spanish *cañon,* represented in English by *ny* (*canyon*).

till, until, 'til • These three words are not different in meaning. Since *'til* in speech sounds the same as *till,* and looks slightly odd on paper, it is rarely used now. Use *till* or *until* according to the stress or the feel of the phrase you want.

Until is most often used at the beginning of sentences or clauses:

> Until he went to college, he never had thought of his speech.
>
> He had never thought of his speech *till* [or: *until*] he went to college.

Time • In subordinate clauses the various time relationships are indicated by the conjunctions *after, *as, as long as, as often as, as soon as, before, since, *till, until, when, whenever, *while.* (See also *Tenses of verbs, *Centuries, *Dates, *Hours.)

Titles of articles, books, etc. •
1. *Formal usage.* In most college writing, in most books, and in some periodicals, the titles of books and the names of magazines and newspapers are put in italics (indicated in manuscript by underlining). Capitals are used for the first word, for all nouns, pronouns, verbs, adjectives, and adverbs, and for prepositions that stand last or that contain more than five letters:

No Place to Hide	*You Can't Take It with You*
Wit and Its Relation to the Unconscious	*Parts of Speech and Accidence*
	The Kansas City Star
The New Yorker	

Often the *the* of magazine and newspaper titles is not regarded as a part of the title and so is not capitalized. In some periodicals the name of the city in a newspaper name is not italicized (the Milwaukee *Sentinel*). Usage is divided on this point. If the name of the city is not part of the name of the newspaper, it would not, of course, be italicized: the London *Times.*

If the official title of a work does not follow these conventions, references to it may use the exact title or standardize it (as, *The Story of a Novel,* which was printed as *the story of a NOVEL*). Library catalogs and some long bibliographies do not use italics and capitalize only first words and proper nouns or adjectives.

Titles of short stories and magazine articles are put in quotation marks when they are used with or near titles of books or names of periodicals. They are often italicized when used without reference to their means of publication, especially in discussion of them as works of literature. Usage is divided on the titles of poems, but academic writing tends to use italics for the titles of separately published poems. In less formal style, the titles of short poems are quoted.

The words *Preface* and *Introduction* are not italicized or quoted, but chapter titles are put in quotation marks. (See

*Chapters, *Quotation marks § 3a. Reference: University of Chicago Press *Manual of Style,* index references.)
2. *Informal usage.* In many magazines (*The New Republic, The Saturday Evening Post,* for example) and in most newspapers, titles of books and names of periodicals are treated as proper names, capitalized but not quoted or italicized.

In Formal papers for college courses and in theses Formal usage should be followed; in other college papers either style may be used, as the instructor prefers.
3. *Typed copy.* In typed copy that is not going to be printed it is simpler to write titles all in capitals (to save backing up and underlining). This is the common form in publishers' letters. (See Ch. 11, "Form of bibliographical entries," p. 428.)

Titles of persons • *The New York Times Style Book* recommends using *Mr., Mrs.,* or *Miss* for persons of every nationality unless a special title seems called for. (See *Abbreviation § 2, *Mr., *Mrs., *Professor, *Reverend. For fuller accounts see the "Forms of Address" sections in *Webster's Seventh New Collegiate Dictionary* and *Webster's New World Dictionary.*)

Titles of papers • Since titles help stir the reader's interest, a striking and easily remembered title is an advantage. But strained titles are often ludicrous, and if no good title comes to mind, it is better just to name the subject of the paper as exactly as possible in a few words and let it go at that. As a rule, titles that give no clue to the subject, such as *The Moving Finger Writes* or *The Greeks Had a Name for It,* are better avoided. Don't postpone writing a paper (or handing one in) to hunt for a clever title. In published work the title is often given by the editor rather than by the writer.

The title is considered a separate part of the paper, and the first sentence should not refer to it by a pronoun. Leave a blank line between the title and the beginning of the text.

to •
1. The confusion of *to* and *too* in writing is conspicuously careless and one of the small matters to be watched in revision of papers.
2. It is generally understood that in expressions like *pages 56 to 89* the last numbered unit is included. Hours are an exception, as in *1 to 3 p.m. Up to* or *till* excludes the last unit.

today •
1. *Today* (like *tonight* and *tomorrow*) is rarely hyphenated.
2. *Today, of today* are often *deadwood, adding nothing to the meaning of a statement already placed in the present:

Economic conditions [of today] are more unsettled than they have been for two generations.

too • When *too* in the sense of *also* comes within a construction, it is usually set off by commas, but in Informal writing it usually is not when it comes at the end:

"I, too, have become a philosopher," she said sadly.—IRWIN EDMAN, *Philosopher's Holiday*, p. 74

I'm going too. [More Formal: I'm going, too.]

toward—towards • These words are identical in meaning, and the choice of one or the other is a matter of taste. The first is the more frequent. (Reference: Bryant, p. 220.)

Transition •
*Revision: Make the transition between these sentences
(or paragraphs) clear and smooth.*   Trans

Amateur writing frequently suffers from a lack of transitions —words or phrases or sentences that show the relation between one statement and another, one paragraph and another, one part of the paper and another. When a sentence or paragraph stands as an isolated unit (as if nothing had preceded it and nothing was to follow it), the reader is bound to be puzzled about its relevance. A lack of transition between one paragraph and another is sometimes a sign of faulty organization, sometimes simply neglect on the part of the writer to provide a signpost that will show the reader where he has been or where he is going. A lack of transition between sentences usually indicates that the writer has not thought through carefully the relationship between consecutive statements.

The most familiar of the transitions that indicate relationships and knit a piece of prose together are connectives and adverbs—*and, but, still, yet, for, because, then, though, while, in order that, first, second, however, moreover, therefore, for example*. Choosing the right one for the relationship to be expressed is rarely a problem, once the need for a transition is recognized; but overuse of the heavier connectives (*however, nevertheless, consequently*) can weigh down the style and make it sound artificial and contrived. Less obtrusive transitions can be made by repeating a key word from sentence to sentence, by using a synonym or a pronoun to echo or pick up the key word, and by binding sentences or parts of sentences together through parallel structures. Whether the transitions are overt or subtle, they are the chief means of making a piece of writing coherent. (See *Coherence.)

(See *Coherence and Ch. 4, "Continuity in paragraphs," pp. 139-143, "Transitions between paragraphs," pp. 149-150, "Transitional paragraphs," p. 151.)

Transitive and intransitive verbs • These are syntactical terms borrowed from Latin grammar to describe whether a verb does or does not take an object in a particular construction. Because a verb which takes an object can usually be put into a passive construction (He was given a book) and one that does not cannot (He slept calmly), it might be assumed that all transitive verbs can be passive and no intransitive ones can. But *It cost a dollar* can't be made passive nor *Her clothes became her.* And verbs like *laugh, look, sleep,* intransitives when used alone, occur in passive constructions: *He was laughed at. She was looked at. The bed was slept in.* A verb is transitive when it is used with an object to complete its meaning: *They fought the whole gang. He was given a book.* A verb is intransitive when it does not have an object: *The choir will sing. The hymn was sung by the choir. They hid in the tall grass.* Many verbs are used in both constructions, often with different meanings: *He wrote two books* (transitive). *She cannot write* (intransitive). Dictionaries note whether a verb is typically used transitively or intransitively, and in what senses. *Lie* and *sit* are intransitive, *lay* and *set* are transitive. *Linking verbs *(be, become, taste* ...) are regarded as intransitive. (References: Curme, *Parts of Speech,* Ch. 4; Jespersen, *Modern English Grammar,* III:16.)

Transpire • Long objected to in the sense of *happen* or *occur* because of its etymology (*trans,* "across"; *spirare,* "breathe"), *transpire* is frequently used Informally to mean *happen* and is understood by many people in no other sense.

Transpose • A change in the order of sentences or paragraphs in copy can be shown by using numbers in the margin opposite the elements to be changed, or by circling and drawing arrows.

The transposition of letters is shown by a curved line:

C o n n e c t i c u t   r e c i e v e

Triads • Parallel series of three units are so common in writing, especially in Formal writing, that they form a definite trait of style. Such a series is called a triad:

The Prince possessed a handsome, florid face, a splendid, if slightly plump, figure, and first-class legs, of which he was inordinately proud.—J. H. PLUMB, "An Oriental Palace for an English King," *Horizon,* Nov. 1962, p. 22

Trite •
*Revision: Replace the trite expression with one that is
simpler and fresher.*

Trite

Trite words are usually worn out figures of speech or phrases: *the picture of health, the order of the day, reign supreme, from the face of the earth, crack of dawn, acid test.* What was once fresh and striking has become stale and hackneyed from being used again and again. This passage compresses a great number of such expressions into small space:

The Blushing Bride

I suppose it is natural that I should have been asked to step into the breach on this happy day, if only because I have had the privilege of knowing Geraldine since she was so high.... Onlookers see most of the game, you know, and it is easy to be wise after the event, but I thought I could see which way the wind was blowing last August.

They say marriages are made in Heaven, well, be that as it may, these two look as happy as the day is long. It was a great pleasure to me to see Hubert give away his one ewe lamb to such a regular chip off the old block as our friend here. Like father like son, they say, and I think his father deserves a pat on the back. As for Geraldine, bless her, she is a real Trojan, and has been a tower of strength to her dear mother, who doesn't look a day older than when I first set eyes on her, far longer ago than either of us cares to remember.

At moments like this, when family ties are stronger than ever, these young things should remember how much they owe to their parents.

One last word, I must not fail to remind Geraldine that the way to a man's heart is his stomach, and to warn Bertrand that the hand that rocks the cradle rules the world.

Now, I mustn't take up any more of your valuable time, I feel sure you will all join me in drinking the health of the happy couple, and wishing that all their troubles may be little ones.—Georgina Coleridge, *I Know What I Like,* p. 41

The author dedicates her book as follows:

Because I know which side my bread is buttered, this *magnum opus* is dedicated to my better half, the master of the house who wears the trousers, and who has proved conclusively that two heads are better than one.—p. 5

(See Ch. 9, "Trite words," p. 345.)

trousers, pants • See *pants, trousers.

Type • Typography is a complex technical field, but many people make a hobby of it, and most writers have some curiosity about it. Here are a few of the fundamental facts:

1. *Type faces.* There are many different type faces, each with its characteristic appearance. They may differ in thickness of line in the letters, in length of ascenders and descenders (as in *h* or *y*), in wideness of letters, in serifs (thin or smaller lines used to finish off a main stroke of a letter, as at the top and bottom of *M*), and in other features. Every type face is made in many standard sizes and style variations. Some popular faces for book and periodical use are set here in 10 point size:

This type face is Caslon.   This type face is Bodoni.
This type face is Garamond.   This type face is Granjon.
This type face is Times Roman.

This *Guide-Index* is set in the following type faces and sizes:

The text is set in 10 point Baskerville Roman.
The quotations are set in 9 point Baskerville Roman.
The footnotes are set in 6 point Bulmer Roman.
The entry words are set in 10 point Baskerville Roman bold.
The subheads are set in 10 point Baskerville italic.

2. *Type style variations.* A given face and size of type is available in several standard variations of style:

Name and example	Abbreviation	Indicated in manuscript by:
ROMAN CAPITALS	Caps.	Three lines underneath
roman lower case	l. c.	Unmarked manuscript
ROMAN SMALL CAPITALS	s. c.	Two lines underneath
ITALIC CAPITALS	Ital. Caps.	One line underneath and labeled "all caps"
italic lower case	ital.	One line underneath
BOLD FACE CAPITALS	b. f. caps	Wavy line underneath and labeled "all caps"
bold face lower case	b. f.	Wavy line underneath

3. *Type measurement.* Type is measured in *points,* a point equaling .0138 or approximately 1/72 of an inch. A square unit of type of any size is an *em.* Space is usually measured in *pica* (12 point) *ems* (1/6 of an inch). Type ranges in size from 4 to 144 points, but the most generally used sizes are those from 6 to 72 points.

This line is set in 6 point type.

This line is set in 10 point type.

This line is set in 14 point type.

(See *Proofreading. References: The University of Chicago Press *Manual of Style* contains much information about type, as do other stylebooks and books on journalism, advertising, and typography.)

-type • This is an overused suffix: *handsome-type man.* (Compare *-wise.)

type of • The idiom *type of* is being shortened colloquially by omitting the *of*: *this type letter.* Although the construction is beginning to appear in print, General usage should still be followed: *this type of letter* (but not: this type of *a* letter). (Reference: Bryant, pp. 221-222.)

Typewritten copy • Manuscript for a printer, business letters and reports, and impersonal writing should be typed. Whenever possible, college papers should be typed. In the United States we are so accustomed to typescript (which is so much more legible than most handwriting) that it can be used in a good deal of personal correspondence. Since there is a convention that longhand shows added courtesy, *social correspondence should usually be handwritten.

In general, typewritten copy follows the customs of good manuscript, but some points need special emphasis. Use only one side of the sheet, leave wide margins (especially at the right side, since letters cannot be compressed as in longhand), keep type clean, and change ribbons regularly. Ordinarily use a black ribbon.

Regular manuscript should be double spaced. Personal writing may be single spaced, and for economy single space is generally used in business writing. If single spaced, the lines should be kept fairly short to make the reading easier. Full, crowded pages are forbidding reading. In typing first drafts, leave plenty of space for revision, perhaps using triple space between lines and extra space between paragraphs.

In single-spaced typing, use double space between paragraphs. For double-spaced typing, make a triple space between paragraphs only if you wish an open appearance or special emphasis on the paragraphs. Indent paragraph first lines from five to eight spaces.

Long quotations may be indicated in double spaced copy by indenting the number of spaces used for paragraphs and single spacing the quoted matter. No quotation marks are used with this style.

The standard typewriter keyboard has no symbol for the figure 1. Use the small *l* (not capital *I*). For a dash use two hyphens not spaced away from the words on each side. Leave a space after all other punctuation marks except at the end of sentences, where two should be used.

Transposed letters should be erased and retyped or corrected by the proofreader's symbol. (See *Transpose.) Strikeovers are often hard to read. A few mistakes can be corrected in ink.

but if there are so many that the page will look messy it should be retyped.

(To type ! and [ ], see *Exclamation mark, *Brackets. See also Ch. 2, "Preparing the manuscript," p. 56.)

U •

1. There are two "long *u*" sounds: /ü/ as in *rule* /rül/, *blew* /blü/, *shoe* /shü/, *true* /trü/, *juice* /jüs/, *move* /müv/, *lose* /lüz/, *booby* /bü′bē/, *hoodoo* /hü′dü/; and /ū/, a diphthong beginning with a /y/ sound and ending with /ü/ as in *use* /ūs/ or /ūz/, also spelled as in *few, cute, beauty, you, hue, nuisance, neuter, view, yew, yule, ewe.*

After *t, d, n, s, st* usage is divided between these two sounds: *tune* /tūn, tün/, *duty* /dū′ti, dü′ti/, *news* /nūz, nüz/, *stew* /stū, stü/. In such words the /ü/ sound is frequent and is increasingly used by educated speakers in spite of widespread prejudice against it. (See Kenyon and Knott § 109 and their entries on particular words of this type.)

2. There are two "short *u*" sounds: /u/ as in *cup* /kup/, *fun* /fun/, *under* /un′dər/, *son* /sun/, *love* /luv/, *come* /kum/, *trouble* /trub′əl/, *does* /duz/, *other* /uᴛʜ′ər/, *blood* /blud/; and /ů/ as in *full* /fůl/, *pull* /půl/, *wood* /wůd/, *woman* /wům′ən/, *wolf* /wůlf/, *should* /shůd/.

3. *U* as in *burn* and *curl* is represented by ė /bėrn, kėrl/.

An unpronounced *u* is sometimes spelled after *g,* as in *guest,* usually in words from French to show the "hard" value of *g.*

The letter *u* is one form of a Latin letter of which the other form is *v*; only within the last few hundred years have the two been consistently differentiated in English.

Umlaut • In some German words, the vowels *a, o,* and *u* are *umlauted* (*ä, ö, ü*). On a typewriter the symbol can be made with the quotation mark. To omit it in German words is to misspell them; *ä, ü,* and *ö* are quite different from *a, o,* and *u.*

Underlining •

Und   *Revision: In longhand and typewritten copy underline words and passages to correspond to the conventions of using italic type.*

These conventions are of great importance in Formal manuscript and in material to be printed. Newspapers have generally abandoned italic type, but most magazines and books use it, and in academic writing—course papers, articles in the

learned journals, monographs, dissertations, reference books—
rather strict conventions are still followed. (See Ch. 10, "Underlining for italics," p. 402.)

Underlining is used:

1. *To indicate titles of books and periodicals.* The complete
title should be underlined; usage is divided on whether the
underscoring should be broken between words or whether it
may be continuous:

I like <u>Barbary</u> <u>Shore</u> the best [<u>Barbary Shore</u>].
He took <u>Time</u> and <u>The</u> <u>Reader's</u> <u>Digest</u> [or: and <u>The Reader's Digest</u>].

(For details of this use see *Titles of articles, books, etc., and
Ch. 11, "Form of bibliographical entries," p. 428. Compare
*Ships' names. Reference: The University of Chicago Press,
A Manual of Style, pp. 46-54.)

2. *For emphasis.* Words that would be heavily stressed if
spoken may be underlined:

He was <u>the</u> man that night.

Any word a writer wishes to emphasize may be underlined
(italicized in print), but this is a rather mechanical form of
emphasis and loses its force if overused. Whole sentences, except in textbooks and manuals, are better not underlined,
since there are usually more intelligent ways of securing emphasis. As Fowler (p. 305) put it: "To italicize whole sentences
or large parts of them as a guarantee that some portion of
what one has written is really worth attending to is a miserable
confession that the rest is negligible." (See *Emphasis § 7,
*Schoolgirl style.)

3. *To mark words and locutions considered not for their
meaning but as words.* This is a common use of underlining
(italicizing) in this and all books on language:

If we take such a sentence as *I am hungry,* neither a grammarian
nor a logician would have any difficulty in pointing out the predicate, though one would say that it was *am hungry* and the other
that it was simply *hungry.*—P. B. BALLARD, *Thought and Language,*
p. 88

4. *To mark foreign words.*

But good clothes were a *sine qua non.*

(See *Foreign words in English.)

Understatement • See *Negatives § 1.

unique • In strict Formal usage *unique* means "single, sole,
unequaled," and consequently is not compared. In General
usage, like so many other words of absolute meaning, it has
become somewhat extended, and as an emphatic *rare,* it is
sometimes found compared with *more* or *most:*

... the more unique his nature, the more peculiarly his own will be the colouring of his language.—OTTO JESPERSEN, *Mankind, Nation and Individual from a Linguistic Point of View,* p. 204

(See *Comparison of adjectives and adverbs § 4.)

United States • We live in *the* United States. The temptation to drop *the* is greatest when *United States* is forced to do duty as an adjective: *Europe needs the money from United States imports.* In such a case it is better to use *American* or *imports of the United States.* (See *American.)

Unity • Gross disregard of unity—including material that is quite unrelated to a paragraph or to a paper or that distracts from its main point—is exasperatingly apparent to a reader. Genuine unity is to be judged in the light of the writer's purpose. The test of unity is found not in any general principles that can be applied in every situation but in appropriateness to the writer's view of his material and his consistent carrying out of his purpose.

(Various matters related to unity are discussed in Ch. 4, "Writing Paragraphs," and Ch. 8, "Revising Sentences.")

unquote • Used orally, *unquote* indicates the end of a quotation, *quote* to begin it. Do not use it in writing.

until, 'til, till • See *till, until, 'til.

up • *Up* is a member of many typical *verb-adverb combinations in general use (*give up, grow up, sit up, use up*). Because they have developed meanings which are not the sum of the meanings of their parts, they are usually entered separately in dictionaries and they behave like independent verbs, including the possibility of being used as passives. *Up* is also an intensive in a number of other combinations to which it contributes no new element of meaning (*divide up, fill up, raise up, join up*). The latter usage is appropriate in General writing but is usually avoided in Formal.

up to • See *to.

Upside-down subordination • See *Subordination § 3.

-us, -ous • See *-ous, -us.

Usage • The view presented in this book is that there are three emphases in the study of current English—on linguistics, on style, and on usage. The same materials are studied and the methods have much in common, but there are characteristic differences in the three emphases, particularly in purposes. *Linguists* are chiefly concerned with the objective observation and analysis of the language—primarily of the spoken language—in order to discover and describe its system or "structure." Students of *style* examine specific examples of language—in our culture especially of written literature—primarily to find the qualities of language that produce an effect on a listener or a reader. Students of *usage* observe specific items in the language—both spoken and written—primarily to ascertain their currency and appropriateness in speech and writing of various sorts.

Some would regard style and usage simply as divisions of linguistics, but while linguistics furnishes much of the data and methods of the other two, and will do so increasingly, style and usage involve some consideration of social attitudes and responses usually not the concern of linguistics. An analysis made by a linguist will usually be more detailed than a student of usage requires, and often more detailed even than a student of style needs. Though linguists recognize the importance of sensitivity to qualities of style and of judging the appropriateness of usage, they seldom consider these their primary concern and feel that preoccupation with such questions may interfere with their descriptive and analytical purpose. Although all people working with current English need a good deal of the same basic training, some division of labor, based on a recognition of the different purposes of the three emphases, will work not only for simplicity but for efficiency.

1. *The varying emphases of usage, style, and linguistics.* Though all three approaches start with the facts of usage, with ways in which the various units are actually used in the language, the emphasis of linguistics is on systematic description, of style on aesthetic judgment, and of usage on socially significant details. In the linguistic approach, the concern is with all the units, from the smallest to the largest, or at least all that seem to fit into a describable structure. In the stylistic approach, the concern is with the units which offer linguistic choices. And in the usage approach, the concern is with the units which have socially significant variants.

Linguistics deals with every detail of the sound system (see *Phonemes) of the language, of word forms, and of sentences. It does the best it can with the meanings of words. Since writing is a secondary and incomplete manifestation of language, linguistics gives it only incidental attention.

Stylistics is less concerned with word forms than with the choice of words and their arrangement in phrases and sentences. It is also concerned with the sounds of the language when they produce effects such as rhyme, *alliteration, onomatapoeia (see *Imitative words and phrases), etc.

Usage study investigates socially significant variations in the units of the language itself and in the transcription of it, units which may extend in size from the smallest to the largest. For variation in individual phonemes, see *A §5, 6, *T, *U, *wh; see also Kenyon and Knott, pp. xxxviii-xlv. In the pronunciation of individual words, there are hundreds of examples of *divided usage; some of the variants are Standard (see *Pronunciation § 4), some are not (*municipal* as /mū'ni si'pəl/, *piano* as/pī a'nə/, etc.). The same is true for word forms (see, for example, the past tense and past participial forms under *Principal parts of verbs; some of these variants are unlabeled, hence Standard, some are labeled *NS*, Nonstandard). Many English constructions, made up of words which in themselves are entirely acceptable in Standard, arrange those words in combinations which are Nonstandard: *We was, He don't have no time, being as, used to could,* etc. And Nonstandard uses a great many words in senses which are unacceptable in Standard. Sometimes the inappropriate usage results from confusion of words of similar sound—*formally, formerly; ingenious, ingenuous; notorious, notable; respectively, respectfully* (for extreme examples, see *Malapropism). One of the functions of dictionary definitions is to discriminate Standard senses of words from Nonstandard ones. It is not surprising that two dictionaries sometimes report different findings.

Usage study is also much concerned with the conventions of writing. Correctness in spelling is entirely a matter of conforming to the prevailing usage in Standard printed material, and much the same is true for capitalization and punctuation. Many errors in writing exist solely because of failure to follow Standard usage in spelling, punctuation, and capitalization, as in the following sentence, where the numbered items deviate from Standard written (though not spoken) usage:

Mary and [1] jane were under the [2] allusion [3], that [4] there father had [5] dyed.

2. *The study of usage.* The study of usage helps us to decide what to say or write in a particular situation. Questions usually arise either from lack of knowledge of what people say or write in a particular variety of English or from uncertainty because of differing practices. Since we are usually less at home in writing than in speaking, the questions often relate to written usage.

The study of usage is based on an accumulation of specific instances and depends on wide observation of what people say and write in various situations to provide a basis for judging the standing of particular words, forms, and constructions. No one person can cover thoroughly this vast field, though he can amass a considerable body of data. Since many people make special studies of individual points and present them in articles—in *American Speech, College English, Word Study,* and other periodicals—a good deal of reliable information accumulates. Four important books on usage are worth studying for their method, data, and conclusions:

Albert H. Marckwardt and Fred G. Walcott in *Facts About Current English Usage* (1938) present not so much a record of actual usage as of attitudes toward it. They include the results of the Leonard questionnaire to editors, teachers, and businessmen asking their judgment of a number of proscribed items and add the record of scholarly studies of those items. They give recommendations based on this material.

C. C. Fries' *American English Grammar* (1940) presents systematically the language found in a large group of letters and considers it in relation to the education and social position of the writers. The study made clear that educated writers of Standard English show more variation in usage than was commonly thought.

George Summey's *American Punctuation* (revised 1949) discusses the practices in punctuation he discovered from studying a large body of printed material. Although Mr. Summey discovered considerable range, he found prevailing practices that could be safely followed by individual writers.

Margaret M. Bryant's *Current American Usage* (1962) is the most recent reliable compilation of evidence on American usage. It contains about 240 entries and is based on hundreds of individual studies.

As a result of these and other usage studies we now have a more accurate picture of what educated users of English say and, more especially, write. Such studies, presenting not a "liberal" but simply a more accurate picture of the language in use, have done a good deal to limit the puristic tendencies of textbooks on grammar and usage.

But recording usage by itself is not enough, partly because there is variation in the matters that are likely to raise questions. Relative frequency of occurrence is an important fact, but it gives only the range of usage. Evaluation of the data and further study are needed. Dictionaries record what their files show on particular words and phrases and give "usage labels" for many, designating them as colloquial or slang or restricted to some occupation. Such books are useful but may not adequately present actual cultivated practice. The *style-books of publishers, such as the *United States Government Printing Office Style Manual* or the Associated Press *Stylebook,* give the choices their publishers have made for printed matter and should be taken into account. The history of a word or construction, in the *Oxford English Dictionary* or a history of the language, is often instructive (**shall—will,* **don't*), because such histories reveal that a good many of the more puristic strictures on usage are of relatively recent origin. Another source of information is the explicit or incidental comments by writers, defending their own preferences or lamenting those of others.

People's attitudes toward usages—which sometimes are not consistent with their own usage—need to be taken into account. Though *disinterested is widely used in the sense of "uninterested" and is so recorded in dictionaries, many people object to it; the same is true of *like as a conjunction, the construction "the *reason is because," and many others. Actual use of *shall* and *will* has not materially changed in recent years, but the attitudes toward the usage have. In fact, most questions are concerned not with differences between Standard and Nonstandard English (*we was,* the *double negative) but with matters of *divided usage within Standard English. A student of usage, then, has not only to observe widely what is said and written but also to note the attitudes of people toward particular items.

And finally he has to use his judgment, based on his accumulated data. Judgments will vary somewhat, depending on the range of the individual's information and to a certain extent on his preferences in language. The best safeguard against avoidable bias is awareness of some principles of selection. Principles of appropriateness are presented in more detail on pp. 25-32. See also *American and British usage, *Divided usage, *Mixed usage.)

used to • Although the spelling *use to* comes closer than *used to* in representing what we say, the *d* is required in writing: *used to.* (See *-ed.) The negative constructions *didn't use to, used not to,* etc., are common in speech but are rarely found in print. (Reference: Bryant, pp. 68-69.)

utilize • *Utilize* means specifically "put to use"; *use* (verb) is often preferable.

V • /v/ as in *very* /ver′ē/, *vivid* /viv′id/, *save* /sāv/; also spelled *ph* in *Stephen* /stē′vən/; and *f* in *of* /ov/. The letter is a variant of *u* (see *U).

Verb-adverb combinations • In *I looked up at the top of the tree,* the verb *look* is used in its ordinary sense and is modified by the adverb *up*. In *I looked up the word in the dictionary, looked up* is a verb meaning "investigated," a meaning not explained by a literal use of the two words. Similarly a man may *break out* (literally) of jail, or *break out* with measles; he can *look after* a departing car, or *look after* the children. In each of these pairs of expressions, the first has a verb modified by an adverb in its ordinary meaning, and the second is really a different verb, with a meaning of its own, composed of two elements. These have become a single word, the parts of which can sometimes have more than one position in a sentence. Compare "I *looked up* the word in a dictionary" and "I *looked* the word *up* in a dictionary."

There are hundreds of such verb-adverb combinations in use, most of them one-syllable verbs with adverbs like *about, around, at, by, down, for, in, out, through, to, up, with.* They are widely used in General English and often give an emphatic rhythm differing from the more Formal *investigate* (*look into*), *sacrifice* (*give up*), *surrender* (*give up*). This pattern is now the most active way of forming new verbs in English. When the combinations develop meanings beyond what their elements imply, they are separately entered in dictionaries. (See *Prepositions § 3b.)

Verb forms • See *Verbs § 3.

Verb stress • See *Noun and verb stress.

verbal, oral • See *oral, verbal.

Verbals • The parts of a verb that function as nouns or adjectives are called *verbals*. *Gerunds* (or verbal nouns) are used in the function of nouns (though they may, like verbs, have a subject or object), *participles* in the function of adjectives, and *infinitives* in the functions of adjectives or nouns:

Gerunds: Swimming is better exercise than *rowing. Having been invited* pleased him enormously.

Infinitives: His only ambition was *to pass.* It was too good *to last. To have asked* for more would have wrecked the whole conference. He had plenty of money *to spend.*

Participles: He reached the float, *swimming* as easily as he had before he had been hurt. *Asked* to take a part, he refused at first but finally accepted. *Having been invited,* he began to make plans.

(For the various uses of verbals see *Gerund, *Infinitives, *Participles.)

Verbs •

1. *Verbs as a part of speech.* If we exclude *be* and the modals, all verbs can be identified by their capacity to add to the base form (*ask, sing, tear*) the suffix *-ing*, the suffix *-s* (when the verb has as its subject a singular noun or the pronouns *he, she, it*), and the suffix *-ed* or the equivalent (but *have + s = has; have + ed = had*). *Ask,* for example, has the forms *ask, asks, asking, asked.* Some verbs use other formal devices as the equivalent of the *-ed—sing, sings, singing, sang, sung; tear, tears, tearing, tore, torn;* and *hit, hits, hitting, hit. Be* has eight forms (*be, am, is, are, was, were, being, been*); *can, may, must,* and other *modal auxiliaries have only one or two forms. We recognize verbs by their form and sentence position even when we don't know their meaning. In *I am sure that his words will coruscate,* we know that *am, will,* and *coruscate* are verbs—*am* and *will* because we have already learned their forms, functions, and meanings, and *coruscate* because it depends on *will,* even if we have no notion of its meaning. As suggested in the first sentence of this paragraph, verbs fall into two classes, a closed one (no new ones are added) whose function is primarily grammatical, and an open one (new ones are constantly added) whose *lexical meaning is important. In *He got hurt, got* performs the grammatical function of showing past tense and passive voice and *hurt* carries the lexical meaning.

2. *Typical function.* The syntactical function of verbs is typically to form the predicate of a clause or sentence—that is, to join with a subject, and perhaps an object, to form a single construction. For convenience we are using *verb* instead of some more specific word like *predicator* to indicate this function as well as to indicate the part of speech.

3. *Details of verb forms.* The following *Index* articles give details of the principal characteristics of verbs:

*Auxiliary verb	*Phrasal verb
*Commands and requests	*Principal parts of verbs
*Gerund	*Progressive verb forms
*Infinitives	*Subjunctives
*Linking verbs	*Tenses of verbs
*Modal auxiliaries	*Transitive and intransitive verbs
*Mood	*Verbals
*Participles	*Voice

4. *Syntax of verbs.* Besides articles on numerous particular verbs (such as *ain't, *be, *do, *can—may, *get, *need, *shall—will), the following articles are especially concerned with the use of verbs in speaking and writing:

*Absolute constructions	*Clauses
*Agreement	*Collective nouns

*Commands and requests
*Conditions
*Dangling modifiers
*Finite verbs
*Fragmentary sentence
*Function words
*Gerund
*Infinitives
*Objects

*Participles
*Passive verbs
*Predicate adjective
*Split infinitive
*Subject and verb
*Subjunctives
*Tenses of verbs
*Verb-adverb combinations
*Voice

(References: Fries, Curme, Jespersen, and all grammars treat verbs; see especially Fries, *AEG*, Ch. 8, and Fries, *Structure*, Chs. 5-7.)

Vernacular • *Vernacular* as applied to English formerly referred to the native, spoken language—as opposed to the literary languages of Latin or Norman French. It now usually means Nonstandard and perhaps Informal English, the native homely, spoken language as contrasted with Formal or literary English, usually with the implication that, though inelegant, the vernacular has more vitality and force. (See *Colloquial English.)

Verse • See *Capital letters § 3, *Poetry.

Verse form • The form of a line of verse is described by telling the arrangement of the stressed syllables (the kind of "foot"), the length of the line (the number of feet), and many other qualities of movement or variation from the typical movement that it shows. This article presents the vocabulary and an outline of the facts necessary for describing verse form.

The feet:

The length of lines:

Iambic ∪ − (An iamb)	*Dimeter:* Two feet
Trochaic − ∪ (A trochee)	*Trimeter:* Three feet
Anapestic ∪∪ − (An anapest)	*Tetrameter:* Four feet
Dactylic − ∪∪ (A dactyl)	*Pentameter:* Five feet
Spondaic − − (A spondee)	*Hexameter:* Six feet

Other facts:

A line is *end-stopped* if its end corresponds with a distinct sense of pause, either the end of a sentence or of a major sentence element; it is *run-on* when the construction is carried over the end of the line.

Alexandrine: A line containing six iambic feet

Anacrusis: An extra unstressed syllable at the beginning of a line

Catalexis: The dropping of the final unstressed syllable

Feminine ending: An extra unstressed syllable at the end

Refrain: A line repeated, typically at the end of each stanza of a poem

A *cesura* (*caesura*) is a rhythmic pause within a line.

Two successive lines rhyming are a *couplet*.

A four-line stanza is a *quatrain,* which may have any rhyme scheme: *abab, abba*; an iambic tetrameter quatrain rhyming *abcb* is the *ballad stanza.*

More complex stanza forms (sonnet, ode, ballade, and so on) are described in books on literature and poetry.

Blank verse is unrhymed iambic pentameter. *Free verse* is verse of varied length lines with a flexible movement, usually unrhymed.

Examples of scansion:

Iambic pentameter (feminine ending):

A thing of beauty is a joy forever

Anapestic tetrameter:

There are brains, though they moulder, that dream in the tomb

Trochaic tetrameter (catalectic), a couplet:

Souls of poets dead and gone,

What Elysium have ye known,

These examples show that scansion tells the typical physical characteristics of verse but does not define the rhythm, which is far more important. For the more distinctive qualities of poetry, such as imagery, tone, color, rhythm (not to mention meaning), see books on poetry and literature.

very •

1. *"Very" as an intensive.* Very is so much used that its intensive force is slight. A writer should make sure that it really adds to the meaning of his phrase.

The *Emporia Gazette* once described its war upon *very* this way:

"If you feel you must write 'very,' write 'damn.'" So when the urge for emphasis is on him, the reporter writes "It was a damn fine victory. I am damn tired but damn well—and damn excited." Then, because it is the Emporia (Kan.) Gazette, the copy desk deletes the profanity and the quotation reads: "It was a fine victory. I am tired but well—and excited." That's how the Gazette attains its restrained, simple, and forceful style. Very simple.

2. *"Very" and past participles.* In Formal English many people will not use *very* with a past participle (He was very ex-

cited), because *very*, now used primarily as an intensive, supposedly marks only a high degree of a *quality*, as in *very happy*, and the verb function of the participle denotes an action rather than a quality. The Formal locution would be: He was *very much* excited.

This distinction, since it is based purely on arbitrary grammatical reasoning, is too insubstantial for users of General English, who use *very* to modify such participles without any qualms (I shall be very pleased to come; We shall be very delighted to have you).

When the President and the trustees finally decided to allow the Psychology Department to sponsor a clinic, Dr. Bonham was very elated.—JAMES REID PARKER, *Academic Procession*, p. 13

viewpoint • *Viewpoint* is a natural and economical substitute for *point of view*. It is not stigmatized in the dictionaries.

Before we condemn him for affectation and distortion we must realize his viewpoint.—E. M. FORSTER, *Aspects of the Novel*, p. 182

viz. • *Viz.* is the abbreviation of the Latin *videlicet* /vǝ del'ǝ-sit/, which means "to wit, namely." *Viz.* exists only in the language of rather Formal documents or reference works. It is usually read "namely." (See *namely and other introductory words.)

Vocabulary • See *Words.

Voice •
1. *Definition and forms. Voice* is a term borrowed from the grammars of the classical languages where it usually differentiates distinctive endings on verbs. In English the term *passive voice* refers to constructions made with the past participle and some form of the verb *be* (*was killed*); all other forms are *active*.

	Active	Passive
Present:	he (is asking) asks	he is asked (is being asked)
Future:	he will ask	he will be asked
Perfect:	he has asked	he has been asked
Infinitives:	to ask, to have asked	to be asked, to have been asked
Participles:	asking, having asked	being asked, asked

Get and *become* are also used, especially in Informal English:

If he should get elected, we'd be lost.
Our house is getting painted.
They had become separated from their guide.

The traditional definition in terms of meaning is often a

useful guide in identifying active and passive verbs. When the subject of a verb is the doer of the action or is in the condition named by its verb, the verb is said to be in the active voice:

> The congregation *sang* "Abide with Me."
>
> They *will go* swimming.   Our side *had been winning.*
>
> Jimmy's father *gave* him a car.   We *rested* an hour.

When the subject of a verb receives the action, the verb is said to be in the passive voice:

> "Abide with Me" *was sung* by the congregation.
>
> Jimmy *was given* a car by his father.
>
> The pit *was dug* fully eight feet deep.
>
> They *had been caught.*

These different expressions of the verb give considerable flexibility in sentence word order. They allow the speaker or writer to emphasize by position the thing that is most important to him:

> The *house* was finished by the crew in record time.
>
> The *crew* finished the house in record time.

Or, more often, they merely allow the speaker to approach the statement from the viewpoint of his thinking about it (the *house* or the *crew,* for example, in the sentences above). The construction in English is more important as a matter of style than of grammar and is one of the devices that make it possible for one's expression to come close to his process of thought.

2. *Use of active verbs.* Active verbs are more common than passive because we are accustomed to the actor-action-goal pattern of expression. In the text of the preceding paragraph, for example, the seven finite verbs (*give, allow, is, allow, is, is, make*) and the three infinitives (*to emphasize, to approach, to come*) are active.

3. *Use of passive verbs.* Passive verbs may occur less frequently, but they have several important uses. (The frequency of the passive construction in Standard writing appears to run from a high of 13 percent in expository writing to as low as one percent in narrative. See Margaret M. Bryant, "The Passive Construction," *College English,* 1960, 21:230.)

The object, the goal, may be more important, in the writer's mind, than the doer:

> The bill *was passed* without opposition.
>
> The well *was drilled* in solid rock.
>
> Our house *was painted* last year.

In indefinite statements the passive is often used when the actors may not be known or are not to be named in the statement:

Much *has been written* on both sides.

Many records *have been set* in past Olympics.

The passive allows various degrees of emphasis by placing the name of the act or of the doer at the end:

Our house *is being painted.* (Active: They *are painting* our house.)

Our house *was painted* by Joe Mead and his brother. (Active: Joe Mead and his brother *painted* our house.)

"Abide with Me" was sung by the choir [that is, not by the congregation].

Sometimes the passive shows a change in the relation between subject and verb (though the shift should not be made within a sentence unless the action is continuous):

We *drove* [active] there and *were taken out* [passive] in a dory.

(For discussion of the object of a passive verb, see *Objects § 1b.)

4. *Overuse of the passive.* (For the objectionable use of passive verbs when active would be more effective, see *Passive verbs.)

(References: Curme, *Syntax,* pp. 102-103; Fries, *AEG,* pp. 188-193; Jespersen, Ch. 12.)

Voiced, voiceless sounds • In voiced sounds the vocal cords vibrate, as in the vowels and *b, d, g, v, z* /zh/, and *th* /ᴛʜ/; *p, t, k, f, s, sh,* and *th* /th/ are the voiceless sounds corresponding to these voiced consonants. In addition there are the voiced consonants *m, n, ng, w, y, r* and the voiceless *h*; some phoneticians would add *j* (voiced) and *ch* (voiceless), though others consider these as combinations of /d/ plus /zh/ and /t/ plus /sh/.

Some nouns and verbs are distinguished by voicing of the consonant in the verb: *use* (noun, /ūs/—verb, /ūz/), *proof—prove* (noun, /prüf/—verb, /prüv/), *grief—grieve* (/grēf/—/grēv/).

A few spelling errors seem to be caused by a confusion between voicing and non-voicing, as *significance* /-kəns/ often appears as *signifigance* /-gəns/.

Vowels • See *Neutral vowel, *Pronunciation, *schwa.

Vulgate English • See *Nonstandard English.

W • /w/ as in *wild* /wīld/, *twinkle* /twing′kḷ/; also spelled as in *quick* /kwik/, *choir* /kwīr/. *W* is silent in *write* /rīt/, *two* /tü/, *sword* /sôrd/, and other words, and spoken though not spelled in *one* /wun/, *once* /wuns/.

The letter, as the name indicates, is two *u*'s—formerly written vv—together.

wake • English is oversupplied with verbs for waking from sleep (intransitive) and waking someone else from sleep (transitive); all are used in each function:

awake (*awaked, awaked* or *awoke, awoke*). Rather Formal; more commonly used intransitively (I *awoke*).

awaken (*awakened, awakened*). Formal.

wake (*waked* or *woke, waked* or *woke* [*woken*]). More widely used than the preceding.

waken (*wakened, wakened*). Less common than *wake*.

The usual solution is the *verb-adverb combination *wake up* (*waked* or *woke up*):

She waked up [woke up] at eleven. She waked [woke] me up at six.

want • The General idiom with *want* has an infinitive:

General: I want you to get all you can from the year's work.
Local: I want for you to get all you can from the year's work.
Local: I want that you should get all you can from the year's work.

Want is Informal for *ought, had better*: *You want to review all the notes if you're going to pass his exam.*

In the sense of *lack* or *need, want* is Formal and suggests British usage: *The letter, though clear, wants correcting.*

Want in, want out without a complementary verb (The dog wants out) seems to be of Scotch rather than German origin and is widely heard in the United States. (See Albert H. Marckwardt, "*Want* with Ellipsis of Verbs of Action," *American Speech*, 1948, 23:3-9.) *Want off* is common in the speech of some areas. (Reference: Bryant, pp. 224-225.)

way, ways • *Way* is Informally used for *away* (way over across the valley). *Way* is used in a number of General and Informal idioms (*in a bad way, out our way,* I don't see how she can act *the way* she does).

Ways is often used in speech for *way* in expressions like *a little ways down the road.*

we •

1. *Indefinite "we."* *We* is frequently used as an indefinite pronoun in expressions like *We find, We sometimes feel,* to avoid passive and impersonal constructions. (See *Reference of pronouns § 3.)

2. *Editorial "we."* In editorial columns and in some other regular departments of periodicals, like "The Talk of the Town" in *The New Yorker,* the writer refers to himself as *we,* which leads to the curious form *ourself.* In some instances the *we* refers to an editorial board that determines the opinions expressed but more often it is a convention. It is less used than formerly.

The usage has passed into Informal writing, especially of a light tone. Used merely to avoid *I, we* is usually conspicuous and to be avoided. (See *I § 2.)

3. *Parental "we."* *We* is used Informally in softened requests, especially to children (We won't lose our mittens, will we?). This is a more effective use than the nurse's "How are we feeling this morning?"—sometimes called the "medical *we.*"

well—good • See *good—well.

wh • *wh* is the English spelling for the sound /hw/: *what* /hwot/ or /hwut/, *when* /hwen/, *wheel* /hwēl/, *whether* /hweŦʜ'ər/, *why* /hwī/. In *who* /hü/, *whole* /hōl/, *whoop* /hüp/, *wholly* /hōl'ē/, and so on, *wh* represents /h/.

when • Most handbooks warn against statements like "Welding is when two pieces of metal are heated and made into one." The reason given is that it is illogical or ungrammatical to equate an "adverbial clause" with a noun. Even the reasoning is fallacious because a clause cannot be classified solely by its introductory word, and in any case usage studies show that *when* (and *where*) clauses are frequently used (1) in noun constructions, as in "Do you have any way of knowing *when she will come?*" in which the *when* clause is the object of *knowing,* and (2) as adjective modifiers, as in "There comes a time *when a man has to be careful of his diet,*" in which the clause modifies *time.*

The objection to the construction is stylistic rather than grammatical and comes from the overuse of *when* clauses in amateurish definitions: *Communism is when all property is owned by all the people together or by the state.* The more Formal pattern would be: *Communism is a system in which all property is owned by all the people together or by the state.*

The construction, then, is to be used with caution rather than shunned altogether. (References: Fries, *AEG,* pp. 233-234; Marckwardt and Walcott, p. 115; Russell Thomas, *College English,* 1949, 10:406-408. Compare *reason is because.*)

when, as, and if • Securities are advertised "when, as, and if issued," and the phrase *when and if* or *if and when* is used in talking about goods whose future is uncertain. It should not be used when the matter is certain, and is generally inappropriate in all nonbusiness contexts.

whence • See *where.

where • *Where* clauses are frequently used to modify nouns, most commonly when some notion of place is involved:

General: This is the place where the trucks stop.
General: He wants a job where he will be with people.
More Formal: He wants a job in which he will be with people.

Where clauses in definitions are subject to the same objections that *when* clauses (see *when) are—that is, they frequently sound amateurish:

Amateurish: Etching is where you cut lines in a copper plate and then print from them.
General: Etching is the process of cutting lines in a copper plate and then printing from it.

English once had *whither*, "place to which"; *whence*, "place from which." They are now rarely used, and *where* has taken their place with help from other words—always with *from* to replace *whence*; often with *to* for *whither*. This pattern of *where* plus a preposition has been completed in Nonstandard: "*Where* is he *at*?" The construction also crops up in Informal speech but not in General or Formal writing. (References: Fries, *AEG*, pp. 234-235; Marckwardt and Walcott, p. 115.)

whether • *Whether* is used in indirect questions: *He asked whether you could come.*

In statements *whether* is used with *or* to indicate two alternatives: *They have never decided whether he committed suicide or was murdered.*

In Formal usage *or not* is frequently used with *whether* to indicate a second alternative when it is simply the negative of the one stated (They have never decided whether or not he was murdered). But in General usage *or not* is frequently omitted (They have never decided whether he was murdered), and should not be used if it will make an awkward statement, as it often will.

General: Whether or not this was the best plan, they went ahead. [Or: *Whether this was the best plan or not, they went ahead.*]
General: It is a sorry state when pupils don't know whether or not to believe their teachers.
Clumsy: It is a sorry state when pupils don't know whether to believe their teachers or not [Omit the *or not*].

(Reference: Fries, *AEG,* pp. 207, 217. See *if § 2, *Conditions.)

which •
1. *Which* refers to things and to groups of people regarded impersonally (The legislature which passed the act . . .). It is no longer used in Standard English to refer to a person or persons.
2. *Which* (like *that* and *this*) frequently has as its antecedent the idea of a phrase or clause:

> Relative pronouns are as troublesome to the inexpert but conscientious writer as they are useful to everyone, *which* is saying much.
> —H. W. Fowler, *A Dictionary of Modern English Usage,* p. 709

As with other uses of pronouns, the reference should be clear. (See *which* in *Webster's Third New International Dictionary*; Bryant, pp. 172-174; and James A. Drake, "How 'Which' Is Used in America Today," *American Speech,* 1960, 35:275-279. Compare *this.)
3. *Whose* is often used as the genitive of *which,* instead of the more cumbersome *of which*:

> This story of the life of General Custer is *Boots and Saddles,* whose author is the General's wife.

4. *And* and *but* are carelessly used to join a *which* clause, which is subordinate, to a main statement.

> *Inaccurate*: He got the contract to install new copper work on the Post Office, and which will require 4500 pounds of lead-coated copper.
> *Accurate*: He got the contract to install new copper work on the Post Office, which will require 4500 pounds of lead-coated copper.

while • *While* most exactly is a connective of time:

> While the rest were studying, he was playing cards.

While also means *though* or *but,* but rather weakly:

> Magazines, newspapers, and scientific books became my chief interest, *while* [More exact: *but*] poems were still a torture to me.

While is occasionally used for *and*:

> The second number was an acrobatic exhibition, *while* [Better: *and*] the third was a lady trapeze artist.

Awhile is an adverb, written as one word: *Awhile ago.* In phrases in which *while* is a noun, the *a* should be written separate: *In a while; After a while.* (Reference: Fries, *AEG,* pp. 236-237.)

Whitespace • Whitespace has the function of a punctuation mark in display matter. It has now taken the place of commas and periods at the ends of lines in envelope addresses, in letter headings, in titles of books and articles, in outlines, in lines that are spaced off in advertisements, posters, etc., in matter set in tables or columns. No punctuation marks are used at the ends of lines in Formal social notes. In indented quotations whitespace has displaced the quote marks. These various uses have helped relieve the spottiness of correspondence and many printed pages.

whither • See *where.

who—whom •
1. *Antecedent of "who."* Who refers to people, to personified objects (a ship, a country), and occasionally to animals:

Diogenes Checkpoints says what is needed is a list of horses who should be out of training.—Audax Minor, *The New Yorker*, Aug. 27, 1938.

Whose (not *of which*) is commonly used as the genitive case of *which*. (Reference: Hall, pp. 320-327. See *which § 3.)
2. *"Who" versus "whom."* In 1928 the *Oxford English Dictionary* said *whom* was "no longer current in natural colloquial speech." The struggle to make writing conform to grammatical rules of case is consequently difficult and full of problems. *Whom* consistently occurs only when it immediately follows a preposition as object (I don't know to whom I should go). But since the preposition often comes last in the expression, in General usage we find *who* (I don't know who I should go to). The most important reason for the development of this usage is that we no longer depend on the form to indicate the case function (except genitive). None of the other relative pronouns show case function by form, nor do the nouns (again, except genitives); the personal pronouns are too few to keep us sensitive to case forms, and two of them (*you, it*) lack an accusative form. Three other factors combine to make this *who* construction usual: (1) the position before the verb—the "subject-territory," (2) the infrequent use of *whom* in speech, and (3) our habit of not using relative pronouns in the object function to introduce clauses (I know the man [whom] you mean).

Formal usage generally keeps the accusative form when the pronoun is used as an object:

Formal: Whom [object of *introduce*] do you introduce to whom [object of the immediately preceding *to*]?
General: Who do you introduce to whom?
Formal: No matter whom [object of *meets*] one meets, the first thing one mentions is the weather.

General: No matter who you meet, the first thing you mention is the weather.

Which you use, then, depends on the variety and tone of the particular piece of writing. In Formal and academic writing and in much General writing, *whom* is what usually gets printed in the object function; in Informal narratives and personal writing, *who* is usually appropriate when the pronoun is used as an object. The unfortunate effect of the excessive attention given to these forms is that when used as an object either one now calls attention to itself in print. Another result is that *whom* is occasionally found in subject function: The man *whom* I know was guilty was exonerated. The same problems affect *whoever*.

3. *"Who" separated from verb*. When *who* is the subject of a verb separated from it by other words, care should be taken to keep the subject form:

He made a list of all the writers who [subject of *were*] he thought were important in the period.

This construction is troublesome, probably because the speaker recognizes that *he thought* restricts *who were important*; he may make an unconscious transformation of *writers he thought were important* into *he thought them important* and turn *them* into *whom* [*whom he thought*].

4. *The number of the verb*. A verb with *who* as its subject has the number of the antecedent of the *who*:

I'm one of the few people who don't [antecedent *people*] like to read many books.

I'm one who doesn't [antecedent *one*] like to read books.

Informally there is a strong tendency to make the verb of the *who* clause agree with the principal subject, which would give *doesn't* in the first sentence above. This is avoided in careful writing. (See *one of those who.)

whose • See *which.

will—shall • See *shall—will.

-wise • This suffix has long had a limited currency in forming adverbs from nouns (*edgewise, lengthwise, slantwise*). Recently it has greatly increased in use, especially in an abstract rather than a spatial sense: *average-wise, budget-wise, legislation-wise, tax-wise*. (It is usually hyphened in these new formations.)

This use of *-wise* occurs chiefly in commercial, journalistic, and political contexts; it carries the connotation of jargon as well as of faddish overuse and hence is inappropriate to college writing in spite of some advantages in economy (*economy-wise*).

with • There is a temptation to use *with* when another preposition or a different construction would be more accurate:

Our outfit was composed of two platoons *with* [Better: *of*] 43 men each.

I'll never forget the farmer who, not seeing the wave, tried to get his few cows to safety and was washed away *with* [Better: *by*] the water.

Americans believe in freedom, but with Germans it is different [Or: *but Germans are different*].

without • Nonstandard for *unless*.

I won't go without you do.

woman • *Woman* is the singular form, *women* the plural. Notice that in the spelling only one letter is altered from singular to plural; in the pronunciation, both syllables have changed vowels. (See also *man, woman.)

Wordiness •

Wdy   *Revision: Compress this passage by replacing the wordy expressions with more compact and exact ones.*

The use of unnecessary words in conveying one's ideas results in flabby writing. The commonest types of wordiness are:

1. *Circumlocution*—the use of several words instead of one exact word:

destroyed by fire often means *burned up* or *burned down*
come in contact with usually means *meet* or *know*
the necessary funds usually means no more than *the money*
in this day and age means *today*
the sort of metal they use for plating the shiny parts of automobiles might mean *chromium*

2. *Long function words*—function phrases that might be replaced by one or by fewer words:

During the time that [*While*] she was in Los Angeles she had at least six different jobs.

(See *Function words § 2.)

3. *Deadwood*—words which add nothing to the meaning:

The cars are neat and graceful [in appearance].
In the majority of cases they do not. [For: *The majority do not.*]

The home of my boyfriend was in a town called Hillsdale. [For: *My boyfriend's home was in Hillsdale.*]

(See Ch. 8, "Economy in sentences," p. 314.)

4. *Formless, fuzzy writing*:

Wordy	*Revised*
It has some of the best ski trails in the country and as far as the other cold weather sports are concerned, they have them too, along with one of the most fashionable hotels in the country.	They have a very fashionable hotel, all the cold weather sports, and some of the best ski trails in the country.

(See also Ch. 8, "Long and short constructions," "Repetition," pp. 317, 320, and specific articles like *case, *Passive verbs, *seem, *there is, there are.)

Word order •

Revision: Change the order of words or other elements so that the meaning is clearer, or the sentence is more natural or more effective.   WO

The order of words and of other locutions in a sentence is the most important device of English grammar to show the relations of words in sentences. It plays a large part in style, especially emphasis. The work done in many languages by inflections (endings) is in English performed largely by *function words (prepositions, auxiliary verbs, and so on—whose function is made clear by their position) and by the word order. Since we pick up the standard word order as we learn to talk, it offers little difficulty. We use the subject-verb-object order of clauses and sentences; we put adjectives before their nouns and relative clauses after their nouns and in general put modifiers near the words modified.

This article is intended to bring the fact of word order to your attention rather than to cover its enormous number of details.

1. *Position changed for emphasis.* As a rule an element taken out of its usual position receives increased emphasis, as when the object is put before both subject and verb:

Object first: That book I read when I was sixteen. (Instead of: *I read that book when I was sixteen.*)

Predicate adjective first: Lucky are the ones who register early. (Instead of: *The ones who register early are lucky.*)

(See Ch. 8, "Position," p. 323.)

2. *Interrupted constructions.* When a word or words interrupt a construction, the effect is usually unhappy unless the interrupting word deserves special emphasis:

Between subject and verb: Newspaper headlines in these trying and confused times are continually intensifying the fears of the American people. [More natural: In these trying and confused times newspaper headlines are. . . .]

Between verb and adverb: He played quietly, efficiently on. He took a pack from his pocket and she took one thoughtfully out. (More natural: He played on, quietly, efficiently. He took a pack from his pocket and she took one out thoughtfully [or: and she thoughtfully took one out].)

(See Ch. 8, "Interrupted movement," p. 310, *Split infinitive.)
3. *Misleading word order.* English usually has a modifier close to the word modified and care must be taken that modifiers separated from their main words do not mislead the reader.

Misleading	*Improved*
I wish to order one of the machines which I saw advertised in *The Saturday Evening Post* sent to the above address.	I wish to order sent to the above address one of the machines which I saw advertised in *The Saturday Evening Post*.
Her uncle, King Leopold, was even unable to influence her.	Even her uncle, King Leopold, was unable to influence her.
This success in villages will probably be duplicated in the cities as time goes on at an accelerated rate.	As time goes on, this success in villages will probably be duplicated at an accelerated rate in cities.
Until recently the chains have been able to get special prices on the goods they buy from producers with little opposition.	Until recently the chains have been able to get with little opposition special prices on the goods they buy from producers.

(See *Ambiguity § 2. References: Margaret M. Bryant, *College English*, 1944, 5:434-438; Fries, *AEG*, Ch. 10; Curme, *Syntax*, Ch. 17; C. Alphonso Smith, *Studies in English Syntax*, Boston, 1906, Ch. 2.)

Words • The framework for the treatment of words and word usage in this book is provided by the opening chapter, "The varieties of English," pp. 2-32.

General questions on the use of words are treated in Ch. 9, "Revising words and phrases." Many specific words that are likely to raise questions have articles of their own (*contact, *drunk, *hope, *however, *notorious, *ye=the . . .). Very often the solution to a question of diction can be found in a good dictionary.

Some of the general discussions about words or their uses will be found under the following in the *Guide*:

Index articles containing general discussions about words or their uses include:

*Abstract and concrete
    words
*Antonym
*Compound words
*Concrete words
*Context
*Contractions
*Counter words
*Division of words
*Double negative
*Ellipsis
*Euphemisms
*Foreign words
    in English
*Function words
*Gobbledygook
*Group words
*Headword

*Homonyms
*Hyphen
*Idiom and idioms
*Linguistics
*Localisms
*Meaning
*namely and other
    introductory words
*Origin of words
*Phrases
*Repetition
*Shoptalk
*Slang
*Suggestion
*Underlining
*Usage
*Wordiness

(See also *Pronunciation, *Spelling, *Style.)

worthwhile • *Worthwhile* is now usually written as one word, occasionally hyphened, rarely as two words.

would—should • See *should—would.

would have, would of • See *have § 3.

writ large • The phrase is "bookish" (see *literary).

Written English • See *Spoken and written English. See also *Experiment in written English, *Factual and imaginative writing, *Style.

Wrong word •

WW
Revision: Replace the word marked with one that says what you mean.

No word is right or wrong in itself. As used here, "wrong word" means that the word does not convey a meaning that makes sense in the context. In this sentence, *comprehensibility* does not make sense: *What he said showed real comprehensibility of the problems in Asia.* The writer probably meant *comprehension.* Errors like this occur when the writer is attempting to use a vocabulary in which he is not at home, when he confuses words of similar sound, or when he simply writes too hurriedly and fails to proofread his work before turning it in. (See *Carelessness.)

X • is an unnecessary letter in English. It spells several sounds transcribed phonetically as /ks/ as in *fox* /foks/, *exclusive* /eks klü′siv/, *exceed* /ik sēd′/; /gz/ as in *exist* /ig zist′/, *exhibit* /ig zib′it/; /ksh/ as in *luxury* /luk′shə rē/; /gzh/ as in *luxurious* /lug zhùr′ē əs/ or /luk shùr′i əs/; /z/ as in *xylophone, Xantippe, Xavier* (not /eks zā′viər/). In British usage *ct* is sometimes spelled *x* as in *inflexion;* and in this country *cks* is spelled *x* for the baseball teams *White Sox* and *Red Sox.*

X
X is also a correction symbol indicating a careless mistake. (See *Carelessness.)

Xmas • *Xmas* is an Informal word seen chiefly in advertising; it is pronounced like *Christmas,* for which it stands. The *X* is from the initial letter of the Greek spelling of *Christ.*

X-ray • *X-ray* is hyphened as a verb and noun; also printed *X ray* as a noun. It is usually capitalized, though as a verb it is sometimes not.

Y • /y/ as in *yes* /yes/, *beyond* /bi yond′/. *Y* also spells /ī/ and /ē/, as in *sky* /skī/, *bloody* /blud′ē/.

A final *y* following a consonant is changed to *i* before a suffix beginning with a vowel except *i: duty—dutiable, try—tries, body—bodies, bodied;* but *play—played, playing, playable, fly—flying.*

ye = the • In Old English the sound of *th* in *thin* was represented by the letter thorn, **þ** . In early printing the letter *y,* which in the type fonts of the time looked most like the thorn, was used to represent it. Consequently we find *ye* (*the*), *yat* (*that*), *yem* (*them*) in early books, and even oftener find the forms in manuscript down to about 1800.

This *y* then represents *th* and is pronounced like *th*. Its use in recent faking of antiquity has not changed this fact: *Ye Olde Coffee Shoppe* is just *The Old Coffee Shop* and should presumably be so pronounced, though there is no telling what pronunciation the proprietor intended.

ye = you • *Ye*, originally the nominative plural and then also the nominative singular of the second person pronoun (now *you*), survived for a long time in poetry and other literature with a tendency to be archaic (sermons, florid oratory). It is now obsolete in writing, though the unstressed pronunciation of *you* ("whad ya think?") is probably much like what *ye* used to represent.

yes • *Yes* and *no* are labeled *adverbs* in dictionaries. They may modify a sentence (Yes, you're right) or may have the value of a coordinate clause (No; but you should have told me) or may stand as complete sentences. ("Do you really intend to go with him?" "Yes.")

Yes and *no* have variants in speech, where there are innumerable substitutes, from *ye-us* to *yop* and the "colloquial nasals," for which there are no satisfactory spellings (*uh-huh, huh-uh, humph, eh,* etc.), not to mention the current slang affirmatives and the longer lived ones like *OK. (See *sure.)

yet • *Yet* is an adverb (The books haven't come yet); it is also used as a *coordinating conjunction, equivalent to *but:*

His speech was almost unintelligible, yet for some unknown reason I enjoyed it.

you • *You* is used as a pronoun of indefinite reference (It's a good book, if you like detective stories) in General writing. Formal English would more often use *one*, though the prejudice against *you* is declining. (See *one, *they.)

When *you* is used in an Informal approach to readers or to an audience, it sometimes may be unintentionally personal (or even insulting) or seem to indicate an invidious distinction between writer and reader (Take, for instance, *your* [better: *our* or *one's*] family problems). In speech the indefinite *you* is distinguished from the personal *you* by the reduced stress on it.

you all • In Southern American *you all*, contracted to *y'all*, is frequently used as the plural of *you*, as in some other regions *you folks* is used. It is also used when addressing one person regarded as one of a group, usually a family. It is sometimes asserted that *you all* is also used as a singular, addressing one. (See *American Speech*, especially volumes 2 and 4.)

There are at least three current locutions that attempt to remedy the lack of distinction between second person singular and plural in English: *youse, you'uns,* and *you all.* Only *you all* has achieved respectability. (References: Mencken, pp. 543, 545-549; George P. Wilson, "You All," *Georgia Review*, 1960, 14:38-54.)

your—you're • In revision, check for careless confusion in the transcription of these words. *Your* is a possessive pronoun (your books); *you're* is a subject and verb (You're all right).

youth • *Youth* is overused in the sense of "young people" and suggests a ministerial style.

you was, you is • *You was* and *you is* are Nonstandard.

youngster, child, kid • See *kid.

Z • /z/ as in *Zion* /zī'ən/, *buzz* /buz/, *busy* /biz'ē/, *shoes* /shüz/. The sound is also spelled *s* as in *desire, x* as in *anxiety, ss* as in *scissors*.

zh • The phonetic symbol representing the sound in *rouge* /rüzh/, *measure* /mezh'ər/, and so on. (See *G § 3.)

& • See *Ampersand.

✓ A "correction symbol" expressing approval of the idea or style.

Acknowledgments

The authors gratefully acknowledge the kindness of authors and publishers in giving permission to reproduce their materials in *Writer's Guide and Index to English*. Where the territory rights are divided among various publishers, the acknowledgment states what permission was granted. An unqualified acknowledgment indicates that world permission was granted.

The American Scholar: selection by Eugene Rabinowitch from *The American Scholar,* Summer 1964.

Appleton-Century-Crofts: selections from *American English Grammar* by Charles Carpenter Fries, copyright 1940, The National Council of Teachers of English and Charles C. Fries; reprinted by permission of Appleton-Century-Crofts.

The Atlantic Monthly: from selections in *The Atlantic Monthly:* "Vive Moi!" by Sean O'Faolain; "The Art of Being Free" by Gerald W. Johnson; "The Power of James R. Hoffa" by A. H. Raskin; "Medical Care for Developing Countries" by Carl E. Taylor; "The National Debt and the Peril Point" by J. David Stern; "Writer versus Bureaucrat in the Soviet Union" by F. D. Reeve; "Born a Square—The Westerners' Dilemma" by Wallace Stegner; "The Death of the Salmon" by Roderick Haig-Brown—all published January 1964. Selections from "Alaska: Last Frontier" by Paul Brooks, September 1962; "Must the Colleges Police Sex?" by John T. Rule, April 1964; "Must We Hate?" by Archibald MacLeish, February 1963; "Man Against Darkness" by W. T. Stace from *Jubilee: One Hundred Years of* The Atlantic, copyright 1948 by The Atlantic Monthly Company.

Barnes and Noble, Inc.: selection from *Semantics, An Introduction to the Science of Meaning* by Stephen Ullmann, 1962.

Brandt & Brandt: selection from *John Brown's Body* by Stephen Vincent Benét, published by Farrar & Rinehart, Inc.; copyright 1927, 1928 by Stephen Vincent Benét.

Cambridge University Press: world rights outside the United States and Canada for selection from "Religion and Science" in *Science and the Modern World* by Alfred North Whitehead, copyright 1925, 1935 by The Macmillan Company; reprinted by permission of The Macmillan Company. Selection from *The Universe Around Us* by Sir James Jeans.

Jonathan Cape, Ltd.: British Empire except Canada for selection from *Green Hills of Africa* by Ernest Hemingway.

Chanticleer Press, Inc.: selection from *Living Mammals of the World* by Ivan T. Sanderson, copyright 1955 by Doubleday and Company, Inc.; reprinted by permission of Chanticleer Press, Inc.

Chicago *Sun-Times:* "My Grandmother . . . The Florida Jailbird" by Francis Fitzgerald, a *New York Herald Tribune* special in the Chicago *Sun-Times,* April 5, 1964; reprinted by permission of the Publishers Newspaper Syndicate. Selections from Chicago *Sun-Times,* February 27, 1964; "Tom Meany Made Sports Field Richer" by Red Smith, September 16, 1964.

Malcolm Cowley: selection from *Exile's Return* by Malcolm Cowley.

Thomas Y. Crowell Company: selection from *Of Whales and Women* by Frank B. Gilbreth, Jr.

Curtis Brown Ltd.: selection from "The Blushing Bride" in *I Know What I Like* by Georgina Coleridge, copyright 1959 by Chatto & Windus Ltd.; copyright 1963 by Georgina Coleridge; reprinted by permission of the author. World exclusive of the United States and Canada for selection from *Hard Lines* by Ogden Nash, copyright 1931 by Ogden Nash; reprinted by permission of Little, Brown and Company and the author.

J. M. Dent & Sons Ltd.: selection from "The Lagoon" in *Tales of Unrest* by Joseph Conrad, copyright 1898, 1920 by Doubleday & Company, Inc.

Dodd, Mead & Co.: selection reprinted by permission of Dodd, Mead & Co. from *The New World,* Vol. 2 of *A History of the English-Speaking Peoples,* by Winston S. Churchill, © 1956 by Winston S. Churchill; also by permission of Cassell and Company Ltd. Selection from *Modern American Painting* by Peyton Boswell, Jr.; reprinted by permission of the publishers, Dodd, Mead & Co.

Doubleday & Company, Inc.: selection from *Good Behaviour: Being a Study of Certain Types of Civility* by Sir Harold George Nicolson.

Duell, Sloan & Pearce, Inc.: selection from *Virgin Spain* by Waldo Frank, copyright 1926, 1942 by Waldo Frank.

E. P. Dutton & Co., Inc.: selection from "Henry James, Preface to the Aspern Papers (1908)" in *Henry James: Selected Fiction,* edited by Leon Edel.

Emporia *Gazette:* selection from an article by William Allen White.

Esquire: selection from "Memoirs of a Six-Months Trainee" by John Berendt, June 1964.

Faber and Faber, Ltd.: world exclusive of the United States for selection from "Gerontion" by T. S. Eliot.

Allan Ferguson: selection from "The Scientist's Need for New Words" by Allan Ferguson in *The Listener,* April 21, 1937.

W. H. Freeman and Co.: selection from *Sets, Logic, and Axiomatic Theories* by Robert R. Stoll.

C. C. Fries: selections from *What Is Good English?* by C. C. Fries.

Funk & Wagnalls Company, Inc.: selections reprinted by permission from the *Funk*

& *Wagnalls Standard® College Dictionary,* copyright 1963 by Funk & Wagnalls Company, Inc.

Harcourt, Brace & World, Inc.: selections from *Poems 1923-1954* by E. E. Cummings, 1954; reprinted by permission of the publishers, Harcourt, Brace & World, Inc. Selections from *Machines That Built America* by Roger Burlingame; (Harvest Books) *Language* by Edward Sapir; *The Modern Temper* by Joseph Wood Krutch; *The Road to Wigan Pier* by George Orwell.

Harper & Row: selection from pp. 262-263 in *Only Yesterday* by Frederick Lewis Allen (Harper & Brothers, 1931). Selections from *Pagan Spain* by Richard Wright; *Personality* by Gardner Murphy, copyright 1947; "Once More to the Lake" in *One Man's Meat* by E. B. White; *Call to Greatness* by Adlai E. Stevenson; from an article by Carl Landauer in *The American Way* by D. C. Coyle and others, copyright 1938 by Harper & Row; *My Life and Hard Times* by James Thurber, copyright 1933 by James Thurber.

Harper's Magazine: from selections in *Harper's Magazine:* "A Draftee's Diary" by Charles Vanderburgh, February 1964; "The Quietmouth American" by Donald Lloyd, September 1963—reprinted by permission of the author; "Speaking for the Working-Class Wife" by Patricia Cayo Sexton, October 1962; book review of *When the Cheering Stopped,* by Paul Pickrel, March 1964, copyright 1964 by *Harper's*

Magazine—reprinted by permission of the author; "An Ex-convict's Scheme for More Practical Prisons" by Hal Hollister, August 1962.

George G. Harrap & Co., Ltd.: selection by E. N. da C. Andrade from *Physics for the Modern World;* additional credit to Barnes and Noble, Inc.

Harvard Educational Review: selection from "Language Disorders in Childhood" by Eric H. Lenneberg, Spring 1964.

Holiday: from selections in *Holiday:* "Deer Stalking in the Highlands" by Neil M. Gunn, January 1957; "Living with a Peacock" by Flannery O'Connor, September 1961; "America Talking" by Bergen Evans, July 1961; "Canadiana: One Man's View" by Mordecai Richler, April 1964; "A Stranger in New York," Part II, by V. S. Pritchett, August 1964.

Holt, Rinehart & Winston, Inc.: from "On Looking Up by Chance at the Constellations" from *Complete Poems of Robert Frost,* copyright 1928 by Holt, Rinehart & Winston, Inc.; copyright renewed © 1956 by Robert Frost; reprinted by permission of Holt, Rinehart and Winston, Inc.

Hutchinson & Co. Ltd.: British Empire for selection from *The Americans* by Oscar Handlin (Atlantic-Little, Brown and Company, 1963); reprinted by permission of the publishers.

Alfred A. Knopf, Inc.: selections from *Indirections* by Sidney Cox; *Poems* by Rex Warner.

Selection reprinted by permission of AAK, Inc. from "A Passion for Ivory" in *Dynasty of Abu* by Ivan T. Sanderson, copyright © 1960 by the Curtis Publishing Co.; renewed 1960, 1962 by Ivan T. Sanderson.

Little, Brown and Company: world exclusive of the British Commonwealth for selection from *The Americans* by Oscar Handlin, copyright © 1963 by Oscar Handlin; reprinted by permission of Atlantic-Little, Brown and Company, publishers. United States and Canada for selection from *Hard Lines* by Ogden Nash, copyright 1931 by Ogden Nash; reprinted by permission of Little, Brown and Company and the author. Selection from *Teacher in America* by Jacques Barzun. United States and Canada for selection from *No Place to Hide* by David Bradley; reprinted by permission of Little, Brown and Company and the author.

McGraw-Hill Book Company: selection from *What to Listen for in Music* by Aaron Copland, copyright 1939, 1957. United States and Canada for *Bears in My Kitchen* by Margaret Merrill, and "Pleasant Agony" in *Still Seeing Things* by John Mason Brown. Selection from *Propaganda and the News* by Will Irwin, copyright 1936; courtesy of McGraw-Hill Book Company, New York.

The Macmillan Company: United States and Canada for selection from "Religion and Science" in *Science and the Modern World* by Alfred North Whitehead, copyright 1925, 1935; used with permission of The Macmillan Company. Selection from *The American Irish* by William V. Shannon, copyright 1963; used with permission of The Macmillan Company. Selections from *The Promise of American Life* by Herbert Croly, copyright 1910; *The Phantom Public* by Walter Lippmann.

The Harold Matson Company, Inc.: selection from "Our Challenging Deserts" by Jack Schaefer in *Holiday*, July 1958, copyright © 1958 by Jack Schaefer; reprinted by permission of the Harold Matson Co., Inc.

G. & C. Merriam Company: selections by permission from *Webster's Seventh New Collegiate Dictionary*, copyright 1963 by G. & C. Merriam Co., publishers of the Merriam-Webster Dictionaries.

The Nation: selection from "Co-existence or No Existence: The Choice Is Ours" by Bertrand Russell, June 18, 1955; reprinted by permission of *The Nation*.

New American Library of World Literature, Inc. (Mentor Books) : selections from *Christopher Columbus, Mariner* by Samuel Eliot Morison; *The Shaping of the Modern Mind* by Crane Brinton.

New Era: selection from "Rogues' Gallery" by Martin Oliver, in 50th Anniversary issue, Summer 1964.

The New Yorker: from selections

in *The New Yorker:* "Evans vs. Evans" by Whitney Balliett, September 21, 1963—reprinted by permission, © 1963, The New Yorker Magazine, Inc.; "Return to the Randolph" by Montgomery Newman, May 11, 1957; "Encounters in Barrios" by Robert Shaplen, September 28, 1963—reprinted by permission, © 1963, The New Yorker Magazine, Inc.; "A Pageant in Sack Suits" by Christopher Rand, January 19, 1957. Selections from articles by Meyer Berger, November 26, 1938; and *The New Yorker* of January 17, 1948, and of February 19, 1949.

The North American Review: selection from "Delusions of a University" by Sheldon Zitner, March 1964; reprinted by permission of the publisher.

Odhams Books, Ltd.: world exclusive of the United States for a selection from *My Early Life* by Winston S. Churchill, copyright by Odhams Books Limited; reprinted by permission of the publishers.

Oxford University Press, Inc.: selections from *American English* by Albert H. Marckwardt; *The Uses of the Past* by Herbert J. Muller.

Partisan Review: selection from "The Making of a Poem" by Stephen Spender, which first appeared in *Partisan Review,* XIII, 3 (Summer 1946) ; reprinted by permission of the publisher and the author.

Penguin Books Ltd.: selection from *England under the Stuarts* by G. M. Trevelyan.

Pocket Books, Inc.: selection from *U. S. Foreign Policy* by Walter Lippmann.

Prentice-Hall, Inc.: selection reprinted with permission of Prentice-Hall, Inc., from *The Open Self* by Charles Morris, © 1958 by Prentice-Hall, Inc., Englewood Cliffs, New Jersey; published by Prentice-Hall, Inc. Selection from *Conserving American Resources* by Ruben L. Parson.

Random House, Inc.: selection from *The Immense Journey* by Loren Eiseley. Selections reprinted from *The American College Dictionary,* copyright 1947, © copyright 1964, by permission of Random House, Inc.

The Reporter: selection from "The Future of Liberalism" by Arthur Schlesinger, Jr., May 3, 1956.

Arnold M. Rose: selection from "Social Problems of the Contemporary World" in *Contemporary Civilization—Issue Three;* published by Scott, Foresman and Company.

Saturday Review: from selections in *Saturday Review:* "Cornelia and the Loves of Charles" by John Ciardi, April 13, 1963; "The Other Island" in *The Water Beetle* by Nancy Mitford, March 19, 1963; "The Creative Dilemma" by Joseph Wood Krutch, February 8, 1964, from *Creative America.*

Scientific American: from selections in *Scientific American:* "Food" by Nevin S. Scrimshaw, September 1963; "The Amateur Scientist: How to collect and preserve the delicate webs of spiders" by C. L. Stong, February 1963; "Education for Development" by Frederick

Harbison, September 1963.

Charles Scribner's Sons: United States only for selection reprinted with the permission of Charles Scribner's Sons from *A Roving Commission: My Early Life,* pp. 29-30, by Winston Churchill, copyright 1930 Charles Scribner's Sons; renewal copyright © 1958 Winston Churchill. Selections from *The Enjoyment of Poetry with Anthology for Enjoyment of Poetry* by Max Eastman; "Haircut" in *Roundup* by Ring Lardner; "The Classical Tradition and Education" by Hugh MacLennan in *Scotchman's Return and Other Essays.* World exclusive of the British Empire for selection from *Green Hills of Africa* by Ernest Hemingway.

Simon and Schuster, Inc.: world exclusive of the British Empire for selection reprinted from *With Malice Toward Some* by Margaret Halsey; by permission of Simon and Schuster, publishers, copyright 1938 by Margaret Halsey.

Social Science Research Council: selection from *Local History— How to Gather It, Write It, and Publish It* by Donald D. Parker; published by Social Science Research Council.

Soil Science: selection from "Interpretive Soil Classification: Timber, Range, and Watershed" by Robert A. Gardner and John L. Retzer, 1949; published by The Williams and Wilkins Co.

Sports Illustrated: selections from "Let's Not Spoil Their Sport" by Andrea Mead Lawrence, *Sports Illustrated,* February 3, 1964, © 1964, Time Inc.; reprinted by permission of the author. Selection from "Just Out from under a Rock" by John Terres, May 4, 1964.

The Times Literary Supplement: selection from "The Language of Scholarship"; reprinted by permission from *The Times Literary Supplement,* August 17, 1956, The Times Publishing Company, Limited.

United Feature Syndicate: selection from "Candle Is Remarkable Invention" by Inez Robb, printed in Seattle *Post-Intelligencer,* February 6, 1954.

University of Chicago Press: "Proofreader's Marks" reprinted from *A Manual of Style,* 11th ed. copyright 1949 by permission of The University of Chicago.

University of Washington Press: selection from *Garden Design* by John A. and Carol L. Grant.

Vanguard Press, Inc.: selection from *Representative Opinions of Mr. Justice Holmes,* edited by Alfred Lief.

The Viking Press, Inc.: selections from "The Squirt and the Monkey" in *Triple Jeopardy* by Rex Stout, copyright 1957; *The Literary Situation* by Malcolm Cowley, reprinted by permission of The Viking Press, Inc.; *Philosopher's Holiday* by Irwin Edman; *Wolf Willow* by Wallace Stegner.

Voice of America: selection from "Biological Clocks" by Victor G. Bruce in *Frontiers of Modern Biology,* edited by Gairdner Moment and sponsored by Voice of America.

John Wiley & Sons, Inc.: selections reprinted by permission from *Shore Processes and Shoreline Development* by Douglas W. Johnson and from *Theories of Perception and the Concept of Structure* by Floyd H. Allport, published by John Wiley & Sons, Inc.

The H. W. Wilson Company: selections from *Readers' Guide to Periodical Literature,* February 10, 1964; reprinted by permission of the publishers.

Woman's Day: selection from "Homily for a Troubled Time" by Bernard DeVoto, January 1951.

The World Publishing Company: from *Webster's New World Dictionary, College Edition,* copyright 1964, by The World Publishing Company, Cleveland, Ohio.

Yale University Press: selections from *The Gentleman from New York: A Life of Roscoe Conkling* by Donald B. Chidsey; *Sweden: The Middle Way* by Marquis W. Childs.

General Index

This index refers only to the *Writer's Guide*. For additional references, see also the alphabetically arranged *Index to English*.

2 3 4 5 6 7 8 9 10 11 12 13 14 15 16 17 18 19 20 21 22 23 24 25 RM 74 73 72 71 70 69 68

Symbols for marking papers